MIRABE TOM. I
MIRABE TOM. II
MIRABE TOM. III
MIRABE TOM. IV
PAUL B. I
PAUL B. II
PAUL B. III
PAUL B. IV
IONAS RERUM HISTORIE III THEIL
MAV HISTORIE
GOLDASTI MONARCH ROM. IMPER. TOM. I
BARONII
AVENTINI GUILIM
WEGELINI RERUM SUEVICAR TOM. III
WEGELINI RERUM SUEVICAR VOL IV
OPERA
I0729528

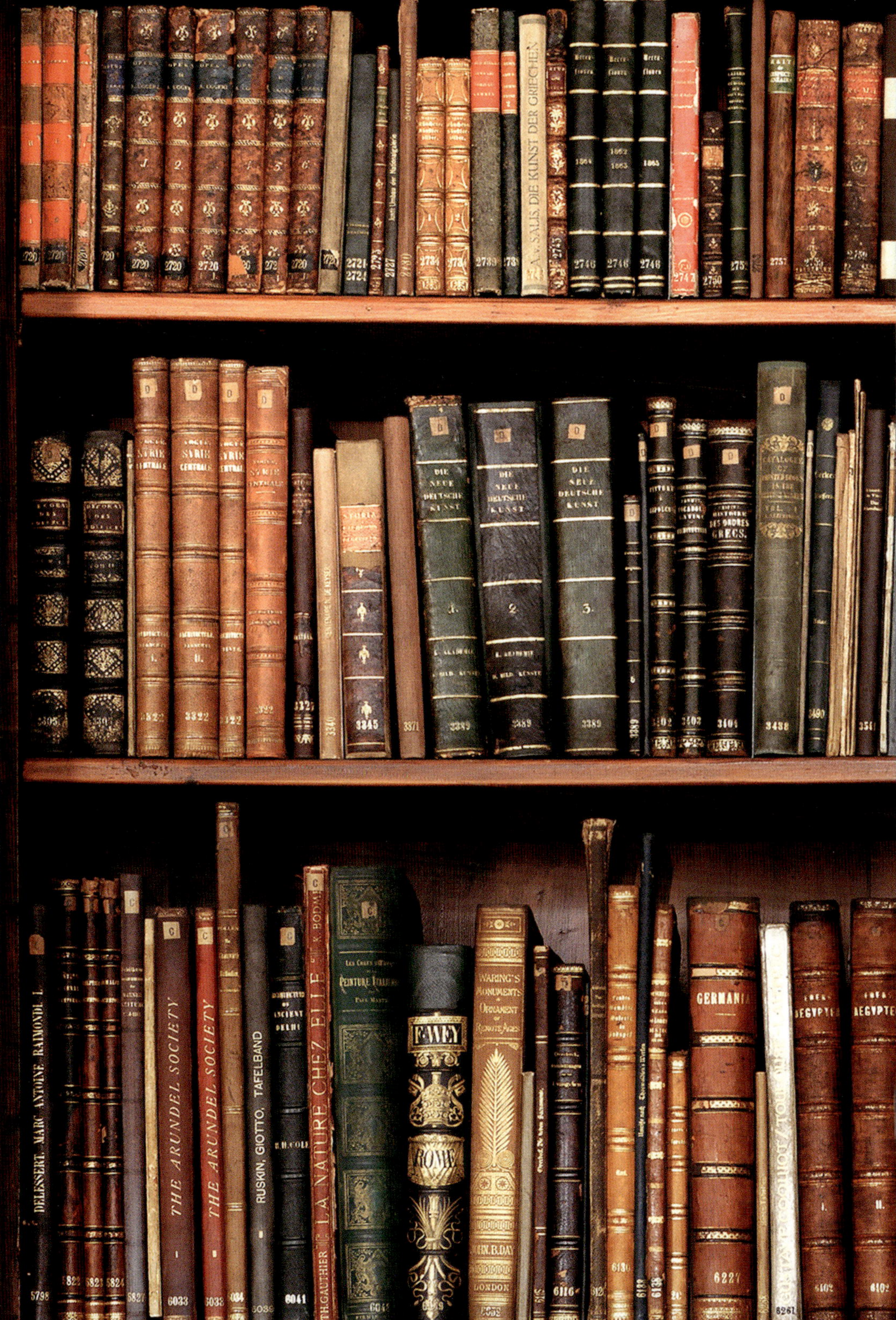

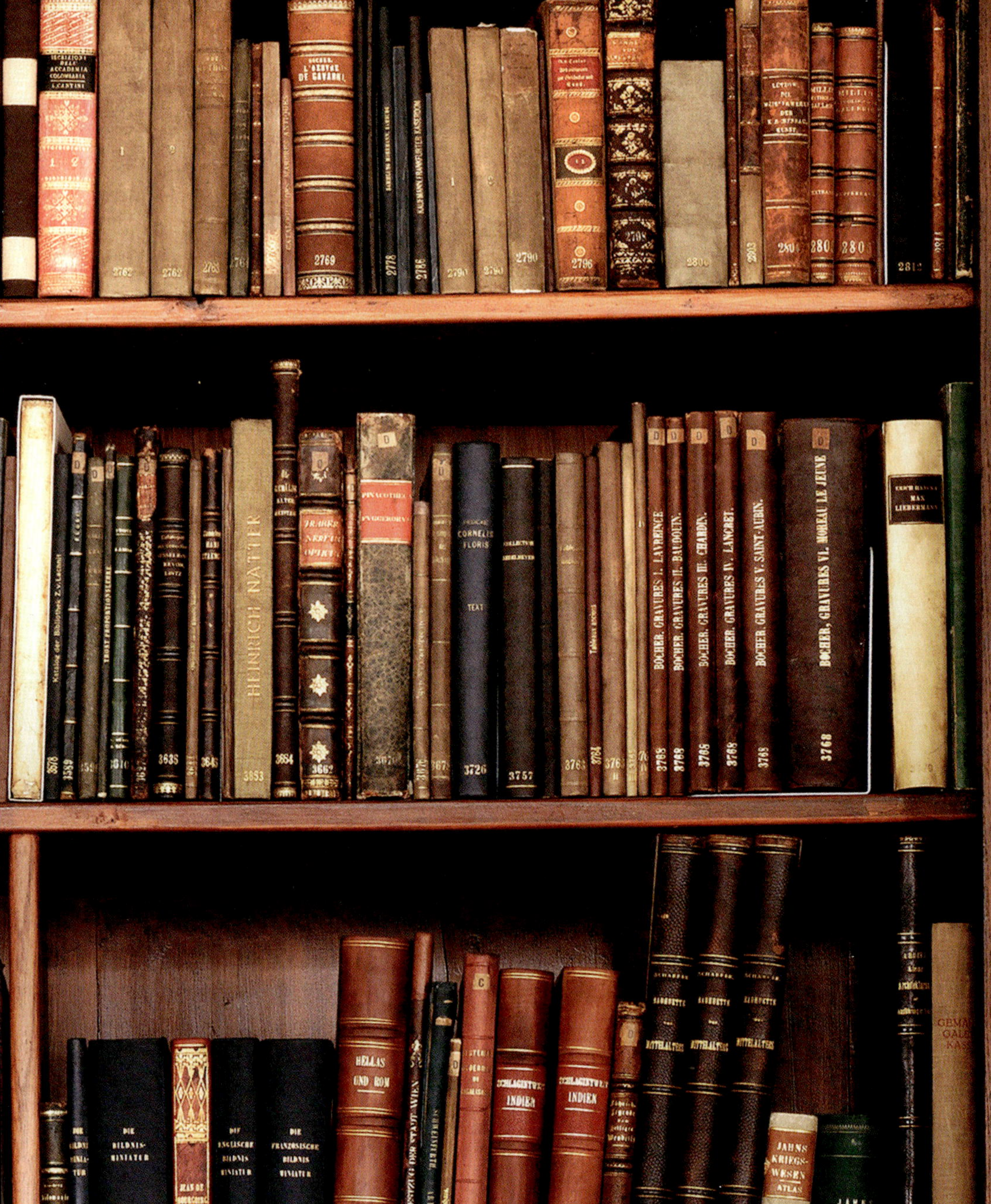

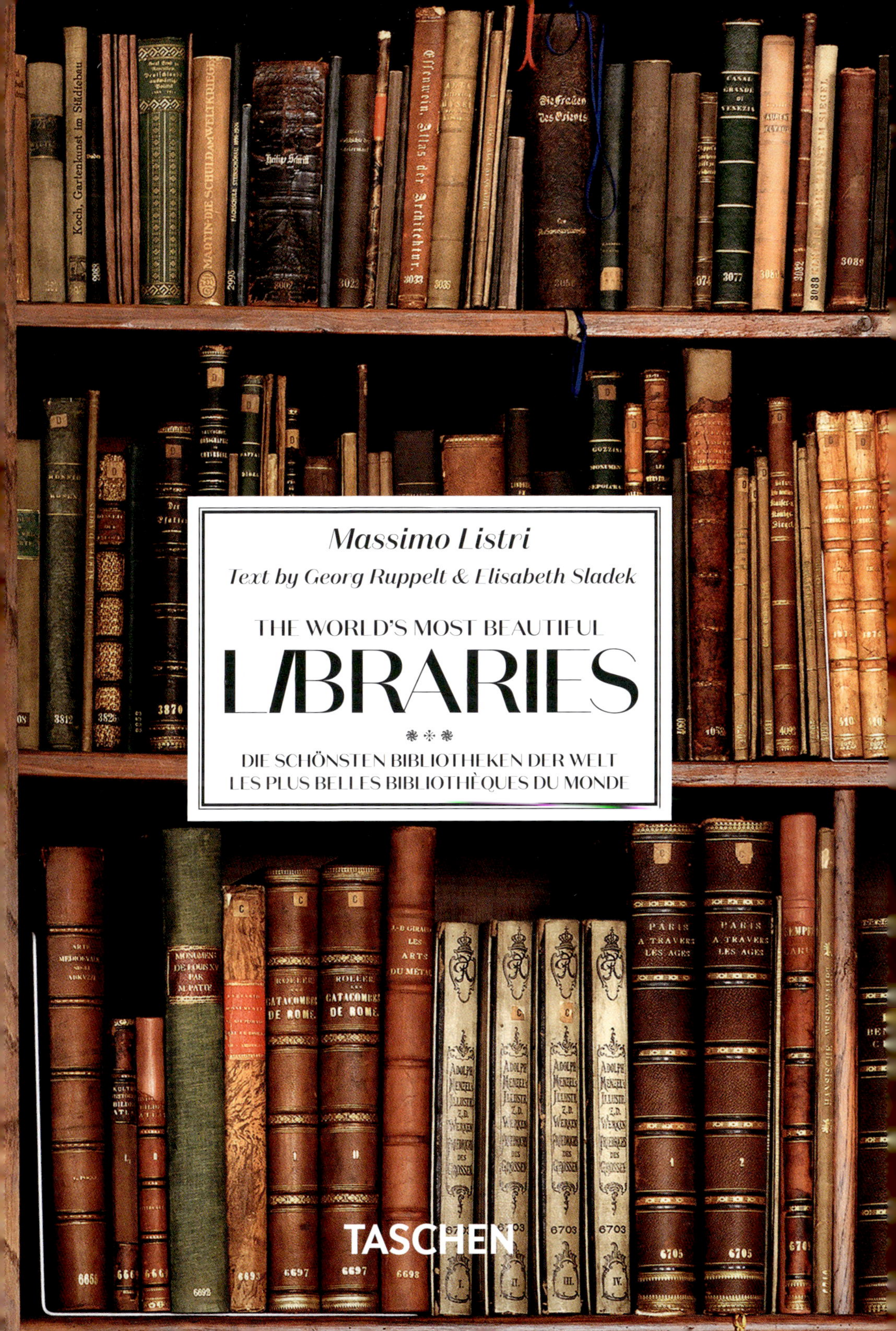

Massimo Listri
Text by Georg Ruppelt & Elisabeth Sladek
THE WORLD'S MOST BEAUTIFUL
LIBRARIES
DIE SCHÖNSTEN BIBLIOTHEKEN DER WELT
LES PLUS BELLES BIBLIOTHÈQUES DU MONDE
TASCHEN

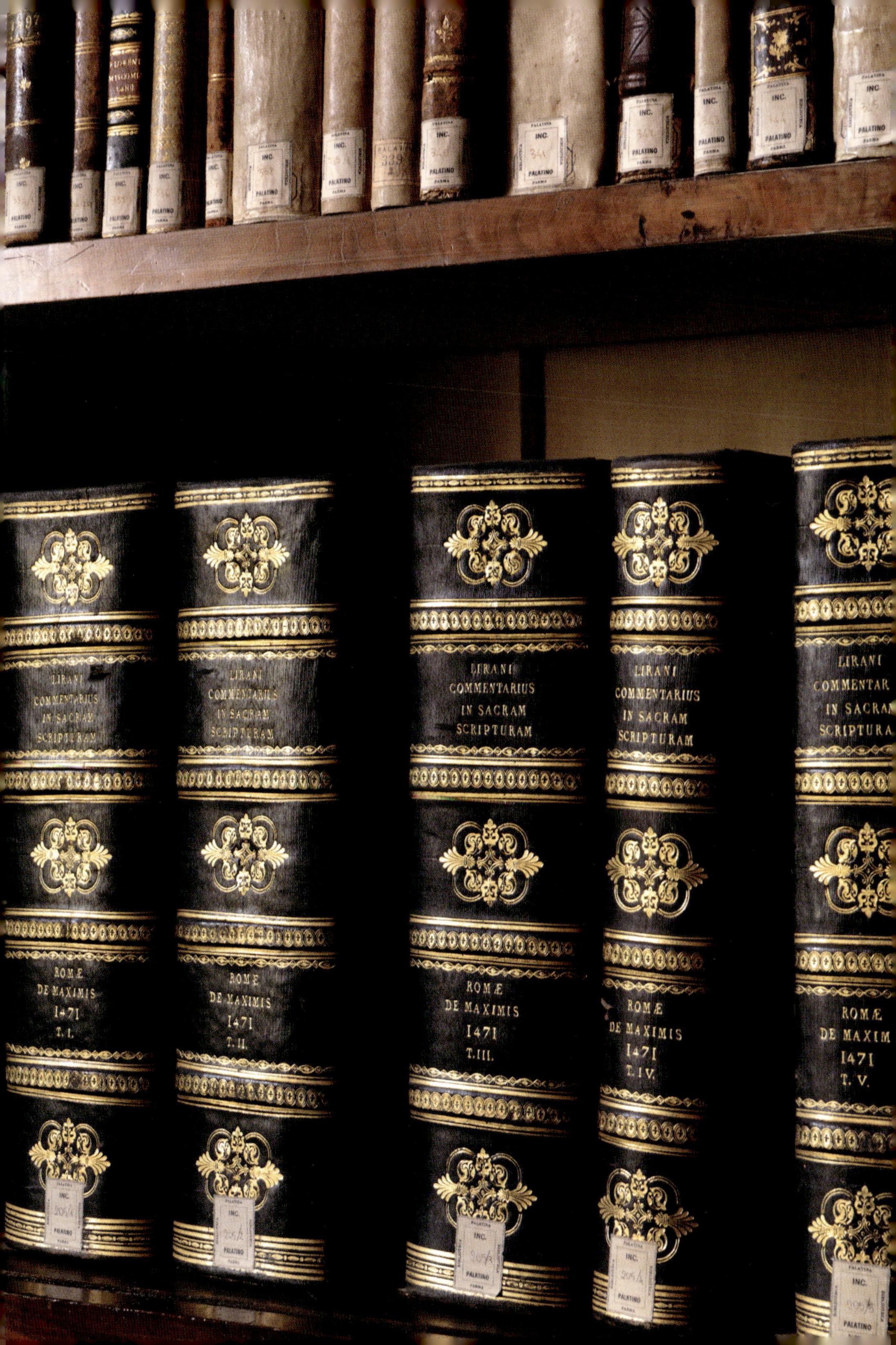

LIRANI
COMMENTARIUS
IN SACRAM
SCRIPTURAM
ROMÆ
DE MAXIMIS
1471
T. III.

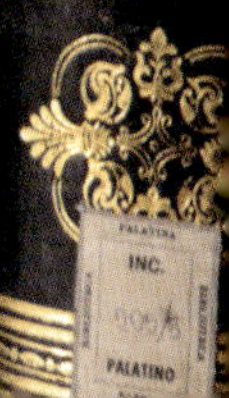

INC.
205/4
PALATINO
PARMA

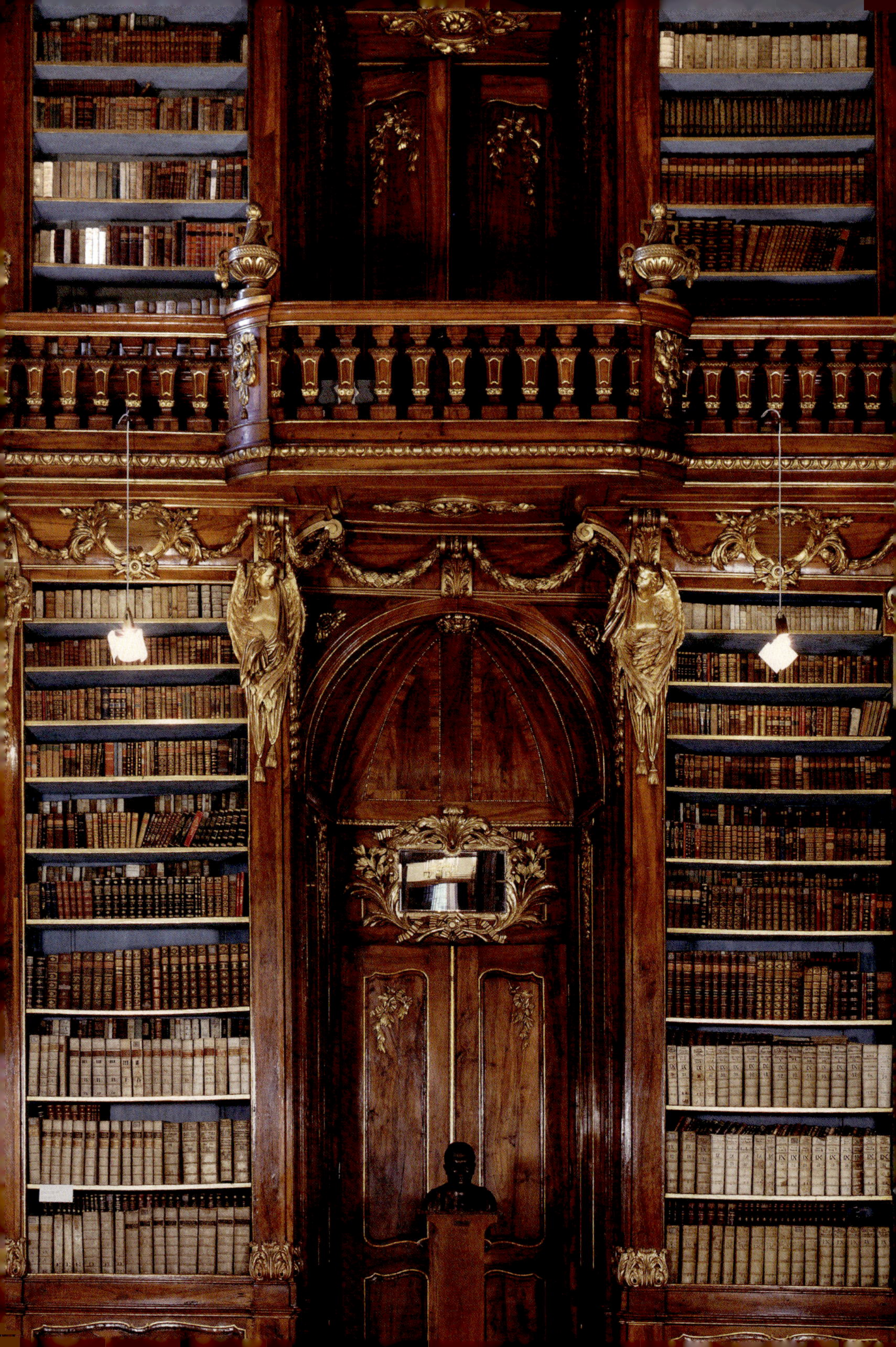

Memory of the World

Georg Ruppelt

Libraries are "well laid-out gardens, in which new flowers spring up around us with every step, embellishing their surroundings and giving off the scent of pleasure".[1]

The metaphor of the library as a garden, which draws an analogy between two of humanity's greatest cultural achievements, is one of the images used by thinkers and literary figures seeking to encapsulate and describe their essence and significance. The comparison of libraries with gardens is especially illuminating and prompts a number of associations. With reference to the biblical account of the origins of humankind in the Garden of Eden, for example, the writer and librarian Jorge Luis Borges (1899–1986) confessed that he had always imagined Paradise as a sort of library, while Giacomo Casanova (1725–1798) compared the time he spent in the Wolfenbüttel library in 1764 with the life of the Blessed.

Gottfried Wilhelm Leibniz (1646–1716; ill. p. 55), who held the post of chief librarian at the court of the prince-elector in Hanover for 40 years and an advisory post at the ducal library in Wolfenbüttel for 25 years, set out in a letter his thoughts on the importance and use of a universal library: "It is the treasury of all the riches of the human mind, to which one resorts for the arts of both peace and war, for the maintenance of the human body, for the knowledge of minerals, plants, animals and the secrets of nature as a whole, for the movements of the stars and for the different regions of the Earth, for civil and military architecture, for embellishments and public facilities, for laws, policing and good government, for ancient and more modern history, for the affairs of princes, for everything beautiful that captivates the human interest, in short for the pleasurable as well as the useful and necessary [...].[2]

Johann Wolfgang von Goethe (1749–1832) offered a description of the essence of large libraries that is both poetic and realistic. Of his visits to Göttingen University library, he wrote: "one feels as in the presence of a great capital, noiselessly yielding its incalculable interest."[3]

The library as Paradise, as Heaven on Earth, as capital from which humankind will profit in the long term and to an ever greater degree, and the library as treasury of the human mind – all these metaphors are reflected in the UNESCO Memory of the World (MoW) programme. Established in 1992 as one of the UNESCO world heritage programmes, the MoW registers valuable holdings of books, manuscripts and other

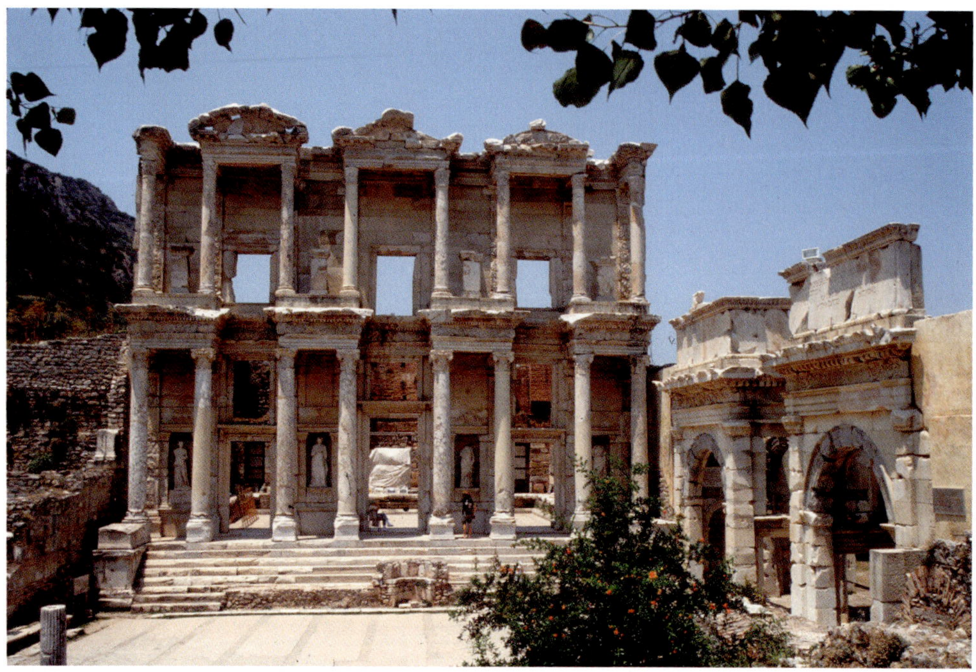

Page 6 Massimo Listri
View into the Strahovská Knihovna, Prague
Blick in die Bibliothek von Strahov
Vue de la bibliothèque de Strahov

Library of Celsus in Ephesus /
Die Celsus-Bibliothek in Ephesus /
La bibliothèque de Celsius à Éphèse,
100–110 AD

documents preserved in libraries, archives and museums which represent the collective
memory of humankind in the various countries. The programme thus exemplifies, in
compact form, the mission and claim of these documentary heritage institutions – and in
particular the libraries – to represent the memory of the world in its totality. At the end of
2015, the MoW Register encompassed 348 documentary items from some 100 countries;
some of these feature in this book in the context of their respective library.

Libraries in history through to the present

The historical and present-day situations of libraries are as diverse as humanity and its
culture. In Europe, the oldest libraries still in existence today date from the Early Middle
Ages, although collections were being assembled in a general manner even before this
period. Collections are defined as libraries when they are housed in rooms marked for this
purpose and for which someone is officially responsible. In this way the Stiftsbibliothek
St Gallen in Switzerland (see pp. 374–383) has existed since the middle of the 8th century,
the Vatican Apostolic library in Rome (see pp. 80–97) since about 800 and the library
of St Peter's Abbey in Salzburg since the middle of the 9th century.

Fourteen hundred years is a short time in the history of humanity, but a long time when measured against the lifespan of an individual. Some 45 generations thus separate us today from the Early Middle Ages, yet only ever three, occasionally four successive generations have had the chance to travel a section of life's path together, to meet each other in person and exchange information directly. For everything that has happened in the more distant past, we must return to written or audiovisual forms of recording and storage. Libraries collect and preserve the knowledge individuals pass on beyond their own lifetime to subsequent generations.

The definition of knowledge and scholarship includes the criterion of unlimitedness. Scholarship knows no national or ethnic borders and no boundaries of religion or language; the bounds of ethics and morality are those it sets for itself. Other limits are imposed upon it only in times of darkness or by inhumane systems.

Just like scholarship, great libraries in principle and ideally recognise no limits – apart from those required by the state, their infrastructure or their specific purpose. Libraries as a whole are a marvel – a marvel because they present, within a relatively small space, the world as it is, as it was and how it (possibly) will be, as well as how it should be and could be. Libraries are repositories of the facts of the real world as well as of the many alternative worlds of the imagination. They thereby preserve the human mind in all its wealth and beauty, its perfection and cruelty, its enlightenment and its darkness. Libraries store in their stacks and storerooms, or on the latest electronic (and in future perhaps also biochemical) data-carriers, the knowledge of God and the world, right and wrong, reality and invention.

Libraries map the minds of many individuals and allow us to sense the intellectual processes of societies and communities, and indeed of humanity as a whole. In our large libraries with their archival function, knowledge is, in principle, stored "for all time". This alone, however, is not enough to make it immediately available: it must be processed and rendered accessible in suitable forms. After knowledge has been created and increased, libraries fulfil a key function by placing this knowledge at our disposal – nowadays by means of a global network. The knowledge accumulated over thousands of years in the past is transmitted in the present so that it can be harnessed for use in the future.

In an age whose storage and communications systems are the largest in the history of humanity, and which continue to grow in orders of magnitude that defy our powers of imagination, in our own age, in other words, libraries as storehouses of memory face enormous challenges. Yet libraries have long since been more than simple repositories of knowledge. They are living centres of intellectual exchange, research, teaching and learning whose doors are firmly open to the world at large. They are places of education and of cultural and scientific transfer within their domain and at the same time open portals to global information. Libraries stand for communication with the past, present and future. Furthermore, libraries were and remain statements of prestige as well as aesthetic and architectural sophistication. These houses of knowledge and its appropriation have inspired secular and spiritual authorities since the Early Modern Era to devote particular attention to their design and décor – as abundantly witnessed by the impressive photographs in this book.

Our own present is no less possessed of this creative urge: "Lately, people all over the world have been building fabulous temples to books", noted the *Frankfurter Allgemeine Sonntagszeitung* in March 2014.[4]

The image of the temple invoked here is another familiar metaphor for libraries. It reflects a feeling of respect and veneration for something more sublime, perhaps not necessarily in the religious or metaphysical sense, but undoubtedly for something that looks beyond the limits of our individual lives. In a veritable declaration of love to libraries, the German physician and entertainer Eckart von Hirschhausen (b. 1967) recently expressed it thus: "We are part of a great work that looks beyond each individual."[5]

And there is something else that people find in the reading-rooms of these book temples: quiet – a quiet that, in the public spaces of our noisy cities, is probably only otherwise found in places of worship outside times of service.

The word "library" comes from the Latin *librarium* and originally meant a bookcase or chest for books. In modern usage it designates a collection of books and media which in most cases does not serve commercial ends and is available either to a restricted circle of users or to the general public for information, study, education and entertainment. The public library service as a whole has to satisfy a vast spectrum of needs, ranging from highly specialised research and scholarship to material for young readers and children of pre-reading age.

The four main tasks which constitute the work of a library have remained fundamentally the same over the millennia – even if many more activities have since clustered around them in the Modern Era. They also apply to the materials involved, be they clay tablets (ill. p. 12), papyri (ill. pp. 14–15), parchments (ill. pp. 20–21), textiles, paper, or electronic or (as we may soon be seeing) biochemical data-carriers. Libraries have firstly to collect information in a planned fashion as texts, images and/or data; secondly, to conserve and protect this information, in whatever form; thirdly, to organise it in such a way that it can be accessed; and fourthly, to make it available and share it.

Ancient Near East and Antiquity

The library system as we have defined it here had its beginnings around 3500 BC, with the emergence of linear script in the advanced civilisations of Mesopotamia, Egypt and China. The development of trade, knowledge and education brought with it the need to preserve sacred and secular writings for posterity, and by the 3rd millennium BC cuneiform clay tablets were already being stored in jars, chests and baskets. Large archives have also been uncovered during excavations at temple sites, and collections of letters and documents relating to business affairs are known from the reign of Hammurabi (1811–1750 BC). It was out of archives such as these that libraries gradually evolved.

The library created by the Assyrian ruler Ashurbanipal (687–627 BC) in his palace in Nineveh is considered the very first to have been assembled in a planned manner and laid out with a view to frequent use. Administrative, medical, as well as religious and literary texts were kept here at the ruler's disposal. Estimated to have contained 28,000 tablets, Ashurbanipal's library also fulfilled – alongside collection and consultation – the third criterion that defines a library, namely organisation. We do not know, however, on what principles this first documented library was organised.

From the wealth of written documents that have been found in tombs, we may also assume the existence of libraries in Ancient Egypt. The Egyptian language had two terms for a library and/or archive,

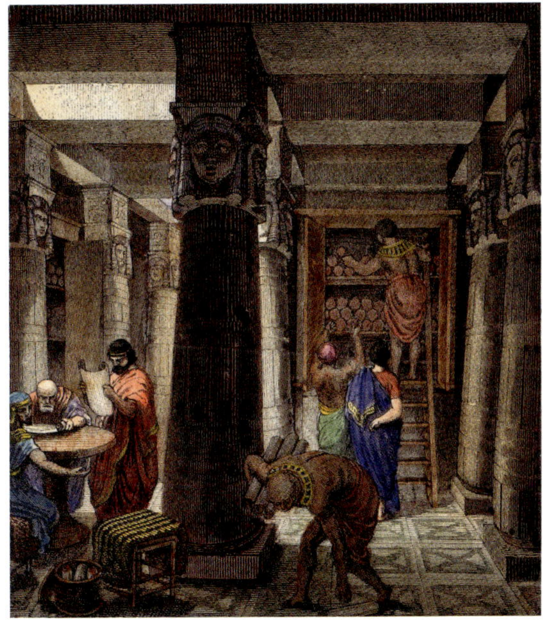

H. Göll, *Hall in the Library of Alexandria / Halle in der alexandrinischen Bibliothek / Hall de la bibliothèque alexandrine*, c. 1880. Coloured woodcut

namely the *House of Books* (also the *House of Books of God*), and the *House of Life*. In the *House of Life*, which was always attached to a temple, scholarly and religious works were compiled, copied and stored. The writings stored in the *House of Books of God* served the practice of the respective cult. Only in the Ptolemaic period (from the 4th century BC) does the term *House of Books* specifically designate a library belonging to a temple.

In a similar fashion to Egypt, libraries in Ancient Greece could be visited in temples or centres of academic study and teaching (gymnasia, academies). Famous private libraries belonging to rulers (Peisistratus) or scholars and authors (Euripides, Aristotle) are also documented.

Through foundations and endowments from Rome's private libraries (ill. p. 8), the creation of public libraries was made possible – the first in 39 BC on the initiative of the Roman statesman Gaius Asinius Pollio (76 BC–5 AD). Core holdings, provided by their founders, were subsequently increased by donations and the copying of borrowed works. Books were arranged and catalogued in systematic order, and as a rule they were accessible to the public in the mornings, but could not be taken out on loan (reference library). Provincial cities were also furnished with sizable libraries. In the decades after the rule of Augustus, a large number of libraries were founded by Rome's emperors. This ancient library tradition was continued in the Byzantine Empire by way of the imperial library

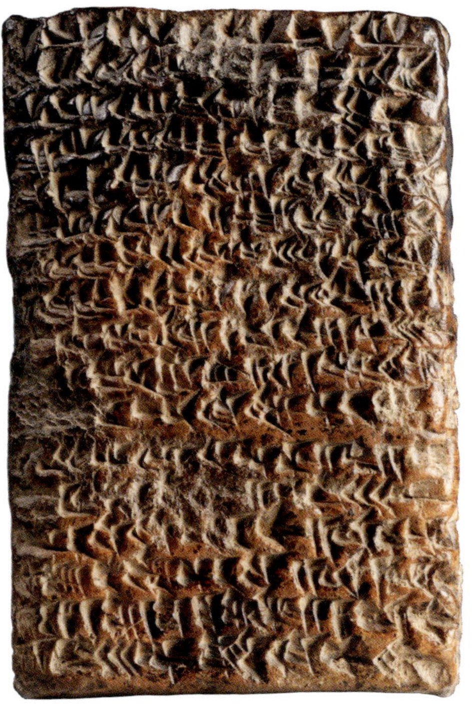

Cuneiform clay tablet / Schreibtafel mit Keilschrift / Tablette en écriture cunéiforme, Babylon,
6–5th century BC, Clay, 7.7 x 5.2 cm / 3 x 2 in.
Berlin, Vorderasiatisches Museum,
Staatliche Museen zu Berlin

founded in 356 AD in Constantinople and only came to an end in 1453 with the city's conquest by the Ottoman Turks.

The largest libraries of Antiquity were established in the Hellenistic period under the Ptolemaic rulers in Alexandria, namely in the Museion, the Alexandrian academic institution, with its 700,000 scrolls (ill. p. 11), and in the Temple of Serapis (the Serapeion), with over 40,000 scrolls. The burning of the Museion library during the war against Caesar in 48/47 BC, the news of which devastated the ancient world, is today considered a legend: it seems more probable that the library was only lost in the 3rd century AD, when the palace quarter was destroyed.

Middle Ages

With the decline of the Roman Empire, the ancient was replaced by the Christian library tradition (ill. p. 17). From the 2nd to the 4th century AD, the codex (the form of book that has prevailed in the Western world ever since; ill. p. 31) steadily replaced the scroll wound around a roller (ill. pp. 14–15). With the consolidation of ecclesiastical power in the 6th century, monasteries became the sole providers of education, with Latin as the language of scholarship (ill. p. 32). In the first monastic library, founded in 540 at Vivarium in southern Italy, the monks were tasked by Cassiodorus (c. 485–580), the former chancellor to the Gothic king Theodoric (451–526), to pursue academic studies and to collect and copy manuscripts. The monastic libraries of Ireland, Scotland and England likewise grew via the production and collection of manuscripts, while missionary activity by Irish and Anglo-Saxon monks in mainland Europe led to the founding of new monasteries and to a flowering of writing, books and libraries, for example, in Luxeuil, Bobbio, Corbie, Echternach and Fulda.

Ecclesiastical education reached a peak under the Carolingians in the 9th century, thanks to the creation of libraries at the imperial court, in bishoprics such as Cologne, Mainz and Würzburg, and above all in the monasteries.

In St Gallen and on Reichenau Island, the abbey libraries flourished together with their scriptoria (writing and copying workshops; ill. p. 28), and so too did the art of illumination. After a period during which many monasteries were plundered and destroyed, libraries and manuscript production along with book illustration saw a fresh upswing under the Ottonians, above all in Regensburg, on Reichenau, in Freising and Hildesheim. In the 11th and 12th centuries, reform efforts, in conjunction with the founding of new monastic orders and the emergence of scholasticism, generated an intellectual momentum – issuing from France – that would also have an impact on libraries.

In the 1200s the relatively homogeneous culture of the Middle Ages began to disintegrate. The establishment of mendicant orders led to a decline in luxury codices in favour of practical manuals for the care of the soul. In the second half of the 13th century, the rise of scholastic teaching and study libraries can be seen as the precursors of modern-day university libraries. Although individual colleges and faculties already held their own collections as early as the 1100s, it was the libraries designed for universities as a whole, such as those in Paris, Oxford, Cambridge, Prague, Heidelberg, Vienna and Erfurt, that proved decisive for the development of the library in the form we know it today.

This future development was determined – initially alongside the Church, but subsequently as the main stimulus – by secular providers of education and culture at the courts and in the cities (ill. p. 37). With the end of the Middle Ages, the monastic and ecclesiastical libraries increasingly declined in significance. Only a few such medieval libraries still survive in their original locations today, many holdings passed into other libraries, such as university libraries or into princely or private collections, or they were lost or their materials reused by bookbinders. This process of the dissolution of monastic libraries reached its climax with secularisation at the start of the 19th century.

Humanism and the Reformation

The age of humanism and the Renaissance (14th to 16th century) consciously drew upon ancient traditions and only to a limited degree upon medieval thinking. In contrast to the Middle Ages, it emphasised the individuality of the person. The scholarly world asserted itself with increasing self-confidence against the Church's claim to intellectual dominance. Thus Ulrich von Hutten (1488–1523) wrote: "Oh century, oh sciences! It is a pleasure to be alive [...]. Studies are blooming, minds are stirring. Barbarism, [...] prepare to be sent packing."[6]

This new intellectual attitude, which looked back into the distant past in order to fashion an entirely different, future-oriented picture of humanity and the world, resulted in Italy first of all in the assembling of large and magnificent private libraries (ill. pp. 58 and 61) such as those of Petrarch (1304–1374), Giovanni Boccaccio (1313–1375), Niccolò Niccoli (1364–1437), Tommaso Parentucelli (1397–1455; later Pope Nicholas V, founder of the Biblioteca Apostolica Vaticana) and Cardinal Basilius Bessarion (1403–1472). Some of these private libraries later evolved into public libraries, such as the Biblioteca Medicea Laurenziana in Florence, the Biblioteca Marciana in Venice (see pp. 98–107) and the above-mentioned Biblioteca Vaticana in Rome (ill. p. 34; see pp. 80–97).

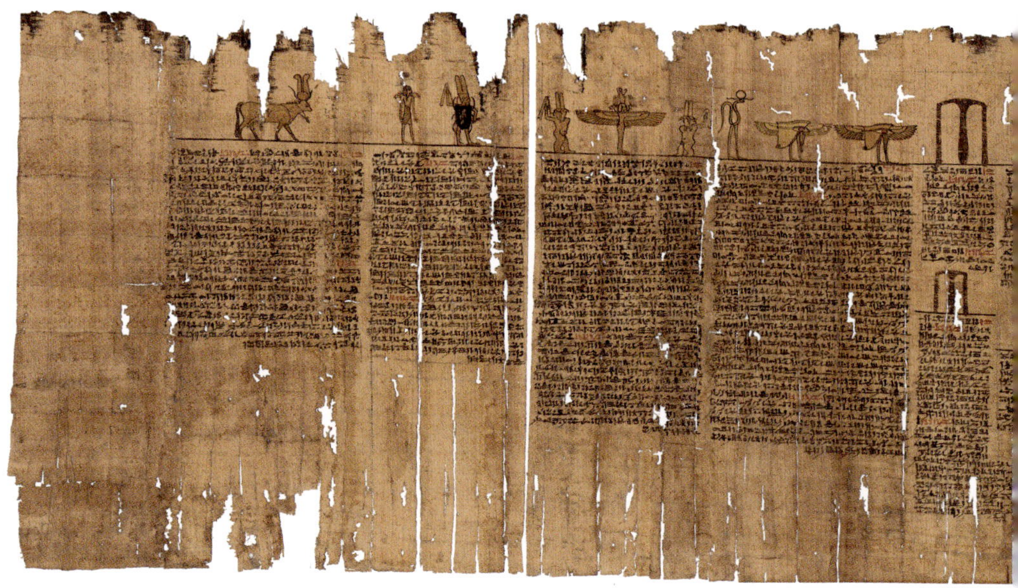

During this period, paper started to replace parchment as the material on which books were written. Above all, however, it was the invention of movable-type printing (ill. p. 42) by Johannes Gutenberg (c. 1400–1468; ill. p. 41) in the mid-1400s which profoundly changed the face of libraries. From about 1500 onwards, the number of printed books overtook the number of manuscript codices in libraries. There was a direct causal link between the rise of book-printing (ill. p. 38) and the spread of the Reformation: without the Reformation, book-printing would probably not have increased at such a rapid pace (ill. p. 45) at this time, just as the extensive and intensive impact of the Reformation is barely conceivable without the vehicle of texts mass-produced at speed.

In his open letter of 1524 addressed "To the Councilmen of All Cities in Germany That They Establish and Maintain Christian Schools", Martin Luther demanded that "no effort or expense should be spared to found good libraries, especially in the larger cities, which can well afford it. [...] This is necessary, not only so that those who are to be our spiritual and temporal leaders may have books to read and study, but that the good books, the arts and the languages that we now have through the grace of God may be preserved and not lost."[7] Reform efforts led to public education, the development of the school system and a new type of library, that of municipal, council and school libraries (as in Nuremberg, Braunschweig, Hanover, Hamburg, Magdeburg and Augsburg, among other places), which in part took over the holdings of monastic and ecclesiastical libraries.

In Catholic areas, Jesuit libraries – such as those in Ingolstadt, Innsbruck, Maria Laach, Münster and Zurich – assumed particular importance. These libraries, like the new university libraries established in the 16th century, presented the bases for religious conflict – the book as spiritual weapon and libraries as arsenals of weaponry.

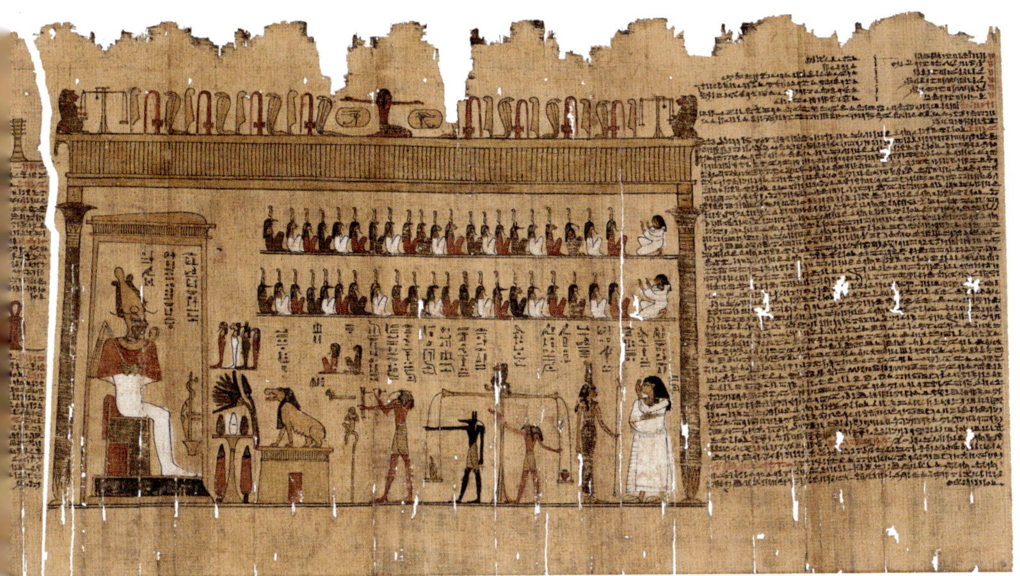

Baroque era

The most important libraries of the 16th and 17th centuries developed out of the collections of books at the courts of the European nobility and were at the same time museums and cabinets of curiosities. The underlying ideas of humanism, various confessional conflicts, but also bibliophile tendencies led to the expansion of the Bibliotheca Palatina in Heidelberg and of the court libraries in Munich and Vienna (see pp. 432–447). One of the most important German libraries founded in the 1600s was that established by Duke Augustus the Younger at Wolfenbüttel. In the following centuries these court libraries, to which only a small number of people were granted access but which could rely on permanent funding by their founders, would become the core of the national, state and regional libraries.

In contrast to the desk libraries that were standard in the Middle Ages, the necessity of housing increasing quantities of books resulted, in the Baroque era, in library halls with wall shelving. The new form of library also corresponded to the Baroque desire for highly visible statements of prestige. Although these well-stocked court libraries were substantially shaped by the interests of their princely owners, they nevertheless served as important resources for research purposes: the sciences, for example, enjoyed a significant rise in the 1600s, also assisted by the academy movement. Model examples of public libraries appeared in Milan (Biblioteca Ambrosiana), Oxford (Bodleian Library) and Paris (Bibliothèque Mazarine, see pp. 274–279), but in comparison with these well-funded libraries, the significance of the university libraries waned.

Book of the Dead of Ta-emetsch-en-Bastet /
Totenbuch der Ta-emetsch-en-Bastet / Livre des
morts de Ta-emetsch-en-Bastet, 332–246 BC

Papyrus, 36.3 x 413.4 cm / 14 ¼ x 162 ¾ in.
Berlin, Ägyptisches Museum und Papyrussammlung,
Staatliche Museen zu Berlin

18th century

Proposals for placing book collecting in libraries on an organised footing, as formulated in the 17th century by Gabriel Naudé (1600–1653) in Paris and Gottfried Wilhelm Leibniz in Hanover and Wolfenbüttel, were partially implemented in the 18th century. For the history of library science internationally, the most important event of this century was the founding of Göttingen University Library, inaugurated in 1735 – two years before the founding of the university itself. In Göttingen the reforms put forward by Leibniz were put into practice for the first time: a fixed budget for the purchase of books, targeted acquisition of the most important academic literature, careful cataloguing, strict procedures governing book movement within the library, convenient daily opening hours, liberal rules of use and the provision of excellent services to scholarship – all of these made Göttingen a model for library development beyond the borders of Germany and Europe.

With the Enlightenment came a shift in attitudes towards education: no longer the domain only of the elite, it was now propagated as a general public asset. One outward sign of this new stance was a weakening in the dominance of Latin as the language of scholarship in favour of the vernacular. The relationship between the demand for reading material and its supply led in the second half of the 18th century to the creation of reading societies and commercial lending libraries, the forerunners of modern public libraries.

One source for our knowledge about Europe's private, ecclesiastical and princely libraries in the 18th century is the travelogue, a new literary genre that developed during this period. Travel accounts were particularly suited to spreading the Enlightenment thinking of their authors, who were usually educated individuals. Some of them used the libraries they visited as a sort of literary salon, in which they met and conversed with prominent local figures.

The libraries sought out by cultural tourists at this time were closer in character to cabinets of artworks and curios than to service facilities. The reason for this was that in addition to the academic interest of scholarly visitors in a library's historical holdings, and in particular its manuscripts and incunabula, other library tourists were more interested in particular curiosities and famous "sights". Thus visitors to the Wolfenbüttel library right up to the 19th century came first and foremost to see a printing error in a Low German Bible of 1731. In the sole surviving copy of the edition, the Sixth Commandment states: "Du solt ehe brechen" ("Thou shalt commit adultery").

When the ecclesiastical libraries were expropriated in the course of the French Revolution and the secularisation of 1803, vast quantities of books passed into state possession from Church principalities and suppressed monasteries, especially in the south of Germany. The Hof- und Staatsbibliothek in Munich profited in particular from this migration of books and became the largest German library of the day, with 500,000 volumes. Many books ended up in paper mills, however, or had their pages recycled as paper bags by shopkeepers. Parchment sheets were used by tailors for patterns and leather bindings as soles for shoes. Two to three million books are thought to have fallen victim to secularisation in this way.

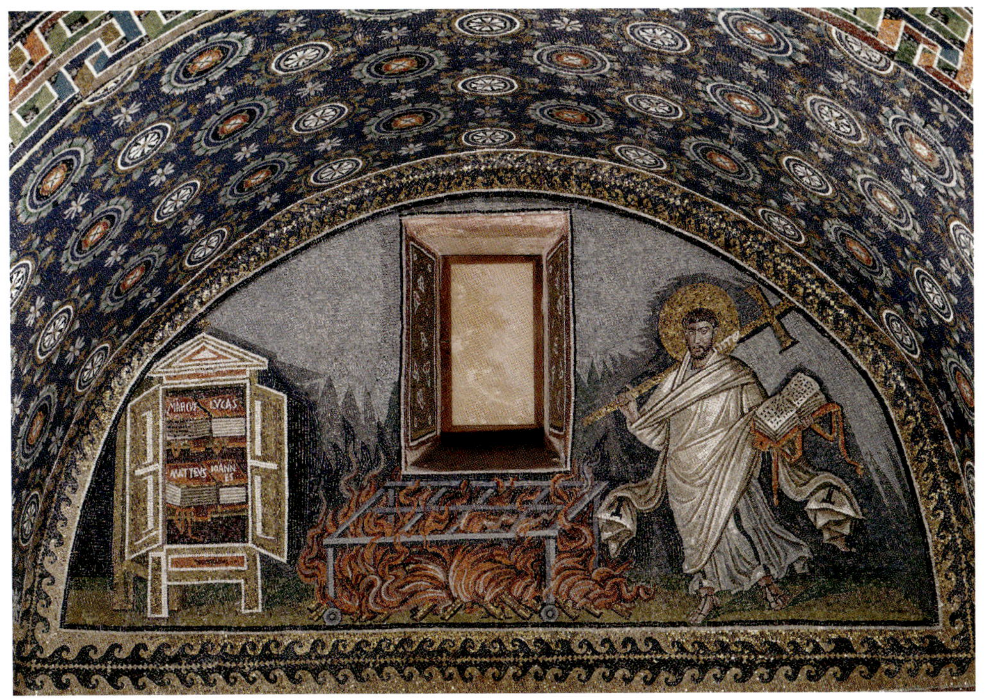

Martyrdom of St Laurence and open bookcase containing the Gospels / Martyrium des Heiligen Laurentius und geöffneter Bücherschrank mit den Evangelien / Martyre de saint Laurent et armoire à livres ouverte montrant les Évangiles, c. 425–430
Mosaic. Ravenna, Mausoleum of Galla Placidia

19th and 20th century

Industrialisation, the rise of the middle classes, the expansion of the sciences and the immense and ongoing increase in book production meant that library holdings in the 19th century were constantly growing. In Washington, Paris and London, national libraries were established in magnificent buildings that brought together the entire national and selected foreign-language literature in one place. Despite certain efforts in 1848, this was not the case in splintered Germany: here, the university libraries gained ever greater importance alongside the state and regional libraries. Increasing specialisation within the sphere of research and scholarship also resulted in the establishment of numerous specialist libraries.

Towards the end of the 19th century many parts of Europe saw the professionalisation of the job of librarian, together with reforms in library staffing and administration and the introduction of supra-regional cataloguing rules. In the Anglo-Saxon and later the Scandinavian countries, forward-looking examples of public libraries were established that served further education, entertainment and information. In the USA, a number of public libraries had already been founded at the start of the 19th century. In the

German-speaking sphere, with its many individual states, such services were at first provided primarily by educational associations and the Churches. The working classes developed their own concept of education, initially socialist in orientation, which in the course of the first half of the 20th century shifted more towards middle-class ideas. From the 19th to the middle of the 20th century, commercial lending libraries also played an initially important, but subsequently dwindling role in the education and entertainment of all strata of society. In Germany, efficient municipally run public libraries were established later than in other European countries.

In the German Empire, Prussia assumed a leading role in the library sphere. Around 1900, the Königliche Bibliothek originally founded in 1659, which was later renamed the Preußische Staatsbibliothek and is today the Staatsbibliothek zu Berlin – Preußischer Kulturbesitz, became the largest library in Germany.

In 1912 the Deutsche Bücherei was founded in Leipzig as an archive library. As in other countries, legal deposit legislation meant that it received a copy of every work published in Germany. After the Second World War, the role of copyright library in the Federal Republic of Germany was assumed by the Deutsche Bibliothek in Frankfurt am Main. Today the Deutsche Nationalbibliothek is represented both in Leipzig and Frankfurt.

The Nationalist Socialist regime imposed changes on Germany's library system as soon as it seized power in 1933. Academic and public libraries alike were affected by racially and politically motivated purges of staff members and by the enforced conformity of professional organisations. The nationwide book burnings of 10 May 1933, when "un-German" books confiscated in particular from public libraries were destroyed in bonfires, will for ever be the most shameful date in German library history (ill. pp. 71 and 73).

Libraries in danger

Libraries have faced dangers for as long as they have existed, whether from war, theft, rodents, microorganisms, water or fire. The destruction – probably apocryphal, as already noted – of the Library of Alexandria by fire in the 1st century BC sent lasting shockwaves through the centuries. In Umberto Eco's 1980 novel *The Name of the Rose* and the film of the same name (1986), this same shock is transported by modern means into our own times.

The fear of fire in libraries, and the preventative steps that were taken to reduce the risk of conflagration, found their way into many of the 18th-century descriptions of library tours mentioned above. In the centuries before electricity, when candles were the sole means of illumination, library windows were built as large as possible in order to let in a maximum amount of daylight. Similar concerns about the risk of fire meant that libraries were also unheated, since open fireplaces were the only form of heating available.

But the fear of fire in libraries is justified even today, despite all our technical safety measures. In September 2004, news of the fire at the Herzogin Anna Amalia library in Weimar was received with horror and dismay in Germany and around the world, but also prompted a wave of assistance. Damage in such cases is caused not just by the flames but also by the measures taken by the fire brigade to put them out. Water is the greatest enemy of library holdings – as damp that leads to the growth of mould, or as rain, damage from flooding, or from the water used to extinguish a blaze.

Many libraries have today put in place, often as part of emergency-management associations also involving other institutions, organisational and technical procedures in the event of their collections becoming saturated with water. These include arrangements with firms having at their disposal large refrigeration chambers, to which saturated library items can be taken in order for them to be shock-frozen prior to treatment at a later date.

Wars and revolutions have likewise always posed a threat to libraries. The earliest Roman libraries were brought back as booty by victorious generals returning from Greece. It was in this way, for example, that the library of Aristotle reached Rome.

Libraries in Germany suffered heavily in the Thirty Years' War as a result of the destruction and

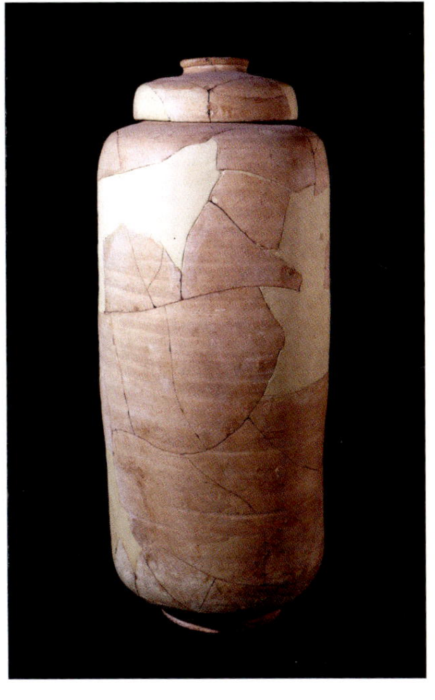

Tall pottery jar used to contain scrolls / Aufbewahrungsgefäß für Schriftrollen / Jarre à manuscrits antiques, Qumran, 1st century AD, Clay, 56 cm / 22 in. London, British Museum

seizure of large and important collections, for example, the forcible removal of the contents of the Heidelberg Bibliotheca Palatina to Rome. The burning of Leuven University Library by German troops in the First World War was perceived worldwide as an act of barbarism; in 1919 an article in the Treaty of Versailles imposed upon Germany the obligation to restore the library.

In Nazi Germany, book theft was committed quite openly and at the same time on a quasi-official basis. The private libraries of Jewish citizens, the majority of whom were murdered with only a few managing to escape into exile, were confiscated and sold or made over to public libraries. The same applied to the libraries of Social Democrat, Communist, trade union, religious, Masonic and other undesirable bodies.

The task of identifying and restituting books that were unlawfully seized between 1933 and 1945, and which are today in the possession of libraries, is still far from complete even in the 2010s. Since 2016 the German Centre for Lost Cultural Property in Magdeburg, the successor to other similar institutions, has been devoting itself internationally to identifying books and works of art that were stolen from German citizens and to restoring them where possible to the lawful heirs of their original owners.

The Second World War left deep scars on many European libraries. Not only the devastation caused directly by the conflict, but also pillaging by the Wehrmacht, SS and individual soldiers led to the destruction or misappropriation of large quantities of books from German-occupied areas. Towards the end of the war and afterwards, library holdings that had been sent for storage to what was then East Germany fell into Soviet hands.

In Germany itself, approximately one-third of pre-war library holdings, including treasures and rarities of the first order, fell victim to the war – in total, some 25 million volumes. Enormous numbers of books have changed owners in this way right up to the present or were destroyed or lost in the chaos of war. The history of the migration of individual books and entire libraries is also a history of the confrontation between power and violence on the one hand, and intellect and culture on the other.

Even without the chaos of war and political oppression, however, libraries have been unashamedly plundered over the course of the centuries, whether out of greed or bibliomania. The holdings of law and theology libraries have always been said to form particular targets for book thieves. While librarians of legal and medical books will confirm this even today, it is no longer as often the case with theological texts.

The fact that some of the most (in)famous book thefts have been attributed to theologians, of all confessions, has perhaps fuelled a prejudice against this professional group. In the 18th century, for example, the later Cardinal Domenico Silvio Passionei (1682–1761; ill. p. 52), a man of great erudition and a passionate bibliophile, assiduously relieved monastic libraries of their treasures. In his position as papal nuncio in Lucerne, he carried out his duty to inspect the Swiss abbeys, and above all their libraries, with great zeal. With the aid of his cassock and an accomplice, strategically positioned beneath the library window to catch the books the nuncio threw out of it, Passionei is alleged to have played a considerable role in reducing the holdings of Swiss monastic libraries. In 1755, Passionei become director of the Vatican library. After his death, his private library of

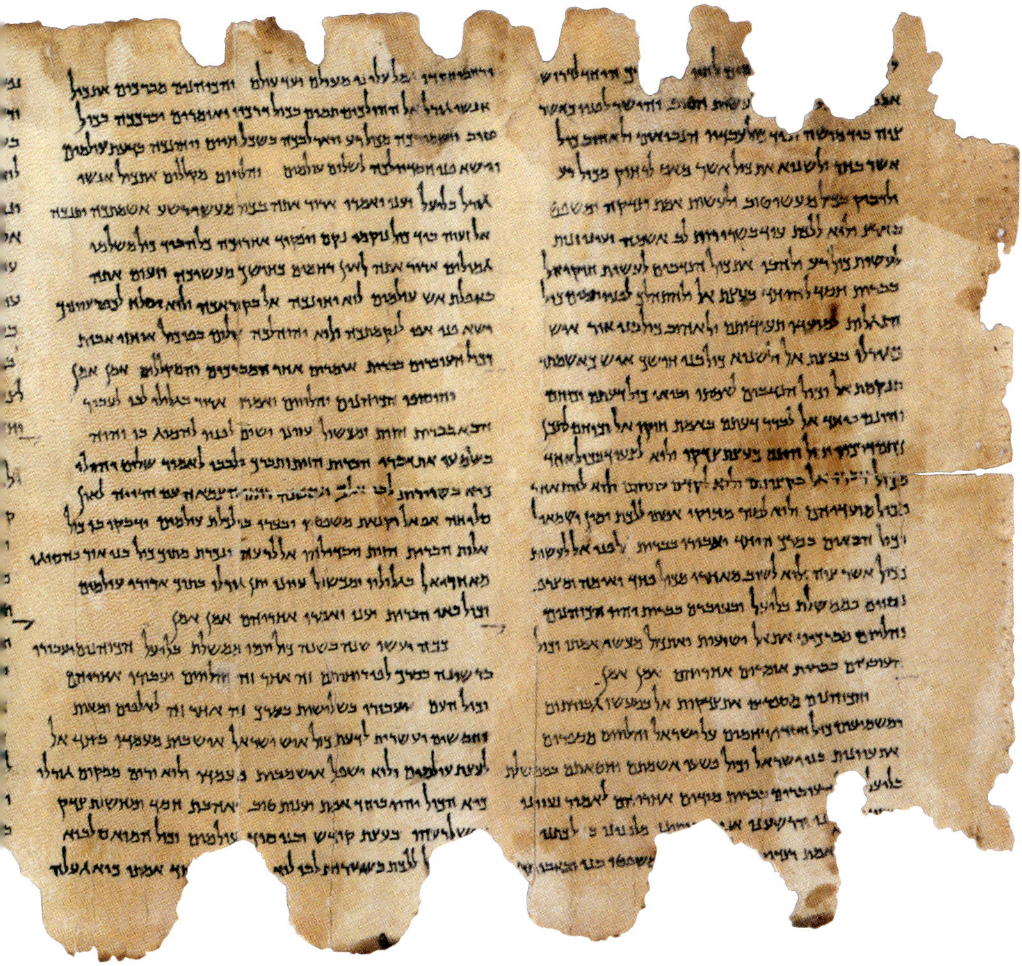

40,000 volumes was purchased by the Pope and made over to the Augustinian Order for the Biblioteca Angelica (see pp. 126–139).

All cases of large-scale thefts from libraries pale, however, in comparison with the greatest "bibliofilou" of all time, Count Guglielmo Brutus Icilius Timeleone Libri Carucci dalla Sommaja (1803–1869). A member of the old Italian aristocracy, he even carried the Latin and Italian word for books (*libri*) in his surname – a legacy from a 14th-century ancestor who adopted it for the purpose of showing himself a booklover. Guglielmo Libri kept the European press as well as many experts, bibliophiles and librarians busy for decades.

Dead Sea Scroll. The Rule of Community / Schriftrolle vom Toten Meer. Sogenannte Gemeinderegel / Rouleau de la mer Morte.

La Règle de la communauté, dit aussi Manuel de discipline, Qumran, 100–75 BC, Vellum, 24 x 250 cm / 9 ½ x 98 ½ in. Jerusalem, The Israel Museum

Born in Florence in 1803, Libri established himself when still a young man as a natural scientist who was known and respected in European academic circles and who corresponded with the leading scholars of his day. At the age of just 20 he was appointed Professor of Physics at the University of Pisa, but after being obliged to leave Italy for political reasons, he subsequently pursued his glittering academic career in France. His four-volume *Histoire des sciences mathématiques en Italie* (1838–1841) remains a standard work even today.

His real passion, however, was building up his private library, which is said eventually to have comprised 40,000 volumes. He also traded on a large scale in autograph and antiquarian books, from which this renowned bibliophile earned considerable sums. Libri's dearest wishes were fulfilled when he was appointed secretary of a commission whose task was to compile and publish a catalogue of all the manuscripts held in French libraries. Libri used his position to appropriate magnificent manuscripts, something made easier by the frequently neglected state of the library catalogues. He erased ownership marks in the volumes he took, making their subsequent identification harder or even impossible.[8] As secretary of the commission, Libri furthermore took the opportunity to efface catalogue entries where these were present. Lastly, he also altered books by giving them new bindings or otherwise disguising them. In 1848, when suspicions of his stealing became so strong that a warrant was issued for his arrest, Libri fled to London with 18 chests of books. Only after much effort did the police succeed in tracking down his library, which had been hidden by his friends. Had Libri remained unchecked for another few months, the scale of his thefts would have equalled that of the confiscations which took place during the French Revolution.

Libri was sentenced in absence to ten years in prison and then to the workhouse and was stripped of all his offices and honorary titles. In England, he managed to sell his collection of stolen books at auctions; his catalogues comprised several thousand items. In France, meanwhile, catalogues were compiled to list the books he had stolen. It was several decades before French libraries were reunited with their most precious holdings. Libri himself squandered his wealth in England and returned penniless to his native Italy one year before his death in 1869.

Books have been stolen for as long as books have existed. Library books today are protected by electronic means. In the past, however, they were quite literally chained to desks as *libri catenati*, or made do with an admonishing inscription on the cover. These so-called "book curses" threatened would-be thieves with the most gruesome worldly and infernal punishments and were intended to discourage them from their potential crime – including that of stealing intellectual property. The modern descendants of the book curse are the copyright notices in books today.

"Habent sua fata libelli" – books have their destiny, and so do libraries too, destinies that are intimately bound up with those of individuals, communities and societies.

Libraries present and future

Some cultural pessimists (or cultural optimists, depending on personal viewpoint) consider that the greatest threat facing libraries since the end of the 20th century – greater even than the most massive thefts or the devastation following upon fire or war – is the IT revolution. But information technology offers immeasurable opportunities for the present and future development of libraries, opportunities that libraries have seized and embraced from an early date.

Individual libraries as well as international and regional library associations guarantee comprehensive access to conventional as well as electronic media and allow research to be conducted and documents to be delivered anywhere in the world. Historical holdings, too, are being made accessible in multiple ways with the aid of the latest data technology and are thus available to a global readership to a degree unknown just a few decades ago. More or less every academic library in the world is now also taking extensive steps to digitise its holdings. Old and new library materials can thus be consulted in principle by everyone everywhere and at any time, even if many copyright issues remain to be resolved in this area. Digitisation is furthermore a means of protecting old and precious holdings, which now only need to be examined in the original in exceptional cases. Equally at risk are the books and journals printed in the 19th and 20th centuries on acidic paper. Libraries are striving to conserve both their contents and their physical fabric by way of modern reproduction and data technologies and through de-acidification.

The resources offered by modern libraries are highly diverse and range from books and manuscripts, computer programs and audiovisual media, to newspapers and magazines, games and access to databases. Libraries provide their users with access – through whatever medium – to research papers, guidebooks, fiction, reference books, specialist literature, picture books and much more besides. Contemporary technologies thereby allow a broad spectrum of individual libraries to connect with each other in a close-knit network, providing common access to local, regional and nationwide collections of information and databases. Separate departments for children and young people, along with music and picture-lending libraries, cater for specific age groups and interests, and special services are also offered to people in hospitals and prisons. Many libraries have thus developed into active centres of the arts and in the case of small communities are often their sole cultural institution. The success of modern libraries, according to the *Frankfurter Allgemeine Sonntagszeitung* in March 2014, lies not in the expansion of their holdings "but primarily in the spaces they offer: reading-rooms, workspaces, group rooms, areas for children and families, newspaper corners and, as in Birmingham, an interior courtyard with table-tennis tables."[9]

Since the 1970s there has been regular talk of the imminent death of the book and hence also of libraries. In many places people were of the opinion that future libraries, if indeed any such were even to exist, would no longer need book stacks. But in many parts of the world in the last few decades, large and architecturally ambitious new libraries have been built and others renovated – and all of them have space for books. They include, for example, the libraries in Alexandria (ill. p. 68), Beijing, Berlin, Cottbus, Delft, Dresden, Hanover, Copenhagen, Leipzig, Osaka, Paris, Stuttgart, Utrecht, Weimar and Zurich.

To a much greater extent than in the older buildings, all of these new libraries offer space for people who want to immerse themselves in their studies or to converse with others (in the corresponding spatial facilities), whether on academic or non-academic matters. Visitors can also seek expert advice from professional librarians on a one-to-one basis – a precious commodity in an age that is increasingly intent on replacing interpersonal contact with technology. Indeed, people have spoken in this context of the "village-well function" performed by libraries. Libraries have long since ceased to be simply lending institutions for books or other media. Today they are cultural and academic centres whose spatial design and technological and logistical systems acknowledge the fact that each one of us is and will remain a *zoon politikon*, that is to say a member of a community. Here the user continues to enjoy access to older as well as to the latest media, and to the virtual worldwide, limitless library. Libraries look back over a long and turbulent past. They shape a present tailored to humankind's needs for information, communication and entertainment, and look ahead to an important role in the future. For humankind – unless it loses its senses entirely – will always want to preserve its Memory of the World.

Notes

1 Stockhausen 1771, pp. IV/V.
2 Heinemann 1894, p. 117.
3 Goethe 1884, p. 245.
4 Kloepfer 2014.
5 *Wir sind Teil eines großen Werkes*, 2015.
6 Hutten 1521.
7 Luther 1962.
8 Willms 1978, p. 107.
9 Kloepfer 2014.

Opposite *Interior view of the Shrine of the Book, in which some of the Qumran scrolls are preserved in a column in the shape of a Torah scroll / Innenansicht des Schreins des Buches, in dem einige der Qumran-Schriftrollen in einer als Torarolle gestalteten Säule aufbewahrt werden / Vue intérieure du Sanctuaire du Livre dans lequel sont conservés plusieurs manuscrits de Qumrân dans une colonne en forme de rouleau de Torah, 1950–1960.* Jerusalem, The Israel Museum

Pages 26–27 Library of the Stiftsbibliothek Kremsmünster, Austria

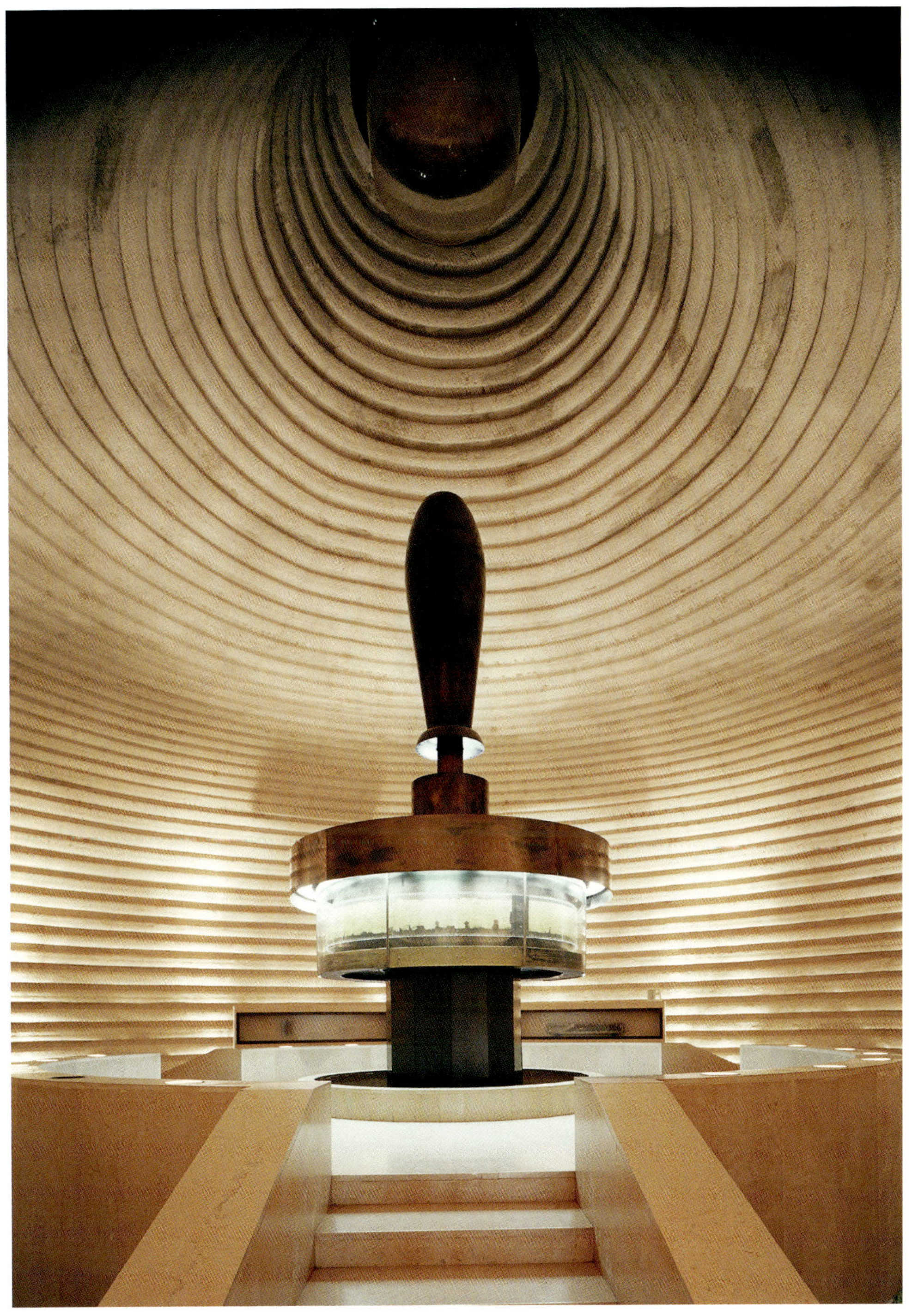

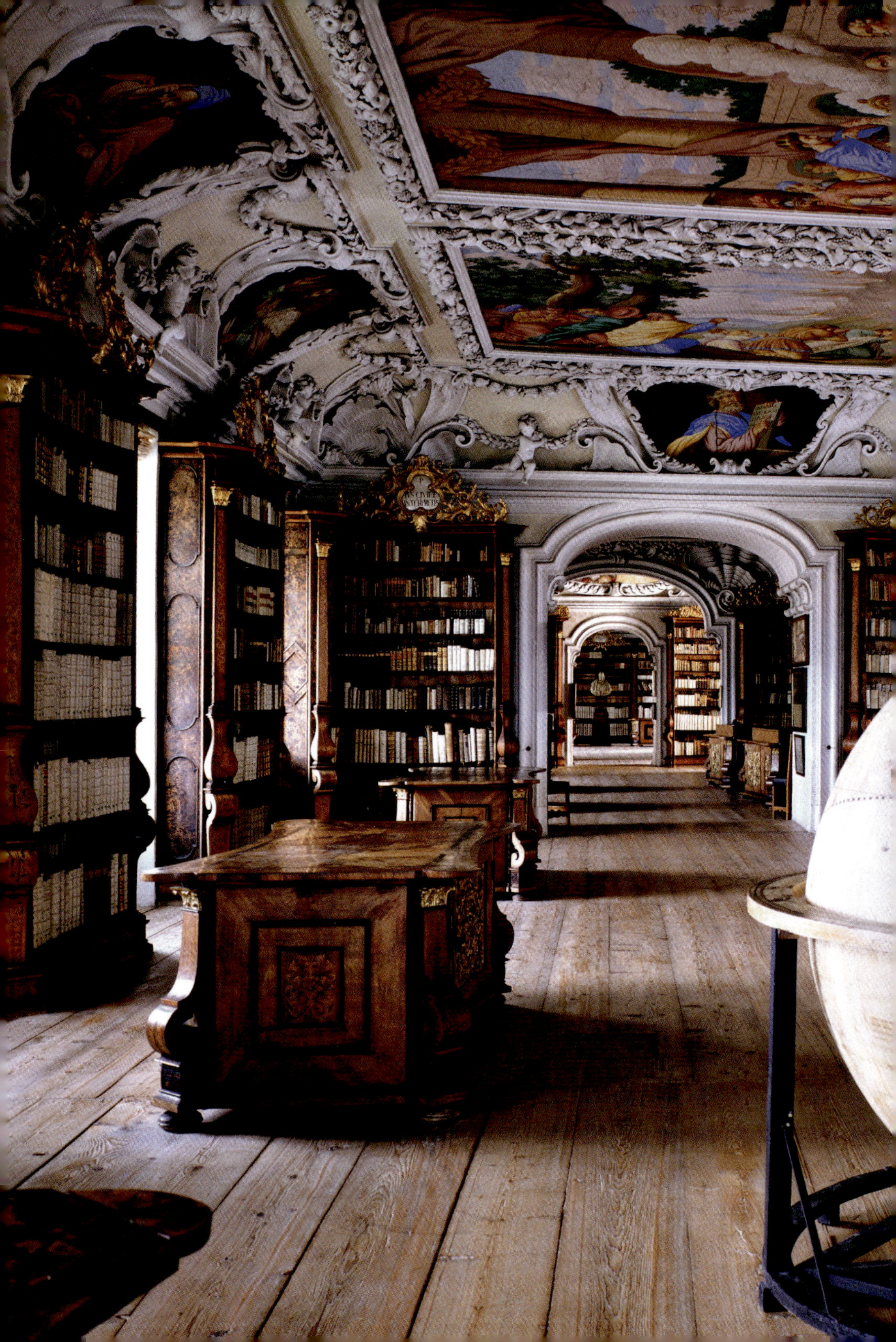

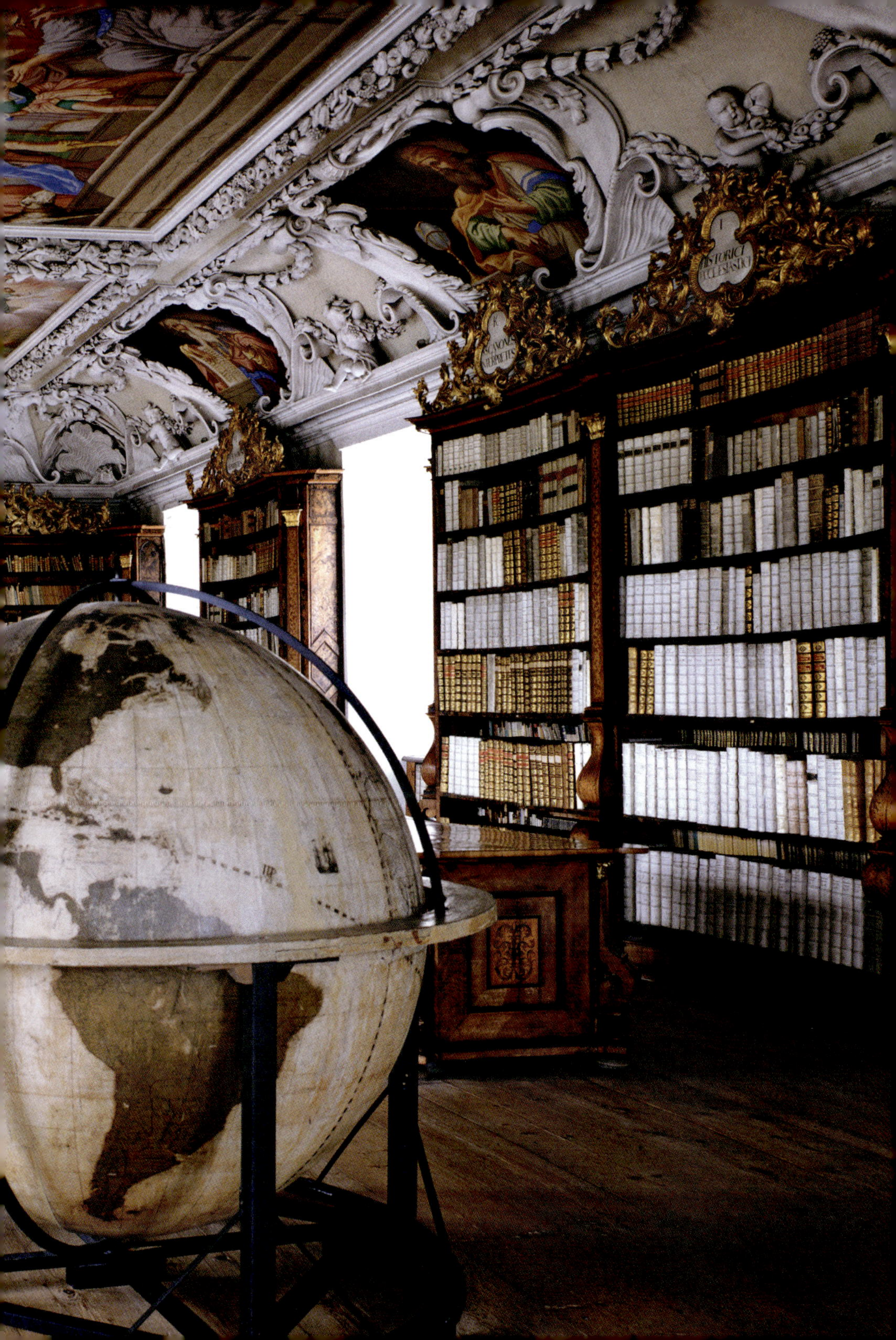

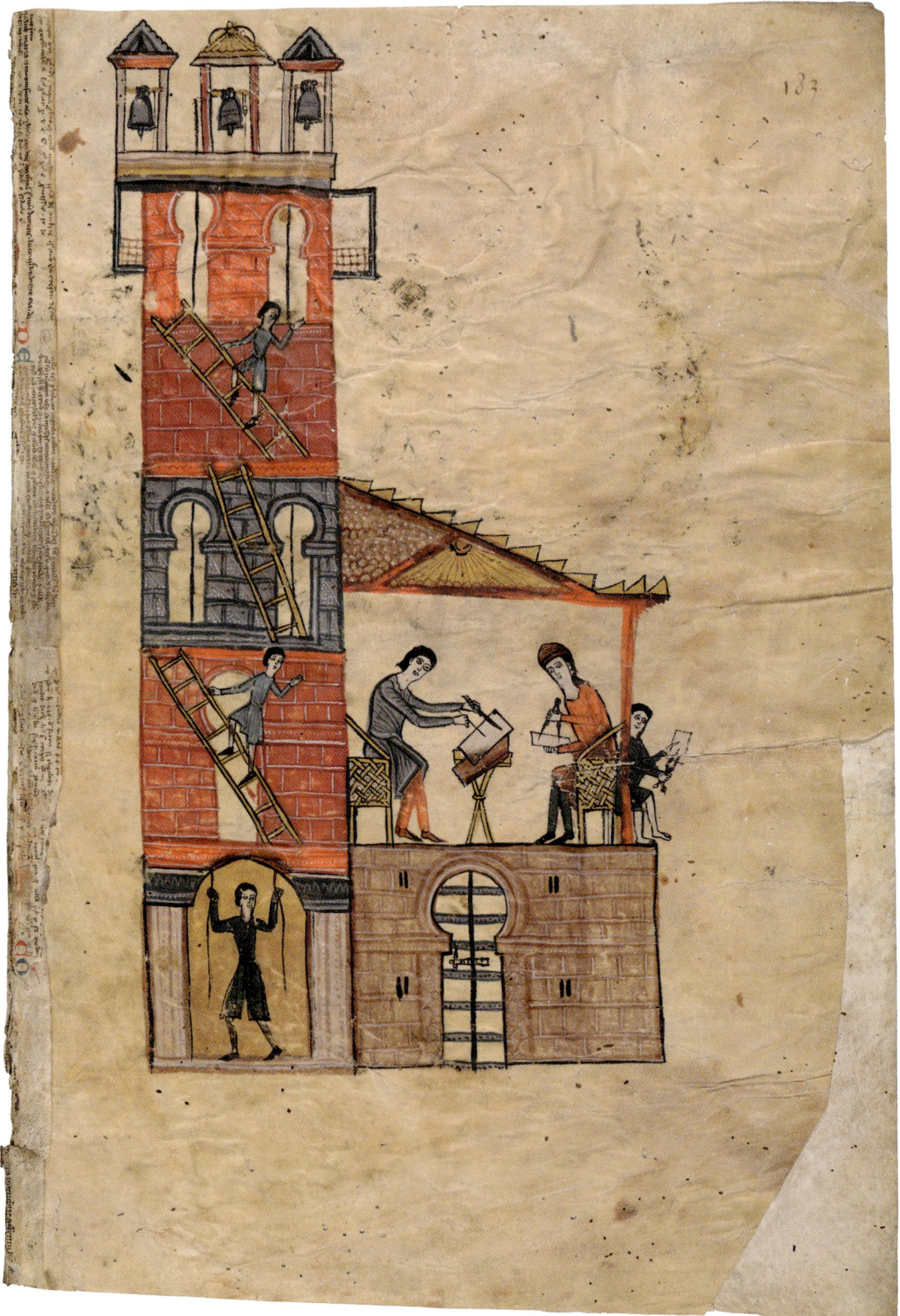

Gedächtnis der Welt

Georg Ruppelt

Bibliotheken sind „wohlangelegte Gärten, wo uns bei jedem Schritte neue Blumen aufsprießen, die die Gegend verschönern und das Vergnügen von sich duften".[1]

Die Metapher von der Bibliothek als Garten, in der zwei der größten Kulturleistungen der Menschheit gleichgesetzt werden, gehört zu den Bildern, mit denen Denker und Literaten das Wesen und die Bedeutung von Bibliotheken erfassen und beschreiben wollten. Der Vergleich von Bibliotheken mit Gärten leuchtet ein und lässt manche Assoziation zu. So liegt etwa der biblische Bericht vom Ursprung der Menschen im Paradiesgarten nahe. Der Schriftsteller und Bibliothekar Jorge Luis Borges (1899–1986) bekannte, dass er sich das Paradies immer als eine Art Bibliothek vorgestellt habe. Mit dem Leben der Seligen verglich Giacomo Casanova (1725–1798) seinen Aufenthalt 1764 in der Wolfenbütteler Bibliothek.

Gottfried Wilhelm Leibniz (1646–1716; Abb. S. 55), der 40 Jahre lang der fürstlichen bzw. kurfürstlichen Bibliothek in Hannover und 25 Jahre im Nebenamt der herzoglichen Bibliothek in Wolfenbüttel vorstand, erläuterte in einem Brief seine Vorstellungen von der Bedeutung und dem Nutzen einer universalen Bibliothek: „Sie ist die Schatzkammer aller Reichtümer des menschlichen Geistes, zu der man seine Zuflucht nimmt für die Künste des Friedens und des Krieges, für die Erhaltung des menschlichen Körpers, für die Kenntnis der Mineralien, Pflanzen, Tiere, überhaupt für die Geheimnisse der Natur, für die Bewegungen der Gestirne, der verschiedenen Regionen der Erde, für bürgerliche und militärische Baukunst, für Verschönerungen und öffentliche Anlagen, für Gesetze, Polizei und gute Staatsordnung, für alte und neuere Geschichte, für die Angelegenheiten der Fürsten, für alles das menschliche Interesse reizende Schöne, kurz für das Angenehme sowohl wie für das Nützliche und Notwendige [...]."[2]

Ebenso poetisch wie realistisch ist die Äußerung Johann Wolfgang Goethes (1749–1832) über das Wesen großer Bibliotheken. Über seinen Aufenthalt in der Göttinger

Beatus of Liébana, *View of the scriptorium tower at Tábara, where parchment sheets are being ruled and trimmed / Blick in den Skriptoriumsturm in Tábara, wo Pergamentseiten liniiert und zugeschnitten werden / Vue du scriptorium du monastère de Tábara où des pages de parchemin étaient lignées et coupées*, Spain, 1220
From: *Codex Las Huelgas*, f. 183
Vellum, 52 x 37 cm / 20 ½ x 14 ½ in.
New York, The Morgan Library & Museum, MS M. 429

Universitätsbibliothek schrieb er: „Man fühlt sich wie in der Gegenwart eines großen Kapitals, das geräuschlos unberechenbare Zinsen spendet."[3]

Die Bibliothek als Paradies, als Himmel auf Erden, als Kapital, von dem die Menschheit auf Dauer und in immer umfangreicherem Maße profitieren werde, und die Bibliothek als Schatzkammer des menschlichen Geistes – all diese Metaphern spiegeln sich im Programm *Memory of the World* (MoW) der UNESCO wider. Das MoW-Programm, das seit 1992 zu den UNESCO-Welterbe-Programmen zählt, listet wertvolle Buchbestände, Handschriften und andere Dokumente aus Bibliotheken, Archiven und Museen auf, die das kollektive Gedächtnis der Menschen in den verschiedenen Ländern repräsentieren. Das Programm bildet damit in kompakter Form den Auftrag und den Anspruch dieser Gedächtniseinrichtungen – und insbesondere auch der Bibliotheken – ab, in ihrer Gesamtheit das Gedächtnis der Welt zu vertreten. 348 eingetragene Dokumente aus rund 100 Staaten umfasste das MoW-Programm Ende 2015; einige von ihnen sind in diesem Buch im Kontext der jeweiligen Bibliothek vertreten.

Bibliotheken in Geschichte und Gegenwart

Die Geschichte und Gegenwart der Bibliotheken sind so vielfältig wie die Menschheit und ihre Kultur. Die ältesten noch existierenden Bibliotheken Europas stammen aus dem frühen Mittelalter, wobei der Beginn einer allgemeinen Sammeltätigkeit schon vorher anzusetzen ist. Als Bibliotheken werden Sammlungen bezeichnet, die über eigene Räume verfügen und für die es einen Verantwortlichen gibt. So bestehen die Stiftsbibliothek St. Gallen in der Schweiz (siehe S. 374–383) seit der Mitte des 8. Jahrhunderts, die Vatikanische Apostolische Bibliothek in Rom (siehe S. 80–97) seit etwa 800 und die Bibliothek der Erzabtei St. Peter in Salzburg seit der Mitte des 9. Jahrhunderts.

14 Jahrhunderte sind eine kurze Zeit in der Menschheitsgeschichte, aber eine lange Zeit gemessen an der Lebensspanne eines Individuums. Etwa 45 Generationen umfassen diese Jahrhunderte seit dem frühen Mittelalter, doch immer nur drei, gelegentlich vier aufeinanderfolgende Generationen hatten die Chance, ein Stück ihres Lebensweges gemeinsam zu gehen, sich zu begegnen und Informationen direkt auszutauschen. Für alles, was sich davor zugetragen hat, muss der Mensch auf schriftliche oder audiovisuelle Aufzeichnung und Speicherung zurückgreifen. Bibliotheken sammeln und bewahren das Wissen, das Menschen über die eigene Lebenszeit hinaus an nachfolgende Generationen weitergeben möchten.

Zur Definition von Wissen und Wissenschaft gehört das Kriterium der Grenzenlosigkeit. Wissenschaft kennt keine nationalen und ethnischen Grenzen, keine Grenzen der Religion und keine der Sprache, und die Grenzen von Ethik und Moral setzt sie sich selbst. Nur in dunklen Zeiten und von inhumanen Systemen werden ihr andere Grenzen gesetzt.

Ebenso wie die Wissenschaft kennen große Bibliotheken im Prinzip und idealerweise keine Grenzen – außer solchen, die ihnen der Etat, die Infrastruktur oder eine Zweckbestimmung setzen. Bibliotheken in ihrer Gesamtheit sind ein Wunder – sie sind ein Wunder,

weil sie auf vergleichsweise kleinem Raum die
Welt abbilden, wie sie ist, wie sie war, wie sie
(möglicherweise) sein wird, aber auch wie sie
sein sollte und wie sie sein könnte. Bibliotheken
sind Speicher für die Tatsachen der realen Welt
ebenso wie für die vielen Alternativwelten der
Fantasie. Sie bewahren dabei den menschlichen
Geist umfassend auf, in all seiner Vielfalt und
Schönheit, in seiner Verkommenheit und Grau-
samkeit, in seinem Licht und seiner Finsternis.
Bibliotheken speichern in ihren Magazinen
und Tresoren oder auf den jeweils neuesten
elektronischen (vielleicht in Zukunft etwa auch
auf biochemischen) Datenträgern das Wissen
um Gott und die Welt, Richtiges und Falsches,
Reales und Erdachtes.

Bibliotheken bilden den Geist vieler Indi-
viduen ab und lassen geistige Prozesse von
einzelnen Gesellschaften sowie Gemeinschaften
oder der ganzen Menschheit erahnen. In unseren großen Bibliotheken mit Archivfunktion
wird Wissen im Prinzip „für die Ewigkeit" ge-
speichert, doch damit allein ist es noch nicht
verfügbar. Es muss in adäquaten Formen auf-
bereitet und zugänglich gemacht werden. Nach
der Wissensschöpfung und Wissensvermehrung
erfüllen Bibliotheken eine Schlüsselfunktion,
indem sie dieses Wissen auch erschließen und

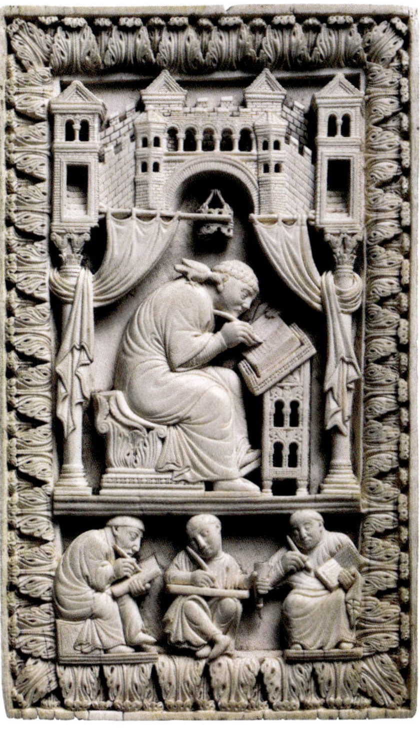

Master of the Vienna Gregory Tablet /
Meister der Wiener Gregorplatte /
Maître de la plaque grégorienne viennoise
*St Gregory and Scribes / Der Heilige Gregor mit
Schreibern / Saint Grégoire et trois scribes*, end
of 10th century, Ivory, 20.5 x 12.5 cm / 8 x 4 ¾ in.
Vienna, Kunsthistorisches Museum,
Kunstkammer

bereitstellen – Letzteres mittlerweile im weltweiten Verbund. Das in Jahrtausenden
akkumulierte Wissen der Vergangenheit wird in der Gegenwart vermittelt und für die
Zukunft nutzbar gemacht.

In einer Zeit, in der die größten Speicher- und Kommunikationsinstrumente der
Menschheitsgeschichte zur Verfügung stehen und in Größenordnungen wachsen, die sich
der Vorstellungskraft entziehen, in unserer Zeit also sind den Bibliotheken als Gedächt-
nisspeicher gewaltige Aufgaben erwachsen. Bibliotheken sind aber seit Langem schon
nicht mehr nur Wissensspeicher. Sie sind lebendige, der Welt zugewandte Stätten des
geistigen Austausches, des Forschens, Lehrens und Lernens. Sie sind Orte der Bildung,
des kulturellen und wissenschaftlichen Transfers in die Region ebenso wie sie weltweit
Portale öffnen zu Informationen. Bibliotheken stehen für die Kommunikation mit Vergangenheit, Gegenwart und Zukunft. Bibliotheken waren und sind darüber hinaus Orte der

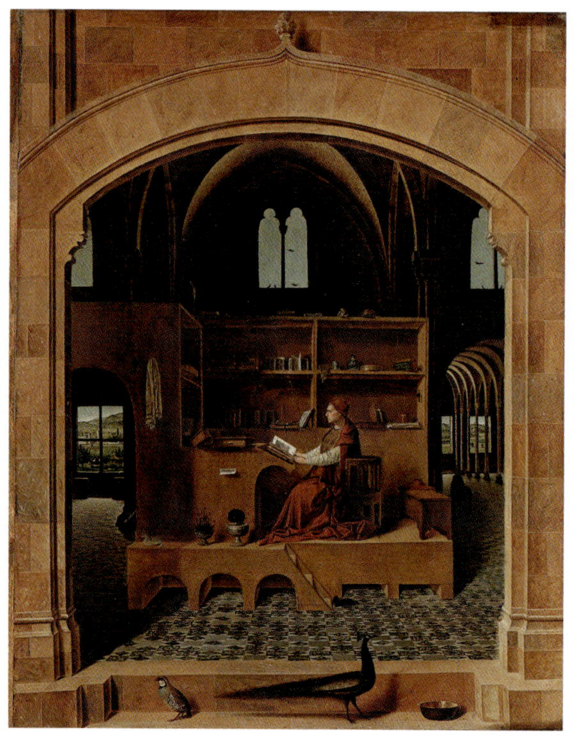

Repräsentation, der Ästhetik und der anspruchsvollen Architektur. Diese Häuser des Wissens und seiner Aneignung haben seit der frühen Neuzeit die weltlichen und geistlichen Mächte bewogen, sie auf besondere Weise gestalten zu lassen. Die eindrucksvollen Bilder des vorliegenden Buches zeigen dies in verschwenderischer Weise.

Unsere Gegenwart ist von diesem Gestaltungswillen nicht ausgenommen. „Überall auf der Welt haben die Menschen den Büchern in jüngster Zeit phantastische Tempel gebaut", hieß es in der *Frankfurter Allgemeinen Sonntagszeitung* im März 2014.[4]

Das Bild vom Tempel, das hier verwandt wird, ist durchaus nicht selten in der Bibliotheksmetaphorik zu finden. Hochachtung, Verehrung für etwas Höheres spiegelt sich darin wider, vielleicht nicht unbedingt im religiös-metaphysischen Sinn, aber durchaus als Blick auf etwas, das über die Grenzen des individuellen Lebens blickt. Der deutsche Arzt, Entertainer und Schriftsteller Eckart von Hirschhausen (geb. 1967) hat es jüngst in einer wahren Liebeserklärung an Bibliotheken so ausgedrückt: „Wir sind Teil eines großen Werkes, das über jeden einzelnen Lesenden hinausweist."[5]

Und noch etwas finden Menschen in den Lesesälen der Büchertempel: Stille – eine Stille, wie man sie sonst in öffentlichen Räumen unserer geräuschvollen Städte wohl nur in Gotteshäusern außerhalb der Gottesdienste antrifft.

Das Wort Bibliothek kommt aus dem Griechischen und meinte ursprünglich eine Bücherkiste für Papyrusrollen. Im heutigen Sprachgebrauch wird damit eine Bücher- und Mediensammlung bezeichnet, die meist nicht kommerziellen Zwecken dient und für Information, Wissenschaft, Bildung und Unterhaltung einem eingeschränkten Benutzerkreis oder der Allgemeinheit zur Verfügung steht. Das öffentliche Bibliothekswesen in seiner Gesamtheit hat die Bedürfnisse hoch spezialisierter Forschung und Wissenschaft ebenso wie die von Kindern im ersten Lese- oder Vorlesealter zu befriedigen.

Die vier Hauptaufgaben, die das Wesen einer Bibliothek ausmachen, sind im Grunde über die Jahrtausende hinweg die gleichen geblieben – mögen sich auch in der Neuzeit

vielfältige andere Tätigkeiten und Aufgaben darum
gruppiert haben. Diese Aufgaben sind unabhängig
von den Materialien, seien es Tontafeln (Abb. S. 12),
Papyri (Abb. S. 14–15), Pergament (Abb. S. 20–21),
Textilien, Papier, elektronische oder vielleicht dem-
nächst auch völlig andere Datenträger. Bibliotheken haben erstens Informationen als Texte, Bilder
oder Daten planvoll zu sammeln; zweitens sie zu
konservieren und zu schützen; drittens sie zu ord-
nen und zu erschließen und viertens sie bereitzu-
stellen und zu vermitteln.

Alter Orient und Antike

Der Beginn dieses so definierten Bibliothekswesens
liegt um 3500 v. Chr., als in den Hochkulturen des
Zweistromlandes, in Ägypten und China die Schrift
ausgebildet wurde. Die Entwicklung des Handels,
des Wissens und der Bildung brachte die Notwendigkeit mit sich, religiöse und profane Niederschrif-
ten für die Nachwelt zu sichern. Keilschriftliche
Tontafeltexte bewahrte man bereits im 3. Jahrtausend v. Chr. in Krügen, Kästen oder Körben auf.

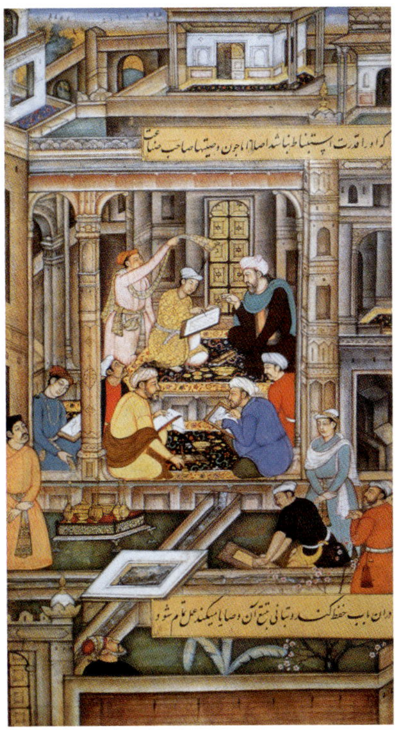

Große Archive fand man auch bei Ausgrabungen von Tempelanlagen; Briefsammlungen
und Geschäftsarchive sind aus der Zeit des Hammurabi (1811–1750 v. Chr.) bekannt. Aus
diesen Archiven entwickelten sich nach und nach Bibliotheken.

Als erste Bibliothek, die planvoll gesammelt und unter dem Gesichtspunkt der
häufigen Benutzung angelegt wurde, gilt die Bibliothek des assyrischen Herrschers
Assurbanipal (687–627 v. Chr.) in seinem Palast in Ninive. In ihr sollten verwaltungstech-
nische und medizinische, aber auch religiöse und literarische Texte für die Herrscher
verfügbar gehalten werden. Die vermutlich 28 000 Tafeln umfassende Bibliothek
Assurbanipals erfüllte – neben Sammlung und Benutzung – auch das dritte Kriterium,
das eine Bibliothek definiert, nämlich die Ordnung. Wir wissen jedoch nicht, nach welchen
Prinzipien die erste nachgewiesene Bibliothek geordnet war.

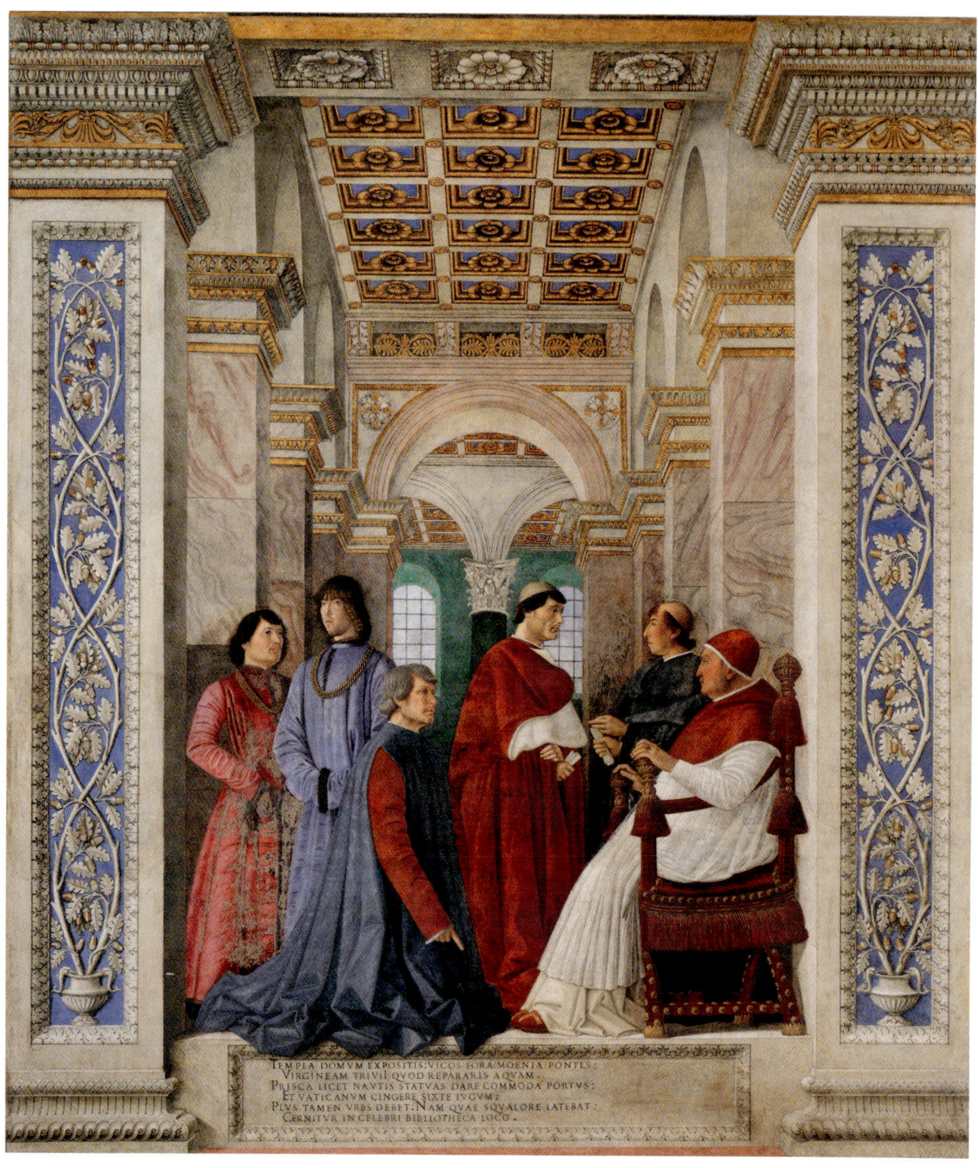

Melozzo da Forlì
*Sixtus IV Appointing Platina as Prefect of the Sistine
Library / Sixtus IV. ernennt Platina zum Präfekten
der vatikanischen Bibliothek / Sixte IV nomme Platina
préfet de la bibliothèque vaticane*, 1476–1481
Fresco, transferred to canvas, 37 x 31.5 cm / 14 ½ x 12 ½ in.
Rome, Vatican City, Pinacoteca

Auch für das alte Ägypten ist die Existenz von Bibliotheken vorauszusetzen; Schrift-
zeugnisse sind in reicher Zahl in Gräbern gefunden worden. Das Ägyptische kannte zwei
Begriffe für Bibliothek und/oder Archiv, nämlich das *Bücherhaus*, auch *Gottes-Bücherhaus*,
und das *Lebenshaus*. Das *Lebenshaus* war immer einem Tempel angegliedert, in dem wis-
senschaftliche und religiöse Werke verfasst, abgeschrieben und gesammelt wurden. Im
Gottes-Bücherhaus wurden die Schriften gesammelt, die der Praktizierung des jeweiligen
Kultes dienten. Erst in ptolemäischer Zeit (ab dem 4. Jahrhundert v. Chr.) bezeichnet
Bücherhaus konkret eine dem jeweiligen Tempel zugehörige Bibliothek.

Im antiken Griechenland standen ähnlich wie in Ägypten Bibliotheken in Tempeln
oder in Stätten zur Verfügung, die der wissenschaftlichen Forschung und Lehre dienten
(Gymnasien, Akademien). Daneben sind berühmte Privatbibliotheken von Herrschern
(Peisistratos) und Gelehrten oder Schriftstellern (Euripides, Aristoteles) bezeugt.

Aus den Privatbibliotheken Roms entstanden durch Stiftung (Abb. S. 8) oder Gründung öffentliche Bibliotheken – die erste 39 v. Chr. auf Veranlassung des römischen Staats-
mannes Gaius Asinius Pollio (76 v. Chr.–5 n. Chr.). Die Stifter stellten einen Grundstock
zur Verfügung, die Bestände wurden durch Schenkungen und Abschreiben geliehener
Exemplare vermehrt. Die Bücher wurden systematisch geordnet aufgestellt und katalogisiert. In der Regel waren sie wohl am Vormittag öffentlich zugänglich, durften aber nicht
ausgeliehen werden (Präsenzbibliothek). Auch Provinzstädte waren mit ansehnlichen
Bibliotheken ausgestattet. Seit Augustus kam es in den folgenden Jahrzehnten zu zahlreichen Bibliotheksgründungen durch die Kaiser. Die antike Bibliothekstradition wurde
im Oströmischen Reich von der 356 n. Chr. gegründeten kaiserlichen Bibliothek in
Konstantinopel fortgeführt und fand ihr Ende erst 1453 durch die Eroberung der Stadt
durch die Türken.

Die größten Bibliotheken des Altertums entstanden in hellenistischer Zeit unter den
ptolemäischen Herrschern in Alexandria (Abb. S. 11), nämlich im Museion, der alexandrinischen Gelehrtenschule, mit 700 000 Buchrollen, und im Serapis-Tempel (Serapeion) mit
über 40 000 Buchrollen. Der Brand der Museionsbibliothek während des Krieges gegen
Caesar 48/47 v. Chr., von dessen Nachricht die antike Welt erschüttert wurde, gilt heute
als Legende. Vielmehr soll die Bibliothek des Museion erst im 3. Jahrhundert n. Chr. bei
der Zerstörung des Palastviertels vernichtet worden sein.

Mittelalter

Mit dem Untergang des Römischen Reiches wurde die antike Bibliothekstradition durch
die christliche abgelöst (Abb. S. 17). Vom 2. bis 4. Jahrhundert n. Chr. setzte sich das Buch
in Form des Kodex (die in der westlichen Welt seitdem vorherrschende Buchform; Abb.
S. 31) gegenüber der um einen Stab gewickelten Buchrolle (Abb. S. 14–15) durch. Mit der
Konsolidierung der kirchlichen Macht im 6. Jahrhundert wurden die Klöster zu alleinigen
Bildungsträgern auf der Grundlage des Lateinischen als Bildungssprache (Abb. S. 32).
In der ersten Klosterbibliothek, die 540 in Vivarium in Süditalien gegründet wurde,

waren die Mönche durch Cassiodorus (um 485–580), vormals Kanzler des Gotenkönigs Theoderich (451–526), zu wissenschaftlichen Studien und zum Sammeln und Abschreiben von Handschriften verpflichtet. Die Klosterbibliotheken in Irland, Schottland und England wuchsen durch diese Handschriftenproduktion und durch das Sammeln dieser Manuskripte. Die Missionierung Mitteleuropas durch irische und angelsächsische Mönche führte auch auf dem Festland zur Gründung von Klöstern und zum Aufblühen des Schrift-, Buch- und Bibliothekswesens, so etwa in Luxeuil, Bobbio, Corbie, Echternach oder Fulda.

Die kirchliche Bildung erreichte im 9. Jahrhundert, zur Zeit der Karolinger, einen Höhepunkt durch das Entstehen von Bibliotheken am Kaiserhof, in Bischofssitzen, wie zum Beispiel in Köln, Mainz oder Würzburg, und vor allem in den Klöstern.

In St. Gallen und auf der Reichenau gelangten die Bibliotheken wie die Skriptorien (Schreibwerkstätten; Abb. S. 28) und damit die Buchkunst zur Blüte. Nach einer Zeit, in der zahlreiche Klöster geplündert und zerstört wurden, erfuhren unter den Ottonen die Bibliotheken und die Handschriftenproduktion sowie die Buchmalerei einen neuen Aufschwung vor allem in Regensburg, auf der Reichenau, in Freising und Hildesheim. Im 11. und 12. Jahrhundert gingen durch Reformbestrebungen, die Gründung neuer Mönchsorden sowie die Herausbildung der Scholastik geistige Impulse von Frankreich aus, die auch Auswirkungen auf das Bibliothekswesen hatten.

Im 13. Jahrhundert begann sich die relativ einheitliche mittelalterliche Kultur aufzulösen. Die Entstehung der Bettelorden bewirkte einen Rückgang der Prachthandschriften zugunsten der für die Seelsorge notwendigen Gebrauchshandschriften. In der zweiten Hälfte des 13. Jahrhunderts entstanden als Vorläufer der heutigen Universitätsbibliotheken scholastische Lehr- und Studienbibliotheken. Einzelne Kollegien und Fakultäten besaßen bereits im 12. Jahrhundert eigene Sammlungen, aber erst die für die Gesamtuniversitäten angelegten Bibliotheken, wie zum Beispiel in Paris, Oxford, Cambridge, Prag, Heidelberg, Wien oder Erfurt, wurden für die Entwicklung des Bibliothekswesens bis zur Gegenwart entscheidend.

Die säkularen Bildungs- und Kulturträger an den Höfen und in den Städten (Abb. S. 37) bestimmten zunächst neben der Kirche, dann aber hauptsächlich die zukünftige Entwicklung des Bibliothekswesens. Mit dem Ende des Mittelalters verloren schließlich die mittelalterlichen Kloster- und Kirchenbibliotheken zunehmend ihre Bedeutung. Heute sind nur noch wenige Kloster- und Kirchenbibliotheken am alten Ort erhalten. Ihre Bestände gelangten in andere Bibliotheken, etwa in Universitätsbibliotheken, oder in fürstliche oder private Sammlungen; sie gingen verloren oder wurden als Material für Buchbinder verbraucht. Dieser Auflösungsprozess der Klosterbibliotheken erreicht seinen Höhepunkt in der Säkularisation Anfang des 19. Jahrhunderts.

Humanismus und Reformation

Das Zeitalter des Humanismus und der Renaissance (14. bis 16. Jahrhundert) griff bewusst
auf antike Traditionen und nur wenig auf die
mittelalterliche Geisteswelt zurück. Anders
als im Mittelalter wurde die Individualität
des Menschen betont. Die Gelehrtenwelt trat
zunehmend selbstbewusst gegenüber dem
geistigen Führungsanspruch der Kirche auf.
So schrieb Ulrich von Hutten (1488–1523):
„O Jahrhundert, o Wissenschaften! Es ist eine
Lust zu leben [...]. Die Studien blühen, die Geister regen sich. Barbarei, nimm dir einen Strick
und mache dich auf Verbannung gefasst."[6]

Diese neue Geisteshaltung, die auf der einen
Seite weit in die Geschichte zurückgriff, um auf
der anderen Seite ein völlig anderes, zukunfts-
orientiertes Menschen- und Weltbild zu ent-
werfen, führte zunächst in Italien zum Aufbau
großer und kostbarer Privatbibliotheken
(Abb. S. 58 und 61), etwa der von Francesco
Petrarca (1304–1374), Giovanni Boccaccio
(1313–1375), Niccolò Niccoli (1364–1437),
Tommaso Parentucelli (1397–1455; später
Papst Nikolaus V., Begründer der Biblioteca
Apostolica Vaticana) und Kardinal Basilius
Bessarion (1403–1472). Aus einigen dieser
Privatbibliotheken entwickelten sich später
öffentliche Bibliotheken, wie die Biblioteca
Medicea Laurenziana in Florenz, die Biblioteca Marciana in Venedig (siehe S. 98–107) oder
die schon genannte Biblioteca Vaticana in Rom (Abb. S. 34; siehe S. 80–97).

In dieser Zeit begann das Papier das Pergament als Beschreibstoff für Bücher abzu-
lösen; vor allem veränderte aber die Erfindung des Buchdruckes (Abb. S. 42) mit bewegli-
chen Lettern um die Mitte des 15. Jahrhunderts das Bild der Bibliotheken entscheidend.
Seit etwa 1500 überstieg die Menge der gedruckten Bücher die der Handschriften in
Bibliotheken. Johannes Gutenbergs (um 1400–1468) Erfindung (Abb. S. 41) und die Verbreitung des Buchdruckes (Abb. S. 38) standen in unmittelbarem Kausalzusammenhang
zur Ausbreitung der Reformation. Kurz gesagt: Ohne die Reformation hätte sich der
Buchdruck wohl nicht in solcher für jenes Jahrhundert rasanten Geschwindigkeit (Abb.
S. 45) ausbreiten können – auf der anderen Seite ist die extensive wie intensive Wirkung

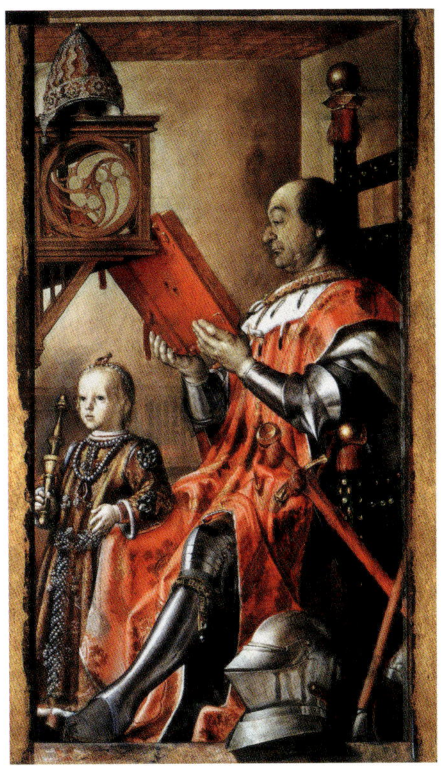

Pedro Berruguete
*Federico da Montefeltro and his Son Guidobaldo /
Federico da Montefeltro mit seinem Sohn
Guidobaldo / Portrait de Federico da Montefeltro
et son fils Guidobaldo*, c. 1476/77
Oil on panel, 138.5 x 82.5 cm / 54 ½ x 32 ½ in.
Urbino, Palazzo Ducale, Galleria Nazionale
delle Marche

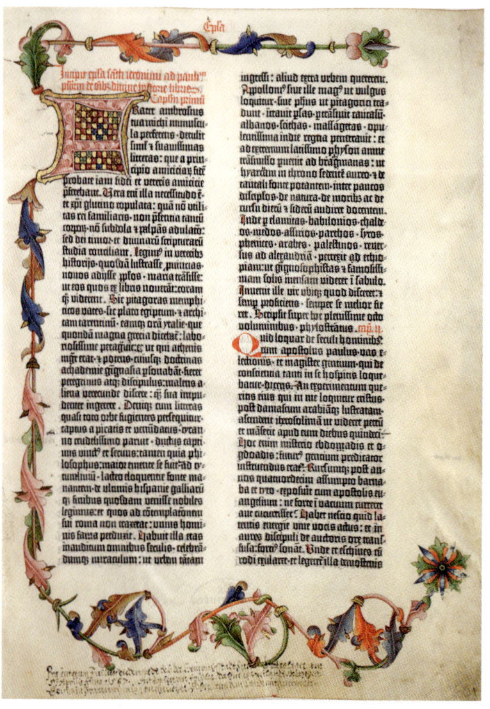

Johannes Gutenberg
*Start of the Book of Genesis / Beginn des
Buches Genesis / Début du Livre de la Genèse*,
c. 1454, vol. I, fol. 1r
Vellum, 40.1 x 29.4 cm / 15 ¾ x 11 ½ in.
Göttingen, Niedersächsische Staats-
und Universitätsbibliothek

der Reformation ohne die Möglichkeit der raschen Massenproduktion von Texten kaum vorstellbar.

Martin Luther forderte 1524 in seiner Sendschrift „An die Ratsherren aller Städte deutsches Lands, daß sie christliche Schulen aufrichten und halten sollen", „daß man Fleiß und Kosten nicht spare, gute Libereien oder Bücherhäuser, besonders in den großen Städten, die solches gut vermögen, zu verschaffen. [...] Und das nicht nur aus dem Grund deswegen, daß diejenigen, die uns geistlich und weltlich vorstehen sollen, zu lesen und studieren haben, sondern daß auch die guten Bücher behalten und nicht verloren werden mitsamt der Kunst und Sprache, die wir jetzt von Gottes Gnaden haben."[7] Die reformatorischen Bemühungen führten zu Laienbildung, Entwicklung des Schulwesens und zu einem neuen Bibliothekstyp, den der Stadt-, Rats- und Schulbibliotheken (wie in Nürnberg, Braunschweig, Hannover, Hamburg, Magdeburg, Augsburg unter anderen), die zum Teil die Bestände von Kloster- und Kirchenbibliotheken übernahmen.

In den katholischen Gebieten gewannen Jesuitenbibliotheken, wie in Ingolstadt, Innsbruck, Maria Laach, Münster und Zürich, besondere Bedeutung. Diese Bibliotheken wie auch die im 16. Jahrhundert gegründeten neuen Universitätsbibliotheken boten die Grundlagen für die religiöse Auseinandersetzung – das Buch als geistige Waffe, die Bibliotheken als Waffenarsenale.

Barock

Im 16. und 17. Jahrhundert entwickelten sich die fürstlichen Büchersammlungen zu den wichtigsten Bibliotheken; sie waren zugleich auch Museen und Kuriositätenkabinette. Die Ideen des Humanismus, konfessionelle Auseinandersetzungen, aber auch bibliophile Neigungen führten zum Ausbau der Bibliotheca Palatina in Heidelberg sowie der Hofbibliotheken in München und Wien (siehe S. 432–447). Als eine der bedeutendsten deutschen Bibliothek ist für das 17. Jahrhundert die von Herzog August dem Jüngeren gegründete

Wolfenbütteler Bibliothek zu nennen. Aus den nur eingeschränkt zugänglichen fürst-
lichen Bibliotheken, die aber auf eine dauerhafte finanzielle Ausstattung durch ihre
Gründer zurückgreifen konnten, gingen in den folgenden Jahrhunderten die National-,
Staats- und Landesbibliotheken hervor.

Während im Mittelalter Pultbibliotheken üblich waren, ließ die Notwendigkeit, die
wachsenden Büchermengen unterzubringen, nun Saalbibliotheken (Wandregalbiblio-
theken) entstehen. Die neue Form der Bibliotheken entsprach überdies dem barocken
Repräsentationsbedürfnis. Obwohl diese gut ausgestatteten Hofbibliotheken stark von
den Interessen der fürstlichen Eigentümer abhängig waren, wurden sie für Forschungs-
zwecke benötigt: Die Wissenschaften erfuhren etwa auch durch die Akademiebewegung
im 17. Jahrhundert einen bedeutsamen Aufschwung. Vorbildliche öffentliche Bibliotheken
entwickelten sich in Mailand (Biblioteca Ambrosiana), Oxford (Bodleian Library) und
Paris (Bibliothèque Mazarine, siehe S. 274–279); gegenüber diesen gut geförderten Bibliotheken trat die Bedeutung der Universitätsbibliotheken zurück.

18. Jahrhundert

Im 18. Jahrhundert wurden die Forderungen nach organisiertem Büchersammeln in Bibliotheken, wie sie im 17. Jahrhundert Gabriel Naudé (1600–1653) in Paris und Gottfried
Wilhelm Leibniz in Hannover und Wolfenbüttel formuliert hatten, teilweise realisiert. Das
bedeutendste Ereignis für die Geschichte des internationalen Bibliothekswesens stellt
im 18. Jahrhundert die Gründung der Universitätsbibliothek Göttingen dar, die 1735 ihren
Betrieb aufnahm – zwei Jahre vor Gründung der Universität selbst. In Göttingen wurden
die Reformideen von Leibniz zum ersten Mal konsequent verwirklicht: ein fester Etat
zum Erwerb von Büchern, gezielte Anschaffung der wichtigsten wissenschaftlichen Literatur, sorgfältige Katalogisierung, ein geregelter Gang des Buches durch die Bibliothek,
günstige tägliche Öffnungszeiten, eine liberale Benutzungsordnung und hervorragende
Dienstleistungen für die Wissenschaft – dies alles ließ Göttingen zum Vorbild für die
Bibliotheksentwicklung über die Grenzen Deutschlands und Europas hinaus werden.

Im Zuge der Aufklärung löste sich die Bildungsidee von den Eliten und wurde als Gut
für die Allgemeinheit propagiert; äußeres Zeichen war die schwindende Dominanz der
lateinischen Sprache in der Wissenschaft zugunsten der Nationalsprachen. Die Wechselwirkung zwischen Lesebedürfnis und Leseangebot führte in der zweiten Hälfte des
18. Jahrhunderts zum Entstehen von Lesegesellschaften und gewerblichen Leihbüchereien, den Vorläufern der späteren Volksbüchereien oder öffentlichen Bibliotheken.

Über den Zustand europäischer Privat- wie kirchlicher oder fürstlicher Bibliotheken
im 18. Jahrhundert werden wir durch eine in jener Zeit sich entwickelnde neue Literatur-
gattung informiert, den Reisebericht. Die Reisebeschreibung eignete sich besonders
für die Verbreitung aufklärerischen Gedankengutes der meist gelehrten Reisenden.
Einige nutzten die besuchte Bibliothek als eine Art literarischen Salon, in dem man mit
den Honoratioren des Ortes zusammentraf und sich unterhielt.

Die von Bildungstouristen aufgesuchten Bibliotheken hatten in dieser Zeit eher den Charakter einer Kunst- oder Wunderkammer als den einer Serviceeinrichtung. Denn neben dem wissenschaftlichen Interesse gelehrter Reisender an historischen Bibliotheksbeständen, insbesondere an Handschriften und Inkunabeln, gab es auch Bibliothekstouristen, die an Sehenswürdigkeiten und Curiosa in den Bibliotheken interessiert waren. So wollten Besucher der Wolfenbütteler Bibliothek bis in das 19. Jahrhundert vor allem einen Druckfehler in einer niederdeutschen Bibel von 1731 sehen. In dem einzig erhaltenen Exemplar des Druckes lautet das sechste Gebot: „Du solt ehe brechen".

Als die kirchlichen Bibliotheken im Zuge der Französischen Revolution und der Säkularisation von 1803 enteignet wurden, kamen besonders in Süddeutschland gewaltige Büchermengen aus den geistlichen Fürstentümern und aufgehobenen Klöstern in staatliches Eigentum. Vor allem die Hof- und Staatsbibliothek München profitierte von dieser Büchermigration und wurde mit 500 000 Bänden die größte deutsche Bibliothek jener Zeit. Viele Bücher allerdings landeten in Papiermühlen, aus anderen machten Krämer Tüten, Pergamentblätter wurden von Schneidern für Schnittmuster, Ledereinbände zum Anfertigen von Schuhsohlen verwandt. Zwei bis drei Millionen Bücher sollen auf diese Weise der Säkularisation zum Opfer gefallen sein.

19. und 20. Jahrhundert

Die Industrialisierung, der Aufstieg des Bürgertums, die Expansion der Wissenschaften und die immens ansteigende Bücherproduktion führten im 19. Jahrhundert zu einer stetigen Bestandserweiterung der Bibliotheken. In Washington, Paris und London entstanden Nationalbibliotheken in repräsentativen Bauten, die das gesamte nationale und ausgewähltes fremdsprachiges Schrifttum an einem Ort des Landes verfügbar machten; im zersplitterten Deutschland gelang dies trotz einiger Bemühungen im Jahre 1848 nicht. Hier gewannen die Universitätsbibliotheken neben den Staats- und Landesbibliotheken immer größere Bedeutung. Zu diesen gesellten sich, bedingt durch die Spezialisierung in Forschung und Wissenschaft, zahlreiche Spezialbibliotheken.

Gegen Ende des 19. Jahrhunderts kam es in vielen Ländern Europas zur Professionalisierung des bibliothekarischen Berufsstandes, zu Personal- und Verwaltungsreformen und zu überregional gültigen Katalogisierungsregeln. In den angelsächsischen und später auch in den skandinavischen Ländern wurden Public Libraries mit Vorbildcharakter gegründet, die der Fortbildung, Unterhaltung und Information dienten. In den USA war bereits zu Anfang des 19. Jahrhunderts eine Vielzahl von Public Libraries etabliert. Im deutschen Sprachraum mit seinen zahlreichen Einzelstaaten wurden diese Aufgaben zunächst vor allem von Bildungsvereinen und den Kirchen übernommen. Die Arbeiterschaft entwickelte einen eigenen Bildungsbegriff, der, zunächst sozialistisch orientiert, sich im Laufe der ersten Hälfte des 20. Jahrhunderts den bürgerlichen Ideen annäherte. Eine zunächst bedeutsame, dann zunehmend weniger wichtige Rolle für Bildung und Unterhaltung aller Bevölkerungsschichten spielten vom 19. bis in die Mitte des

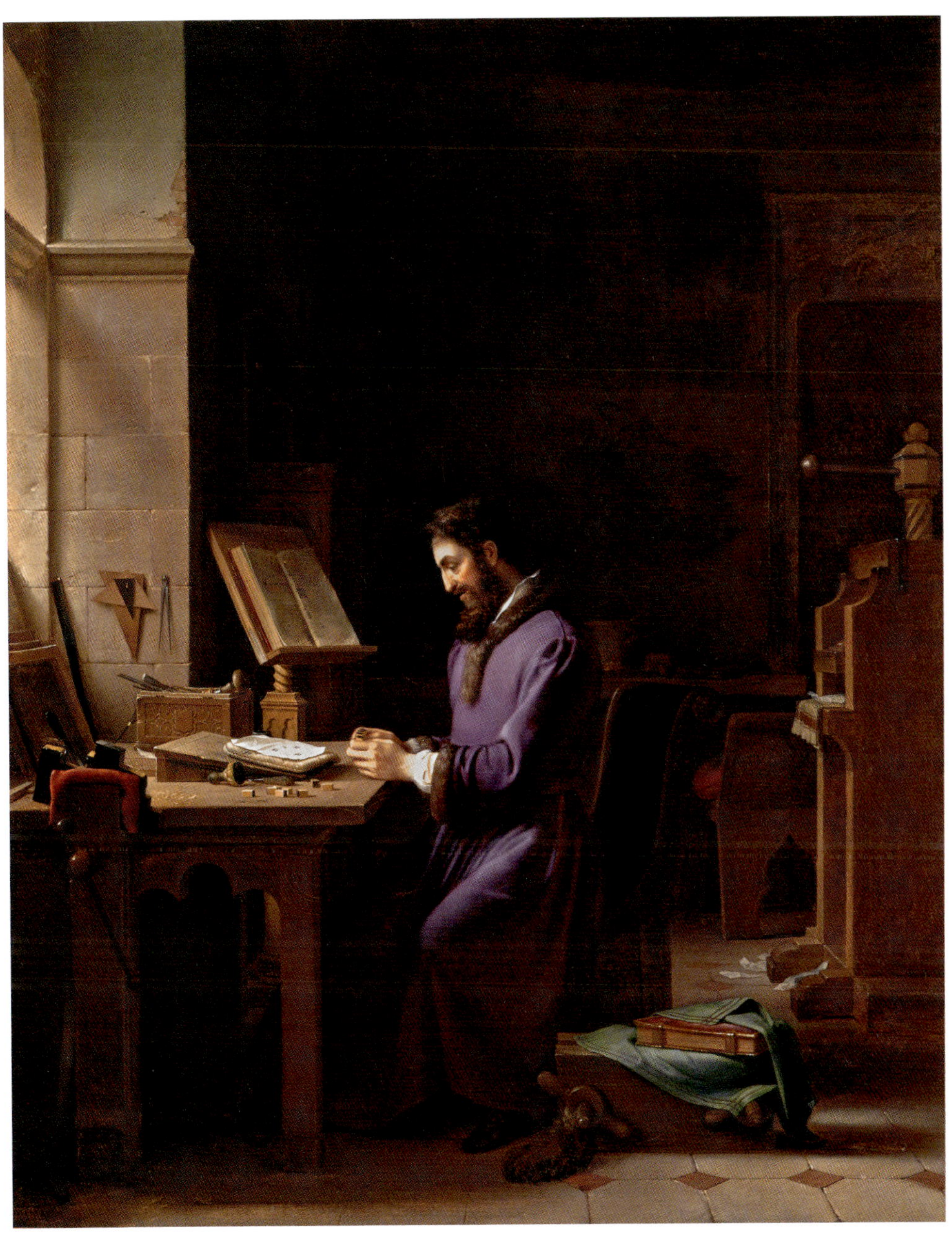

Jean-Antoine Laurent
Gutenberg Inventing the Printing Press /
Gutenberg bei der Erfindung des Buchdrucks /

Gutenberg inventant l'imprimerie, c. 1830
Oil on canvas, 98 x 79 cm / 38 ½ x 31 in.
Grenoble, Musée de Grenoble

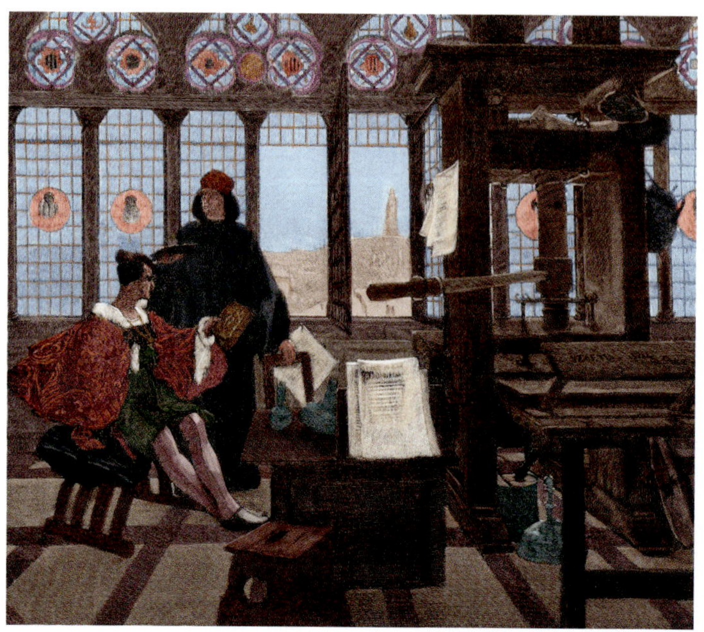

20. Jahrhunderts auch gewerbliche Leihbüchereien. Leistungsfähige öffentliche Bibliotheken in kommunaler Trägerschaft entstanden in Deutschland später als in anderen europäischen Ländern.

Im Deutschen Reich übernahm Preußen eine Leitfunktion im Bibliothekswesen. Die 1659 gegründete Königliche Bibliothek (später Preußische Staatsbibliothek, heute Staatsbibliothek zu Berlin – Preußischer Kulturbesitz) wurde um 1900 zur größten deutschen Bibliothek.

1912 wurde die Deutsche Bücherei in Leipzig als Archivbibliothek gegründet. Ein Pflichtexemplargesetz regelte nun wie in anderen Staaten die Abgabe eines Exemplars von jedem in Deutschland produzierten Verlagsprodukt. Diese Funktion übernahm nach dem Zweiten Weltkrieg für die Bundesrepublik die Deutsche Bibliothek in Frankfurt/Main – heute ist die Deutsche Nationalbibliothek sowohl in Leipzig wie Frankfurt vertreten.

Der Zugriff des nationalsozialistischen Staates auf das Bibliothekswesen erfolgte unmittelbar nach der Machtübernahme 1933. Von den personellen Säuberungen aus rassistischen oder politischen Gründen wurden wissenschaftliche wie öffentliche Bibliotheken gleichermaßen tangiert; dies gilt auch für die Gleichschaltung der berufsständischen Organisationen. Der Tag der Bücherverbrennung am 10. Mai 1933, an dem auch und vor allem Bücher aus deutschen öffentlichen Bibliotheken verbrannt wurden, wird für immer das schmachvollste Datum für das deutsche Bibliothekswesen sein (Abb. S. 71 und 73).

Anonymous
Jean Grolier de Servières (seated), a bibliophile with an extensive collection of books, and Aldus Manutius, a printer in Venice who introduced major innovations in printing / Jean Grolier de Servières (sitzend), ein Bibliophiler, der über eine umfangreiche Büchersammlung verfügte, mit Aldus Manutius, einem Drucker in Venedig, der wichtige Neuerungen im Druckwesen einführte / Jean Grolier de Servières (assis), un bibliophile qui possédait une riche bibliothèque, avec Aldus Manutius, un imprimeur vénitien qui introduisit des innovations majeures dans le domaine de l'imprimerie
Coloured engraving, From: *El Mundo Ilustrado*, 1880

Bibliotheken in Gefahr

Seit es Bibliotheken gibt, sind diese auch bedroht, sei es durch Kriege, Diebstahl, Nage-
tiere, Mikroorganismen, Wasser oder Feuer. Der wohl legendäre Brand der Bibliothek von
Alexandria im 1. Jahrhundert v. Chr. durchzieht wie ein andauernder Schock die Jahrhunderte. Umberto Ecos Roman *Der Name der Rose* (1980) und der gleichnamige Film von
1986 haben diesen Schock mit modernen Mitteln in das 20. Jahrhundert transportiert.

Die Furcht vor Feuersbrünsten und die Vorkehrungen, die getroffen werden, um Bib-
liotheken davor zu schützen, spielen in vielen der oben erwähnten Beschreibungen von
Bibliotheksreisen aus dem 18. Jahrhundert eine wichtige Rolle. Die Angst vor Feuer führte
vor der Elektrifizierung zu Bibliotheksbauten mit möglichst großen Fenstern, um viel
Lichteinfall zu haben, aber auch dazu, dass man Räume nicht zu heizen wagte, denn für
Beleuchtung und Wärme standen nur Kerzen und Kaminfeuer zur Verfügung.

Doch auch in der Gegenwart hat die Angst vor Feuer trotz aller technischen Siche-
rungsmaßnahmen ihre Berechtigung. Der Brand der Weimarer Herzogin Anna Amalia
Bibliothek im September 2004 löste in Deutschland wie in der Welt Entsetzen, aber auch
eine Welle der Hilfsbereitschaft aus. Dabei entstehen Schäden nicht nur durch das Feuer,
auch die Rettungsmaßnahmen durch die Feuerwehr können schlimme Auswirkungen
haben. Wasser ist der größte Feind der Bibliotheksbestände – als Feuchtigkeit, die zur
Schimmelbildung führt, als Regenwasser, als Folge von Überschwemmungen oder eben
als Löschwasser.

Viele Bibliotheken treffen heute, oft in Notfallverbünden gemeinsam mit anderen
Einrichtungen, organisatorische und technische Vorsorge zur Behandlung durchnässten
Bibliotheksgutes; dazu gehören auch Vereinbarungen mit Unternehmen, die über große
Gefrierkammern verfügen, in die durchnässtes Bibliotheksgut verbracht werden kann,
um schockgefrostet und später behandelt zu werden.

Seit jeher haben auch Kriege und Unruhen Bibliotheken gefährdet. Die ältesten römischen Bibliotheken waren Beutegut der siegreichen Feldherren, die aus dem griechischen
Osten heimkehrten. So gelangte etwa die Bibliothek des Aristoteles nach Rom.

In Deutschland erlebte das Bibliothekswesen im Dreißigjährigen Krieg einen schweren
Rückschlag durch Zerstörung und Verschleppung großer und bedeutender Sammlungen,
so etwa durch die Entführung der Heidelberger Bibliotheca Palatina nach Rom. Die Vernichtung der Universitätsbibliothek von Löwen im Ersten Weltkrieg durch deutsche Truppen
galt weltweit als barbarischer Akt; 1919 wurde das Deutsche Reich in einem eigenen Para-
grafen des Versailler Vertrages zur Wiederherstellung der Bibliothek in Löwen verpflichtet.

Im nationalsozialistischen Deutschland wurde Bücherdiebstahl ganz öffentlich und
gleichsam von Staats wegen begangen. Privatbibliotheken jüdischer Bürger, von denen
die meisten ermordet wurden und wenige ins Exil gelangen konnten, wurden konfisziert
und verkauft oder öffentlichen Bibliotheken übereignet. Dies gilt ebenso für Bibliotheken
sozialdemokratischer, kommunistischer, gewerkschaftlicher, kirchlicher, freimaureri-
scher und anderer missliebiger Einrichtungen.

Die Identifizierung und Restitution der 1933 bis 1945 geraubten Bücher im Bestand der Bibliotheken ist auch im zweiten Jahrzehnt des 21. Jahrhunderts längst nicht abgeschlossen. Das Deutsche Zentrum für Kulturgutverluste in Magdeburg als Folgeeinrichtung anderer Institutionen widmet sich seit 2016 international der Aufgabe, Kunstwerke und Bücher zu identifizieren, die von Deutschen geraubt wurden, und sie, wenn möglich, zu restituieren.

Der Zweite Weltkrieg hat Spuren der Verwüstung in vielen europäischen Bibliotheken hinterlassen. Direkte Kriegseinwirkungen, aber auch die Raubzüge von Wehrmacht und SS oder einzelner Soldaten führten zur Vernichtung oder Entwendung großer Büchermengen aus den von Deutschland besetzten Gebieten. Gegen Ende des Krieges und danach wurden nach Ostdeutschland ausgelagerte deutsche Bibliotheksbestände in großem Umfang Beutegut der Sowjetarmee.

In Deutschland selbst fielen etwa ein Drittel des Vorkriegsbibliotheksbestandes, darunter Kostbarkeiten und Raritäten ersten Ranges, dem Krieg zum Opfer – insgesamt etwa 25 Millionen Bände. Bis in unsere Gegenwart haben auf diese Weise enorme Büchermengen ihre Besitzer gewechselt oder sind in Kriegswirren vernichtet worden oder verschwunden. Die Geschichte der Migration einzelner Bücher oder ganzer Bibliotheken ist auch eine Geschichte der Auseinandersetzung zwischen Macht und Gewalt auf der einen und Geist und Kultur auf der anderen Seite.

Doch auch ohne Kriegswirren und politischen Terror sind Bibliotheken im Laufe der Jahrhunderte auf eklatante Weise beraubt worden – aus Habgier oder Bibliomanie. Seit jeher wird behauptet, dass besonders die Bestände von juristischen und theologischen Bibliotheken dem Zugriff von Dieben ausgesetzt seien. Bestätigt wird dies heute noch von Bibliothekaren für juristische und medizinische Bücher, kaum jedoch für theologische. Vielleicht hat die Tatsache, dass einige der berühmtesten Diebstähle auf das Konto von Theologen aller Bekenntnisse gingen, ein Vorurteil gegenüber dieser Berufsgruppe begründet.

So erleichterte der spätere Kardinal Domenico Silvio Passionei (1682–1761; Abb. S. 52), ein Mann von hoher Gelehrsamkeit und ein leidenschaftlicher Bibliophile, im 18. Jahrhundert Klosterbibliotheken um die Verantwortung für ihre Bücherschätze. Als er noch päpstlicher Nuntius in Luzern war, kam er seiner Inspektionsaufgabe gegenüber den schweizerischen Abteien und vor allem gegenüber deren Bibliotheken gern und ausgiebig nach. Passionei soll mithilfe seiner Soutane und eines Fängers, der unter einem Fenster der jeweiligen Bibliothek bereitstand, um die vom Nuntius aus dem Fenster geworfenen Bücher aufzufangen, erheblich zum Bestandsabbau der schweizerischen Klosterbibliotheken beigetragen haben. 1755 wurde Passionei Direktor der Vatikanischen Bibliothek. Nach seinem Tod wurde Passioneis 40 000 Bände umfassende Privatbibliothek vom Papst aufgekauft und dem Augustinerorden für die Biblioteca Angelica überantwortet (siehe S. 126–139).

Alle Fälle von Diebstählen aus Bibliotheken in großem Stil verblassen angesichts des größten „Bibliofila" aller Zeiten, des italienischen Grafen Guglielmo Brutus Icilius

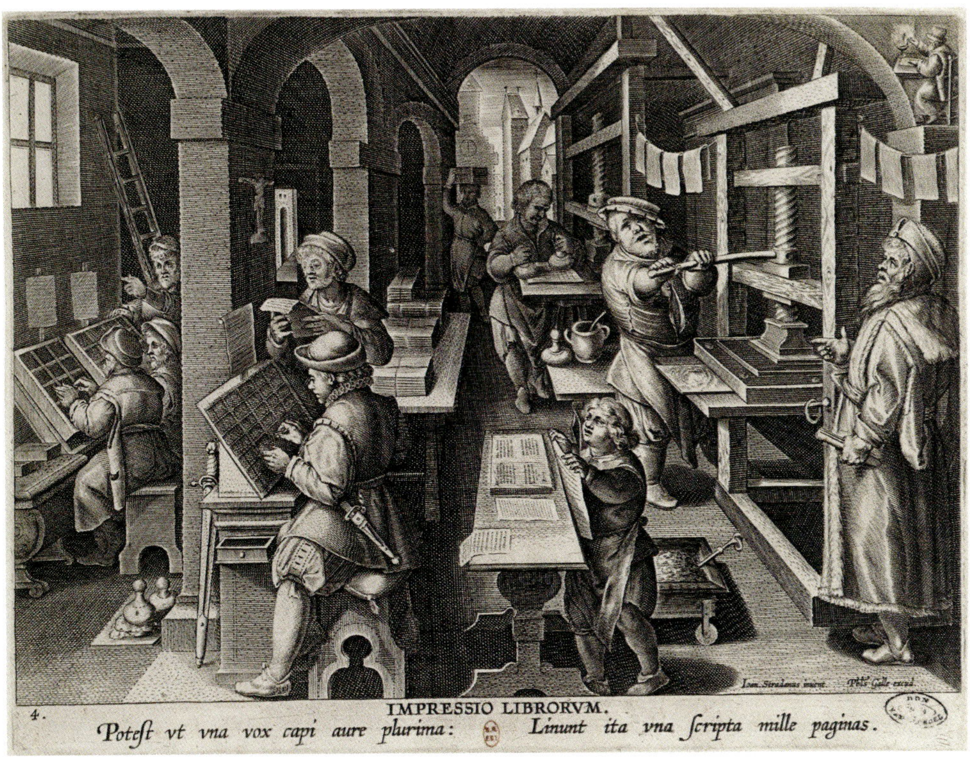

Jan van der Straet, called Stradanus
*Impressio Librorum / The Invention of Book Printing /
Die Erfindung der Buchdruckkunst / L'invention de
l'imprimerie, c. 1591*

Copper engraving, 20.4 x 26.7 cm / 8 x 10 ½ in.
From: *Nova Reperta*, c. 1591, pl. 4
Paris, Bibliothèque nationale de France

Timeleone Libri Carucci della Sommaia (1803–1869). Dieser Mann aus altem Adel, der das lateinische bzw. italienische Wort für Bücher als Familienname trug – ein Erbe von einem seiner Vorfahren aus dem 14. Jahrhundert, der sich auch namentlich als Bücherliebhaber zu erkennen geben wollte –, Libri also beschäftigte über Jahrzehnte die europäische Presse, viele Gutachter, Bücherfreunde und Bibliothekare.

Der 1803 in Florenz geborene Libri war schon als junger Mann ein in der europäischen Gelehrtenwelt bekannter und anerkannter Naturwissenschaftler, der mit den bedeutendsten Gelehrten seiner Zeit korrespondierte. Bereits mit 20 Jahren wurde er Physikprofessor an der Universität Pisa und setzte, nachdem er Italien aus politischen Gründen hatte verlassen müssen, seine glänzende wissenschaftliche Karriere in Frankreich fort. Berühmt wurde seine Geschichte der mathematischen Wissenschaften in Italien, noch heute ein Standardwerk.

Seine ganze Leidenschaft aber galt dem Aufbau seiner Bibliothek, die schließlich 40 000 Bände umfasst haben soll. Nebenher betrieb er einen umfangreichen Handel mit

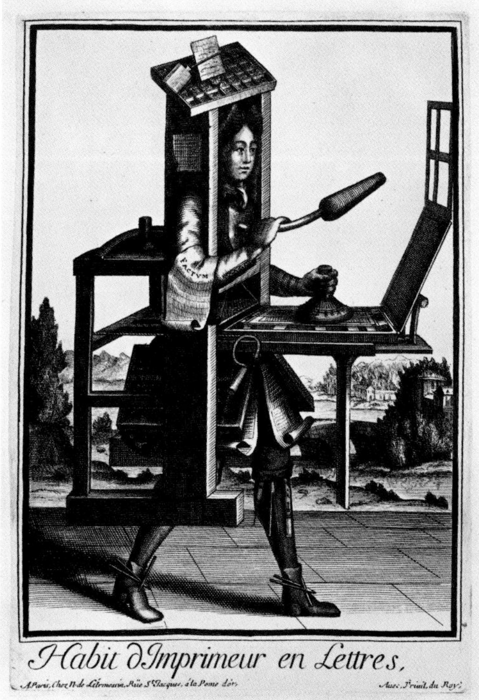

Nicolas de Larmessin
*A Mobile Book-Printer / Ein mobiler Buchdrucker /
Habit d'imprimeur en lettres*, 1695
From: *Allegorien der Handwerke und Gewerbe*, 1695
Copper engraving

Autografen und antiquarischen Büchern, aus dem der ausgewiesene Bibliophile erhebliche Einkünfte erzielte. Am Ziel seiner Wünsche war Libri, als er zum Sekretär einer Kommission bestellt wurde, die die Redaktion und Publikation eines Kataloges aller Handschriften vorsah, die sich in den Bibliotheken Frankreichs befanden. Libri nutzte seine Position, um sich eine kostbare Handschriftensammlung anzueignen, was durch die häufig verwahrloste Katalogsituation in den Bibliotheken erleichtert wurde. Besitzvermerke in den Bänden löschte er, was deren spätere Identifikation erschwerte oder unmöglich machte.[8] Als Sekretär der Kommission hatte Libri zudem die Möglichkeit, in den Katalogen, so welche vorhanden waren, die Einträge zu löschen. Schließlich veränderte er die Bücher auch durch neue Einbände oder sonstige Fälschungsmaßnahmen. Als sich 1848 der Verdacht gegen ihn so verstärkte, dass er angeklagt wurde, floh Libri mit 18 Bücherkisten nach London. Seine Bibliothek, die von Freunden versteckt wurde, konnte die Polizei nur mit Mühe finden. Wäre Libri noch einige Monate unbehelligt geblieben, hätten seine Diebstähle vom Umfang her den Konfiszierungen während der Französischen Revolution entsprochen. Libri wurde in Abwesenheit zu zehn Jahren Kerkerhaft und anschließender Verbringung in ein Arbeitshaus verurteilt und sämtlicher seiner Posten und Ehrenämter enthoben. In England verkaufte Libri seine zusammengestohlene Sammlung auf Auktionen; seine Kataloge umfassten mehrere Tausend Nummern. Unterdessen stellte man in Frankreich Kataloge der von ihm gestohlenen Bücher zusammen. Es sollte noch Jahrzehnte dauern, bis die französischen Bibliotheken wieder in den Besitz ihrer kostbarsten, von Libri gestohlenen Bestände gelangten. Libri selbst verschleuderte sein Vermögen in England und kehrte völlig verarmt 1868 in seine Heimat Italien zurück.

Bücherdiebstähle gibt es, seitdem Bücher existieren. Heute werden Bücher in Bibliotheken elektronisch gesichert. Früher kettete man Bücher an Lesepulten fest, *libri catenati* genannt, oder man begnügte sich mit einer Inschrift auf dem Buchdeckel, dem sogenannten Bücherfluch. Mit diesem sollte der mögliche Dieb – auch der des geistigen

Eigentums – von seiner potenziellen Schandtat abgehalten werden. Ihm wurden die
grässlichsten weltlichen und höllischen Strafen angedroht. Späte Nachkommen der
Bücherflüche sind die Vermerke über Urheberrechte in unseren modernen Büchern.
„Habent sua fata libelli" – Bücher haben ihre Schicksale, so auch Bibliotheken, und ihre
Schicksale sind auf das Innigste mit dem Schicksal einzelner Menschen wie mit dem
von Gesellschaften oder Gemeinschaften verbunden.

Mit Bibliotheken in die Zukunft

Mehr noch als durch die größten Bücherdiebstähle, mehr als durch Feuersbrünste oder
Kriegseinwirkungen sehen manche Kulturpessimisten – oder je nach Standpunkt auch
Kulturoptimisten – Bibliotheken durch die informationstechnische Revolution seit dem
Ende des 20. Jahrhunderts bedroht. Doch diese bietet unermessliche Entwicklungschan-
cen gerade für deren Gegenwart und Zukunft. Die Bibliotheken haben sich der Heraus-
forderung früh gestellt und diese Chancen ergriffen.

Die einzelnen Bibliotheken sowie internationale und regionale Bibliotheksverbünde
garantieren einen umfassenden Zugriff auf konventionelle wie elektronische Medien
und ermöglichen weltweite Recherchen und Dokumentenlieferungen. Auch die alten
Bestände der Bibliotheken werden mithilfe modernster Datentechnik auf vielfältige
Weise erschlossen und stehen so in bis vor wenigen Jahrzehnten undenkbarem Maße
den Benutzern in aller Welt zur Verfügung. Dazu gehören auch umfangreiche Digitali-
sierungsmaßnahmen in wohl allen wissenschaftlichen Bibliotheken der Welt. Altes und
neues Bibliotheksgut wird auf diese Weise im Prinzip für jedermann an jedem Ort und
zu jeder Zeit bereitgestellt, auch wenn auf diesem Gebiet noch viele Fragen, wie etwa des
Urheberrechts, zu klären sind. Die Digitalisierung dient darüber hinaus dem Schutz alter
und kostbarer Bestände, die nun nur noch in besonderen Fällen im Original eingesehen
werden müssen. Auch die auf säurehaltigem Papier gedruckten Bücher und Zeitschriften
des 19. und 20. Jahrhunderts sind äußerst gefährdet. Man versucht, dieser Gefahr durch
Sicherung der Inhalte mithilfe moderner Reproduktions- und Datentechnik und durch
Entsäuerung zu begegnen.

Das Angebot moderner Bibliotheken ist vielseitig. Es umfasst gedruckte Bücher und
Handschriften, Computerprogramme und audiovisuelle Medien, Zeitungen und Zeitschriften, Spiele und Zugang zu Datenbanken. Bibliotheken stellen ihren Benutzern For-
schungsliteratur, Ratgeber, Belletristik, Lehrbücher, Fachliteratur, Bilderbücher und
vieles mehr – durch welches Medium auch immer – zur Verfügung. Ein breites Spektrum
unterschiedlicher Bibliotheken bildet ein engmaschiges Informationsnetz, das durch
zeitgemäße Techniken die Bibliotheken untereinander verbindet und den gemeinsamen
Gebrauch lokaler, regionaler und überregionaler Informationssammlungen und Datenbanken ermöglicht. Durch Sonderabteilungen für Kinder und Jugendliche, Musikbib-
liotheken und Artotheken berücksichtigen sie besondere Interessen; mit speziellen
Serviceleistungen sprechen sie auch Gruppen wie Kranke und Gefangene an. So haben

sich viele Bibliotheken zu aktiven kulturellen Zentren entwickelt, in kleineren Gemeinden oft die einzige kulturelle Einrichtung am Ort. Das Erfolgskonzept moderner Bibliotheken, so die *Frankfurter Allgemeine Sonntagszeitung* im März 2014, liege überdies nicht in der Ausweitung der Bestände, „sondern zunächst im Raumangebot: Lesesäle, Arbeitsplätze, Gruppenräume, Platz für Kinder und Familien, Zeitungsecken – und, wie in Birmingham, ein Innenhof mit Tischtennisplatte".[9]

Seit den 1970er-Jahren ist oft die Rede vom baldigen Ende der Bücher und damit auch der Bibliotheken. Vielerorts war man der Meinung, dass künftige Bibliotheken, wenn es denn in Zukunft überhaupt noch welche geben sollte, keine Büchermagazine mehr benötigen würden. Doch in vielen Teilen der Welt sind in den letzten Jahrzehnten große und architektonisch ambitionierte Bibliotheken neu errichtet und andere umgebaut worden – und alle haben sie Platz für Bücher. Zu ihnen gehören beispielsweise die Bibliotheken in Alexandria (Abb. S. 68), Berlin, Cottbus, Delft, Dresden, Hannover, Kopenhagen, Leipzig, Osaka, Paris, Peking, Stuttgart, Utrecht, Weimar oder Zürich.

Alle diese neuen Bibliotheken bieten zudem viel mehr als ältere Bauten Platz für Menschen, die sich in ihre Studien versenken oder sich in entsprechenden Räumlichkeiten mit anderen austauschen wollen. Der Besucher findet hier außerdem individuelle Beratung durch Fachleute – im Gespräch von Mensch zu Mensch – ein hohes Gut in einer Zeit, die den zwischenmenschlichen Kontakt in zunehmendem Maße durch Technik zu ersetzen gewillt ist. Man hat in diesem Zusammenhang auch von der „Dorfbrunnenfunktion" der Bibliotheken gesprochen. Bibliotheken sind schon seit Langem nicht mehr nur Leihanstalten für Bücher oder andere Medien, sondern kulturelle und wissenschaftliche Zentren, die der Tatsache durch räumliche, technische und logistische Angebote Rechnung tragen, dass der Mensch ein *zoon politikon*, ein Gemeinschaftswesen, ist und bleiben wird. Hier stehen dem Besucher nach wie vor sowohl die älteren wie auch die neuesten Medien zur Verfügung, und er hat Zugang zur virtuellen weltweiten, unendlichen Bibliothek.

Bibliotheken blicken auf eine lange, bewegte Vergangenheit zurück. Sie gestalten eine dem Menschen und seinen Informations-, Kommunikations- und Unterhaltungsbedürfnissen angemessene Gegenwart, und sie gehen einer bedeutenden Zukunft entgegen, denn die Menschheit wird nie auf ihr Gedächtnis, auf ihr „Memory of the World" verzichten wollen.

Anmerkungen

1   Stockhausen, 1771, S. IV/V.
2   Heinemann 1894, S. 117.
3   Goethe 1801, S. 97.
4   Kloepfer 2014.
5   *Wir sind Teil eines großen Werkes*, 2015.
6   Hutten 1521.
7   Luther 1899, S. 49.
8   Willms 1978, S. 107.
9   Kloepfer 2014.

Opposite Agostini Ramelli
Bookwheel / Das Bücherrad / La roue à livres
From: *Le diverse et artificiose machine*, 1588,
p. 317, fig. CLXXXVIII
Copper engraving
New Haven, Yale University

Pages 50–51 View into the Biblioteca Palafoxiana
in Puebla, Mexico

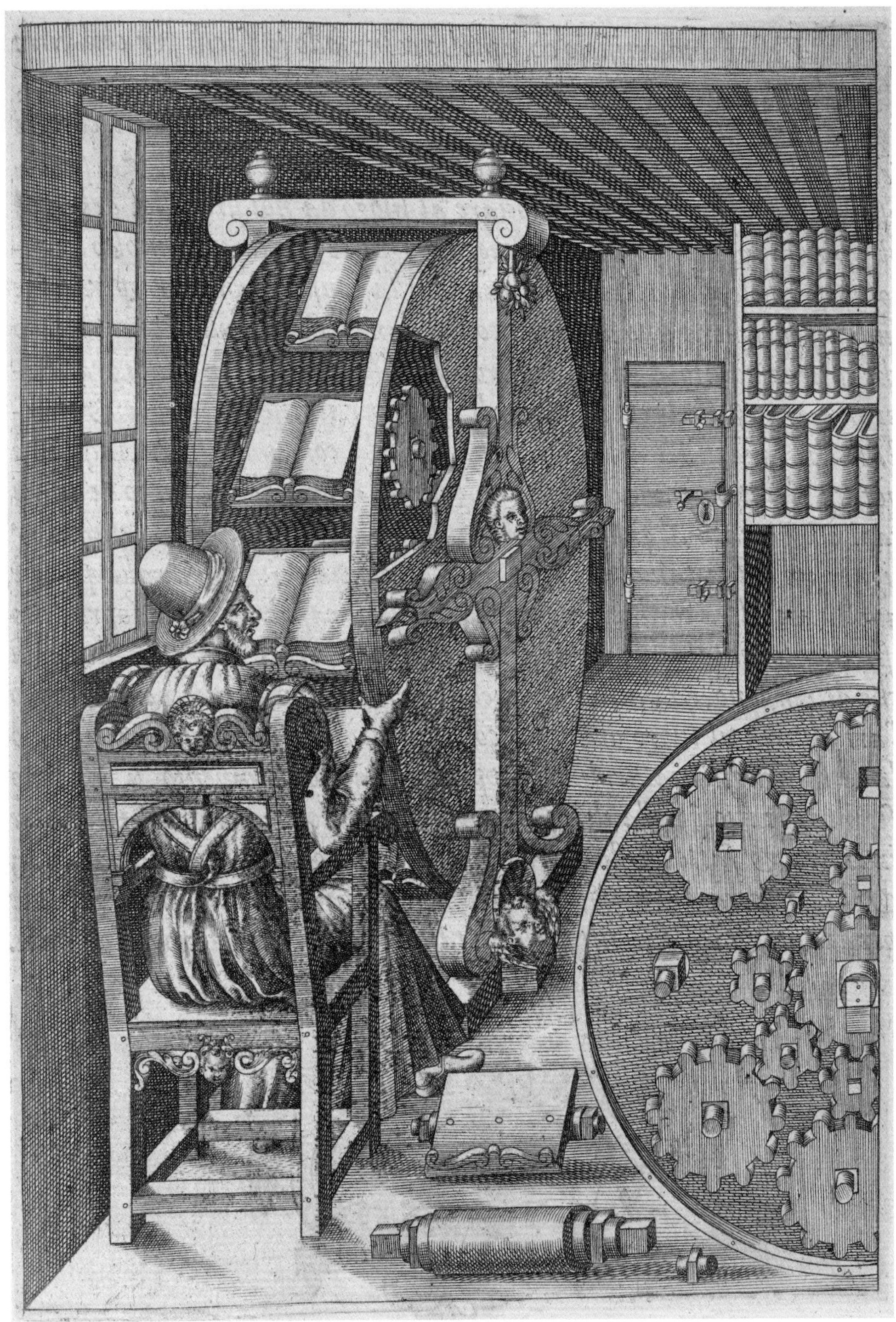

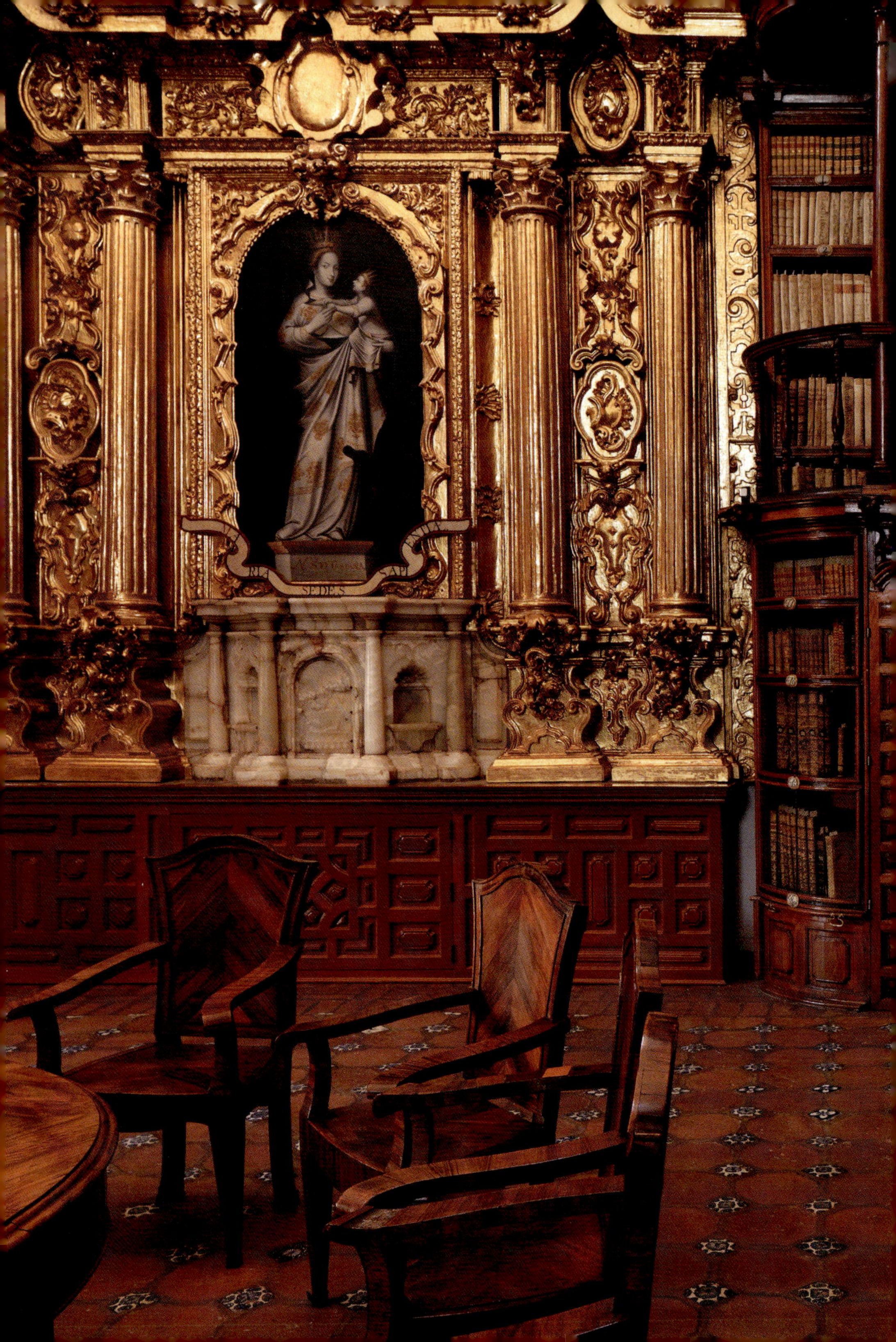

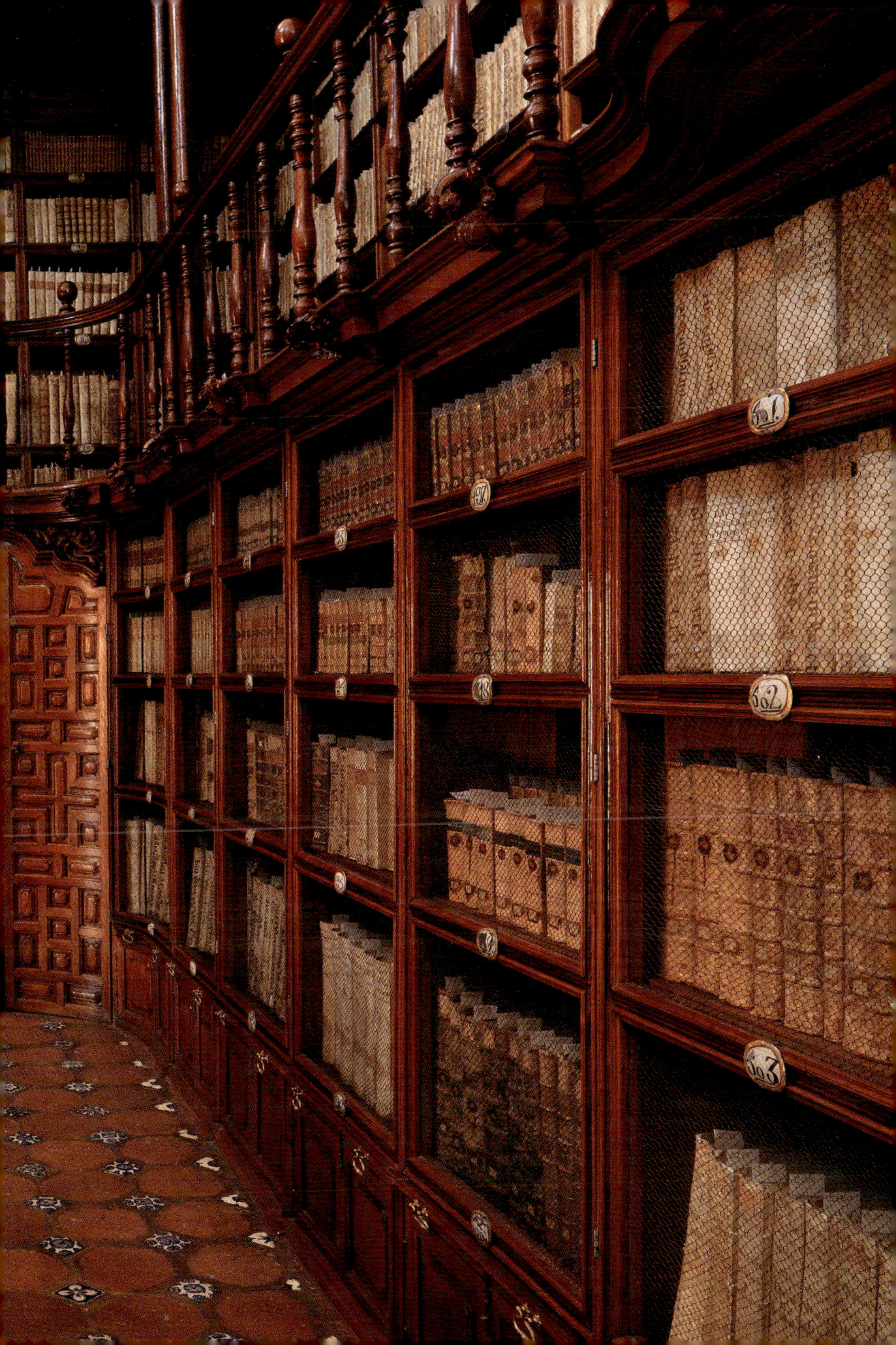

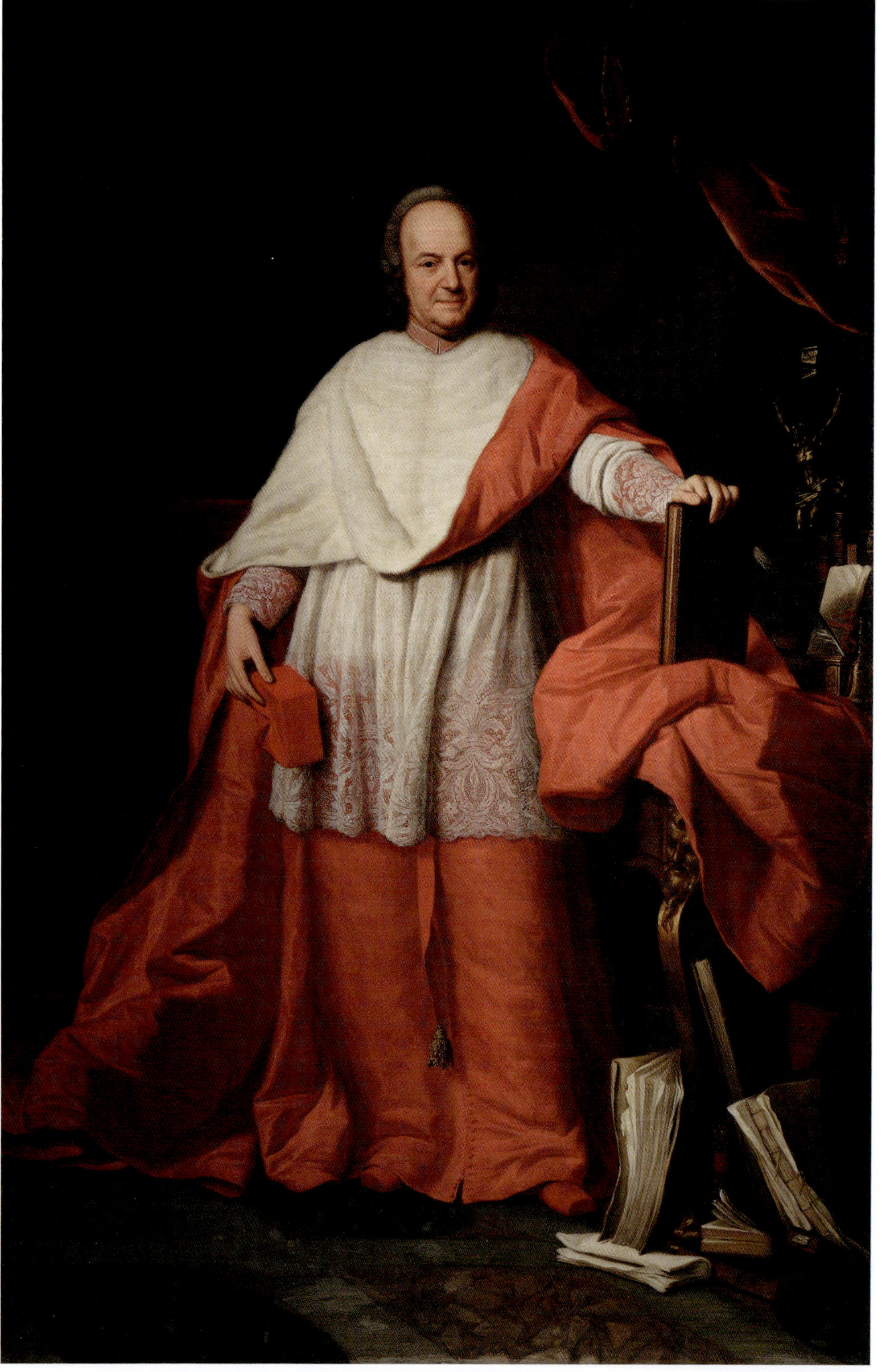

Mémoire du monde

Georg Ruppelt

Les bibliothèques sont « *des jardins d'agrément où de nouvelles fleurs, qui embellissent la région et embaument le plaisir, éclosent à chacun de nos pas* ».[1]

Comparer une bibliothèque à un jardin, assimiler ainsi deux des plus grandes prouesses culturelles de l'humanité, est une image que penseurs et gens de lettres aiment employer pour définir et décrire les bibliothèques. La métaphore semble évidente et suscite bien des associations. Le récit biblique de l'origine des êtres humains au jardin d'Éden s'en approche. L'écrivain et bibliothécaire Jorge Luis Borges (1899–1986) reconnut s'être imaginé le paradis comme une sorte de bibliothèque. Giacomo Casanova (1725–1798), quant à lui, compara son séjour à la bibliothèque de Wolfenbüttel en 1764 à une vie de bienheureux.

Gottfried Wilhelm Leibniz (1646–1716 ; ill. p. 55), qui dirigea la bibliothèque princière de Hanovre pendant 40 ans et en parallèle pendant 25 ans la bibliothèque ducale de Wolfenbüttel, détailla dans une lettre son idée de l'importance et de l'utilisation d'une bibliothèque universelle : « Elle est la salle du trésor de toutes les richesses de l'esprit humain, où l'on se réfugie pour s'instruire sur les arts de la paix et de la guerre, la protection du corps humain, les minéraux, les plantes, les animaux et surtout sur les secrets de la nature, le mouvement des constellations, les diverses régions de la terre, l'architecture civile et militaire, les embellissements et les structures publiques, les lois, la police et le bon ordre politique, l'histoire antique et moderne, les affaires personnelles des princes, et tout ce qui ravit l'intérêt humain. En bref, elle sert tant le plaisir que l'utile et l'indispensable [...]. »[2]

La formule de Johann Wolfgang Goethe (1749–1832) sur l'existence des grandes bibliothèques est aussi poétique que réaliste. Il évoque ainsi son séjour à la bibliothèque universitaire de Göttingen : « Je me sentais en présence d'un énorme capital, qui rapporte sans bruit des intérêts incalculables. »[3]

La bibliothèque en tant que paradis sur terre, salle du trésor de l'esprit humain, capital dont l'humanité profiterait durablement – et en proportion toujours croissante… Toutes ces métaphores se reflètent dans le Registre de la Mémoire du Monde, programme de l'UNESCO intitulé *Memory of the World* (MoW). Partie intégrante des programmes patrimoniaux de l'UNESCO depuis 1992, le Registre de la Mémoire du Monde répertorie collections, manuscrits et autres documents de grande valeur des bibliothèques, archives et musées de divers pays qui constituent la mémoire collective des habitants de la planète. Ce programme répond sous forme compacte aux exigences de ces institutions gardiennes de la mémoire et remplit le contrat des bibliothèques en représentant la mémoire du monde dans sa globalité. Fin 2015, le Registre de la Mémoire du Monde indexait 348 documents d'une centaine de pays, certains d'entre eux sont cités dans le présent ouvrage.

Bibliothèques d'hier et d'aujourd'hui

Au passé comme au présent, le visage des bibliothèques possède autant de riches facettes que l'humanité et ses cultures. Les plus anciennes d'Europe encore existantes datent du haut Moyen Âge, mais le fait de collecter les écrits remonte à bien plus longtemps. Le terme « bibliothèque » désigne ici des collections abritées en un lieu spécifique et pour lesquelles il existe un ou une responsable en titre. La bibliothèque de Saint-Gall Suisse (voir p. 374–383) existe depuis le milieu du VIIIe siècle, la bibliothèque apostolique du Vatican, dite la Vaticane (voir p. 80–97), depuis 800 environ, et la bibliothèque de l'abbaye Saint-Pierre à Salzbourg depuis le milieu du IXe siècle.

Par rapport à l'histoire de l'humanité, quatorze siècles, c'est peu. Par rapport à la vie d'un individu en revanche, c'est beaucoup. Depuis l'époque médiévale, cela représente 45 générations. Sauf qu'à chaque fois trois, voire quatre générations successives uniquement ont la chance de partager un bout de vie commune, de franchir des étapes significatives ensemble, de se rencontrer et d'échanger directement des informations. Pour tout ce qui s'est passé auparavant, les êtres humains doivent s'en remettre à ce qui a été consigné par écrit ou enregistré sur supports audiovisuels. Les bibliothèques compilent et conservent le savoir au-delà de ce qui se transmet d'une génération à l'autre.

L'un des critères permettant de définir la science et les connaissances est leur immensité. La science ne connaît aucune frontière nationale ou ethnique, aucune barrière de langue ou de religion. Elle seule se fixe les limites de l'éthique et de la morale. Ce n'est que dans les temps sombres et sous des régimes inhumains que d'autres frontières lui sont assignées.

À l'image de la science, les grandes bibliothèques ne connaissent dans l'idéal et en principe pas de frontières – hormis celles posées par leur budget, leur infrastructure ou leur vocation finale. Globalement, les bibliothèques tiennent du miracle. Un miracle, car elles représentent sur une assez petite surface le monde tel qu'il est, tel qu'il était, tel qu'il sera (éventuellement), tel qu'il devrait être et tel qu'il pourrait être. Ces lieux sauvegardent les faits du monde réel ainsi que ses diverses alternatives imaginées. Ils immortalisent l'esprit humain dans toute sa diversité et sa beauté, dans sa déchéance et sa cruauté, sa face sombre et sa face lumineuse. Dans leurs magasins, réserves, trésors et même sur les supports de données électroniques les plus récents (peut-être biochimiques à l'avenir), les bibliothèques sauvegardent le savoir sur Dieu et le monde, le bien et le mal, le réel et l'imaginaire.

Les bibliothèques reflètent l'esprit
de nombreux individus et laissent
entrevoir le processus intellectuel de
sociétés, de communautés élargies et
de l'humanité tout entière. Dans nos
immenses bibliothèques à fonction
d'archives, le savoir est en principe
conservé « pour l'éternité ». Mais cela
ne le rend pas pour autant disponible.
Pour ce faire, il doit être mis à disposition sous une forme adéquate. Après la
production d'un savoir et sa multipli-
cation, les bibliothèques remplissent
une fonction clé : celle de révéler et de
procurer ces connaissances – ce qui est
désormais réalisé à échelle mondiale.
Le savoir du passé accumulé au fil des
siècles est partagé au présent et rendu
utilisable pour l'avenir.

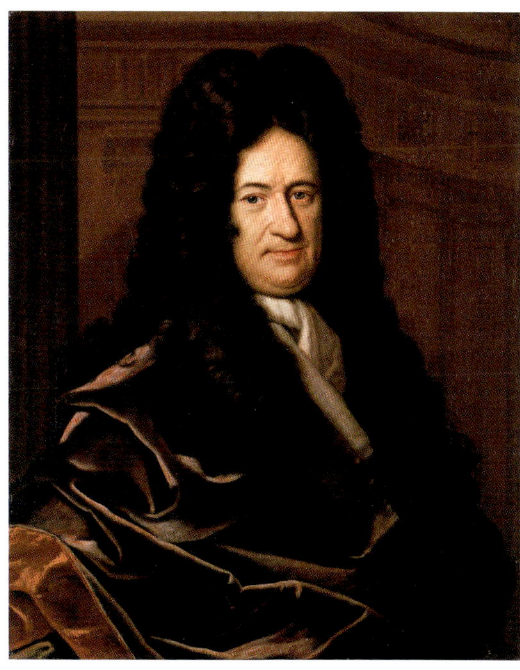

À une époque où les plus grands
moyens de communication et de sauvegarde de l'histoire de l'humanité existent et
s'accroissent dans des proportions se dérobant à notre imagination, à l'époque que nous
vivons donc, la tâche considérable des bibliothèques va bien au-delà du registre de la
mémoire. Depuis longtemps même, elles ne sont pas uniquement des consignes du savoir.
Ce sont des sites vivants et tournés vers le monde, des sites d'échange intellectuel, de
recherche, d'enseignement et d'apprentissage. Ce sont des lieux d'éducation, de transmission culturelle et scientifique à échelle locale ainsi que des portails d'information à échelle
internationale. Les bibliothèques sont les garantes d'un lien entre le passé, le présent et
le futur. Elles sont en outre des lieux d'apparat, d'esthétique et d'architecture de prestige.
Ces demeures du savoir et de leur appropriation ont incité, depuis les débuts de l'époque
moderne, les puissances laïques et religieuses à les aménager de façon remarquable. Les
splendides photographies présentées dans cet ouvrage en témoignent avec prodigalité.

Cette volonté créatrice n'est pas l'apanage du passé. L'hebdomadaire *Frankfurter
Allgemeine Sonntagszeitung* signalait en mars 2014 : « Dernièrement, les habitants de
toute la planète ont érigé de formidables temples à la faveur des livres. »[4]

Page 52 Domenico and Giuseppe Duprà
Cardinal Domenico Silvio Passionei, c. 1750
Oil on canvas, 249 x 165 cm / 98 x 65 in.
Fossombrone, Pinacoteca Civica "A. Vernarecci"

Above Bernhard Christoph Francke
Wilhelm von Leibniz, c. 1695
Oil on canvas, 81 x 66 cm / 31 ⅞ x 26 in.
Braunschweig, Herzog Anton Ulrich-Museum

L'image du temple utilisée ici revient fréquemment dans la littérature ayant trait aux bibliothèques. Elle reflète estime et considération pour quelque chose de supérieur, pas nécessairement au sens religieux et métaphysique, mais plutôt dans le sens d'un regard qui transcende les limites d'une vie humaine. Le médecin et conférencier allemand Eckart von Hirschhausen (né en 1967) a récemment fait une véritable déclaration d'amour aux bibliothèques en écrivant : « Nous faisons partie d'un immense ouvrage, qui s'élève au-dessus de chaque lecteur ou lectrice. »[5]

Et les êtres humains trouvent encore autre chose dans les salles de lecture des temples dédiés au livre : la quiétude. Un calme introuvable dans les bruyants espaces publics urbains – si ce n'est dans les lieux de culte en dehors des offices religieux.

Le terme « bibliothèque » vient du grec et désignait à l'origine une boîte renfermant des rouleaux de papyrus. L'usage actuel renvoie à une collection de livres et autres supports, à usage non commercial en général, donnant accès pour un cercle restreint d'utilisateurs et utilisatrices ou pour le grand public à des renseignements, des connaissances scientifiques, de l'instruction et du divertissement. Globalement, la bibliothèque publique a pour vocation de satisfaire tant la soif de savoir et de recherche spécialisée que le besoin des enfants qui apprennent tout juste à lire ou en découvrent les joies.

Les quatre missions principales d'une bibliothèque restent pour l'essentiel inchangées, à travers les millénaires – quelles que soient les multiples activités parallèles qui s'y sont rattachées de nos jours. Elles sont indépendantes des matériaux utilisés : tablettes d'argile (ill. p. 12), papyrus (ill. p. 14–15), parchemin (ill. p. 21), textile, papier, supports électroniques voire bientôt biochimiques. La première mission est de rassembler de façon systématique les informations sous forme de textes, images et données ; la seconde de conserver et protéger ces documents ; la troisième de classer et ainsi d'identifier les documents ; la quatrième de les mettre à disposition pour qu'ils remplissent leur objectif de transmission.

Proche-Orient ancien et Antiquité

L'essence de la bibliothèque ainsi définie remonte à 3500 avant notre ère, lorsque l'écriture est inventée dans les civilisations de Mésopotamie, de Chine et d'Égypte. L'expansion du commerce, des connaissances et de l'instruction entraîne la nécessité de consigner par écrit et pour la postérité des textes religieux et profanes.

Dès le IIIe siècle avant notre ère, on conserve des tablettes d'argile comportant des textes cunéiformes dans des jarres, coffrets et paniers. On retrouve aussi des archives volumineuses lors de fouilles effectuées auprès des temples. Des lettres et des archives

Jean Chevret
Encyclopaedic cosmological diagram with a didactic function. Thoughts on the planned construction of a new Bibliothèque de la République / Kosmologisch-enzyklopädisches Diagramm mit didaktischer Funktion. Überlegungen zum geplanten Neubau einer Bibliothèque de la République / Diagramme cosmologique-encyclopédique à fonction didactique. Considérations sur la construction envisagée d'une Bibliothèque de la République, 1791
Copper engraving
Paris, Bibliothèque nationale de France

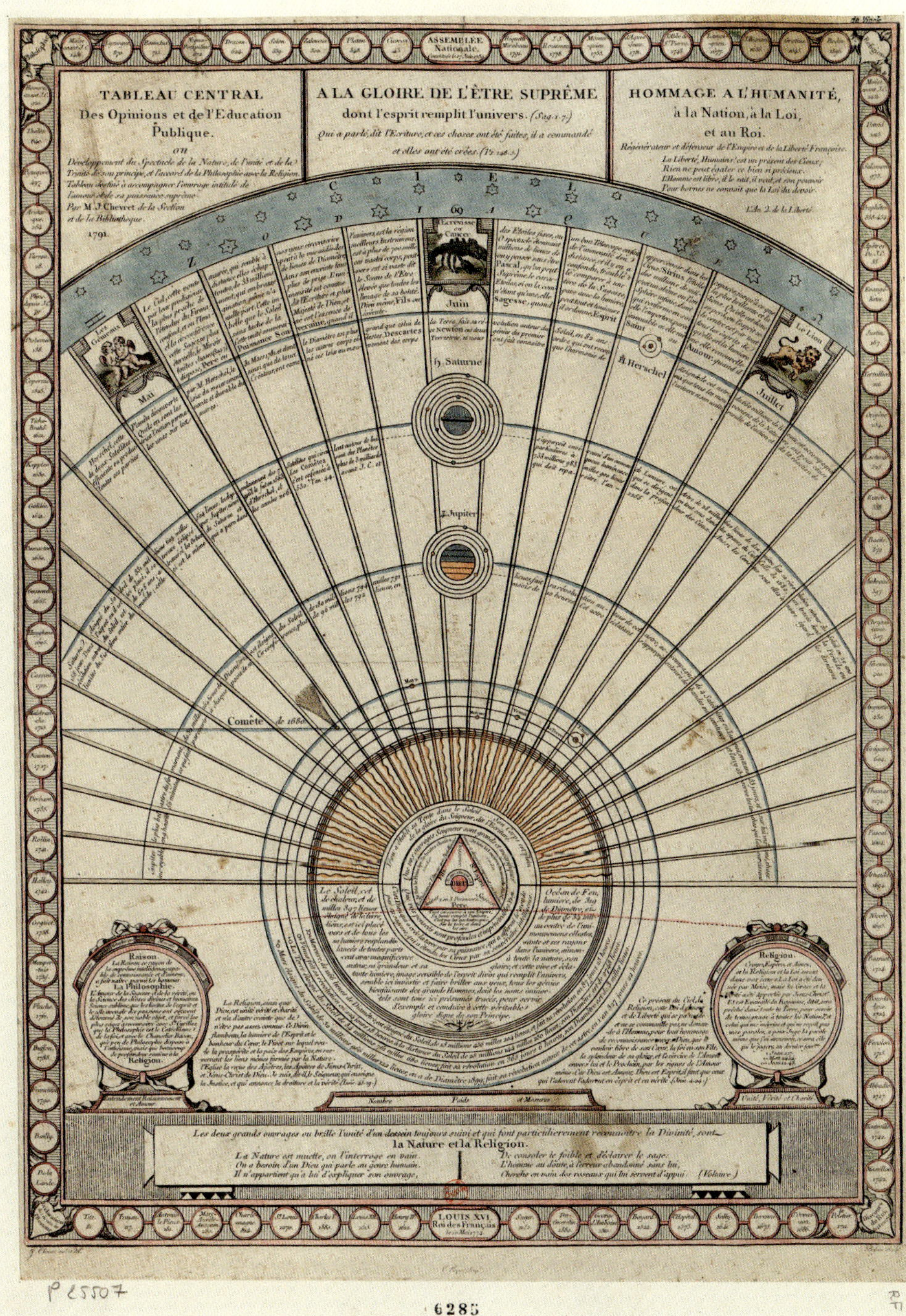

TABLEAU CENTRAL
Des Opinions et de l'Education Publique.
ou
A LA GLOIRE DE L'ÊTRE SUPRÊME
dont l'esprit remplit l'univers.
HOMMAGE A L'HUMANITÉ,
à la Nation, à la Loi, et au Roi.
ASSEMBLÉE Nationale.
LOUIS XVI. Roi des François.
Juin
Mai
Juillet
Les Gémeaux
Le Lion
Saturne
Jupiter
Comète de 1680
Herschel
Raison
Religion
Le Soleil
DIEU
Les deux grands ouvrages où brille l'unité d'un dessein toujours suivi et qui font particulierement reconnoître la Divinité, sont la Nature et la Religion.
Nombre Poids et Mesures

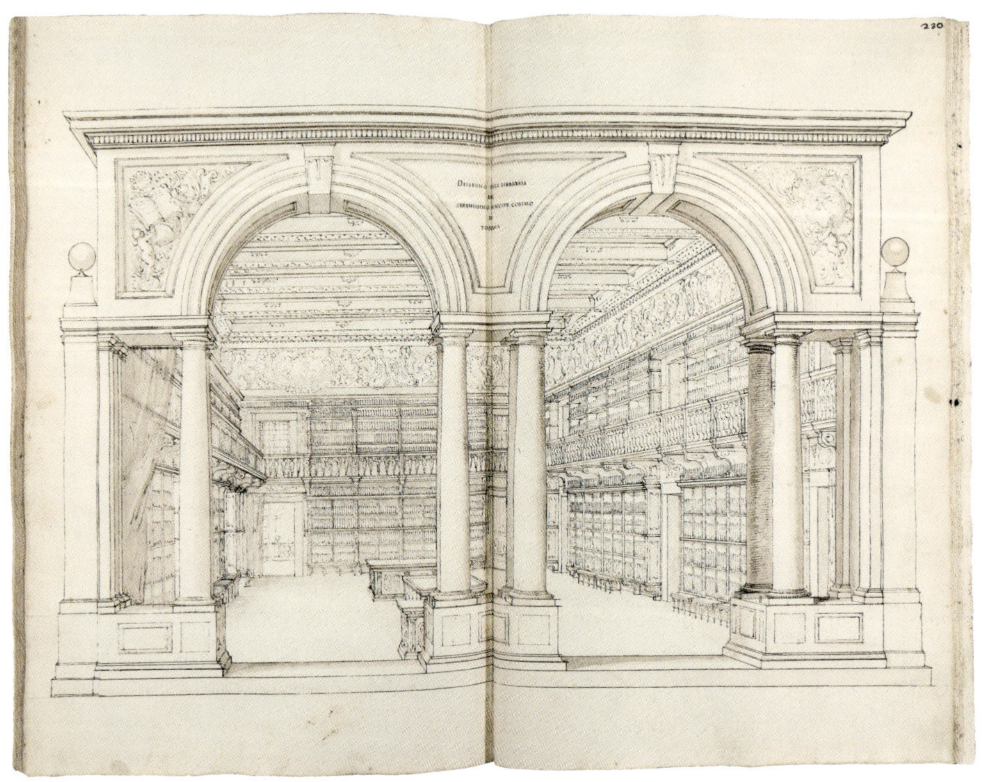

Diacinto Maria Marmi
View of the Library of Cosimo III de' Medici /
Blick in die Bibliothek Cosimos III. de' Medici /
Vue intérieure de la bibliothèque de Cosme III

de Médicis, last third of the 17th century
Pen and watercolor, 43.5 x 45 cm / 17 ⅛ x 17 ¾ in.
Florence, Biblioteca Nazionale Centrale di Firenze,
Magl. II.I. 380, fol. 229v–230r

administratives du temps d'Hammourabi (1811–1750 av. J.-C.) existent encore. Ces
archives se sont peu à peu muées en bibliothèques.

La toute première bibliothèque constituée de façon systématique et dans l'optique d'une
utilisation fréquente est celle du roi d'Assyrie Assourbanipal (687–627 av. J.-C.) dans son
palais à Ninive. Elle doit abriter des documents administratifs et médicaux ainsi que des
textes religieux et littéraires que le souverain pourra consulter. Estimée à 28 000 tablettes,
la bibliothèque d'Assourbanipal remplissait – outre le collectage et la consultation – le troisième critère définissant une bibliothèque, celui du classement. Nous ne connaissons toutefois pas les principes qui présidaient au classement de la première bibliothèque attestée.

On suppose également l'existence de bibliothèques dans l'Égypte antique.
On a retrouvé des inventaires en très grand nombre dans les tombes. Les Égyptiens
employaient deux dénominations pour les bibliothèques et/ou archives : la *maison des
livres*, également dite *maison divine des livres*, et la *maison de vie*. La maison de vie était

toujours adjointe à un temple où des ouvrages scientifiques et religieux étaient composés, copiés et collectés. Dans la *maison divine des livres*, en revanche, on rassemblait les écrits servant la pratique du culte en question. Ce n'est qu'à l'ère ptolémaïque (à partir du IVe siècle av. J.-C.) que le terme « maison des livres » décrivit concrètement la bibliothèque appartenant à l'un des temples.

Dans la Grèce antique, les bibliothèques étaient, tout comme en Égypte, installées dans les temples ou sur des sites servant à l'enseignement et à la recherche scientifiques (lycées, académies). En outre, l'existence de bibliothèques privées de souverains (Pisistrate) et d'érudits ou d'écrivains (Euripide ou Aristote) est attestée.

À Rome, des établissements publics naquirent des bibliothèques privées par le fait de fondation (ill. p. 8) ou mécénat, la première étant celle créée en 39 avant J.-C. à l'instigation de l'homme politique romain Caius Asinius Pollio (76–5 av. J.-C.). Les instigateurs mettaient un stock de base à disposition, les fonds s'accroissaient par le biais de donations et la copie d'exemplaires empruntés. Les livres étaient rangés de façon systématique et inventoriés. En règle générale, ils étaient accessibles au public dans la matinée, mais leur emprunt n'était pas permis (lieux de consultation). Même les villes de province bénéficiaient de tels établissements prestigieux. Dans les décennies qui suivent le règne d'Auguste, les empereurs fondent de nombreuses bibliothèques. Cette tradition classique se perpétue sous Byzance, avec la constitution d'une bibliothèque impériale en 356 après J.-C. à Constantinople. La prise de la ville par les Ottomans y met fin en 1453.

Les plus vastes bibliothèques de l'Antiquité sont érigées à l'époque hellénistique sous les rois lagides à Alexandrie (ill. p. 11), au sanctuaire des muses, le Musée, l'école d'érudits alexandrins comptant 700 000 rouleaux, et dans le temple dédié à Serapis (le Sérapeion) comptant plus de 40 000 rouleaux. L'incendie de la bibliothèque du Musée, survenu durant la guerre civile contre César (48–47 av. J.-C.) et dont la nouvelle ébranla le monde antique, n'est en fait qu'une légende. Il est bien plus probable qu'elle a été anéantie au IIIe siècle après J.-C., lors de la destruction des quartiers royaux.

Moyen Âge

À la chute de l'Empire romain, la tradition des bibliothèques antiques est relayée par la tradition chrétienne (ill. p. 17). Du IIe au IVe siècle après J.-C., le livre sous forme de codex (depuis lors, forme prépondérante dans le monde occidental ; ill. p. 31) prend le pas sur le volume enroulé autour d'une baguette (ill. p. 14–15). Avec la consolidation de la puissance chrétienne au VIe siècle, les monastères deviennent les seuls centres d'instruction, le latin étant la langue de base pour l'éducation (ill. p. 32). Dans la première bibliothèque monastique, fondée en 540 à Vivarium dans le sud de l'Italie, Cassiodore (vers 485–580), auparavant préfet du prétoire de Théodoric le Grand (451–526), roi des Ostrogoths, exige que les moines se consacrent à l'étude scientifique, à la constitution et à la copie de manuscrits. Les bibliothèques monastiques en Irlande, Écosse et Angleterre prospèrent notamment grâce à la production et à la collection de tels manuscrits. L'évangélisation de l'Europe centrale par les moines irlandais et anglo-saxons conduit sur le continent à la fondation de couvents et à l'épanouissement de tout ce qui se rapporte à l'écriture, au livre et au lieu qui l'abritait. Luxeuil, Bobbio, Corbie, Echternach et Fulda en sont de bons exemples.

L'instruction chrétienne atteint son apogée au IXe siècle sous les Carolingiens grâce à la création de bibliothèques au sein des cours impériales et des sièges d'évêché comme Cologne, Mayence et Wurtzbourg, et surtout au sein des monastères.

Les abbayes de Saint-Gall et de l'île de Reichenau voient l'essor des bibliothèques, et leurs ateliers de copie sont appelés scriptoriums (ill. p. 28). Ainsi, l'art du livre prospère. Après une époque pendant laquelle d'innombrables temples sont pillés et détruits, les bibliothèques et la production de manuscrits et de miniatures connaissent un nouvel élan sous les Ottoniens, en particulier à Ratisbonne (aujourd'hui Regensburg), sur l'île de Reichenau, à Freising et à Hildesheim.

La volonté de réforme traversant les XIe et XIIe siècles, la création de nouveaux ordres monastiques et la naissance de la scolastique sont autant d'impulsions spirituelles venues de France qui influèrent sur la vie des bibliothèques.

Au XIIIe siècle, la culture médiévale assez homogène commence à se déliter. La création des ordres mendiants entraîne le recul des livres de prestige au profit des écrits pratiques nécessaires à l'assistance spirituelle. Ancêtres des bibliothèques universitaires actuelles, des bibliothèques d'étude et d'enseignement scolastique voient le jour dans la seconde moitié du XIIIe siècle. Les collèges et facultés possèdent déjà leurs propres collections au XIIe siècle, mais c'est l'organisation des bibliothèques pour l'ensemble du corps universitaire (comme celles de Paris, Oxford, Cambridge, Prague, Heidelberg, Vienne ou Erfurt) qui déterminera véritablement l'évolution des bibliothèques jusqu'à aujourd'hui.

Les centres éducatifs et culturels laïcs introduits dans les cours et dans les villes marquent (ill. p. 37), tout d'abord avec l'Église puis de façon dominante, l'évolution future des bibliothèques. Les bibliothèques monastiques et adjointes à des églises médiévales perdent leur importance à la fin du Moyen Âge. Rares sont celles qui subsistent sur leur lieu d'origine. Leurs collections parviennent dans d'autres bibliothèques, universitaires, princières ou privées. Elles ont été perdues ou récupérées pour fabriquer des reliures. Le processus de délitement des bibliothèques monastiques culmine pendant la sécularisation, au début du XIXe siècle.

Humanisme et Réforme

L'ère de l'humanisme et de la Renaissance (du XIVe au XVIe siècle) recourt délibérément aux codes de l'Antiquité et très peu à l'univers de pensée médiéval. On accorde bien plus d'importance à l'individualité humaine qu'au Moyen Âge. Le monde savant s'affirme avec de plus en plus d'assurance contre la volonté de guide spirituel incarnée par l'Église. Cela pousse Ulrich von Hutten (1488–1523) à écrire : « Ô siècle, ô sciences ! Vivre est un désir [...]. Les études fleurissent, les esprits s'échauffent. Barbarie, prends une corde et bannis-toi d'ici. »[6]

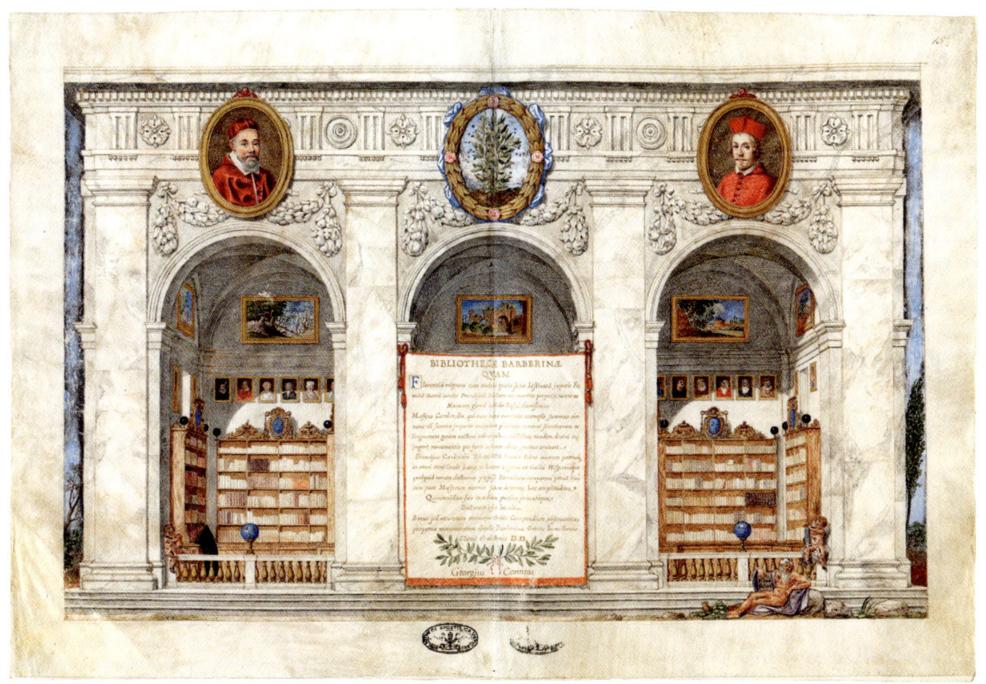

Jean de Saillant, *Idealized View of the Barberini Library / Idealansicht der Biblioteca Barberini / Vue idéale de la bibliothèque Barberini*, c. 1638

Tempera on vellum
Rome, Vatican City, Biblioteca Apostolica
Vaticana, Barb. lat. 4357 ff. 14v-15r

Ce nouvel état d'esprit qui, d'une part, se réfère à l'histoire pour, d'autre part, projeter une toute nouvelle image de l'homme et du monde axée sur le futur, conduit d'abord en Italic à la construction de bibliothèques privées (ill. p. 58 et 61) vastes et prestigieuses, comme celles de Francesco Petrarca (dit Pétrarque, 1304–1374), Giovanni Boccaccio (dit Boccace, 1313–1375), Niccolò Niccoli (1364–1437), Tommaso Parentucelli (1397–1455 ; le futur pape Nicolas V, fondateur de la bibliothèque apostolique vaticane) et du cardinal Basilius Bessarion (1403–1472). Plusieurs de ces bibliothèques privées ouvrent par la suite au public, à l'instar de la Biblioteca medicea laurenziana à Florence, la Biblioteca marciana à Venise (voir p. 98–107) ou la Vaticane à Rome, mentionnée plus haut (ill. p. 34 ; voir p. 80–97).

Arrive le moment où le papier éclipse le parchemin en tant que support d'écriture. C'est surtout l'invention de l'imprimerie à caractères mobiles (ill. p. 42) qui bouleverse l'univers du livre dans le courant du XVe siècle. À partir de 1500, le nombre de volumes imprimés supplante le nombre de manuscrits dans les bibliothèques. L'invention de Johannes Gutenberg (vers 1400–1468 ; ill. p. 41) et la propagation de cette technique (ill. p. 38) sont en rapport direct avec la diffusion de la Réforme. En fait, sans la Réforme, l'imprimerie ne se serait pas répandue à une vitesse aussi extraordinaire pour l'époque (ill. p. 45). Et inversement, la portée si intense et extensive de la Réforme est à peine imaginable sans la possibilité de reproduction de livres rapide et massive.

Dans un écrit de 1524, Martin Luther recommande « aux conseillers de toutes les villes allemandes de construire et entretenir des écoles chrétiennes », « de ne pas épargner le labeur et les coûts pour ériger de bonnes librairies ou bibliothèques publiques, en particulier dans les grandes villes qui en ont la possibilité. [...] Et ce, non seulement parce que ces bibliothèques doivent être à la disposition des futurs guides laïcs et spirituels, mais parce que les bons livres doivent perdurer et ne pas disparaître, tout comme l'art et la langue que la Grâce de Dieu nous a donnés. »[7] Ces efforts réformateurs instaurent l'instruction laïque, le développement de l'école et un nouveau type de bibliothèque rattachée à la ville, à la mairie ou à l'école (à Nuremberg, Brunswick, Hanovre, Hambourg, Magdebourg et Augsbourg notamment) qui reprennent une partie des fonds des bibliothèques de couvents et d'églises.

En territoire catholique, les bibliothèques jésuites acquièrent de l'importance, en témoignent celles d'Ingolstadt, Innsbruck, Maria Laach, Münster et Zurich. Ces établissements, ainsi que les bibliothèques universitaires fondées au XVIe siècle, posent les jalons du débat sur la religion – le livre devient arme intellectuelle, les bibliothèques des arsenaux.

La période baroque

Aux XVIe et XVIIe siècles, les collections princières deviennent des institutions de première importance. Elles servent à la fois de musées et de cabinets de curiosités. La pensée humaniste, la réflexion sur le religieux et la bibliophilie entraînent la construction de la Bibliotheca Palatina à Heidelberg et des bibliothèques de cour à Munich et à Vienne (voir p. 432–447). La bibliothèque de Wolfenbüttel, créée par le duc Auguste II, est des plus éminentes pour le XVIIe siècle. En Allemagne, au cours des siècles suivants, les bibliothèques nationales, d'État et de Land se constituent à partir des bibliothèques princières dont l'accès était limité mais qui disposaient d'un apport financier durable par leurs fondateurs.

Alors que les bibliothèques à pupitre prévalaient au Moyen Âge, la nécessité de ranger la quantité toujours croissante de livres suscite l'aménagement de salles (avec des étagères le long des murs). Ce nouvel agencement correspond d'ailleurs au besoin de représentation de l'époque baroque. Même si ces bibliothèques de cour richement dotées dépendent fortement de l'intérêt de leurs propriétaires princiers, elles sont utilisées à des fins de recherche. La création d'académies au XVIIe siècle redonne un nouvel essor significatif aux sciences. Des bibliothèques publiques montrent l'exemple à Milan (Biblioteca Ambrosiana), Oxford (Bodleian Library) et Paris (Bibliothèque Mazarine, voir p. 274–279). Face à ces établissements très fournis, les bibliothèques universitaires perdent de l'importance.

Master of the Dresden Prayer Book
Nebuchadnezzar Presiding over the Burning of Books /
Nebukadnezar verbrennt die Heiligen Bücher /

Nabuchodonosor brûle les livres sacrés, c. 1490–1497
From: Isabella Breviary, MS 18851, fol. 111v
London, The British Library

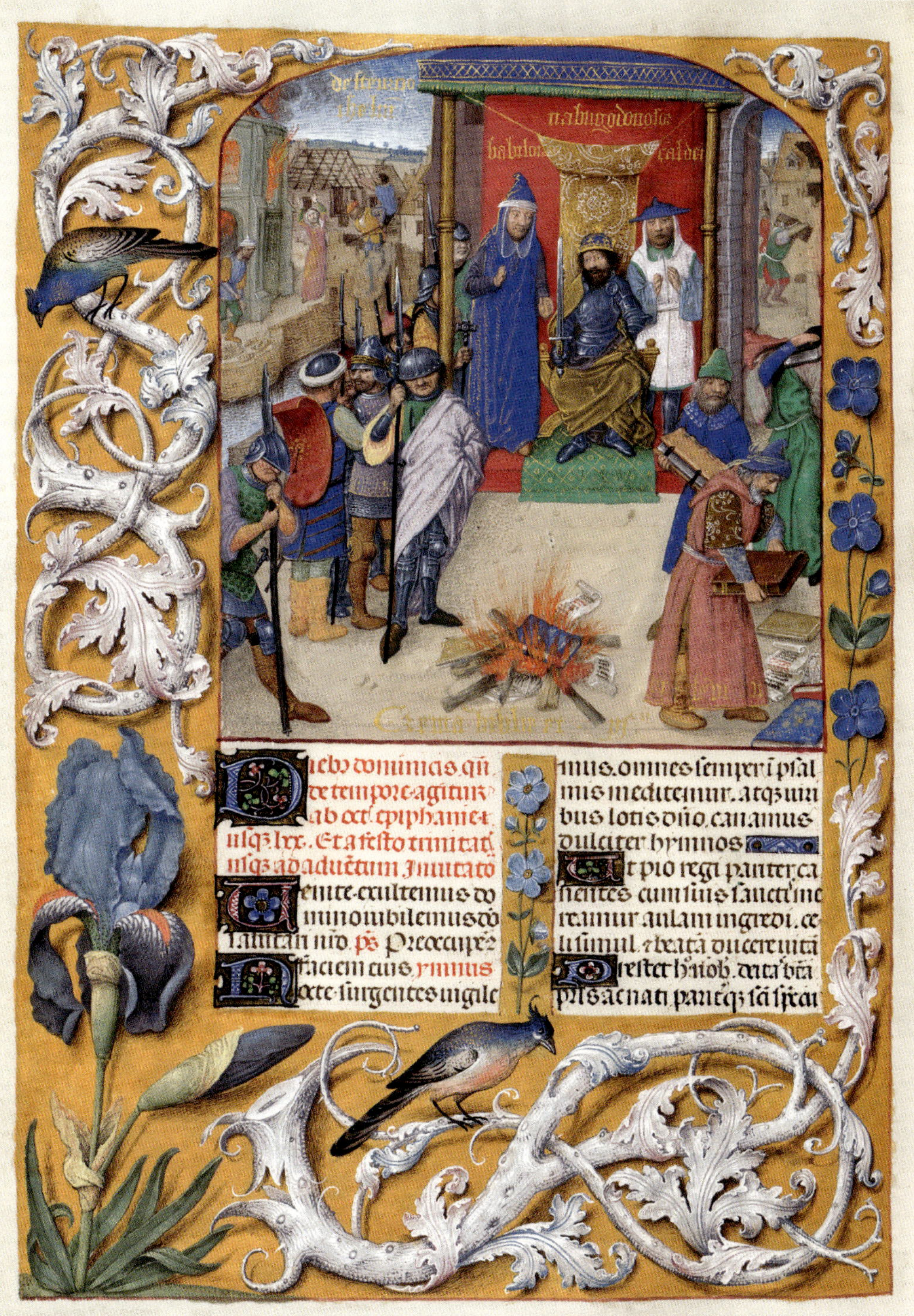

Diebus dominicis, quando de tempore agitur, ab oct. epiphanie usque lxx. Et a festo trinitatis usque ad aduentum. Inuitato-
[Ven]ite. exultemus do-
mino iubilemus do-
minum nostrum. ps. Preoccupe-
mus faciem eius. ymnus
Nocte surgentes uigile-
mus. omnes semper in psal-
mis meditemur. atque uiri-
bus totis dño. canamus
dulciter hymnos
Et pio regi pariter ca-
nentes cum suis sancti, me-
reamur aulam ingredi. ce-
lis simul. z beata ducere uita
Prestet hoc nob. deitas bea
pris ac nati pariterque sca spirita

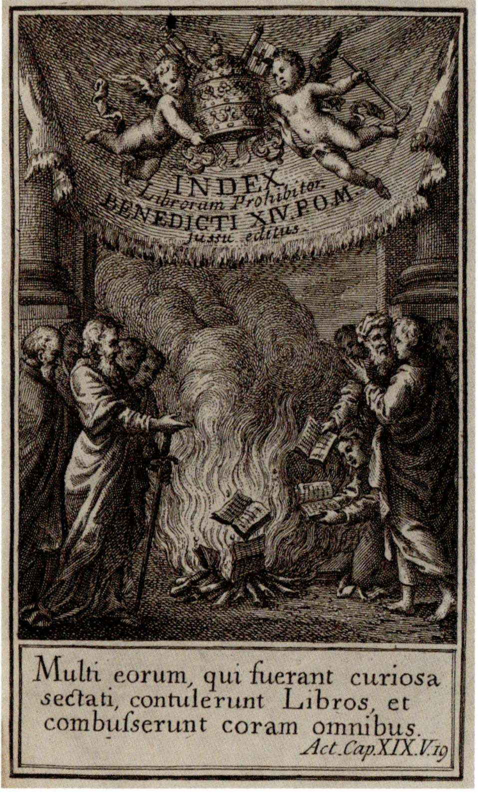

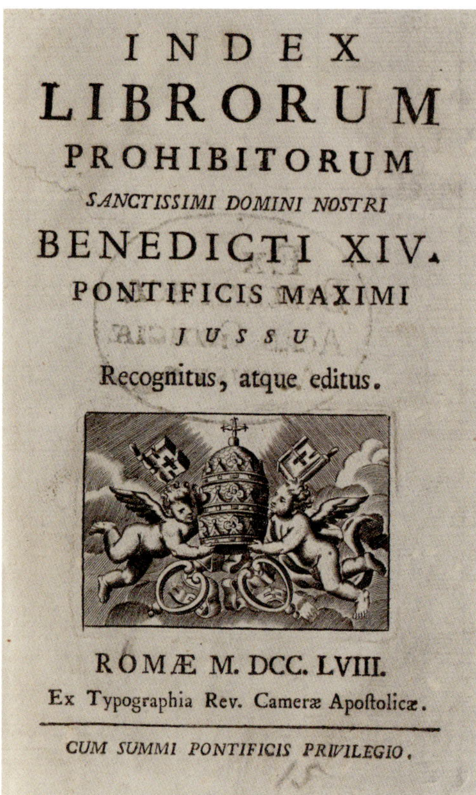

XVIIIᵉ siècle

Au XVIIIᵉ siècle, les exigences pour des collections organisées, telles que Gabriel Naudé
(1600–1653) à Paris et Gottfried Wilhelm Leibniz à Hanovre et Wolfenbüttel les avaient
formulées au siècle précédent, sont en partie remplies. L'événement le plus marquant
dans l'histoire internationale des bibliothèques n'est autre que la fondation de la bibliothèque universitaire de Göttingen, mise en service en 1735 – deux ans avant la fondation
de l'université. Les idées réformatrices de Leibniz sont pour la première fois appliquées
à Göttingen : budget fixe alloué à l'acquisition de livres, achat ciblé d'ouvrages scientifiques primordiaux, entretien minutieux du catalogue, circulation suivie des ouvrages
dans le bâtiment, horaires d'ouverture quotidiens pratiques, règlement d'usage libéral
et services exceptionnels pour la science. Tout ceci érige Göttingen en modèle d'élaboration de bibliothèques au-delà des frontières allemandes et européennes.

Frontispiece and title page of / Frontispiz und
Titelblatt des / Frontispice et couverture
*de l'*Index Librorum Prohibitorum, Rome 1758
Dallas, Southern Methodist University

Au siècle des Lumières, l'instruction n'est plus un privilège réservé aux élites, elle se
propage comme un bien bénéfique à tous. Ce changement se perçoit dans l'usage du latin,
langue autrefois dominante dans le domaine scientifique, qui recule au profit des langues
nationales. En outre, l'interaction entre « besoin de lire » et « possibilité de lire » condi-
tionne la création de sociétés de lecture et de librairies de prêt dans la seconde moitié du
XVIIIe siècle, les ancêtres de nos bibliothèques nationales ou publiques.

L'état des bibliothèques européennes privées, royales ou ecclésiastiques au XVIIIe siècle
nous est décrit grâce à un nouveau genre littéraire en plein essor à cette époque : le récit
de voyage. Ce type de récit convenait tout particulièrement à la propagation de l'héritage
des Lumières par des voyageurs, la plupart du temps érudits. Certains d'entre eux se
servaient des bibliothèques pour y rencontrer les notables locaux et s'entretenir de divers
sujets comme dans les salons littéraires.

Les édifices visités par les voyageurs savants ressemblent à des cabinets d'art ou
de curiosités plutôt qu'à des établissements délivrant des services. Outre les voyageurs
savants férus d'histoire à l'affût de fonds spécifiques, manuscrits et incunables en particulier, il y a ces touristes de bibliothèques désireux d'admirer les *curiosa* et autres volumes
étonnants. Ainsi, certains visiteurs de la bibliothèque de Wolfenbüttel traquent jusqu'au
XIXe siècle une célèbre faute d'imprimerie enfouie dans une bible en bas-allemand de 1731.
Dans l'unique exemplaire conservé, le sixième commandement est ainsi formulé : « Du solt
ehe brechen [Tu commettras l'adultère] ».

À la suite de la Révolution française et de la sécularisation menée en 1803, les bibliothèques rattachées aux églises deviennent propriété de l'État. Dans le sud de l'Allemagne
notamment, des quantités considérables de livres sont confisquées aux nobles ecclésiastiques et dans les couvents démantelés. Cette migration de livres profite à la bibliothèque de
Munich (Hof- und Staatsbibliothek München). Avec ses 500 000 volumes, elle devient la plus
grande bibliothèque allemande de son temps. Beaucoup de livres ont néanmoins échoué
dans les moulins à papier, d'autres ont été transformés en sachets par les épiciers. Des
feuillets de parchemin ont servi de patron aux tailleurs, les reliures en maroquin à la fabri-
cation de semelles. Deux à trois millions de livres ont ainsi été victimes de la sécularisation.

XIXe et XXe siècles

L'industrialisation, l'ascension de la bourgeoisie, l'expansion des sciences et la production
de livres toujours plus faramineuse conduit au XIXe siècle à l'agrandissement constant
des fonds de bibliothèques. À Washington, Paris et Londres, des bibliothèques nationales
sont installées dans des bâtiments de prestige qui rendent disponibles dans un même
lieu toute la littérature nationale et une sélection de littérature étrangère. Ceci ne
réussit pas dans l'Allemagne éclatée, malgré les efforts déployés en 1848. De ce côté du
Rhin, les bibliothèques universitaires acquièrent toujours plus d'importance face aux
bibliothèques d'État et de Land. À celles-ci s'ajoutent de très nombreuses bibliothèques
spécialisées, reflétant l'avancement toujours plus pointu de la recherche et de la science.

Vers la fin du XIXe siècle, le corps de métier de bibliothécaire se professionnalise dans de très nombreux pays d'Europe. Des réformes concernant le personnel et l'administration sont engagées, et des lois de catalogage valides sont instaurées au-delà des régions. Dans les pays anglo-saxons tout d'abord et les pays scandinaves par la suite, des Public Libraries sont créées à titre d'exemple. Elles contribuent à l'éducation et au divertissement ainsi qu'au relayage de l'information. Aux États-Unis, un grand nombre de Public Libraries s'est déjà établi au début du XIXe siècle. Dans l'espace germanophone comptant de nombreux États isolés, ces fonctions sont tout d'abord assurées par les instituts d'étude et les églises. Le milieu ouvrier développe sa propre conception de l'instruction, qui suit tout d'abord un courant socialiste avant de se rapprocher de la pensée bourgeoise dans la première moitié du XXe siècle. Le rôle éducatif et divertissant que jouaient les librairies de prêt auprès de toutes les couches de la société perd son importance significative entre le XIXe siècle et 1950 environ. Des bibliothèques publiques performantes à responsabilité municipale se constituent en Allemagne plus tard que dans les autres pays d'Europe. Sous l'Empire allemand, la Prusse endosse un rôle phare dans le développement des bibliothèques. La bibliothèque royale fondée en 1659 (future Preußische Staatsbibliothek qui deviendra Staatsbibliothek zu Berlin – Preußischer Kulturbesitz) est, vers 1900, la plus vaste bibliothèque d'Allemagne.

En 1912 est créée une bibliothèque d'archives à Leipzig sous le nom de Deutsche Bücherei. Une loi commune à d'autres pays exige la remise d'un exemplaire de chaque publication allemande. Cette charge incombe à la Deutsche Bibliothek de Francfort-sur-le-Main après la Deuxième Guerre mondiale. La Deutsche Nationalbibliothek est aujourd'hui représentée à Leipzig et à Francfort.

L'État nazi s'empara des bibliothèques dès la prise de pouvoir en 1933. Les purges touchant le personnel pour des raisons politiques ou racistes affectèrent tant les bibliothèques spécialisées que publiques, et les organisations professionnelles furent également mises au pas. Le 10 mai 1933, jour des autodafés qui vit la destruction de livres aussi et surtout issus de bibliothèques publique allemandes, reste à jamais une date de la honte pour la bibliophilie allemande (ill. p. 71 et 73).

Bibliothèques en danger

D'une manière ou d'une autre, les bibliothèques sont menacées depuis leur création, par des facteurs aussi divers que la guerre, le vol, les rongeurs, les micro-organismes, l'eau ou le feu. Le très légendaire incendie de la bibliothèque d'Alexandrie, au Ier siècle avant notre ère, traverse les siècles comme un choc pérenne. Le roman d'Umberto Eco *Le Nom de la rose* (1980) et le film éponyme (1986) ont transposé par des moyens modernes ce choc au XXe siècle. La peur des grands incendies et les mesures préventives engagées pour protéger les établissements jouent un rôle important dans plusieurs des cercles de bibliothèques du XVIIIe siècle évoqués ci-dessus. Cette peur du feu amène, avant l'avènement de l'électricité, à pourvoir les salles de nombreuses fenêtres afin d'y faire entrer le

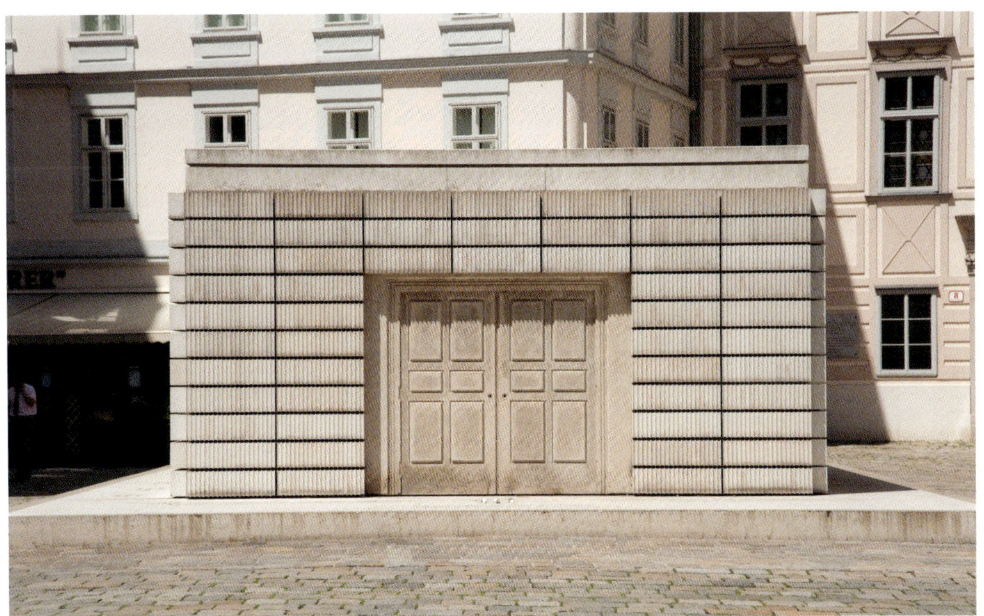

Rachel Whiteread
Memorial to the Austrian Jewish victims of the Holocaust / Mahnmal für die österreichischen jüdischen Opfer der Schoah / Monument à la mémoire des victimes juives autrichiennes de l'Holocauste, 2000, Vienna

The outside surfaces of the cube are structured as walls of library shelves lined with books, their spines facing inwards / Die Außenflächen des Kubus sind wie Bibliothekswände ausgeformt, deren Bücher mit den Buchrücken nach innen zeigen / Les faces extérieures du cube sont modelées comme des murs de bibliothèque tournés vers l'extérieur

plus de lumière possible. On n'ose alors pas chauffer ces salles puisque les seuls moyens à disposition pour éclairer comme pour chauffer sont les candélabres et les cheminées.

Malgré les mesures de sûreté appliquées de nos jours, l'angoisse de l'incendie est encore justifiée. La bibliothèque de la duchesse Anne-Amélie à Weimar, qui succomba aux flammes en septembre 2004, provoqua l'effroi dans le monde entier, mais aussi une vague de solidarité. Les dégâts ne sont pas dus qu'aux flammes. Les gestes de sauvegarde effectués par les pompiers peuvent également avoir de graves conséquences. L'eau, sous ses divers aspects – humidité entraînant la moisissure, eau de pluie, inondations ou même eau d'extinction propulsée en cas d'incendie –, est la plus grande ennemie des fonds de bibliothèques.

Afin de restaurer le patrimoine documentaire immergé, beaucoup de bibliothèques adoptent de nos jours des mesures techniques et des plans d'action, souvent dans le cadre de consortiums d'urgence en association avec d'autres institutions. Il existe, par exemple, des accords avec des entreprises disposant de vastes salles réfrigérées où les objets immergés peuvent être stockés. Ils subissent alors un processus de congélation ultra rapide qui facilitera leur restauration par la suite.

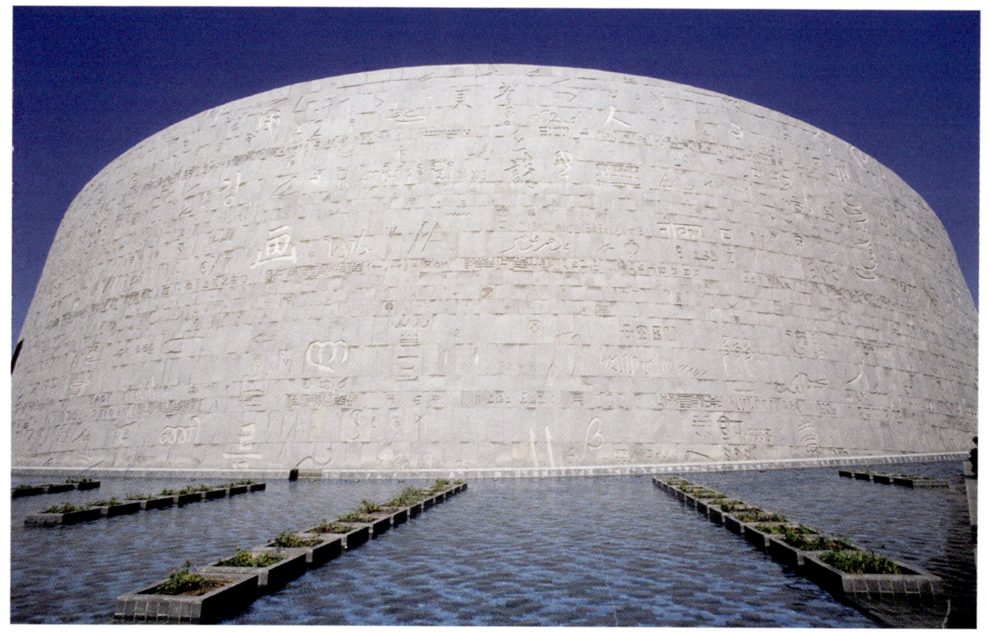

*Bibliotheca Alexandrina, south façade /
Südfassade / façade sud*

Architects: Snöhetta and Hamza Associates,
built 1995–2002. Photograph, 2005

Autres sinistres menaçant les bibliothèques depuis la nuit des temps : les faits de
guerre et les soulèvements. Les premières bibliothèques de la Rome antique contenaient
le butin de guerre des généraux victorieux en territoire grec. C'est ainsi que la bibliothèque d'Aristote s'est retrouvée à Rome.

Les bibliothèques d'Allemagne essuyèrent de lourdes pertes par destruction et dépla-
cement de collections prestigieuses durant la guerre de Trente ans. Le détournement à
Rome de la Biblioteca Palatina de Heidelberg est un exemple notable. La destruction de la
bibliothèque universitaire de Louvain durant la Première Guerre mondiale par les troupes
allemandes est considérée comme un acte de barbarie. Le traité de Versailles, signé en
1919, engagea l'Allemagne à reconstituer les collections de cet édifice anéanti.

Sous l'Allemagne nazie, le vol de livres était commis au vu et au su de tous, et même
par l'État. Les collections privées de citoyens juifs, exterminés pour la plupart et exilés
pour quelques autres, ont été confisquées et vendues, parfois remises à des bibliothèques
publiques. Le même sort a été réservé aux bibliothèques des sociaux-démocrates, com-
munistes, ouvriers, membres du clergé, francs-maçons et autres catégories en disgrâce
auprès du régime.

L'identification et la restitution de livres volés dans les stocks patrimoniaux entre
1933 et 1945 sont loin d'être achevées en cette deuxième décennie du XXIe siècle. Le
centre allemand contre la perte de biens culturels de Madgebourg (Deutsche Zentrum für

Kulturgutverluste) se consacre, depuis 2016 et à l'échelle internationale, à l'identification de livres et d'œuvres d'art spoliés par les Allemands et, si possible, à leur restitution.

Plusieurs bibliothèques européennes portent les stigmates de la Deuxième Guerre mondiale. Les faits de guerre directs, comme les razzias conduites par la Wehrmacht, la SS ou des soldats isolés, ont provoqué la destruction et la spoliation de quantité de livres dans les territoires occupés par l'Allemagne. Vers la fin de la guerre et plus tard, les fonds stockés en Allemagne de l'Est ont en majeure partie intégré les possessions de l'Armée soviétique.

En Allemagne, près d'un tiers des fonds existant avant les événements, soit 25 millions de volumes comprenant des ouvrages rares et précieux, sont à ajouter aux pertes de guerre. Jusqu'à aujourd'hui, des montagnes de livres ont ainsi changé de propriétaire ou ont été détruites ou perdues dans les affres de la guerre. L'histoire de la migration de chacun de ces livres et des bibliothèques en général est aussi en rapport avec les thèmes « pouvoir et violence », d'un côté, et « génie et culture », de l'autre.

Néanmoins, même en temps de paix et sans terreur politique, les bibliothèques ont été pillées de façon éclatante, par cupidité ou bibliomanie. On affirme même depuis des siècles que les collections judiciaires et théologiques sont la cible toute trouvée des bandits. Les bibliothécaires actuels confirment cette tendance pour les livres de droit et de médecine, mais à peine pour les documents théologiques. Ce préjugé se justifierait-il par le fait que de nombreux vols notables ont été imputés aux théologiens de toutes les confessions ?

Le futur cardinal Domenico Silvio Passionei (1682–1761 ; ill. p. 52), personnage fort cultivé et bibliophile passionné, allégea par exemple moult bibliothèques monastiques de leur précieux contenu. Alors qu'il était nonce apostolique à Lucerne, il s'acquitta avec dévotion et bonne grâce de sa charge dans les abbayes de Suisse, et tout particulièrement dans leurs bibliothèques. Protégé par sa soutane et assisté d'un chasseur qui se serait tenu au-dessous des fenêtres des bibliothèques qu'il inspectait, Passionei a largement contribué à amoindrir les stocks des bibliothèques monastiques suisses. Il fut nommé directeur de la bibliothèque vaticane en 1755. Après sa mort, le pape racheta sa bibliothèque privée dénombrant 40 000 volumes et la remit aux Augustins s'occupant de la bibliothèque Angélique (voir p. 126–139).

Le « bibliofilou » qui détrône tous les autres gentlemen voleurs de livres n'est autre que le comte italien Guglielmo Brutus Icilius Timeleone Libri Carucci della Sommaia (dit Guillaume Libri, 1803–1869). Issu de la haute noblesse, Libri avait pour nom de famille le mot signifiant « livre » en latin et en italien – héritage de l'un de ses ancêtres du XIVe siècle qui voulut officialiser sa bibliophilie. Pendant des décennies, Libri donna du fil à retordre à la presse européenne, à de nombreux experts, bibliophiles et bibliothécaires.

Né à Florence en 1803, le scientifique qu'était Libri fut très tôt réputé auprès des cercles érudits européens. Il correspondait d'ailleurs avec les personnages les plus éminents de son époque. Il fut nommé professeur de physique à l'université de Pise à vingt ans seulement. Contraint de quitter l'Italie pour des raisons politiques, il poursuivit une brillante carrière scientifique en France. Sa célèbre *Histoire des sciences mathématiques en Italie* est aujourd'hui encore considérée comme un ouvrage majeur.

Sa passion véritable allait toutefois à l'élaboration de sa bibliothèque qui finit par atteindre 40 000 volumes. Il exerçait en parallèle un commerce considérable d'autographes et de livres antiques dont il tira un profit énorme. Le vœu de Libri fut exaucé lorsqu'il fut nommé secrétaire d'une commission qui présidait à la rédaction et à la publication d'un catalogue visant à recenser tous les manuscrits des bibliothèques de France. Libri usa de son poste pour s'approprier une collection de manuscrits inestimables. L'entreprise fut facilitée par la négligence affectant souvent les catalogues de bibliothèque à l'époque. Il effaça les marques de possession inscrites sur les ouvrages, ce qui compliqua ou rendit impossible l'identification de volumes subtilisés.[8] En tant que secrétaire de la commission, Libri avait en outre la possibilité d'effacer les entrées dans les catalogues qui passaient entre ses mains. Il parvint également à altérer les livres en effectuant de nouvelles reliures ou divers actes de falsification. Lorsque les soupçons se renforcèrent en 1848 au point qu'il fut inculpé, Libri s'enfuit à Londres avec 18 caisses de livres. La police eut beaucoup de difficultés à retrouver sa bibliothèque, dissimulée par des amis. Quelques mois de liberté de plus auraient suffi pour que la somme de ses larcins égale celle des confiscations effectuées pendant la Révolution française.

Libri fut condamné par contumace à dix ans de réclusion et à servir dans une maison de travail. Il fut destitué de ses charges et fonctions honorifiques. Il vendit aux enchères, en Angleterre, l'ensemble de ses collections volées. Ses catalogues affichaient plusieurs milliers d'entrées. Entre-temps, des inventaires furent dressés outre-Manche afin de retrouver les livres spoliés. Des décennies se sont écoulées avant que les bibliothèques françaises soient de nouveau en possession de leurs livres dérobés par Libri. Ce dernier dilapida sa fortune en Angleterre et, ruiné, revint en Italie, un an avant sa mort en 1869.

Le vol de livres existe depuis qu'il y a des livres. Ils sont à l'heure actuelle munis d'une protection électronique. Autrefois, ils étaient enchaînés à leur pupitre, ces fameux *libri catenati*, ou bien l'on se bornait à écrire un sort sur leur couverture. Cette inscription sortilège était censée empêcher le voleur potentiel (bafouant également la propriété intellectuelle) de commettre un acte honteux. Le sort le menaçait des punitions terrestres et infernales les plus atroces. Les phrases concernant les droits d'auteur publiées dans nos livres d'aujourd'hui sont les rejetons des sorts de protection.

« Habent sua fata libelli » – les livres ont leur destin, les bibliothèques aussi. Ce destin est intimement lié au sort de chaque individu, de la société et de ses communautés.

Le devenir des bibliothèques

À en croire certains pessimistes (ou optimistes culturels, tout dépend du point de vue), la révolution informatique menacerait les bibliothèques depuis la fin du XXe siècle, plus encore que le vol massif de livres, plus encore que les incendies ou les actes de guerre. Pourtant, ces nouvelles technologies leur offrent des pistes de développement incommensurables pour aujourd'hui et pour demain. Très tôt, les bibliothèques ont fait face au défi afin de saisir leur chance.

Qu'elles soient indépendantes ou regroupées sous forme de consortium régional ou international, les bibliothèques garantissent un accès vaste aux médias conventionnels et électroniques ainsi que des recherches et une livraison de documents mondiales. Les outils de bureautique les plus modernes profitent même aux fonds anciens qui sont mis en valeur de diverses manières et se retrouvent à la disposition de milliers d'utilisateurs de par le monde. Leur portée était encore insoupçonnée il y a quelques décennies. Les mesures de numérisation colossales appliquées dans toutes les bibliothèques scientifiques de la planète font partie de ces nouveaux moyens. La dématérialisation permet à chacun de consulter à toute heure et en tout lieu des fonds documentaires anciens et nouveaux – même si bien des questions sur le droit d'auteur restent à résoudre dans ce domaine.

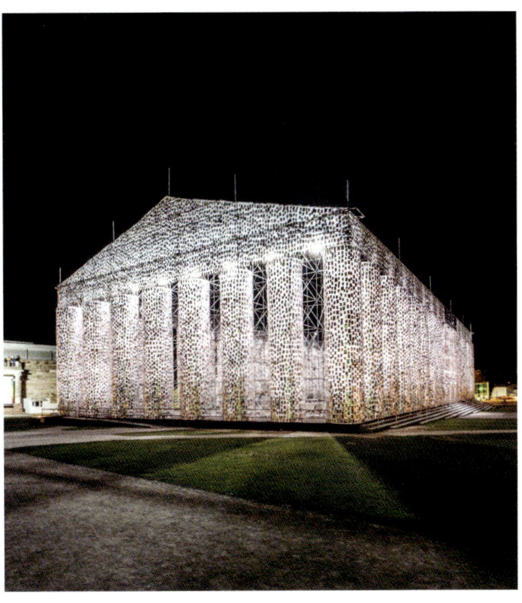

Marta Minujín, *The Parthenon of Books*, 2017
Kassel, documenta 14
The installation takes a symbolic stance against the banning of texts and the persecution of their authors /
Die Installation setzt ein Zeichen gegen das Verbot von Texten und die Verfolgung ihrer Verfasser / L'installation tire la sonnette d'alarme contre l'interdiction de textes et la persécution de leurs auteurs

De plus, la numérisation sert la protection des collections antiques et inestimables, car l'original ne peut être consulté que dans des cas bien précis. Les livres et journaux des XIXe et XXe siècles imprimés sur papier acide sont en grand danger. On s'efforce de pallier ce problème en les désacidifiant et en sécurisant leur contenu à l'aide des moyens de reproduction et de bureautique modernes.

L'offre des bibliothèques contemporaine est plurielle. Elles abritent des livres imprimés et des manuscrits, des programmes d'ordinateur et des supports audiovisuels, des journaux et des revues, des jeux et un accès aux banques de données. Les bibliothèques proposent des documents de recherche, des conseils, de la littérature générale et spécialisée, des manuels d'enseignement, des livres d'images et bien plus encore … sur de très divers supports.

L'éventail formé par diverses bibliothèques compose un solide réseau de renseignement. Les bibliothèques sont reliées entre elles grâce aux techniques d'aujourd'hui, et l'utilisation commune de banques de données et de collections locales, régionales et transrégionales est enfin possible. Les sections spécialisées permettent aux bibliothèques de cultiver des centres d'intérêt très différents (sections Petite Enfance, Jeunesse, Musique, Artothèque, etc.). Elles touchent un très large public par le biais de services permettant le prêt dans les hôpitaux et dans les prisons. Certaines bibliothèques sont devenues de véritables centres culturels. Dans les petites communes, elles sont souvent le seul établissement culturel de proximité. D'après le *Frankfurter Allgemeine Sonntagszeitung* en mars 2014, la recette du succès des bibliothèques contemporaines ne réside pas dans l'agrandissement des collections « mais dans l'aménagement du lieu et la fourniture de salles de lecture, postes de travail, salles de réunion, de l'espace pour les enfants et les familles, des coins presse et, comme à Birmingham, une cour intérieure avec tables de ping-pong ».[9]

Depuis les années 1970, il est souvent question de la mort du livre et de la fin des bibliothèques. D'aucuns ont prétendu que les bibliothèques du futur, dans le cas où elles ne disparaîtraient pas, n'auraient plus besoin de réserves de livres. Pourtant, au cours des dernières décennies, de majestueuses bibliothèques à l'architecture ambitieuse ont vu le jour dans de très nombreux endroits de la planète, sans parler des extensions réalisées. Toutes font la part belle au livre papier. Les bibliothèques d'Alexandrie (ill. p. 68), Berlin, Cottbus, Delft, Dresde, Hanovre, Copenhague, Leipzig, Osaka, Paris, Pékin, Stuttgart, Utrecht, Weimar ou Zurich peuvent en témoigner.

En outre, ces établissements récents offrent, bien plus que les anciens, de la place aux personnes souhaitant s'immerger dans leurs études ou échanger des idées dans un espace adéquat – sur le plan scientifique ou non. Le conseil y est délivré de vive voix par des spécialistes, fait ultra-précieux à l'heure où le dialogue entre les êtres humains tend à être supplanté par les échanges virtuels. À cet égard, la mission des bibliothèques a été aussi comparée à celle que le puits du village incarnait dans le passé.

Il est loin le temps où les bibliothèques s'apparentaient à un mont-de-piété pour livres et autres supports. Elles sont désormais de véritables centres scientifiques et culturels, qui tiennent compte du fait que l'être humain est et restera un animal civique – le fameux *zoon politikon* d'Aristote – à travers leurs infrastructures et offres techniques et logistiques. Hier comme aujourd'hui, les visiteurs disposent des médias traditionnels comme des médias les plus récents et ont accès à une bibliothèque connectée, à la portée infinie.

L'histoire des bibliothèques est riche et mouvementée. Elles composent une réalité adaptée aux êtres humains et à leurs besoins en information, communication et divertissement. Un brillant avenir les attend. Car – à moins qu'elle ne perde la tête – l'humanité ne voudra jamais renoncer à sa mémoire collective, à son registre de la mémoire.

Notes

1 Stockhausen, 1771, p. IV/V.
2 Heinemann 1894, p. 117.
3 Goethe 1801, p. 97.
4 Kloepfer 2014.
5 *Wir sind Teil eines großen Werkes*, 2015.
6 Hutten 1521.
7 Luther 1899, p. 49.
8 Willms 1978, p. 107.
9 Kloepfer 2014.

Opposite *Books are Weapons in the War of Ideas*
Anti-Nazi propaganda poster "Books cannot be killed by fire" / Anti-Nazi Propaganda-Plakat „Bücher können nicht durch Feuer vernichtet werden" / Affiche de propagande antinazie « Les livres ne peuvent pas être détruits par le feu » (Franklin Roosevelt), 1942
Universal History Archive

Pages 74–75 Library of the Stiftsbibliothek Sankt Gallen, Switzerland

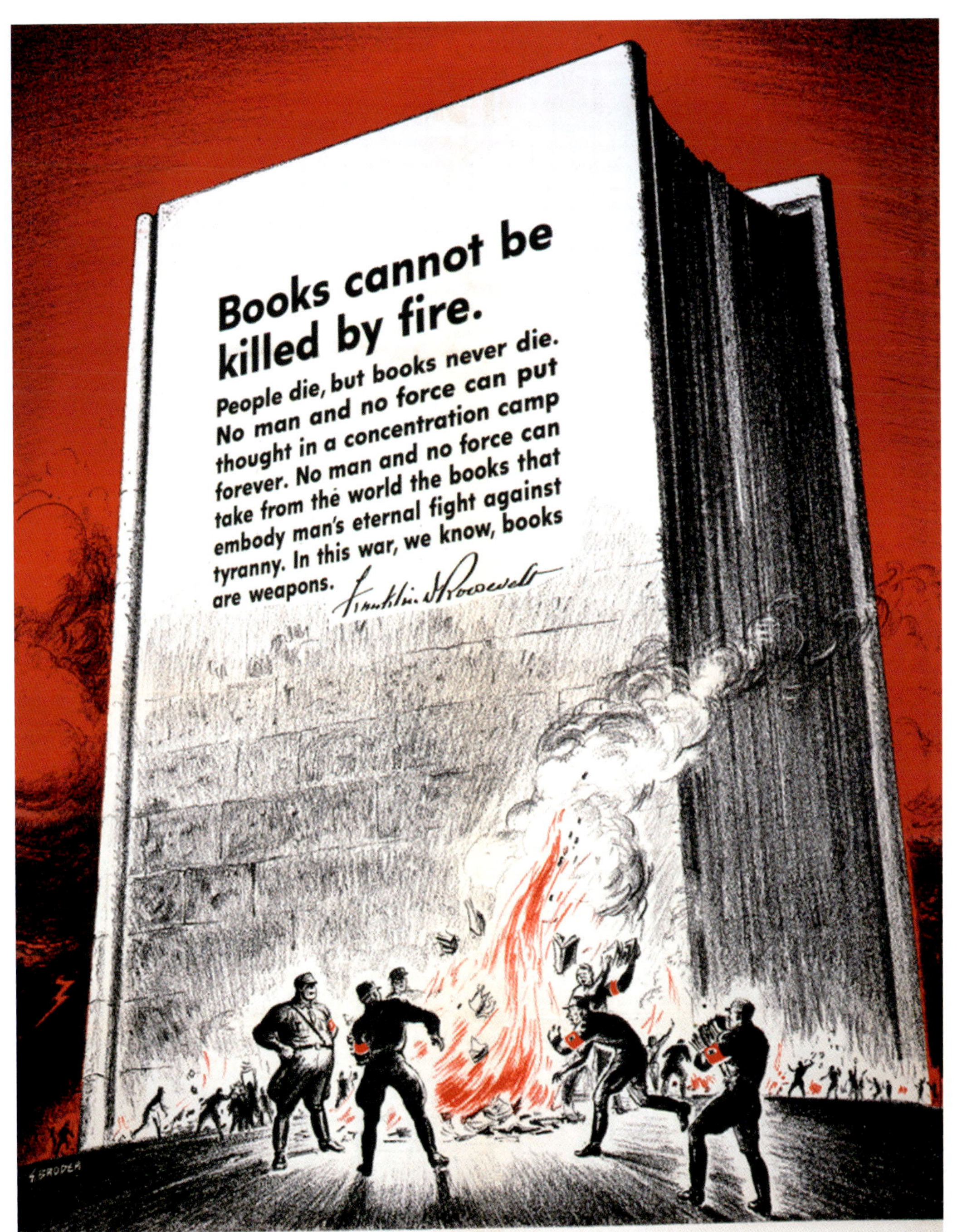

Books cannot be killed by fire.
People die, but books never die. No man and no force can put thought in a concentration camp forever. No man and no force can take from the world the books that embody man's eternal fight against tyranny. In this war, we know, books are weapons.
Franklin D Roosevelt
BOOKS ARE WEAPONS IN THE WAR OF IDEAS

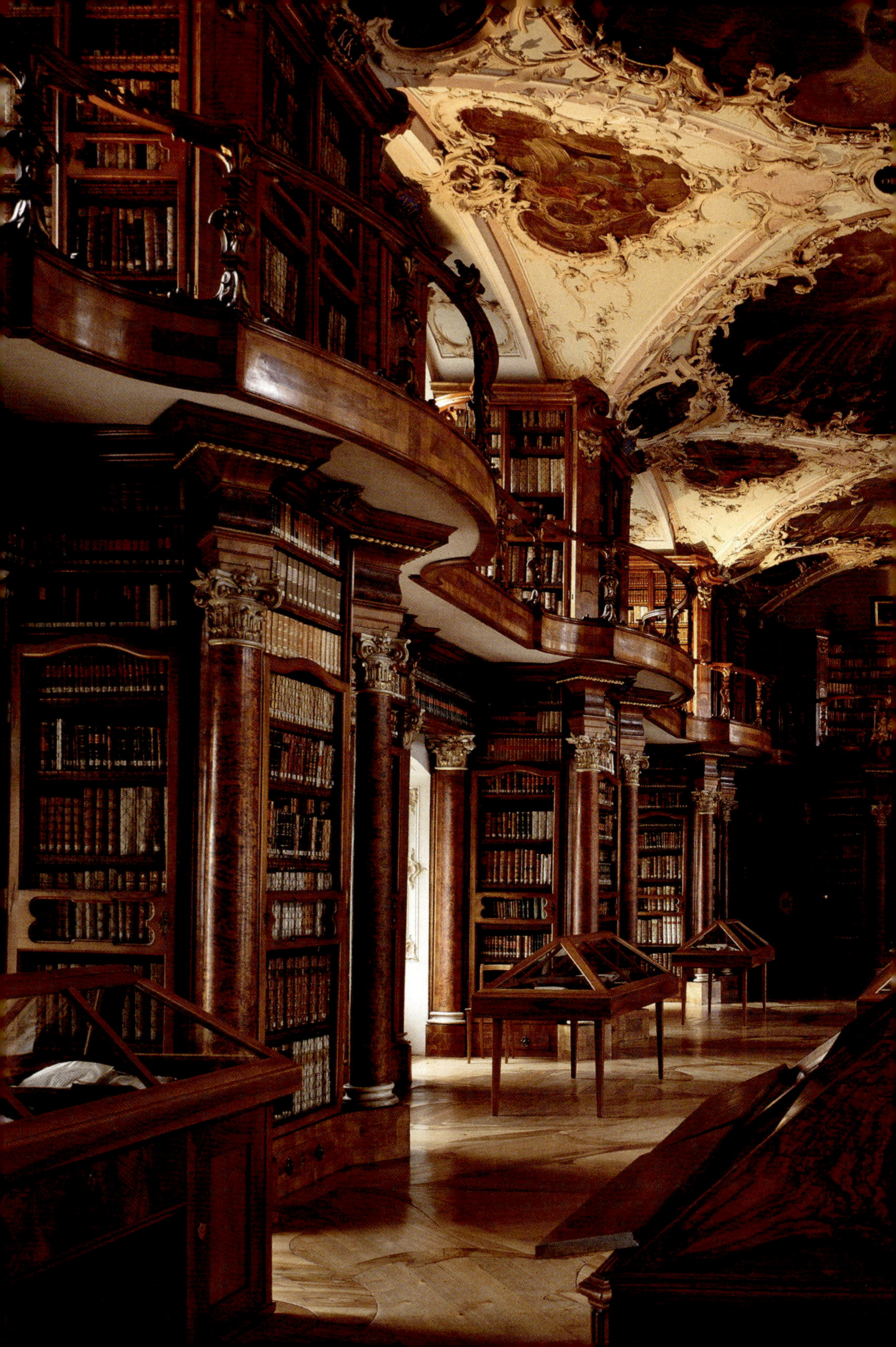

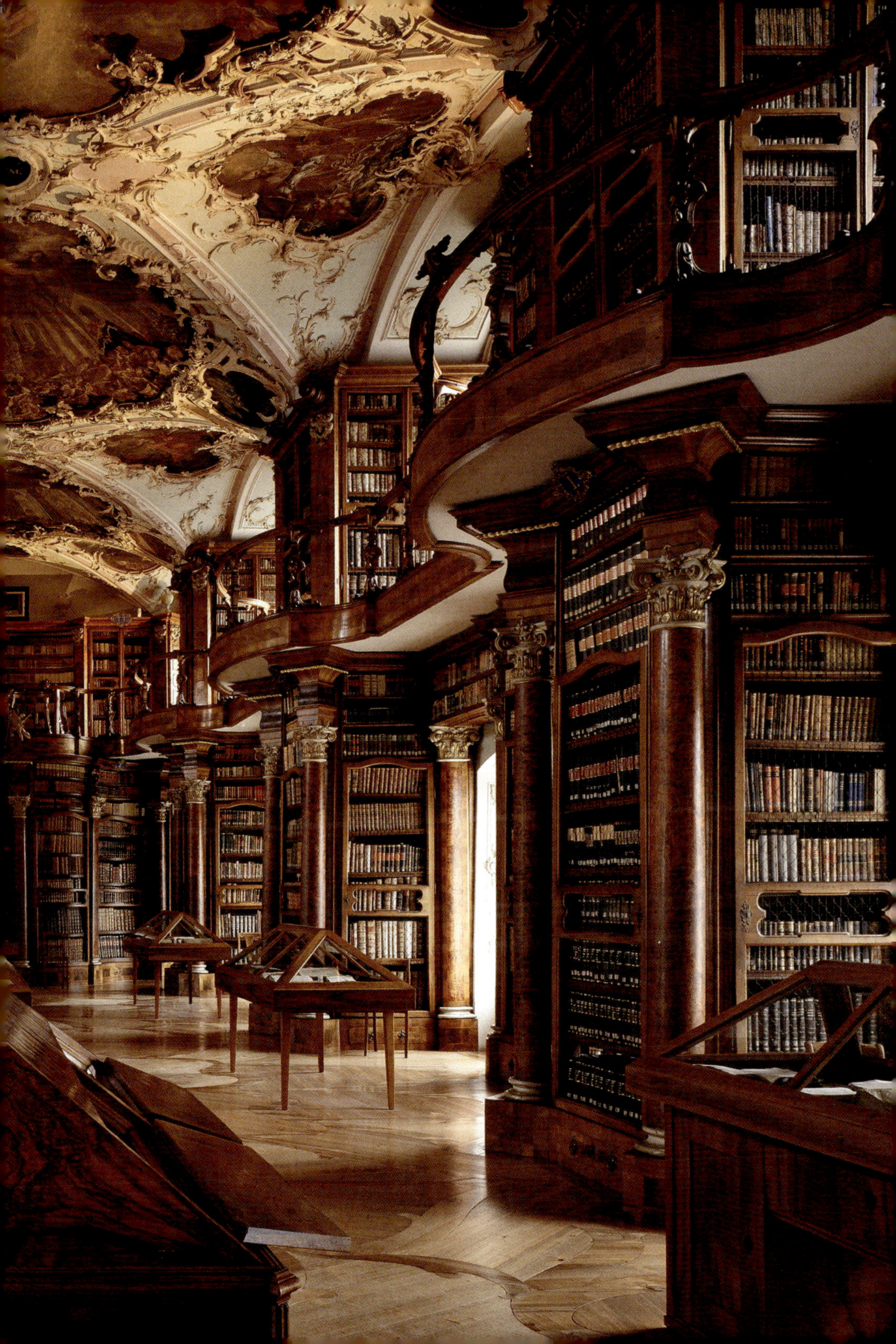

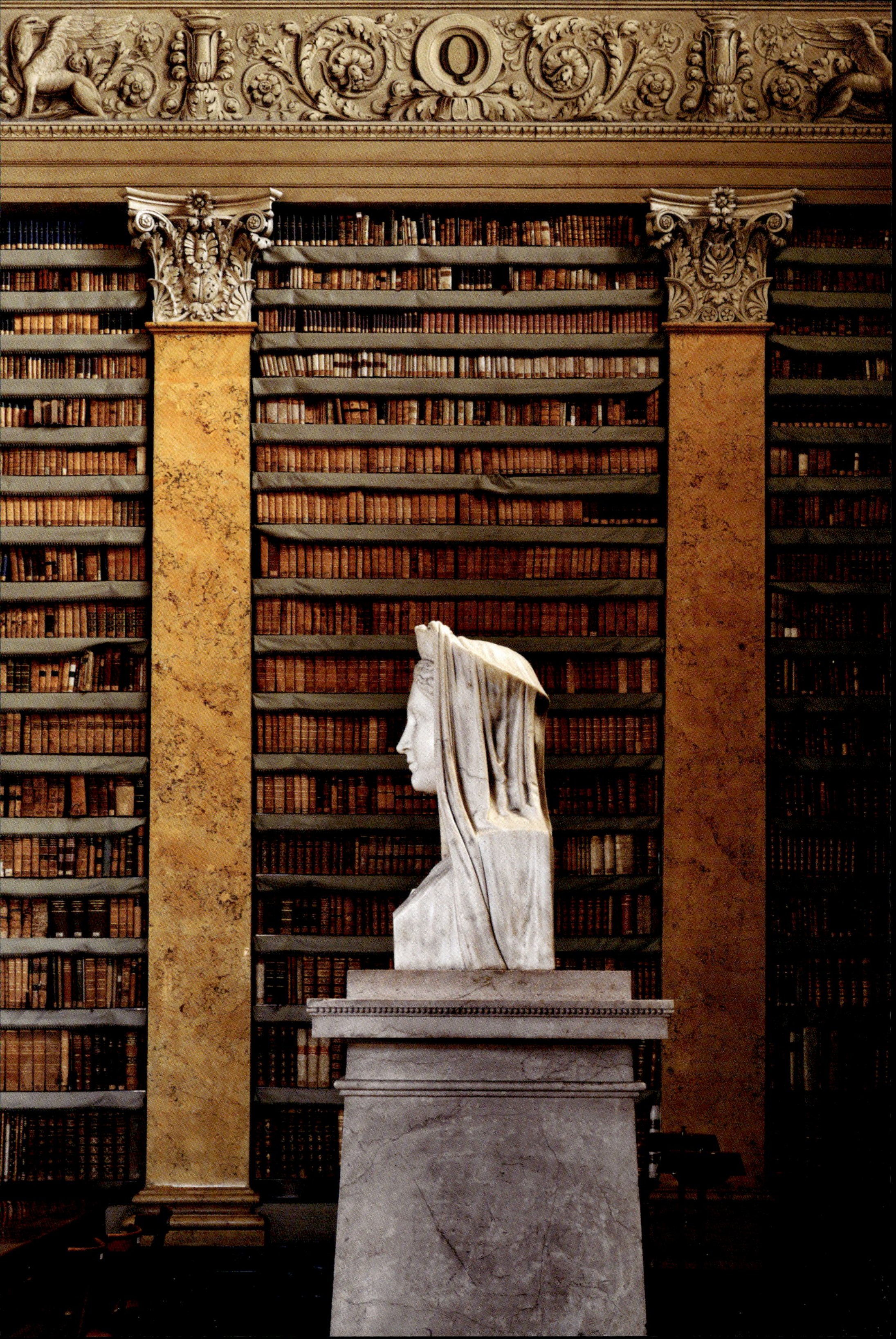

SOUTHERN EUROPE

Italy
Spain
Portugal

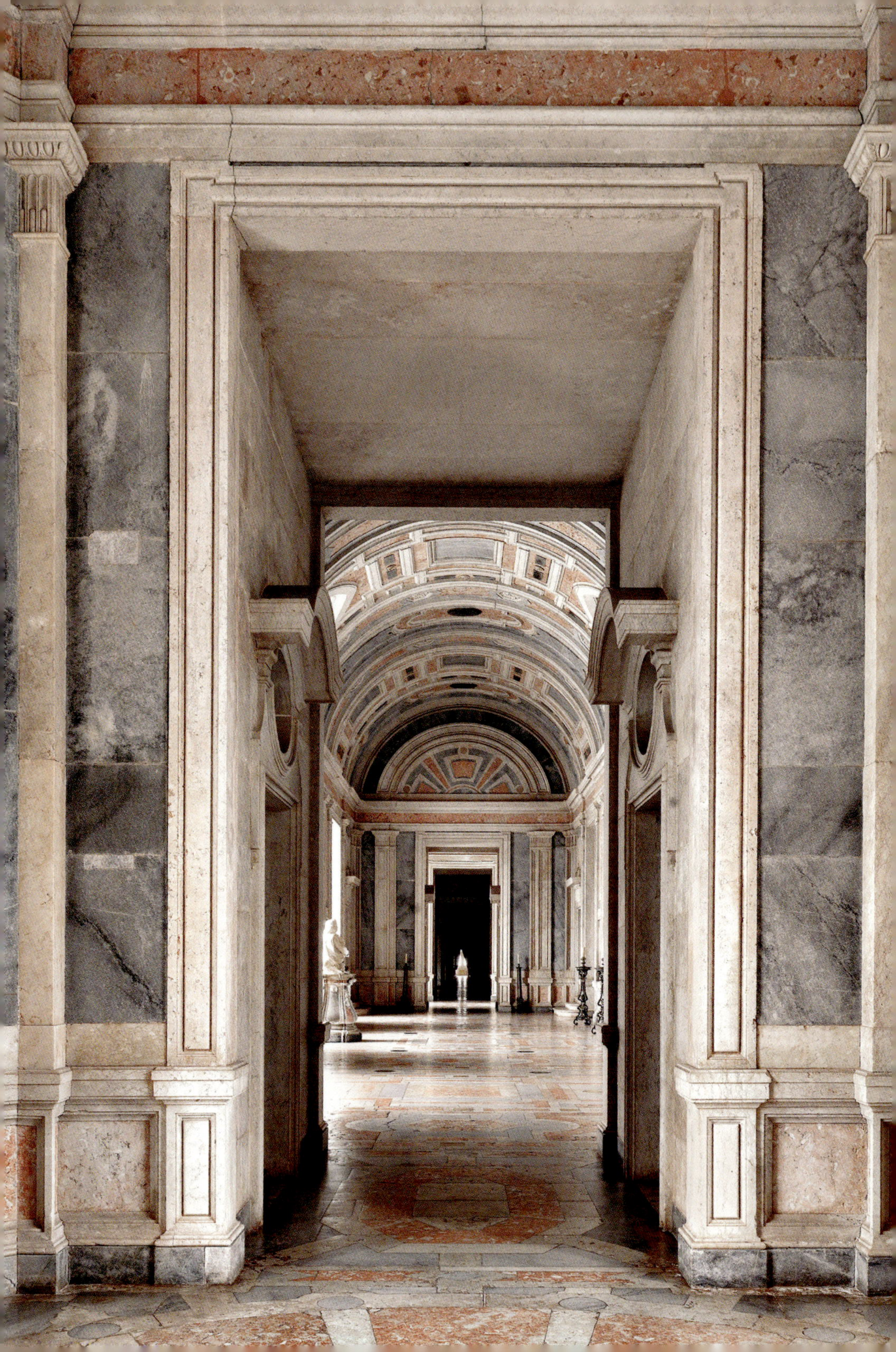

ITALY

SPAIN

PORTUGAL

Text by Elisabeth Sladek

Page 76 Biblioteca Palatina, Parma, Italy
Opposite Biblioteca do Convento de Mafra, Portugal

Biblioteca Apostolica Vaticana

The books and papers which belonged to the early popes, who took up residence in Rome in the 4th century, were stored in a *scrinium* (a case or chest) and from the 8th century onwards were maintained by a librarian with this special responsibility. The eventful history of the papacy in the Middle Ages interrupted the continuous development of this first collection, however, and most of these holdings were subsequently scattered. Around 1450 Pope Nicholas V (1397–1455), as part of his project to rebuild the papal palace in the spirit of the Renaissance, established a new library, whose holdings were also to be made accessible to the scholarly public. By 1475 the Vatican library already occupied four rooms on the ground floor, which at the behest of Sixtus IV (1414–1484) were decorated by the most celebrated painters of the day. The same pope also appointed as librarian the erudite humanist Bartolomeo Platina (1421–1481; ill. p. 34), who wrote the *Lives of the Popes* on the basis of the Vatican manuscripts he catalogued.

The history of the Vatican Library as we know it today dates back to Sixtus V (1521–1590), who initiated the construction of a new building to house the collection, which by that time contained over 20,000 volumes. The site chosen was Bramante's Cortile del Belvedere at the centre of the Vatican complex, which had served the Renaissance popes as an open-air space where tournaments and festivities could be held. This courtly tradition was radically terminated by the construction of the library building, which not only ran right across the courtyard, but also symbolised a new moral authority at the heart of the Apostolic Palace. According to the plans drawn up by the architect Domenico Fontana (1543–1607), the Vatican's printing press was also to be accommodated in the new building, wholly in the spirit of the Counter-Reformation. The library room on the top floor, named the Salone Sistino (Sistine Hall) after its founder, measures an imposing 70 x 15 metres (230 x 49 feet) and became the yardstick for later libraries, including the Imperial Court Library in Vienna. With the ambitious fresco programme decorating its walls and twin vaulted ceilings, the Sistine Hall sits firmly within the tradition of centres of learning and the libraries of secular princes. The most valuable manuscripts and books were housed in wooden cabinets along the walls; in contrast to the earlier organisation of the codices into a Latin and a Greek library, the holdings are today catalogued according to subject area. With the opening of a reading room for printed books in 1892, the library was opened up to a wider circle of readers. The Vatican Library is today run by a Prefect, under the titular direction of a Cardinal Librarian.

⁂

Founded c. 1450; new library built in 1587–1588 by Domenico Fontana
Holdings c. 2,400,000 items, of which c. 1,800,000 manuscripts and printed works
Type of library research library
Highlights *Codex Vaticanus*, 4th century (Vat. Gr. 1209), one of the oldest extant manuscripts of the Greek Bible; *Vergilius Vaticanus*, c. 400 (Vat. Lat. 3225); *Lorsch Gospels*, before 814 (Pal. Lat. 50); *La Commedia (Dante Urbinate) (Codex urbinate latino 365) – The Divine Comedy*, with miniatures by Gugliemo Giraldi, c. 1480 (Urb. Lat. 365)

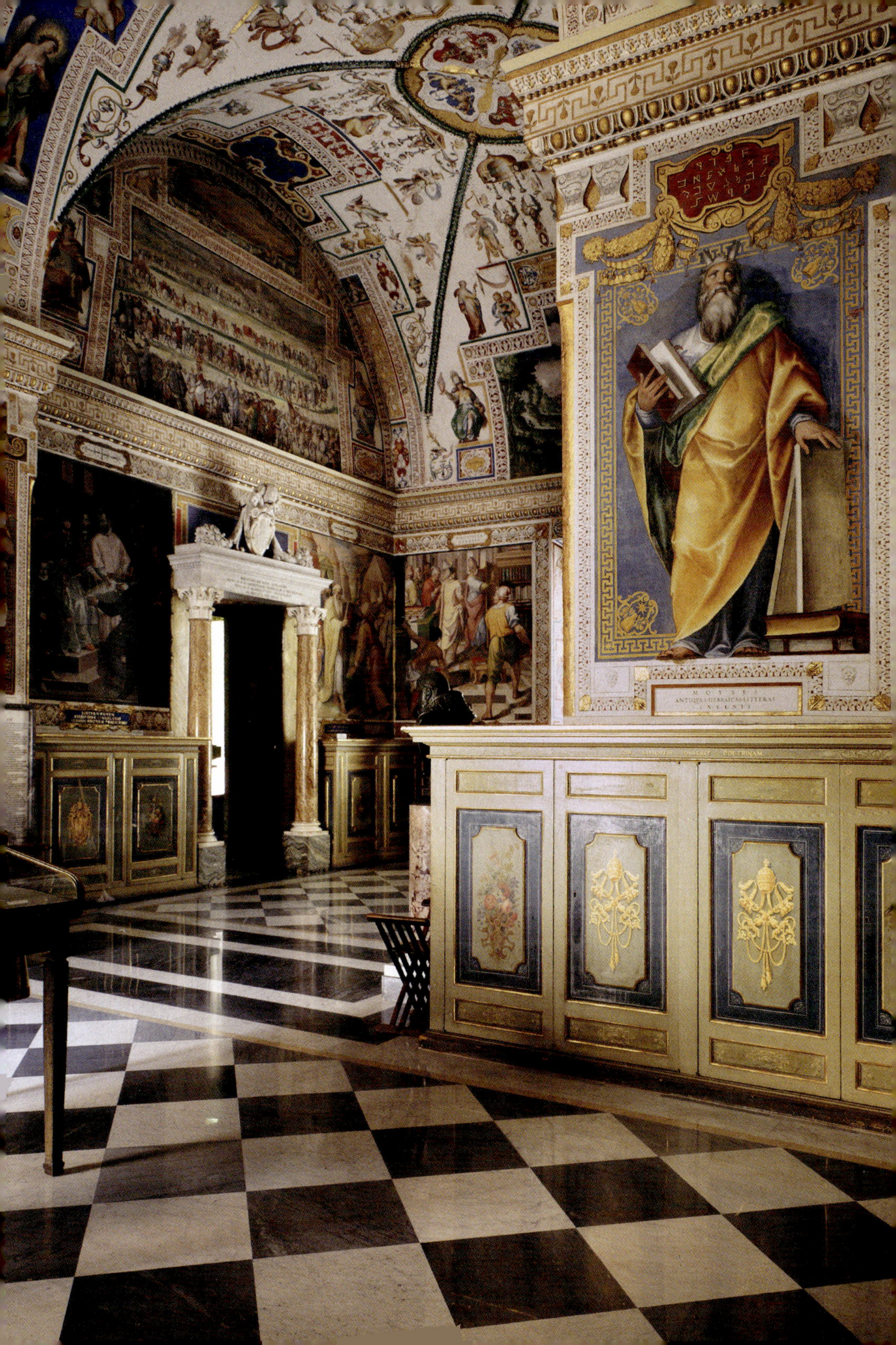

Seit die Päpste im 4. Jahrhundert in Rom ihre Residenz einrichteten, ist ein *scrinium*, ein Bücherschrein, überliefert, in dem Schriften und Dokumente gesammelt und von einem seit dem 8. Jahrhundert belegten Bibliothekar verwaltet wurden. Die wechselhafte Geschichte des Papsttums im Mittelalter verhinderte aber die kontinuierliche Entwicklung dieser Sammlung, die großteils verloren ging. Um 1450 gründete Nikolaus V. (1397–1455) im Vatikan, wo er eine im Geist der Renaissance erneuerte Residenz der Päpste zu gestalten begann, eine auch dem gelehrten Publikum geöffnete Bibliothek. 1475 erstreckte sie sich bereits über vier Säle im Erdgeschoss der päpstlichen Residenz, die im Auftrag Sixtus' IV. (1414–1484) von den bekanntesten Malern der Zeit prächtig ausgestattet wurden. Er berief den gelehrten Humanisten Bartolomeo Platina (1421–1481) zum Bibliothekar (Abb. S. 34), der anhand der von ihm katalogisierten Büchersammlung unter anderem sein Werk zur Papstgeschichte verfasste.

Die Geschichte der Vatikanischen Bibliothek, wie wir sie heute kennen, geht auf Sixtus V. (1521–1590) zurück, der einen Neubau für die bereits auf mehr als 20 000 Bände angewachsene Sammlung in Angriff nahm. Er wählte dazu den Belvederehof Bramantes im Zentrum der Vatikanischen Paläste, der den Päpsten der Renaissance als Turnier- und Festplatz gedient hatte. Mit dieser höfischen Tradition wurde durch den Bibliotheksbau radikal gebrochen, der nicht nur als architektonischer Riegel quer das Platzareal durchschnitt, sondern auch als neue moralische Instanz im Zentrum der Papstresidenz zu begreifen war. Nach dem Plan des Architekten Domenico Fontana (1543–1607) sollte ganz im Sinne der Gegenreformation gemeinsam mit der Bibliothek auch die Vatikanische Druckerei in dem neuen Gebäude untergebracht werden. Der zweischiffige, nach seinem Gründer Salone Sistino benannte Bibliothekssaal im Obergeschoss wurde mit seiner imposanten Größe von 70 x 15 Metern zum Maßstab späterer Bibliotheksneubauten – so zum Beispiel der Kaiserlichen Hofbibliothek in Wien. Das anspruchsvolle Freskenprogramm dieses Saals stellt die Bibliothek der Päpste in die Tradition von Herrscherbibliotheken und Stätten der Gelehrsamkeit. Die wertvollsten Handschriften und Bücher waren entlang der Wände in Holzschränken untergebracht. Im Unterschied zu der früheren Aufteilung der Kodizes in eine lateinische und eine griechische Bibliothek setzte sich nun eine neue Ordnung nach Sachgebieten durch. Mit der Errichtung des Druckschriftenlesesaals im Jahr 1892 wurde die Bibliothek einem weiteren Lesekreis zugänglich gemacht. Sie wird heute von einem Präfekten geführt, dem ein Kardinal-Bibliothekar vorsteht.

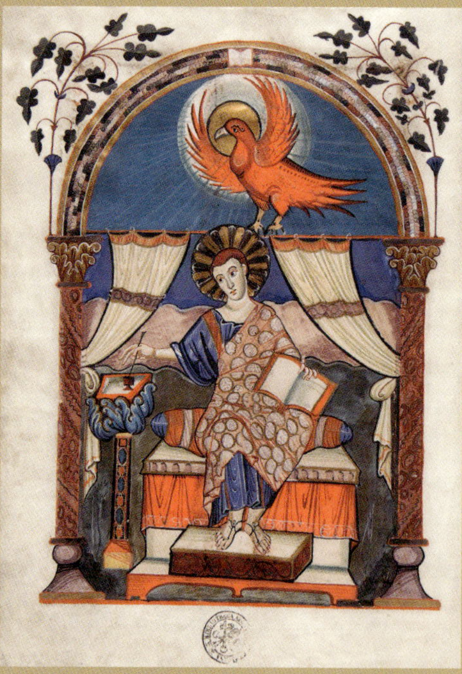

Lorsch Gospels, before 814, sig. Pal. Lat. 50, fol. 67v: *John the Evangelist*

Dante Alighieri, *La Commedia (Dante Urbinate) – The Divine Comedy*, with miniatures by Gugliemo Giraldi, c. 1480, sig. Urb. Lat. 365, fol. 97r: *Dante and Virgil have arrived on the shores of Mount Purgatory and meet the wise Cato*

Dès leur installation à Rome au IVe siècle
de notre ère, les papes se transmettent un
scrinium, sorte d'écrin rassemblant des écrits
et des documents, qui sera administré par un
bibliothécaire attitré à partir du VIIIe siècle.
L'histoire mouvementée de la papauté au Moyen
Âge empêche l'agrandissement de cette collection, dont la plus grande partie sera perdue.
Vers 1450, Nicolas V (1397–1455) crée une bibliothèque au Vatican, où il entreprend de rénover
la résidence papale dans le style Renaissance.
Il souhaite également ouvrir la bibliothèque au
public instruit. En 1475, elle s'étend déjà sur
quatre salles du premier niveau de la résidence,
que Sixte IV (1414–1484) fait admirablement
décorer par les meilleurs peintres de son temps.
C'est ce même pape qui nomme l'humaniste
érudit Bartolomeo Platina (1421–1481 ; ill. p. 34)
bibliothécaire. Ce dernier rédigea notamment
un ouvrage sur l'histoire de la papauté en utili-
sant la collection de livres qu'il avait indexée.

L'histoire de la Vaticane telle qu'on la
connaît aujourd'hui remonte à Sixte Quint
(1521–1590), qui initia la construction d'une aile
pour abriter environ 20 000 volumes. Pour ce
faire, il choisit la cour du Belvédère de Bramante
au centre du palais, que les papes de la Renaissance avaient convertie en aire de tournois et
de jeux. Le choix était en rupture radicale avec
la tradition. Il ne s'agissait pas seulement d'une
barre architectonique coupant la place en deux,
mais aussi d'une nouvelle instance morale au
cœur du palais. D'après les plans de l'architecte
Domenico Fontana (1543–1607), l'imprimerie
vaticane devait, dans l'esprit de la Contre-
Réforme, trouver elle aussi sa place dans le nouveau bâtiment. La salle de bibliothèque à double
vaisseau située à l'étage supérieur se nomme
Salone Sistino en hommage à son fondateur.
De par ses dimensions imposantes (70 x 15 m),
elle a servi de modèle de référence, notamment
pour la bibliothèque impériale de Vienne. Le
programme ambitieux des fresques inscrit la
Vaticane dans la tradition des bibliothèques
privées et des centres d'érudition. Les manuscrits et ouvrages les plus précieux ont trouvé

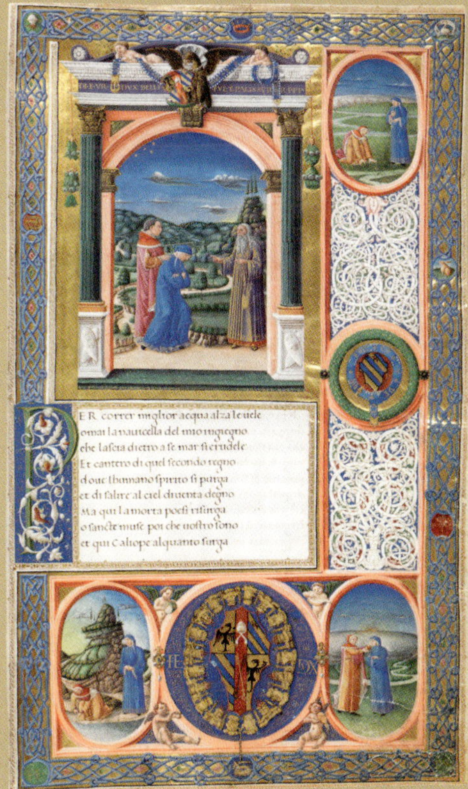

refuge dans les cabinets en bois le long des
murs. À l'origine, les codex étaient répartis en
deux bibliothèques (une latine et une grecque) ;
aujourd'hui, l'ordonnancement est thématique.
En 1892, la création d'une salle de lecture dédiée
aux imprimés, permit d'élargir la fréquentation
de la bibliothèque. Celle-ci est aujourd'hui
administrée par un préfet, placé sous l'autorité
d'un cardinal bibliothécaire.

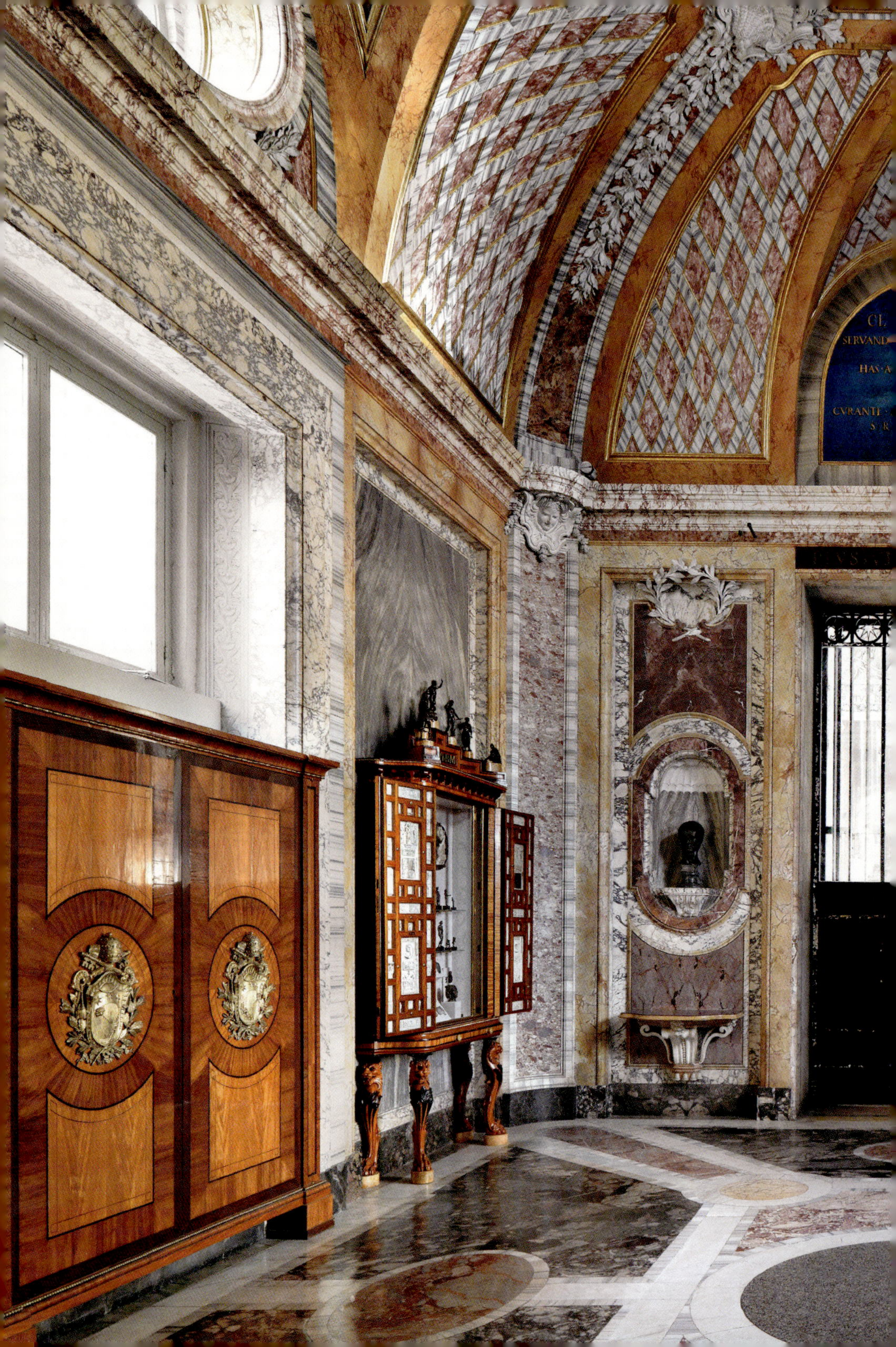

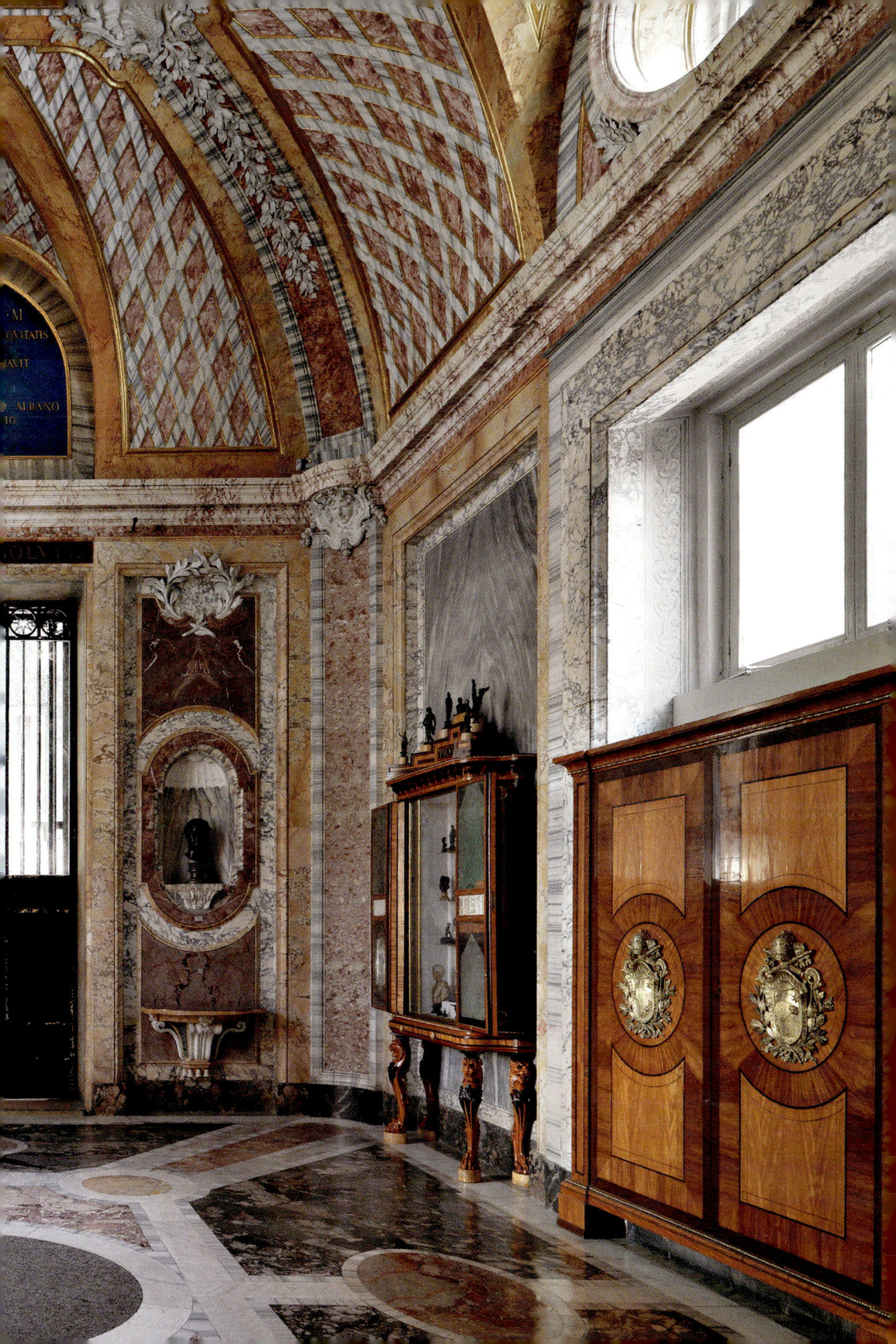

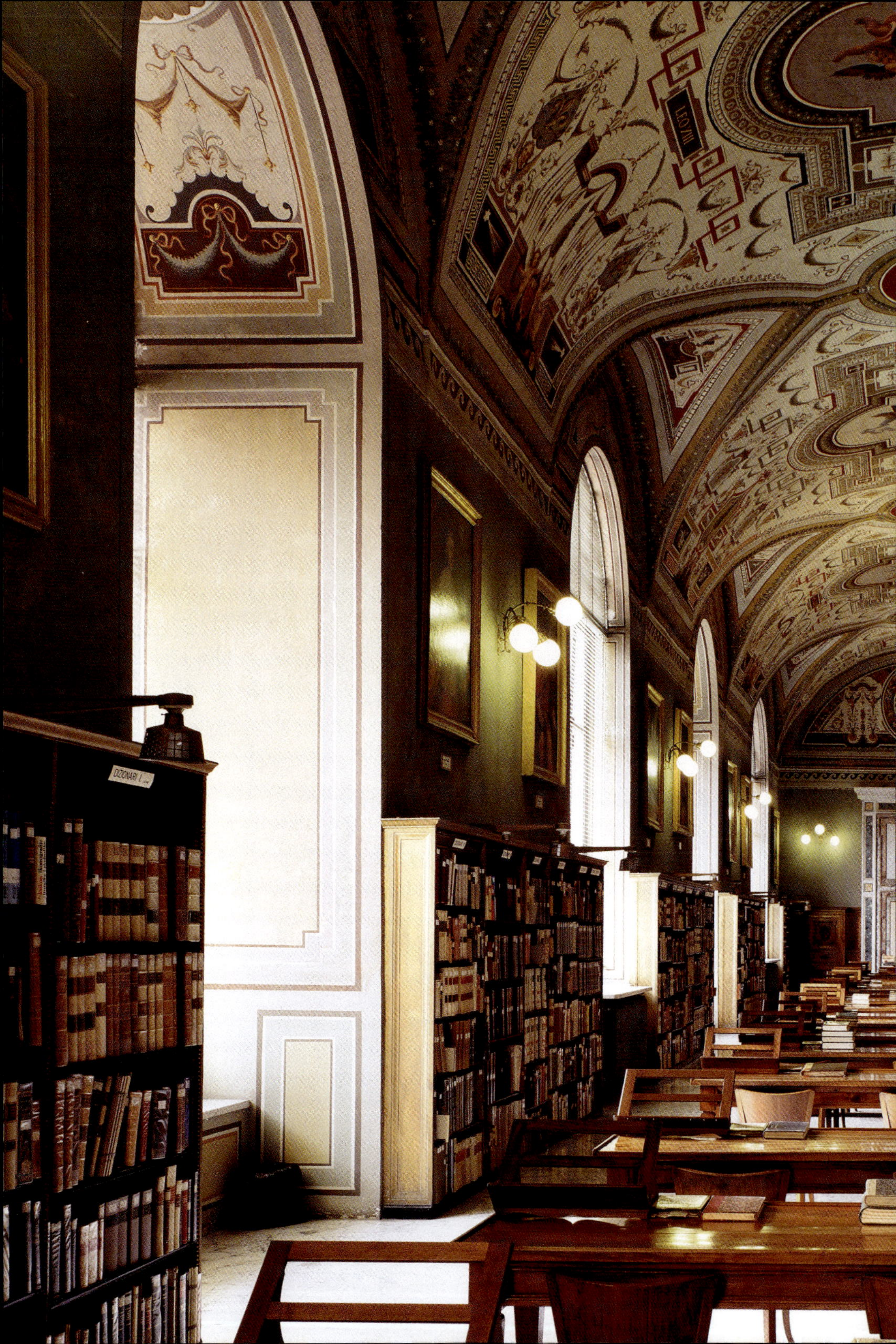

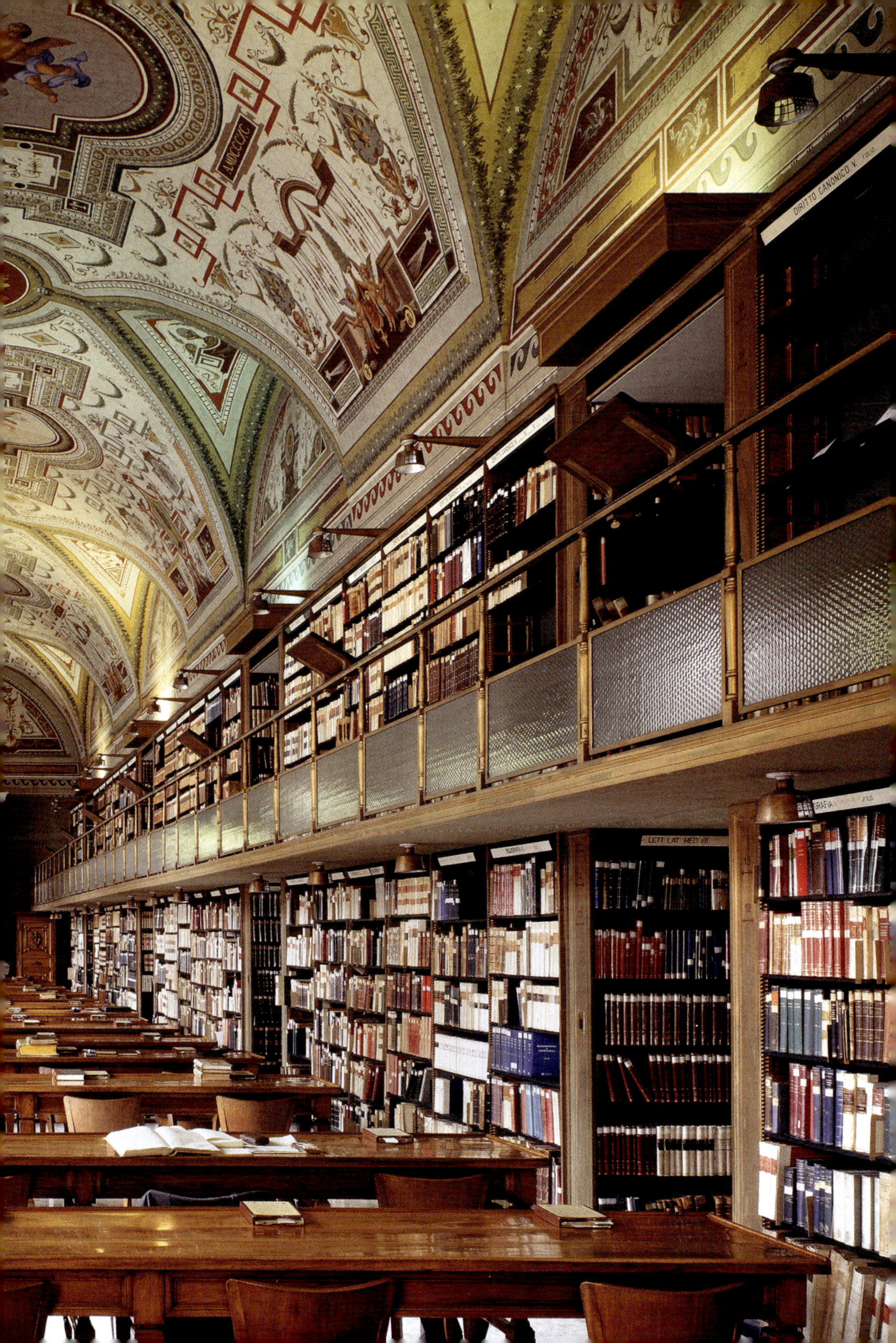

DIRITTO CANONICO V.
LETT. LAT. MED. III.

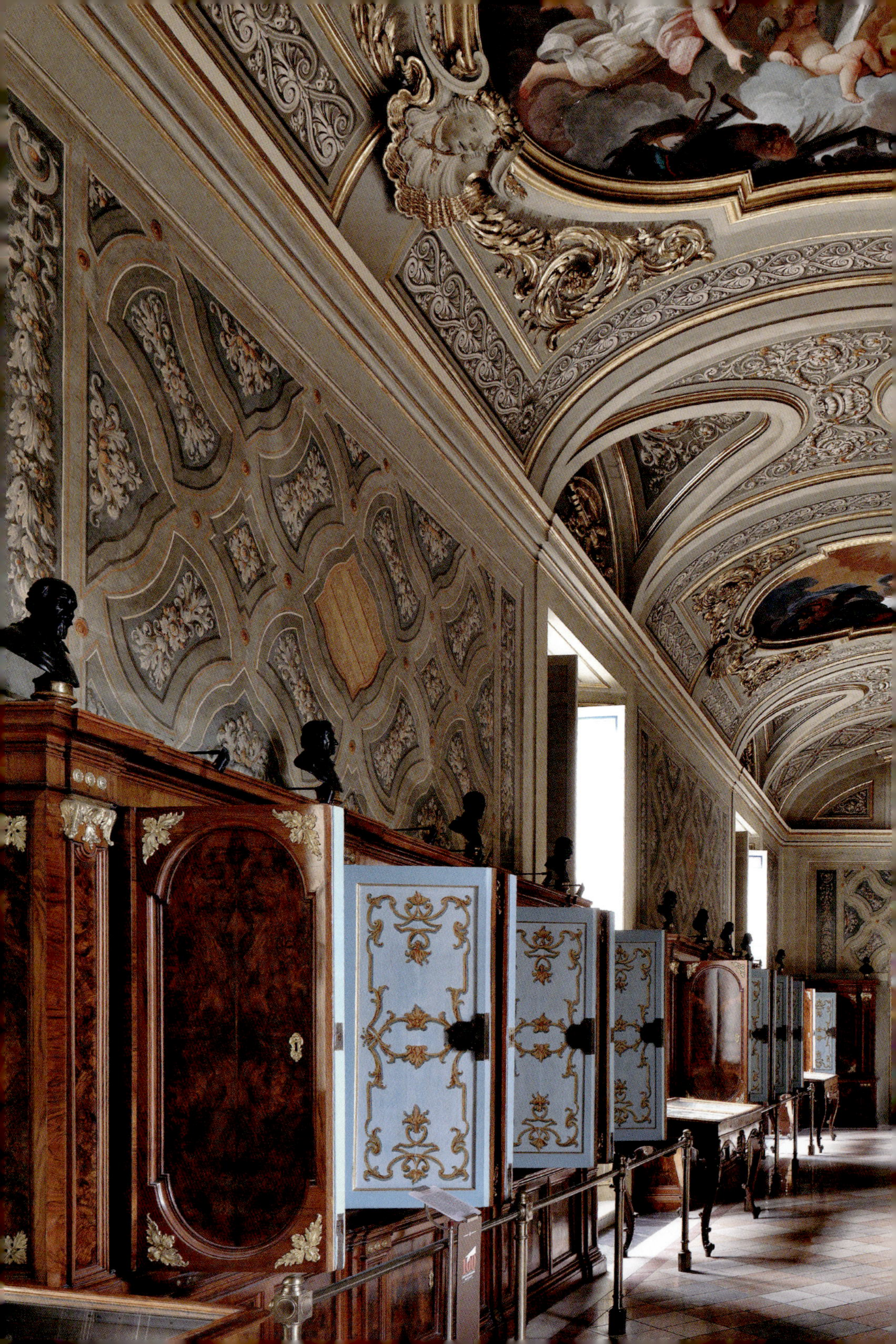

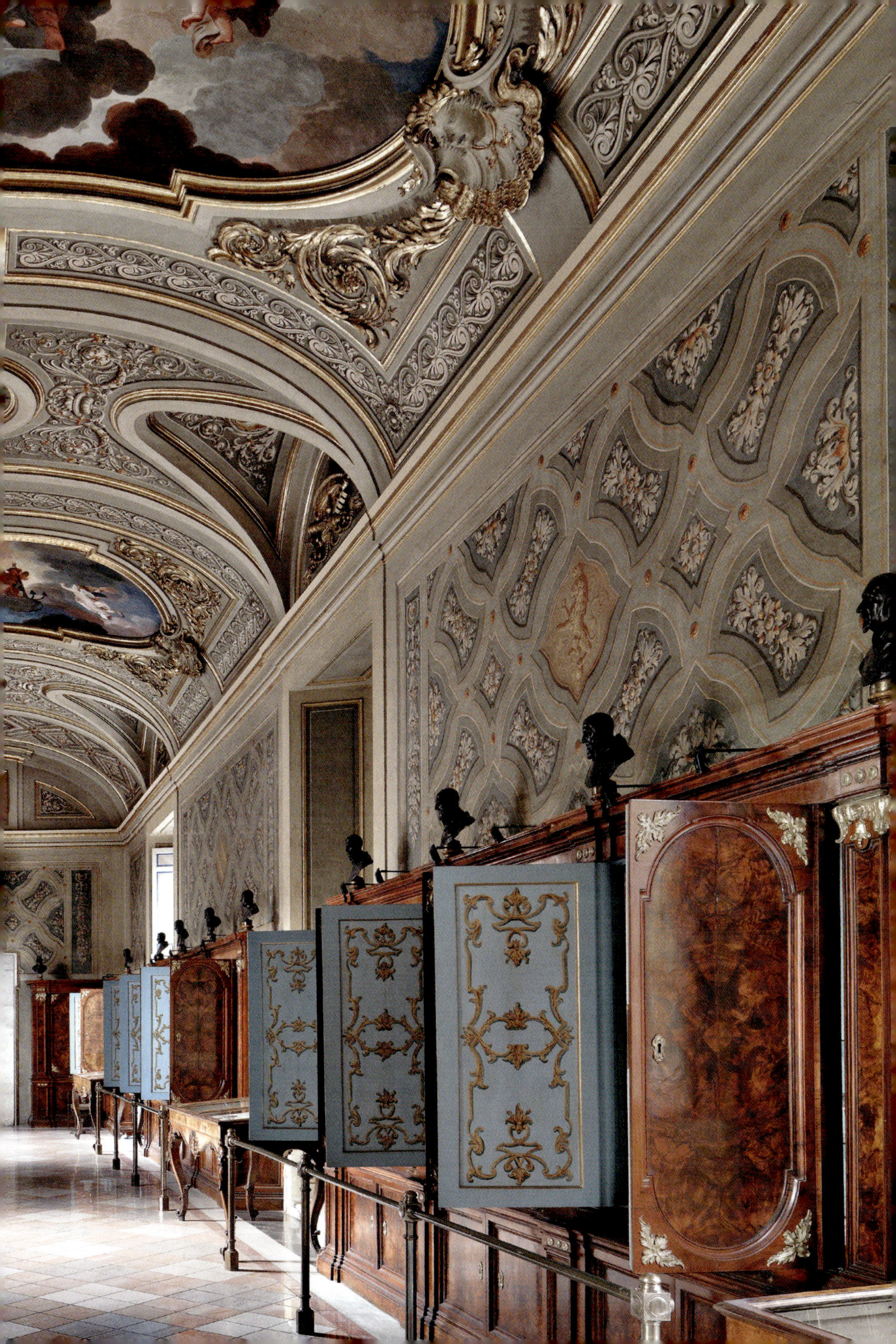

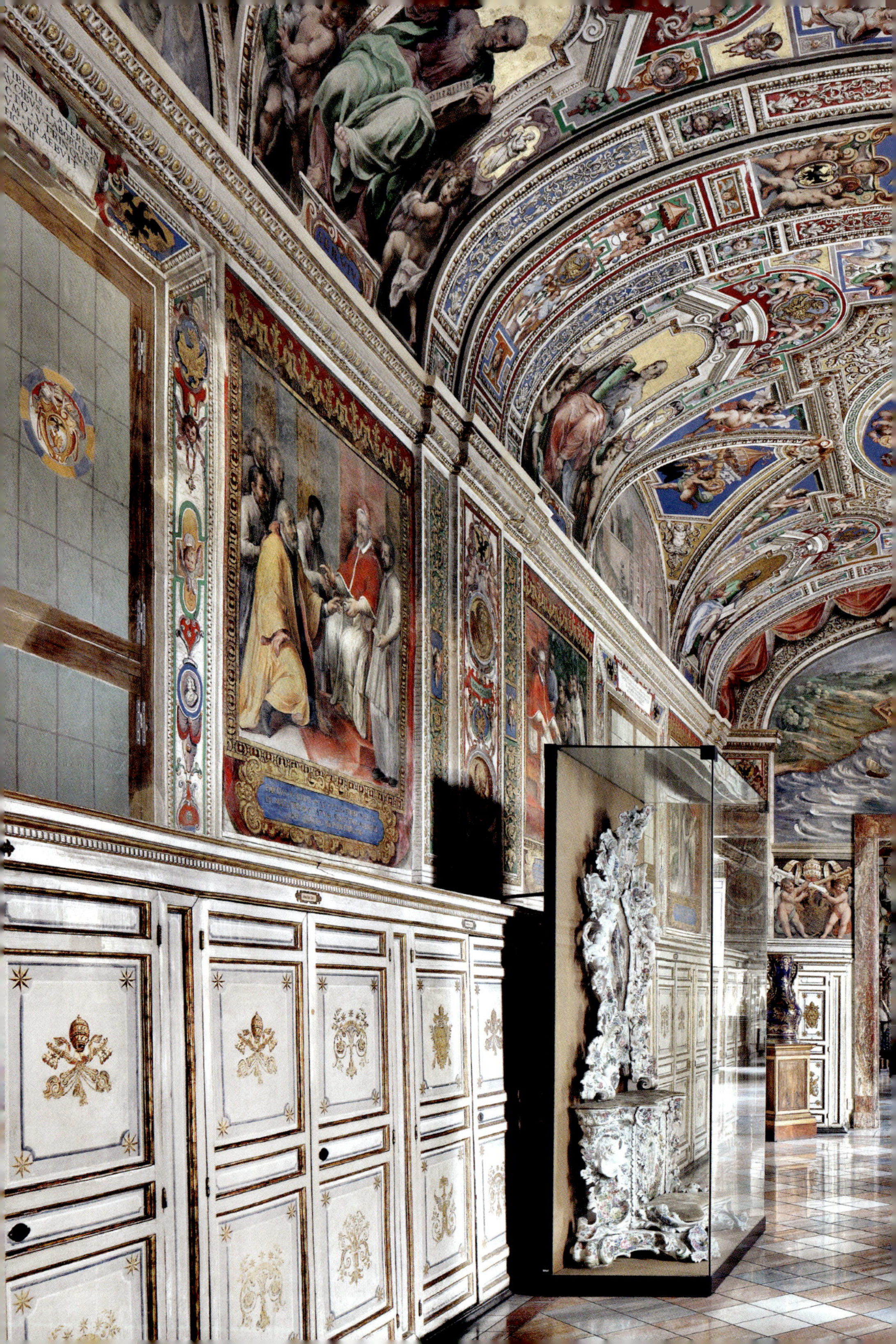

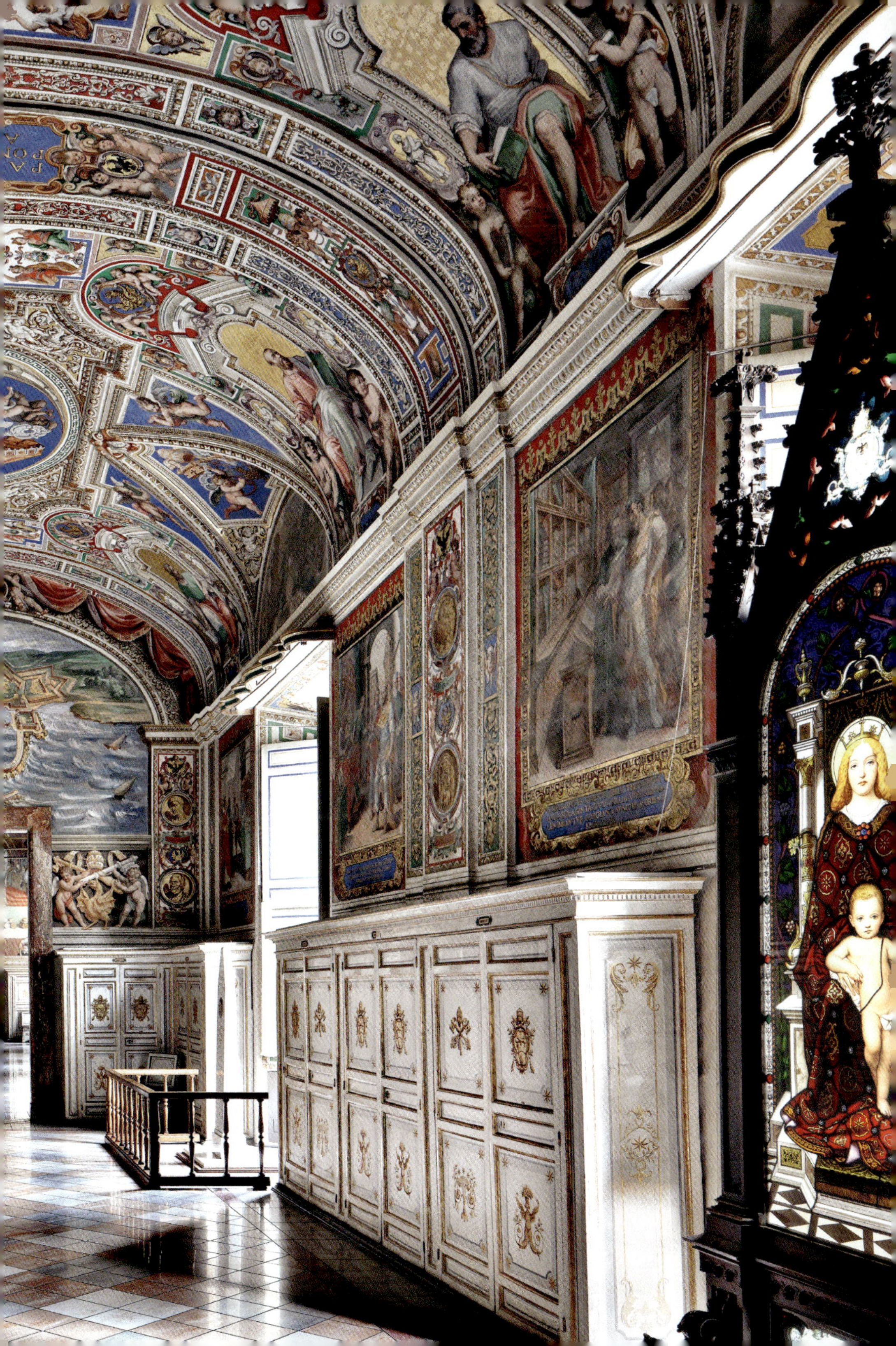

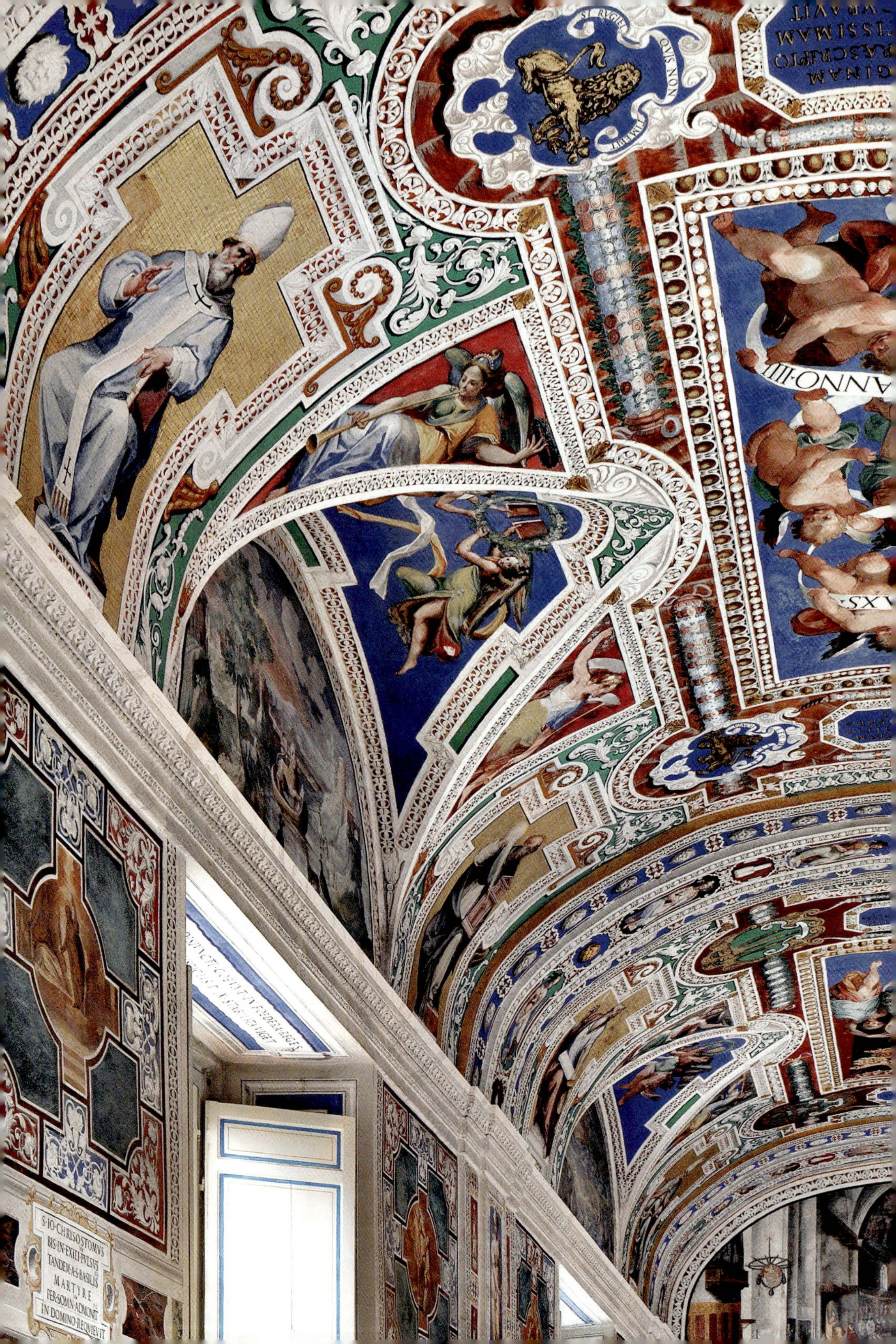

SI RVGIET ... QVIS NON ... TIMEBIT
ANNO IIII
S. IO. CHRYSOSTOMVS
BIS IN EXILI PVLSVS
TANDEM A S BASILIS
MARTYRE
PER SOMN ADMONT
IN DOMINO REQVIEVIT

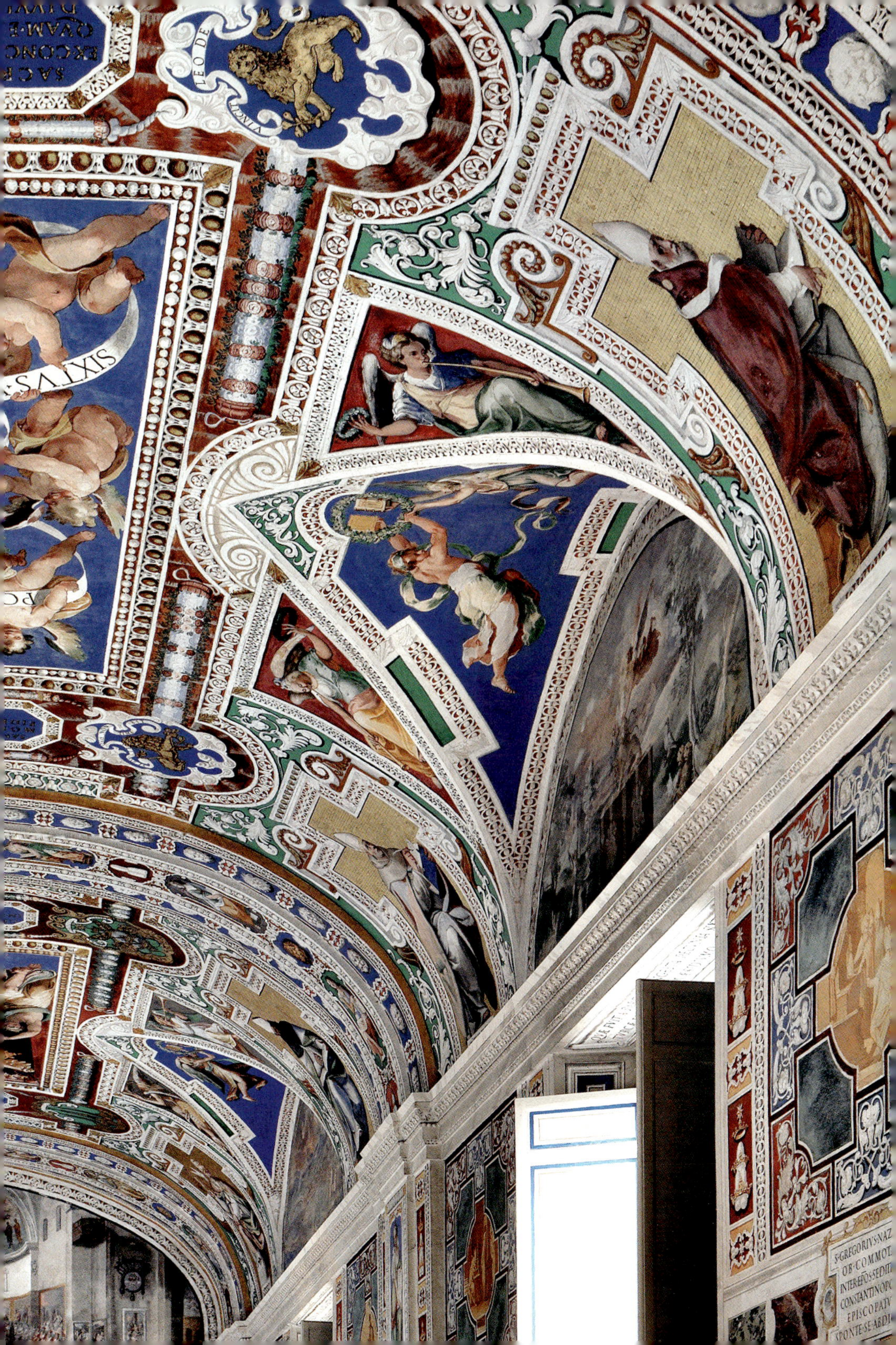

LEO DE
VINCIT
SIXTVS
S·GREGORIVS·NAZ
OB·COMMOT
INTER·EÕS·SEDIT
CONSTANTINOP
EPISCOPATV
PONTE·SE·ABDI

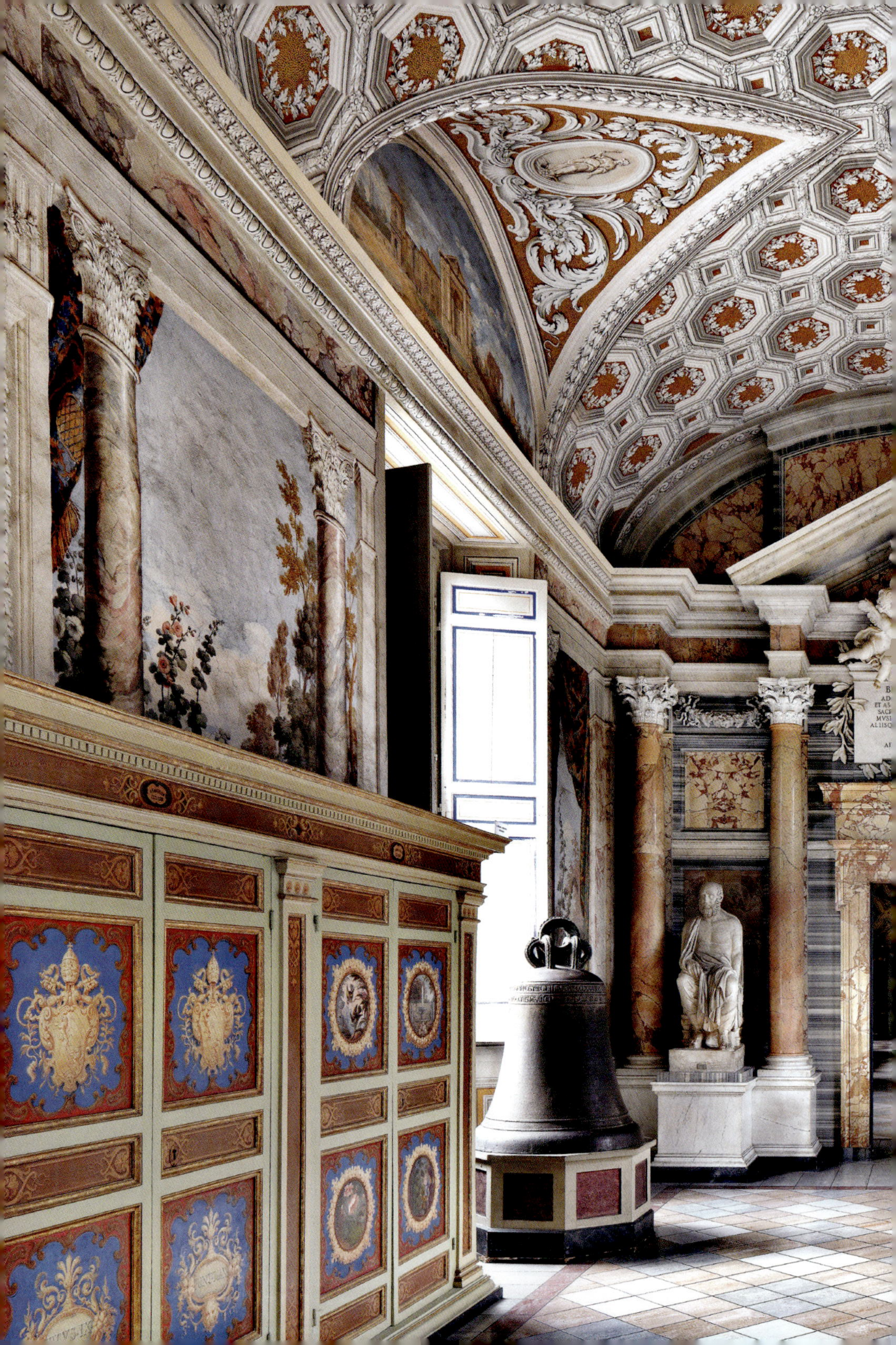

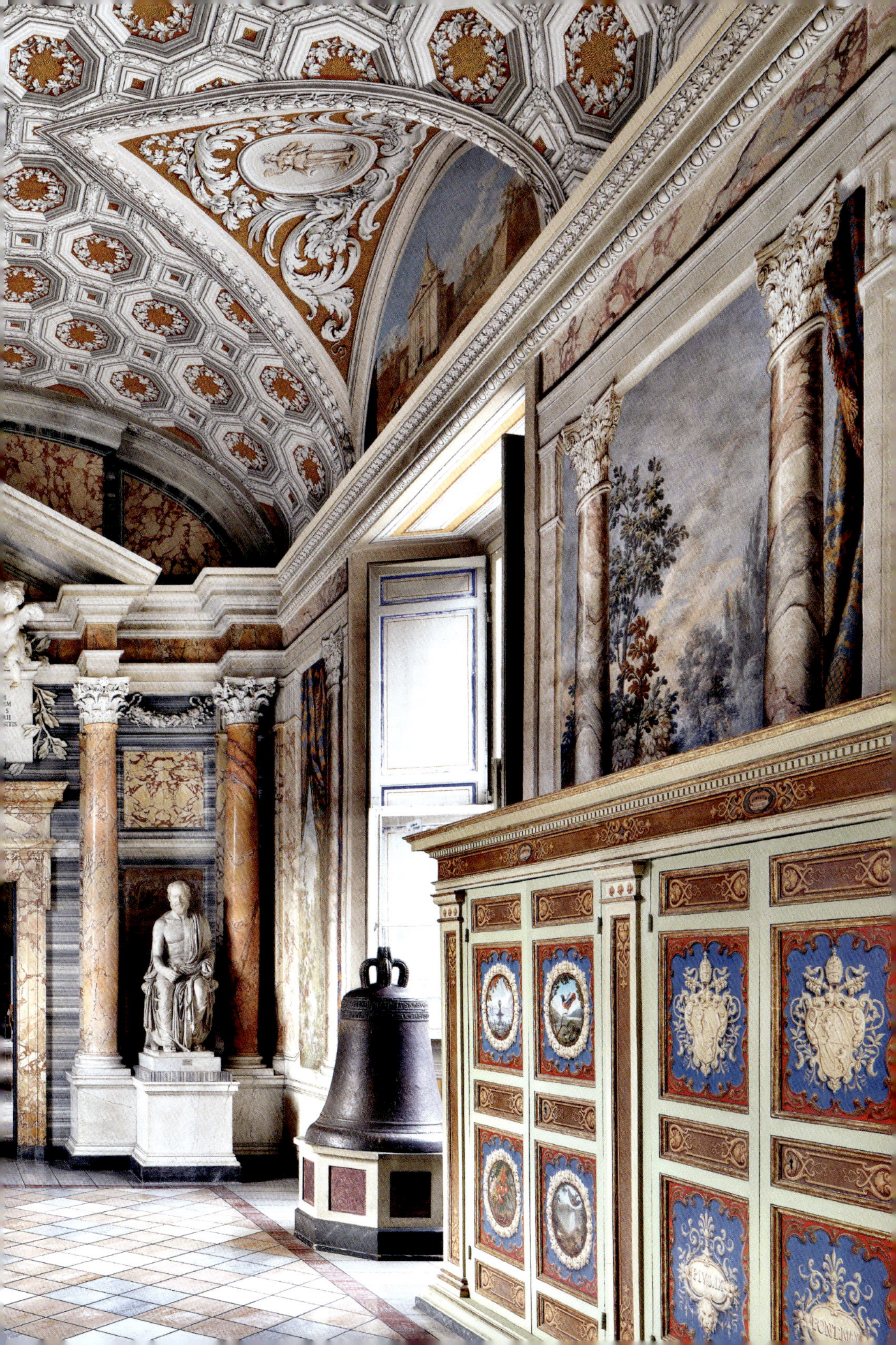

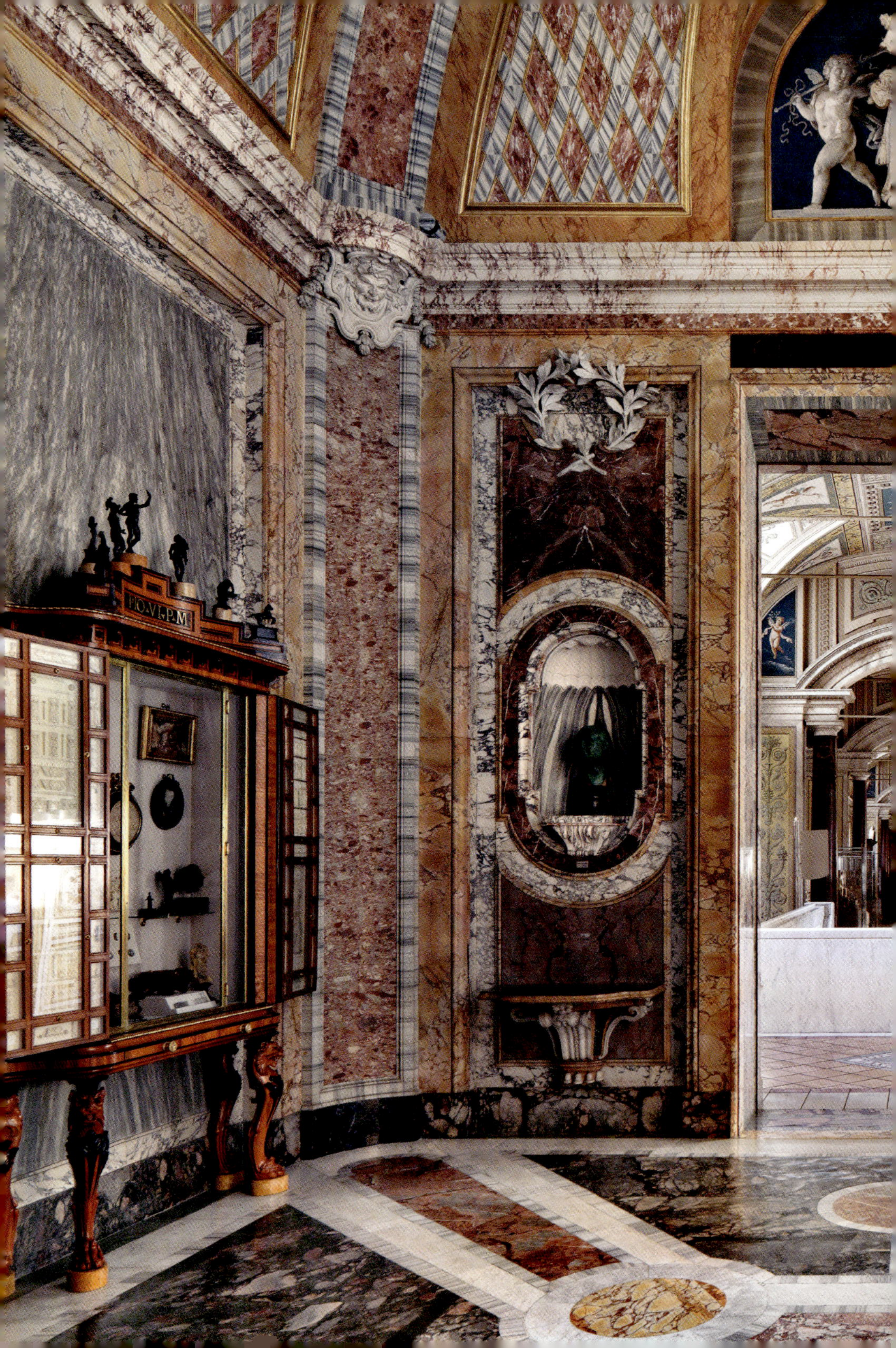

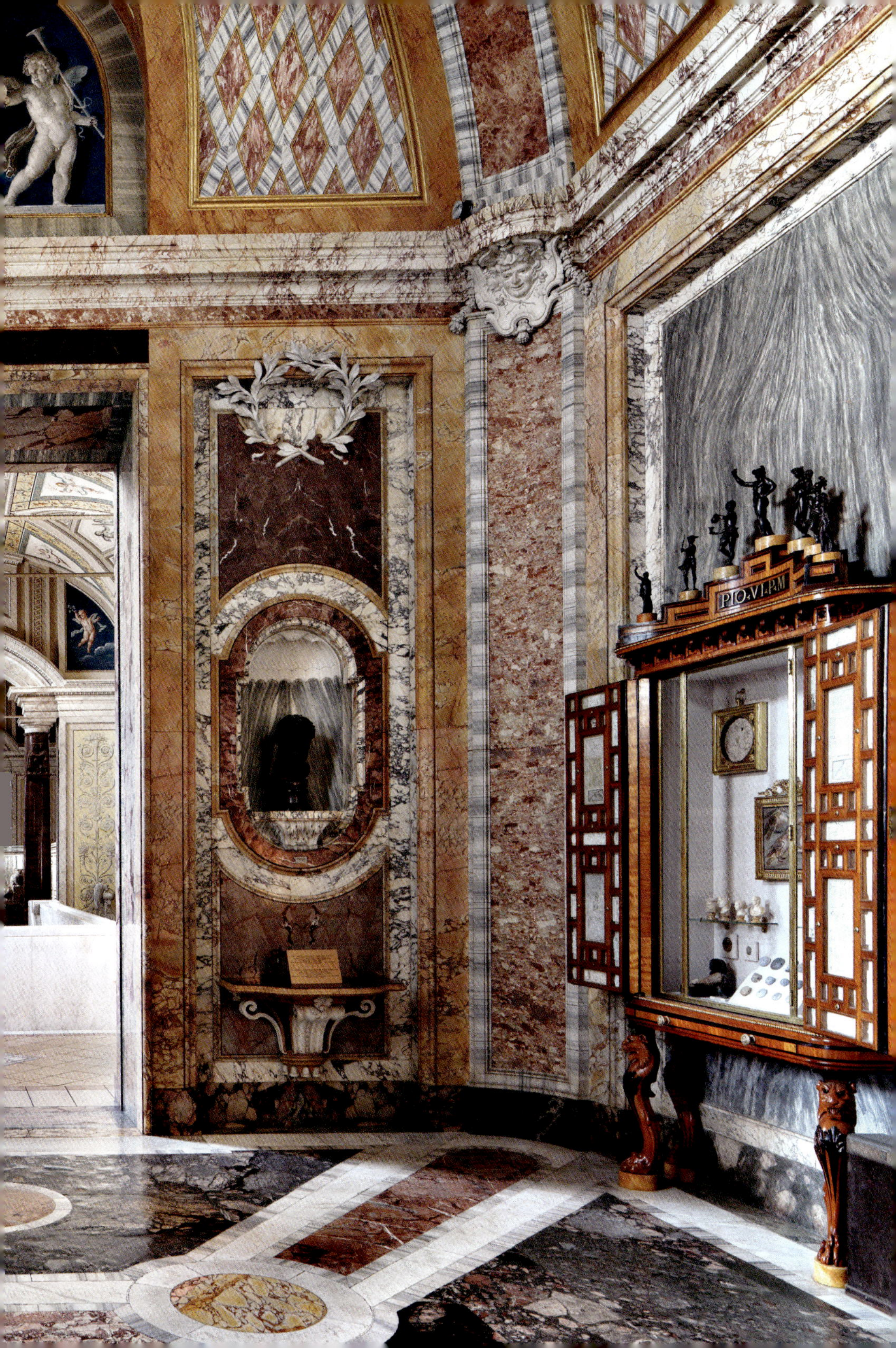

PIO.VI.P.M

Biblioteca Nazionale Marciana

The Biblioteca Nazionale Marciana (National Library of St Mark's) is named after the patron saint of Venice and owes its establishment to endowments by famous benefactors. Francesco Petrarca (1304–1374), who is commemorated by a statue in today's reading room, called for a public library in Venice as early as 1362 and bequeathed his famous collection of manuscripts to the city to this end. In 1468 Cardinal Basilius Bessarion (1403–1472), who like Petrarch wished to give Venice an intellectual centre, followed suit and presented the city with 750 codices and 250 manuscripts from his widely admired private collection. As today's library was only built after 1536 as part of the remodelling of St Mark's Square, the collection was provisionally housed in St Mark's Basilica, where it was known as the Biblioteca Nicena. In 1530 the Republic of Venice appointed the humanist and scholar Pietro Bembo (1470–1547) as its librarian. In the wake of the enclosure of St Mark's Square by buildings in a uniform architectural style, the collection – now called the Libreria di San Marco – found a home befitting its importance in the wing, 21 arcaded bays in length, opposite the Doge's Palace. Offices for the Procurators of San Marco were located on the ground floor and a new mint was installed on the lagoon side, the old one having burned down. The commission for this prestigious project was awarded to architect and sculptor Jacopo Sansovino (1486–1570), who held the post of chief architect and superintendent of San Marco, and was completed after his death by Vincenzo Scamozzi (1548–1616). In collaboration with the most admired Venetian artists of the day, Sansovino created a magnificent building whose monumental rooms provided a fitting framework not only for precious books but also for choice works of art. From 1597 the collection of ancient Greek statuary belonging to the patriarch of Aquileia, Giovanni Grimani (1506–1593), was exhibited in the classically orchestrated vestibule, which served for academic assemblies and as a venue for the Scuola di San Marco. Some of these statues can still be seen there today. The decoration of the vestibule and in particular the library, with its 21 allegorical ceiling paintings and portraits of philosophers on the walls, was carried out by Paolo Veronese (1528–1588), Jacopo Tintoretto (1519–1594) and Titian (1490–1576), with the latter responsible for the coordination of the works as a whole. The marble floor of the vestibule invites the visitor to linger with its centralised pattern, while the black and white lozenge pattern of the library floor creates an illusionistic sense of depth. The library, which was originally furnished with monumental

Founded 1536 on the basis of older holdings; the Libreria di San Marco built 1537–1553 by Jacopo Sansovino and completed 1582–1588 by Vincenzo Scamozzi

Holdings c. 1 million volumes, of which 13,000 manuscripts

Type of library national library

Highlights The illustrated editions of the *Iliad* belonging to Cardinal Bessarione: *Homerus Venetus A*, 10th century (Cod. Gr. Z. 454) and *Homerus Venetus B*, 11th century (Cod. Gr. Z. 453); *Map of the World (Mappamondo)* by Fra Mauro, c. 1450; *Breviario Grimani*, a book of hours decorated with Flemish miniatures, before 1520 (Cod. Lat. I, 99); *Codice Latino* III, 177, end of the 15th century; first printed edition of the *Veduta di Venezia* by Jacopo de' Barbari, Venice, 1500

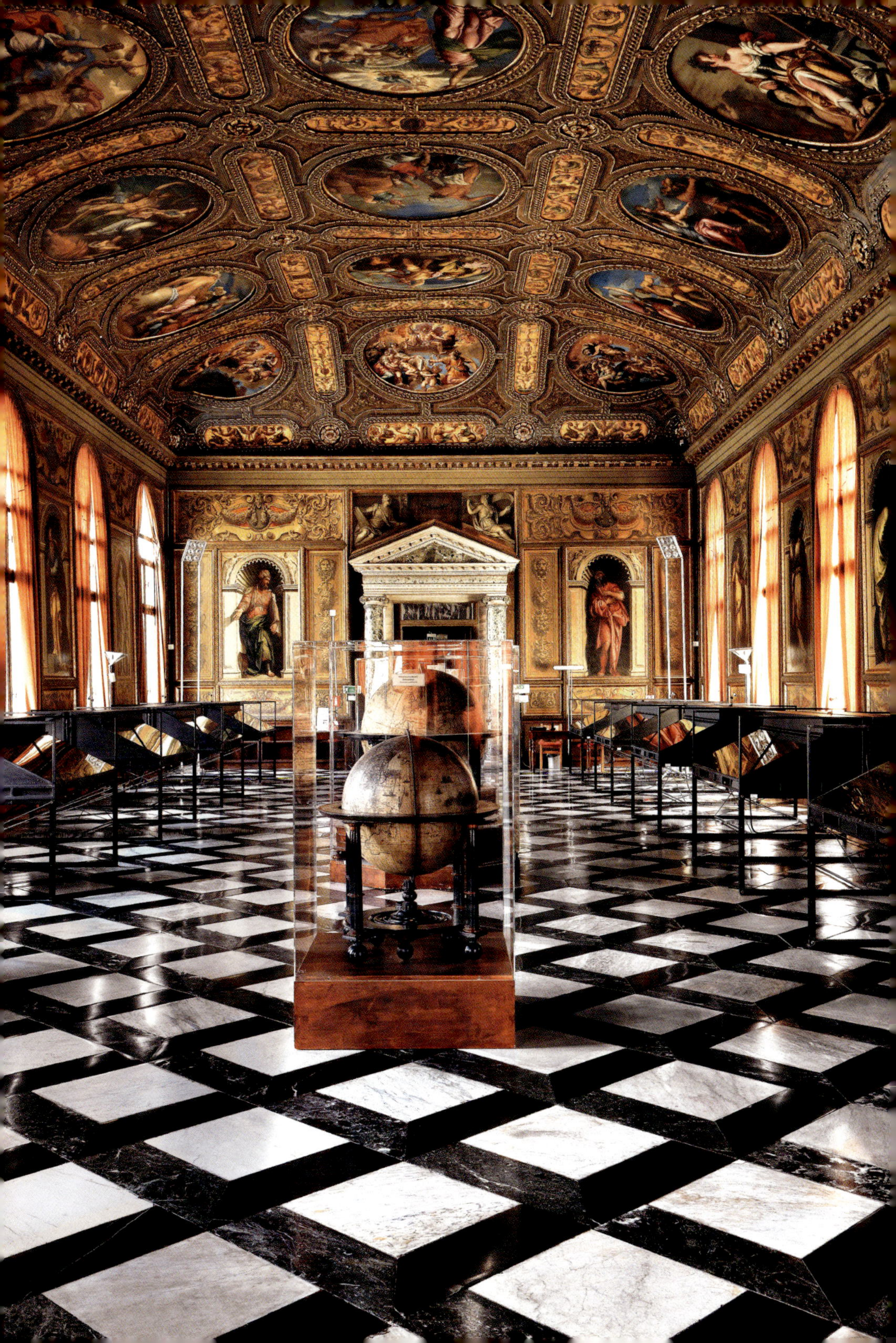

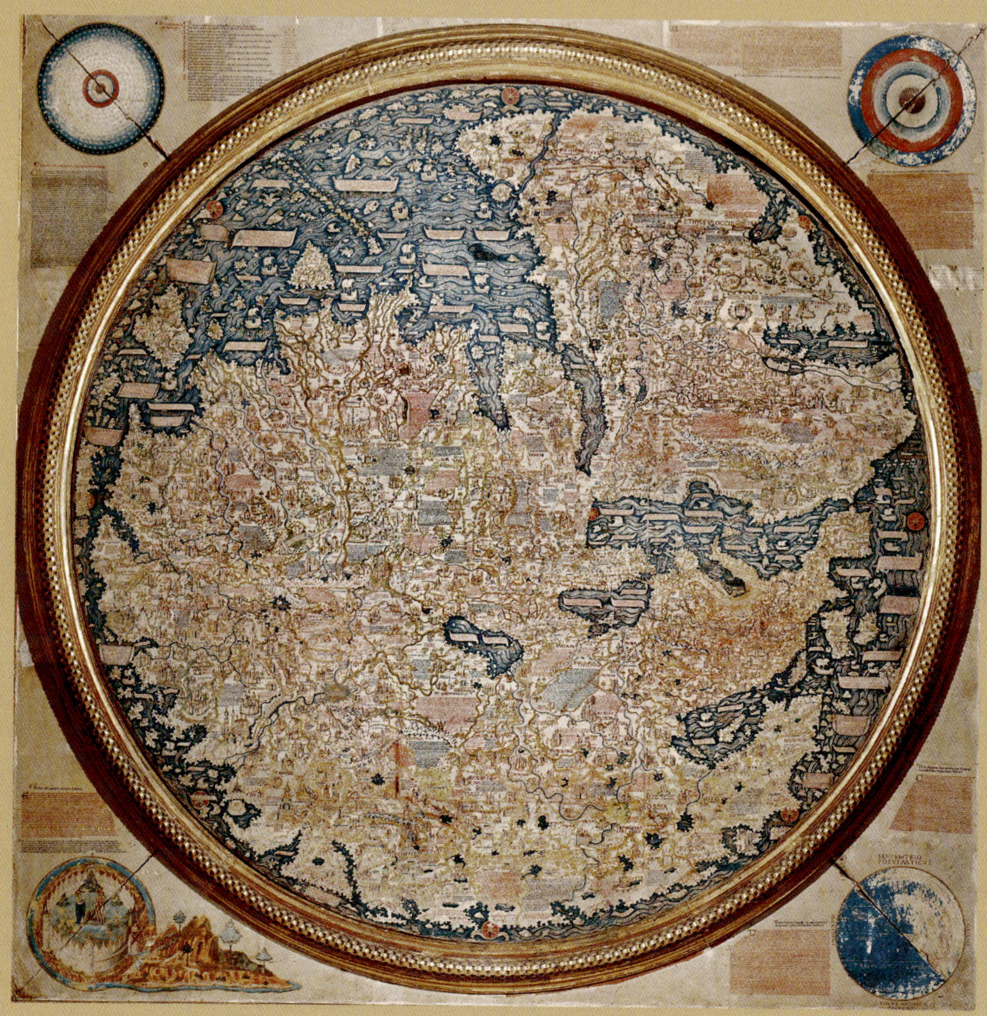

walnut desks and impressive wall cabinets, began operating in 1553. As the number of books grew, there was less and less space for the paintings and other works of art also displayed in the hall. These were therefore moved to the Doge's Palace and replaced by shelves extending right up to the ceiling, which by around 1700 held 10,000 books. In 1811, after the fall of the Venetian Republic, the entire library moved to the Doge's Palace, where it remained until 1904. Today the collection, which has grown to one million volumes, is housed between the Libreria and the Palazzo della Zecca, the government mint also built by Sansovino, whose three-storey-high inner courtyard, glazed over in 1904, currently serves as the reading room. The library in the 16th century was a centre of humanist studies, with a conspicuous number of Greek and Oriental manuscripts thanks to Bessarion's bequest. Its holdings decisively expanded after 1603, however, when the Republic of Venice passed a law that required one copy of every book printed on Venetian soil to be deposited with the Biblioteca Marciana.

Die nach dem Schutzheiligen der Republik Venedig benannte Bibliothek verdankt ihr Entstehen den Stiftungen berühmter Mäzene. Bereits 1362 hatte Francesco Petrarca (1304–1374), an den eine Statue im Zentrum des heutigen Lesesaals erinnert, den Bau einer öffentlichen Bibliothek angeregt und im Hinblick darauf seine berühmte Handschriftensammlung der Stadt vermacht. Dieser Schenkung folgte 1468 jene des Kardinals Basilius Bessarion (1403–1472), der mit seiner nicht nur in Humanistenkreisen geschätzten Sammlung von 750 Kodizes und 250 Handschriften ebenso wie Petrarca der Stadt ein intellektuelles Zentrum geben wollte. Da der heutige Bibliotheksbau aber erst ab 1536 im Rahmen der Neugestaltung des Markusplatzes entstand, war die ursprünglich als Biblioteca Nicena bezeichnete Sammlung bei der Basilika San Marco provisorisch untergebracht. 1530 ernannte die Republik Venedig den Humanisten und Gelehrten Pietro Bembo (1470–1547) zu ihrem Bibliothekar. Im Zuge der Umfassung des Markusplatzes mit einheitlich gestalteten Gebäuden fand die als Libreria di San Marco bezeichnete Sammlung in dem heute 21 Fensterachsen langen Flügel gegenüber dem Dogenpalast einen ihrer Bedeutung entsprechenden Standort. Dort entstanden auch Räumlichkeiten für die Prokuratoren von San Marco im Erdgeschoss sowie an der Seite zur Lagune die nach einem Brand neu zu errichtende Münze. Der Auftrag für das prestigeträchtige Projekt erging an den obersten Baumeister von San Marco, den Architekten und Bildhauer Jacopo Sansovino (1486–1570), und wurde nach seinem Tod von Vincenzo Scamozzi (1548–1616) fertiggestellt. Sansovino schuf in Zusammenarbeit mit den angesehensten venezianischen Künstlern einen von höchstem Anspruchsniveau geprägten Prachtbau, in dessen monumentalen Sälen

nicht nur den wertvollen Büchern, sondern auch ausgewählten Kunstschätzen ein adäquater Rahmen geschaffen wurde. Im klassisch instrumentierten Vestibül, das akademischen Versammlungen sowie der Scuola di San Marco als Tagungsort diente, war seit 1597 die Antikensammlung aus dem Besitz des Patriarchen von Aquileia, Giovanni Grimani (1506–1593) ausgestellt, die teilweise heute noch dort zu sehen ist. An der Ausstattung des Vestibüls und vor allem des Bibliothekssaals mit 21 allegorischen Deckenbildern und Philosophenporträts an den Wänden arbeiteten Paolo Veronese (1528–1588), Jacopo Tintoretto (1519–1594) und Tizian (1490–1576), dem die Koordination der Arbeiten oblag. Während das prachtvolle Marmorpaviment des Vestibüls mit seinem zentralisierten Dekor zum Verweilen einlädt, verleiht das schwarz-weiße Rhombenmuster dem ehemals mit monumentalen Nussholztischen und prächtigen Wandschränken ausgestatteten Prunksaal der Bibliothek illusionistische Tiefe. 1553 konnte schließlich der Bibliotheksbetrieb

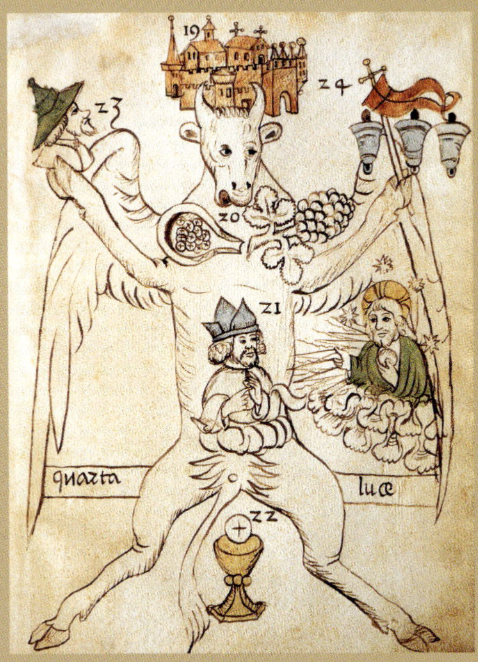

Fra Mauro, *Map of the World*, c. 1450

Codice Latino III, 177, end of the 15th century, sig. Lat. III, 177 (= 2176), fol. 44: *The Antichrist*

aufgenommen werden. Allerdings verdrängten
die stetig anwachsenden Bestände zunehmend Gemälde und andere hier ausgestellte
Kunstwerke. Sie wurden in den Dogenpalast
gebracht und durch bis an die Decke reichende
Bücherregale ersetzt, die die um 1700 gezählten
10 000 Bücher fassen konnten. Nach dem Fall
der Republik Venedig gelangte 1811 die gesamte
Bibliothek in den Dogenpalast, wo sie bis 1904
verblieb. Heute befindet sich die auf eine Million
Bücher angewachsene Sammlung sowohl in der
Libreria als auch vor allem in der ebenfalls von
Sansovino errichteten Münzstätte, deren drei-
geschossiger, 1904 gedeckter Innenhof aktuell
als Lesesaal dient. Während die Sammlung im
16. Jahrhundert ein Zentrum humanistischer
Studien war, das dank Bessarions Stiftung über
einen klaren Schwerpunkt an griechischen
und orientalischen Handschriften verfügte,
erlaubte ein von der Republik Venedig 1603
erlassenes Gesetz eine entscheidende Ausweitung der Bestände. Seither musste für jedes
auf venezianischem Boden gedruckte Buch
ein Pflichtexemplar an die Biblioteca Marciana
abgeliefert werden.

❋ ❖ ❋

La bibliothèque qui doit son nom à saint Marc,
le patron de la République de Venise, est née de
la générosité de mécènes célèbres. Dès 1362,
Francesco Petrarca (dit Pétrarque, 1304–1374),
dont on voit la statue au centre de l'actuelle
salle de lecture, suggéra la construction d'une
bibliothèque publique avec l'objectif d'abriter
sa fameuse collection de manuscrits qu'il offrit
à la ville. Une autre donation suivit en 1468, celle
du cardinal Basilius Bessarion (1403–1472), qui
souhaitait, tout comme Pétrarque, doter la ville
d'un précieux centre intellectuel avec sa collection de 750 codex et 250 manuscrits - admirée
au-delà des cercles humanistes. Le bâtiment
actuel, érigé dans le cadre de la rénovation de
la place Saint-Marc, date de 1536. La collection
à l'origine appelée Biblioteca Nicena fut
entreposée temporairement près de la basilique
Saint-Marc. La République de Venise désigna

l'humaniste et érudit Pietro Bembo (1470–1547)
comme premier bibliothécaire en 1530. Dans le
cadre de l'harmonisation architecturale de la
place Saint-Marc, la collection, alors intitulée
Libreria di San Marco, trouva un domicile digne
d'elle dans une aile percée de vingt-et-une
fenêtres en face du palais des Doges. Autour de
cette même place s'élevèrent au rez-de-chaussée des locaux destinés aux procurateurs de
Venise et, côté lagune, pour remplacer l'ancien
anéanti par un incendie, l'hôtel de la monnaie.
La prestigieuse commande échut à l'architecte
et sculpteur Jacopo Sansovino (1486–1570),
protomaestro de la basilique Saint-Marc.
À la mort de ce dernier, elle fut achevée par
Vincenzo Scamozzi (1548–1616). En collaboration avec les artistes vénitiens les plus
doués et les plus en vue, Sansovino conçut un
bâtiment exceptionnel et magnifique dont les
salles monumentales n'abritent pas seulement
des livres précieux, mais constituent un cadre
adéquat pour une sélection d'œuvres d'art. Le
vestibule au décor classique, qui servait de salle
de congrès aux assemblées académiques telles
que la Scuola di San Marco, accueillit en 1597
la collection de statues antiques du patriarche
d'Aquilée Giovanni Grimani (1506–1593), qui
reste de nos jours en partie visible. L'aména
gement intérieur du vestibule et de la salle de
bibliothèque incomba à Véronèse (1528–1588),
Le Tintoret (1519–1594) et Titien (1490–1576),
du reste chargé de coordonner les travaux.
Ils parèrent le plafond de 21 allégories, et les
murs de portraits de philosophes. Tandis que
le somptueux dallage en marbre aux motifs
concentriques du vestibule invite à la contemplation, le motif de losanges blancs faussement
surélevés sur fond noir crée un effet de perspective dans la salle de bibliothèque, autrefois
meublée de tables monumentales en noyer et
d'étagères magnifiques. Le bâtiment prend
enfin ses fonctions de bibliothèque en 1553. Or,
les fonds littéraires qui s'étoffent sans cesse
éclipsent de plus en plus les peintures et autres
œuvres d'art exposées. Ces dernières sont
transférées au palais des Doges et remplacées

par des rayonnages allant jusqu'au plafond pour héberger les 10 000 livres dénombrés vers 1700. Après la chute de la République de Venise en 1811, la bibliothèque au complet rejoint le palais des Doges et y reste jusqu'en 1904. Enrichie d'un million de livres, la collection occupe de nos jours non seulement le Palazzo de la Libreria, mais aussi « l'hôtel de la monnaie », c'est-à-dire le bâtiment adjacent à trois étages également érigé par Sansovino, dont la cour intérieure couverte en 1904 sert de salle de lecture. Tandis que la collection du XVIe siècle représentait un centre d'études humanistes, disposant surtout, grâce au legs de Bessarion, de manuscrits grecs et orientaux, la République de Venise par une loi promulguée en 1603 permit un enrichissement déterminant des fonds de bibliothèque. Par cette loi, un exemplaire de chaque ouvrage imprimé sur le sol vénitien devait rejoindre les étagères de la Marciana.

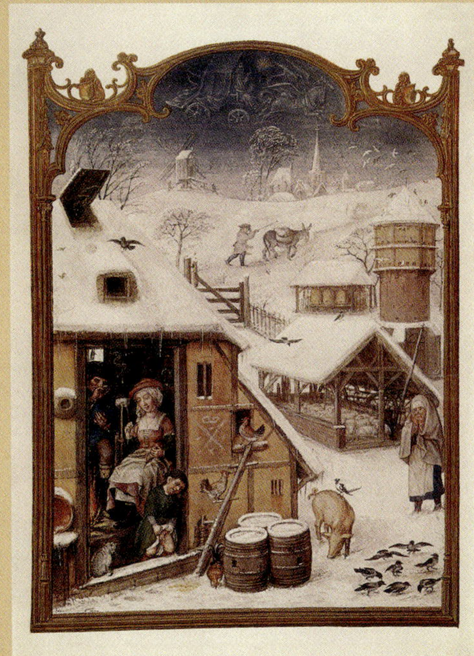

Breviario Grimani, before 1520,
sig. Cod. Lat. I, 99, fol. 2v: *The Month of February*

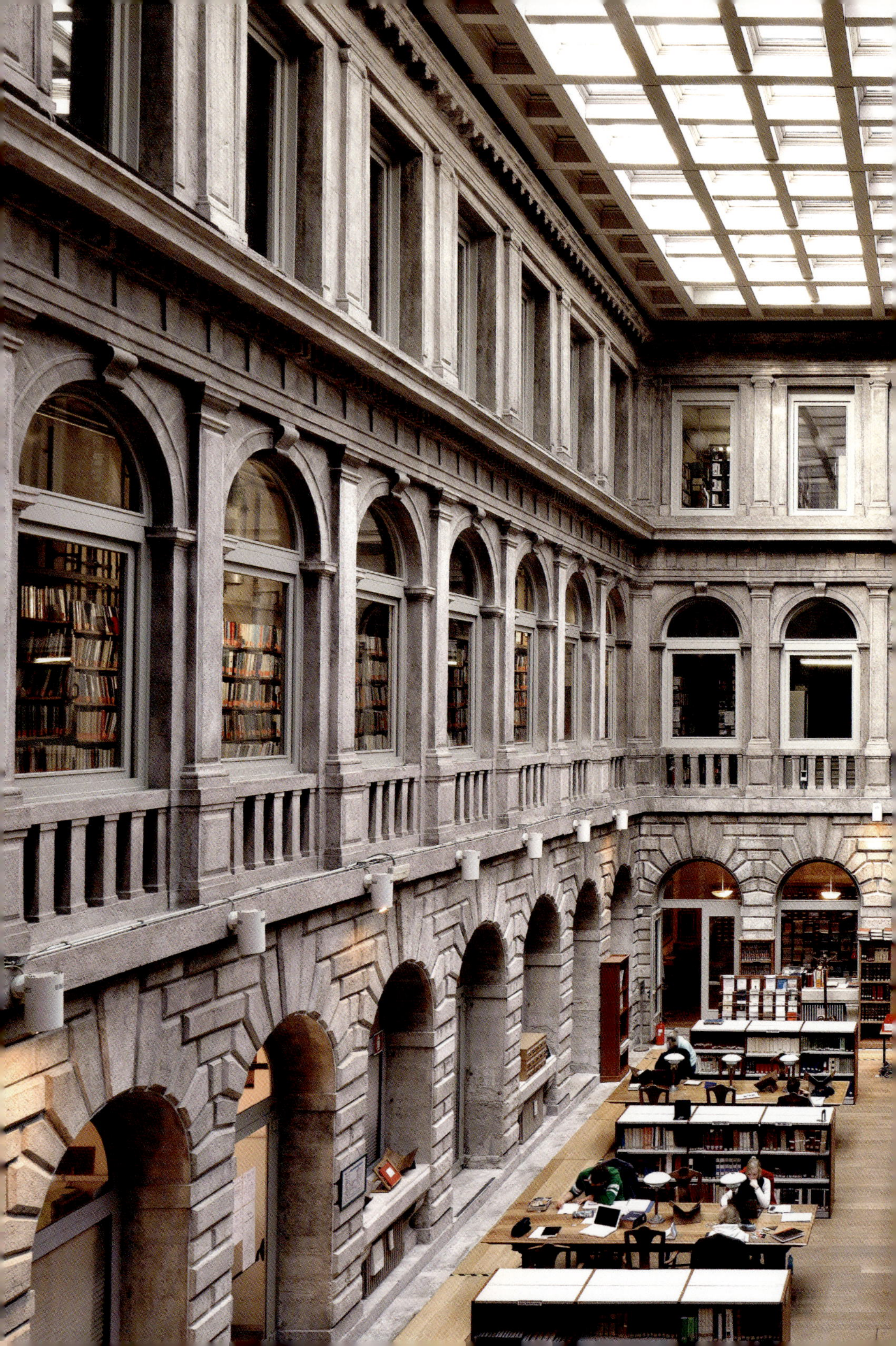

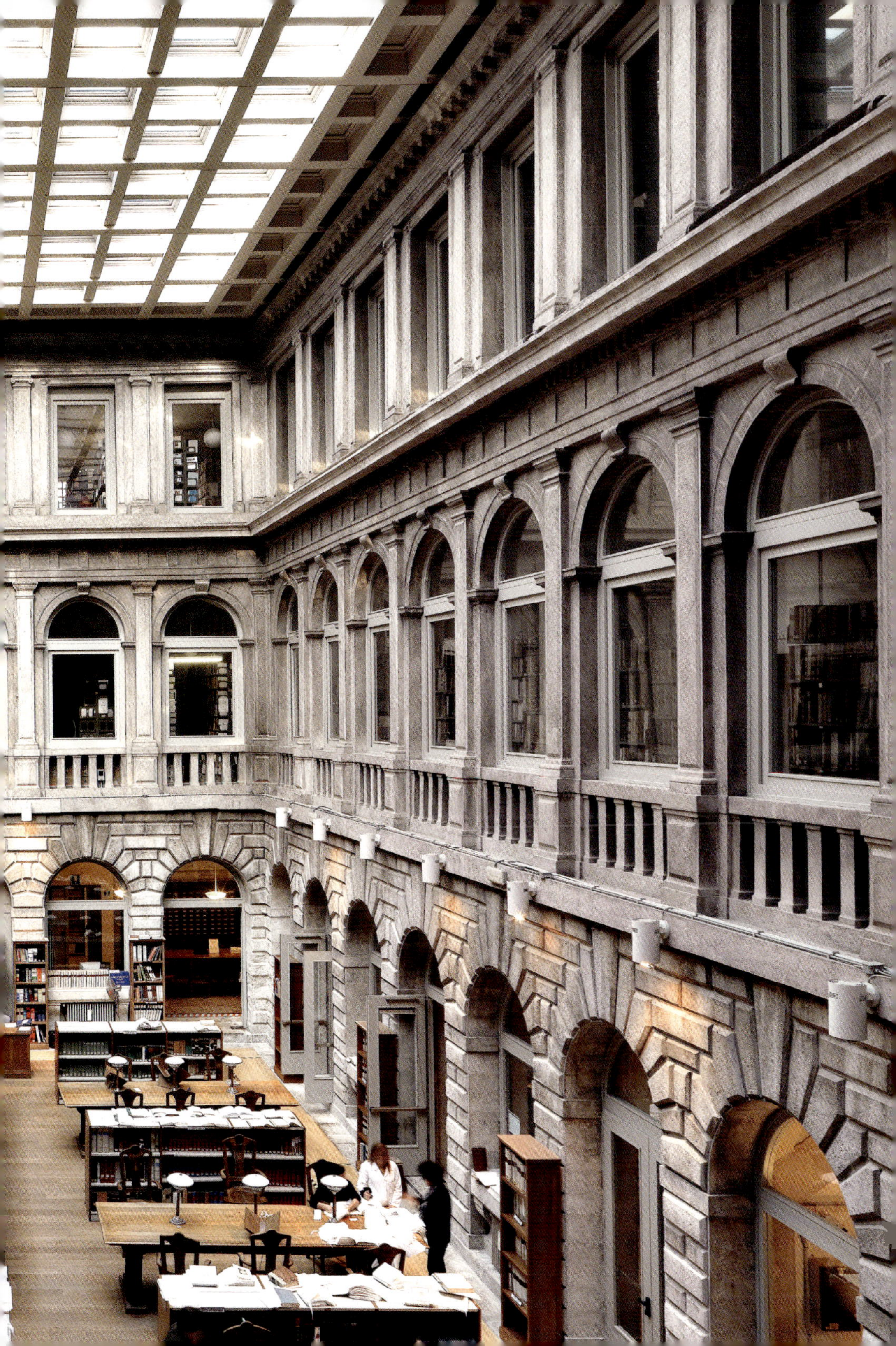

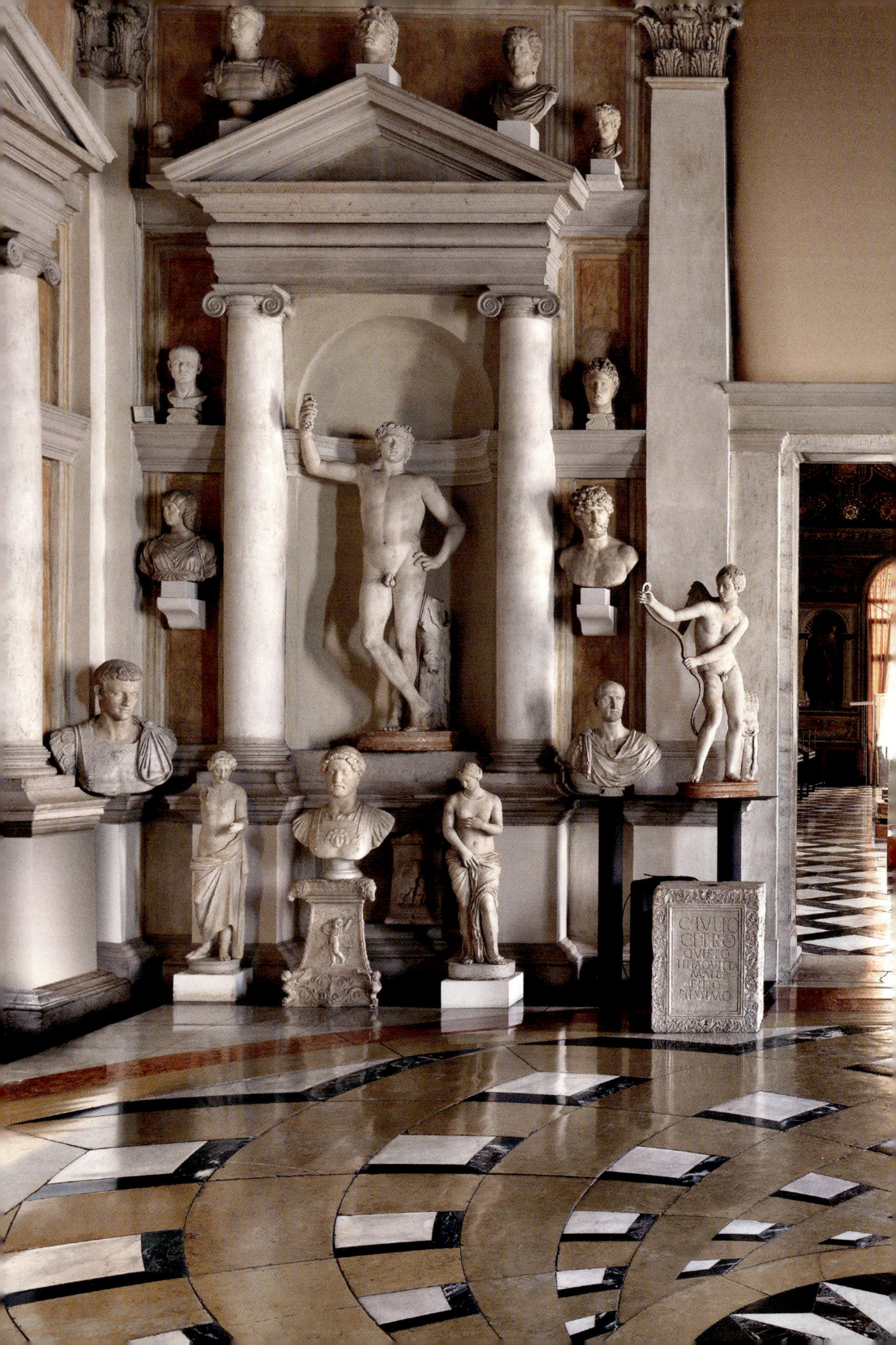

C IVLIO
CETEO
QVIETO
IVLIA QVIETA
MATER
FILIO
PIISSIMO

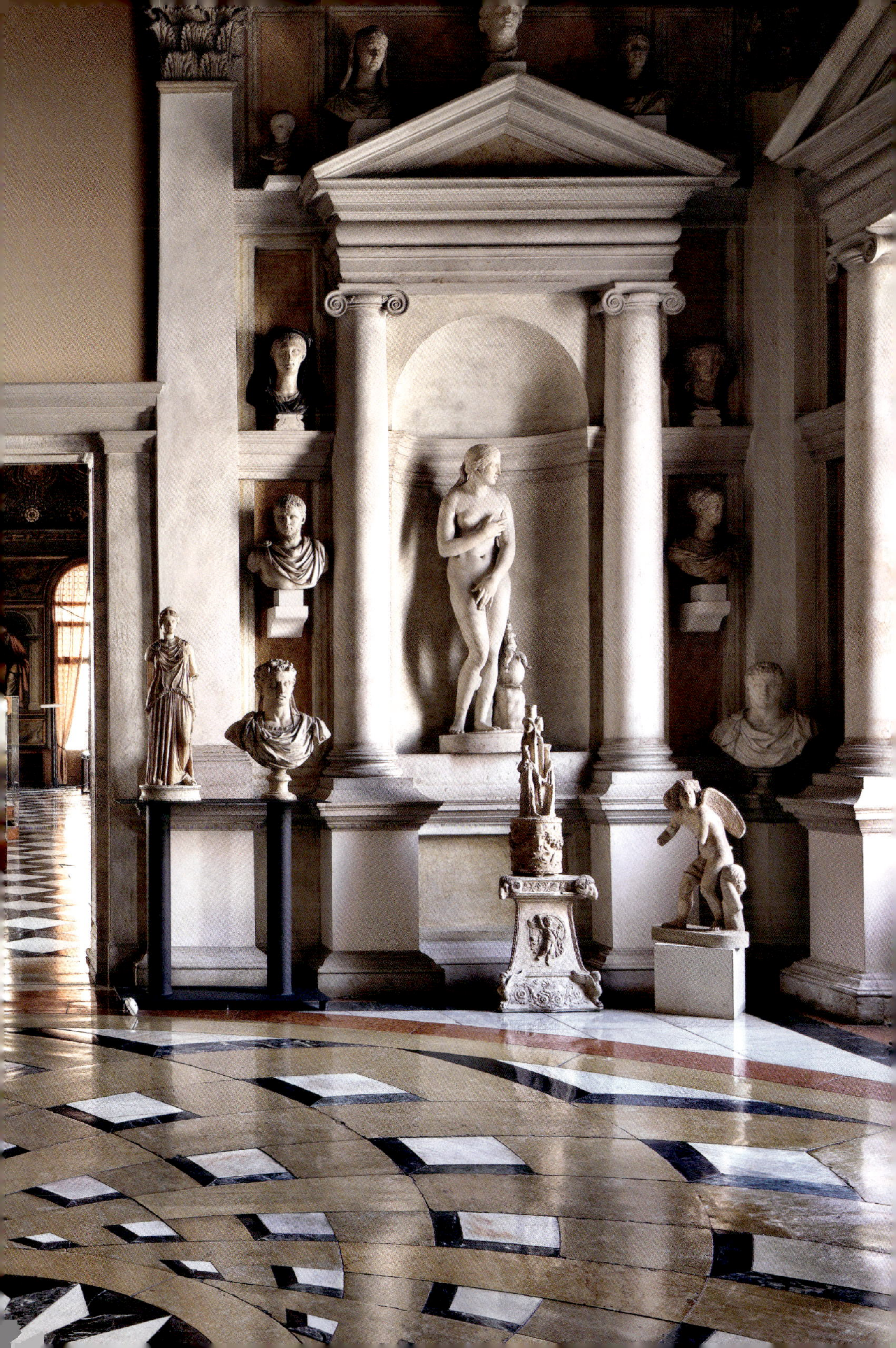

Biblioteca Statale Oratoriana dei Girolamini

Preserved in the form of this library is not only a historical monument of unique beauty but also an exceptionally rich collection of manuscripts, incunabula, rare editions and old musical scores. Philosophy, Christian theology, Church history and spiritual music are all prominently represented in the library's holdings. The Biblioteca dei Girolamini is the oldest library in Naples and has been open to the public since its foundation in 1586. Together with the church associated with it, the library forms part of a monumental architectural complex directly opposite the cathedral in the centre of the city. With its interior courtyards, bounded by the wings of the monastery and planted with orange trees, it retains a tranquil atmosphere of seclusion and contemplation. The Neapolitan Oratorians modelled themselves on the religious congregation founded by St Philip Neri (1515–1595) in Rome, where the latter also began to build up the Biblioteca Vallicelliana from his base at San Girolamo della Carità (whence the name Girolamini by which the Oratorians were also known). Alongside the communal reading of religious texts, music – with its power to uplift – was a fundamental component of the spiritual exercises recommended by St Philip Neri. It is from the Oratorians, in fact, that the oratorio takes its name, as a distinct form of musical meditation upon sacred texts. The importance of music in Oratorian spirituality is directly reflected in the substantial holdings of music manuscripts in the Biblioteca dei Girolamini (some 6,500 musical compositions from the 16th–19th centuries), which include valuable Baroque scores by Alessandro Scarlatti (1660–1725) and Giovanni Paisiello (1740–1816). The reading room today occupies the former refectory, where the Neapolitan Fathers read and discussed sacred texts. The magnificent library hall rises through three storeys and was built as part of an ambitious suite of rooms, whose interiors are decorated in the Neapolitan Late Baroque style. While architects Arcangelo (1648–1735) and Marcello Guglielmelli were creating this light-filled spatial ensemble in the years 1726–1736, the library was being used as a place of study by illustrious individuals such as the philosopher Giambattista Vico (1668–1744), whose bequest of books and papers is now housed in its own room. It was in this library that Vico wrote his major work, *Scienza Nuova* (*New Science*), first published in 1725 and reprinted in a second, revised edition in 1730.

❊❊❊

Founded 1586; national library since 1866
Holdings c. 160,000 volumes
Type of library formerly a monastic library; today a research library under the aegis of the Ministero per i beni e le attività culturali
Highlights Cino da Pistoia, *Lectura codicem*, illuminated manuscript, 14th century; Giovanni Boccaccio, *Teseidea*, manuscript illustrated with pen, 15th century (Ms. C.F. 2.8)

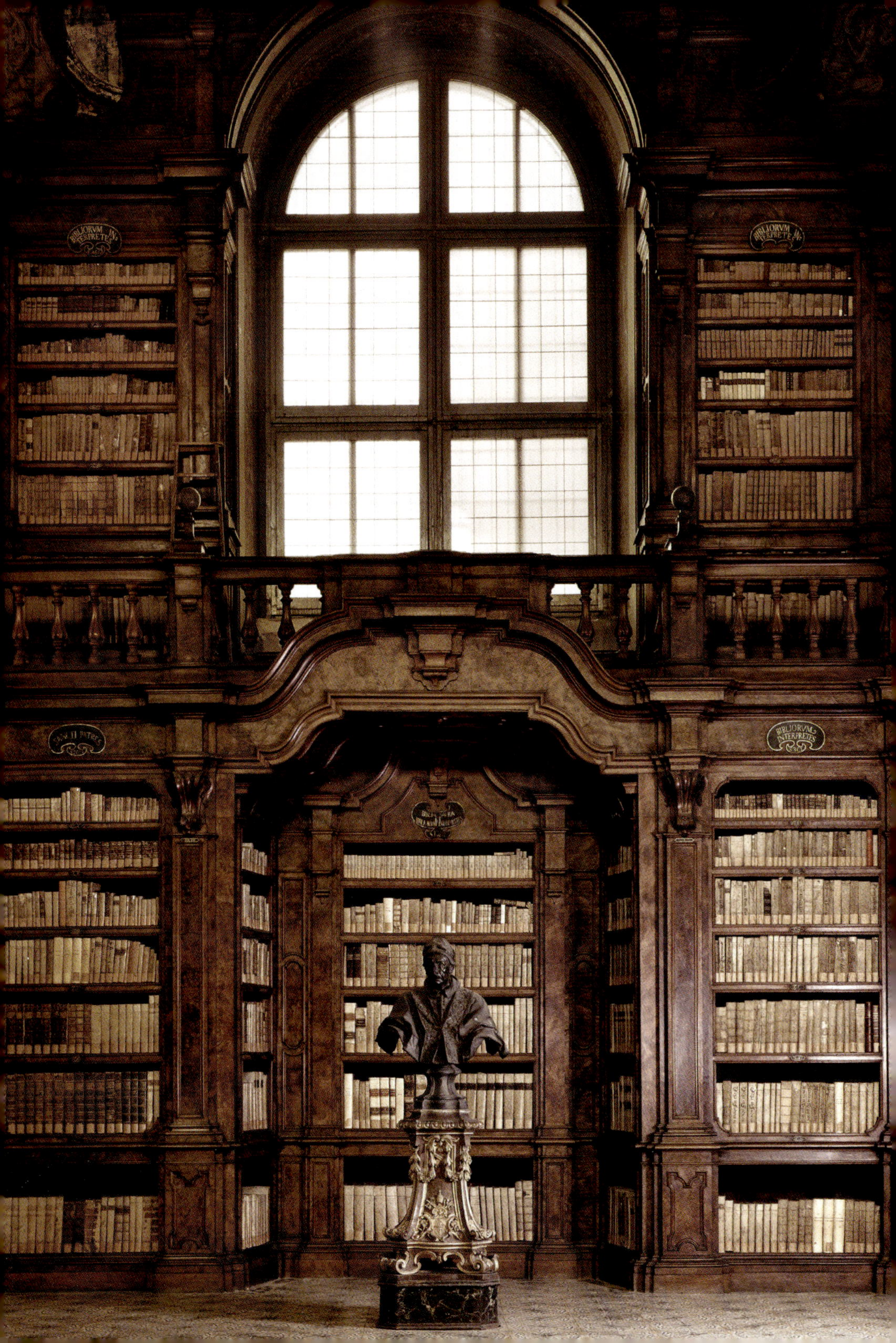

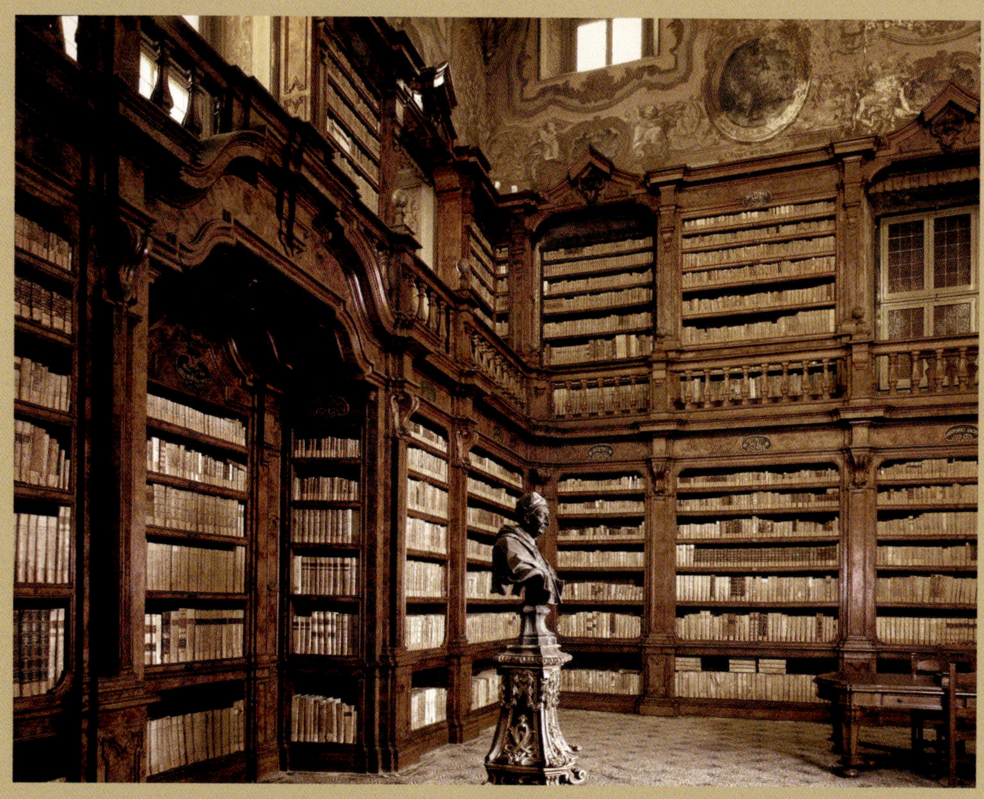

In dieser Bibliothek hat sich nicht nur ein historisches Baudenkmal von einzigartiger Schönheit erhalten, sondern auch ein außergewöhnlich reicher Schatz an Manuskripten, Inkunabeln, seltenen Editionen und alten Notenbüchern. Ihre Bestände haben christliche Theologie und Philosophie, Kirchengeschichte und geistliche Musik als inhaltlichen Schwerpunkt. Sie ist die älteste Bibliothek Neapels und seit ihrer Gründung im Jahr 1586 für das Publikum geöffnet. Obwohl sie mit der zugehörigen Kirche Teil eines monumentalen, zentral dem Dom gegenübergelegenen Gebäudekomplexes ist, erlauben die von den Klostertrakten umschlossenen Innenhöfe, die mit Orangenbäumen bestanden sind, Abgeschlossenheit und Einkehr. Der neapolitanischen Niederlassung der auch als Girolamini bezeichneten Oratorianer diente die römische Kongregation als

Vorbild, wo damals noch ihr Gründer, Filippo Neri (1515–1595), wirkte und dort – ausgehend von der namensgebend gewordenen Kirche San Girolamo della Carità – die Biblioteca Vallicelliana aufzubauen begann. Für die von Filippo Neri geprägte Spiritualität der Oratorianer war die gemeinsame Lektüre religiöser Texte ebenso wie die Musik mit ihrer erhebenden Wirkung grundlegend, was einer eigenen Form von musikalischer Andacht – ebenden Oratorien – den Namen gab. Der reiche Bestand an Musikmanuskripten in dieser Bibliothek (etwa 6 500 musikalische Werke aus dem 16. bis 19. Jahrhundert) hängt auch mit der speziellen Form hier gepflegter Andacht und Unterhaltung zusammen. Exemplarisch erwähnt seien wertvolle barocke Originalpartituren, etwa von Alessandro Scarlatti (1660–1725) oder Giovanni Paisiello (1740–1816). Als heutiger

Lesesaal dient das ehemalige Refektorium
der Patres, wo nach dem Vorbild Filippo Neris
heilige Schriften vorgetragen und diskutiert
wurden. Der prächtige, über drei Geschosse
reichende Büchersaal entstand als Teil einer
großzügig konzipierten Raumfolge, die in den
Stilformen des neapolitanischen Spätbarocks
ausgestattet ist. Als Arcangelo (1648–1735) und
Marcello Guglielmelli dieses lichtdurchflutete
Raumensemble in den Jahren 1726 bis 1736
errichteten, galt die Bibliothek illustren Persönlichkeiten wie dem Philosophen Giambattista
Vico (1668–1744), dessen gesamten Nachlass die
Bibliothek in einem eigenen Raum beherbergt,
als Studienort. 1725 war die erste und 1730 die
überarbeitete zweite Version seines hier an der
Bibliothek verfassten Hauptwerkes *Scienza
Nuova* (Neue Wissenschaft) erschienen.

❋⁙❋

Cette bibliothèque n'est pas uniquement
un monument historique d'une beauté
exceptionnelle, c'est aussi un extraordinaire
trésor de manuscrits, incunables, éditions
rares et partitions anciennes. Son contenu a
essentiellement trait à la théologie chrétienne
et à la philosophie, à l'histoire de l'Église et à la
musique spirituelle. Il s'agit de la toute première
bibliothèque napolitaine, ouverte au public dès
sa fondation en 1586. Même si son bâtiment
et l'église dont elle dépend font partie d'un
ensemble architectural situé au cœur de Naples,
à deux pas de l'imposante cathédrale, les cours
intérieures ceintes de galeries notamment fleu-
ries d'orangers offrent un sentiment de retrait
et de recueillement. La congrégation romaine de
l'oratoire servit de modèle au site napolitain des
Pères oratoriens, également appelés Girolamini.
À l'époque, leur fondateur Philippe Néri (1515–
1595) œuvrait encore à Rome et notamment à
la construction de la Bibliothèque vallicelliane
depuis l'église San Girolamo della Carità – qui
inspira l'appellation de l'ordre. Pour les Oratoriens, marqués par la personnalité de leur fondateur, la lecture collective de textes religieux et
l'élévation spirituelle engendrée par la musique
étaient essentielles à leur spiritualité, ce qui
donna naissance à une forme particulière de
prière musicale : l'oratorio. L'inestimable fonds,
riche en manuscrits musicaux (près de 6 500
en tout datant du XVIe au XIXe siècle), est aussi
lié à cette forme particulière de prière et de
divertissement sacré alors en usage. Il importe
de mentionner quelques partitions originales
baroques de grande valeur comme celles
d'Alessandro Scarlatti (1660–1725) ou de Giovanni
Paisiello (1740–1816). La salle de lecture actuelle
n'est autre que l'ancien réfectoire des Pères, où
les Saintes Écritures étaient récitées et com-
mentées suivant l'exemple de Philippe Néri. Le
splendide Cabinet des livres, s'élevant sur trois
niveaux, s'inscrit dans une enfilade de salles aux
dimensions généreuses et décorées dans le goût
du baroque napolitain tardif. Lorsqu'Arcangelo
(1648–1735) et Marcello Guglielmelli ont érigé
cet ensemble architectural baigné de lumière
dans les années 1726 à 1736, la bibliothèque
servit de lieu d'étude à d'illustres personnages
comme le philosophe Giambattista Vico
(1668–1744), dont la succession entière est
conservée dans une salle à part. Une première
version de son ouvrage majeur *Scienza Nuova*
(Nouvelle science), rédigé dans cette bibliothèque, fut publiée en 1725. Une seconde version
retravaillée fut publiée en 1730.

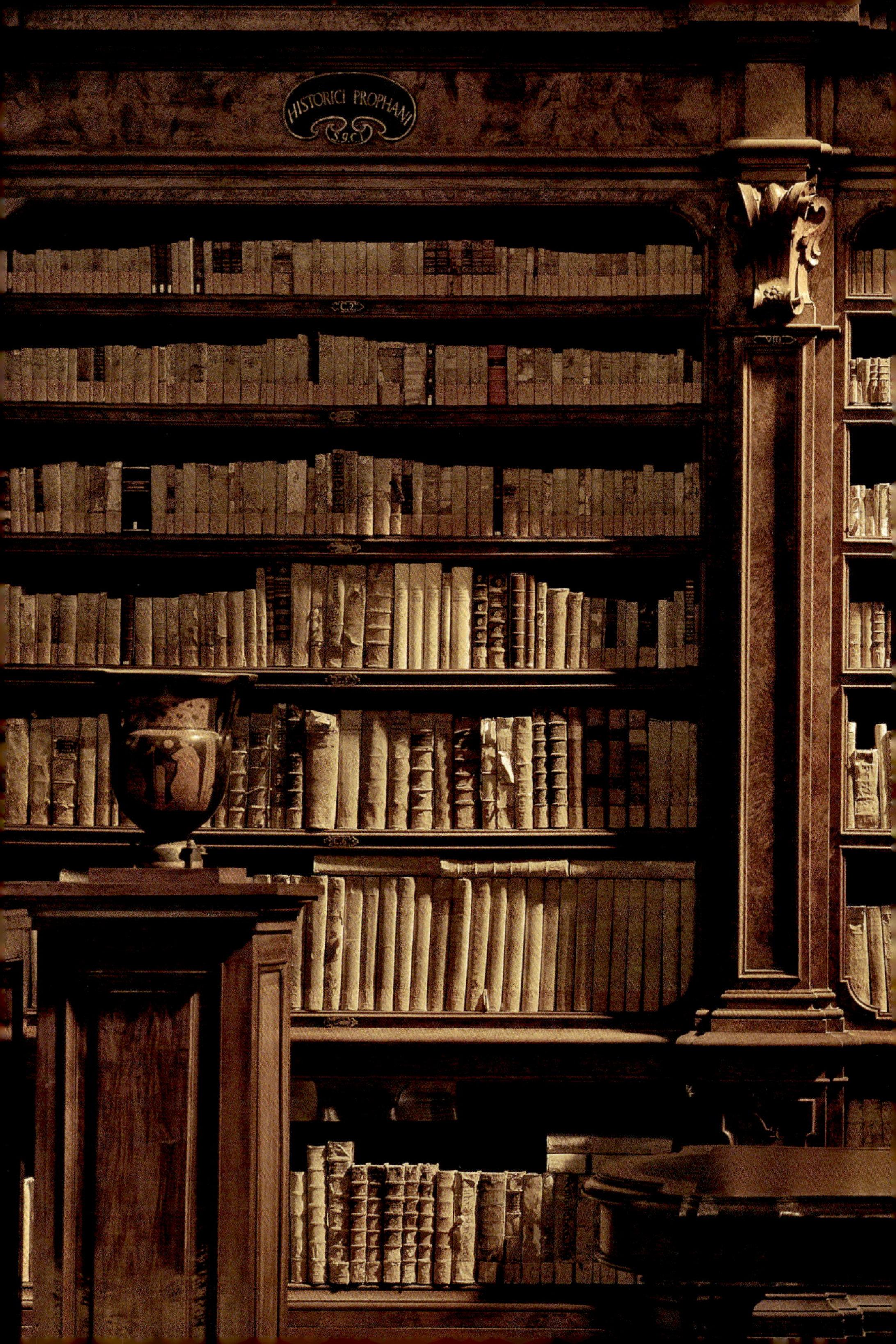

HISTORICI PROPHANI
S.9.C.V
HISTORICI PROPHANI

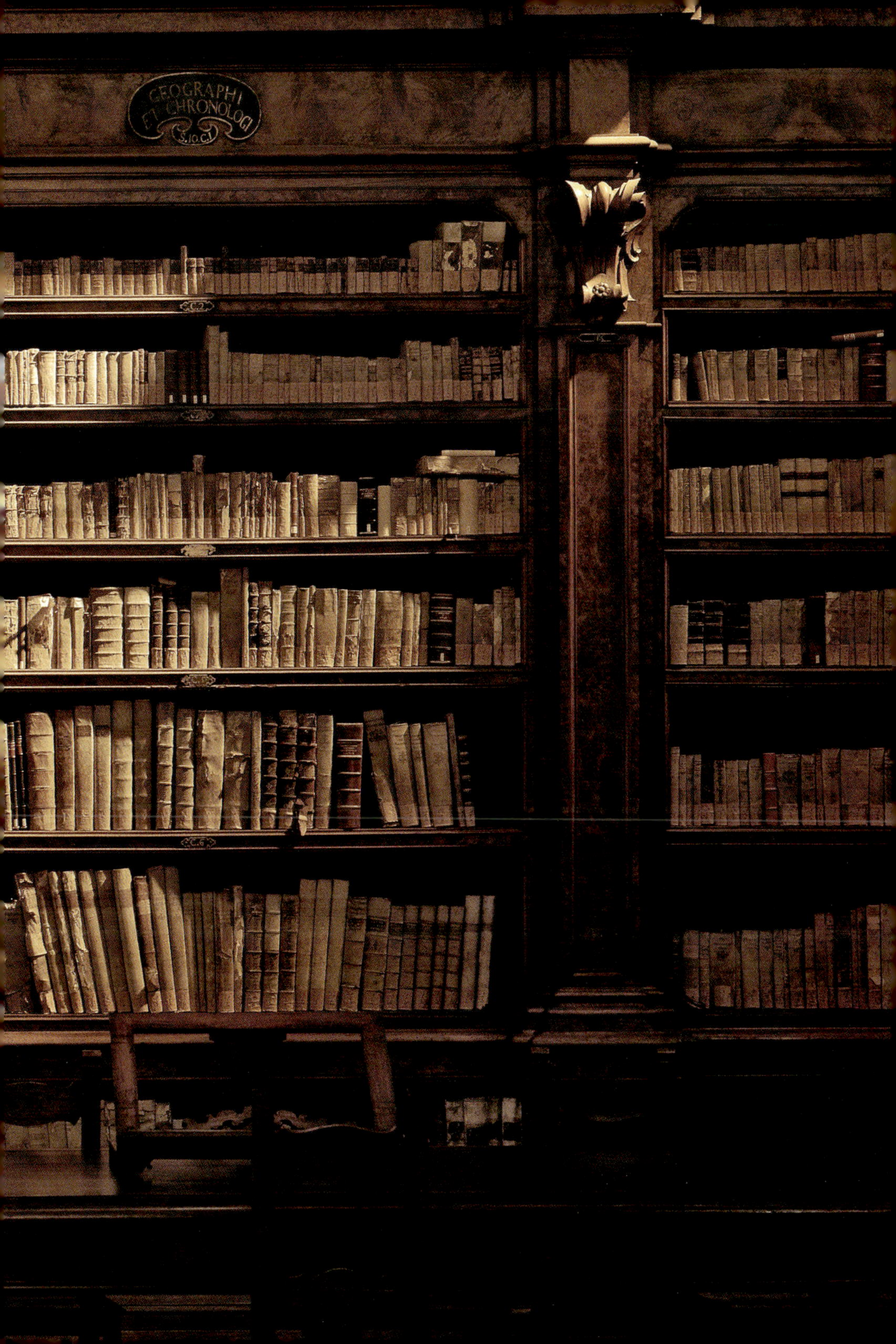

GEOGRAPHI
ET CHRONOLOGI
S. Io. C.
GEOGRAPHI
ET CHRONOLOGI
S. Io. C.

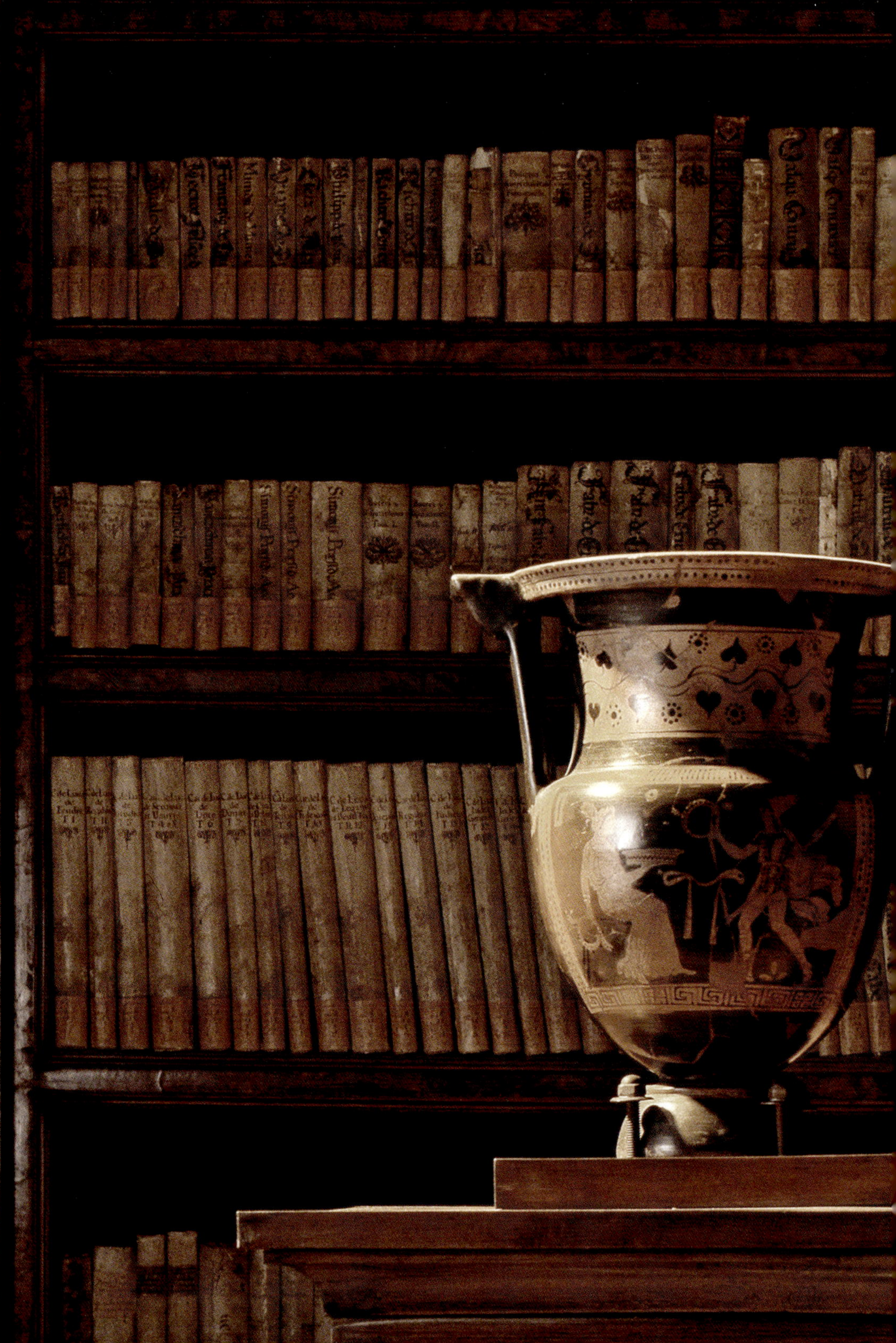

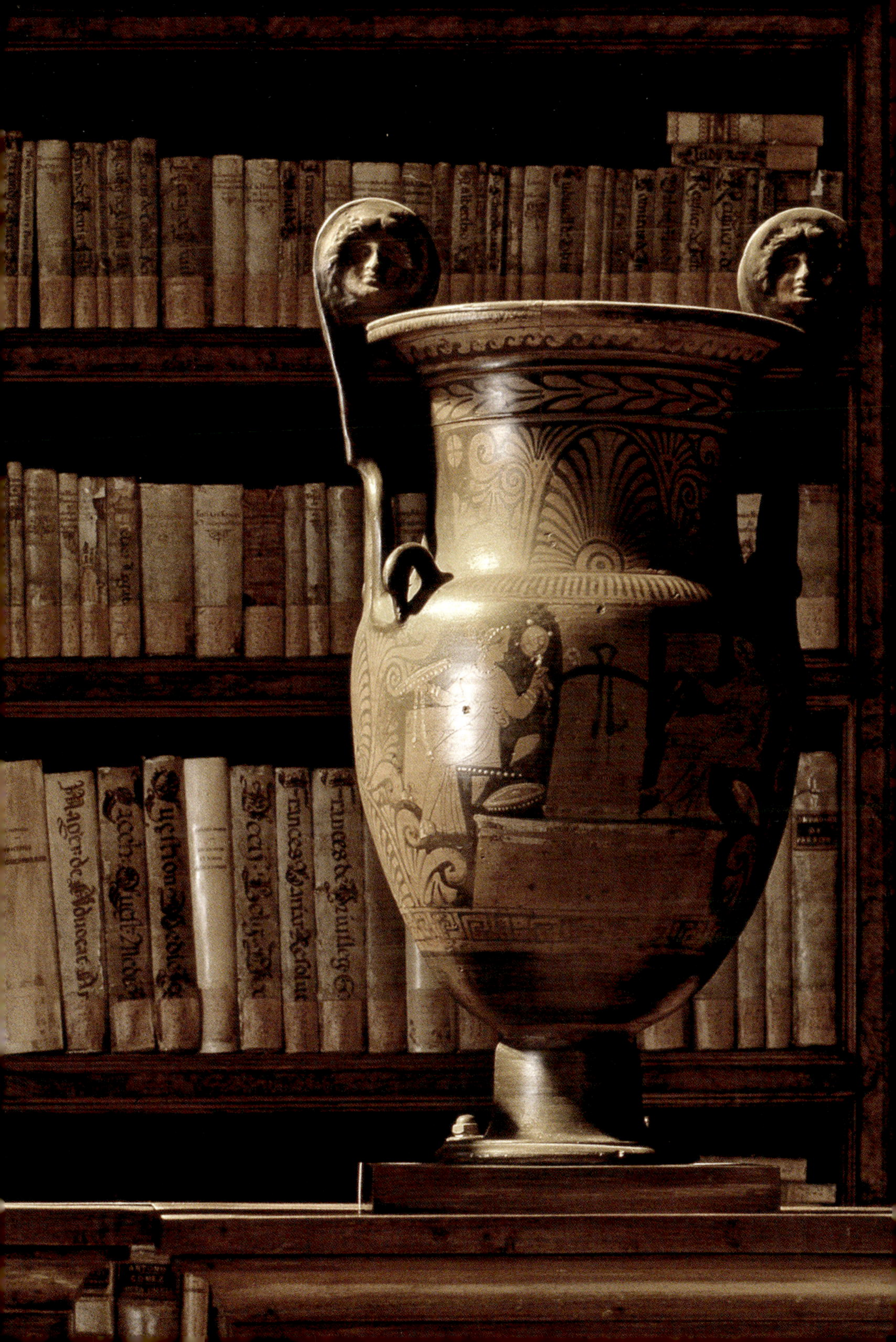

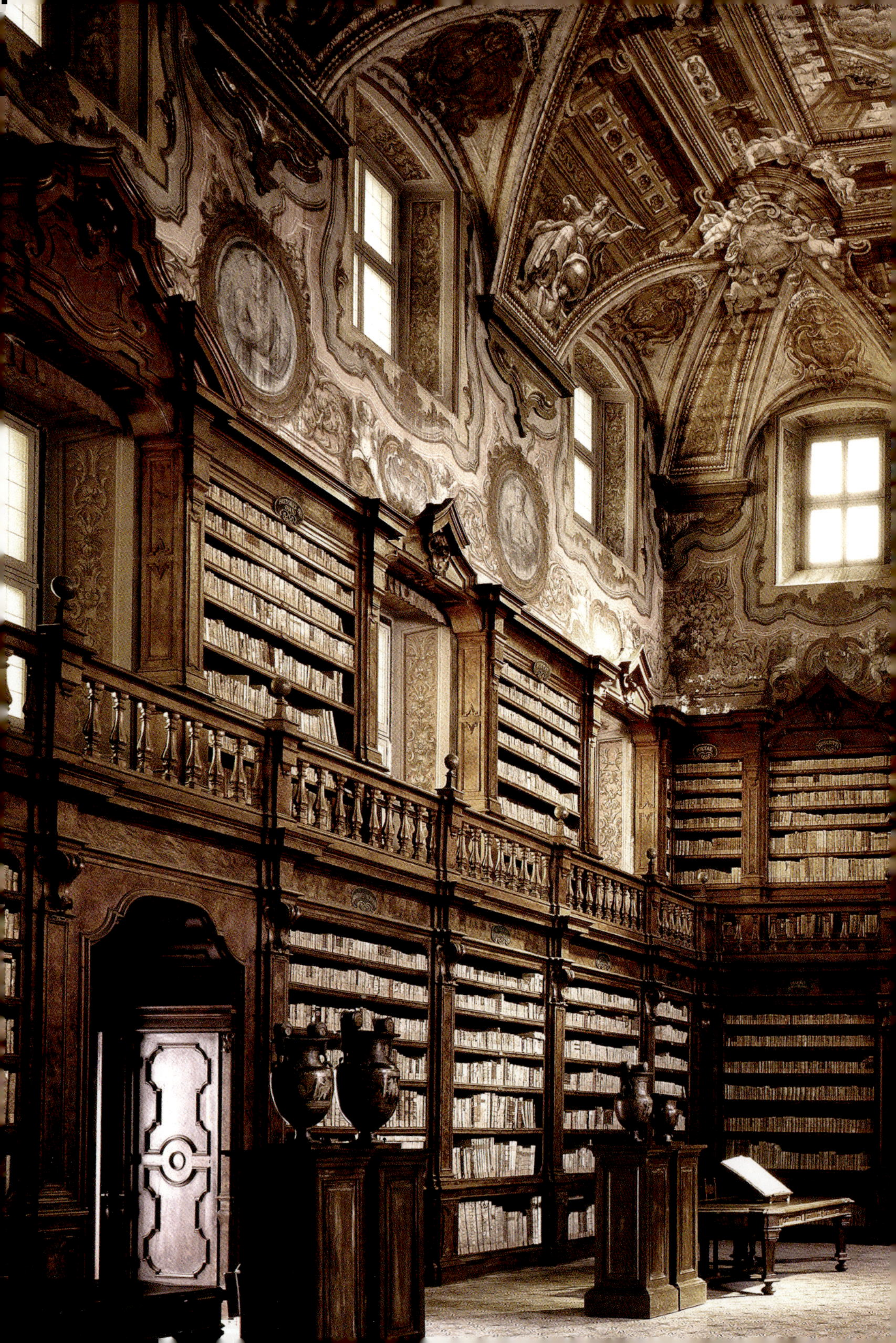

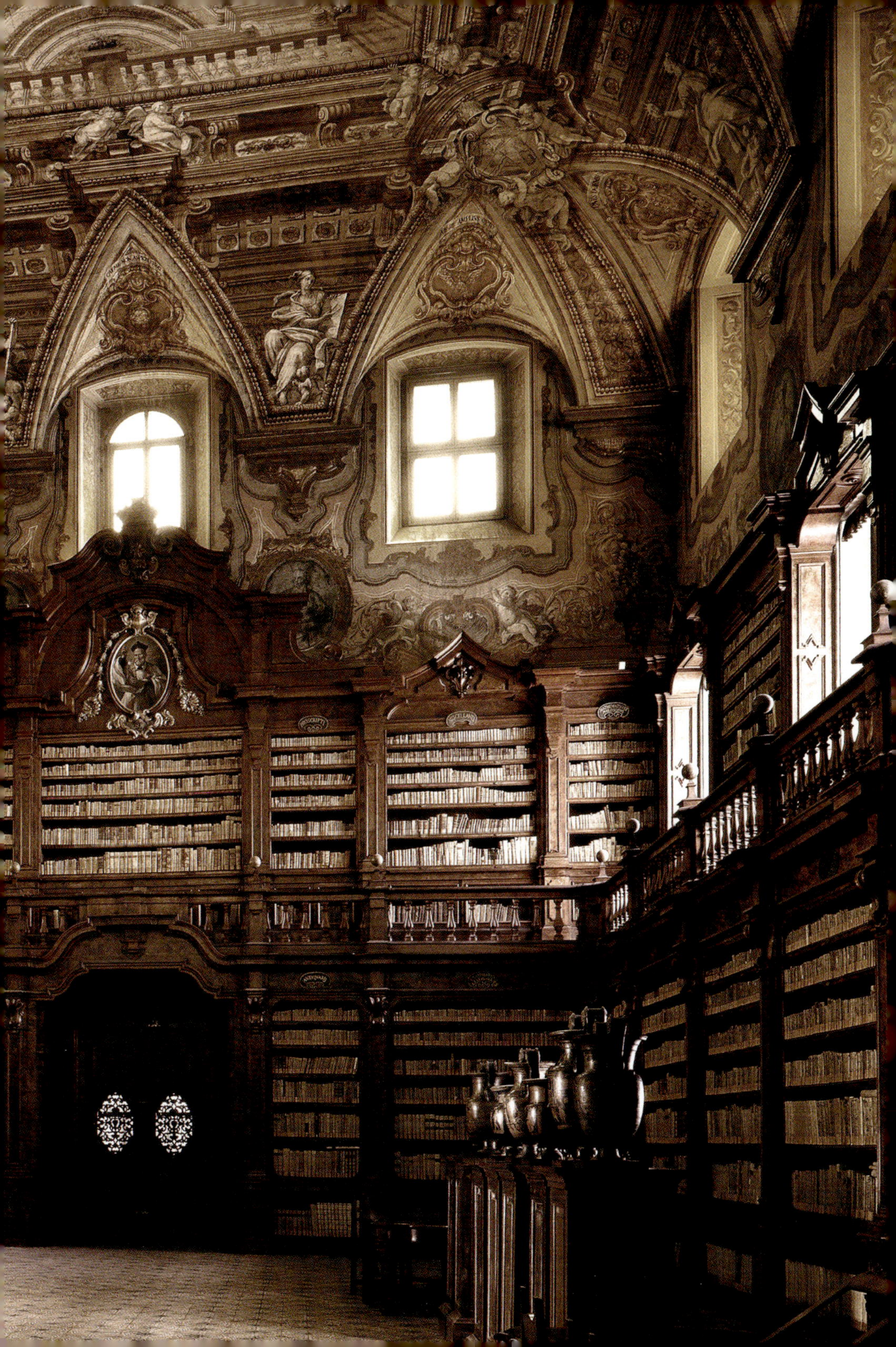

Biblioteca Riccardiana

The library of the Riccardi banking family, together with the adjacent hall of mirrors and the art collections in the Palazzo Medici Riccardi, were sights no illustrious visitor to Florence failed to admire. Johann Caspar Goethe (1710–1782) saw the library during a trip to Italy in 1740 and praised its holdings enthusiastically in his diary (*Viaggio per l'Italia*). In May 1938 the library's magnificent interior was the setting for an evening gala attended by Mussolini and Hitler. After Gabriello Riccardi (1606–1675) was elevated to the nobility by Grand Duke Ferdinando II de' Medici and invested with feudal fiefdoms, he and his heir Francesco Riccardi (1648–1719) proceeded to create a new residence worthy of the family's high rank. In 1659 Gabriello purchased from the Grand Duke the prestigious palace originally built in the mid-15th century by Michelozzo (1396–1472) for the patriarch of the Medici family, Cosimo the Elder (1389–1464). The Riccardis set about building a new complex that was twice the size and which preserved the old palace inside it like a relic. The latter's Renaissance forms were restated on the new façade fronting on to via Ginori. The library is located on the *piano nobile* of this new wing, which also houses the living quarters of the banking family. Medici court artists Ferdinando Tacca (1619–1686) and Pier Maria Baldi (1630–1686) were responsible for the architectural concept and interior decoration. In 1665 Gian Lorenzo Bernini (1598–1680), probably the most famous artist of his day, was a guest in the new palace; over the following years he would train Baldi, before the latter embarked on the construction of the library in 1670–1678. The fittings were designed by Giovan Battista Foggini (1652–1725) according to the instructions of Francesco Riccardi, who like his uncle was an enthusiastic book collector. In 1685 the magnificent ceiling fresco by Luca Giordano (1634–1705) concluded the interior decoration. The Libreria Riccardi provided a fitting framework for the family's valuable collection of books, whose original core was built up by Riccardo Romolo Riccardi (1558–1612), the founder of the banking dynasty. Among the jewels of the collection are illuminated medieval codices of imperial provenance (such as the Psalter of Frederick II) and *de luxe* editions dating from the 15th century. Galileo Galilei consulted the books of the Libreria Riccardi and benefited from the family's patronage in particular during his trial in 1633. Contemporary inventories allow us to reconstruct the library's historical holdings, which in 1810 comprised 17,900 volumes. In 1813 the Libreria Riccardi was acquired by the City of Florence and is today a public institution.

✳✳✳

Founded 1600; built 1670–1678 by Pier Maria Baldi; sold to the City of Florence in 1813
Holdings c. 81,000 volumes
Type of library formerly the library of an aristocratic family; today a public municipal library
Highlights *Illuminated Psalter of Frederick II*, 1235 (Ricc. 323); *Illuminated Lives of St Margaret and St Agnes*, end of the 13th century (Ricc. 453); Piero della Francesca, transcription and illustration of the writings of *Archimedes*, c. 1450 (Ricc. 106); Bartolomeo Ammannati, *Sketchbook*, 1545–1570 (Ricc. 120)

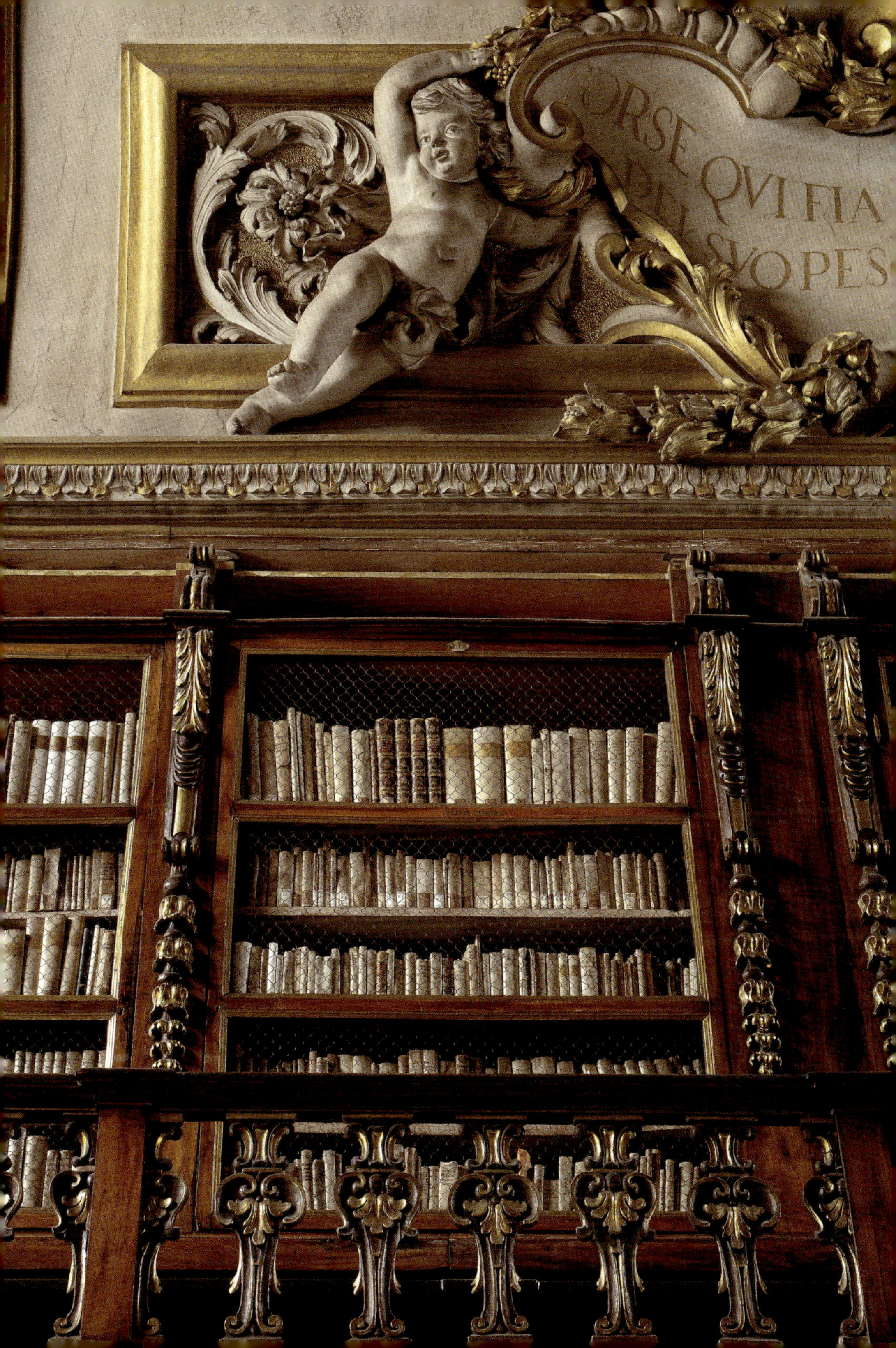
ORSE QVI FIA
DEL SVO PES

Die Bibliothek der Bankiersfamilie Riccardi gehörte mit der angrenzenden Spiegelgalerie und den Kunstsammlungen des Palastes zu jenen Sehenswürdigkeiten, die sich kein illustrer Reisender in Florenz entgehen ließ. Johann Caspar Goethe (1710–1782) pries nach seinem Besuch im Jahr 1740 begeistert ihre Bestände und berichtet davon im Tagebuch seiner Italienreise (*Viaggio per l'Italia*). Benito Mussolini und Adolf Hitler nutzten die repräsentativen Räumlichkeiten, um sich hier im Mai 1938 zu einem Gala-Abendessen zu treffen. Seit Gabriello Riccardi (1606–1675) von Großherzog Ferdinand II. von Medici in den Adelsstand erhoben und mit Feudalherrschaften belehnt worden war, schufen er und sein Erbe Francesco Riccardi (1648–1719) eine neue Familienresidenz, die dieser Würde entsprach. Prestigeträchtig war bereits der Palast, den Gabriello 1659 dem Großherzog abkaufte. Ihn hatte der Patriarch der Familie Medici, Cosimo der Ältere (1389–1464), ab 1444 von Michelozzo (1396–1472) errichten lassen. Er wurde wie eine Reliquie im neuen Gebäude, das die Riccardi auf das Doppelte vergrößerten, beibehalten. Seine Renaissanceformen wurden auch an der neuen Außenfront zur Via Ginori beibehalten. Die Bibliothek befindet sich im *piano nobile* dieses neuen Traktes, der auch die Wohnräume der Bankiersfamilie beherbergt. Höchstes Anspruchsniveau galt auch für dessen Baukonzept und Ausstattung, für die die Hofkünstler der Medici Ferdinando Tacca (1619–1686) und Pier Maria Baldi (1630–1686) verantwortlich zeichnen. Bereits 1665 war im neuen Palast der Familie Riccardi der wohl berühmteste Künstler seiner Zeit zu Gast, Gian Lorenzo Bernini (1598–1680). Er sollte Baldi in den Folgejahren unterweisen, bevor dieser in den Jahren 1670 bis 1678 die Errichtung der Bibliothek in Angriff nahm. Ihr Mobiliar gestaltete Giovan Battista Foggini (1652–1725) nach den Anweisungen Francesco Riccardis, der ebenso wie seine Ahnen ein begeisterter Büchersammler war. Mit seinem prächtigen Deckenfresko schloss Luca Giordano (1634–1705) bis 1685 die Ausstattung

der Libreria Riccardi ab. Hier war der wertvollen Büchersammlung des Hauses, als deren Gründer Riccardo Romolo Riccardi (1558–1612) gilt, ein adäquater Rahmen gegeben. Illuminierte mittelalterliche Handschriften kaiserlicher Provenienz (wie der Psalter Friedrichs II.) zählen ebenso wie Prachtausgaben des 15. Jahrhunderts zu den Kostbarkeiten der Sammlung. Galileo Galilei nutzte die Bestände der Libreria Riccardi und profitierte von der Schirmherrschaft der Familie insbesondere während seines Prozesses im Jahr 1633. Zeitgenössische Inventare erlauben es, die historische Büchersammlung zu rekonstruieren. 1810 enthielt sie 17 900 Bände. 1813 wurde die Bibliothek von der Stadt Florenz erworben, heute ist sie eine staatliche Einrichtung.

❋ ❖ ❋

À l'instar de la galerie des glaces attenante et de la collection d'art du palais, la bibliothèque de la famille de banquiers Riccardi faisait partie des curiosités qu'aucun illustre voyageur de passage à Florence ne voulait manquer. Enthousiasmé par son contenu qu'il découvrit en 1740, Johann Caspar Goethe (1710–1782) en vante les mérites dans son carnet de voyage en Italie (*Viaggio per l'Italia*). En mai 1938, les locaux de cérémonie ont servi de cadre à une rencontre entre Benito Mussolini et Adolf Hitler lors d'un repas de gala. Anobli par le grand-duc Ferdinand II de Médicis et doté de seigneurie féodale, Gabriello Riccardi (1606–1675) créa avec son héritier Francesco Riccardi (1648–1719) une nouvelle résidence familiale à la hauteur de son titre. Le palais que Gabriello acheta au grand-duc en 1659 était déjà prestigieux. Il fut construit par Michelozzo (1396–1472) à la demande de Côme l'Ancien (1389–1464), patriarche de la famille de Médicis. Les Riccardi doublèrent la surface des locaux et conservèrent le bâtiment original en relique dans le nouveau. La nouvelle façade donnant via Ginori conserva aussi son allure Renaissance. La bibliothèque se trouve au *piano nobile* de la nouvelle aile, qui abrite également les appartements privés de la famille. Les artistes de la cour des Médicis Ferdinando Tacca (1619–1686) et Pier Maria Baldi (1630–1686) furent chargés de l'architecture et de l'aménagement. Dès 1665, Gian Lorenzo Bernini (dit Le Bernin, 1598–1680), l'un des artistes les plus célèbres de son temps, séjourna dans le palais des Riccardi. Il avait pour mission de former Baldi, avant que celui-ci n'entreprenne la construction de la bibliothèque dans les années 1670–1678. Giovan Battista Foggini (1652–1725) conçut le mobilier suivant les instructions de Francesco Riccardi qui était, tout comme ses aïeux, un fervent collectionneur de livres. Luca Giordano (1634–1705) paracheva l'aménagement de la Libreria Riccardi en 1685 avec sa somptueuse peinture de plafond. Le

trésor littéraire familial, qui porte le nom de son fondateur Riccardo Romolo Riccardi (1558–1612), bénéficiait enfin d'un écrin digne de son immense valeur. Elle est notamment due à des manuscrits médiévaux illuminés de provenance impériale (comme le psautier de Frédéric II) et à des éditions de luxe du XVe siècle. Galileo Galilei, dit Galilée, consulta les fonds de la Libreria Riccardi et bénéficia de la protection de la famille durant le procès qui lui fut intenté en 1633. Les inventaires actuels permettent de reconstituer la collection historique. En 1810, elle comprenait 17 900 volumes. La Ville de Florence en a fait l'acquisition en 1813 ; la bibliothèque appartient désormais à l'État.

Illuminated Psalter of Frederick II, 1235, sig. Ricc. 323, fol. 14v–15r: *Annunciation and Nativity*

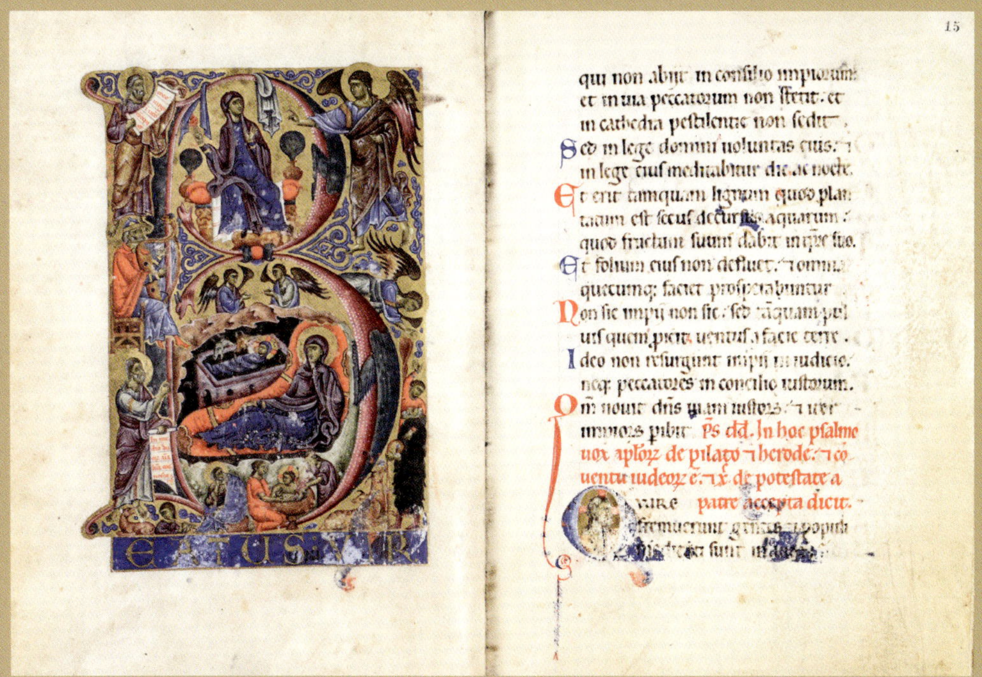

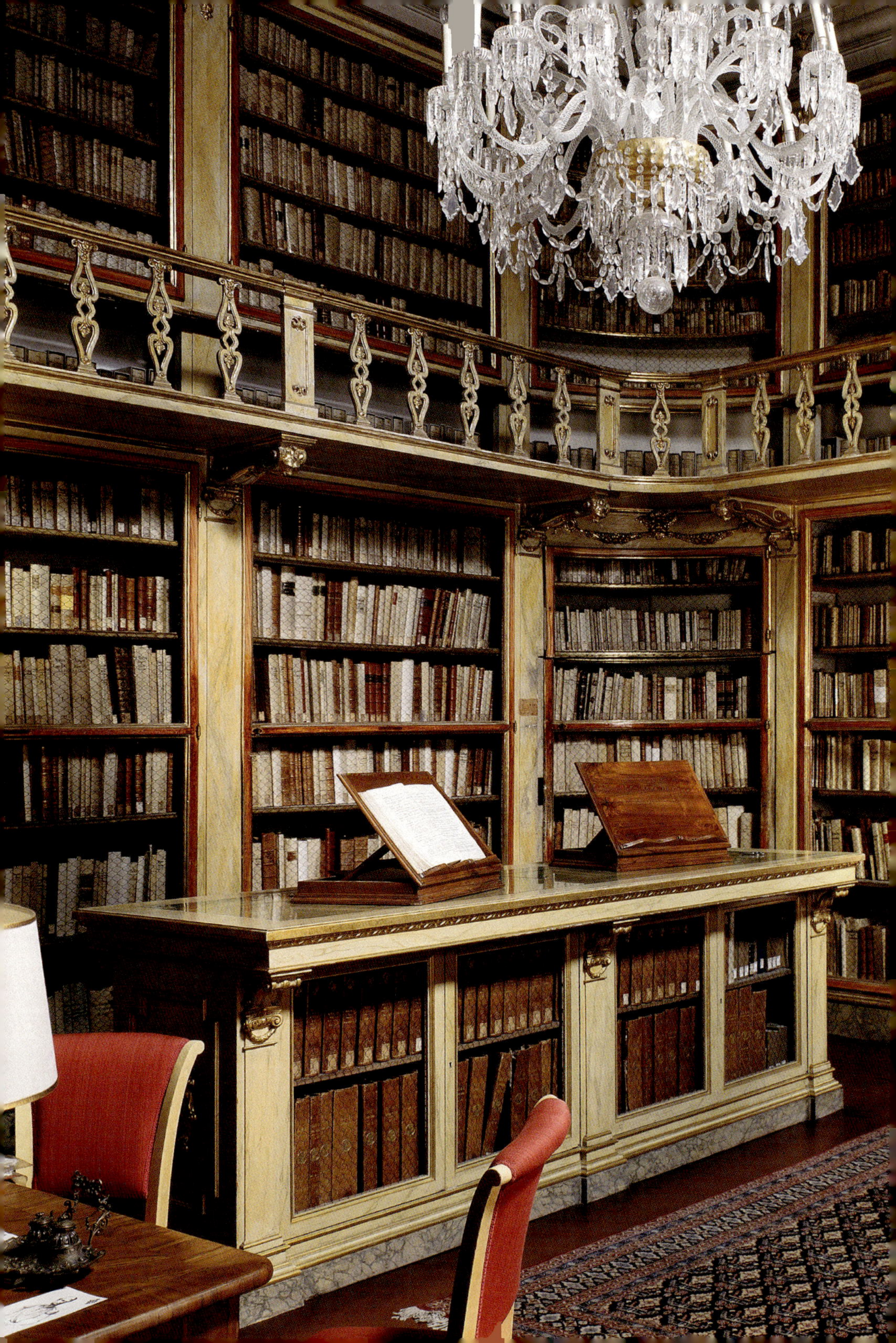

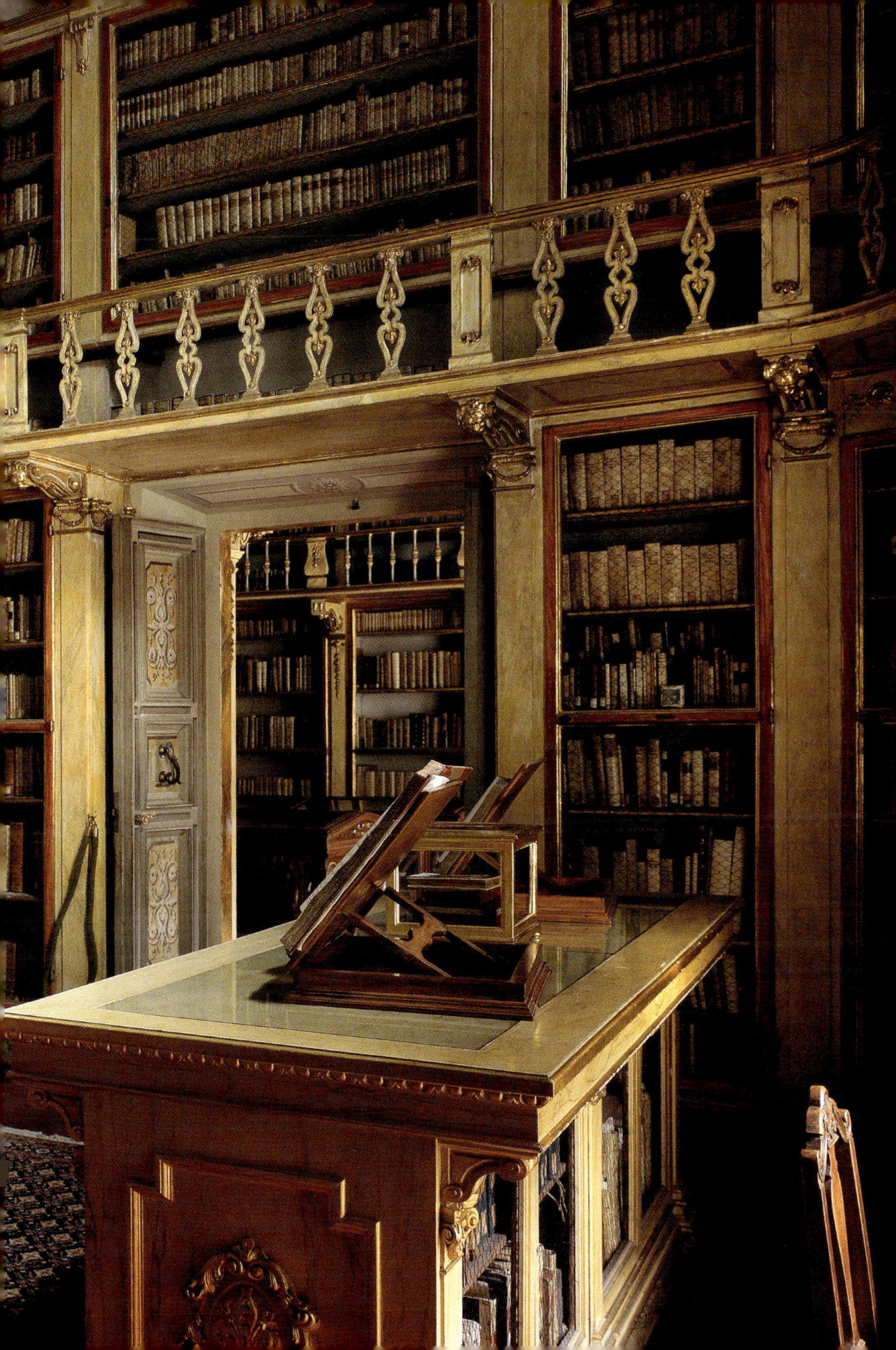

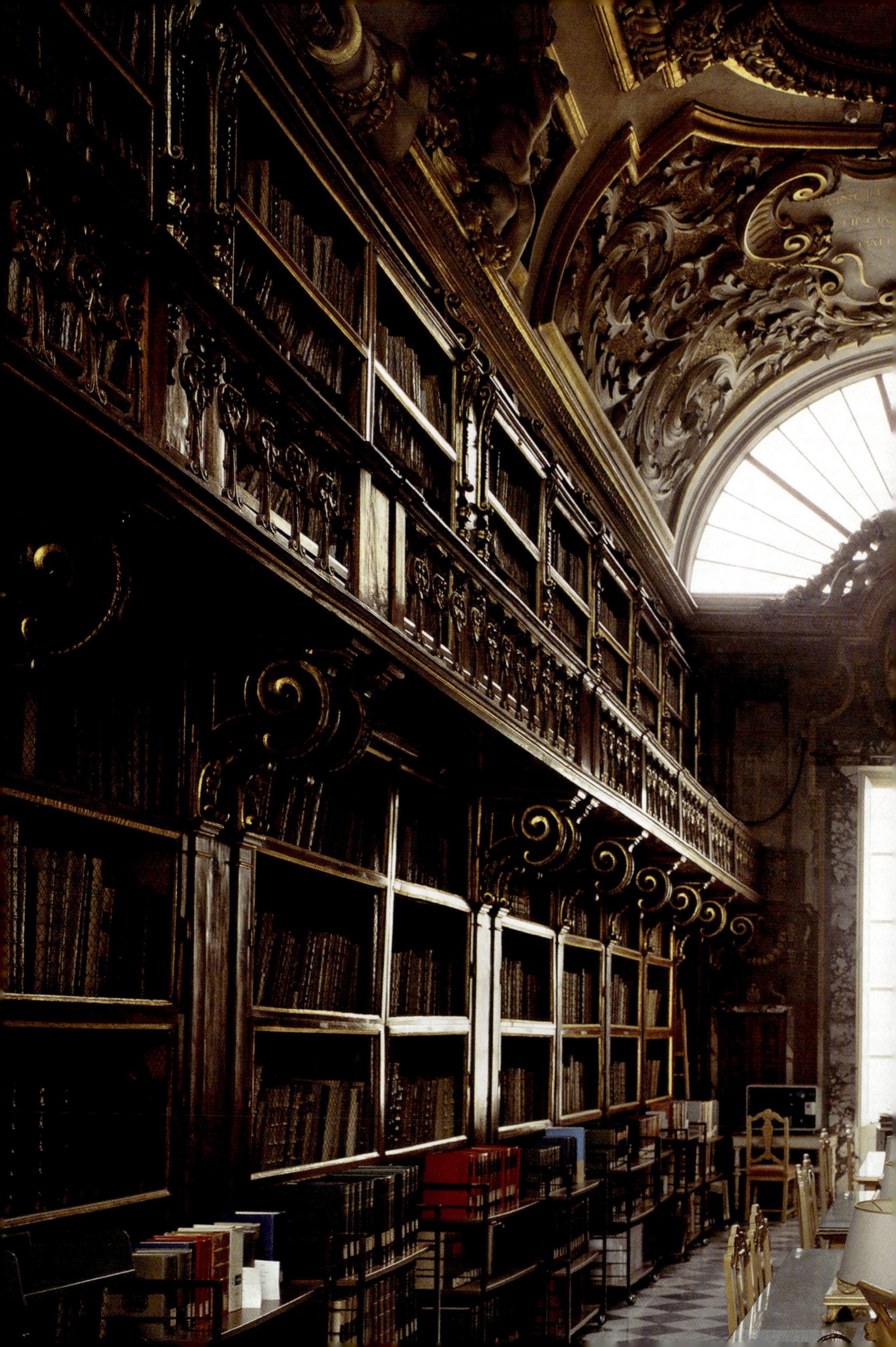

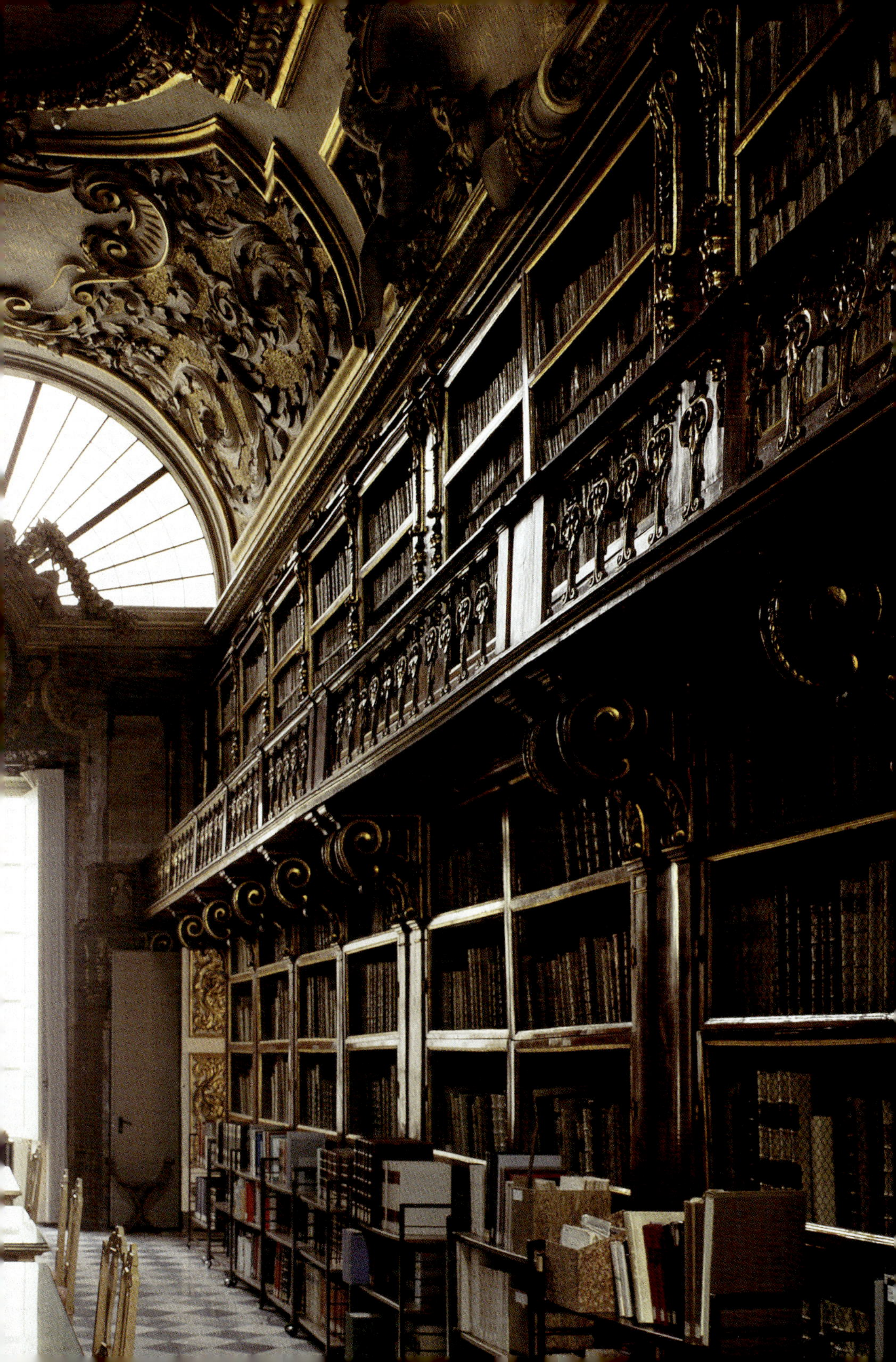

Biblioteca Angelica

The Biblioteca Angelica, which is situated not far from the Piazza Navona in Rome, traces its origins back to the library assembled by the Hermits of St Augustine, who first arrived here in 1286. These holdings, which originally served for monastic study, grew with the increasing importance of the monastery, which lay adjacent to the church of Sant'Agostino in a privileged location among the palaces of the old nobility and thereby enjoyed links with Rome's leading families. These latter not only decorated the church in a lavish manner but also supported the library with targeted donations and by way of bequests of valuable manuscripts and codices. The collection only assumed enduring substance from 1604, however, when Cardinal Angelo Rocca (1546–1620) – a highly erudite Augustinian who was in charge of the Vatican printing press during the pontificate of Sixtus V – transferred his celebrated collection of 20,000 scholarly volumes to the monastery. A first, large library hall, completed in 1614, was built to house them and was open to the public right from the start. This was unusual in Counter-Reformation papal Rome but typical of an Augustinian library, in which – wholly in the spirit of the founder's values – a broad spectrum of theological, legal, philosophical, literary and scientific writings were available to readers, including some that were banned or otherwise difficult to get hold of. The Biblioteca Angelica's most dazzling acquisition in this respect was the library of Cardinal Domenico Silvio Passionei (1682–1761; ill. p. 52), who was linked with Jansenist circles in Rome. His collection of over 60,000 printed works, most of them purchased during his travels as papal nuncio through Protestant Europe, was acquired by the Angelica in 1762 and doubled the library's holdings. Also of interest is the geography collection, the core of which goes back to the bequest of Lucas Holstenius (1596–1661). Work was completed in 1763 on the new library hall, in which over 100,000 books from the *fondo antico* are housed today. It is the work of architect Luigi Vanvitelli (1700–1773), whom the Augustinians had commissioned to remodel both the church and the monastery.

⁂

Founded 1604 as regards earlier holdings; from 1614 Augustinian reference library; since 1873 owned by the Italian State
Holdings c. 200,000 volumes
Type of library formerly a monastic library; today a research library under the aegis of the Ministero per i beni e le attività culturali
Highlights *Codex Angelicus*, 1029–1039 (Ms. 123); Pietro da Eboli, *De balneis puteolanis*, 13th century (Ms. Lat. 1474); *Book of Hours*, 1476–1500 (Ms. 976); Ludovico Ariosto, *Orlando Furioso di Ludovico Ariosto ristampato et con diligentia da lui corretto*, Ferrara, 1521; Camillo Agrippa, *Trattato di scientia d'arme, con un dialogo di filosofia*, Rome, 1553; Gerard van Keulen, *Collection of Nautical Maps*, 1709–1713 (CGR 3/7)

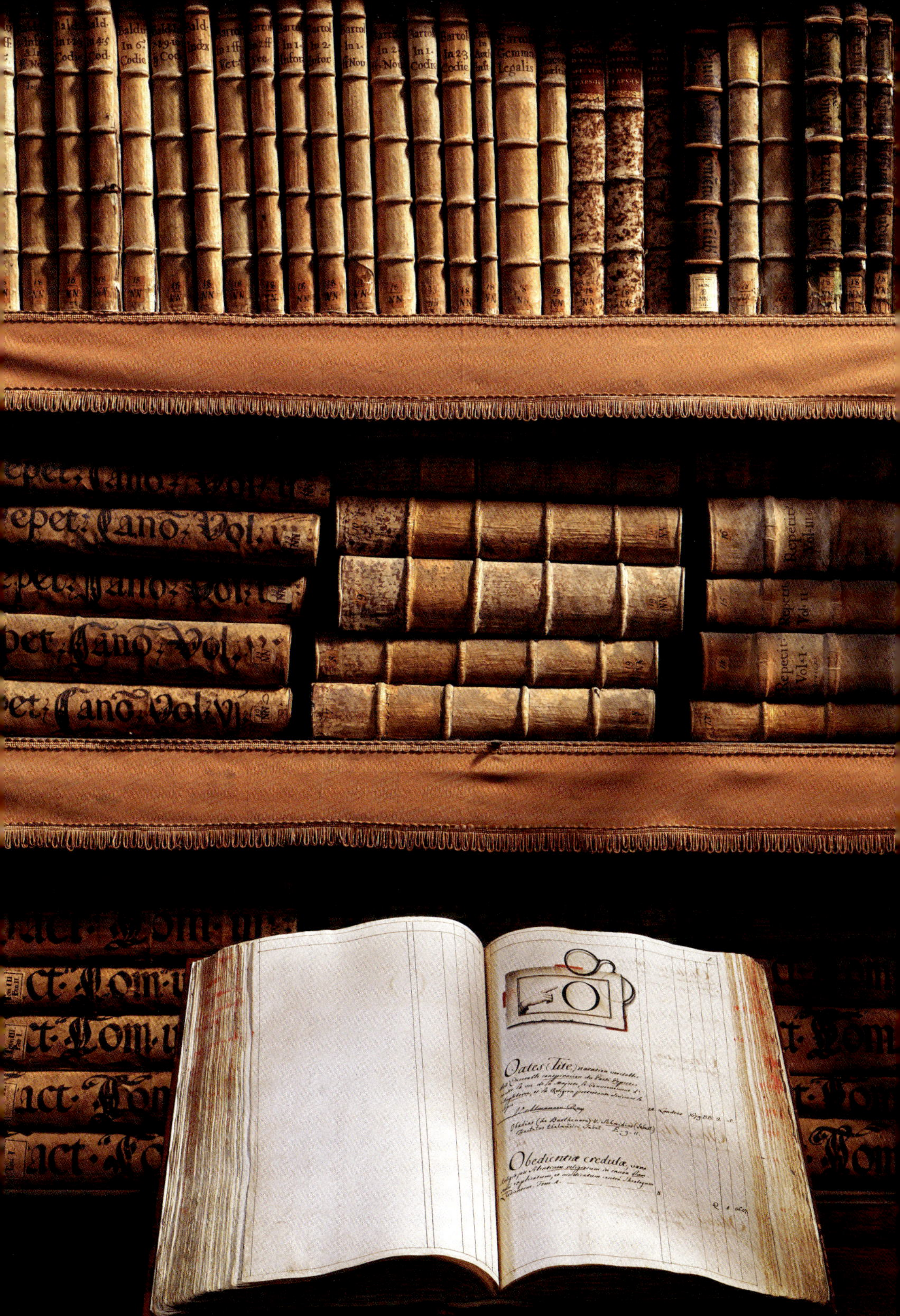

Unweit der Piazza Navona in Rom hat sich die Ordensbibliothek der Augustiner erhalten, die dort bereits seit 1286 eine Niederlassung besaßen. Die hauseigenen Buchbestände wuchsen mit der zunehmenden Bedeutung dieses neben der Kirche Sant'Agostino gelegenen Klosters, das aufgrund seiner privilegierten Lage inmitten alter Adelspaläste Kontakte zu den bekanntesten römischen Familien unterhielt. Sie statteten nicht nur die Kirche reich aus, sondern förderten auch die Bibliothek mit gezielten Zuwendungen und durch Nachlässe wertvoller Handschriften und Kodizes. Eine solide Basis erhielt die Sammlung aber erst mit der Stiftung Kardinal Angelo Roccas (1546–1620), eines hoch gebildeten Augustiners, der während des Pontifikats von Sixtus V. die vatikanische Druckerei geleitet hatte. Der Gelehrtenwelt war seine an die 20 000 Bände zählende Büchersammlung wohlbekannt, die ab 1604 in den Besitz des Augustinerklosters überging. Dafür wurde ein erster großer Bibliothekssaal errichtet, der seit seiner Fertigstellung im Jahr 1614 der Öffentlichkeit zugänglich war. Das war ungewöhnlich im päpstlichen Rom der Gegenreformation und programmatisch für eine Augustinerbibliothek, in der ganz im Sinne der Wertlehre ihres Gründers ein weites Spektrum an theologischen, juristischen, philosophischen, literarischen und wissenschaftlichen Schriften den Lesern zur Verfügung stand, die mitunter verboten oder andernorts nur schwer zu finden waren. Der brisanteste Erwerb im Jahr 1762 war in diesem Sinne wohl jener der Bibliothek des Kardinals Domenico Silvio Passionei (1682–1761; Abb. S. 52), der dem Umfeld der römischen Jansenisten verbunden war. Sie verdoppelte den Bestand der Angelica mit über 60 000 Drucken, die der Kardinal großteils während seiner Reisen als päpstlicher Nuntius durch die protestantischen Länder Europas erworben hatte. Von Interesse ist außerdem die Sammlung zur Geografie, deren Grundstock auf den Nachlass von Lucas Holstenius (1596–1661) zurückgeht. 1763 war der neue Bibliothekssaal vollendet, in dem noch heute über 100 000 Bücher des *fondo antico* aufgestellt sind. Sein Architekt ist Luigi Vanvitelli (1700–1773), den die Augustiner mit dem Umbau von Kirche und Konvent beauftragt hatten.

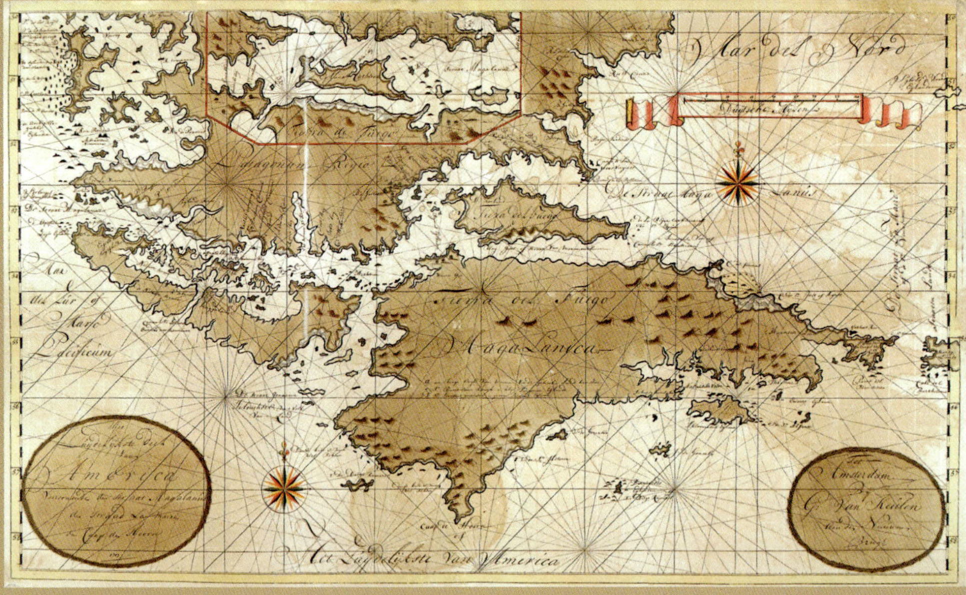

La bibliothèque des Augustins se trouve à Rome, non loin de la Piazza Navona, où l'ordre disposait déjà d'un site dès 1286. Le fonds d'origine privée s'étoffa à mesure que le monastère jouxtant l'église Sant'Agostino s'agrandissait. Du fait de sa situation privilégiée tout près des palais de l'ancienne noblesse romaine, les Augustins entretenaient des liens avec les familles les plus en vue. Elles ne dotèrent pas uniquement l'église avec générosité, mais aussi la bibliothèque, grâce à des dons ciblés et des legs de manuscrits et de codex précieux. La collection bénéficia d'une solide assise avec la donation du cardinal Angelo Rocca (1546–1620), un augustin très cultivé qui avait dirigé l'imprimerie vaticane sous le pontificat de Sixte Quint. Riche d'au moins 20 000 volumes, la bibliothèque des Augustins acquit en 1604 la collection qui la rendit célèbre auprès de l'élite mondiale. Pour l'abriter, une première grande salle fut construite et ouverte au public dès son achèvement en 1614. La bibliothèque augustine avait un dessein inhabituel sous la Contre-Réforme de la Rome papale : celui de mettre à disposition, dans le souhait d'érudition de son fondateur, tout un éventail d'écrits théologiques, juridiques, philosophiques, littéraires et scientifiques parfois interdits ou difficiles à trouver ailleurs. À cet égard, l'acquisition la plus surprenante est celle de 1762. Le legs du cardinal Domenico Silvio Passionei (1682–1761 ; ill. p. 52), qui était lié aux jansénistes romains, fit en effet doubler le fonds de la bibliothèque Angelica. Le cardinal laissait plus de 60 000 imprimés – pour la plupart acquis durant ses voyages en tant que nonce papal à travers les contrées protestantes d'Europe. La collection géographique dont le noyau remonte à la succession de Lucas Holstenius (1596–1661) est également digne d'intérêt. La nouvelle salle achevée en 1763 continue d'abriter plus de 100 000 volumes du *fondo antico*. Son architecte n'est autre que Luigi Vanvitelli (1700–1773) auquel les Augustins avaient également commandé la réfection de l'église et du couvent.

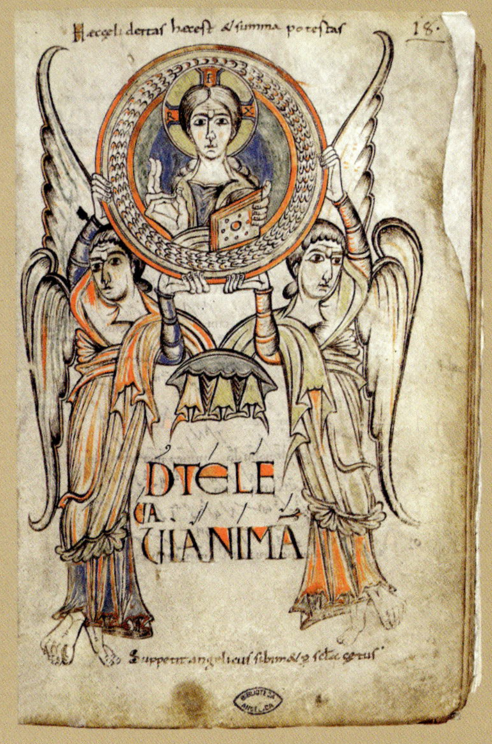

Gerard van Keulen, *Collection of Nautical Maps*, 1709–1713, sig. CGR 3/7: *Strait of Magellan*

Graduale Troppario (Codex Angelicus), 1029–1039, sig. Ms. 123, fol. 18r: *Pantocrator*

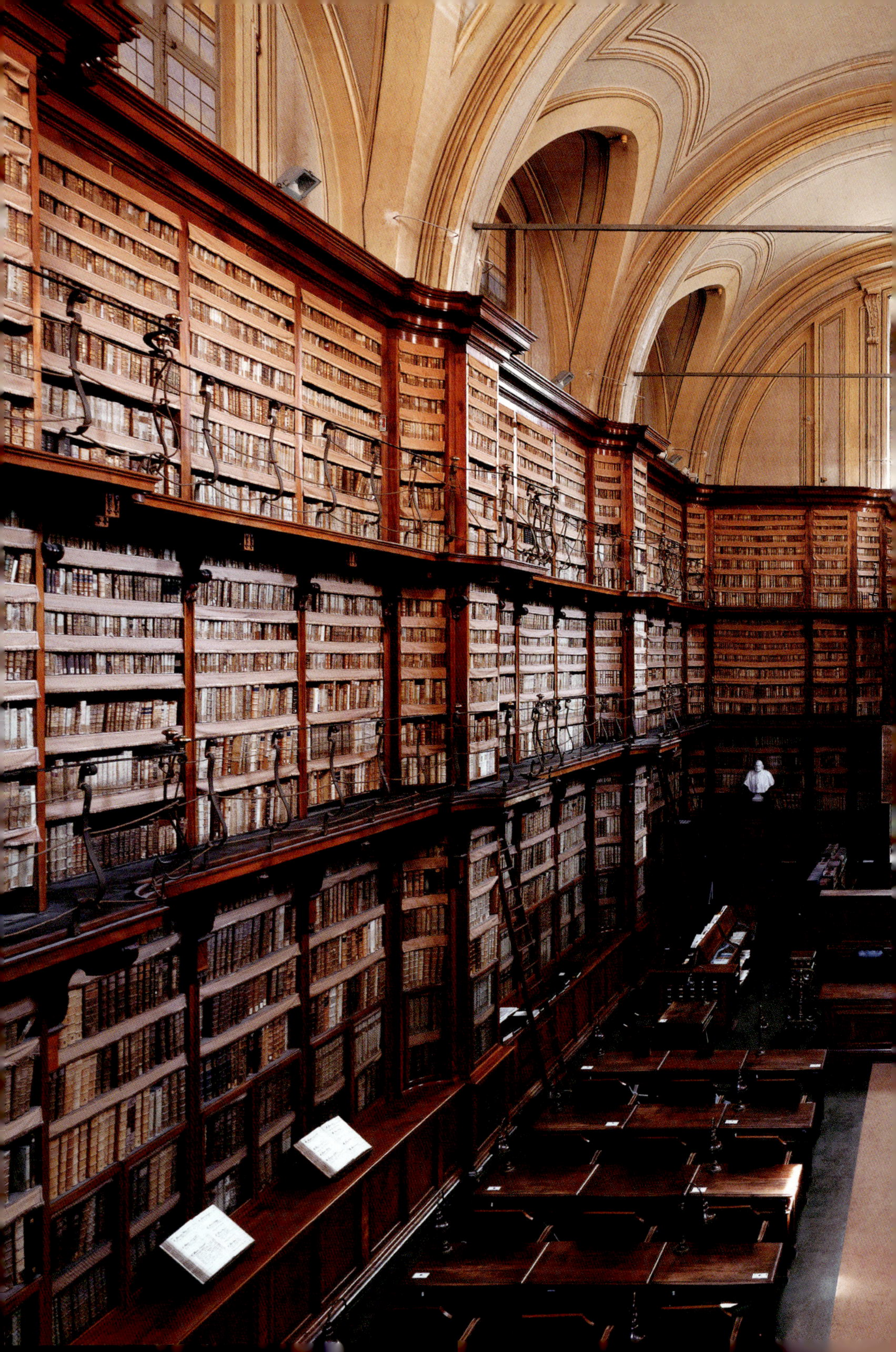

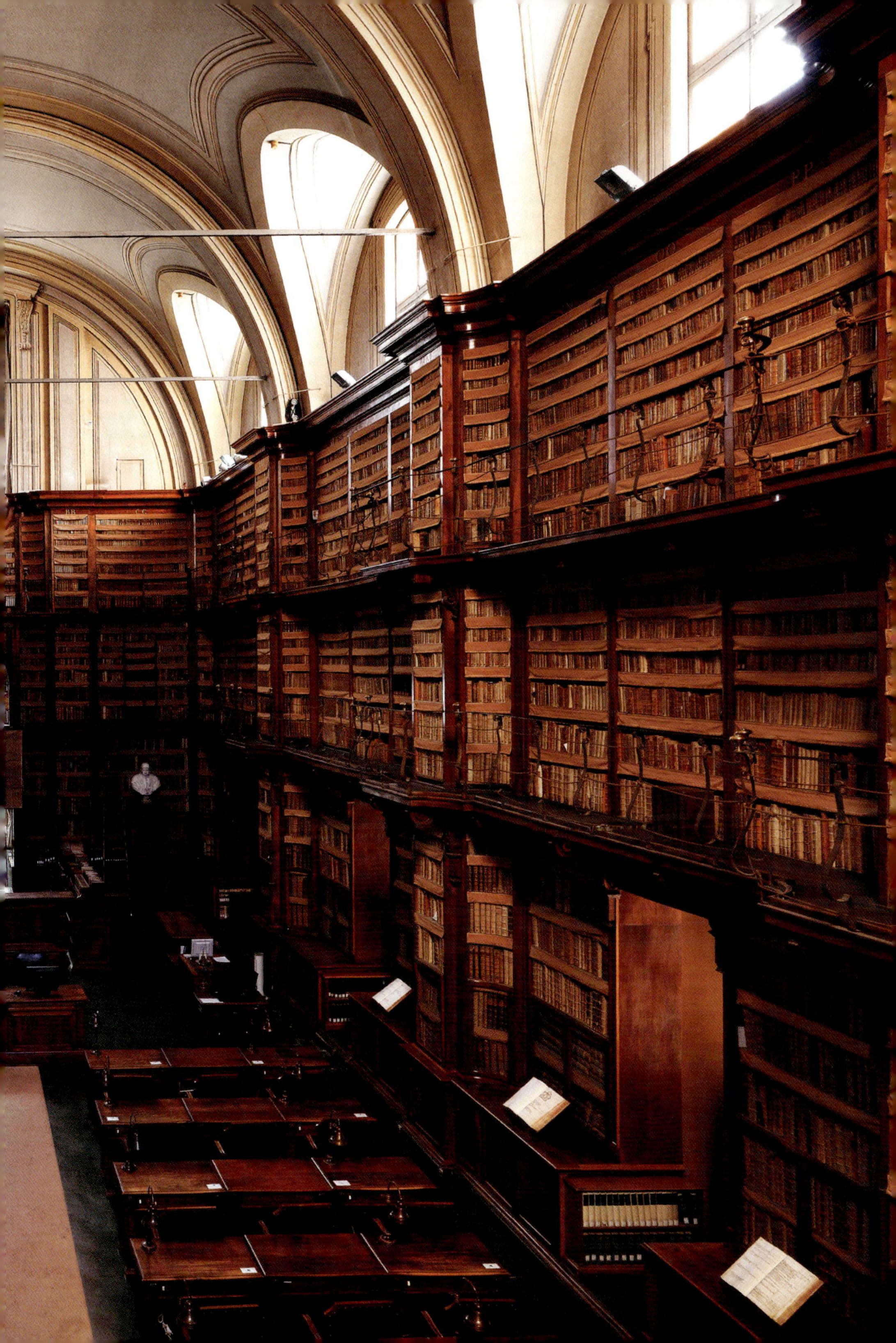

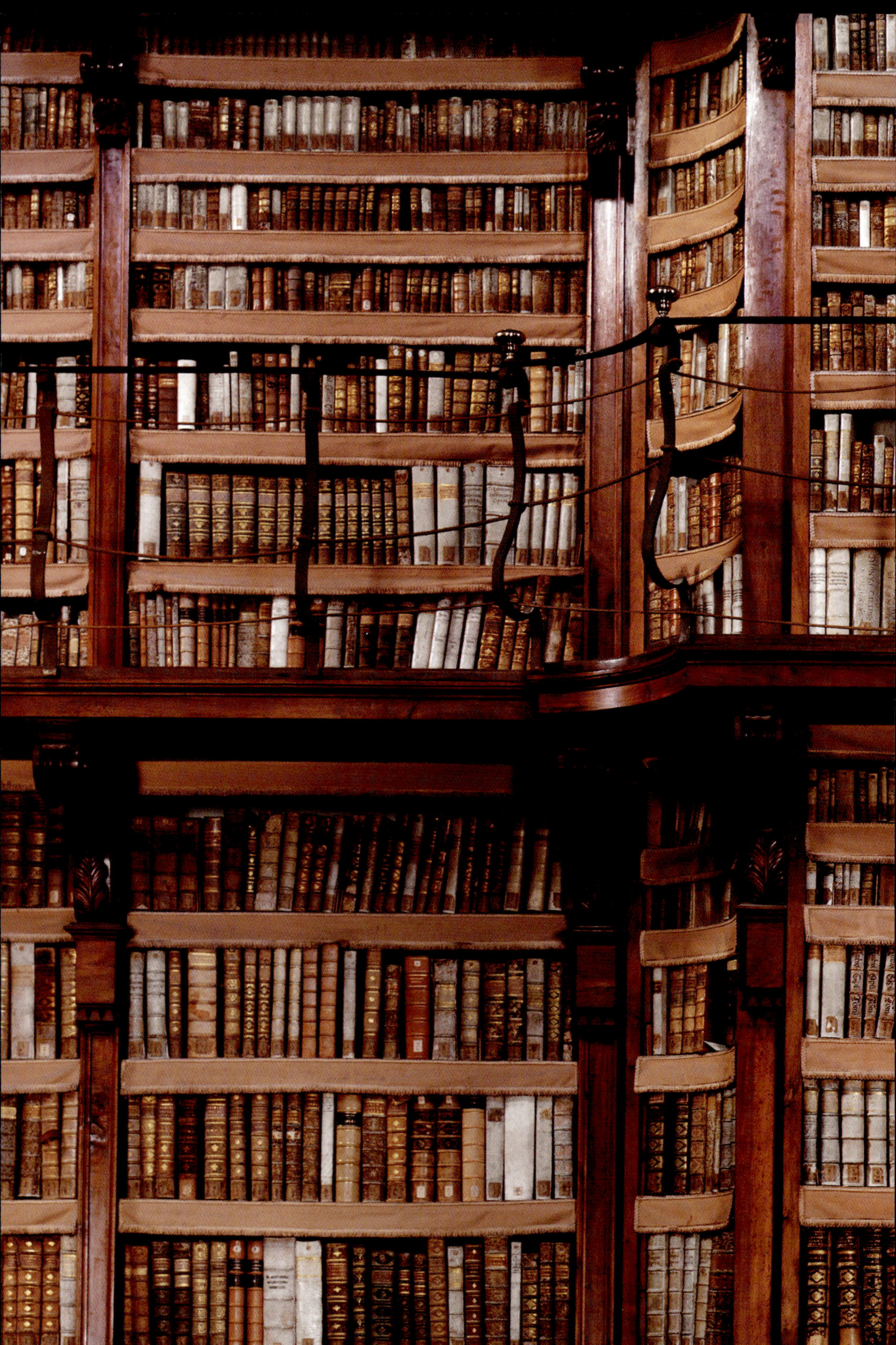

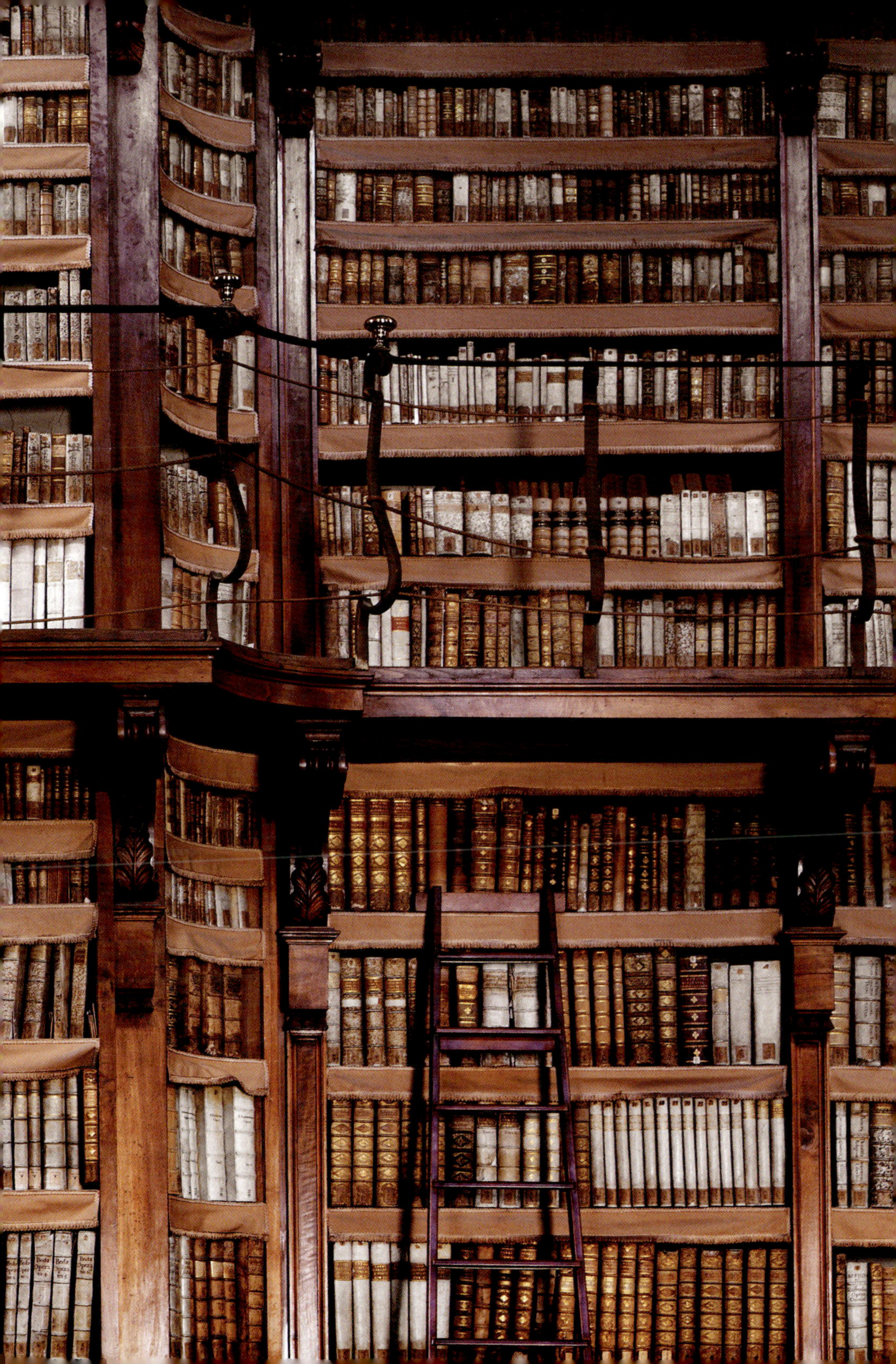

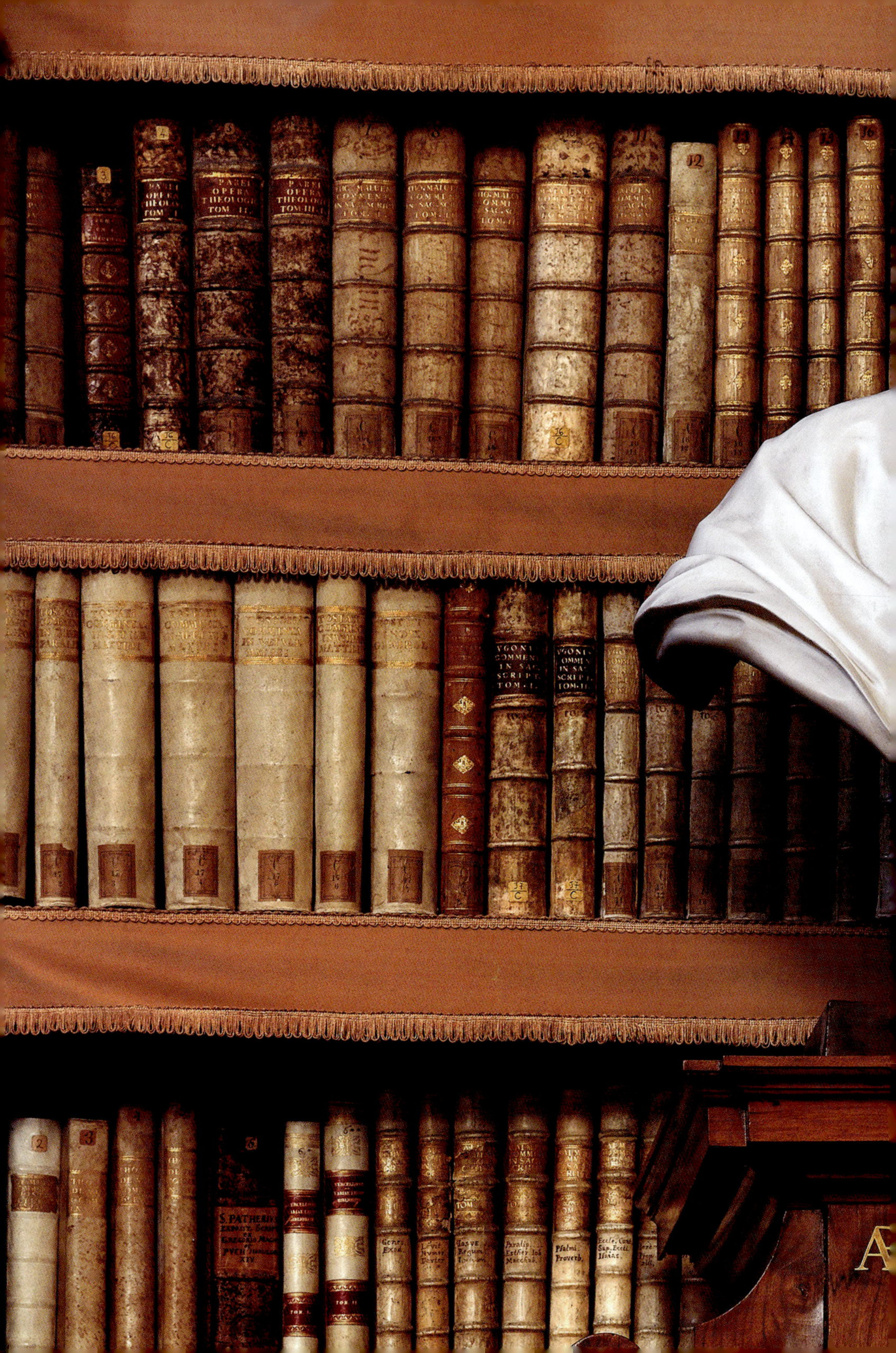

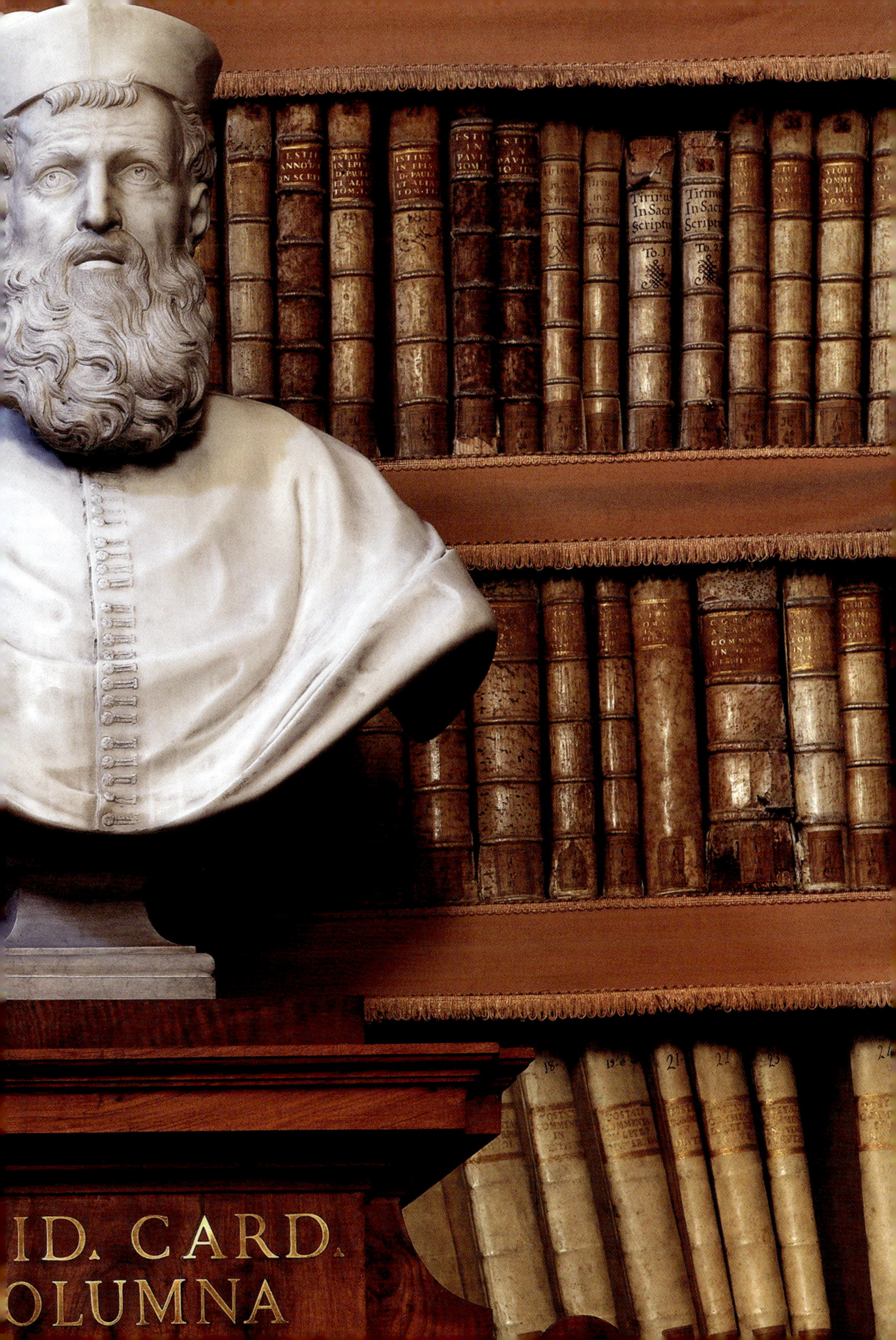
ID. CARD.
OLUMNA

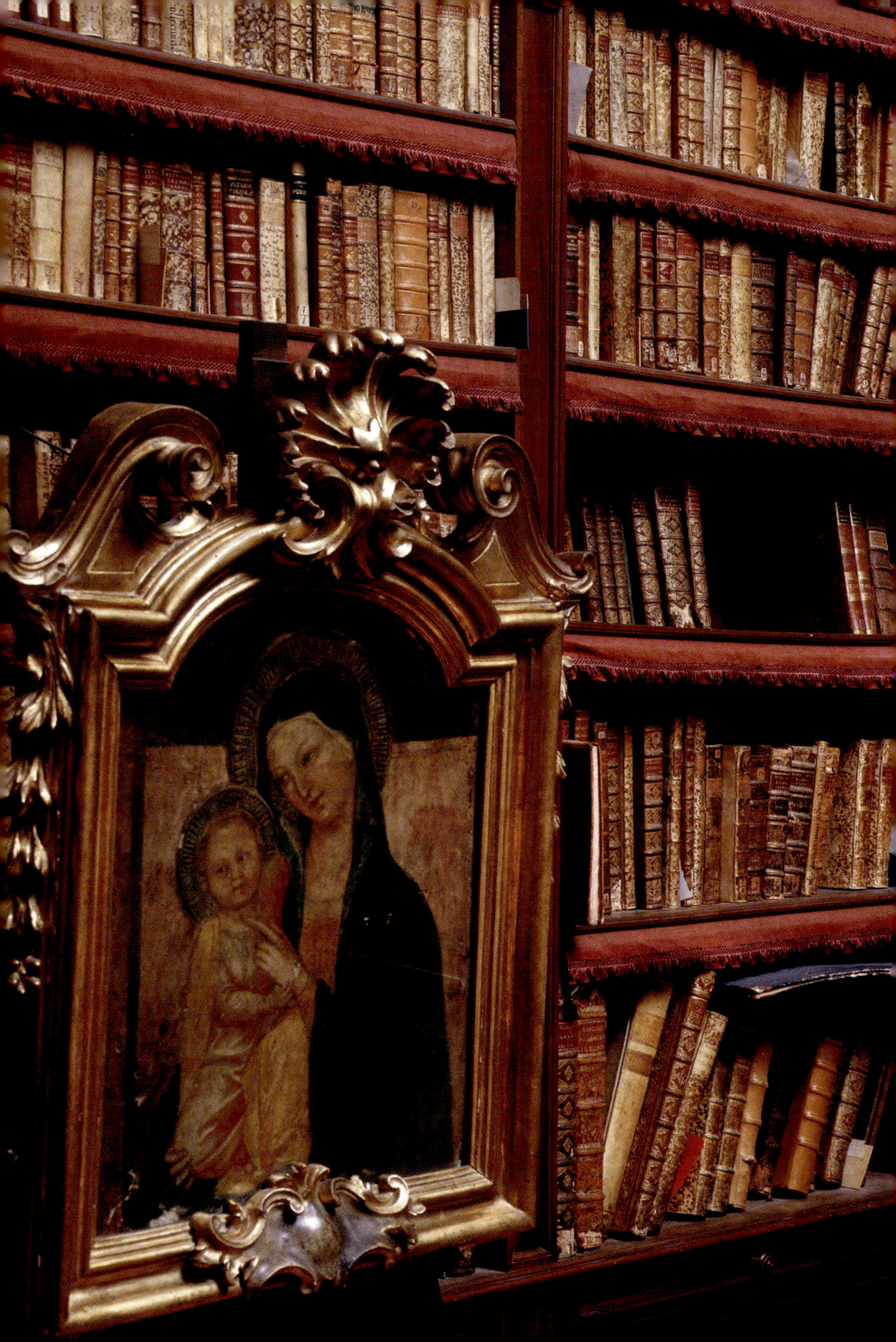

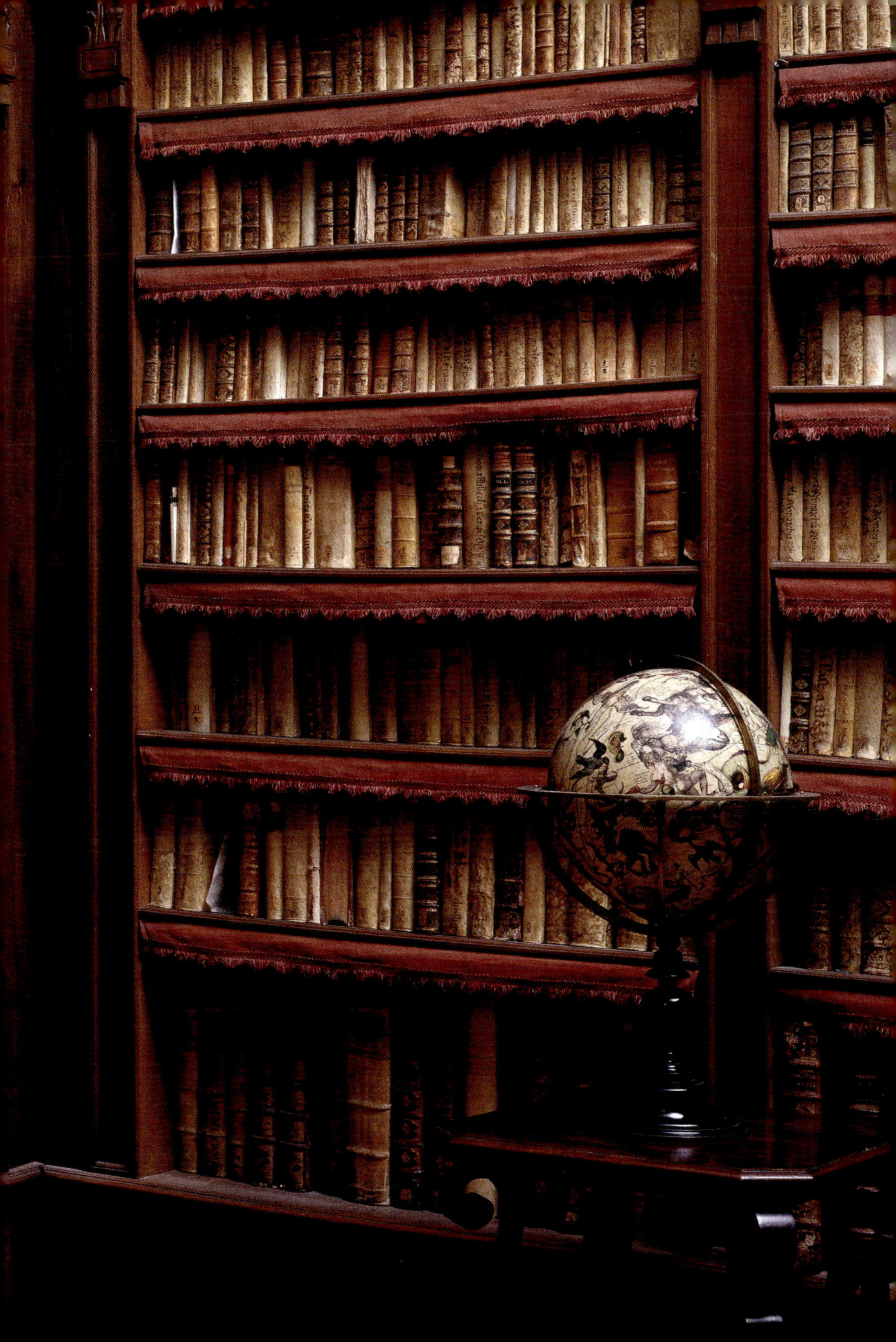

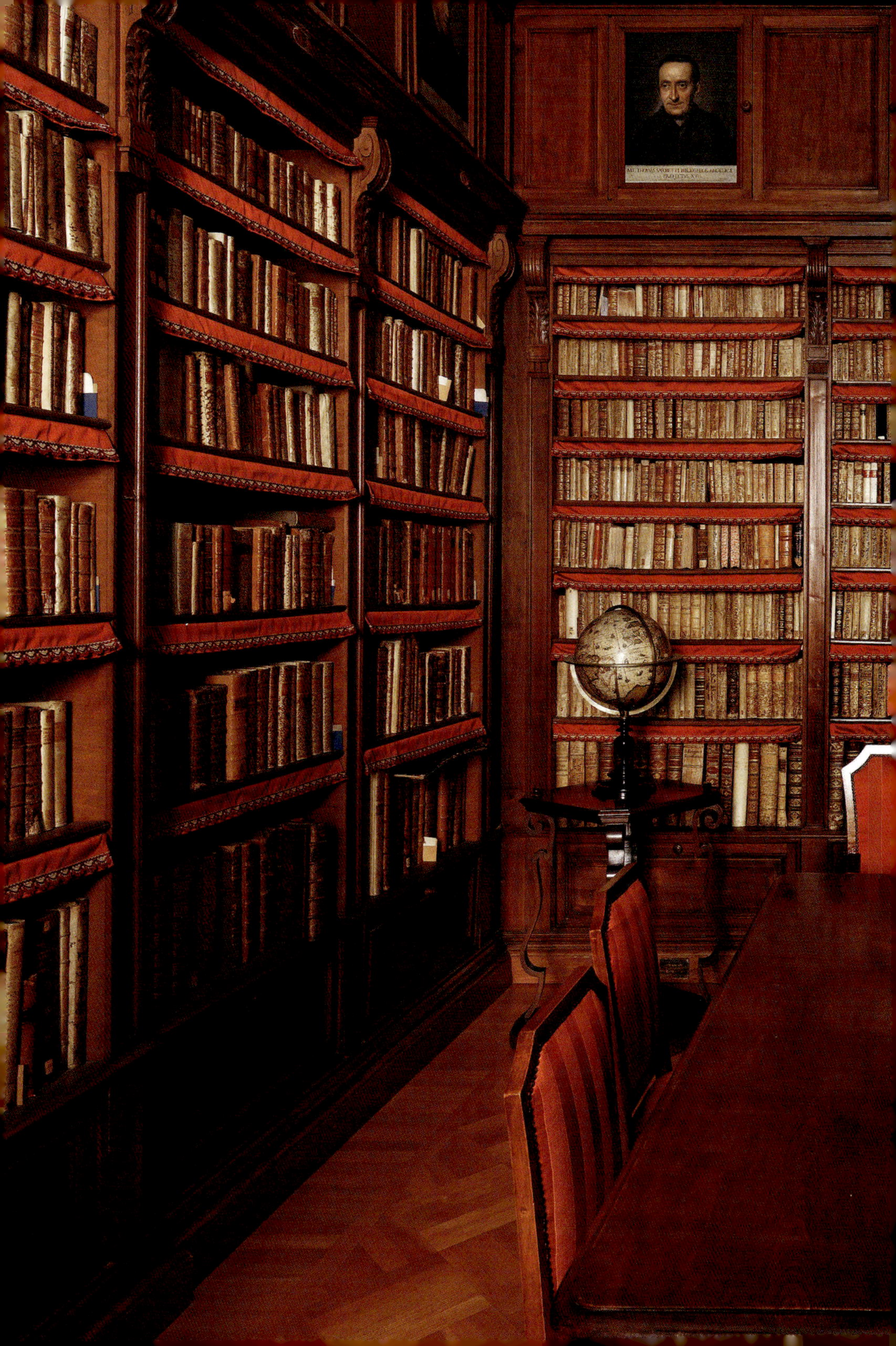

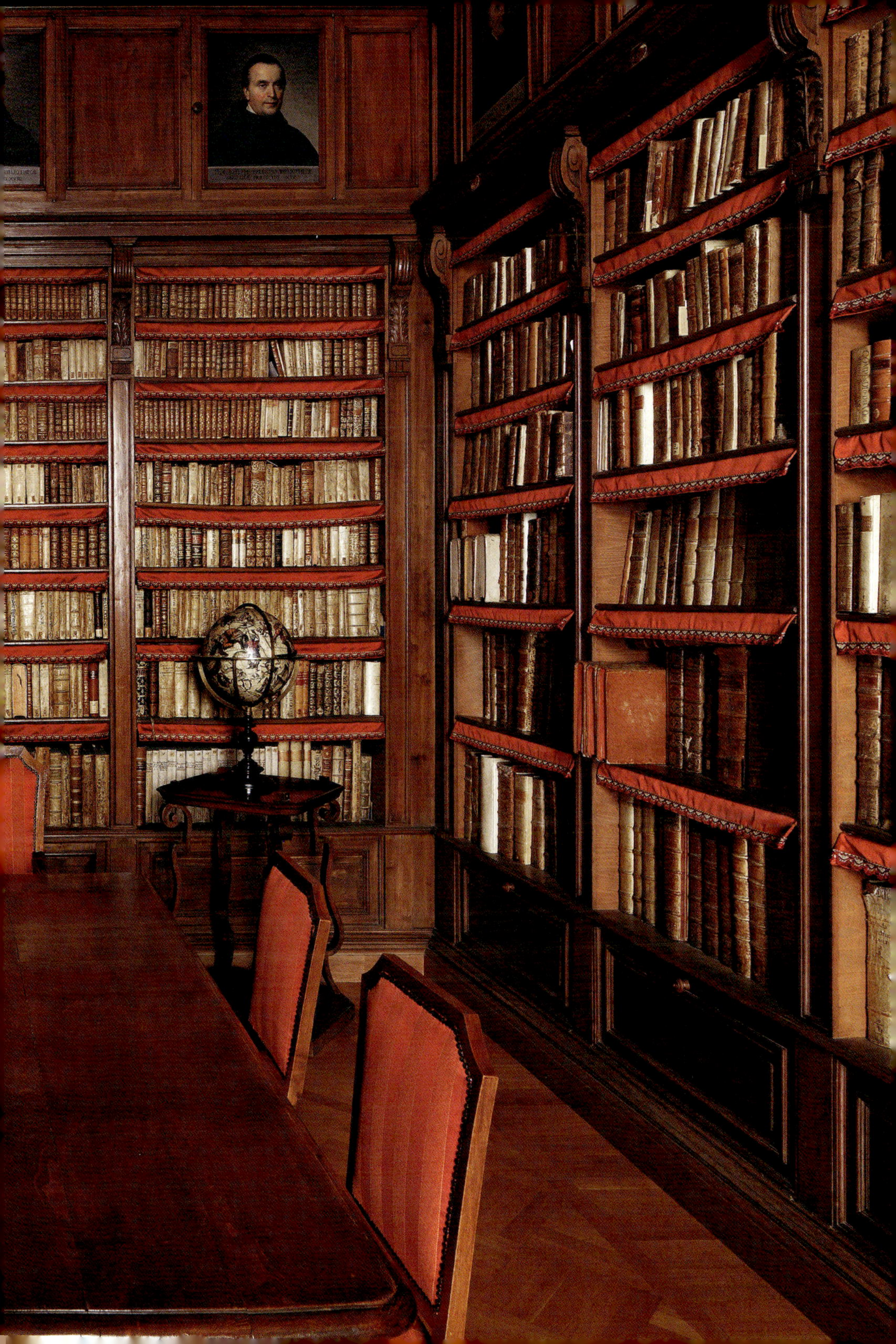

Biblioteca Civica Gambalunga

Rimini's Biblioteca Civica Gambalunga is one of the oldest public libraries in Italy. For its founder, the jurist Alessandro Gambalunga (c. 1554–1619), it became a monument to the humanism he embraced. The library has been housed since its foundation in the magnificent, classically inspired palace built for Gambalunga between 1610 and 1614 in the historical heart of the city, where Rimini's oldest patrician families had their residences. Within this noble setting, the universal scholar pursued his activities as a patron of the arts. He assembled around him a circle of academics and writers and allocated generous funds to his private library. His books were managed by a full-time librarian and were accessible to anyone who wished to consult them. The library was continuously expanded in all areas and upon its founder's death already comprised some 2,000 volumes, many of them Venetian in provenance. Gambalunga's acquisitions included legal works, Latin and Greek classics, modern Italian authors, travelogues, treatises on grammar, poetry and rhetoric, manuals of theology and history, and scientific writings in particular in the fields of medicine and astronomy. An in-house book-binding workshop meant that all the volumes were given uniform bindings. In 1617 Alessandro Gambalunga stipulated in his will that his library should pass to the city of Rimini after his death and should remain accessible to the public. The original holdings today on display on the *piano nobile*, still in their 17th-century bookcases, continue to pay tribute to an extraordinary patron, who made provision during his lifetime for the preservation and expansion of his library long after his death. In the 18th century the library saw its holdings substantially expanded thanks to Giuseppe Garampi (1725–1792), the Rimini-born Prefect of the Vatican Secret Archives. Garampi not only arranged for rare works from old monastery collections to be deposited with the library, but bequeathed to it his own estate, which contained precious medieval manuscripts and incunabula. Luigi Tonini (1807–1874), who was in charge of the Gambalunga from 1840 to 1874, compiled a catalogue of the library in five volumes and expanded its holdings with manuscripts, parchments, maps and archaeological finds.

***

Founded before 1619; owned by the municipality of Rimini since 1619
Holdings c. 280,000 volumes, of which c. 60,000 rare and old books and manuscripts
Type of library originally a private library, today a civic library
Highlights parchment codex of *La Commedia (Dante Gradenighiano)*, transcribed by Giacomo Gradenigo, 14th century (Sc-Ms. 1162); Vespasiano da Bisticci, *Comentario de'gesti e fatti e detti dello invictissimo Signore Federigo Duca d'Urbino*, with miniatures by Francesco d'Antonio del Chierico, 15th century (Sc-Ms. 94); Francesco Petrarca, *I trionfi*, illuminated codex, 15th century (Sc-Ms. 92)

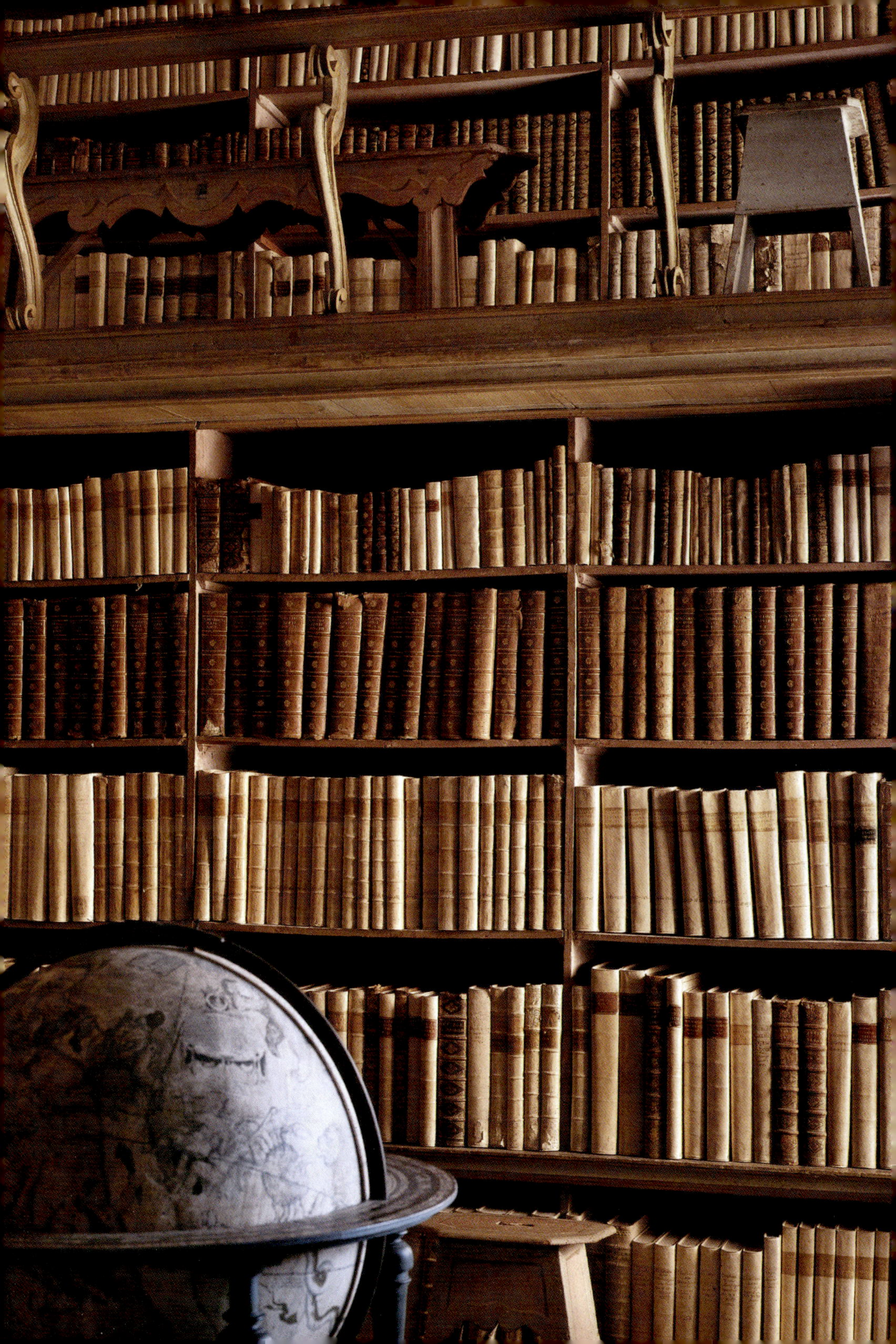

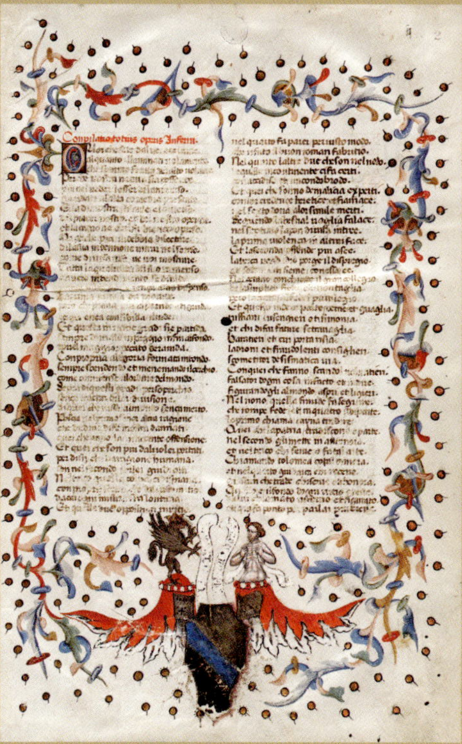

Mit der Stadtbibliothek von Rimini hat sich eine der ältesten öffentlichen Bibliotheken Italiens erhalten. Für ihren Gründer, den Rechtsgelehrten Alessandro Gambalunga (um 1554–1619), wurde sie zum Denkmal gelebten Humanismus. Seit ihrer Gründung befindet sich die Bibliothek in dem prächtigen, klassisch inspirierten Palast, den Gambalunga in den Jahren 1610 bis 1614 im historischen Stadtkern von Rimini errichten ließ, wo der alteingesessene Adel zu Hause war. In diesem noblen Rahmen entfaltete der universell interessierte Gelehrte seine Mäzenatentätigkeit. Er versammelte einen Kreis von Wissenschaftlern und Literaten um sich und förderte seine Privatbibliothek großzügig. Die Bücher standen bereits damals mithilfe eines hauptamtlich tätigen Bibliothekars jedem an ihrer Benutzung Interessierten zur Verfügung. Der Bestand wurde mit universellem Anspruch laufend erweitert und zählte beim Tod des

Gründers wohl bereits an die 2 000 Bände, viele davon mit venezianischer Provenienz. Zu Gambalungas Anschaffungen zählten rechtswissenschaftliche Werke, lateinische und griechische Klassiker, moderne italienische Autoren, Reiseberichte, Abhandlungen über Grammatik, Dichtung und Rhetorik, Handbücher zur Theologie und Geschichte sowie wissenschaftliche Schriften aus den Gebieten Medizin und Astronomie. Eine Buchbinderwerkstatt im Hause sorgte für prachtvolle einheitliche Bindungen. Im Jahr 1617 verfügte Alessandro Gambalunga in seinem Testament, dass die Bibliothek nach seinem Ableben der Stadt Rimini übergeben werden und öffentlich zugänglich bleiben sollte. Der im *piano nobile* des Palastes in Mobiliar aus dem 17. Jahrhundert ausgestellte Originalbestand gibt noch heute Zeugnis von einem außergewöhnlichen Mäzen, der weit über seinen Tod hinaus für den Bestand und die Weiterentwicklung dieser Bibliothek vorgesorgt hatte. Dem ebenfalls aus Rimini stammenden Präfekten der vatikanischen Geheimarchive, Giuseppe Garampi (1725–1792), ist eine wesentliche Erweiterung der Bibliothek im 18. Jahrhundert zu verdanken. Er ließ ihr Zimelien aus alten Klosterbeständen und schließlich seinen Nachlass zukommen, der kostbare mittelalterliche Manuskripte und Inkunabeln enthielt. Von 1840 bis 1874 übernahm Luigi Tonini (1807–1874) die Leitung der Bibliothek Gambalunga. Er verfasste einen fünfbändigen Bibliothekskatalog und erweiterte den Bestand um Manuskripte, Pergamentschriften, Karten und archäologische Funde.

Dante Alighieri, *La Commedia (Dante Gradenighiano) – The Divine Comedy*, 14th century, sig. Sc-Ms. 1162, fol. 2r
Francesco Petrarca, *I trionfi*, 15th century, sig. Sc-Ms. 92, fol. 1r

La bibliothèque municipale de Rimini est l'une des plus anciennes bibliothèques publiques d'Italie. Son fondateur, le jurisconsulte Alessandro Gambalunga (vers 1554–1619), l'envisageait comme l'incarnation de l'humanisme. Elle se trouve, depuis sa création, au sein du somptueux palais d'inspiration classique des Gambalunga, érigé entre 1610 et 1614 dans le centre historique de Rimini où les familles de l'ancienne noblesse étaient bien établies depuis longtemps. C'est dans cet auguste cadre que l'érudit universaliste pratiqua son activité de mécène. Il s'entoura de scientifiques et de lettrés et entretint sa bibliothèque privée avec largesse. Déjà à l'époque, grâce à l'aide d'un bibliothécaire professionnel, les livres étaient tenus à la disposition de toute personne intéressée. Les aspirations universelles de leur fondateur ont contribué à l'étoffement constant du fonds, qui comptait déjà 2 000 ouvrages à sa mort – beaucoup provenant de Venise. Ses acquisitions consistaient en ouvrages de jurisprudence, classiques latins et grecs, auteurs italiens contemporains, récits de voyage, traités de grammaire, de poésie et de rhétorique, manuels de théologie et d'histoire sans oublier des écrits scientifiques de médecine et d'astronomie. La reliure uniforme et élégante des ouvrages a été exécutée par un atelier à demeure. Alessandro Gambalunga prescrivit dans son testament de 1617 que la bibliothèque revienne à la Ville de Rimini après sa mort et qu'elle reste ouverte au public. Le fonds original situé à l'étage noble du palais présenté dans un mobilier XVIIe siècle témoigne aujourd'hui encore de la volonté d'un mécène extraordinaire qui avait anticipé le sort de sa collection et de cette bibliothèque bien après sa disparition. L'extension substantielle de la bibliothèque au XVIIIe siècle a été permise par Giuseppe Garampi (1725–1792), préfet des archives secrètes du Vatican, également originaire de Rimini. Il y fit venir ses imprimés illustrés, issus d'anciens fonds monastiques, et son héritage qui contenait de précieux manuscrits et incunables médiévaux. De

1840 à 1874, Luigi Tonini (1807–1874) fut chargé de la direction de la bibliothèque Gambalunga. Ce dernier rédigea un catalogue en cinq tomes et agrandit le fonds au moyen de manuscrits, de parchemins, de cartes et de découvertes archéologiques.

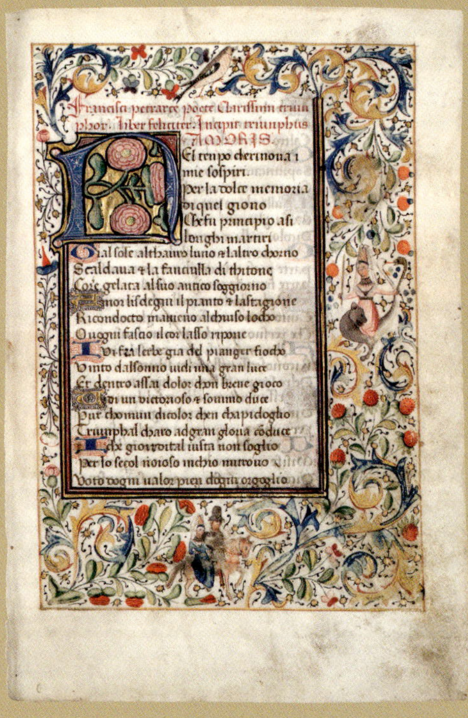

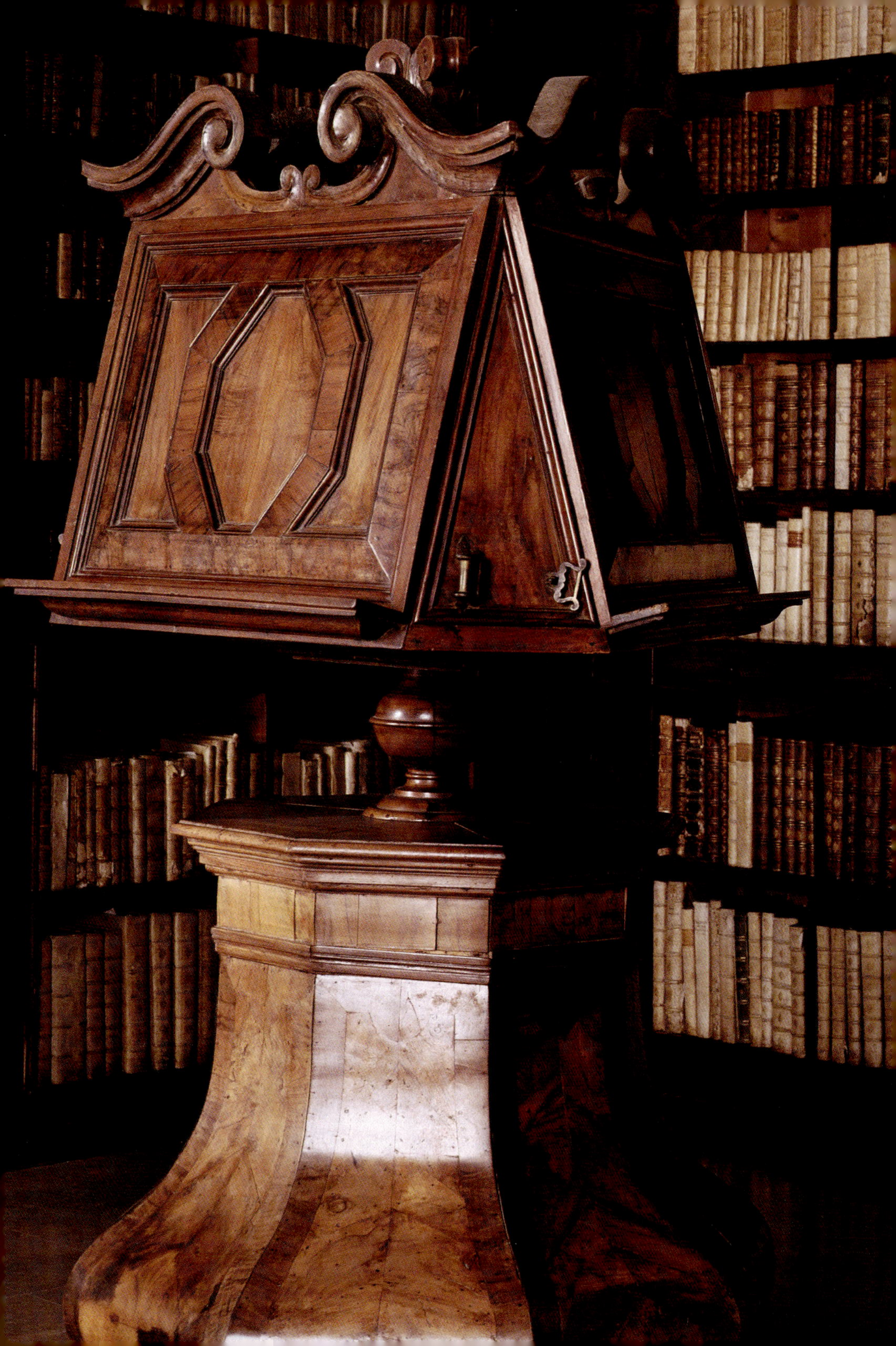

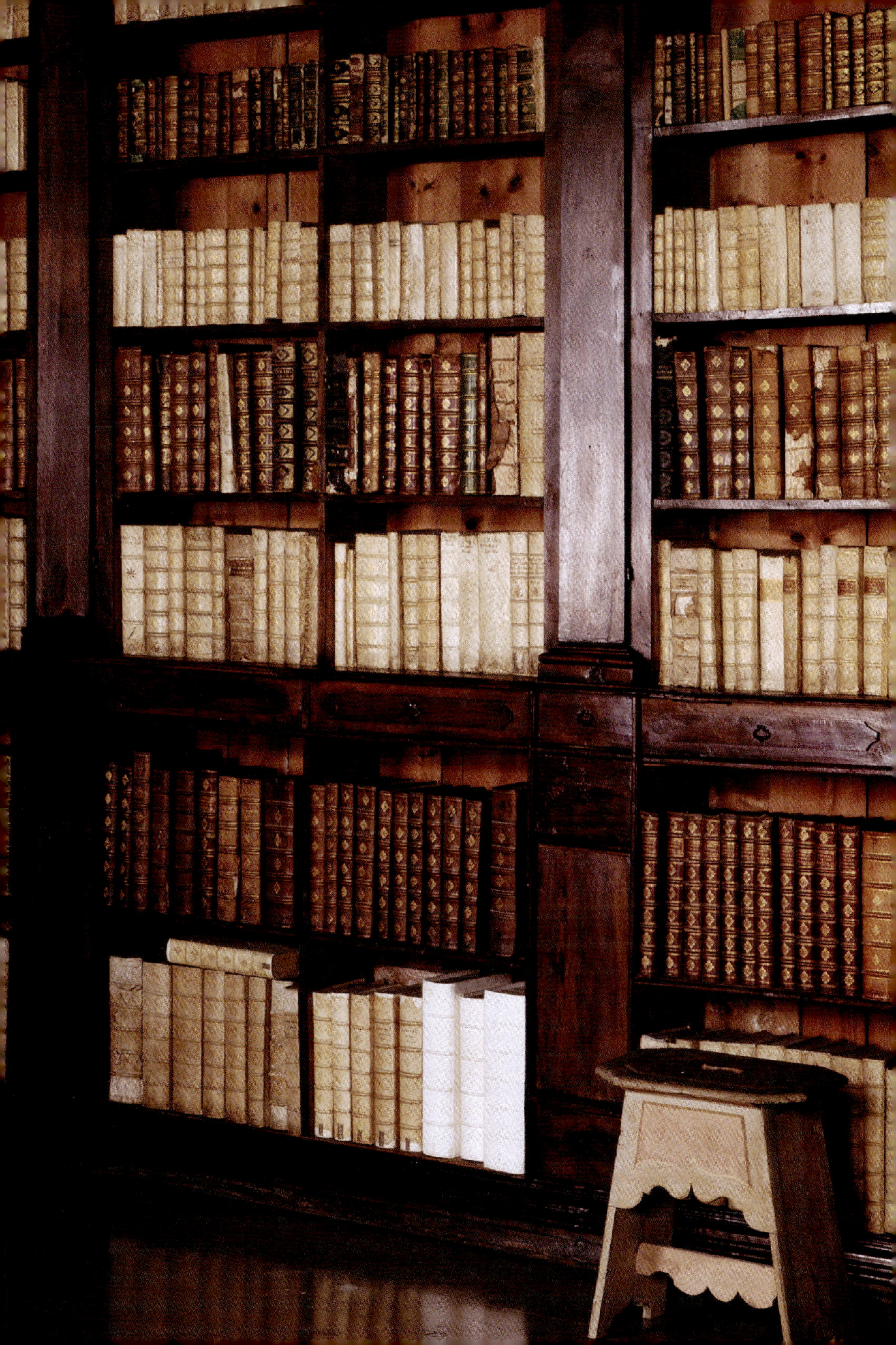

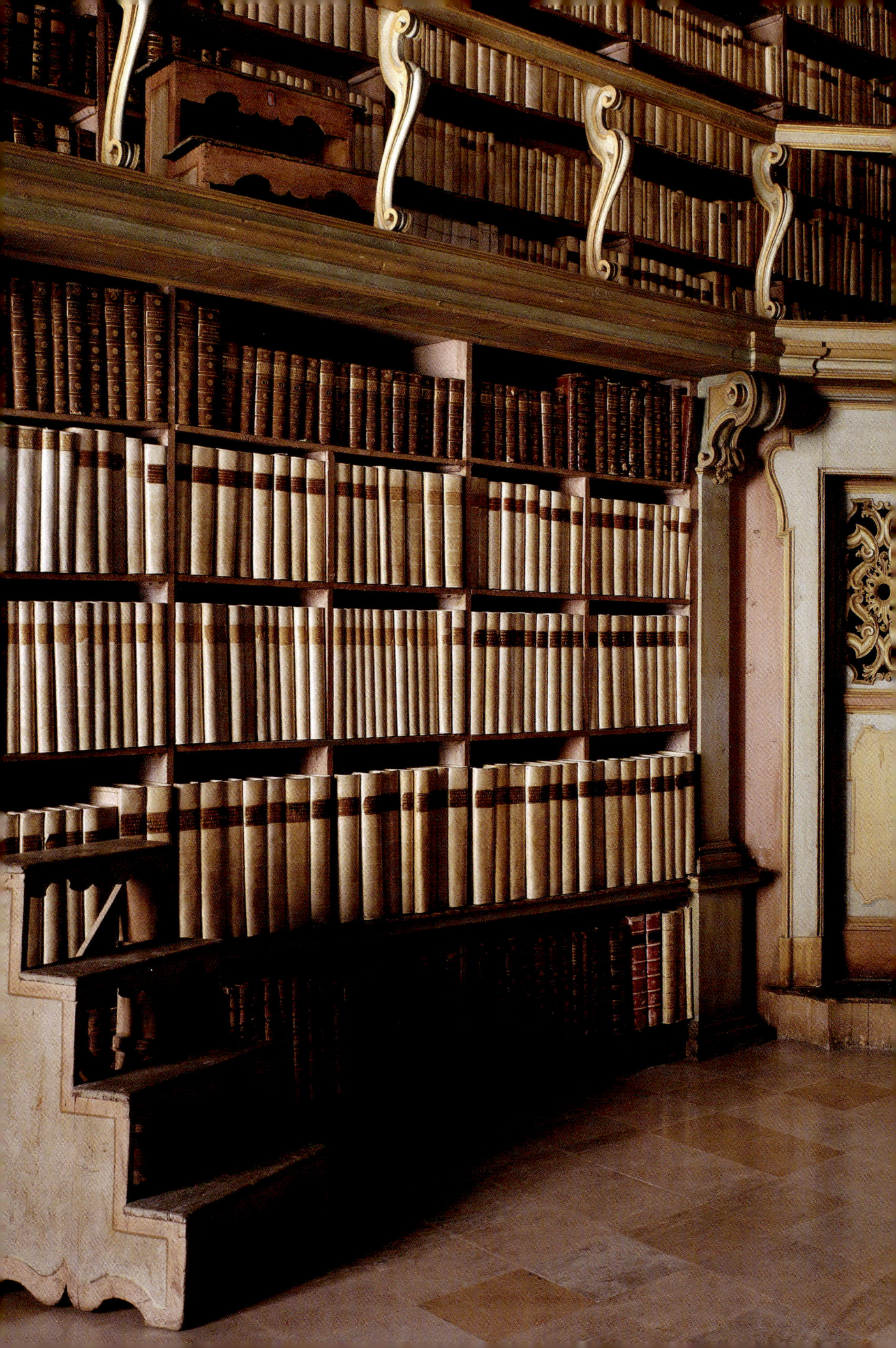

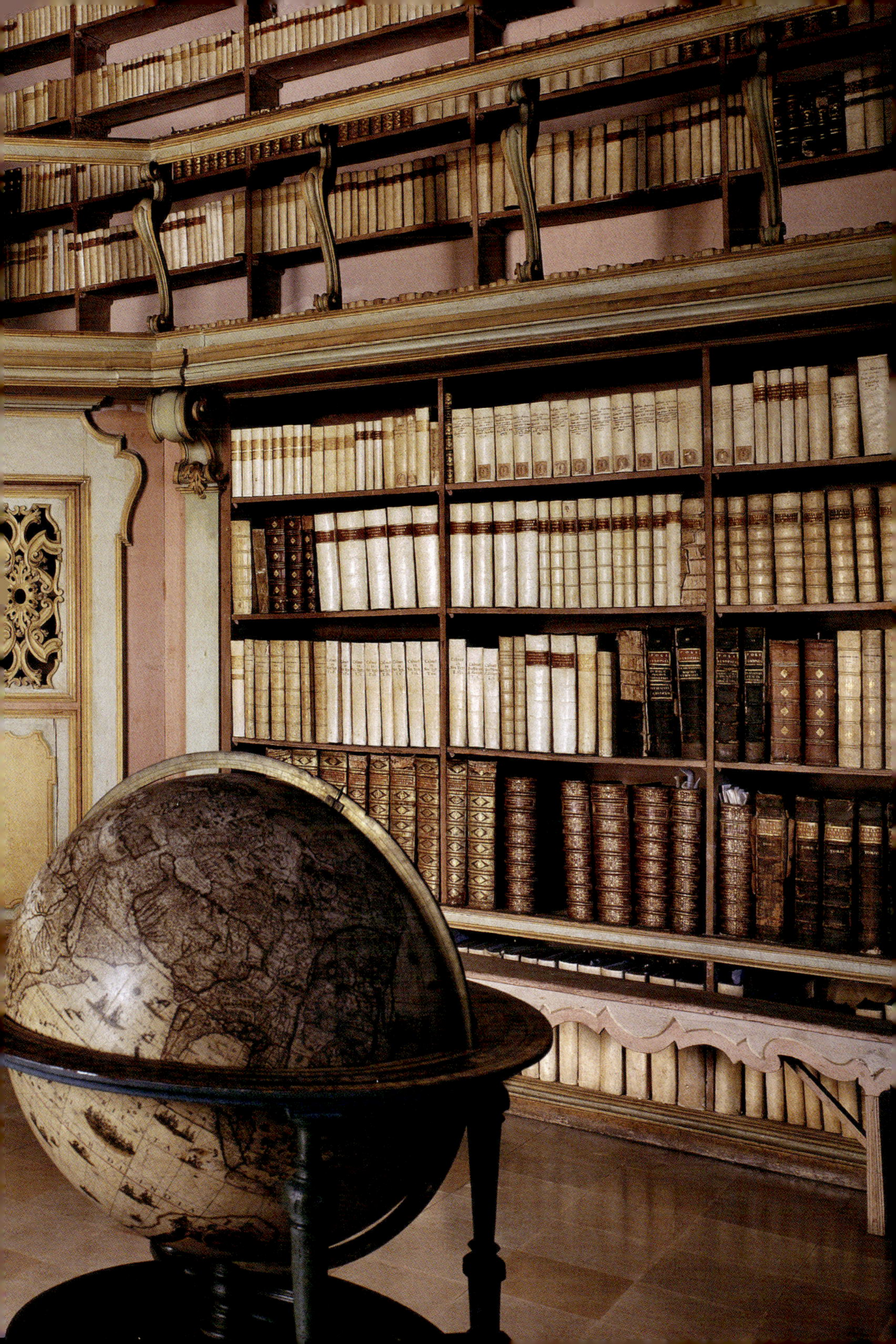

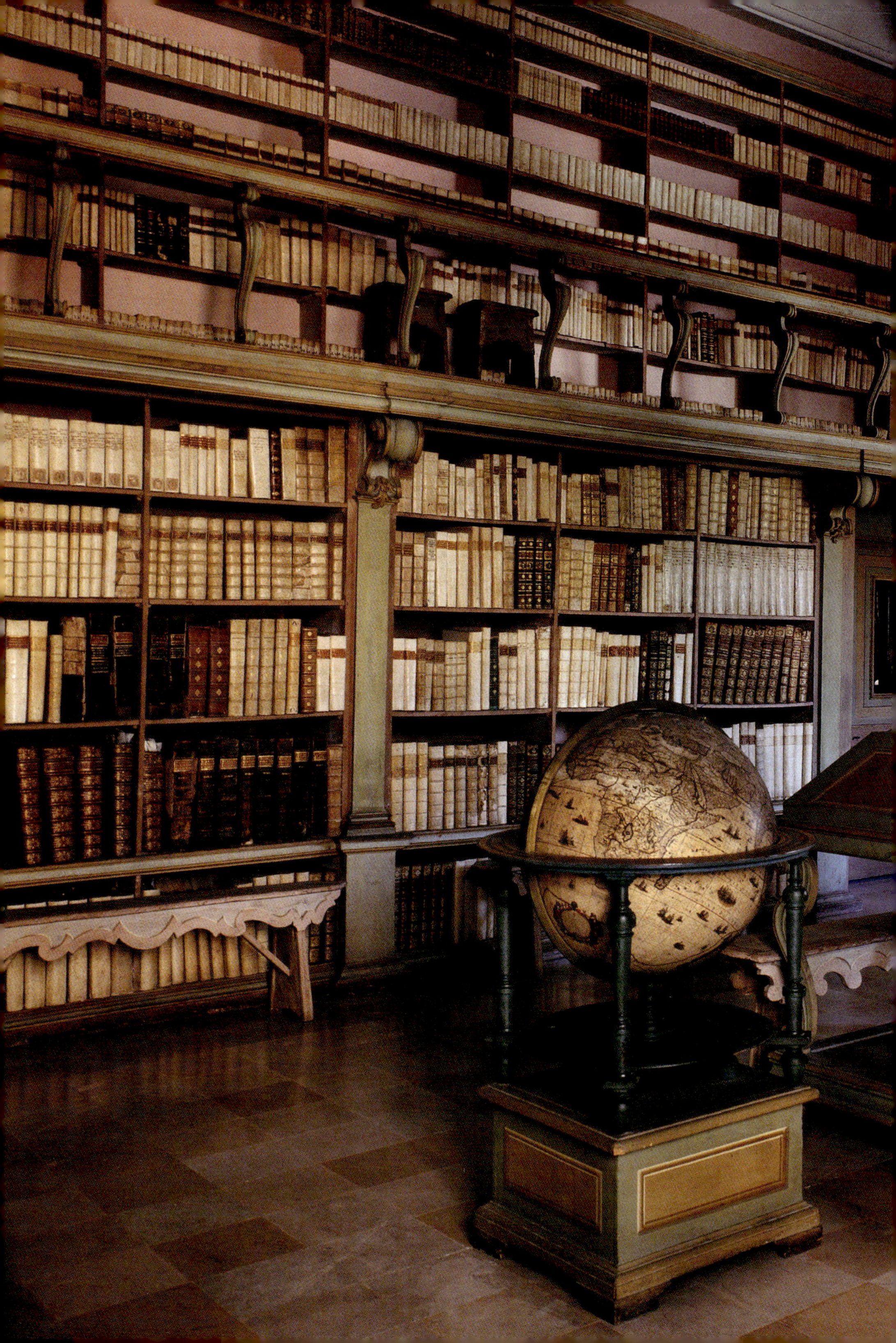

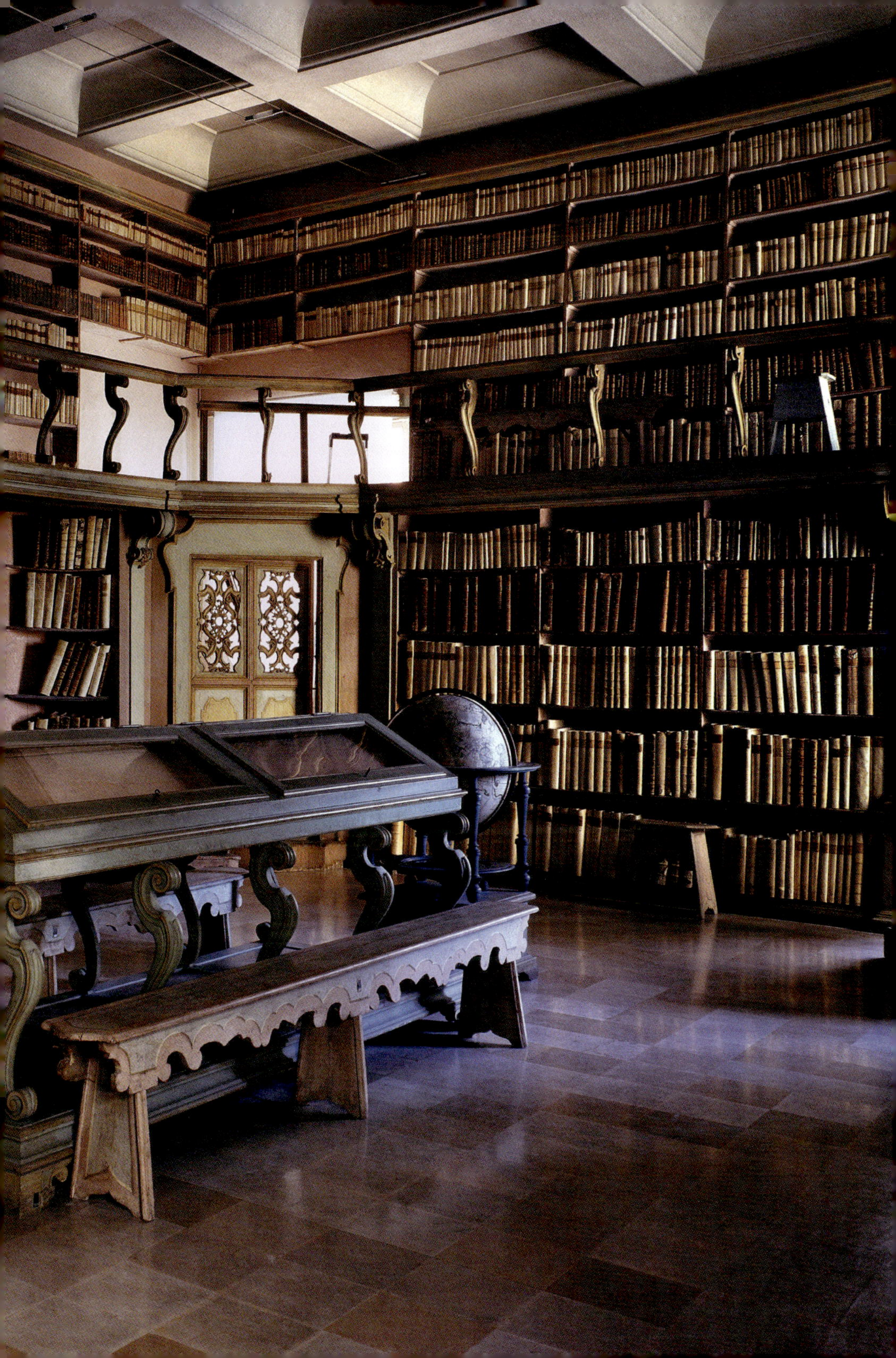

Biblioteca Casanatense

When Cardinal Girolamo Casanata (1620–1700) bequeathed his vast collection of 25,000 volumes, together with an endowment fund, to the Dominican Order, the foundations were laid for a unique centre of learning in matters of faith. One whole wing of the convent of Santa Maria sopra Minerva was adapted to accommodate the library, which opened to the public in 1701. The convent itself, which was founded in 1266 and is located not far from the Pantheon in the centre of Rome, has gone down in history as the site of the trials mounted by the relentless Roman Inquisition – including those against Giordano Bruno (1548–1600) and Galileo Galilei (1564–1642). Casanata was himself a papal Inquisitor and a member of the Dominican Order. He was particularly interested in writings on theology – with an emphasis on the works of Thomas Aquinas (c. 1225–1274) – and law, whereby all areas of knowledge were represented in his intellectually highly sophisticated library right from the outset. Other holdings include rare editions from various Roman private collections. In 1708, 191 unique works of botany entered the library from the collection of Giovanni Battista Trionfetti (1656–1708), formerly a professor at the Botanical Garden at Rome's La Sapienza University. The Biblioteca Casanatense's close association with the Inquisition, and in this context with the Sacred Congregation of the Index, that is the Vatican censors, explains its high proportion of Protestant writings in German along with rare polemical pamphlets and broadsheets from the early years of the Reformation, as well as documents in Hebrew and Greek, scientific treatises, and in general those writings that came under suspicion of heresy and were passed on to the theologians working in the library for critical scrutiny. Among these books classified as "heretical" are some with a significant provenance, such as the Biblioteca Palatina and the Fugger library. Following the suppression of the Jesuit Order in 1773, major holdings from their adjacent building passed to the Dominicans. It rapidly became clear that the cloister wing originally assigned to the library was too small and that more space was needed. A new room, almost twice the size, was completed in 1725 and – with its imposing shelves carrying 60,000 volumes – remains virtually unchanged today. The original arrangement of the books according to a historical system of classification, on the other hand, has not survived into the present.

* * *

Founded 1701, and until 1873 Dominican reference library; run by the Italian government since 1885

Holdings c. 400,000 objects, of which 350,000 books

Type of library formerly a monastic library; today a research library under the aegis of the Ministero per i beni e le attività culturali

Highlights *Historia plantarum*, c. 1395–1400 (Ms. 459); *Theatrum sanitatis*, 14th century (Ms 4182); Georg Bartisch, *Ophthalmodouleia, das ist Augendienst*, Dresden, 1583; *Indo-Portuguese Album of Drawings, Illustrating Customs and Traditions of Asia and Africa*, with short statements in Portuguese, 1540 (Ms. 1889)

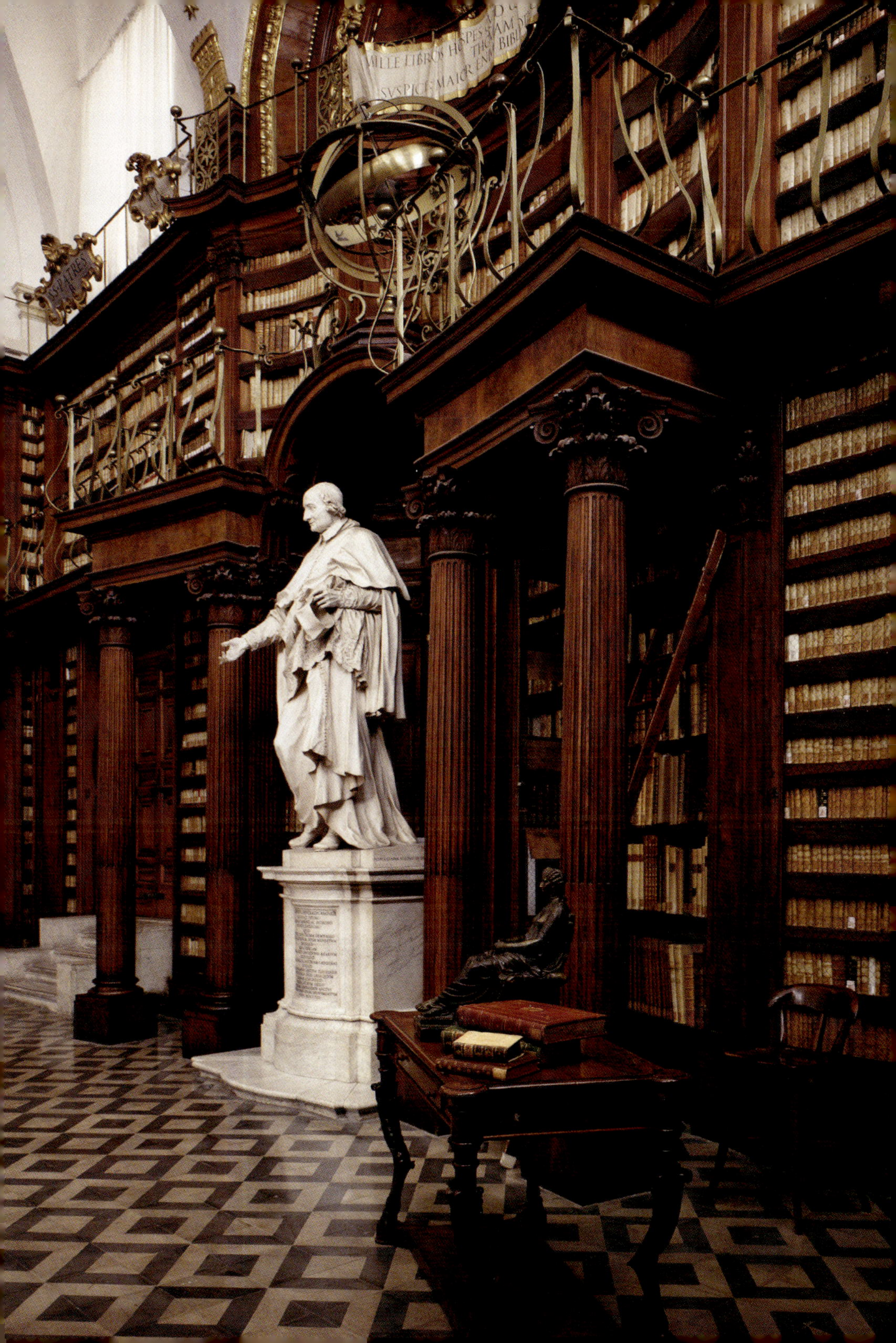

Als Kardinal Girolamo Casanate (1620–1700) seine reiche, 25 000 Bände umfassende Sammlung samt Stiftungskapital dem Dominikanerorden überließ, war der Grundstein für ein einzigartiges Kompetenzzentrum für Glaubensfragen gelegt. Für die Unterbringung der seit ihrer Gründung dem Publikum geöffneten Bibliothek wurde ein Trakt jenes im Zentrum Roms unweit des Pantheons gelegenen, bereits 1266 gegründeten Klosters von Santa Maria sopra Minerva adaptiert; das Kloster war als Schauplatz unerbittlicher Inquisitionsprozesse in die Geschichte eingegangen – etwa gegen Giordano Bruno (1548–1600) oder Galileo Galilei (1564–1642). Auch Casanate selbst war päpstlicher Inquisitor und Angehöriger des Predigerordens der Dominikaner. Sein besonderes Interesse galt den Schriften zur Theologie – mit einem Schwerpunkt auf Thomas von Aquin (um 1225–1274) – und der Rechtswissenschaften, auch wenn von Anfang an alle Wissensgebiete in

dieser intellektuell höchst anspruchsvollen Bibliothek vertreten waren. Seltene Buchausgaben stammen aus verschiedenen Privatbibliotheken Roms. 1708 gelangten 191 einzigartige botanische Werke in die Bibliothek, die aus der Privatsammlung von Giovanni Battista Trionfetti (1656–1708) stammten, der als Professor beim Botanischen Garten der römischen Universität La Sapienza tätig war. Aus der engen Beziehung der Casanatense zur Inquisition und in diesem Zusammenhang zur Indexkongregation, dem *Sant'Uffizio*, also der Zensurbehörde des Vatikans, erklären sich der hohe Anteil der vorhandenen Reformationsschriften in deutscher Sprache sowie seltene Streit- und Flugschriften aus der Frühzeit der Reformation, hebräische und griechische Schriftdokumente, aber auch wissenschaftliche Abhandlungen und allgemein jene Schriften, die im Verdacht der Häresie standen und an die an der Bibliothek tätigen Theologen zur kritischen Prüfung weitergeleitet wurden. Unter diesen als „ketzerisch" eingestuften Büchern finden sich mitunter bedeutende Provenienzen, wie die Bibliotheca Palatina oder die Fuggerbibliothek. Nach Auflösung des Jesuitenordens im Jahr 1773 gelangten aus dessen nahe gelegenem Professhaus wichtige Bestände an die Dominikaner. Bereits bald nach der Gründung der Bibliothek erwies sich eine Erweiterung des ursprünglichen Büchersaals als notwendig, der 1701 in einem Gebäudeflügel am Minervakreuzgang errichtet worden war. Der fast doppelt so große neue Raum war 1725 vollendet und hat sich bis heute mit seinen imposanten, 60 000 Bände fassenden Bücherregalen unverändert erhalten. Die ursprüngliche Aufstellung der Bücher nach historischer Wissenschaftssystematik hat sich hingegen nicht bis in die heutige Zeit erhalten.

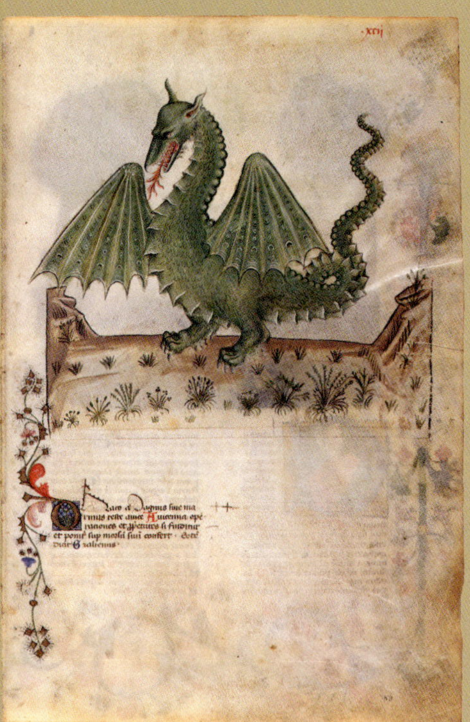

Historia plantarum, c. 1395–1400, sig. Ms. 459, fol. 89r

George Bartisch, *Ophthalmodouleia, das ist Augendienst*, Dresden, 1583, p. 146: *Application of Medicine into the Eyes*

Lorsque le cardinal Girolamo Casanate
(1620–1700) lègue sa collection de 25 000
volumes et le capital de la fondation à l'ordre
des Dominicains, il pose la pierre angulaire d'un
centre de compétences singulier en faveur de
la question religieuse. Une aile du couvent de la
Minerve, fondé en 1266 et situé dans le centre
de Rome non loin du Panthéon, est aménagée
afin d'abriter la bibliothèque dès le début
accessible au public. Le couvent est notamment
entré dans l'histoire pour son rôle joué dans
les impitoyables procès de l'Inquisition – par
exemple contre Giordano Bruno (1548–1600)
ou Galilée (1564–1642). Casanate était à la fois
inquisiteur et membre de l'ordre des Dominicains. Il s'intéressait tout particulièrement aux
écrits théologiques – en mettant l'accent sur
Thomas d'Aquin (vers 1225–1274) – et au droit,
même si la bibliothèque d'un très haut niveau
intellectuel couvre d'emblée tous les domaines
du savoir. Des éditions rares proviennent de
diverses bibliothèques privées de Rome. 191
ouvrages exceptionnels de botanique arrivent
en 1708 de la collection privée de Giovanni
Battista Trionfetti (1656–1708), alors professeur
au jardin botanique de l'université La Sapienza
de Rome. Les liens étroits entre Casanatense
et l'Inquisition et, à cet égard, la congrégation
de l'Index, le Saint-Office, l'autorité de censure
du Vatican, expliquent l'abondance d'écrits
se rapportant à la Réforme protestante en
langue allemande ainsi que la présence de rares
pamphlets et feuilles datant des débuts de la
Réforme, de documents en hébreux et en grec,
d'études scientifiques et, plus généralement,
d'écrits soupçonnés d'hérésie remis aux théologiens actifs dans les bibliothèques afin d'être
examinés de près. Parmi ces ouvrages classés
« hérétiques », certains proviennent d'endroits
aussi importants que la Bibliothèque palatine ou
la bibliothèque de Fugger. Après la dissolution
de l'ordre des Jésuites en 1773, les Dominicains
reçoivent des fonds considérables issus du
lieu attenant où ils professaient. Peu après la
fondation de la bibliothèque, une extension de
la pièce établie en 1701 dans une aile latérale au

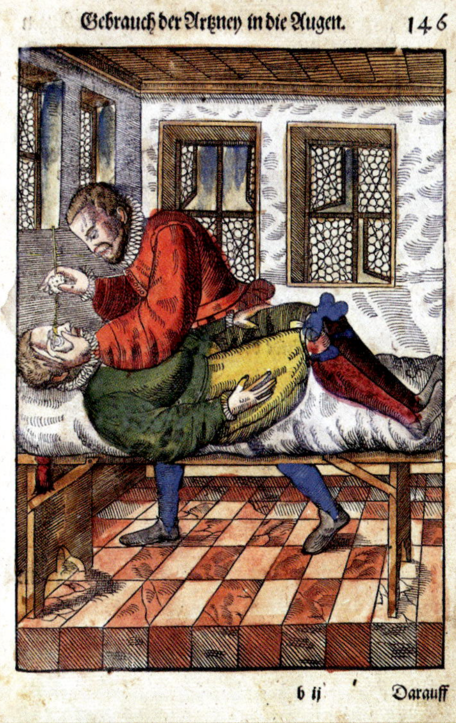

niveau du cloître de Minerve s'avère nécessaire.
La nouvelle salle aux dimensions doublées est
achevée en 1725. Ses imposants rayonnages
supportant 60 000 volumes ont été conservés
en l'état. En revanche, la répartition originelle
des livres suivant une systématique scientifique
historique n'a pas été maintenue.

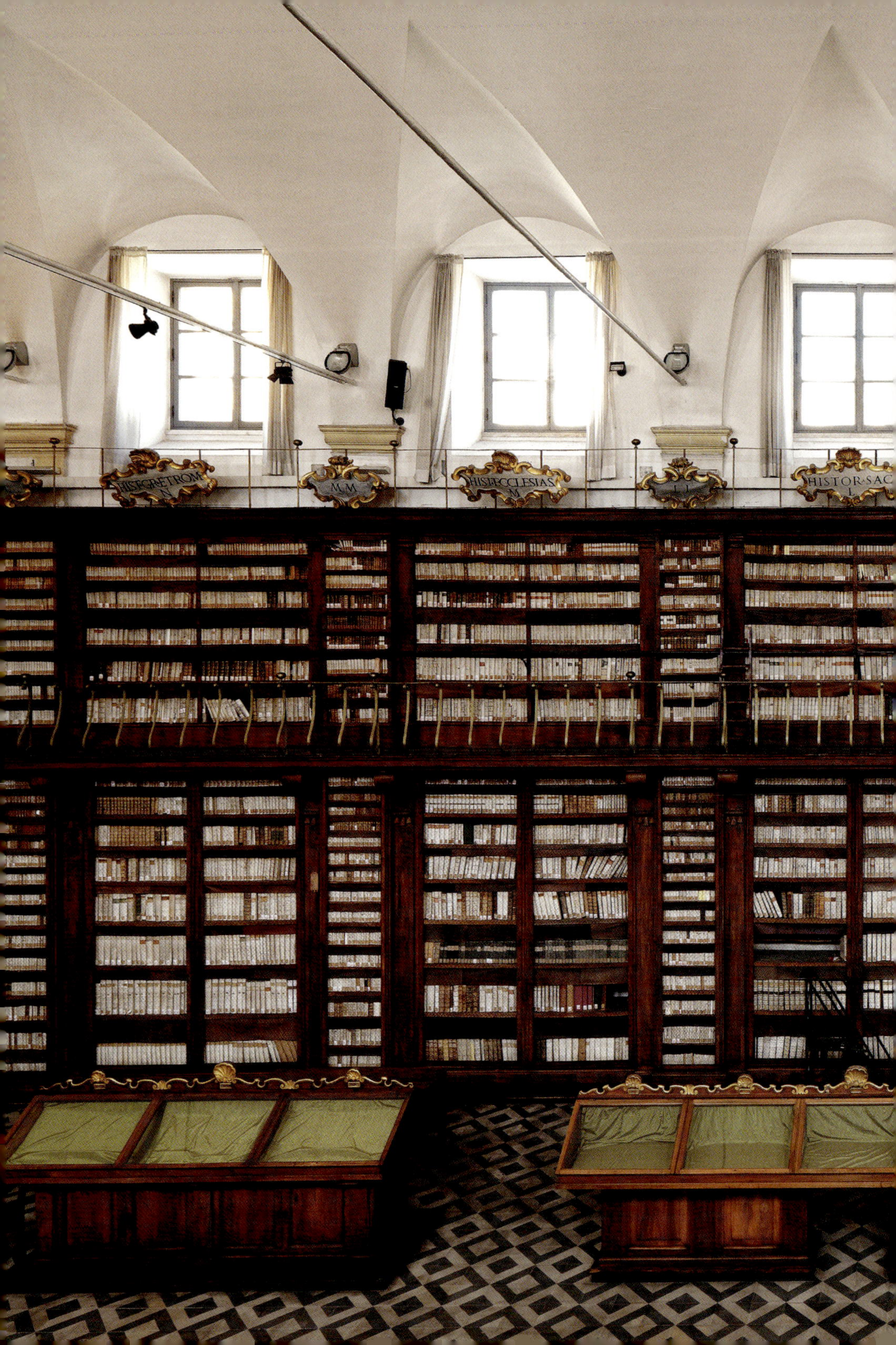

HIST.GRÆT.ROM
N
M.M
HIST.ECCLESIAS
M
L.L
HISTOR.SAC
L

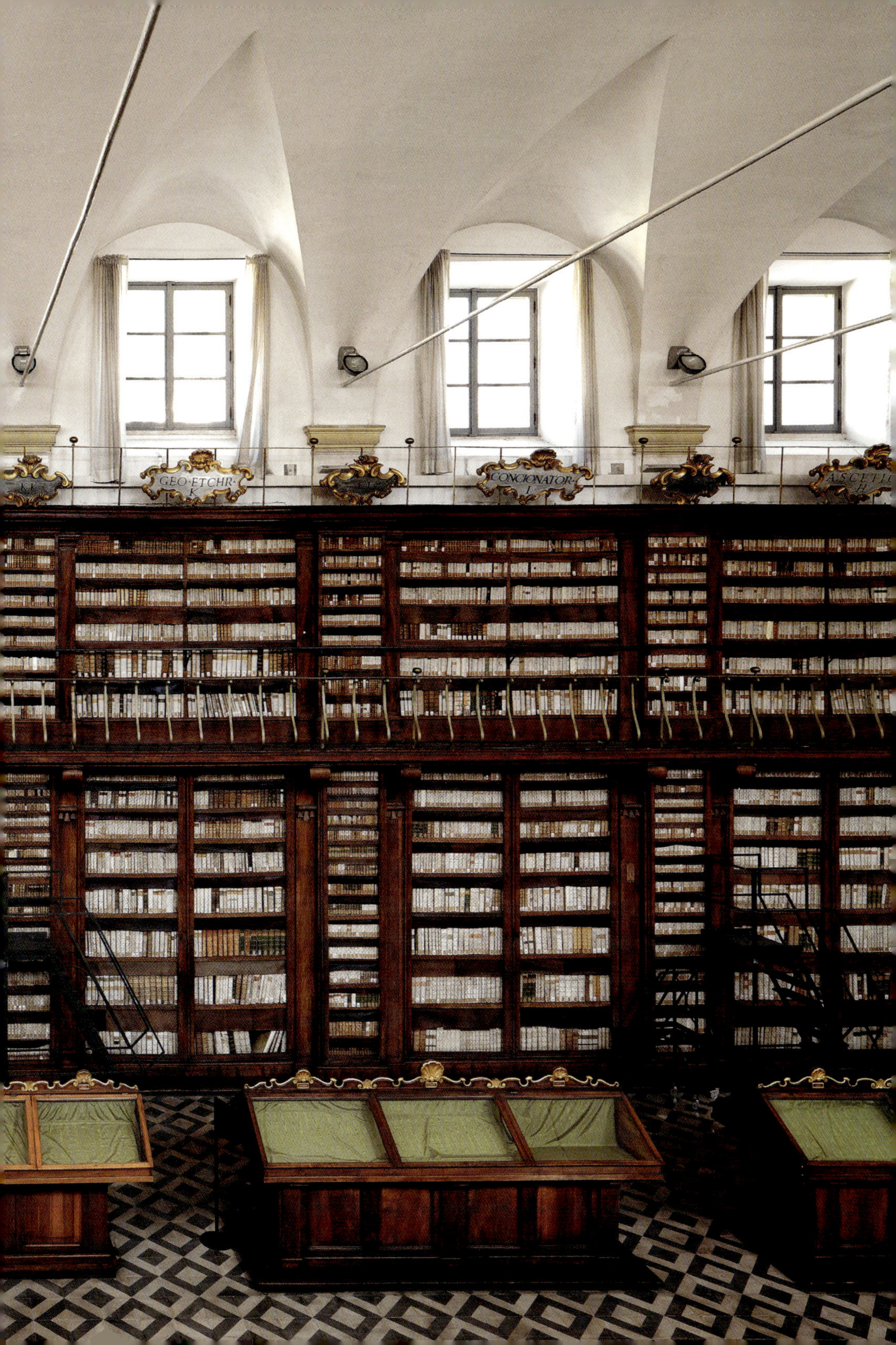
GEO·ETCHR·
CONCIONATOR·
ASCETI

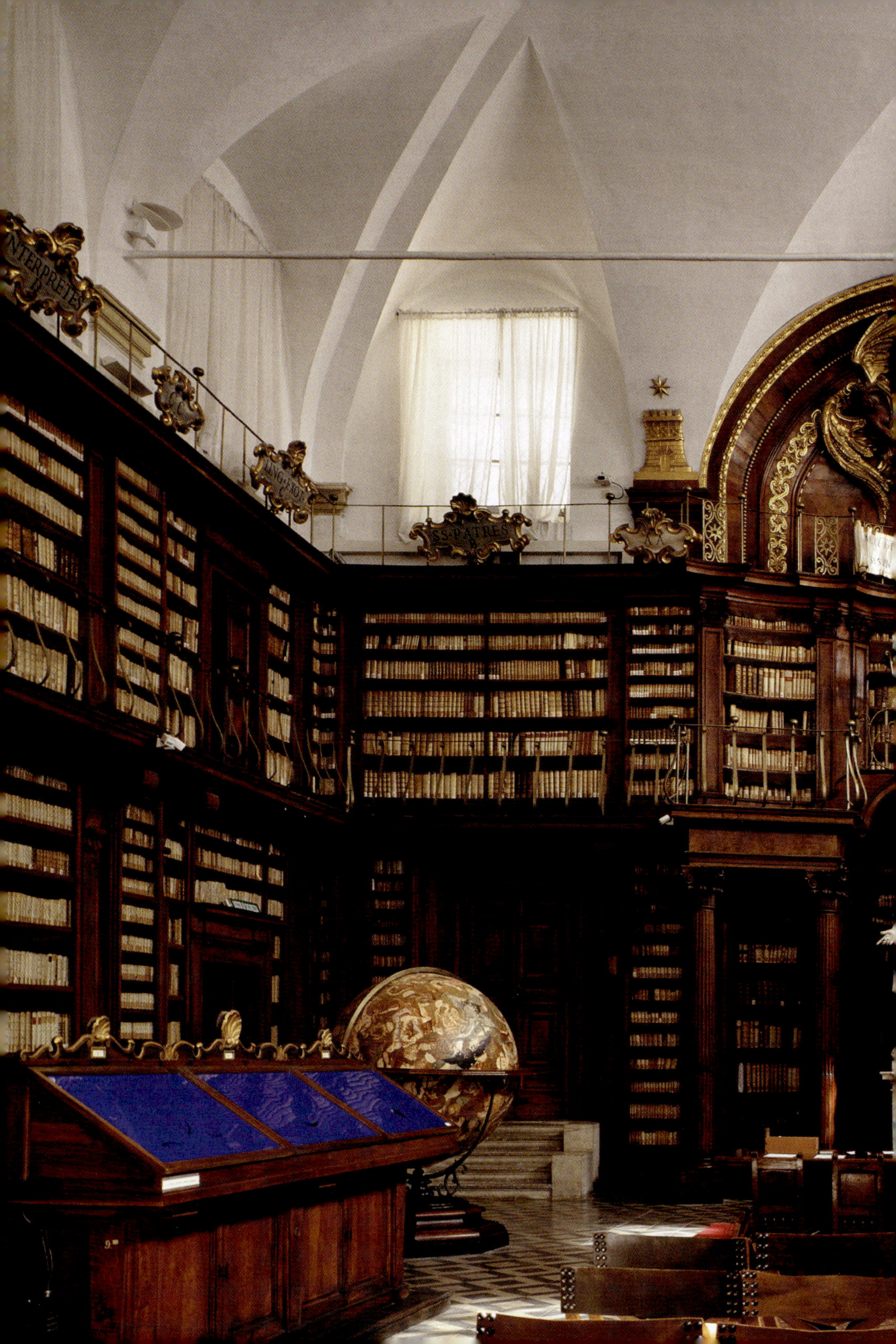

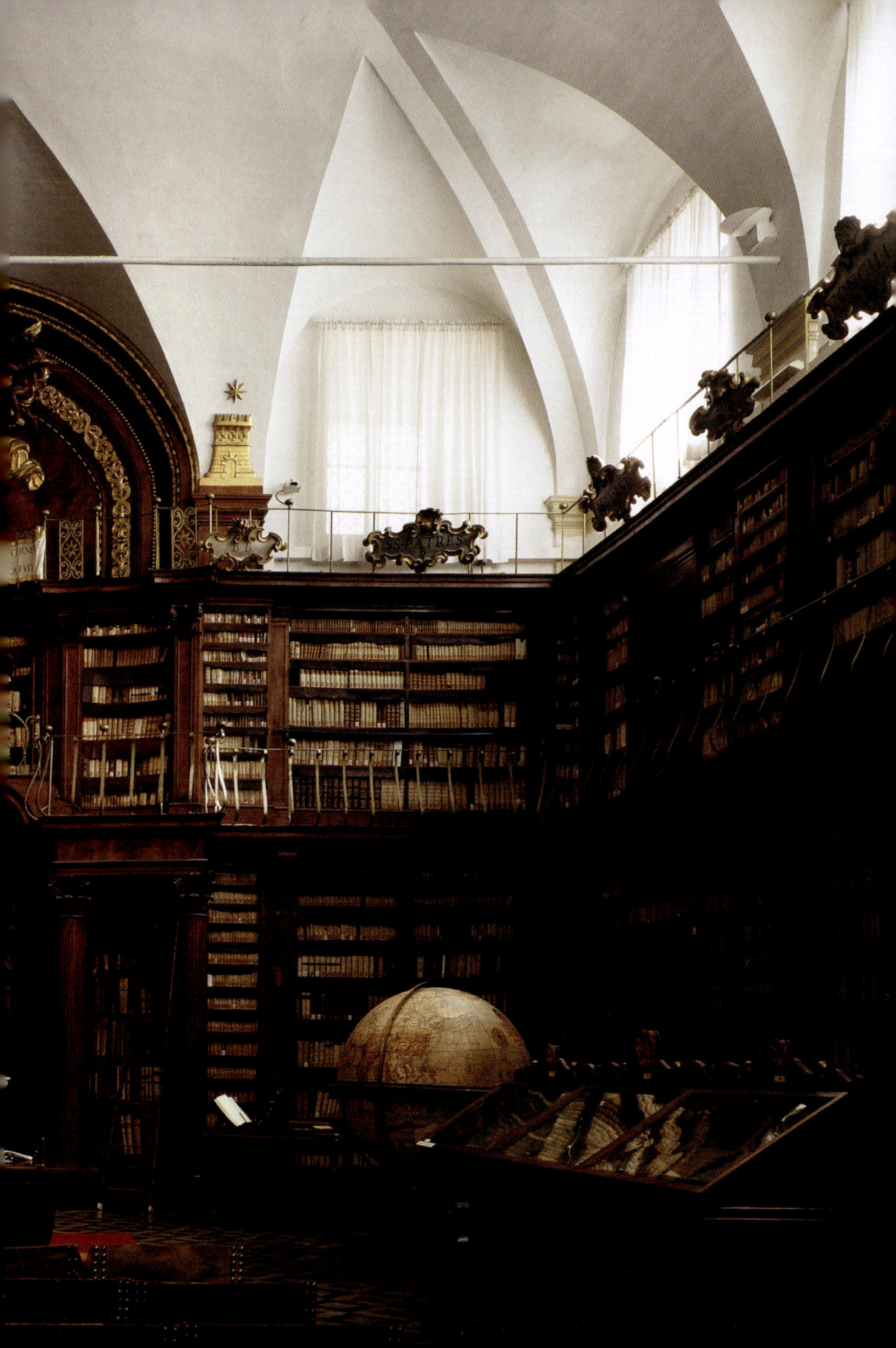

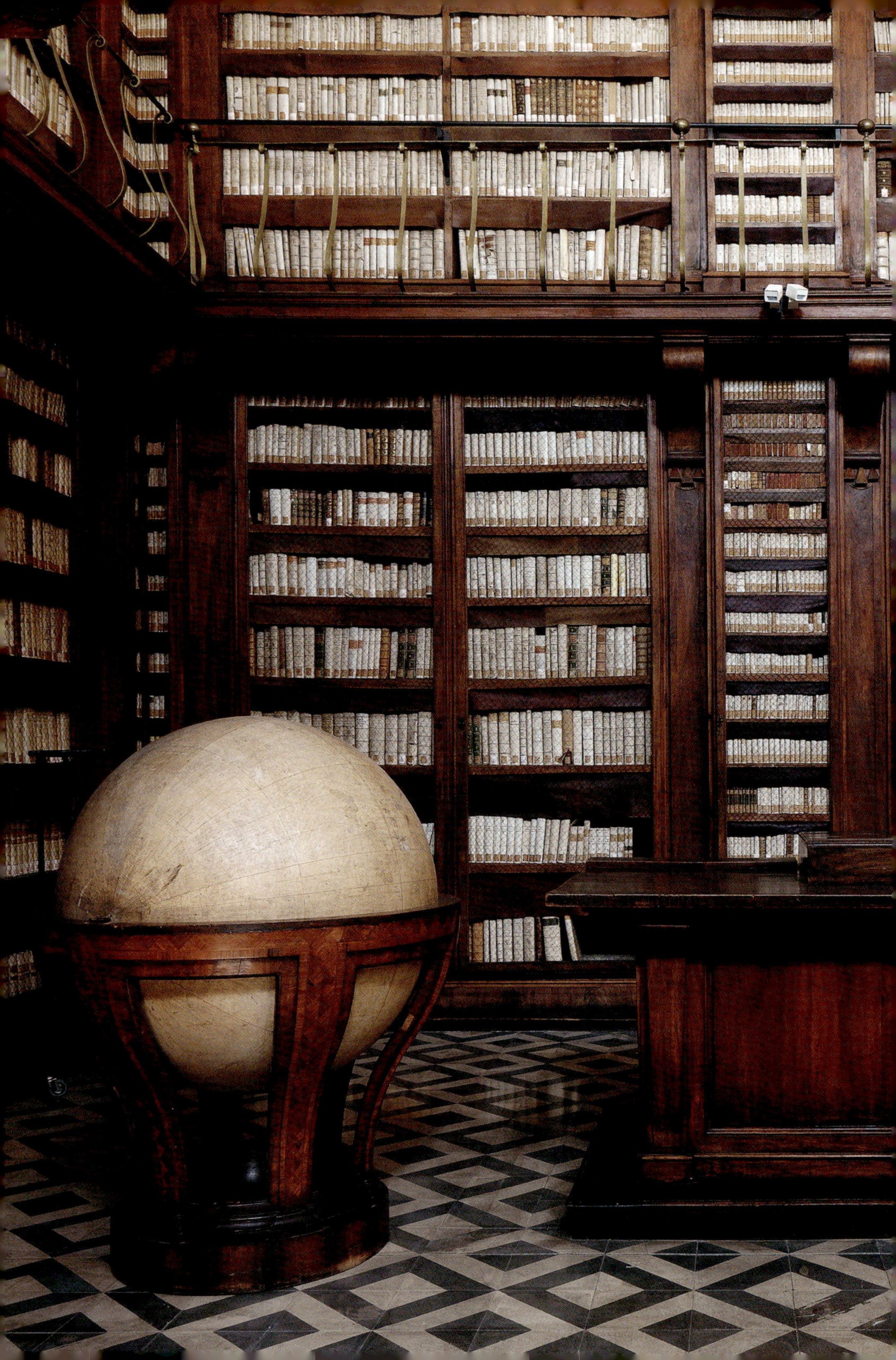

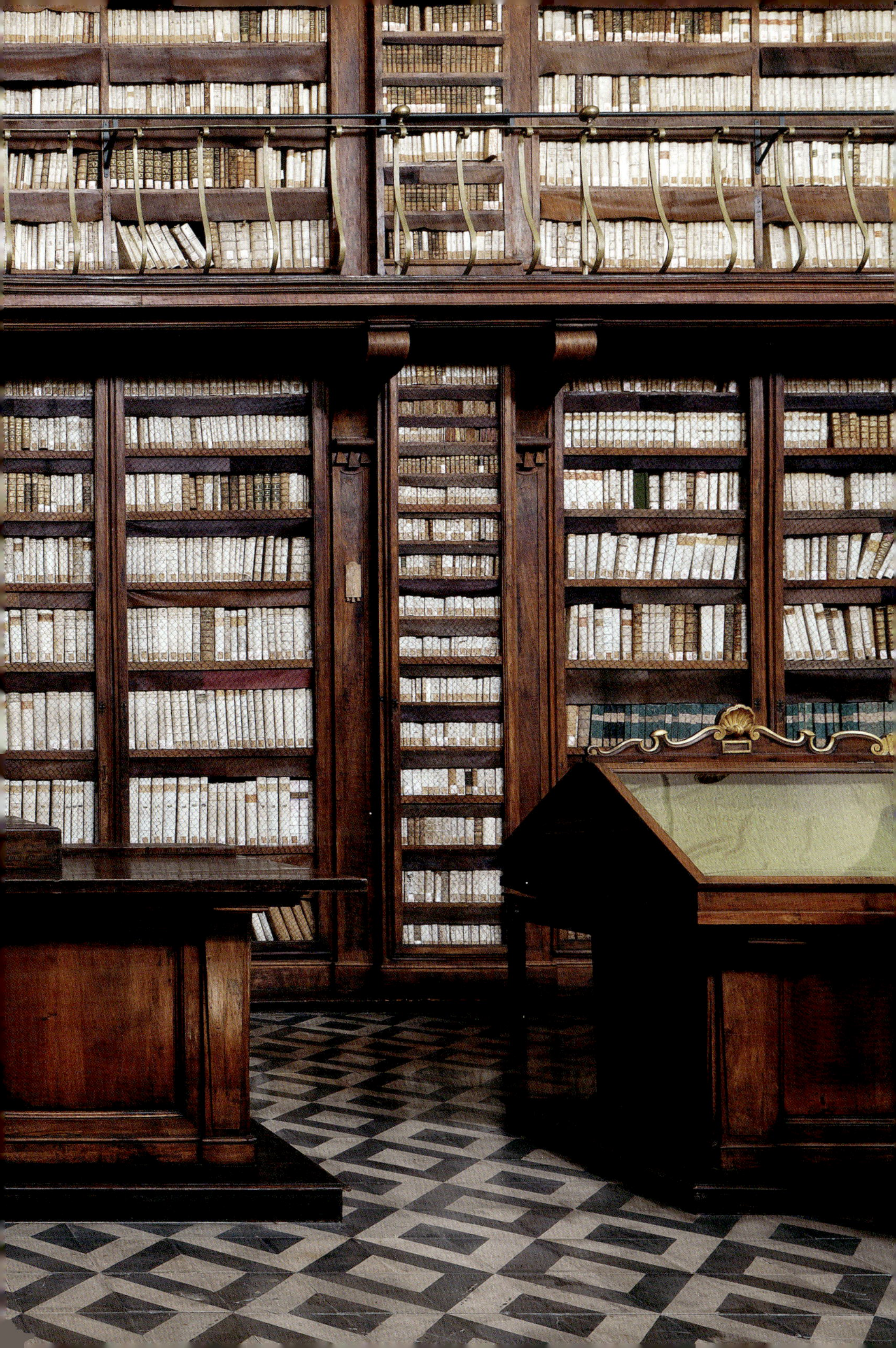

Biblioteca comunale di Imola

The Franciscan library in Imola's public library is a jewel of early neoclassical architecture and interior décor. Designed by Cosimo Morelli (1732–1812), this elegant room on a square ground plan rises through two storeys to a vaulted coffered ceiling. A continuous balcony demarcates the two levels and provides access to the books on the upper storey. With his understated Classicist style, Morelli – a native of Imola who remained closely tied to the city all his life – was one of the most successful architects of his day in the Papal States, to which Imola at the time belonged. At the nucleus of today's Biblioteca comunale is the library formerly belonging to the Franciscan Friars Minor, which was housed in the monastery. Around 1750, an endowment by a Franciscan friar by the name of Giuseppe Maria Setti made it possible to plan a new monastery library. First of all, an imposing staircase was built up to the monastery's first floor, where the new library was to be created. The erudite programme of mural decorations in the stairwell and the Franciscan library was executed by painters Alessandro della Nave (c. 1732/36–1821) and Antonio Villa (1750–1827). It includes profile portraits of famous men from Antiquity to the Renaissance, emblems of the arts and sciences, and cartouches with Latin mottos. The subjects of the books, which are carefully arranged by area of knowledge, are written in cartouches above the shelves, which hold 10,000 books dating from the 15th to the 19th century. Spiral staircases concealed in the corners of the room connect the library's two levels. This modern and functional library did not remain the property of the Franciscans for long, however, but was transferred to municipal ownership in 1799 following the occupation of the Papal States by the French. The library's holdings were considerably expanded during this period following the dissolution of other monastery libraries belonging to the Capuchins, Jesuits, Dominicans and other religious houses in and around Imola.

❀ ❖ ❀

Founded c. 1750, Aula Magna built 1761–1768 by Cosimo Morelli
Holdings c. 450,000 volumes
Type of library originally a monastic library, today a public library
Highlights illuminated *English Psalter*, 13th century (Ms.111); Dante Alighieri, *La Commedia – The Divine Comedy* (fragments of *Inferno*), illuminated by Maestro delle Vitae Imperatorum, first half of the 15th century (Ms. 76); *Hebrew Bible* from Toledo, second half of the 15th century (Ms. 77)

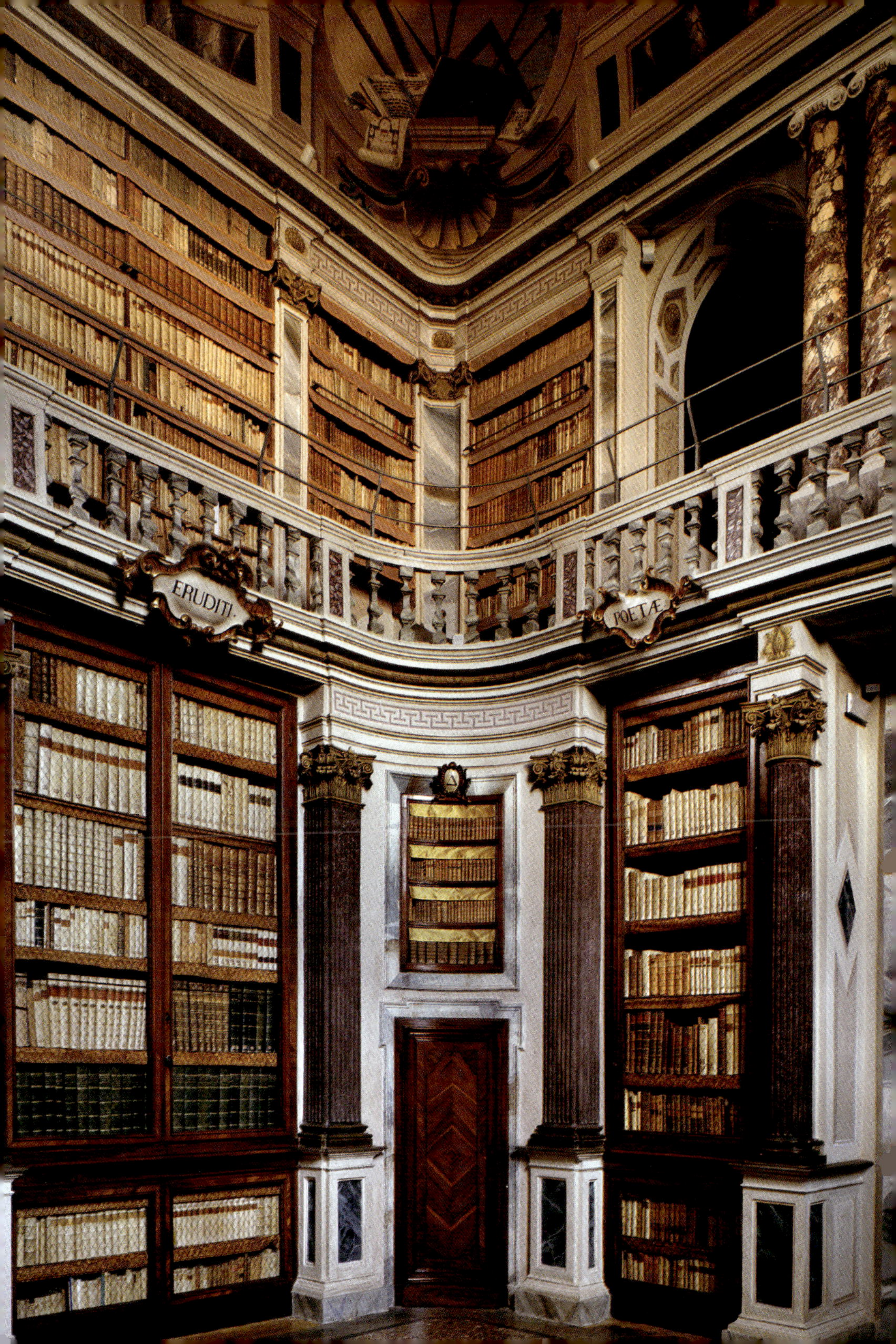

ERUDITI
POETÆ

Die Franziskaner-Bibliothek in der Stadtbibliothek von Imola ist ein Juwel frühklassizis-
tischer Architektur und Einrichtung, das sich
unverändert erhalten hat. Der Entwurf dieses
eleganten, über quadratischem Grundriss errichteten und mit einer flachen Kassettenkup-
pel überwölbten Raumes, dessen Geschosse
von einer umlaufenden Balkongalerie getrennt
sind, stammt von Cosimo Morelli (1732–1812).
Sein zurückhaltender, klassisch geprägter Stil
machte ihn zu einem der erfolgreichsten Architekten seiner Zeit im Kirchenstaat, zu dem
Imola damals gehörte. Morelli stammte aus
Imola und war auch zeitlebens an diese Stadt
gebunden. Ursprünglich war die Bibliothek
Eigentum der Franziskaner, ihre Bestände wurden in deren Kloster aufbewahrt. Die Stiftung
eines Franziskanerbruders namens Giuseppe
Maria Setti machte es um 1750 möglich, eine
neue Klosterbibliothek zu planen. Zunächst
wurde eine imposante Freitreppe errichtet, die
das Obergeschoss des Klosters erschloss, wo

der neue Bibliothekssaal eingerichtet werden
sollte. Das gelehrte Programm der Wand-
dekorationen vom Treppenhaus und von der
Franziskaner-Bibliothek wurde von den Malern Alessandro della Nave (um 1732/36–1821)
und Antonio Villa (1750–1827) ausgeführt. Zu
sehen sind Profilporträts berühmter Männer
von der Antike bis in die Neuzeit, Embleme der
Wissenschaften und Künste und Kartuschen
mit Merksprüchen in lateinischer Sprache.
Die Thematik der rigoros nach Wissensgebie-
ten geordneten Bücher ist auf Kartuschen
vermerkt, die über den Regalen angebracht
sind, in denen 10 000 Bücher aus dem 15. bis
19. Jahrhundert Aufstellung gefunden haben.
In den Eckräumen verborgene Wendeltreppen sorgen für die Verbindung zwischen den
beiden Bibliotheksgeschossen. Diese moderne
und funktionale Bibliothek blieb den Franziskanern allerdings nicht lange erhalten, da
sie im Zuge der französischen Besetzung
des Kirchenstaates bereits 1799 dem Kloster

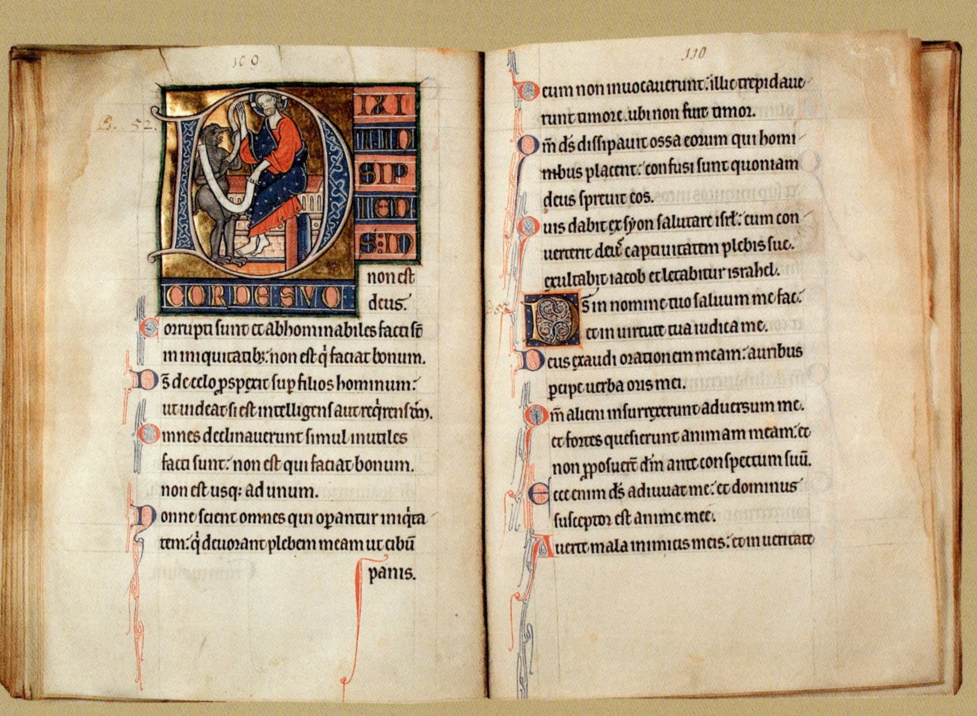

enteignet und der Stadt übertragen wurde.
Die Bestände der Bibliothek erfuhren
damals durch die zeitgleiche Auflösung der
alten Klosterbibliotheken der Kapuziner,
Jesuiten, Dominikaner und anderer kirchlicher
Vereinigungen in Imola und Umgebung eine
beträchtliche Erweiterung.

* * *

La bibliothèque Franciscaine de la bibliothèque
municipale d'Imola est un joyau du premier
classicisme, conservée sans aucune modifica-
tion. L'architecte Cosimo Morelli (1732–1812)
est à l'origine de cette salle élégante bâtie sur
plan carré, surmontée d'une coupole plate
à caissons et dont les niveaux sont séparés
par une galerie circulaire. Son style classique
empreint de retenue fit de Morelli l'un des
architectes les plus fameux de son temps dans
les États pontificaux dont Imola faisait partie à
l'époque. Natif de cette ville, Morelli lui resta lié
toute sa vie durant. À l'origine, la bibliothèque
appartenait aux Franciscains, les fonds étaient
conservés dans le monastère. Le don d'un Frère
franciscain nommé Giuseppe Maria Setti permit
la conception d'une nouvelle bibliothèque
monacale vers 1750. Fut alors construit un
imposant escalier à perron ayant pour fonction
de relier l'étage supérieur, qui accueillerait la
salle de bibliothèque. Les peintres Alessandro
della Nave (vers 1732/36–1821) et Antonio Villa
(1750–1827) réalisèrent le décor de la cage
d'escalier et de la Bibliothèque franciscaine
en se conformant à un savant programme. Y
sont représentés des hommes de profil, ayant
marqué l'histoire (de l'Antiquité à l'époque
moderne), des emblèmes des sciences et des
arts, et des devises en latin sur cartouche. Les
10 000 livres provenant du XVe au XIXe siècle
ont trouvé refuge sur des étagères surmontées

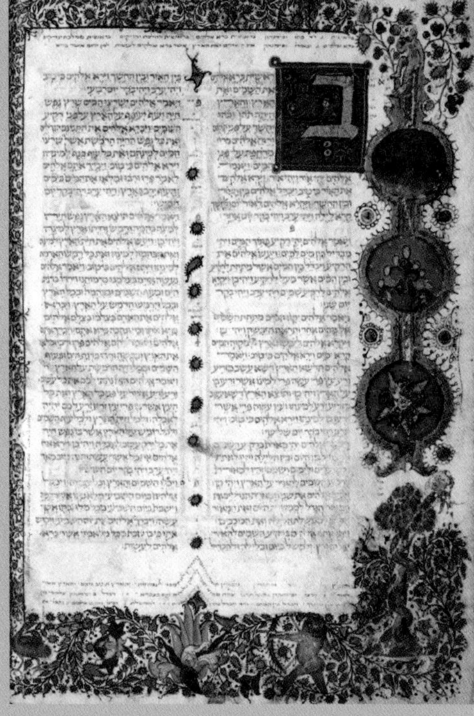

de cartouches signalant l'ordre scientifique
rigoureux selon lequel ils sont rangés. Le lien
entre les deux niveaux se fait par des escaliers
en colimaçon dissimulés dans les coins de la
pièce. Les Franciscains ne profitèrent pas
longtemps de cette bibliothèque moderne et
fonctionnelle, devenue propriété de la Ville à la
suite de leur expropriation en 1799 dans le cadre
de l'annexion française de l'État pontifical. La
confiscation des biens de bibliothèques des
Ordres supprimés à la même époque (Capucins,
Jésuites, Dominicains et autres congrégations
religieuses d'Imola et des environs) eut pour
résultat d'agrandir considérablement les fonds
désormais municipaux.

Illuminated *English Psalter*, 13th century,
sig. Ms. 111, fol. 109v–110r: *Initial D with
The Temptation of Christ*

Hebrew Bible from Toledo, second half of the
15th century, sig. Ms. 77, fol. 13r: *Book of Genesis*

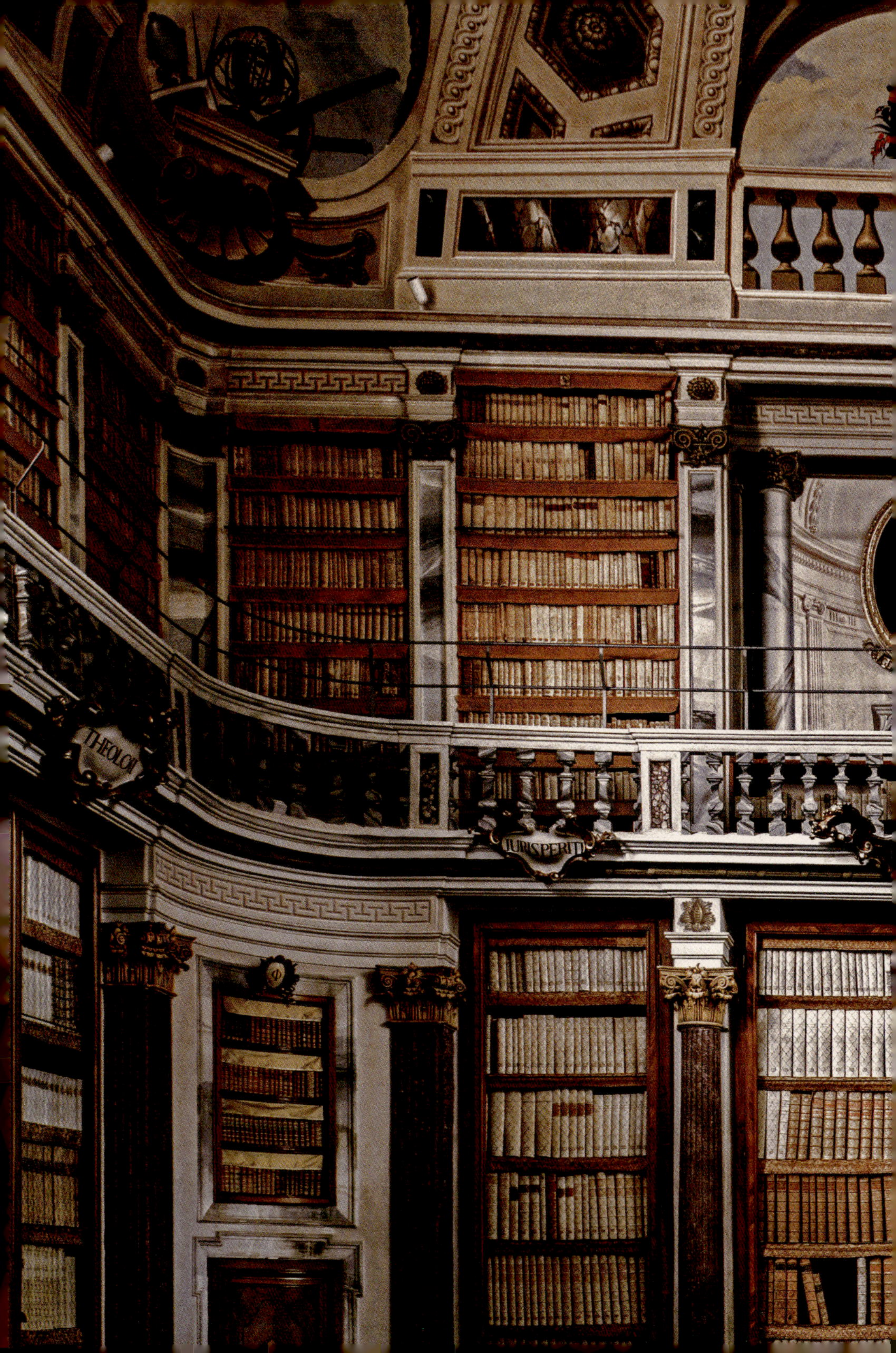

THEOLO
JURISPERITI

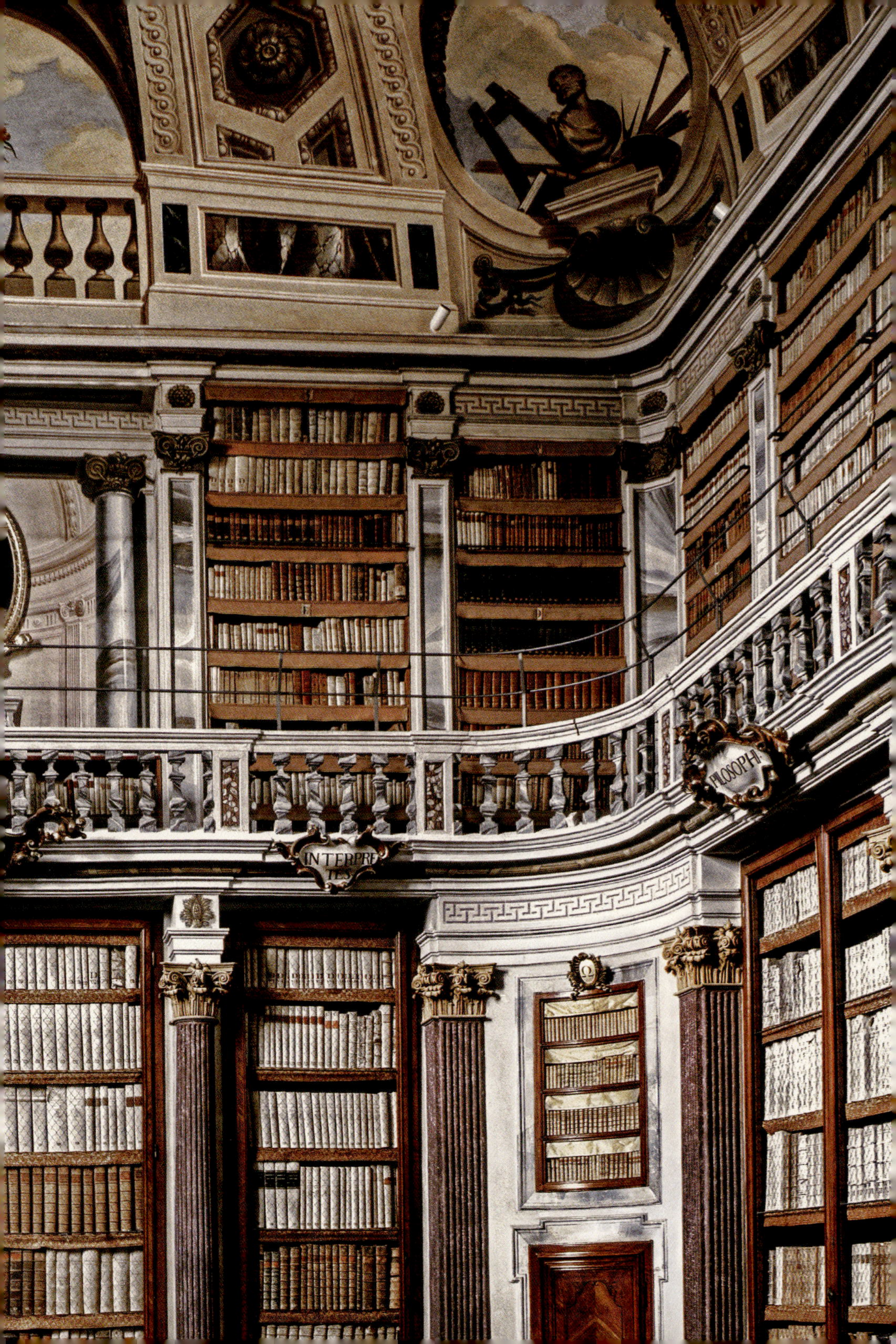

PHILOSOPHI
INTERPRE
TES

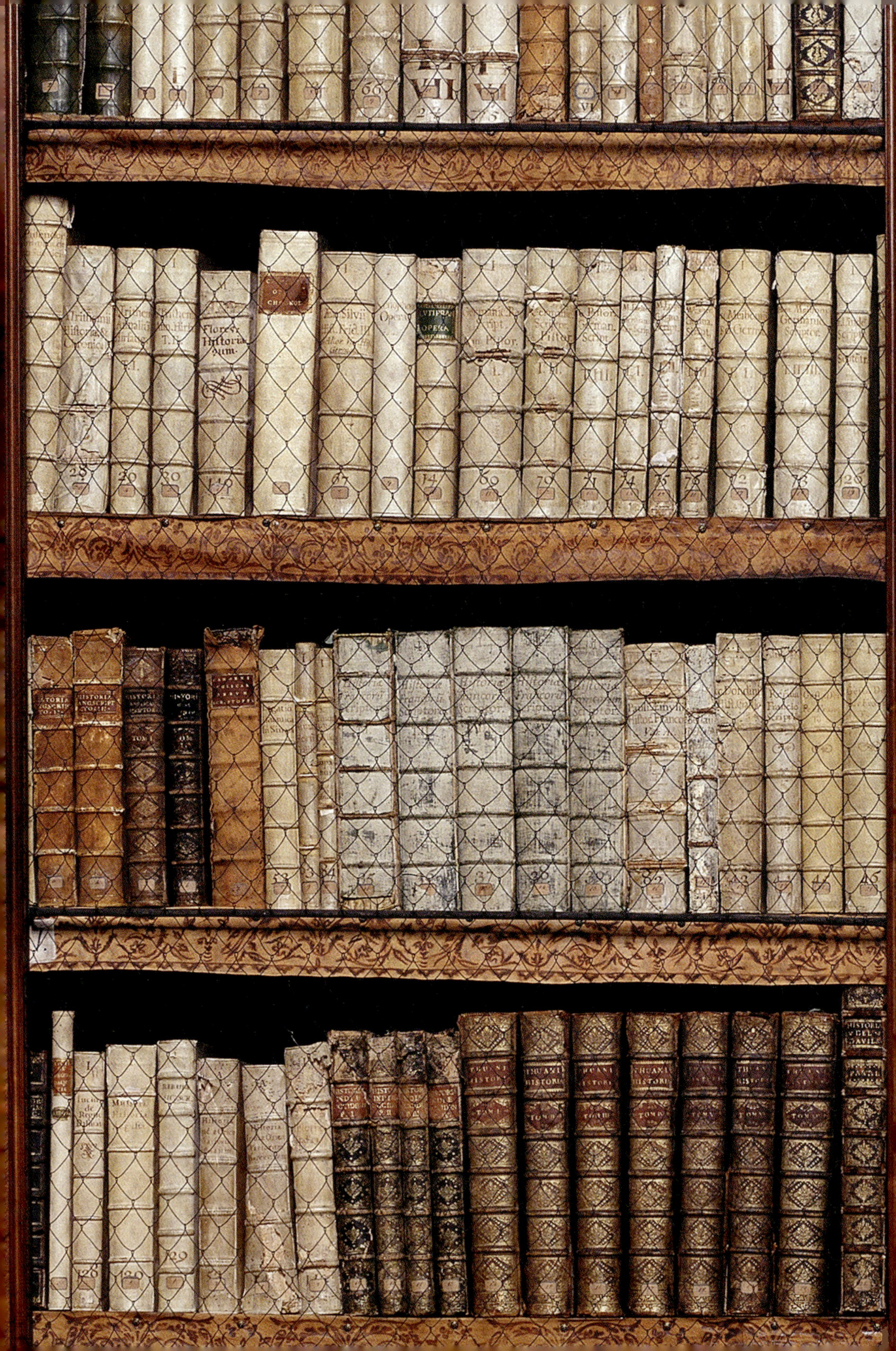

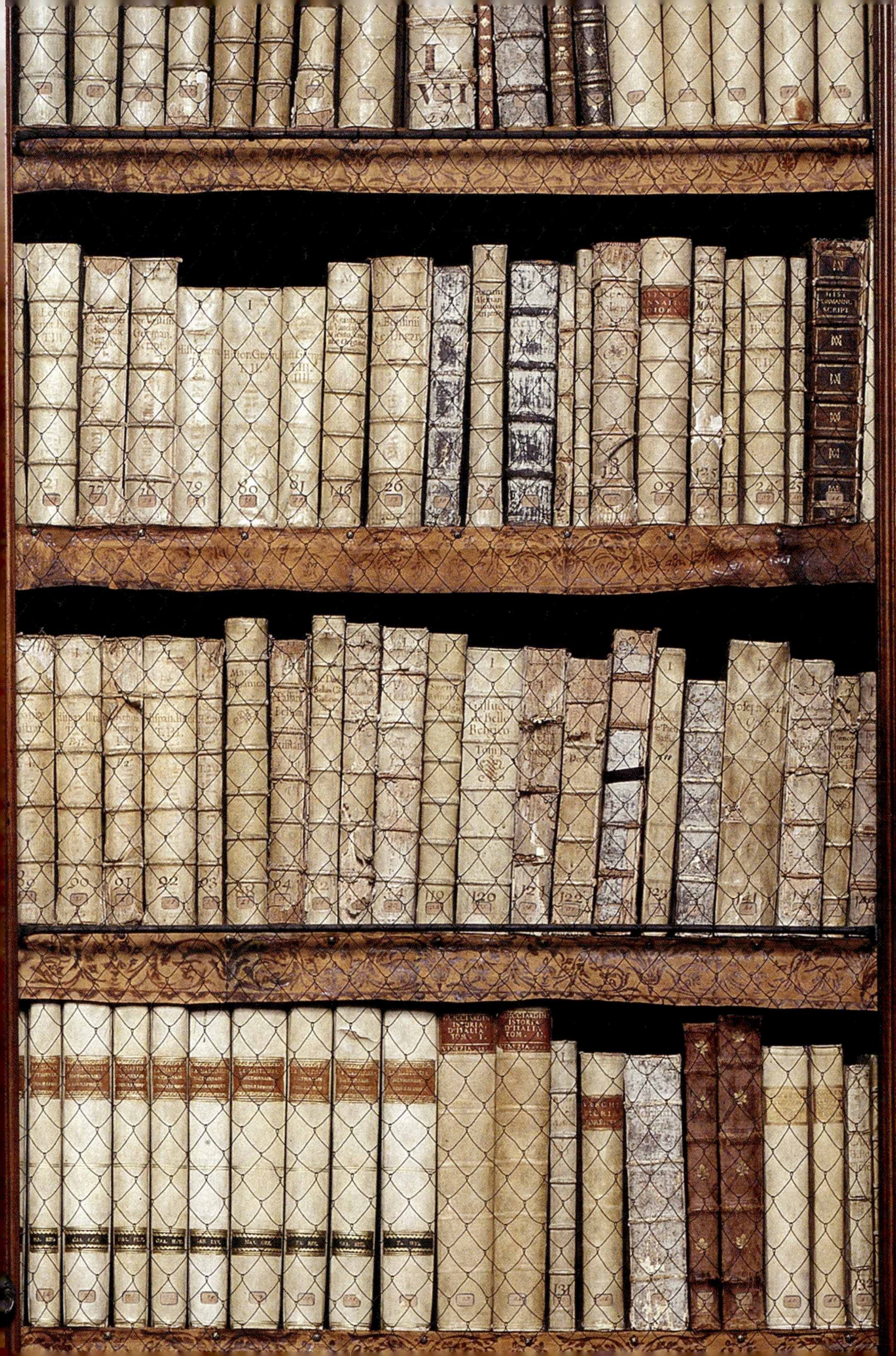

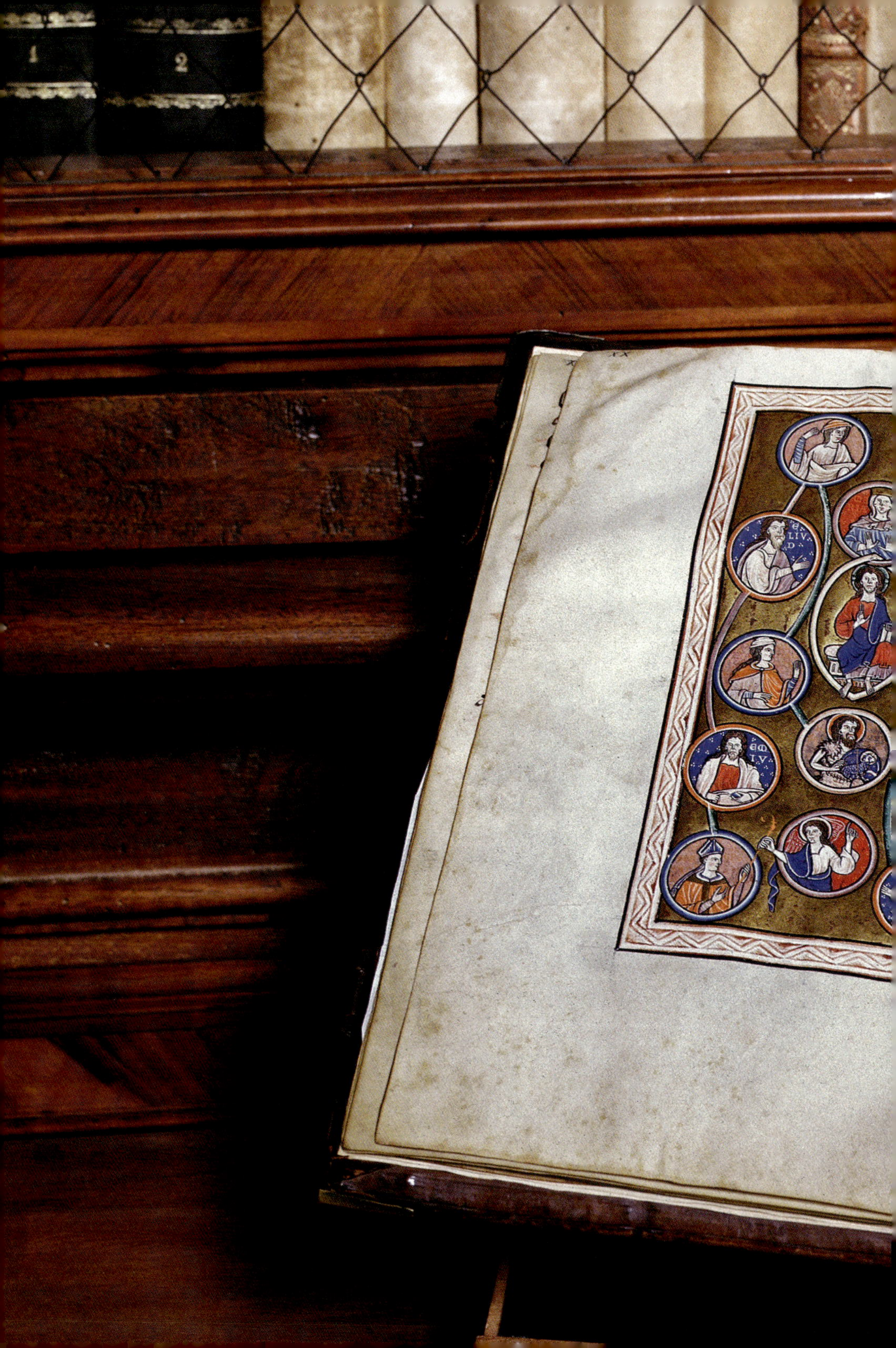

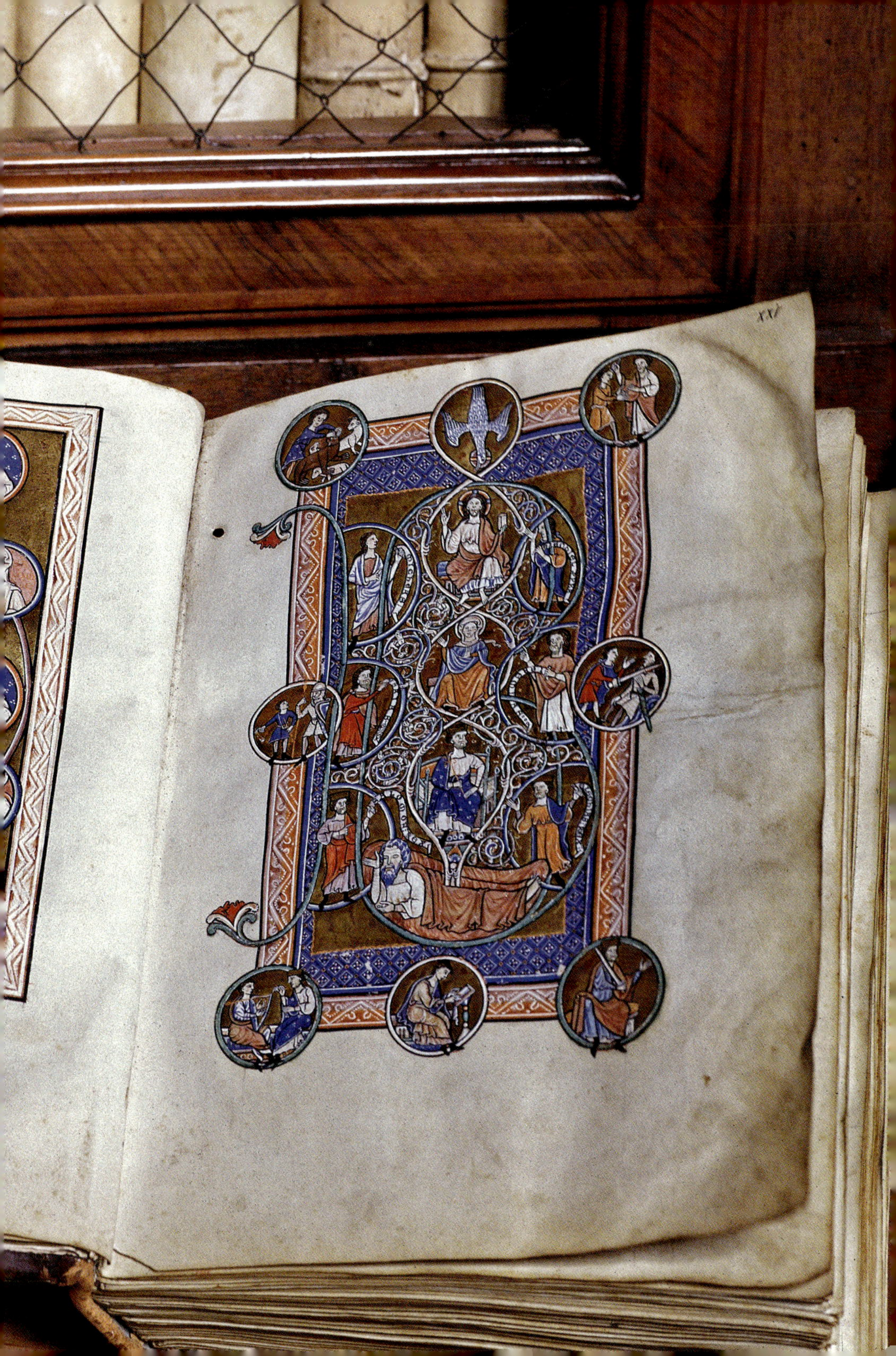

Biblioteca Palatina

In 1734, when the Bourbon King Charles III (1716–1788) transferred the valuable Farnese collection of books and art he had inherited from his mother from Parma to his residence in Naples, the palace of the dukes of Parma, previously famed for its cultural life, was left without a library. This loss was felt particularly keenly in the age of the Enlightenment, with its cultivation of wide-ranging interests, when a library was considered an integral component of every noble palace. Philip of Bourbon (1720–1765) and his son and successor Ferdinand (1751–1802), together with their first minister Guillaume du Tillot (1711–1774), a politician steeped in the ideas of the Enlightenment, were probably conscious of this fact when, in 1761, they commissioned the Theatine monk Paolo Maria Paciaudi (1710–1785) to build up a collection of books intended for the use and benefit of the public. Paciaudi did for Parma what Gabriel Naudé had done in the 17th century for Mazarin and other high-ranking patrons. He was a library specialist with a network of international (and in particular French) contacts and maintained close relations with the world of academia, politics and the nobility. These enabled him to make strategic acquisitions, out of which the "Bibliotheca Regia Parmensis" effectively arose *ex novo*. The volumes that entered the collection during this period were given leather bindings bearing the three fleur-de-lys of the Bourbon coat of arms. Paciaudi also compiled a detailed card catalogue that made the holdings easy to access. The new library was housed in a long connecting corridor in the Palazzo della Pilotta, which Ennemond Alexandre Petitot (1727–1801) furnished in 1769 with bookshelves in the neoclassical style. Numerous iconographical allusions characterise the Biblioteca Palatina (to which a museum of antiquities, an academy of art and a painting gallery were at that time also attached) as a temple of the arts, sciences and letters presided over by the eponymous Apollo Palatinus. In a bas-relief in the vestibule, Apollo invites us to consult the library in the words of Horace: "Scripta Palatinus quaecumque recepit Apollo" ("whichever writings Palatine Apollo has received"). The library was officially inaugurated in 1769, in a ceremony attended by Emperor Joseph II (1741–1790) in person. Under his grand-niece Marie Louise (1791–1847), who ruled Parma from 1818, the Palatina was further expanded, in particular by a barrel-vaulted room designed by Nicola Bettoli (1780–1854) and built in 1830–1833, with an elegant shelving system which completely fills the walls. Antonio Canova (1757–1822) created a lasting memorial to the patroness with a portrait bust in classic white marble.

※✳※

Founded 1761; book gallery 1769 by Ennemond Alexandre Petitot; Salone Maria Luigia reading room 1830–1833 by Nicola Bettoli
Holdings c. 708,000 volumes
Type of library formerly the library of a prince, today a public research library
Highlights Saint Ildephonsus from Toledo, *De virginitate Sanctae Mariae*, c. 1100 (Ms. Parm. 1650); *Tehillim* (psalters), c. 1300 (Ms. Parm. 1870); Piero della Francesca, *De prospectiva pigendi*, second half of the 15th century (Ms. Parm. 1576)

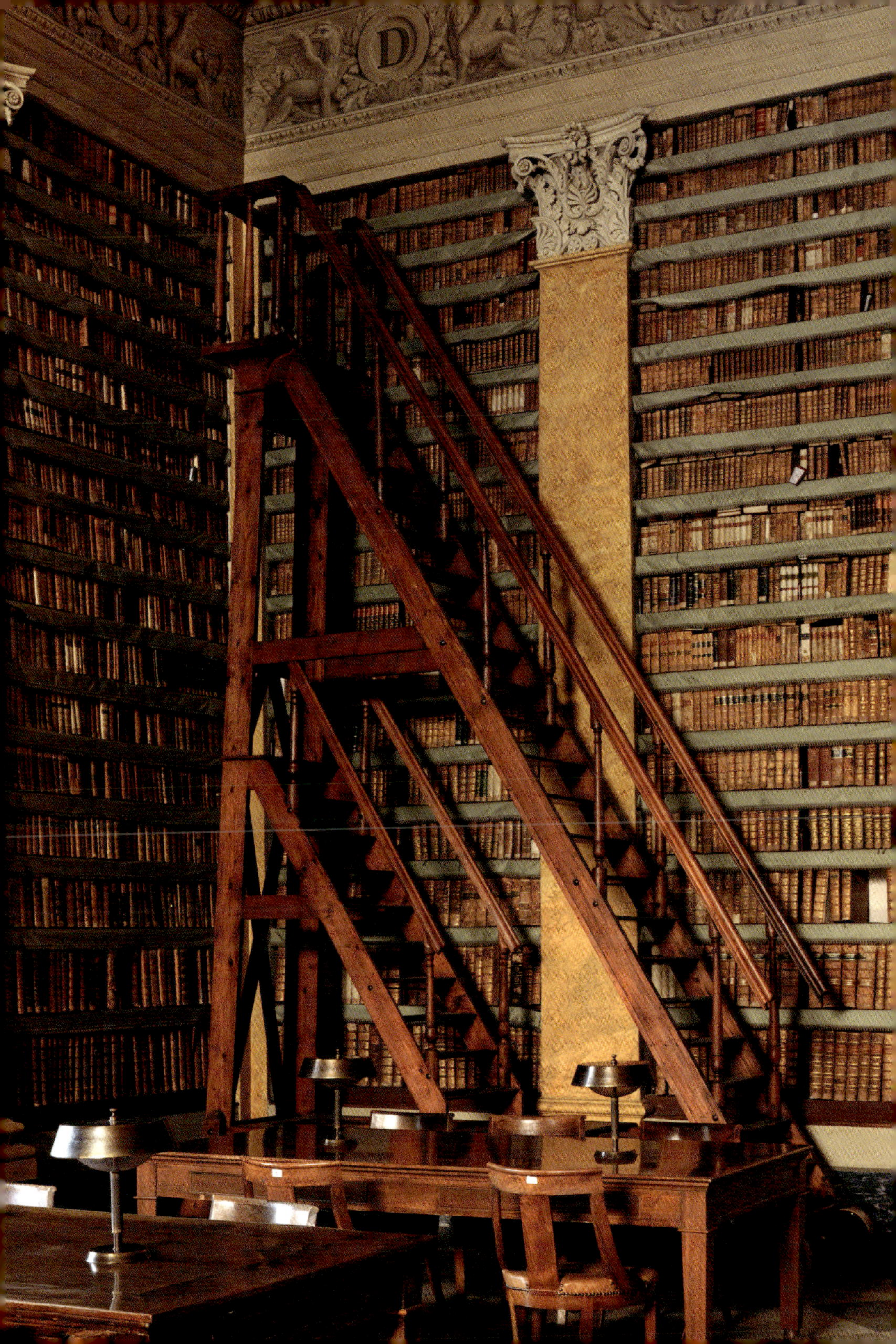

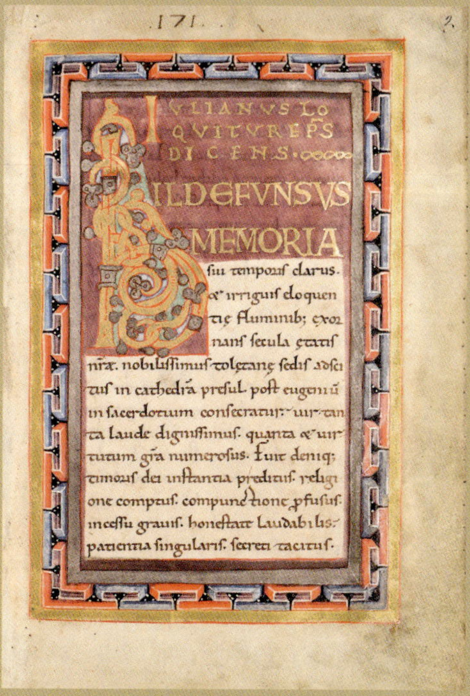

Als der Bourbonenkönig Karl III. (1716–1788) die wertvolle Bibliothek der Farnese samt zugehöriger Kunstsammlung als mütterliches Erbe 1734 aus Parma nach Neapel schaffte, wo er residierte, blieb die ehemals für ihr Kulturleben gerühmte Residenz der Herzöge von Parma ohne Bibliothek. Eine solche galt hingegen ganz besonders im Zeitalter der Aufklärung und der vielfach kultivierten Interessen als integraler Bestandteil jedes Fürstenhofes. Diese Tatsache war Philipp (1720–1765) und seinem Sohn und Nachfolger Ferdinand von Bourbon (1751–1802) sowie deren von der Aufklärung geprägtem Premierminister Guillaume du Tillot (1711–1774) wohl bewusst, als sie 1761 den Theatinermönch Paolo Maria Paciaudi (1710–1785) mit dem Ankauf einer Büchersammlung beauftragten, die dem öffentlichen Wohl zugedacht war. Paciaudi leistete für Parma, was Naudé im 17. Jahrhundert für Mazarin und andere fürstliche Auftraggeber geschaffen hatte. Er war ein Bibliothekenspezialist mit internationalen, vor allem französischen Kontakten, der ein enges Netzwerk zur Welt der Gelehrten, der Höfe und der Politik unterhielt. Diese Kontakte ermöglichten es ihm, gezielt Ankäufe zu tätigen, aus denen die „Bibliotheca Regia Parmensis" praktisch *ex novo* entstand. Kostbare Ledereinbände mit den drei Lilien des Bourbonenwappens kennzeichneten die damals in die Bibliothek eingegangenen Bände. Ein von Paciaudi verfasster Zettelkatalog erschloss sie in vorbildlicher Weise. Sie fanden in einem mächtigen Verbindungskorridor des Palazzo della Pilotta Aufstellung, den Ennemond Alexandre Petitot (1727–1801) bis 1769 dem Zweck entsprechend mit Bücherregalen in klassizistischem Stil ausgestattet hatte. Vielfache ikonografische Anspielungen wiesen die Biblioteca Palatina, der damals auch ein Antikenmuseum, eine Kunstakademie und eine Pinakothek angeschlossen wurden, als Olymp der Künste, Wissenschaften und Literatur aus, in den der namensgebende Apollo Palatinus einführte, und zwar mit Horaz' Worten: „Scripta Palatinus quaecumque recepit Apollo" (Schriften in der Obhut von Apollo Palatinus). Kaiser Joseph II. (1741–1790) wohnte sogar persönlich der feierlichen Eröffnung dieser Institution im Jahr 1769 bei. Unter seiner Großnichte Maria Ludovica (1791–1847), die ab 1818 Parma regierte, erfuhr die Palatina vielfache Förderung und Erweiterung. Insbesondere wurde in den Jahren 1830 bis 1833 ein von Nicola Bettoli (1780–1854) gestalteter, tonnengewölbter Büchersalon angebaut, dessen elegantes Regalsystem die gesamten Wände einnimmt. Dort setzte Antonio Canova (1757–1822) der Mäzenin mit einer Porträtbüste in klassisch weißem Marmor ein unvergängliches Denkmal.

Saint Ildephonsus from Toledo, *De virginitate Sanctae Mariae*, c. 1100, sig. Ms. Parm. 1650, fol. 2r
Piero della Francesca, *De prospectiva pingendi*, second half of the 15th century, sig. Ms. Parm. 1576, fol. 61r: *Perspective studies of the human head and cranium*

Lorsque Charles III d'Espagne (1716–1788) fit venir en 1734 à Naples, où il résidait, la précieuse collection de livres de la maison Farnese ainsi que la collection d'art, reçues en héritage maternel, la résidence des ducs de Parme, autrefois célèbre pour sa vie culturelle, se retrouva privée de bibliothèque. Cette situation était bien singulière à l'époque des Lumières, du temps où les cours princières vénéraient la culture sous toutes ses facettes. Philippe (1720–1765) et son fils et successeur Ferdinand de Bourbon (1751–1802) ainsi que Guillaume du Tillot (1711–1774), leur Premier ministre et admirateur des Lumières, en étaient tout à fait conscients lorsqu'ils mandatèrent le moine théatin Paolo Maria Paciaudi (1710–1785) en 1761 pour acheter une collection de livres qui servirait l'intérêt général. Paciaudi fut à Parme ce que Naudé fut à Mazarin et à d'autres commanditaires au XVIIe siècle. Ce spécialiste des bibliothèques entretenait des liens à un niveau international, en particulier avec la France, dans le domaine des lettres, des cours et de la politique. Il réalisa des achats bien ciblés grâce à ces contacts et créa la « Bibliotheca Regia Parmensis » quasiment à partir de rien. Les volumes arrivés à cette époque portent l'emblème de la maison de Bourbon, trois lys, sur leurs précieuses reliures en cuir. Paciaudi sut les mettre en valeur au moyen d'un catalogue à fiches mobiles exemplaire. Ils rejoignirent un hall impressionnant du Palazzo della Pilotta, qu'Ennemond Alexandre Petitot (1727–1801) aménagea pour l'inauguration de 1769 avec des étagères de style néoclassique. De nombreuses allusions iconographiques font de la Biblioteca Palatina, autrefois rattachée à un musée d'objets antiques, à une académie des arts et à une pinacothèque, un temple des arts, des sciences et des lettres où l'on se retrouve introduit par Apollon Palatin qui cite Horace : « Scripta Palatinus quaecumque recepit Apollo » (écrits dont Apollon Palatin a reçu la garde). L'empereur Joseph II (1741–1790) en personne assista à la fête donnée pour inaugurer l'institution en 1769. Sa petite-nièce Marie-Louise d'Autriche (1791–1847), qui régna sur Parme à partir de 1818, impulsa un bel essor à la bibliothèque. Ainsi, les ouvrages rejoignirent, dans les années 1830–1833, un élégant système d'étagères occupant la totalité des parois d'un salon coiffé d'une voûte en berceau conçue par Nicola Bettoli (1780–1854). Antonio Canova (1757–1822) rendit un hommage impérissable à la mécène dans ce salon, en sculptant un portrait en buste de style classique dans du marbre blanc.

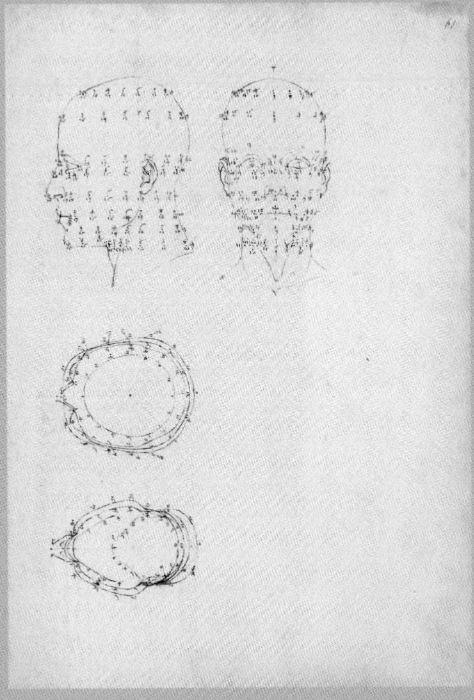

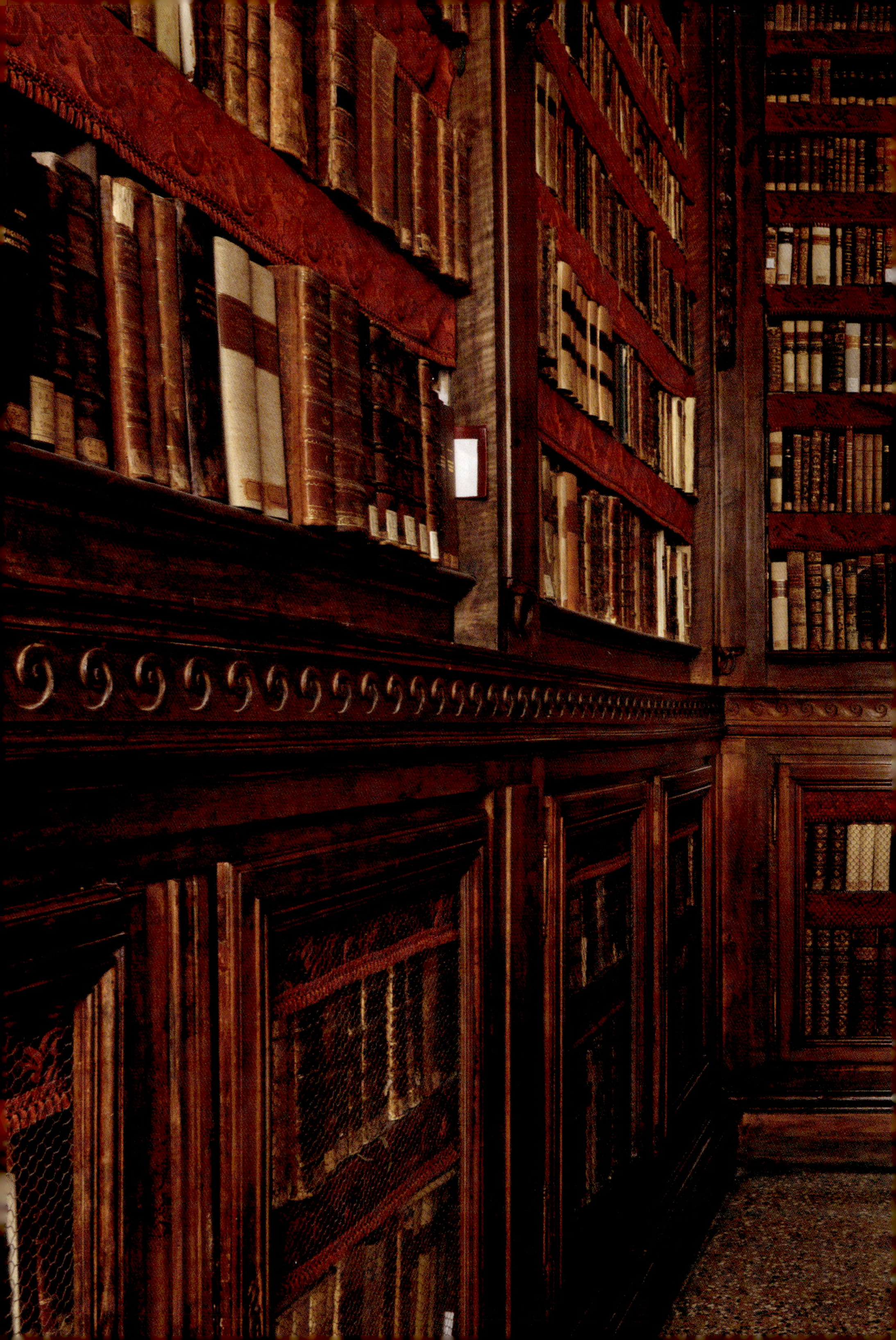

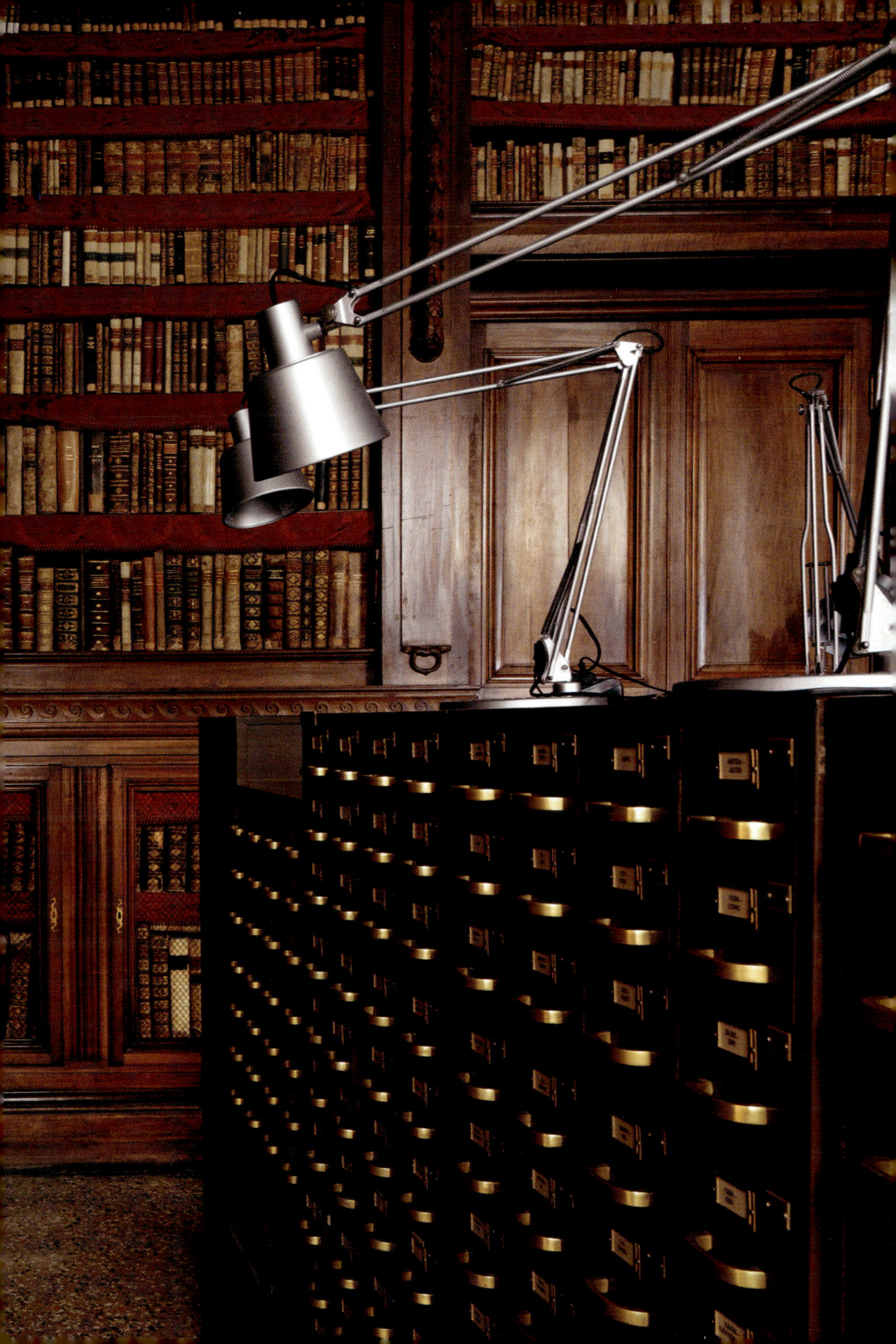

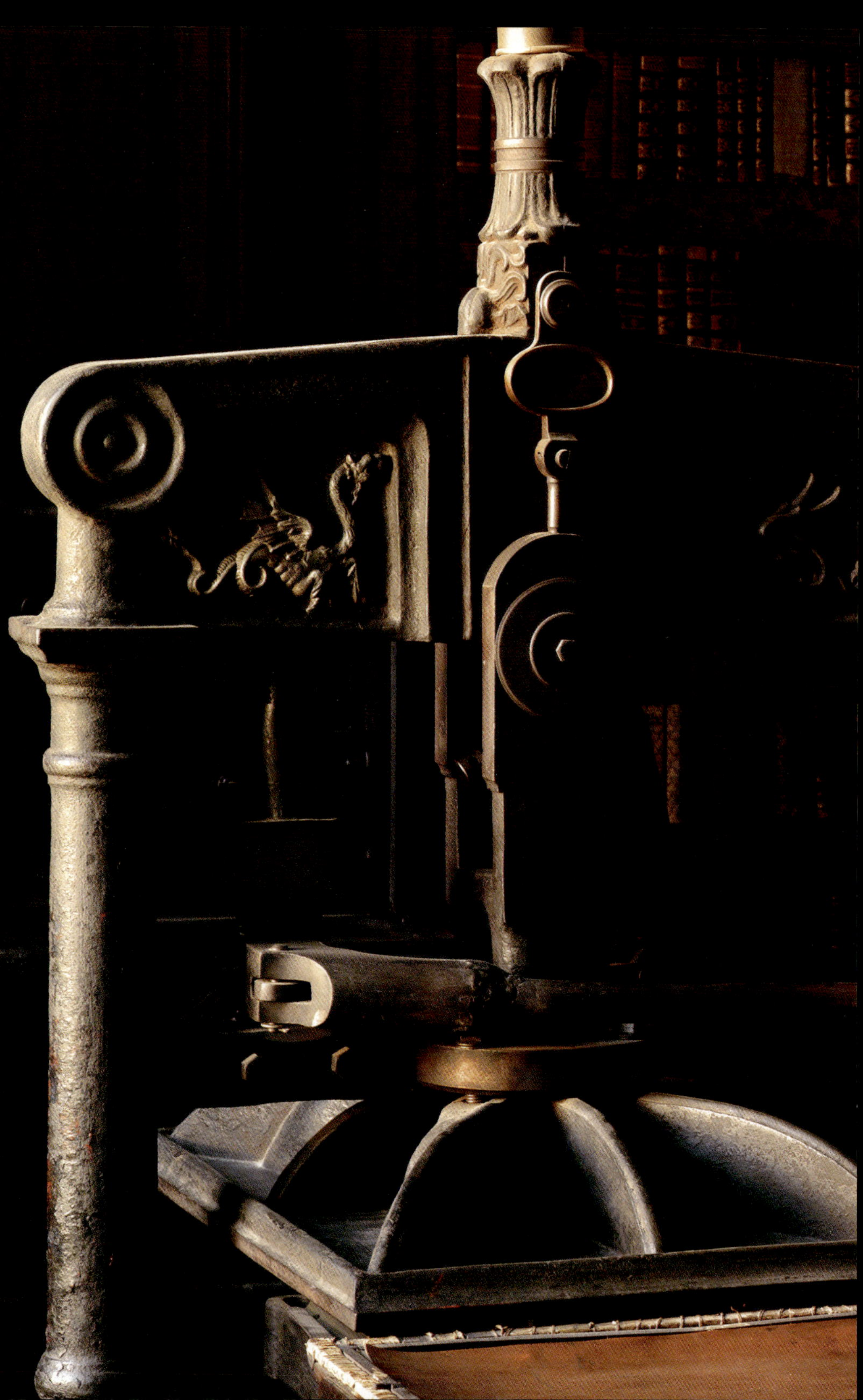

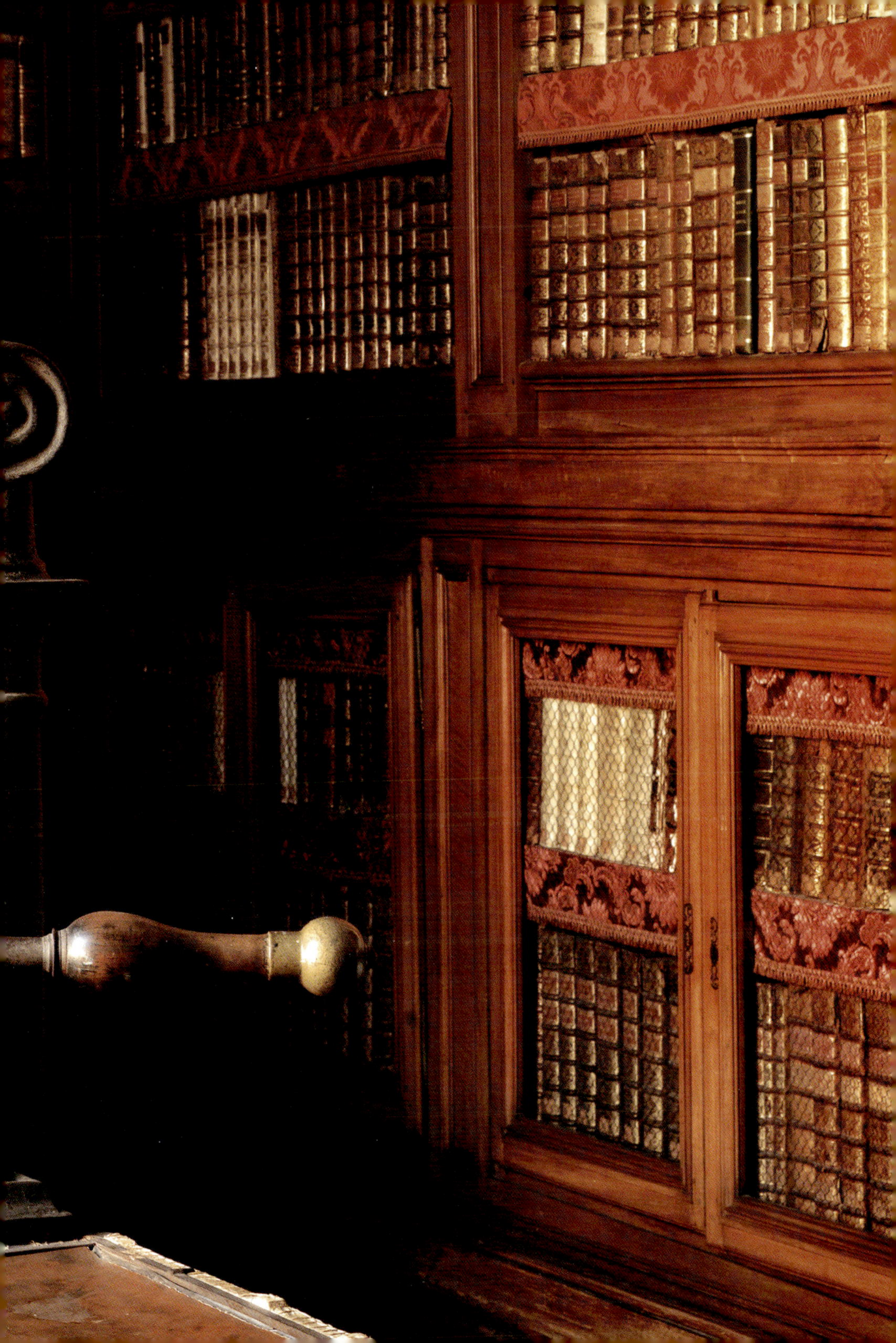

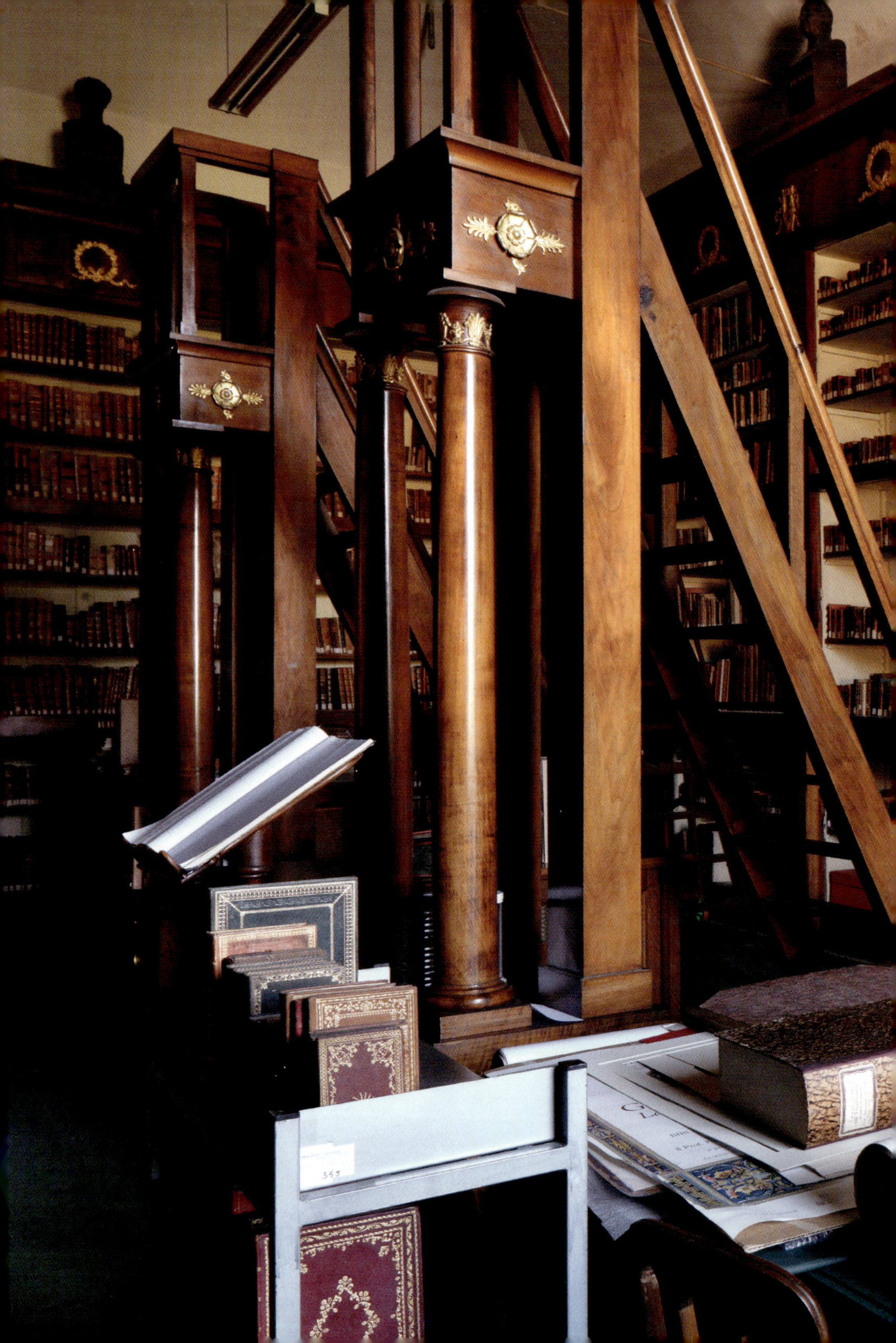

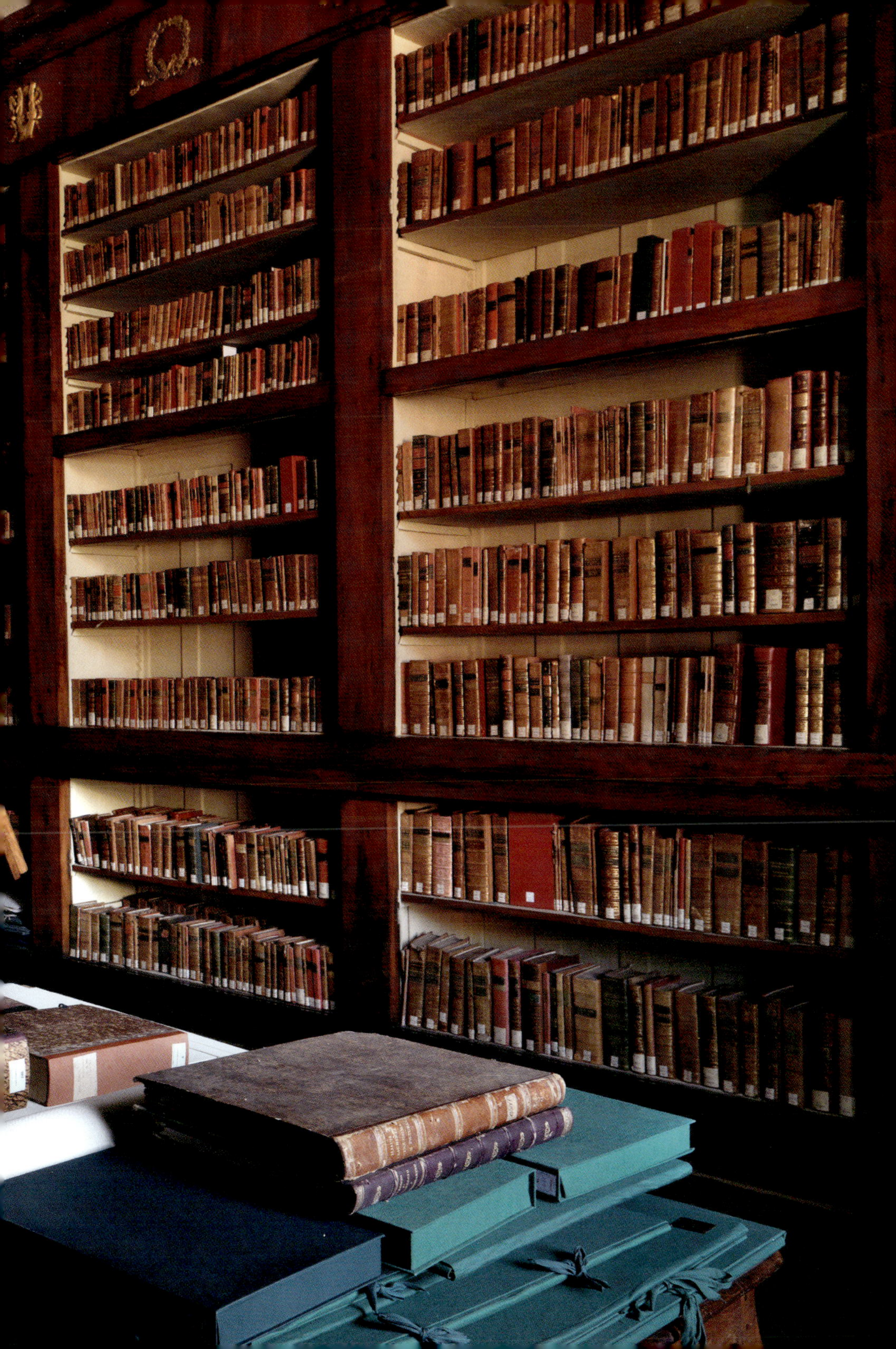

Biblioteca Nazionale Braidense

The Braidense was conceived from its foundation in 1770 as a public educational establishment covering a broad range of fields. Within the wider context of libraries in and around Milan, it stood at the opposite end of the spectrum to the older Ambrosiana, with its emphasis on functioning as a museum and most especially by being managed by members of the clergy. As with the Ambrosiana, however, other educational institutions were also attached to the Braidense, albeit in this case with no religious affiliations: the Brera Art Gallery, the Academy of Fine Arts, the Lombard Institute of Science and Letters, the Observatory and the Botanical Gardens. From 1773 these were installed, together with the library, in the former Jesuit College in Milan's Brera district. The fact of their casting off the traditional monopoly on education which was kept in the hands of the clergy can be traced back to the Habsburgs, who as rulers of Lombardy founded these public institutes in their capital and whose educational policies were influenced by the ideas of the early Enlightenment. Thus it was on the initiative of the Habsburgs that the Braidense's core holdings, which essentially consist of the collection of Count Carlo Pertusati (1674–1755), were purchased from Milan private ownership. Another example of the modern cultural and educational policy pursued by Empress Maria Theresa (1717–1780) was the acquisition of a significant body of medical and natural scientific works, in order to supplement the Braidense's existing nucleus of primarily historical and literary works and to furnish other centres of learning in Austrian Lombardy with the latest scientific discoveries. This private collection of some 20,000 books and writings was assembled by the Bern doctor and naturalist Albrecht von Haller (1708–1777). Further holdings came from the Imperial Court Library in Vienna and from old abbeys and monastic libraries dissolved during this period. It was through these channels that the Milan library acquired its valuable collection of illuminated manuscripts, such as those from the Charterhouse at Pavia and the monastery of Sant'Ambrogio. After Emperor Joseph II expressed his disappointment at seeing the Braidense still unfinished on a visit to Milan in 1782, the completion of the library was substantially accelerated and in 1786 it finally opened its doors to the public. After the departure of the Austrians, in 1880 the Braidense became a national library owned by the Italian State.

✳✳✳

Founded 1770; national library since 1880
Holdings over 800,000 volumes
Type of library national library
under the aegis of the Ministero per i beni
e le attività culturali
Highlights *Manuscript with the Hagiographic Legend of Josephat and Barlaam*, 15th century (AC.XI.37); *Carthusian Missal*, 15th century (Ms. AG. XII.1); René Descartes, *Opera philosophica*, Frankfurt a. M., 1692; August Johann Rösel von Rosenhof, *Historia naturalis ranarum nostratium*, Nuremberg, 1758 (D-XVII-11077)

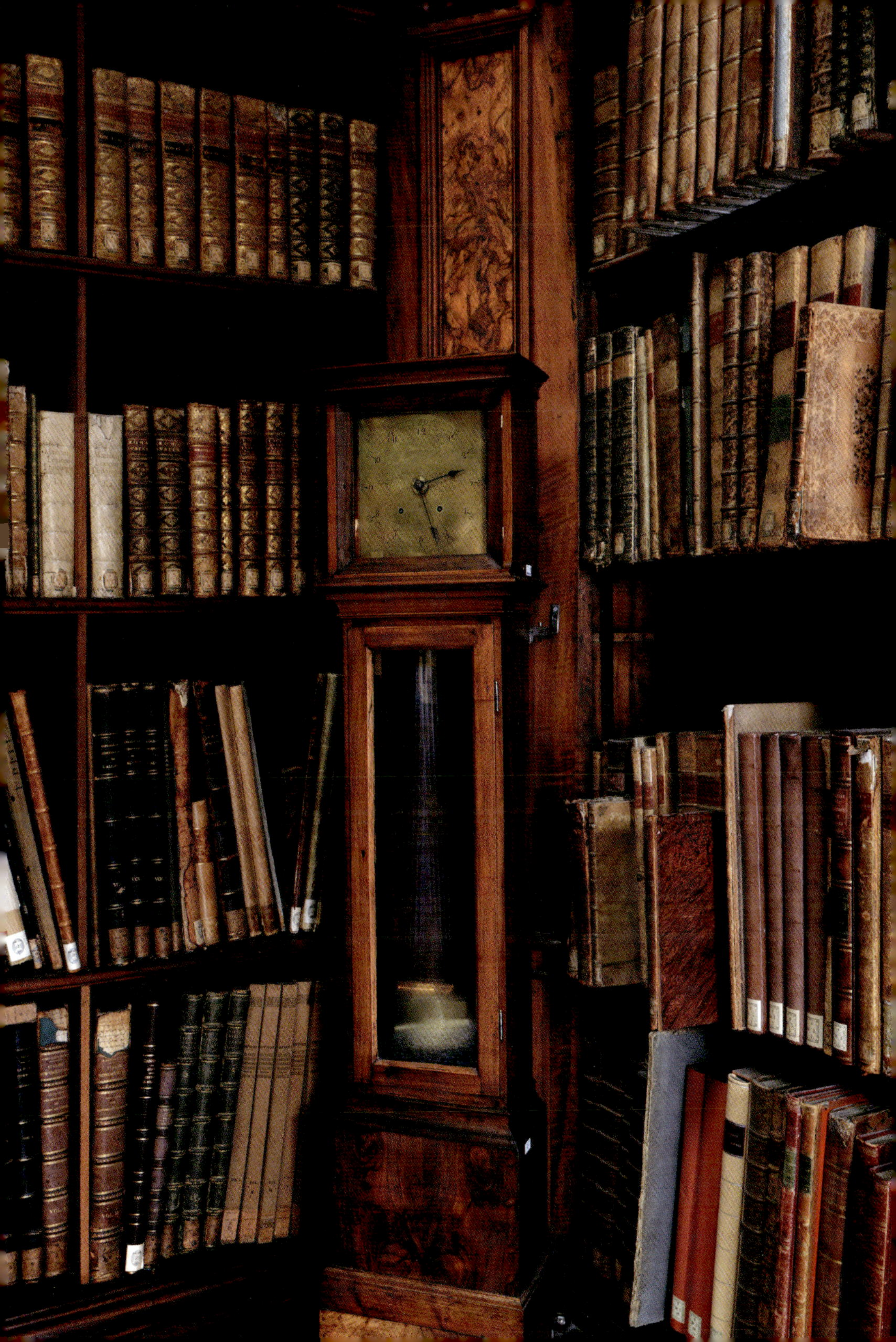

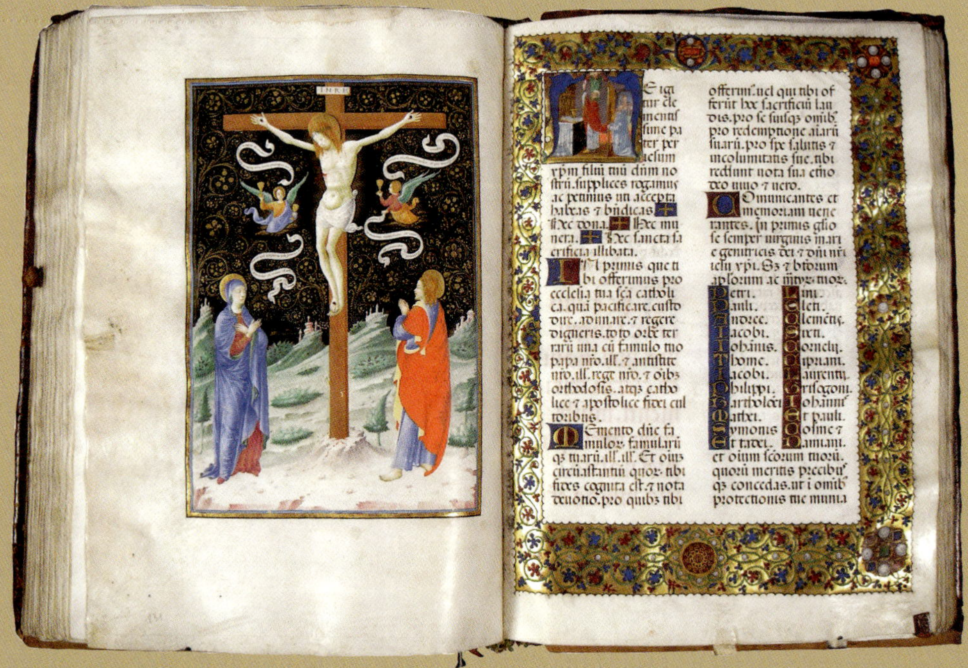

Die Biblioteca Braidense ist seit ihrer Gründung im Jahr 1770 als öffentliche Bildungsstätte mit breit gefächerter Kompetenz konzipiert, was sie in der Mailänder Bibliothekenlandschaft zum Gegenpol der älteren, museal ausgerichteten und vor allem geistlich geführten Ambrosiana werden ließ. Wie bereits im Fall der Ambrosiana sind auch der Braidense weitere, hier nicht geistliche Bildungsinstitutionen angeschlossen, die ab 1773 gemeinsam mit der Bibliothek in das mächtige Gebäude des ehemaligen Jesuitenkollegs im Stadtviertel Brera einzogen: die Pinakothek, die Kunstakademie, die Akademie der Geisteswissenschaften sowie ein Observatorium und der Botanische Garten. Dass das traditionelle Bildungsmonopol des Stadtklerus durchbrochen wurde, geht auf die von der frühen Aufklärung geprägte Bildungspolitik der Habsburger zurück, die als Landesherren der Lombardei in deren Hauptstadt diese öffentlichen Einrichtungen gründeten. Ihrer Initiative ist es zu verdanken, dass der Kernbestand der Bibliothek, der im Wesentlichen die

Büchersammlung des Senatspräsidenten Carlo Pertusati (1674–1755) umfasste, aus Mailänder Privatbesitz angekauft und umfassend ergänzt wurde. Beispielhaft für die moderne von Kaiserin Maria Theresia (1717–1780) propagierte Kulturpolitik war auch der Ankauf eines bedeutenden medizinisch-naturwissenschaftlichen Bestandes, der die bis dahin überwiegend historisch und literarisch ausgerichtete Bibliothek ergänzen sowie auch andere Bildungsstätten der österreichischen Lombardei mit den neuesten wissenschaftlichen Erkenntnissen ausstatten sollte. Diese vom Berner Arzt und Naturforscher Albrecht von Haller (1708–1777) zusammengestellte Privatsammlung umfasste etwa 20 000 Bücher und Schriften. Weitere Bestände kamen aus der Kaiserlichen Hofbibliothek in Wien sowie aus damals aufgelösten alten Abteien und Ordensbibliotheken. Der reiche Bestand wertvoller illuminierter Handschriften, etwa aus der Kartause von Pavia oder dem Kloster Sant'Ambrogio, gelangte auf diesem Weg in die Mailänder Bibliothek. Den entscheidenden

Anstoß für die Öffnung der Bibliothek gab schließlich die Mailandreise Kaiser Josefs II. im Jahr 1782, der sich enttäuscht zeigte, die Braidense noch nicht fertiggestellt zu sehen. 1786 konnte die Bibliothek schließlich dem Publikum geöffnet werden. Nach dem Abzug der Österreicher wurde die Braidense 1880 zur Nationalbibliothek erklärt.

❋ ✳ ❋

Dès sa fondation en l'an 1770, la bibliothèque de Brera est conçue comme un établissement d'enseignement public aux vastes compétences, ce qui fait d'elle, dans le paysage milanais, l'antithèse de l'Ambrosiana, son aînée au dessein plus muséal, du reste dirigée par des instances spirituelles. À l'instar de son pendant, cette bibliothèque est rattachée à des institutions d'enseignement – non cléricales dans le cas présent – qui investissent dès 1773 l'imposant bâtiment de l'ancien collège de Jésuites dans le quartier de Brera : la pinacothèque, l'académie des arts, l'académie des sciences humaines, un observatoire et un jardin botanique. La rupture avec le traditionnel monopole que le clergé de la ville exerçait sur l'enseignement s'explique par la politique que les Habsbourg, très marqués par les Lumières, ont menée en fondant ces institutions publiques dans la capitale lombarde. Cette famille alors à la tête de la Lombardie prit l'initiative d'acheter le noyau de la bibliothèque, qui se composait essentiellement de la collection du président du Sénat Carlo Pertusati (1674–1755), à des privés milanais et de l'enrichir considérablement. Autre exemple de politique culturelle moderne menée par l'impératrice Marie-Thérèse (1717–1780) : l'achat d'un fonds significatif en médecine et sciences naturelles afin, d'une part, d'enrichir la bibliothèque essentiellement dédiée

à l'histoire et à la littérature et, d'autre part, de doter les autres sites d'enseignement de la Lombardie autrichienne des dernières avancées scientifiques. Cette collection privée rassemblée par le médecin et chercheur bernois Albert de Haller (1708–1777) comptait près de 20 000 écrits et livres. D'autres fonds sont parvenus de la bibliothèque de la cour impériale de Vienne ainsi que de bibliothèques d'anciennes abbayes et ordres supprimés. C'est ainsi que le fonds de manuscrits enluminés de grande valeur, en provenance de la Chartreuse de Pavie ou du monastère Sant'Ambrogio, a trouvé le chemin de la bibliothèque milanaise. Lors de sa venue à Milan en 1782, l'empereur Joseph II s'est montré déçu que la bibliothèque ne soit pas encore prête. Sa déception fit l'effet d'un coup de fouet, et la bibliothèque de Brera ouvrit au public en 1786. Elle est devenue bibliothèque nationale en 1880 après le retrait des Autrichiens.

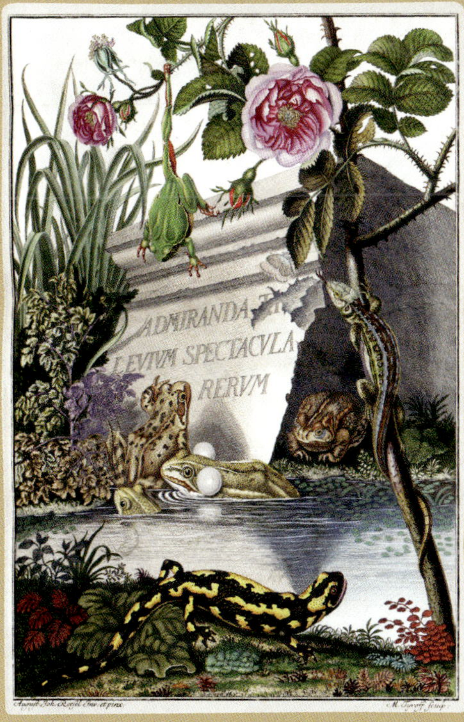

Carthusian Missal, 15th century, sig. Ms. AG. XII.1, fol. 131v–132r: *Crucifixion of Christ*

August Johann Rösel von Rosenhof,
Historia naturalis ranarum nostratium, Nuremberg, 1758: *Frontispiece*

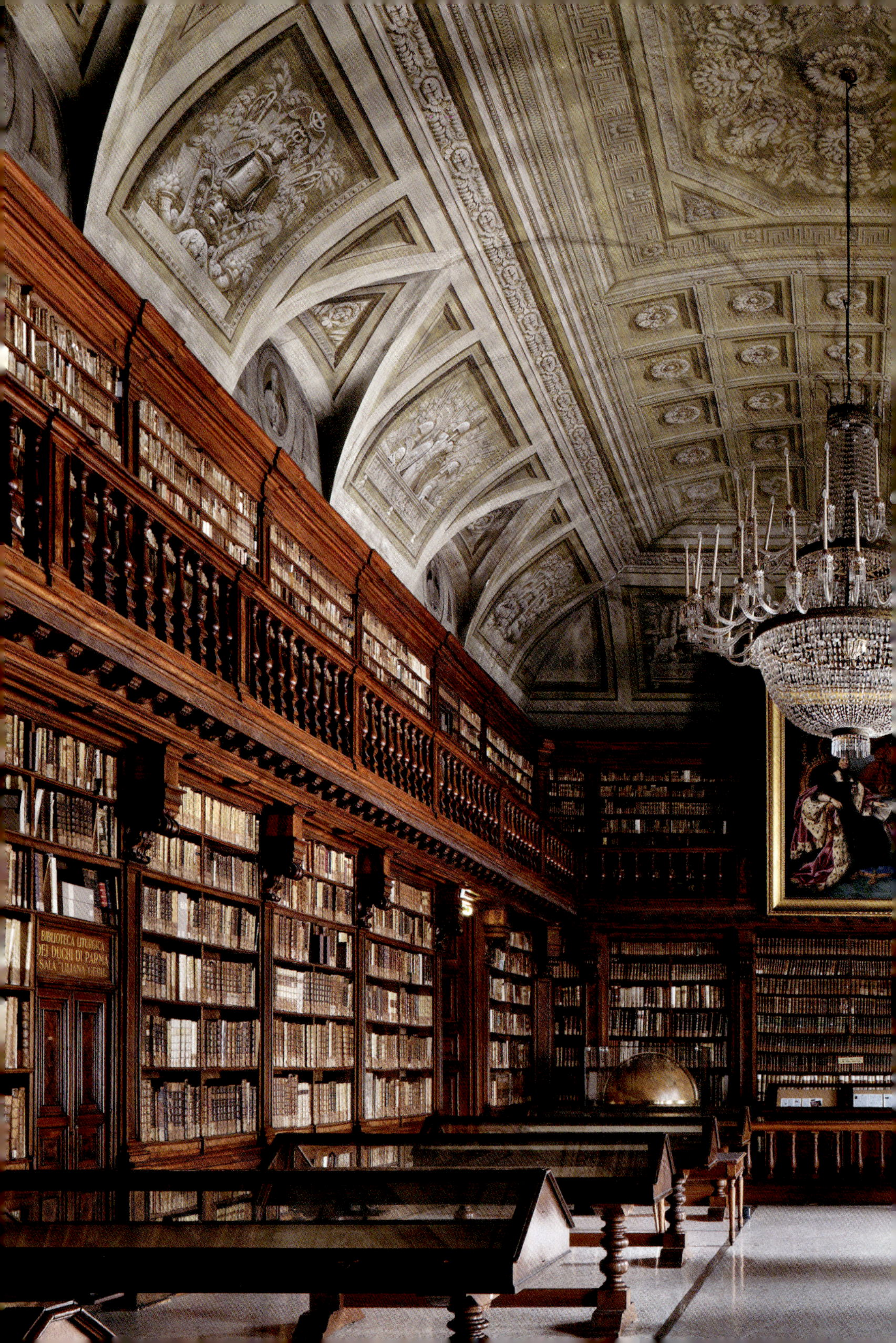

BIBLIOTECA LITURGICA
DEI DUCHI DI PARMA
SALA LILIANA GERLI

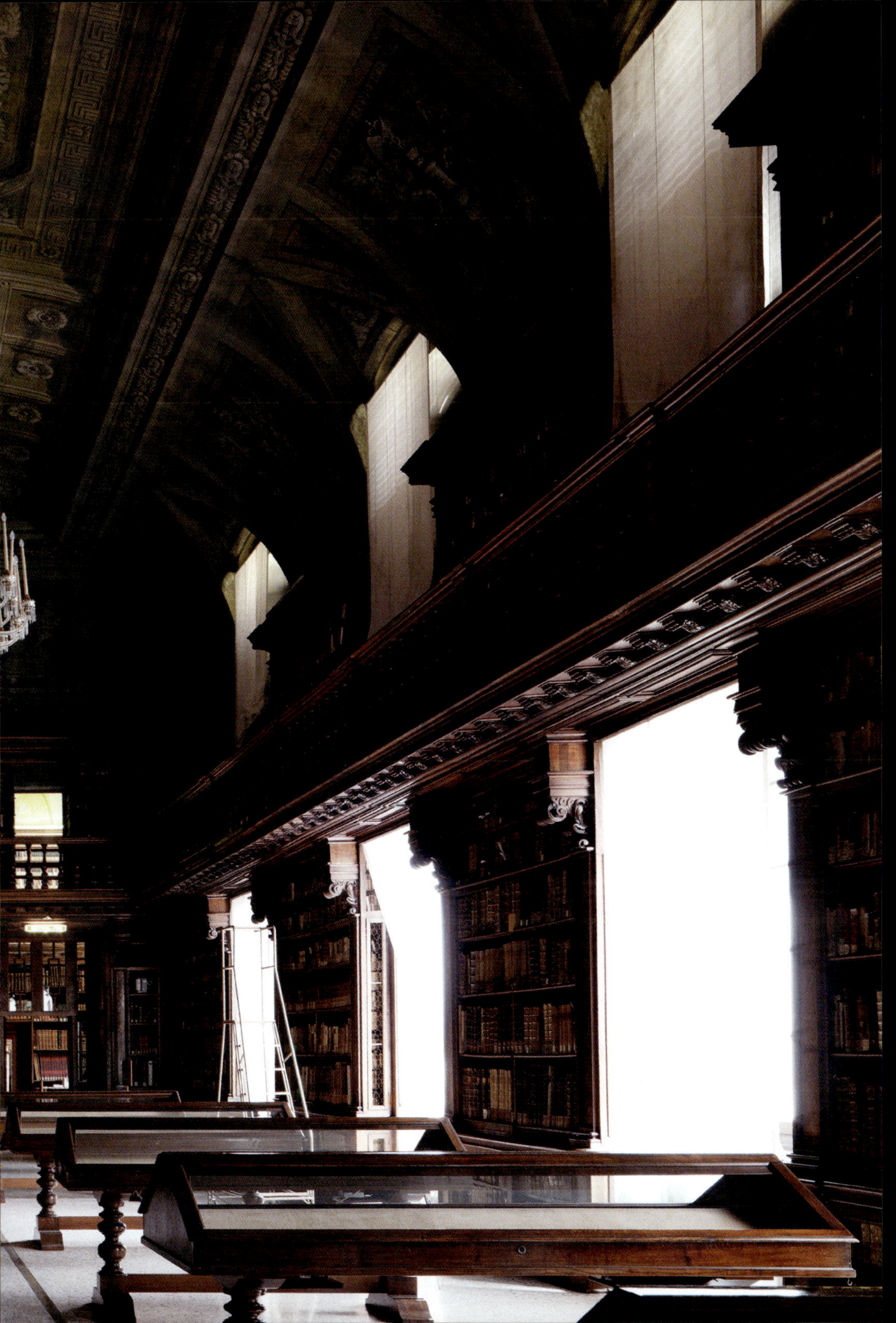

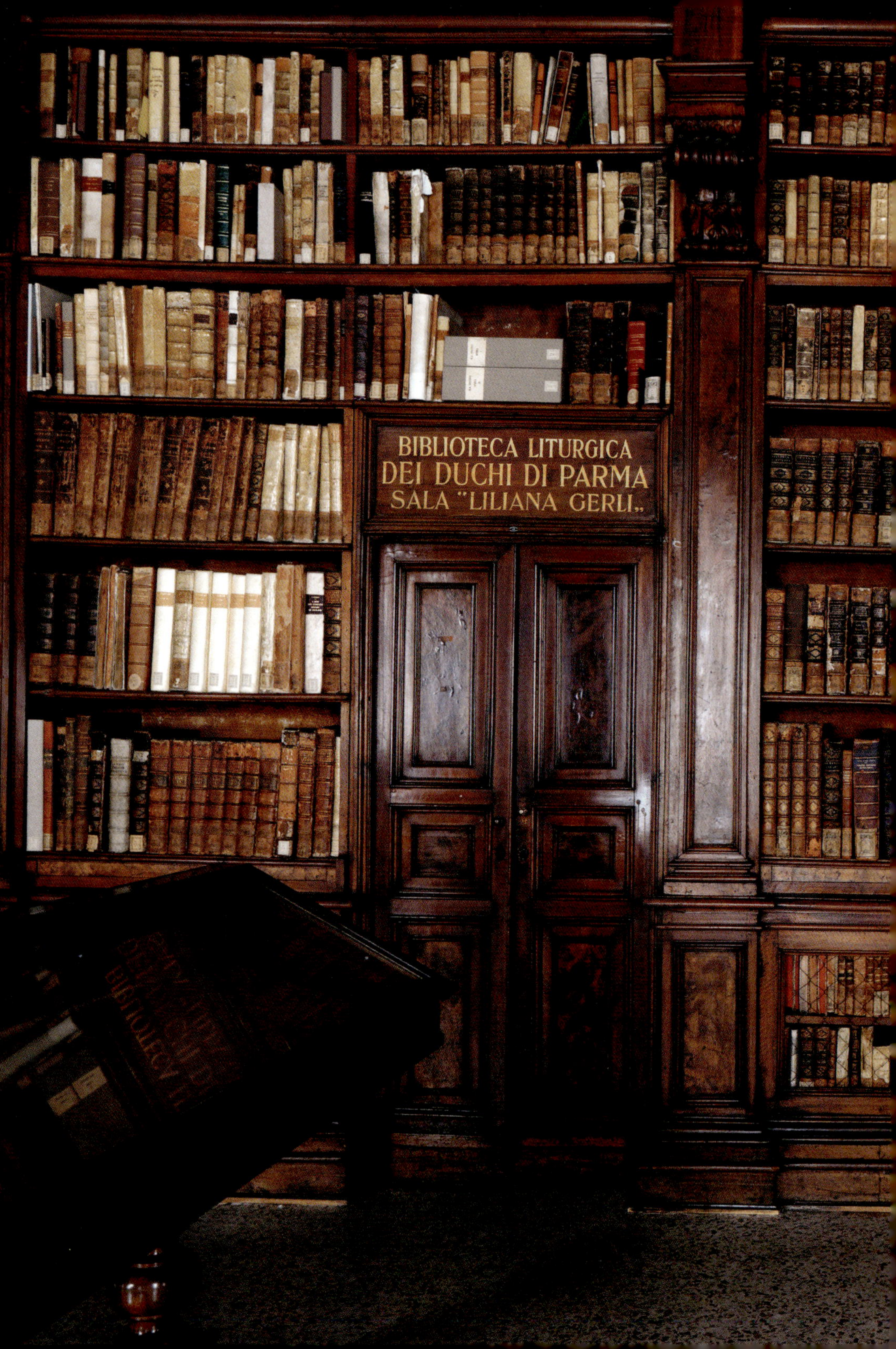
BIBLIOTECA LITURGICA
DEI DUCHI DI PARMA
SALA "LILIANA GERLI,,

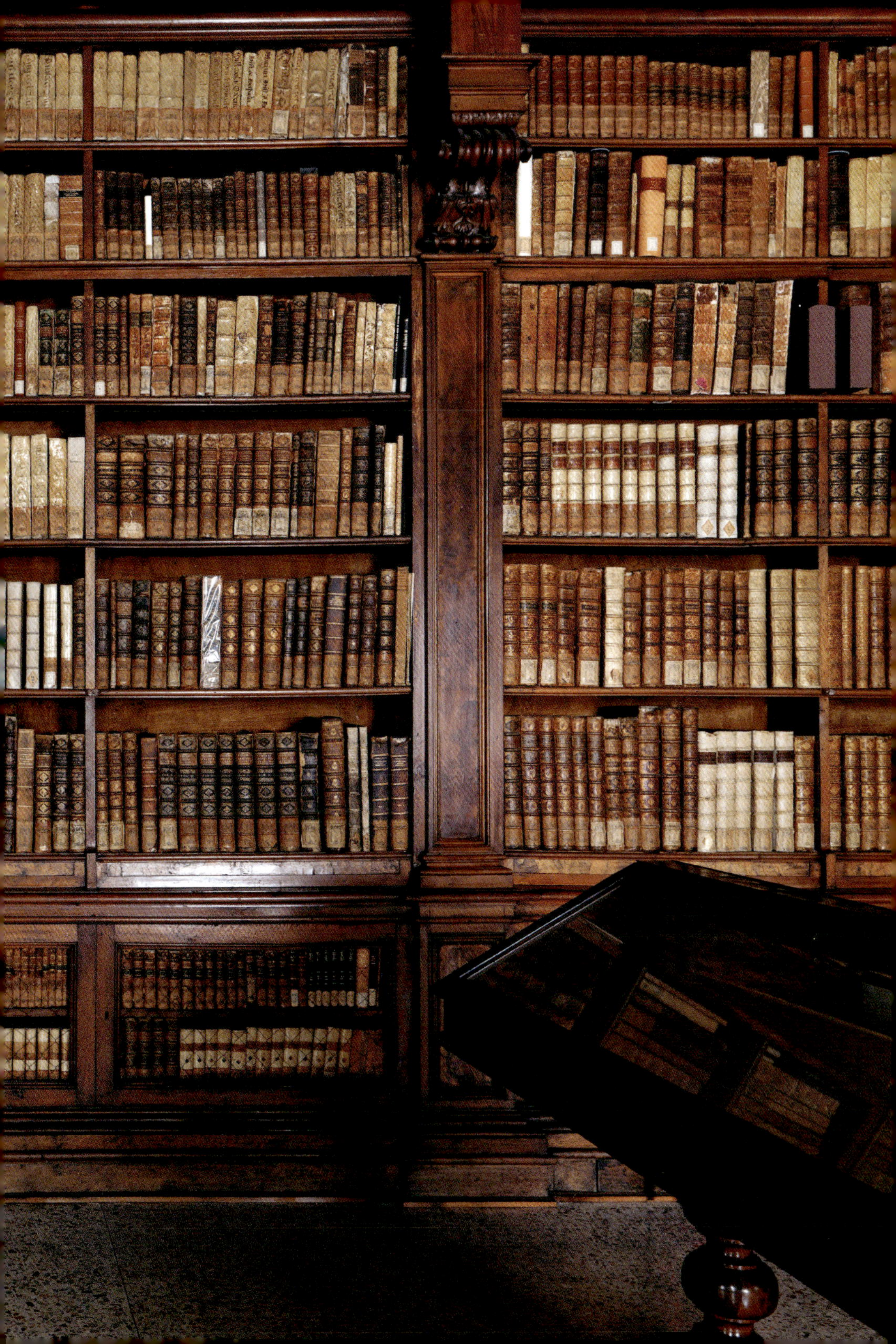

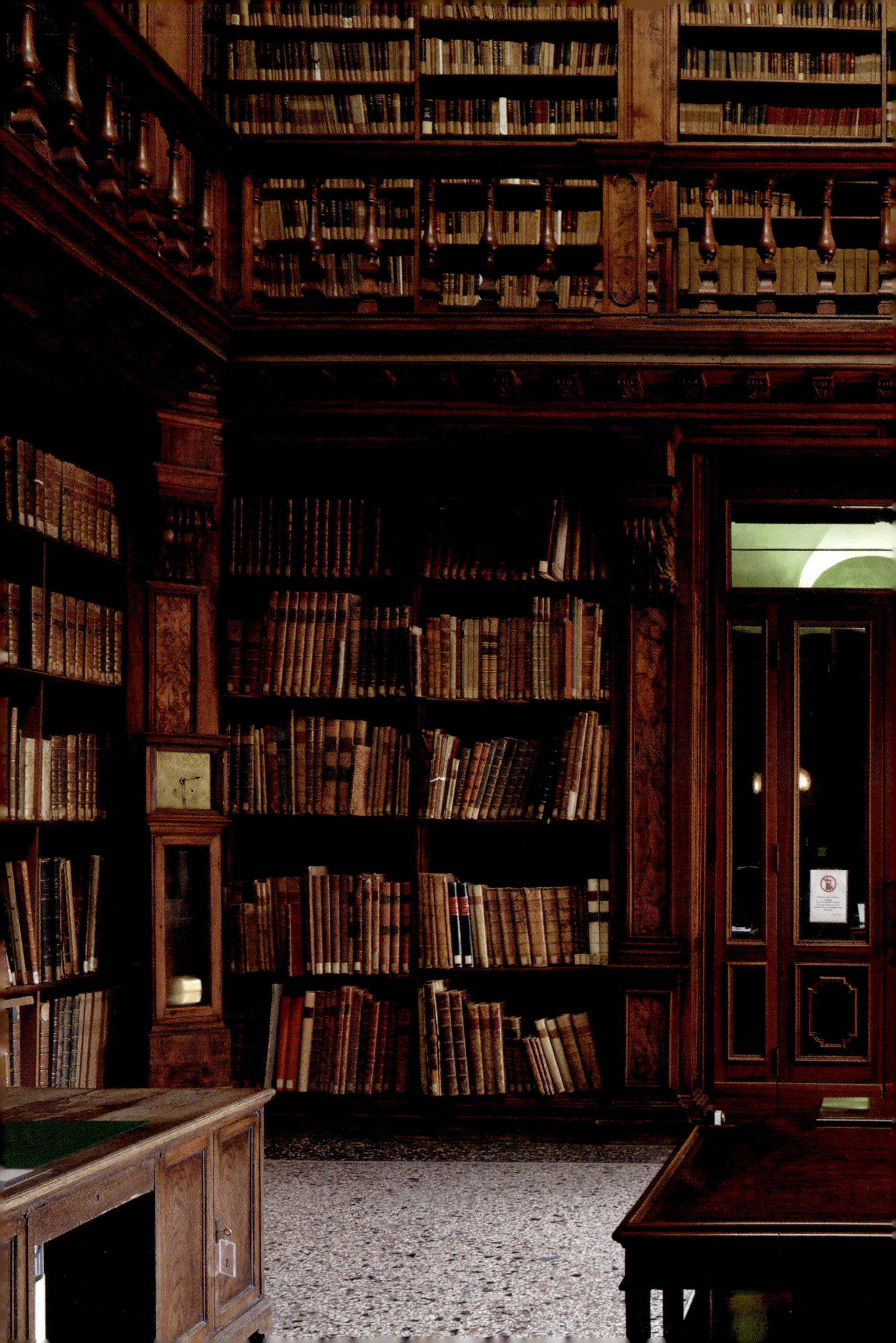

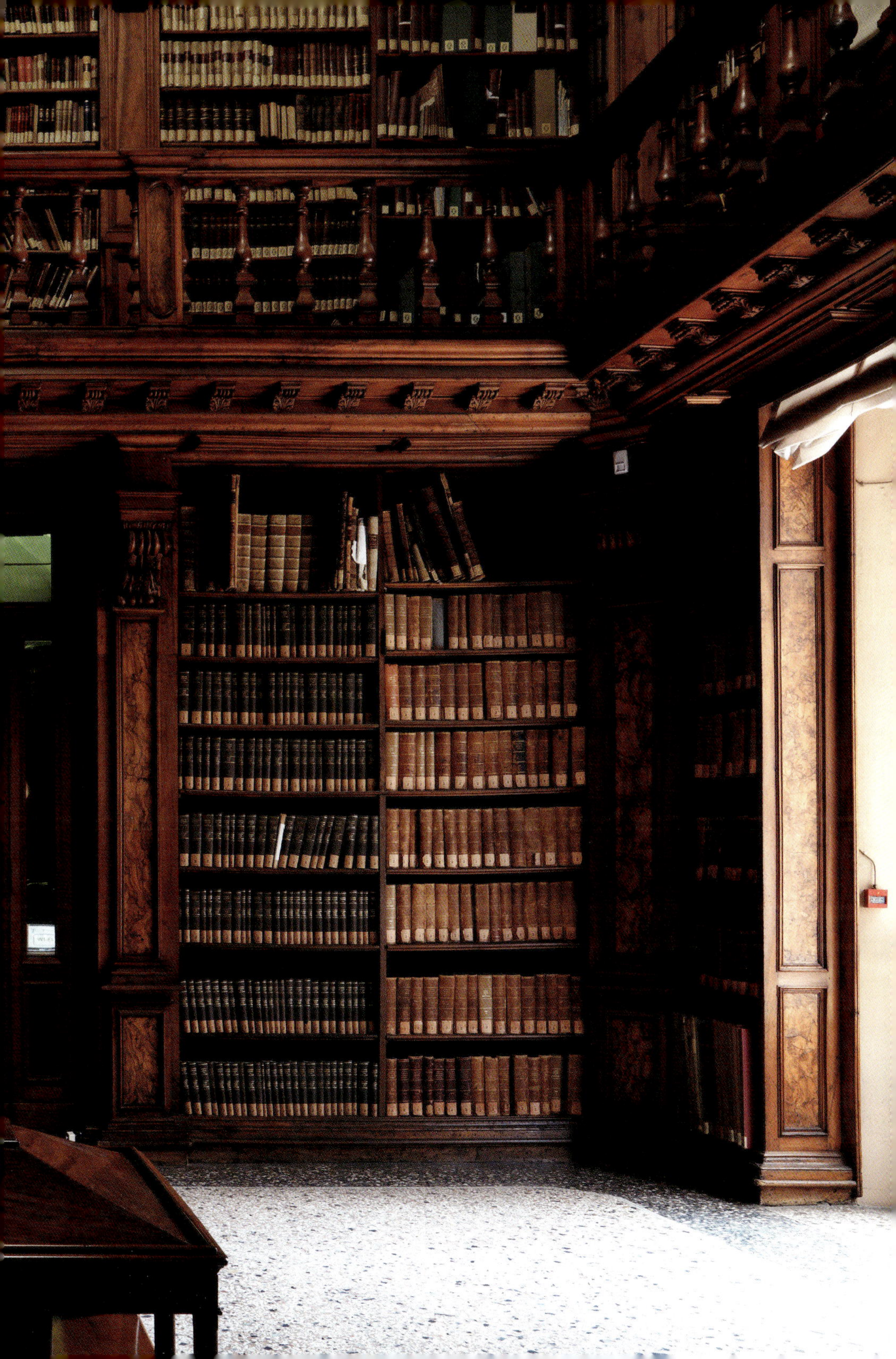

Real Biblioteca del Monasterio de San Lorenzo de El Escorial

Philip II (1527–1598) ruled one of the largest global empires in history. His royal monastery and palace of El Escorial, built in the mountains outside Madrid, remains its enduring witness: a gigantic complex laid out around a large number of courtyards in allusion to the Temple of Solomon, with the palace church in the centre, El Escorial testifies in impressive fashion to the Habsburgs' understanding of themselves as sovereigns appointed "by the Grace of God". For 30 years Philip II ruled the Kingdom of Spain, with its territories around the globe, and did so largely from the Escorial which consequently served multiple functions – as a shrine and memorial to royal dignity, a statement of the Tridentine creed, a centre of power and administration, a place of education and a private retreat. The fact that the king now resided in just one place and governed from there was an entirely new departure for the Spanish monarchy, which up until then had operated out of various palaces and centres of learning around the country. The Escorial, however, would become Philip's sole place of work, thinking and study, even though he had been born and grew up in Valladolid. He seems to have embarked on the plans for the project following the death of his father, Emperor Charles V (1500–1558). A royal library was an integral part of the design, and in line with Philip's wishes it was conceived as the main national library of the Spanish Kingdom. Already in 1555 the royal chronicler, Juan Páez de Castro (c. 1510–1570), had petitioned the monarch regarding the urgent construction of a library, in which the kingdom's most precious books and most recent scholarly writings might be brought together. At the time these were still scattered in the libraries of private palaces, monasteries and universities across the various Spanish provinces. Páez de Castro's *Memorial a Felipe II sobre la utilidad de juntar una biblioteca* is still preserved today in the collections of the Real Biblioteca Monasterio Escorial. While the royal advisors had certainly hoped that Spain's new central library would be based in one of the royal or university cities rather than in the isolated Escorial, Philip had the Salón Principal of the library, which was built directly above the main entrance and prominently facing the front façade of the church, designed as one of the most magnificent rooms in his palace. The determination that the library's artistic decoration should rival the wealthiest and most modern libraries in Europe – such as the Marciana of the Doges in Venice – was expressed right from the start by the humanists in the royal circle. In his fresco paintings for the vault, whose iconographical scheme was conceived by court historiographer José de Sigüenza (1544–1606), Pellegrino Tibaldi (1527–1596) made reference to the frescos by Michelangelo in the Sistine Chapel. The classically elegant interior furnishings, including the wall cabinets which were an innovation for

Founded 1563 (date foundation stone laid), built to plans by Juan Bautista de Toledo, completed by Juan de Herrera
Holdings c. 70,000 books
Type of library royal library
Highlights Beatus de Liébana, *Commentaria in Apocalypsin (Commentary on the Apocalypse)*, c. 950–955 (Ms. &-II-5); *Codex Aureus Escorialiensis,* 1045/46 (Cod. Vitrinas 17*)*; Ibn al-Durayhim al-Mawsili, *Libro de la utilidad de los animales,* 1354 (Ms. Árabes 898)

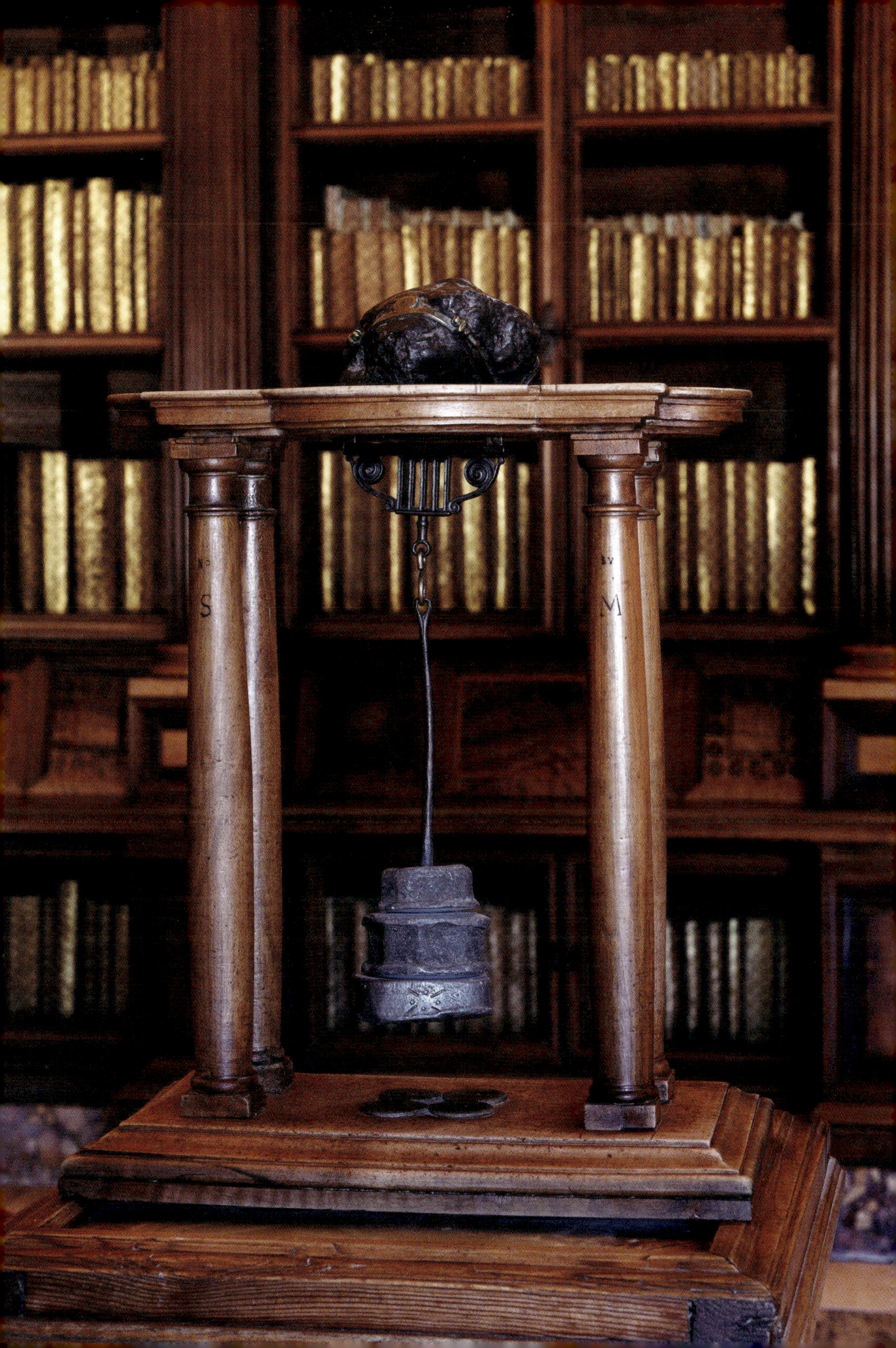

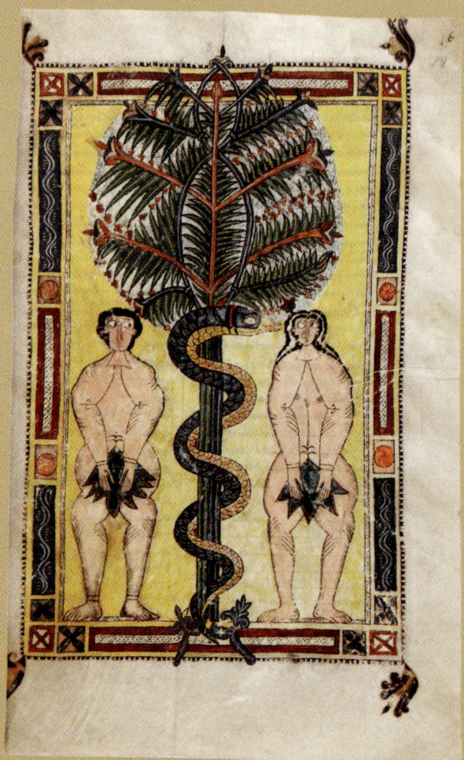

themselves in the monastery attached to his new palace. Issuing from their ranks was not only the architect Antonio de Villacastín (1512–1603), but also the scholars of the king's closest circle. In 1566 Philip's valuable private library was installed at the Escorial. Among its almost 1,000 volumes were some of the oldest manuscripts in the collection, including the *Codex Aureus*. Humanists such as Ambrosio de Morales (1513–1591) in turn contributed towards ensuring that the most precious books held in other parts of the country were relocated to the king's library. Royal envoys abroad, above all in Venice, France and Flanders, were also tasked with making acquisitions. By the time the palace was ready for habitation in 1571, it housed 4,000 volumes and the most modern scientific equipment. The king's personal armillary sphere has stood in the library hall since 1593.

❀❖❀

Philipp II. (1527–1598) herrschte über eines der größten Weltreiche der Geschichte. Seine in den Bergen unweit von Madrid errichtete Klosterresidenz El Escorial ist dessen steinerner Zeuge: eine gigantische, in Anspielung auf den salomonischen Tempel in zahlreiche Höfe gegliederte Anlage mit der Palastkirche im Zentrum, die das Selbstverständnis der „von Gottes Gnaden" zur Herrschaft berufenen Habsburger eindrucksvoll vor Augen führt. Denn das weltumspannende Königreich Spanien wurde von Philipp II. 30 Jahre lang weitgehend vom Escorial aus regiert. Diesem war daher vielfältige Bestimmung zugedacht: als Weihestätte und Memorial königlicher Würde, Manifest tridentinischer Gesinnung, Macht- und Verwaltungszentrum, Ausbildungsstätte und Rückzugsort. Bahnbrechend neu war für die spanische Monarchie, dass der König nun an einem einzigen Ort residierte und von dort aus waltete, hatte es doch bis dahin

libraries of the day, were designed by the royal court architect Juan de Herrera (1530–1597), who in 1567 succeeded Juan Bautista de Toledo (c. 1515–1567) as artistic director. The classification system goes back to the first librarian, court theologian Benedictus Arias Montanus (1527–1598), who like other humanists attached to the court taught at the Escorial's own college. In collaboration with Sigüenza, he was also responsible for the particular way in which the books were displayed, namely with their fore-edges – all of them gilt – facing outwards, thereby lending the room a note of uniform appearance. The lattice doors were only added in the 18th century, as originally the wall cabinets were open-fronted. Two years after construction had begun (the foundation stone was laid in April 1563), the first deliveries of books were already arriving. They were initially intended for the Hieronymite monks who, at the king's request, had installed

Beatus de Liébana, *Commentaria in Apocalypsin*, c. 950–955, sig. Ms. &-II-5, fol. 18r: *The Fall of Mankind*
Beatus de Liébana, *Commentaria in Apocalypsin*, c. 950–955, sig. Ms. &-II-5, fol. 120r: *Hay and Grape Harvest*

landesweit eine Vielzahl von Residenzen und
Kompetenzzentren gegeben. Philipps Ort
des Schaffens, Denkens und Forschens sollte
aber ausschließlich der Escorial sein – obwohl
er doch selbst in Valladolid geboren und
aufgewachsen war –, und dessen Planung
scheint er bereits seit dem Tod seines Vaters
Kaiser Karl V. (1500–1558) betrieben zu haben.
Integraler Bestandteil des Entwurfs war eine
königliche Bibliothek, die nach dem Wunsch
Philipps als zentrale Nationalbibliothek des
spanischen Königreiches konzipiert wurde.
Bereits 1555 hatte der königliche Chronist Juan
Páez de Castro (um 1510–1570) dem Monarchen
seinen Appell zur dringlichen Errichtung einer
Bibliothek überreicht, in der die wertvollsten
Bücherschätze und aktuellsten Wissensvorräte
des gesamten Landes zusammengeführt werden sollten. Denn diese waren bis dahin in den
Büchersammlungen von Privatpalästen, Klöstern und Universitäten über die verschiedenen
Provinzen des Landes verstreut. Das *Memorial
a Felipe II sobre la utilidad de juntar una
biblioteca* hat sich bis heute in den Sammlungen der Real Biblioteca Monasterio Escorial
erhalten. Freilich hatten sich die königlichen
Berater als Basis der Zentralbibliothek
Spaniens nicht den isoliert gelegenen Escorial,
sondern eine der Residenz oder Universi-
tätsstädte gewünscht, doch Philipp ließ den
direkt über dem Haupteingang – prominent
der Kirchenfassade gegenüber – gelegenen
Salón Principal der Bibliothek zu einem der
prächtigsten Räume seiner Klosterresidenz
gestalten. Der künstlerische Wettstreit mit
den reichsten und modernsten europäischen
Bibliotheken – wie der Marciana der Dogen in
Venedig – wurde bereits von den Humanisten
im Umkreis des Königs thematisiert. In der Fres-
kodekoration des Gewölbes, für deren ikonogra-
fisches Programm der Hofhistoriograf José de
Sigüenza (1544–1606) verantwortlich zeichnet,
nahm Pellegrino Tibaldi (1527–1596) auf
Michelangelos Sixtinische Kapelle Bezug. Das
klassisch edle Mobiliar mit den für zeitgenössische Bibliotheken neuartigen Wandschränken

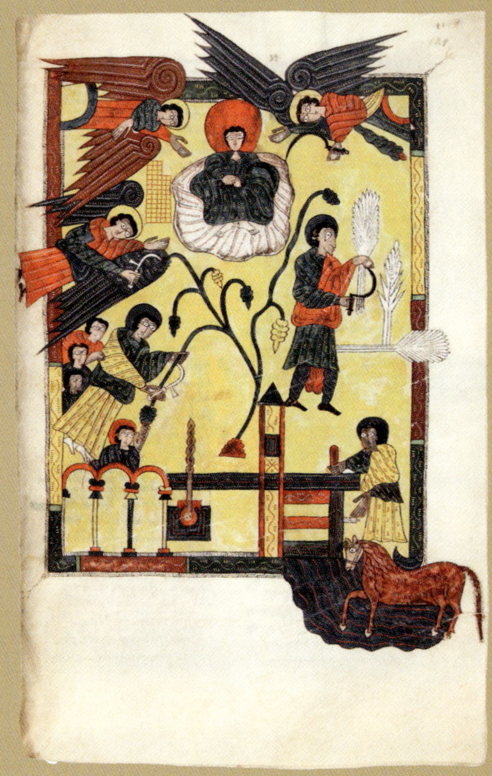

wurde vom königlichen Hofarchitekten Juan de
Herrera (1530–1597) entworfen, der 1567 Juan
Bautista de Toledo (um 1515–1567) als künstleri-
scher Leiter gefolgt war. Die thematische Anordnung der Bücher geht auf den Hoftheologen und
ersten Bibliothekar Benedictus Arias Montanus
(1527–1598) zurück, der am palasteigenen Kolleg
lehrte, wie auch andere Humanisten aus dem
königlichen Umkreis. Auch hatte er gemeinsam
mit Sigüenza die spezielle Aufstellung der
Bücher betreut, die mit ihrer nach außen gerich-
teten, durchweg in Gold gehaltenen Schnittseite
dem Raum eine einheitliche Note verleihen. Die
Gittertüren wurden erst im 18. Jahrhundert
hinzugefügt, ursprünglich standen die Wandschränke offen. Zwei Jahre nach Baubeginn – die
Grundsteinlegung fand im April 1563 statt – sind
bereits die ersten Bücherlieferungen des Königs
dokumentiert. Sie waren zunächst für die

Mönche des Hieronymitenordens bestimmt, die nach dem Willen des Königs das Kloster seiner neuen Residenz besiedelten. Aus ihren Reihen stammten nicht nur der Baumeister Antonio de Villacastín (1512–1603), sondern auch die Gelehrten aus dem engsten Umkreis des Königs. 1566 gelangte die wertvolle Privatbibliothek des Königs in den Escorial, unter deren nahezu 1 000 Bänden sich die ältesten Handschriften der Sammlung befanden, wie etwa der *Codex Aureus*. Humanisten wie Ambrosio de Morales (1513–1591) trugen dazu bei, die wertvollsten Bücher des Landes der Bibliothek des Königs zuzuführen. Königliche Gesandte wirkten im Ausland, vor allem in Venedig, Frankreich und Flandern. Als der Palast 1571 bezogen wurde, standen bereits 4 000 Bände und modernstes wissenschaftliches Gerät bereit; die persönliche Armillarsphäre des Königs befindet sich seit 1593 im Büchersaal.

✳ ✳ ✳

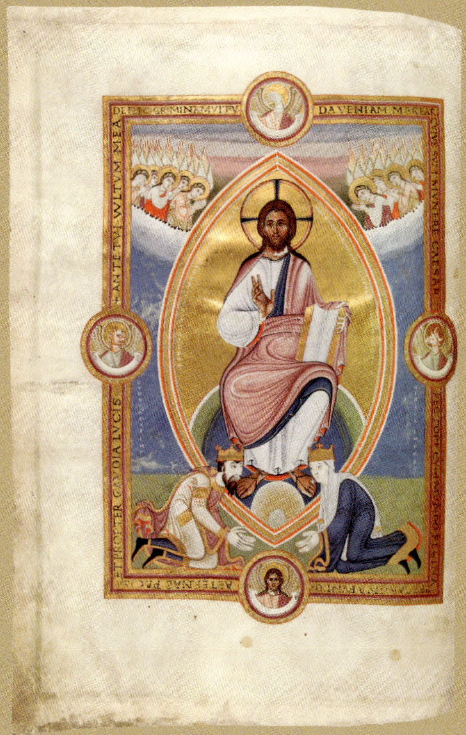

Philippe II (1527–1598) gouverna l'un des empires les plus vastes au monde. Sa résidence monastique dite « El Escorial », située sur les hauteurs proches de Madrid, en est le témoignage en pierre. Ce complexe architectural gigantesque, allusion au temple de Salomon, est quadrillé de cours. L'élément central est l'église palatiale, dont la monumentalité fait ressentir la « grâce de Dieu » qui a appelé un Habsbourgeois au pouvoir. Trente années durant, Philippe II dirigea l'Empire mondial d'Espagne principalement depuis ce site qui avait plusieurs vocations : lieu de culte et de souvenir de la grandeur royale, manifeste défendant l'esprit tridentin, centre de pouvoir et d'administration, lieu de formation et de retraite. Grande nouveauté pour la monarchie espagnole : le roi prenait toutes les décisions depuis un seul et même endroit, alors qu'auparavant il régnait depuis moult résidences et centres de gouvernance répartis dans tout le pays. Bien que natif de Valladolid, Philippe II choisit le site de l'Escurial comme lieu unique pour l'exécutif, la méditation et la recherche. Il semblerait qu'il en avait formulé le vœu et les plans dès la mort de son père, l'empereur Charles Quint (1500–1558). La bibliothèque royale faisait partie intégrante des plans, étant donné que Philippe l'envisageait comme la bibliothèque centrale du royaume d'Espagne. Déjà en 1555, le chroniqueur officiel de la cour, Juan Páez de Castro (vers 1510–1570), avait sommé le monarque d'ériger au plus tôt un bâtiment qui rassemblerait les trésors écrits les plus somptueux aux côtés des savoirs actuels du pays tout entier. Car ces derniers se trouvaient jusqu'alors dispersés dans les différentes collections des palais privés, couvents et universités de diverses provinces. La Real Biblioteca Monasterio Escorial abrite aujourd'hui encore le *Memorial a Felipe II sobre la utilidad de juntar una biblioteca*. À l'évidence, les conseillers du roi ne voyaient pas d'un bon œil l'idée d'une bibliothèque principale dans un lieu aussi retiré. Au site de l'Escurial, ils auraient préféré une grande ville ou une ville universitaire. Le monarque édifia le Salón

Principal face à l'entrée principale – répondant
ainsi à la façade de l'église. Ce Salón est l'une
des salles les plus prodigieuses de la résidence
monacale. Les humanistes gravitant autour
du roi évoquaient déjà le parfum de rivalité
artistique planant entre les bibliothèques les
plus richement dotées et les plus modernes
d'Europe (dont la Marciana des Doges de
Venise). Les fresques au plafond voûté sont
l'œuvre de Pellegrino Tibaldi (1527–1596), qui
s'inspira du décor de la chapelle Sixtine, et
attestent en outre du responsable de leur iconographie, l'historien de cour José de Sigüenza
(1544–1606). L'architecte de cour Juan de Herrera (1530–1597), qui remplaça Juan Bautista de
Toledo (vers 1515–1567) à la direction artistique
en 1567, conçut le mobilier noble d'esprit
classique et les armoires à livres, une nouveauté
pour l'époque. Le classement thématique des
livres est l'œuvre du théologien officiel de la
cour et premier bibliothécaire, Benedictus
Arias Montanus (1527–1598), qui enseignait au
collège du palais à l'instar d'autres humanistes
du cercle royal. Avec son collègue Sigüenza, il
se chargea de la disposition originale des livres,
dont la tranche dorée tournée vers l'extérieur
confère une touche homogène à la pièce. À
l'origine les armoires n'étaient pas closes ; les
grilles ont été ajoutées au XVIIIe siècle. On
rapporte que les premières caisses de livres
arrivèrent deux ans après le début des travaux
(la pose de la première pierre eut lieu en avril
1563). Elles étaient destinées aux moines de
l'ordre des Hiéronymites qui habitaient alors,
volonté du roi oblige, le couvent de la nouvelle
résidence royale. Parmi ces moines on trouve
non seulement le maître d'œuvre Antonio de
Villacastín (1512–1603), mais aussi des érudits
du plus proche entourage royal. La prestigieuse
collection personnelle du roi, un millier de
volumes environ, rejoignit l'Escurial en 1566.
Elle comprenait les manuscrits les plus anciens
de la bibliothèque dont le *Codex Aureus*. La
collection de la bibliothèque royale s'est, par la
suite, enrichie grâce aux ouvrages les plus précieux du pays remis par des humanistes comme

Ambrosio de Morales (1513–1591). En outre,
des envoyés royaux œuvraient à l'étranger, et
notamment à Venise, en France et en Flandre.
Au moment d'emménager dans le palais en
1571, on dénombrait déjà 4 000 volumes et des
ustensiles scientifiques très élaborés. On note
la présence de la sphère armillaire personnelle
du roi dans la bibliothèque dès 1593.

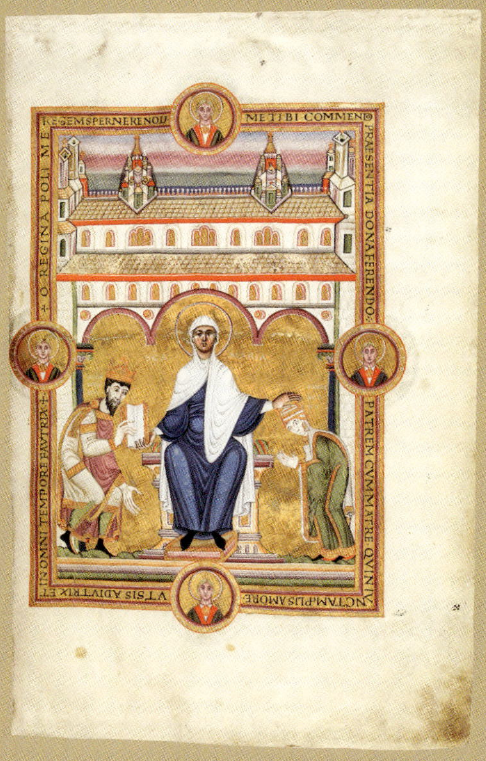

Codex Aureus Escorialiensis, 1045/46,
sig. Cod. Vitrinas 17, fol. 2v: *Pantocrator*
Codex Aureus Escorialiensis, 1045/46,
sig. Cod. Vitrinas 17, fol. 3r: *Dedication page*

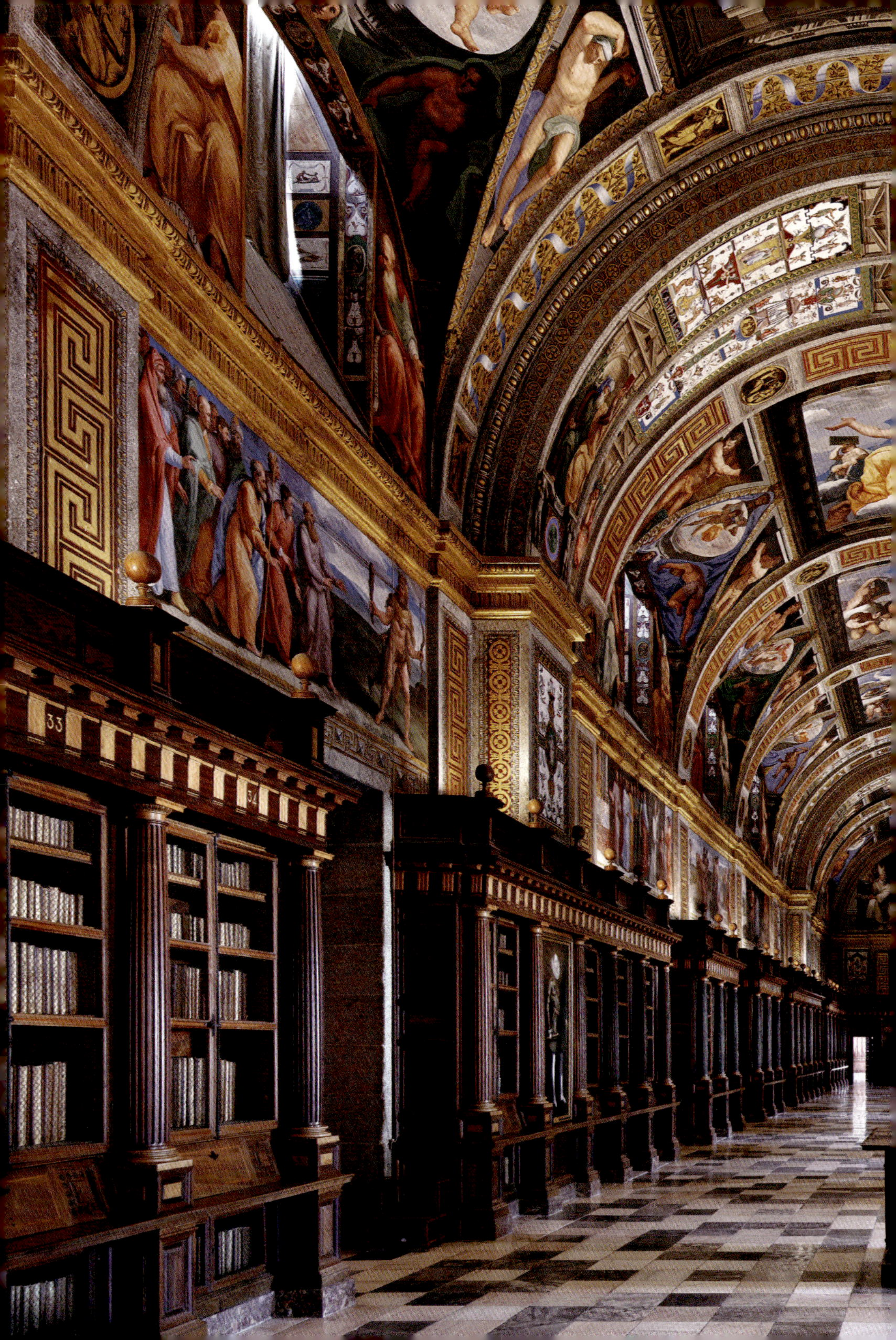

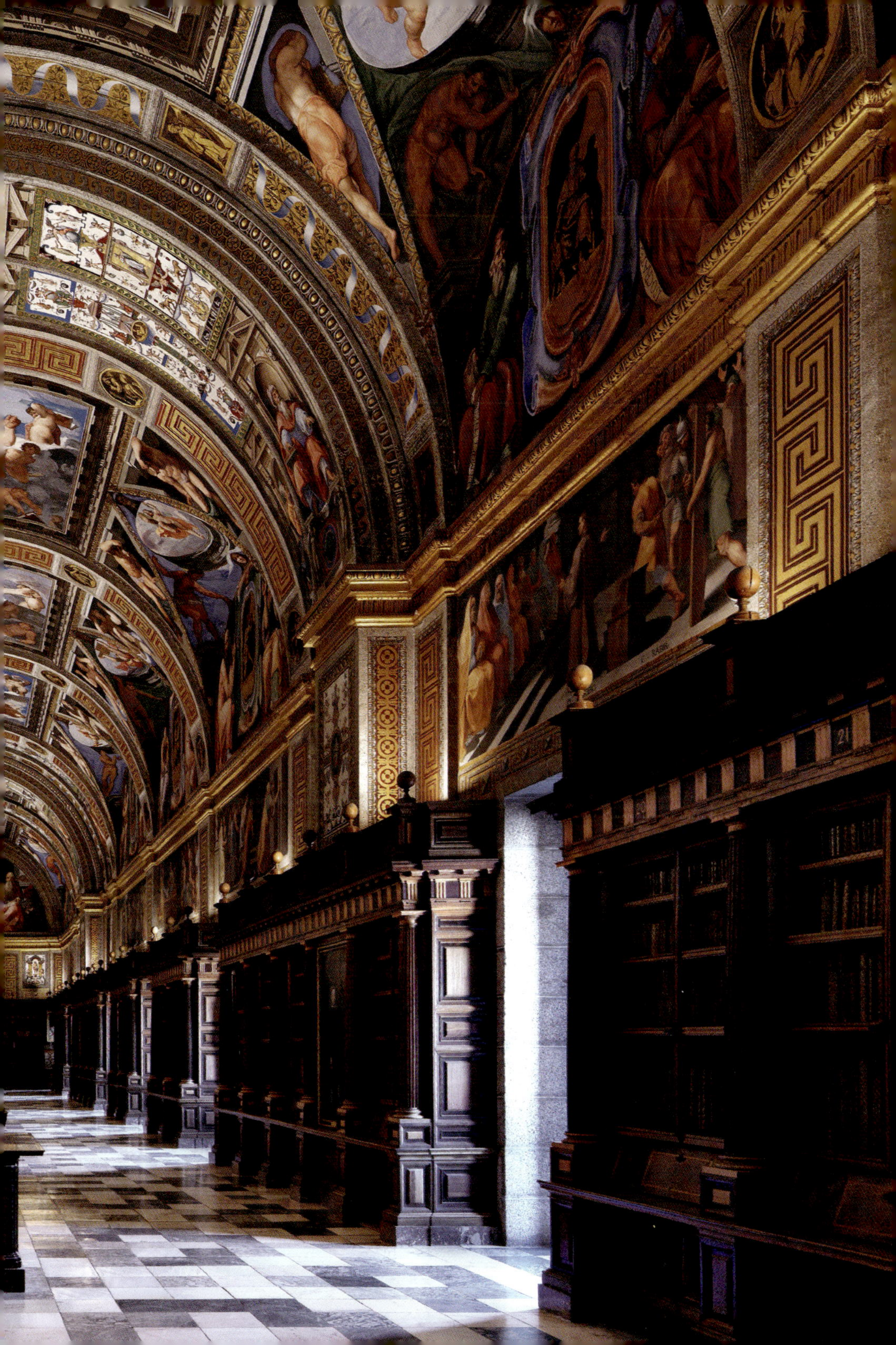

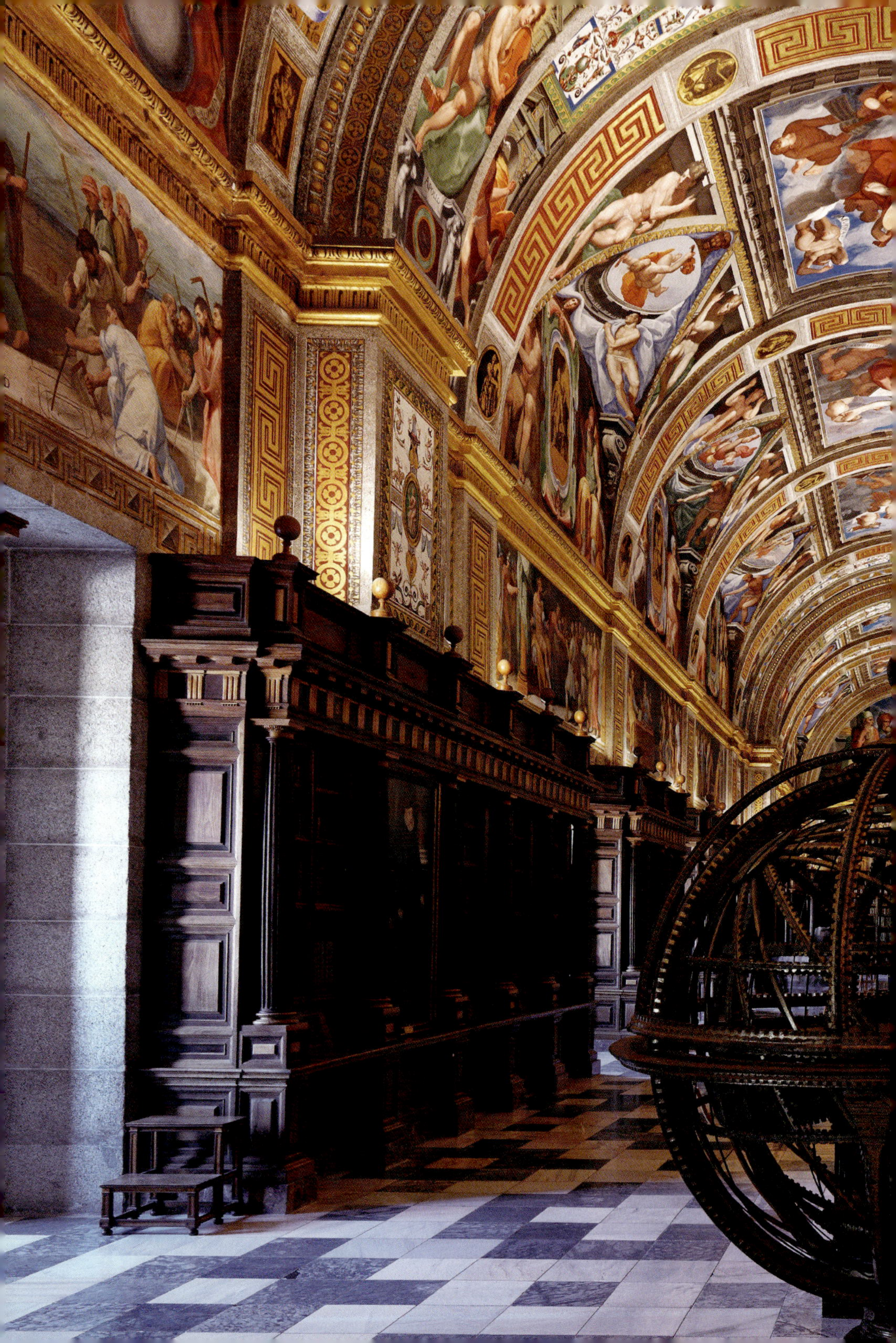

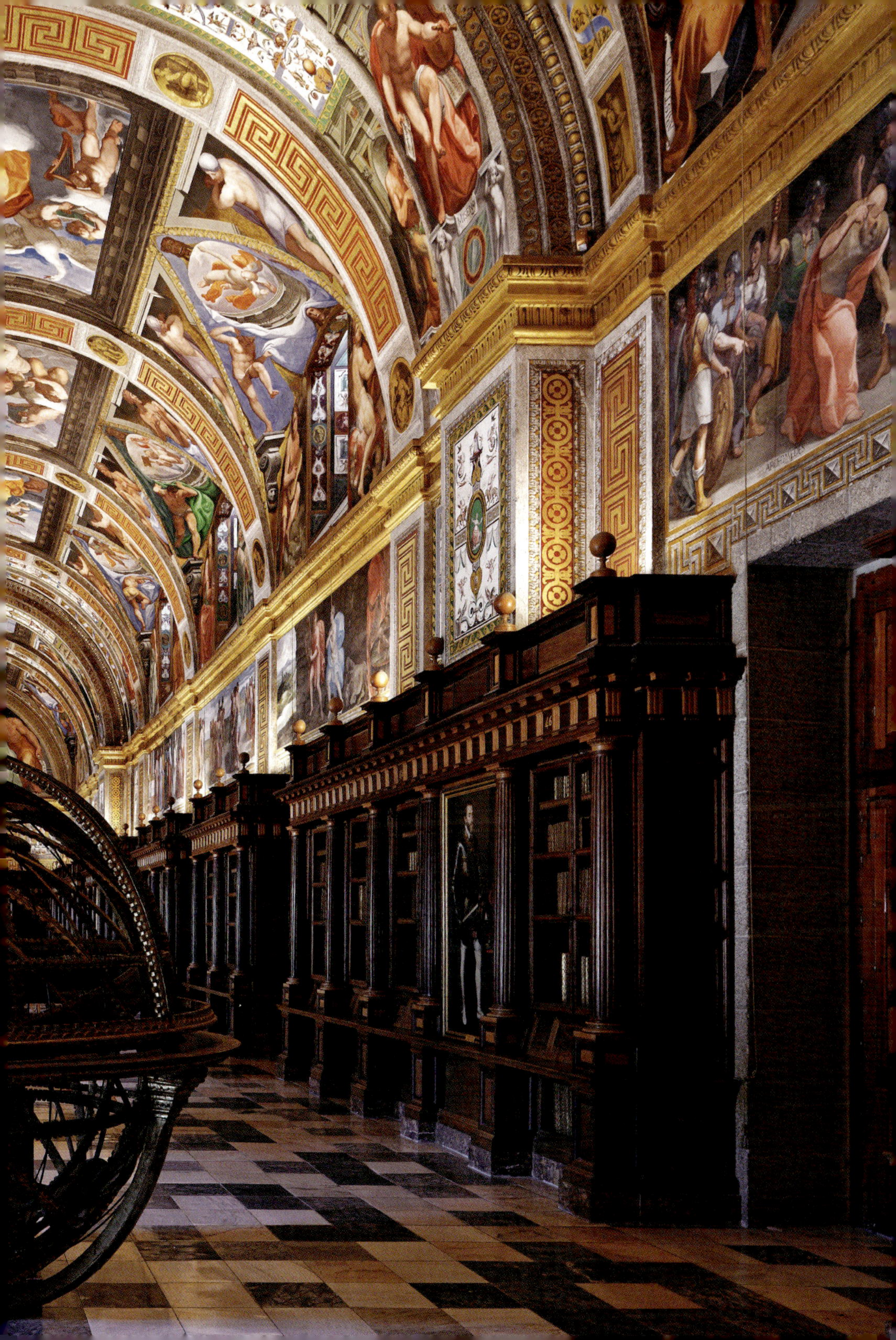

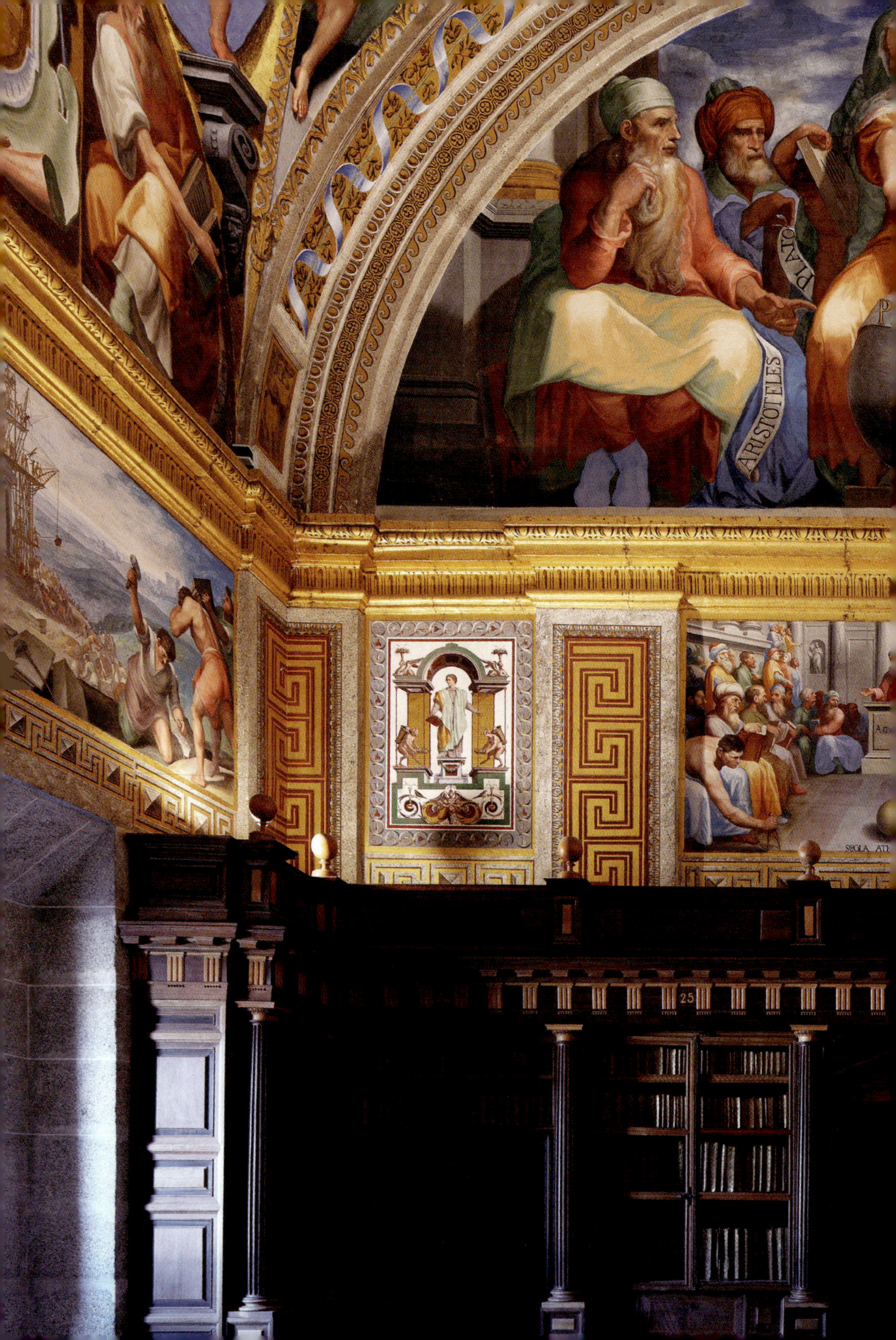

PLATO
ARISTOTELES
SCOLA ATE

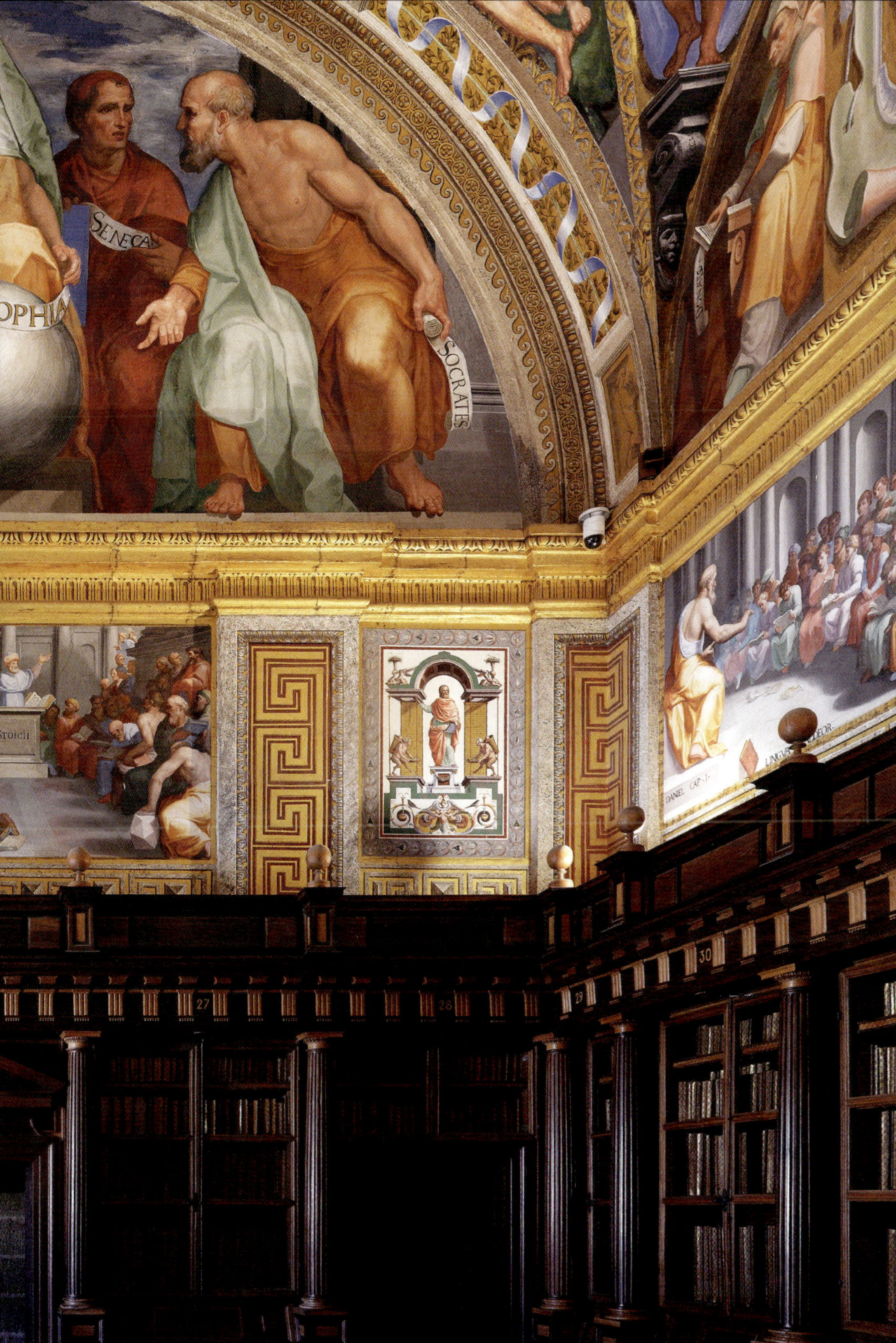
SENECA
SOCRATES
OPHIA
Stoici
DANIEL CAP. I.
27
28
29
30

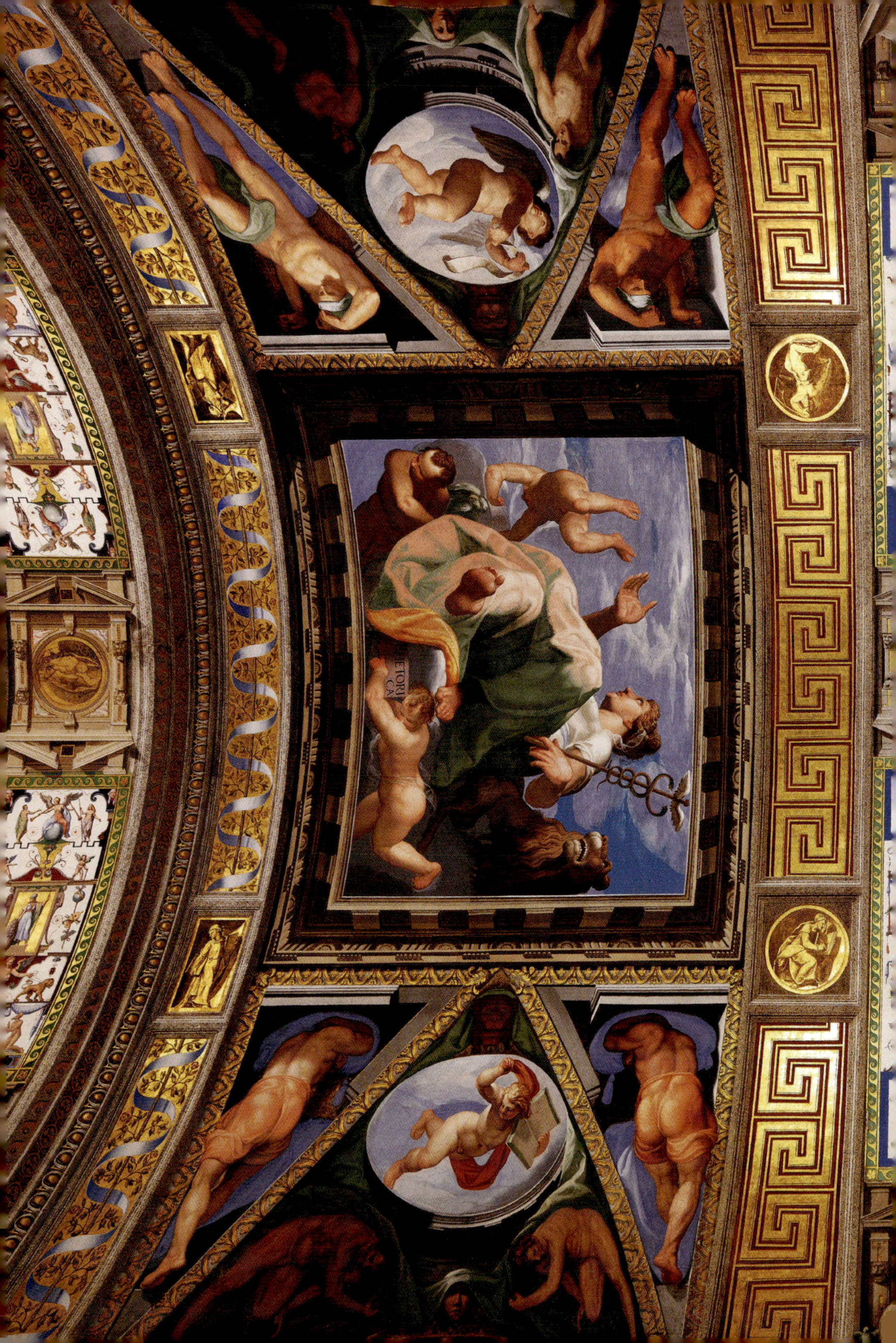

ETORI
CA

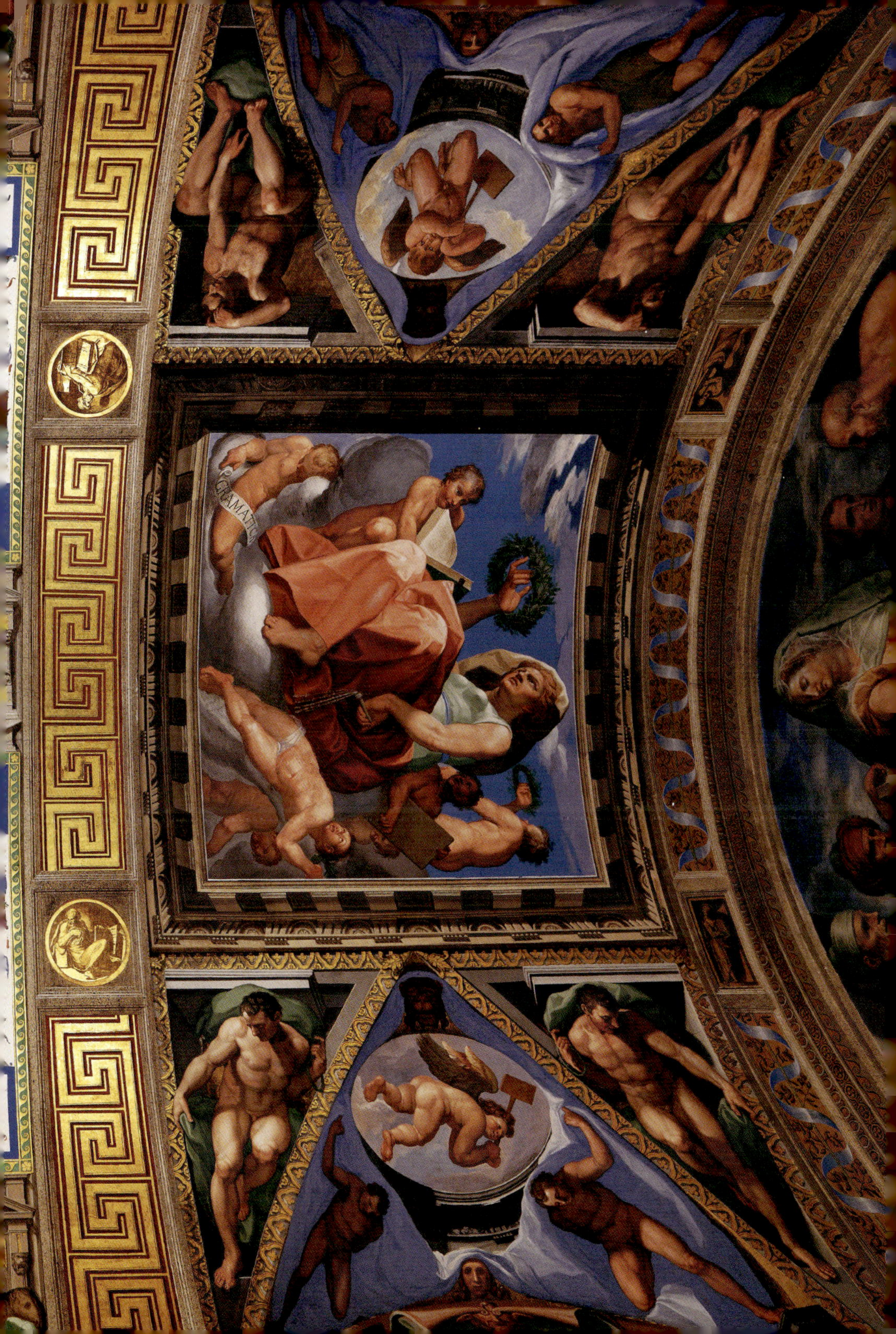

GRAMATICA

Archivo General de Indias

The General Archive of the Indies houses all the historical documents relating to the Spanish colonial empire that was erroneously identified as "India" by Christopher Columbus (1451–1506) and which later became known as the Indies. The archive was founded in 1785 as one of the administrative reforms decreed by the Bourbon Charles III (1716–1788) and overseen by "Indies minister" José Bernardo de Gálvez y Gallardo (1720–1787). The aim was to facilitate the running of Spain's overseas territories by bringing together all the pertinent documents in one place. The earliest forerunner of the General Archive of the Indies may be considered the Real Consejo de Indias (Royal Council of the Indies), founded in 1519, which was in overall charge of the executive, legislative and military affairs of the Americas, although without having a central base. The choice of Seville as the seat of the General Archive of the Indies was directly connected with the Andalusian city's traditional role as the main hub of Spanish maritime trade. From 1503, all such trade was regulated by the Casa de Contratación, a sort of chamber of commerce, which fell in turn under the jurisdiction of the Council of the Indies. The Casa de Contratación was also a centre of navigation for all the Spanish colonies, which is one of the reasons so many of the great voyages of discovery started from Seville, including those undertaken by Amerigo Vespucci (1451–1512) and Ferdinand Magellan (1480–1521). Alongside the library assembled by Columbus, which his son bequeathed to Seville cathedral in 1539 as a collection under the name of the Bibliotheca Colombina (and which is today part of the General Archive of the Indies), the city already held a substantial wealth of historical documents relating to the Spanish Empire even before the Archive was founded. It therefore seemed sensible that the remaining documents and maps scattered in other parts of Spain should all be brought to Seville, where – wholly in the spirit of the Enlightenment, whose ideas the Spanish monarch embraced – they would be accessible to scholars and the authorities alike. The ambitious project was placed in the hands of the erudite Dominican Juan Bautista Muñoz (1745–1799), who was considered the most important Spanish cosmographer of his day. He organised the wide-ranging material, which came from the royal archives in Simancas as well as from the "Indies" ministry, consulates and other institutions, according to a coherent system that is still in place today. His scholarly efforts also yielded the most comprehensive work on the history of the Spanish colonial empire, which was commissioned by the Spanish crown in 1779. Against the backdrop of the war between Spain and England that broke out the same year, Muñoz's *Historia del Nuevo Mundo* (1793) was intended to set straight, from

Founded 1785; today the central archives of the Spanish State; Casa Lonja built by Juan de Herrera from 1572
Holdings c. 43,000 volumes
Type of library research archive and library
Highlights *Inter caetera*, 1493, papal bull issued by Pope Alexander VI with the division of the world into Spanish-ruled and Portuguese-ruled hemispheres (MP-Bulas y Breves, 1); *Tratado de Tordesillas (The Treaty of Tordesillas between Spain and Portugal)*, 1494 (Patronato, 1, N.6, R.1)

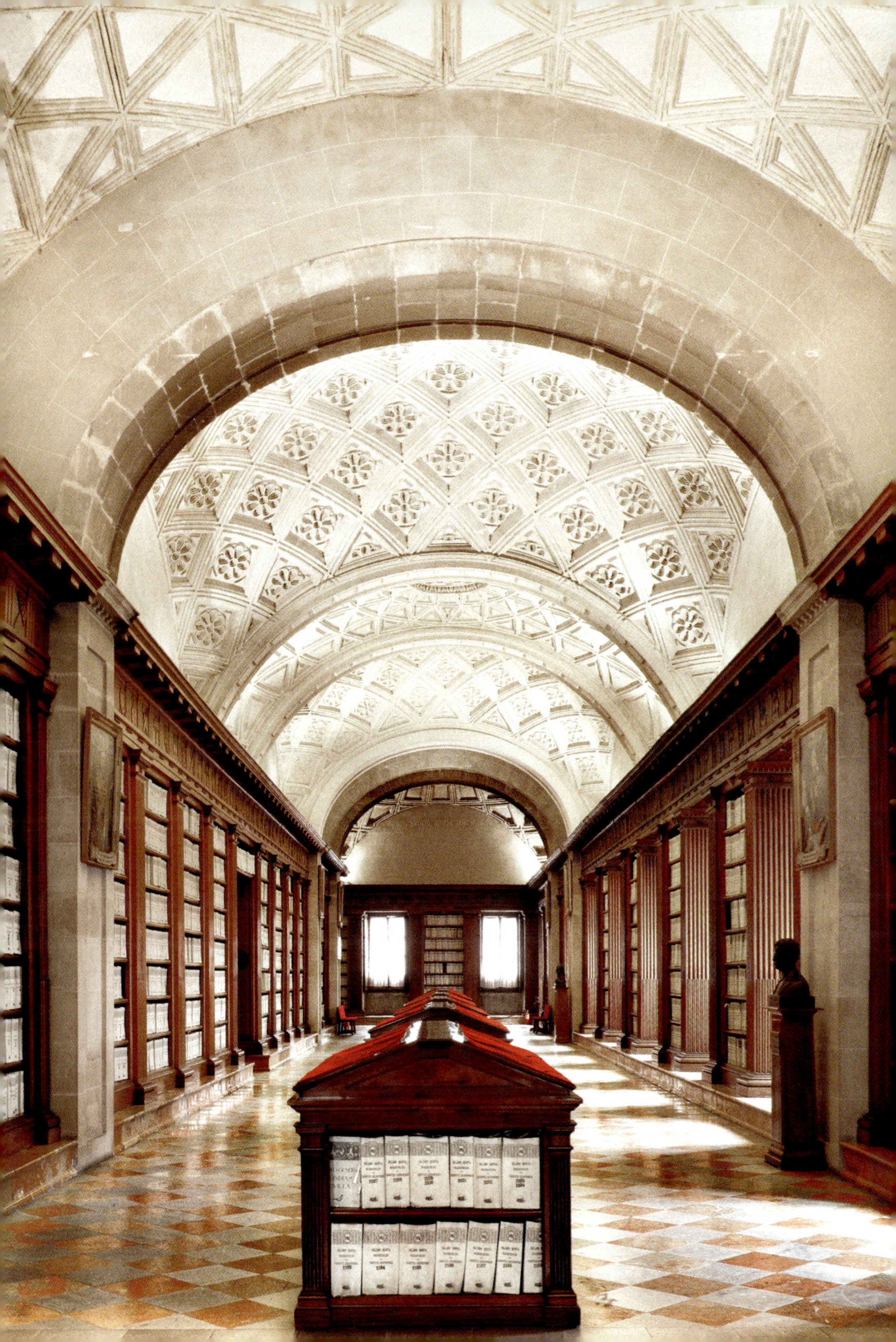

a patriotic Spanish perspective, the widely accepted version of the Spanish conquest and colonisation of the New World given by Scottish historian William Robertson in his *History of America*, published in 1777. The General Archive of the Indies was housed in the Lonja de Mercaderes, the former merchants' exchange that occupied a privileged location between the cathedral and the Alcázar. The Casa Lonja had been commissioned by Philip II and constructed from 1572 by Juan de Minjares (1520–1599) and Alonso de Vandelvira (1544–1627) using plans by the royal architect Juan de Herrera (1530–1597). The creation of the Archive was accompanied by the construction of the magnificent staircase leading up to the first floor, where the Archive is housed in long corridors vaulted with magnificent coffered ceilings. In 1987 both the building and the General Archive of the Indies were incorporated into the UNESCO list of World Heritage Sites.

❋ ❖ ❋

„Indienarchiv" wird jene Bibliothek genannt, in der alle historischen Schriftstücke zum spanischen Kolonialreich – von Kolumbus (1451–1506) fälschlicherweise, später aber aus Tradition als „Indien" bezeichnet – zusammengeführt wurden. Seine Gründung im Jahr 1785 versteht sich als eine der Verwaltungsreformen, die der Bourbone Karl III. (1716–1788) in Angriff nahm und durch seinen „Indienminister" José Bernardo de Gálvez y Gallardo (1720–1787) ausführen ließ. Ziel war es, durch das Zusammenführen aller verfügbaren Akten die Verwaltung der Überseeterritorien zu erleichtern. Als ältester Vorläufer des „Indienarchivs" gilt der Real Consejo de Indias, der bereits 1519 als höchste Autorität in Verwaltungs-, Justiz- und Militäraufgaben der amerikanischen Länder gegründet worden war, ohne allerdings über einen zentralen Sitz zu verfügen. Dass gerade die andalusische Stadt Sevilla als Sitz des „Indienarchivs" gewählt wurde, hat mit ihrer jahrhundertealten Tradition als Hauptumschlagplatz des spanischen Seehandels zu tun.

Die Geschäfte wurden seit 1503 über die Casa de Contratación, eine Art von Handelskammer, abgewickelt. Ihr stand der „Indienrat" vor, der sich auch als Navigationszentrum aller spanischen Überseeterritorien verstand. Dies war unter anderem ein Grund, weswegen die großen historischen Seereisen zumeist in Sevilla starteten, so etwa die des Amerigo Vespucci (1451–1512) oder des Ferdinand Magellan (1480–1521). Gemeinsam mit der Bibliothek des Kolumbus, die dessen Sohn als Sammlung mit dem Namen Bibliotheca Colombina 1539 der Kathedrale gestiftet hatte (und die heute Teil des „Indienarchivs" ist), verfügte die Stadt bereits vor der Gründung des „Indienarchivs" über einen umfassenden Bestand an historischen Dokumenten zum spanischen Kolonialreich. Es erschien daher naheliegend, gerade hier die restlichen, über Spanien verstreuten Schriftstücke und Pläne zusammenzuführen und ganz im Sinne der Aufklärung, von deren Ideen auch der spanische Monarch geprägt war, der Verwaltung und Forschung verfügbar zu machen. Mit der Durchführung des anspruchsvollen Projektes wurde der gelehrte Dominikaner Juan Bautista Muñoz (1745–1799) betraut, der als bedeutendster spanischer Kosmograf seiner Zeit galt. Er gab dem vielfältigen Material, das aus den königlichen Archiven in Simancas ebenso wie aus dem Staatssekretariat der „indischen" Provinzen sowie anderen Instituten stammte, eine sinnvolle und bis heute gültige Ordnung. Seinen Forschungen entsprang aber auch das umfassendste Werk zur Geschichte des spanischen Kolonialreichs, mit dem er 1779 von der spanischen Krone beauftragt worden war. Vor dem Hintergrund des im selben Jahr ausgebrochenen spanisch-englischen Konfliktes verstand sich seine *Historia del Nuevo Mundo* (1793) als spanische Gegenbetrachtung zu der bis dahin gültigen und ab 1777 veröffentlichten *History of America* des Schotten William Robertson. Sitz des „Indienarchivs" wurde die traditionsreiche Händlerbörse von Sevilla (Lonja de Mercaderes), die der königliche Architekt Juan de Herrera (1530–1597) ab 1572

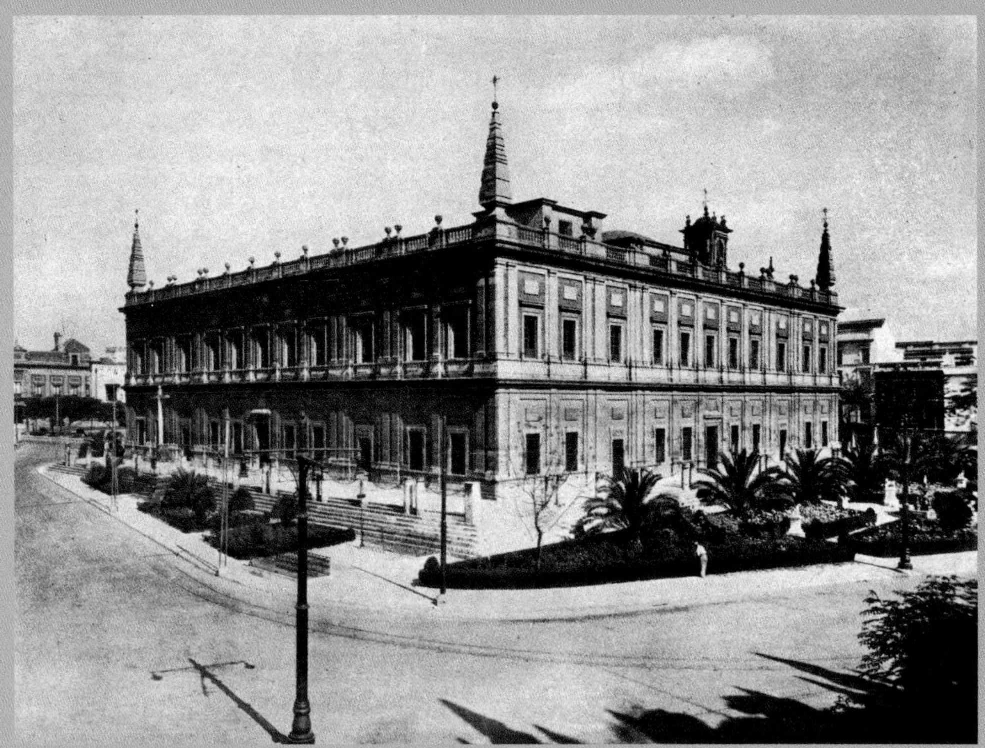

Archivo General de Indias, view from the outside

an privilegierter Stelle zwischen der Kathedrale und dem Alcázar im Auftrag Philipps II. plante. Zeitgleich zur Einrichtung des „Indienarchivs" erhielt der von Juan de Minjares (1520–1599) und Alonso de Vandelvira (1544–1627) ausgeführte Bau seine repräsentative Freitreppe, die das Obergeschoss erschließt. Dort ist in langen Gängen, die mit prächtigen Kassettendecken überwölbt sind, das Archiv untergebracht. 1987 wurden sowohl das Gebäude als auch das „Indienarchiv" von der UNESCO zum Weltkulturerbe erklärt.

✳✳✳

La bibliothèque nommée « Archives des Indes » rassemble tous les écrits et fragments historiques relatifs à l'Empire colonial espagnol que Christophe Colomb qualifia de façon erronée d'« Indes », appellation qui cependant perdura. Elle fut fondée en 1785 dans le cadre d'une réforme administrative entreprise par Charles III d'Espagne (1716–1788) et menée par son « secrétaire des Indes » José Bernardo de Gálvez y Gallardo (1720–1787). Son but, en centralisant tous les documents disponibles, était d'alléger l'administration des territoires d'outre-mer. L'ancêtre des « Archives des Indes » n'est autre que le Real Consejo de Indias. Sans disposer de siège central, ce conseil existant depuis 1519 faisait autorité dans l'administration, la juridiction et les actions militaires des missions conduites sur le continent américain. La capitale andalouse fut choisie pour siège en raison de sa réputation historique de port de marchandises et de plateforme du négoce espagnol. Les affaires se réglaient depuis 1503 au sein d'une sorte de chambre de commerce nommée Casa de Contratación. Celle-ci était chapeautée par le « Conseil des Indes », qui se considérait aussi comme le centre de navigation de tous les territoires espagnols d'outre-mer. Cela explique en partie pourquoi bon nombre de grands voyages historiques eurent Séville pour lieu de départ, comme par exemple ceux d'Amerigo Vespucci (1451–1512) et de Ferdinand Magellan (1480–1521). La Ville disposait déjà (avant la fondation des « Archives des Indes ») de fonds extraordinaires, riches en informations sur les colonies espagnoles, notamment avec la bibliothèque de Christophe Colomb, une collection nommée Bibliotheca Colombina que son fils offrit à la cathédrale en 1539 et qui a rejoint les « Archives des Indes ». Il semblait donc approprié d'y rassembler les autres écrits et plans dispersés dans toute l'Espagne et, tout à fait dans l'esprit des Lumières qui avait marqué le monarque espagnol, de les mettre à disposition de l'administration et de la recherche. Le dominicain lettré Juan Bautista Muñoz (1745–1799), réputé comme le plus grand cosmographe espagnol de son temps, eut pour charge de mener à bien l'ambitieux projet. Il administra les diverses ressources en provenance des archives royales de Simancas, du secrétariat national des provinces « indiennes »

et d'autres institutions et leur conféra leur ordonnancement actuel. Ses recherches ont aussi donné naissance à l'ouvrage le plus complet sur l'histoire de l'Empire colonial espagnol, que la Couronne lui commanda en 1779. Étant donné qu'un conflit hispano-anglais éclata la même année, son *Historia del Nuevo Mundo* (1793) peut se lire comme une réaction patriotique espagnole à l'*History of America* de l'Écossais William Robertson, publiée en 1777 et encore en usage à l'époque. Les « Archives des Indes » élurent domicile à la Bourse de commerce de Séville dite aussi Lonja de Mercaderes, conçue par l'architecte de cour Juan de Herrera (1530–1597) à partir de 1572 sur un emplacement privilégié entre la cathédrale et l'Alcázar sur commande de Philippe II. Au moment même où les « Archives des Indes » sont installées, l'édifice réalisé par Juan de Minjares (1520–1599) et Alonso de Vandelvira (1544–1627) se voit doté d'un escalier monumental permettant d'accéder à l'étage supérieur. C'est dans des galeries parées de splendides voûtes à caissons que les archives furent transférées. Le bâtiment et les « Archives des Indes » font partie du patrimoine de l'humanité de l'UNESCO depuis 1987.

Tratado de Tordesillas, 1494,
sig. Patronato, 1, N.6, R.1, fol. 3

Dom Joham per g̃ça de ds
Rey de purtugual e dos alguarues daquem e dalem mar em a
fríca e Snõr de guinee. A quanto esta nossa carta uirem fa
zemos sabr que p̃ Ruy de sousa Snõr das villas de sagre e bi
rugel E dom Joham de sousa seu filho nosso almotacee moor. E Johan̄
ado anes dalmada Cõr des frõís cuuees em nossa corte e do nosso desembargo. todos do
nosso consselho que enuiamos com nossa embaixada e poder aos muy altos e muy excelentes
e poderosos dom fernando e dona Jsabel per graça de ds Rey e Raynha de castella de liam da
ragũ de ezilia degrada e c̃ nossos muyto amados e prezados Jrmãaos. sobre a deferẽ
ça do que anos e aelles pertençe. do que tee sete dias do mes de Junho dafeitura desta Capi
tulaçom estaua por descobrir no mar oceano. foy tractado e capitulado por nos e ẽ nosso
nome per v̄tude de nosso poder com os dittos Rey e Raynha de castella nossos Jrmãaos e
com dom anrriqueanrrĩqz seu mordomo moor e dom gotere de caidenes Comendador moor
de liam e seu contador moor. E o doutor Ro maldonado todos do seu consselho E em seu no
me p̃ v̄tude do seu poder. Na qual dita capitulaçã os ditos nossos embaixadores e procu
radores antre as outras cousas prometerã que dentro de certo termo em ella contheudo
Nos outorguariamos confirmariamos Juraríamos retificariamos e aprouariamos a dita
Capitullaçã p̃ nossa pesoa E querendo nos asy e comprindo todo oque asy ẽ nosso no
me foy assentado capitulado e outorgado acerca do suso dito. Mandamos traz ante nos
a dita scriptura da dita Capitulaçõ e asento pa a ueer e examinar. o theor da qual de
v̄bo a uerbo he este que se segue. **Em nome de dos** todo poderosso padre
filho e spũ sancto tres pesoas realmente distintas e apartidas e hũa soo essencia di
uina. Manifesto e notoryo seia A todos quantos este pub̃co stormento virem como
na uilla de toidesilhas a sete dias do mes de Junho anno do nascemento de nosso
Snõr Jhũ xpõ de mil quatrcentos nouenta e quatro annos em presença de nos os secre
tarios scripuãaes e notarios pub̃cos adiante scriptos stando presentes os honrrados dõ
anrriqueanrrĩqz mordomo moor dos muy altos e muy poderosos prinçepes os Snõres
dom fernando e dona Jsabel p graça de ds Rey e Raynha de castella de liam daragũ
de ezilia de grada e c̃ E dom gotere de caidenes contador moor dos dittos Snõres
Rey e Raynha E o doutor Ro maldonado todos do consselho dos ditos Snõres Rey e
Raynha de castella de lion daragam de ezilia de grada e c̃ seus procuradores abas
tantes de hũa parte. E os honrrados Ruy de sousa Snõr de sagres e de birugel

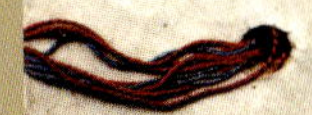

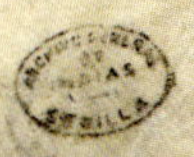

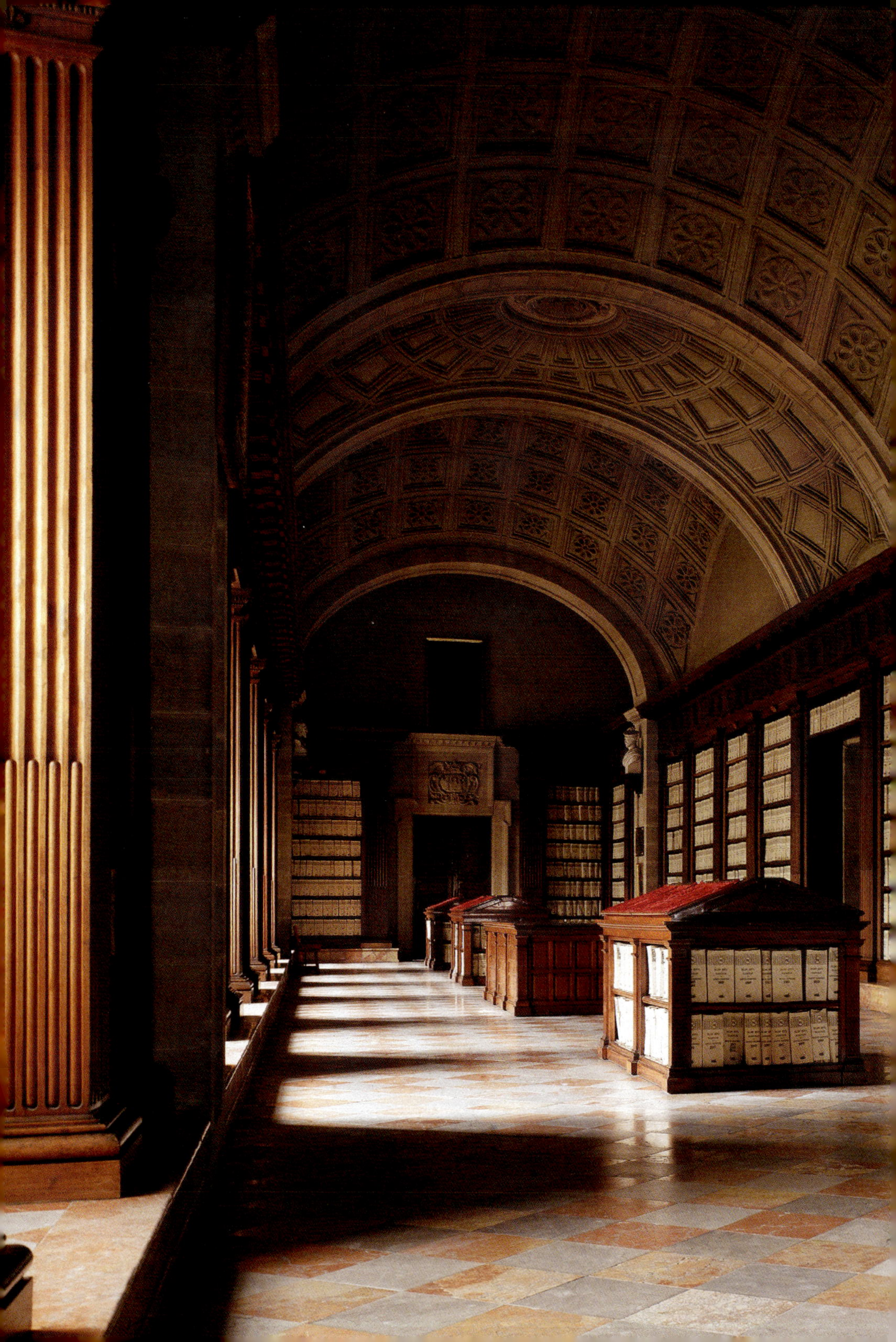

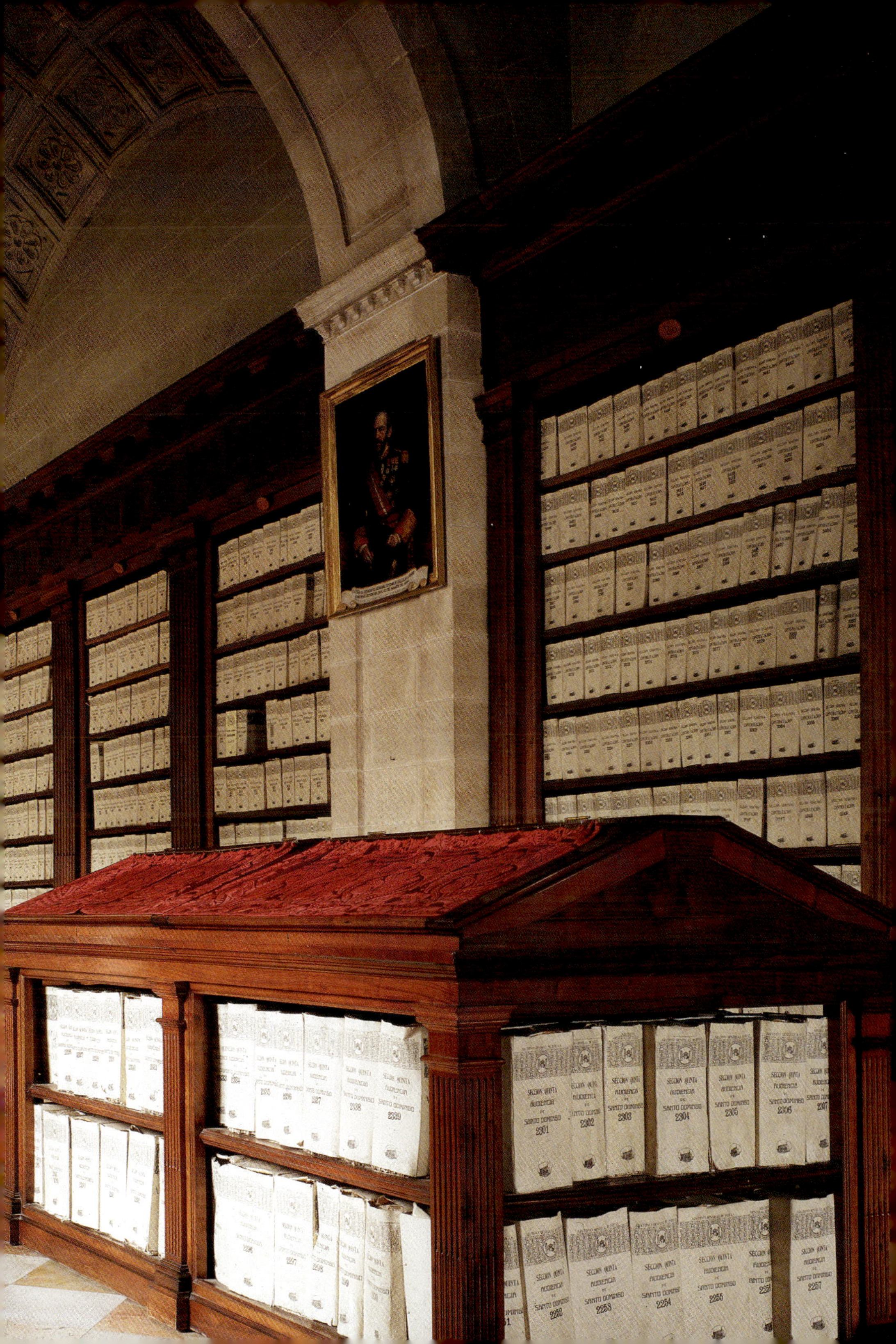

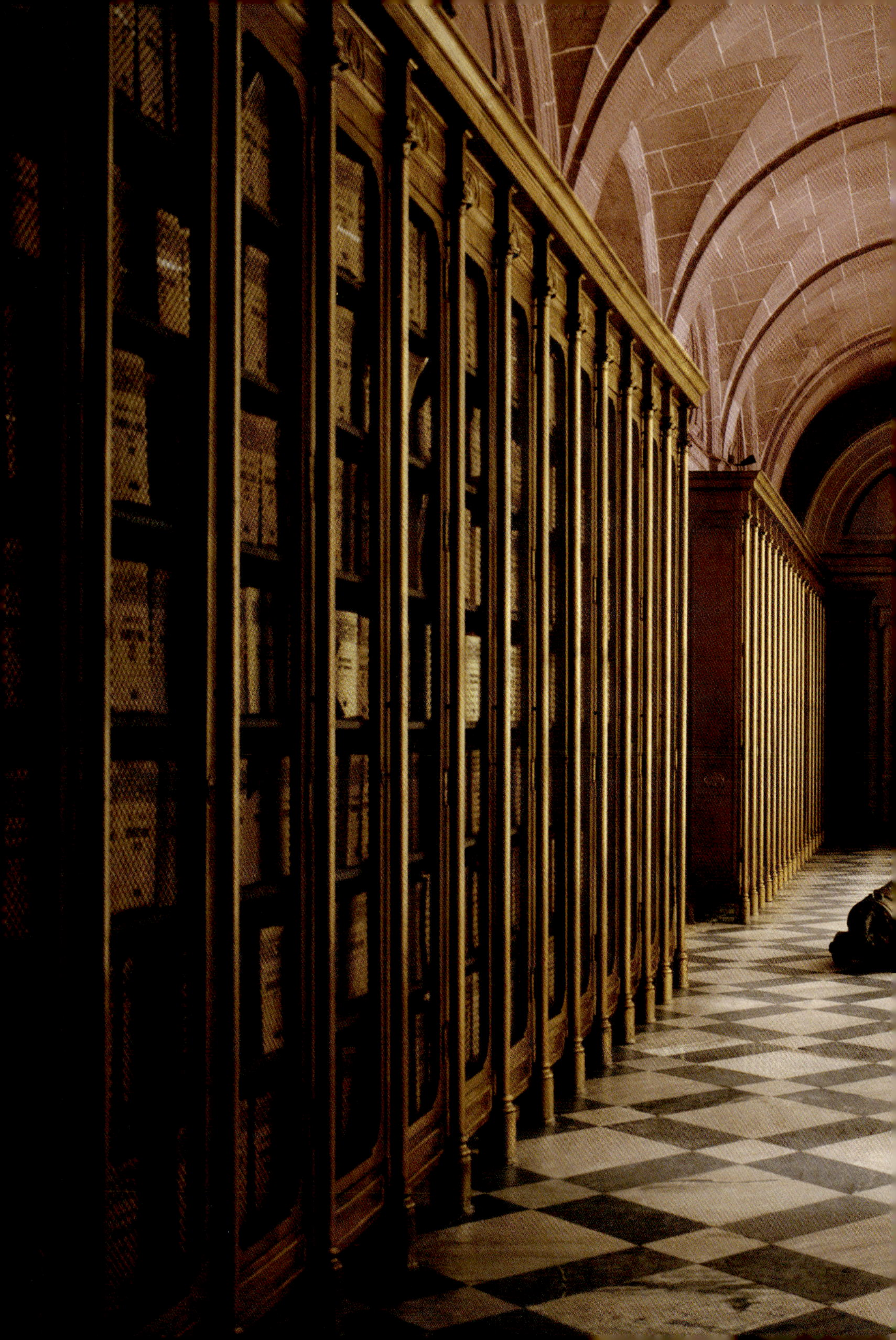

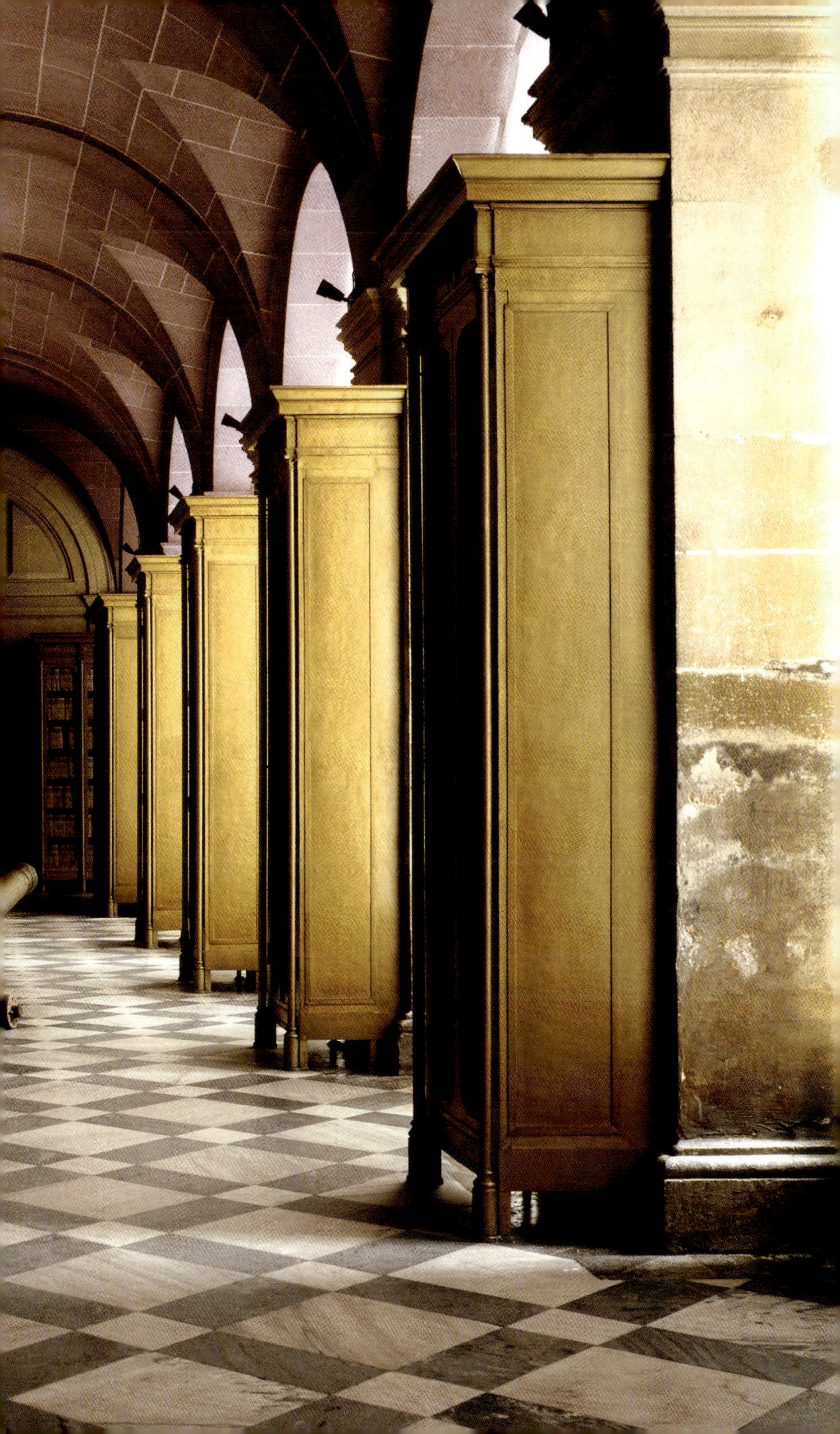

Biblioteca Joanina

Built on the site of a Moorish citadel, parts of which can still be seen on the north side of the complex, the Biblioteca Joanina has been considered a fortress of knowledge and learning since its foundation by John (João) V (1689–1750) of the ruling house of Braganza, after whom it is named. Its origins date back to 1537, when John III (1502–1557) decided that his royal palace at Coimbra – originally built during the Umayyad caliphate and home to the kings of Portugal since the 12th century – should become the new seat of the University of Lisbon. In addition to the rooms designated for lectures and classes, the king allocated a cloakroom just off today's Grand Hall (Sala dos Capelos) for use as the university library, which at that time comprised some 100 codices. At the same time he appointed the historian Fernão Lopes Castanheda (c. 1500–1559) as its first librarian. As the royal residence was gradually relinquished, the university expanded to fill the whole of the former fortified *alcáçova*. St Peter's College was also established in the western Gerais wing of the four-winged complex. The decision by John V to build a new library was probably prompted by an acute shortage of space, and in fact the proposals for an extension put forward by the rector were rejected in favour of the king's ambitious scheme to create a brand-new structure in the Baroque style at the centre of the royal complex. The foundation stone was laid on 17 July 1717 and by 1728 the library was largely finished. In line with the plans drawn up by John V in consultation with a team of artists and consultants, the library took the shape of a tall new building erected on top of the old prison built in the 14th century by John I (1357–1433). Entry is gained from the south side via the Minerva Steps, named after the goddess of wisdom. Above the stacks in the basement and the professors' offices on the mezzanine, the books are housed in three magnificent rooms that have the character of a palace library. Their iconography and décor culminate in an imposing portrait of the royal patron by court artist Domenico Duprà (1689–1770). Under the supervision of sculptor Claude de Laprade (1682–1728), who was responsible for the sculptural decoration, artists and artisans worked according to directions from the king in order to ensure that his grandiose vision was realised. Allegories of royal magnanimity and far-sightedness are found throughout the entire decorative programme, which is exemplified in cartouches with inscriptions, sculptural features, magnificent wood-carvings and illusionistic ceiling frescos with large numbers of figures. The bookcases, which extend right up

Founded 1717; built 1717–1728 by Gaspar Ferreira
Holdings c. 250,000 volumes
Type of library royal library in a university setting
Highlights *Tábuas dos roteiros da Índia de D. João de Castro (Charts of the Rutters of Dom João de Castro)*, mid-16th century, collection of watercolour illustrations (Cofre 33); Pietro Andrea Mattioli, *Kreutterbuch des hochgelehrten und weitberühmten Herrn D. Petri Andreae Matthioli* (Herbal), Frankfurt a. M., 1590; Fernão Mendez Pinto, *Peregrinaçao* (Japanese travelogue, 1578), first published by Pedro Craesbeeck, Lisbon, 1614

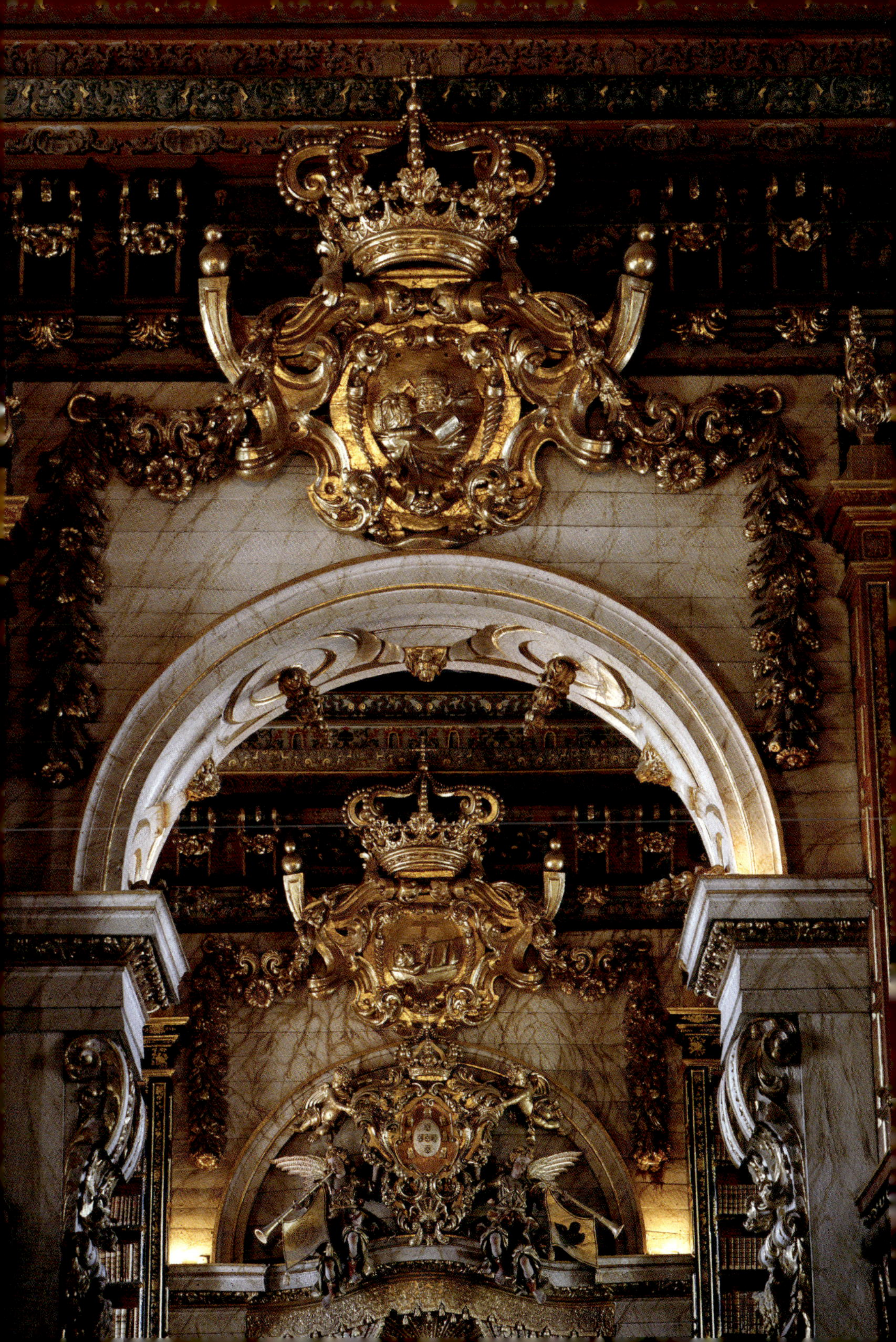

to the ceiling and are divided into two storeys by galleries, were carved by Gaspar Ferreira (active in Coimbra from 1718, died 1761), who also oversaw the building works, and were decorated by Manuel da Silva with chinoiseries lavishly detailed in gold. The desks crafted by Francesco Realdino from precious exotic woods also date from the same period. Painters António Simões Ribeiro (died 1755) and Vicente Nunes were summoned from Lisbon to create the ceiling paintings that harmoniously conclude the library's imposing interiors. In order to facilitate scholarly research on a broad scale in the spirit of the Enlightenment, the library's holdings were increased substantially. Alongside books on the humanities, theology, philosophy and law, sections on medicine, geography and history were established. Despite his energetic personal commitment, however, John V did not succeed in his enlightened aim to lay down the fundamental reforms for this conservative institution and make the library, together with the new reference materials it contained, accessible to the public. This was only achieved in 1772 under Joseph I (1714–1777) and his powerful minister, the Marquis of Pombal. John nevertheless created a monument for posterity in the Joanine Library that today bears his name.

❋❋❋

Auf den Grundfesten einer arabischen Zitadelle errichtet, die sich in Teilen noch an der Nordseite des Gebäudekomplexes erhalten hat, gilt die Bibliothek seit ihrer Gründung durch Johann (João) V. (1689–1750) aus dem Haus Braganza, nach dem sie benannt ist, als Hochburg des Wissens und der Lehre. Ihre Geschichte reicht bis in das Jahr 1537 zurück, als die portugiesischen Könige, die seit dem 12. Jahrhundert in dem prächtigen, ursprünglich von den Umayyaden errichteten Kastell residierten, den Sitz der Universität von Lissabon nach Coimbra verlegten. Neben dem „Studium Generale" mit seinen Lehr- und Studiensälen wurde auch dessen Bibliothek,

die damals etwa 100 Kodizes umfasste, in den Königspalast integriert. Johann III. (1502–1557) wies ihr die Garderobe zu, die zu Seiten des großen Salons liegt, der heute als Sala dos Capelos oder Doktorensaal bezeichnet wird. Gleichzeitig ernannte er den Historiker Fernão Lopes Castanheda (um 1500–1559) zum ersten Bibliothekar. Im Zuge der Auflösung der Königsresidenz weitete die Universität ihren Sitz auf das gesamte Areal des ehemaligen Alcáçova aus. Im sogenannten Gerais, dem Westtrakt der Vierflügelanlage, entstand außerdem das Sankt Peterskolleg. Akuter Platzmangel war in der Folge mit ein Grund, weswegen der barocke Bibliotheksneubau in Angriff genommen wurde. Die Erweiterungspläne für die Bibliothek vonseiten des Rektors wurden von den hochgesteckten Bauplänen des Königs übertrumpft, der einen Neubau im Zentrum des Hofareals wünschte. Die Grundsteinlegung fand am 17. Juli 1717 statt, 1728 war die Bibliothek im Wesentlichen vollendet. Gemäß Joãos Plänen, die er gemeinsam mit einem Team von Künstlern und Beratern erarbeitete, entstand dort auf den Grundmauern eines von Johann I. (1357–1433) im 14. Jahrhundert errichteten Gefängnisses der hoch aufragende Neubau, der über die nach der Göttin der Weisheit benannte Minerva-Treppe im Süden erschlossen wird. Über den Depoträumen im Bereich der Fundamente und den Büroräumen der Professoren im Mezzanin wurde eine Folge von drei Büchersälen angeordnet, die den Charakter einer Palastbibliothek haben. Ikonografie und Dekor kulminieren im raumbeherrschenden Porträt des Auftraggebers, einem Werk des königlichen Hofmalers Domenico Duprà (1689–1770). Um höchstes Anspruchsniveau zu gewährleisten, arbeiteten Bauleitung und Kunsthandwerker nach königlicher Weisung, koordiniert von dem Bildhauer Claude de Laprade (1682–1728), der für den Skulpturenschmuck verantwortlich zeichnet. Allegorien königlicher Freigiebigkeit und Weitsicht prägen das gesamte dekorative Programm, das in

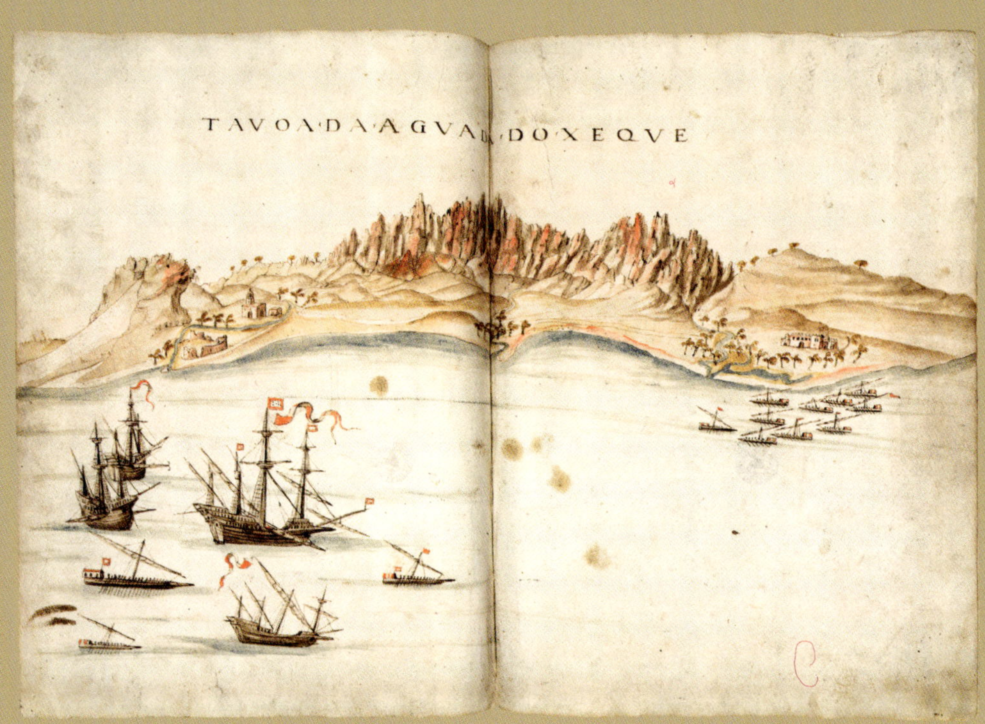

Tábuas dos roteiros da Índia de D. João de Castro, mid-16th century, sig. Cofre 33, fol. 64–65: *Tavoa de Aguada do Xeque*

den Inschriftenkartuschen, der Bauplastik, den prächtigen Schnitzwerken und den vielfigurigen illusionistischen Deckenfresken exemplifiziert wird. Die bis zur Decke reichenden Bücherschränke, die von umlaufenden Galerien in zwei Geschosse getrennt sind, wurden von Gaspar Ferreira (in Coimbra tätig ab 1718, gestorben 1761), der auch für die Bauleitung verantwortlich war, geschnitzt und von Manuel da Silva mit kostbar in Gold gefassten Chinoiserien dekoriert. Auch die von Francesco Realdino aus wertvollen exotischen Hölzern gefertigten Arbeitstische entstammen der Bauzeit. Die aus Lissabon berufenen Maler António Simões Ribeiro (verstorben 1755) und Vicente Nunes fertigten die Deckenmalereien, die die imposante Raumfolge harmonisch abschließen. Um eine im Sinne der Aufklärung breit angelegte Forschungstätigkeit zu ermöglichen, wurde der Buchbestand damals um ein Vielfaches erweitert. Neben Büchern zu den humanistischen Wissenschaften, Theologie, Philosophie und Recht entstanden neue Abteilungen zu Medizin, Geografie und Geschichte. In seiner Zielsetzung, die konservativ ausgerichtete Institution grundlegend zu reformieren und nicht nur neuen Lehren, sondern im Sinne der Aufklärung auch der Öffentlichkeit verfügbar zu machen, ist Johann V. aber trotz seines persönlichen Engagements gescheitert. Diese Reformen konnten erst 1772 unter Joseph I. (1714–1777) und seinem mächtigen Minister, dem Marquis von Pombal, verwirklicht werden. In dem später nach ihm benannten Bibliotheksbau hat er sich aber für die Nachwelt ein Denkmal gesetzt.

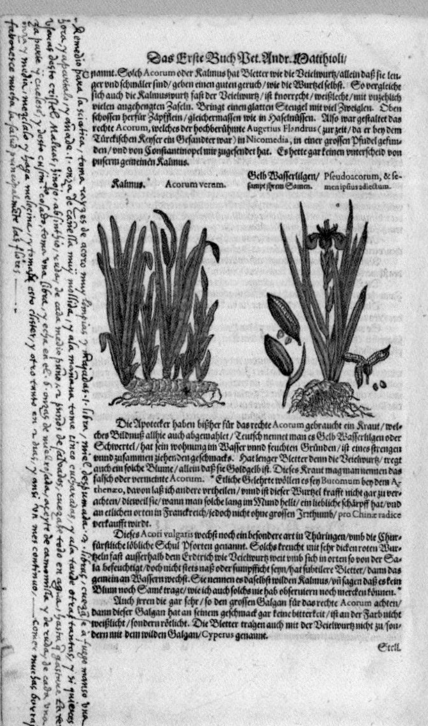

Érigée sur les fondements d'une citadelle arabe, dont certaines parties ont été conservées comme le côté nord de l'enceinte, la bibliothèque se veut, depuis sa fondation par Jean V de Portugal de la Maison de Bragance (1689–1750), le bastion du savoir et de l'érudition. Son histoire remonte à l'année 1537, lorsque les rois du Portugal, qui résidaient depuis le XIIe siècle dans le magnifique château fort à l'origine édifié par les Umayyades, décidèrent de transférer le siège de l'université de Lisbonne à Coimbra. Outre l'université médiévale avec ses salles d'étude et d'enseignement, la bibliothèque, qui comptait alors près de cent codex, fut intégrée au palais royal. Jean III de Portugal (1502–1557) lui assigna le vestiaire jouxtant le grand salon aujourd'hui appelé Sala dos Capelos (ou salle des doctorants). Il en profita pour nommer l'historien Fernão Lopes Castanheda (vers 1500–1559) premier bibliothécaire. Dans le cadre de la suppression de la résidence royale, le siège de l'université s'étendit à la totalité de l'ancienne *alcáçova*. Dans l'aile occidentale nommée Gerais de l'édifice à plan carré, on bâtit de surcroît le collège Saint-Pierre. En raison d'un sérieux manque de place, on décida la construction d'un nouveau bâtiment baroque pour la bibliothèque. Les projets d'agrandissement du recteur pour cette dernière furent toutefois contrecarrés par les ambitions de la royauté qui projetait un nouveau bâtiment au centre de la cour. La première pierre fut posée le 17 juillet 1717, la bibliothèque quasiment achevée en 1728. Suivant les plans de Jean, qu'il élabora avec une équipe d'artistes et de conseillers, on éleva à cet endroit, sur les fondations d'une prison érigée par Jean Ier (1357–1433) au XIVe siècle, le nouveau bâtiment d'une belle hauteur avec accès au sud par les escaliers dits « de Minerve » en hommage à la déesse romaine de la sagesse. Au-dessus des salles de dépôt situées au sous-sol et des bureaux des professeurs à l'entresol fut aménagée une enfilade de trois salles de lecture qui présente les caractéristiques d'une bibliothèque palatiale. Le décor iconographique culmine dans le portrait du commanditaire qui domine l'enfilade, une œuvre du peintre de cour Domenico Duprà (1689–1770). Afin de garantir une excellence d'exécution, le maître d'ouvrage et les artisans d'art ont travaillé sous l'égide du roi, orchestrés par le sculpteur Claude de Laprade (1682–1728) qui était responsable de l'ensemble du décor sculpté. La libéralité et la clairvoyance royales s'illustrent dans le décor tout entier par le biais d'allégories dans les formes architecturales, les inscriptions sur cartouche, l'ouvrage délicatement sculpté et les trompe-l'œil à personnages multiples. Les corps de bibliothèque grimpant jusqu'au plafond et séparés par une coursive sont de Gaspar Ferreira (actif à Coimbra à partir de 1718, décédé en 1761), qui était également maître d'ouvrage. L'œuvre sculptée et les précieuses incrustations d'or dans le goût chinois sont de Manuel da Silva. Les tables de travail que Francesco Realdino a réalisées

dans des bois exotiques de grande valeur
datent aussi de l'époque de la construction. Les
fresques du plafond, exécutées par les peintres
António Simões Ribeiro (décédé en 1755) et
Vicente Nunes que l'on a fait venir de Lisbonne,
parachèvent l'harmonie des trois salles. Afin
d'offrir une activité de recherche digne des
Lumières, le fonds littéraire fut alors considérablement augmenté. Outre les ouvrages relatifs
aux humanités, à la théologie, à la philosophie
et au droit, de nouvelles sections dédiées à la
médecine, à la géographie et à l'histoire ont
été créées. Malgré toute l'énergie déployée,
Jean V de Portugal échoua dans sa mission
personnelle qui ne consistait pas seulement à
remanier l'institution conservatrice au moyen
de nouveaux enseignements, mais aussi à
la rendre accessible à tous dans l'esprit des
Lumières. Ces réformes n'ont pu se faire qu'en
1772, sous Joseph Ier de Portugal (1714–1777) et
son puissant ministre, le marquis de Pombal.
Il n'en demeure pas moins que l'édifice qui
porte son nom est une réussite, un monument
pour la postérité.

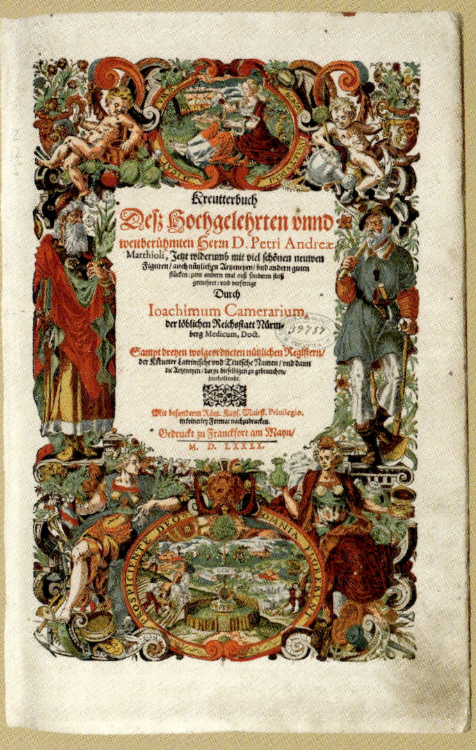

Pietro Andrea Mattioli, *Kreutterbuch*,
Frankfurt a. M., 1590, p. 3, left: *Sweet flag (Acorus
calamus)*, right: *Yellow flag (Iris pseudacorus)*

Pietro Andrea Mattioli, *Kreutterbuch*,
Frankfurt a. M., 1590: *Frontispiece*

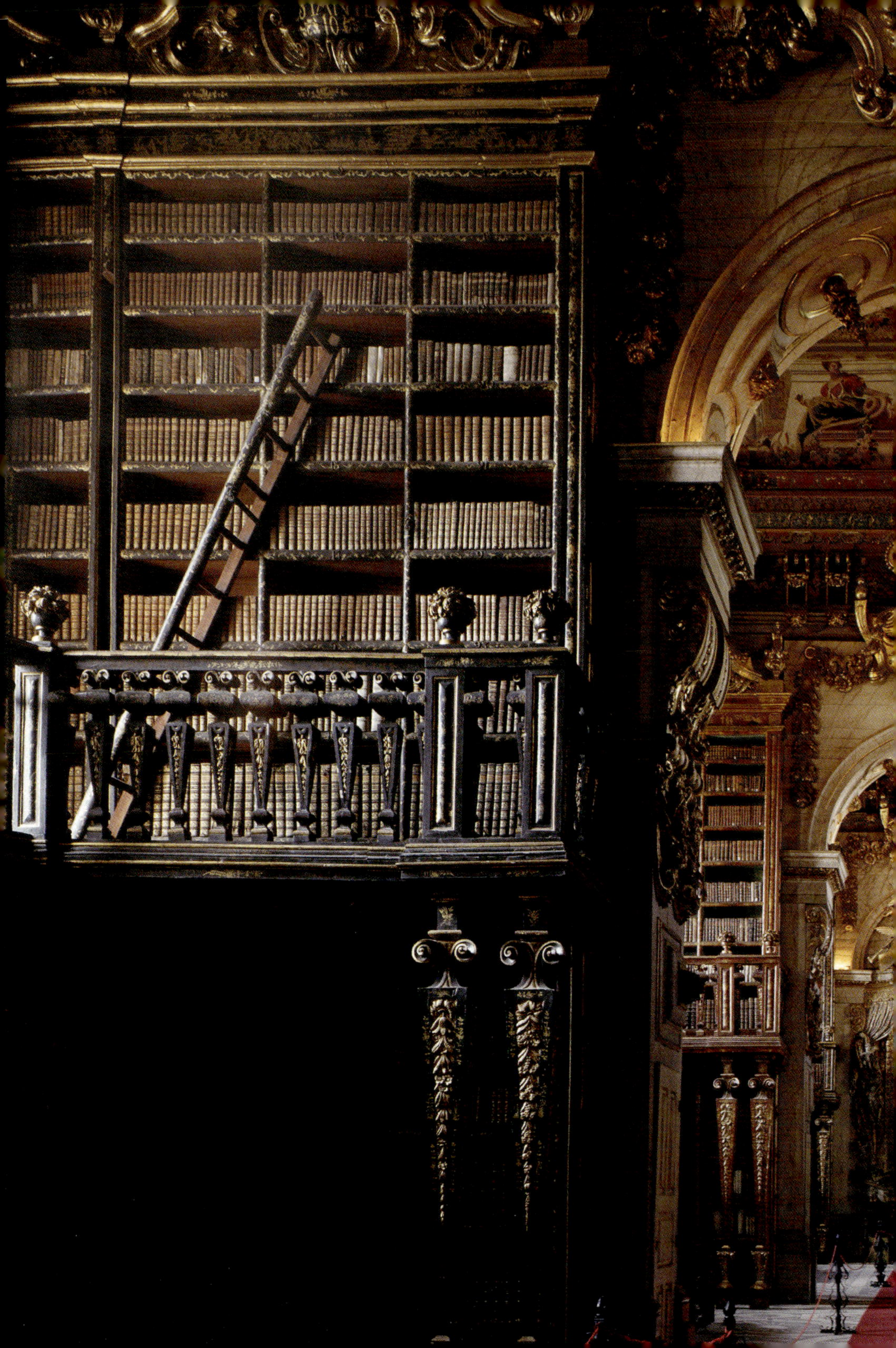

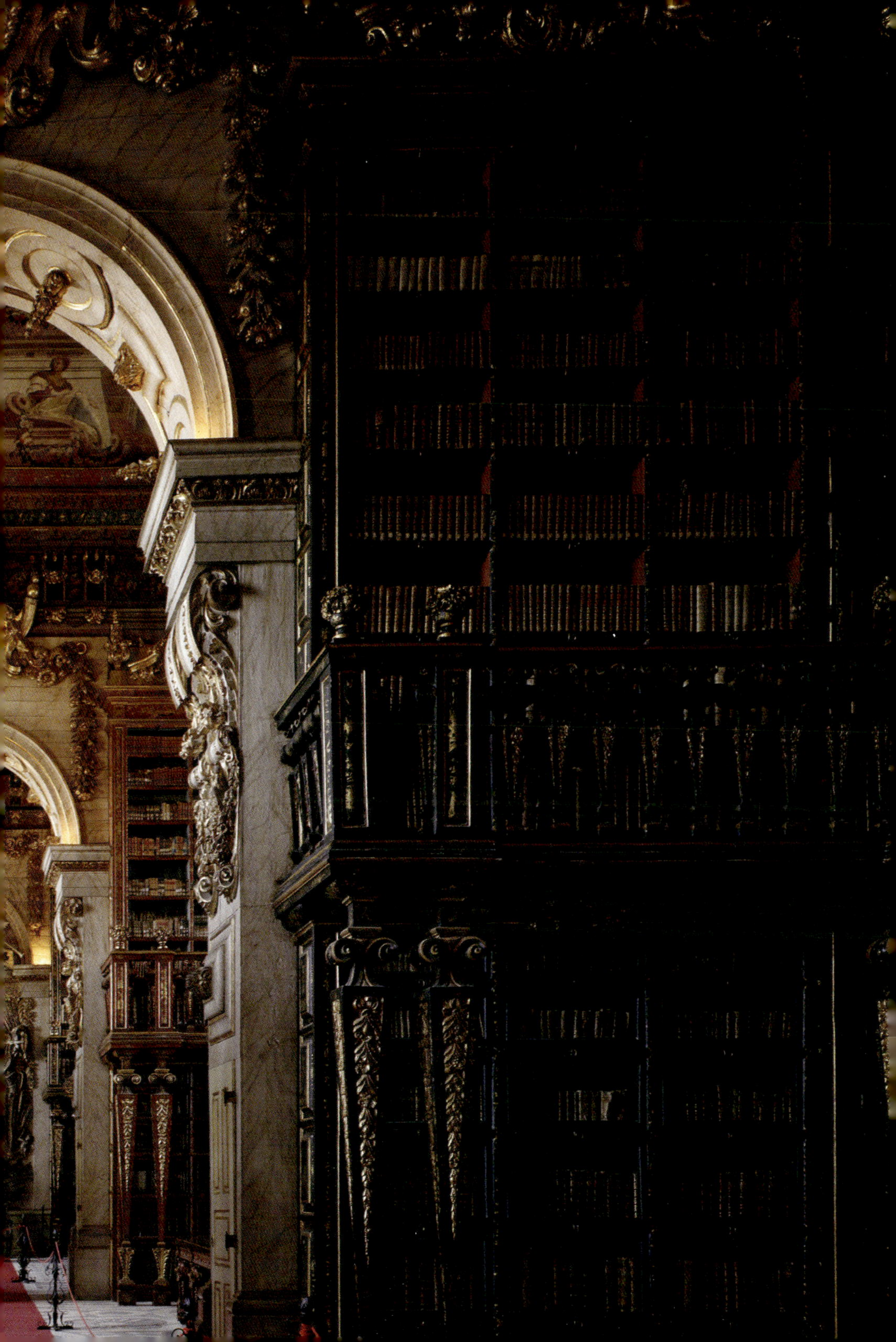

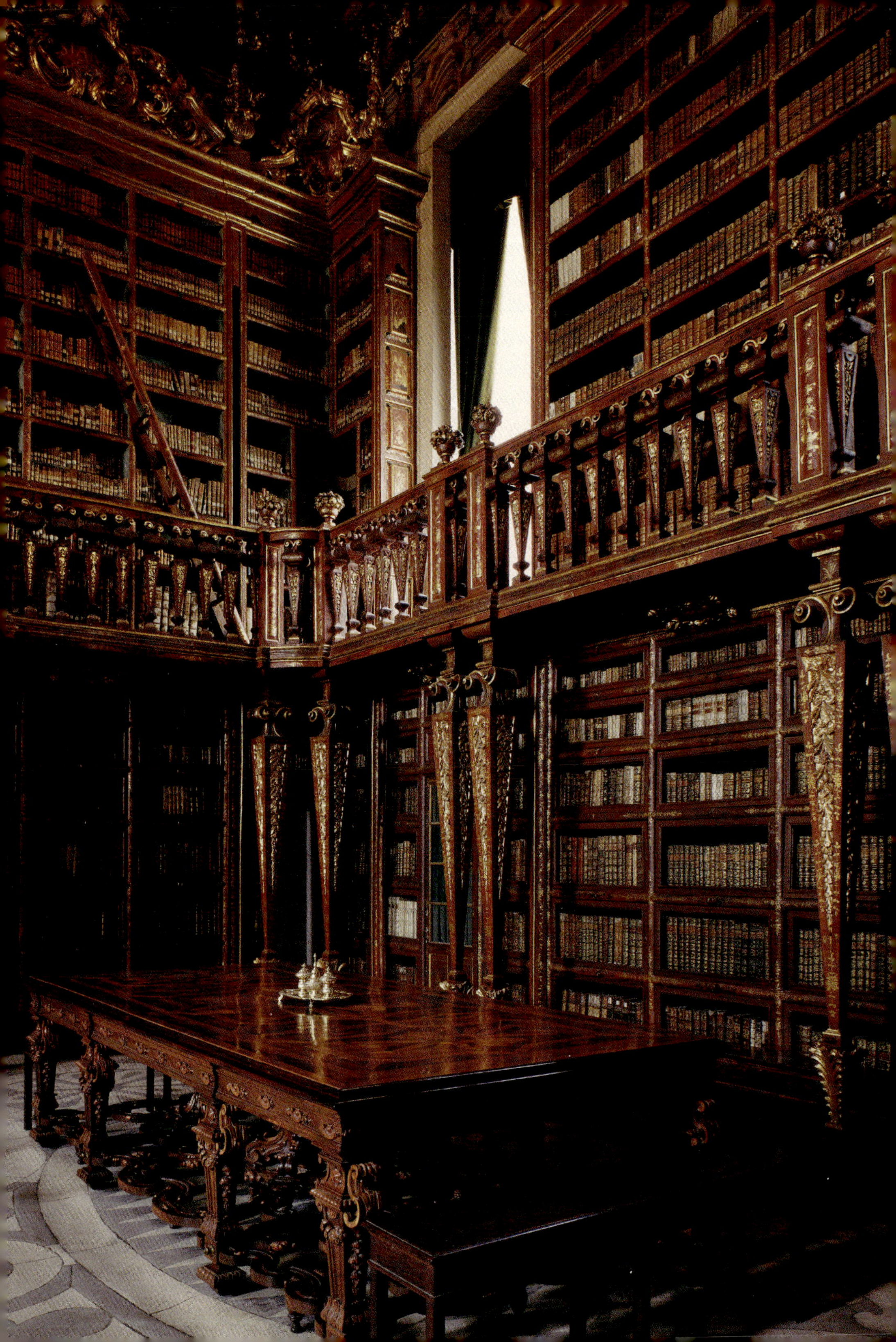

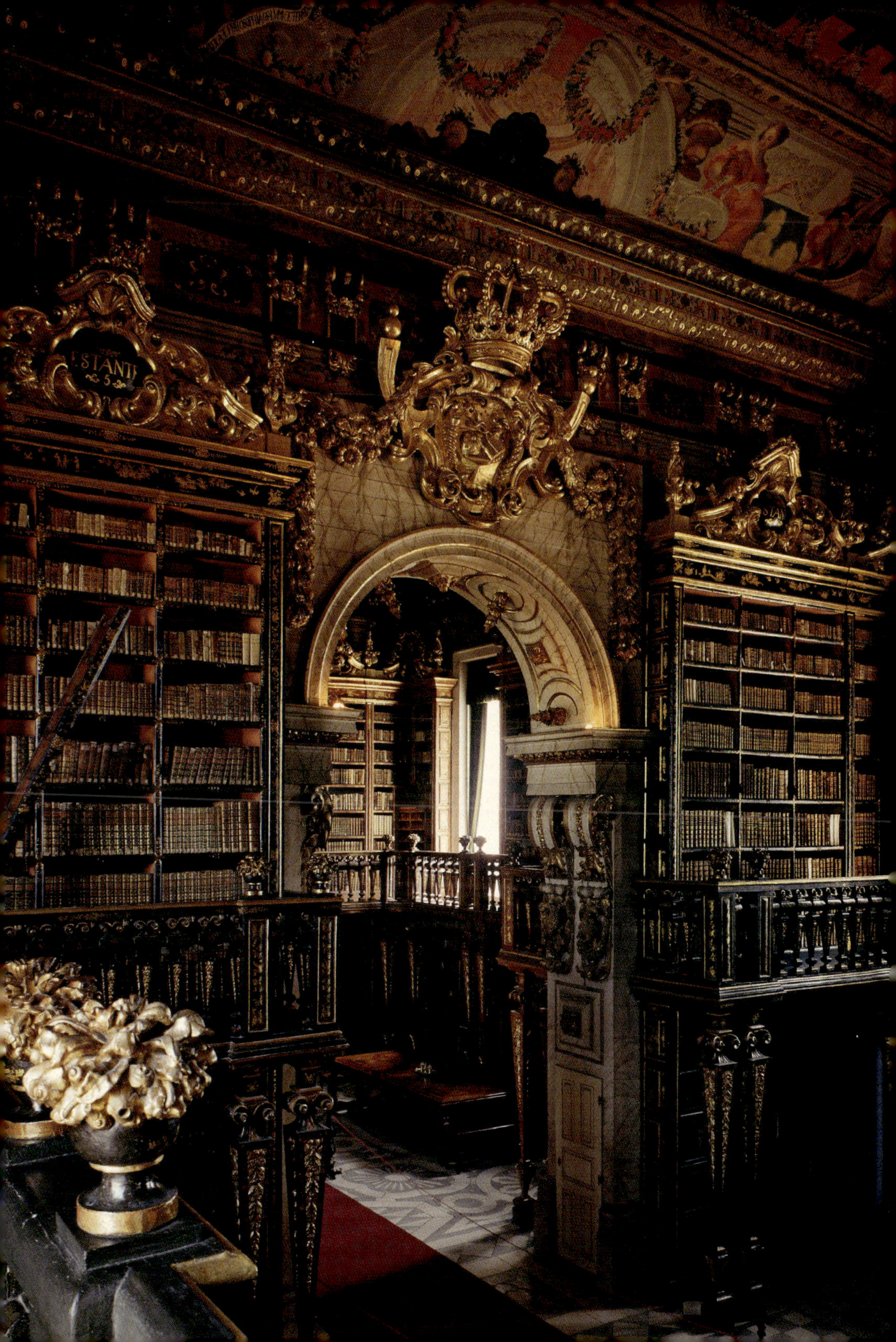

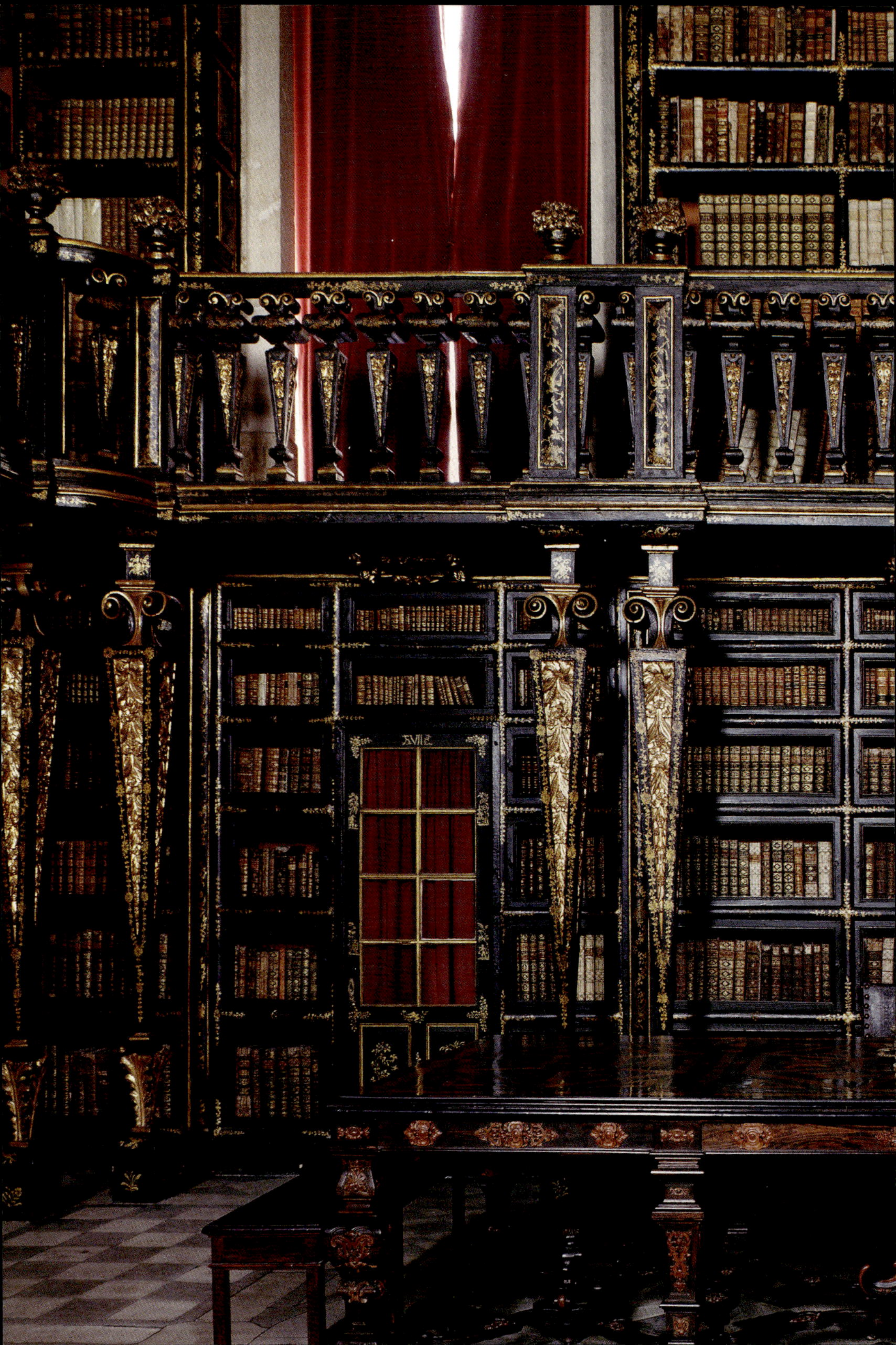

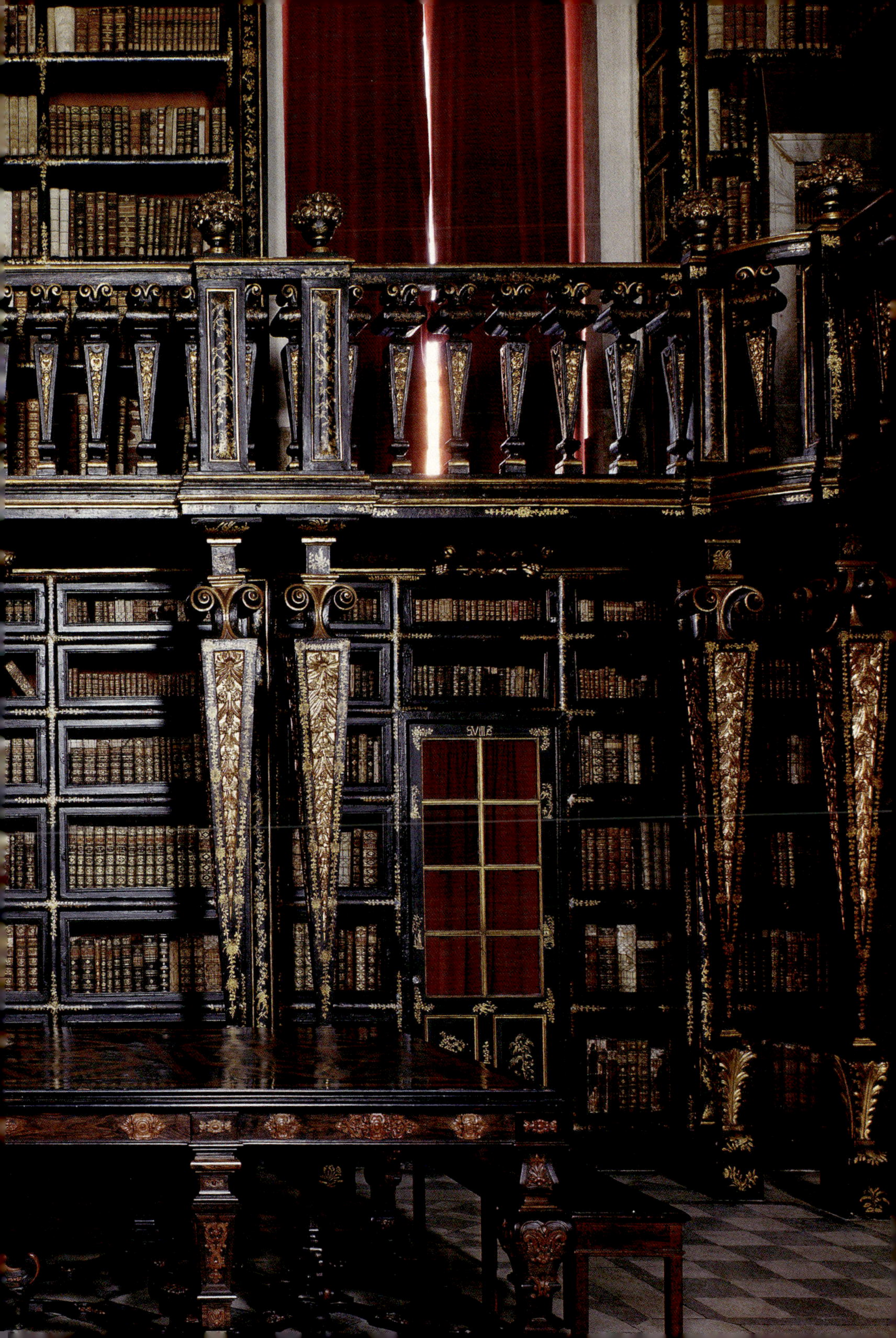

Biblioteca do Convento de Mafra

The Mafra Palace library is considered one of the most magnificent Rococo library buildings in the world. Designed in the style of a monumental hall by royal court architect Manuel Caetano de Sousa (1742–1802) and situated in the west wing of the vast palace of the Portuguese kings, the library was completed in 1771 and today serves as a museum, with its historical appearance intact. Coffered barrel vaults and a central cupola soar overhead, reflecting the daylight generously entering through numerous windows. Galleries with high balustrades run round all sides of the room, whose walls are lined with bookcases, lending it a compact, homogeneous appearance despite its size. In the absence of gilded and painted decoration, which was not part of the original design, light colours dominate, and together with the lavish, polychrome marble floor, they bring out the finely worked Rococo ornamentation to great effect. For the carvings, the most precious woods from the Portuguese colonies were used. The historical holdings, inventoried by the monks in the convent attached to the palace, include a number of valuable, unique manuscripts such as musical works composed especially for the famous six organs in the palace basilica. Amongst these are scores by the royal music teacher João de Sousa Carvalho (1745–1799) and his pupil Marcos Portugal (1762–1830). Alongside Coimbra, the Mafra was the second of the magnificent libraries completed during the reign of Joseph I (1714–1777), who here again fulfilled the wishes of his father, John V (1689–1750), by finishing this building project. In 1711 the Portuguese king, who had married Archduchess Maria Anna Josepha (1683–1754), a daughter of Emperor Leopold I (1640–1705), vowed to build a palace and convent dedicated to St Anthony should he be blessed with a male heir. The foundation stone for the new royal residence, designed on a grand scale by the Swabian architect and goldsmith Johann Friedrich Ludwig (1673–1752), was laid in 1717. Situated outside the royal capital of Lisbon and instead set in the royal hunting grounds at Mafra, the palace incorporated a Capuchin monastery and a palace church as part of a single complex built around several courtyards, on the model of the Escorial in Spain. It not only surpassed the Spanish example in scale, but was also quite different in its décor, which in Mafra is sumptuously opulent, in contrast to the Escorial. The gigantic project was made financially possible by the enormous quantities of gold arriving from the Portuguese colony of Brazil and the building work was accomplished within a short space of time by the use of a conscripted workforce of thousands of labourers and members of the military. The church was consecrated in 1730 and 300 Capuchin monks were provided with accommodation in the wings

Founded 1717 by John V; built 1771 by Manuel Caetano de Sousa
Holdings c. 36,000 volumes
Type of library royal library, today national museum
Highlights *Heures Chrétiennes (Book of Hours)*, c. 1400–1420 (Cod. Ms. Parchment. BPNM Safe box 22); *Officium defunctorum*, c. 1480–1490 (Cod. Ms. Parchment. BPNM Safe box 32); *Papal Bull Benedictus XIV for the Library of Mafra*, 1754 (BPNM, Safe box n. 62, register 3711)

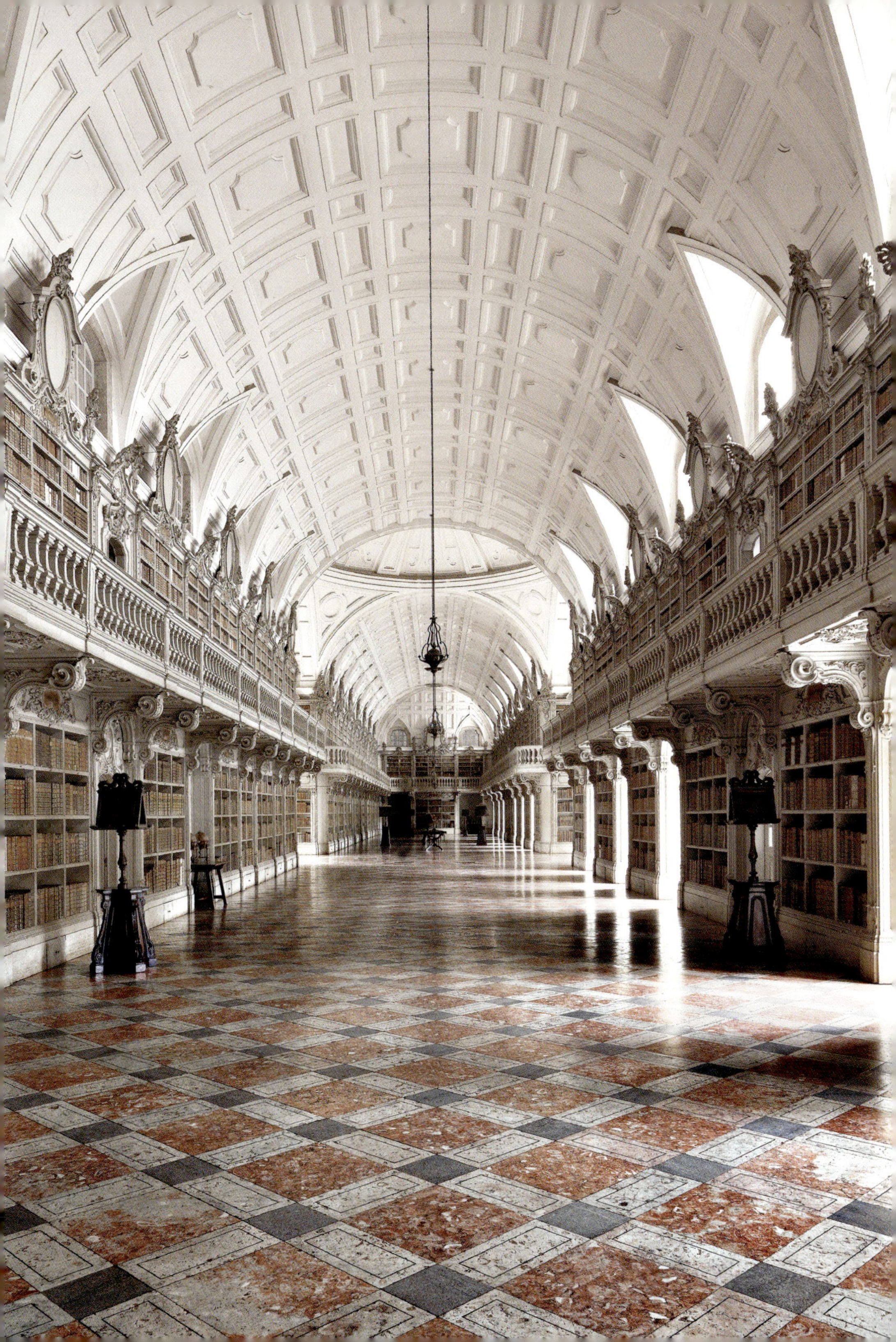

on either side of it. In 1745 Pope Benedict XIV
(1675–1758) issued a papal bull granting special
rights to the Royal Library of Mafra, including
permission to house titles on the Index of
Prohibited Books and to grant access to them
at the king's discretion. The building project
would earn the Portuguese kings of the House of
Braganza the title of "Most Faithful Majesty".

❋⋇❋

Die Palastbibliothek von Mafra gilt als eine der
prächtigsten Rokokobibliotheken der Welt.
Als monumentaler Saalraum vom königlichen
Hofarchitekten Manuel Caetano de Sousa
(1742–1802) entworfen, bewahrt die 1771 fertiggestellte und heute museal genutzte Bibliothek
ein intaktes Erscheinungsbild. Kassettierte
Tonnen und eine Mittelkuppel überwölben den
im Westflügel des weitläufigen Palastes der portugiesischen Könige eingerichteten Büchersaal
und reflektieren das großzügig über zahlreiche
Fenster einfallende Licht. Umlaufende Galerien
mit hohen Balustraden säumen den von Wandregalen umgebenen Raum und verleihen ihm
trotz seiner Größe ein kompaktes, einheitliches
Aussehen. Durch den ursprünglich nicht
geplanten Verzicht auf Vergoldung und gemalte
Dekoration dominieren helle Farbtöne, die
gemeinsam mit der Polychromie des aufwen-
digen Marmorfußbodens die fein gearbeiteten
Dekorationen im Stil des Rokoko wirkungsvoll
zur Geltung bringen. Edelste Hölzer aus den
portugiesischen Kolonien wurden für die
Schnitzarbeiten verwendet. Im historischen,
von den Mönchen des palasteigenen Klosters
inventarisierten Buchbestand finden sich
wertvolle Unikate, wie etwa die speziell für
die berühmten sechs Orgeln der Palastkirche
komponierten Musikwerke. Zu diesen gehören
die Partituren des königlichen Musiklehrers
João de Sousa Carvalho (1745–1799) und seines
Schülers Marcos Portugal (1762–1830). Mit
der Fertigstellung dieses Prachtraums – neben
Coimbra die zweite unter der Herrschaft
Josefs I. (1714–1777) vollendete Prunkbiblio-
thek – hatte der portugiesische König auch

in Mafra dem ausdrücklichen Wunsch seines
Vaters Johann V. (1689–1750) Folge geleistet,
dessen Baupläne zu verwirklichen. 1711 hatte der
mit Erzherzogin Maria Anna Josefa (1683–1754),
einer Tochter Kaiser Leopolds I. (1640–1705),
verheiratete Monarch gelobt, eine dem Heiligen
Antonius geweihte Klosterresidenz zu stiften,
falls ihm männlicher Nachwuchs geboren würde.
1717 erfolgte die Grundsteinlegung für den vom
schwäbischen Baumeister und Goldschmied
Johann Friedrich Ludwig (1673–1752) großzügig
entworfenen Klosterpalast. Außerhalb der
Residenzstadt Lissabon sollte inmitten der
königlichen Jagdreviere in Mafra eine prachtvolle königliche Residenz entstehen, die nach
dem Vorbild des spanischen Escorial mit einem
Kapuzinerkloster sowie einer Palastkirche zu
einer einzigen mehrhöfigen Anlage vereint
wurde. Nicht nur die Ausmaße übertrafen aber
die spanische Klosterresidenz bei Weitem, auch
die Ausstattung ist im Unterschied zu dieser
in Mafra prunkvoll opulent. Unermessliche
Goldschätze aus der portugiesischen Kolonie
Brasilien hatten die Verwirklichung des gigan-
tischen Bauvorhabens ermöglicht, das in kurzer
Zeit Gestalt annahm. Die Kirche konnte bereits
1730 geweiht und 300 Kapuzinermönche in
den ihr zu Seiten gelegenen Gebäudeflügeln
untergebracht werden. 1745 erließ Papst
Benedikt XIV. (1675–1758) eine Bulle, die der
königlichen Bibliothek von Mafra Sonderrechte
einräumte, unter diesen die Erlaubnis, auf den
Index der verbotenen Bücher gesetzte Schriften
zu verwahren und gemäß königlicher Weisung
zu verwalten. Den portugiesischen Königen
des Hauses Braganza sollte das Bauprojekt den
Titel „Allergläubigste Könige" einbringen.

❋⋇❋

La bibliothèque du palais de Mafra est l'une
des bibliothèques de style rocaille les plus
opulentes au monde. Construite sur les plans
de l'architecte de la cour royale Manuel Caetano
de Sousa (1742–1802), cette bibliothèque à
la salle de lecture monumentale et à l'usage
dorénavant muséal est restée intacte depuis

son achèvement en 1771. La salle de lecture, aménagée dans l'aile est du vaste palais royal portugais, est coiffée de voûtes à caissons et d'une coupole centrale. Ce système permet aussi de renvoyer la lumière, abondante grâce aux nombreuses fenêtres. La salle comprend une galerie circulaire marquée d'une haute balustrade, tandis que les murs sont tapissés de rayonnages. Cette balustrade a l'intérêt de conférer une allure homogène et compacte à la pièce aux dimensions considérables. En l'absence de dorures et décorations peintes (pourtant prévues à l'origine), les tons clairs prédominent. Associés à la polychromie du sol en marbres élaborés, ces tons soulignent la finesse du décor en style rocaille. Les boiseries ont été sculptées dans des matériaux très nobles en provenance des colonies portugaises. Le fonds historique (dont l'inventaire fut dressé par les moines du couvent intégré au palais) inclut des pièces uniques de très grande valeur. En font partie les œuvres de musique composées pour les six fameux orgues de l'église palatiale et les partitions du maître de musique de la famille royale, João de Sousa Carvalho (1745–1799), et de son élève Marcos Portugal (1762–1830). Cette salle d'apparat – seconde bibliothèque princière après celle de Coimbra achevée sous le règne de Joseph Ier (1714–1777) – permit au roi du Portugal de concrétiser, à Mafra également, les projets de construction ordonnés par son père Jean V (1689–1750) et, ainsi, d'exaucer ses vœux. En 1711, le souverain marié à l'archi-duchesse Marie-Anne d'Autriche (1683–1754), une fille de l'empereur Léopold Ier (1640–1705), avait promis de créer une résidence monacale dédiée à saint Antoine dans le cas où elle lui donnerait un héritier. La première pierre de la magnifique résidence monacale, conçue par le maître d'œuvre et orfèvre souabe Johann Friedrich Ludwig (1673–1752), fut posée en 1717. Cette résidence d'été en dehors de Lisbonne, la résidence principale, devait être bâtie dans le domaine de chasse nommé Mafra. Façonnée à l'image de l'Escurial en Espagne, cette nouvelle résidence disposerait d'un couvent de capucins

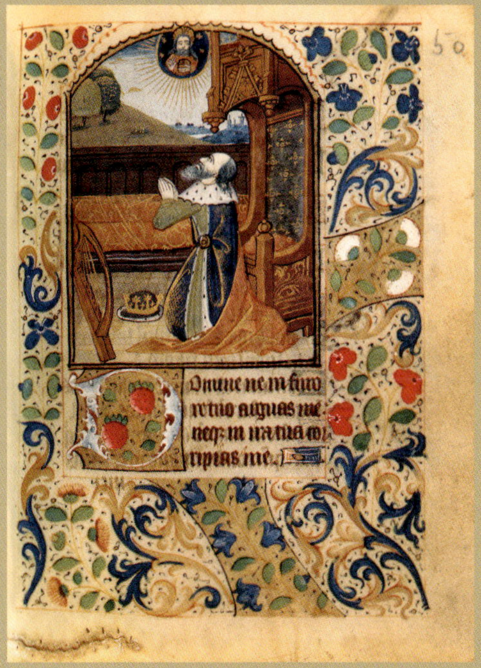

et d'une église palatiale jouxtant un complexe architectural à cours multiples. La résidence de Mafra outrepasse son modèle espagnol par ses dimensions, mais aussi par son aménagement intérieur d'une somptuosité exubérante. Des trésors originaires du Brésil, alors sous domination portugaise, ont permis la réalisation de ce projet titanesque, qui a rapidement pris forme grâce au travail de milliers de forçats et de militaires. 300 capucins emménagèrent dans les ailes contiguës à l'église à l'occasion de son inauguration en 1730. En 1745, le pape Benoît XIV (1675–1758) édicta une bulle autorisant la bibliothèque royale de Mafra à conserver les livres interdits à l'Index et à les administrer selon les ordres de la royauté. Ce projet de construction valut aux rois portugais de la Maison de Bragance le titre de « Très Fidèles ».

Officium defunctorum, c. 1480–1490,
sig. Cod. Ms. Parchment. BPNM Safe box 32, fol. 50

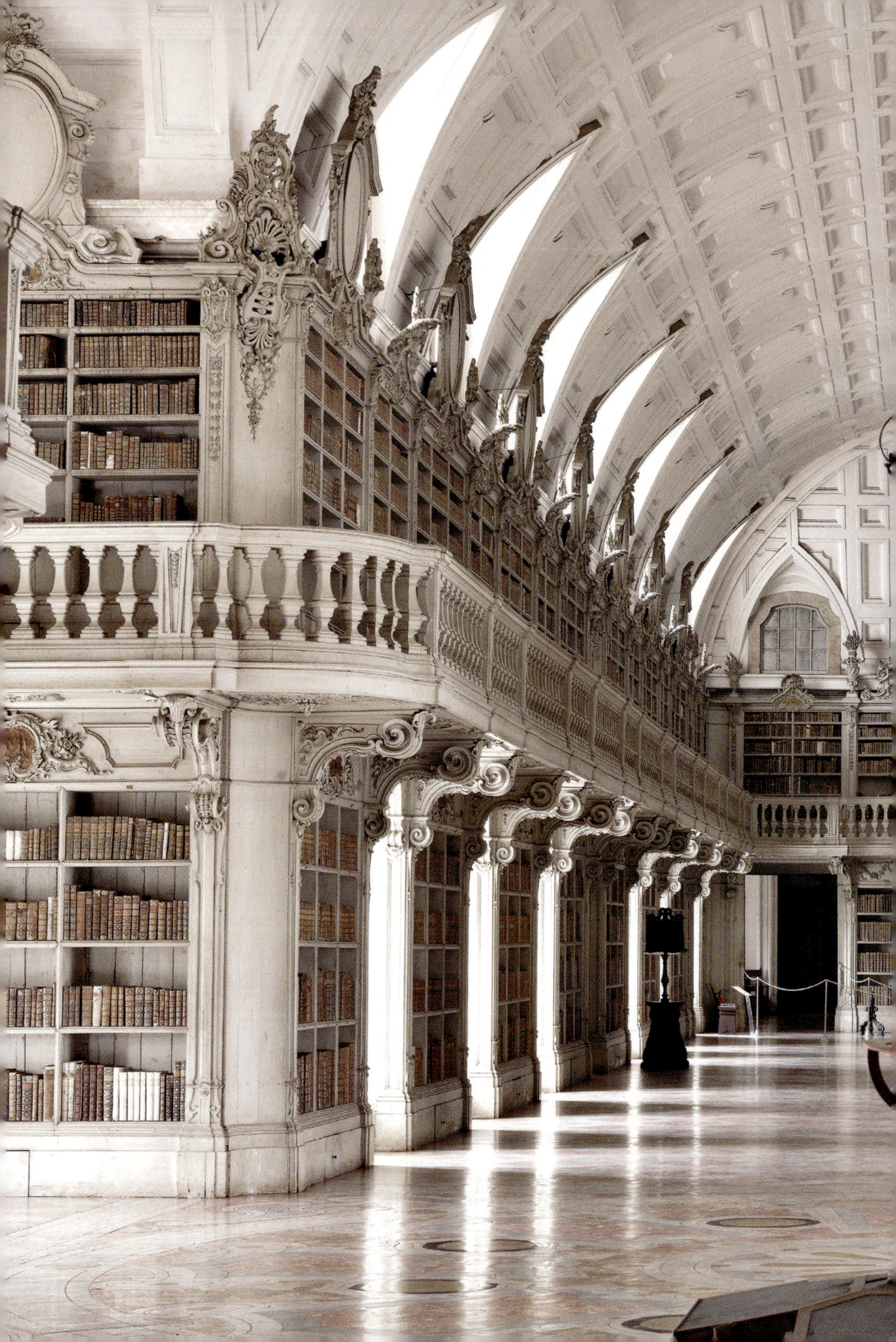

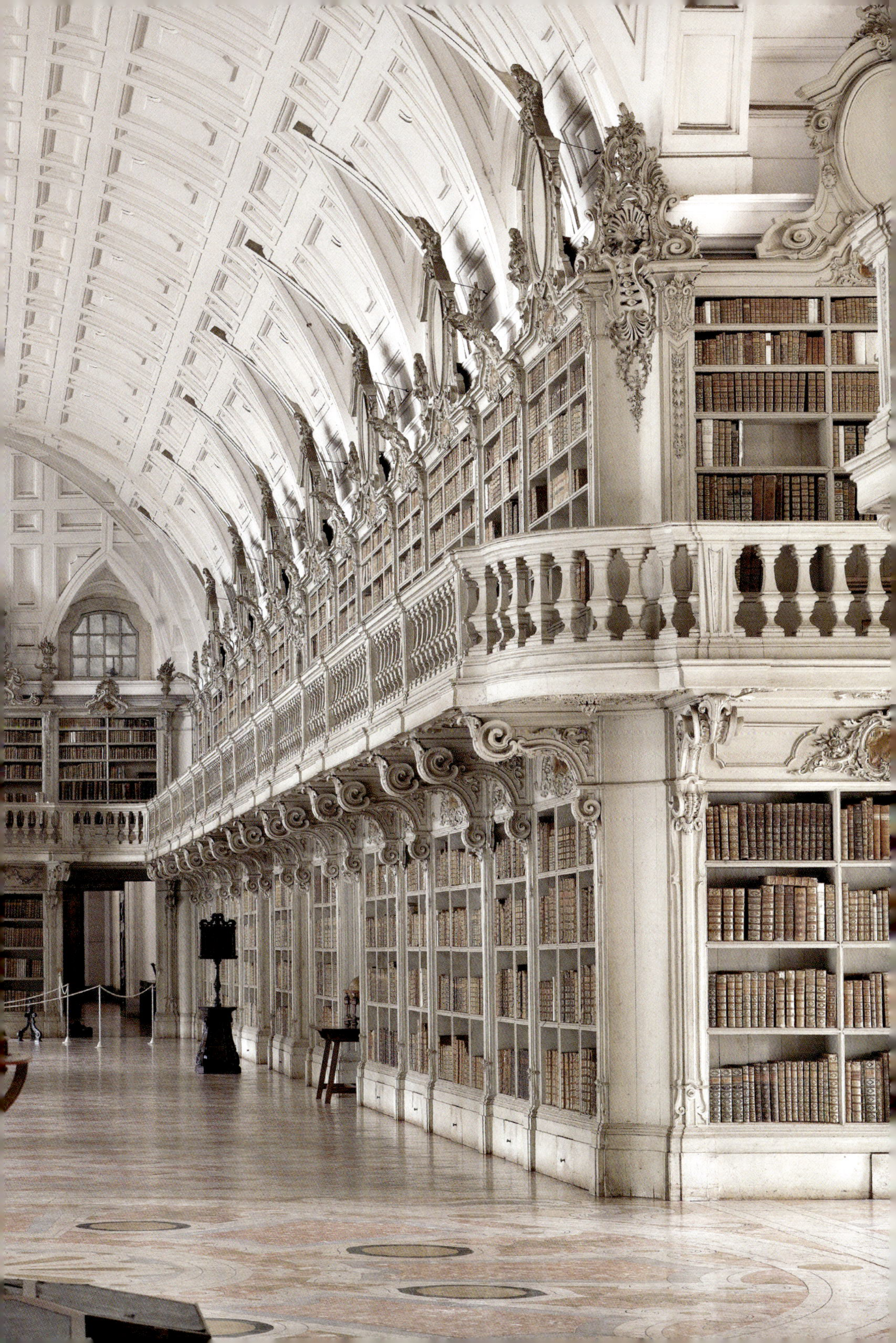

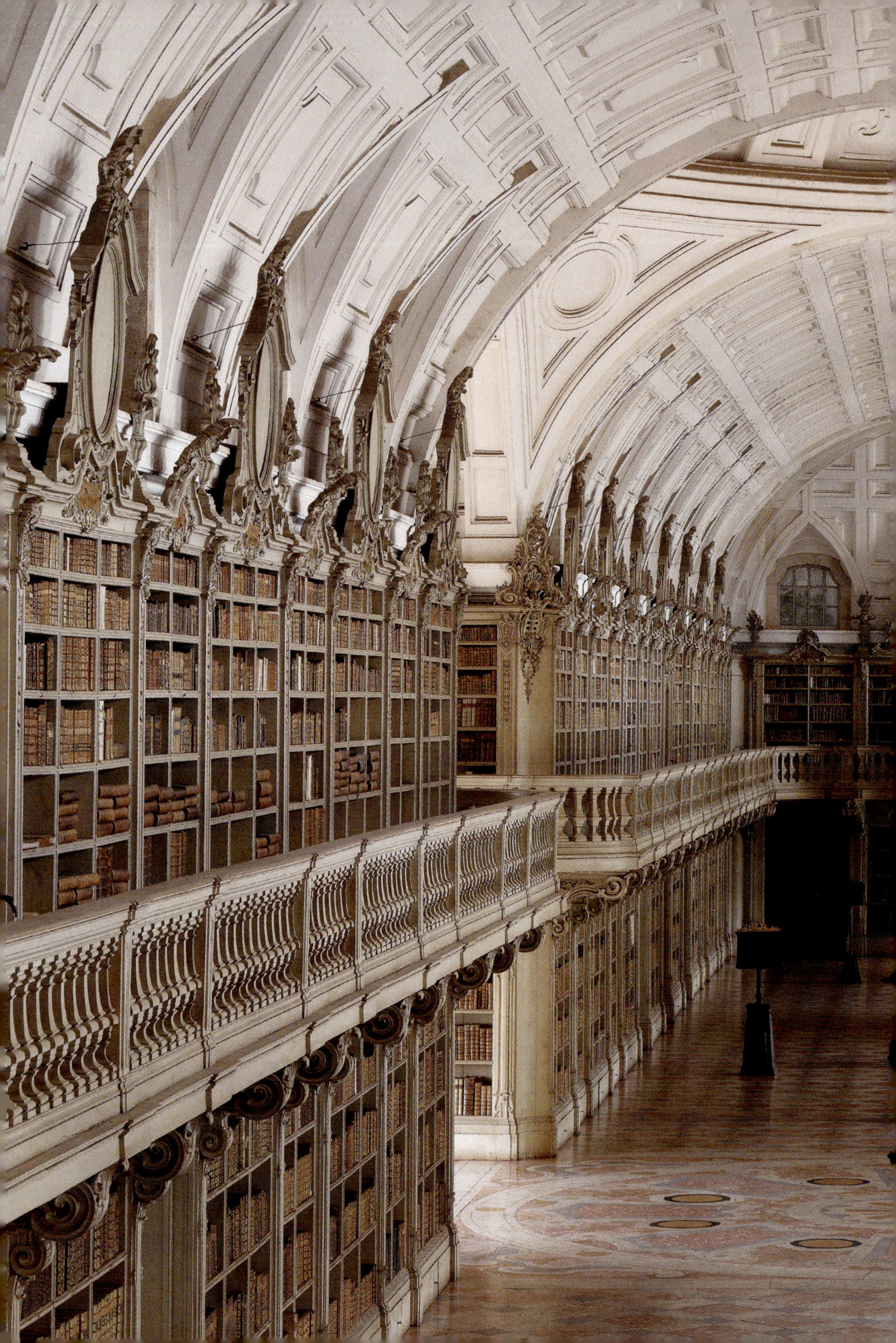

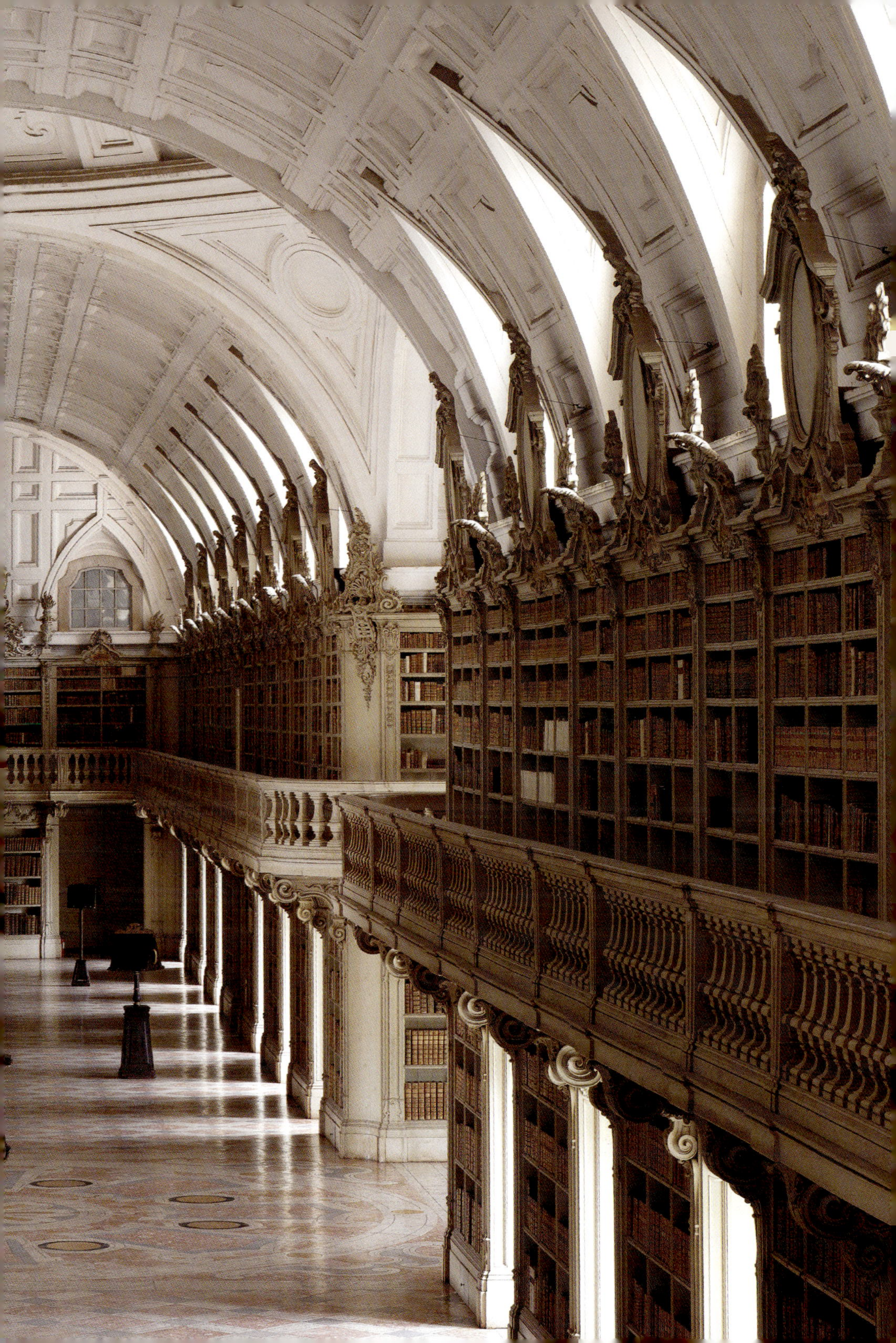

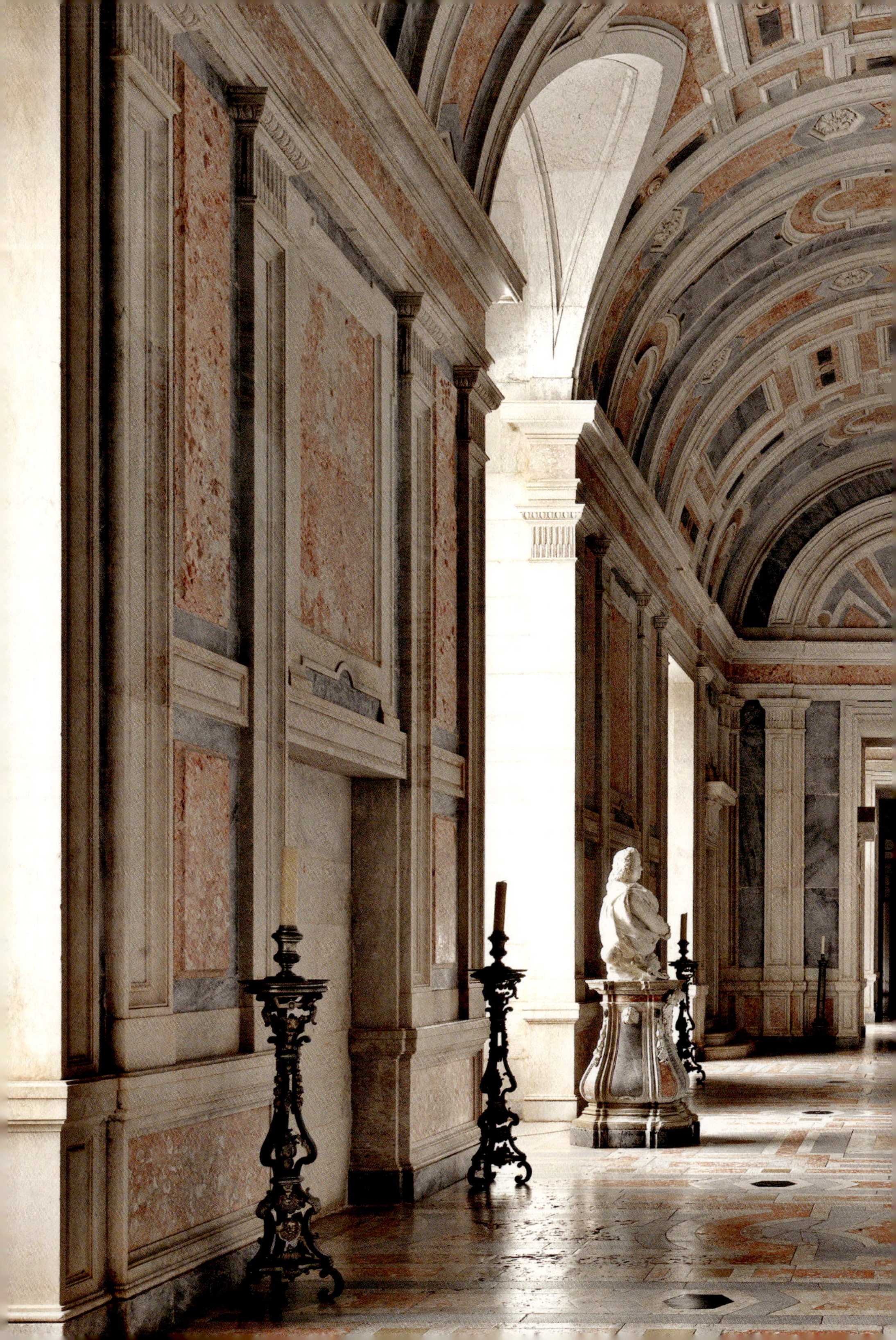

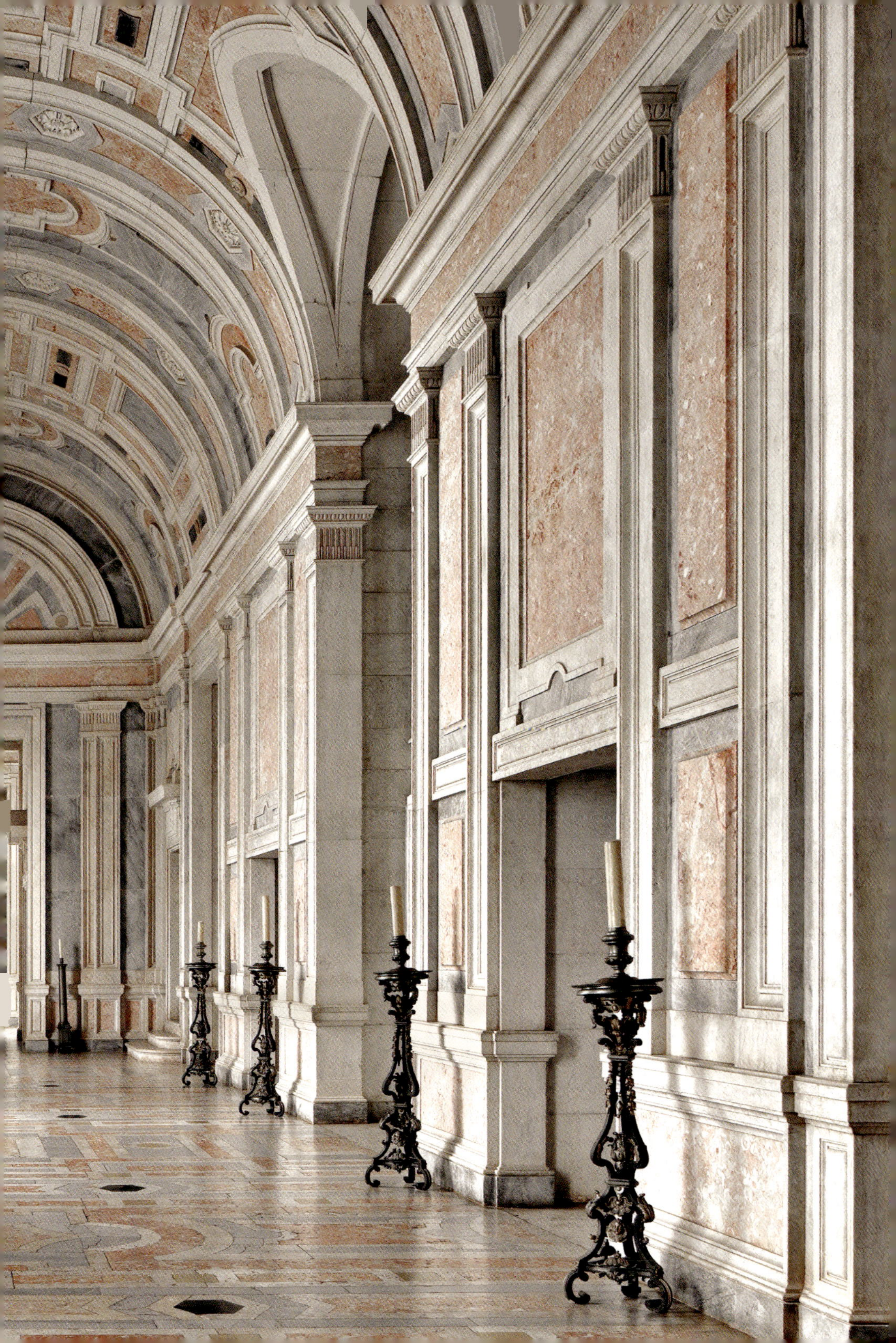

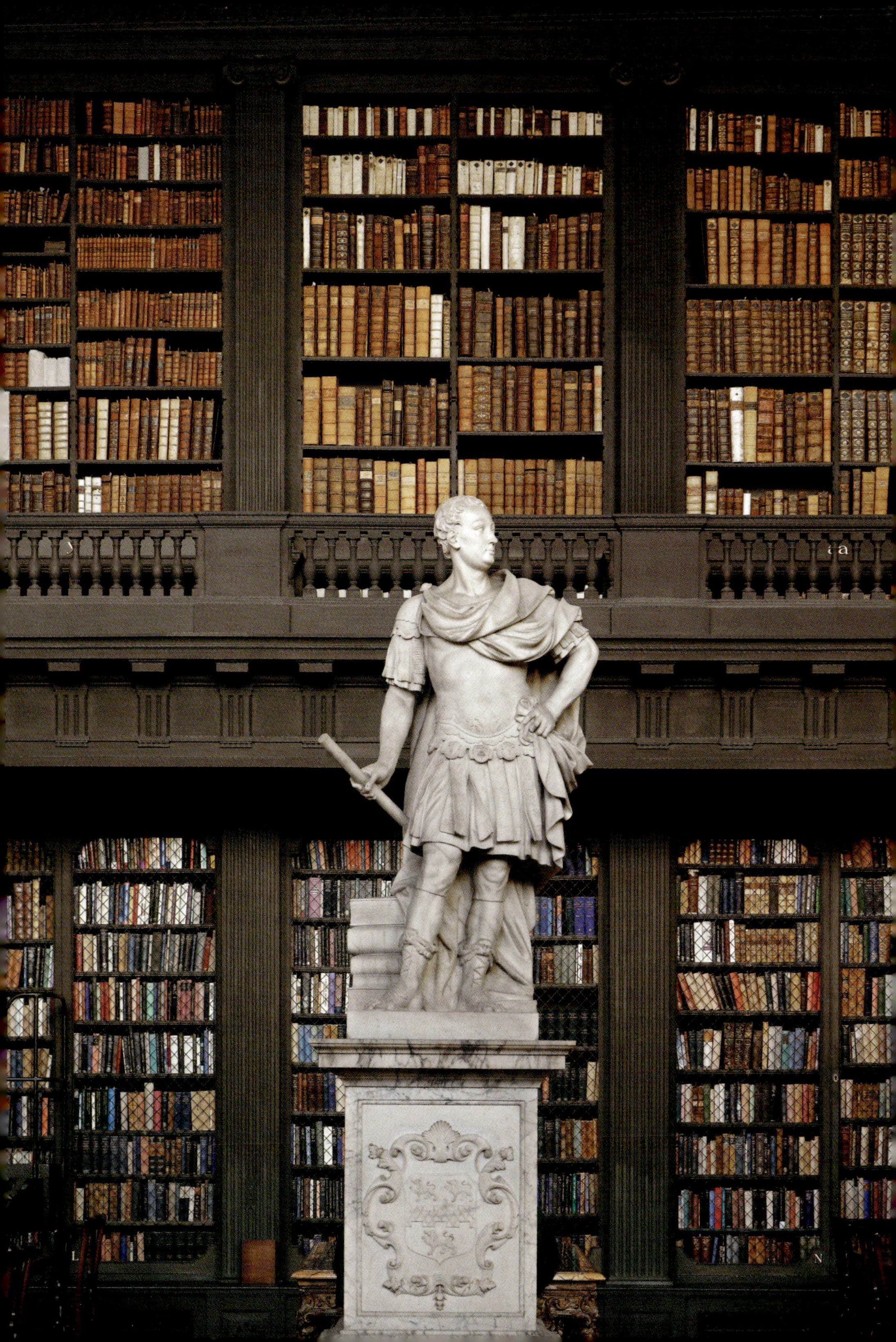

WESTERN & NORTHERN EUROPE

Ireland

England

France

The Netherlands

Sweden

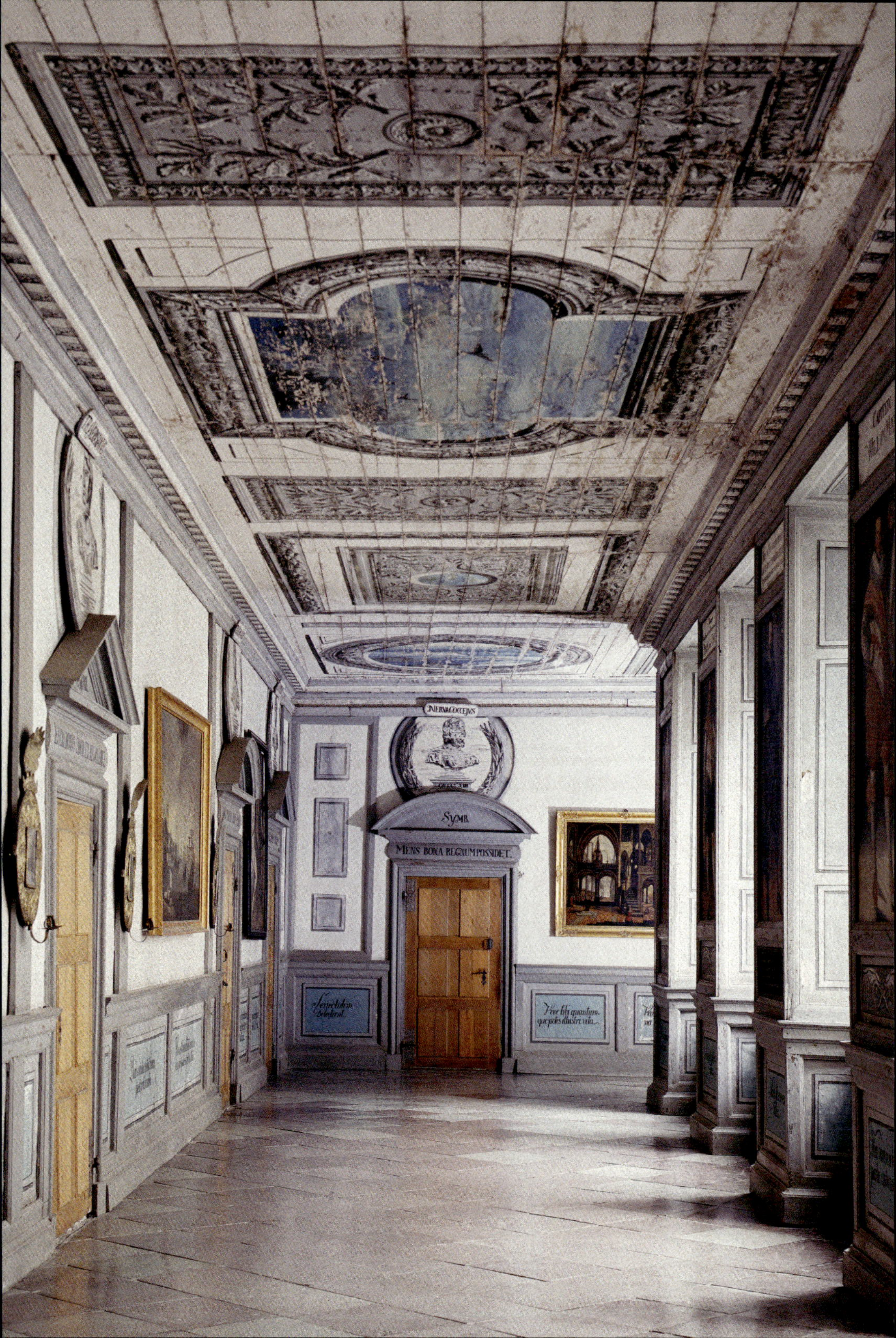

NERVA COCCEJVS
SYMB.
MENS BONA REGNVM POSSIDET.

IRELAND

ENGLAND

FRANCE

THE NETHERLANDS

SWEDEN

Text by Elisabeth Sladek

Page 236 The Codrington Library, Oxford, England
Opposite Skoklosters Slotts Bibliotek, Sweden

Trinity College Library

As the largest library in the country, with five million volumes, Trinity College Library is not only a symbol of the country's written culture but also the shrine of such national emblems as the Trinity College harp on show in the Long Room. Following the Christianisation of the island by missionary monks in the 5th century, scriptoria were established within the monasteries from the time of the early Middle Ages where monks recorded and handed down the knowledge and artistic endeavour of late Antiquity. Early medieval codices such as the *Book of Kells* and the *Book of Durrow* – both today housed in Trinity College Library – bear witness, in their magnificent illustrations, to a high artistic standard whose influence, along with that of monastic scholarship, would be felt far beyond the bounds of Ireland. The classic period of Irish literature that blossomed from about 1200 came to an end with the colonising actions taken by the English queens Mary (1516–1558) and Elizabeth I (1533–1603) and the upheavals that ensued. This also cast a shadow over the early years of Trinity College Library, which were marked by reformist and reorganisational measures that duly hampered its early development. Elizabeth I founded Trinity College in 1592 as a centre of Protestant scholarship on the remains of an abandoned Catholic priory. She thereby created a new centre of learning for the intellectual elite, and one that operated within the framework of the University of Dublin rather than within the monastic culture of the past. Owing to lack of space, the first library, built immediately after the foundation of the College, had to give way at the start of the 18th century to a new building designed by chief engineer and surveyor-general Thomas Burgh (1670–1730). Today known as the Old Library, this building was begun in 1712 and completed two years after Burgh's death. It includes a central hall of spectacular length, aptly known as the Long Room; the originally flat ceiling of this single-storey room was raised in 1858 and replaced by the barrel-vaulted ceiling clad in oak that can still be seen today, creating space for an upper gallery. The Long Room's oak shelves are today lined with 200,000 of the library's oldest volumes. Among the busts of philosophers, writers, academics and patrons mounted between the massive bookcases are a number of famous individuals who once studied in this very library, including Oscar Wilde (1854–1900) and Samuel Beckett (1906–1989).

✳✳✳

Founded 1592; 1712–1730 construction of the Old Library with the Long Room by Thomas Burgh (completed 1732)
Holdings c. 5 million volumes
Type of library university library
Highlights *Book of the Dead*, Egyptian papyrus containing a canon of spells and instructions, 3rd century BC (MS 1664); *Book of Kells*, c. 800 (MS 58), *Book of Durrow*, c. 650–700 (MS 57)

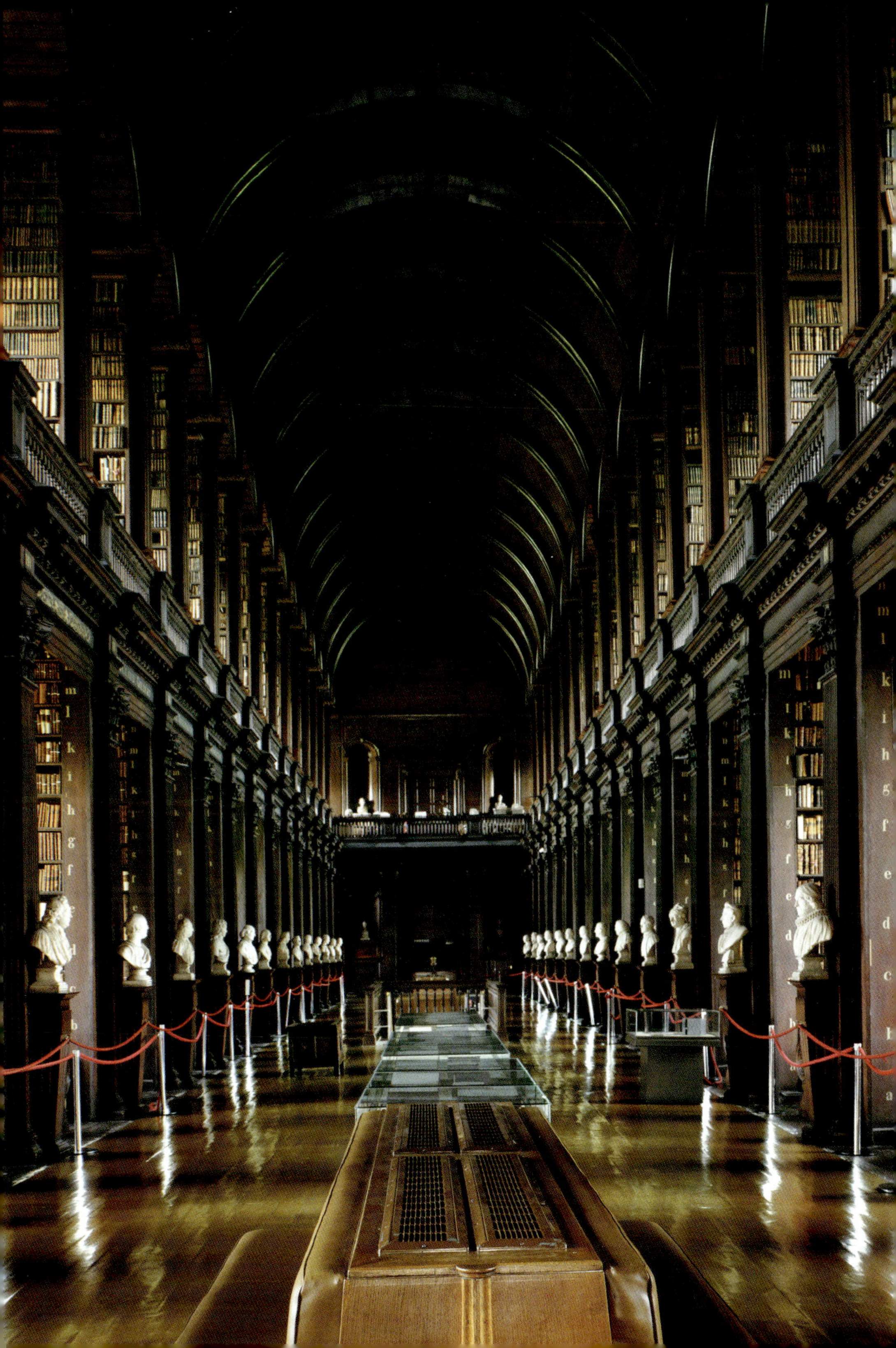

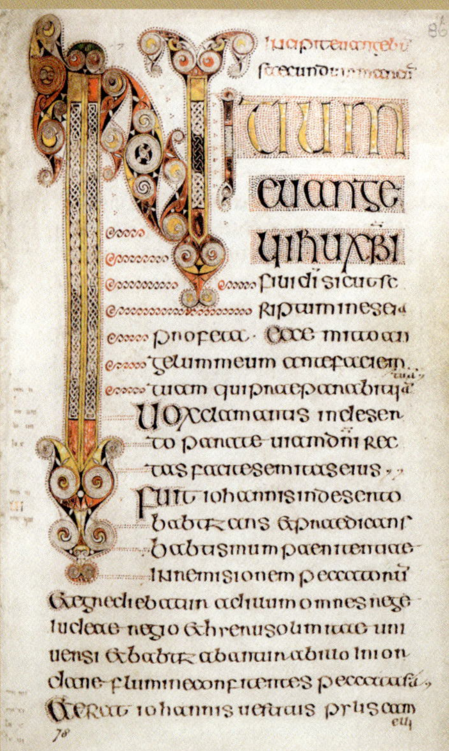

Als größte Bibliothek des Landes ist die Trinity College Library mit ihren fünf Millionen Bänden nicht nur ein Wahrzeichen der Schriftkultur des Landes, sondern auch ein Schrein identitätsstiftender Symbole des Landes – wie zum Beispiel der wahrscheinlich aus dem 15. Jahrhundert stammenden keltischen Harfe. Bereits im Frühmittelalter entstanden auf der von Wandermönchen christianisierten Insel im Rahmen von Klöstern Skriptorien, in denen Wissen und Kunst der Spätantike tradiert wurden. Frühmittelalterliche Kodizes wie das *Book of Kells* oder das *Book of Durrow* – beide befinden sich heute in der Bibliothek des Trinity College – zeugen mit ihren prächtigen Illustrationen von einem hohen künstlerischen Standard, der von den Inselklöstern gemeinsam mit der dort gepflegten Gelehrsamkeit weit über die Grenzen Irlands hinaus wirken sollte. Die ab 1200 einsetzende klassische

Periode irischer Literatur fand mit den Kolonialisierungsmaßnahmen der englischen Königinnen Maria I. Tudor (1516–1558) und Elisabeth I. (1533–1603) und den ihnen folgenden Tumulten ein vorläufiges Ende. Sie haben auch die von Reformations- und Reorganisationsmaßnahmen geprägten Gründungsjahre der Trinity College Library überschattet und zunächst in ihrem Wirken eingeschränkt. Als Elisabeth I. das Trinity College im Jahr 1592 über den Resten eines verlassenen katholischen Augustinerklosters als Stätte protestantischer Gelehrsamkeit gründete, setzte sie der alten Klosterkultur eine neue Ausbildungsstätte der intellektuellen Elite entgegen, die nun im Rahmen der Universität von Dublin wirkte. Das unmittelbar nach der Gründung des College errichtete erste Bibliotheksgebäude musste wegen Platzmangels zu Beginn des 18. Jahrhunderts einem Neubau weichen, dessen Raumbild sich im Wesentlichen in der heutigen Old Library erhalten hat. Ab 1712 schuf der Chefingenieur des britischen Königs, Thomas Burgh (1670–1730), einen Bibliothekssaal von spektakulärer Länge, der bis heute als Long Room bezeichnet wird. 1858 wurde die ursprünglich eingeschossige Halle um ein Obergeschoss erweitert und mit der noch heute sichtbaren hölzernen Tonne gewölbt. In den aus Eichenholz geschnitzten Bücherregalen des Schauraums sind heute 200 000 Bände aus Altbestand untergebracht. Zwischen den mächtigen Bücherregalen angeordnete Büsten von Philosophen, Schriftstellern, Wissenschaftlern und Förderern weisen die Universitätsbibliothek von Dublin als „Pantheon des Geistes" aus. Zu ihren Studenten zählten Oscar Wilde (1854–1900) und Samuel Beckett (1906–1989).

Book of Durrow, c. 650–700,
sig. MS 57, fol. 86r: *The opening words
of the Gospel of St Mark*

Book of Kells, c. 800, sig. MS 58, fol. 34r:
*The monogram representing Christ "Chi Rho",
from the Gospel of St Matthew*

La plus grande bibliothèque du pays avec ses cinq millions de volumes, la Trinity College Library est non seulement le berceau de la culture écrite, mais aussi l'écrin d'un des symboles identitaires de l'île, tels la harpe celtique datant probablement du XVe siècle. Dès le haut Moyen Âge, les *scriptoria* sont le lieu de transmission du savoir et de l'art de l'Antiquité tardive sur l'île christianisée par des moines itinérants. Des codex somptueusement illustrés, comme le *Livre de Kells* et le *Livre de Durrow* – deux joyaux du haut Moyen Âge exposés à la Trinity College Library –, témoignent des critères artistiques élevés qui prévalaient à l'époque et qui rayonnèrent bien au-delà des frontières maritimes de l'île où l'érudition était entretenue également dans les monastères. Les actions colonisatrices des reines Marie Tudor (1516–1558) et Élisabeth Ire (1533–1603) d'Angleterre – et les remous qui s'ensuivirent – mirent un terme provisoire à la période classique de la littérature irlandaise amorcée dès 1200 ap. J.-C. Elles assombrirent aussi les années de constitution de la Trinity College Library, les réformes et mesures de réorganisation ayant pour effet de restreindre son influence. De fait, lorsqu'Élisabeth Ire fonde Trinity College en 1592 sur les ruines d'un monastère catholique augustin abandonné pour donner une assise à l'érudition protestante, le nouvel établissement (aujourd'hui intégré à l'université de Dublin) s'oppose à la vieille culture monacale. La première bibliothèque, édifiée sans attendre à la suite de la création du College, doit, par manque de place, s'effacer au début du XVIIIe siècle derrière un nouveau bâtiment dont la facture est conservée dans l'Old Library. À partir de 1712, l'ingénieur en chef de la cour d'Angleterre Thomas Burgh (1670–1730) conçoit une salle de bibliothèque d'une longueur spectaculaire, appelée Long Room. En 1858, cette salle immense à niveau unique est surélevée d'un étage et dotée d'une voûte en berceau en bois encore visible de nos jours. Les étagères en hêtre sculpté de cette étonnante salle accueillent aujourd'hui 200 000 volumes du fonds d'origine. Devant d'imposants rayonnages s'alignent des bustes de philosophes, écrivains, scientifiques et mécènes qui élèvent la bibliothèque de l'université de Dublin, où Oscar Wilde (1854–1900) et Samuel Beckett (1906–1989) ont étudié, au rang de « Panthéon de l'esprit ».

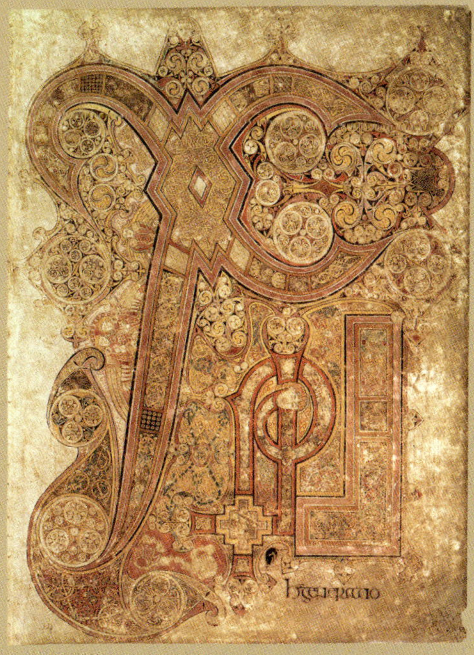

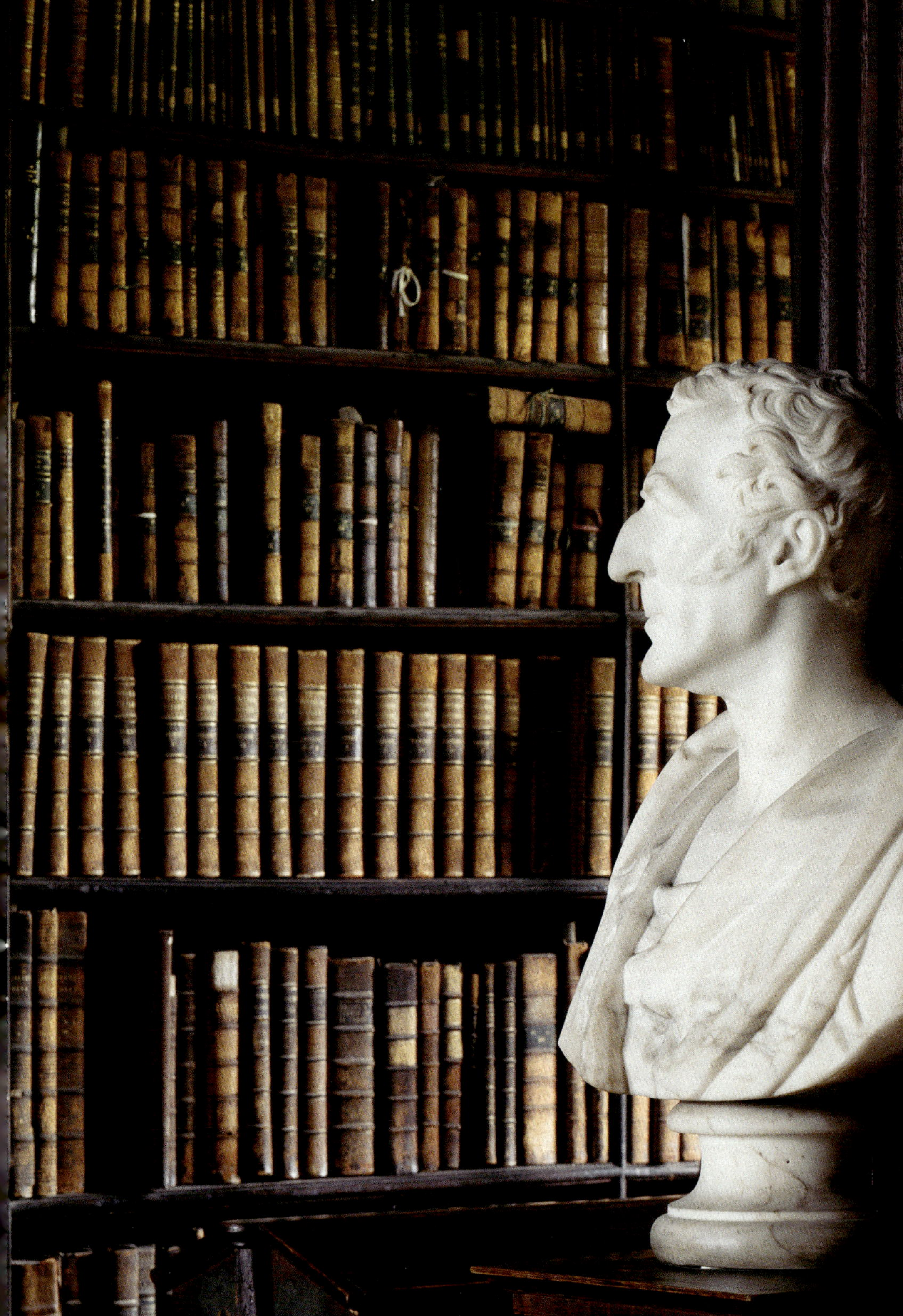

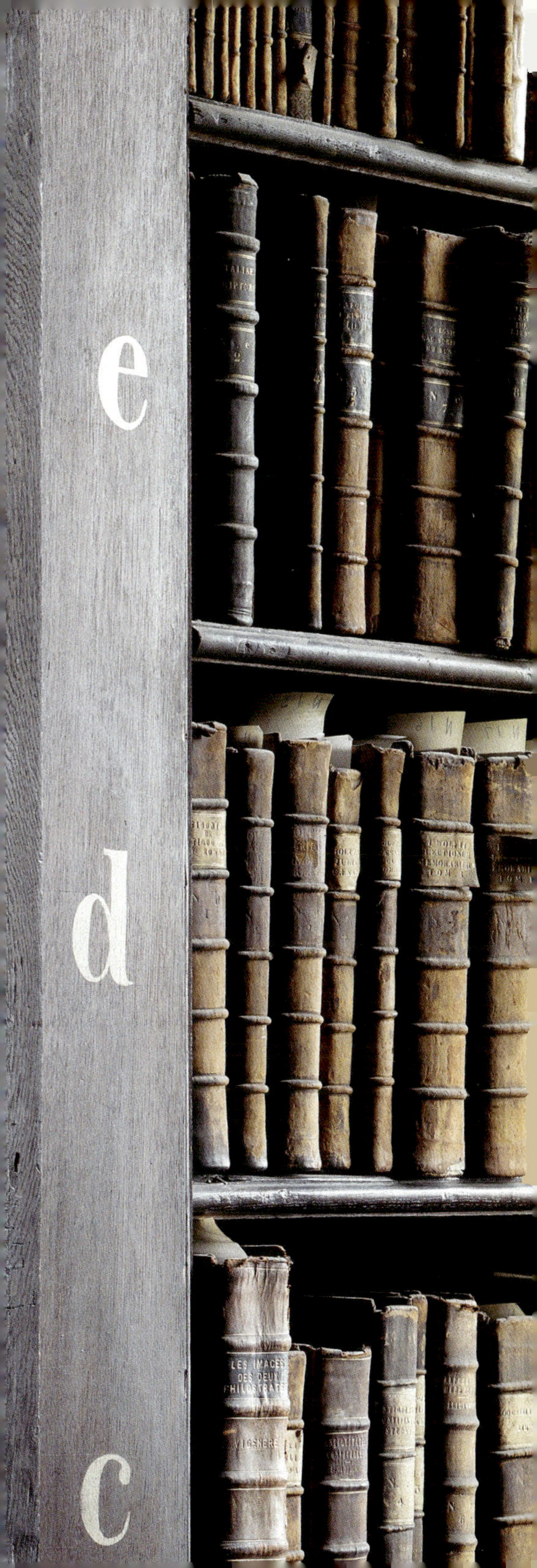

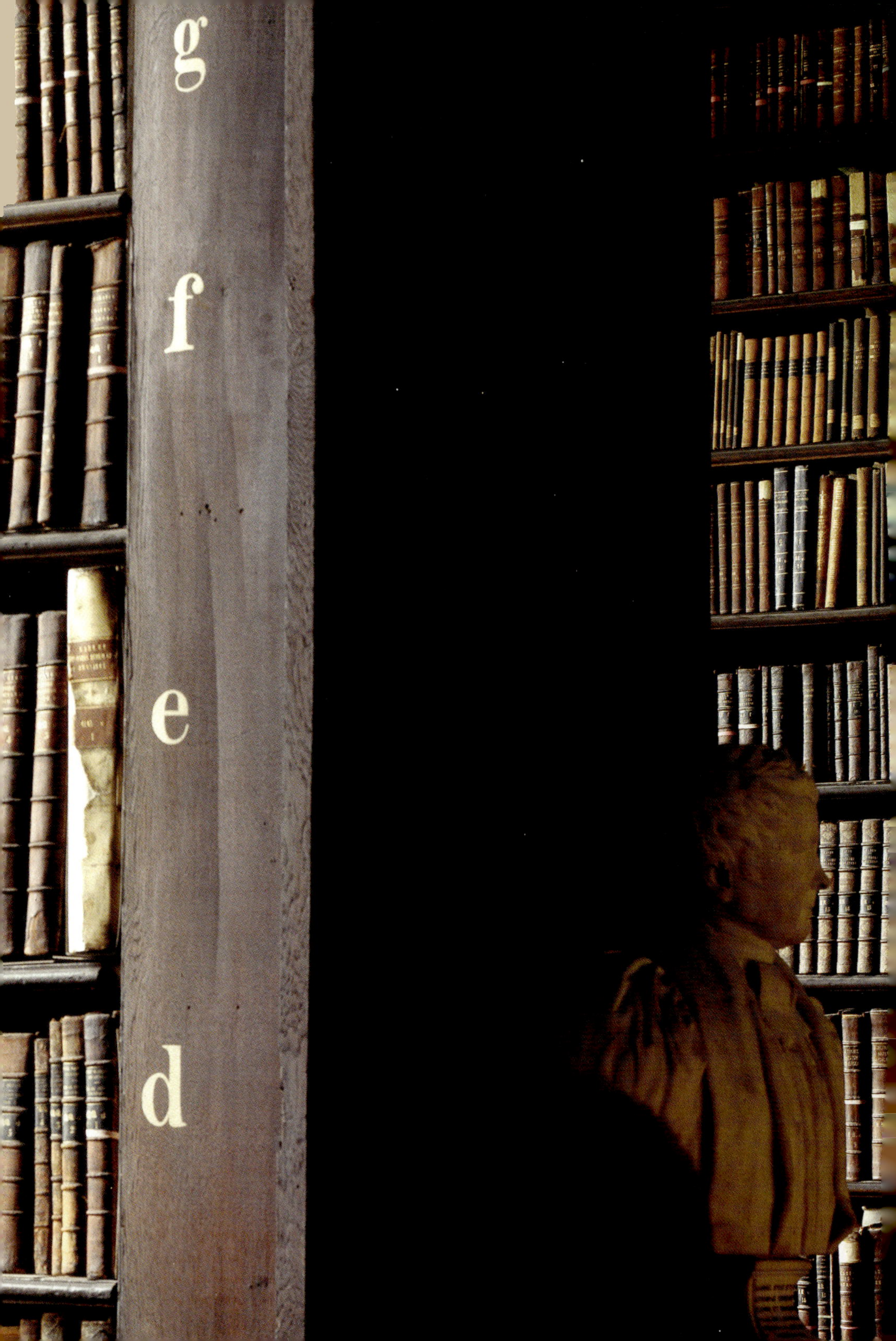

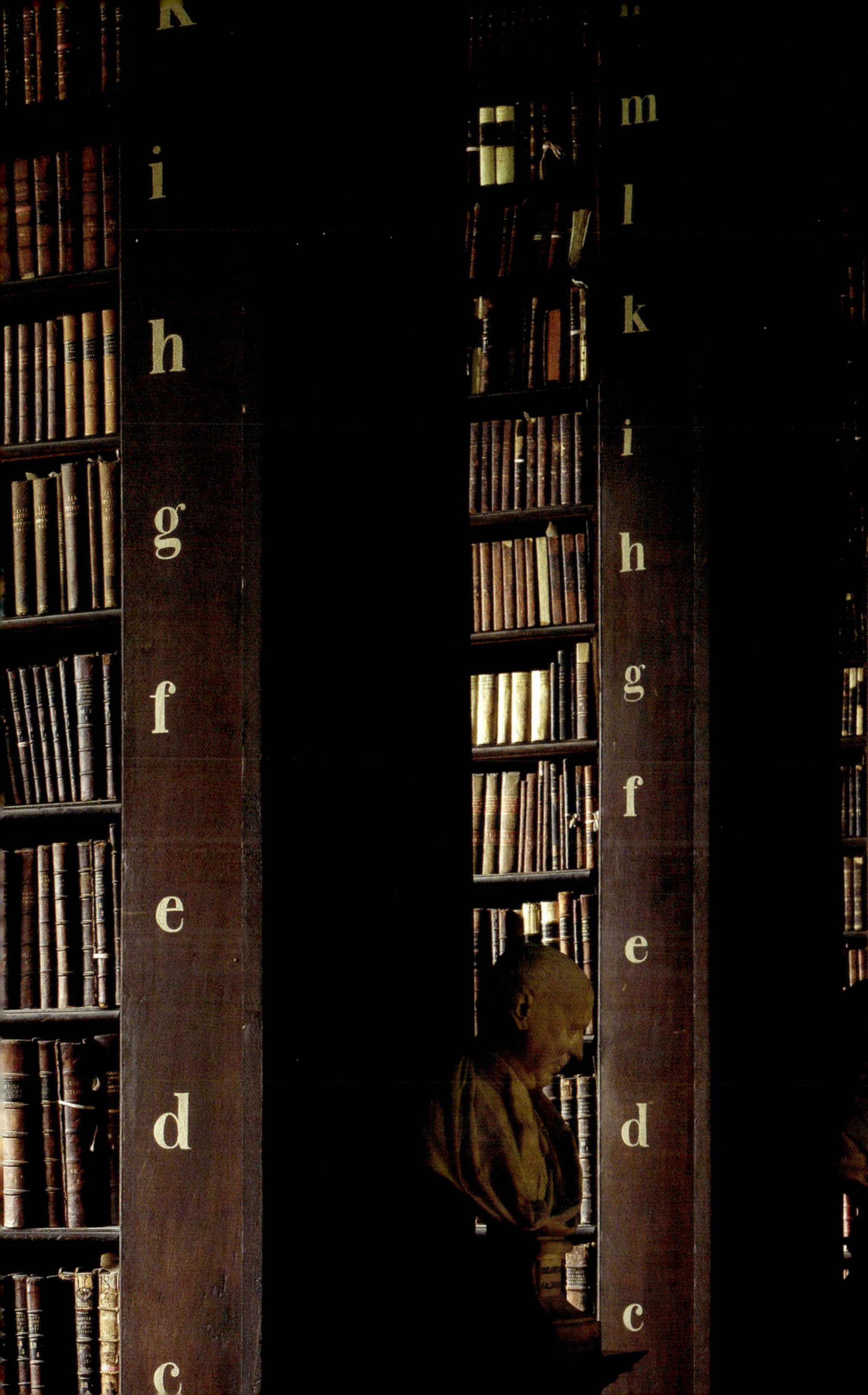

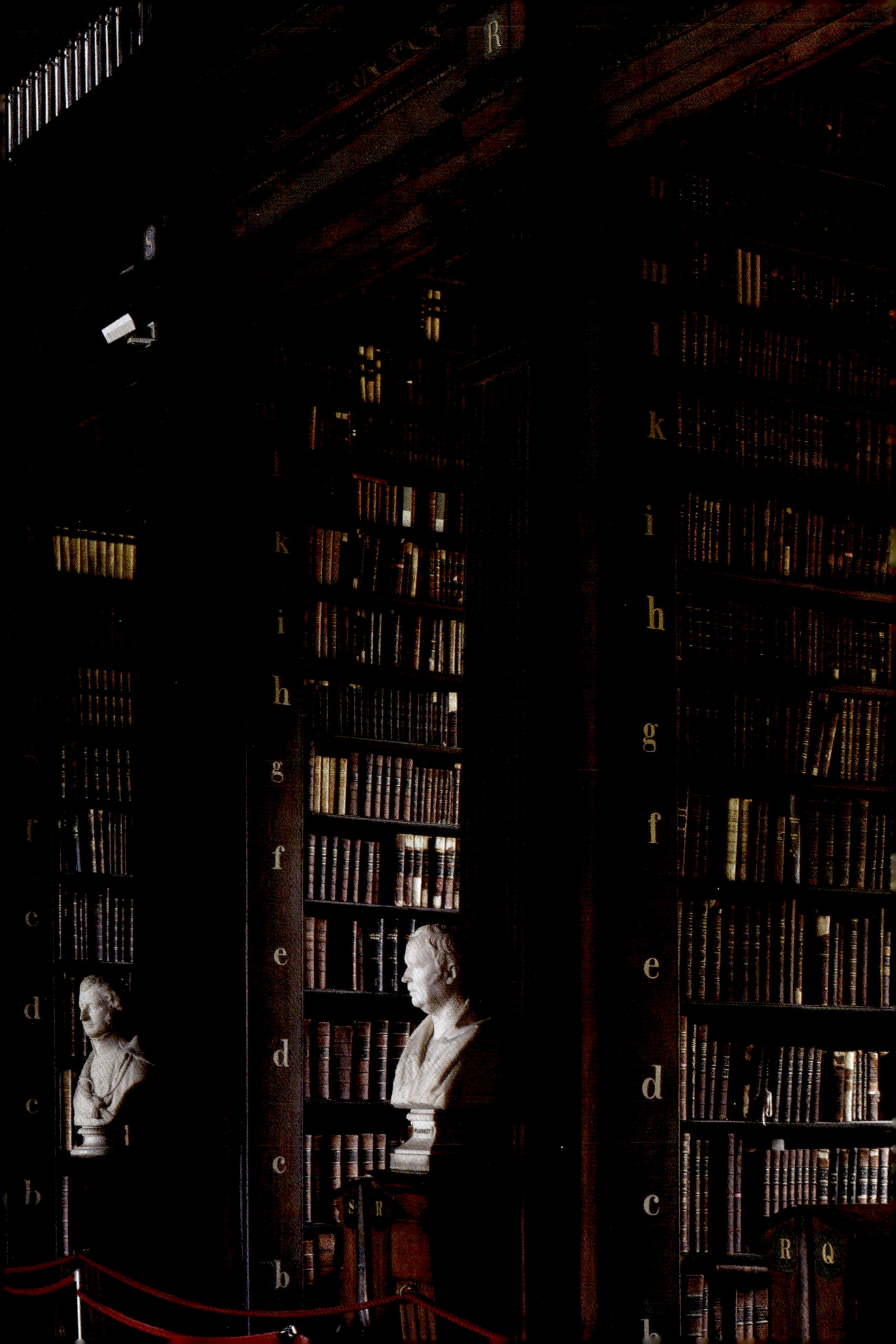

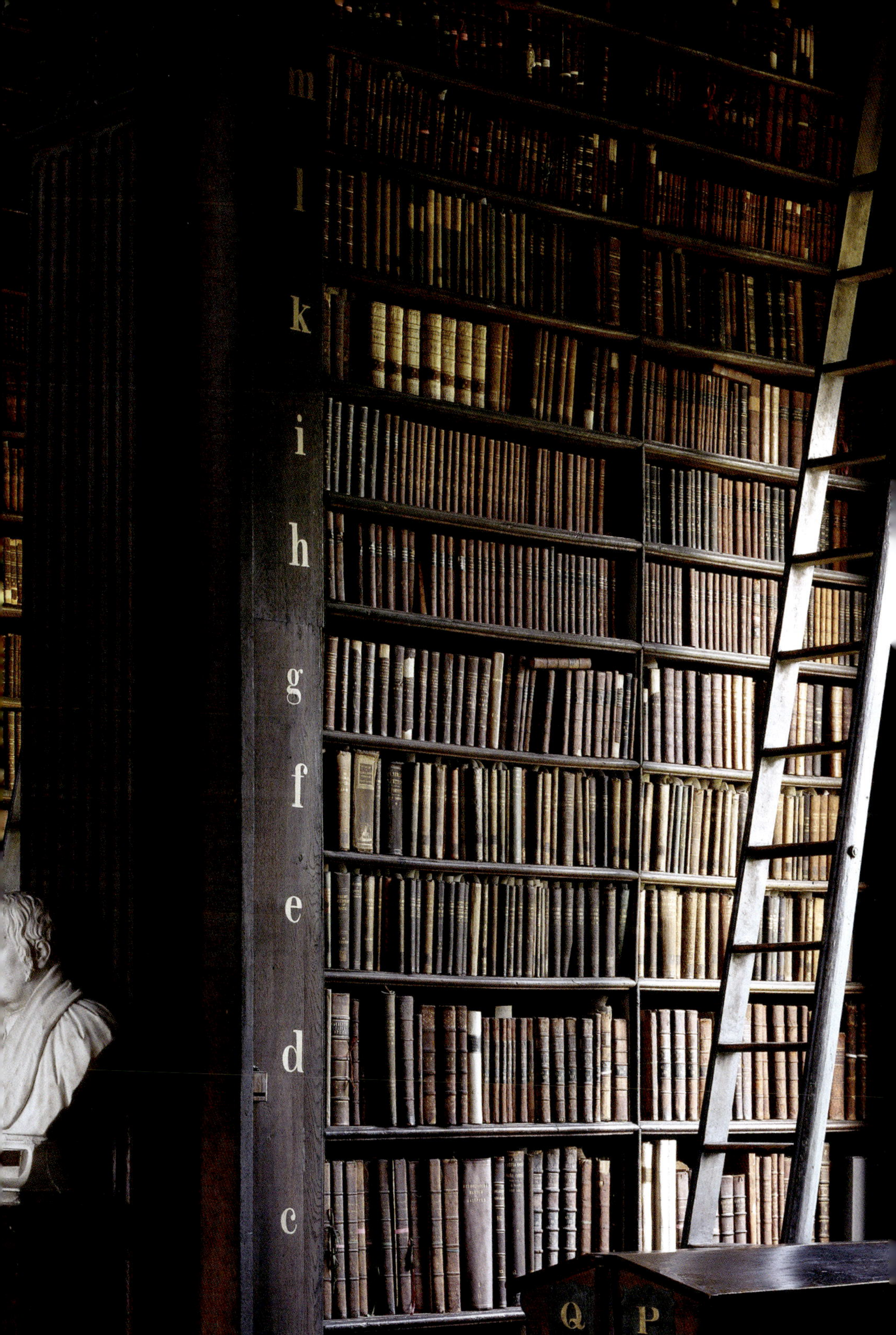
m
l
k
i
h
g
f
e
d
c
Q P

Marsh's Library

Narcissus Marsh (1638–1713) was an Oxford-educated scholar and clergyman whose interest lay in mathematics in particular and the natural sciences in general. His prominence in academic circles was reflected in his membership of numerous learned societies. Along with Jonathan Swift (1667–1745) and others, Marsh was among the founding members of the Dublin Philosophical Society. Marsh moved to Ireland from England in 1679, in order to take up the post of Provost of the prestigious Trinity College in Dublin and it was here that his idea of creating his own library began to take root. It was to be accessible to all, clearly catalogued and easy to consult – criteria inadequately met, in Marsh's view, by the library at Trinity College, but of fundamental importance to users. Against the backdrop of the bitter rifts that were developing between Ireland's Catholics and Protestants in the late 17th century, and which were naturally therefore at the forefront of his mind, Marsh wished above all that his library should become a centre of learning on the principles of the Protestant faith. Holdings in various areas, such as the valuable collection of oriental manuscripts, were bequeathed to the Bodleian Library in Oxford, where Marsh's career had begun. In 1691 he was appointed Archbishop of Dublin and took up residence in St Sepulchre's palace. Its rooms were soon found insufficient to house his collection of books, which had meanwhile grown to several thousand volumes. In 1701, therefore, he commissioned the Surveyor General of Ireland, Sir William Robinson (1645–1712), to build a new library right beside St Patrick's cathedral. The interior of the library, with its dark oak bookcases surmounted by ornamental gables and carved bishop's insignia, has remained unchanged right up to the present. The shelves house some 25,000 books, all of them in essence chosen by Marsh or acquired as part of entire collections, such as those of Edward Stillingfleet (1635–1699) and Élie Bouhéreau (1643–1719), Marsh's first librarian. In 1707 the Irish Parliament granted the library the permanent status of a public charitable institution, governed by a board of trustees made up of the reigning archbishop and representatives of the Irish church authorities.

❋ ✳ ❋

Founded 1701
Holdings c. 25,000 volumes
Type of library originally a private library; Protestant research library
Highlights *Codex Kilkenniensis*, 15th century; *Irish primer*, prepared for Elizabeth I at her request, 16th century; *Vocabularium Latinum et Hibernum*, compiled by Richard Plunkett, 1662; Demosthenes, *All the Orations of Demosthenes, Pronounced to Excite the Athenians against Philip King of Macedon*, edited in 1756 by Thomas Leland, Dublin, 1792

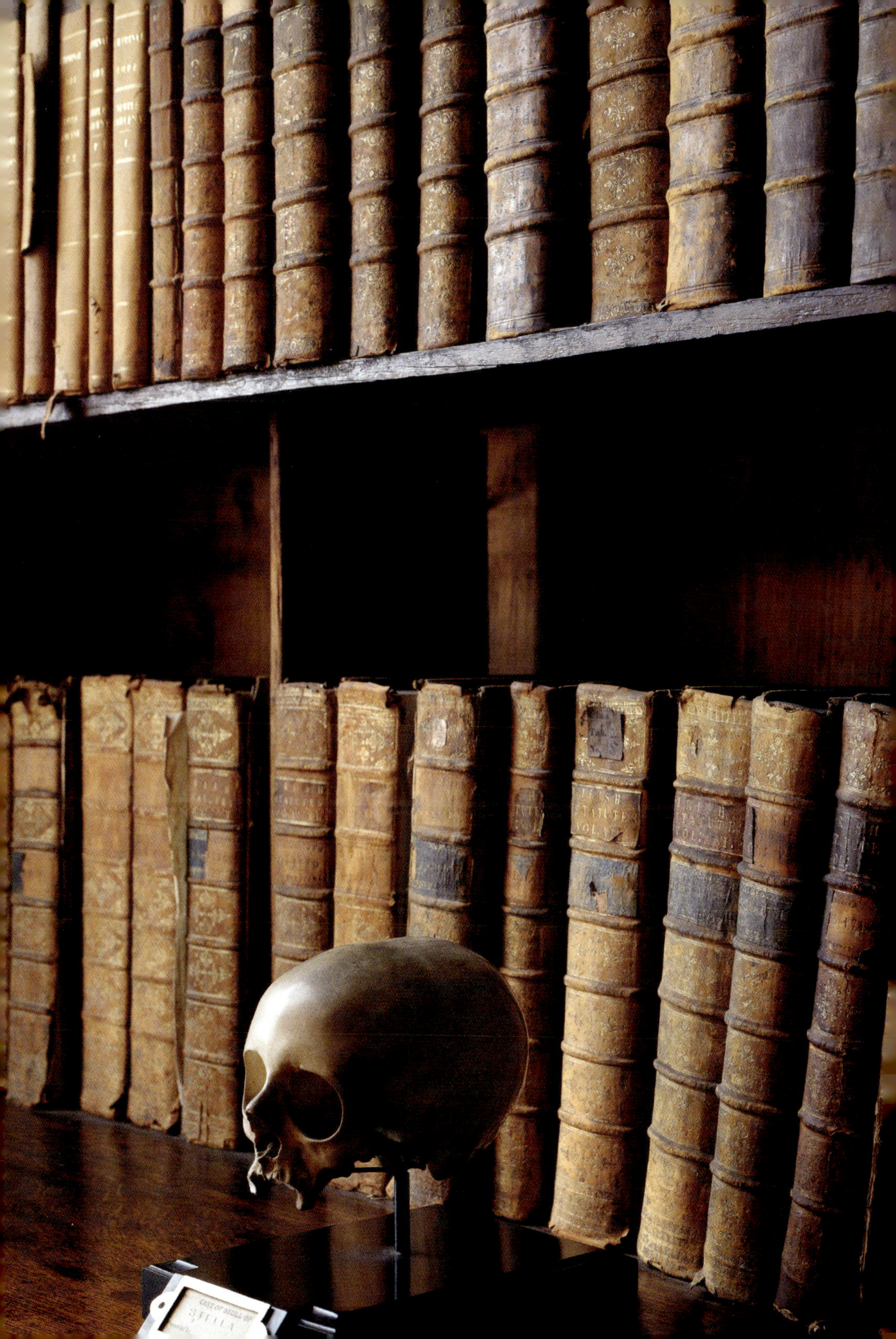

Narcissus Marsh (1638–1713) war ein in Oxford ausgebildeter und dort bereits als Kleriker tätiger Gelehrter, dessen besonderes Interesse der Mathematik und allgemein den Naturwissenschaften galt. Seine brillante wissenschaftliche Laufbahn fand in der Mitgliedschaft zahlreicher gelehrter Gesellschaften Ausdruck. Bei der Dublin Philosophical Society war Narcissus Marsh zusammen mit Jonathan Swift (1667–1745) und anderen Gründungsmitglied. Als Marsh im Jahr 1679 von England nach Irland übersiedelte, um in Dublin die Leitung des prestigeträchtigen Trinity College zu übernehmen, begann seine Idee zu reifen, eine eigene Bibliothek zu gründen. Sie sollte allgemein zugänglich, klar erfasst und leicht zu konsultieren sein. Denn diese Kriterien erschienen ihm in der Bibliothek des College nur unzureichend gelöst, jedoch grundlegend für den Benutzer. Vor allem sollte seine Bibliothek aber vor dem

Hintergrund herber konfessioneller Auseinandersetzungen, die Irland am Ende des 17. Jahrhunderts erschütterten und sein Geistesleben entsprechend prägten, ein Kompetenzzentrum für protestantische Glaubensgrundlagen werden. Bestände unterschiedlicher Thematik, wie etwa seine kostbare Sammlung orientalischer Handschriften, vermachte Marsh der Bodleian Library in Oxford, wo seine Laufbahn begonnen hatte. Bald reichten die Räumlichkeiten des erzbischöflichen St.-Sepulchre-Palastes, den Marsh seit seiner Ernennung zum Erzbischof von Dublin 1691 bewohnte, nicht mehr aus, um seine mittlerweile auf mehrere Tausend Bände angewachsene Büchersammlung unterzubringen. 1701 ließ er daher vom Generalinspekteur des englischen Königs für Irland, William Robinson (1645–1712), in unmittelbarer Nähe der Saint-Patrick-Kathedrale das neue Bibliotheksgebäude errichten. Sein Interieur hat

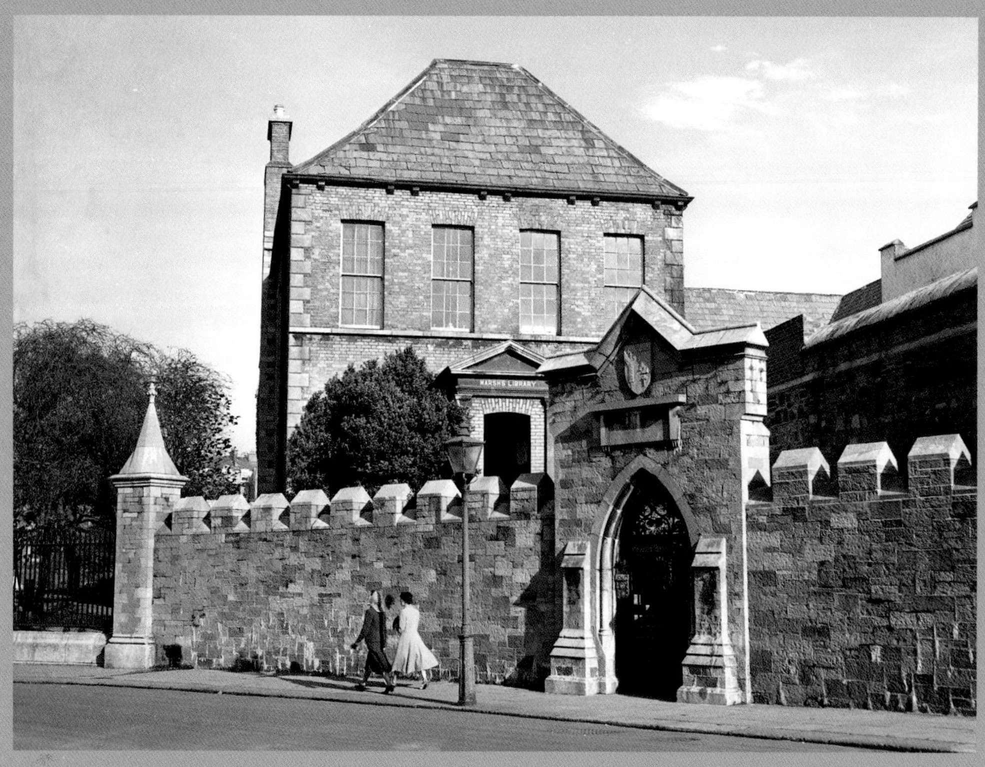

sich mit den von Ziergiebeln und geschnitzten
Bischofsinsignien überragten Bücherregalen
aus dunklem Eichenholz bis heute unverändert
erhalten. In diesen sind rund 25 000 Bücher
ausgestellt, die im Wesentlichen von Marsh
selbst ausgewählt beziehungsweise als kom-
plette Sammlungen erworben wurden – wie jene
von Edward Stillingfleet (1635–1699) und Élie
Bouhéreau (1643–1719), seinem ersten Bibliothekar. 1707 gewährte das irische Parlament
der Bibliothek den immerwährenden Status
einer öffentlich gemeinnützigen Einrichtung,
die von den jeweils amtierenden Erzbischöfen
und Autoritäten der irischen Kirche verwaltet
werden sollte.

❈∗❈

Narcissus Marsh (1638–1713), grand érudit,
s'intéressait aux sciences naturelles en général
et aux mathématiques en particulier. Ses
multiples adhésions aux sociétés savantes s'en
font l'écho. Formé à Oxford, c'est là que débute
sa brillante carrière d'ecclésiastique. Il est
cofondateur avec Jonathan Swift (1667–1745) de
la Dublin Philosophical Society. Lorsque Marsh
quitte l'Angleterre pour l'Irlande en 1679 afin
de reprendre la direction du prestigieux Trinity
College de Dublin, l'idée de posséder sa propre
bibliothèque germe en lui. Il l'imagine accessible
à tous, clairement agencée et facile à consulter.
Car il lui semble que ces critères justement
cruciaux pour les utilisateurs font défaut à la
bibliothèque universitaire. Il lui importe avant
tout que sa bibliothèque devienne un centre de
compétences pour le fondement de la foi protestante, étant donné les âpres conflits religieux
qui secouent l'Irlande vers la fin du XVIIᵉ siècle
et qui marquent sa vie spirituelle. Il a légué des
fonds relatifs à d'autres thématiques comme sa
précieuse collection de manuscrits orientaux
à la bibliothèque bodléienne d'Oxford où sa
carrière a démarré. Bientôt, la place disponible
dans le palais archiépiscopal St Sepulchre
que Marsh occupait depuis sa nomination
d'archevêque de Dublin en 1691 ne suffit plus
à abriter la collection qui s'est entre-temps

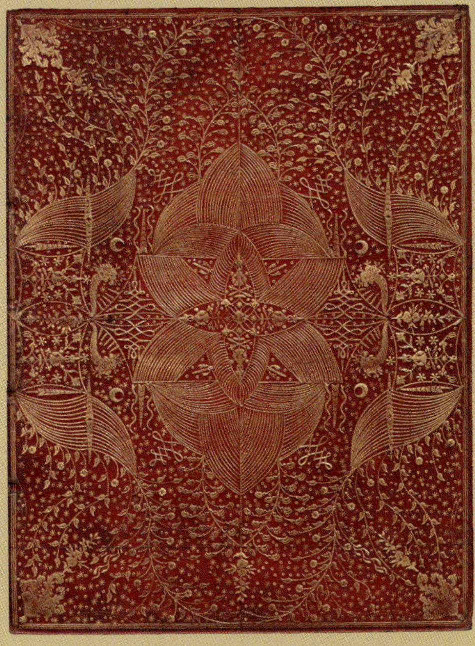

considérablement agrandie et compte plusieurs
milliers de volumes. Il fait alors ériger en 1701
par l'inspecteur général du roi d'Angleterre
pour l'Irlande, William Robinson (1645–1712), un
nouveau bâtiment dans le voisinage direct de la
cathédrale Saint-Patrick. Son intérieur aux étagères en bois de chêne foncé ornées de frontons
et de mitres sculptées (l'insigne des évêques)
est resté intact jusqu'à nos jours. Ces rayonnages accueillent près de 25 000 livres, des
intégrales pour l'essentiel choisies par Marsh,
ainsi que par Edward Stillingfleet (1635–1699) et
Élie Bouhéreau (1643–1719), son premier bibliothécaire. En 1707, le Parlement irlandais vote
une loi conférant à la bibliothèque un statut
perpétuel d'institution d'utilité publique et en
confie la gestion aux évêques en fonction et aux
autorités de l'Église anglicane d'Irlande.

Dublin, Marsh's Library, c. 1947–1959

Demosthenes, *All the Orations of Demosthenes,*
Pronounced to Excite the Athenians against
Philip King of Macedon, edited by Thomas Leland,
Dublin, 1792: *Book binding*

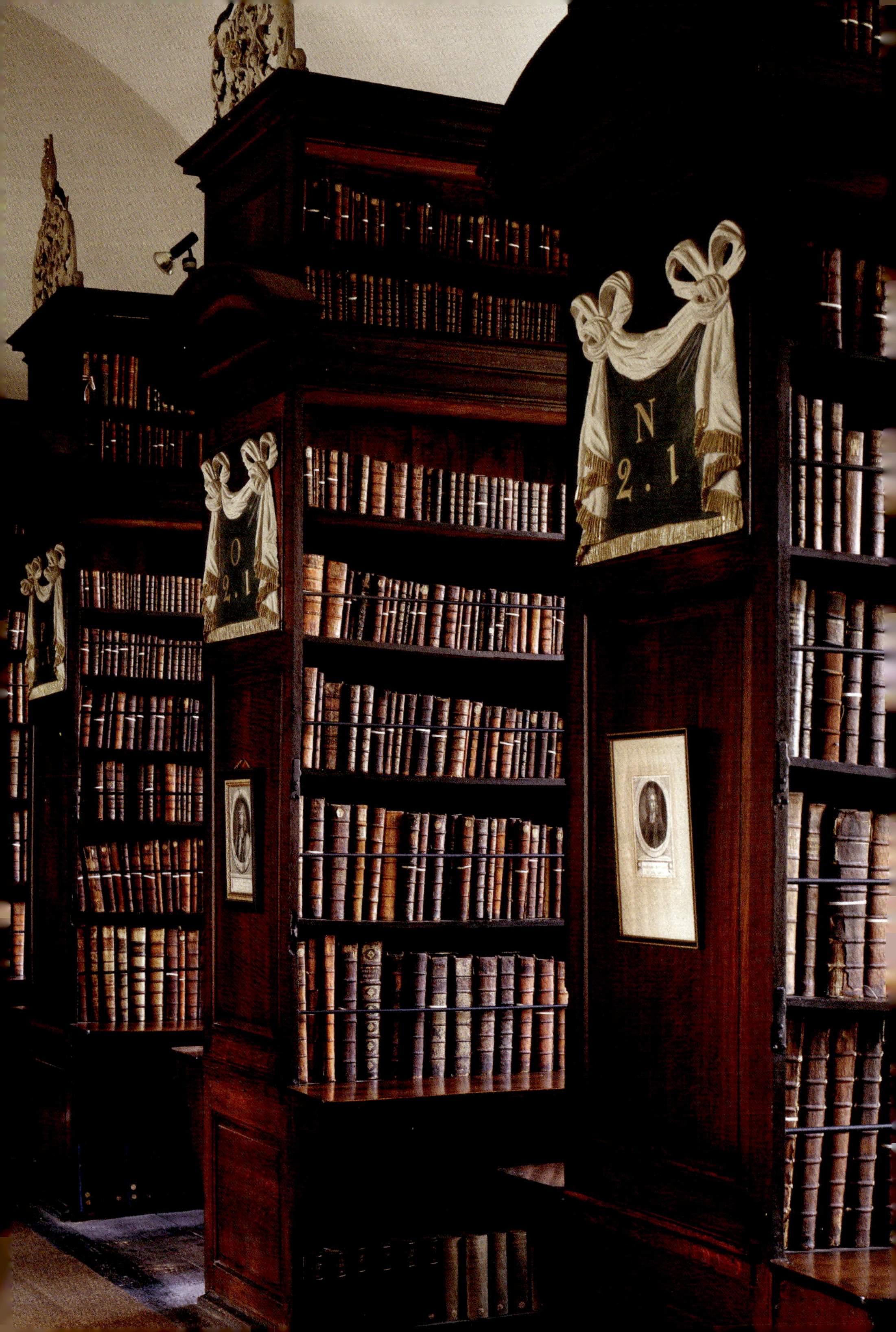
N
2. 1
0.
2. 1

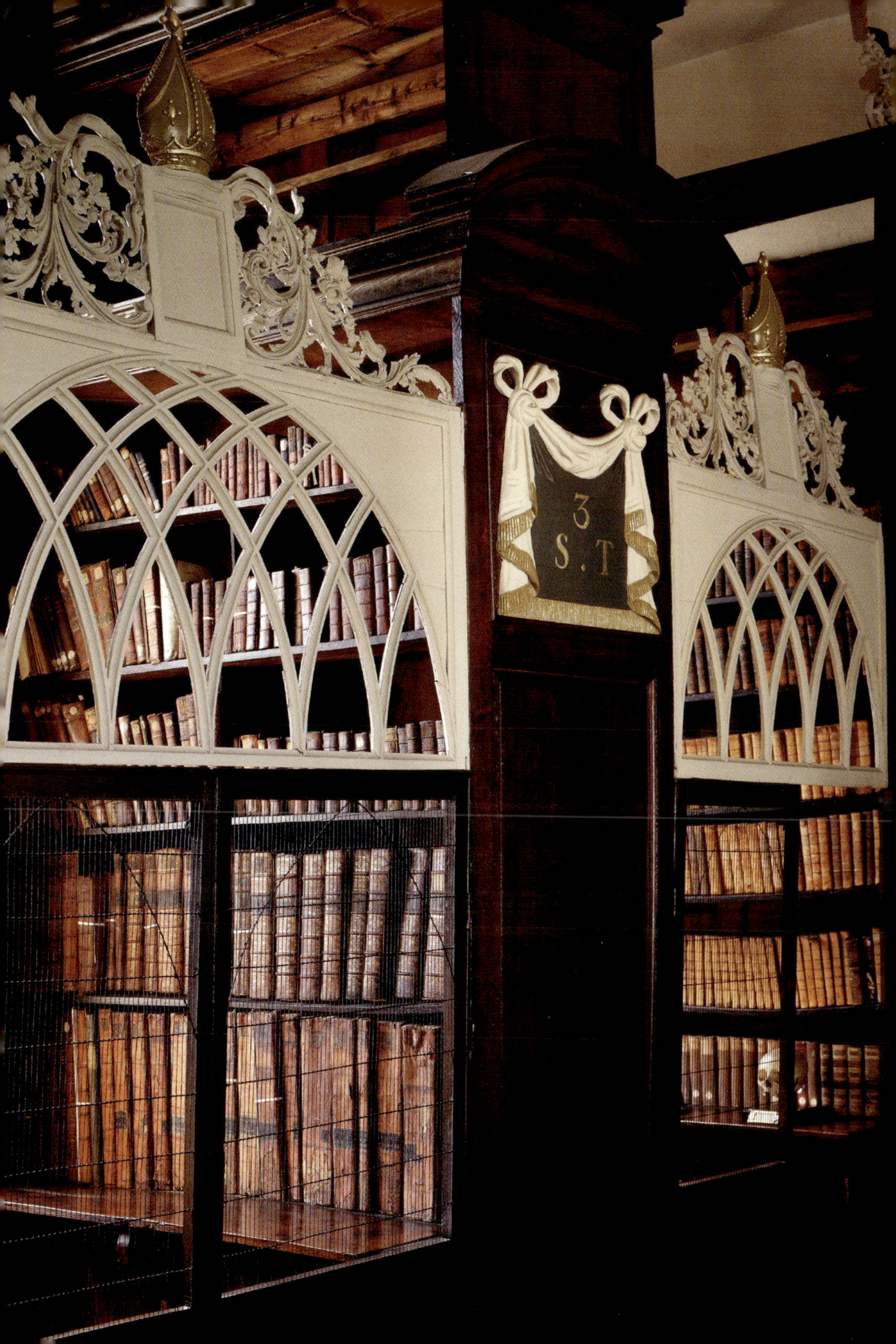
3
S . T

The Codrington Library

The University of Oxford – one of the oldest in the world – has shaped intellectual life in Britain since the late Middle Ages. Its architecture still bears extensive witness to the Gothic period, when research and teaching first flowered here, and in 1438 King Henry VI (1421–1471) awarded All Souls College its first statutes. The college owes its prime location in the centre of the university complex, and the virtually unchanged front façade, to its influential patron Henry Chichele (c. 1364–1443), who as Archbishop of Canterbury was the spiritual head of the country and who is considered the real founder of the college. In line with his ideas, All Souls College was to be an institute of advanced study, at which scholars who had already studied elsewhere could further their knowledge in the areas of civil and canon law, theology and medicine. Like earlier colleges before it, All Souls was reserved for the clergy and as such aimed to produce a highly qualified and learned clerical "militia". From the time of the Reformation, however, this primarily theological mission was overtaken by academic concerns in terms of national importance. In the course of the Reformation, numerous medieval manuscripts were removed from the old library, with some of them ending up in the Plantin Moretus Museum in Antwerp. After the Renaissance, law and history became specialised areas within the library's holdings. The building was furnished according to the latest standards and replaced its medieval desk library with an early shelving system contemporaneously with other Oxford colleges, even before the building of the new Great Library. The benefactor of the Great Library, Christopher Codrington (1668–1710), had himself been a Fellow of All Souls before being appointed Governor of the Antilles, part of the British Empire, which he sought to rule according to Enlightenment principles. His statue (1734) by Henry Cheere (1703–1781) in the middle of the library, which portrays him as a Roman general, may allude to this role. Codrington's legacy consisted of funds to build and run a new library, together with the bequest of his own private collection of 12,000 books. Construction began in 1716 on the basis of plans by Nicholas Hawksmoor (1661–1736). The resulting structure, which today survives almost exactly as it was built, represented something entirely new in the history of library architecture. The building housing the library – which, contrary to tradition, is laid out on the ground floor (with a basement) – blends into its surroundings as part of a larger scheme, begun in 1703, to transform the medieval structure into a regular complex constructed around a double courtyard. With a view to stylistic uniformity, Hawksmoor originally planned his new building wholly in the Late Gothic style. In the end, however, he was required, in line with the brief given to him by the College, to employ Classicist forms in the interior. The result is an elongated

Founded 1438; Great Library: 1716–1751 to designs by Nicholas Hawksmoor
Holdings c. 185,000 volumes
Type of library study library
Highlights *Amesbury Psalter*, 13th century (Ms 6); Sir Christopher Wren, *Warrant Designs for St Paul's Cathedral*, c. 1675 (Wren II:10-14); Ferdowsi, *Shahnama* ("The Book of Kings"), the national epic poem of Persia, copy of the early 18th century (MS 289)

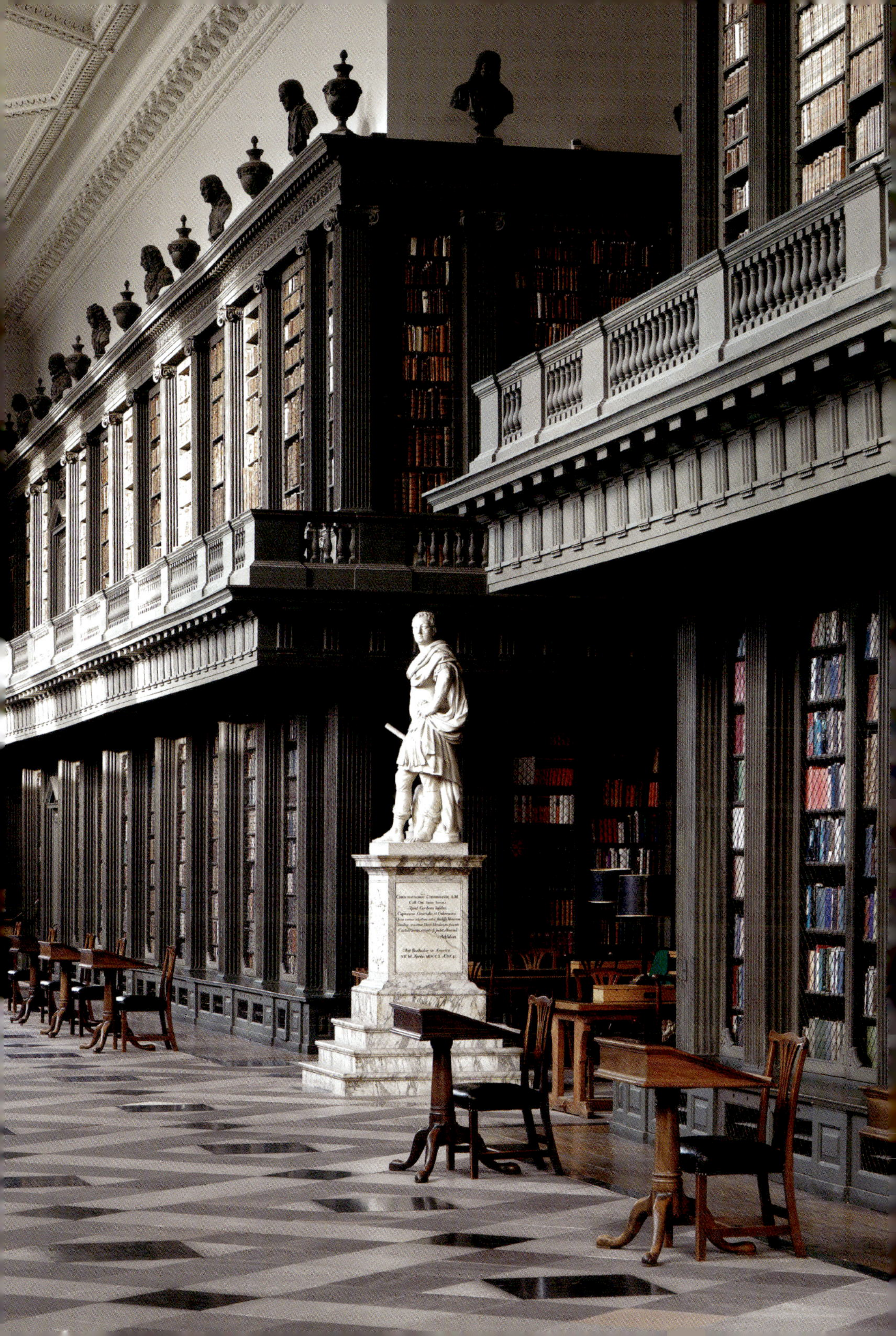

room of exceptional homogeneity and elegance, lined with bookshelves on all sides. The classical Palladian windows on the short walls correspond to Late Gothic tracery windows on the exterior façades, just as the simple neoclassical rounded-arch windows on the south front relate to the pointed arches on the courtyard façade, which communicate with the architecture of the Gothic chapel opposite. The bookcases in dark olive green, divided into two levels by an upper gallery, are conceived as Classical architectural façades and lend the room coherence. Their palette is taken up by the polychrome tiled floor. The freestanding furniture, in particular the small desks on tripod feet, were reproduced after historical originals.

❋❋❋

Seit dem ausgehenden Mittelalter prägt die Universität von Oxford, die zu den ältesten der Welt zählt, das Geistesleben Großbritanniens. Ihr Erscheinungsbild verdankt sie im Wesentlichen der Gotik, als Forschung und Lehre hier zu einer ersten Blüte gelangt waren. 1438 verlieh König Heinrich VI. (1421–1471) dem All Souls College seine ersten Statuten. Die bevorzugte Lage im Zentrum des Universitätskomplexes und die bis heute nahezu unveränderte Fassadenfront verdankt das Kolleg seinem einflussreichen Stifter Henry Chichele (um 1364–1443), der als Erzbischof von Canterbury zur geistlichen Autorität des Landes geworden war und als eigentlicher Gründer des Kollegs gilt. Seinen Vorstellungen entsprechend sollte im All Souls College eine Eliteschule für höhere Studien entstehen, an der bereits anderenorts ausgebildete Akademiker ihre Kenntnisse in Theologie, Zivil- und Kirchenrecht sowie Medizin vertiefen konnten. Wie auch ältere Kollegien zuvor war das All Souls College ursprünglich als geistliche Einrichtung entstanden und zielte als solche auf die Ausbildung eines hoch qualifizierten, mit den „Waffen des Geistes" gerüsteten Klerus. Ab der Reformation sollte jedoch die akademische Komponente gegenüber der vorzugsweise theologischen Zielsetzung an Gewicht und

nationaler Bedeutung gewinnen. Aus der alten Bibliothek wurden im Zuge der Reformation zahlreiche mittelalterliche Manuskripte entfernt. Einige davon gelangten in das Plantin-Moretus-Museum in Antwerpen. Ab der Neuzeit wurden Recht und Geschichte zu Sammlungsschwerpunkten der nach den jeweils aktuellsten Standards ausgestatteten Bibliothek. Die mittelalterliche Pultbibliothek war – gleichzeitig mit anderen Colleges in Oxford – einem frühen Regalsystem gewichen, noch bevor der Neubau der Great Library in Angriff genommen wurde. Ihr Stifter Christopher Codrington (1668–1710) war selbst Absolvent des Kollegs gewesen, bevor er die zum britischen Imperium zählenden Antillen als Gouverneur nach den Prinzipien der Aufklärung zu regieren versuchte. Auf diese Rolle mag sein Standbild (1734) von Henry Cheere (1703–1781) im Zentrum der Bibliothek, das ihn als römischen Feldherrn zeigt, hinweisen. Seine Stiftung beinhaltete die Errichtung und den Betrieb einer neuen Bibliothek sowie seine eigene 12 000 Bände zählende Büchersammlung. Nach Plänen von Nicholas Hawksmoor (1661–1736) entstand ab 1716 ein bis heute nahezu unverändert erhaltener, in der Architekturgeschichte neuartiger Bibliotheksbau. Das Gebäude dieser Bibliothek, die entgegen der Tradition im (unterkellerten) Erdgeschoss angelegt wurde, fügt sich in die Neugestaltung des gesamten Baukomplexes seit 1703, die das mittelalterliche Baugefüge zu einer regelmäßigen Doppelhofanlage formte. Im Hinblick auf stilistische Einheitlichkeit plante Hawksmoor ursprünglich auch seinen Neubau zur Gänze im Stil der Spätgotik. Den Innenraum hatte er schließlich nach den Vorgaben der Auftraggeber in klassizistischen Formen zu gestalten. Es entstand ein lang gestreckter, allseits von Bücherschränken umfasster Saalraum von außergewöhnlicher Einheitlichkeit und Eleganz. Den klassischen Serliana-Fenster der Schmalseiten entsprechen spätgotische Maßwerkfenster an den Außenfronten, den klassizistisch schlichten Rundbogenfenstern der Südfront Spitzbögen an der Hoffassade, die mit der Architektur der gegenüberliegenden gotischen Kapelle kommunizieren. Die in dunklem Olivgrün gehaltenen Bücherschränke mit geschosstrennender Galerie sind als klassische Architekturfronten konzipiert und verleihen dem Raum Geschlossenheit. Ihre Farbigkeit wird von dem polychromen Steinboden aufgenommen. Das freistehende Mobiliar, insbesondere die Pulttischchen auf Dreifüßen, wurde originalen Vorlagen nachgebildet.

✳ ✳ ✳

Parmi les plus anciennes au monde, l'université d'Oxford marque la vie intellectuelle de la Grande-Bretagne depuis le Moyen Âge tardif. Elle doit son allure principalement à l'époque gothique, qui fit d'elle l'un des fleurons de la recherche et de l'enseignement. L'All Souls College acquit ses premiers statuts en 1438 grâce au roi Henri VI (1421–1471). Il doit son emplacement privilégié au cœur d'un complexe universitaire et sa façade quasiment inchangée à un donateur influent nommé Henry Chichele (vers 1364–1443). Fondateur officiel de l'All Souls College, et archevêque de Canterbury, cet homme bénéficiait d'une réelle autorité spirituelle sur tout le pays. L'All Souls College fut pour lui l'occasion de créer une école d'élite où des académiciens formés ailleurs pourraient approfondir leurs connaissances en théologie, droit civil et religieux et médecine. À l'instar d'autres collèges plus anciens, l'All Souls College était un établissement spirituel ayant pour vocation de former au mieux le clergé et le munir de « l'arme du savoir ». Dès la Réforme cependant, les composants académiques prirent le pas sur l'objectif théologien visé et gagnèrent du poids à l'échelle nationale. Dans le sillage de la Réforme, de nombreux manuscrits médiévaux disparurent. Certains d'entre eux atterrirent dans le musée Plantin-Moretus à Anvers. Au cours des siècles suivants, le droit et l'histoire devinrent des points forts de la collection de la bibliothèque alors enrichie selon les standards de l'époque moderne. La bibliothèque à pupitre médiévale céda le pas à un système de rayonnages ancien, changement connu à la même époque par d'autres établissements d'Oxford, mais avant que les travaux de la Great Library ne débutent. Son mécène, Christopher Codrington (1668–1710), étudia à l'All Souls College avant de devenir gouverneur et d'essayer de diriger, selon des principes éclairés, les Antilles qui appartenaient à la Couronne britannique. Placé au centre de la bibliothèque, son portrait en pied, réalisé par Henry Cheere (1703–1781) et le représentant en seigneur romain, tend à rappeler ce rôle. Son mécénat incluait la construction et l'entretien d'une nouvelle bibliothèque ainsi que le legs de ses propres collections s'élevant à 12 000 volumes. Les plans de Nicholas Hawksmoor (1661–1736) donnèrent naissance dès 1716 à un bâtiment novateur dans l'histoire de l'architecture et peu changé au fil des siècles. Contrairement à la tradition, les livres sont rangés au premier niveau (au-dessus d'un sous-sol), le nouveau bâtiment s'inscrit dans un processus de réaménagement entamé en 1703. L'ensemble médiéval fut repris et réorganisé afin d'obtenir un bâtiment régulier à double cour. Dans un objectif d'unité stylistique, Hawksmoor avait prévu un édifice tout en style gothique tardif. Mais il dut se plier aux directives des commanditaires et concevoir l'intérieur selon le modèle classique. Il en résulte une salle allongée dont les murs sont couverts d'armoires d'une élégance et d'une harmonie extraordinaires. Les serliennes classiques des petits côtés correspondent aux encadrements de fenêtre gothique perpendiculaire sur la façade extérieure. Les arcades de fenêtre typiques du classicisme correspondent aux ogives côté cour qui semblent justement répondre à l'architecture de la chapelle gothique située en face. Les armoires teintées vert olive foncé s'articulent sur deux niveaux. Elles sont pensées comme des éléments d'architecture classique et confèrent une exceptionnelle uniformité à la pièce. Leur teinte est assortie aux tons polychromes du sol carrelé. Le mobilier et notamment les pupitres sur trépied sont des répliques d'originaux.

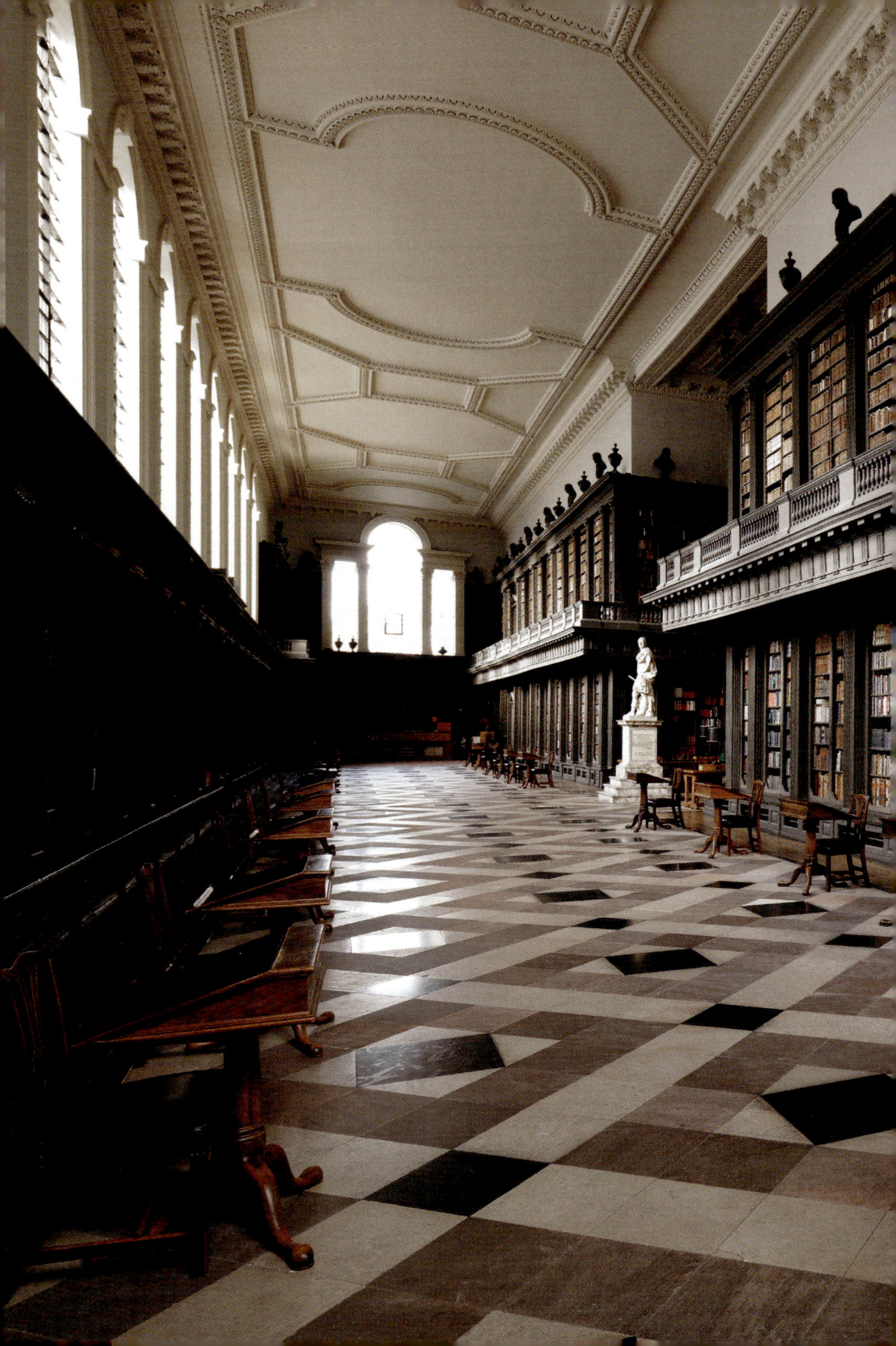

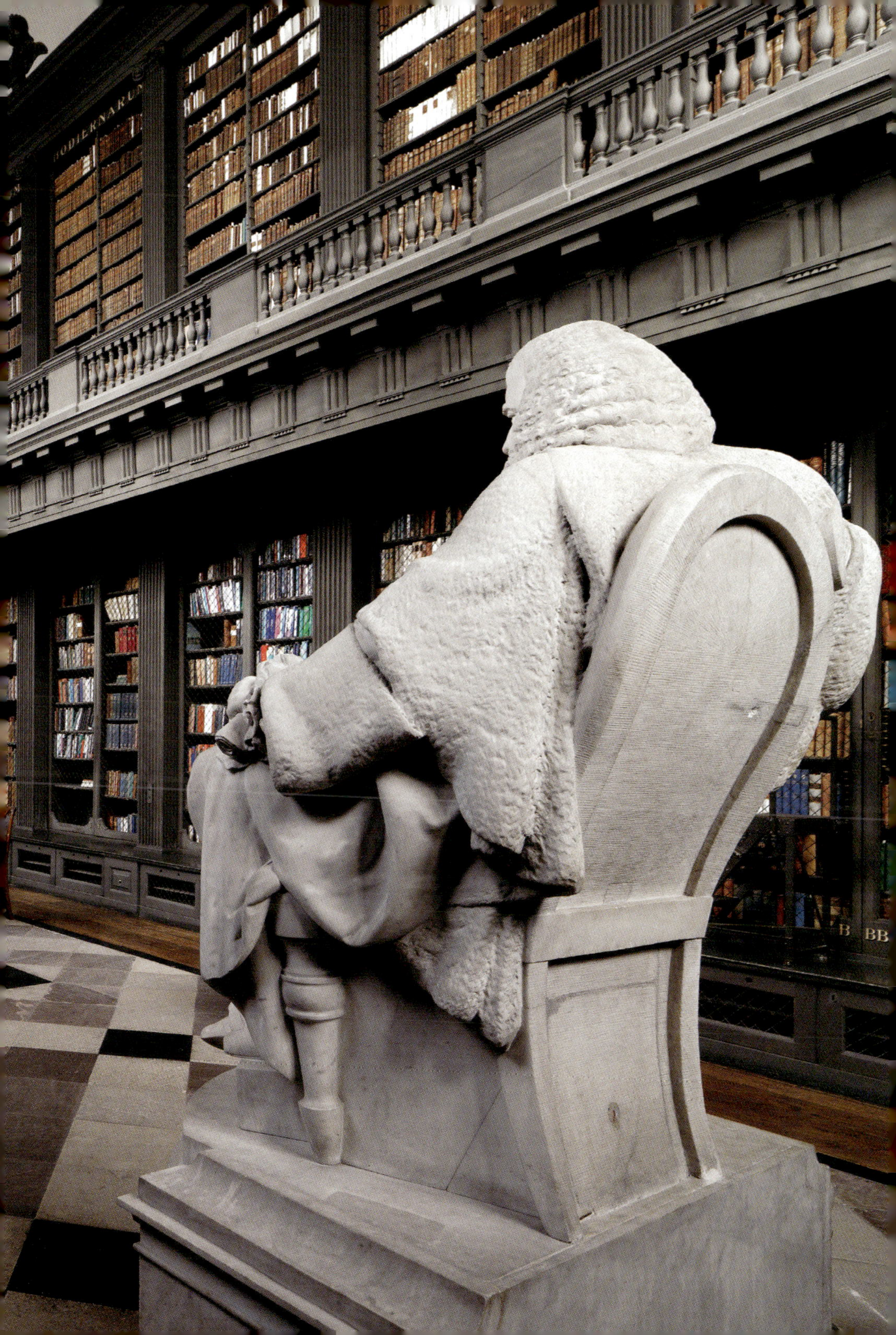

Eastnor Castle Library

Eastnor Castle in the county of Herefordshire conceals a particular gem in the form of its country-house library. The books are embedded in a cosy atmosphere among furnishings that evoke the Italian Renaissance. The room is known as the Long Library on account of its elongated proportions. The decoration was carried out around 1866 under the third Earl Somers (1819–1883), who chose the already successful interior designer George Edward Fox (1833–1908) to create the library rooms at his country seat. A few years earlier, Augustus Welby Northmore Pugin (1812–1852) had placed his characteristic Gothic Revival stamp on the decoration at Eastnor. This style is best preserved in the Gothic Drawing Room. Robert Smirke (1780–1867), the architect of Eastnor, was himself an early champion of the Gothic Revival, but looked back to even earlier styles when he was commissioned by the first Earl Somers to design a country residence in keeping with the family's new status. Smirke chose the medieval Norman Revival style from the time of King Edward I (1239–1307) for this castle built on the border with Wales (which the Norman Edward I had conquered for the English crown). The imposing crenellated complex with its fortified towers and keep was built between 1810 and 1824. Thanks to the cast-iron used in its construction, which was modern for the time, Eastnor Castle survives essentially unaltered today. Within this architectural context, the library – whose fixtures and fittings were purchased by its owner while on the Grand Tour – is conceived as a fundamentally new creation. Its two chimney breasts were designed in the Italian Renaissance style by George Edward Fox, who had studied in Italy, and are correspondingly made of Istrian stone. All around the room, thousands of volumes line the walls in shelving purchased in Italy by Henry Bathurst-Somers. The bookcases are distinguished by fine inlay-work in precious woods, while the book bindings in antique leather with gilt tooling reinforce the impression of magnificence. Above the bookcases, which reach to just under half the height of the room, the upper part of the walls is hung with sumptuous Flemish tapestries showing scenes from the life of Catherine de' Medici (1519–1589). The tapestry cycle, with its large figures portrayed in an antique setting and style of dress, came from Mantua. Scholarly themes are also found on the coffered ceiling, for example, in the representations of Virtues and Vices. Only the writing desk beside the short wall of the Long Library points to the room's true function as a place of study and reading. Overall, however, drawing-room elements predominate: there are sofas grouped around the massive fireplaces, with armchairs, settles, side tables and other furnishings scattered throughout the room, which also includes a piano. The upholstery, Indian carpets and drapes are all characterised by warm colours. Tall French windows ensure a generous amount of natural lighting, while artificial light is provided by

Founded 1812; Long Library from 1860 after designs by George Edward Fox
Type of library private library
Highlights José de Acosta, *The Naturall and Morall Historie of the East and West Indies,* London, 1604; François Le Gouz de la Boullaye, *Les voyages et observations du sieur de la Boullaye Le Gouz,* Paris, 1657; Charles Darwin, Phillip Parker King, Robert Fitzroy, *Narrative of the Surveying Voyages of His Majesty's Ships Adventure and Beagle, between the years 1826 and 1836, Describing their Examination of the Southern Shores of South America, and the Beagle's Circumnavigation of the Globe,* London, 1839–1840, 3 vols.

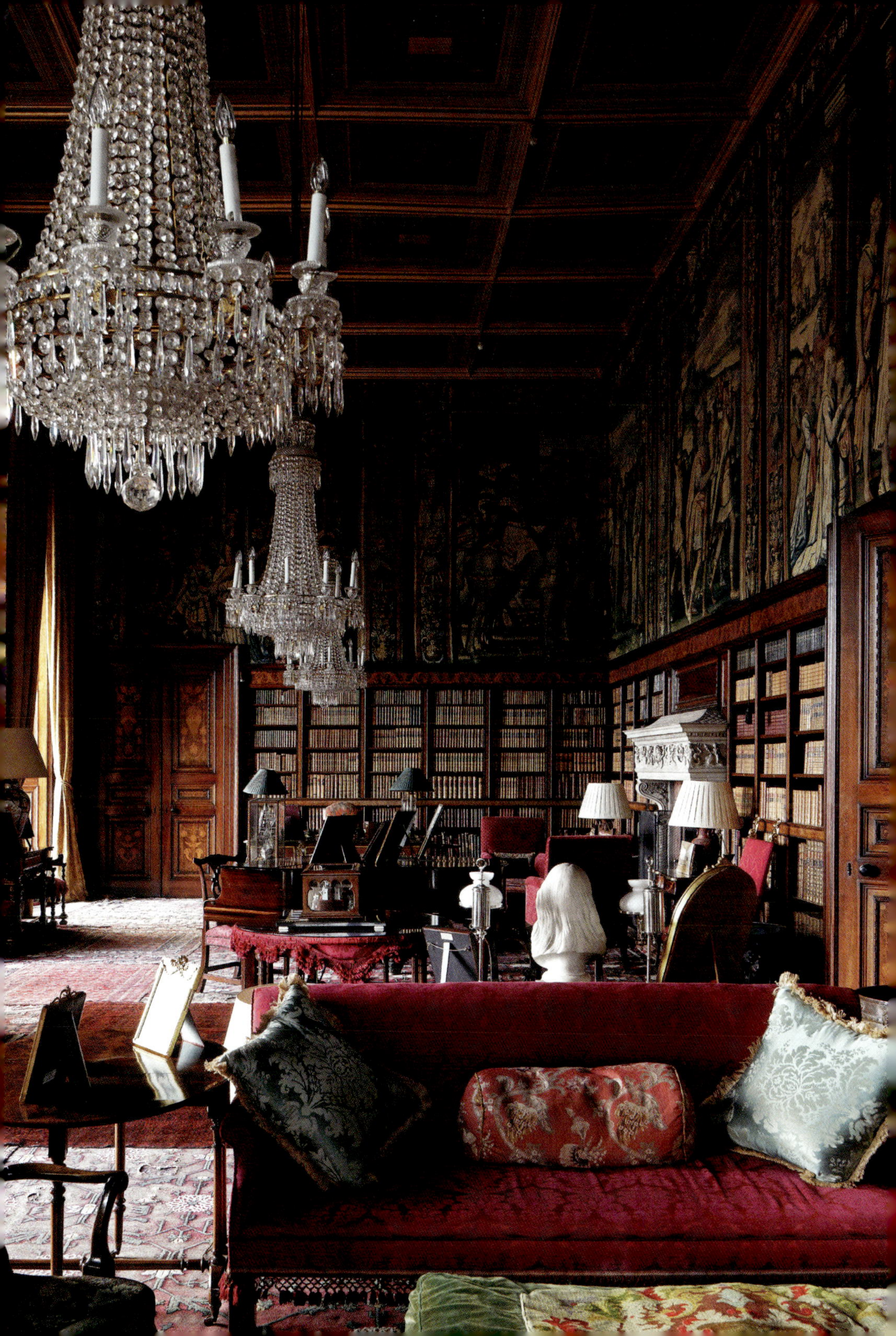

impressive crystal chandeliers in conjunction with floor and table lamps located all around the room. Eastnor Castle, idyllically situated within an English landscape garden, is still in private hands today and is successfully run as an event location and tourist attraction by James Felton Somers Hervey-Bathurst, a descendant of the Somers-Cock family and the Barons Somers who founded Eastnor. English Heritage has listed Eastnor Castle as a Grade 1 historic building.

※∗※

Das Eastnor Castle in der Grafschaft Herefordshire birgt mit seiner Landhausbibliothek ein besonderes Juwel. Sie ist eingebettet in ein wohnliches Ambiente mit Versatzstücken, die die italienische Renaissance evozieren. Die lang gestreckten Raumproportionen haben ihr die Bezeichnung „Long Library" eingebracht. George Edward Fox (1833–1908) war, als er um 1866 nach Eastnor berufen wurde, um im Auftrag des dritten Earl Somers (1819–1883) die Bibliotheksräume seines Landsitzes zu gestalten, bereits ein erfolgreicher Innenarchitekt. Vor ihm hatte Augustus Welby Northmore Pugin (1812–1852) die Innenraumgestaltung von Eastnor in den für ihn charakteristischen neugotischen Formen geprägt. Sie haben sich am besten im sogenannten Gothic Drawing Room erhalten. Als früher Verfechter des Gothic Revival galt auch bereits der Architekt von Eastnor, Robert Smirke (1780–1867). Allerdings griff er noch auf ältere Stilformen zurück, als er vom ersten Earl Somers den Auftrag erhielt, eine dem neuen Status gemäße Familienresidenz zu konzipieren. Er wählte den normannischen Stil der Epoche König Eduards I. (1239–1307) für die an der Grenze zu Wales (das der Normanne Eduard I. für die englische Krone erobert hatte) errichtete Burg. Von 1810 bis 1824 entstand eine mächtige, zinnenbewehrte Anlage mit Wehrtürmen und einem Bergfried, die sich dank ihrer für die Zeit modernen Gusseisenkonstruktion bis heute im Wesentlichen unverändert erhalten hat. In diesem baulichen Kontext versteht sich die Bibliothek mit ihren vom Auftraggeber im Laufe der Grand Tour erworbenen Versatzstücken als grundlegend neue Schöpfung. Ihre beiden Kamine wurden von dem in Italien ausgebildeten George Edward Fox im italienischen Renaissancestil entworfen, als Material wurde entsprechend Pietra d'Istria verwendet. Rings um den Saal sind Tausende Bücher in Wandregalen untergebracht, die Henry Bathurst-Somers in Italien erworben hatte. Die Regale zeichnen sich durch feine Einlegearbeiten in wertvollen Holzsorten aus. Die antiken Lederbindungen der Bücher mit Golddekor verleihen den Regalwänden zusätzliche Preziosität. Die Wandregale nehmen knapp die untere Hälfte der Raumhöhe ein, während kostbare flämische Tapisserien die obere Hälfte der Wände prachtvoll verkleiden. Der großfigurige Zyklus mit antik verbrämten Szenen aus dem Leben Katharina de' Medicis (1519–1589) stammt aus Mantua. Gelehrte Themen sind auch an der Kassettendecke zu finden, etwa in den Darstellungen von Tugenden und Lastern. Einzig der Schreibtisch an der Stirnseite der Long Library verweist auf ihre eigentliche Funktion, nämlich die des Studiums und der Lektüre. Im Allgemeinen überwiegen aber Salonelemente, zu denen auch ein Klavier gehört. Um die mächtigen Kamine sind Sofas angeordnet. Außerdem sind über den ganzen Salon Lehnstühle, Wandbänke und komplementäres Kleinmobiliar verteilt. Warme Farben prägen die Bezüge sowie die in Indien gewobenen Teppiche und die Draperien. Der Raum ist großzügig durch hohe Türfenster belichtet, während imposante Kristallüster und allerorts angeordnete Tisch- und Stehlampen für künstliche Beleuchtung sorgen. Noch heute befindet sich das idyllisch inmitten eines englischen Landschaftsgartens gelegene Eastnor Castle in Privatbesitz und wird von James Felton Somers Hervey-Bathurst, einem Nachfahren der Barone Somers-Cocks, die Eastnor gegründet haben, erfolgreich als Eventlocation und Touristenattraktion geführt. English Heritage hat Eastnor Castle als historisches Gebäude ersten Ranges gelistet.

La bibliothèque du château d'Eastnor situé dans le comté d'Herefordshire est un remarquable joyau. L'aménagement de son intérieur évoquant la Renaissance italienne invite à la détente. Ses dimensions en longueur lui ont valu l'appellation de « Long Library ». Lorsque le comte Somers (1819–1883), troisième du nom, fit venir George Edward Fox (1833–1908) à Eastnor vers 1866 pour aménager les salles de bibliothèque de son domaine, celui-ci était déjà un décorateur renommé. L'intérieur d'Eastnor était alors très empreint de néo-gothique, forme caractéristique du prédécesseur de Fox, Augustus Welby Northmore Pugin (1812–1852). C'est dans le Gothic Drawing Room que cet héritage s'est le mieux conservé. L'architecte d'Eastnor, Robert Smirke (1780–1867), était lui aussi l'un des premiers défenseurs du néo-gothique. Il recourut néanmoins à d'autres styles plus anciens, lorsque le premier comte Somers lui confia la charge de concevoir une résidence familiale en conformité avec son nouveau statut. Il choisit le style normand de l'époque du roi Édouard Ier (1239–1307) pour créer une forteresse située non loin de la frontière avec le pays de Galles (que le Normand Édouard Ier avait conquis pour la Couronne d'Angleterre). Un ensemble crénelé imposant avec donjon et tours de défense fut bâti entre 1810 et 1824. Il s'est maintenu jusqu'à aujourd'hui grâce à l'utilisation de la fonte, un élément de construction moderne pour l'époque. Dans ce contexte architectural, la bibliothèque dotée d'éléments de décor acquis par le commanditaire durant son Grand Tour s'apparente à une création tout à fait inédite. Ses deux cheminées en *pietra d'Istria* style Renaissance italienne sont de George Edward Fox, qui avait lui-même été formé en Italie. La salle est ceinte d'étagères qui hébergent des milliers de livres acquis par Henry Bathurst-Somers durant son séjour en Italie. Ces étagères se distinguent par leur fine marqueterie en bois précieux. La reliure antique dorée des ouvrages confère un caractère encore plus précieux aux étagères. Ces dernières habillent la partie inférieure de la pièce tandis que des tapisseries flamandes d'une valeur

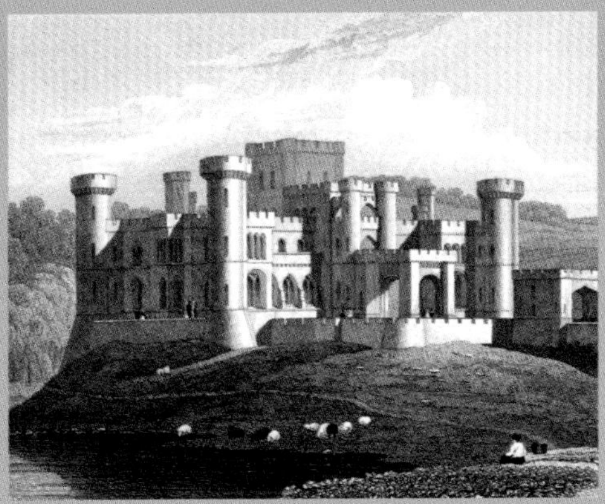

Eastnor Castle, 1826

inestimable ornent un peu plus de la moitié des murs, en partie supérieure. En provenance de Mantoue, ces tapisseries bordées de motifs antiques illustrent, grandeur nature, des scènes de la vie de Catherine de Médicis (1519–1589). Le plafond à caissons affiche lui aussi des thèmes savants. En témoignent la figuration des vices et des vertus. Seul le bureau placé tout au fond de la Long Library rappelle sa fonction première, celle d'un espace dédié à l'étude et à la lecture. Les autres éléments de mobilier, dont un piano à queue, évoquent plutôt une atmosphère de salon. Agrémentés çà et là de confortables fauteuils, d'un coffre-banc et de petit mobilier complémentaire, plusieurs canapés sont disposés autour des imposantes cheminées. Les tentures comme les draperies et les tapis tissés en Inde présentent des couleurs chaudes. La pièce est baignée d'une lumière généreuse grâce à de hautes portes-fenêtres. Des lustres en cristal majestueux et diverses lampes de bureau et luminaires diffusent l'éclairage artificiel. Niché au cœur d'un jardin paysager idyllique à l'anglaise, le château d'Eastnor est une propriété privée. Il est actuellement administré par James Felton Somers Hervey-Bathurst, un descendant des barons Somers-Cocks, les fondateurs de la lignée Eastnor. Le domaine est devenu un site touristique, servant aussi de lieu événementiel. L'English Heritage a classé le château d'Eastnor monument historique de premier rang.

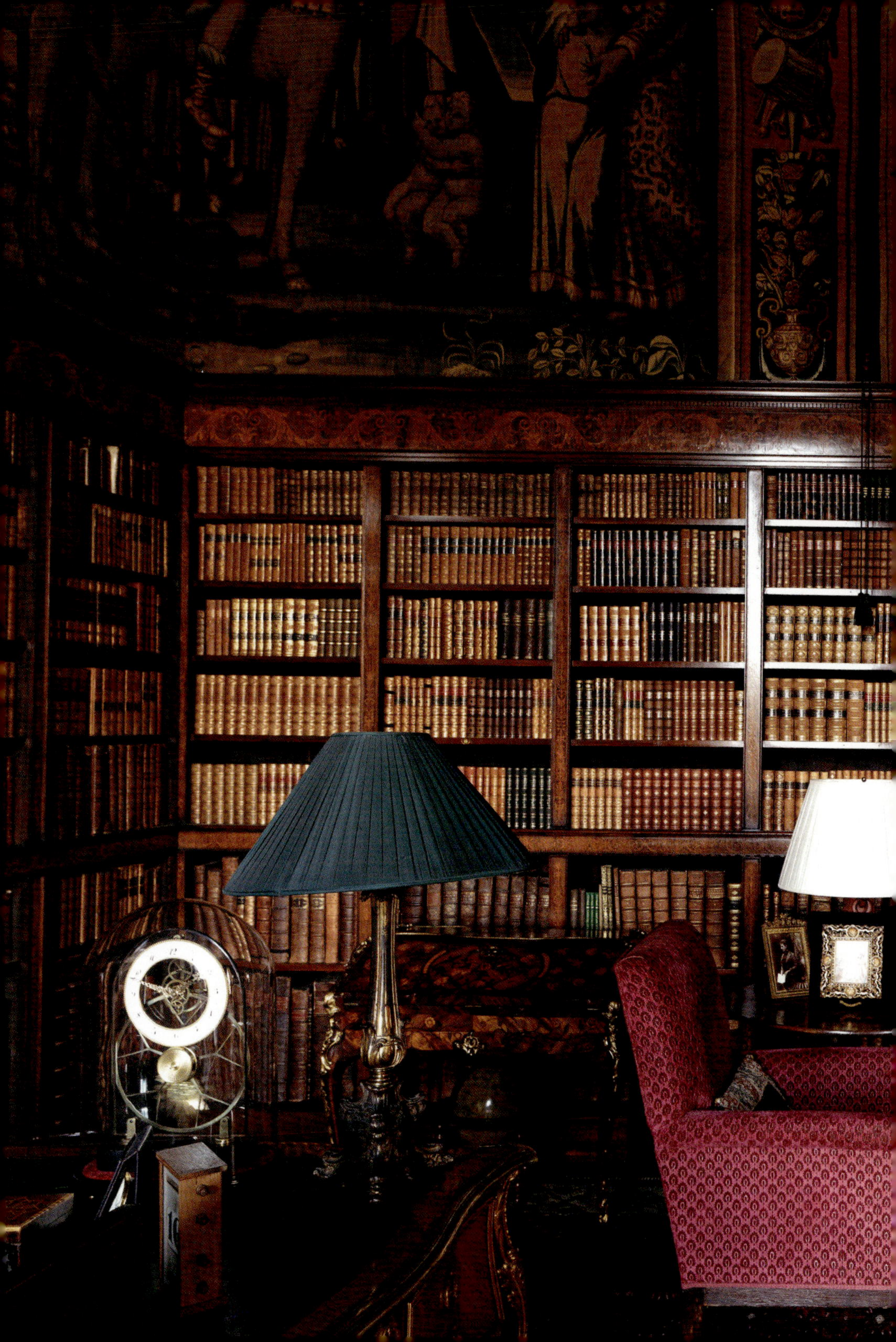

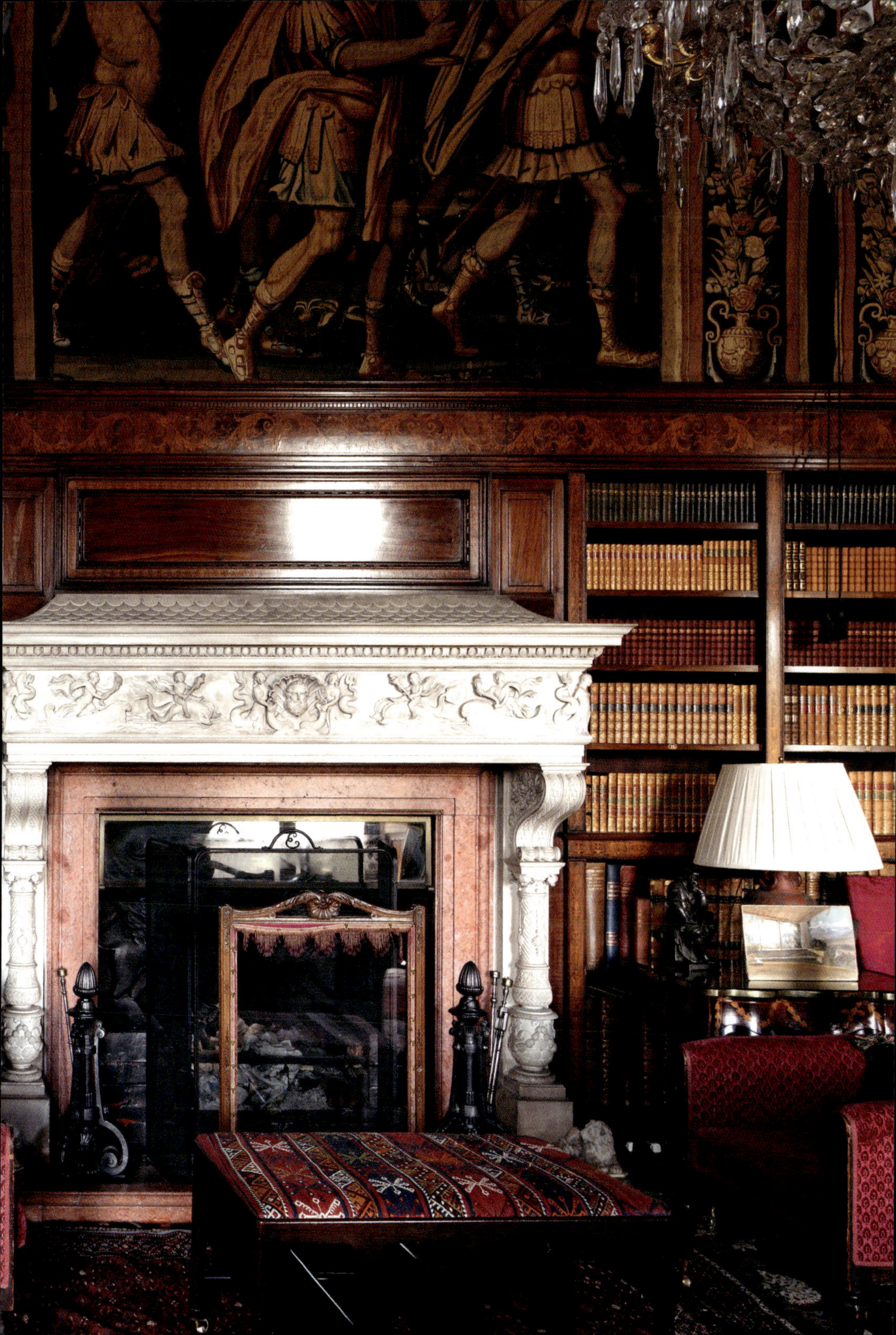

Bibliothèque Sainte-Geneviève

The former monastic library owes its name to Geneviève, the patron saint of Paris, who in 512 was buried next to the 6th-century monastery founded by the Merovingians, in the church that now bears her name. Documentary information about the library only surfaces from 1148, however, when the influential Abbot Suger of Saint-Denis (1081–1151) dispatched Augustinian canons to Sainte-Geneviève and charged them with running the monastery library and a scriptorium. A number of manuscripts from these historical holdings, with the abbey's ownership mark, still survive today. A library catalogue from the 13th century shows that at this stage the library already contained 226 codices. Important centres of scholarship began to develop not only in Sainte-Geneviève but also in the nearby abbeys of Saint-Germain-des-Prés and in particular Saint-Victor. These would lay the foundation stone of intellectual life in the so-called Quartier Latin, the student quarter which in the Middle Ages sprang up around the university outside Paris's city walls. The Bibliothèque Sainte-Geneviève continues to serve the purposes of study today as the Paris 1 Panthéon-Sorbonne university library, with holdings that have meanwhile grown to two million media units. In 1624 Louis XIII (1601–1643) refounded the library, whereby it not only gained in prestige as a "royal" library, but also in substance. Donations from private individuals and institutional bodies enriched its holdings, which from now on assumed an encyclopaedic range, while its catalogue was conceived on the model of the king's private library. The library was opened to the public from the early 18th century and with its 60,000 printed works and 2,000 manuscripts even became an attraction for scholarly tourists. Its public mission may have been one of the reasons why the Bibliothèque Sainte-Geneviève survived the Revolution years intact, although the abbey in which it was housed was dissolved and converted into a school, parts of which are still preserved in today's Lycée Henri IV. The new abbey church that had been built by Jacques-Germain Soufflot (1713–1780) from 1764, on top of the Sainte-Geneviève hill, was turned into the secular Panthéon, the national hall of fame. The library, still housed in the remains of the old abbey, was renamed the "Bibliothèque du Panthéon", and valuable books from dissolved monasteries and confiscated private libraries were transferred here. These events from the Revolutionary period are still reflected in the different provenances of the holdings. In 1844 work began on a new library building opposite the Panthéon, designed by Henri Labrouste (1801–1875); when it opened in 1851, the reading room contained 65,000 volumes with a further 40,000 in the ground-floor stacks. Groundbreaking features included not only the iron-frame construction that was a prerequisite for the gas lighting, and which

Founded new foundation in 1624 of the monastic library documented since 1148; building 1844–1851 by Henri Labrouste
Holdings c. 2 million media units
Type of library study library; formerly monastic library, today university library
Highlights *Bible Manerius*, 1185–1195 (Ms. 008); *Chroniques de Saint-Denis*, 1275–1280 (Ms. 782); Manuel Philè, *De animalium proprietate*, 1566 (Ms. 3401)

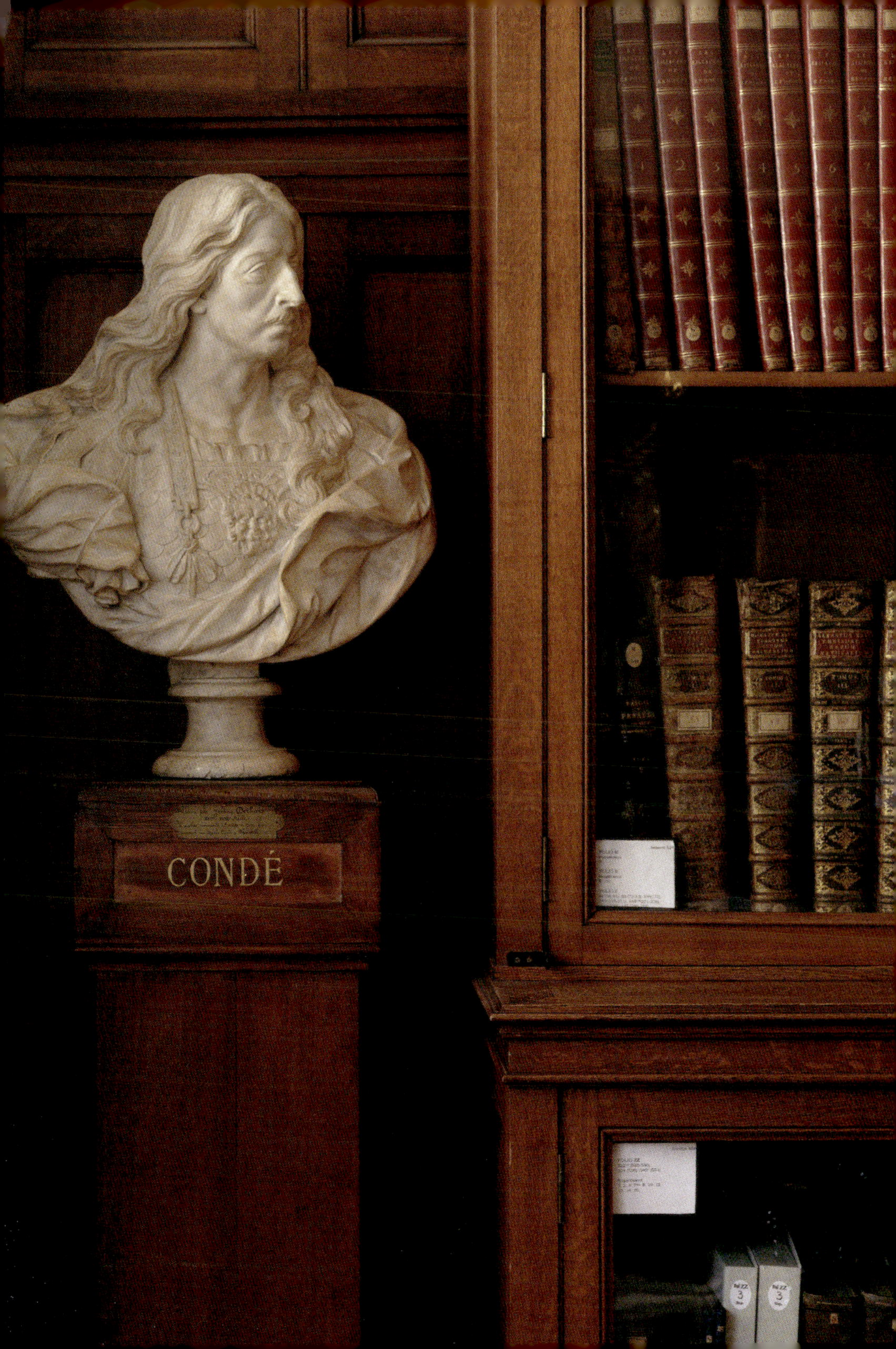

CONDÉ

was here visibly employed in a monumental hall for the first time, but also the typology of the design: an independent library building with book stacks at ground level and a reading room lit from all sides, with books running all the way round the walls and a gallery on the upper level. Interior and façade would exercise a great influence upon later library buildings; in Paris, Labrouste was subsequently commissioned to design a new reading room for the Bibliothèque Nationale.

❊❊❊

Ihren Namen verdankt die ehemalige Klosterbibliothek der Schutzpatronin von Paris, die 512 in der nach ihr benannten Kirche neben der Abtei, einer merowingischen Gründung des 6. Jahrhunderts, begraben wurde. Dokumentarische Angaben zur Bibliothek finden sich aber erst ab 1148, als der einflussreiche Abt Suger von Saint-Denis (1081–1151) Augustiner-Chorherren nach Sainte-Geneviève berief und mit dem Betrieb der Klosterbibliothek und eines Skriptoriums beauftragte. Einige Handschriften dieses Altbestandes haben sich mit dem zeitgenössischen Besitzvermerk der Abtei bis heute erhalten. Er umfasste laut einem Bücherkatalog des 13. Jahrhunderts bereits 226 Kodizes. Aber nicht nur in Sainte-Geneviève, sondern auch in den nahe gelegenen Abteien Saint-Germain-des-Prés und vor allem Saint-Victor begannen sich bedeutende geistige Zentren herauszubilden, die den Grundstein legen sollten für das intellektuelle Leben des sogenannten Quartier Latin, des im Mittelalter rund um die Universität entstandenen Studentenviertels außerhalb der Stadtmauern von Paris. Eine Bestimmung, der die Bibliothèque Sainte-Geneviève noch heute als Studienbibliothek der Universität Paris I Panthéon Sorbonne nachkommt, und zwar mit einem auf zwei Millionen Medieneinheiten angewachsenen Bestand. Als königliche Neugründung durch Ludwig XIII. (1601–1643) im Jahr 1624 gewann die Bibliothek nicht nur an Prestige, denn sie wurde nun zur „königlichen" Bibliothek, sondern auch

an Substanz. Stiftungen von privater und institutioneller Seite bereicherten ihre Bestände, die ab nun enzyklopädisch ausgerichtet waren. Ihr Katalog wurde nach dem Vorbild der königlichen Privatbibliothek konzipiert. Seit dem frühen 18. Jahrhundert war die Bibliothek der Öffentlichkeit zugänglich und galt mit ihren 60 000 Druckwerken und 2 000 Manuskripten sogar als Attraktion für Bildungsreisende. Dieser Öffentlichkeitsanspruch mag unter anderem ein Grund dafür gewesen sein, dass die Bibliothèque Sainte-Geneviève die Revolutionsjahre unbeschadet überstanden hat, während das sie beherbergende Kloster aufgelöst und zur Schule umgewidmet wurde. Teile davon sind im heutigen Lycée Henri IV erhalten. Die von Jacques-Germain Soufflot (1713–1780) ab 1764 am Gipfel des Genoveva-Hügels neu errichtete Abteikirche wurde zur nationalen Ruhmeshalle des Panthéon. Die noch immer in Resten der alten Abtei untergebrachte Bibliothek wurde zur neuen „Bibliothèque du Panthéon", der nun wertvolle Bücherschätze aus aufgelösten Klöstern und konfiszierten Privatbibliotheken zugewiesen wurden. Über die unterschiedlichen Provenienzen der Bestände lassen sich noch heute diese umwälzenden Ereignisse erschließen. Als Henri Labrouste (1801–1875) ab 1844 einen Neubau gegenüber dem Panthéon errichtete, wurden bei der Inbetriebnahme der Bibliothek im Jahr 1851 im Lesesaal 65 000 und in den Erdgeschossmagazinen 40 000 Bände gezählt. Bahnbrechend war nicht nur die hier erstmals in einem monumentalen Saalraum sichtbar inszenierte Technik des Gusseisenbaus – Letzterer war eine Vorgabe für die Gasbeleuchtung –, sondern auch die Typologie der Konstruktion: ein unabhängiger Bibliotheksbau mit Büchermagazinen im Erdgeschoss und einem allseits durchlichteten Lesesaal mit umlaufenden Wandregalen und Galerien im Obergeschoss. Innenraum und Fassade sollten großen Einfluss auf spätere Bibliotheksbauten ausüben; in Paris wurde Labrouste in der Folge mit dem Ausbau der Nationalbibliothek beauftragt.

Cette ancienne bibliothèque monastique doit son nom à la patronne de Paris, inhumée en 512 de notre ère dans l'église éponyme érigée près de l'abbaye fondée au VIᵉ siècle par les Mérovingiens. Les premiers documents en attestant remontent à 1148, l'année où Suger, le puissant abbé de Saint-Denis (1081–1151), fit venir des chanoines réguliers de Saint-Augustin à Sainte-Geneviève pour leur confier la direction de la bibliothèque et d'un atelier de copistes. Quelques manuscrits du fonds initial portant le sceau de l'abbaye existent encore aujourd'hui. Le catalogue dressé au XIIIᵉ siècle prouve que ce fonds comptait déjà 226 codex. Sainte-Geneviève n'était pas l'unique centre d'érudition à l'époque. Les abbayes voisines aussi, Saint-Germain-des-Prés et Saint-Victor notamment, contribuèrent à poser les jalons de la vie intellectuelle du Quartier latin – nom donné au quartier étudiant entourant l'université médiévale implantée au-delà de l'enceinte de Paris. La bibliothèque Sainte-Geneviève perdure par le fait d'un décret. Cette bibliothèque encyclopédique, attachée à l'université Panthéon Sorbonne, Paris 1, s'enorgueillit d'un fonds porté à deux millions de documents. Elle acquit, lors du décret de Louis XIII (1601–1643) ordonnant la nouvelle fondation d'une bibliothèque royale en 1624, d'une part un statut prestigieux, d'autre part de la substance. Enrichie par maints dons privés et institutionnels, elle a pris une allure encyclopédique. Son catalogue est conçu suivant le modèle de la bibliothèque royale privée. À son ouverture au public au début du XVIIIᵉ siècle, la bibliothèque Sainte-Geneviève disposant de 60 000 imprimés et de 2 000 manuscrits devient un aimant pour les voyageurs en quête de savoir. C'est probablement cette volonté d'ouverture au public qui la sauve de la Révolution, alors que le monastère qui l'abrite est démantelé avant d'être converti en école. Certaines parties sont d'ailleurs conservées au lycée Henri-IV. La nouvelle abbatiale, construite peu avant au sommet de la butte Sainte-Geneviève (à partir de 1764 par Jacques-Germain Soufflot), est

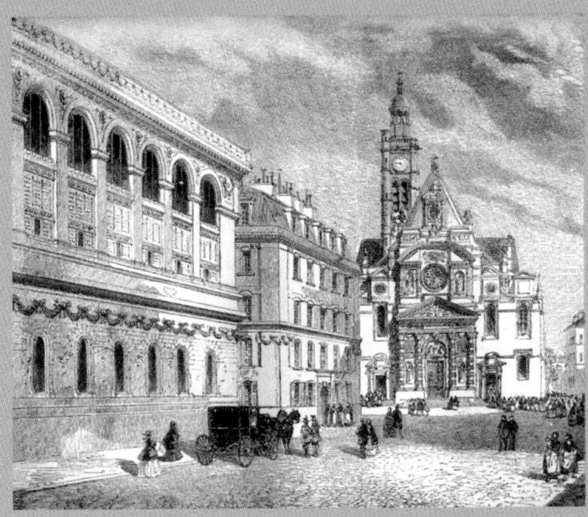

Library Sainte-Geneviève and Saint-Étienne du Mont, Paris, 1878, in: Henri Gourdon de Genouillac, *Paris à travers les siècles*, 1878, vol. III, p. 278

en fait le fameux temple honorifique national appelé Panthéon. Les restes de l'ancienne abbaye encore en ruines constitueront la « bibliothèque du Panthéon » et seront complétés des trésors inestimables en provenance de couvents détruits et de collections privées confisquées. L'étendue du fonds actuel de provenance disparate révèle l'impact de ces événements révolutionnaires. Dans le nouveau bâtiment, élevé face au Panthéon dès 1844 par Henri Labrouste (1801–1875) et mis en service en tant que bibliothèque en 1851, on dénombre 65 000 volumes dans la salle de lecture et 40 000 dans les magasins du rez-de-chaussée. L'édifice est novateur à plusieurs égards, d'une part pour l'usage apparent de la fonte dans la salle monumentale – découlant d'une directive concernant l'éclairage au gaz –, d'autre part pour sa typologie de construction présentant un bâtiment de bibliothèque à part entière, avec magasins de livres au rez-de-chaussée et salle de lecture baignée de lumière mais garnie de rayonnages et d'une galerie en mezzanine. La façade et l'agencement intérieur eurent une belle postérité sur d'autres bâtiments de bibliothèques. Peu de temps après, Labrouste fut chargé des plans de la construction de la Bibliothèque nationale de Paris.

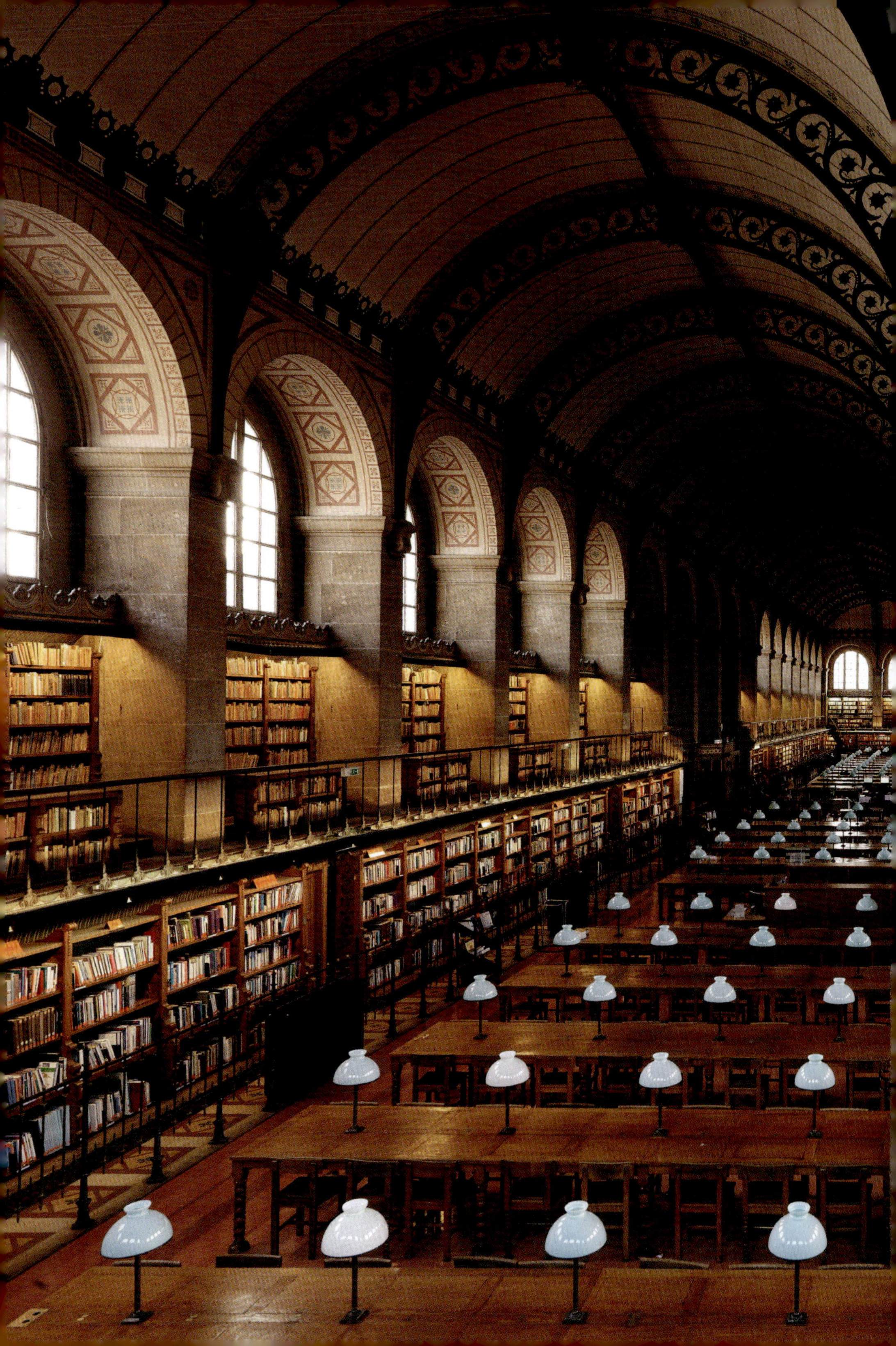

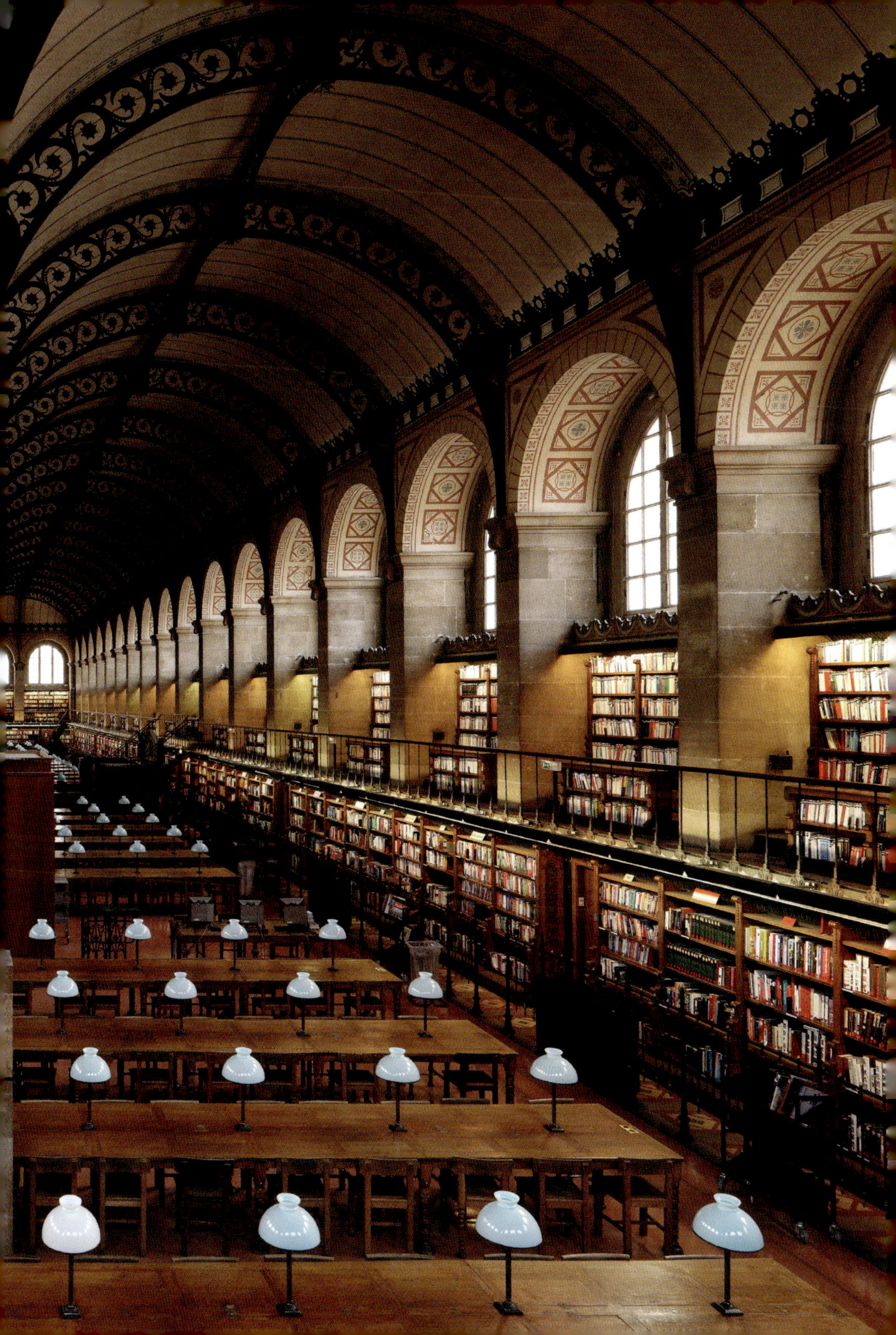

Bibliothèque Mazarine

Just as it was in the 17th century, when it was originally founded as a private library, the Bibliothèque Mazarine remains one of the most exclusive and best-stocked research libraries in a historical setting. Attached to the prestigious Institut de France since 1945, the Bibliothèque Mazarine owes its interior fittings and its exclusive location to the cardinal and French royal minister Jules Mazarin (1602–1661). Cardinal Mazarin opened his private collection of books to scholars from 1649 and in his final years set up an educational foundation to ensure its preservation as an academic resource. The library was housed during Mazarin's lifetime in a magnificent galleried room in his Rue Richelieu residence, before moving to its present home in the Collège des Quatre Nations in 1691. Work on the new college started the year after Mazarin's death, in accordance with the provisions made in his will, and was completed in 1688. Built by Louis Le Vau (1612–1670) as a teaching institute and research library, the complex also contains Mazarin's burial chapel. The Collège was also assured of attention by its prominent position on the banks of the River Seine, directly opposite the royal palace of the Louvre. The collection owes the quality of its holdings and the fact that these were made accessible to the public to its first librarian, Gabriel Naudé (1600–1653), whose services Mazarin engaged from 1643 to build up his private library, before this became France's oldest public library. Mazarin thereby followed in the footsteps of other illustrious individuals, such as Cardinal Francesco Barberini (1597–1679), nephew of Pope Urban VIII (1568–1644), who had likewise sought Naudé's advice following the publication of his groundbreaking work on the theory of library science, *Advis pour dresser une bibliothèque* (1627). In order to fulfil its highest purpose, namely the public good (*bien publique*), a library in the views of Naudé had to guarantee unlimited access to knowledge. To this end it needed to be well organised, laid out according to a logical system and catalogued in full detail. The holdings assembled on behalf of Cardinal Mazarin by Gabriel Naudé and subsequently by his successor, François de la Poterie (librarian from 1653 until 1689), embrace not only a complete spectrum of contemporary academic works – including those on the index of books banned by the Catholic Church – but also rare editions and precious manuscripts, which today represent some of the library's particular treasures. By 1652 Cardinal Mazarin's library already boasted 40,000 books, which form the nucleus of today's holdings of 600,000 volumes and can be recognised not least by their magnificent morocco bindings stamped in gold with the Cardinal's insignia.

* * *

Founded 1643; since 1691 housed in the Collège des Quatre-Nations, by Louis Le Vau
Holdings c. 600,000 volumes
Type of library originally a cardinal's library, today a research library
Highlights *Bréviaire Oderisius (Breviary from Monte Cassino)*, 1099–1105 (Ms 364); *Heures à l'usage de Paris (Hours of Charles of France)*, 1465 (Ms 473)

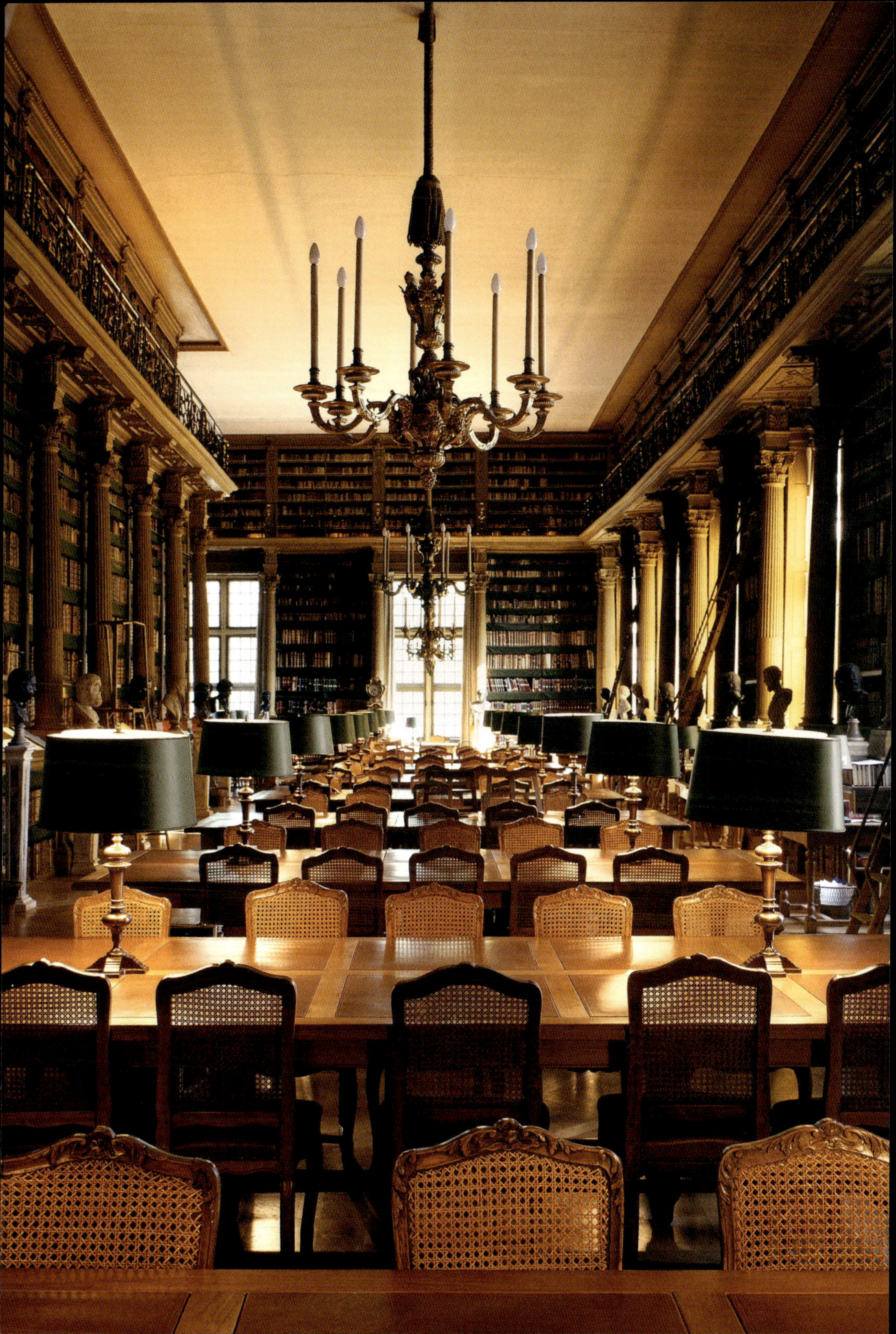

Noch heute zählt die Bibliothèque Mazarine, die seit 1945 Teil des prestigeträchtigen Institut de France ist, wie zur Zeit ihrer Gründung als Privatbibliothek Mazarins zu den exklusivsten und bestsortierten historischen Forschungsstätten. Die Exklusivität der Lage und ihr Mobiliar verdankt sie dem Kardinal und Minister des französischen Königs Jules Mazarin (1602–1661), der seine private Büchersammlung bereits ab 1649 der Forschung geöffnet und zu seinem Lebensende als wissenschaftliches Institut etabliert hat. Sie war zunächst in einem prachtvollen Galerieraum seines Stadtpalastes in der Rue Richelieu untergebracht, bevor sie gemäß der testamentarischen Verfügung ihres Gründers 1691 in das Collège des Quatre Nations übersiedelte, wo sie sich noch heute befindet. Dieses war ein Jahr nach dem Ableben Mazarins nach dessen Intentionen von Louis Le Vau (1612–1670) als Wissenschaftskolleg und Forschungsbibliothek gemeinsam mit seiner Grabkapelle errichtet und 1688 eröffnet worden. Aufmerksamkeit sicherte dem Collège auch seine prominente Lage am Ufer der Seine gegenüber dem Königspalast des Louvre. Die Qualität und öffentliche Verfügbarkeit der Bestände verdankt die Sammlung ihrem ersten Bibliothekar Gabriel Naudé (1600–1653), den Mazarin ab 1643 zunächst mit dem Aufbau seiner Privatbibliothek beauftragt hatte, bevor diese zur ältesten öffentlichen Bibliothek Frankreichs werden sollte. Damit schloss er an einschlägige Erfahrungen illustrer Persönlichkeiten an, denen der französische Gelehrte seit der Veröffentlichung seines bahnbrechenden Werkes zur Theorie des Bibliothekswesens im Jahr 1627 mit dem Titel *Advis pour dresser une bibliothèque* ein bevorzugter Berater war – etwa Kardinal Francesco Barberini (1597–1679), Neffe von Papst Urban VIII. (1568–1644). Um ihrem höchsten Ziel, dem öffentlichen Wohl (*bien publique*) gerecht zu werden, hatte die Bibliothek eine uneingeschränkte Verfügbarkeit des Wissens zu garantieren, wohl organisiert, gemäß einer sinnhaften Systematik aufgestellt und mittels aussagekräftiger Kataloge erschlossen

zu sein. Ihre im Auftrag Kardinal Mazarins von Gabriel Naudé und seinem Nachfolger François de la Poterie (Bibliothekar von 1653 bis 1689) zusammengestellten Bestände umfassen nicht nur ein komplettes Spektrum zeitaktueller wissenschaftlicher Werke – die auch jene einschließen, die damals auf dem Index der von der katholischen Kirche verbotenen Bücher standen –, sondern auch seltene Ausgaben und kostbare Manuskripte, die noch heute zu den besonderen Schätzen der Bibliothek zählen. Kardinal Mazarins Bibliothek umfasste 1652 bereits 40 000 Bücher, die den Kernbestand der heute auf 600 000 Werke erweiterten Sammlung bilden. Er ist nicht zuletzt an den kunstvollen Bindungen in Maroquinleder mit den prächtig in Gold geprägten Emblemen des Kardinals zu erkennen.

❊ ❊ ❊

Rattachée au prestigieux Institut de France en 1945, la bibliothèque privée du cardinal Mazarin s'inscrit aujourd'hui encore, tout comme à l'époque de sa fondation, parmi les centres de recherche historiques les plus exceptionnels et les mieux assortis. Elle doit sa situation sensationnelle et son mobilier à Jules Mazarin (1602–1661), cardinal et « principal ministre de l'Estat » sous Louis XIV, qui permit aux savants de consulter sa collection de livres personnelle dès 1649 avant d'en faire un institut scientifique vers la fin de sa vie. La bibliothèque vit le jour rue de Richelieu, dans une splendide galerie de l'hôtel particulier de Mazarin. Elle rouvrit en 1691 quai de Conti, où elle se trouve toujours, du fait de son rattachement au collège des Quatre-Nations selon les dispositions testamentaires de son fondateur. La construction du collège est entamée un an après le décès de Mazarin, qui avait laissé à Louis Le Vau (1612–1670) le soin d'ériger un institut scientifique et une bibliothèque de recherche ainsi qu'une chapelle funéraire. Il fut inauguré en 1688. De par sa localisation rive gauche, face au palais du Louvre, le collège accaparait l'attention. Sa qualité et sa mise à disposition au public,

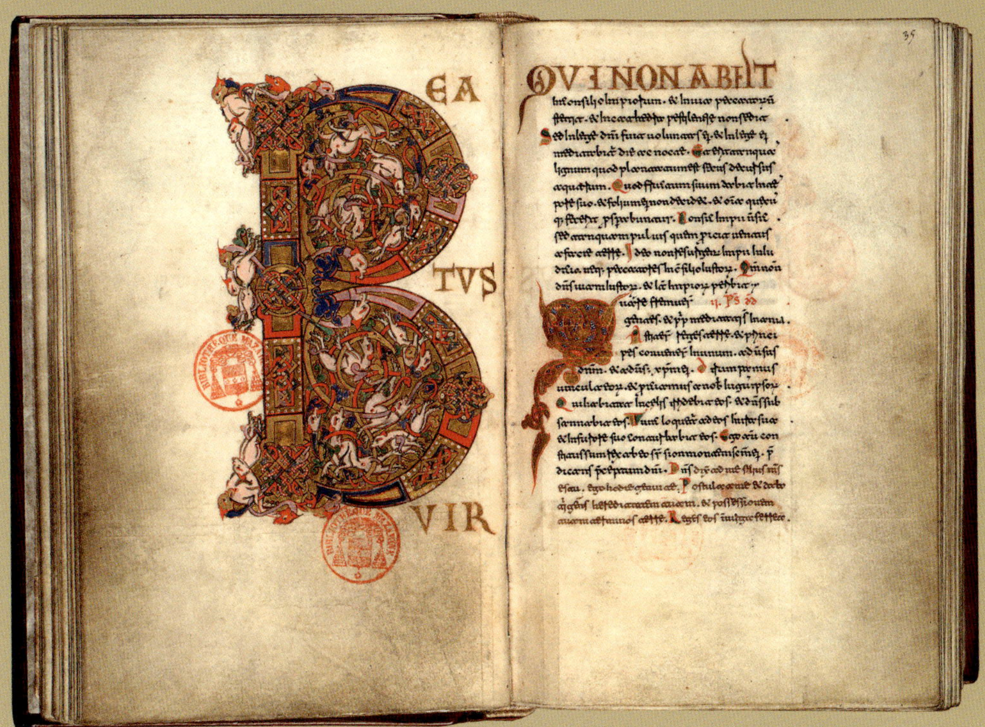

la collection les doit à son premier bibliothécaire Gabriel Naudé (1600–1653). Mazarin le
sollicita en 1643 pour constituer sa bibliothèque
personnelle, qui devint alors la plus ancienne
bibliothèque publique de France. Naudé noua,
grâce à des rencontres pertinentes, des liens
avec des personnages illustres comme le
cardinal Francesco Barberini (1597–1679), neveu
du pape Urbain VIII (1568–1644), dont il était
devenu le conseiller favori après la publication
en 1627 de son ouvrage révolutionnaire concernant l'agencement des bibliothèques intitulé
Advis pour dresser une bibliothèque. Afin de
remplir son but ultime, rendre justice au bien
public, une bibliothèque se doit de garantir un
accès illimité au savoir, d'être parfaitement
organisée, présentée selon une systématique
sensée et mise en valeur au moyen de catalogues judicieux. Ses fonds constitués du vivant
du cardinal Mazarin par Gabriel Naudé mais
aussi du temps de son successeur, François
de la Poterie (bibliothécaire de 1653 à 1689),
englobent la gamme complète des ouvrages
scientifiques de leur époque – incluant ceux mis
à l'index par l'Église catholique –, ainsi que des
éditions rares et des manuscrits inestimables
qui constituent aujourd'hui encore le trésor de
la bibliothèque. En 1652, la bibliothèque du cardinal Mazarin avoisinait déjà les 40 000 livres –
le noyau de base des 600 000 ouvrages de la
collection actuelle. Ce fonds est notamment
reconnaissable à sa prestigieuse reliure en
maroquin où les armes du cardinal se présentent à l'or repoussé.

Bréviaire Oderisius, 1099–1105,
sig. Ms. 364, fol. 34v–35r: *Initial B*

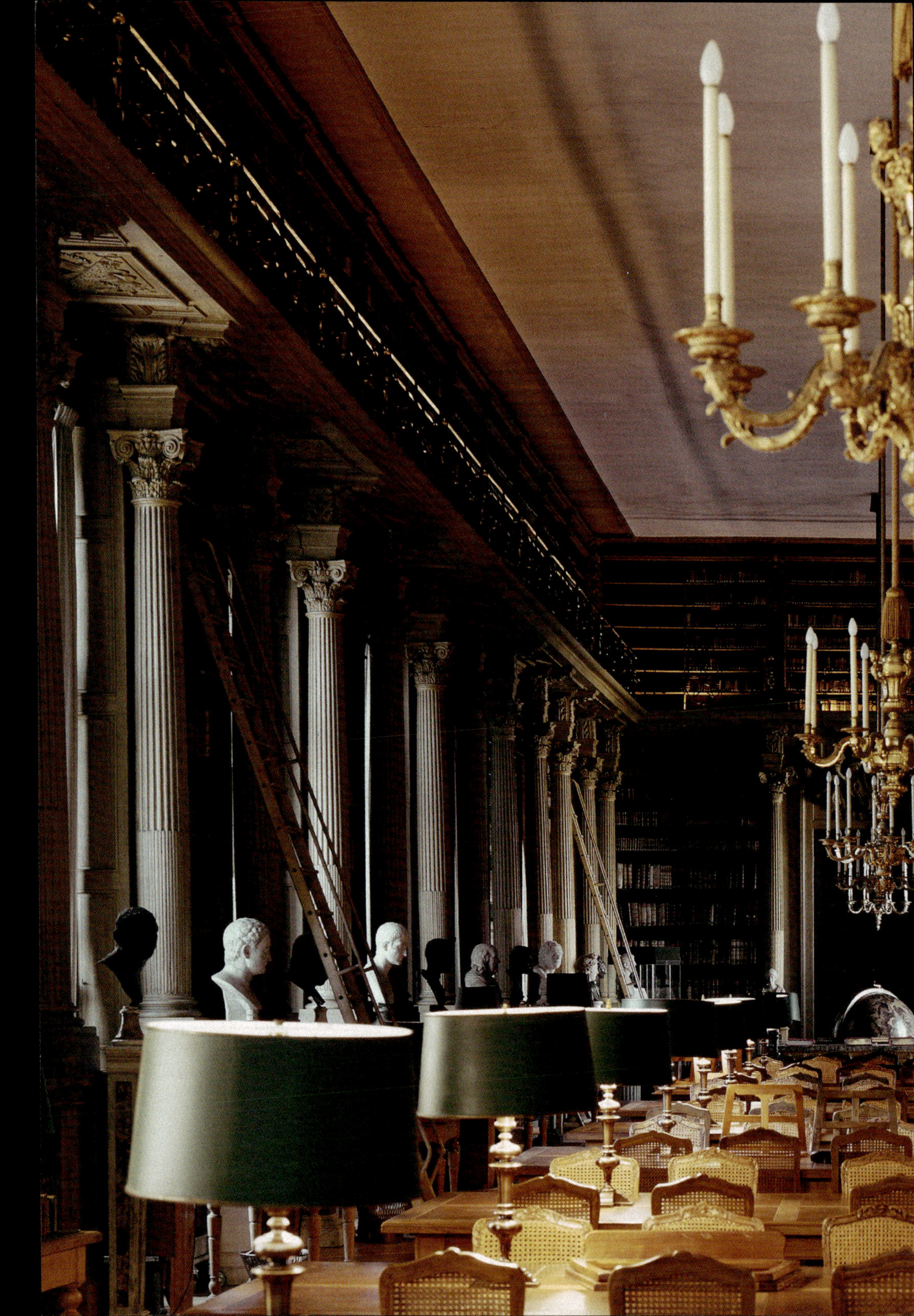

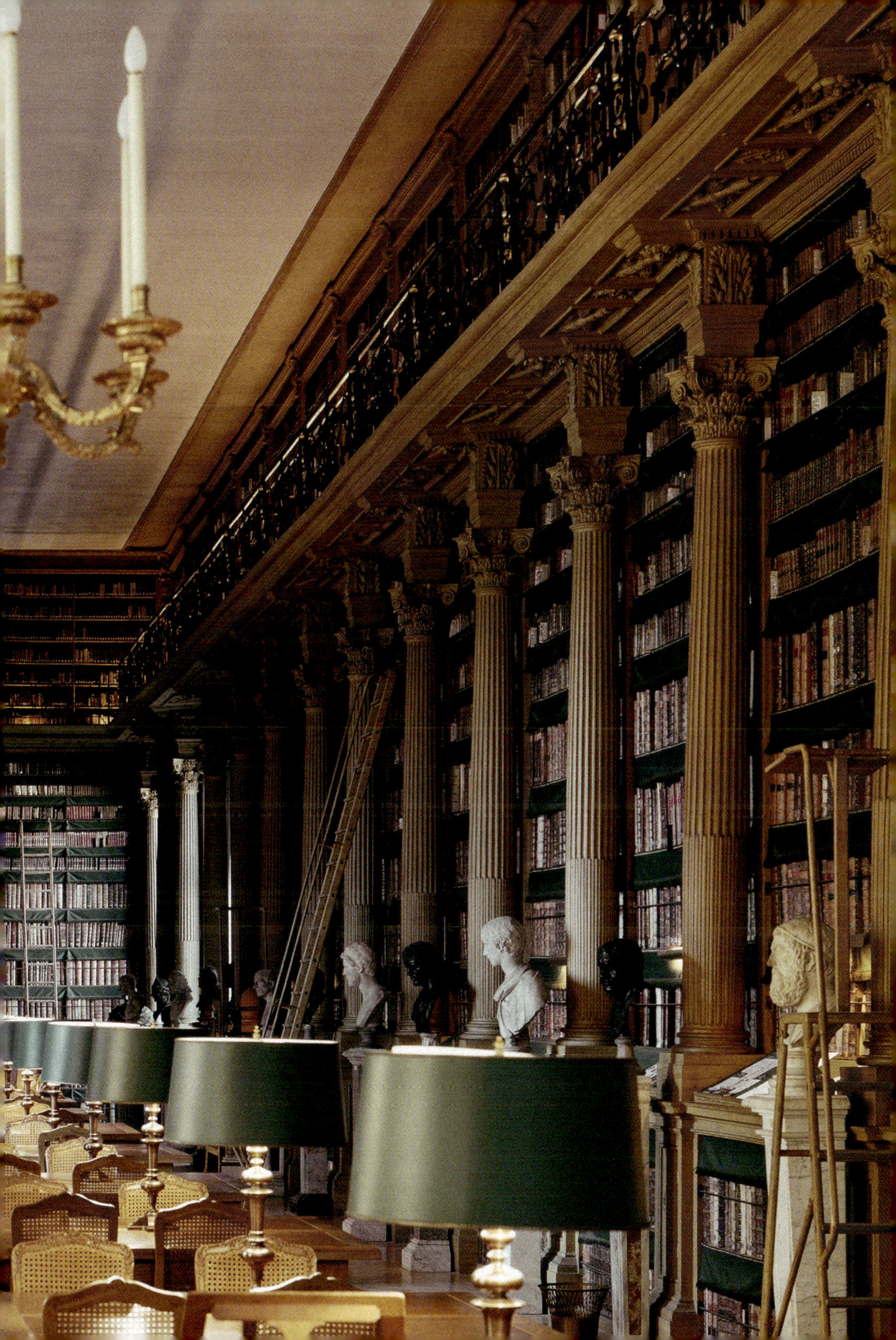

Bibliothèque du Château de Chantilly

Henry of Orléans, Duke of Aumale (1822–1897), son of the "citizen king" Louis Philippe (1773–1850) and grandson and universal heir of the last prince of the house of Condé-Bourbon, was an enthusiastic collector of art and books. He was inspired most of all though by the idea of reviving the history of his illustrious house, of which he was the last representative, in its collections. Like the Chantilly palace, which had served this subsidiary branch of the French royal family as a residence since the 1400s, over the course of the centuries these collections had been broken up, confiscated and even destroyed. Henry was forced to go into exile several times and saw his family estates appropriated by his political opponents. He circumvented a renewed threat to disperse his life's work by bequeathing all his collections to the French State, on the condition that they remained undivided and were administered by the Académie française, of which he was a member. Against this unstable background, which he would endure all his life, in 1875 the Duke commissioned Honoré Daumet (1826–1911) to rebuild the Grand Château at Chantilly, which had been destroyed during the French Revolution. Daumet specialised in historical reconstructions, or more accurately, in new buildings in a historical style. In the Grand Château he created a series of museum galleries and reception rooms, along with a theatre he later, in 1888–1889, converted into a library and which has been known ever since as the Bibliothèque du Théâtre. The library is not open to the public. Its rooms contain work-related publications consulted by the Duke and his reference library of some 30,000 volumes. The family archives were also reorganised and are today housed in the Tour des Chartes.

However, Henry kept the much older nucleus of the family library near his own apartments in the Petit Château. In 1876–1877 this originally private Cabinet des Livres was furnished by Daumet with metal shelves which are accessed via a gallery. The books are arranged by size, binding and subject. An easel painting by Gabriel Ferrier (1847–1914) shows the Duc d'Aumale in his library, in the company of his acquisitions advisor, Alfred-Auguste Cuvillier-Fleury (1802–1887). Duke Henry compiled the first catalogue of his library himself. Probably his most famous ancestor, the Grand Condé, can be seen above the fireplace in the portrait bust by Antoine Coysevox (1640–1720). Today the Cabinet des Livres is also regularly used for special exhibitions inspired by the books in the collection. The library and its valuable holdings, including some 1,500 manuscripts, fall under the aegis of the Institut de France.

❋❋❋

Founded probably 1848, on the basis of the core holdings of the Condé family library; Cabinet des Livres created in 1876–1877 in the Petit Château, Bibliothèque du Théâtre created in 1888–1889 in the Grand Château; both built by Honoré Daumet

Holdings c. 60,000 volumes

Type of library formerly the private library of Duke d'Aumale; today a research library under the aegis of the Institut de France

Highlights *Registrum Gregorii* (fragment including miniature of Otto II), 983 (Ms. 14 bis); *Psalter of Queen Ingeborg of Denmark*, c. 1200 (Ms. 9); Limburg Brothers, *Les très riches heures du Duc de Berry*, 1411–1416 (Ms. 65); Jean Fouquet, *Hours of Étienne Chevalier*, 1452–1460 (Ms. 71)

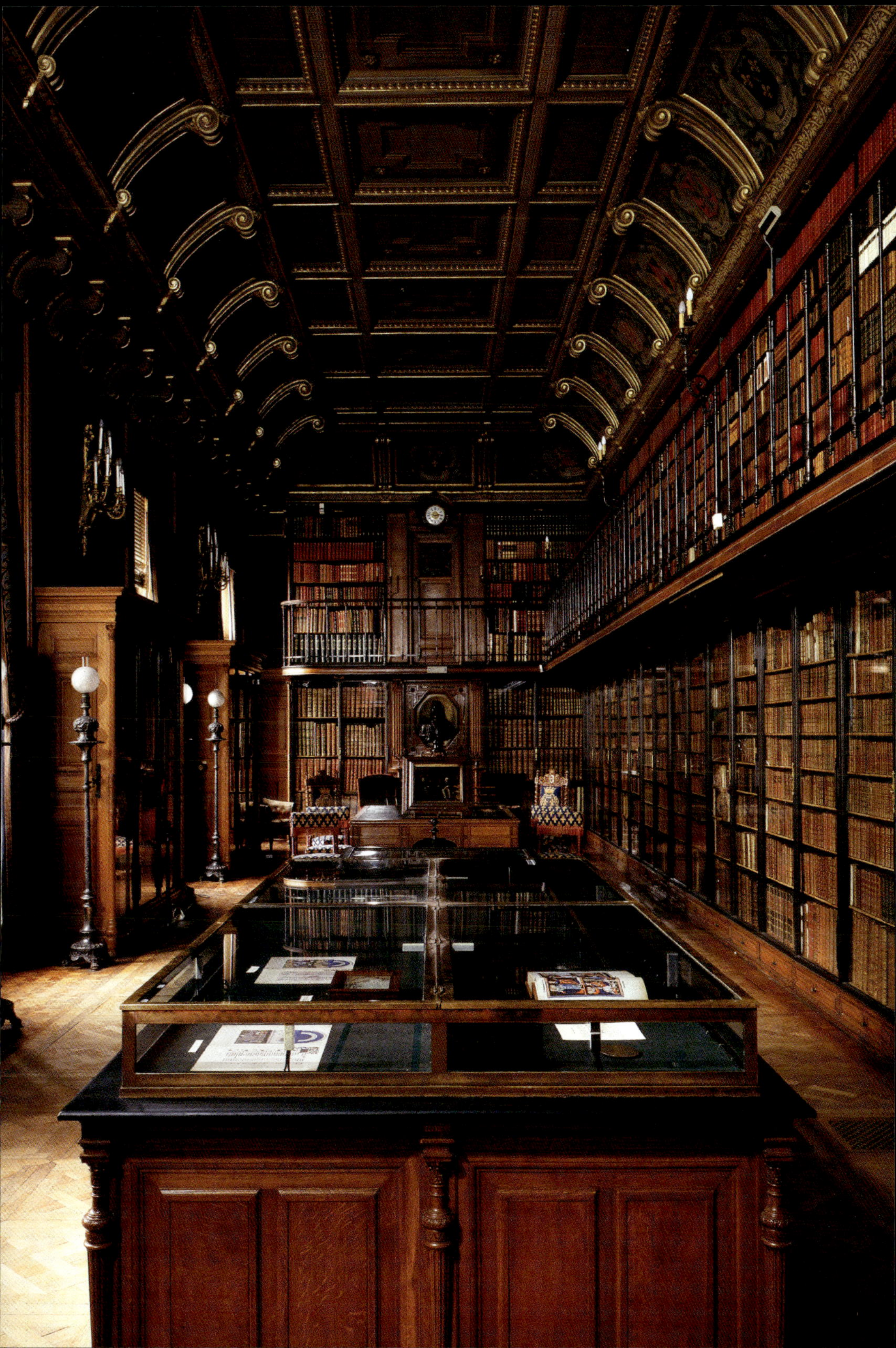

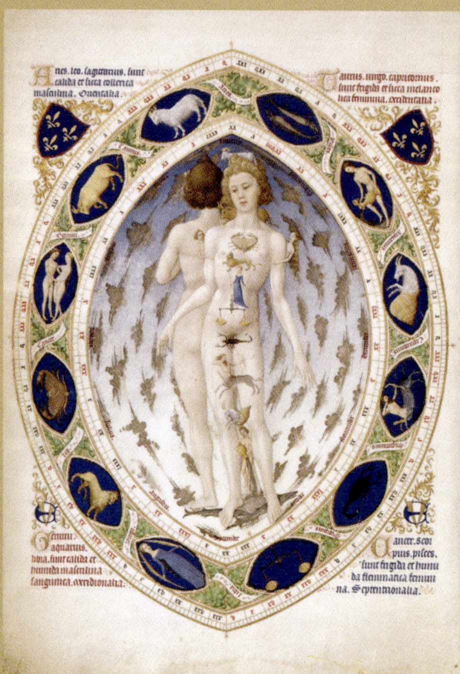

Limburg Brothers, *Les très riches heures*
du Duc de Berry, 1411–1416, sig. Ms. 65, fol. 14v:
The Anatomical Zodiac Man

Henri d'Orléans, Duc d'Aumale (1822–1897),
Sohn des „Bürgerkönigs" Louis Philippe
(1773–1850) und Enkel sowie Universalerbe
des letzten Prinzen aus dem Geschlecht
Condé-Bourbon, war nicht nur ein begeisterter
Kunst- und Büchersammler, sondern vor allem
von der Idee beseelt, die Geschichte seines
ruhmvollen Hauses, dessen letzter Vertreter
er war, in dessen Sammlungen neu erstehen
zu lassen. Sie waren ebenso wie das Schloss
Chantilly, das dieser Nebenlinie des französischen Königshauses seit dem 15. Jahrhundert
als Residenz diente, im Zuge der Geschichte
verstreut, konfisziert oder auch zerstört worden. Er selbst war mehrmals zu Exilaufent-
halten gezwungen und durch seine politischen
Gegner der Familiengüter enteignet worden.
Einer erneuten Auflösung seines Lebenswerkes
entzog er sich durch die Schenkung aller

Sammlungen an den französischen Staat, mit
der Auflage, dass sie ungeteilt und von der
Académie française (der er ebenfalls ange-
hörte) betreut blieben. Vor diesem instabilen
Hintergrund, der sein gesamtes Leben prägen
sollte, beauftragte er 1875 Honoré Daumet
(1826–1911), einen Architekten, der sich auf
historische Rekonstruktionen beziehungsweise
Neufassungen in historischem Stil spezialisiert
hatte, mit dem Wiederaufbau des in der Revolution zerstörten Großen Schlosses von Chantilly.
In diesem entstanden eine Reihe musealer
Schauräume und Empfangssalons sowie das
Theater, das Daumet aber später, in den Jahren
1888 bis 1889, zu einem Bibliotheksraum
umbaute, der seither Bibliothèque du théâtre
genannt wird. Die Bibliothek ist nicht öffentlich
zugänglich. In ihren Sälen befinden sich die
Arbeitsmaterialien des Duc d'Aumale und seine
an die 30 000 Bände zählende Handbibliothek.
Damals wurde auch das Familienarchiv neu
geordnet. Es ist heute in dem Tour des Chartes
untergebracht. Die historische Bibliothek des
Hauses bewahrte Henri d'Orléans aber in der
Nähe seiner Wohnräume im Kleinen Schloss
auf. Dieses ursprünglich private Cabinet des
livres wurde von Honoré Daumet in den Jahren
1876 bis 1877 mit Metallregalen ausgestattet,
die über eine Galerie zu erreichen sind. Die
Bücher sind nach Größe, Einband und Themen
geordnet. Auf dem Staffeleibild von Gabriel
Ferrier (1847–1914) ist der Duc d'Aumale in dieser Bibliothek dargestellt, in Begleitung seines
Beraters in Akquisitionsfragen, Alfred-Auguste
Cuvillier-Fleury (1802–1887). Den ersten Katalog seiner Bibliothek erstellte der Duc d'Aumale
persönlich. Sein wohl berühmtester Vorfahre,
der Grand Condé, ist in Antoine Coysevox'
(1640–1720) Porträtbüste auf dem Kaminsims
zu sehen. Heute dient das Bücherkabinett
des Duc d'Aumale im Kontext des Museums
ausgewählten Sonderausstellungen zum
Thema der Bibliophilie als Ausstellungsort.
Seine kostbaren Buchbestände mit etwa
1 500 Handschriften werden vom Institut de
France verwaltet.

Henri d'Orléans, duc d'Aumale (1822–1897),
fils de Louis-Philippe (1773–1850) le « roi bour-
geois », petit-fils et héritier universel du dernier
prince de la célèbre lignée Condé-Bourbon ne
se contenta pas d'être un collectionneur fervent
d'art et de littérature. Il s'enthousiasmait aussi
à l'idée de faire revivre dans ses collections
l'histoire de sa glorieuse famille, dont il était le
dernier représentant. Au cours de l'histoire,
ses collections ont été dispersées, confisquées,
voire détruites, au même titre que le château de
Chantilly, résidence attitrée de cette branche de
la Maison royale de France depuis le XVe siècle.
Le duc d'Aumale fut contraint plusieurs fois
à l'exil et dépossédé des biens familiaux par
ses opposants politiques. Il éluda une ultime
liquidation de sa fortune en offrant l'ensemble
de ses collections à l'État français à la condition
qu'elles restent indivisées et à la charge de
l'Académie française (dont il était membre).
C'est dans ce contexte tourmenté – qui marqua
toute sa vie – qu'il chargea, en 1875, Honoré
Daumet (1826–1911) de la reconstruction du
« Grand Château » de Chantilly, détruit à la
Révolution. Cet architecte était un spécialiste
de la reconstruction historique ou, plus précisé-
ment, de la rénovation dans le goût historisant.
Il en résulta une série de salles d'apparat et de
salons de réception muséaux ainsi qu'un théâtre
que Daumet convertit en salle de bibliothèque
dans les années 1888–1889. Alors nommée
bibliothèque du théâtre, elle n'est pas ouverte
au public. Ses salles abritent les documents
de travail du duc d'Aumale et sa collection de
manuscrits comptant 30 000 volumes. Les
archives de la famille furent aussi réorganisées
à l'époque. Elles se trouvent de nos jours dans
la Tour des Chartes. Henri d'Orléans conservait
toutefois la bibliothèque historique de la famille
non loin de ses appartements dans le « Petit
Château ». En 1876–1877, Honoré Daumet
équipa ce salon privé, nommé à l'origine cabinet
des livres, de rayonnages en métal accessibles

par une galerie. Les livres sont répartis par
dimensions, reliures et thèmes. Sur la peinture
de chevalet de Gabriel Ferrier (1847–1914), le
duc d'Aumale est représenté dans sa bibliothèque, accompagné de son conseiller en
acquisitions, Alfred-Auguste Cuvillier-Fleury
(1802–1887). Le duc d'Aumale a lui-même dressé
le premier catalogue de sa bibliothèque. Son
ancêtre légendaire, le Grand Condé, est présent
grâce au portrait en buste d'Antoine Coysevox
(1640–1720) placé sur le manteau de cheminée.
Dans le musée actuel, le cabinet des livres
du duc d'Aumale sert de lieu d'expositions
temporaires sélectives ayant trait à la bibliophilie. Ses fonds inestimables incluant quelque
1 500 manuscrits sont administrés par l'Institut
de France.

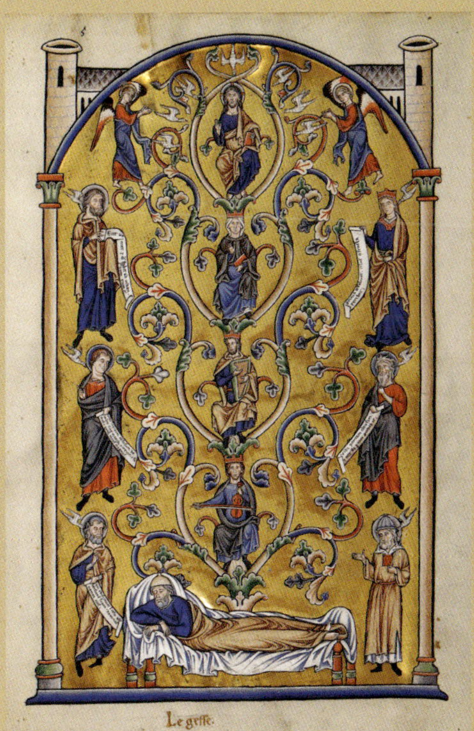

Psalter of Queen Ingeborg of Denmark,
c. 1200, sig. Ms. 9, fol. 14v: *Jesse Tree*

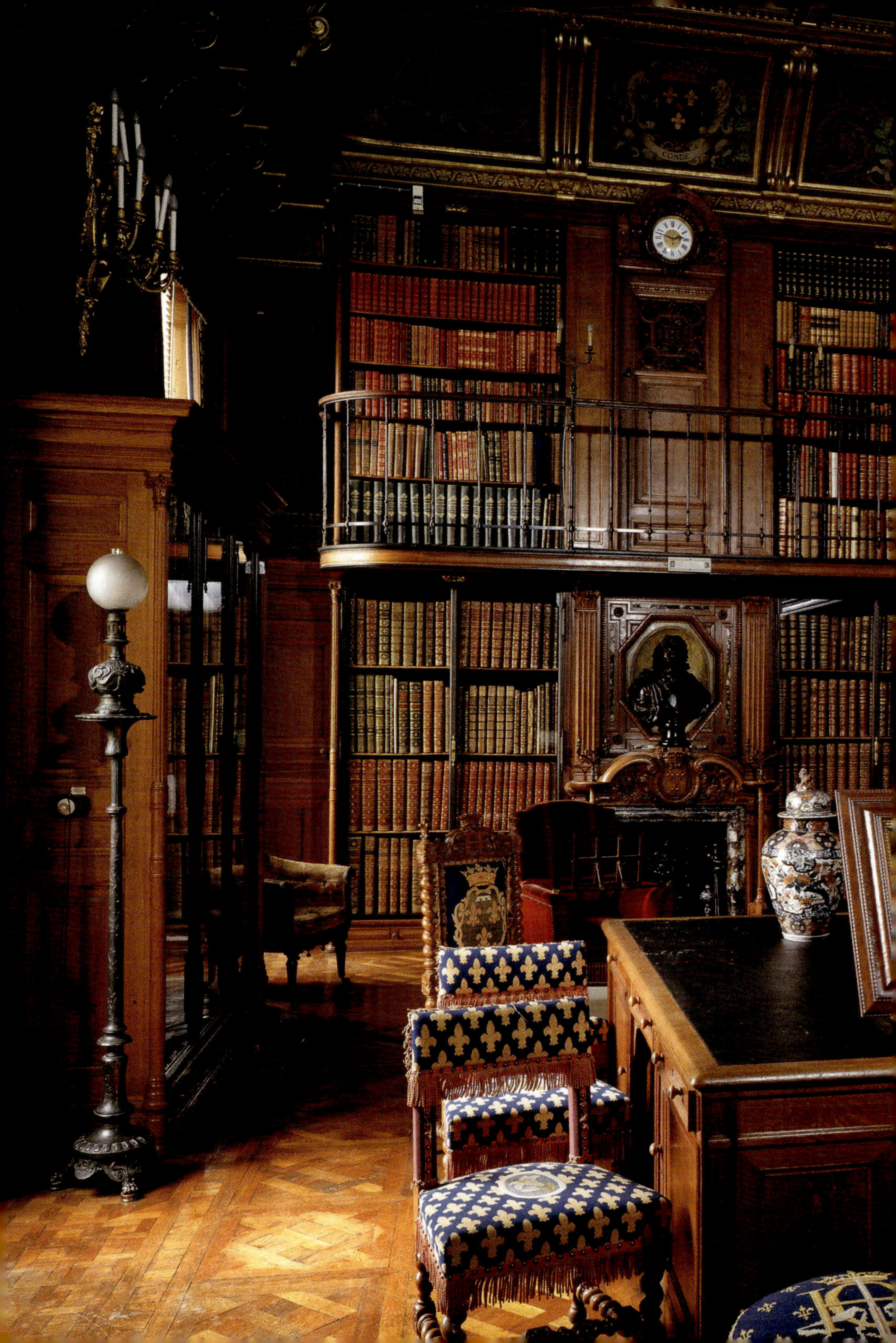

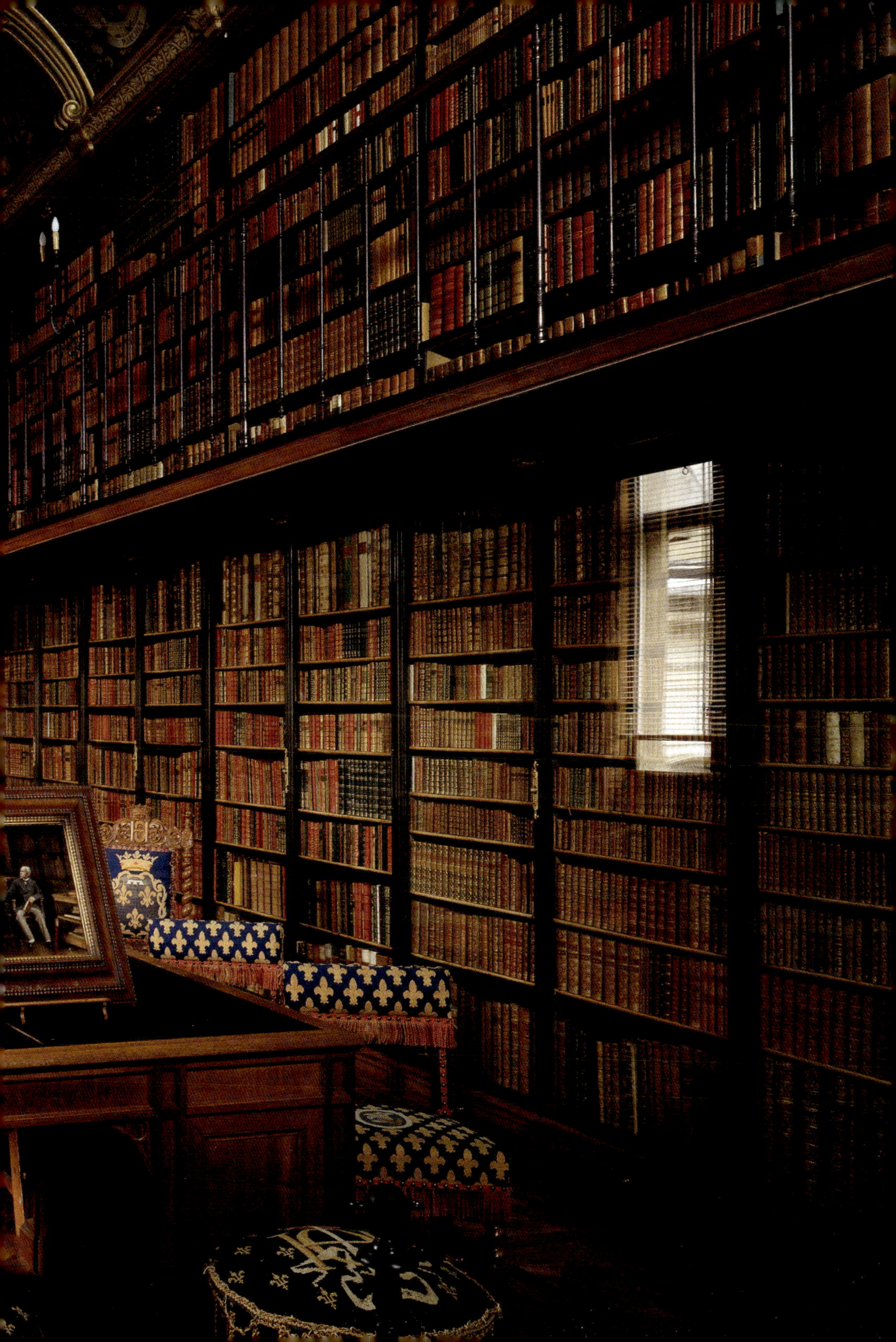

Bibliothèque Paul Marmottan

The Bibliothèque Paul Marmottan is a unique resource in several respects for research on the Napoleonic era. Its collection of books sheds light on Napoleon's life and works, its collection of periodicals allows us to see how he was perceived by his contemporaries, and its collection of engravings illustrates the development and spread of what has gone down in art history as the Empire style. The man who founded the library was not satisfied with reconstructing the Napoleonic era through historical written and visual sources, however, but wanted to enable it to be experienced in a three-dimensional manner. The books about Napoleon were to be displayed in the atmosphere of his day, but they were also to be read and absorbed in the intellectual spirit of his day. This ambitious project was realised by Paul Marmottan (1856–1932), who upon the death of his father in 1883 became heir to an industrial empire. At that time he left the firm and began to devote himself exclusively to his passion for collecting, alongside considerable academic research. Between 1890 and 1920 he had his private residence in the Bois de Boulogne decorated according to his own ideas, including the remodelling of the library as a harmonious ensemble in the style of Napoleon. As in the imperial library at Compiègne, which is laid out in a similar fashion, Marmottan based the furnishings in his library on those of the "Premier Empire". Since Marmottan also lived and worked in his house, however (his desk still stands unaltered in the library today), practical concerns and modern ideas did become superimposed at times upon its aesthetic aims. These latter were represented by a rich collection of paintings, statues and decorative works of applied art. Marmottan also sought to revive the spirit of the Empire by citing Napoleonic residences in the furnishings and colour schemes of his interiors, right down to the smallest details. In the Blue Salon, for example, he reconstructed a mural from the royal palace of Caserta, from where Joseph Bonaparte (1768–1844) and Joachim Murat (1767–1815) ruled the Kingdom of Naples. Connections with Italy are present even in the garden, in the shape of umbrella ferns. In 1934 both his Bois de Boulogne home and his Paris residence – today the Musée Marmottan Monet – were opened to the public, in accordance with his wishes. The library today falls under the aegis of the Institut de France.

* * *

Founded 1883; since 1934 library of the Académie des Beaux-Arts, under the aegis of the Institut de France; run by the Fondation Marmottan
Holdings c. 16,000 volumes, 6,000 prints
Type of library originally a private library, today a research library and part of a museum
Highlights *Quintus Horatius Flaccus* (Horace, *Complete works*), illustrated by Charles Percier, 1799; Martin-Guillaume Biennais, *Recueil des ordres français et étrangers. Dessins originaux de Biennais*, 1808; *Cassette de sa Majesté Impératrice et Reine Marie-Louise* (royal account book), 1810–1814

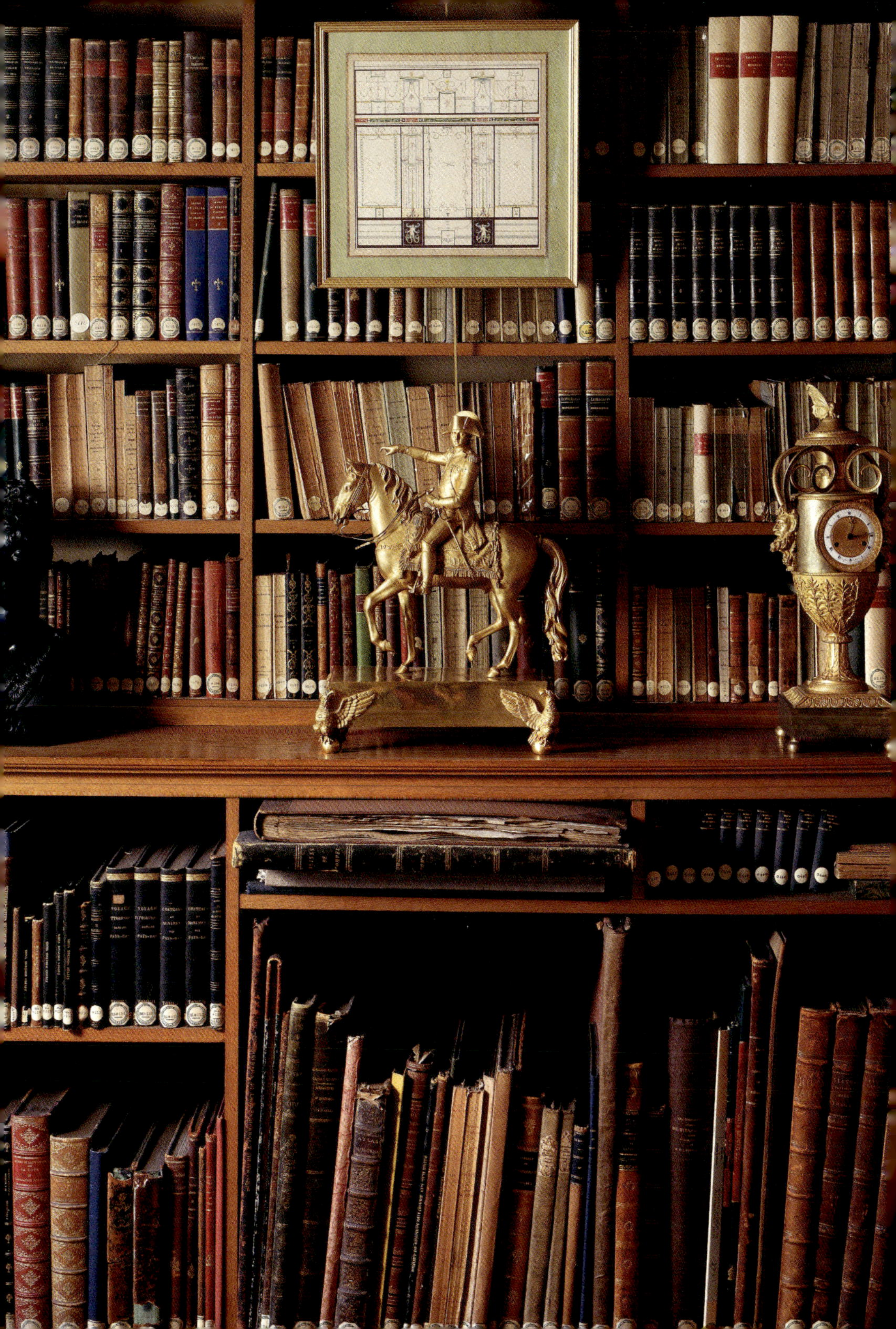

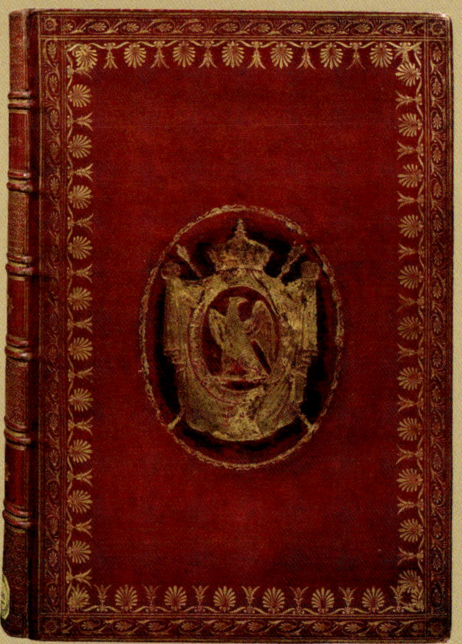

Die Bibliothek Paul Marmottan ist eine einzig-
artige Forschungsstätte zur Epoche Napoleons,
und das in mehrfacher Hinsicht. Ihre Bücher-
sammlung beleuchtet Napoleons Wirken, ihre
Zeitschriftensammlung seine zeitgenössische
Rezeption, während die Kupferstichsammlung
Entwicklung und Ausbreitung des als „Premier
Empire" in die Geschichte eingegangenen
Zeitstils dokumentiert. Historische Text- und
Bildquellen reichten aber dem Gründer der
Sammlung nicht aus, die Epoche Napoleons
zu rekonstruieren, er wollte sie vielmehr drei-
dimensional erlebbar machen. Die Bücher zur
Geschichte Napoleons sollten nicht nur in der
Atmosphäre seiner Zeit aufgestellt, sondern
im Geist der Zeit rezipiert werden. Dieses ehr-
geizige Projekt verwirklichte Paul Marmottan
(1856–1932), der eigentlich Erbe eines Industrie-
imperiums war, erst ab 1883, als sein Vater starb.
Damals trat er aus der Firma aus und begann,
sich ausschließlich seiner Sammelleidenschaft
zu widmen, die von einer beachtlichen Forschungstätigkeit begleitet war. In den Jahren
zwischen 1890 und 1920 stattete er seinen
Wohnsitz am Bois de Boulogne nach eigenen

Ideen aus. Das Raumensemble der Bibliothek
ließ er im Stil Napoleons anlegen. In der Ausstattung der Bibliothek orientierte er sich an
Originalen des „Premier Empire", wie etwa am
Schloss von Compiègne, das eine vergleichbare
Disposition zeigt. Da Paul Marmottan aber in
seinem Palais auch wohnte und arbeitete – sein
Schreibtisch hat sich in der Bibliothek unverändert erhalten –, überlagerten praktische
Aspekte und zeitbedingte Sichtweisen mitunter
museale Intentionen. Diese wurden in der
reichen Sammlung von Gemälden, Statuen und
dekorativem Kunsthandwerk überreich eingebracht. Auch in der Ausstattung und Farbigkeit
der Salons war Paul Marmottan bestrebt, den
Geist des Empires durch Zitate napoleonischer
Residenzen wiederzubeleben, was bis in Details
zu verfolgen ist. Im Blauen Salon rekonstruierte
er eine aus dem Königspalast von Caserta über-
nommene Wanddekoration. Von dort aus hatten
Joseph Bonaparte (1768–1844) und Joachim
Murat (1767–1815) das Königreich Neapel regiert.
Sogar im Garten vermitteln Schirmföhren
Assoziationen zu Italien. 1934 wurde das Palais
ebenso wie der Pariser Stadtpalast, in dem sich
das Musée Marmottan Monet befindet, gemäß
dem Wunsch seines Gründers der Öffentlichkeit
zugänglich gemacht. Die Bibliothek dient heute
als Forschungsstätte des Institut de France.

❋⁜❋

À maints égards, la bibliothèque Paul
Marmottan est un site de référence exceptionnel
sur l'époque napoléonienne. La collection de
livres renseigne sur la geste de Napoléon, les
revues sur la façon dont ses contemporains le
percevaient tandis que les estampes retracent
la naissance et la diffusion du style de l'époque
entré dans l'histoire sous le nom de « Premier

Quintus Horatius Flaccus, illustrated by
Charles Percier, 1799: *Book binding*
Martin-Guillaume Biennais, *Recueil des
ordres français et étrangers*, 1808, p. 9
Martin-Guillaume Biennais, *Recueil des ordres
français et étrangers*, 1808, p. 49

Empire ». Rassembler des sources historiques textuelles et iconographiques afin de reconstituer l'époque napoléonienne ne suffisait pas au fondateur qui tenait à la faire revivre en trois dimensions. Ainsi, les ouvrages sur l'Empire devaient se présenter dans une atmosphère historique afin d'être perçus dans le goût même de l'époque. Cet ambitieux projet, l'héritier Paul Marmottan (1856–1932) le concrétisa en 1883, à la mort de son père, directeur d'une grande société industrielle. Il quitta alors son poste pour s'adonner exclusivement à sa passion de collectionneur qui s'accompagnait de considérables recherches. De 1890 à 1920, il aménagea son domicile situé au bois de Boulogne selon son goût personnel. Les pièces de la bibliothèque bénéficient d'un décor impérial et de mobilier Premier Empire authentique, évoquant celui du château de Compiègne à la disposition similaire. Comme Paul Marmottan habitait et travaillait dans cet hôtel particulier – son secrétaire demeure tel quel dans la bibliothèque –, des

aspects pratiques se sont greffés au décor d'ailleurs fidèle à l'époque et aux intentions muséales. Ces dernières se ressentent clairement dans la précieuse collection de toiles, statues et objets d'art décoratifs. Dans le salon aussi, Paul Marmottan fit tout pour donner vie à l'Empire, d'une part avec des coloris et un mobilier spécifiques, d'autre part en citant les résidences des napoléonides, et ce, par d'infimes détails. Le décor mural du salon bleu par exemple est identique à celui de l'une des pièces du palais royal de Caserte, résidence depuis laquelle Joseph Bonaparte (1768–1844) et Joachim Murat (1767–1815) ont dirigé le royaume de Naples. Même les pins parasols du jardin rappellent l'Italie. La demeure de Paul Marmottan ainsi que l'hôtel particulier parisien qui abrite aujourd'hui le musée Marmottan Monet ont été ouverts au public en 1934, conformément au vœu de son fondateur. La bibliothèque sert désormais de centre de recherches à l'Institut de France.

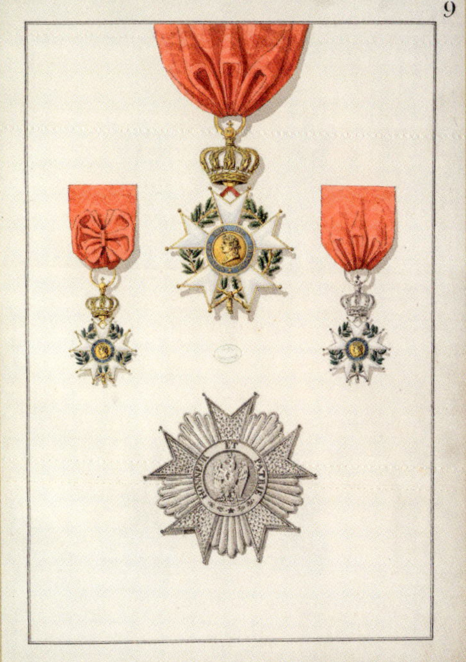

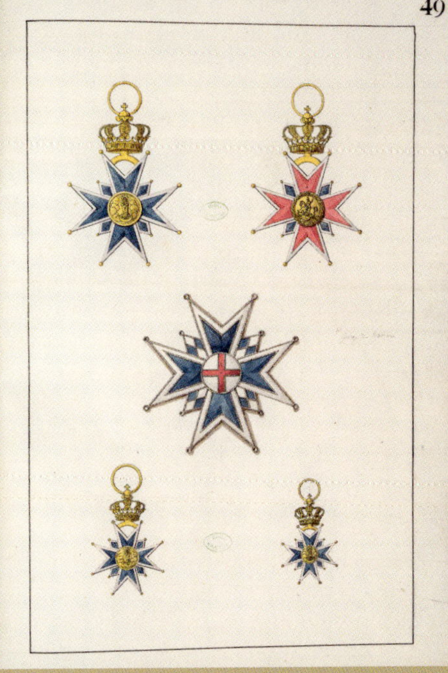

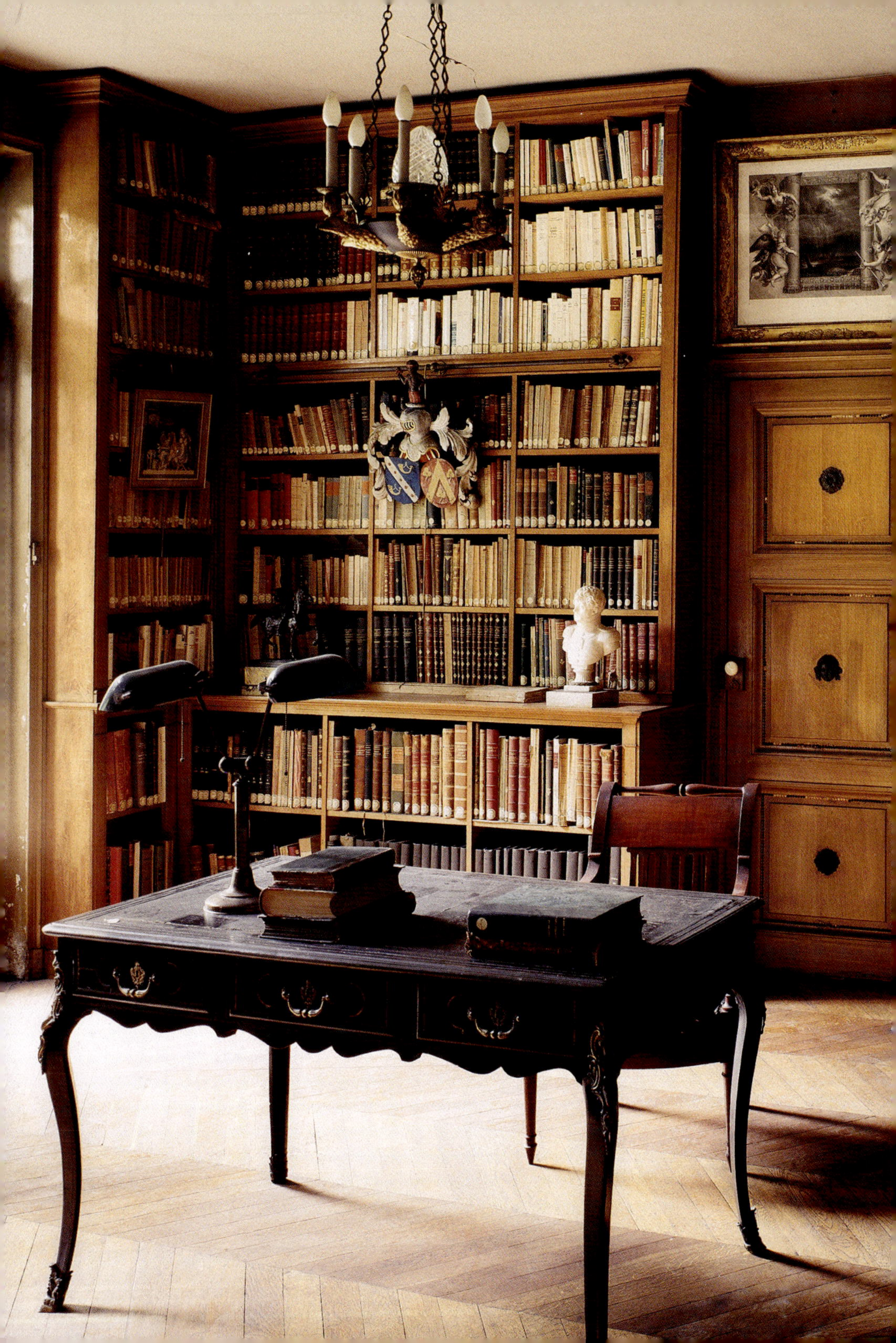

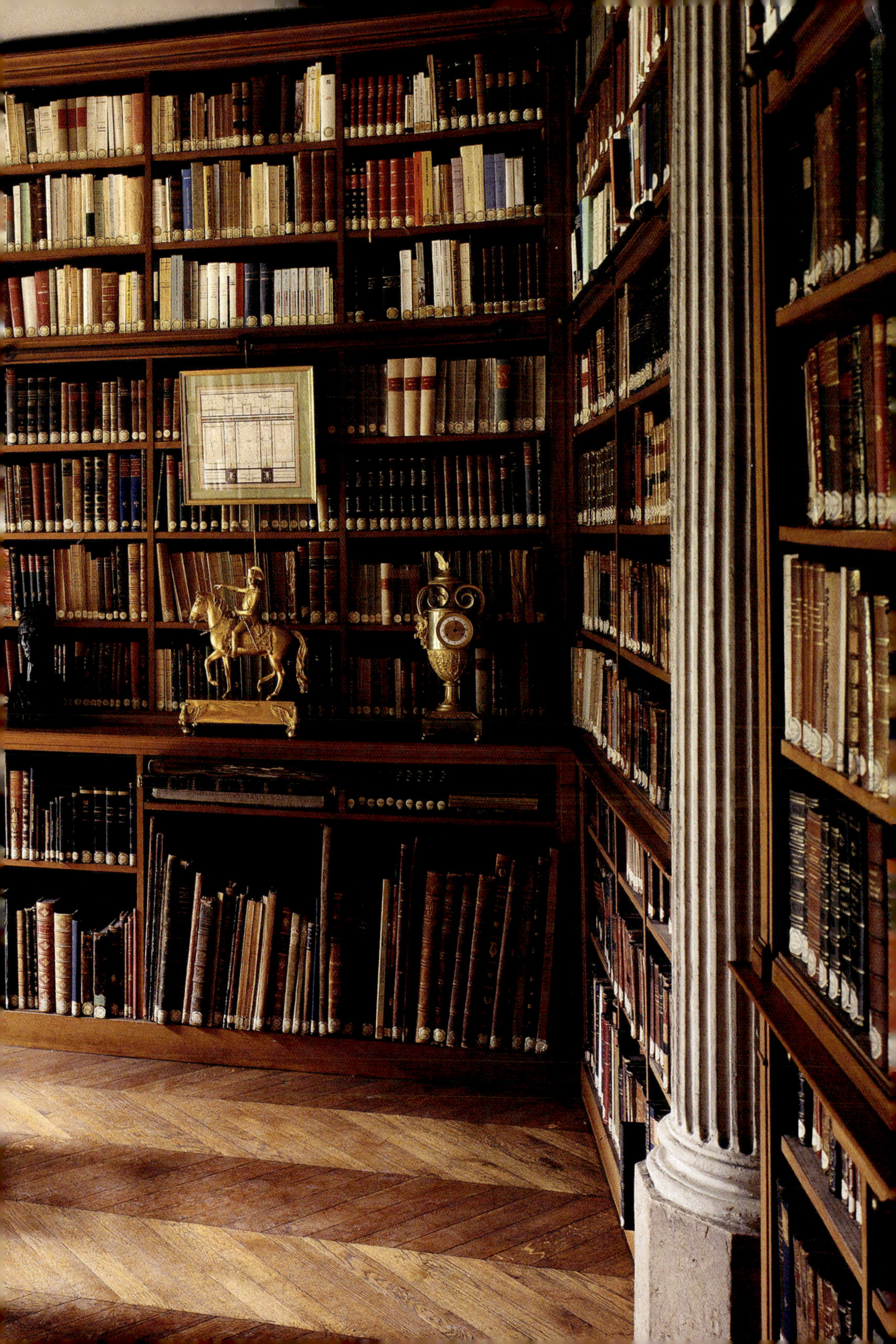

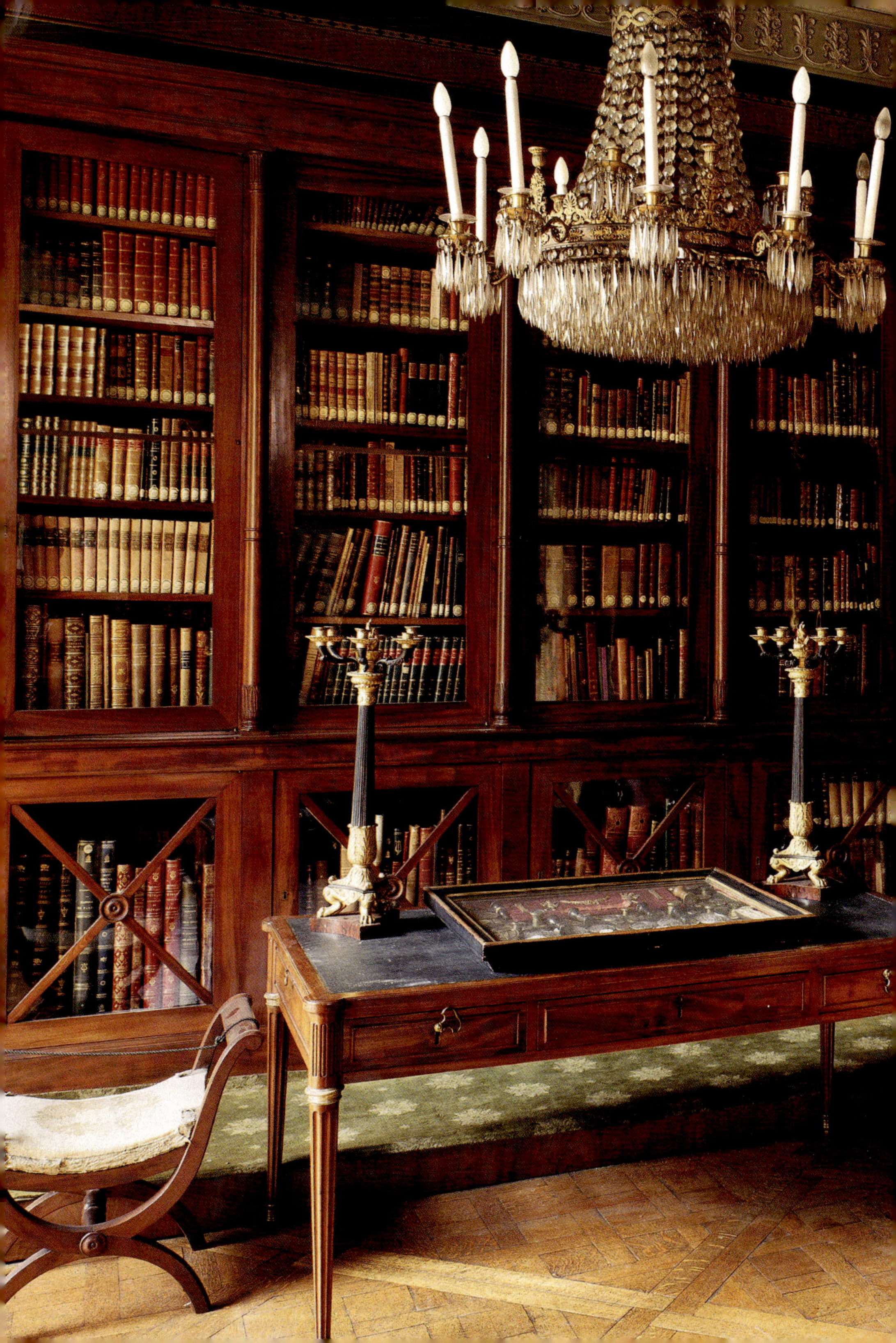

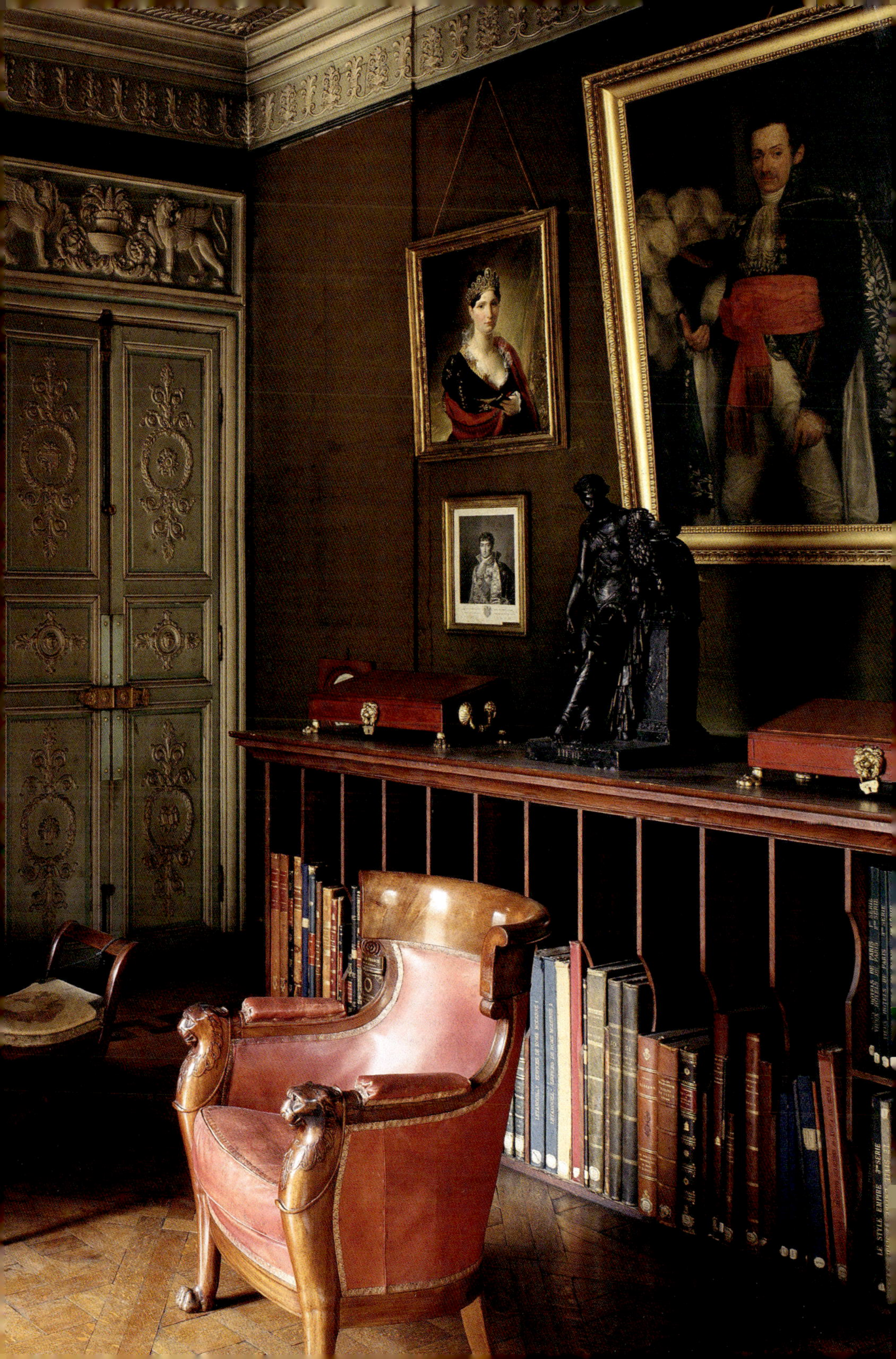

VIEUX HÔTELS DE PARIS
VIEUX HÔTELS DE PARIS
LE STYLE EMPIRE 5e SÉRIE

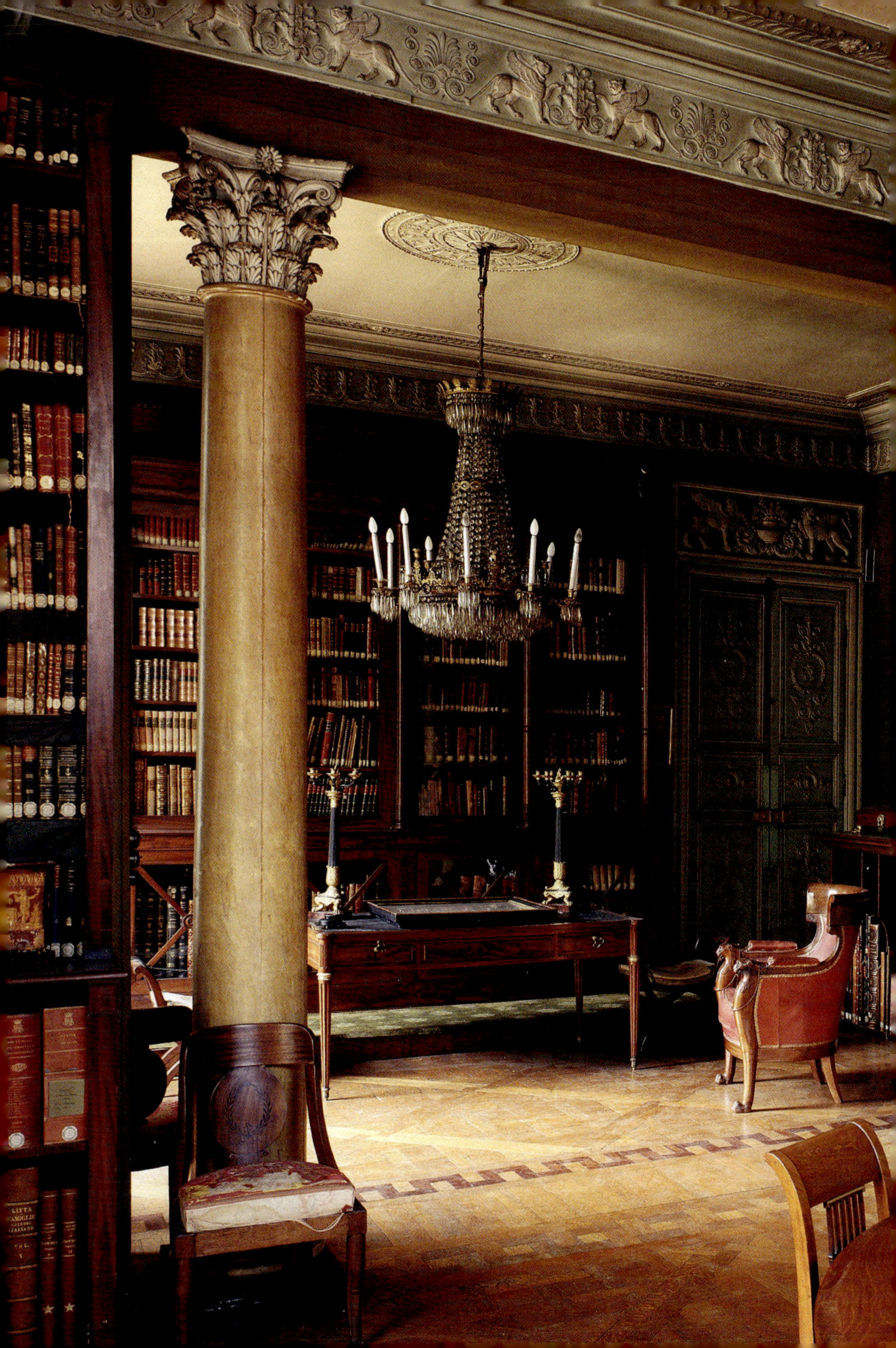

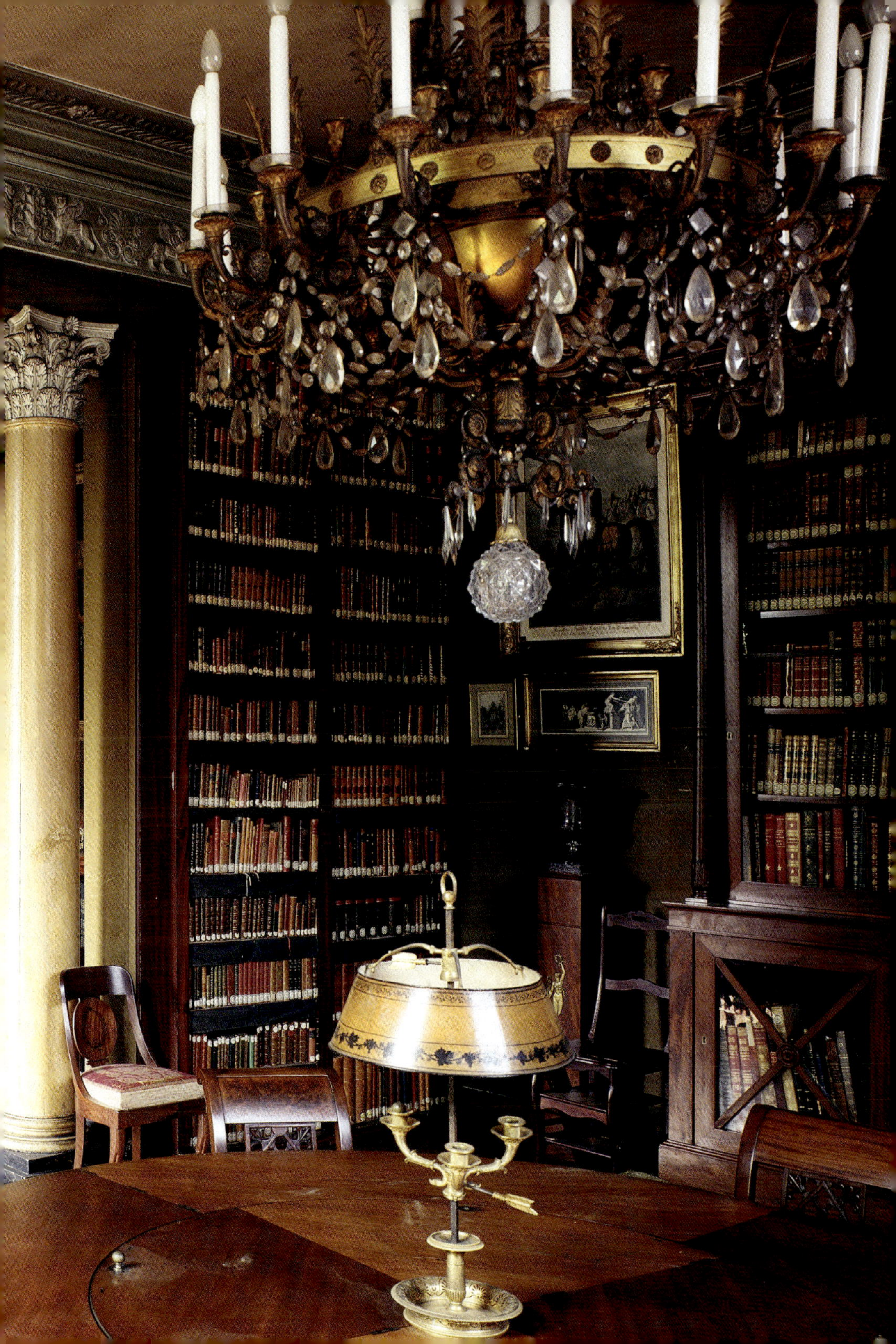

Rijksmuseum Research Library

The Rijksmuseum Research Library in Amsterdam is one of the largest art libraries in the world. From auction catalogues to rare periodicals, a treasury of books has been collected and stored here without interruption since 1885. The library's holdings are thematically related to the museum's collections, which comprise some one million objects, including paintings and sculptures, as well as works of applied art and artefacts of historical interest. Situated inside the main Rijksmuseum building, the reading room's dual function of ordering and storing books is clearly reflected in its design. The visitor is greeted by a closed-shelf library with an integrated reading area, generously lit by natural light arriving via the glazed ceiling and high windows, which lend visual breadth to the shaft-like room. The technique of iron construction that became fashionable in the second half of the 19th century made it possible to build bookshelves up to spectacular heights using filigree and space-saving ironwork structures. The spiral staircases in the corners of the reading room – probably impracticable for anyone who suffers from vertigo – bear witness to this radical development. The problems of climate control in rooms of this kind mean that only a few such closed-stack libraries survive. The Rijksmuseum Research Library, which preserves its 19th-century ambience intact, is therefore a particular gem. In their thorough restoration of the historical Rijksmuseum complex, which was originally built between 1876 and 1885 by Petrus Josephus Hubertus, called Pierre Cuypers (1827–1921), the Spanish architectural team of Cruz y Ortiz (Antonio Cruz, b. 1948, and Antonio Ortiz, b. 1947) paid particular attention to the preservation of the reading room and its functionality. The library's holdings on art and cultural history, iconography, the history of collecting and more recently the history of photography are being constantly expanded. Special collections include the library of the Association of Friends of Asiatic Art (complementing the museum's collection of Asian art, with its origins in Holland's colonial empire) and that of the Dutch Royal Archaeological Society.

❋❋❋

Founded c. 1885; library built 1876–1885 by Pierre Cuypers
Holdings c. 450,000 volumes
Type of library national library, research library
Highlights Andreas Vesalius, *De humani corporis fabrica libri septem*, Basel, 1555; Wenzel Jamnitzer, *Perspectiva corporum regularium*, Nuremberg, 1568; Joseph Friedrich von Racknitz, *Darstellung und Geschichte des Geschmacks der vorzüglichsten Völker in Beziehung auf die innere Auszierung der Zimmer und auf die Baukunst*, 4 vols., Leipzig, 1796–1798

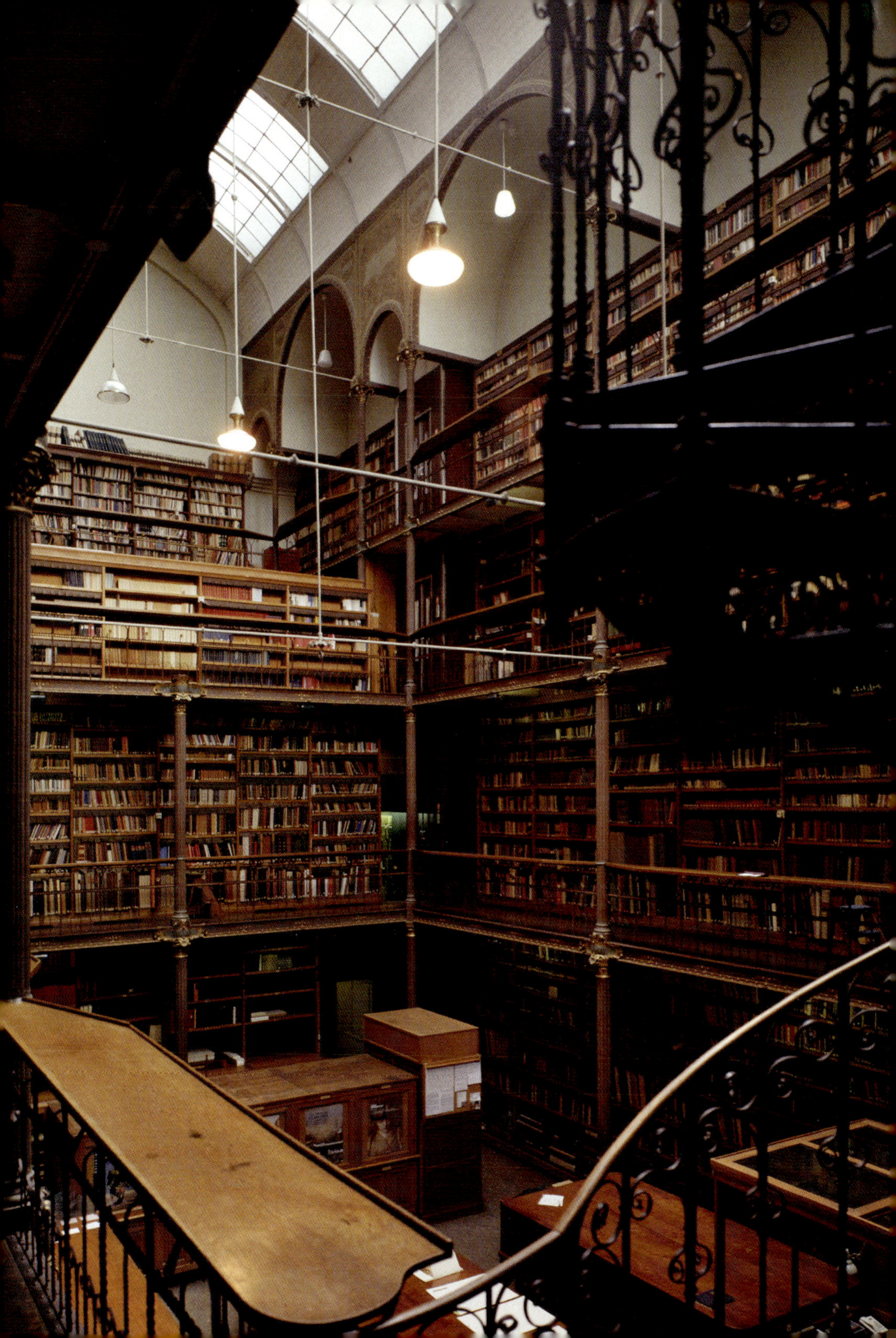

Die Bibliothek des Rijksmuseums in Amsterdam zählt weltweit zu den größten Forschungsbibliotheken zum Thema Kunst. Vom Auktionskatalog bis zum seltenen Periodikum wurde hier seit 1885 ohne Unterbrechung ein Bücherschatz gesammelt und aufbewahrt, der thematisch an die Kollektionen des Museums gebunden ist. Diese umfassen rund eine Million Objekte, zu denen Gemälde und Skulpturen ebenso wie Kunsthandwerk und historisch interessante Artefakte zählen. In der Tat spiegelt der Studiensaal, der direkt im Museumsgebäude liegt, diese Doppelfunktion des ordnenden Bewahrens deutlich sichtbar wider. Es ist eine Magazinbibliothek mit integriertem Lesebereich, die sich dem Betrachter eröffnet, großzügig durch Deckenlicht und hoch liegende Fenster erhellt, was dem schachtartigen Raum optische

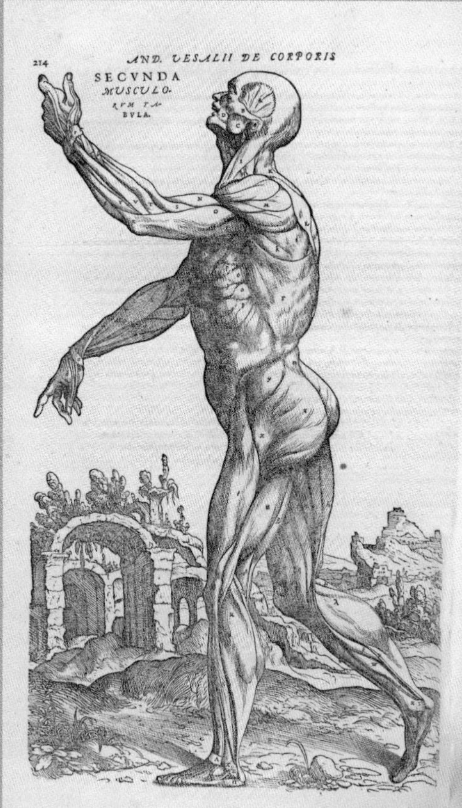

Weite verleiht. Die in der zweiten Hälfte des 19. Jahrhunderts in Mode gekommene Technik der Eisenkonstruktion machte es möglich, spektakuläre Höhen mittels filigraner und raumsparender Konstruktionen baulich zu bewältigen. An den – wohl nur für schwindelfreie Benutzer praktikablen – Wendeltreppen in den Ecken ist die radikale Höhenentwicklung der Bücherregale zu ermessen. Die prekären klimatischen Bedingungen so gestalteter Räume ließen nur wenige Magazinbibliotheken überleben, jene des Rijksmuseums mit ihrem intakt bewahrten 19.-Jahrhundert-Ambiente ist daher ein ganz besonderes Juwel. In der durchgreifenden Restaurierung des historistischen Baukomplexes, der von 1876 bis 1885 von Petrus Josephus Hubertus, genannt Pierre Cuypers (1827–1921), errichtet wurde, schenkte das spanische Architektenteam Cruz y Ortiz (Antonio Cruz, geb. 1948, und Antonio Ortiz, geb. 1947) der Erhaltung des Bibliotheksraumes und seiner Funktionalität besonderes Augenmerk. Seine Büchersammlung zur Kunst- und Kulturgeschichte, zur Ikonografie, zur Sammlungsgeschichte und neuerdings zur Geschichte der Fotografie wird ständig erweitert. Spezialsammlungen sind jene der Vereinigung der Freunde asiatischer Kunst – ein Sammelschwerpunkt des Museums, der im Kolonialreich der Niederlande seinen Ursprung hat – und jene der Königlichen Gesellschaft für Archäologie.

✳✳✳

La bibliothèque du Rijksmuseum d'Amsterdam compte parmi les plus grandes bibliothèques de recherche dans le domaine de l'art. Elle abrite, sans discontinuer depuis 1885, un trésor documentaire allant des catalogues de vente aux enchères aux périodiques les plus rares en concordance avec la thématique des collections exposées dans le musée. Ces collections composées de peintures, sculptures, artisanat et objets d'intérêt historique englobent près d'un million de pièces. La salle d'étude, située dans le musée, est le reflet clair et net de la fonction duelle de la conservation méthodique.

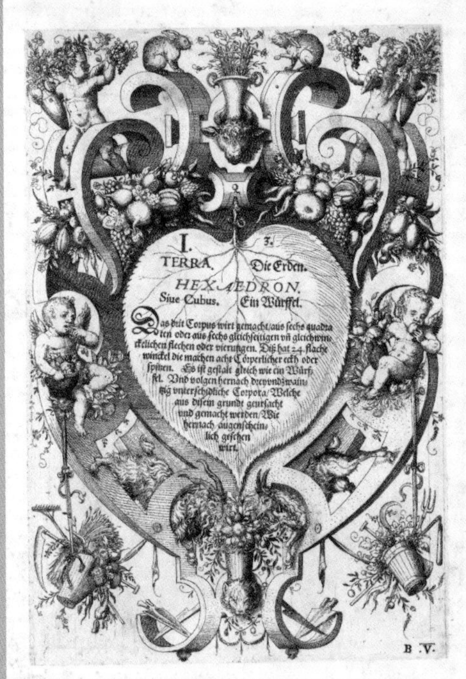

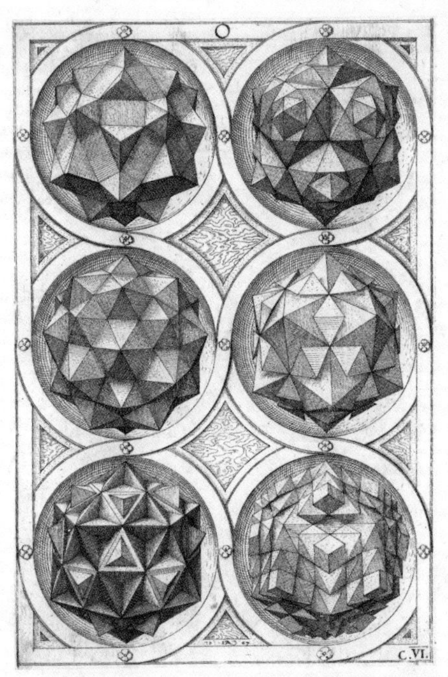

Il s'agit d'un magasin de livres avec coin lecture intégré, généreusement baigné de lumière par une ouverture zénithale et des fenêtres haut placées qui confèrent un caractère immense à une salle plutôt étroite en réalité. L'architecture de fer, devenue à la mode dans la seconde moitié du XIXe siècle, permit en effet de conquérir des hauteurs spectaculaires et d'économiser de l'espace au moyen d'édifices à la structure robuste mais élancée. La hauteur colossale des rayonnages se mesure au nombre de volées des escaliers en colimaçon, seulement praticables par les visiteurs ne craignant pas le vide. Il se trouve que peu de dépôts de livres aménagés dans cet esprit ont survécu à la précarité des conditions climatiques inhérentes à un tel espace. L'ambiance XIXe siècle restée intacte dans la salle du Rijksmuseum en fait un joyau très singulier. L'équipe d'architectes espagnols Cruz y Ortiz (Antonio Cruz, né en 1948, et Antonio Ortiz, né en 1947), chargée de la restauration complète du bâtiment historique construit entre 1876 et 1885 par Petrus Josephus Hubertus (dit Pierre Cuypers, 1827–1921), rendit un bel hommage à l'état de conservation de la salle de bibliothèque ainsi qu'à sa fonctionnalité. Les fonds ayant trait à l'histoire de l'art et de la culture, à l'iconographie, à l'histoire des collections et, depuis peu, à l'histoire de la photographie ne cessent de s'accroître. L'Association des amis de l'art asiatique – un point fort du musée né sous l'Empire colonial néerlandais – et la Société royale d'archéologie disposent toutes deux de collections spéciales abritées sur place.

Andreas Vesalius, *De humani corporis fabrica libri septem*, Basel, 1555, p. 214

Wenzel Jamnitzer, *Perspectiva corporum regularium*, Nuremberg, 1568, sig. 3091 5, p. 16, pl. B. V.

Wenzel Jamnitzer, *Perspectiva corporum regularium*, Nuremberg, 1568, sig. 3091 5, p. 23, pl. C. VI.

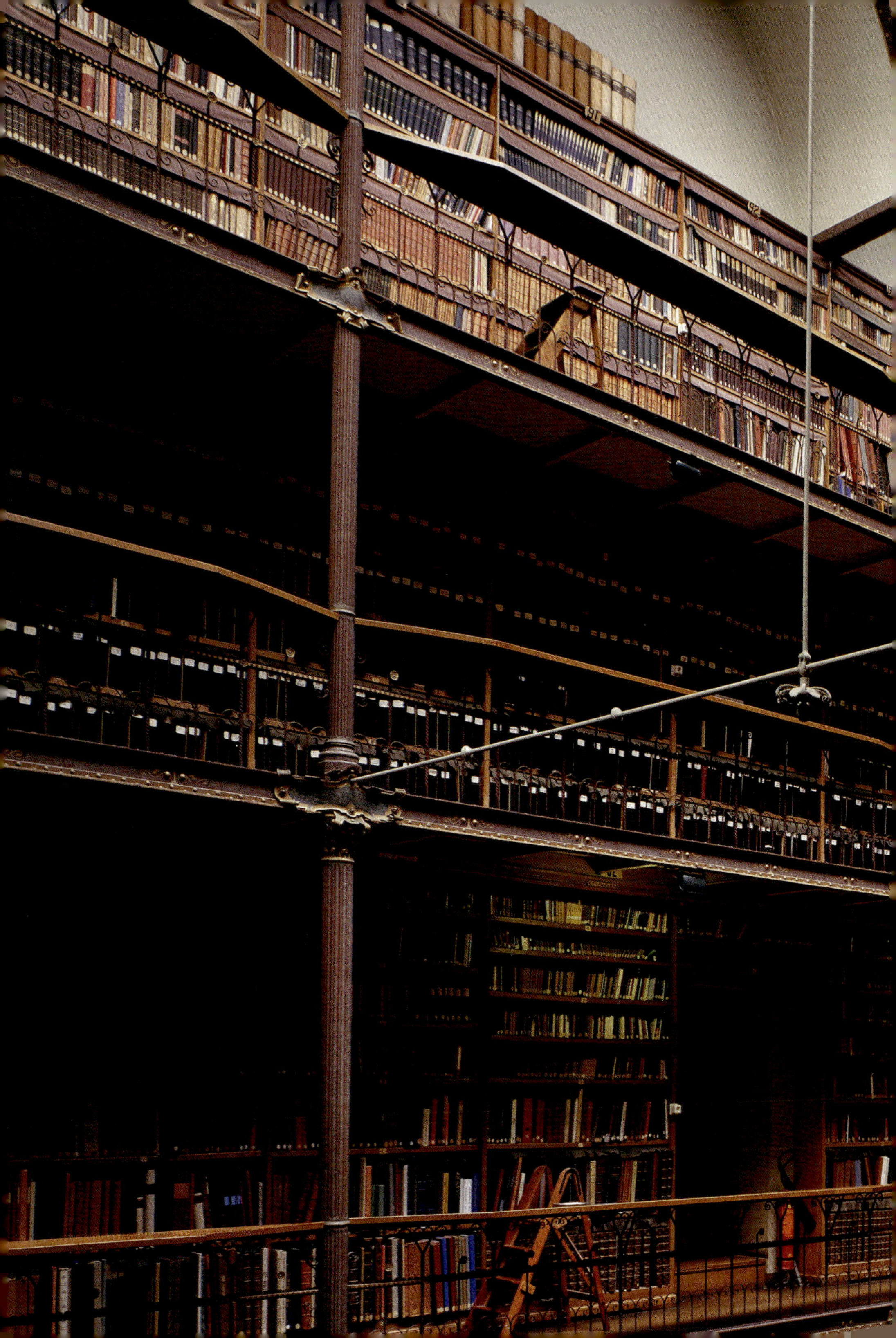

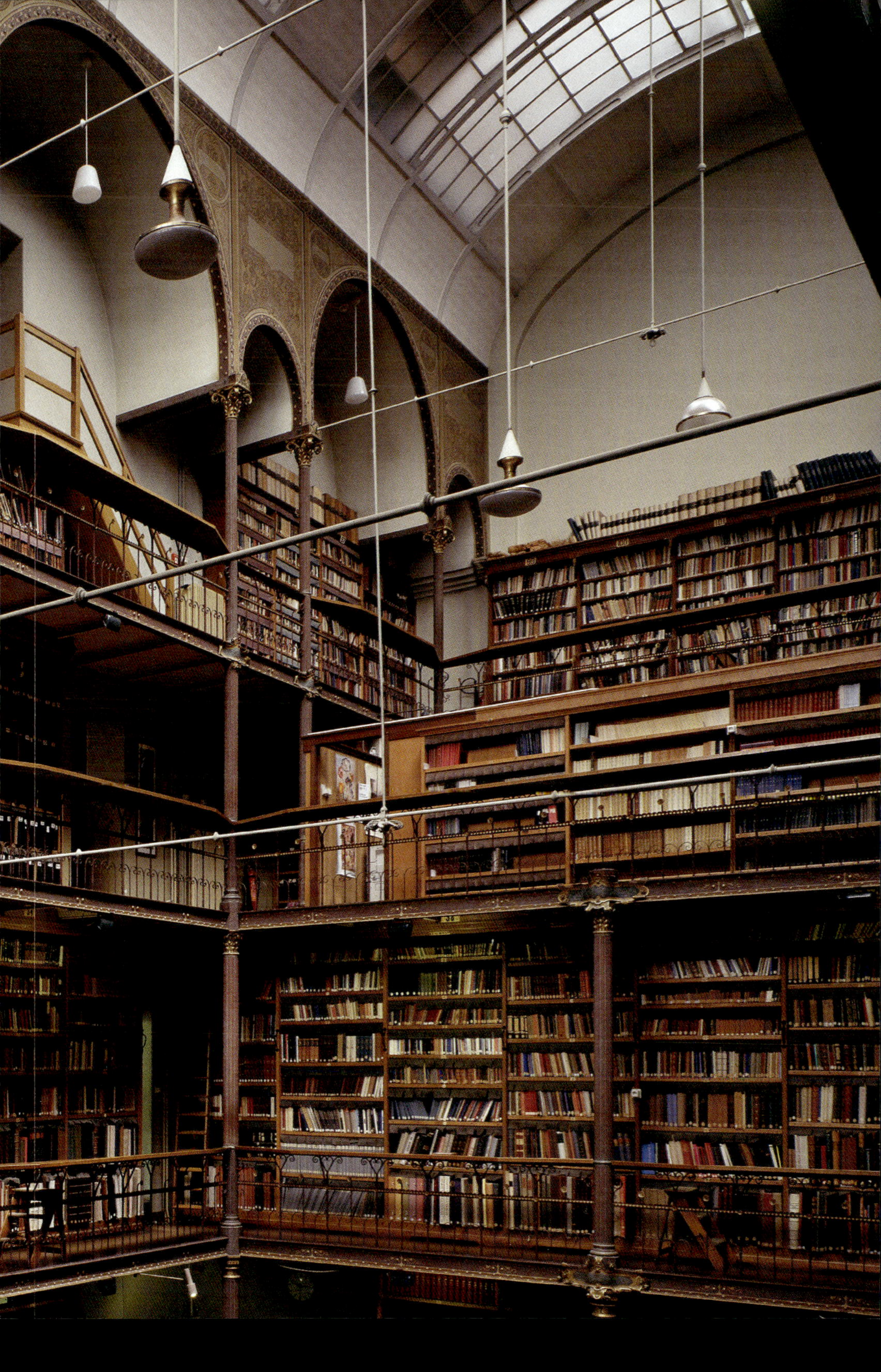

Skoklosters Slotts Bibliotek

The collections in Skokloster Castle bear historical witness to the Thirty Years' War (1618–1648), when Sweden had risen to become one of the most powerful countries in Europe. The war earned Skokloster's builder, the influential field marshal Carl Gustaf Wrangel (1613–1676), both his elevation to the nobility and offices such as that of Governor General of Swedish Pomerania, making him a rich man. Wrangel converted his wealth into prestigious residences and vast collections consisting to a large extent of booty, as evidenced by his country estates in Germany and Sweden, his mansion near the royal palace in Stockholm, and Skokloster Castle, which from 1654 up until his death in 1676 Wrangel transformed into a magnificent residence and his personal art gallery. To this end he employed the leading artists of the day. The plans for the castle, a defensive four-winged complex with corner towers, were drawn up by royal architect Nicodemus Tessin the Elder (1615–1681), whose original scale model is still preserved in the Skokloster collections. Actual construction was carried out under Casper Vogell (1600–1663), whom Wrangel knew from earlier commissions for the Swedish king in Germany. Wrangel's art treasures and precious books were subsequently preserved and enriched for a further 300 years by the Brahe family, his descendants through marriage. In 1967 the castle, which had been inhabited only sporadically since first being built, was sold to the state and in 1971 declared part of Sweden's cultural heritage and opened to the public as a museum. Alongside the historical collection of books, today displayed as part of the museum interior, the rooms of the castle are also home to some 1,000 paintings (of which 770 belong to Wrangel's original holdings), valuable furnishings, silver, glass, textiles, natural history specimens and a splendid armoury. The patron, who was well-versed in architectural theory, had the library installed on the top floor of the east wing in line with recommended practice. Treatises on architecture, books of models and technical literature of all kinds, written primarily in Latin and German, together with maps and travelogues, testify to his specific interests in these areas. In 1665 his collection of books – previously divided between several residences – was brought together at Skokloster, organised and displayed according to subject area and type of book, and catalogued. At Wrangel's death it comprised 2,400 volumes. Today the collection is housed in seven rooms and incorporates seven libraries from related aristocratic families. The largest of these libraries, with almost 9,000 volumes, is that of Count Carl Gustaf Bielkes (1683–1754), one of Sweden's most avid book collectors of the 18th century. The fresco paintings decorating the rooms date from the 19th century.

❋ ⁎ ❋

Founded 1665 on the basis of older holdings; built from 1654 by Casper Vogell after the architectural model by Nicodemus Tessin the Elder; the library's current interior dates from the first half of the 19th century
Holdings c. 30,000 volumes
Type of library aristocratic family library
Highlights Quintus Curtius Rufus, *Les faiz et conquestes d'Alexandre le Grant*, French translation of *Historia Alexandri magni Macedonum*, by Vasca De Lucena, c. 1470; Per Brahe, *Lutbok*, 1620; Johann Wilhelm, *Architectura civilis*, Frankfurt a. M., 1649

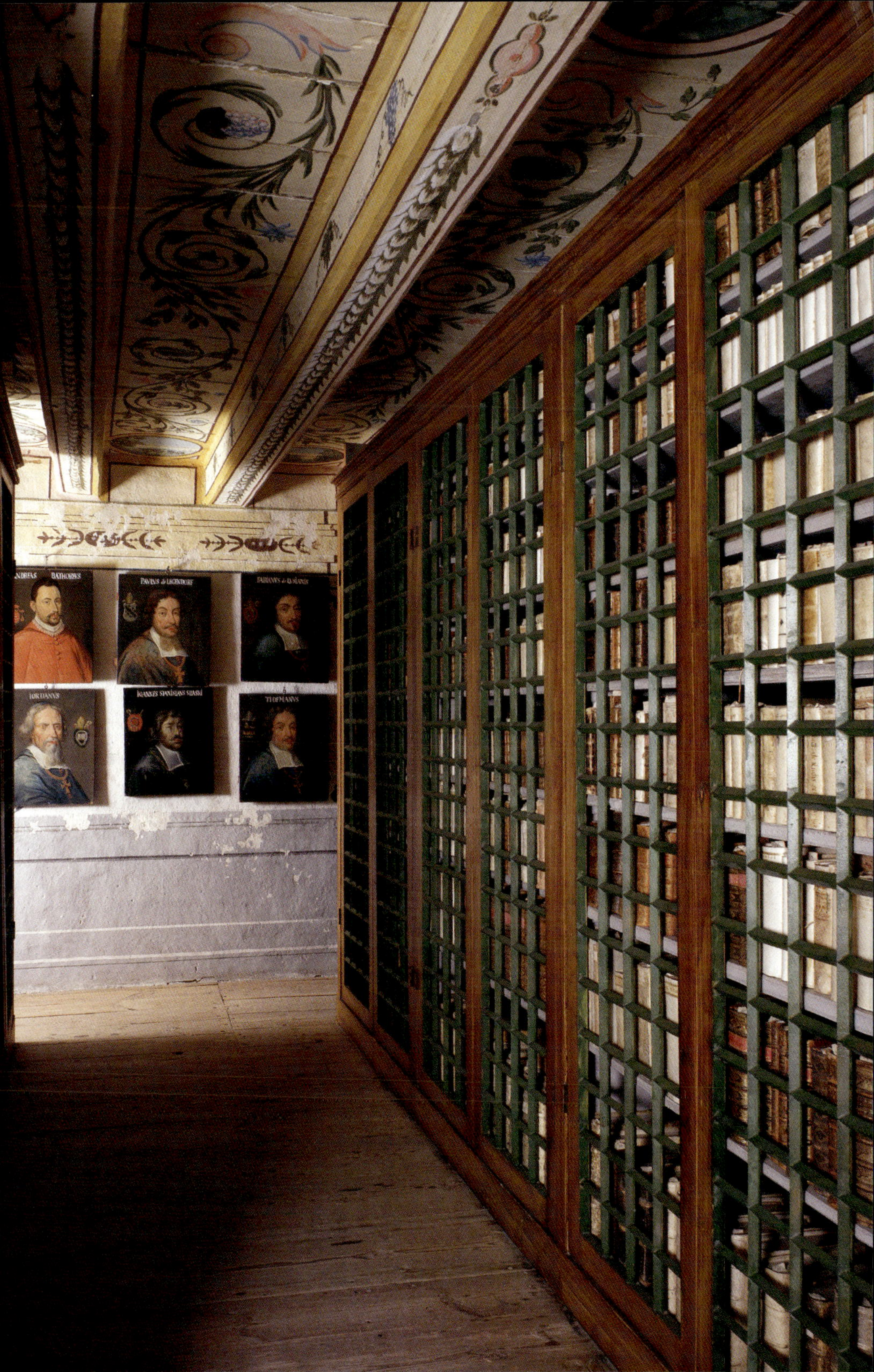

Schloss Skokloster ist ein historisches Zeitzeugnis des Dreißigjährigen Krieges (1618–1648), in dessen Folge Schweden zu einem der mächtigsten Länder Europas geworden war. Seinem Bauherrn, dem einflussreichen Feldmarschall Carl Gustav Wrangel (1613–1676), brachte der Krieg nicht nur die Erhebung in den Adelsstand, sondern auch ertragreiche Ämter wie jenes des Generalgouverneurs von Schwedisch-Pommern. Seinen damals erworbenen Reichtum setzte er in prestigeträchtige Bauten und gewaltige, zu guten Teilen aus Kriegsbeute stammende Sammlungen um. Davon zeugen Landsitze in Deutschland und Schweden, ein Stadtpalais in der Nähe des Königspalastes in Stockholm und Schloss Skokloster, das er ab 1654 bis zu seinem Tod 1676 zu einer prächtigen Residenz und seiner persönlichen Kunstkammer gestaltete. Höchstes Anspruchsniveau galt auch für die von ihm beschäftigten Künstler. Der königliche Architekt Nicodemus Tessin d. Ä. (1615–1681) zeichnet für den Umbau des Schlosses, einer wehrhaften Vierflügelanlage mit Ecktürmen, verantwortlich. Sein originales Architekturmodell hat sich noch heute in dessen Sammlungen erhalten. Den Baumeister Casper Vogell (1600–1663) kannte Carl Gustav Wrangel aus früheren Aufträgen für den schwedischen König in Deutschland. Wrangels Kunst- und Buchschätze in Skokloster wurden über fast 300 Jahre von der mit ihm verschwägerten Familie Brahe bewahrt und weiter bereichert, bevor das seit seiner Entstehung nur sporadisch bewohnte Schloss 1967 an den Staat verkauft, 1971 zum Kulturerbe erklärt und als Museum der Öffentlichkeit zugänglich gemacht wurde. In seinem Inneren sind neben der museal erhaltenen historischen Büchersammlung an die 1 000 Gemälde (770 umfasste bereits der Altbestand Wrangels), wertvolle Möbel, Silber, Glas, eine Textiliensammlung, Naturalienkabinette und eine reiche Waffenkammer aufbewahrt. Die Bibliothek ließ der in Architekturtheorie belesene Auftraggeber deren Vorgaben entsprechend im Obergeschoss des Ostflügels einrichten. In ganz Europa angekaufte Architekturtraktate, Modellbücher und allerlei technische Literatur, vor allem in lateinischer und deutscher Sprache, aber auch Pläne und Reisebeschreibungen zeugen noch heute von diesen spezifischen Interessen. 1665 wurde die bis dahin auf verschiedene Wohnsitze aufgeteilte Büchersammlung in Skokloster zusammengeführt, nach Themenbereichen und Buchtypen geordnet aufgestellt und katalogisiert. Bei Wrangels Tod umfasste sie 2 400 Bände. Heute ist die aus insgesamt sieben verwandtschaftlich verbundenen Fürstenbibliotheken bestehende Sammlung in sieben Räumen untergebracht und gemäß ihren unterschiedlichen Provenienzen sortiert. Unter diesen stellt die Bibliothek Graf Carl Gustaf Bielkes (1683–1754) mit ihren 9 000 Bänden die umfangreichste dar. Er war einer der größten schwedischen Büchersammler des 18. Jahrhunderts. Die Ausstattung der Räume mit Freskenmalereien stammt aus dem 19. Jahrhundert.

✸✜✸

Le château de Skokloster offre un témoignage de l'époque de la guerre de Trente Ans qui fit de la Suède l'un des plus puissants pays d'Europe. La guerre ne permit pas seulement à l'influent seigneur et feld-maréchal Carl Gustaf Wrangel (1613–1676) d'être anobli, mais aussi de remplir des fonctions lucratives comme celle du gouverneur-général de Poméranie suédoise. Il convertit sa richesse issue de butin de guerre en édifices prestigieux et collections impressionnantes. En témoignent diverses propriétés situées en Allemagne et en Suède, un hôtel particulier érigé dans le voisinage du palais royal à Stockholm et le château de Skokloster qu'il transforma, de 1654 à sa mort en 1676, en résidence de luxe et en galerie d'art personnelle. Les hommes dont il s'entoura pour réaliser ce projet excellaient dans leur art. Responsable des plans, l'architecte de cour Nicodème Tessin l'Ancien (1615–1681) proposa un château fortifié sur plan carré avec quatre tours d'angle. La maquette originale est conservée dans les collections actuelles. Carl Gustaf Wrangel fit

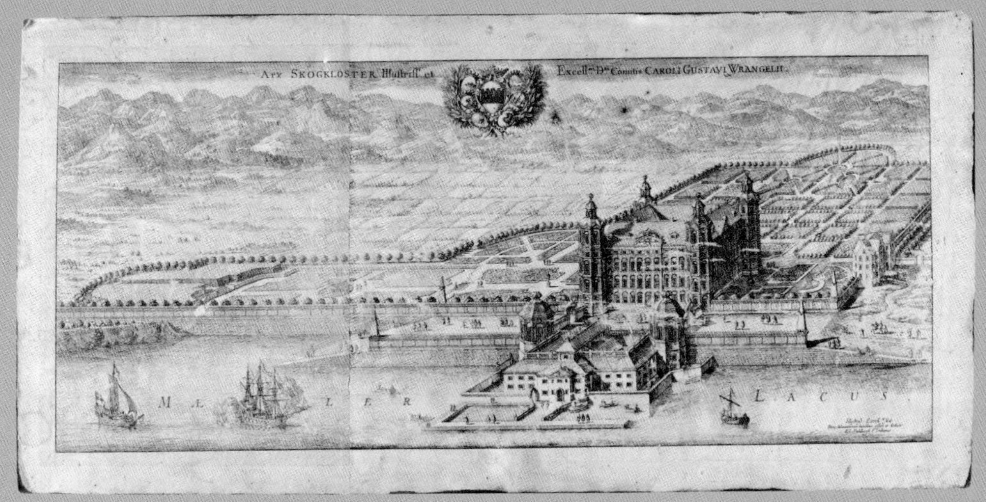

la connaissance du maître d'œuvre Casper Vogell (1600–1663) par le biais d'autres commandes réalisées pour le roi de Suède en Allemagne. Près de 300 ans durant, la famille Brahe, parente par alliance du feld-maréchal, conserva et enrichit les trésors d'art et de littérature de Wrangel à Skokloster, avant que le château – peu habité depuis son édification – soit vendu à l'État en 1967 et déclaré patrimoine culturel en 1971. Il est ouvert au public sous forme de musée. Outre le fonds de livres présenté de façon muséale, il abrite 1 000 peintures (la collection de Wrangel en comportait déjà 770), des meubles de grande valeur, de l'argenterie et de la verrerie, une collection de textiles, un cabinet de curiosités naturelles et une chambre d'armes bien fournie. Le commanditaire très instruit en théorie d'architecture fit aménager, conformément aux directives en vigueur, la bibliothèque

à l'étage supérieur de l'aile est. Des traités d'architecture achetés dans toute l'Europe, des recueils de modèles ainsi que d'instructions techniques, notamment en langues latine et allemande, ainsi que des descriptions de voyage renseignent sur les centres d'intérêt du propriétaire. La collection de livres, jusqu'alors répartie en divers lieux, fut rassemblée à Skokloster en 1665, agencée par thèmes et types d'ouvrages, puis indexée. Elle comptait 2 400 volumes à la mort de Wrangel. La collection actuelle, complétée par les bibliothèques particulières de ses sept parents, occupe sept pièces, chacune correspondant à un parent. Avec ses 9000 volumes, la bibliothèque du comte Carl Gustaf Bielkes (1683–1754) est la plus importante des sept. C'était l'un des plus grands collectionneurs suédois du XVIIIᵉ siècle. Le décor peint dans les pièces date du XIXᵉ siècle.

Arx Skokloster, in: Erik Dahlberg,
Suecia Antiqua et Hodierna, 1710, pl. 140

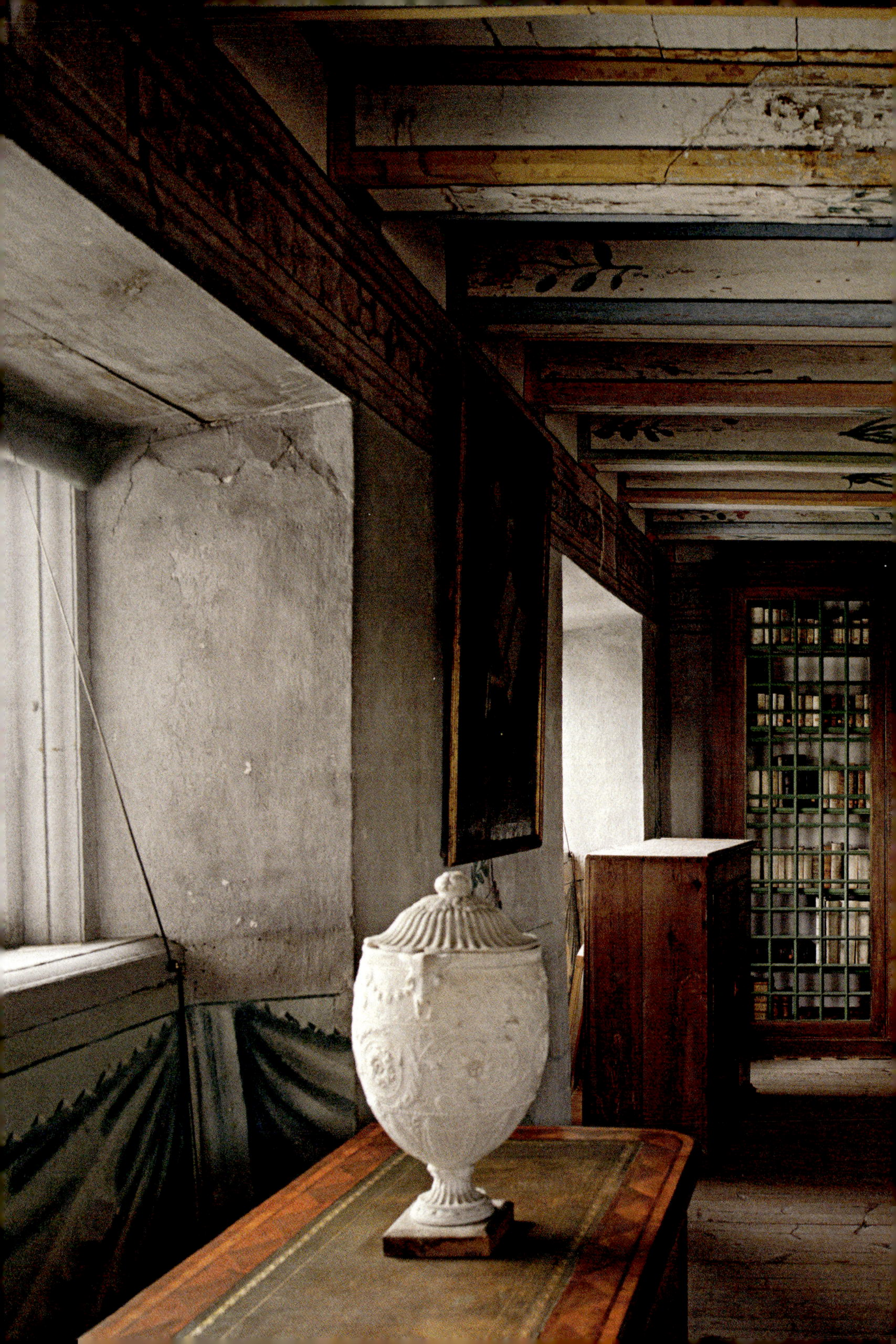

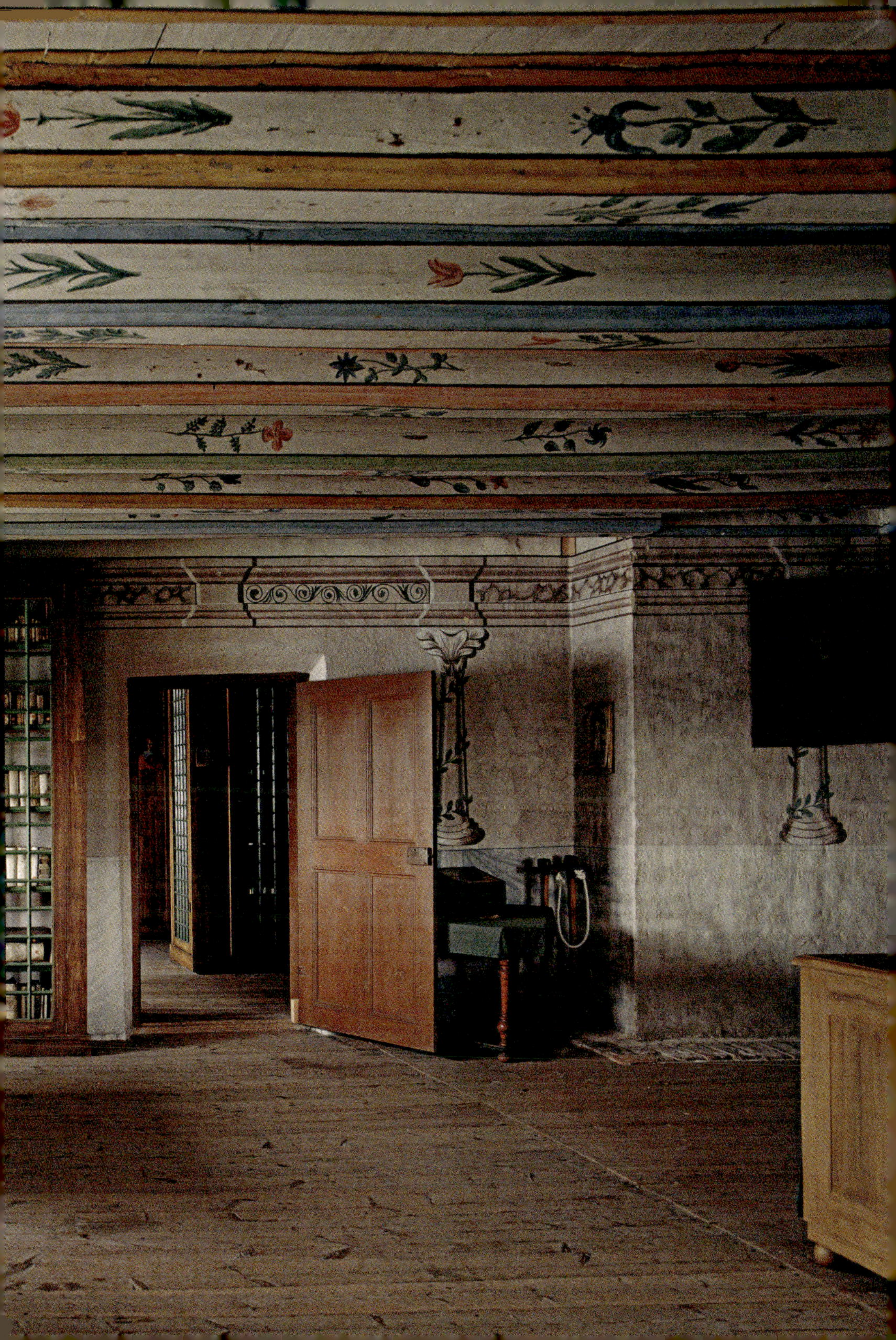

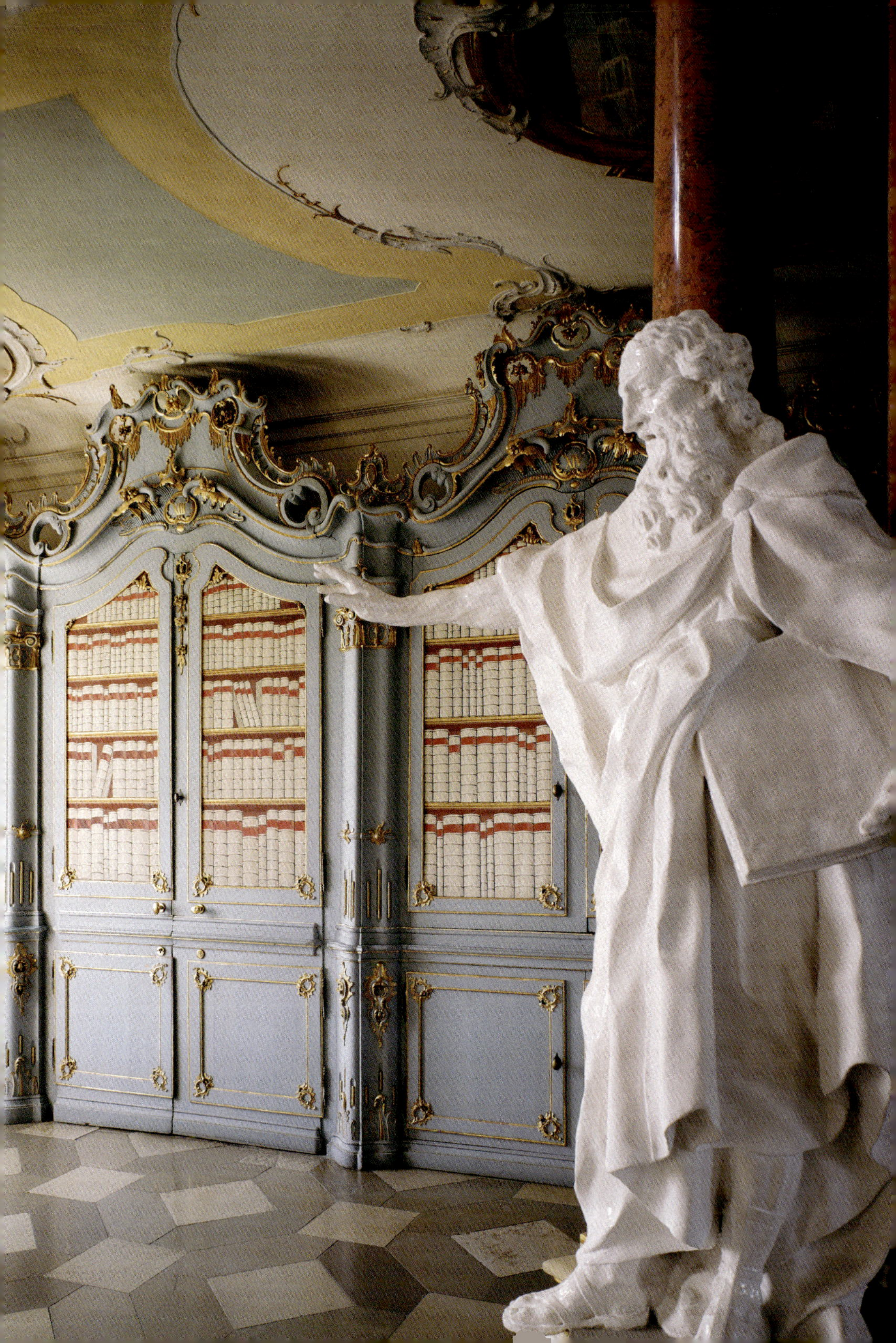

CENTRAL EUROPE

Germany

Switzerland

Austria

Czech Republic

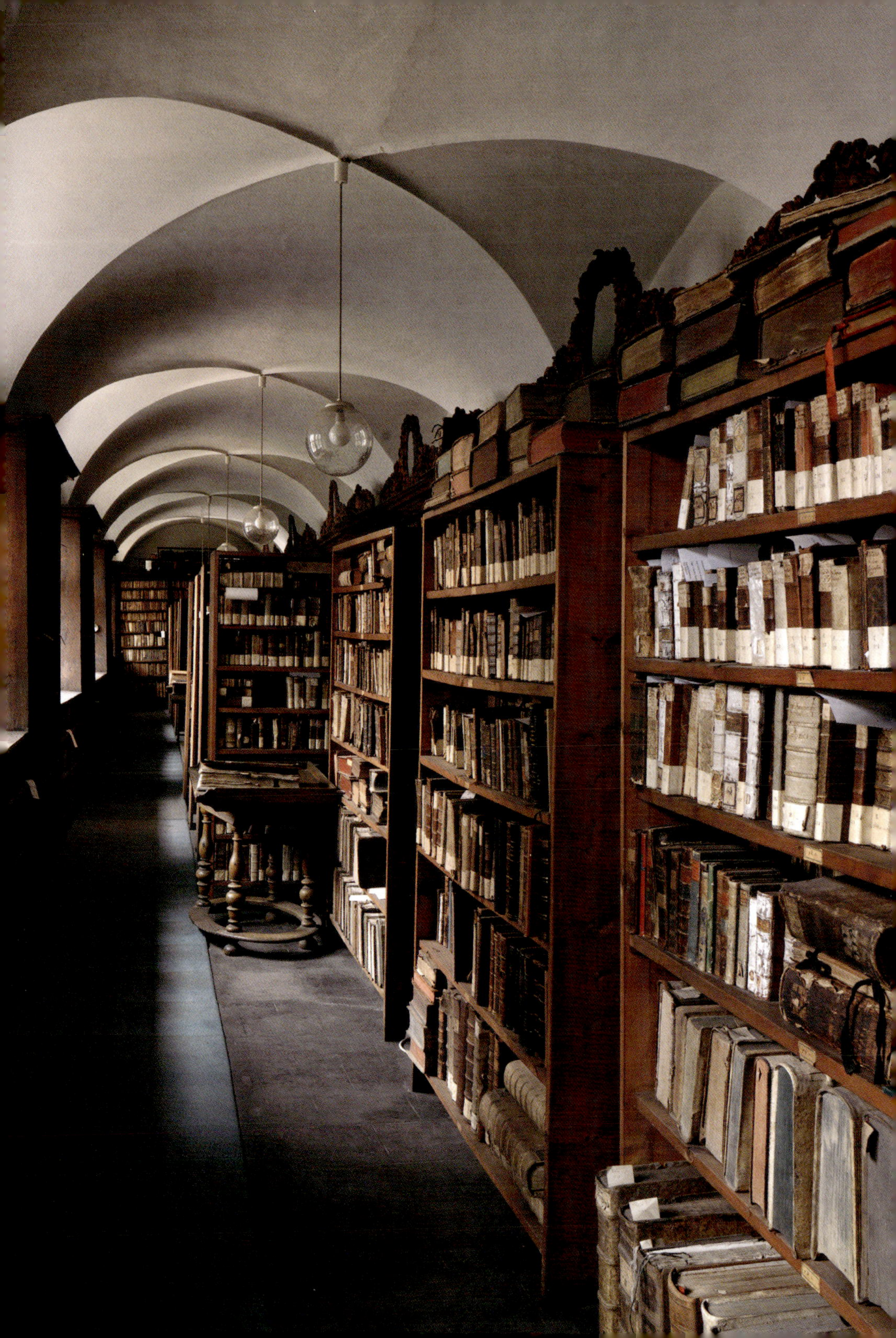

GERMANY

SWITZERLAND

AUSTRIA

CZECH REPUBLIC

Text by Elisabeth Sladek

Page 308 Library Hall in Kloster Schussenried,
Bad Schussenried, Germany

Opposite Knihovna Kláštera Augustiniánu
sv. Tomáše, Prague, Czech Republic

Klosterbibliothek Ottobeuren

The Baroque library at Ottobeuren, with its collection of some 15,000 books, was created during the period in which the fortunes of the abbey were at their height. The monastery itself dates back significantly earlier, however, to Carolingian times. It was founded around 764 by the counts of Silach to serve their family and was settled by Benedictine monks. These came from the Benedictine abbeys of Sankt Gallen and Reichenau, where important centres of Christianisation and early medieval culture had already been established a few decades earlier. In 972 Emperor Otto I (912–973) made Ottobeuren an imperial abbey (a status it enjoyed until its temporary dissolution in 1802), and thereby guaranteed not only its financial and territorial independence but also a continuity of cultural, intellectual and spiritual activity within its walls. This found expression in a collection - today scattered all over the world – of exquisite medieval manuscripts, some of them transcribed and illuminated in Ottobeuren's own workshops. One example still housed in the library today is the *Isingrim Missal*, dating from the 12th century. The foundation of a school of oriental studies at Ottobeuren in 1543 suggests that the monastery library at that time also included substantial holdings of oriental writings. As a cultural centre in the age of humanism, the abbey even had its own printing press from the 16th century onwards, while Ottobeuren Abbey supplied teachers to Salzburg's Benedictine university on several occasions. The knowledge and glorification of God as the ultimate aim of all scholarly activity is proclaimed by the monumental ceiling fresco by Elias Zobel (1677–1718) in the library. It was produced as part of the comprehensive remodelling of the imperial abbey in the Baroque style, undertaken from 1711 by Abbot Rupert II Ness (1670–1740). The library hall was completed in 1718 "as a palace of the Muses, a bulwark of religion and a monument to itself" according to the inscription still visible today. With its statue of Pallas Athene in the centre and its 15,000 volumes bound in white pigskin on white bookshelves along the walls, the library has come down to us as a unified Baroque ensemble. The room is divided into two storeys by a columned gallery, above which magnificent cartouches framed in stucco relief testify to the former arrangement of the books by subject. Their vegetal ornament flows seamlessly into that of the ceiling, symmetrically structured by the stucco decoration of Johann Baptist Zimmermann (1680–1758).

❋ ❖ ❋

Founded c. 764; library hall from 1718
Holdings c. 15,000 volumes
Type of library monastic library, academic library
Highlights *Isingrim-Missale* (MS. 01), 12th century

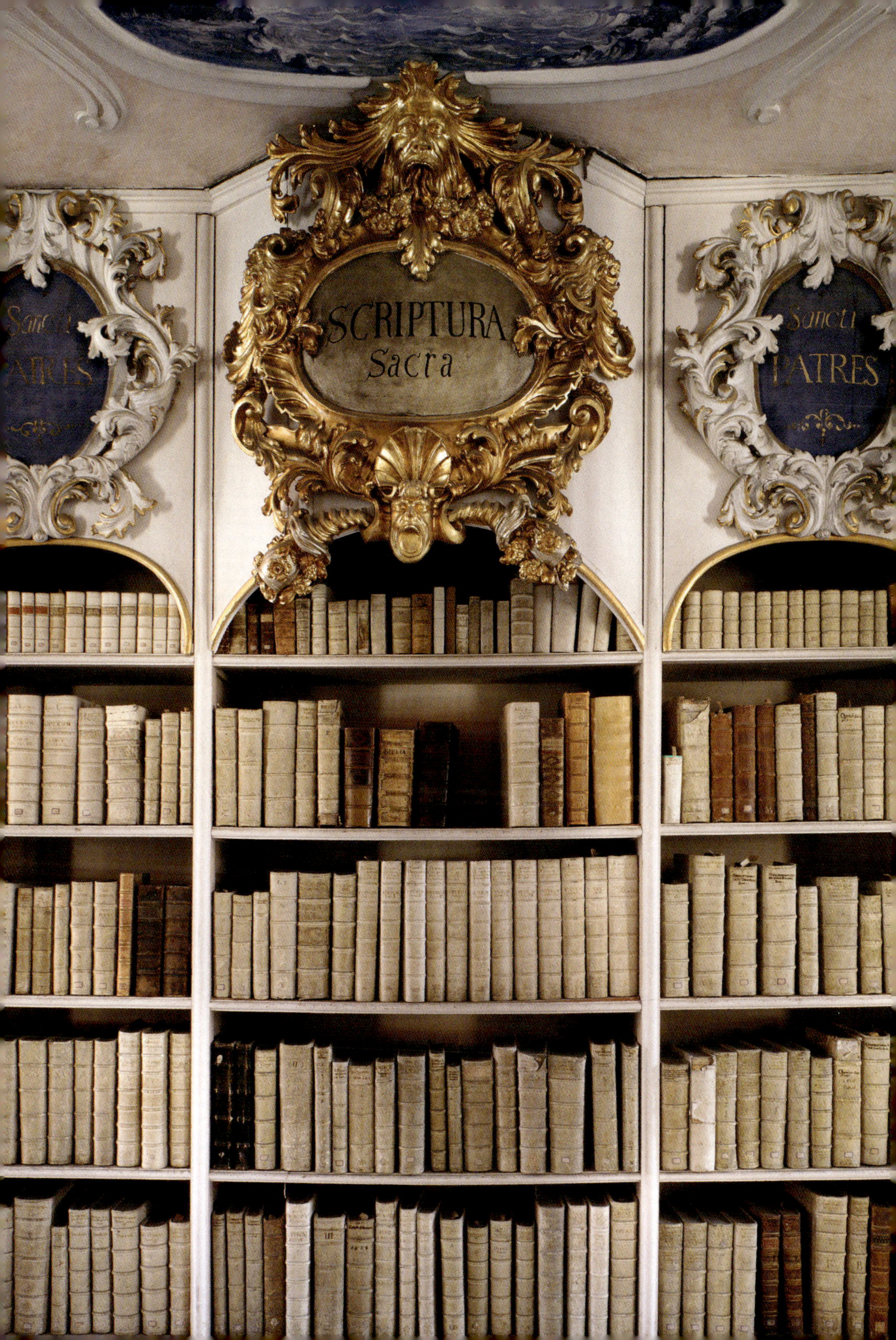

Sancti PATRES
SCRIPTURA Sacra
Sancti PATRES

Die Barockbibliothek des Klosters Ottobeuren stammt mit ihrem um die 15 000 Bände zählenden Buchbestand aus der Blütezeit der Abtei, deren Geschichte aber bereits in karolingischer Zeit einsetzt. Um 764 war sie von den Grafen Silach als deren Hauskloster gegründet und von Benediktinermönchen besiedelt worden. Diese kamen aus den Benediktinerabteien Sankt Gallen und Reichenau, wo sich bereits einige Jahrzehnte zuvor wichtige Zentren der Christianisierung und Pflegestätten frühmittelalterlicher Kultur etabliert hatten. Als Kaiser Otto I. (912–973) im Jahr 972 das Kloster zur Reichsabtei erhob – die es bis zu seiner vorübergehenden Auflösung 1802 blieb –, garantierte er über dessen wirtschaftliche und territoriale Unabhängigkeit auch eine Kontinuität geistigkulturellen Schaffens. Sie fand Niederschlag in einer heute in alle Welt verstreuten Sammlung kostbarer mittelalterlicher Handschriften, die teilweise in der hauseigenen Schreib- und Malschule entstanden sind. Das aus dem 12. Jahrhundert stammende *Isingrim-Missale* in der Ottobeurer Bibliothek ist das einzig dort

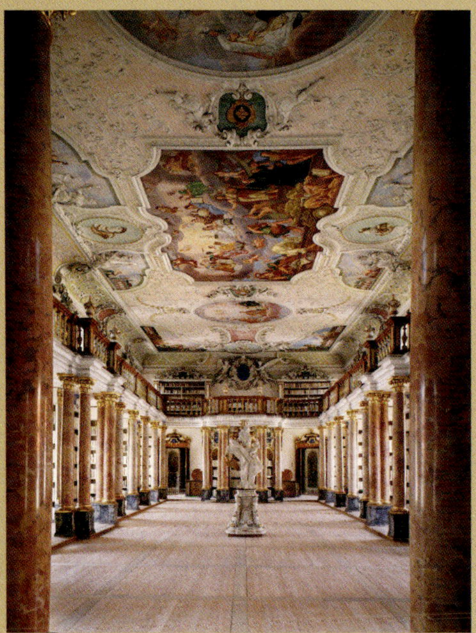

erhaltene Beispiel dafür. Die Gründung der Ottobeurer Akademie zur Pflege der orientalischen Sprachen im Jahr 1543 lässt auf ehemals bedeutende Bestände orientalischer Schriften in der Klosterbibliothek schließen. Als kulturelles Zentrum zur Zeit des Humanismus betrieb das Kloster ab dem 16. Jahrhundert sogar eine hauseigene Druckerei. Mehrfach entsandte die Abtei Ottobeuren Hochschullehrer an die Benediktineruniversität Salzburg. Dass das Ziel aller wissenschaftlichen Tätigkeit letztlich in Gotteserkenntnis und Gottesverherrlichung liege, erläutert das monumentale Deckenfresko von Elias Zobel (1677–1718) im Büchersaal. Es entstand im Zuge der umfassenden Barockisierung des kaiserlichen Reichsstiftes, die Abt Rupert II. Neß (1670–1740) ab 1711 in Angriff nahm. „Den Musen als Palast, der Religion als Bollwerk und sich selbst als Denkmal […]“, ließ Abt Rupert 1718 den barocken Bibliothekssaal errichten, der bis heute zusammen mit dieser Inschrift ein homogenes Bild seiner Entstehungszeit bewahrt hat. Dazu zählen neben dem Standbild der Pallas Athena in seinem Zentrum auch die in weißes Schweinsleder gebundenen 15 000 Bücher, die in weißen Bücherregalen entlang der Wandflächen des durch eine Säulengalerie in zwei Geschosse geteilten Saalraums aufgestellt sind. Auf die ehemals thematische Anordnung der Bücher verweisen die prächtigen stuckgerahmten Kartuschen, deren vegetabiles Ornament in jenes der Decke übergeht, wo Johann Baptist Zimmermann (1680–1758) mit seinen Stuckdekorationen eine einheitliche Raumgliederung geschaffen hat.

❋❖❋

Avec son fonds de 15 000 volumes, la bibliothèque baroque du monastère d'Ottobeuren date de la période florissante de l'abbaye dont l'histoire remonte à l'époque carolingienne. Vers 764 de notre ère, le comte Silach fonda un premier monastère, qui fut par la suite peuplé de moines bénédictins en provenance des abbayes de Saint-Gall et de Reichenau, où des centres de christianisation et de transmission

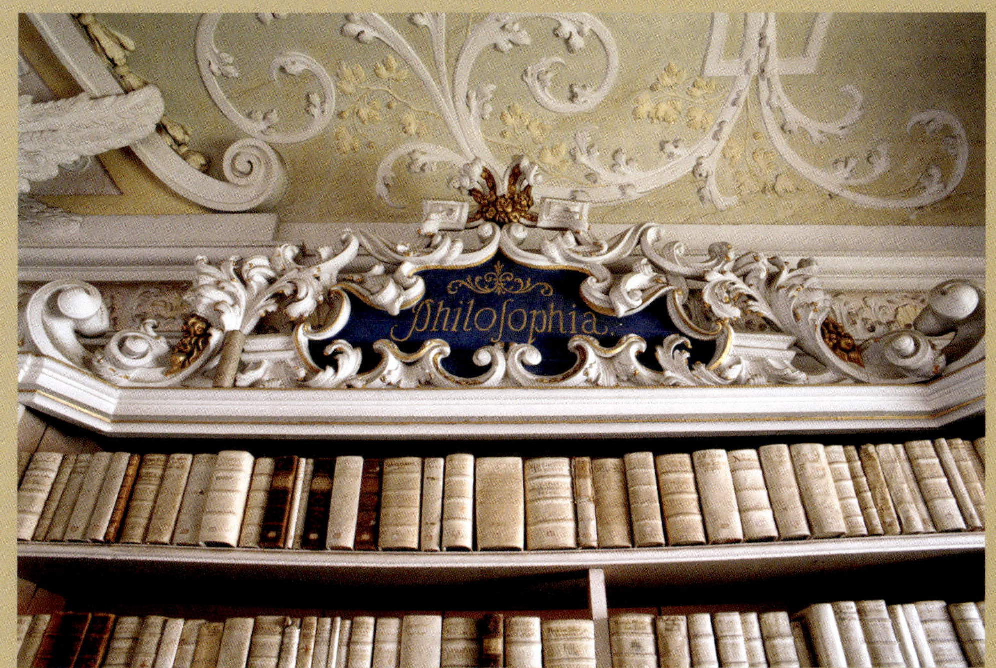

de la culture médiévale s'étaient créés quelques décennies auparavant. Lorsque l'empereur Othon Ier (912–973) fit du monastère une abbaye impériale – appellation qu'elle conserva jusqu'à sa suppression temporaire en 1802 –, il garantit son indépendance économique et territoriale ainsi qu'une continuité de création culturelle et spirituelle. Celle-ci s'incarne dans une collection de manuscrits médiévaux inestimables – aujourd'hui dispersés dans le monde entier. Certains d'entre eux, comme le *Missel d'Isingrim* datant du XIIe siècle, ont été rédigés et enluminés à Ottobeuren même. Enfin, la création en l'an 1543 de l'Académie d'Ottobeuren de langues orientales laisse présumer que la bibliothèque contenait autrefois des fonds importants d'écrits orientaux. Le monastère eut même sa propre imprimerie dès le XVIe siècle, ce qui confirme la place culturelle qu'il occupait au temps des humanistes. L'abbaye d'Ottobeuren envoya plusieurs de ses professeurs qualifiés à l'université bénédictine de Salzbourg. Transmettre que la finalité première de toutes

les activités scientifiques est la connaissance de Dieu et son apologie trouve son illustration dans la fresque monumentale d'Elias Zobel (1677–1718) qui couronne la bibliothèque. Elle date de la rénovation complète de l'édifice impérial, menée dans le goût baroque et entreprise en 1711 par Rupert II Ness (1670–1740). En 1718, l'abbé Rupert fit édifier une bibliothèque, parfaitement préservée, définie par une inscription « palais pour les muses, bastion pour la religion, mémorial pour moi-même ». Une statue de Pallas Athéna se tient en son centre, elle est entourée de 15 000 ouvrages reliés en porc blanc, tous soigneusement rangés dans les corps de bibliothèque blancs qui longent les murs d'une salle divisée en deux niveaux par une galerie soutenue par des colonnes. Les cartouches somptueusement moulurés témoignent de l'ancienne répartition des ouvrages, l'ornementation végétale va même jusqu'à se mêler au plafond que le stucateur Johann Baptist Zimmermann (1680–1758) décora en harmonie avec la forme simple et homogène de la pièce.

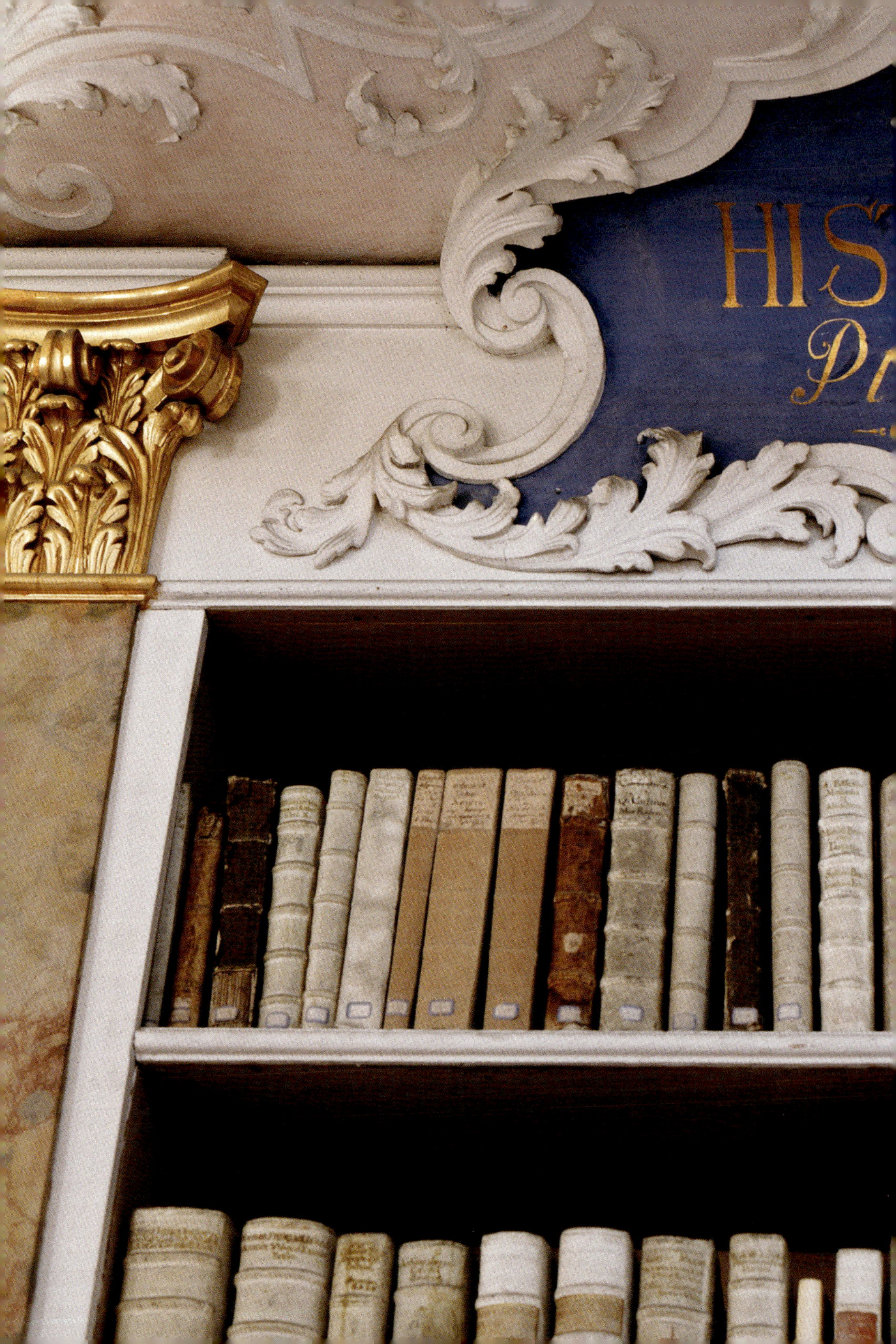

HIS
P

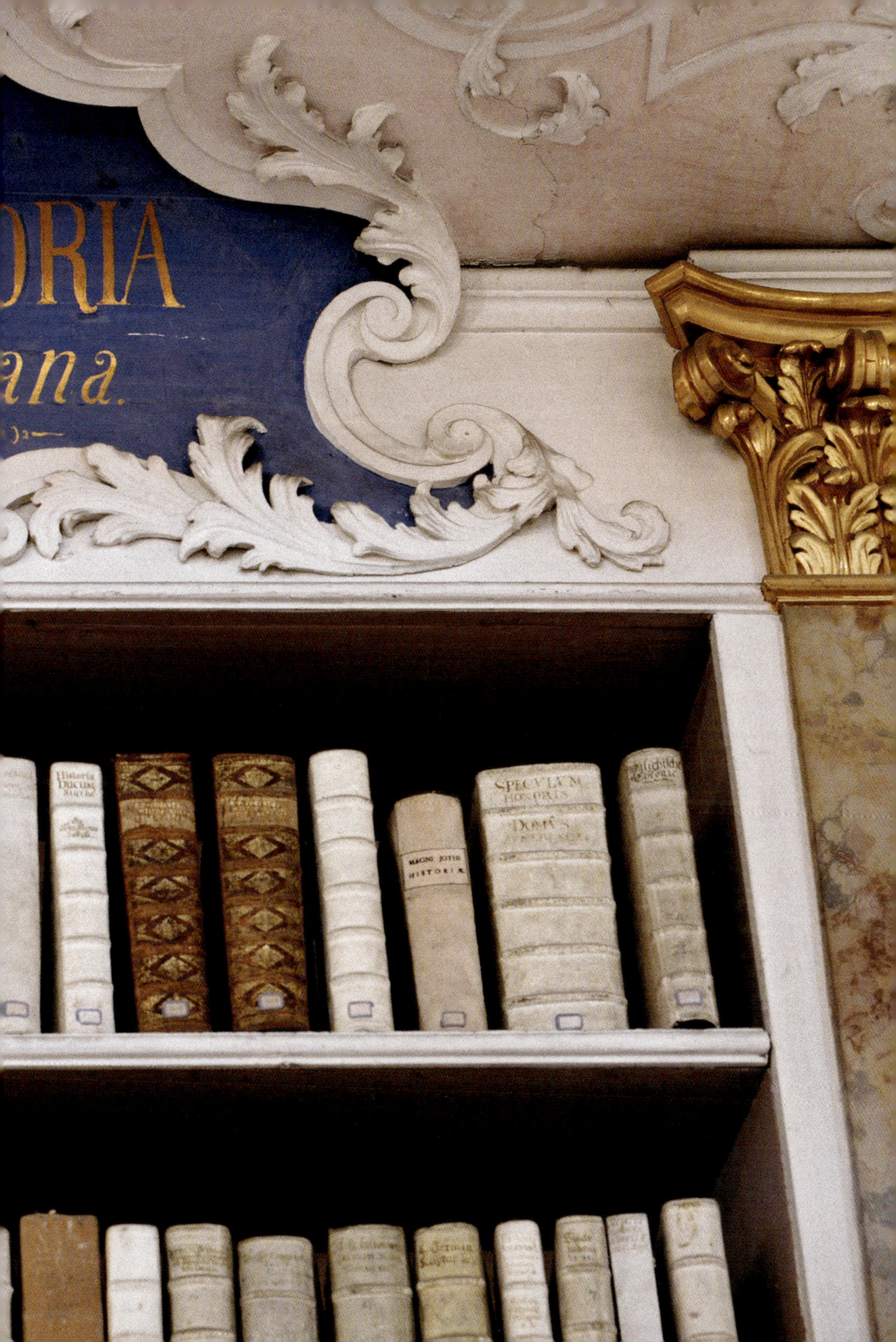

ORIA
ana.
Historia
Ducum
MAGNI JOTIE
HISTORIA
SPECVLVM
DOMŜ

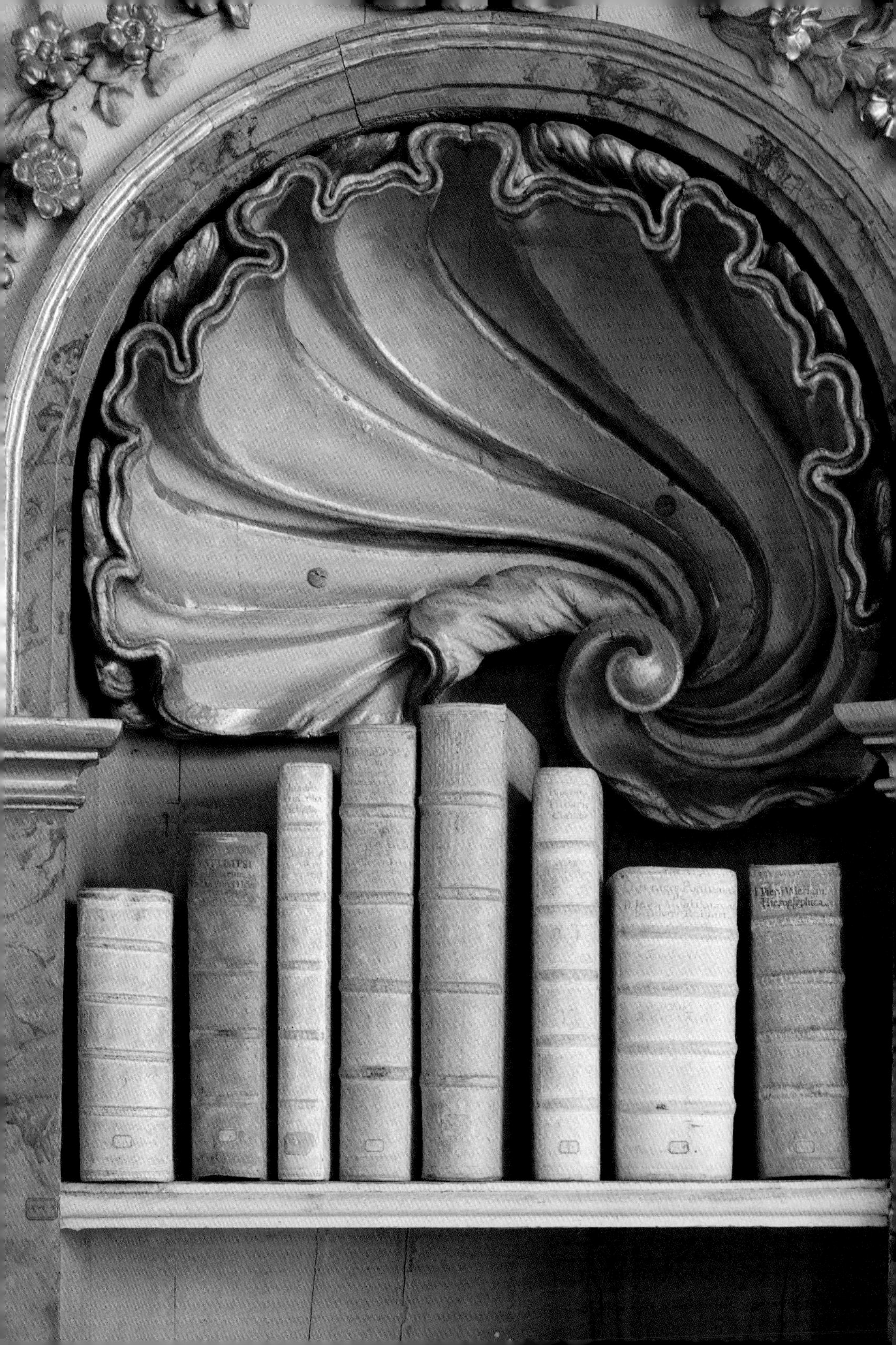

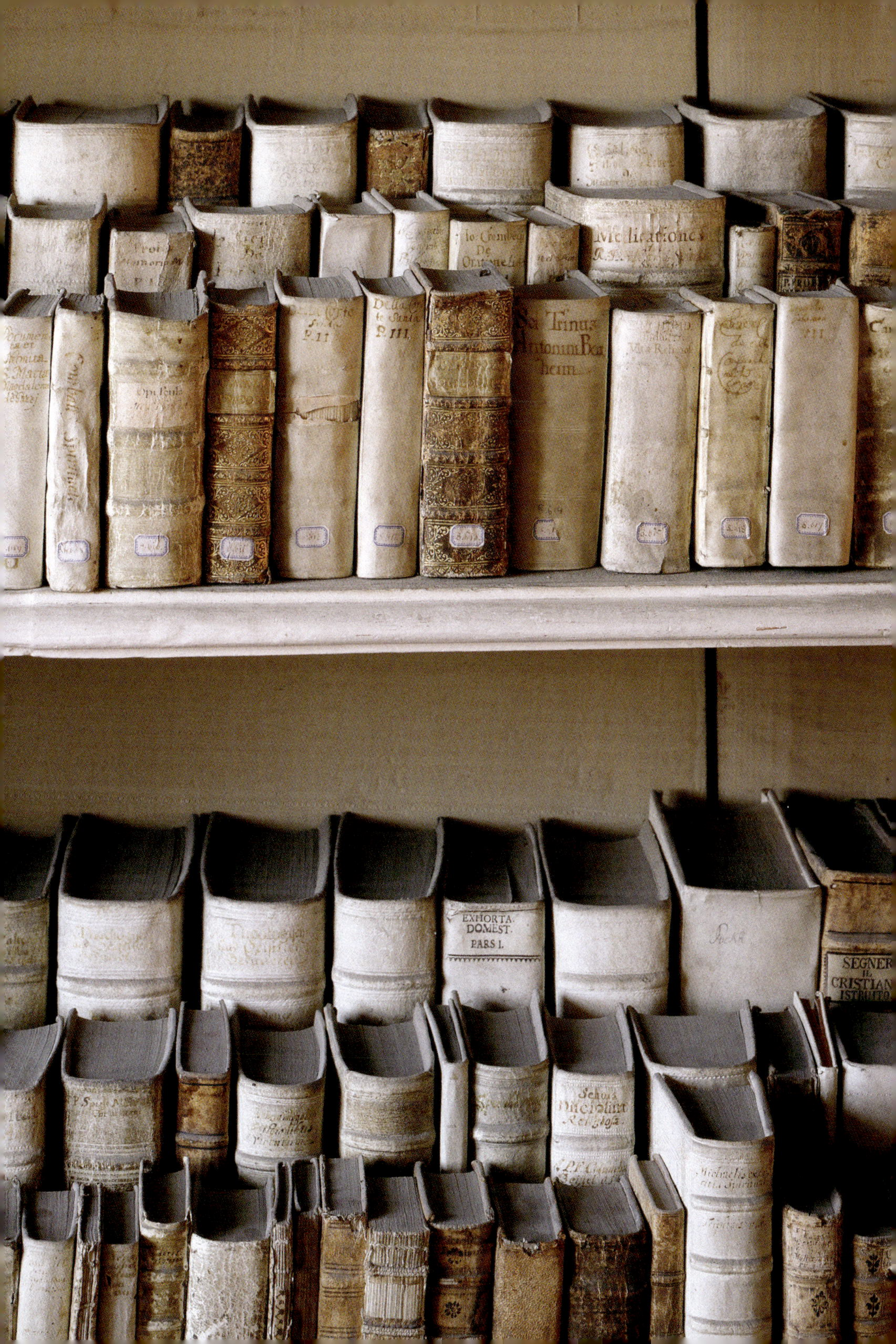

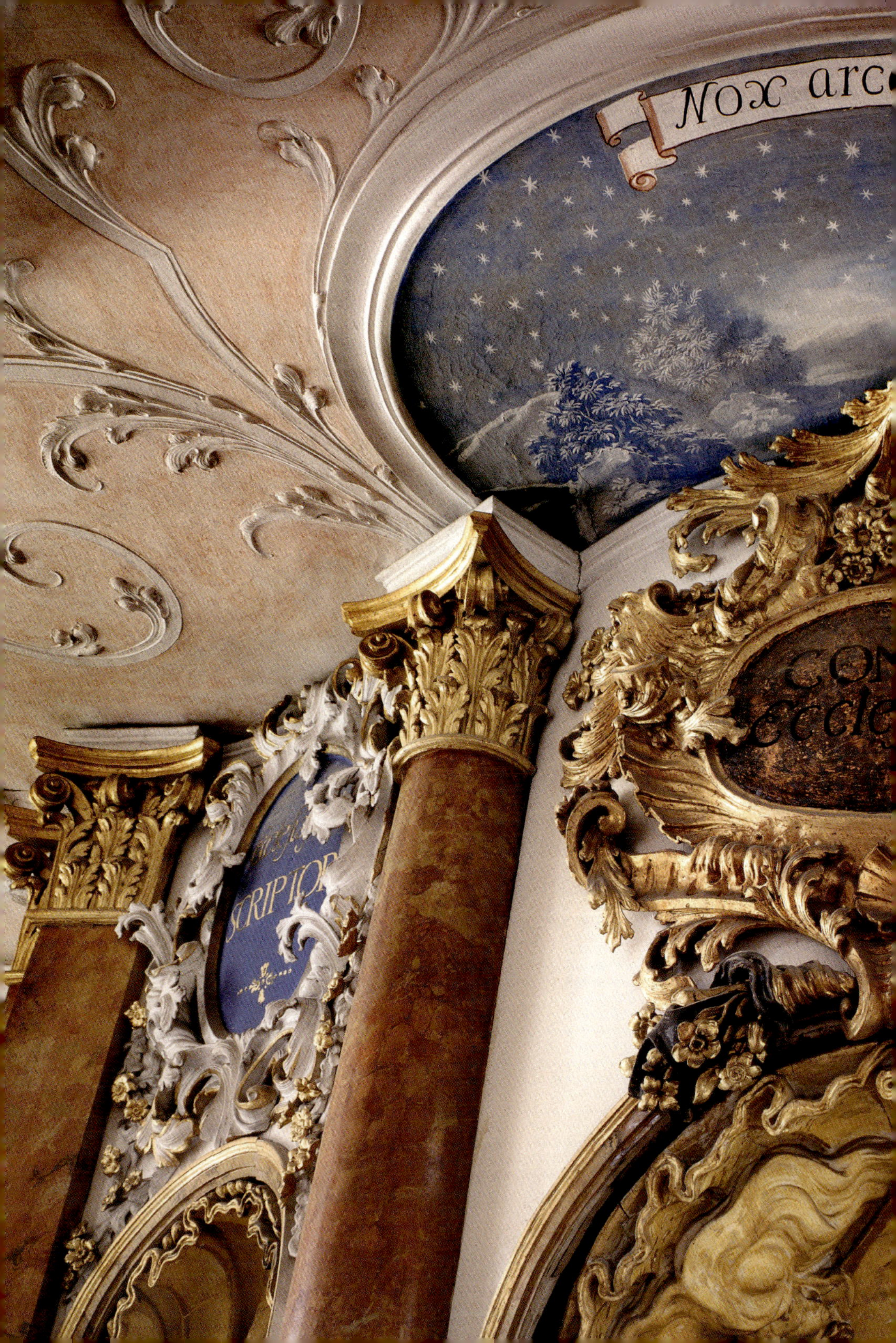

Nox arc
SCRIPTOR
CON
ecclef

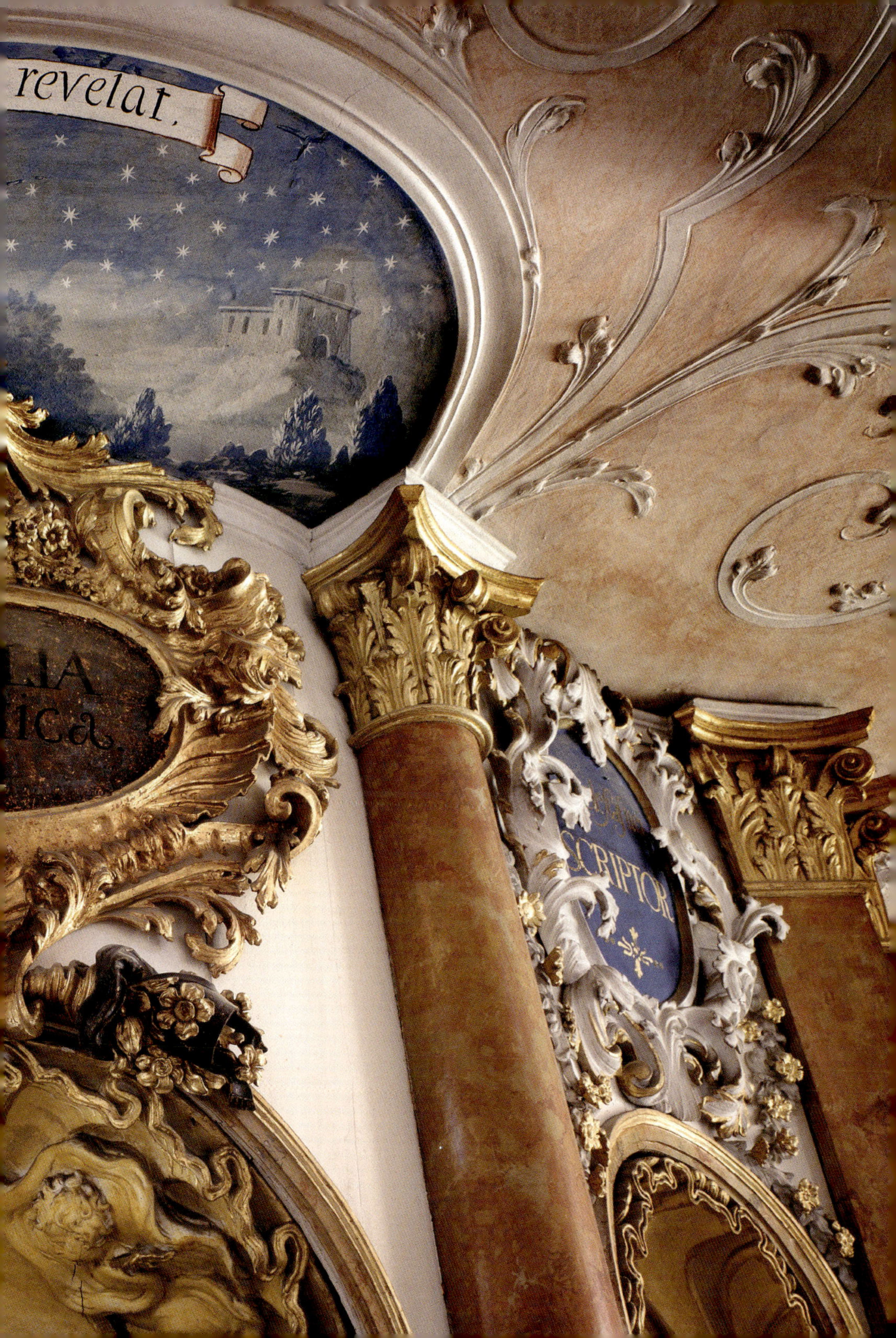

revelat.
LIA
ica
SCRIPTOR

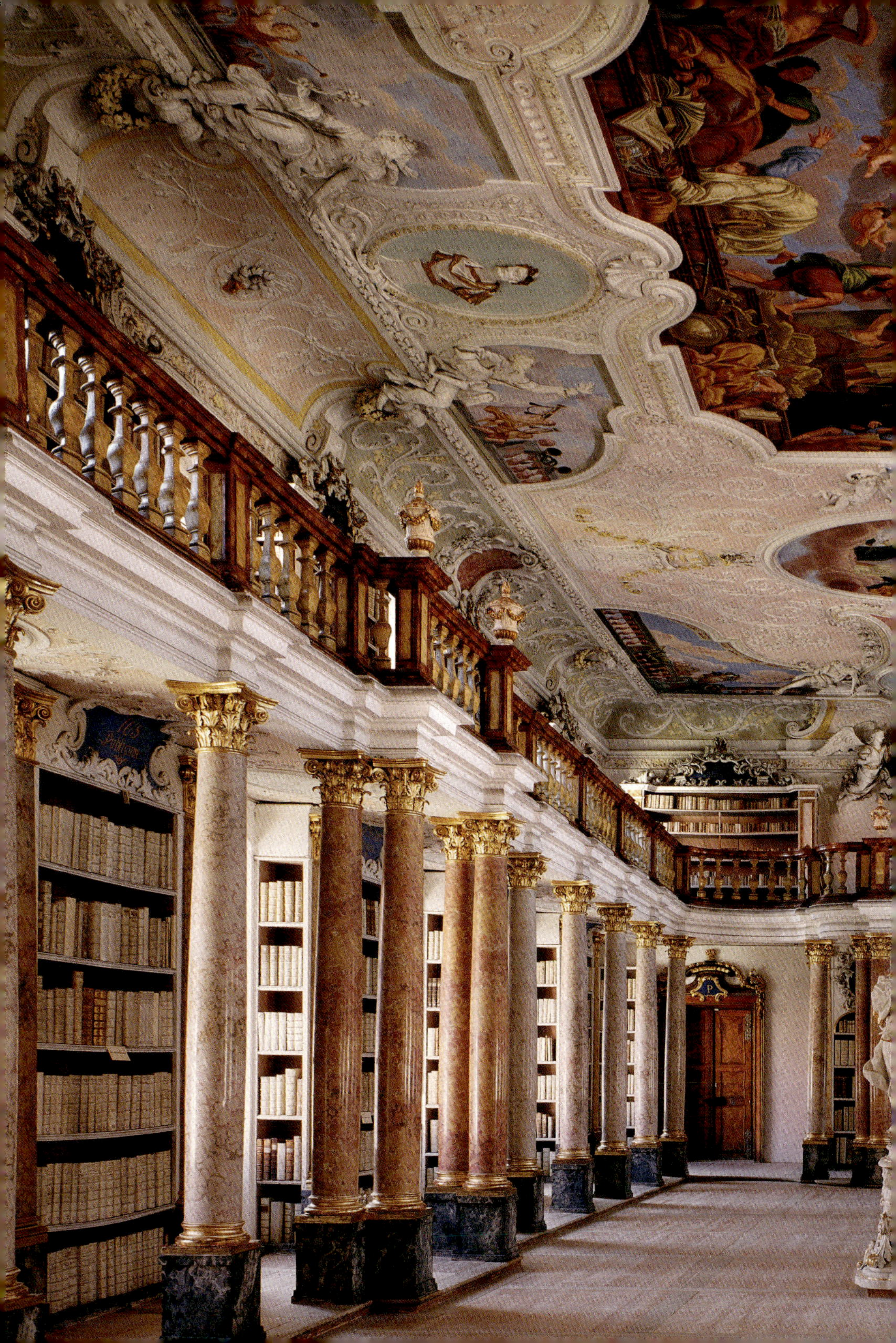

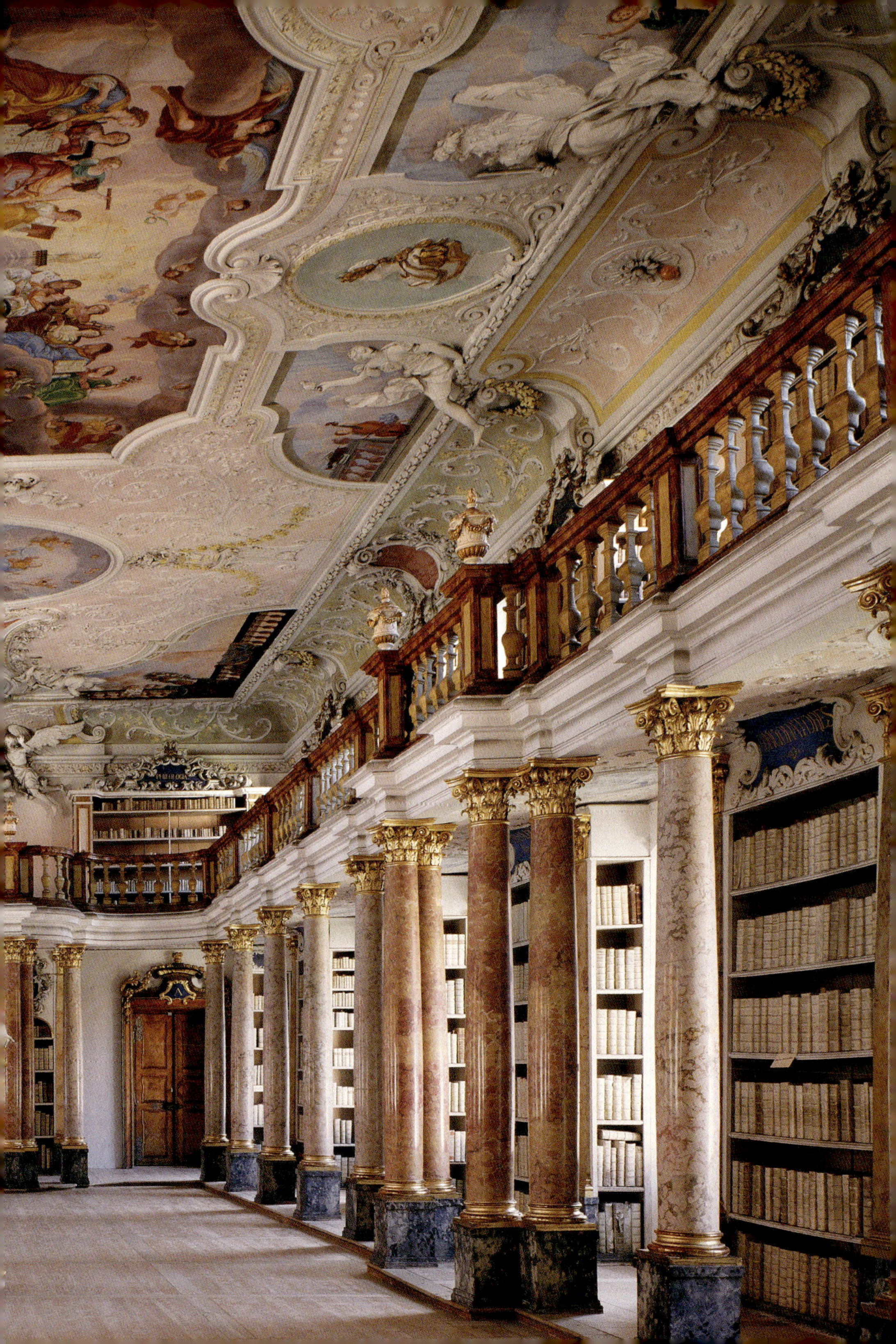

Klosterbibliothek Metten

It is rare to find monastery libraries with an unbroken tradition in Germany. The Reformation, peasant revolts, the Thirty Years' War and secularisation frequently resulted in collections being lost and buildings being assigned new functions. Such was the fate of the library at St Michael's Abbey in Metten, whose historical holdings were dispersed when the monastery was suppressed in 1803. Under King Ludwig I of Bavaria (1786–1868), however, the Benedictine abbey was reopened and a new library established, allowing Metten to resume a tradition that had begun with the founding of the original monastery by Gamelbert around 766. Metten was at that time part of a network of monasteries funded by the Agilolfing rulers, for the purpose of hastening the colonisation of their territories between the Bavarian Forest and the Danube plain. In 792 Charlemagne (747–814) promoted the monastery to a royal abbey and awarded it extensive landholdings and privileges. The commanding position of the imposing architectural complex is a reminder even today of the influence Metten exercised over the local town and its surroundings. The political importance claimed by the abbey is also reflected in the comprehensive renovations that were undertaken after the upheavals of the Thirty Years' War. Under Abbot Roman Märkl (1659–1744), the church was renovated and the monastery transformed into a prelate's palace. Taking pride of place among its official reception rooms is the library, whose interior decoration is based on a sophisticated theological scheme. The main hall of the three-room library suite was converted from an existing gallery, whose central pillars were transformed into mighty pairs of atlantes by Franz Josef Holzinger (1691–1775). In the rooms at either end, the function of architectural support is assumed by angels. The allegorical pairing of knowledge and faith at the library entrance makes it clear to the visitor that true understanding can be gained through divine revelation and inspiration alone. Contrary to the constraints already broken elsewhere by the ideas of the early Enlightenment, the cultivation of the arts and sciences in this "Temple of Wisdom" is open only to those who place their trust in divine inspiration. In the ceiling frescos by Innozenz Anton Warathy (1694–1758) these principles are set out in programmatic fashion, for example, in the scene featuring Thomas Aquinas. It can be assumed that the themes illustrated on the ceiling were reflected in the subjects of the books on the shelves below. The Metten monks taught the doctrines at the heart of the library's decoration both at the school attached to the abbey, and also at the universities in Freising and Salzburg. Metten Abbey also maintained contacts with the Bavarian Academy of Sciences in Munich.

❋⁎❋

Founded 766; library rooms 1722–1726
Holdings c. 200,000 volumes
(current stock from 1830 onwards)
Type of library monastic library, library of the St Michaels Gymnasium grammar school
Highlights *Mettener Antiphonar*, c. 1437; Hartmann Schedel, *Liber Chronicarum (Nuremberg Chronicle)*, Nuremberg, 1493

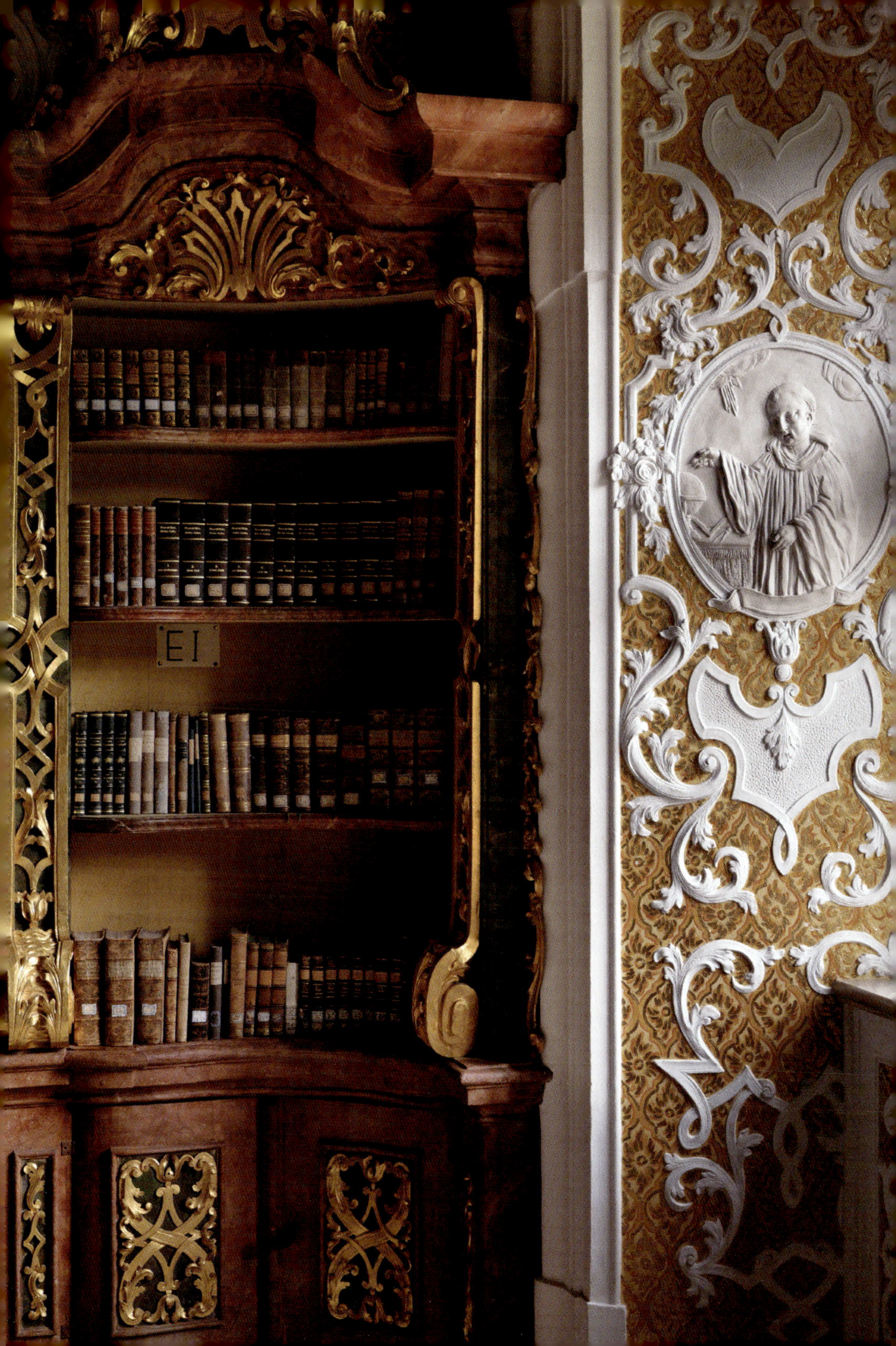

EI

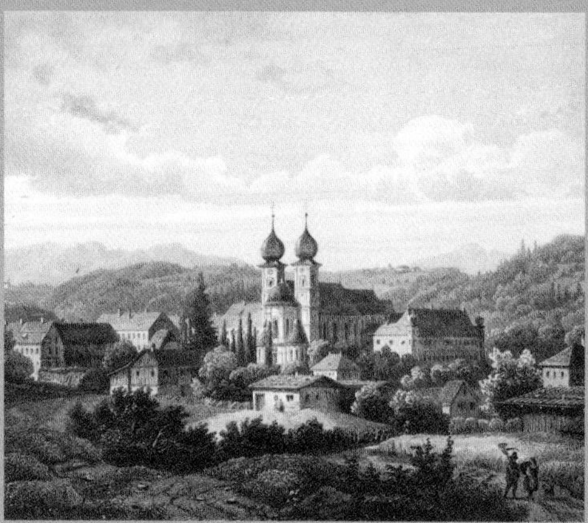

Benedictine Abbey Metten, *view from the west*, c. 1880, in: Hermann von Schmid (ed.), *Das Königreich Bayern. Seine Denkwürdigkeiten und Schönheiten*, Munich, 1879–1881

In Deutschland gibt es nur wenige Klosterbibliotheken mit ungebrochener Tradition. Reformation, Bauernkriege, Dreißigjähriger Krieg und Säkularisation haben häufig zum Verlust der Bestände oder zur Umwidmung der Gebäude geführt. Das Kloster St. Michael in Metten verlor seine alten Buchbestände im Zuge der Verstaatlichung 1803, wurde aber als Benediktinerabtei (mit einer ebenfalls neu begründeten Bibliothek) bald nach der Säkularisierung durch den bayerischen König Ludwig I. (1786–1868) wiedereröffnet. Damit konnte ideell an eine Tradition angeschlossen werden, die mit der Gründung des Benediktinerklosters durch Gamelbert um 766 begonnen hatte. Es war Teil eines Netzes von Klosterniederlassungen, die von den Agilolfingern gefördert wurden, da sie zur Kolonisation ihrer Herrschaftsgebiete zwischen Bayerischem Wald und Donauebene beitrugen. Karl der Große (747–814) erhob das Kloster zur Abtei und belehnte diese mit ausgedehntem Landbesitz und königlichen Privilegien. Die beherrschende Lage des imposanten Baukom

plexes erinnert noch heute an die Herrschaft, die das seit 792 königliche Kloster über den Ort Metten und seine Umgebung ausgeübt hat. Der Herrschaftsanspruch des Klosters prägte auch dessen umfassende Renovierung nach den Wirren des Dreißigjährigen Krieges, im Zuge derer Abt Roman Märkl (1659–1744) die Kirche erneuern und das Kloster zu einer prunkvollen Prälatenresidenz ausbauen ließ. Unter den Repräsentationsräumen kommt seither der Bibliothek, deren Gestaltung ein raffiniertes theologisches Programm zugrunde liegt, erstrangiger Stellenwert zu. Auf den Umbau eines älteren zweischiffigen Saalraumes weisen die mächtigen Atlantenpaare, die Franz Josef Holzinger (1691–1775) anstelle der älteren Pfeiler im Hauptsaal der dreiteiligen Raumfolge geschaffen hat. In den Nebenräumen übernehmen Engel die Funktion von Raumstützen. Bereits am Eingang wird dem Besucher mittels allegorischer Koppelung von Wissenschaft und Glauben verdeutlicht, dass die Gewinnung wahrer Erkenntnis nur durch die göttliche Offenbarung und Inspiration zu erlangen sei. Die Pflege der Wissenschaften steht in diesem „Tempel der Weisheit" – entgegen den von der Frühaufklärung damals bereits aufgebrochenen Beschränkungen – nur jenen offen, die sich der göttlichen Inspiration anzuvertrauen wissen. In den Deckenfresken von Innozenz Anton Warathy (1694–1758) werden diese Prinzipien auf programmatische Weise vor Augen geführt, etwa in der Szene mit Thomas von Aquin. Die Deckenbilder standen gewiss ehemals mit der Anordnung der Bücher in einem inhaltlichen Zusammenhang. Die im Ausstattungsprogramm der Bibliothek dargelegten Grundsätze wurden von den Mönchen aus Metten nicht nur an der traditionsreichen klostereigenen Schule, sondern auch an den Hochschulen in Freising und Salzburg unterrichtet. Kontakte bestanden ebenfalls mit der Bayerischen Akademie der Wissenschaften in München.

En Allemagne, il est rare de trouver une bibliothèque monastique restée intacte et entretenue
depuis ses origines. La Réforme, les guerres des
Paysans, la guerre de Trente Ans et la sécularisation ont souvent causé la perte des fonds ou
la récupération des lieux à d'autres usages. La
nationalisation de 1803 notamment entraîna la
perte de l'ancien fonds de livres du monastère
Sankt Michael de Metten, qui rouvrit grâce à
la volonté de Louis Iᵉʳ de Bavière (1786–1868)
sous la forme d'une abbaye bénédictine (alors
dotée d'une nouvelle bibliothèque). Ainsi, sa
perpétuation pouvait être mise en rapport
avec la tradition qui commença à la fondation,
vers 766 par Gamelbert, du monastère bénédictin. Ce dernier faisait partie d'un réseau de
monastères patronné par les Agilolfides, qui
contribuèrent à la colonisation de leurs terres
entre la forêt de Bavière et la plaine du Danube.
Charlemagne (747–814) promut le monastère
au rang d'abbaye et lui inféoda un vaste
territoire ainsi que des privilèges royaux. La
situation de l'imposant ensemble architectural
rappelle aujourd'hui encore cette suprématie
exercée sur Metten et ses environs par le
monastère devenu royal en 792. La prétention
à la domination du monastère se ressent aussi
dans la rénovation complète entreprise suite
aux troubles de la guerre de Trente Ans, au
moment où Roman Märkl (1659–1744) rénova
l'église et aménagea le monastère en luxueuse
résidence de prélat. Dès lors, la bibliothèque
dont la conception répondait à un programme
théologique mûrement réfléchi rejoignit les
pièces d'apparat de tout premier ordre. Les
puissants couples d'atlantes sculptés par Franz
Josef Holzinger (1691–1775) à l'emplacement
des piliers de la salle principale sur les trois
pièces communicantes rappellent la structure
à deux vaisseaux de la précédente salle. Dans
les pièces adjacentes, des anges endossent la
fonction de soutien. Dès qu'il franchit le seuil,
où les allégories de la connaissance et de la foi
sont associées, le visiteur comprend que le

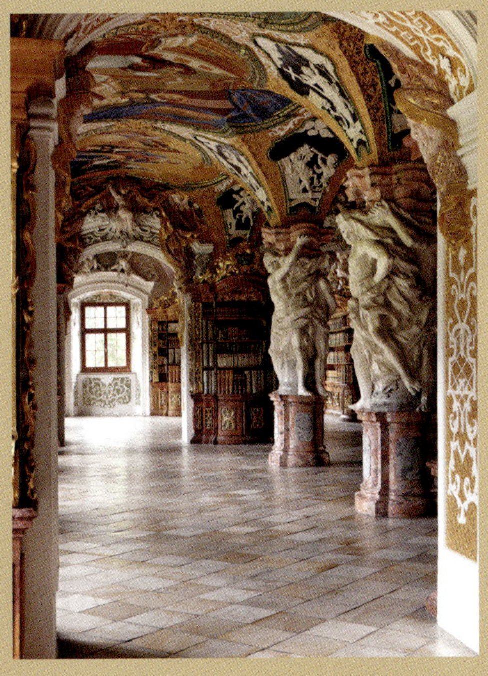

savoir véritable ne s'acquiert que par le biais
de l'inspiration et de la révélation divine. En
effet, à l'opposé des limitations émises par les
Lumières dont le mouvement s'ébauchait alors,
ce « temple de la sagesse » affirme que la seule
manière d'entretenir le savoir et les sciences
est de s'en remettre à l'inspiration divine. Ces
principes sont savamment décrits dans les
plafonds peints par Innozenz Anton Warathy
(1694–1758), notamment dans la scène figurant
Thomas d'Aquin. Tout porte à croire que l'ordre
des représentations picturales correspondait
autrefois à l'agencement des livres selon leur
contenu. Les moines de Metten enseignaient
les principes figurés dans le programme de
décoration de la bibliothèque non seulement au
sein de l'école monacale de tradition séculaire,
mais encore dans les universités de Freising et
de Salzbourg. Ils étaient également en contact
avec l'Académie bavaroise des sciences située
à Munich.

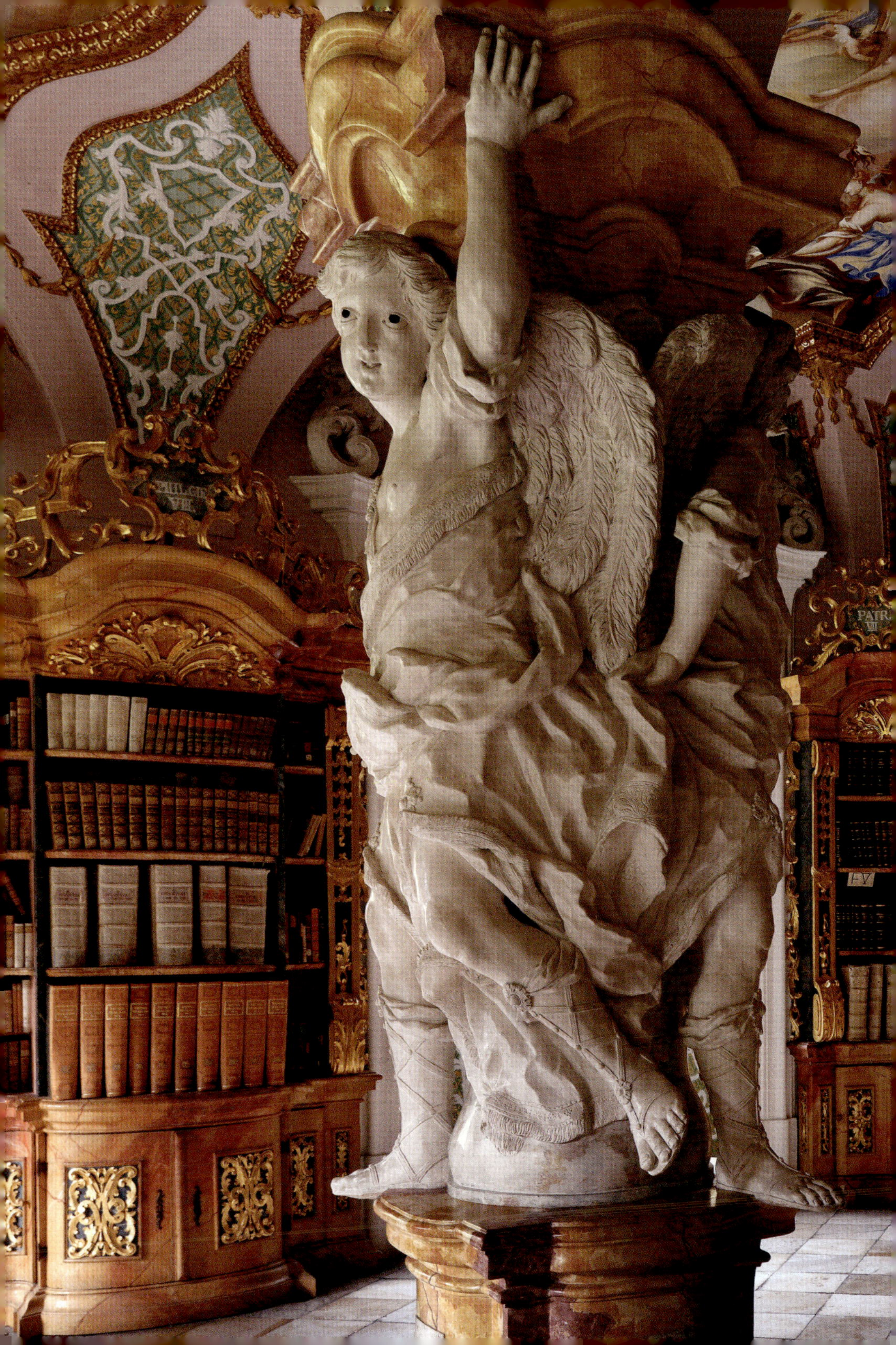

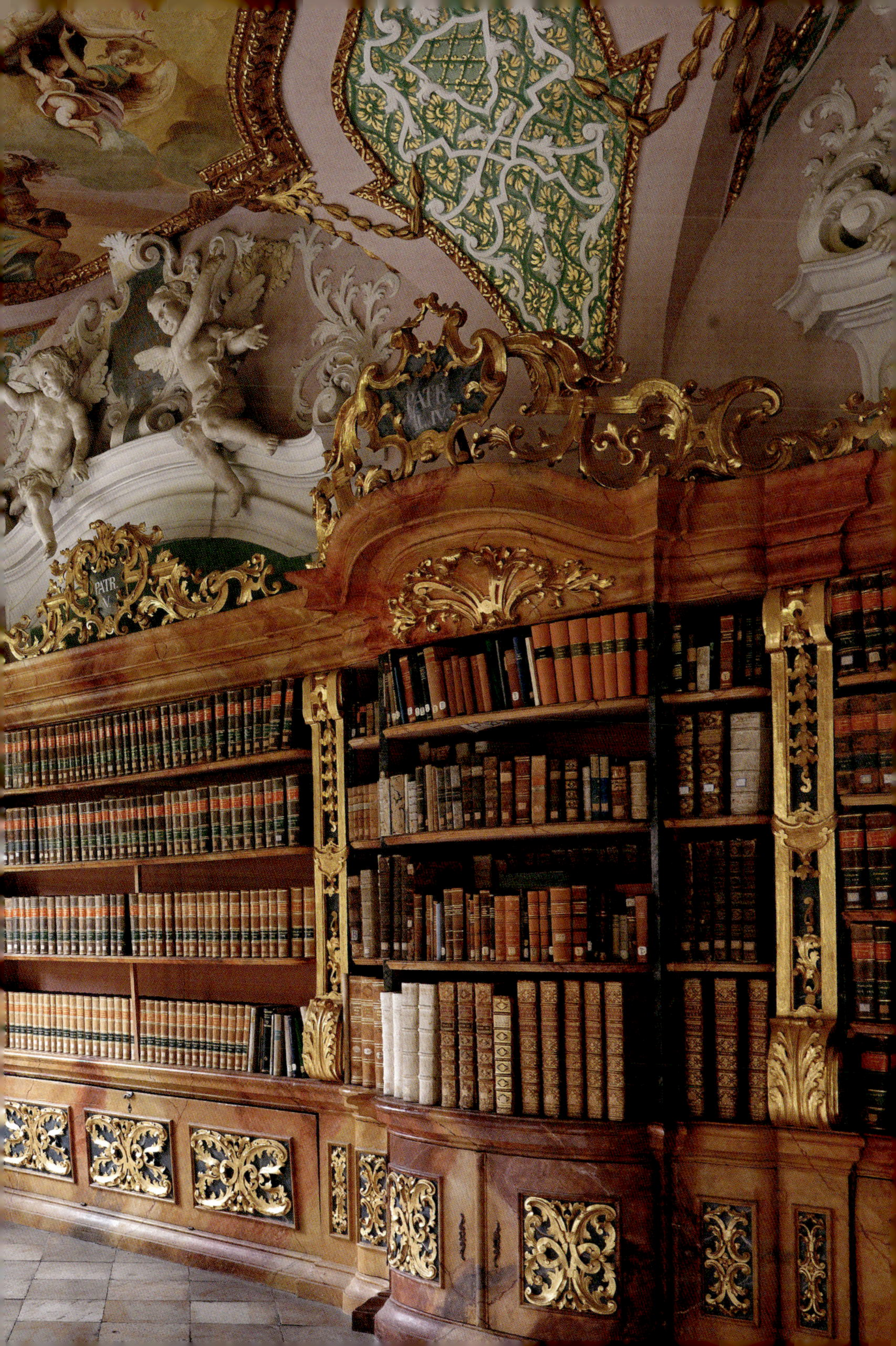

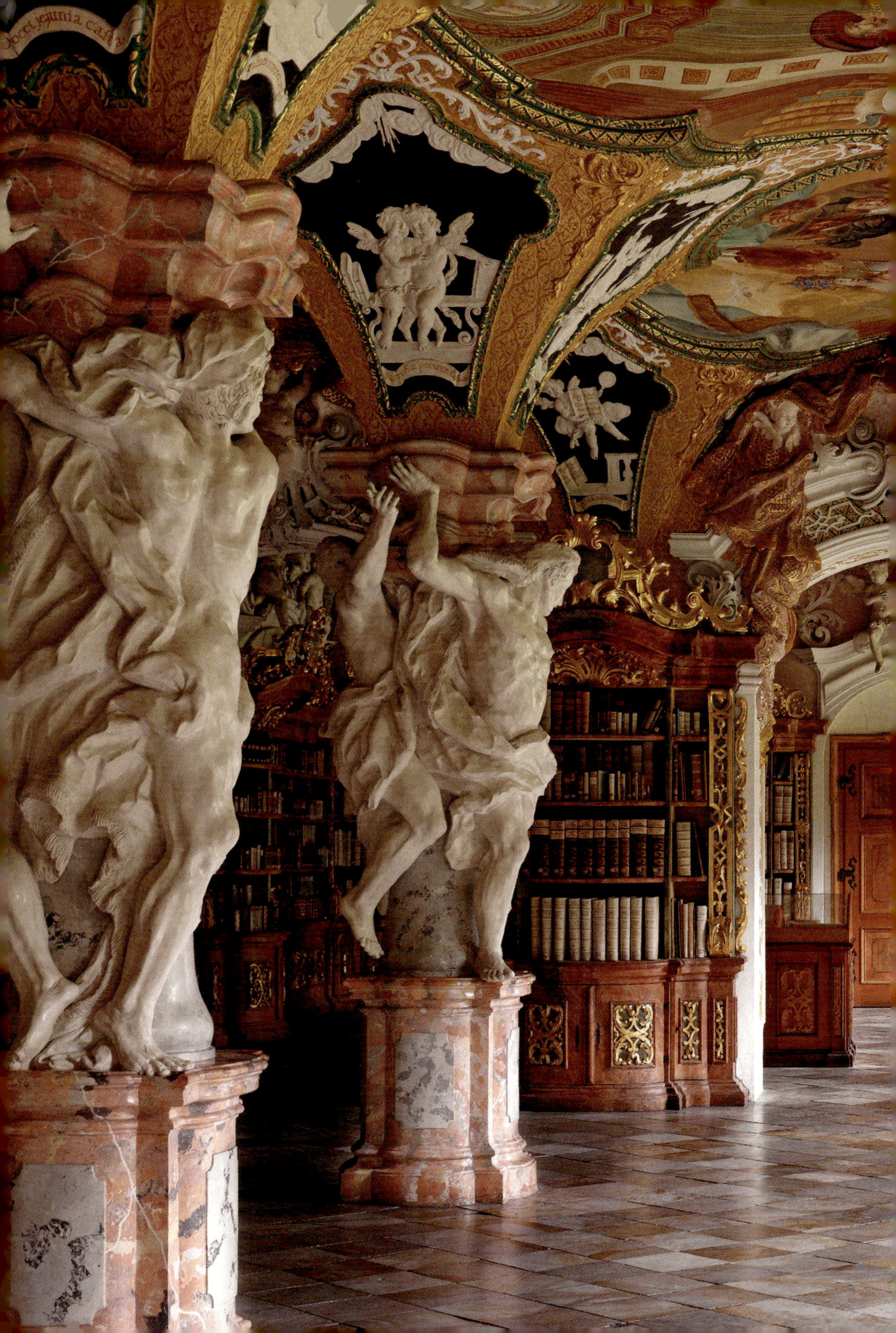

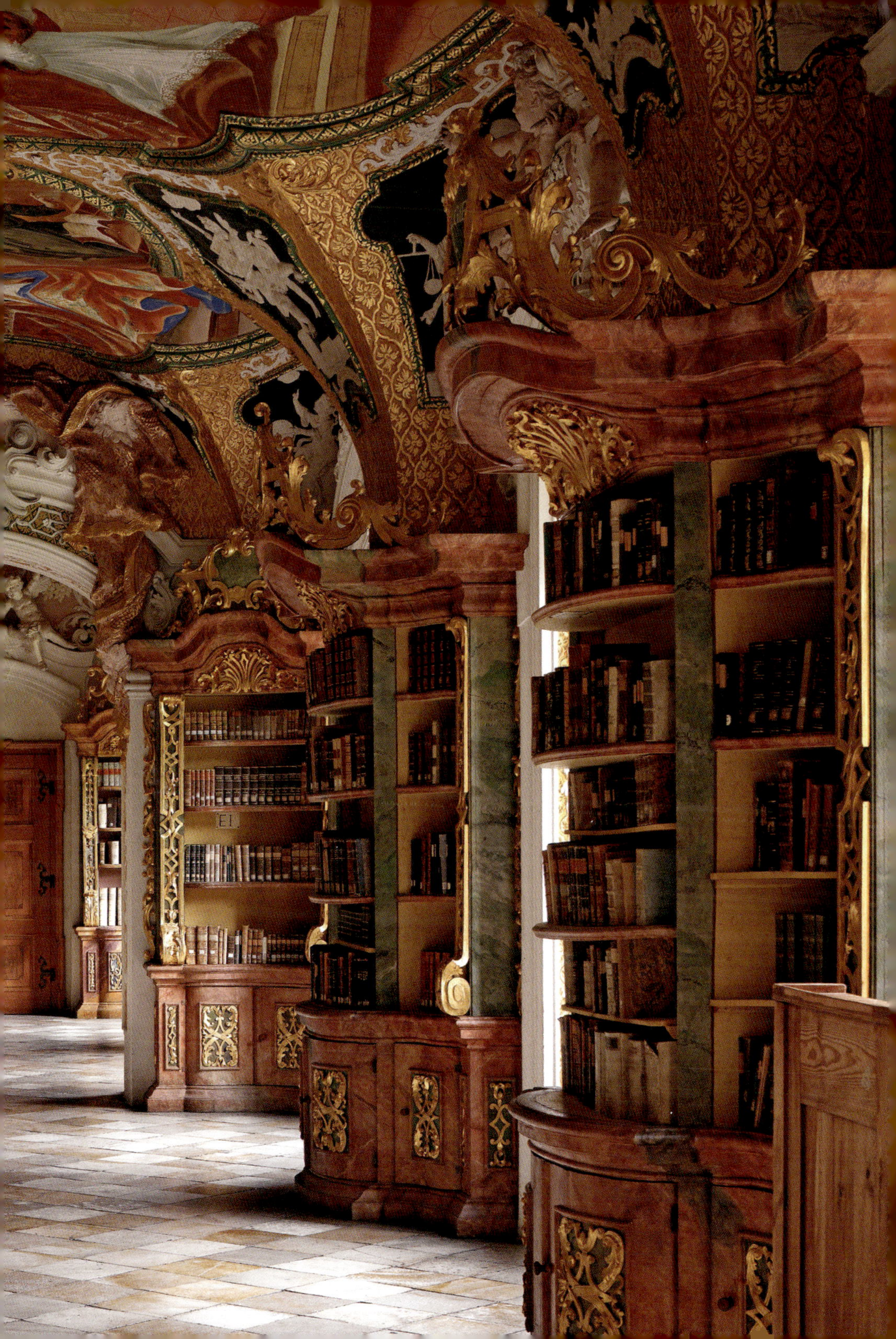

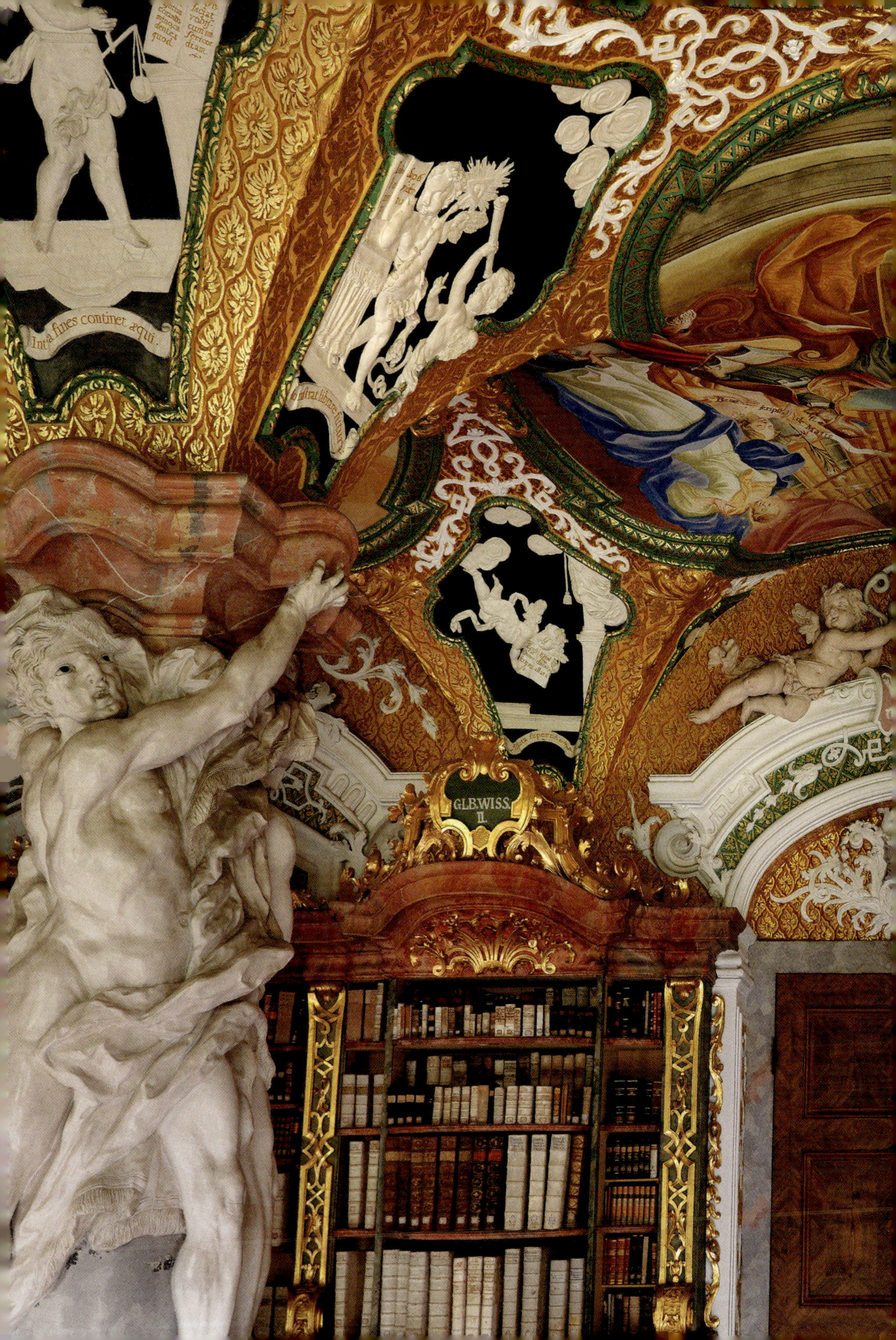

Intra fines continet æqui.
GL.B.WISS.
II.

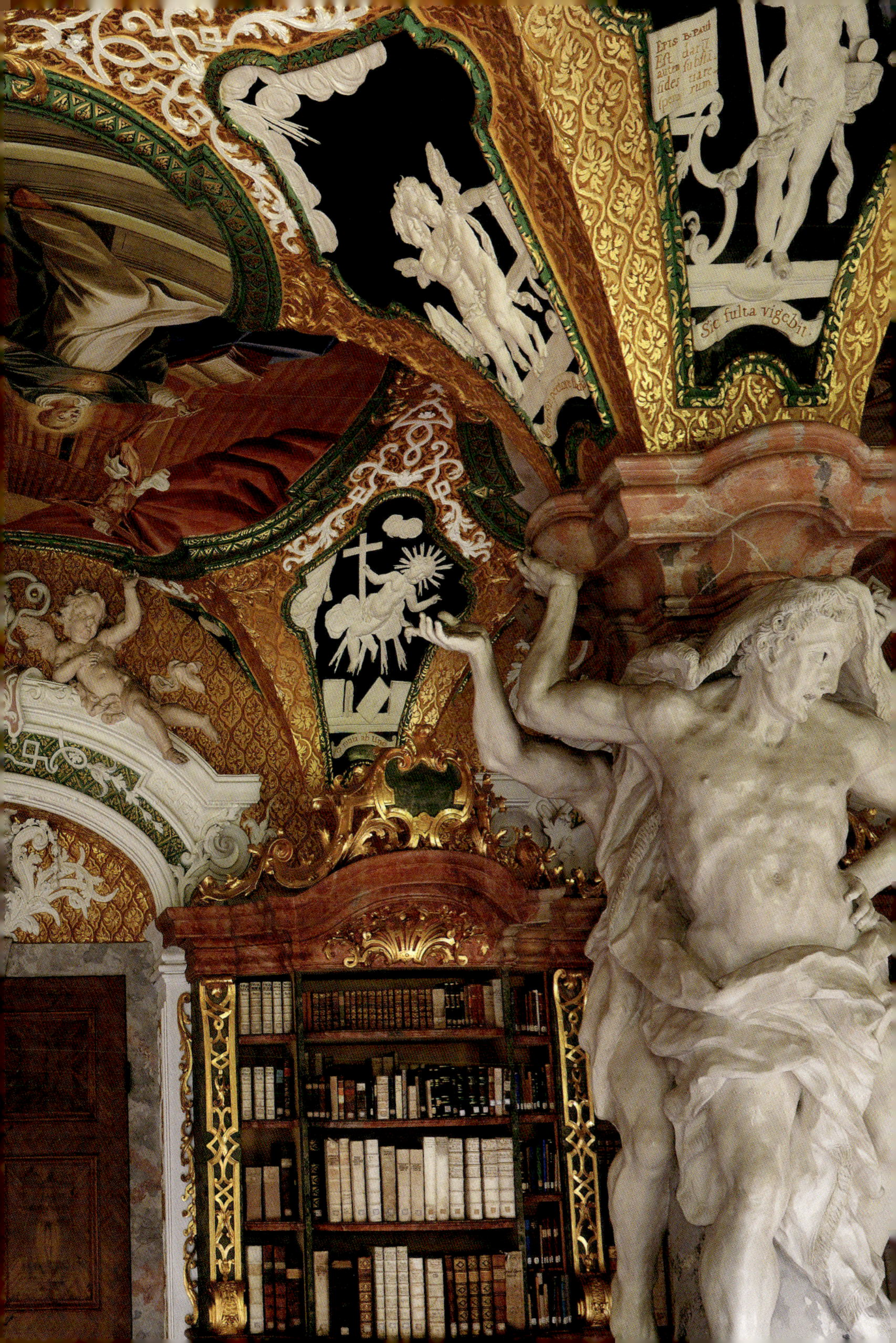
EPIS B:PAUL
Est autem
fides
Sic fulta vigebit.

Klosterbibliothek Wiblingen

Founded and funded with generous endowments by the counts of Kirchberg, and run with energy and efficiency by Benedictine monks from Sankt Blasien in the Black Forest, Wiblingen Abbey acquired a considerable reputation over the course of its more than 700-year history. Wiblingen, situated in the Upper Swabian region of Further Austria and influenced by the Melk Reform, became a particular centre of scholarship, maintaining a school and an important library, a large part of the manuscript holdings of which were produced in the convent's own scriptorium. The monastery continued to enjoy prosperity and high regard as a spiritual centre in the 16th century, after it passed as an imperial fief to the Fugger family, under whom it was substantially renovated. Wiblingen Abbey reached its greatest height in the 18th century, however, after being granted the privileged status of imperial immediacy by the Habsburgs. Between 1714 and 1783 the complex of buildings that had sprung up on top of the monastery's Romanesque foundations was replaced by a unified Baroque ensemble. The model for the new abbey, which was laid out on a huge rectangular ground plan enclosing several courtyards and with the church in the centre, can be found in the monastery and royal palace of El Escorial (1563–1584). This latter served as the benchmark for many monasteries remodelled at this time in Habsburg territories, such as Klosterneuburg Abbey near Vienna, with its wholly comparable structure. When Christian Wiedemann (1680–1739) was commissioned by Abbot Meinrad Hamberger (1700–1762) to transform the traditional monastic library into a magnificent architectural showcase, he created one of the most important testaments to the Rococo in southwest Germany. From it we can gauge the proximity in the Baroque era between spiritual leadership and the trappings of a princely lifestyle, as claimed by Baroque prelates who were at the same time territorial rulers. The library was completed between 1737 and 1744 as a lavish hall richly decorated with Rococo ornament, in which the visitor has to look twice to spot the bookshelves recessed into the walls. The interior is dominated by the imitation marble colonnade in colourful red and blue, which supports a gallery whose decorative balustrade leads the eye upwards to the illusionistic ceiling painting. Here Franz Martin Kuen (1719–1771) has brought together earthly and divine wisdom in a magnificent

Founded 1093; suppressed 1806; library built 1737–1744 by Christian Wiedemann
Holdings c. 950,000 volumes (as Ulm University Library); 15,000 volumes (stock in 1757)
Type of library monastic library; today a public reference library belonging to Ulm University
Highlights Nicolaus Kessler, *Opera Antonii Mancinelli Veliter in cum quibusdam in locis comentaria explanatio(n)e Ascensii*, Basel, 1508; Peter Quentel, *Dionysii Carthusiani Eruditissima simul et utilissima super omnes S. Dionysii Areopagitae libros commenataria, studiosis omnibus hactenus multum desiderata, sed nunc primum utilitati publicae donata*, Cologne, 1536; Lucantonio Giunta (Tommaso Giunti), *Paulo lll Pont. Max., Pontificale Romanum*, Venice, 1543

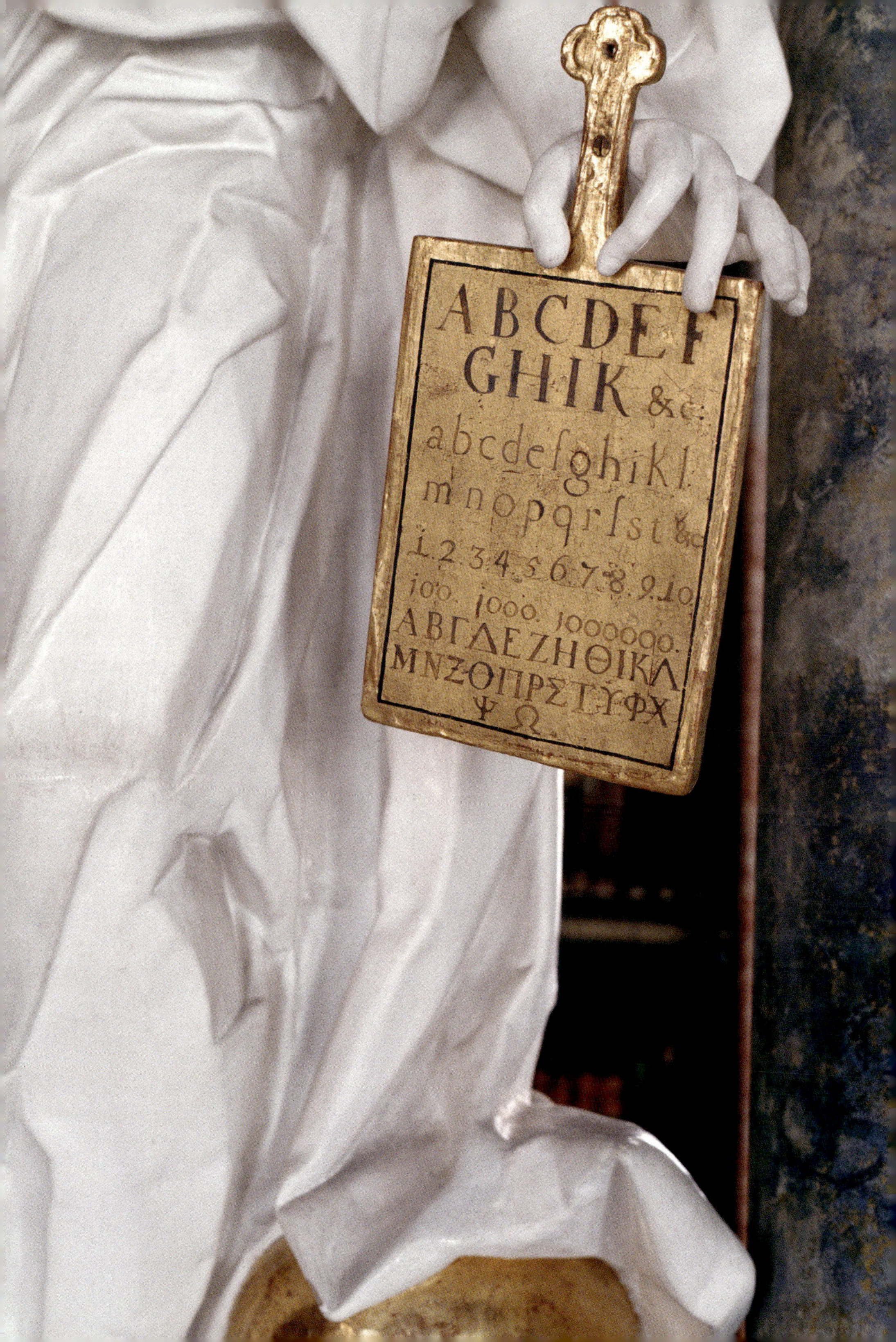

ABCDEF
GHIK &c
abcdefghikl
mnopqrlst &c
1.2 3 4 5 6 7 8.9.10.
100. 1000. 1000000.
ΑΒΓΔΕΖΗΘΙΚΛ
ΜΝΞΟΠΡΣΤΥΦΧ
ΨΩ

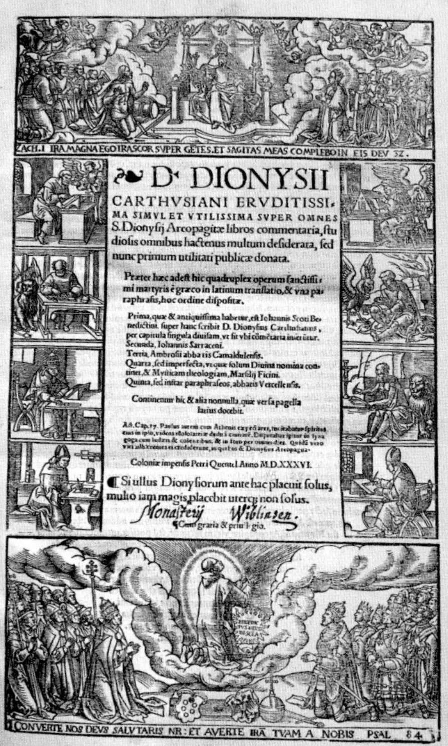

Peter Quentel, *Dionysii Carthusiani Eruditissima simul et utilissima super omnes S. Dionysii Areopagitae libros commenataria*, Cologne, 1536: *Frontispiece*

view of the heavens. In the room below, the daylight arriving from all sides dissolves the spatial limits of this "Treasury of Wisdom and Knowledge" ("Schatzhaus der Weisheit und des Wissens"), as the library is described in the cartouche above its entrance. Allegorical figures in lively poses animate the interior and, with their porcelain-like surfaces and richly gilded attributes, make the colourful room gleam. In 1757 the library held some 15,000 books. In the wake of secularisation in 1806, its holdings were incorporated into other institutions, and the abbey itself became a royal residence belonging to the kingdom of Württemberg.

* * *

Während seines über 700-jährigen Bestehens hatte sich das als Stiftung der Grafen von Kirchberg großzügig dotierte und von Mönchen aus Sankt Blasien im Schwarzwald dynamisch geführte Benediktinerkloster Wiblingen einen weit ausstrahlenden Ruf erworben. Als von Melk beeinflusstes Reformkloster der österreichischen Vorlande wurde es mit seiner Schule und der bedeutenden Bibliothek, die dem hauseigenen Skriptorium einen Großteil ihres Handschriftenbestandes verdankt, zu einer Stätte besonderer Gelehrsamkeit. Wohlstand und hohes geistliches Ansehen prägten das Kloster auch im 16. Jahrhundert, nachdem es als kaiserliches Lehen an die Familie der Fugger gefallen und von diesen weitgehend erneuert worden war. Seine Blüte erlebte es aber als reichsunmittelbares Stift des Kaiserreiches der Habsburger im 18. Jahrhundert, als man den über romanischen Grundfesten gewachsenen Gebäudekomplex zwischen 1714 und 1783 zu einer einheitlichen barocken Anlage erneuerte. Das Vorbild der einem gewaltigen Rechteck eingeschriebenen, mehrhöfigen Anlage mit der Kirche im Zentrum war die Klosterresidenz des Escorial (1563–1584). Sie stand vielen Klostererneuerungen in habsburgischen Territorien Pate, in den gleichen Jahren etwa auch der strukturell durchaus vergleichbaren Abtei Klosterneuburg bei Wien. Als Christian Wiedemann (1680–1739) von Abt Meinrad Hamberger (1700–1762) den Auftrag erhielt, die traditionsreiche Klosterbibliothek in einen prächtigen Schauraum zu verwandeln, schuf er eines der bedeutendsten Zeugnisse des südwestdeutschen Rokoko. An diesem ist zu ermessen, wie nahe sich fürstliche Repräsentation, die die Barockprälaten als Territorialherren für sich beanspruchten, und geistliche Sendung im Barock standen. So entstand in den Jahren 1737 bis 1744 ein mit Rokokoornamenten reich dekorierter Festsaal, in dem man erst auf den zweiten Blick die in die Wand eingelassenen Bücherregale zu erkennen vermag. Im Vordergrund steht die farbenprächtige Kolonnade aus rotem und blauem Kunstmarmor,

auf der ein emporenähnliches Balkongeschoss
ruht, von dessen kunstreichen Balustern der
Blick unmittelbar auf jene der illusionistischen
Deckenmalerei gelenkt wird. Dort hat Franz
Martin Kuen (1719–1771) irdische und göttliche
Weisheit in einem prachtvollen Himmelsaus-
blick zusammengeführt. Im darunterliegenden
Saal löst das reichlich einfallende Licht die
räumlichen Grenzen des „Schatzhauses der
Weisheit und des Wissens" – wie auf der Kartu-
sche über dem Eingang vermerkt ist – auf. Den
Festsaal beleben allegorische Figuren mit ihren
weit ausholenden Gesten und bringen mit ihrer
porzellangleichen Oberfläche und den reich
vergoldeten Attributen den farbenprächtigen
Raum zum Glänzen. Hier wurden im Jahr 1757
an die 15 000 Bücher gezählt. Sie gelangten im
Zuge der Säkularisation 1806 an verschiedene
Institutionen, während das Kloster zur Schloss-
residenz im Königreich Württemberg wurde.

✳✳✳

Richement doté à sa fondation par les comtes de
Kirchberg, puis dirigé avec dynamisme par des
moines de Saint-Blaise en Forêt-Noire, le monastère bénédictin de Wiblingen se forgea, au cours
de ses 700 ans d'existence, une belle renommée.
En tant que monastère réformateur influencé
par Melk et appartenant aux territoires de
l'Autriche antérieure, Wiblingen fut un centre
d'érudition particulièrement important grâce
à son école et à sa vaste bibliothèque, dont la
plupart des manuscrits sortaient de son propre
scriptorium. Le monastère connut la prospérité
et jouit d'une haute estime sur le plan intellectuel, même une fois tombé dans le fief impérial
de la famille Fugger, qui le rénova d'ailleurs
de fond en comble au XVIe siècle. Il prospéra
toutefois davantage au XVIIIe siècle, en tant
que monastère placé sous autorité impériale,
quand on décida de moderniser les bâtisses
aux fondations romanes. La transformation
en un complexe baroque homogène eut lieu
de 1714 à 1783. Le plan carré massif, englobant
plusieurs cours et une église en son centre, est
naturellement repris à l'Escurial (1563–1584),

qui servit à l'époque de modèle de rénovation
à moult monastères habsbourgeois. Le plan
de l'abbaye de Klosterneuburg près de Vienne
fournit un exemple similaire. Lorsque Christian
Wiedemann (1680–1739) exécuta la commande
passée par Meinrad Hamberger (1700–1762),
visant à transformer la bibliothèque monacale
séculaire en écrin luxueux, il donna naissance
à l'un des plus beaux chefs-d'œuvre rococo de
l'Allemagne du Sud-Ouest. Cet édifice montre à
quel point la représentation princière, revendi-
quée par les prélats sous forme de domination
territoriale, et la mission spirituelle étaient liées
au XVIIIe siècle. Ainsi, une salle de cérémonie à
la riche ornementation rococo a été construite
entre 1737 et 1744. Les rayonnages destinés aux
livres ne se repèrent pas à première vue. Au premier plan se trouve une colonnade bigarrée, en
faux marbre rouge et bleu, sur laquelle repose
l'étage supérieur clos par une balustrade dont
le décor dirige le regard vers le trompe-l'œil au
plafond. Franz Martin Kuen (1719–1771) y a peint
la sagesse divine et profane dans une fresque
de toute beauté. Dans la partie inférieure de la
salle, l'abondante lumière dissout les frontières
spatiales du « Schatzhaus der Weisheit und des
Wissens » (temple de la sagesse et du savoir),
comme il est écrit sur le cartouche au-dessus de
l'entrée. La salle dans son ensemble est mise en
mouvement par les gestes amples des figures
allégoriques. Son éclat rappelant celui de la
porcelaine et la dorure des attributs disséminés
dans la pièce la font briller de mille feux. La
pièce comptait près de 15 000 livres en 1757. Ces
derniers passèrent d'institution en institution
lors de la sécularisation de 1806, tandis que le
monastère fut rattaché au palais résidentiel du
royaume du Wurtemberg.

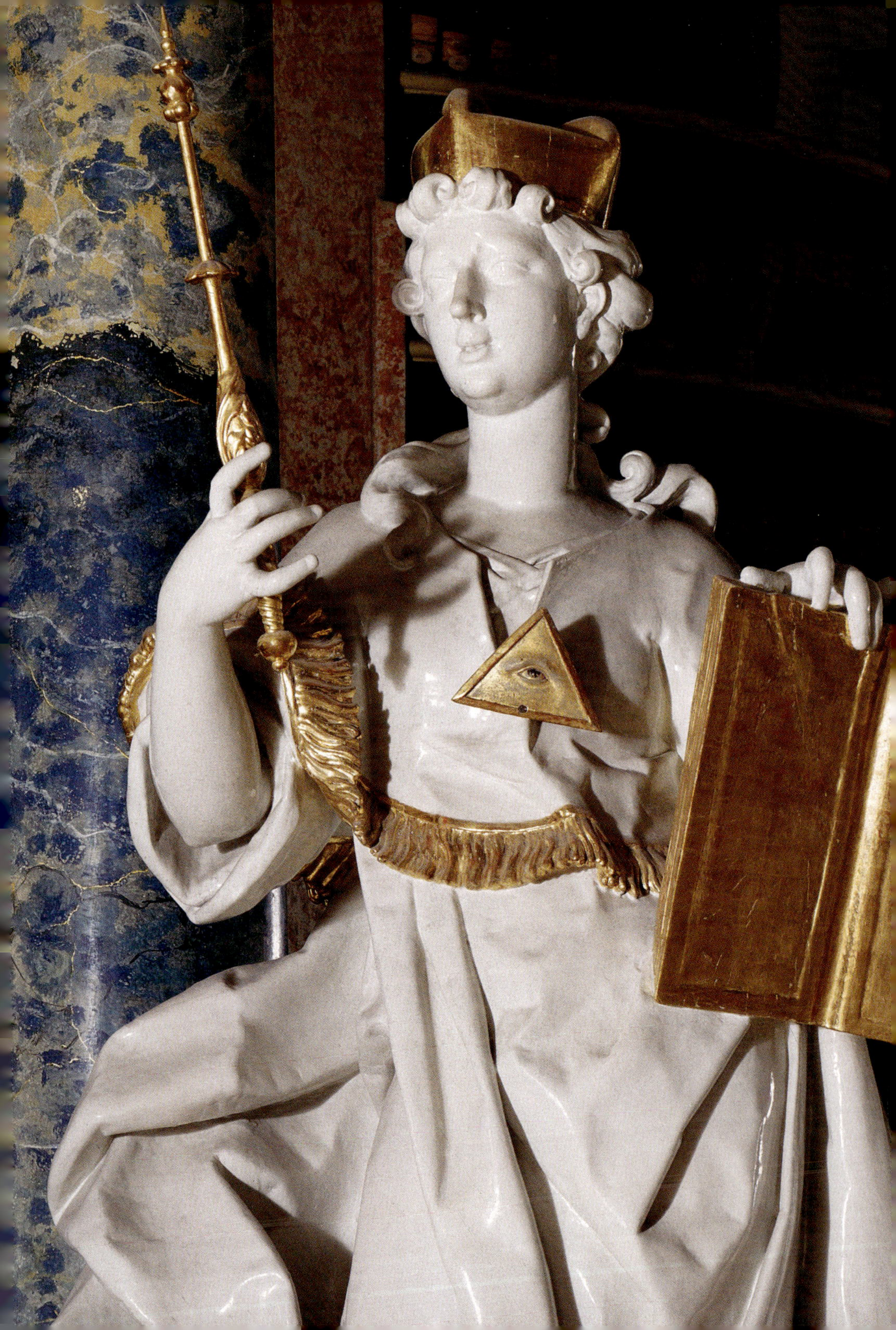

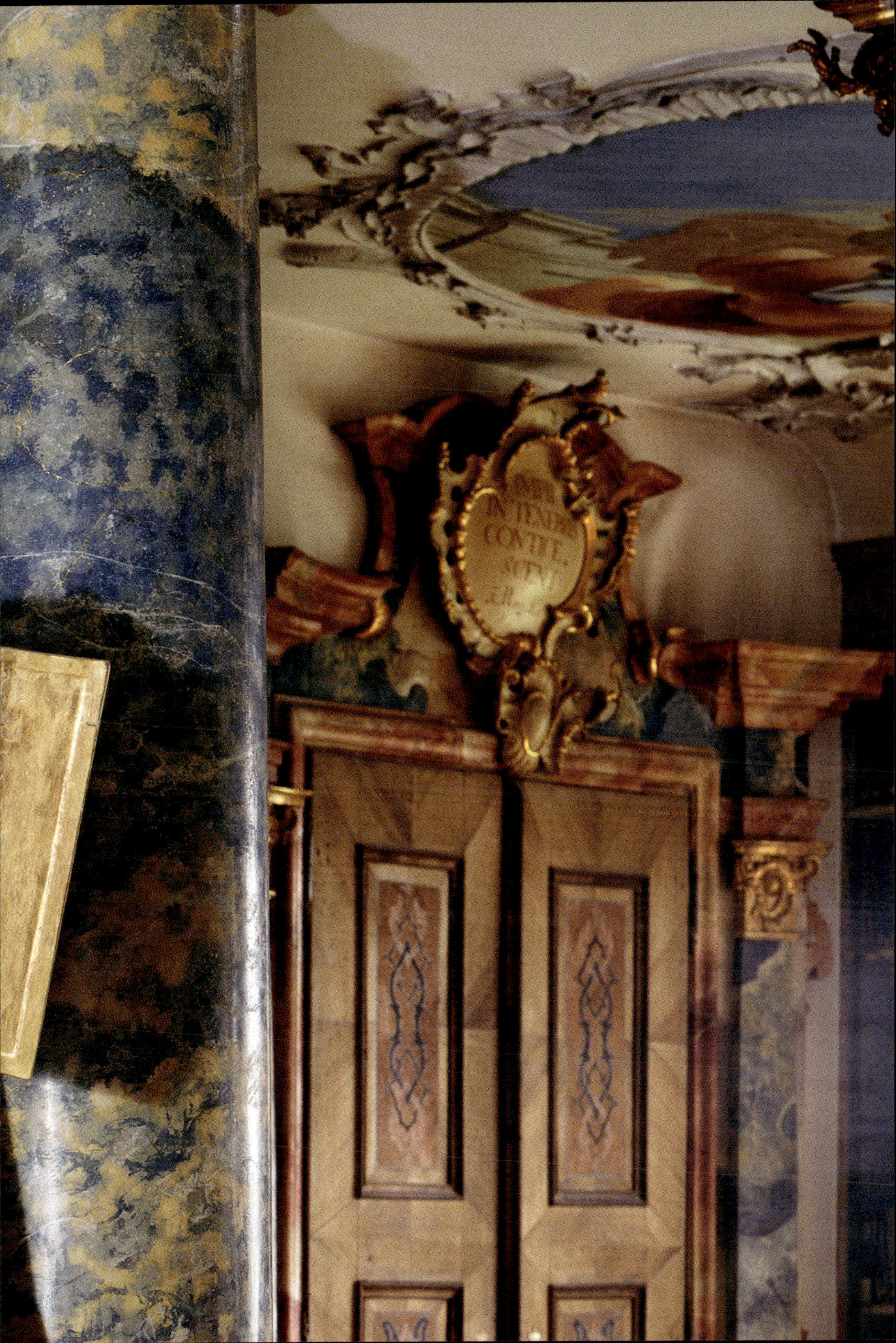

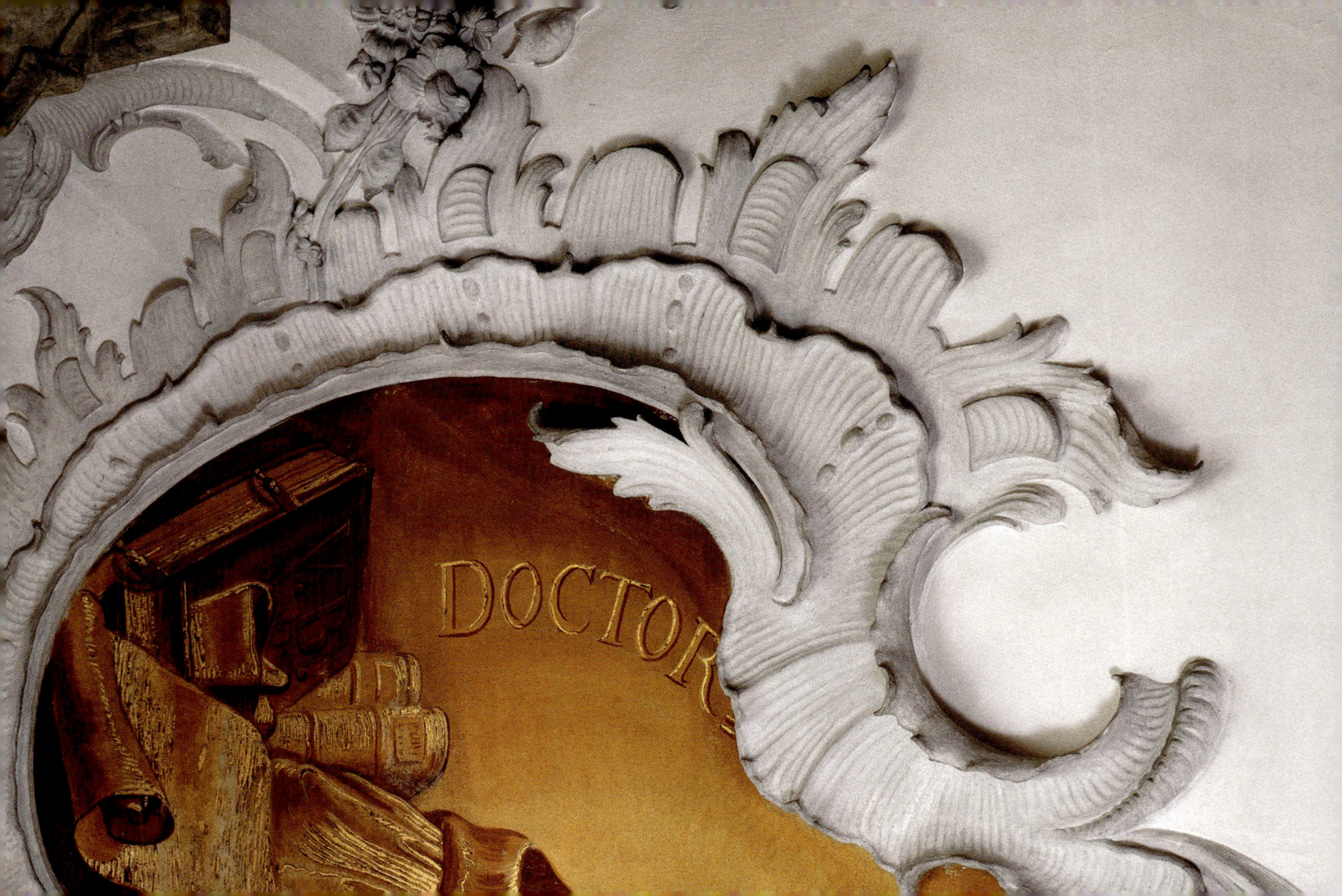
DOCTOR

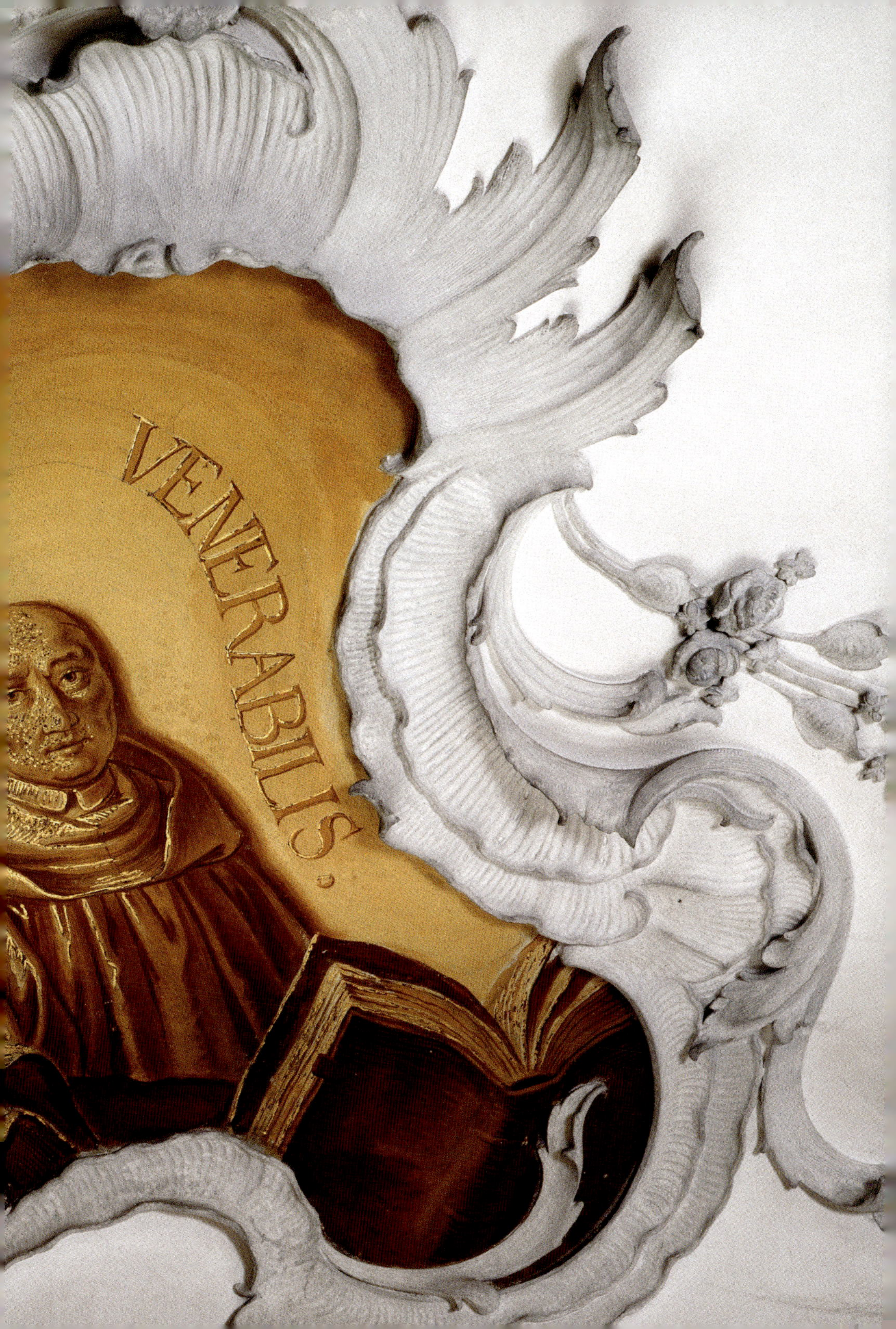

VENERABILIS.

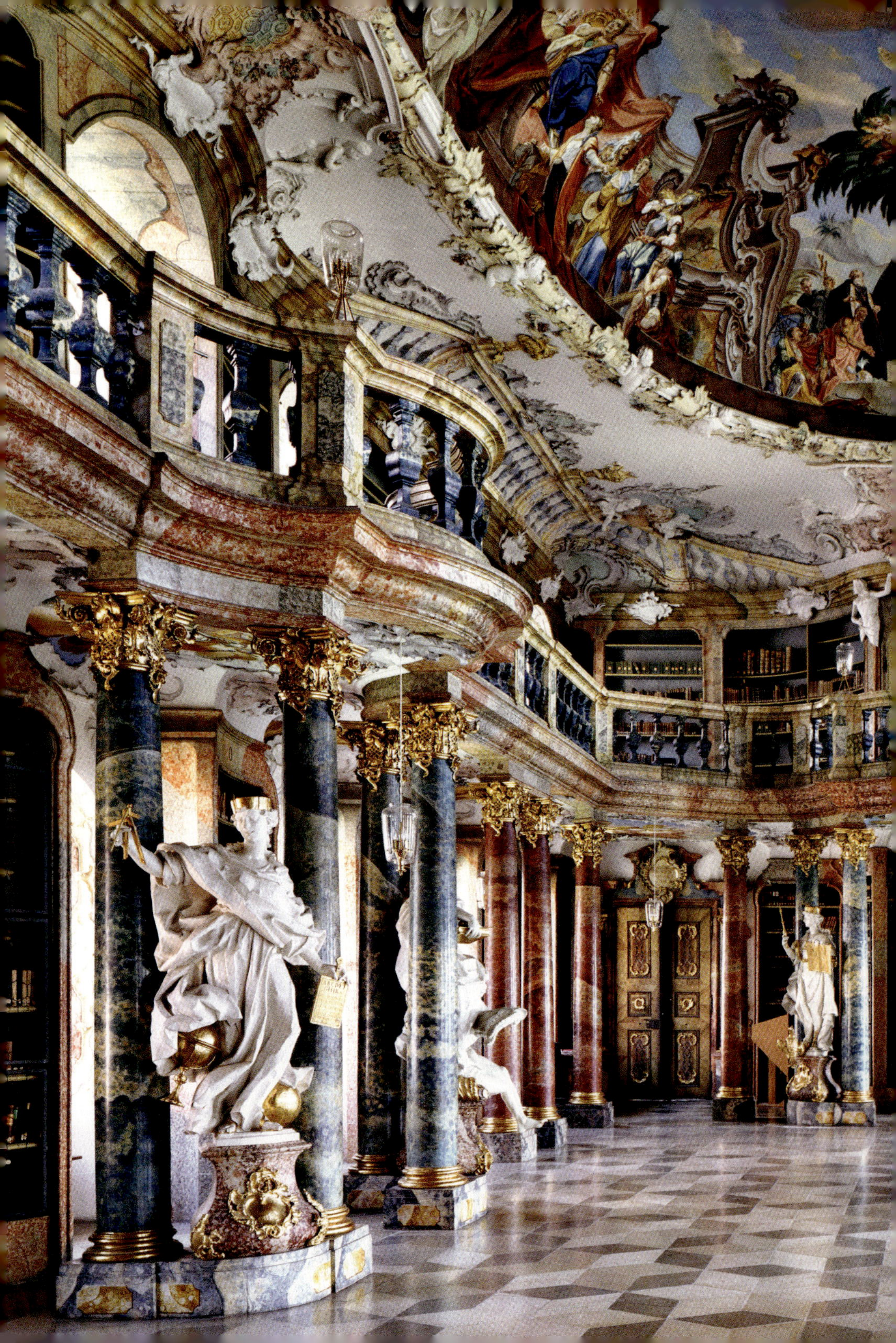

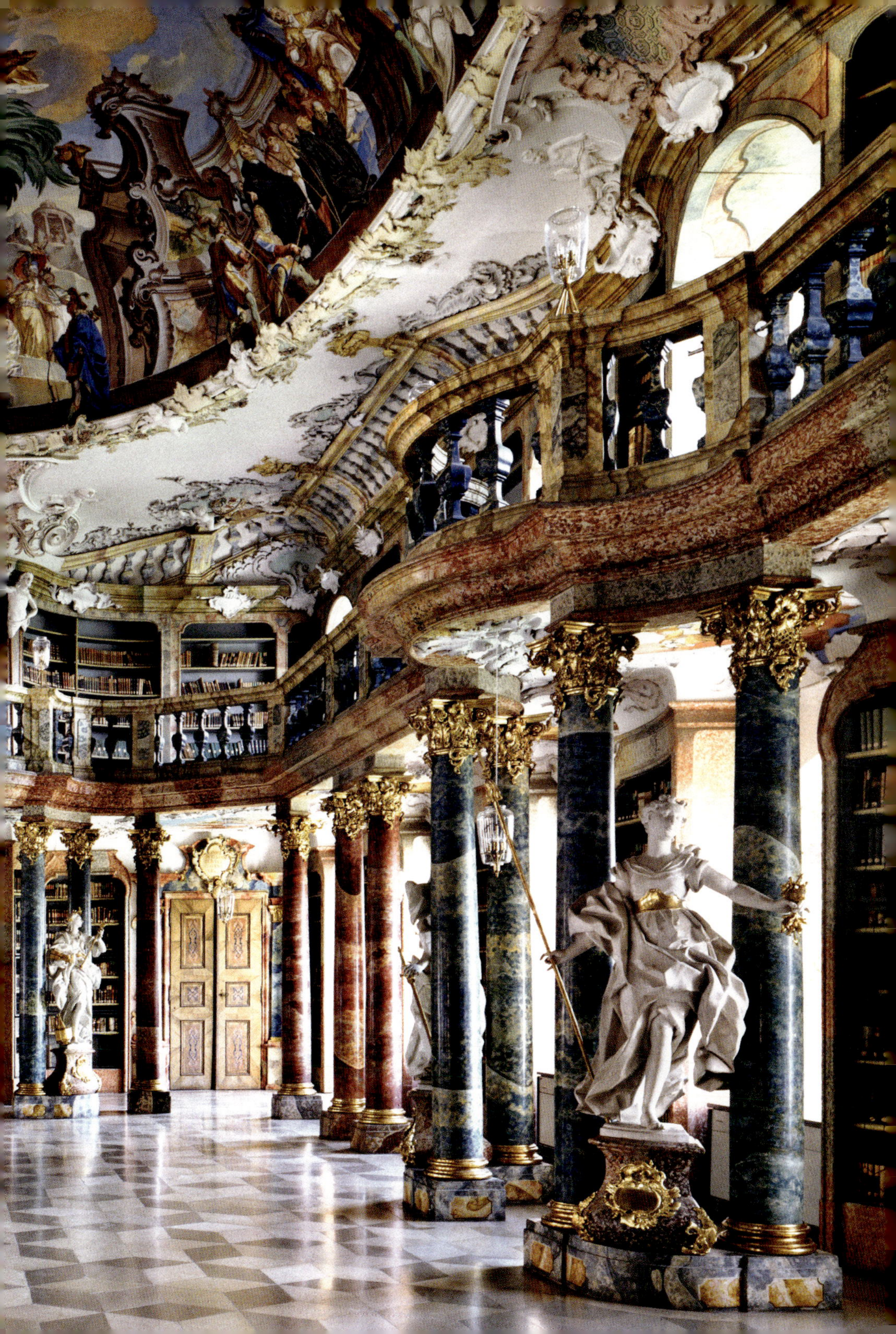

Stiftsbibliothek Waldsassen

The Cistercian nunnery of Waldsassen Abbey is home to a veritable banqueting hall of books, which captivates visitors with its expressive and larger than life-size atlantes. On their shoulders these figures support the upper gallery, reached via hidden spiral staircases in the corners of the room and which allows access to the bookshelves that extend right up to the ceiling. In their manner of dress, gestures and attributes, the figures introduce a moralising theme whose details relate to books and how they may be used. While the personifications of ignorance in its various guises appear to be condemned to bearing the weight of the architectural construction, the representations of philosophers and Church doctors on the upper level allude to the content and tradition of the library's treasures. The portrait busts of famous ancient philosophers and personalities testify to the fact that valuable knowledge from the past was preserved in monastic libraries for centuries. Church fathers, whose writings and commentaries probably made up the library's main holdings, are represented in portrait medallions. Lastly, cartouches set above the shelves are marked with inscriptions which indicate the different subjects of the books on display. In the ceiling frescos by Karl Hofreiter, literary scholarship is situated in the context of the intellectual culture of the Cistercians, represented by scenes from the life and works of Bernard of Clairvaux (1091–1153), during whose lifetime the abbey was founded. This decorative scheme was designed by Eugen Schmid (1688–1744), who worked here as librarian before his election as abbot (1724–1744) and who organised the books by a method of differentiation on the

basis of his own great learning. In the wake of secularisation and the dissolution of the abbey in 1803, the library's holdings, which by then numbered around 19,000 volumes, were largely lost. Part of its collection of books – above all, the works of theology – was transferred to the newly founded Regional Library in Amberg, and these today once again fill the abbey library's shelves. Since 1865, Cistercian nuns have fulfilled the educational mission of their Order, specifically with a school for girls housed at the abbey. Waldsassen, which was established as a Cistercian foundation in 1133 by Margrave Diepold III (1075–1146) following his meeting with Bernard of Clairvaux, has long been a centre of study. The founder's close links with the Staufers meant that just a few years later, in 1147, King Conrad III (1093–1152) granted the abbey the privilege of Imperial immediacy. In 1185 Pope Lucius III (c. 1097–1185) placed the abbey under the protection of the Roman Curia and confirmed its territorial possessions, acquired through the energetic pursuit of colonising and economic activities. Waldsassen's abbots systematically expanded

Founded 1133; library hall 1724–1726 by Johann Karl Stilp
Holdings c. 2,000 volumes (on permanent loan from Amberg Provinzialbibliothek)
Type of library monastery (today nunnery) library
Highlights *Amberger Malerbüchlein*, 15th century (MS 77, part of a composite manuscript: fol. 217r–226v); Stephan Fridolin, *Schatzbehalter der wahren Reichtümer des Heils*, Nuremberg, 1491; Johann Jacob Scheuchzer, *Physica sacra (Kupfer-Bibel)*, Augsburg/Ulm, 1733

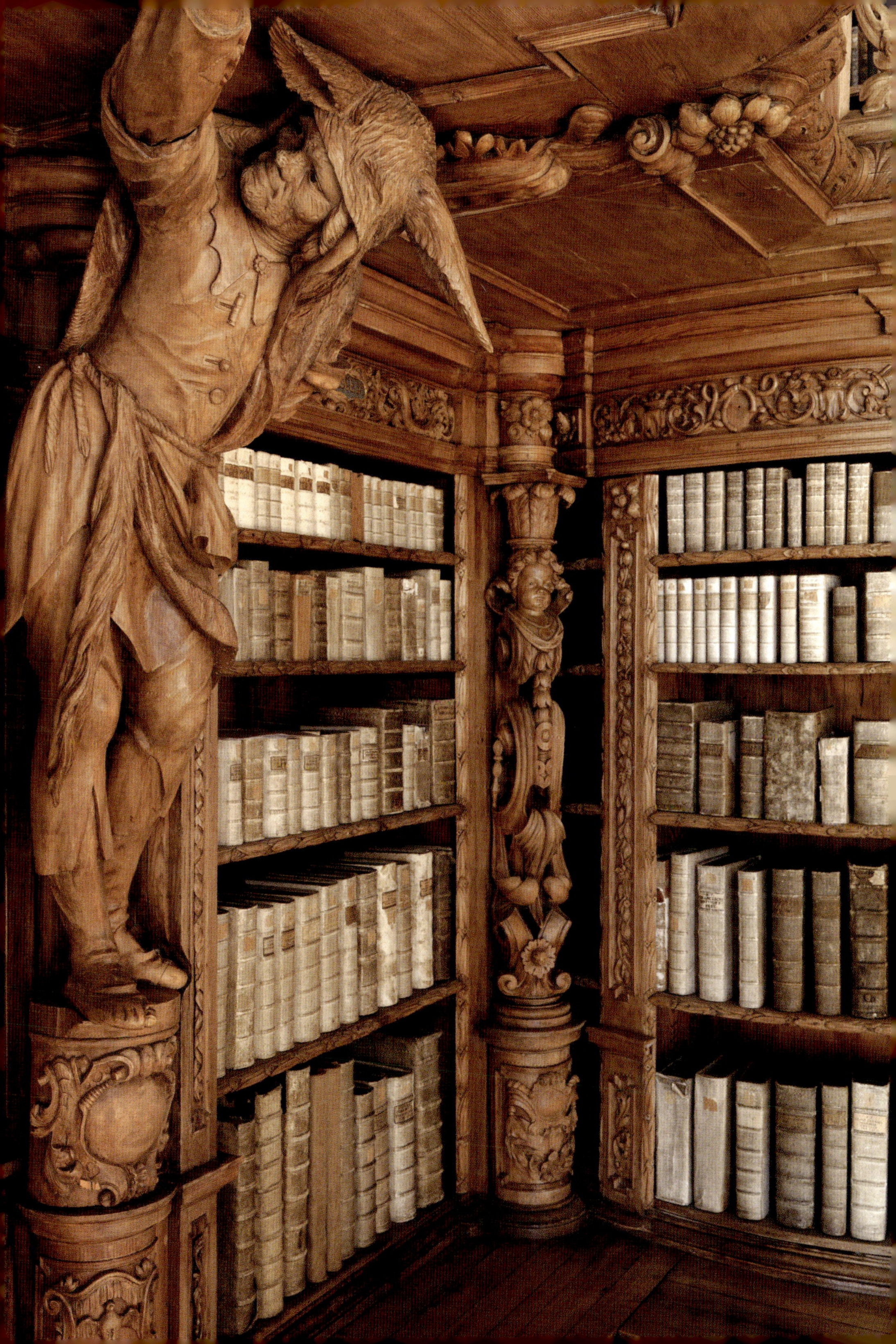

these territories into a self-contained area under their dominion, known as the Stiftland on the Bavarian side and the Egerland on the Bohemian side. Its border location and a series of religious conflicts meant that the wealthy abbey was repeatedly destroyed and plundered. The library, institutionalised in 1433, was consequently only able to start operating properly towards the end of the 16th century, in what was at that time a Lutheran monastery under Wittelsbach rule. A first inventory dates from 1585. Today's library is housed in the west wing of the monastery complex, which was rebuilt from the ground up between 1681 and 1687. Its interiors were decorated between 1724 and 1726. Complementing the magnificent wood carvings by Johann Karl Stilp (1668–1735) is the stucco work on the walls and ceiling by Jacopo Appiani (1687–1742), the ornament in which takes up that of the wood carvings and thereby sets a homogeneous, festive stamp on the room as a whole.

❊ ❊ ❊

In der Zisterzienserinnenabtei Waldsassen hat sich ein regelrechter Festsaal der Bücher erhalten, der den Besucher mit seinen überlebensgroßen, ausdrucksstarken Atlanten in den Bann schlägt. Auf ihren Schultern tragen sie die Galerie, die – über verborgene Wendeltreppen in den Ecken erreichbar – das Obergeschoss der bis zur Decke reichenden Bücherregale erschließt. In ihrer Kostümierung, Gestik und den Attributen eröffnen die Figuren dem Betrachter ein moralisierendes Programm, das thematisch auf Bücher und deren Nutzen bezogen ist. Während die Personifikationen von Ignoranz in ihren verschiedenen Ausprägungen zum Tragen des baulichen Konstrukts verdammt erscheinen, spielen im Obergeschoss Abbilder von Philosophen und Kirchenlehrern auf Inhalt und Tradition der Bücherschätze an. Die Porträtbüsten von Philosophen und Persönlichkeiten der Antike verweisen darauf, dass in den Klosterbibliotheken wertvolles Wissen aus dem Altertum über

die Jahrhunderte tradiert wurde. Kirchenlehrer, deren Schriften und Kommentare wohl den Hauptbestand der Bibliothek ausgemacht haben dürften, sind in den Bildnismedaillons dargestellt. Über den Regalen angebrachte Kartuschen mit Inschriften informieren schließlich über die dort versammelten Themen. In den Deckenfresken von Karl Hofreiter wird das Bücherwissen in den Kontext der Geisteskultur der Zisterzienser gestellt. Für diese stehen Szenen aus dem Leben und Wirken des Bernhard von Clairvaux (1091–1153), zu dessen Lebzeiten die Abtei gegründet worden war. Verantwortlich für dieses Programm war Eugen Schmid (1688–1744), der vor seiner Wahl zum Abt (1724–1744) hier als Bibliothekar wirkte. Sein profundes Wissen erlaubte eine differenzierte Aufstellung der Bücher, deren Anzahl bis 1803 auf 19 000 Exemplare anwuchs. Im Zuge der Säkularisierung und Aufhebung der Abtei im Jahr 1803 ging die Sammlung größtenteils verloren. Jene Buchbestände, die an die damals neu gegründete Provinzialbibliothek in Amberg überstellt wurden – vor allem theologische Literatur –, füllen heute wieder die Regale. Seit 1865 kommen Zisterzienserinnen dem Bildungsauftrag ihres Ordens nach, und zwar in einer im Kloster untergebrachten Realschule für Mädchen. Ein Bildungszentrum war das 1133 von Markgraf Diepold III. (1075–1146) nach seinem Zusammentreffen mit Bernhard von Clairvaux als Zisterzienserniederlassung gegründete Kloster bereits seit Langem. Die enge Verbindung des Gründers zu den Staufern bewirkte, dass das Kloster bereits 1147 von König Konrad III. (1093–1152) mit dem Privileg der Reichsunmittelbarkeit ausgestattet wurde. 1185 stellte Papst Lucius III. (um 1097–1185) das Kloster unter den Schutz der römischen Kurie und bestätigte dessen durch rege kolonisatorische und wirtschaftliche Tätigkeit erworbenen Territorialbesitz. Diesen bauten die Waldsassener Äbte systematisch zu einem geschlossenen Herrschaftsgebiet aus, dem sogenannten Stiftland auf bayerischer und dem Egerland auf

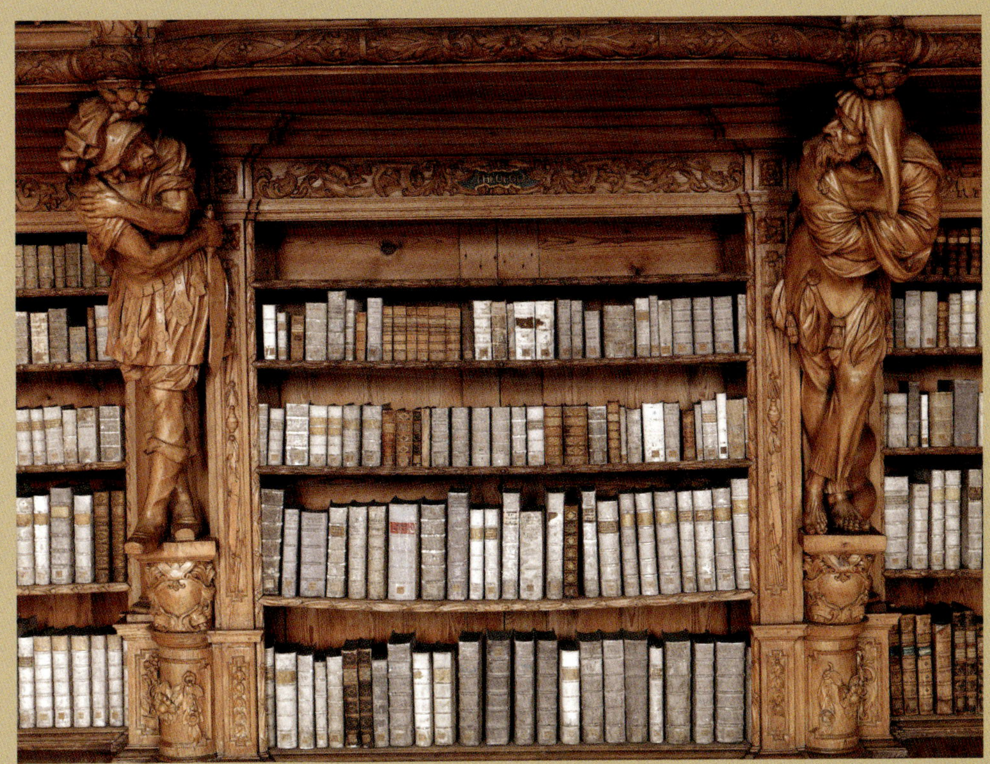

böhmischer Seite. Bedingt durch die Grenzlage und Religionskriege wurde das reiche Kloster wiederholt zerstört und geplündert. Die ab 1433 institutionalisierte Bibliothek konnte daher erst gegen Ende des 16. Jahrhunderts ihren Betrieb aufnehmen, in einem damals lutherischen Kloster unter der Herrschaft der Wittelsbacher. Ein erstes Inventar stammt aus dem Jahr 1585. Die heutige Bibliothek entstand im Westflügel der in den Jahren 1681 bis 1687 von Grund auf neu errichteten Klosteranlage. Ihre Ausstattung erfolgte in den Jahren 1724 bis 1726. Den prächtigen Schnitzwerken von Johann Karl Stilp (1668–1735) stellen sich die Stuckaturen von Jacopo Appiani (1687–1742) zur Seite, die deren Ornamentik an Wand und Gewölbe weiterführen und dem Raum einen einheitlichen Festsaalcharakter verleihen.

❋ ❋ ❋

L'abbaye cistercienne de Waldsassen, aujourd'hui occupée par des religieuses de cet ordre, renferme une bibliothèque d'apparat de toute beauté. Ses atlantes plus grands que nature et aux traits si expressifs ont de quoi stupéfier les visiteurs d'emblée. Ils portent sur leurs épaules la galerie que l'on atteint par des escaliers en colimaçon dissimulés dans les coins. La galerie est bordée d'étagères montant jusqu'au plafond. Le costume, la gestuelle et les attributs de ces personnages connotent tout un programme moralisateur dont la thématique renvoie aux livres et à leur utilisation. Tandis que les diverses incarnations de l'ignorance semblent condamnées à porter la structure architecturale de la bibliothèque, des illustrations de philosophes et d'érudits religieux rassemblées dans la partie supérieure évoquent le contenu et la tradition des trésors situés dans cette pièce. Les portraits en buste

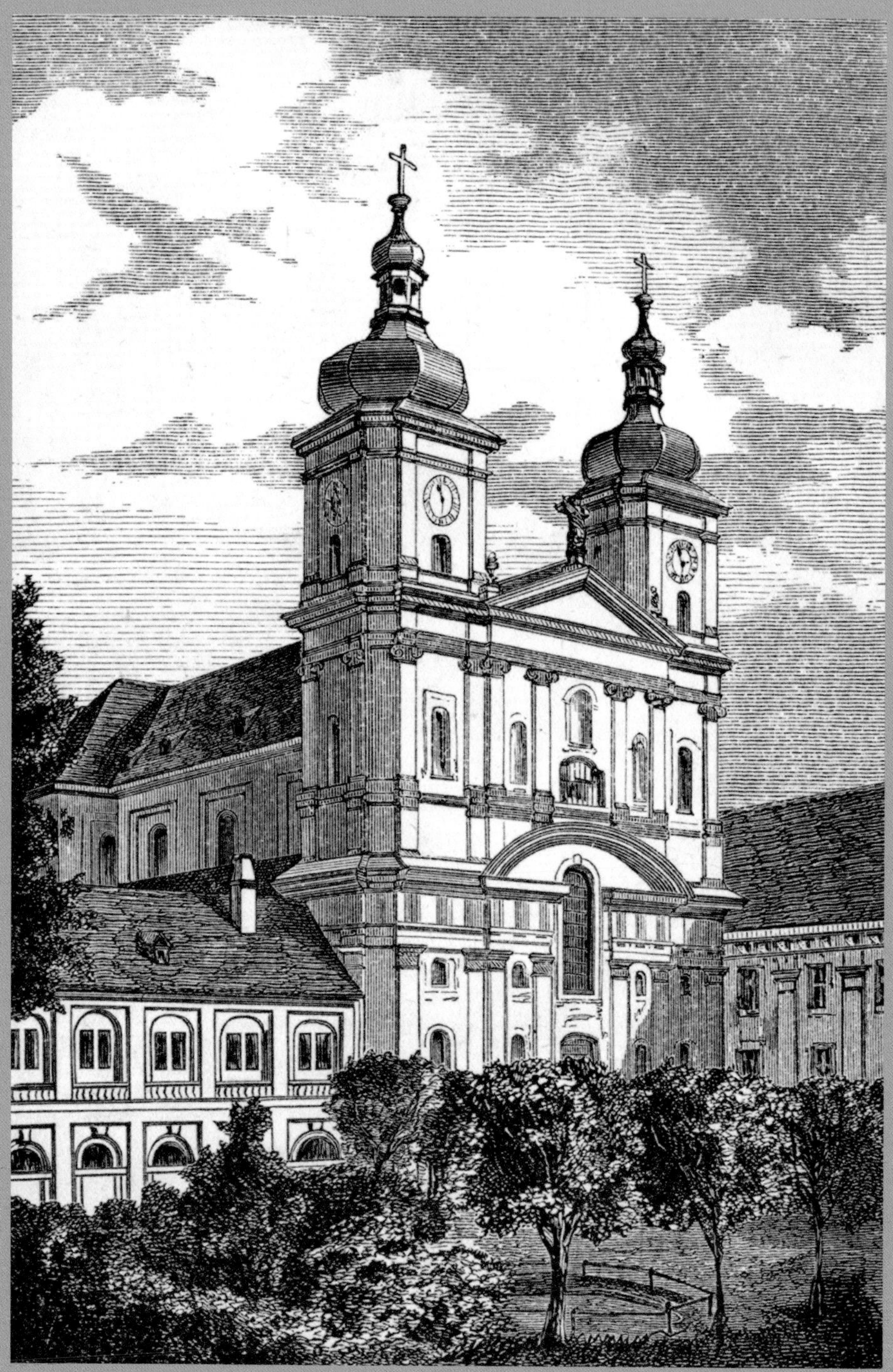

de philosophes et de personnalités antiques rappellent que les bibliothèques monacales sont depuis des siècles un lieu de transmission de précieux savoirs. Les Pères de l'Église, dont les écrits et les commentaires composent probablement l'essentiel du fonds de la bibliothèque, sont représentés dans les portraits en médaillons. Des inscriptions sur cartouches placés sur les étagères informent sur les thèmes traités par les livres rassemblés en dessous. Au plafond, les fresques de Karl Hofreiter replacent le savoir écrit dans le contexte intellectuel de la culture des Cisterciens, avec des scènes de la vie et de l'œuvre de Bernard de Clairvaux (1091–1153), du vivant duquel l'abbaye a été fondée. On doit ce programme iconographique à Eugen Schmid (1688–1744), qui occupa la fonction de bibliothécaire avant d'être élu abbé de Waldsassen (1724–1744). L'étendue de ses connaissances permit une présentation subtile de la collection qui comptait 19 000 volumes au moment de la sécularisation et du démantèlement de l'abbaye en 1803, date à laquelle la collection fut en grande partie perdue. À l'époque transféré à l'abbaye régionale d'Amberg nouvellement créée, le fonds composé pour l'essentiel de livres théologiques a aujourd'hui regagné les étagères de Waldsassen. Les cisterciennes perpétuent la mission éducative de leur ordre depuis 1865, actuellement avec une école de filles située dans le couvent. Fondé en 1133 par le margrave Diepold III (1075–1146) après sa rencontre avec Bernard de Clairvaux, le

monastère cistercien de Waldsassen est depuis longtemps un centre éducatif. En 1147, le roi Conrad III (1093–1152) plaça le monastère sous immédiateté impériale, un privilège sûrement dû au lien étroit que le fondateur entretenait avec la Maison Staufer. En 1185, le pape Lucius III (vers 1097–1185) plaça le monastère sous la protection de la curie romaine, confirmant ainsi ses possessions territoriales, acquises par une ardente activité économique et colonisatrice. Les abbés de Waldsassen étendirent ces territoires de façon systématique en un domaine souverain indépendant, le Stiftland en Bavière et l'Egerland en Bohême. En raison des guerres de religion et de la situation transfrontalière, la riche abbaye fut maintes fois détruite et pillée. Par conséquent, la bibliothèque institutionnalisée en 1433 fut uniquement mise en service vers la fin du XVIe siècle – dans ce qui était alors un monastère protestant dirigé par la Maison de Wittelsbach. Le premier inventaire date de 1585. La bibliothèque actuelle occupe l'aile occidentale du couvent rebâti de fond en comble entre 1681 et 1687. Son aménagement intérieur suivit entre 1724 et 1726. Le décor en stuc de Jacopo Appiani (1687–1742) complète les magnifiques sculptures en bois de Johann Karl Stilp (1668–1735). Les moulures et l'ornementation au plafond citent des éléments de la partie inférieure. Ainsi, le décor de la voûte s'unit aux parois pour conférer une touche homogène à cette superbe salle d'apparat rendant hommage à l'univers du livre.

View of the convent church of Waldsassen, in: Franz Benno Fuchssteiner, *Beschreibung der Klosterkirche zu Waldsassen*, Amberg, 1872

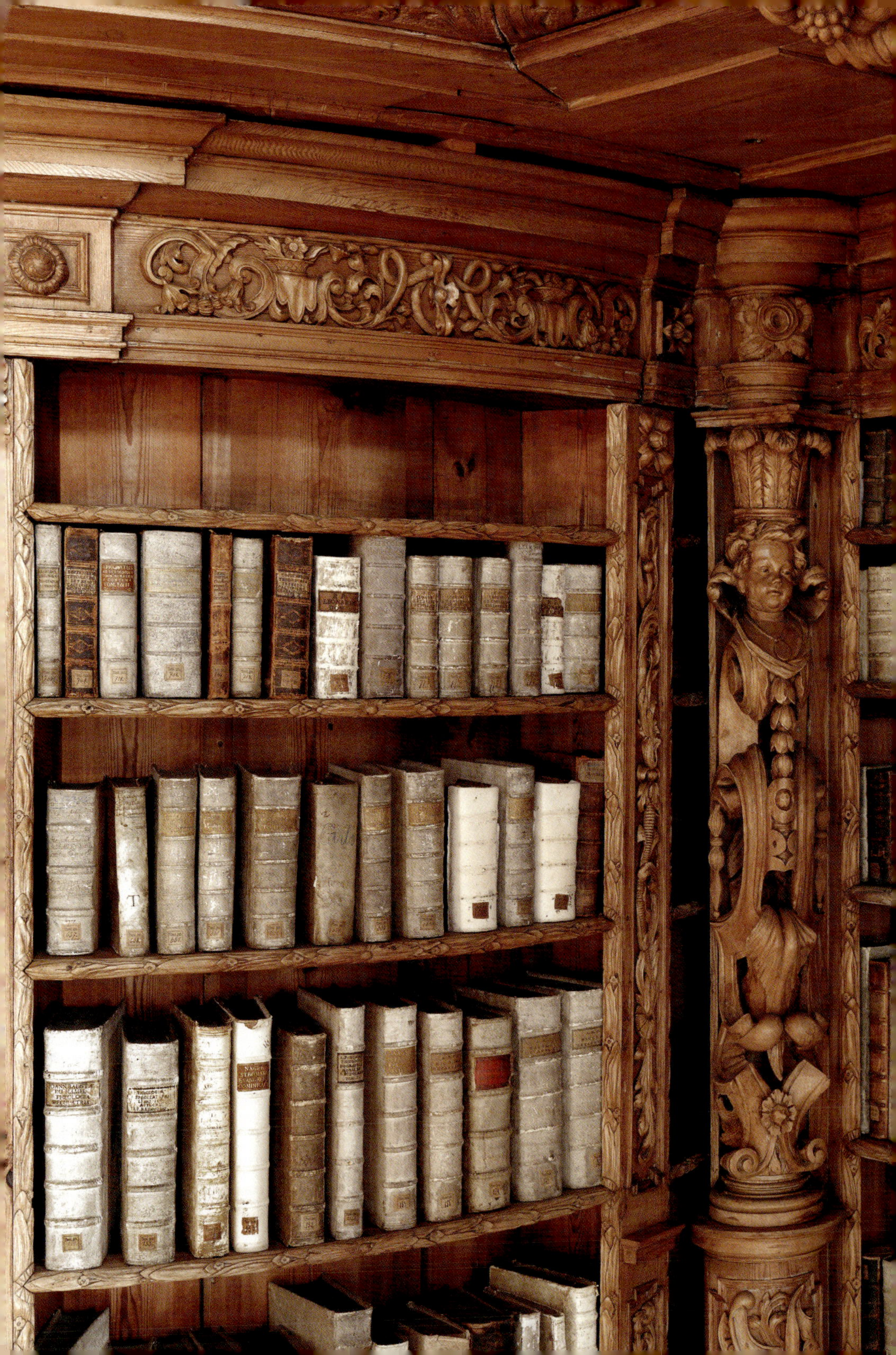

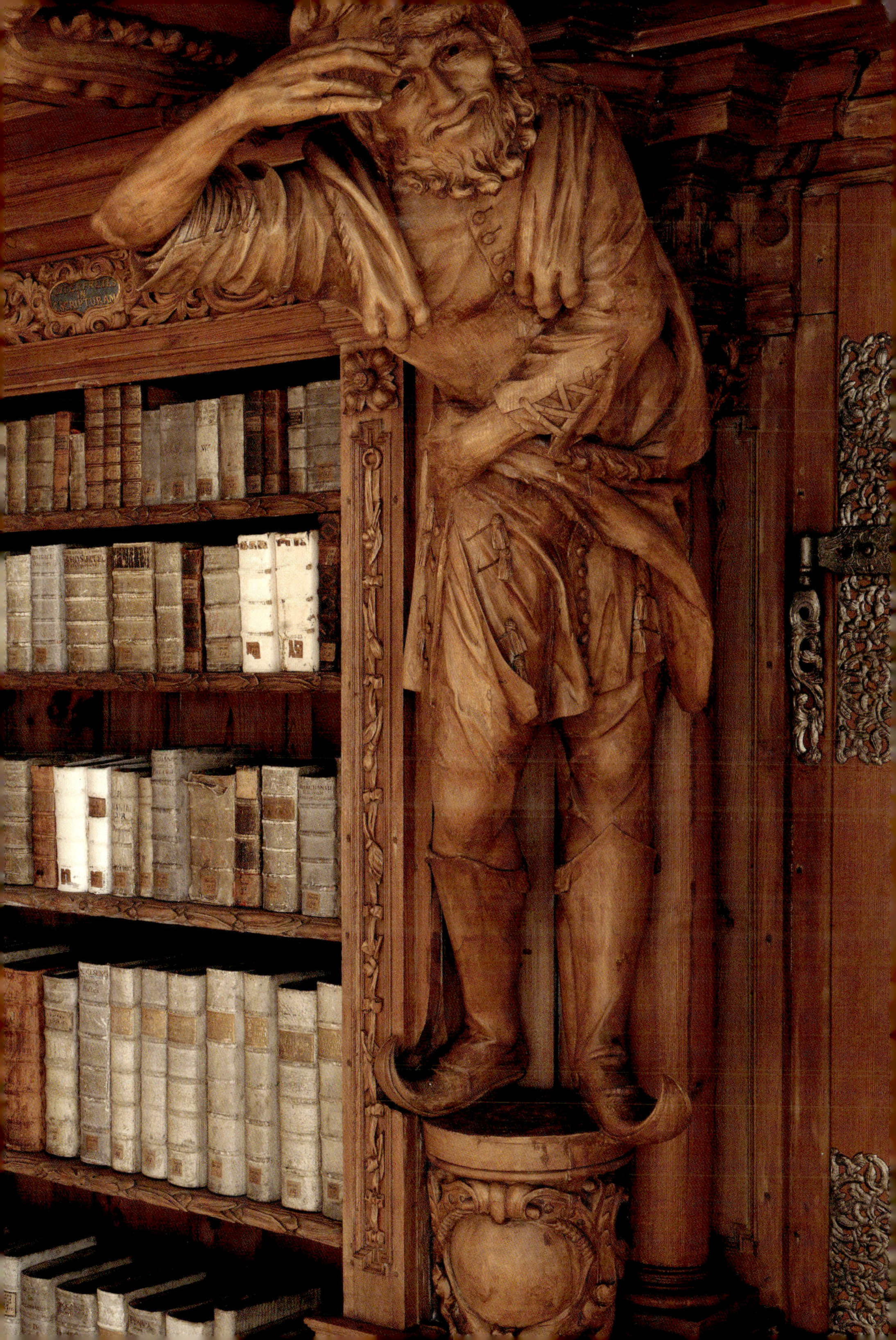

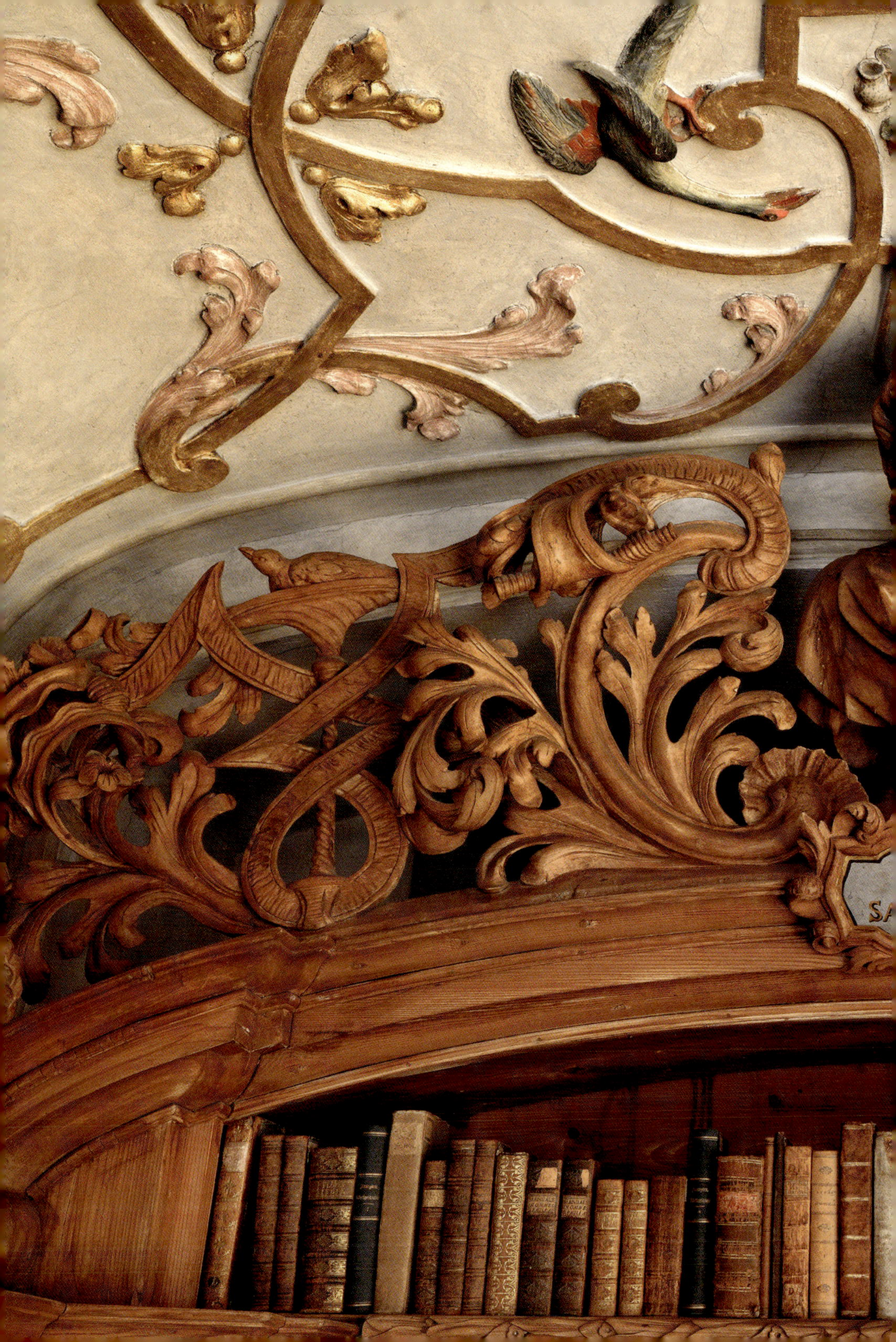

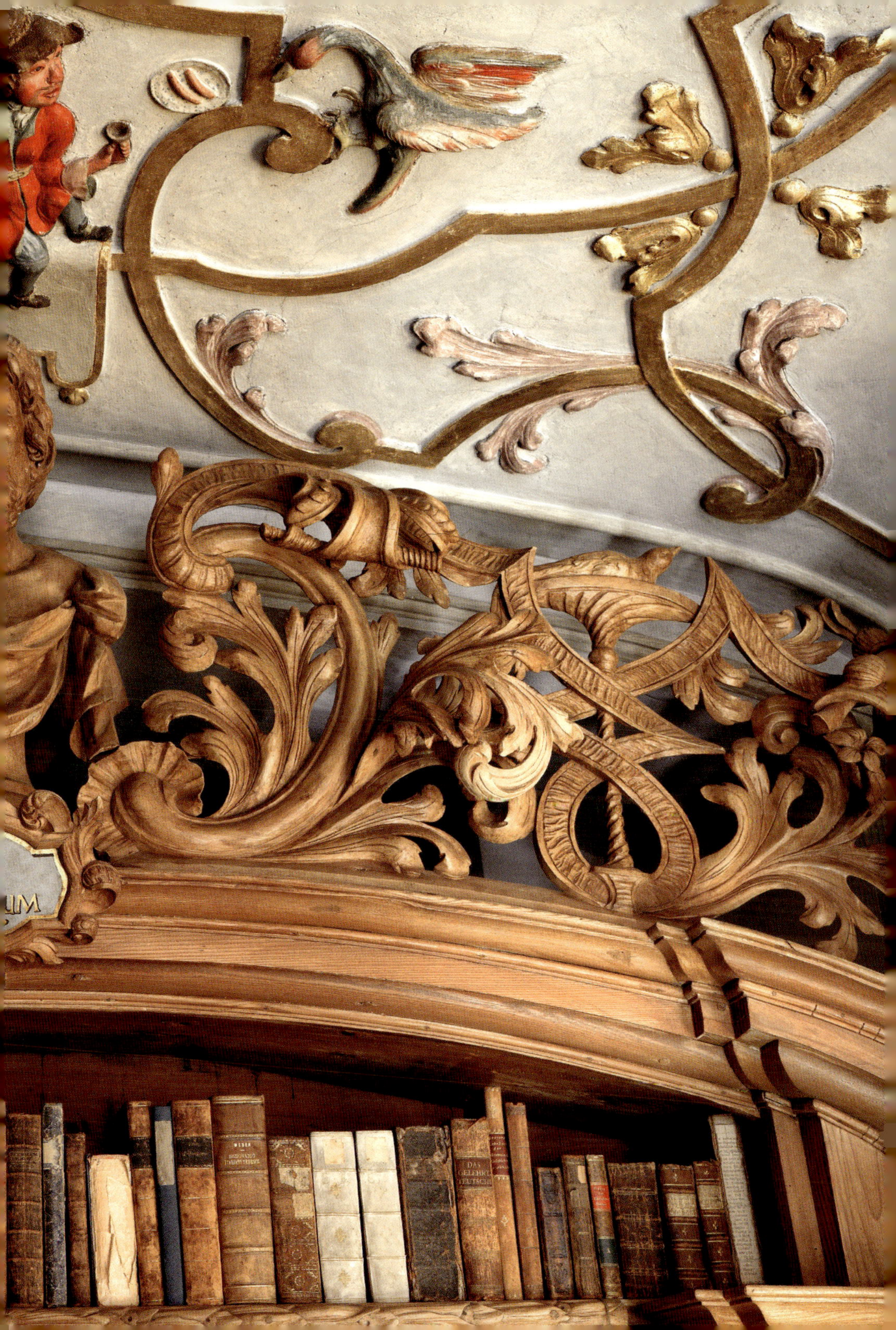

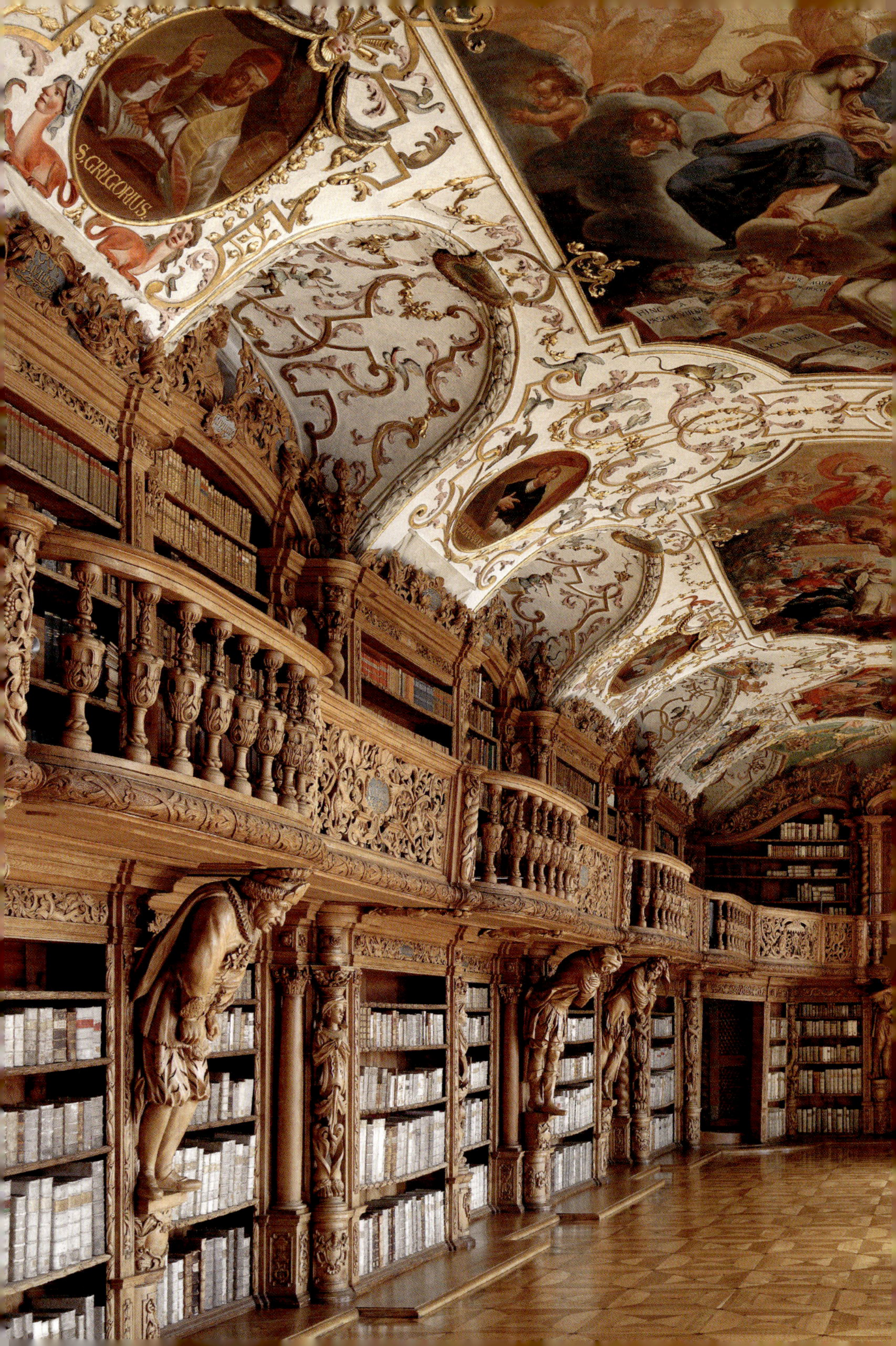

S. GREGORIUS

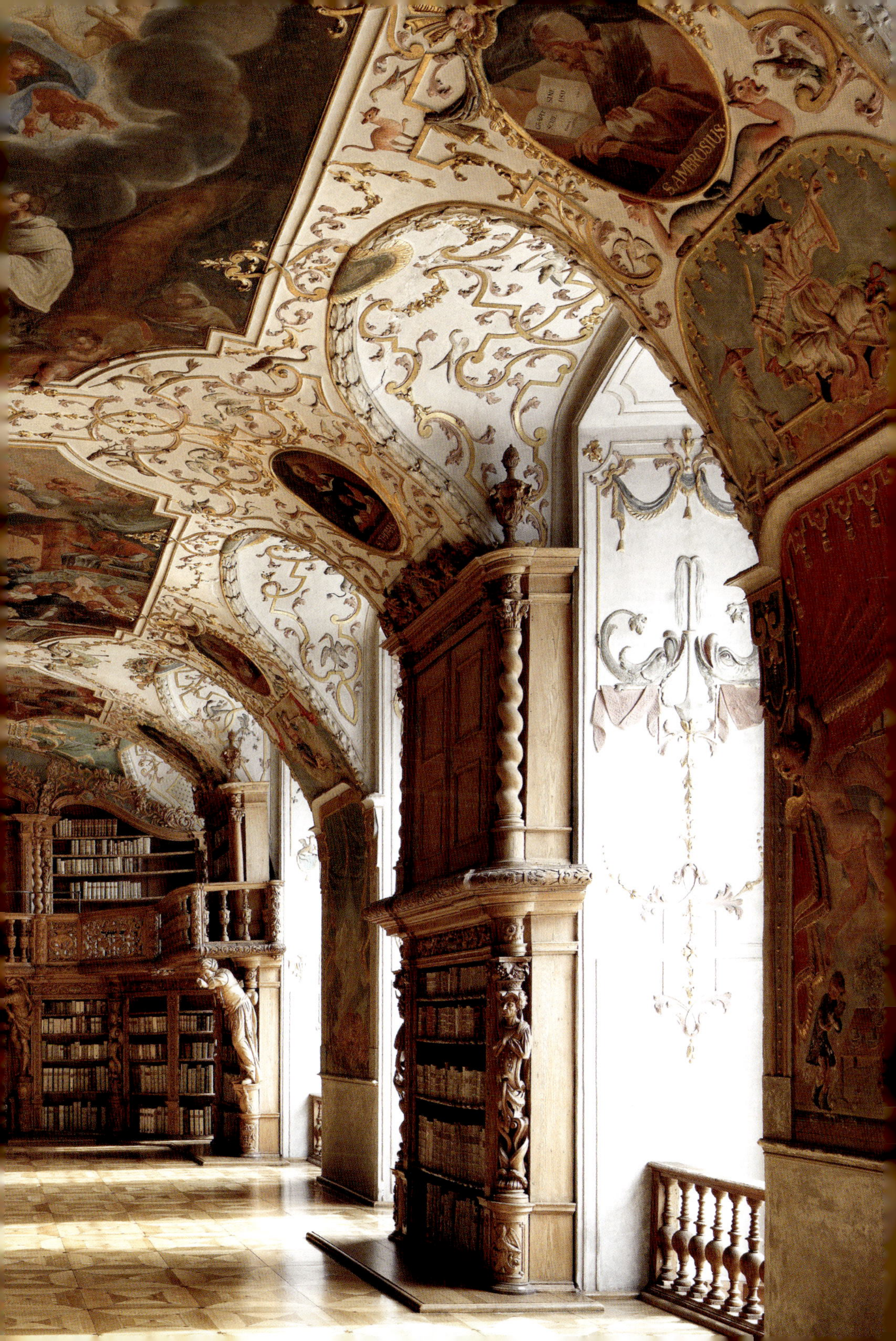

Bibliothekssaal Kloster Schussenried

From the library hall in today's museum complex we may gauge the size and importance of the Premonstratensian abbey that existed at Schussenried for over 600 years before being dissolved in 1803. The monastery was founded in 1183 thanks to a private endowment and was run by the Premonstratensians as a wealthy and powerful imperial abbey. It formed both the spiritual and secular hub of the extensive lands attached to it, and from 1512 held complete jurisdiction over its territory. A wide range of subjects was taught at the monastery school and some of the canons were themselves practising academics and musicians. These activities were facilitated too by the well-stocked library, which probably comprised around 15,000 volumes in around 1750 and was considered a kind of treasury of the knowledge of its day. This wealth of learning is referred to in the ceiling frescos completed in 1757 by Franz Georg Hermann (1692–1768), where – in richly populated allegorical scenes – the various forms and branches of knowledge are submitted to the judgement of divine wisdom in the centre. Portraits of several Premonstratensian scholars can also be recognised among the groups. The sculptures by Fidel Sporer (1731–1811), made between 1764 and 1766, likewise relate to the books and their contents in their arrangement around the room. Thus the representations of the Church Fathers and Doctors of the Church on the ground floor counterpoint the false teachers, represented in figural groups of putti, on the gallery. An organ was later installed between the bookshelves, allowing music recitals. When the abbey buildings passed to the kingdom of Württemberg a few years after the monastery's dissolution, the books in its once so famous library had already largely vanished. An impression of the vast collection can be gained from the bookcases rising up through two storeys, whose historical décor of *trompe l'œil* book spines blends harmoniously with the overall colour scheme. In their uniformity, the painted spines become part of the decorative scheme that extends to the room as a whole, and which, in conjunction with the library's harmonious proportions and good lighting, conveys the impression of a stateroom of the most impressive kind. The Rococo ornamentation in stucco, painting and sculpture fuses the room into a unified artistic whole. Built to plans by Dominikus Zimmermann (1685–1766), the library was originally conceived as the centre of a new abbey complex, laid out around several courtyards, that was to emerge from a major programme of renovations carried out between 1754 and 1762. In the end, however, only a third of the scheme was completed under monastery architect Jakob Emele (1707–1780). The library is situated in the northern wing of the three-sided Neues Kloster, which has the church at its centre.

***

Founded 1183; suppressed in 1803; library hall 1754–1762 after plans by Dominikus Zimmermann
Type of library monastic library, today a museum (under the aegis of the Staatliche Schlösser und Gärten Baden-Württemberg)

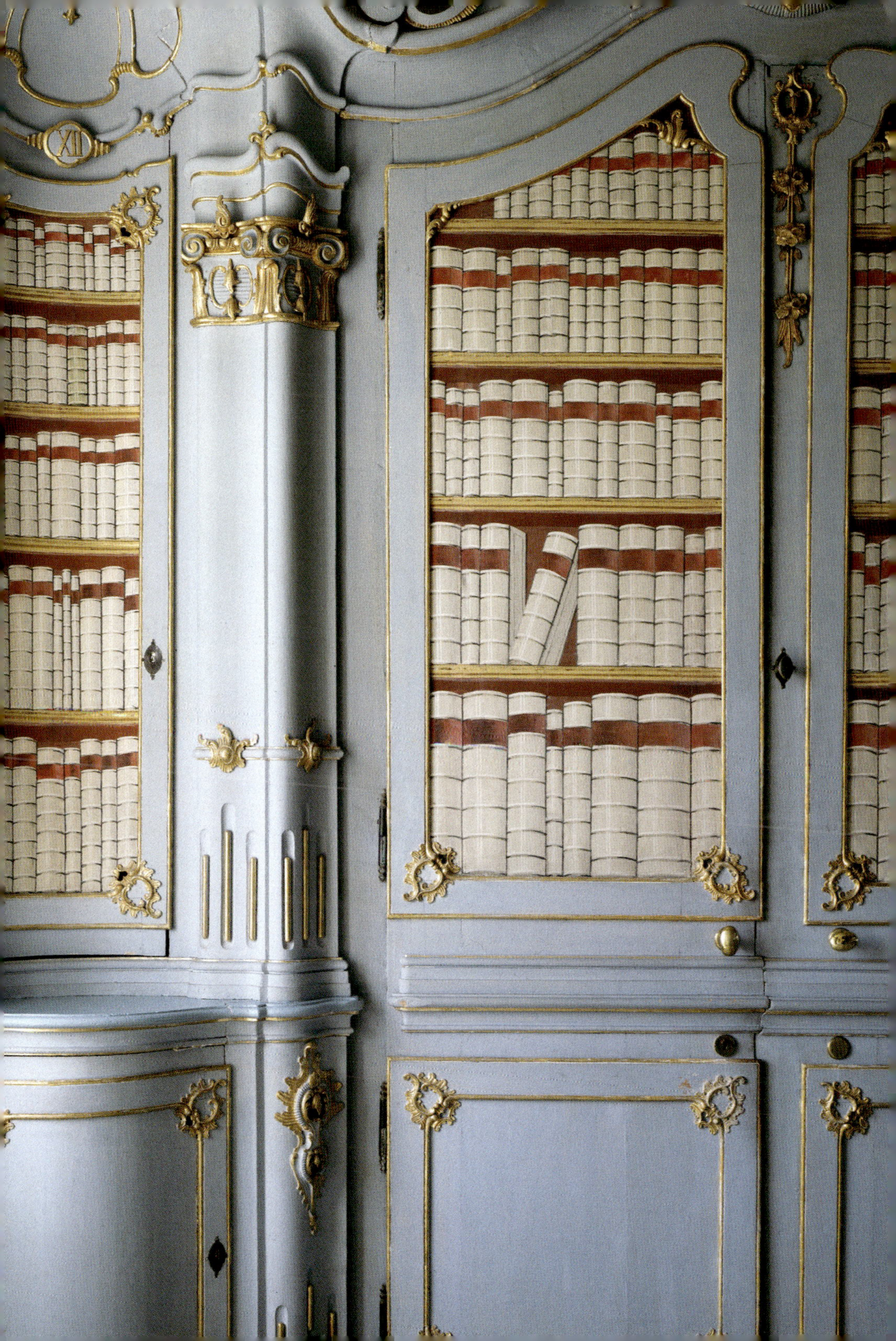

Am Bibliothekssaal im heutigen Museumskomplex kann man die Größe und Bedeutung des nach über 600-jährigem Bestehen 1803 aufgelösten Chorherrenstifts der Prämonstratenser ermessen. Es entstand dank einer privaten Stiftung im Jahr 1183 und wurde von den Prämonstratensern als wohlhabende und mächtige Reichsabtei geführt. Sie war geistlicher und weltlicher Mittelpunkt des ihr angeeigneten Territoriums, innerhalb dessen ihr ab 1512 auch die gesamte Gerichtsbarkeit unterstand. An ihrer Klosterschule boten die Chorherren ein weites Spektrum an Fächern im Unterricht an. Einige unter ihnen waren auch selbst wissenschaftlich oder als Musiker tätig. Dies war auch dank der gut sortierten Bestände der (vermutlich gegen Mitte des 18. Jahrhunderts um die 15 000 Bände zählenden) Bibliothek möglich, die als regelrechte Schatzkammer des Wissens ihrer Zeit galt. Eine später zwischen die Bücherregale eingebaute Orgel erlaubte außerdem Musikaufführungen. Auf den reichen Bücherschatz verweisen die 1757 vollendeten Deckenfresken von Franz Georg Hermann (1692–1768), wo in figurenreichen allegorischen Szenen die verschiedenen Wissensformen oder Wissenschaftssparten vor Augen geführt und der göttlichen Offenbarung im Zentrum anheimgestellt werden. In diesen Gruppen sind auch einige Wissenschaftler aus dem Prämonstratenserorden zu erkennen. Auch die rund um den Saal angeordneten, von 1764 bis 1766 entstandenen Skulpturen von Fidel Sporer (1731–1811) weisen auf die Bücher und deren Inhalte hin. Den Darstellungen der Kirchenväter und Kirchenlehrer im Erdgeschoss sind die Figurengruppen der Irrlehrer auf der Galerie als Puttengruppen gegenübergestellt. Als ein paar Jahre nach der Auflösung des Klosters die Konventsgebäude an das Königreich Württemberg fielen, waren die Bestände der einst so berühmten Bibliothek bereits großenteils verschollen. Einen Eindruck der einst riesigen Sammlung geben die über zwei Geschosse geführten Wandschränke der Bibliothek mit ihrer historischen Bemalung, die harmonisch auf die Raumfarben abgestimmt ist. In ihrer Einheitlichkeit wurden die gemalten Buchrücken selbst Teil der den gesamten Raum gestaltenden Dekoration, die zusammen mit dessen ausgewogenen Proportionen und der guten Durchlichtung die Idee eines Festsaals mit hohem Repräsentationswert vermittelt. Rokokoornamente in Stuck, Malerei und Skulptur bilden ein gattungsübergreifendes künstlerisches Ensemble. Der Bibliothekssaal war nach den Plänen von Dominikus Zimmermann (1685–1766) als eigentliches Zentrum der in den Jahren 1754 bis 1762 erneuerten Klosteranlage konzipiert. Er befindet sich im Nordflügel des mehrhöfig geplanten, vom Klosterbaumeister Jakob Emele (1707–1780) aber nur zu etwa einem Drittel ausgeführten Baukomplexes, dessen Dreiflügelanlage die Kirche zum Zentrum hat.

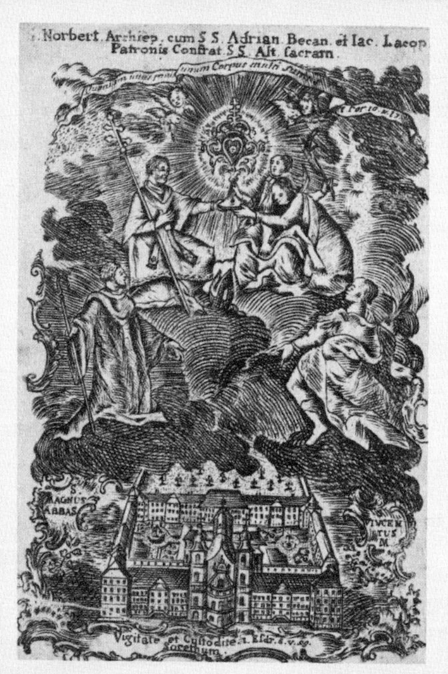

Idealised view of Schussenried Abbey on a Sakramentsbruderschaft admission form, c. 1760
Ideal map of the monastery of Schussenried, 1763

La bibliothèque de l'abbaye des Prémontrés
est englobée aujourd'hui dans un contexte
muséal. Née d'une donation privée en l'an 1183
et distinguée par un privilège impérial, l'abbaye
fut dirigée par les Prémontrés avec grand
succès. Après 600 ans d'existence, l'abbaye fut
dépossédée de ses biens en 1803. Elle représentait le centre géographique et spirituel du
territoire qui lui avait été imparti, territoire du
reste soumis à son entière juridiction à partir
de 1512. Les chanoines enseignaient quantité
de matières diverses à l'école monacale.
Certains d'entre eux étaient aussi musiciens
ou scientifiques. Cette palette de compétences
était facilitée par la bibliothèque – véritable
trésor du savoir à son époque – très bien
achalandée avec ses fonds variés comptant
vraisemblablement 15 000 volumes dans le
courant du XVIIIᵉ siècle. Ensuite, un orgue fut
inséré entre les rayonnages afin d'organiser des
concerts dans l'ambiance splendide de la bibliothèque. Le plafond que Franz Georg Hermann
(1692–1768) acheva de peindre en 1757 atteste
de la richesse littéraire de ce trésor, avec des
scènes allégoriques foisonnant de personnages
qui figurent la science et le savoir sous diverses
formes et laissent à tout un chacun le choix de
croire ou non à la révélation divine, au centre.
On distingue dans les groupes de personnages
quelques scientifiques de l'ordre des Prémontrés. Les sculptures de Fidel Sporer (1731–1811),
réparties dans toute la salle et réalisées entre
1764 et 1766, font aussi référence aux livres et à
leur contenu. Les figures de groupes symboli-
sant l'hérésie prennent la forme de putti sur la
balustrade et font face à la représentation des
Pères de l'Église et de la doctrine religieuse.
À peine quelques années après la suppression
du monastère, tandis que les bâtiments du
couvent revenaient au royaume de Wurtemberg, les fonds de la collection d'antan

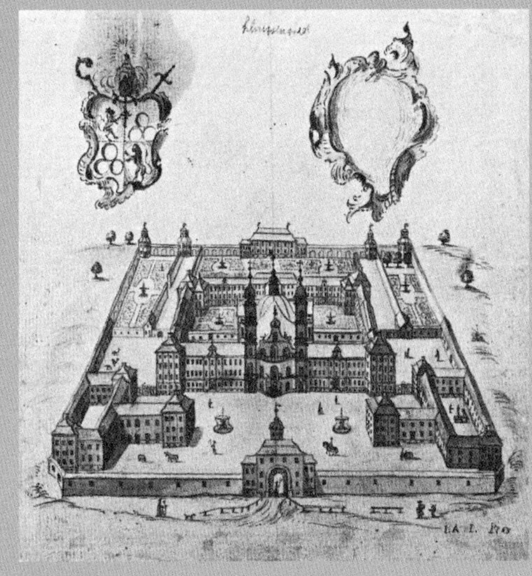

si célèbres disparurent en grande partie. Les
armoires, qui longent sur deux niveaux les murs
de la bibliothèque et dont l'ornementation
historique s'accorde harmonieusement avec le
code couleur de la salle, donnent une idée des
innombrables volumes qu'elles contenaient
auparavant. Grâce à leur apparence homogène,
les reliures peintes des volumes sont devenues
partie intégrante du décor qui transforme cette
pièce baignée de lumière et aux proportions
équilibrées en une salle de cérémonie haute-
ment représentative. Ornements rocaille, stucs,
fresques et ouvrages sculptés, tout contribue
à faire de la pièce un bijou artistique du genre.
Dominikus Zimmermann (1685–1766) conçut
la bibliothèque comme centre et noyau du
nouveau monastère dans les années 1754–1762.
Elle se trouve dans l'aile nord de l'ensemble
architectural, imaginé par le maître d'œuvre
Jakob Emele (1707–1780). Le projet qui devait
s'articuler autour de plusieurs cours ne fut
exécuté qu'au tiers, et l'église occupe désormais
le centre de l'ensemble à trois ailes.

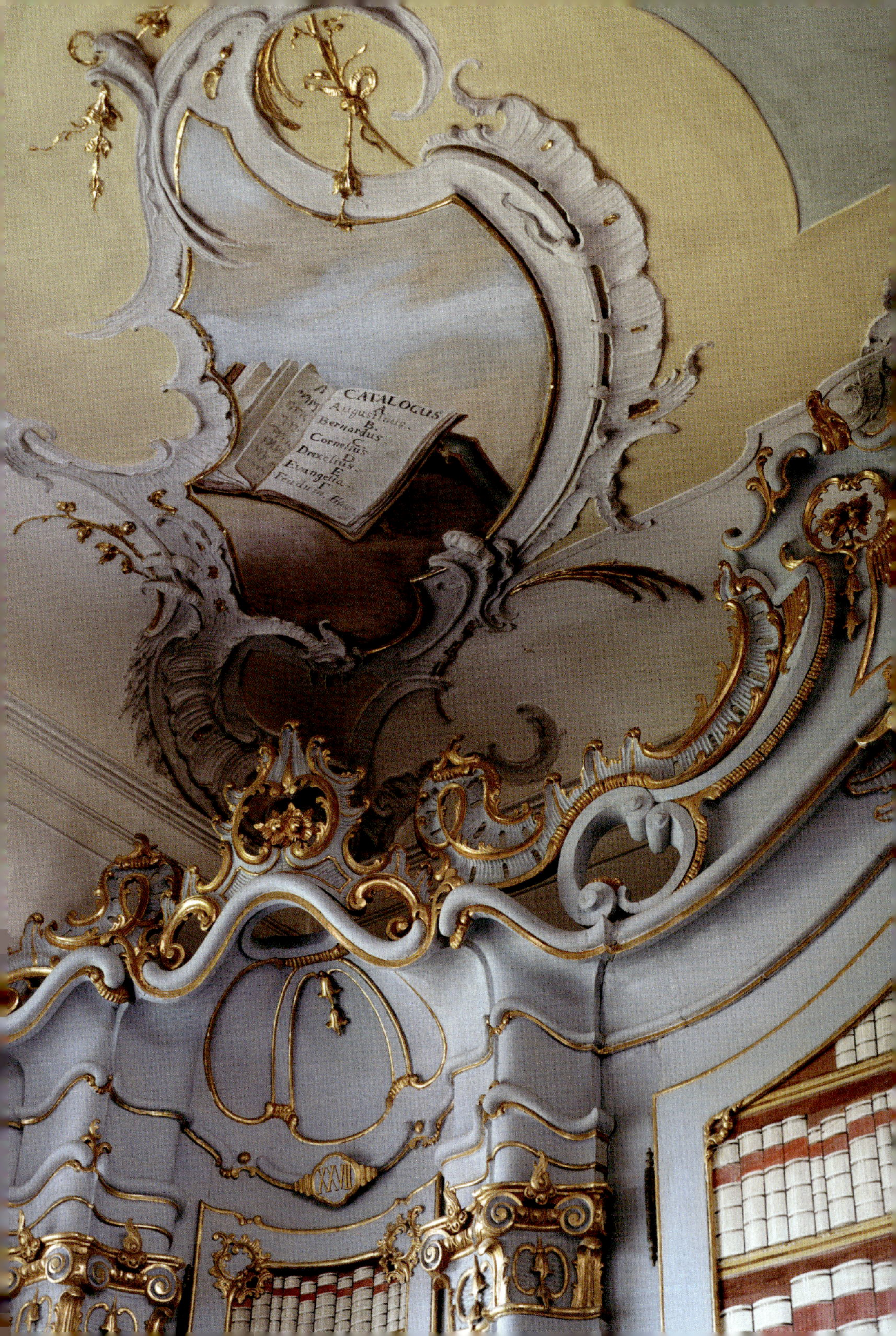

CATALOGUS
A.
Augustinus.
B.
Bernardus
C.
Cornelius
D.
Drexelius.
E.
Evangelia.
F.
Feuda m. Bav.

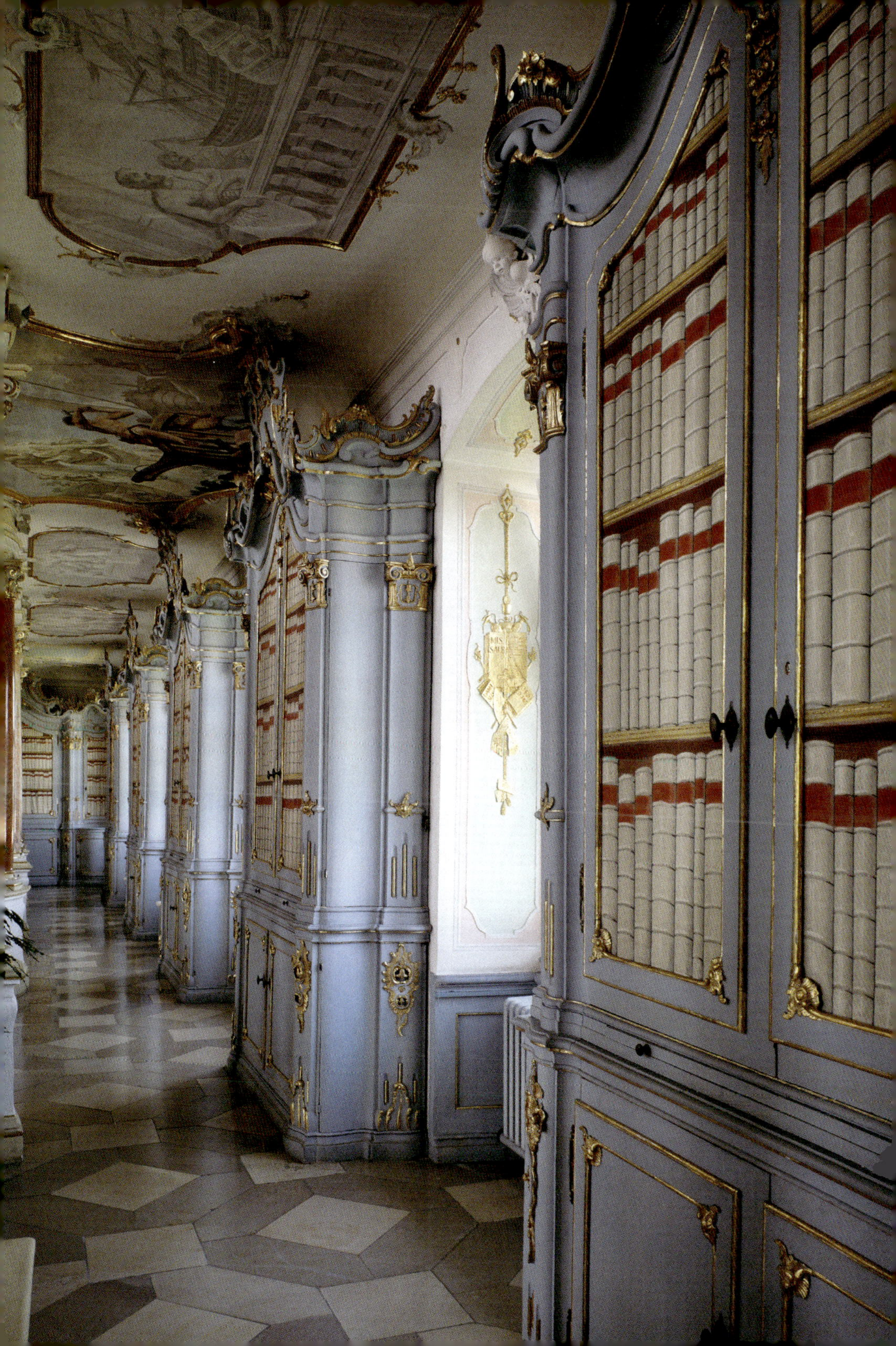

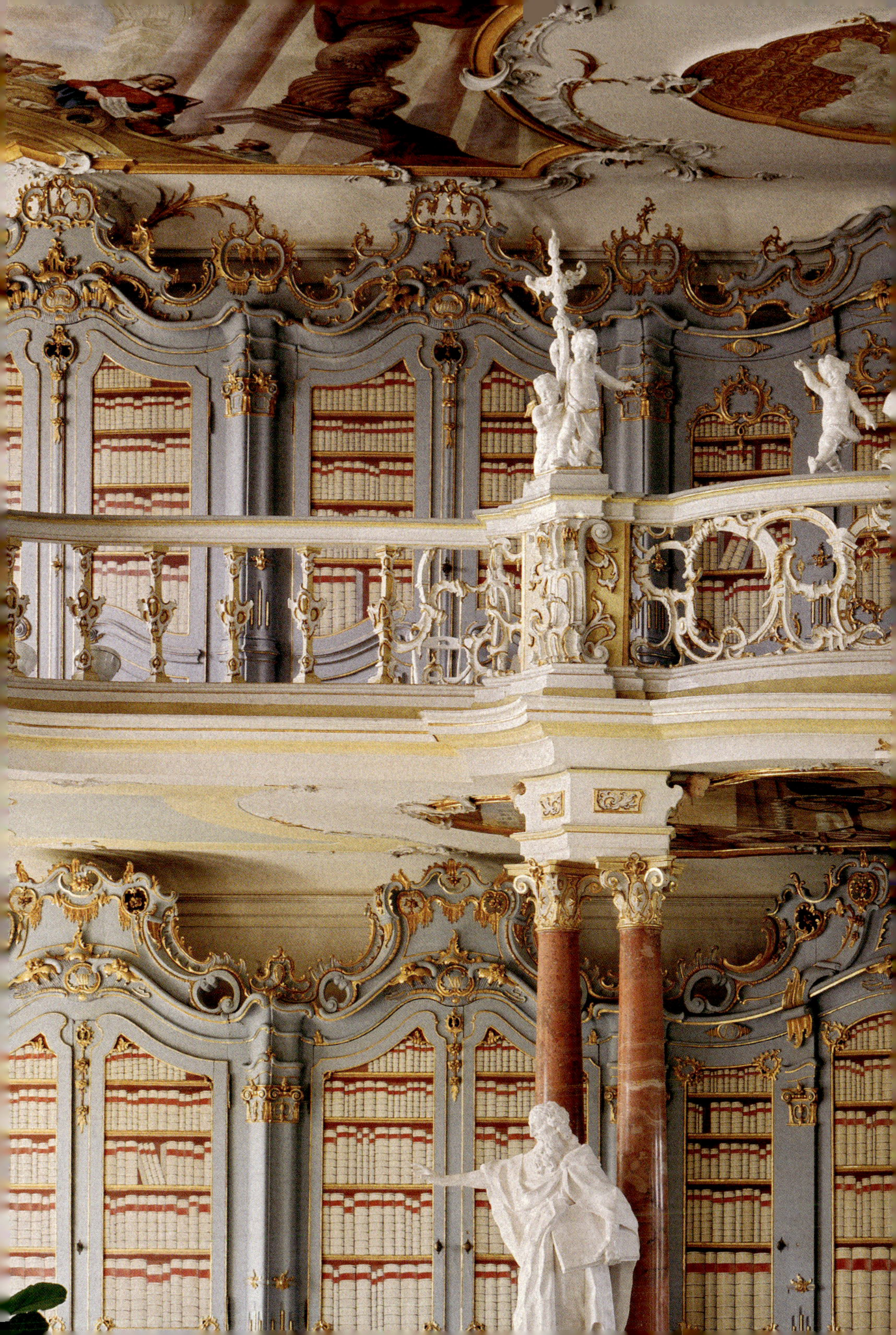

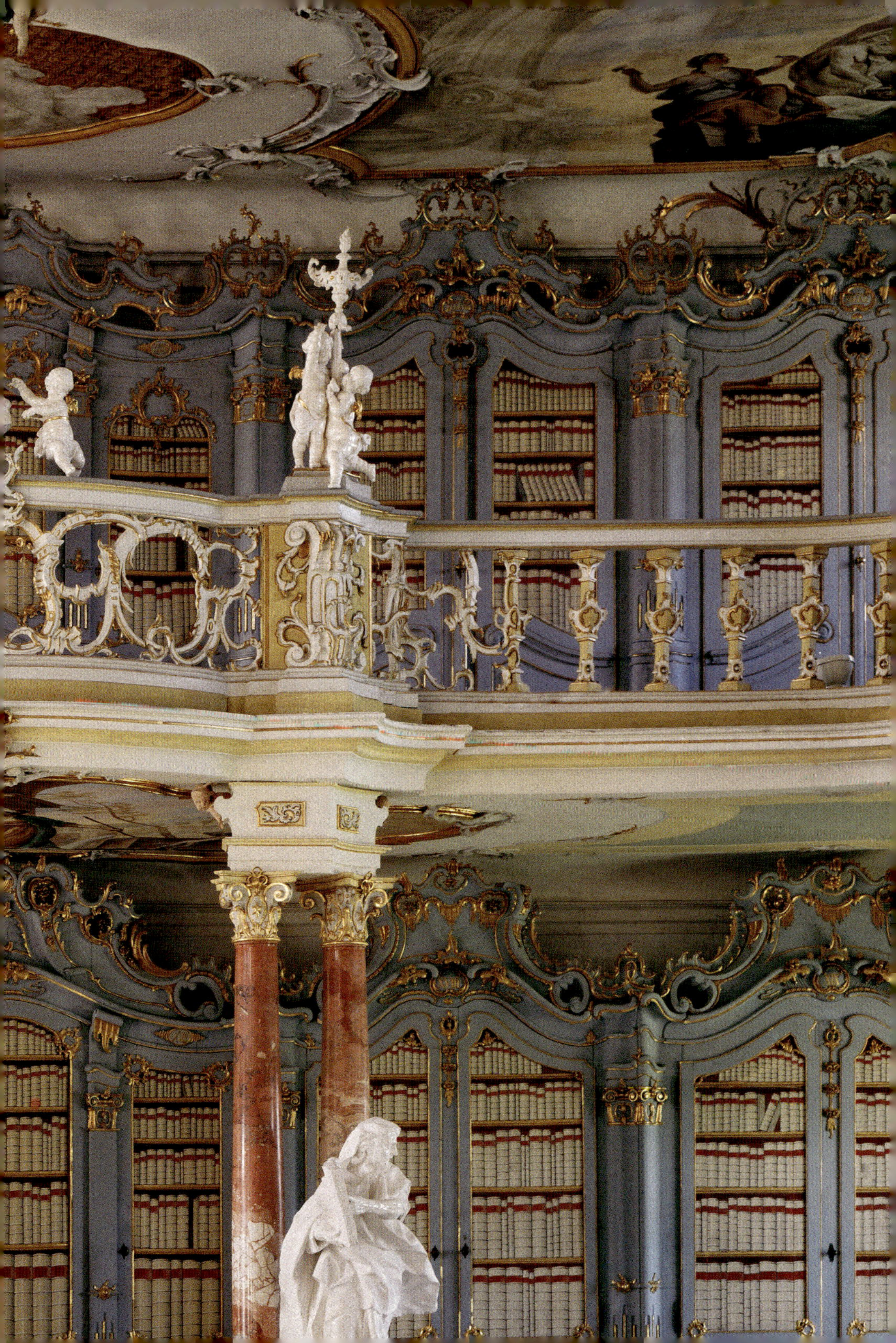

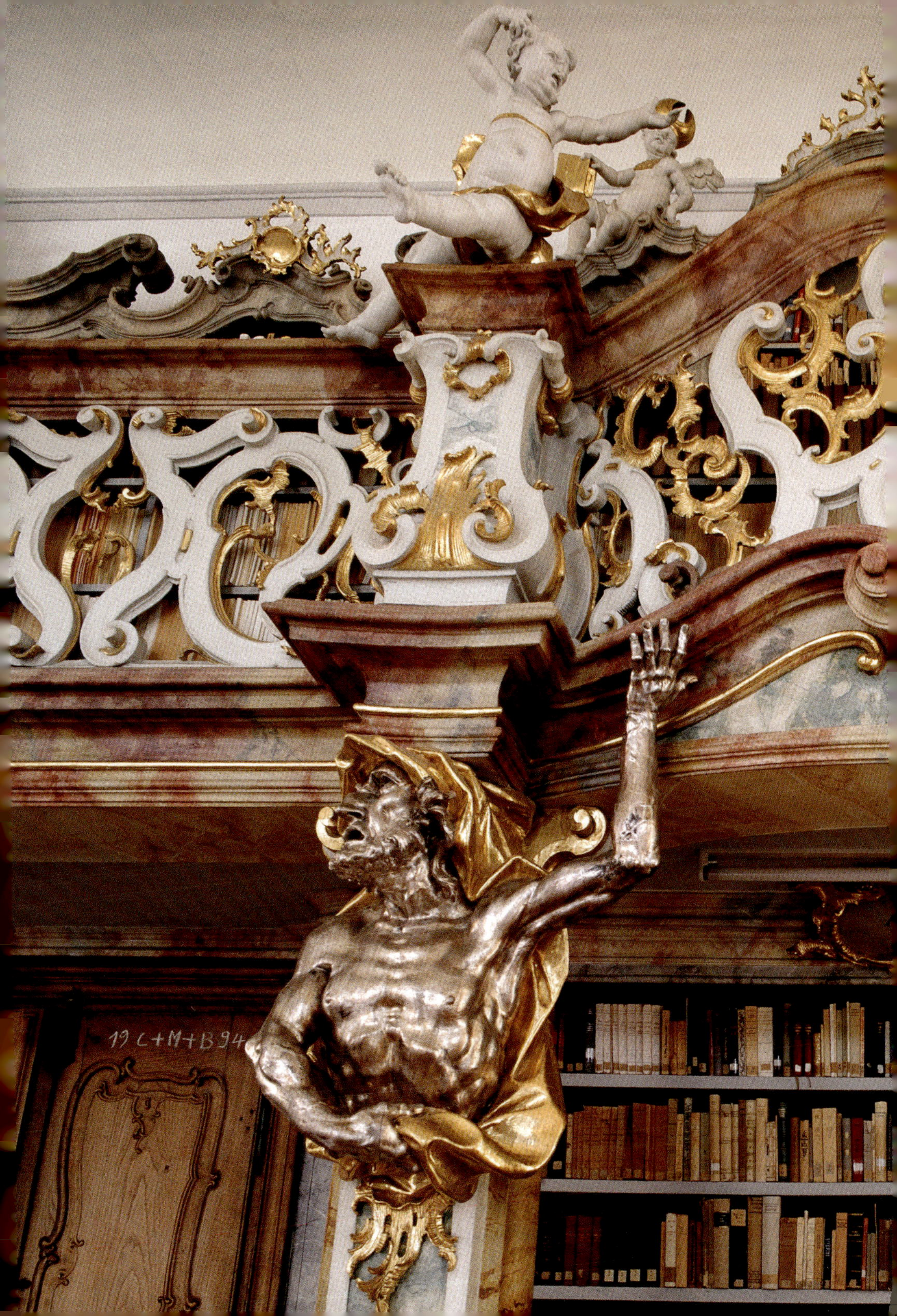

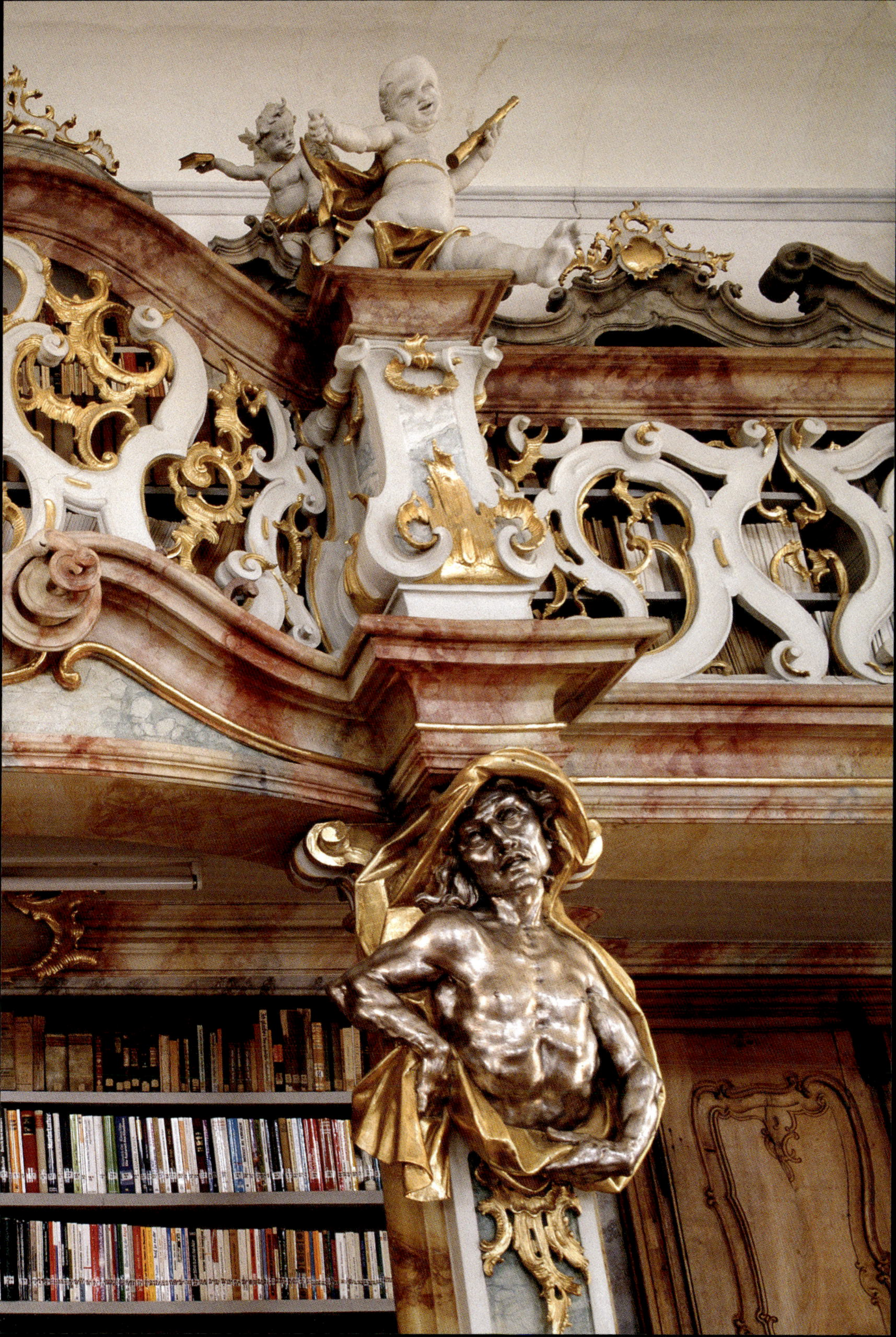

Klosterbibliothek Fürstenzell

Despite its eventful past, the library building of the former Cistercian abbey of Fürstenzell has come down to us as a magnificent testament to Rococo interior design. Its origins date back to the High Middle Ages, when the monastery was founded in 1274 by Cistercians from Aldersbach Abbey under the patronage of Duke Henry XIII of Lower Bavaria (1235–1290; hence the name Fürstenzell, meaning "prince's cell"). Since an important scriptorium was already flourishing at Aldersbach, we may assume that the monks brought this tradition with them to Fürstenzell. The Cistercians attached great importance to written culture and learning: for them, writing was the most important medium of the genesis and spread of their Order. Their religious buildings, which took Protestant as well as Catholic forms, subsequently developed in many cases into centres of education whose influence spread far beyond the monastic world. Cistercian libraries were a resource not just for novices in training, but also as a basis of missionary work and further instruction of the general populace, particularly since Cistercian abbeys were usually some distance from large conurbations. The secularisation of many monasteries in 1803 spelled an abrupt end to institutions that had been built up over centuries. Fürstenzell was among those sup-pressed: its collection of books was dispersed and the library room that had been completed only shortly beforehand was stripped of its function. Some of the holdings passed into the Bavarian Court Library, others to the University of Landshut, but the rest were lost. The books lining the historical shelves in the photographs are of more recent provenance, since after its dissolution the monastery passed into private

hands and from 1931 was occupied by Marist Fathers. In 2007 the building complex was bought by a commercial enterprise. The gener-ously proportioned library hall exudes the air of a Rococo ballroom with its pastel colours, lavish use of silver and gilt and magnificent woodcarv-ings. These are joined by expressive sculptures produced around 1765 by Joseph Deutschmann (1717–1787). The bookcases extend over two storeys, with access to the upper level via an airy balcony that runs all the way around the room and which is reached by two open-sided staircases. The balcony seems to be supported by twelve atlantes, the well-modelled busts of which contrast with the elegant rocaille motifs of their pilasters. The balustrade is composed of diaphanous rocaille ornament in white and gold, on top of which pairs of playful putti inject a lively note into the library with their energetic gestures. Referring to the subjects of the books below, they personify allegories of the arts and sciences, the elements, virtues and vices. Missing from the room today, following their removal in the 19th century, are the ceiling frescos by Matthäus Günther (1705–1788) and Johann Jakob Zeiller (1708–1783), which were painted at the same time as the rest of the inter-ior and complemented the library's artistic pro-gramme. The library room was created under Fürstenzell's penultimate abbot, Otto Prasser (1761–1792), as part of a renovation of the church and monastery in the palatial Baroque style.

❊⊹❊

Founded 1274; dispersed 1803;
library hall 1765 by Joseph Deutschmann
Type of library monastic library,
today preserved as a historical private interior

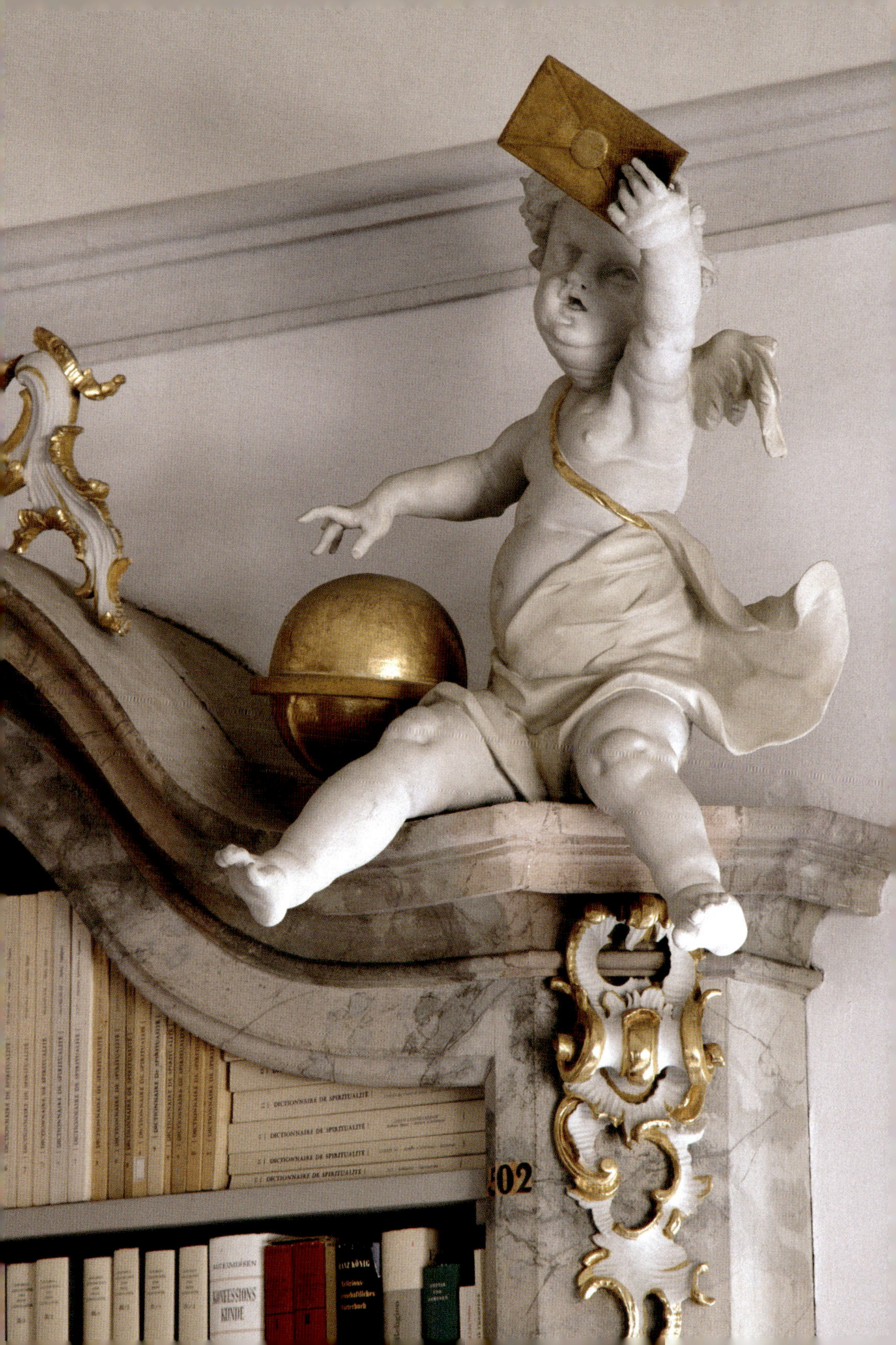

DICTIONNAIRE DE SPIRITUALITÉ
DICTIONNAIRE DE SPIRITUALITÉ
DICTIONNAIRE DE SPIRITUALITÉ
DICTIONNAIRE DE SPIRITUALITÉ
402
GOTTUMISSEN KONFESSIONS KUNDE
FRANZ KÖNIG Religionswissenschaftliches Wörterbuch

Die Bibliothek der ehemaligen Zisterzienserabtei Fürstenzell hat sich trotz ihrer wechselhaften Geschichte als prachtvoller Schauraum des Rokoko erhalten. Ihre Ursprünge reichen in das Hochmittelalter zurück, als Fürstenzell unter dem Schutz Herzog Heinrichs XIII. von Niederbayern (1235–1290) – auf den sich der Ortsname bezieht – im Jahr 1274 von Zisterziensern aus dem Kloster Aldersbach gegründet wurde. Da dort bereits ein bedeutendes Skriptorium bestand, ist anzunehmen, dass die Mönche diese Tradition auch auf ihr neues Kloster in Fürstenzell übertrugen. Zisterzienser pflegten die Schriftkultur und Gelehrsamkeit in ganz besonderer Weise, für sie bildete die Schrift das wichtigste Medium ihrer Genese und ihrer Behauptung. Ihre nicht nur katholischen, sondern auch protestantischen Klöster entwickelten sich in der Folge häufig zu Bildungszentren mit einem weit über die monastische Welt hinausstrahlenden Wirkungsbereich. Die Büchersammlungen der Zisterzienser dienten neben der Ausbildung der Novizen auch der Missionierung und Weiterbildung der Bevölkerung, und das umso mehr, als ihre Klöster meist abseits der großen Ballungszentren lagen. Die Säkularisierung zahlreicher Klöster im Jahr 1803 setzte vielen dieser über die Jahrhunderte aufgebauten Institutionen ein jähes Ende. So wurde auch mit der Aufhebung des Klosters Fürstenzell sein Buchbestand zerstreut, und der erst kurz zuvor eingerichtete Bibliothekssaal verlor seine Funktion. Teile der Bestände gelangten in die Bayerische Hofbibliothek, andere an die Universität Landshut, der Rest ist verloren. Die auf den Fotos in den historischen Regalen sichtbaren Bücher sind neuerer Provenienz, da das Kloster nach seiner Auflösung zunächst Privatbesitz war und ab 1931 von Maristenpatres bewohnt wurde. 2007 kam der Baukomplex in den Besitz einer Unternehmensgesellschaft. Als Festsaal des Rokoko wirkt der großzügig angelegte Bibliotheksraum durch seine pastelltonige Farbigkeit, die reichen Gold- und Silberfassungen sowie die prächtigen Schnitzwerke. Ihnen stellen sich ausdrucksstarke Skulpturen zur Seite, die Joseph Deutschmann (1717–1787) um 1765 geschaffen hat. Die über beide Geschosse reichenden Bücherschränke entlang der Wände werden durch eine luftige, rund um den Raum geführte Empore erschlossen, auf die man über zwei Freitreppen gelangt. Sie ruht scheinbar auf zwölf Hermenpilastern, deren expressive Büsten mit der Eleganz der Rocaillemotive kontrastieren. Diaphanes Rocailleornament in Weiß und Gold bildet die Balustrade, auf der Puttenpaare im Spiel mit ihren raumgreifenden Gesten die Bibliothek beleben. Unter Hinweis auf die Themen der Bücher verkörpern sie Allegorien der Wissenschaften und der Künste, der Elemente sowie der Tugenden und Laster. Es fehlen die zeitgleich mit der übrigen Ausstattung entstandenen und im 19. Jahrhundert zerstörten Deckenfresken von Matthäus Günther und Johann Jakob Zeiller, die den Raum ehemals künstlerisch und inhaltlich vervollständigten. Der Erneuerung der Bibliothek stellte sich jene von Kirche und Konvent zur Seite, der unter dem vorletzten Abt des Klosters, Otto Prasser (1761–1792), barocken Residenzcharakter erhielt.

❊ ❊ ❊

Malgré son histoire mouvementée, la bibliothèque de l'ancienne abbaye cistercienne de Fürstenzell a conservé sa splendeur rococo. Ses origines remontent à l'époque médiévale. Elle fut fondée par des Cisterciens du monastère d'Aldersbach en 1274, sous les auspices du duc de Basse-Bavière Henri XIII (1235–1290) – à qui la localité doit le nom de « Fürstenzell » (« cellule du prince »). Comme un *scriptorium* se trouvait déjà sur place, il est à supposer que les moines ont perpétué leur tradition dans le nouveau monastère. Aux yeux des Cisterciens, l'érudition et la culture écrite témoignent de leur vocation première. De ce fait, leurs couvents, catholiques aussi bien que protestants, devenaient souvent des centres de formation dont l'influence et le rayonnement se ressentaient bien au-delà du monde monacal. Les Cisterciens utilisaient leurs collections de livres pour former les novices, ainsi que pour évangéliser et

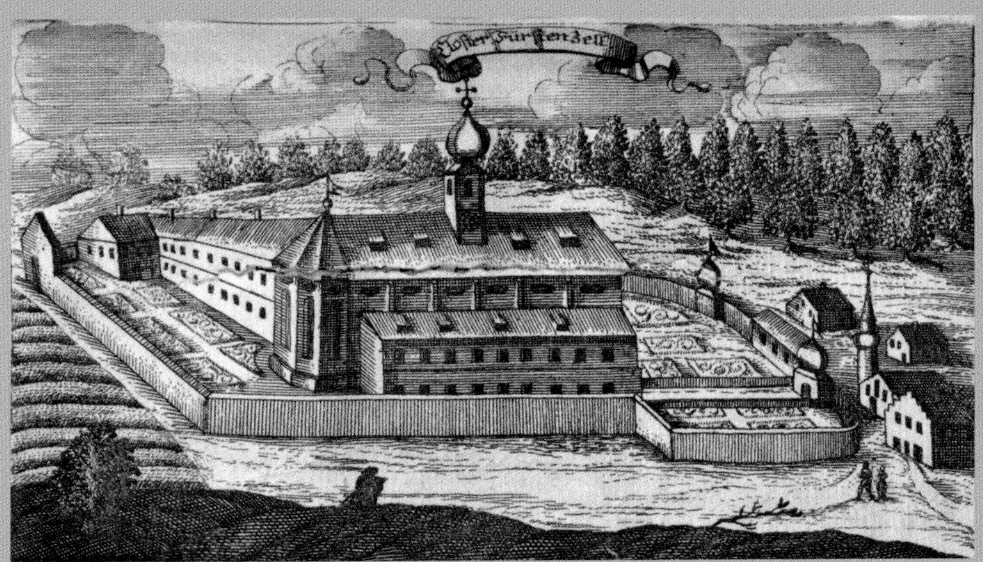

instruire la population, et ce, d'autant plus que leurs filiales se situaient souvent à l'écart des grandes villes. La sécularisation d'innombrables monastères en 1803 mit fin à bon nombre de ces institutions construites au fil des siècles. C'est ainsi que le fonds de Fürstenzell fut dispersé lors de la suppression de l'abbaye et que la bibliothèque complétée peu avant perdit sa fonction. Une partie des ouvrages arriva à la bibliothèque de la cour de Bavière, d'autres atterrirent à l'université de Landshut, le reste est perdu. Les livres visibles sur les étagères d'origine sont plus récents, déposés par des occupants ultérieurs. Juste après sa suppression, le monastère devint propriété privée avant d'être habité par des pères maristes à partir de 1931. Depuis 2007, l'ensemble architectural est la propriété d'une entreprise privée. Avec ses tons et marbrures pastel, ses applications d'or et d'argent et ses splendides ouvrages sculptés, la bibliothèque au décor opulent a maintenu l'effet d'un chef-d'œuvre rococo. Elle est flanquée d'impressionnantes sculptures réalisées vers 1765 par Joseph Deutschmann (1717–1787). Les rayonnages ornant les murs sur deux niveaux sont agrémentés d'une galerie spacieuse et circulaire, accessible par deux escaliers ouverts. Elle semble reposer sur douze atlantes dont les bustes expressifs contrastent avec l'élégance des motifs rocaille. La balustrade aux ornements rocaille blanc et or ajourés est surmontée de couples de putti qui animent la pièce avec leurs gestes emphatiques. En se référant au thème des livres, ces putti incarnent des allégories des sciences et des arts et les vertus et les vices. Peints par Matthäus Günther et Johann Jakob Zeiller, les plafonds qui couronnaient la pièce d'un point de vue artistique et intellectuel ont disparu. Réalisées en même temps que le reste du décor, ces fresques ont été détruites au XIXe siècle. L'église et le couvent ont contribué à la rénovation de la bibliothèque, qui prit une allure de résidence baroque sous l'avant-dernier abbé Otto Prasser (1761–1792).

Johann Ulrich Kraus, *Abbey Fürstenzell*,
in: Anton Wilhelm Ertl, *Chur-Baierischer Atlantis. Zweyter Theil*, Nuremberg, 1690, pl. 26

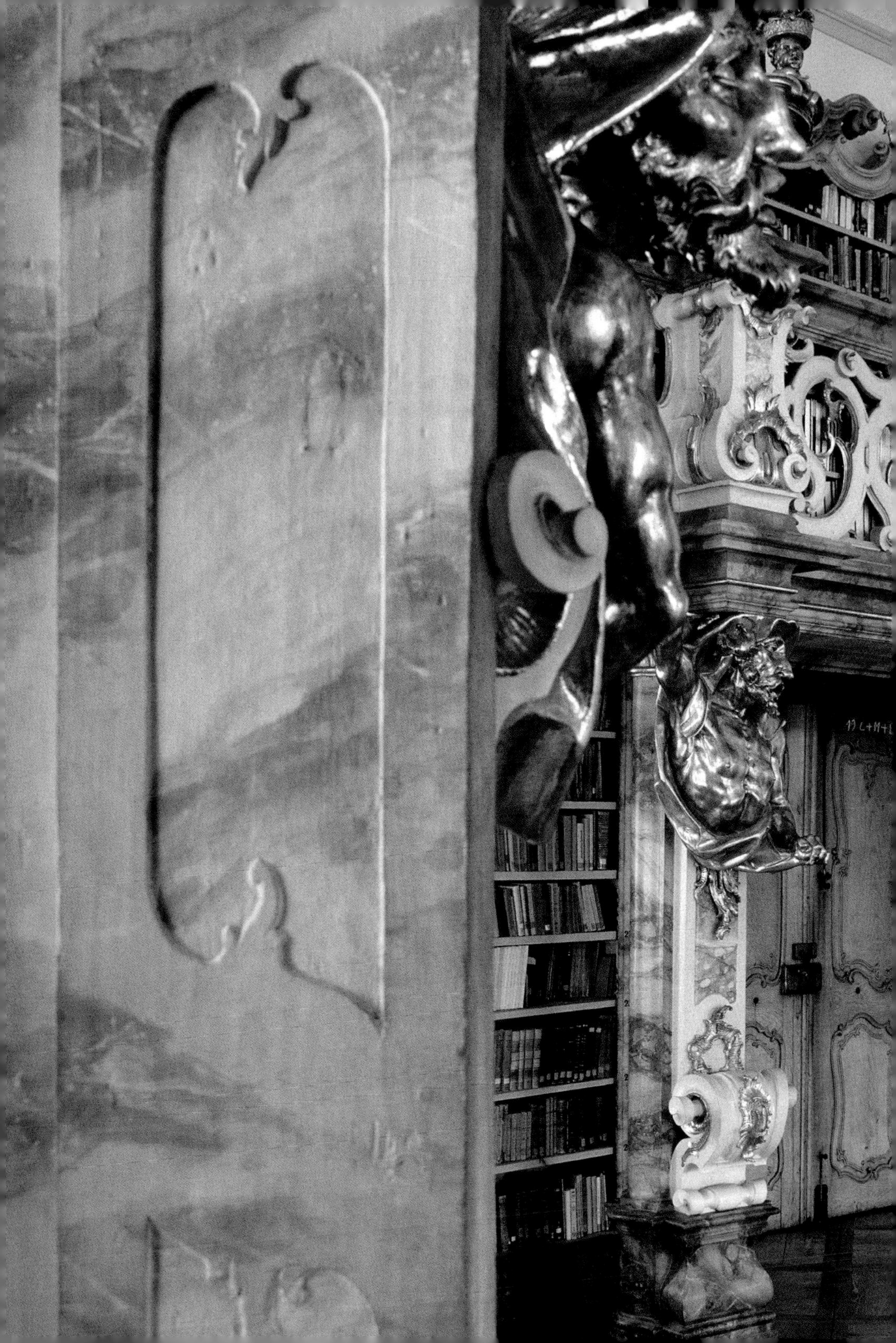

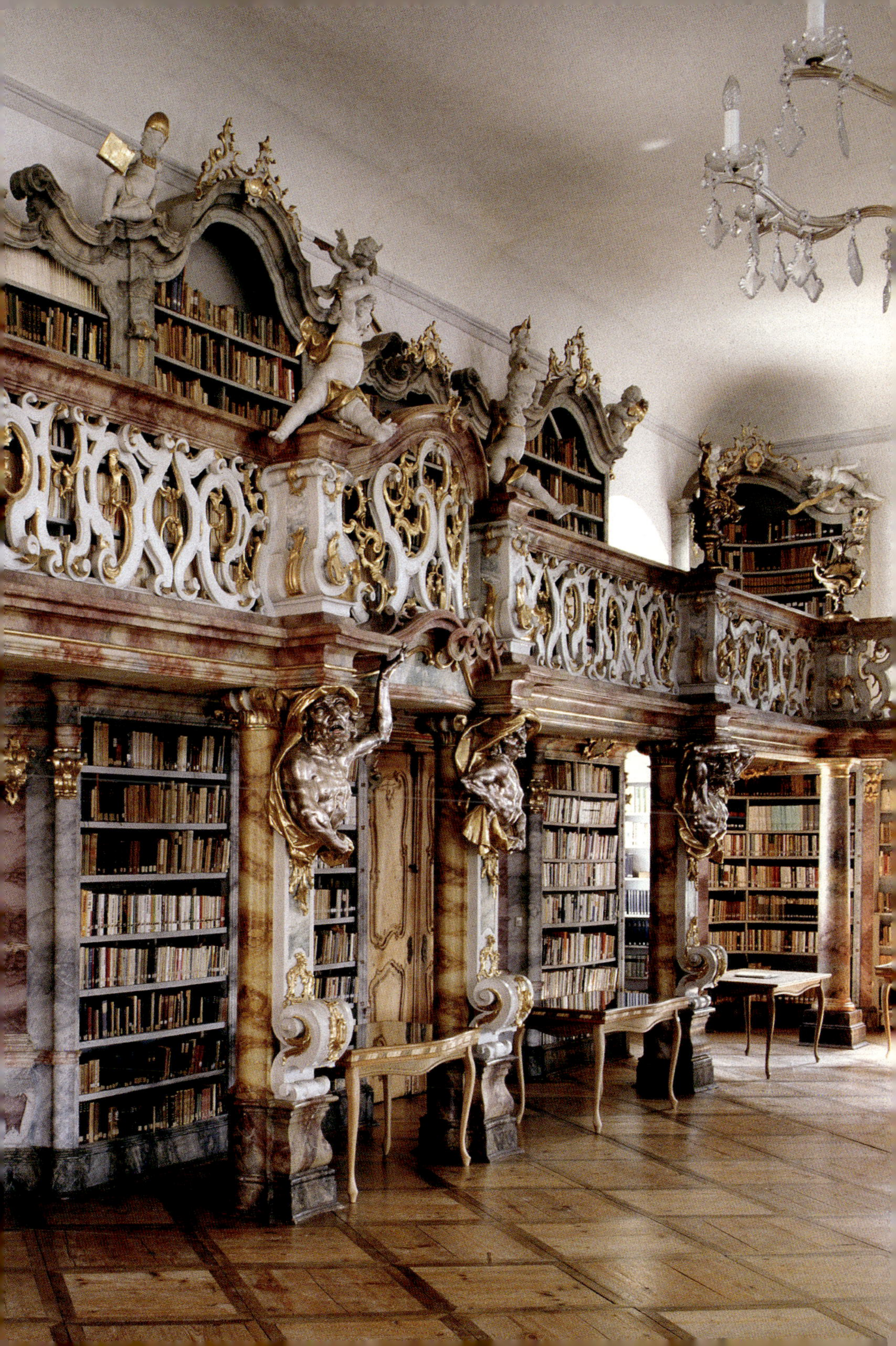

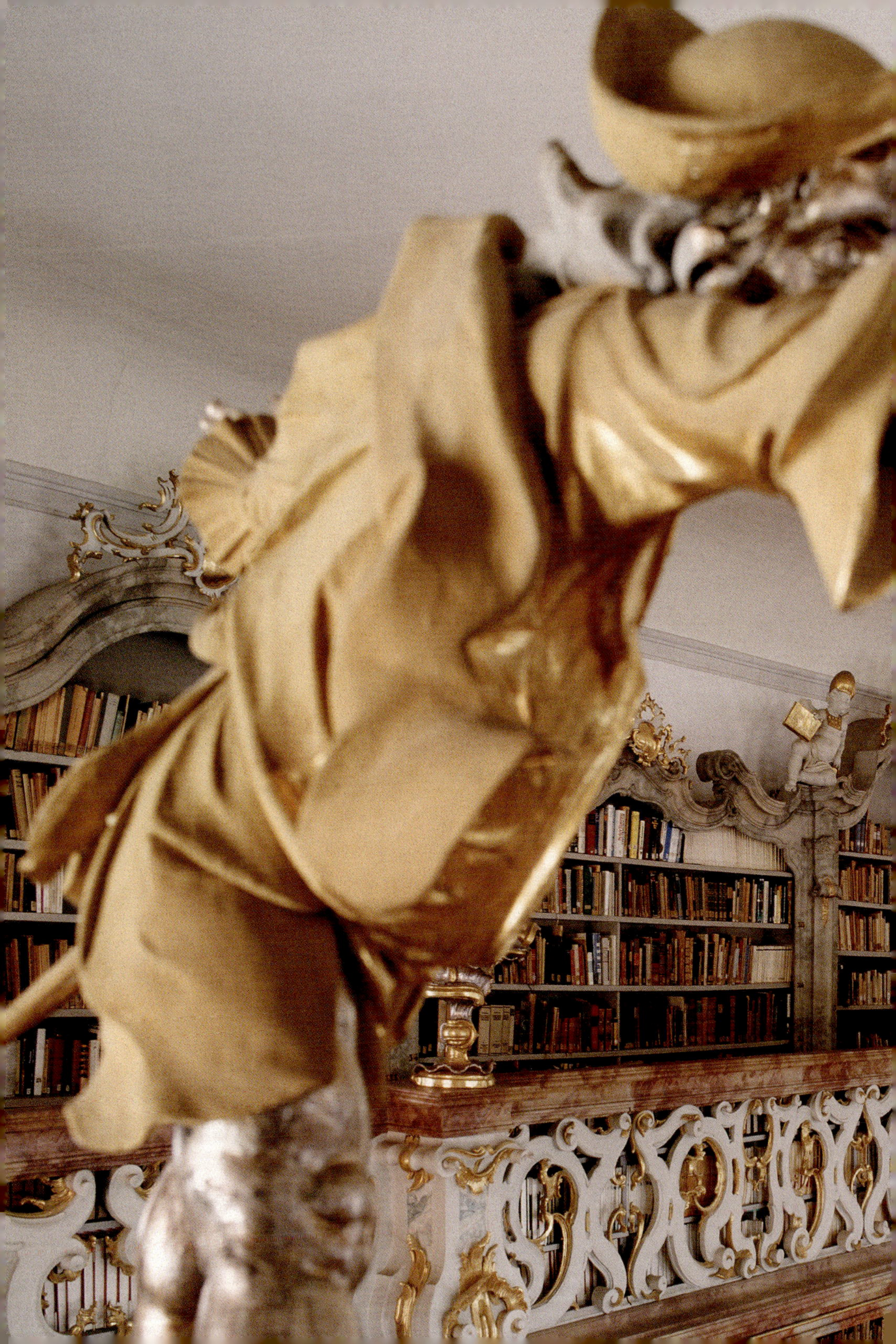

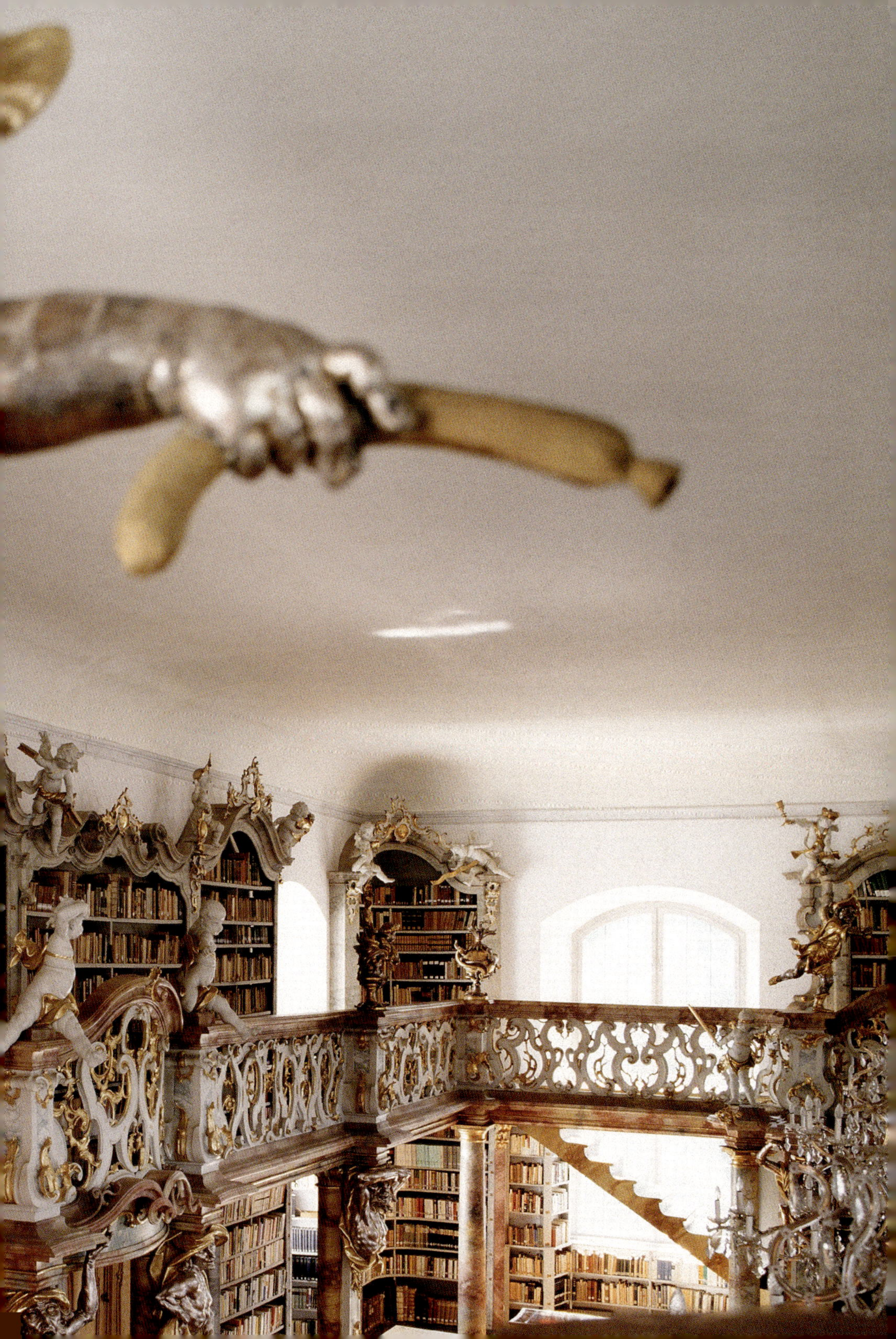

Stiftsbibliothek Sankt Gallen

The Rococo library in the former Abbey of St Gallen is described as a "sanctuary of the soul", ΨΥΧΗΣ ΙΑΤΡΕΙΟΝ, in the Greek inscription in a cartouche above its entrance. Together with the church, it lay at the spiritual heart of one of the most important and scholarly monasteries in western Europe. The abbey's first economic, religious and spiritual flowering began in the 9th century. The instructions laid down by Benedict of Nursia (c. 480–547) in the Rule of the Order he founded, namely that the monks should be employed at certain times in devout reading, were observed at St Gallen for almost 1,100 years. Founded in 612 by the Irish monk Gallus (c. 550–640), from 747 the abbey followed the Rule of St Benedict, which required the contemplative study of religious texts. There is no documentary evidence that the original Merovingian monastery contained a library, but much to suggest that it housed a scriptorium, and it is therefore probable that these two rooms were housed in the same building from the Carolingian era onwards. This is suggested by the architectural plan of the convent, drawn up around 819 at the request of Abbot Gozbert (r. 816–837) and still housed in the library today, which reproduces the ideal appearance of a monastery in the Carolingian era. The plan shows the library and scriptorium occupying a two-storey building situated directly beside the apse and transept of the new abbey church built under the same Abbot Gozbert. Around the middle of the 9th century, 426 titles, arranged by general subject, were already available for consultation in this library. Today's library arose as part of the Baroque remodelling of the abbey under Abbot Cölestin Gugger von Staudach (1701–1767), which involved the sacrifice of the large Renaissance library. Located in the west wing of the quadrangle, the magnificent new library aptly testifies to the superior status of an imperial abbey and provides a fitting home for its treasury of books and manuscripts. Built by Peter Thumb (1681–1766) between 1758 and 1767, the interior is indebted to the tradition of the pilaster hall developed by Vorarlberg architects in the Baroque era, but is lent contemporary new accents in its decoration. The stucco work carried out by masters of the Wessobrunn School is characterised by its Rococo ornament, whilst the richly decorated bookcases advance and recede in a sinuous line along the sides of the room and extend upwards through two storeys, completely concealing the rising walls. The value and influence of the various texts are thematised in the ceiling paintings: the central fields are devoted to the first four ecumenical councils and are accompanied by portraits of the Church Fathers in subsidiary fields, while the fund of knowledge residing in the library finds expression in allegories of the sciences, executed in grisaille. In 1983 the library was added to the UNESCO World Heritage list.

* * *

Founded 612; Benedictine monastery from 747; royal abbey until 1805; library built 1758–1767 by Peter Thumb
Holdings c. 170,000 volumes
Type of library originally a monastic library, today a public reference library
Highlights *Carolingian Plan of the Convent*, Reichenau/St Gallen, 819 or c. 827/830 (Cod. Sang. 1092); *Folchart-Psalter (Psalterium Gallicanum with Cantica)*, St Gallen, 872–883 (Cod. Sang. 23); *Codex sangallensis 857* (collection of Middle High German epic and chivalric poems, including the important Manuscript B version of the *Nibelungenlied*), 13th century (Cod. Sang. 857)

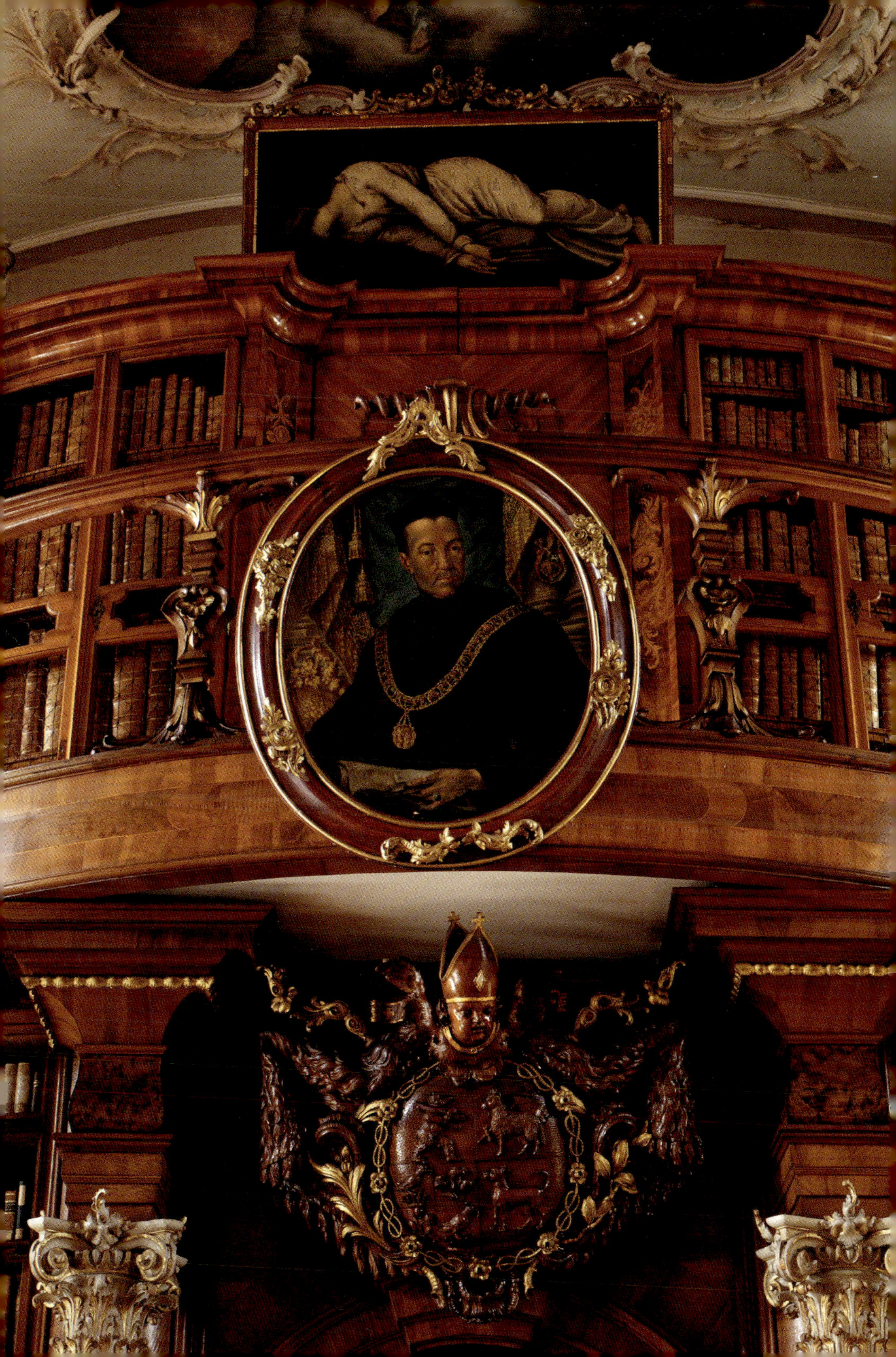

Als „Heilstätte der Seele", ΨΥΧΗΣ ΙΑΤΡΕΙΟΝ, wird die Rokokobibliothek der ehemaligen Fürstabtei Sankt Gallen in einer über deren Eingangsportal angebrachten Kartusche bezeichnet. Neben der Kirche war sie das ideelle Zentrum eines der bedeutendsten und gelehrtesten Klöster des Abendlandes, das seine erste wirtschaftliche, religiöse und geistige Blüte im 9. Jahrhundert erlebte. Hier wurde nahezu 1100 Jahre lang eingelöst, was Benedikt von Nursia (um 480–547) der von ihm gegründeten Ordensgemeinschaft zur Regel gemacht hatte, nämlich „zu bestimmten Stunden mit heiliger Lesung beschäftigt zu sein". Seit dem Jahr 747 befolgte das vom irischen Mönch Gallus (um 550–640) 612 gegründete Kloster Sankt Gallen die Benediktsregel, die ein kontemplatives Bücherstudium vorsieht. Da kein Bücherraum für die merowingische Gründung, sehr wohl aber ein Skriptorium nachweisbar ist, waren diese beiden Räume seit karolingischer Zeit wahrscheinlich gemeinsam in einem eigenen Gebäude untergebracht. Das legt der um 819 im Auftrag des Sankt Galler Abtes Gozbert (reg. 816–837) entstandene und noch heute in der Stiftsbibliothek aufbewahrte Klosterplan nahe, der das Aussehen eines idealen Klosters zur Karolingerzeit wiedergibt. Bibliothek und Skriptorium sind in einem zweistöckigen Raumensemble verzeichnet, das direkt an Apsis und Querhaus der damals ebenfalls von Abt Gozbert errichteten Abteikirche anschließt. In dieser Bibliothek waren um die Mitte des 9. Jahrhunderts bereits 426 Titel nach Fachgebieten geordnet greifbar. Anstelle der großen Renaissancebibliothek, die dem Neubau geopfert wurde, ließ Fürstabt Cölestin Gugger von Staudach (1701–1767) im Westflügel des Klostergevierts den heutigen Bibliothekssaal errichten. Es entstand ein Raum mit hohem, einer Reichsabtei adäquatem Repräsentationswert, der darüber hinaus für deren Handschriften- und Bücherschatz eine angemessene Aufbewahrungsstätte ist. Im Raumtypus ist die von Peter Thumb (1681–1766) in den Jahren 1758 bis 1767 erbaute Wandpfeilerhalle einer von Vorarlberger Barockbaumeistern entwickelten Tradition verpflichtet, die in der Ausstattung zeitgemäß neue Akzente erhielt. Die von Meistern der Wessobrunner Schule ausgeführte Stuckdekoration ist von Rokokoornamenten geprägt. Die reich dekorierten Bücherschränke überziehen in konvex-konkaven Schwingungen über zwei Geschosse reichend das gesamte aufgehende Mauerwerk. Wert und Wirkung der Schriftquellen sind in den Deckenbildern thematisiert. Den zentralen Darstellungen der vier ersten ökumenischen Konzile sind jene der Kirchenväter beigeordnet, während das der Bibliothek innewohnende Wissen in den Grisaillemalereien mit Allegorien der Wissenschaften Ausdruck findet. 1983 wurde die Bibliothek in das Weltkulturerbe der UNESCO aufgenommen.

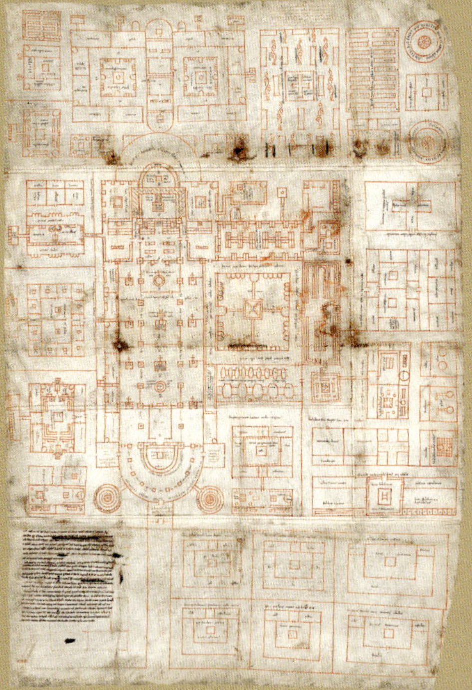

Plan of St Gallen monastery,
Reichenau/St Gallen, 819 or c. 827/830,
sig. Cod. Sang. 1092

Johann Hädener, *The monastery of St Gallen after his new building*, c. 1790

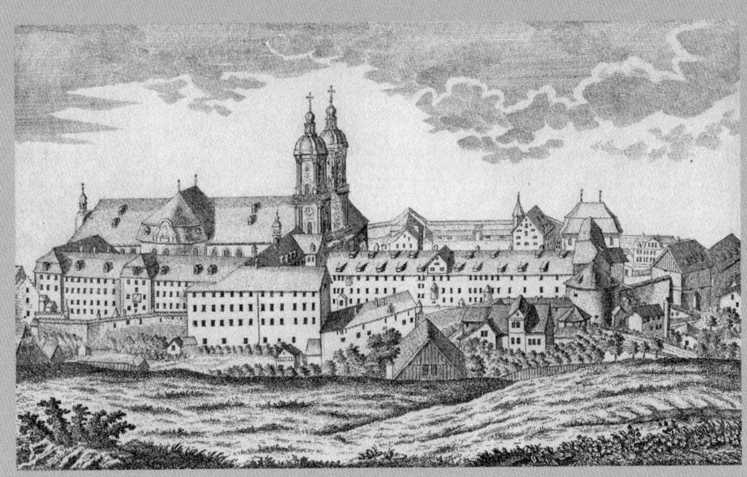

D'après l'inscription située au-dessus de la porte d'entrée « ΨΥΧΗΣ ΙΑΤΡΕΙΟΝ », la bibliothèque rococo de l'ancien couvent de Saint-Gall se veut comme une pharmacie de l'âme. Outre l'église, la bibliothèque était le noyau spirituel de l'un des couvents les plus importants et les plus doctes d'Occident. Ce couvent connut son premier essor économique, religieux et spirituel au IXe siècle. C'est là que fut honorée, pendant plus d'un millénaire, une prescription qui fit la règle de l'ordre fondé par Benoît de Nursie (vers 480–547), à savoir « consacrer certaines heures [...] à la lecture des choses divines ». Depuis l'an 747, le couvent Saint-Gall, fondé par un moine irlandais prénommé Gallus (vers 550–640) en 612, suivait la règle de saint Benoît qui recommande une étude contemplative des livres. L'existence d'un *scriptorium* est attestée dès la fondation mérovingienne, mais il ne reste aucune trace d'un magasin des livres. Il semblerait donc qu'à l'époque carolingienne les deux salles aient été rassemblées en un bâtiment à part. C'est ce que laisse supposer le plan de Saint-Gall, indicateur de l'idéal monastique du temps des Carolingiens. Toujours conservé dans la bibliothèque de l'abbaye actuelle, il fut commandé vers 819 par Gozbert (abbé de Saint-Gall de 816 à 837). La bibliothèque et le *scriptorium* sont indiqués sur un édifice à deux niveaux dans le prolongement direct de l'abside et du transept de l'église abbatiale également commandée par l'abbé Gozbert. Dans le courant du IXe siècle, cette bibliothèque disposait déjà de 426 ouvrages répartis par thèmes. Sacrifiant la vaste bibliothèque Renaissance, le prince-abbé Célestin Gugger de Staudach (1701–1767) fit ériger une nouvelle bibliothèque dans l'aile ouest du monastère. Sa salle devint alors un haut-lieu de conservation de manuscrits et de trésors littéraires, digne de cette abbaye impériale. Dans la réalisation, qui s'étend de 1758 à 1767, du hall à piliers et colonnes engagées, Peter Thumb (1681–1766) reste fidèle à la tradition développée par les maîtres de l'art baroque vorarlbergeois, tout en insérant des accents contemporains. Le décor exécuté par les maîtres-stucateurs de l'école de Wessobrunn est dans le goût rococo. Les corps de bibliothèque richement ornés occupent toute la surface offerte par les parois dont l'élan concave-convexe est conservé sur les deux niveaux. Les fresques du plafond thématisent l'importance et l'effet des sources de l'écriture. Les représentations centrales figurant les quatre premiers conciles œcuméniques sont attribuées aux Pères de l'Église, tandis que le savoir inhérent à la bibliothèque est exprimé en grisaille sous forme d'allégories. L'UNESCO a porté cette bibliothèque sur la liste du patrimoine mondial en 1983.

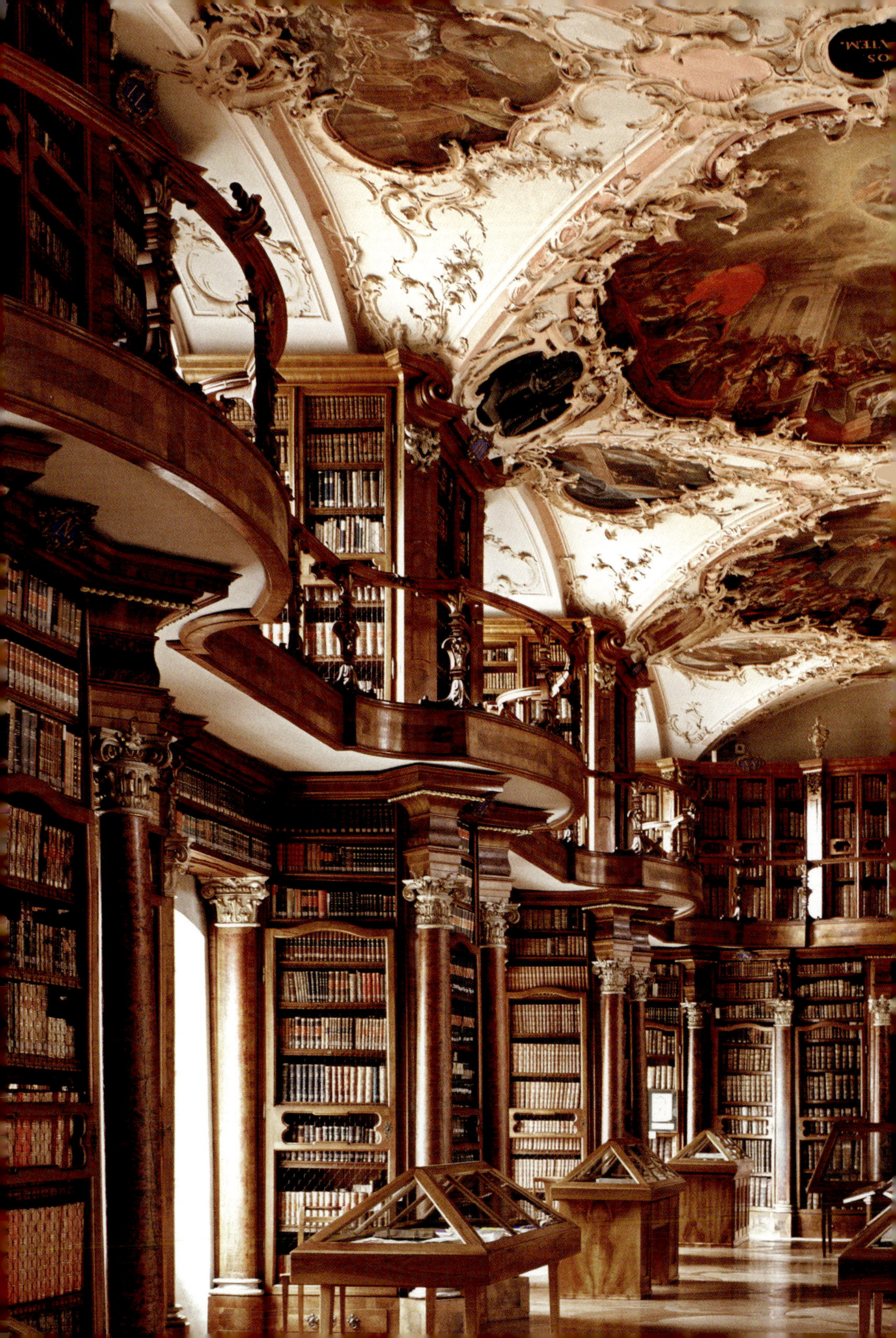

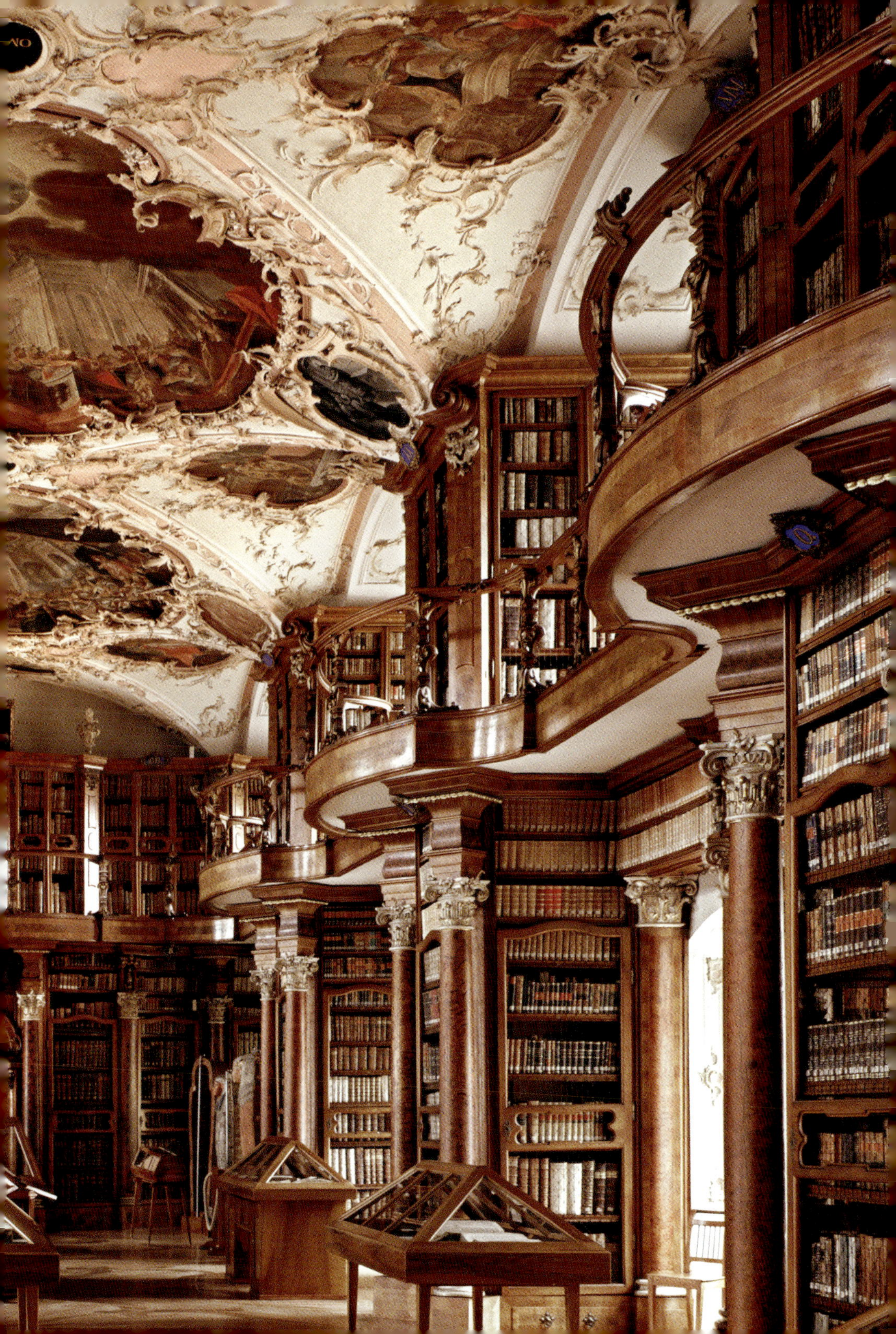

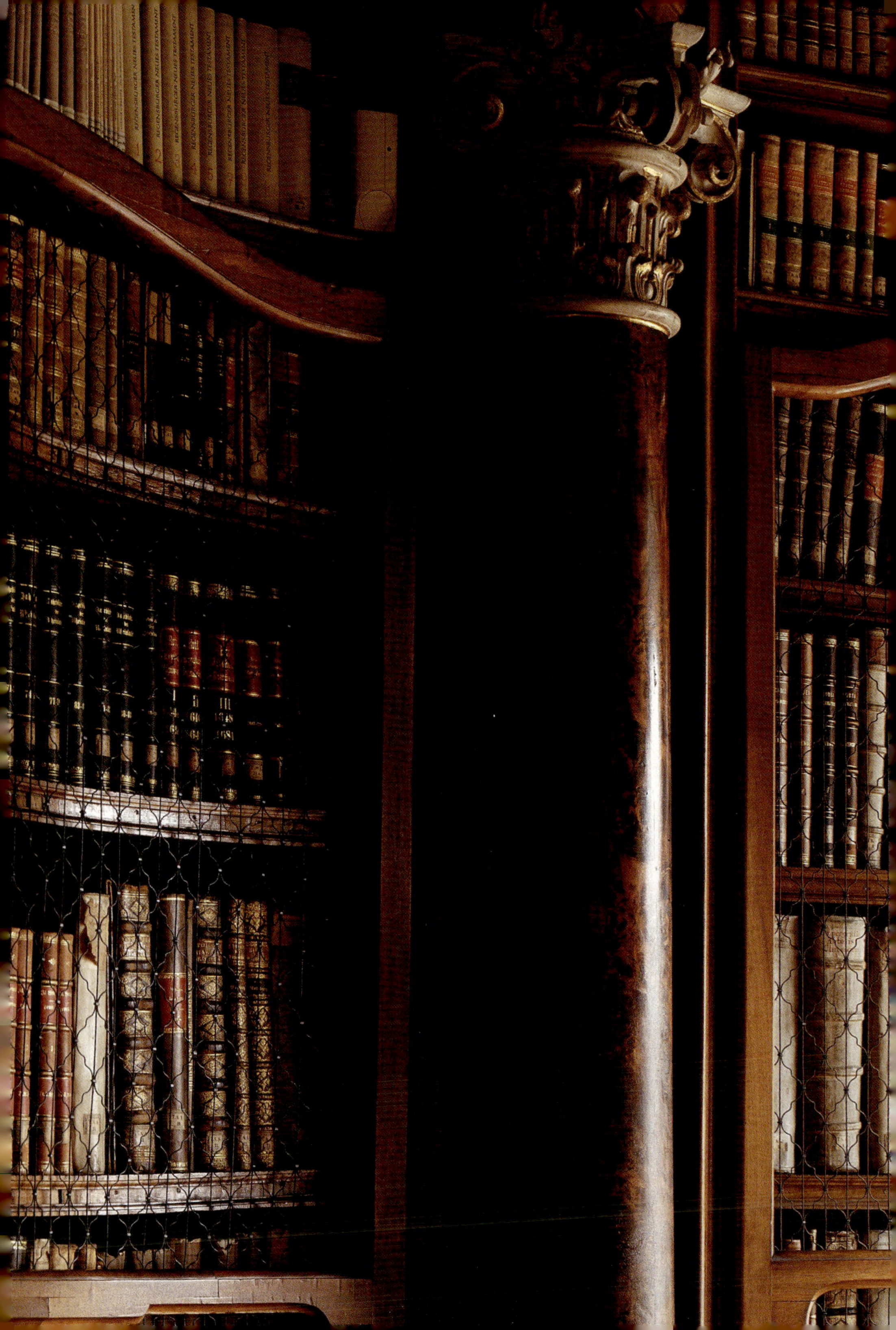

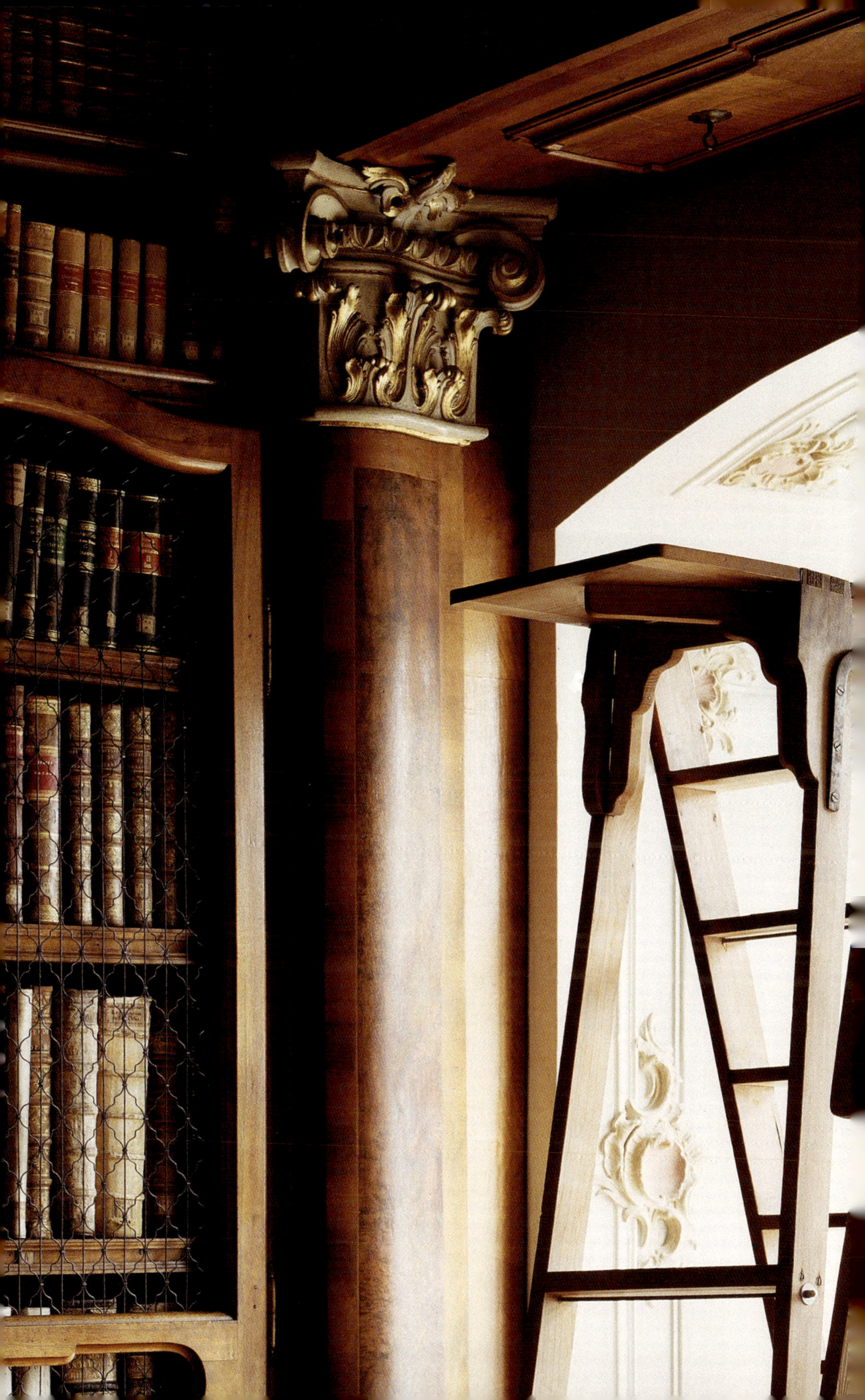

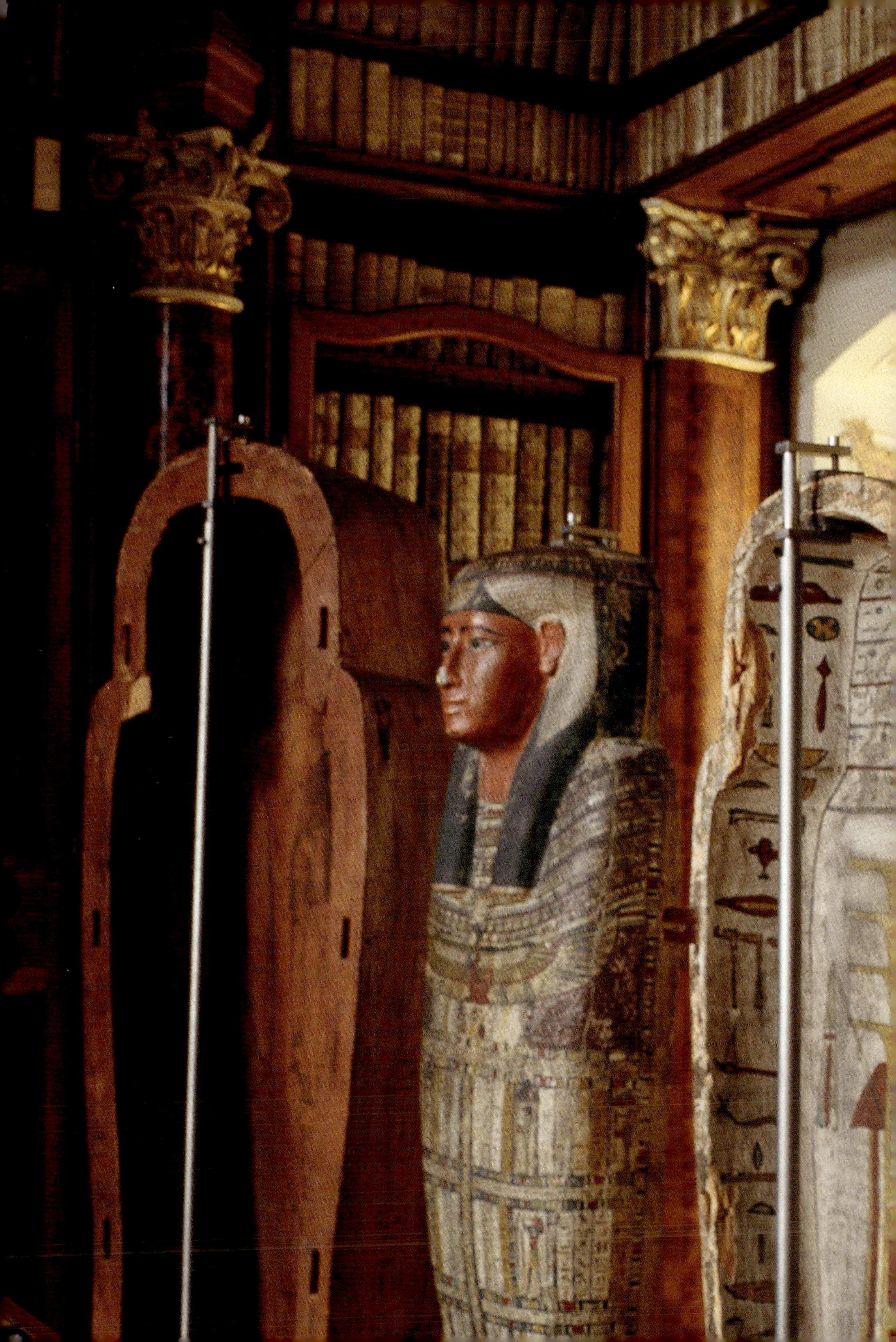

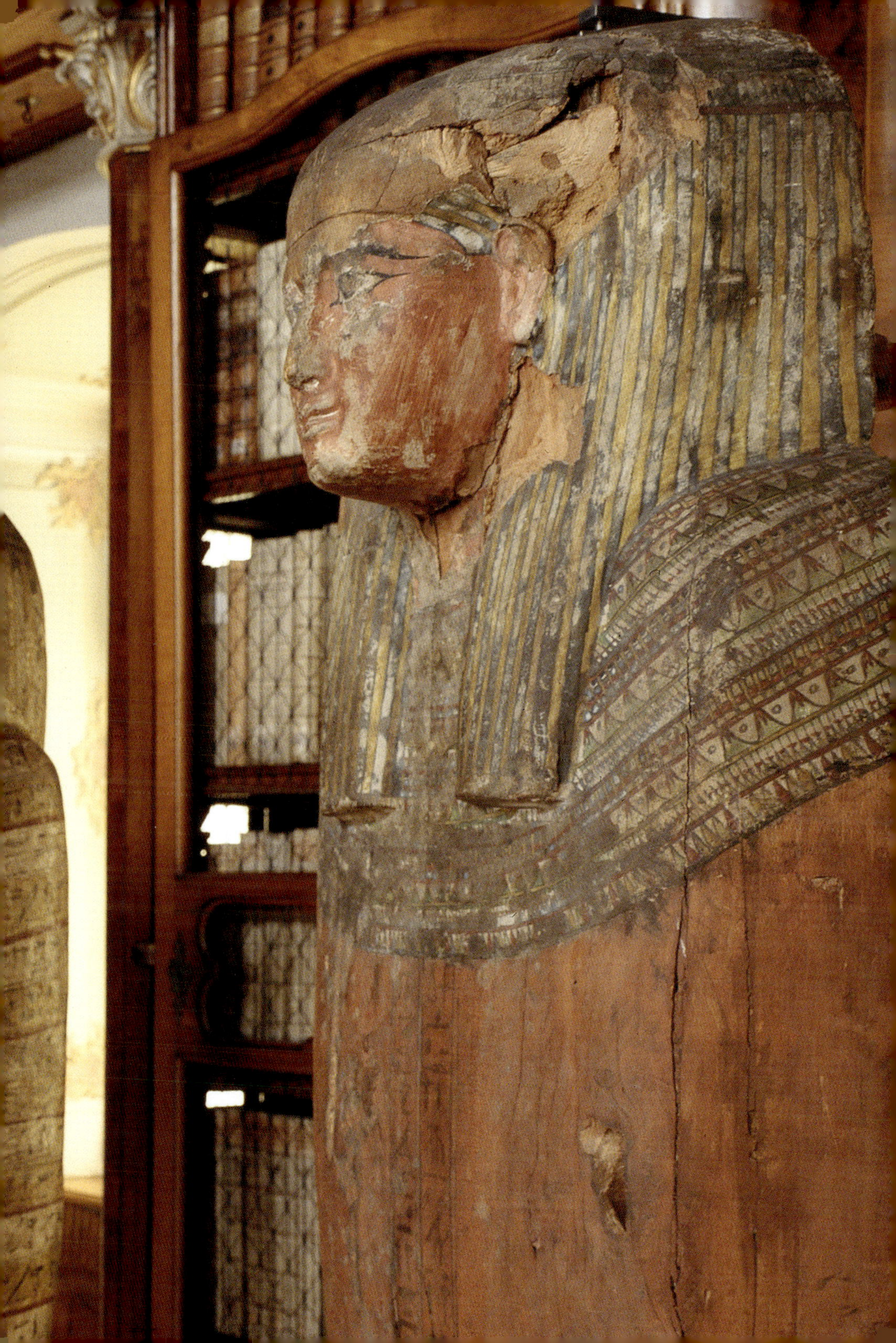

Stiftsbibliothek Kremsmünster

Kremsmünster Abbey, which looks back on more than 1,000 years of unbroken history, is not only one of the oldest but also one of the largest monasteries in Austria. The same is also true of its library, which houses some 170,000 books. The Benedictine monastery was founded in 777 by Tassilo III, Duke of Bavaria (c. 741–c. 796), and quickly became a centre of cultural and economic activity, initially within the Bavarian Lombard and subsequently the Carolingian sphere of influence. It was during the Carolingian era, in 789, that the abbey also opened a school, assuming an educational role that it maintains to this day. The very oldest manuscripts in the library, including the complete copy of the *Codex Millenarius*, likewise date from the 8th century. The rapid growth in valuable manuscript holdings can be linked to the abbey scriptorium which flourished from the middle of the 12th century. As an imperial Habsburg abbey, Kremsmünster also benefited from endowments from the 13th century onwards. Its current appearance is stamped by the comprehensive Baroque remodelling of the church and monastery that was carried out under Abbot Erenbert Schrevogel (1634–1703). The medieval abbey was thereby transformed into a palatial complex in the Baroque style, laid out around six courtyards and incorporating sumptuous reception rooms for the emperor's use. The library was likewise redesigned by architect Carlo Antonio Carlone (c. 1635–1708), with work starting in 1670. Carlone created a magnificent suite of rooms in which clever visual axes suggest a symmetrical layout along an axis that in reality is impossible to contrive. The rooms are divided into sections devoted to a particular area of knowledge, illustrated accordingly in the programme of ceiling paintings and author portraits and reflected in the book titles. The Greek Room, which is decorated with portraits of Classical Greek authors, takes up in its ceiling fresco the theme of the reciprocal relationship between original and translation. The adjacent Latin Room presents wisdom as the foundation of just rule by way of the example of King Solomon. In the Benedictine Room, finally, worldly wisdom gives way to the grace of God. That the Church alone conveys divine wisdom is made clear in the adjoining chamber. The observatory tower with its own library, completed in 1758, reflects the particular emphasis at Kremsmünster Abbey upon the study of the natural sciences.

✳✳✳

Founded 777; library built by Carlo Antonio Carlone from 1670

Holdings c. 170,000 volumes, of which 831 incunabula

Type of library monastic library, in-house reference library

Highlights *Codex Millenarius Maior* (gospels), c. 800 (CC Cim. 1); *Vaticina Pontificum* (prophecies concerning the Papacy), c. 1410–1415 (CC Cim. 6); Bartholomaeus Platina, *De honesta voluptate* (cook book), Venice, 1498

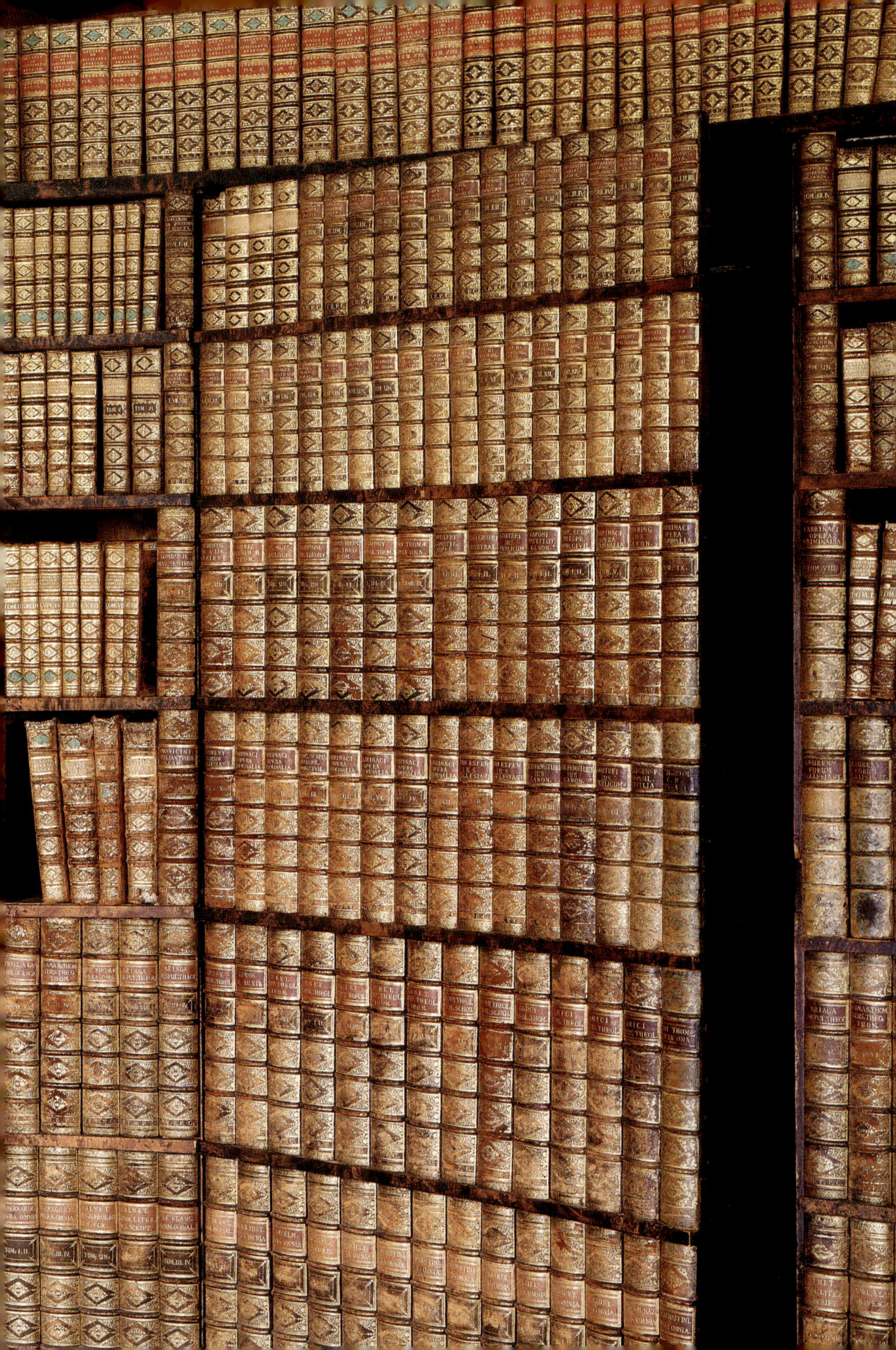

Kremsmünster zählt nicht nur zu den ältesten Stiften Österreichs, die auf eine mehr als tausendjährige Kontinuität zurückblicken, sondern auch zu seinen größten, was in gleicher Weise für die Bibliothek mit ihren etwa 170 000 Büchern gilt. Seit seiner Gründung im Jahr 777 durch den Bayernherzog Tassilo III. (um 741–um 796) war das Kloster ein kulturelles und wirtschaftliches Zentrum, zunächst im bayerisch-langobardischen, danach im karolingischen Einflussbereich, dem es seine lange Schulfunktion verdankt, die es seit 789 wahrnimmt. Aus dem 8. Jahrhundert stammen auch die ältesten Bestände der Bibliothek, unter diesen der vollständig erhaltene *Codex Millenarius*. Einer ab der Mitte des 12. Jahrhunderts florierenden Schreibschule ist das rasche Anwachsen des wertvollen Handschriftenbestandes zu verdanken. Als Reichsabtei der Habsburger erfuhr Kremsmünster seit dem 13. Jahrhundert

Förderungen. Das heutige Erscheinungsbild ist von den umfassenden barocken Erneuerungen geprägt, die Abt Erenbert Schrevogel (1634–1703) an Kirche und Kloster vornehmen ließ. Die mittelalterliche Anlage wurde in einen barocken Repräsentationsbau verwandelt, dessen sechshöfiger Entwurf auch prunkvolle Empfangsräume für den Kaiser vorsah. In gleicher Weise wurde die Bibliothek von Carlo Antonio Carlone (um 1635–1708) ab 1670 zu einer prächtigen Raumfolge gestaltet, die dank raffinierter Blickachsen eine in der Realität nicht zu bewerkstellende Achsialität der Anlage suggeriert. Die einzelnen Raumabschnitte der Bibliothek bilden thematische Einheiten, die im Programm der Deckenbilder und Autorenporträts exemplifiziert und in den Buchtiteln eingelöst werden. Der mit Porträts klassischer griechischer Autoren ausgestattete Griechensaal thematisiert im Deckenfresko die Wechselwirkung zwischen Original und Übersetzung. Der Lateinersaal genannte Folgeraum führt am Beispiel Salomons die Weisheit als Grundlage gerechten Regierens vor Augen. Dieser Ansatz wird im Benediktinersaal überwunden, wo die göttliche Gnade weltliche Weisheit ersetzt. Dass es allein die Kirche ist, die göttliche Weisheit vermittelt, wird im Kabinett klargestellt. Die mit einer eigenen Bibliothek ausgestattete Sternwarte ist seit 1758 Ausdruck der in Kremsmünster in besonderer Weise gepflegten naturwissenschaftlichen Forschungen.

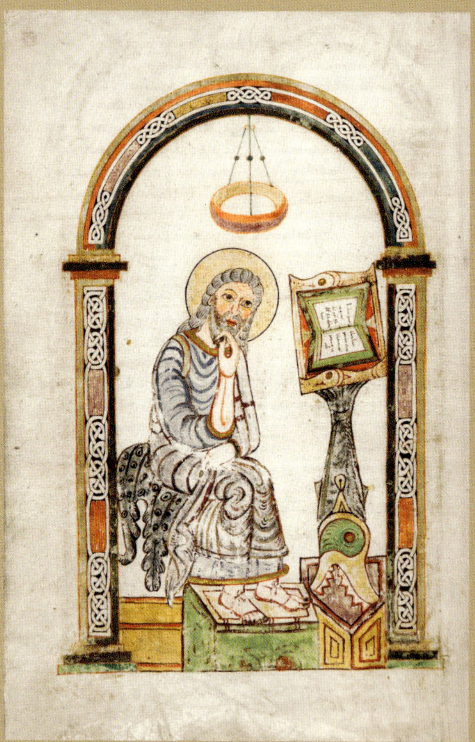

Codex Millenarius Maior, c. 800,
sig. CC Cim. 1, fol. 17v

Codex Millenarius Maior, c. 800, sig. CC Cim 1:
Renaissance treasure binding with the standing figure of Christ as Salvator Mundi. Chased, partially gilded silver and semi-precious stones, c. 1595

Sur pied depuis plus d'un millénaire,
Kremsmünster compte parmi les plus
anciennes abbayes d'Autriche, et les plus
importantes, ce qui vaut aussi pour la
bibliothèque et ses quelque 170 000 livres.
Depuis sa construction en 777 de notre
ère par le duc Tassilon III de Bavière (vers
741–vers 796), le monastère a servi de
centre culturel et économique ; tout d'abord
en Bavière langobarde, puis en territoire
carolingien, à qui il doit sa fonction d'école
qu'il perpétue depuis 789. Les fonds les plus
anciens de la bibliothèque, dont le *Codex
Millenarius* intégralement conservé, remontent
au VIIIe siècle. L'école d'écriture qui a prospéré
dès le courant du XIIe siècle a permis la
rapide expansion d'un fonds de manuscrits
inestimables. En tant qu'abbaye impériale des
Habsbourg, Kremsmünster fut choyée dès le
XIIIe siècle. Son aspect actuel est marqué par
les rénovations baroques effectuées sur l'église
et le monastère à l'initiative de l'abbé Erenbert
Schrevogel (1634–1703). L'ensemble médiéval
fut transformé en bâtiment d'apparat baroque,
articulé autour de six cours et prévoyant des
appartements somptueux à l'intention de l'empereur. Dans une même veine, la bibliothèque
de Carlo Antonio Carlone (vers 1635–1708)
assura, dès 1670, une succession de pièces
munificentes, où la finesse des angles de vue
suggère l'axialité de l'ensemble – néanmoins
peu marquante dans la réalité. Chaque section
de la bibliothèque forme une unité dont le
thème est illustré au plafond par un trompe-
l'œil et explicité par les titres contenus dans
cet espace. La salle grecque agrémentée de
portraits d'auteurs grecs classiques s'illustre
au plafond par une fresque représentant
le phénomène de passation entre original
et traduction. La salle suivante dénommée
« latine » démontre, à l'appui de Salomon, que
la sagesse est à la base d'une gouvernance
juste. Cette approche est détrônée dans la salle
bénédictine où la grâce divine supplante la
sagesse profane. Le cabinet montre clairement
que l'Église est la seule à pouvoir véhiculer la

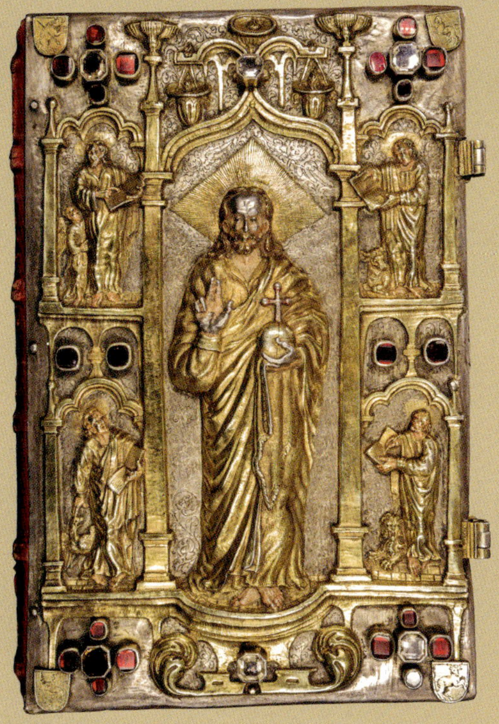

sagesse divine. L'observatoire pourvu de sa
propre bibliothèque témoigne, depuis 1758, des
recherches scientifiques que Kremsmünster
affectionnait tout particulièrement.

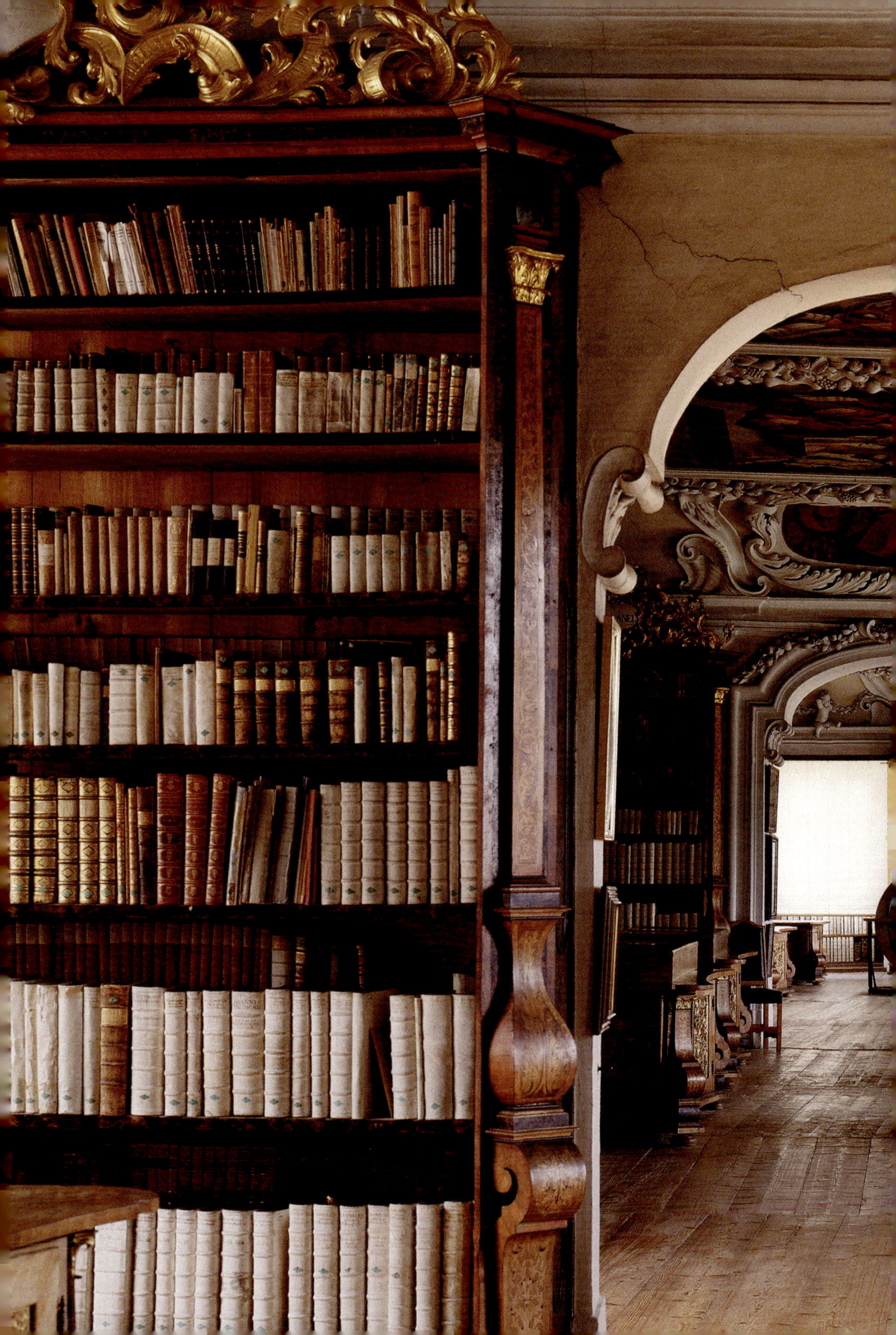

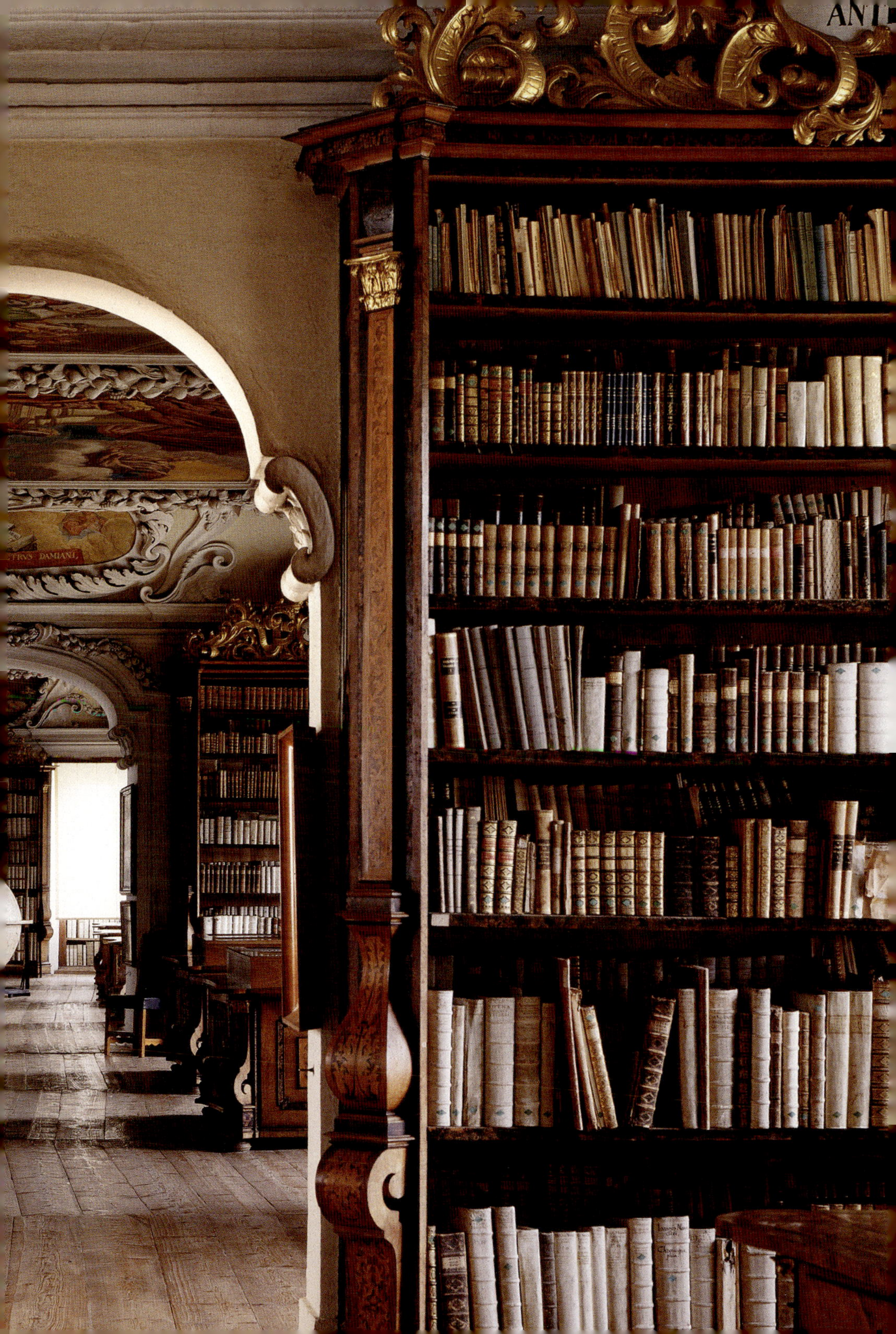

TRVS DAMIANI
ANT

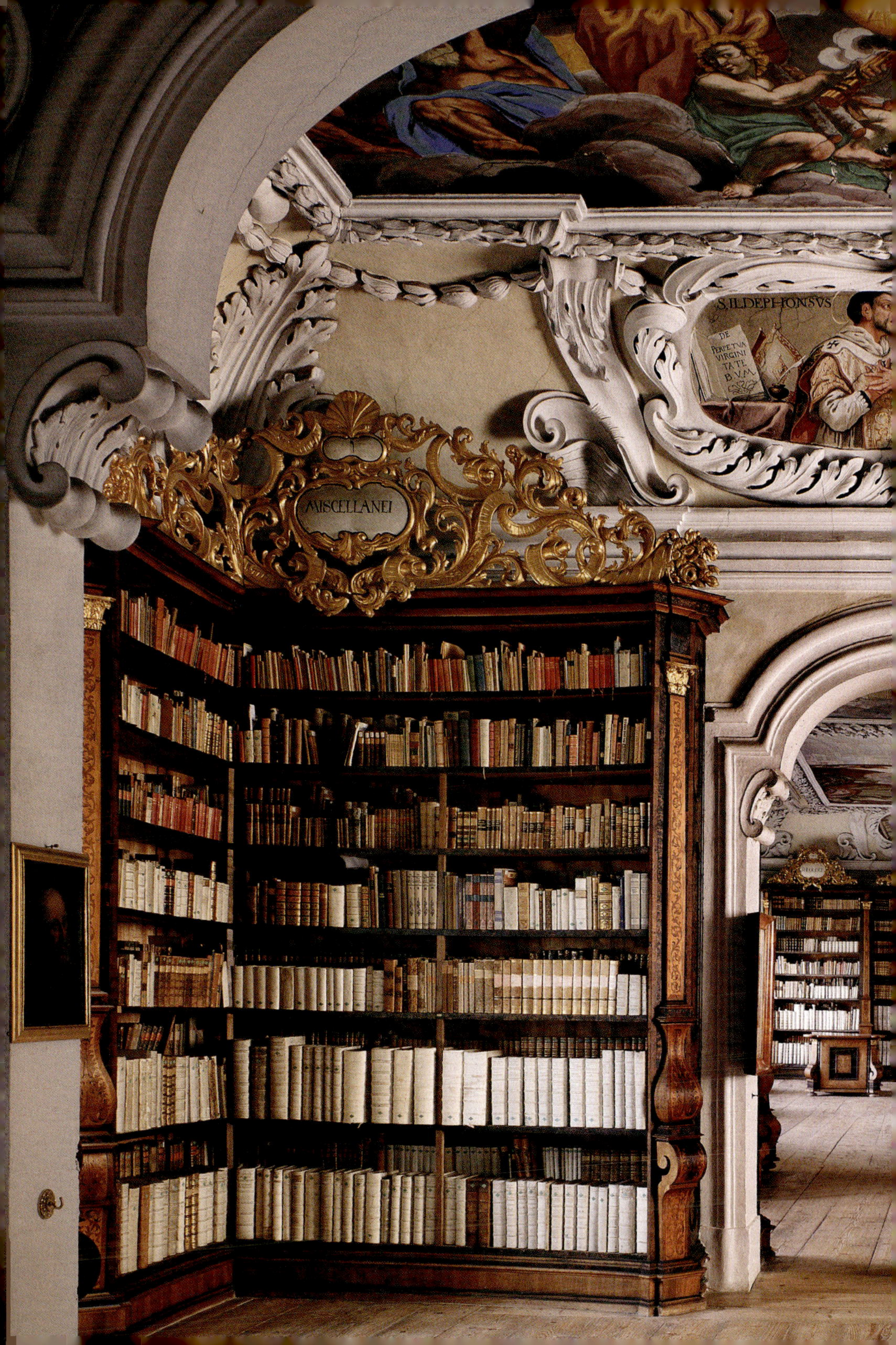
MISCELLANEI
S. ILDEPHONSVS
DE PERPETVA VIRGINITATE B. V. M.

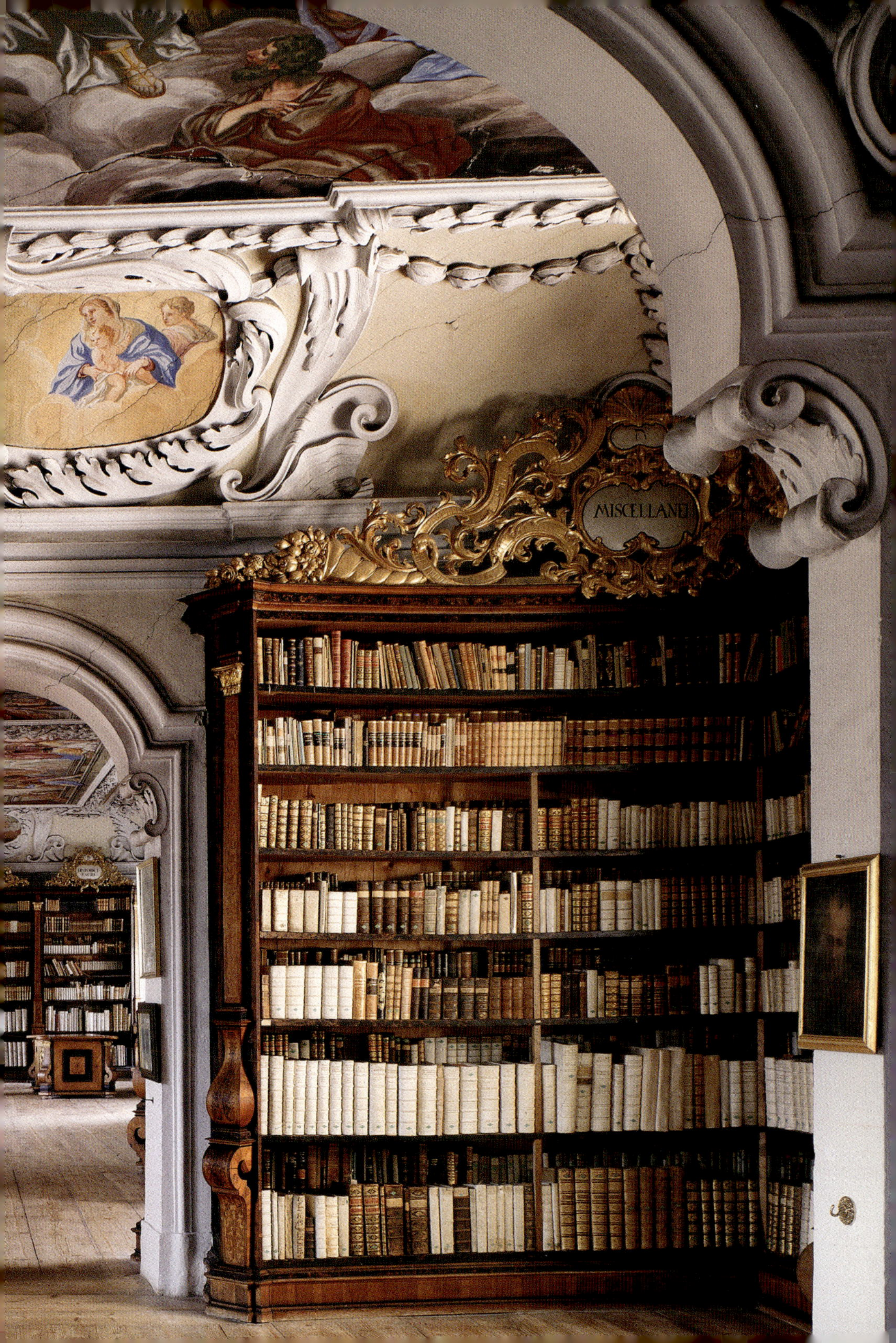

MISCELLANEI

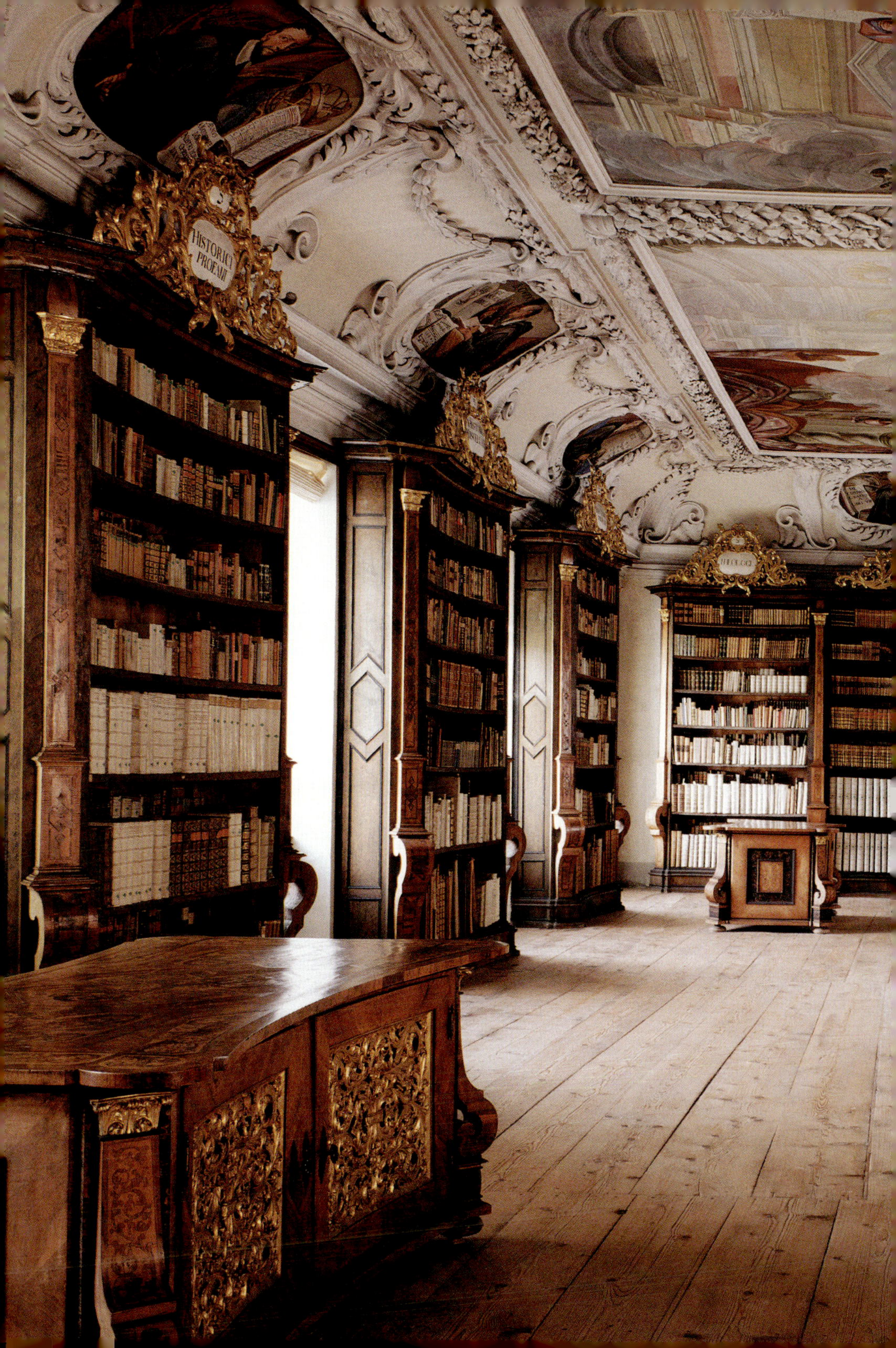

HISTORICI
PROFANI
THEOLOG

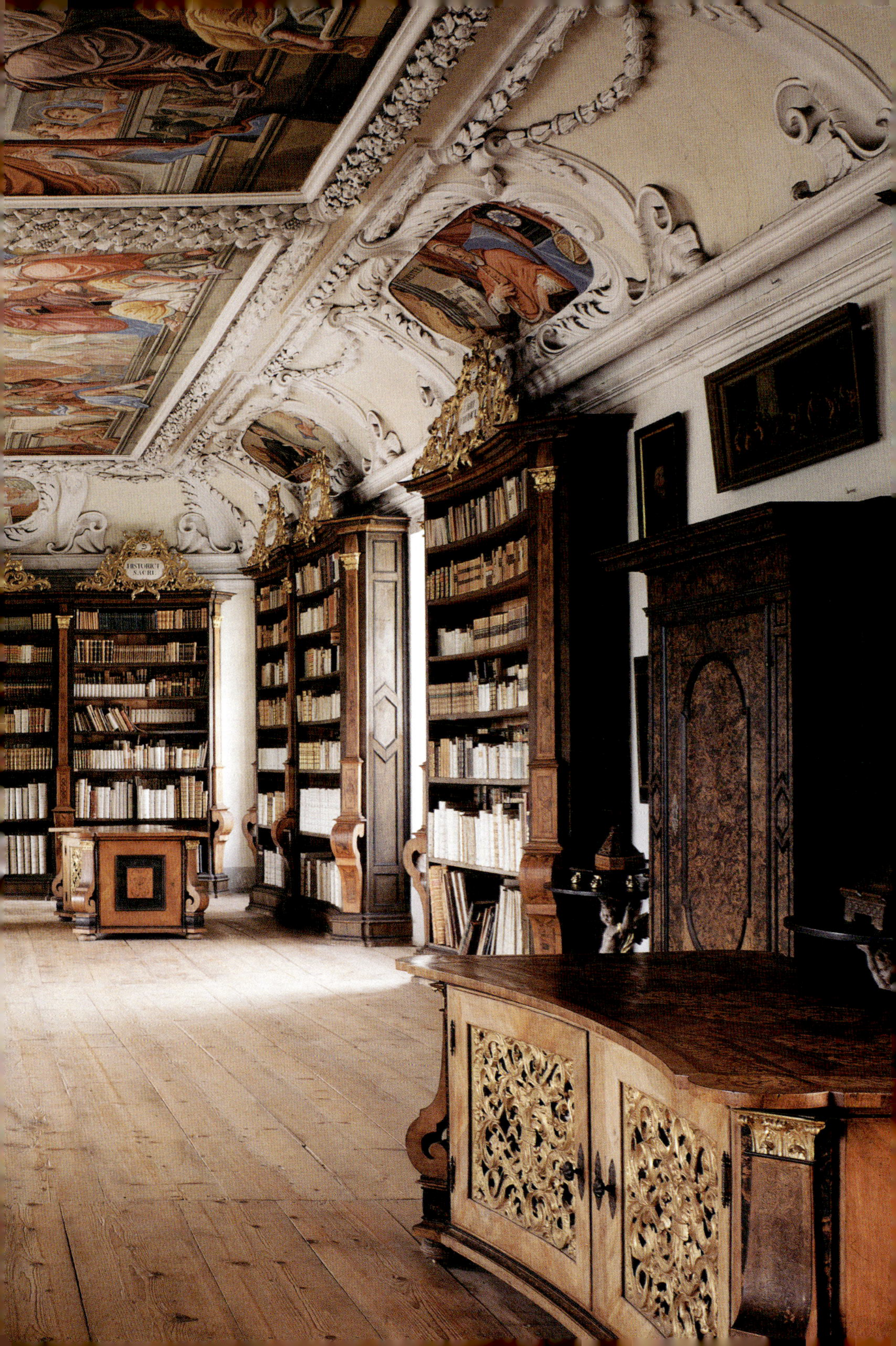

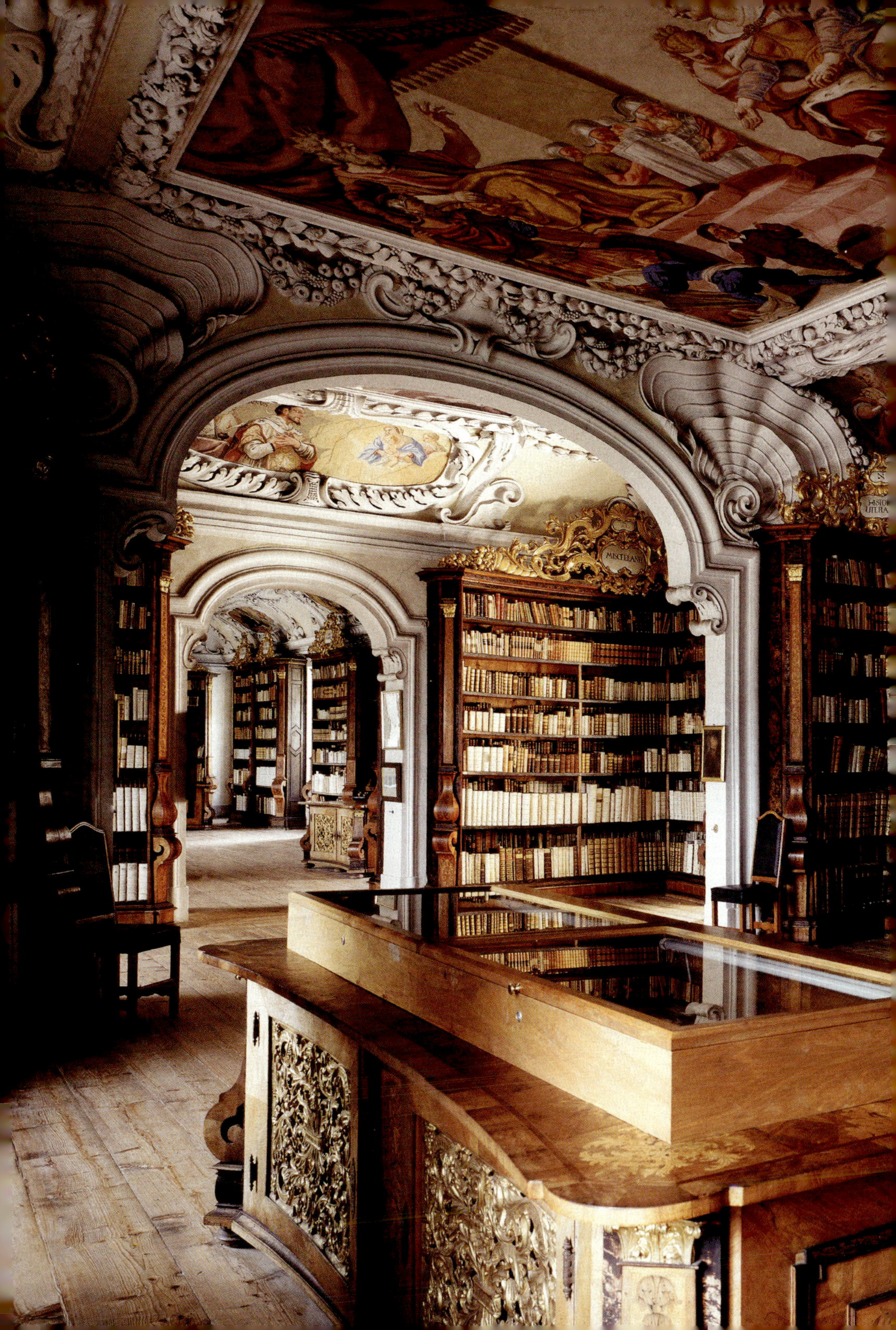

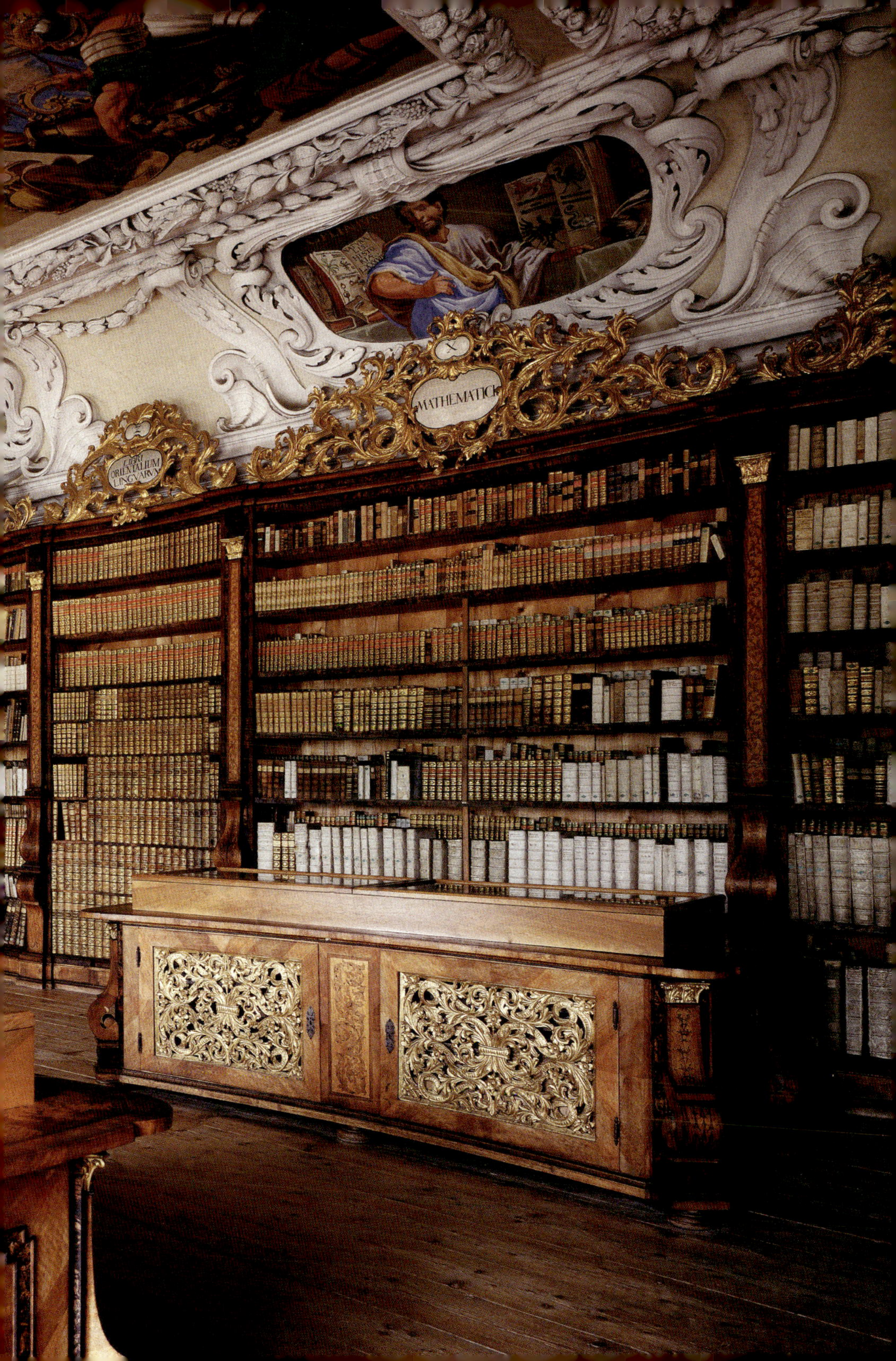
LIBRI ORIENTALIUM LINGVARVM
MATHEMATIC

Stiftsbibliothek Admont

Books have been collected, written and preserved in the Benedictine monastery in Admont, in the Austrian province of Styria, for almost a millennium. The oldest holdings go back to the time of Archbishop Gebhard of Salzburg (c. 1010–1088), who founded the abbey in 1074 and endowed it with substantial landholdings and profitable shares, reallocated from an earlier foundation by Hemma of Gurk. Gebhard also donated books to Admont's new monastic library, including two of its finest manuscripts: the three-volume *Admont Giant Bible*, also known as the *Gebhard Bible*, and a lavishly illuminated book of Gospels. These books – like Admont's first monks – came from the archbishopric of St Peter's in Salzburg, where a centre of manuscript production and illumination had been established in the 7th century. This tradition was taken up at Admont, whose scriptorium developed into a major centre of literary and scholarly activity that continued after its separation from St Peter's. A scriptorium also operated in the affiliated Benedictine nunnery, founded in 1120 and existing in parallel with the monastery until the Reformation. The library at Admont Abbey was first assigned its own room, the Armarium, around the middle of the 12th century, by which time it already comprised some 200 manuscripts – the majority of which are still housed there today. The names of the librarians in charge of the collection were recorded from the 12th century on, while inventories of the books have likewise come down to us from the 14th century onwards. Today Admont Abbey is home to some 1,400 precious manuscripts, of which more than half date from the Middle Ages and the very earliest from the 8th century, plus more than 930 early printed works. For conservation reasons, these treasures are housed in their own climate-controlled environment separate from the main body of the library, which today contains around 200,000 printed books. With its centuries-old tradition, Admont Abbey may be seen as a historic monument of book culture and it is therefore no surprise that its books should be housed in what is perhaps the grandest monastic library of them all. It was modelled on the Imperial Court Library in Vienna, from where its architect, Josef Hueber (1715–1787), also came, and aspired to a similar magnificence. The long interior is spanned by a ceiling made up of seven circular vaults and divided by a vertically accentuated central hall into three harmoniously proportioned spaces, within which the books are grouped clearly by subject, wholly in the spirit of the Enlightenment. In the central hall, beneath the ceiling fresco of *Divine Wisdom* by Bartolomeo Altomonte (1694–1783), the bookcases display numerous editions of the Bible and the writings of the Church Fathers. In the galleries on either side, the ceiling frescos portray the various areas of human knowledge, to which the subjects of the books below again correspond. The library's decoration is further complemented by impressive sculptures by Josef Stammel (1695–1765), who worked for Admont Abbey for many years. The white and gold bookcases along the walls are filled with approximately 70,000 printed works.

***

Founded 1074; library hall 1764–1773 by Josef Hueber
Holdings c. 200,000 volumes
Type of library monastic library, reference library
Highlights *Admont Giant Bible (Gebhard Bible)*, c. 1070 (C); *Book of Gospels*, end of the 11th century (Codex 511); *Responsorium Graduale (Catholic Liturgical Book)*, second half of the 15th century (Codex 305)

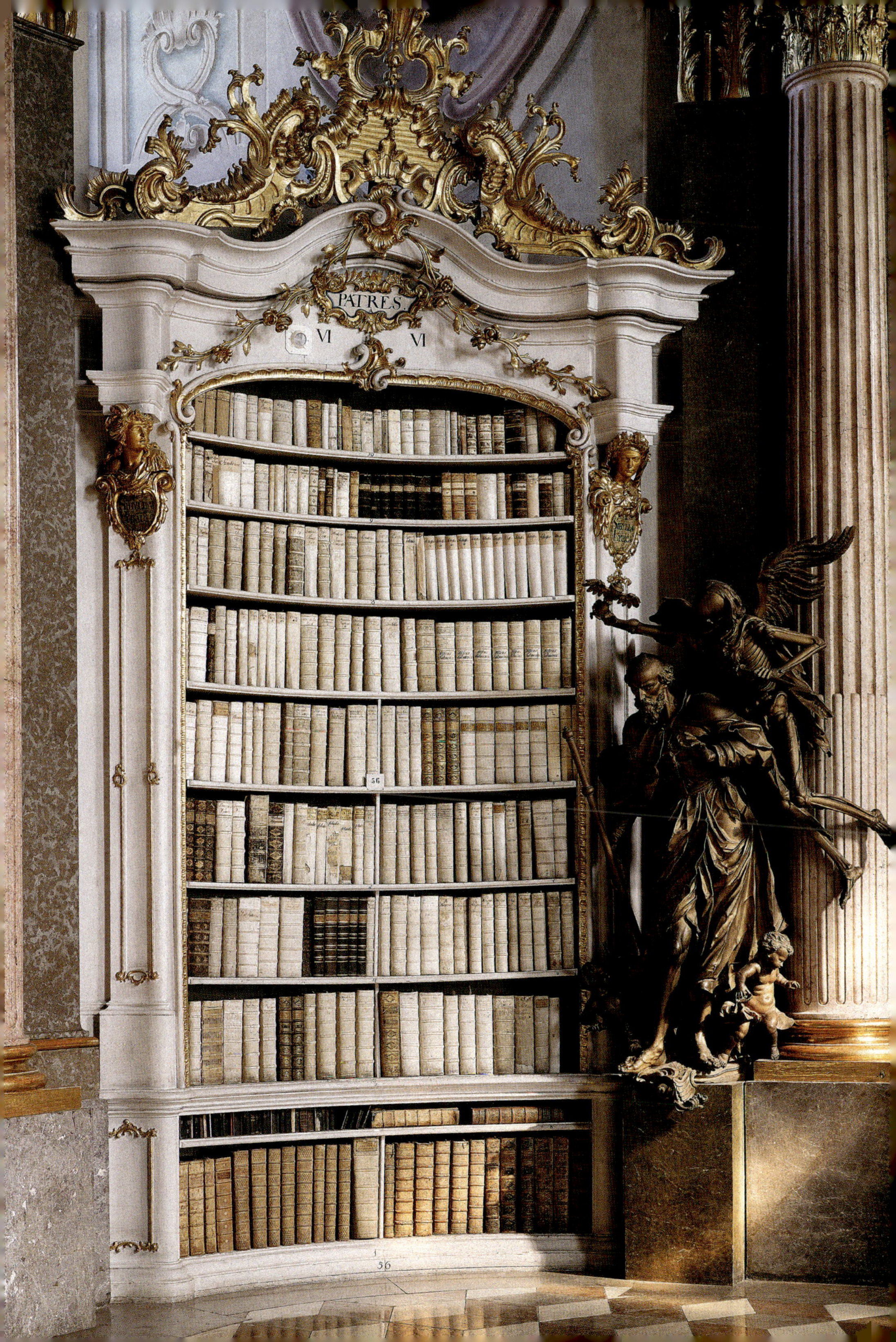
PATRES
VI   VI
56

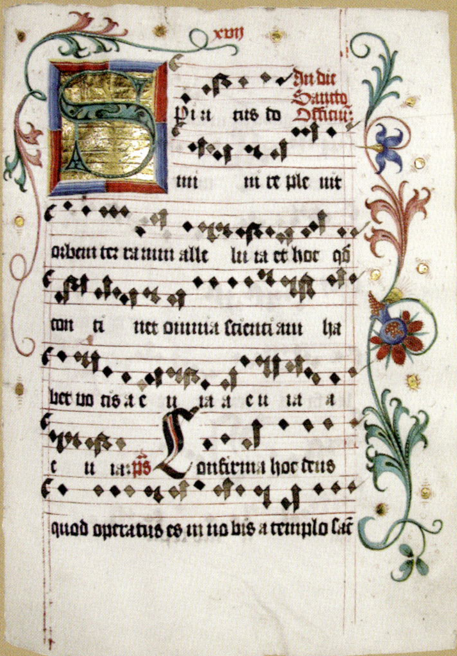

Seit fast einem Jahrtausend werden im Benediktinerstift Admont Bücher gesammelt, geschrieben und bewahrt. Der älteste Bestand geht auf Erzbischof Gebhard von Salzburg zurück (um 1010–1088), der die obersteirische Ordensniederlassung 1074 eröffnet und dank einer Stiftung der Hemma von Gurk mit ausgedehnten Grundherrschaften und ertragreichen Beteiligungen reich ausgestattet hat. Aus seinem Besitz stammen einige der Prunkstücke der seit Anbeginn vorhandenen Bibliothek, wie die dreibändige Riesenbibel (die sogenannte *Gebhardsbibel*) sowie ein prächtig mit Buchmalereien ausgestattetes Evangeliar. Sie kommen, ebenso wie die ersten Mönche, aus dem Erzstift St. Peter in Salzburg, wo sich bereits seit dem 7. Jahrhundert ein Zentrum der Buchmalerei und der Schreibkunst etabliert hatte. Diese Tradition führte Stift Admont weiter und entwickelte in seinem Skriptorium auch nach der Ablösung von St. Peter eine bedeutende literarische und wissenschaftliche Tätigkeit. Sie wurde auch von den Nonnen des seit 1120 und bis in

die Reformationszeit parallel bestehenden Frauenklosters mitgetragen. Um die Mitte des 12. Jahrhunderts brachte man den bereits auf rund 200 Handschriften angewachsenen Buchbestand – der sich mehrheitlich noch heute im Stift befindet – erstmals in einem eigenen Raum, dem Armarium, unter. Die Sammlung wurde von seit dem 12. Jahrhundert namentlich überlieferten Bibliothekaren betreut. Bücherverzeichnisse haben sich ab dem 14. Jahrhundert erhalten. Heute ist Stift Admont im Besitz von 1400 wertvollen, zur Hälfte noch aus dem Mittelalter, ab dem 8. Jahrhundert stammenden Handschriften und 930 Frühdrucken – Preziosen, die aus konservatorischen Gründen getrennt von den rund 200 000 Druckwerken der Bibliothek aufbewahrt werden. Angesichts dieser Tradition, die Stift Admont als historisches Monument der Buchkultur ausweist, verwundert es nicht, gerade hier den vielleicht größten klösterlichen Bibliothekssaal vorzufinden. Höchstes Anspruchsniveau galt schließlich auch für dessen Vorbild, das in der Kaiserlichen Hofbibliothek in Wien zu fassen ist. Von dort kam auch der Architekt Josef Hueber (1715–1787). Das von sieben Kuppeln überwölbte Raumgebilde wird durch den vertikal akzentuierten Mittelsaal in drei harmonisch proportionierte Raumabschnitte gegliedert, die ganz im Sinne der Aufklärung eine übersichtliche Aufstellung der Bücher nach Themen ermöglichen. So kommen etwa im Mittelsaal, in dessen Kuppelfresko Bartolomeo Altomonte (1694–1783) die göttliche Weisheit dargestellt hat, verschiedene Ausgaben der Heiligen Schrift und der Kirchenväter zur Aufstellung. Die Deckenfresken der seitlichen Säle stellen hingegen die verschiedenen Stufen menschlicher Erkenntnis dar, was wiederum die darunter aufgestellten Bücher thematisiert. In eindrücklicher Weise setzen auch die von dem Stiftsbildhauer Josef Stammel (1695–1765) geschaffenen Skulpturen die Thematik der Bücher plastisch um. In den weiß-goldenen Bücherschränken entlang der Wände befinden sich an die 70 000 Druckwerke.

Le couvent bénédictin d'Admont rassemble, produit et préserve des livres depuis près d'un millénaire. Son fonds le plus ancien remonte à l'archevêque Gebhard de Salzbourg (vers 1010–1088) qui permit l'installation de la congrégation en Haute-Styrie en 1074, lui accordant, grâce à un don de sainte Emma de Gurk, une vaste seigneurie foncière. Certains joyaux comme la Bible géante en trois tomes, dite *Bible de Gebhard*, ainsi qu'un évangéliaire somptueusement enluminé lui appartenaient. Ils constituent le noyau fort de la bibliothèque d'origine. À l'instar des premiers moines, ils proviennent de l'archevêché de Saint-Pierre de Salzbourg, où un centre de réalisation de manuscrits et d'enluminures se créa dès le VIIe siècle. L'abbaye d'Admont perpétua la tradition et développa dans un *scriptorium*, même lorsqu'il fut détaché de Saint-Pierre, des activités scientifiques et littéraires importantes, auxquelles participèrent également les religieuses. Elles étaient installées, dès 1120 jusqu'à la Réforme, dans une partie du couvent attenant à celui des moines. Vers le milieu du XIIe siècle, le fonds, déjà riche de presque 200 manuscrits – la plupart encore présents dans l'abbaye –, fut pour la première fois logé dans une pièce à part, nommée *armarium*. La collection fut confiée, durant ce même siècle, à des bibliothécaires qui se transmettaient la charge de l'un à l'autre. L'existence de catalogues est attestée dès le XIVe siècle. À ce jour, l'abbaye d'Admont possède 1400 manuscrits de grande valeur, pour la moitié médiévaux, remontant jusqu'au VIIIe siècle, ainsi que 930 incunables. Pour des raisons de conservation, ces précieux ouvrages sont séparés des 200 000 autres volumes. Au vu de cette tradition qui confère à l'abbaye d'Admont le statut de monument historique de la culture livresque, on ne s'étonnera pas de se trouver dans, semble-t-il, la plus grande bibliothèque monastique. Sa réalisation répond à des critères aussi exigeants que ceux qui ont donné naissance à son modèle : la bibliothèque de la cour impériale de Vienne, d'où l'architecte Josef Hueber (1715–1787) était originaire.

L'espace coiffé de sept coupoles est divisé en trois sections aux proportions harmonieuses du fait de l'accent placé sur la verticalité dans l'espace médian. Cet agencement permet une répartition limpide des livres par thèmes, conformément à l'esprit des Lumières. Ainsi, la pièce centrale, dont le plafond de Bartolomeo Altomonte (1694–1783) exalte la sagesse divine, abrite diverses éditions des Saintes Écritures et des écrits des Pères de l'Église. Les trompe-l'œil des salles contiguës affichent pour leur part les différentes étapes de l'acquisition du savoir, ce qui correspond au thème des livres exposés. Les sculptures réalisées par le sculpteur sur bois Josef Stammel (1695–1765) illustrent aussi de façon impressionnante les sujets traités dans les volumes. Enfin, quelque 70 000 imprimés sont hébergés dans les rayonnages blanc et or qui ornent les murs de la salle d'apparat.

Responsorium Graduale, second half of the 15th century, sig. Codex 305, fol. 1r

Book of Gospels, end of the 11th century, sig. Codex 511, fol. 132v: *Luke the Evangelist*

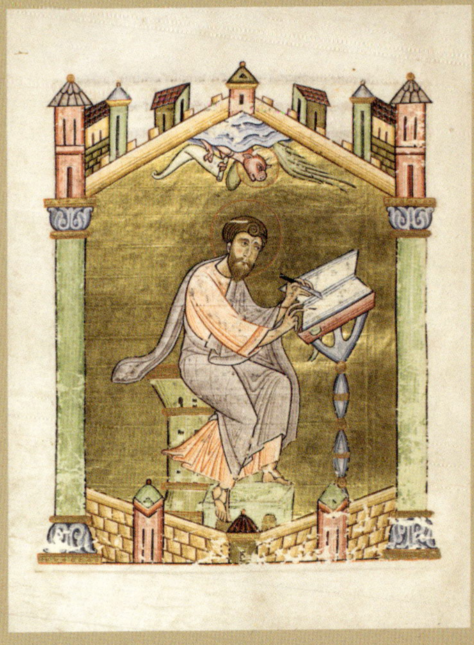

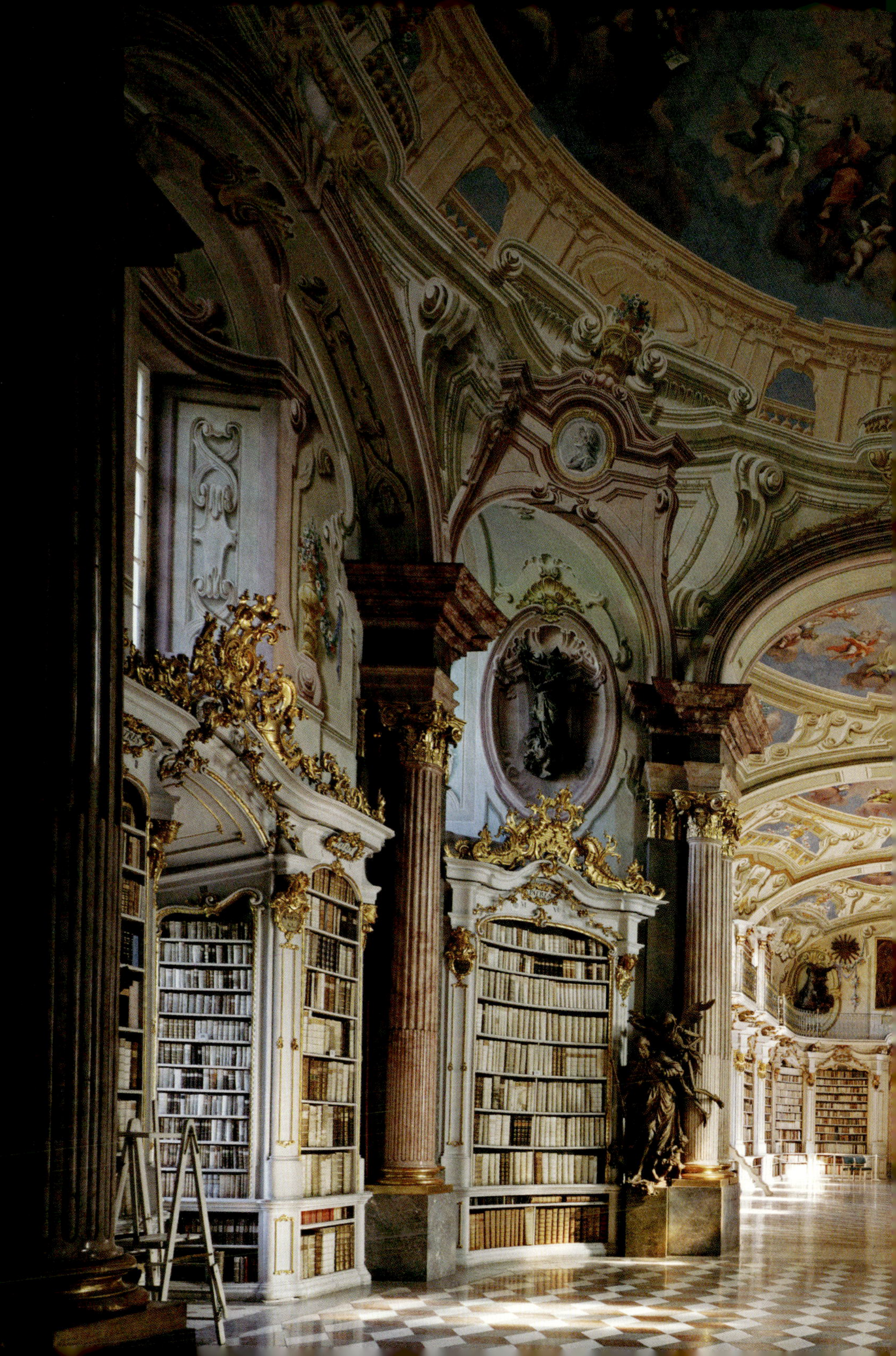

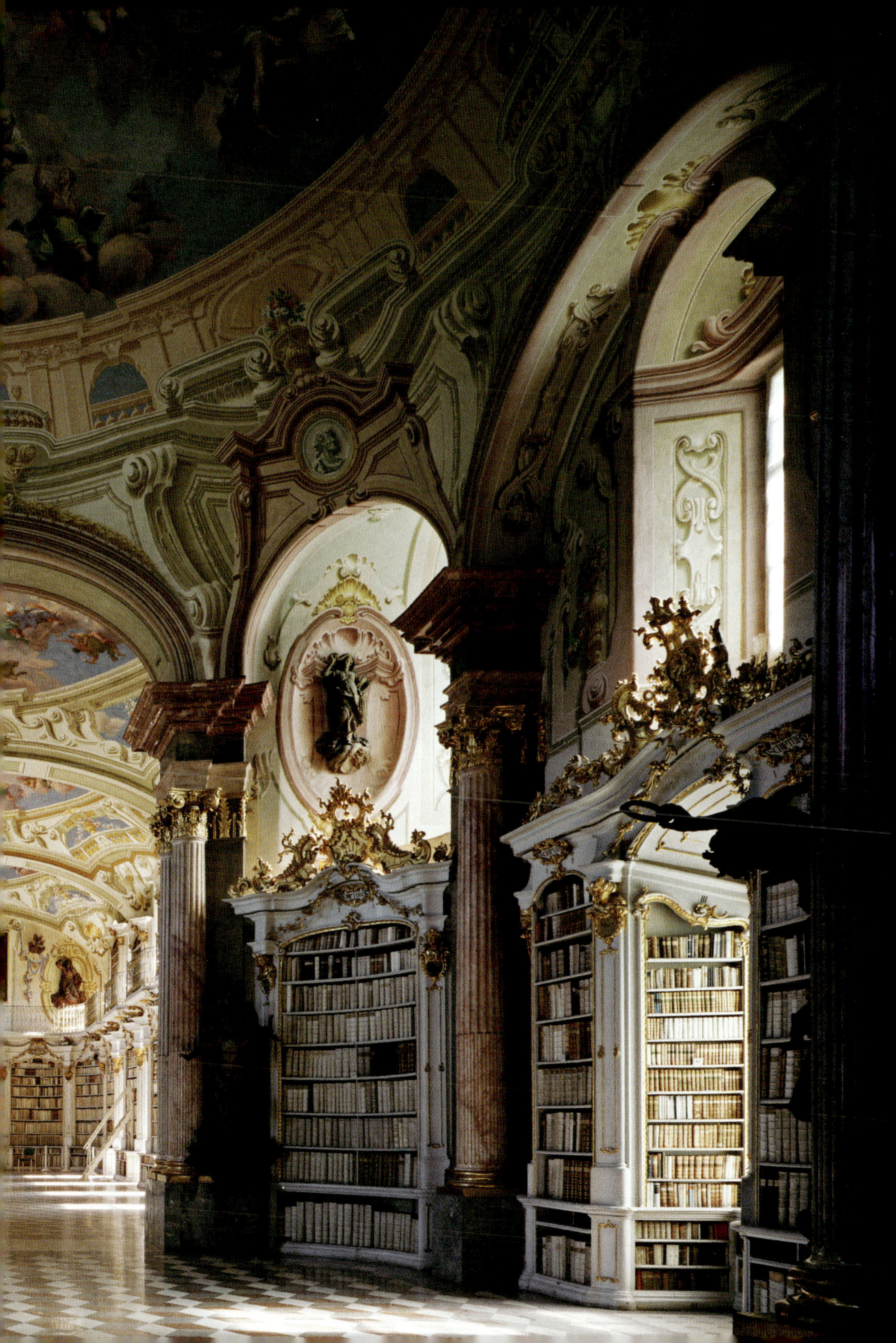

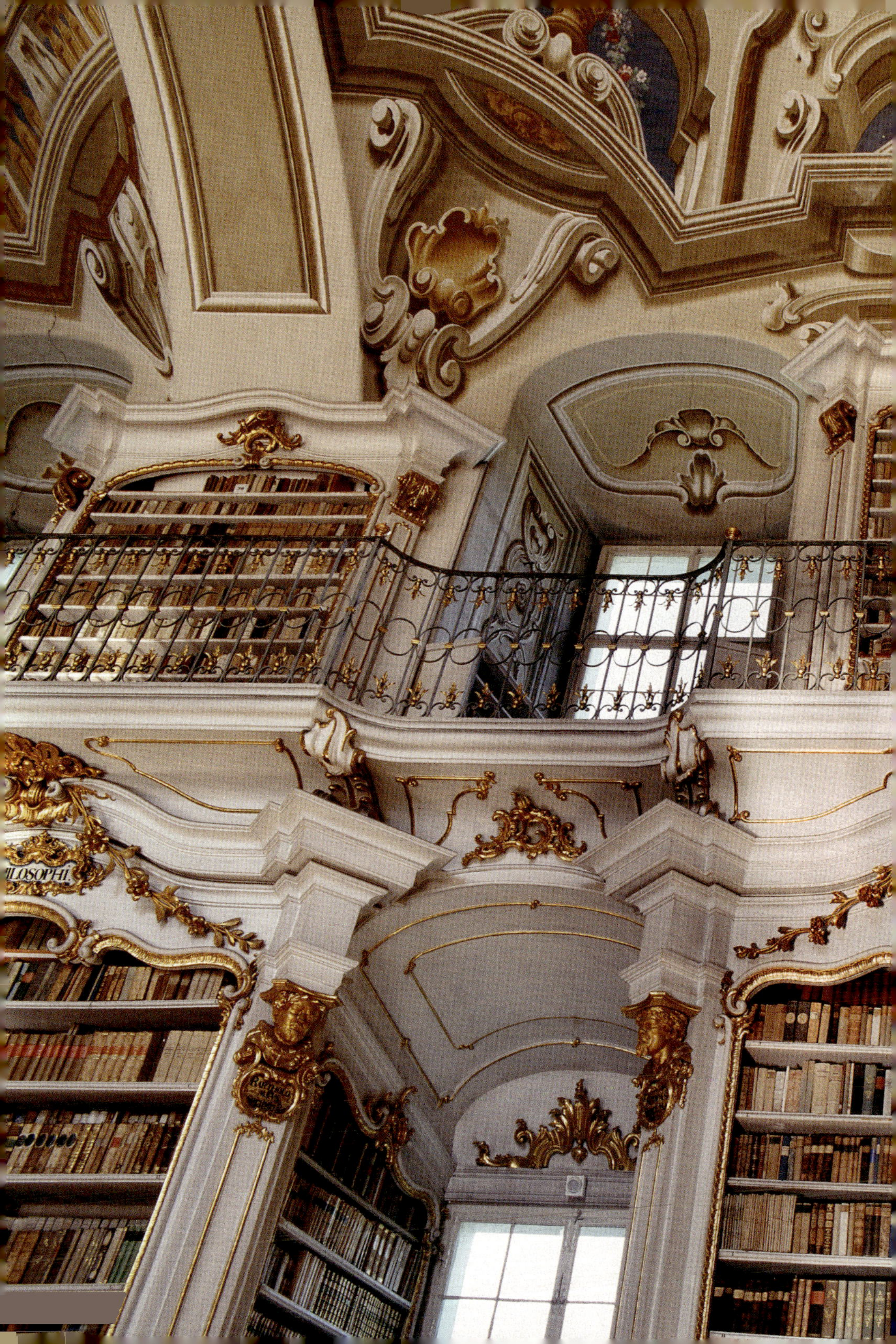

PHILOSOPHI.

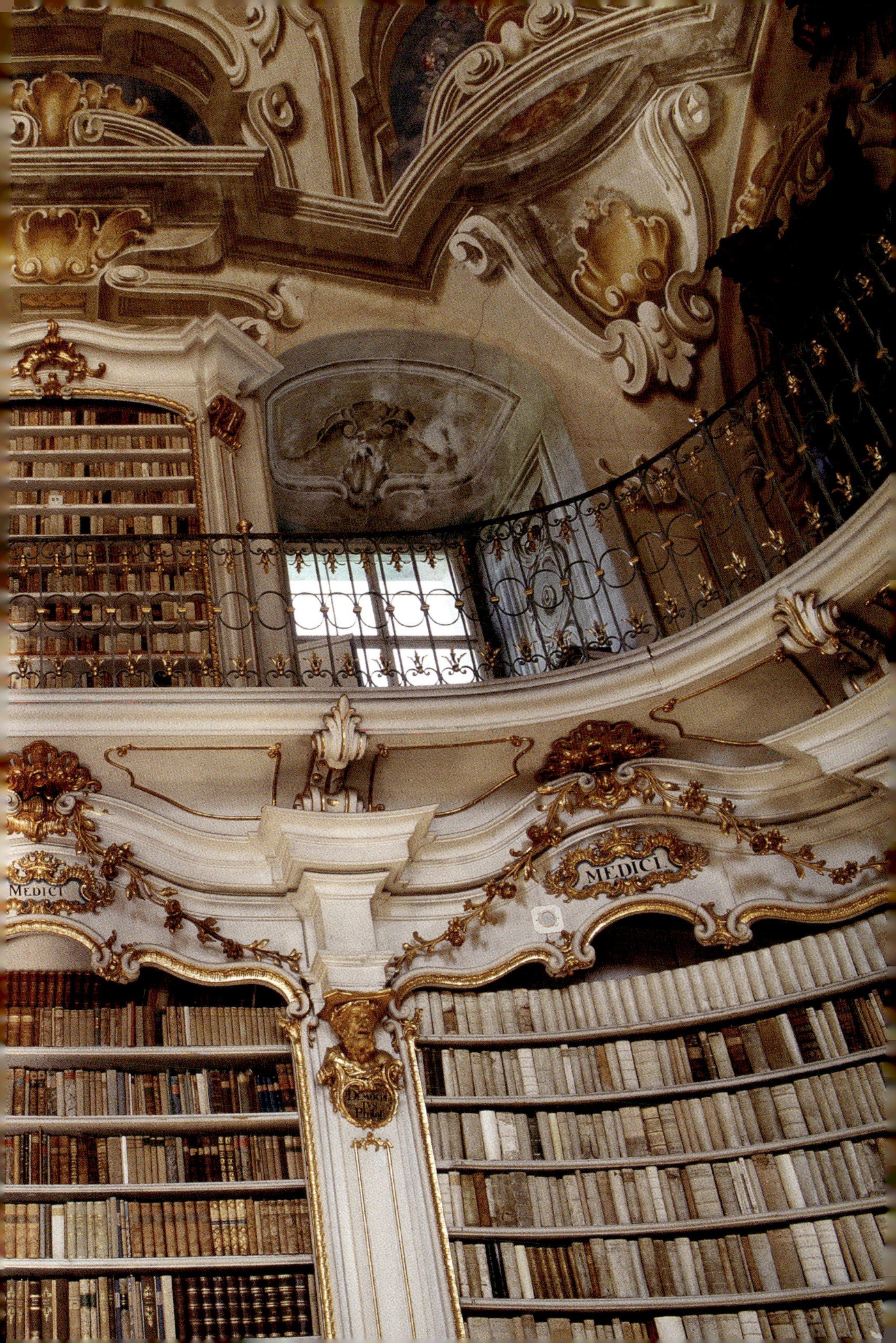

MEDICI
MEDICI

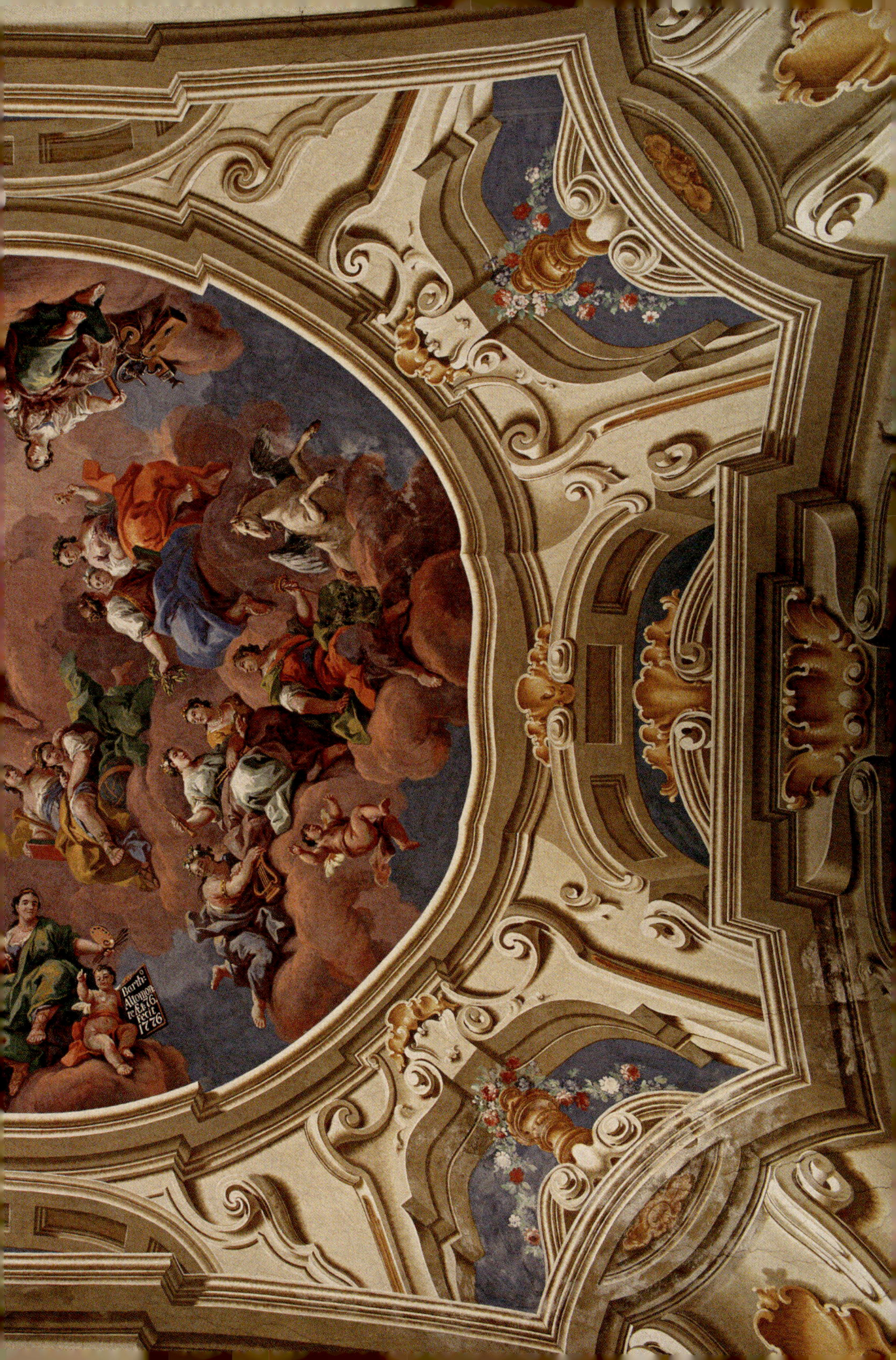

Barth:
Altomon-
te Æt. 76.
fecit
1776

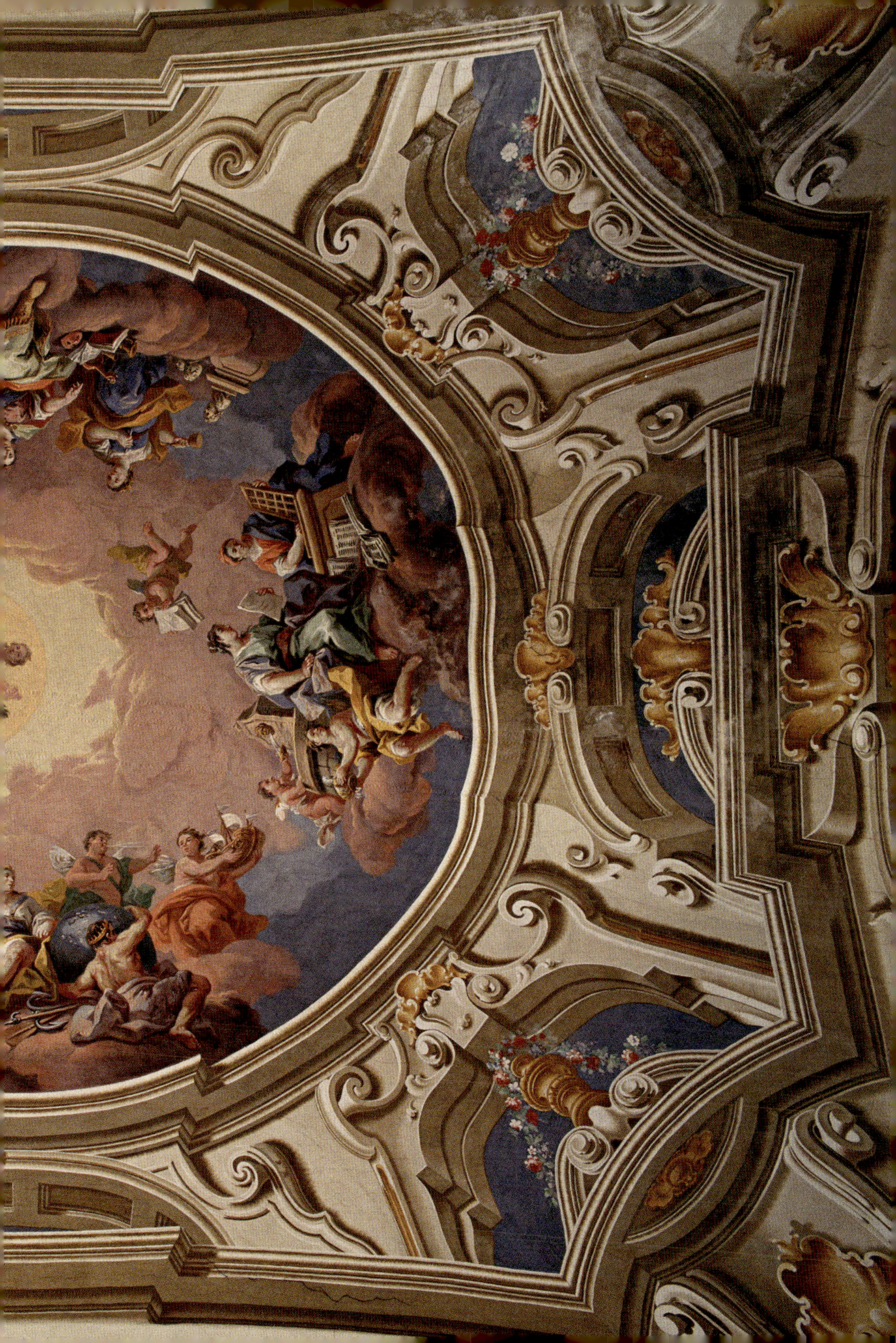

Stiftsbibliothek Melk

A library has flourished continuously at Melk Abbey for over a millennium. When the Babenberg margraves built their first castle on Melk's rocky outcrop, with its commanding position overlooking the River Danube, they also founded an abbey there. Documented from around 985, the canonry consisted not only of the tombs of the Babenberg dynasty, still visible in the church, but also a treasury of Carolingian manuscripts, fragments of which are today preserved in Melk Abbey library. These include the oldest known Latin edition of the *Doctrina apostolorum* (Cod. 597) and a copy of Virgil's *Aeneid* (Fragment 104). In 1089 the Babenbergs relinquished the castle entirely to the abbey, which now became a Benedictine monastery and rapidly embarked on an early phase of cultural and economic growth. The monks arriving from the mother abbey at Lambach brought new holdings into the library, including the *Rule of Benedict* (Cod. 1942), upon which life in the monastic community was based. The scriptorium, whose extensive production included the *Melk Annals*, likewise absorbed traditions from the older scriptoria at Lambach and Admont. In the early 15th century Melk Abbey became the starting point and hub of a far-reaching monastic reform movement, known as the Melk Reform. The abbey's close links with Vienna University during this period also benefitted the library, which received substantial new accessions. Melk became a lively centre of exchange and book production in the service of reform, as illustrated, for example, by the *Melk Missal* of 1490. The abbots of the Baroque era embraced new maxims and perceived themselves as princes of the Church. This was particularly true of the imperial prelate Abbot Berthold Dietmayr (1670–1739), who transformed Melk Abbey from a late medieval fort into a stately Baroque palace worthy of serving the emperor as a temporary residence. The magnificent monastery complex (in whose design Abbot Dietmayr probably had a major hand) is rightly considered the crowning achievement of its architect, Jakob Prandtauer (1660–1726). The south façade, over 330 yards long, dominates the town of Melk, while the west façade – incorporating the two towers of the abbey church and, beside it, the imperial reception rooms and the library – overlooks the Danube valley. The library rooms were completed in 1735, and 16,000 books, grouped by subject and still displayed in their original positions, are housed in the grand Prunksaal alone. The system by which they are classified is set out by librarian Martin Kropff in his book *Bibliotheca Mellicensis*, printed in 1747.

***

Founded 1089; library built 1702–1735 after plans by Jakob Prandtauer
Holdings c. 100,000 volumes, of which 750 incunabula
Type of library monastic library, school library, academic library
Highlights *Beda Venerabilis* (commonly used texts in daily Benedictine life), St Germain d'Auxerre (?), first half of the 9th century (Cod. 412); Virgil, *Aeneid*, France, mid-9th century, with 12th-century additions (Fragment 104); *Psalterium*, Würzburg, c. 1255–1260 (Cod. 1903)

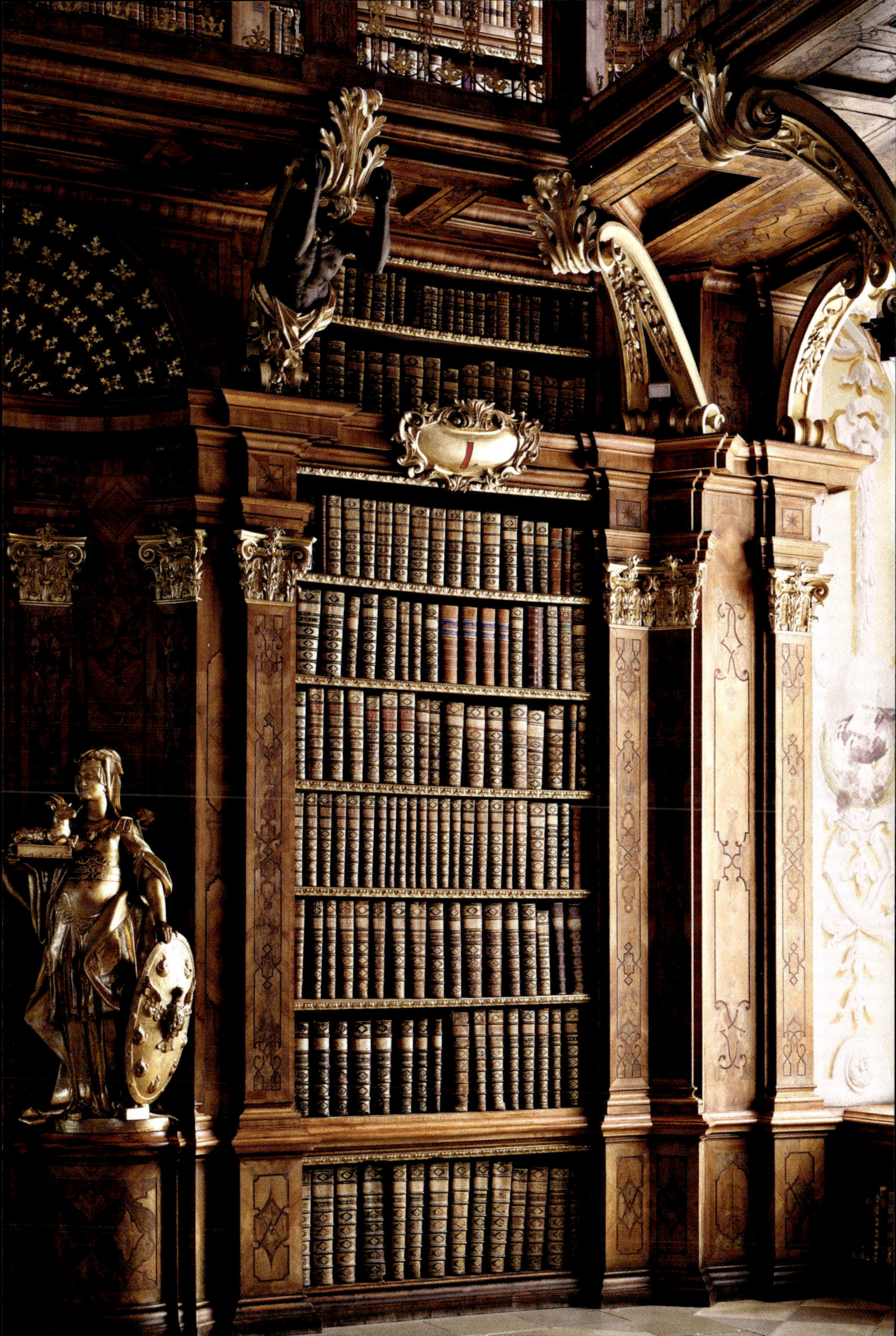

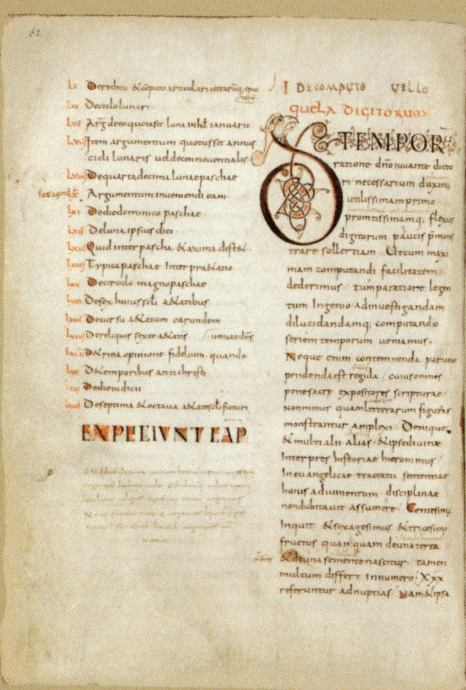

In Stift Melk hat sich eine seit über tausend Jahren kontinuierlich geführte Bibliothek erhalten. Als die Markgrafen der Babenberger ihre erste Residenz auf dem in beherrschender Lage über der Donau gelegenen Burgfelsen von Melk bezogen, richteten sie dort auch ein seit etwa 985 bezeugtes Kanonikerstift ein. Dieses betreute nicht nur die Begräbnisstätte ihrer Dynastie, die sich in der Klosterkirche erhalten hat, sondern auch einen wertvollen Bücherschatz karolingischer Handschriften – darunter die älteste lateinische Ausgabe der *Doctrina apostolorum* (Cod. 597) oder eine Ausgabe von Vergils *Aeneis* (Fragment 104) –, die sich heute noch in Fragmenten in der Stiftsbibliothek befindet. Mit der Berufung der Benediktiner im Jahr 1089 gelangte das Stift, dem ab diesem Zeitpunkt die gesamte Burg überlassen war, in kurzer Zeit zu einer ersten kulturellen und wirtschaftlichen Blüte. Aus dem Mutterkloster Lambach brachten die Benediktiner neue Bestände in die Bibliothek,

unter diesen die für das Leben der Klostergemeinschaft vorbildliche *Benediktsregel* (Cod. 1942). Auch beeinflussten Traditionen aus Lambach und Admont das jüngere Skriptorium in Melk, aus dessen reicher Produktion unter anderem die *Melker Annalen* hervorgingen. Im frühen 15. Jahrhundert wurde das Kloster zum Ausgangsort und Zentrum einer weit wirksamen Reformbewegung, die der Bibliothek, die damals enge Beziehungen zur Wiener Universität unterhielt, umfangreiche Neuzugänge brachte. Im Dienste der Reform wurde Melk zu einem regen Zentrum des Austausches und der Produktion von Büchern – verwiesen sei auf das *Melker Missale* von 1490. Neue Maximen galten für die Äbte des Barock, die sich als geistliche Fürsten verstanden, was insbesondere auf den kaiserlichen Prälaten Berthold Dietmayr (1670–1739) zutrifft. Er ließ die spätmittelalterliche Klosterfestung in einen barocken Repräsentationsbau verwandeln, der würdig war, dem Kaiser als zeitweilige Residenz zu dienen. Mit seiner über 300 Meter langen, den Ort beherrschenden Südfront, der weithin das Donautal überragenden Westfront mit der Doppelturmfassade der Stiftskirche und den ihr zuseiten angeordneten Prunksälen des Kaisers und der Bibliothek gilt der prachtvolle Klosterkomplex zu Recht als (von Abt Dietmayr wohl entscheidend mit geplantes) Meisterwerk des Architekten Jakob Prandtauer (1660–1726). 1735 waren die Bibliotheks-säle bezugsfertig, allein im Prunksaal sind 16 000 nach Themengruppen geordnete Bücher in ihrer Originalaufstellung zu sehen. Das ihr zugrunde liegende Konzept führte der Bibliothekar Martin Kropff in seiner 1747 gedruckten *Bibliotheca Mellicensis* aus.

Beda Venerabilis, St Germain d'Auxerre (?), first half of the 9th century, sig. Cod. 412, fol. 62v
Psalterium, Würzburg, c. 1255 1260, sig. Cod. 1903, fol. 61r

L'abbaye de Melk possède une bibliothèque dont l'histoire s'étale sur plus d'un millénaire. Lorsque les margraves de Babenberg investissent leur première résidence à Melk, sur un roc surplombant le Danube, ils en profitent pour fonder une abbaye de chanoines, dont l'existence est attestée depuis 985 environ. Cette dernière recèle d'une part les sépultures de la dynastie, toujours présentes dans l'église du monastère, d'autre part un incroyable trésor de manuscrits carolingiens (dont la plus vieille édition latine de la *Doctrina apostolorum* (Cod. 597) ainsi qu'une édition de l'*Énéide* de Virgile (Fragment 104)). Ce trésor perdure de façon fragmentée dans la bibliothèque de l'abbaye. Avec l'arrivée des Bénédictins en 1089, l'abbaye – qui administre alors la bourgade tout entière – connut en peu de temps une période florissante sur les plans culturel et économique. Les Bénédictins amenèrent avec eux des fonds de la bibliothèque du monastère de Lambach, dont des ouvrages indispensables à la vie en communauté monastique comme *La Règle de saint Benoît* (Cod. 1942). Les traditions de Lambach et d'Admont influencèrent également le jeune *scriptorium* de Melk dont la riche production donna notamment naissance aux *Annales de Melk*. Au début du XVe siècle, le monastère devint l'épicentre d'un mouvement réformiste de grande envergure, qui, grâce aux liens étroits qu'il entretenait avec l'université de Vienne, dota la bibliothèque de nombreuses nouvelles acquisitions. Il suffit de se référer au *Missel de Melk* de 1490 pour mesurer combien ce lieu était un centre d'échange et de production livresque dynamique au service de la Réforme. À l'époque du Baroque, les abbés suivirent de nouvelles maximes. Ils se voyaient comme des princes spirituels, ce qui vaut surtout pour le prélat impérial Berthold Dietmayr (1670–1739). Il transforma la forteresse monacale médiévale en château baroque digne d'accueillir temporairement l'empereur en résidence. L'ensemble décidé par l'abbé Dietmayr et conçu par l'architecte Jakob Prandtauer (1660–1726) est un somptueux joyau d'art baroque s'étendant sur

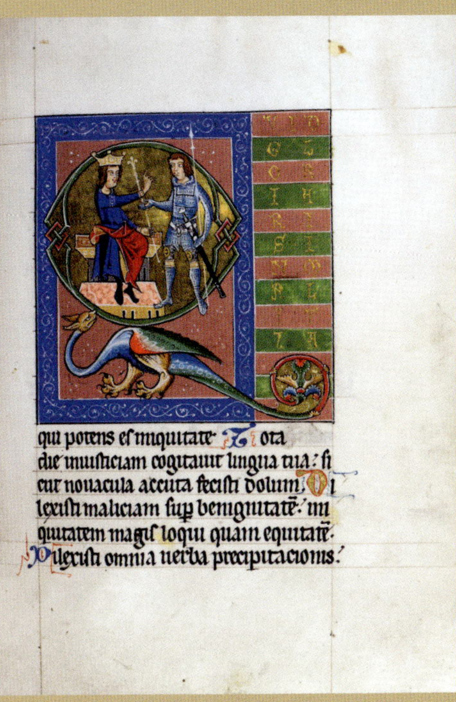

plus de 300 mètres de longueur, surplombant le sud et la vallée du Danube avec une façade occidentale. Il inclut un portail à deux tours au niveau de l'église abbatiale, des appartements impériaux et une bibliothèque. Les salles de la bibliothèque furent achevées en 1735. La salle d'apparat renferme à elle seule 16 000 livres ordonnancés par thème, toujours visibles dans leur disposition originale. Le bibliothécaire Martin Kropff exposa dans son *Bibliotheca Mellicensis*, imprimé en 1747, le concept qui visait à mettre la bibliothèque en valeur.

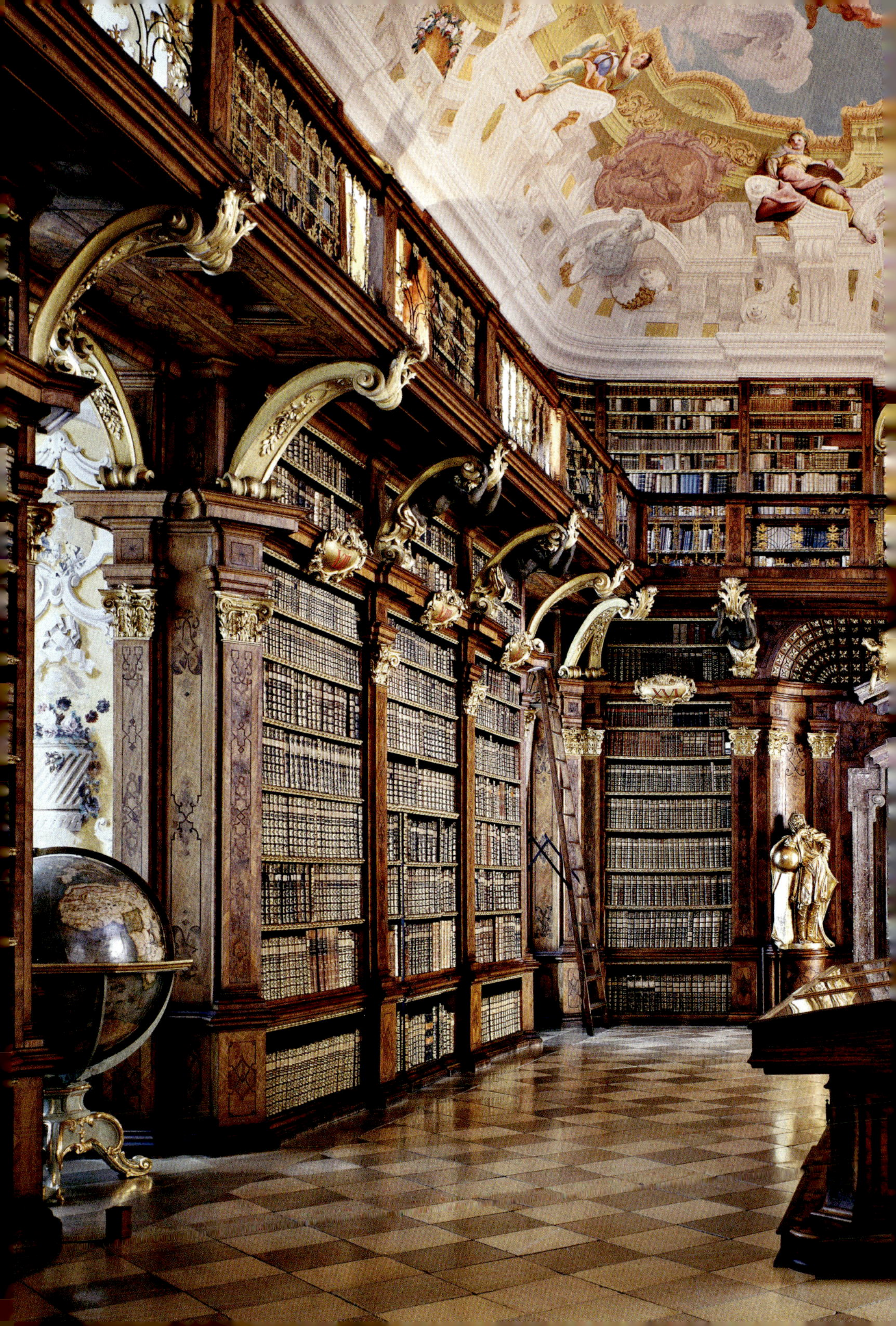

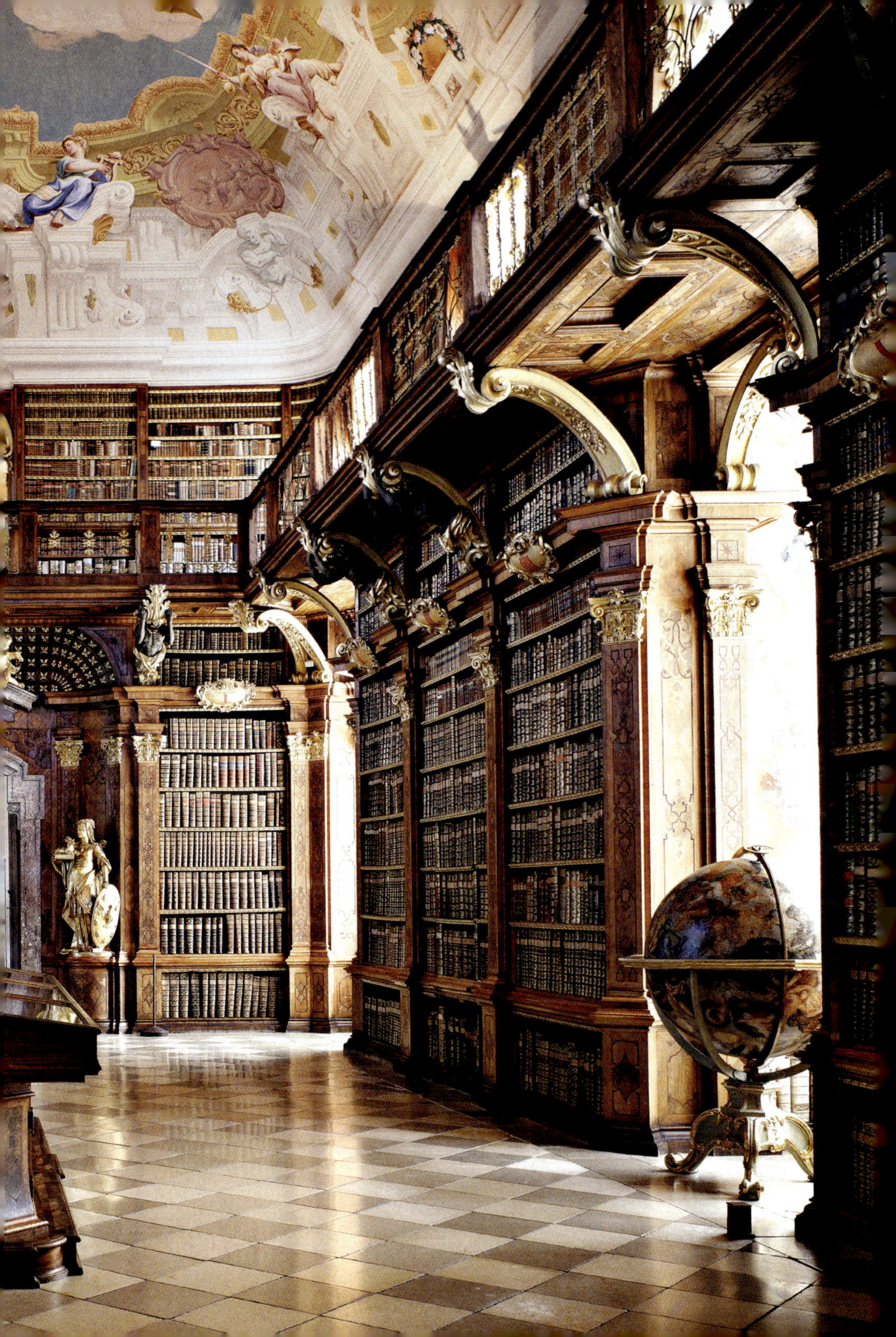

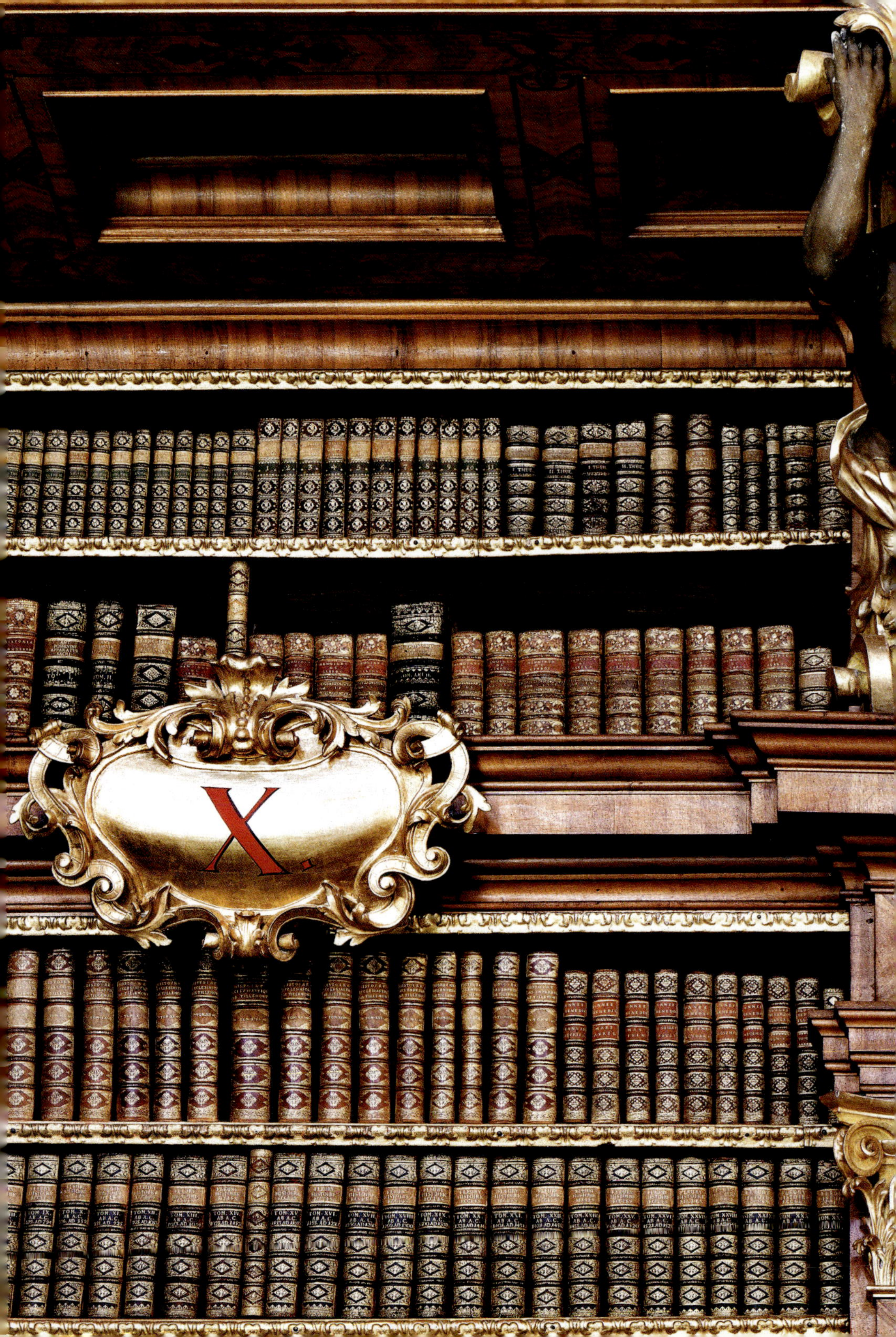

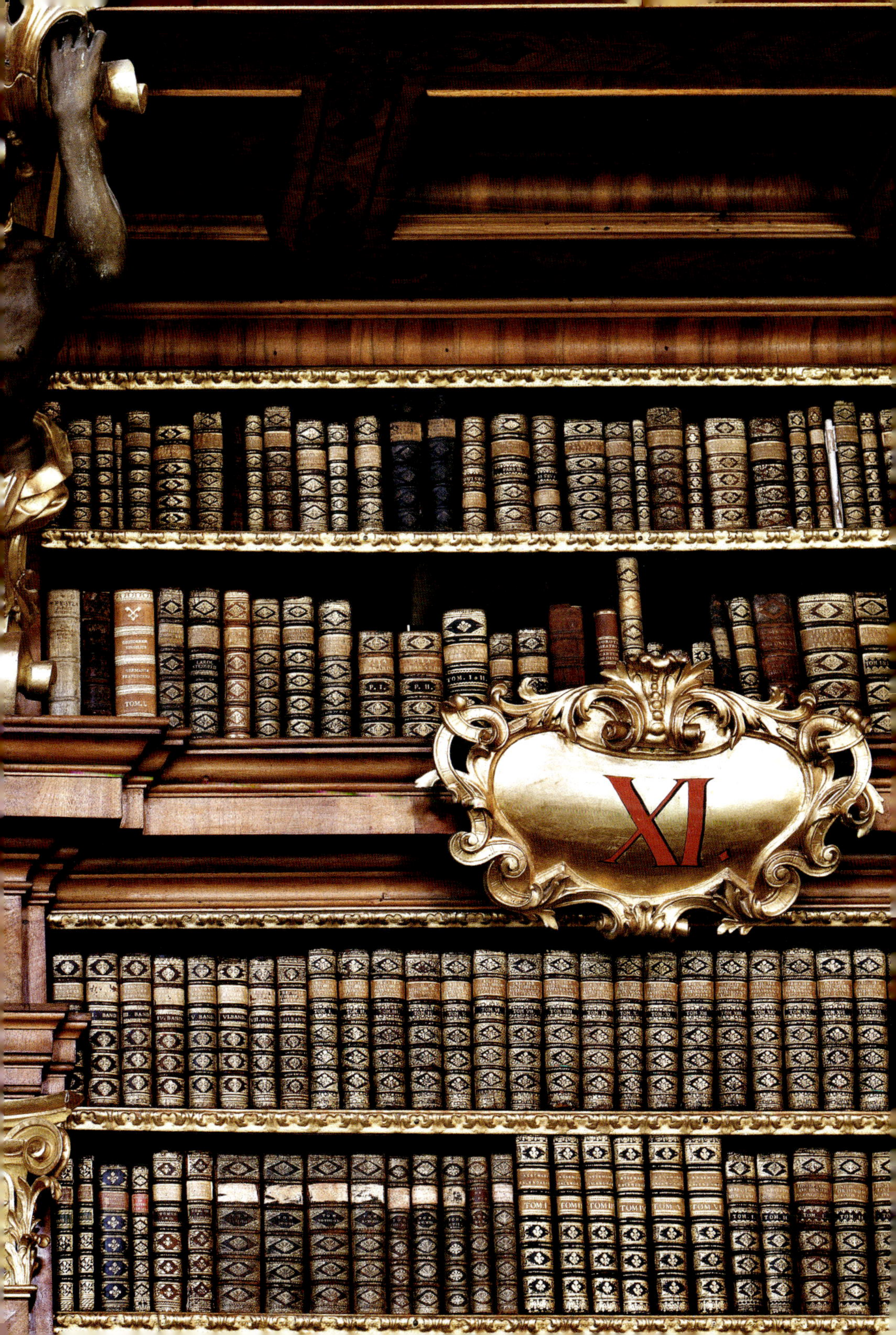

Stiftsbibliothek Seitenstetten

The massive quadrangle of Seitenstetten Abbey, which was rebuilt in its present form between 1718 and 1742 by monastery architect Josef Munggenast (1680–1741), still conveys a sense of its fortified medieval nucleus. With the assistance of the see of Passau and its bishop Ulrich I (c. 1027–1121), a canonry was first founded here around 1112 and settled in 1114 by Benedictine monks from Göttweig. Extensive landholdings, and a secure income from iron mines and saltworks, enabled the abbey to establish itself in the Middle Ages as an important economic and cultural centre. A monastery school operated here from the 12th century onwards, but although the abbey also maintained a library, it was destroyed by fire on several occasions. Systematic steps to build up a library were only taken as a consequence of the reform movement initiated at Melk, which spread to Seitenstetten in 1437 and which placed study and learning at the centre of monastic life. The manuscripts acquired in the wake of this spiritual renewal today represent the library's oldest holdings. Even earlier liturgical manuscripts, originally also kept at Seitenstetten, have today passed into other collections, such as the Morgan Library in New York. The core holdings of the abbey library nevertheless date largely from the Baroque era; the collections of sermons dominating the acquisitions of the early 17th century were joined from the middle of that century by works on theology, philosophy and church history. The introduction of white bindings during these years suggests that an impressive visual impact was already one of the considerations in the way the books were displayed. Josef Munggenast, who as the successor to Jakob Prandtauer (1660–1726) was responsible for the remodelling of a series of medieval monasteries in the Danube region, transformed the Romanesque and early Gothic abbey into a magnificent complex enclosing several courtyards. With its grand reception rooms it offered the prelates of the Baroque era an architectural framework befitting their status. Particular importance was thereby attached to the library, which rises through two storeys in the south wing. The monumental ceiling fresco by Paul Troger (1698–1762) depicts the Book with the Seven Seals described in the Revelation of St John. The clear layout of the approximately 17,000 books in the main hall, located there since 1763, results from their uniform bindings and lettering as well as their strict arrangement by size. The adjoining rooms, housing the reference library, study room, natural history collection and coin collection, were completed in 1777.

※∴※

Founded c. 1109; library built 1718–1742 after plans by Josef Munggenast
Holdings c. 90,000 volumes, of which 277 incunabula and 270 medieval manuscripts
Type of library monastic library, school library, academic library
Highlights *Codex Seitenstettensis of Plutarch*, second half of the 10th century, with supplements of the early 14th and the second half of the 15th century (Cod. 34); *Bible*, manuscript with parts from the 12th century (Cod. 79); Caspar Plautz, *Nova typis transacta navigatio*, Linz, 1621

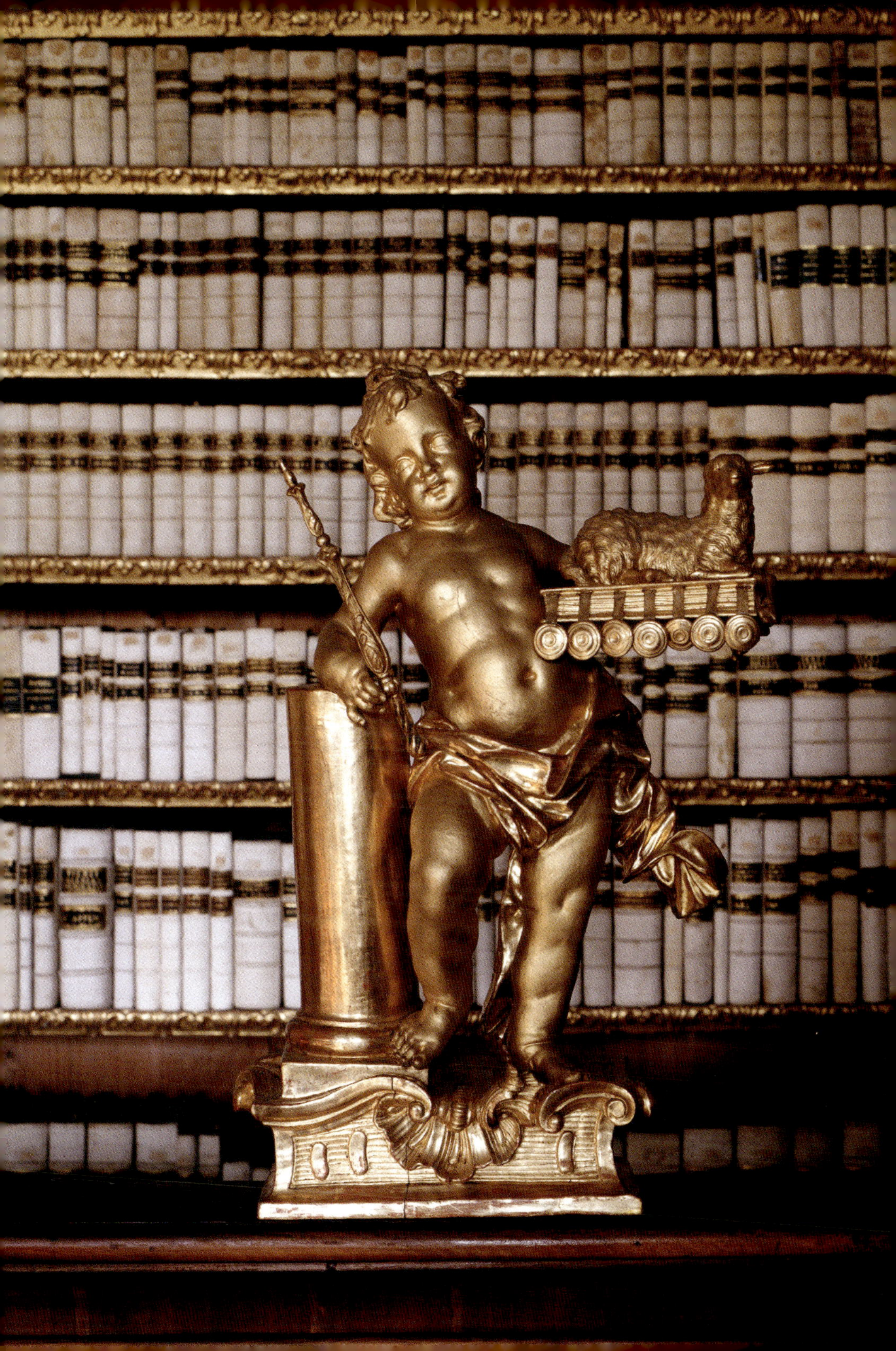

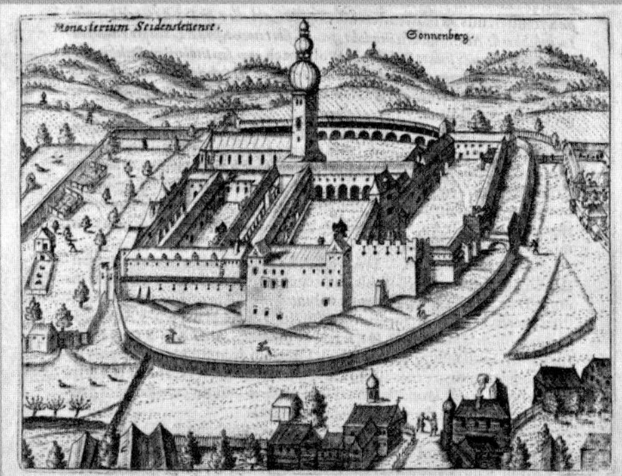

Das mächtige Geviert des in seiner heutigen Gestalt vom Stiftsarchitekten Josef
Munggenast (1680–1741) zwischen 1718 und
1742 erneuerten Benediktinerklosters lässt
noch die mittelalterliche Wehranlage in seinem
Kern erahnen. Unter dem Einfluss des Bistums
Passau und seines Bischofs Ulrich I. (um 1027–
1121) war hier um 1112 ein erstes Kanonikerstift
gegründet und 1114 mit Benediktinern aus
Göttweig besiedelt worden. Reicher Grundbe-
sitz und gesicherte Einkünfte aus Eisengruben
und Salzwerken machten das Stift im Mittelalter zu einem bedeutenden wirtschaftlichen und
zivilisatorischen Zentrum, das bereits ab dem
12. Jahrhundert eine Klosterschule betrieb.
Der systematische Aufbau einer Bibliothek,
die zwar vorhanden war, aber mehrfach durch
Brände vernichtet wurde, ist erst jener von
Melk ausgehenden und ab 1437 in Seitenstetten
wirksamen Reformbewegung zu verdanken,
die Textstudium und Wissenschaft in den Mittelpunkt des klösterlichen Lebens stellte. Die
im Zuge dieser spirituellen Erneuerung angeschafften Handschriften stellen heute den
ältesten Bestand in der Bibliothek dar. Ältere,
gleichwohl aus Seitenstetten stammende
liturgische Handschriften sind aus dem Kloster
in verschiedene andere Bibliotheken gelangt, so
zum Beispiel in die Morgan Library in New York.
Der die Stiftsbibliothek prägende Grundbestand entstammt jedoch großteils dem Barock.
Zu der im frühen 17. Jahrhundert schwerpunkt-
mäßig angeschafften Predigtliteratur kamen ab

der Mitte des Jahrhunderts Werke zur Theologie, Philosophie und Kirchengeschichte hinzu.
Ab diesen Jahren angefertigte, einheitlich
weiße Bindungen lassen bereits eine repräsentative Aufstellung der Bücher vermuten. Josef
Munggenast, der in der Nachfolge Jakob
Prandtauers (1660–1726) für den Umbau einer
Reihe mittelalterlicher Klöster im Donauraum
verantwortlich war, baute den romanisch-
frühgotischen Klosterbezirk zu einer groß-
zügigen mehrhöfigen Anlage um. Sie bot den
Prälaten des Barocks mit ihren Prunkräumen
einen adäquaten repräsentativen Rahmen.
Unter diesen kommt der Bibliothek, die sich
im Südtrakt über zwei Geschosse erstreckt,
ein besonderer Stellenwert zu. Paul Trogers
(1698–1762) monumentales Deckenfresko
stellt das Buch mit den sieben Siegeln nach der
Geheimen Offenbarung des Johannes dar.
Die seit 1763 bestehende übersichtliche Anordnung der rund 17 000 Bücher im Hauptsaal wird
nicht nur durch deren einheitliche Bindung
und Beschriftung, sondern auch die konse-
quente Anordnung nach Formaten bewirkt.
Ab 1777 war auch die an den Hauptraum
anschließende Raumfolge mit der Handbibliothek, dem Studierzimmer, der Naturalien-
sammlung und dem numismatischen Kabinett
fertig eingerichtet.

✳✳✳

Le puissant carré dont la forme actuelle est
de l'architecte du monastère Josef Munggenast
(1680–1741), réalisé entre 1718 et 1742, laisse
entrevoir la structure de la forteresse médiévale. Sous l'influence de l'évêché de Passau
et d'Ulrich Ier (vers 1027–1121), une abbaye de
chanoines fut érigée vers 1112, puis investie
par les bénédictins de l'abbaye de Göttweig en
1114. La vaste seigneurie foncière et les revenus
assurés par les mines de fer et le travail du sel
firent de l'abbaye un centre économique et
civilisateur majeur. Elle administra une école
dès le XIIe siècle. L'aménagement systématique
d'une bibliothèque – préexistante certes,
mais maintes fois réduite à néant par des

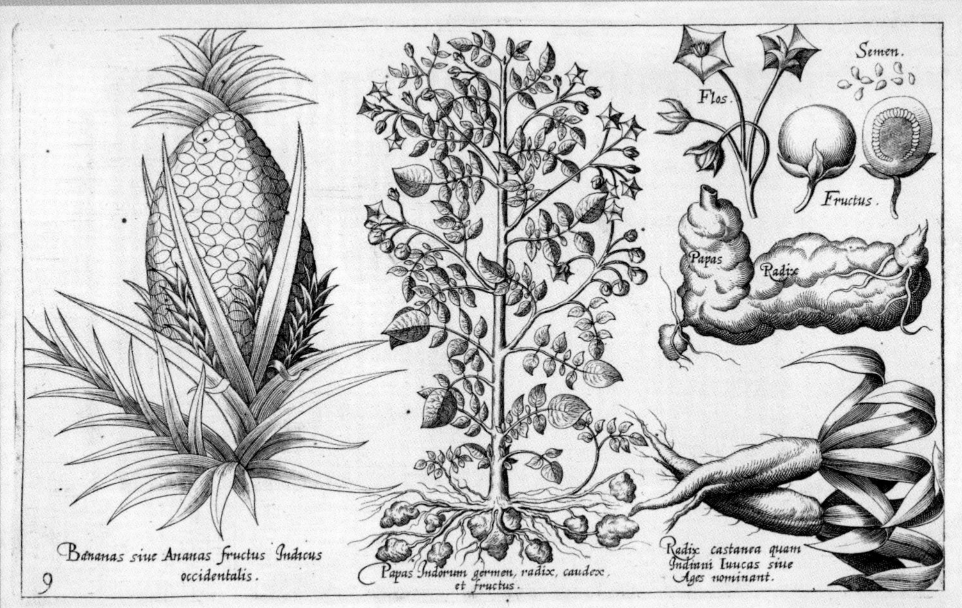

incendies – est dû au mouvement réformateur amorcé à Melk qui influença Seitenstetten dès 1437. Celui-ci plaçait l'étude des textes et la science au premier plan de la vie monacale. Les manuscrits réalisés suivant l'impulsion de ce renouveau spirituel constituent le fonds le plus ancien de la bibliothèque. Certains manuscrits liturgiques plus anciens encore et également réalisés à Seitenstetten sont parvenus dans d'autres bibliothèques, telles que la Morgan Library à New York. Le fonds de base caractéristique de la bibliothèque de Seitenstetten provient toutefois principalement du Baroque. Les ouvrages de prédication datant surtout du début du XVIIe siècle furent rapidement complétés par des ouvrages de théologie, de philosophie et d'histoire religieuse. La reliure blanche uniforme exécutée à partir de cette période indique l'important rôle représentatif accordé aux livres. Josef Munggenast, responsable de la réfection d'une série de monastères médiévaux dans la région du Danube à la suite de Jakob Prandtauer (1660–1726), convertit le domaine monastique roman pré-gothique en un complexe à plusieurs cours dont les salles d'apparat correspondaient aux aspirations des prélats de l'époque baroque. L'une de ces salles majestueuses n'est autre que la bibliothèque. Occupant une place de choix dans l'aile sud, elle s'étend sur deux niveaux. La peinture de plafond monumentale réalisée par Paul Troger (1698–1762) présente le Livre des sept sceaux issu de l'Apocalypse de saint Jean. Les quelque 17 000 ouvrages ont été placés dans la salle principale en 1763. L'effet d'optique créé par l'uniformité des reliures et inscriptions ainsi que la répartition systématique par format est très impressionnant. Les pièces attenantes (la salle de lecture, la salle d'étude, le Cabinet de curiosités naturelles et le Cabinet de numismatique) furent également aménagées en 1777.

Carolus Stengel, _Seitenstetten Abbey_, in: _Monasteriologia_, Augsburg, 1638, p. 21

Caspar Plautz, _Nova typis transacta navigatio_, Linz, 1621, pl. 9: _Ananas comosus_ (left), _Papas Indorum ist Solanum tuberosum_ (centre and upper right), _Radix castanea ist Manihot esculenta_ (lower right)

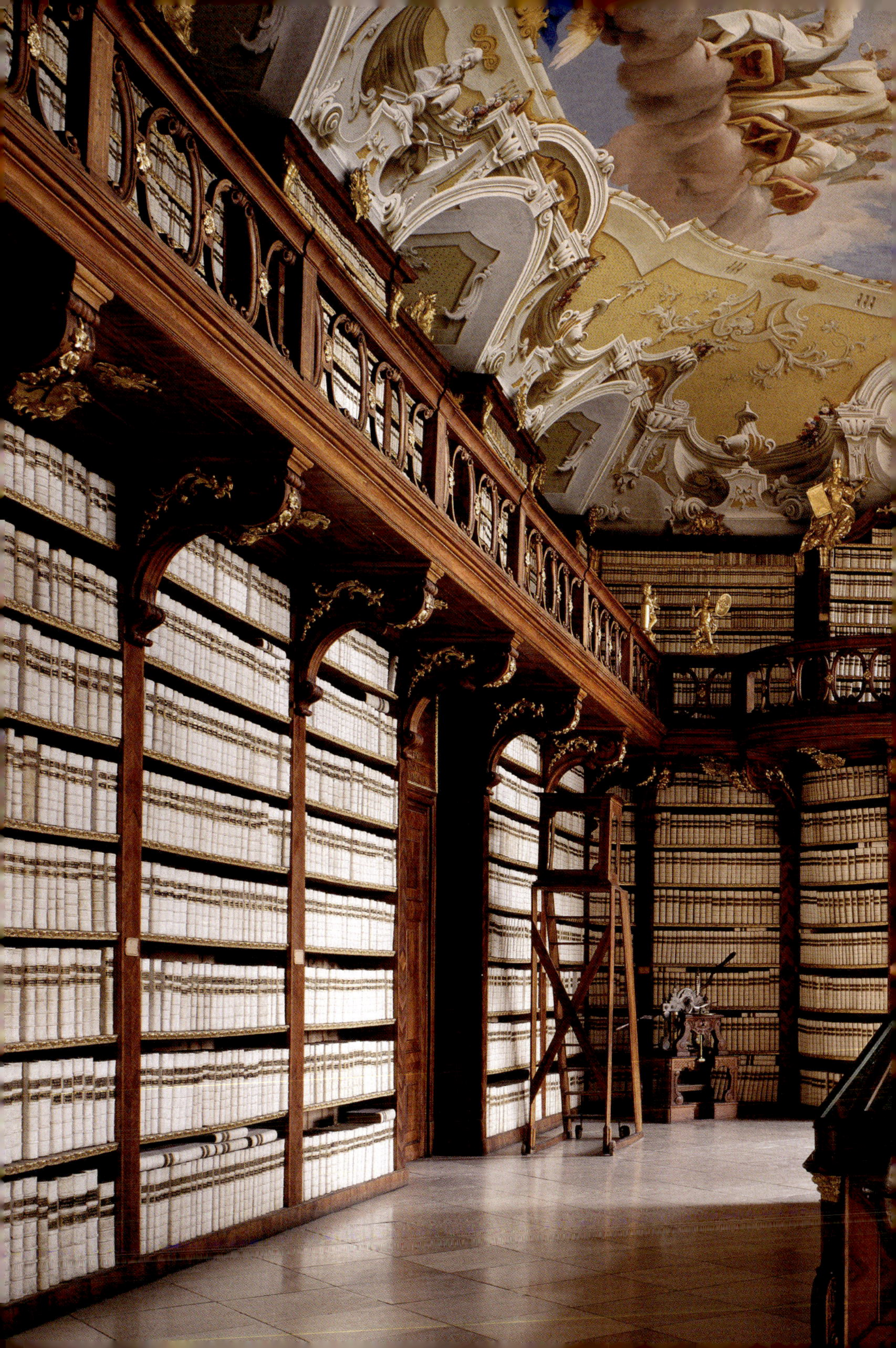

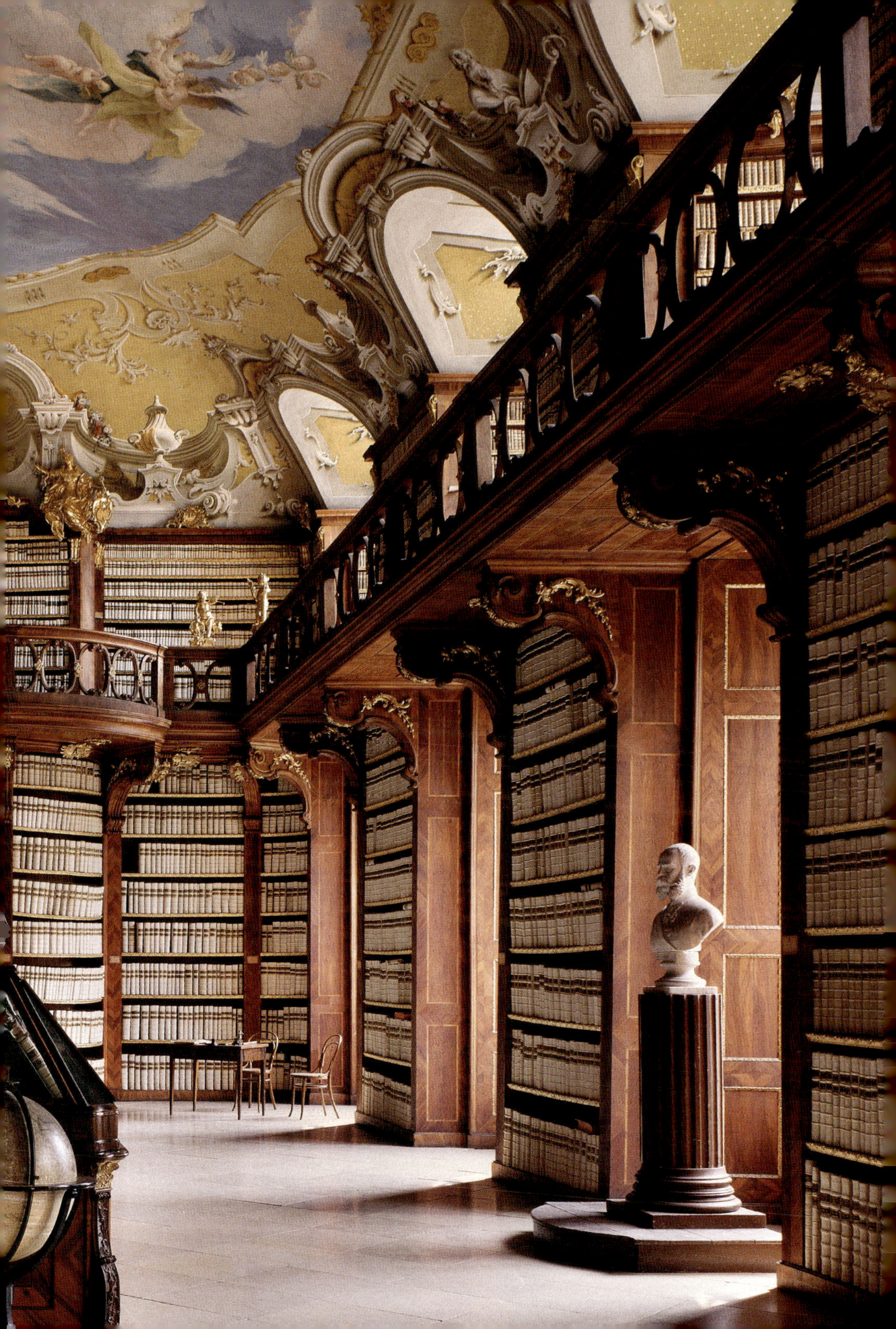

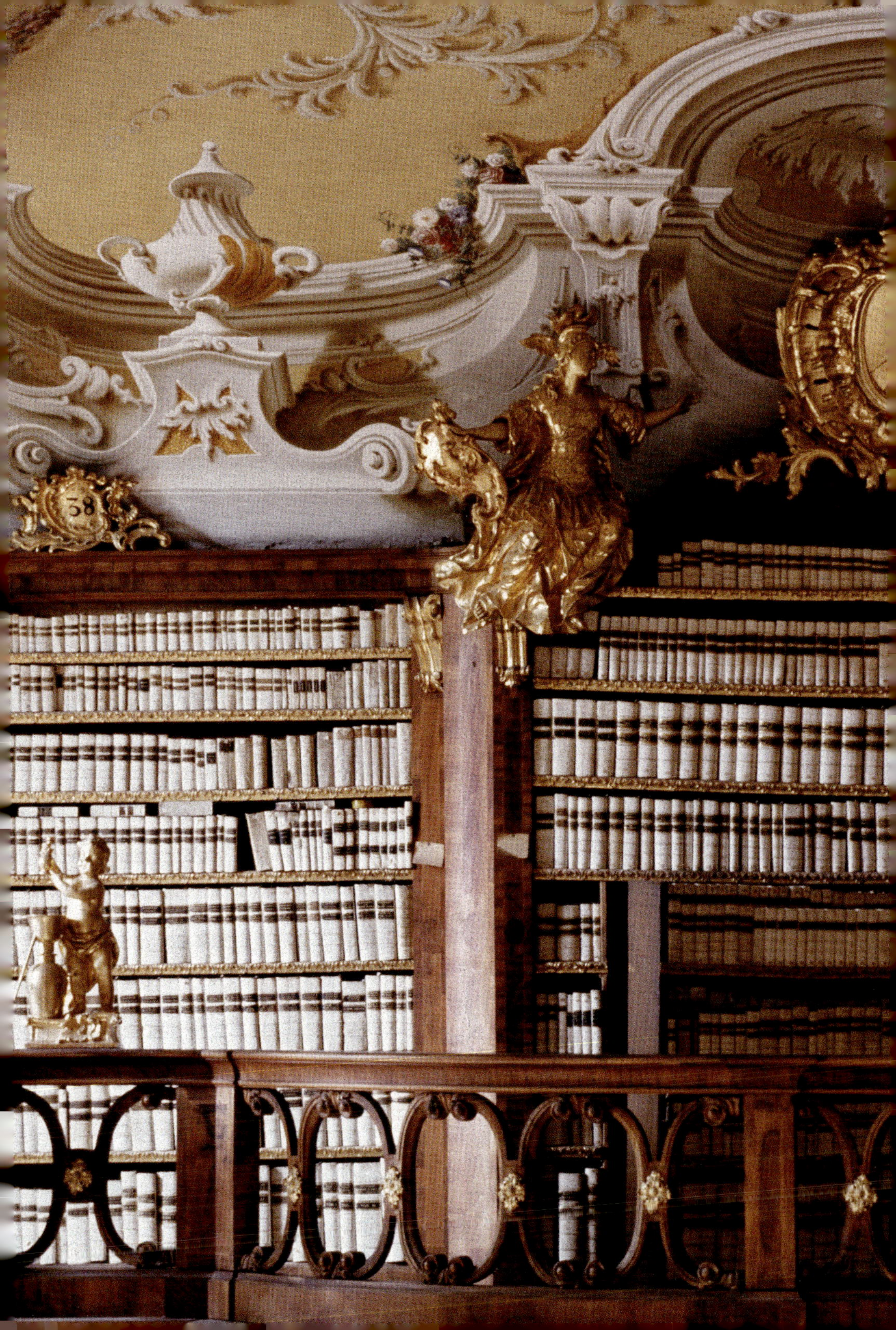

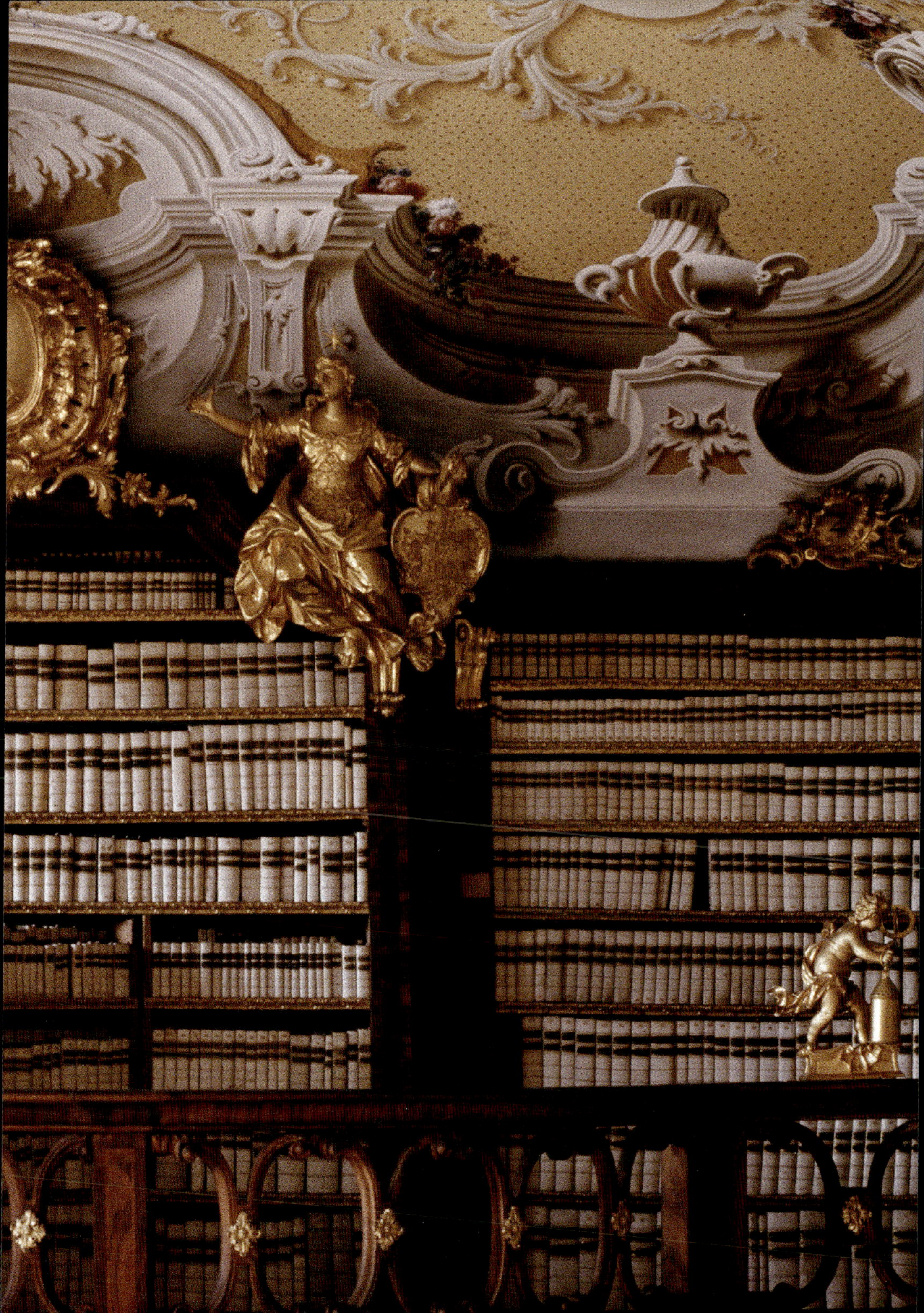

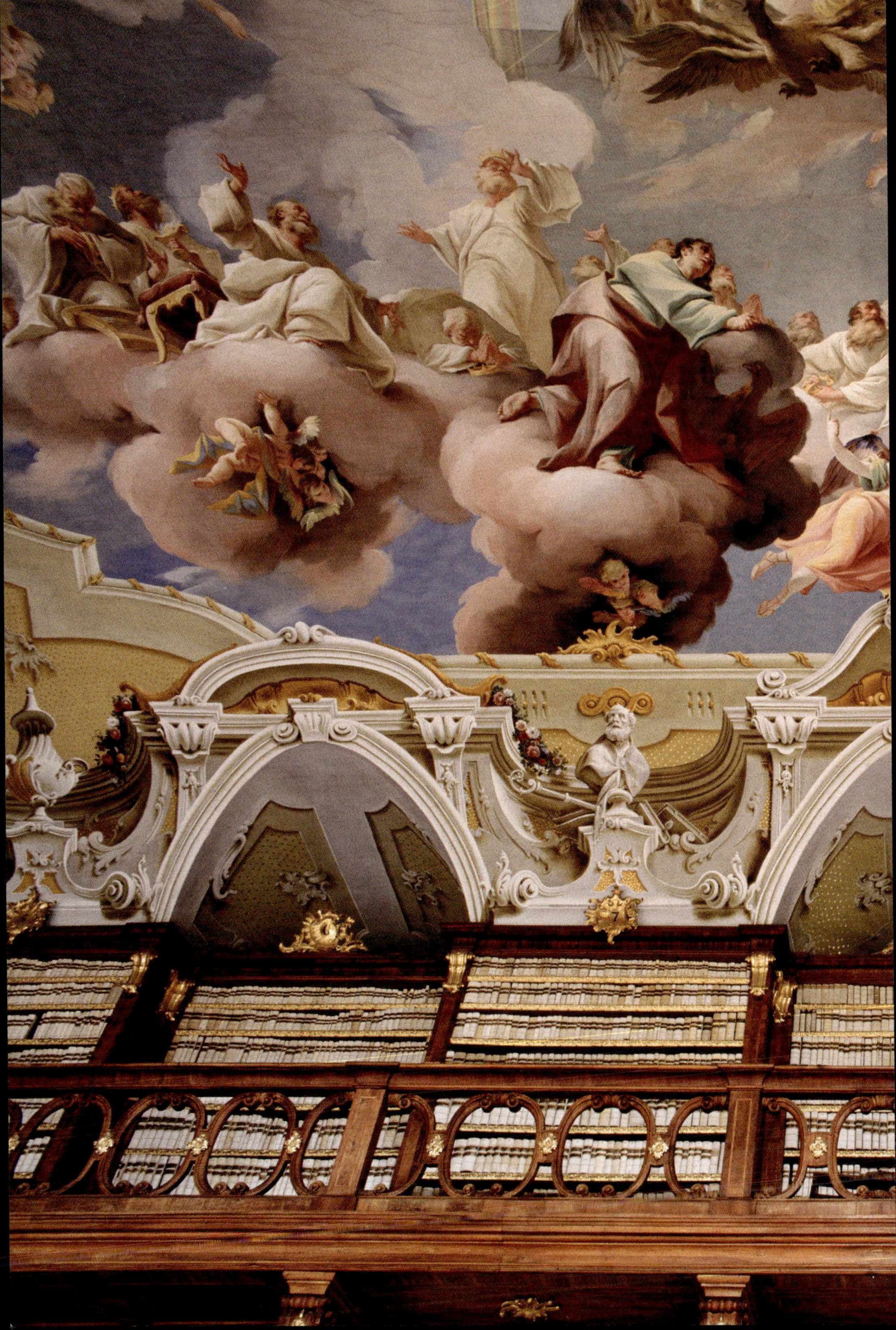

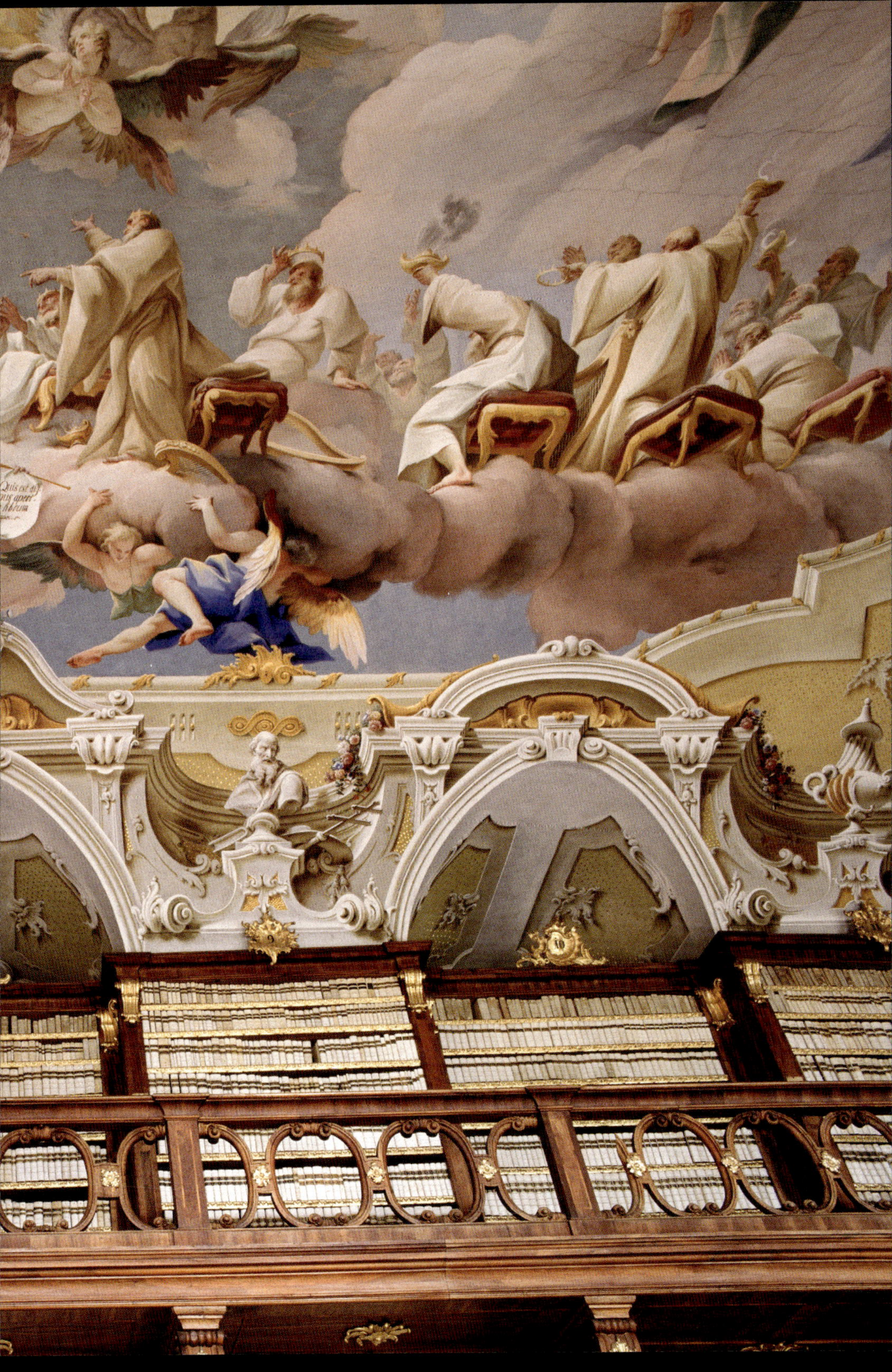

Stiftsbibliothek Zwettl

Zwettl Abbey was founded in 1138 by Hadmar and Gertrud of Kuenring and was chosen as the family abbey and burial place of this powerful noble house. It was settled at their request by Cistercian monks from Heiligenkreuz Abbey, which the ruling margraves of Austria had founded five years earlier and designated as the burial place of several Babenbergs. Like Heiligenkreuz, Zwettl was built in accordance with strict Cistercian principles. It lay in an isolated location not far from the border with Bohemia, in the heart of an unpopulated forested region at a bend of the River Kamp. Imperial privileges and royal protection meant that the abbey complex developed and grew continuously from the middle of the 12th century up until its last major renovation in 1720–1740. This stability encouraged a flourishing scriptorium, whose wide-ranging production, particularly busy in the 12th century, continued right up to the Early Modern Era, and also facilitated a continuous growth in the abbey's collection of books. The collection increased steadily from the 12th century onwards with no major losses, while many of the liturgical manuscripts, annals and inventories in the abbey's library and archives originated in its own scriptorium. The library was initially housed in the armarium between the chapterhouse and the church, but in 1495 was assigned its own room east of the cloister, where some 500 chained books and around 1,000 codices were accommodated. Librarians are documented by name from 1300 onwards. In the 17th century it became necessary to build two new rooms to house the rapidly expanding collection. The large library hall still visible today was constructed between 1730 and 1732; two storeys in height and with its long walls completely lined with bookshelves, it lies on the north side of the east courtyard within the area reserved for the monks. From the very beginning, therefore (and until 2009, when it was separated out of the monastic enclosure), the library was only accessible to a limited public, since it fulfilled the function of a study room for the monks in line with Cistercian tradition. Decorative gilding and figural herms complement the naturally warm hues of the wooden bookcases, which contain over 28,000 books organised by subject. In the compartments of the vault, Paul Troger (1698–1762) created an allegory of monastic education in scenes from the life of Hercules.

❋❋❋

Founded 1139; large library hall built 1730–1732 by Josef Munggenast
Holdings c. 55,000 volumes, of which around 370 incunabula
Type of library monastic library, academic library
Highlights *Liber fundatorum monasterii Zwetlensis* (book of the founders and benefactors of Zwettl Abbey; also known as the *Bärenhaut*, or "bearskin", after its boar-skin binding), 1310/11, with supplements of 1311–1314, 1320 (StiAZ 2/1); Florian Paucke, *Hin und her. Hin süsse, und vergnügt. Her bitter und betrübt*, c. 1775 (StiBZ 420)

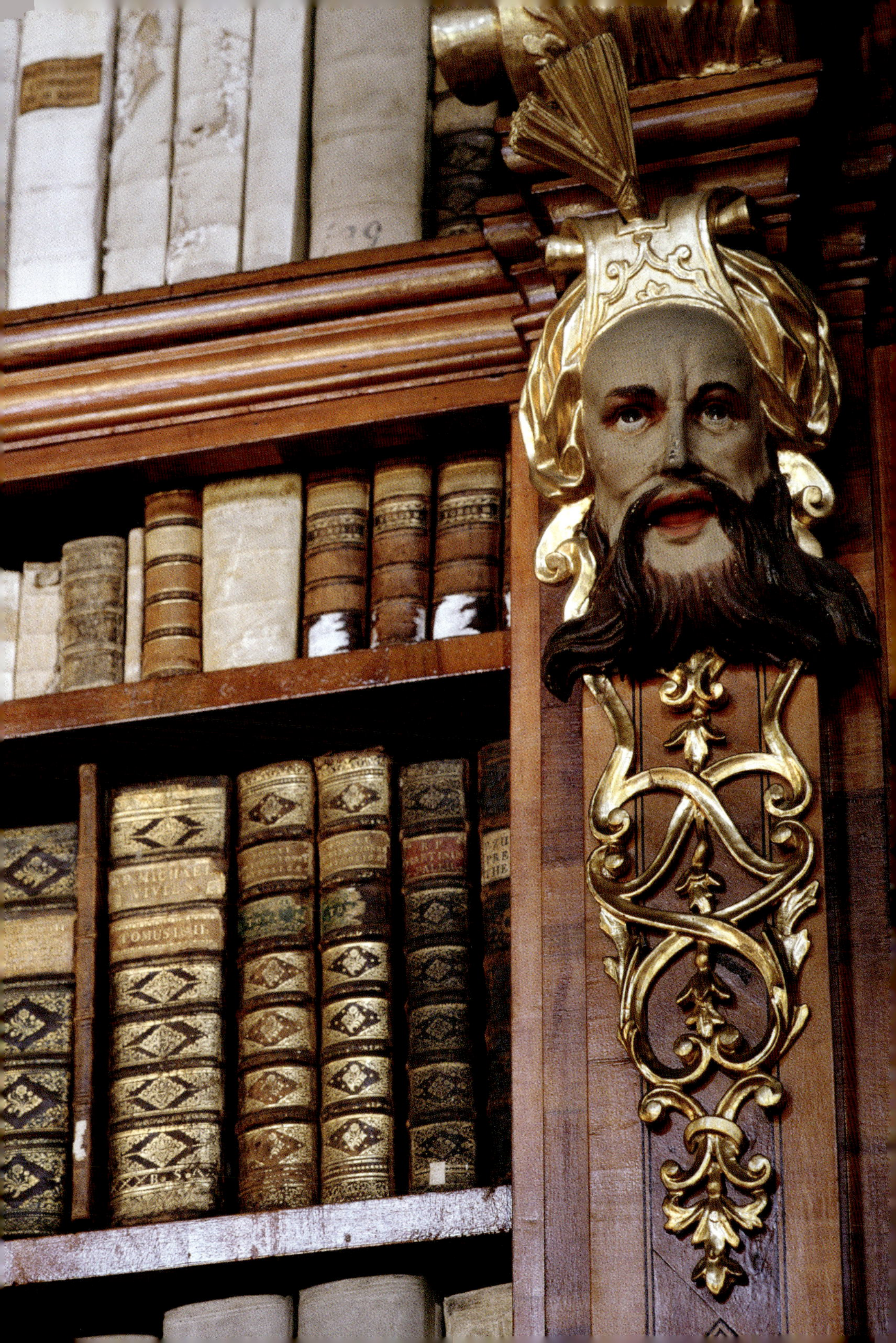

Das Zisterzienserstift Zwettl wurde von Hadmar und Gertrud von Kuenring im Jahr 1138 gegründet und als Grablege und Hauskloster dieses mächtigen Adelsgeschlechts gewählt. Sie beriefen Zisterziensermönche aus dem Kloster Heiligenkreuz, das die regierenden Markgrafen von Österreich fünf Jahre zuvor gegründet und zur Grablege einiger Babenberger bestimmt hatten. Wie das Gründungskloster ist auch Zwettl nach den für Zisterzienser verbindlichen Vorgaben errichtet. Es liegt in Abgeschiedenheit unweit der böhmischen Grenze inmitten eines unerschlossenen Waldgebietes in einer Flussschleife des Kamp. Dank kaiserlichen Privilegs und königlichen Schutzes konnten die Gebäude des Stiftes von der Mitte des 12. Jahrhunderts an bis zur letzten großen Umgestaltung der Jahre 1720 bis 1740 kontinuierlich entwickelt und ausgebaut werden. Diese Stabilität begünstigte nicht nur eine umfassende, im 12. Jahrhundert besonders rege (und bis in die frühe Neuzeit nachzuvollziehende) Skriptorentätigkeit, der die Klosterbibliothek und das Archiv liturgische Handschriften, Annalen

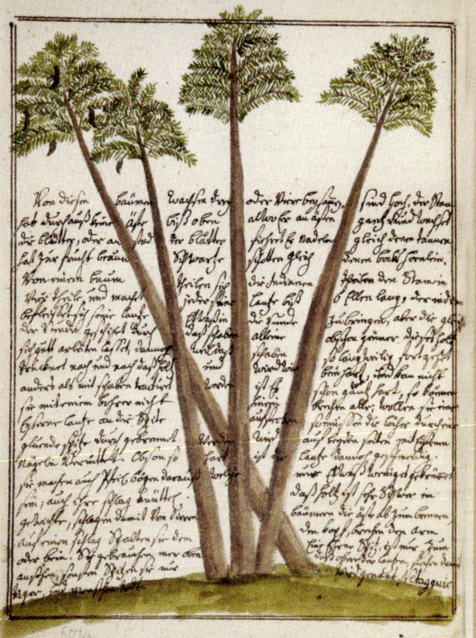

und Verzeichnisse verdanken, sondern auch ein stetes Anwachsen der Büchersammlung, die sich ab dem 12. Jahrhundert ohne wesentliche Verluste kontinuierlich entwickeln konnte. Sie war zunächst im Armarium zwischen Kapitelsaal und Kirche untergebracht, seit 1495 aber in einem eigenen Saal östlich des Kreuzgangs, wo sich etwa 500 Kettenbücher und um die 1 000 sonstige Kodizes befanden. Seit 1300 sind Bibliothekare namentlich überliefert. Das rasante Anwachsen der Buchbestände im 17. Jahrhundert erforderte die Errichtung zweier neuer Büchersäle. Von 1730 bis 1732 wurde schließlich der große, über zwei Geschosse reichende und an seinen Längsseiten komplett von Bücherregalen eingenommene Bibliothekssaal errichtet, der sich im Nordflügel des östlichen Konventhofes im Klausurbereich der Mönche befand. Er war daher von Anfang an (und bis 2009, als er aus der Klausur ausgegliedert wurde) nur einem beschränkten Publikum zugänglich, da er gemäß der Ordenstradition die Funktion eines Studierzimmers der Mönche erfüllte. Die Bücherschränke sind in warmen Holztönen gehalten, teils in Gold gefasst und mit Hermen figural dekoriert. Sie beherbergen über 28 000 Bücher, die in thematische Abteilungen gegliedert sind. In den Gewölbekompartimenten hat Paul Troger (1698–1762) mit Szenen aus dem Leben des Herkules eine Allegorie auf die klösterliche Bildung geschaffen.

✳ ✳ ✳

L'abbaye cistercienne de Zwettl fut fondée par Hadmar et Gertrud de Kuenring en 1138, puis choisie comme couvent familial et caveau de cette puissante famille noble. Ils firent venir des moines de l'abbaye cistercienne de Heiligenkreuz, que les margraves administrant l'Autriche avaient fondée cinq ans plus tôt et désignée comme lieu de sépulture de la Maison de Babenberg. À l'instar de l'abbaye-mère, le plan du monastère de Zwettl répondait aux besoins et prescriptions de la doctrine cistercienne. Isolée, nichée au creux d'un méandre de la Kamp, l'abbaye se trouve au cœur d'une

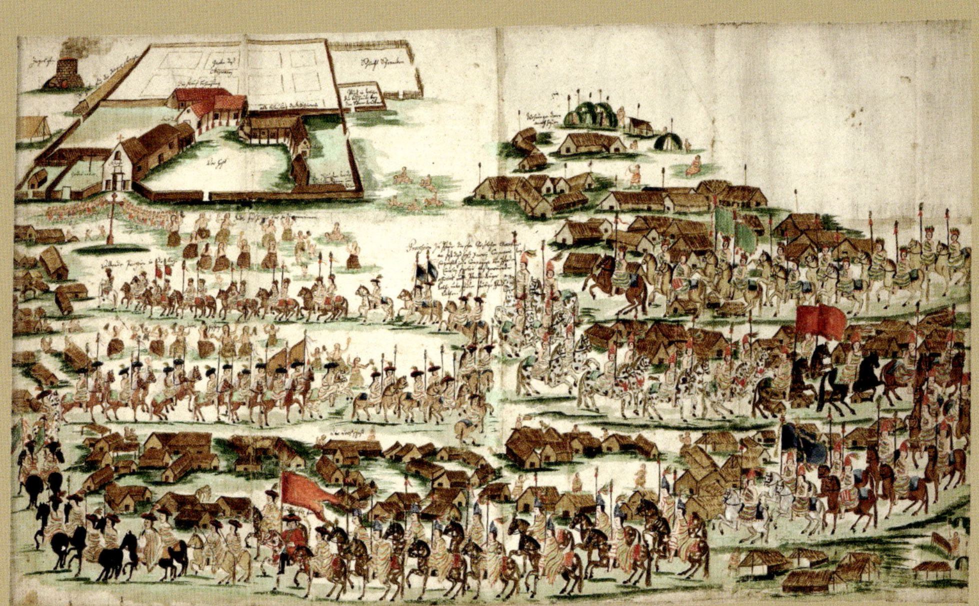

forêt sauvage, non loin de la frontière avec la Bohême. Sous protection royale et dotés de privilèges impériaux, les bâtiments furent augmentés et aménagés en continu depuis le milieu du XIIe siècle jusqu'à la dernière rénovation, entreprise entre 1720 et 1740. D'une part, cette stabilité favorisa l'activité du *scriptorium*, particulièrement intense au XIIe siècle et dont on suit les traces jusqu'à l'époque moderne, notamment grâce au contenu de la bibliothèque ou des archives possédant des manuscrits liturgiques, des annales et des catalogues. D'autre part, l'accroissement continu de la collection de livres s'en trouva encouragé. Aucune perte fondamentale n'a été signalée depuis la fondation. La collection fut tout d'abord installée dans l'*armarium*, entre l'église et la salle capitulaire. Elle disposait de sa propre salle à l'est du cloître, dès 1495. On pouvait alors y trouver près de mille codex et quelque 500 livres enchaînés (*liber catenatus*). La charge de bibliothécaire se transmettait nommément depuis 1300. La croissance effrénée du fonds exigea la construction de deux salons supplémentaires au XVIIe siècle. Enfin, une

immense salle de bibliothèque s'étendant sur deux niveaux et intégrant tous les rayonnages dans sa longueur fut érigée en 1730–1732. Elle se trouvait dans l'aile nord de la cour orientale du couvent, dans la clôture monastique. Dès les débuts (et jusqu'à son extraction de la clôture en 2009), son accès resta donc très limité, selon la tradition de l'ordre qui voulait qu'elle remplisse la fonction de chambre d'étude des moines. Les étagères de la bibliothèque ont été réalisées dans des bois aux tons chauds. Elles sont parées d'hermès et de dorures et accueillent plus de 28 000 livres, répartis en sections thématiques. Paul Troger (1698–1762) illustra les voûtes du plafond au moyen de scènes tirées de la vie d'Hercule et réalisa une allégorie de l'éducation monacale.

Florian Paucke, *Hin und her. Hin süsse, und vergnügt. Her bitter und betrübt*, c. 1775, sig. StiBZ 420, fol. 504a: *Norway Spruce (Picea abies)*

Florian Paucke, *Hin und her. Hin süsse, und vergnügt. Her bitter und betrübt*, c. 1775, sig. StiBZ 420: *Paucke Scroll*

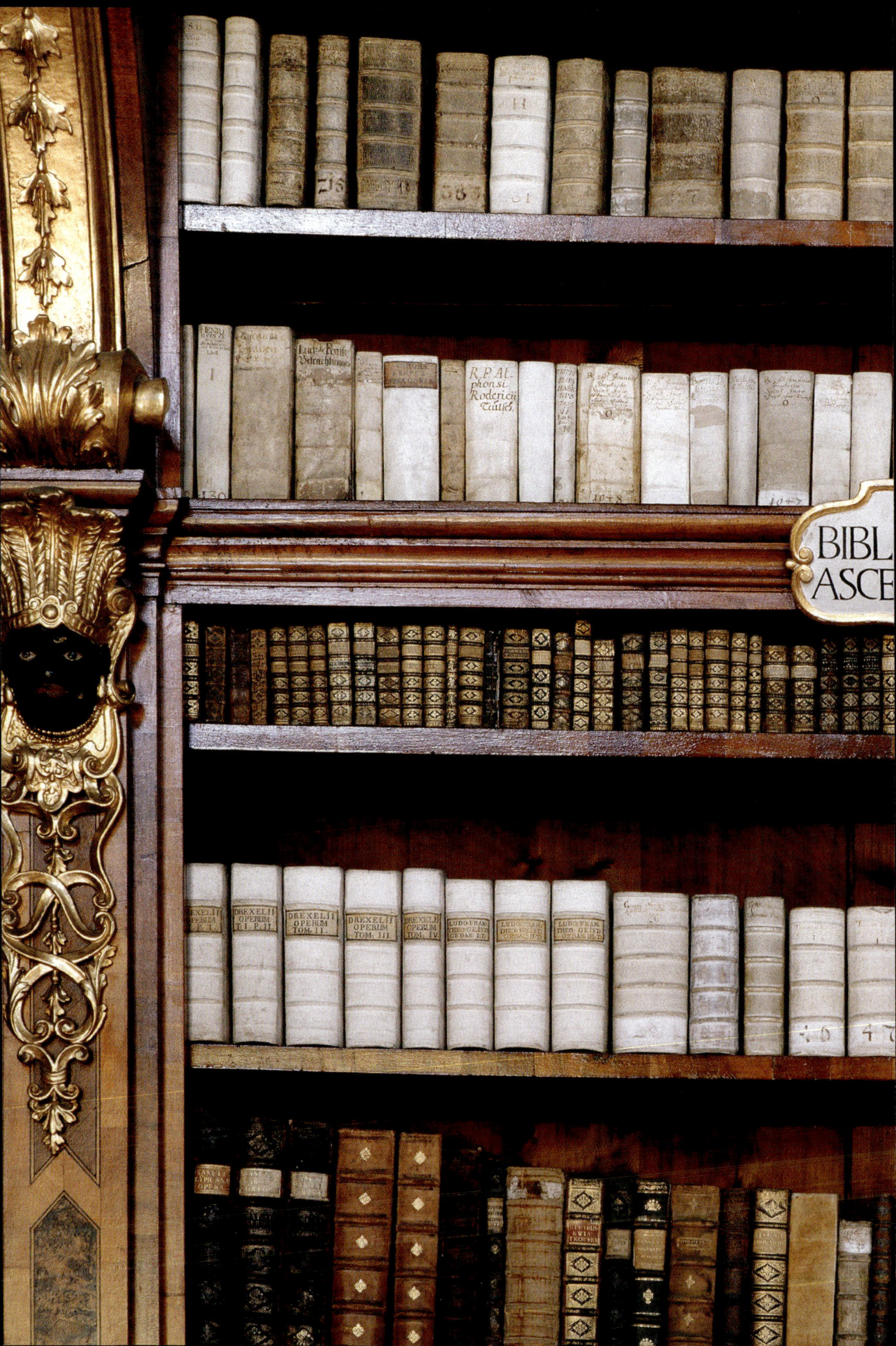
R.P. Alphonsi Roderici Teütsch.
BIBL
ASCE
DREXELII OPERUM T.I. P.I.
DREXELII OPERUM T.I. P.II.
DREXELII OPERUM TOM. II.
DREXELII OPERUM TOM. III.
DREXELII OPERUM TOM. IV.
LUDO. FRAN. THEO. GEST. GEDAN. II.
LUDO. FRAN. THEO. GEST. GEDAN. IV.
LUDO. FRAN. THEO. GEST. GEDAN. II.

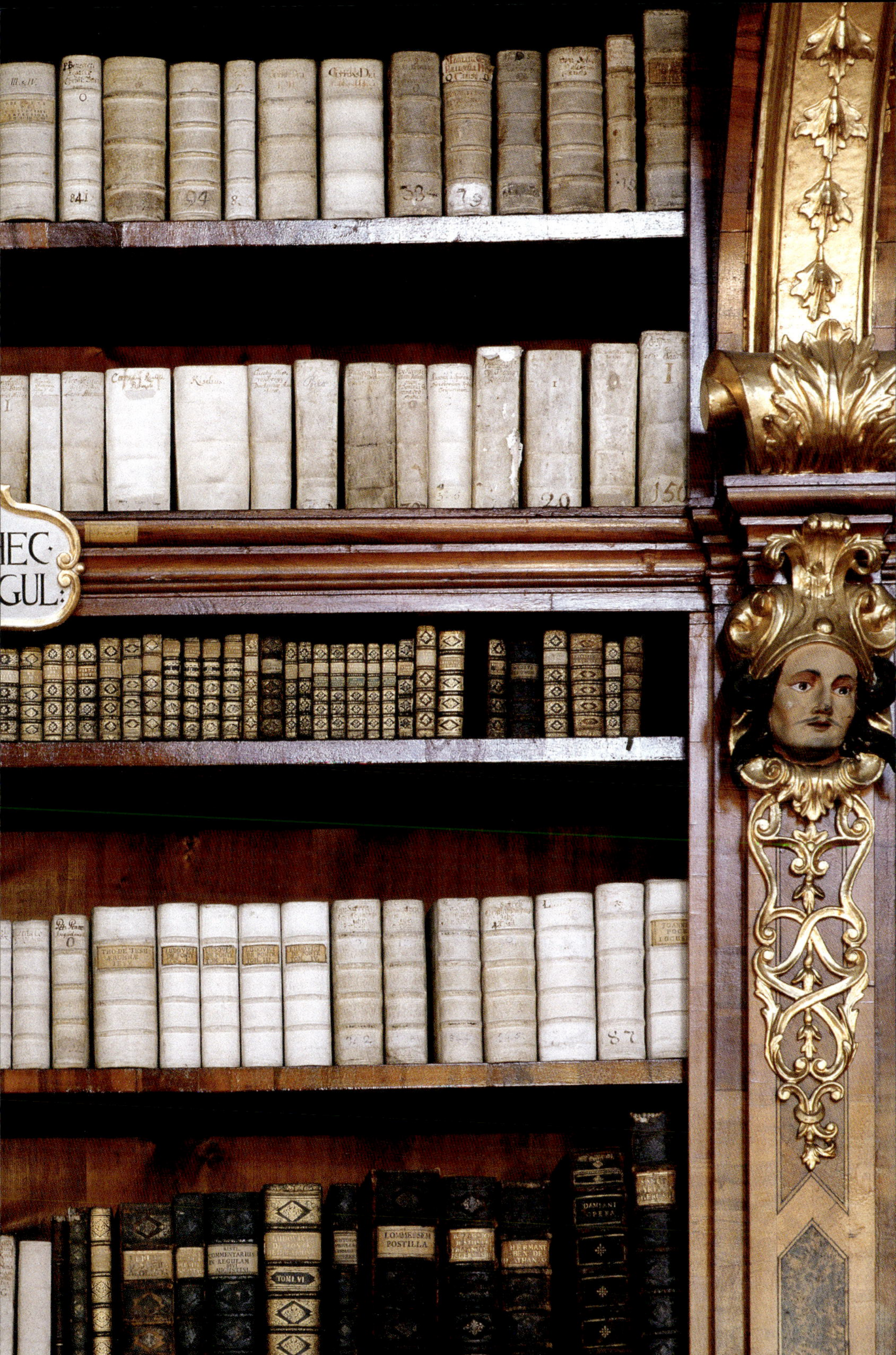

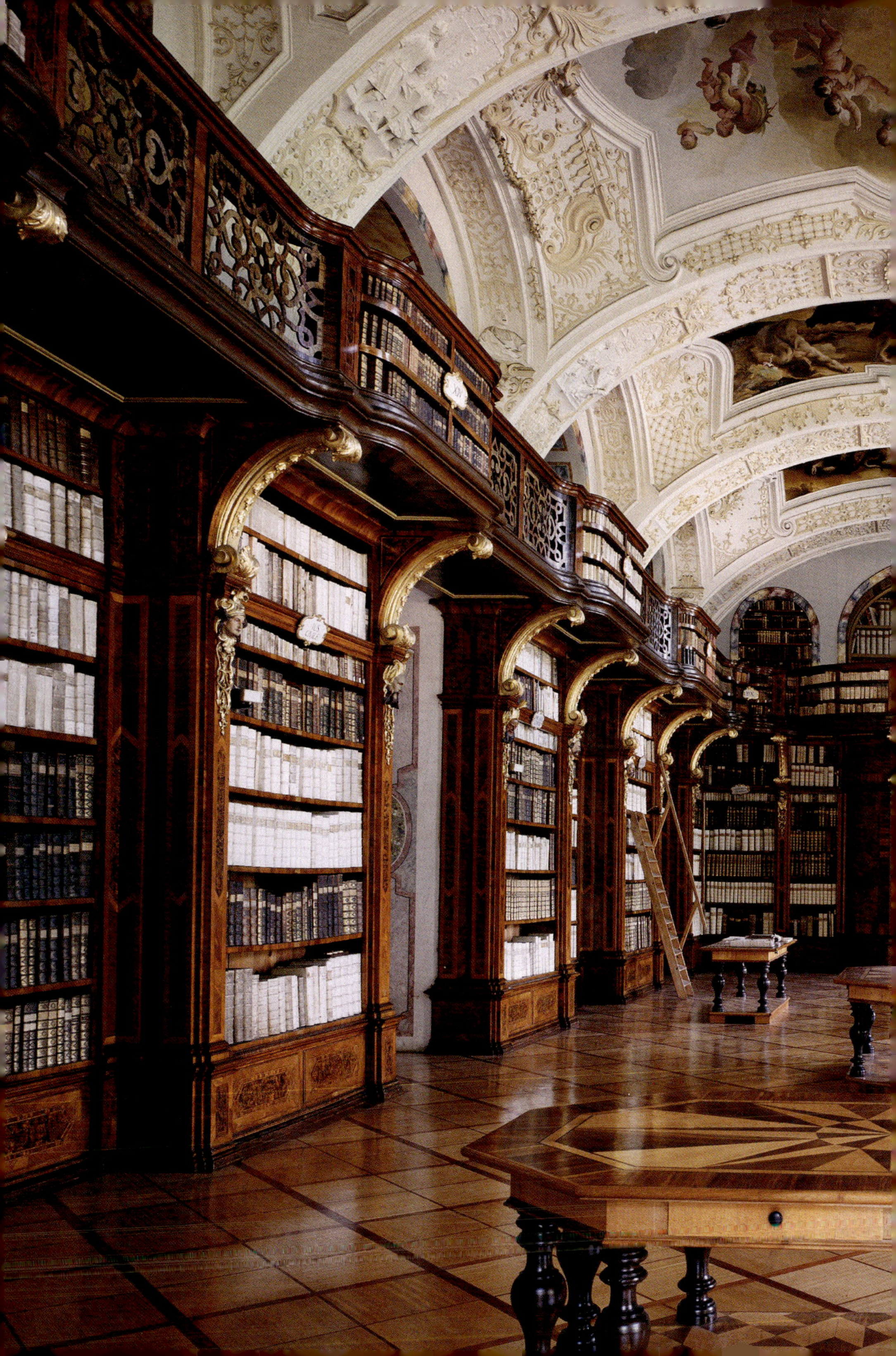

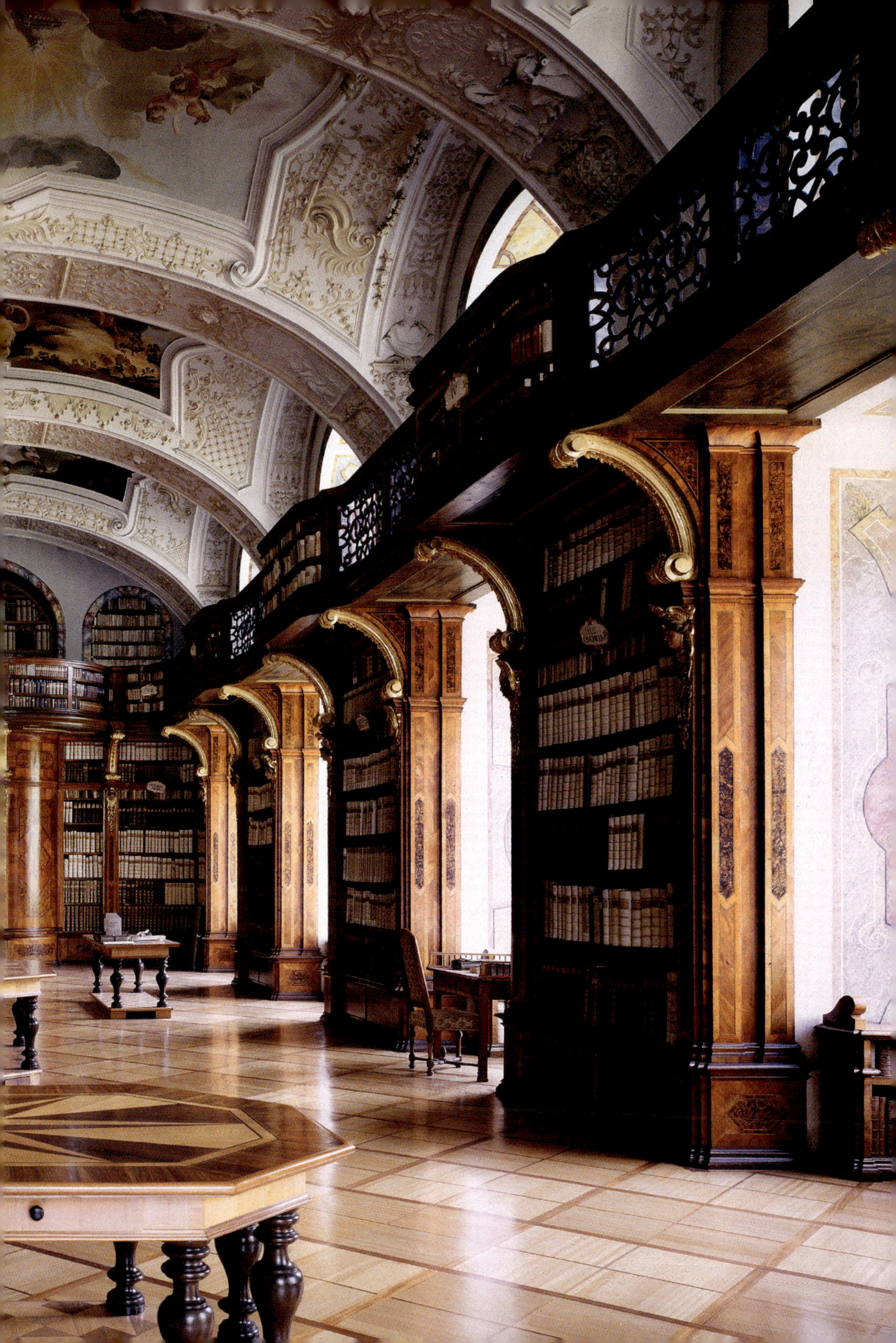

Österreichische Nationalbibliothek

The history of the Österreichische National-bibliothek and its collections is inseparable from that of the Habsburg Empire. It begins in the Late Middle Ages, when magnificent manuscripts and incunabula were housed in cabinets of curiosities and the arts as treasuries in the various imperial palaces. The range of the Habsburgs' political network can be read in the provenances of the earliest manuscripts, which come from Bohemia, Burgundy, France and Italy. From the second half of the 14th century onwards, court miniaturists began producing copies and translations of valuable codices for the Habsburgs' own collection. The holdings of books assembled in Vienna's Hofburg palace and adjacent premises – such as the Minorite monastery – were systematically organised and expanded from the time of the Renaissance by humanists such as Johannes Cuspinian (1473–1529) and later Conrad Celtis (1459–1508). The court library, which was first called the Biblioteca Regia by Celtis in 1504, began to transform itself from a repository of treasures to a place of knowledge and cultural memory. The books were displayed in company with atlases, maps, astronomical instruments and globes, which are today exhibited in their own museum. The accession of important libraries assembled by scholars and containing large numbers of printed works, such as the library of Tycho Brahe (1546–1601), made it imperative for the institution to be run by a full-time librarian with the appropriate expertise. From 1575, the date of the official founding of the Kaiserliche Hofbibliothek, this post was filled by Hugo Blotius (1533–1608), who compiled an inventory complete with an index of authors and subjects. Not until 1681,

however, was the library given a central building by Emperor Leopold I (1640–1705). Even so, it only received an architectural framework befitting its value and scope in the age of Absolutism, when Charles VI (1685–1740) built the Prunksaal (State Hall) on the foundations of Leopold's library and stables complex; some 200,000 books from the 16th to the 19th century are still displayed here today. Designed by the imperial court architect Johann Bernhard Fischer von Erlach (1656–1723) and completed by his son, the library building (1722–1736) occupies the whole of one side of modern-day Josefsplatz within Vienna's Hofburg palace. The dominant space inside the court library, which was originally only accessible from the rooms of the Hofburg palace, is the oval of the domed hall, only a hint of which can be seen behind the central projection on the building's exterior, while the cupola itself consciously

Founded 1575 as an imperial court library, assembled from the collections of various previous libraries; since 1920 the National Library; since 1945 the Austrian National Library

Holdings c. 7 million individual items, of which 3 million printed works

Type of library national library of the Federal Republic of Austria

Highlights *The Vienna Genesis*, 6th century (Cod. theol. gr. 31); *Prague Wenceslas Bible*, 1390–1400, 6 vols. (Cod. 2759–Cod. 2764); *Golden Bull*, Prague, 1400 (Cod. 338 Han); *Black Hours of Galeazzo Maria Sforza*, Milan/Ghent, 1466–1476 (Cod. 1856); *Hours of Mary of Burgundy*, 1470–1480; *Ambraser Heldenbuch*, Eisack, Italy, 1504–1517

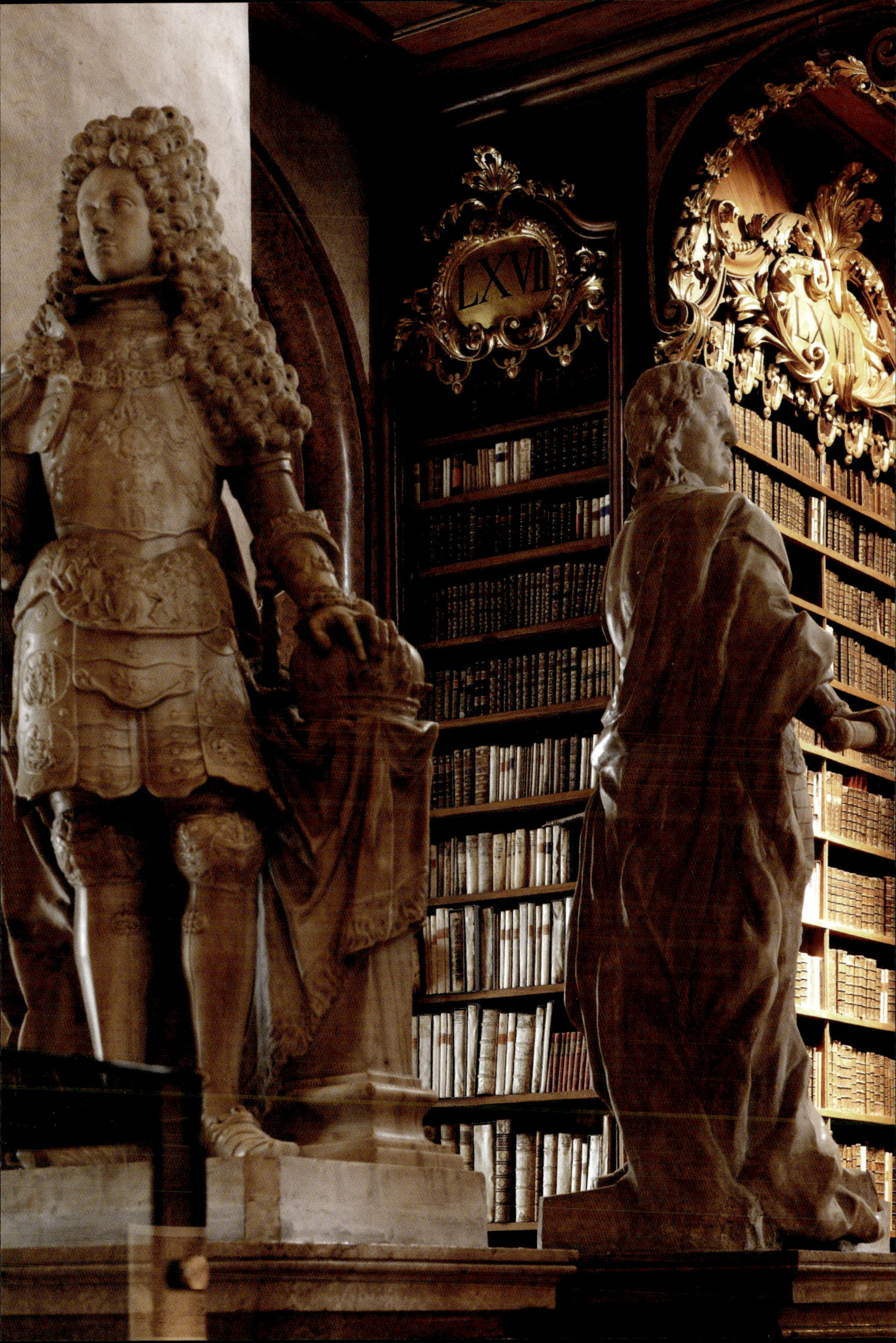

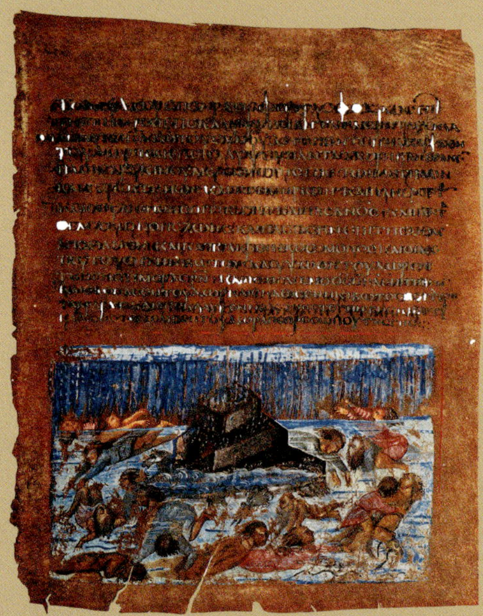

nachzuvollziehen, die aus Böhmen, Burgund, Frankreich und Italien stammen, während Hofminiatoren seit der zweiten Hälfte des 14. Jahrhunderts für hauseigene Kopien und Übersetzungen wertvoller Kodizes sorgten. Ab der Renaissance erfuhren die in der Wiener Hofburg und in anliegenden Gebäuden – etwa dem Minoritenkloster – versammelten Buchbestände durch die Berufung von Humanisten wie Johannes Cuspinian (1473–1529) und später Conrad Celtis (1459–1508) eine systematische Ordnung und Erweiterung. Die von diesem 1504 erstmals als Biblioteca Regia bezeichnete Hofbibliothek begann, sich von einem Hort von Schätzen zu einem Ort des Wissens und kulturellen Gedächtnisses zu wandeln. Den Büchern wurden Atlanten, Landkarten, astronomische Instrumente und Globen zur Seite gestellt, die heute in einem eigenen Museum ausgestellt sind. Der Zugang bedeutender Gelehrtenbibliotheken mit zahlreichen Druckwerken, wie zum Beispiel jener von Tycho Brahe (1546–1601), erforderte die fachkundige Betreuung der Institution durch einen hauptamtlichen Bibliothekar. Ab 1575 nahm Hugo Blotius (1533–1608) dieses Amt wahr, der ein Inventar samt Autoren- und Themenindex anlegte. Auf die institutionelle Gründung folgte erst im Jahr 1681 die Stiftung eines zentralen Bibliotheksgebäudes durch Kaiser Leopold I. (1640–1705). Einen ihrem Wert und Umfang entsprechenden Rahmen erhielt die Kaiserliche Hofbibliothek aber erst zur Zeit des Absolutismus, als Karl VI. (1685–1740) auf den Fundamenten von Leopolds Bibliotheks- und Reitstallgebäude jenen Prunksaal anlegen ließ, in dem noch heute rund 200 000 Bücher aus dem 16. bis 19. Jahrhundert ausgestellt sind. Der vom kaiserlichen Hofarchitekten Johann Bernhard Fischer von Erlach (1656–1723) entworfene und von seinem Sohn fertiggestellte

takes up sacred forms of expression. Emperor Charles VI is glorified as *Hercules Musarum* in the central sculpture by Antonio Corradini (c. 1668–1752), and as patron of the arts and sciences in the ceiling fresco by Daniel Gran (1694–1757). During the Enlightenment the library was run according to modern academic principles by court librarian Gerard van Swieten (1700–1772) and subsequently by his son Gottfried (1733–1803) and furnished with a card catalogue, an indexing system that was previously unknown.

❋ ❋ ❋

Die Geschichte der Österreichischen Nationalbibliothek und ihrer Sammlungen ist untrennbar mit jener des Habsburgerreiches verbunden. Sie beginnt im Spätmittelalter, als erlesene Handschriften und Inkunabeln im Kontext von Kunst- und Wunderkammern untergebracht wurden, die sich als kaiserliche Schatzkammern an den verschiedenen Residenzorten des Reiches befanden. Das politische Netzwerk der Habsburger ist in den Provenienzen der frühesten Handschriften

The Vienna Genesis, 6th century, sig. Cod. theol. gr. 31, fol. 2r: *The Deluge*
Black Hours of Galeazzo Maria Sforza, Milan/Ghent, 1466–1476, sig. Cod. 1856, fol. 119r–120v

Bibliotheksbau (1722–1736) nimmt die gesamte
Front des heutigen Josefsplatzes in der Wiener
Hofburg ein. Der beherrschende Raum der
zunächst ausschließlich von den Räumen der
Hofburg aus zugänglichen Hofbibliothek ist
das am Außenbau hinter dem Mittelrisalit nur
zu erahnende Oval des Kuppelsaales, welcher
bewusst auf sakrale Ausdrucksmöglichkeiten
zurückgreift. Dort wird Kaiser Karl VI. in der
zentralen Skulptur Antonio Corradinis (um
1688–1752) als Herkules der Musen und im
Deckenfresko Daniel Grans (1694–1757) als
Schirmherr der Künste und Wissenschaften
glorifiziert. Zur Zeit der Aufklärung wurde
die Bibliothek von den Präfekten Gerard van
Swieten (1700–1772) und in Nachfolge von seinem Sohn Gottfried (1733–1803) nach modernen wissenschaftlichen Prinzipien betrieben
und über einen bis dahin unbekannten Zettelkatalog erschlossen.

❊ ❊ ❊

L'histoire de la Bibliothèque nationale d'Autriche et de ses collections est indissociable
de l'histoire de l'Empire des Habsbourg. Elle
commence vers la fin du Moyen Âge, lorsque
des manuscrits et des incunables de choix sont
présentés dans des cabinets d'art et de curiosités attachés aux salles du Trésor impérial dans
plusieurs résidences de l'Empire. Grâce à leur
réseau politique, les Habsbourg obtiennent très
tôt des manuscrits en provenance de Bohême,
de Bourgogne, de France et d'Italie. En outre,
depuis la seconde moitié du XIVe siècle, des
miniaturistes officiels se chargent d'effectuer
des copies et des traductions de codex de
toute beauté. Dès la Renaissance, les fonds
littéraires rassemblés dans le palais impérial et
les bâtiments adjacents – comme le couvent des
Frères mineurs – sont l'objet d'un classement
systématique et d'une augmentation grâce à
la vocation d'humanistes tels que Johannes
Cuspinian (1473–1529) et Conrad Celtis

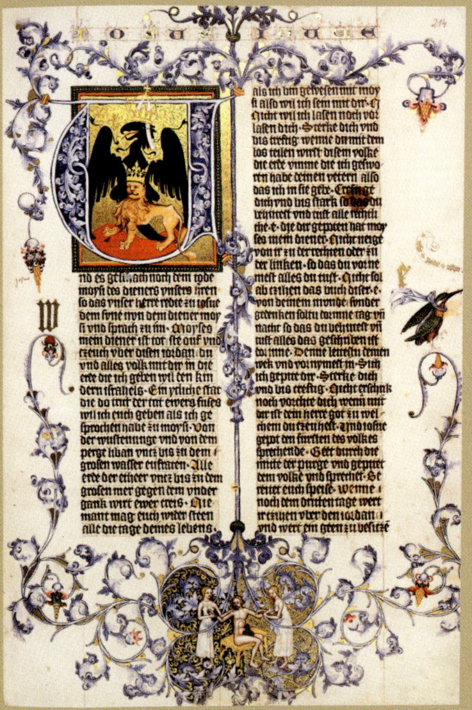

et l'expertise d'un bibliothécaire attitré. Hugo Blotius (1533–1608) assuma cette charge dès 1575 et dressa un inventaire complet des auteurs et des sujets traités. En 1681 seulement, l'empereur Léopold Ier (1640–1705) donna suite à la fondation institutionnelle en faisant ériger un bâtiment central de bibliothèque. La bibliothèque impériale reçut un écrin à la hauteur de sa valeur et de son envergure sous le règne absolutiste de Charles VI (1685–1740), qui fit ériger une salle d'apparat sur les fondations de la bibliothèque et les écuries de Léopold. Cette salle abrite aujourd'hui encore 200 000 livres datant du XVIe au XIXe siècle. Le bâtiment de bibliothèque, conçu par l'architecte officiel de la cour impériale Johann Bernhard Fischer von Erlach (1656–1723) et réalisé par son fils (entre 1722 et 1736), occupe tout le fond de l'actuelle Josefsplatz à Vienne. Tout d'abord accessible par la résidence de l'empereur uniquement, son joyau est la salle ovale correspondant à l'avant-corps central qui laisse à peine entrevoir la coupole et dont le trompe-l'œil recourt manifestement aux moyens d'expression sacrés. L'empereur Charles VI y est glorifié à plusieurs reprises, dans les sculptures centrales d'Antonio Corradini (vers 1688–1752) en Hercule des Muses, et dans la fresque de plafond de Daniel Gran (1694–1757) en patron des arts et de la science. Au temps des Lumières, la bibliothèque fut administrée par les préfets Gerard (1700–1772) et Gottfried van Swieten (1733–1803) selon des principes économiques modernes ; un catalogue à fiches au format absolument inédit assura d'ailleurs sa mise en valeur.

(1459–1508) par la suite. La bibliothèque de la cour, nommée Biblioteca Regia pour la première fois en 1504 par ce dernier, de châsse à trésors devient lieu du savoir et de la mémoire culturelle. Atlas, cartes géographiques, instruments de mesure astronomique et globes sont associés aux livres ; ils sont de nos jours exposés dans un musée à part. L'accès aux bibliothèques érudites abritant de nombreux imprimés comme celui de Tycho Brahe (1546–1601) exigeait la compétence

Prague Wenceslas Bible, 1390–1400, sig. Cod. 2759, fol. 214r

Prague Wenceslas Bible, 1390–1400, sig. Cod. 2760, fol. 27r

ich sie geben in ewer hende. U
Und die kinder israhels leiten
hute vm vnd vimme die stat ga
baa. Und zu dem dritten male
als sie zu einem male vñ tzwir
hetten getan. furten sie gegen
beniamyn ir her. Sunder ouch
die kinder beniamyn kunlich
ous der stat wischten. und vli
hende die widersachen verre
iagten sie also das sie vorwun
ten ous yn. Als an dem ersten
und an dem andern tage. und
weichende durch tzwen wege
kerende die rucke. der do einer
gienk gegen bethel der ander
gegen gabaa. und vilen wol

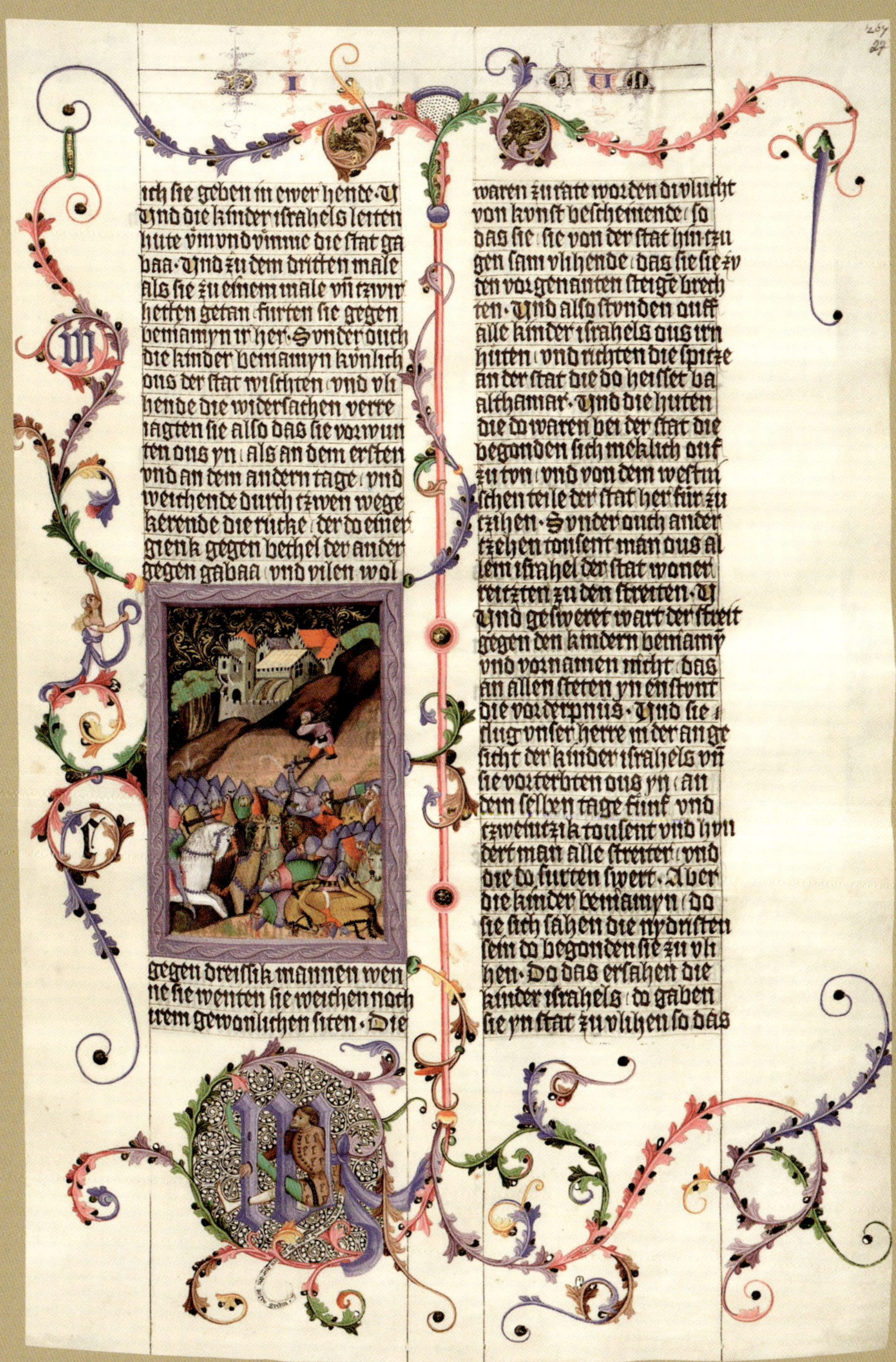

gegen dreissik mannen wen
ne sie weinten sie weichen noch
trem gewonlichen siten. Die

waren zu rate worden di vlucht
von kunst beschemende. so
das sie. sie von der stat hin tzu
gen sam vlihende. das sie sie zu
den vorgenanten steige brech
ten. Und also stunden ouff
alle kinder israhels ous irn
huten. und richten die spitze
an der stat die do heisset ba
althamar. Und die huten
die do waren bei der stat die
begonden sich meklich ouff
zu tun. und von dem westin
schen teile der stat her kir zu
tzihen. Sunder ouch ander
tzehen tousent man ous al
lem israhel der stat wonet
reitzten zu den streiten. U
Und gesweret wart der streit
gegen den kindern beniamy
und vornamen nicht das
an allen steten yn einstunt
die vorderpnus. Und sie
slug unser herre in der an ge
sicht der kinder israhels vn
sie vorterbten ous yn. An
dem selben tage funk vnd
tzweintzik tousent und hun
dert man alle streiter. und
die do furten swert. Aber
die kinder beniamyn. do
sie sich sahen die nydristen
sein do begonden sie zu vli
hen. Do das ersahen die
kinder israhels. do gaben
sie yn stat zu vlihen so das

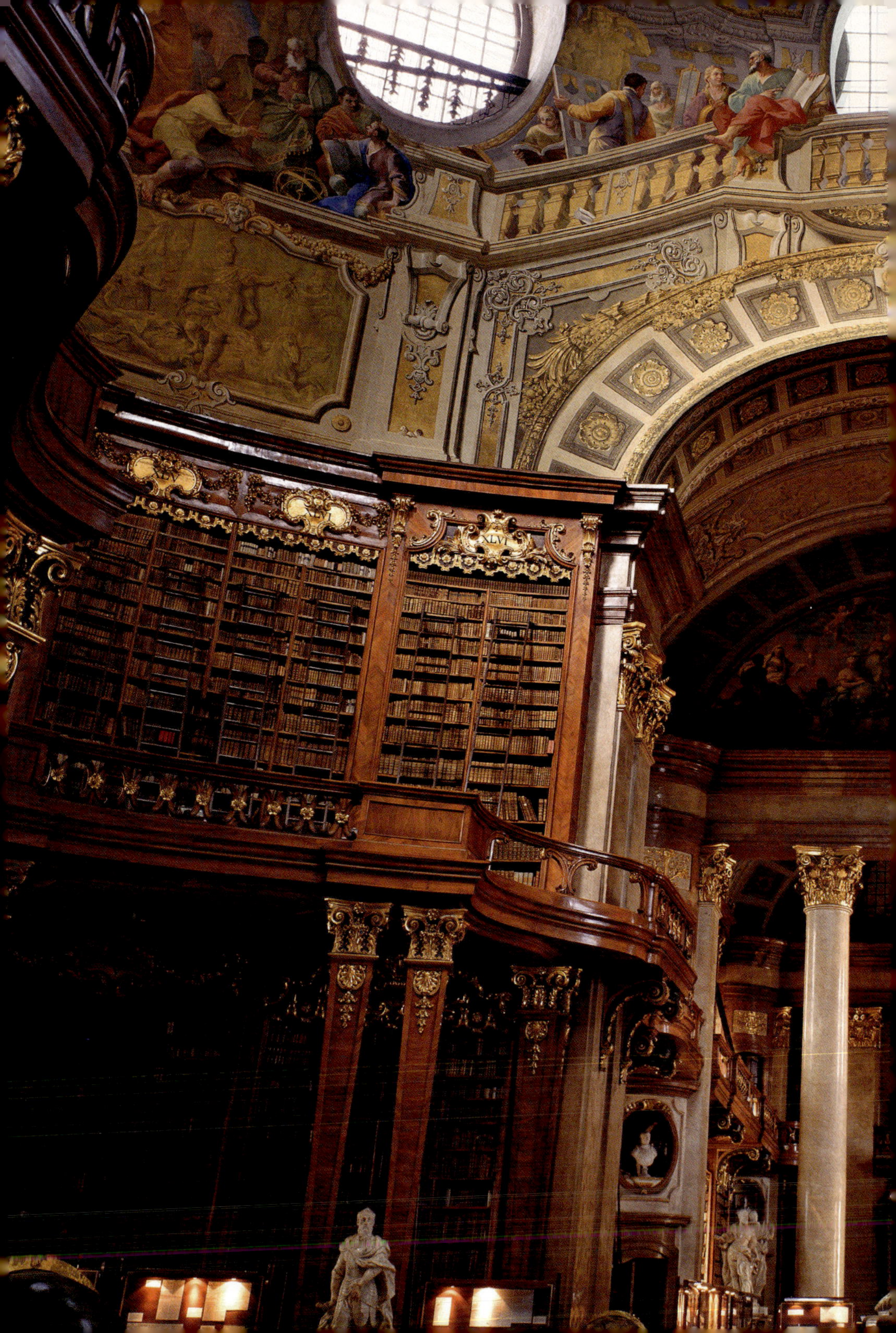

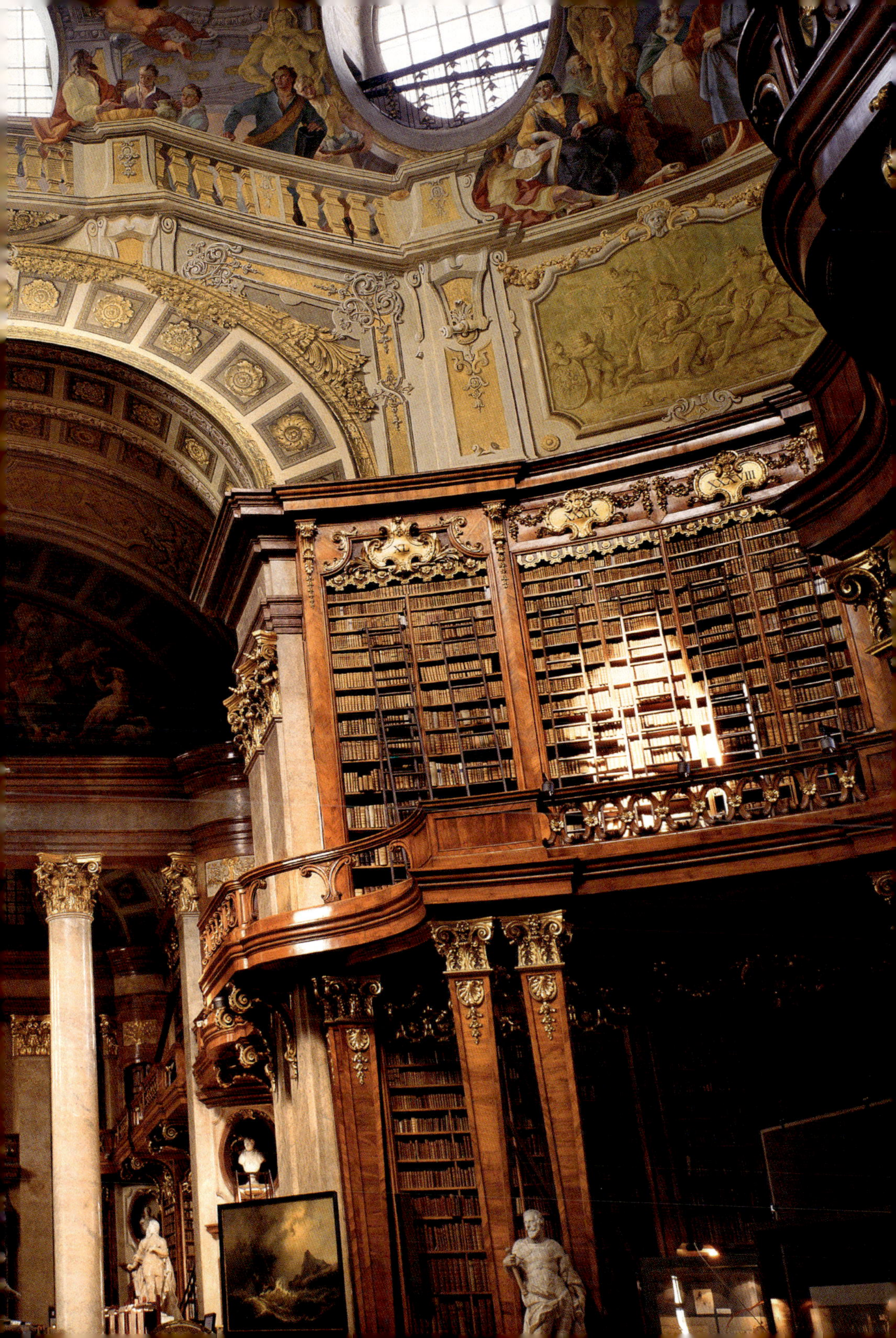

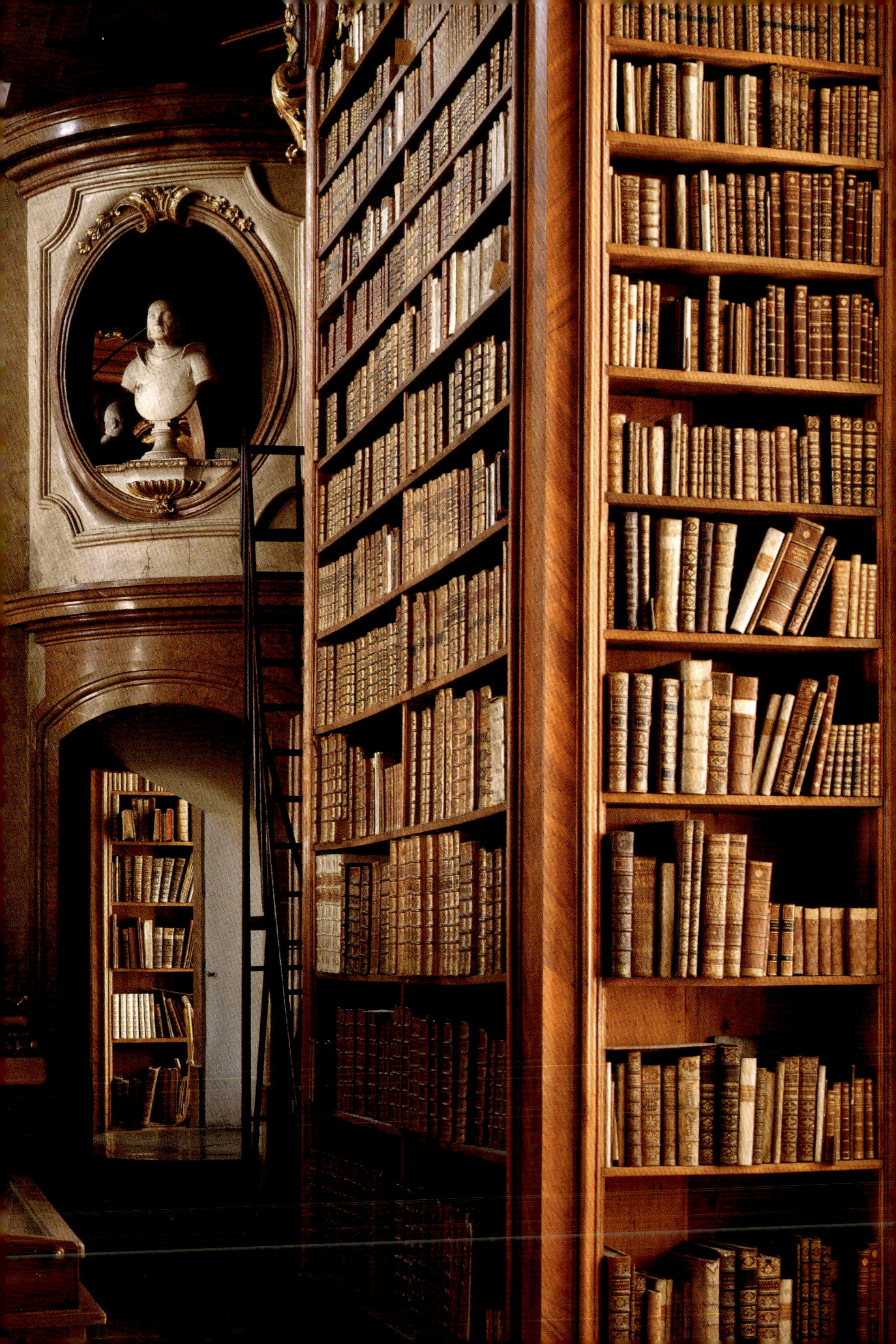

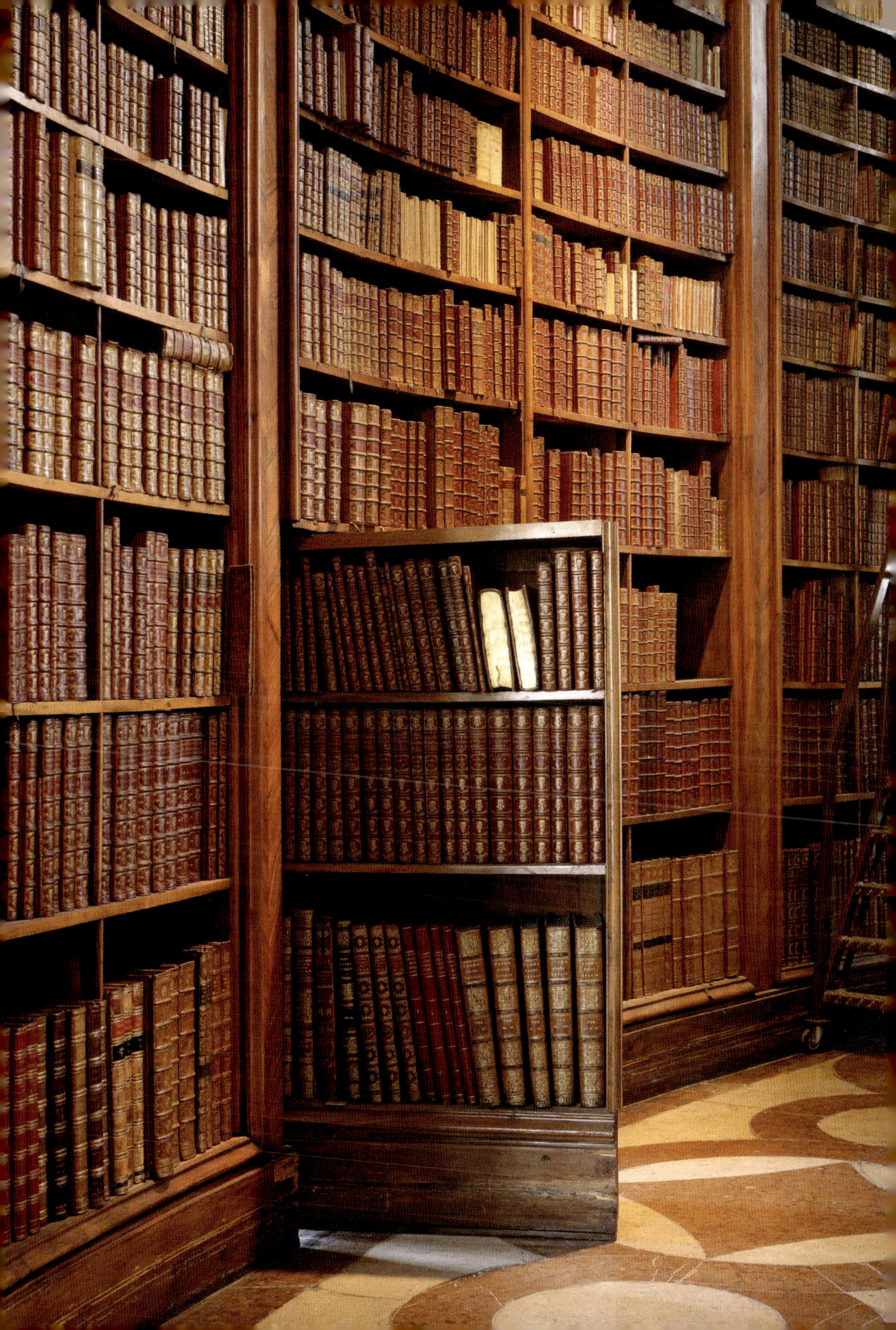

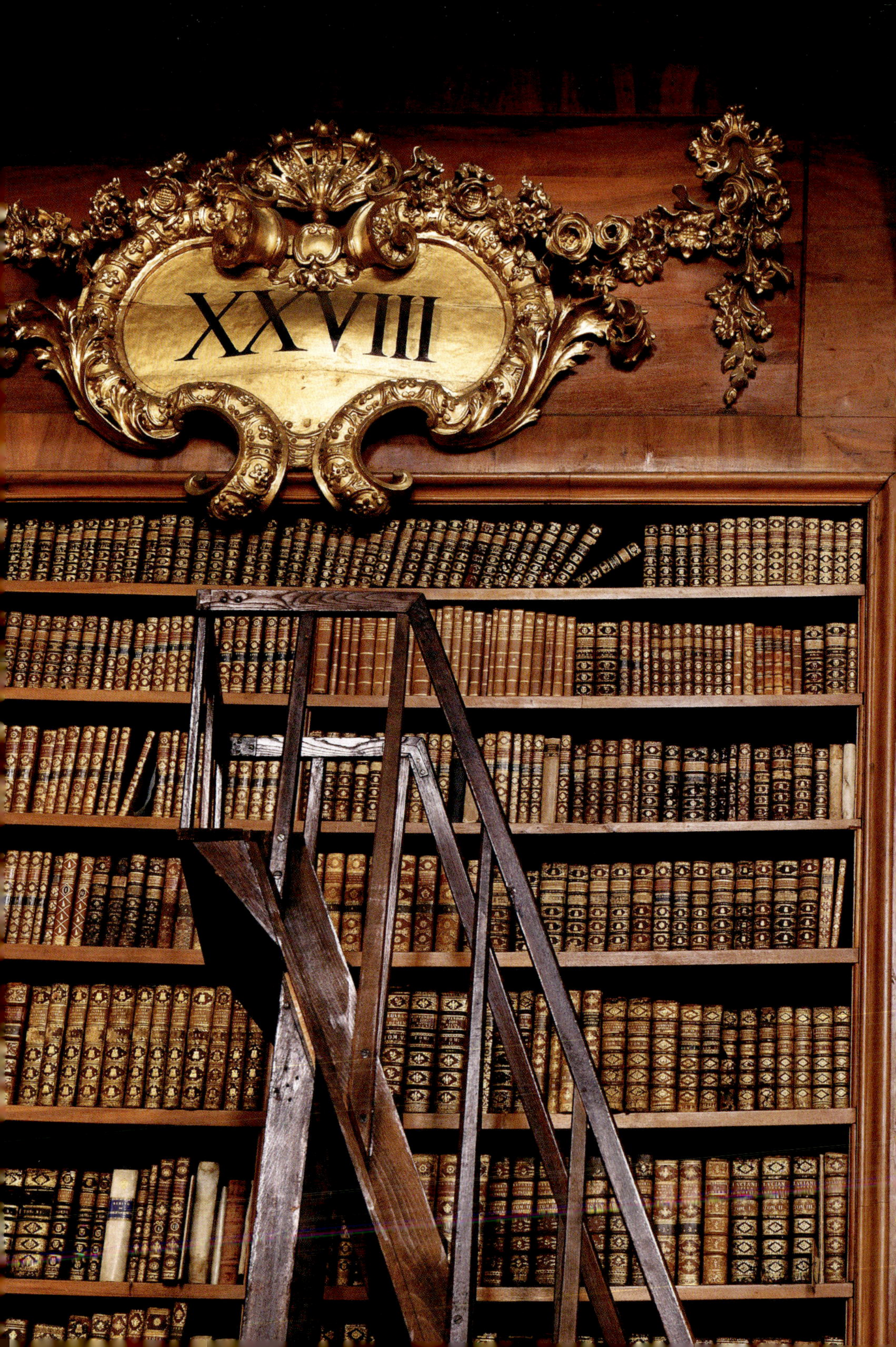

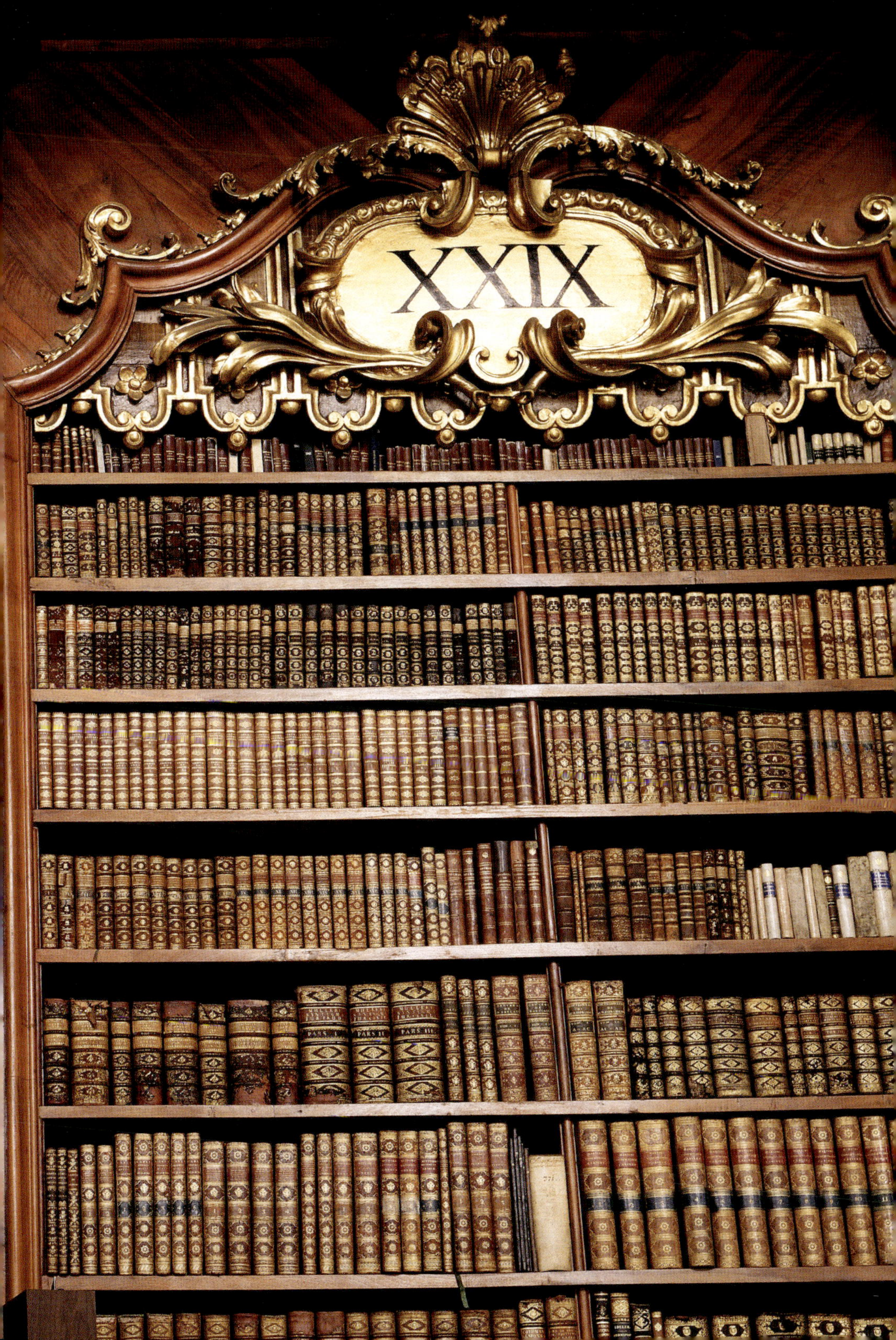
XXIX

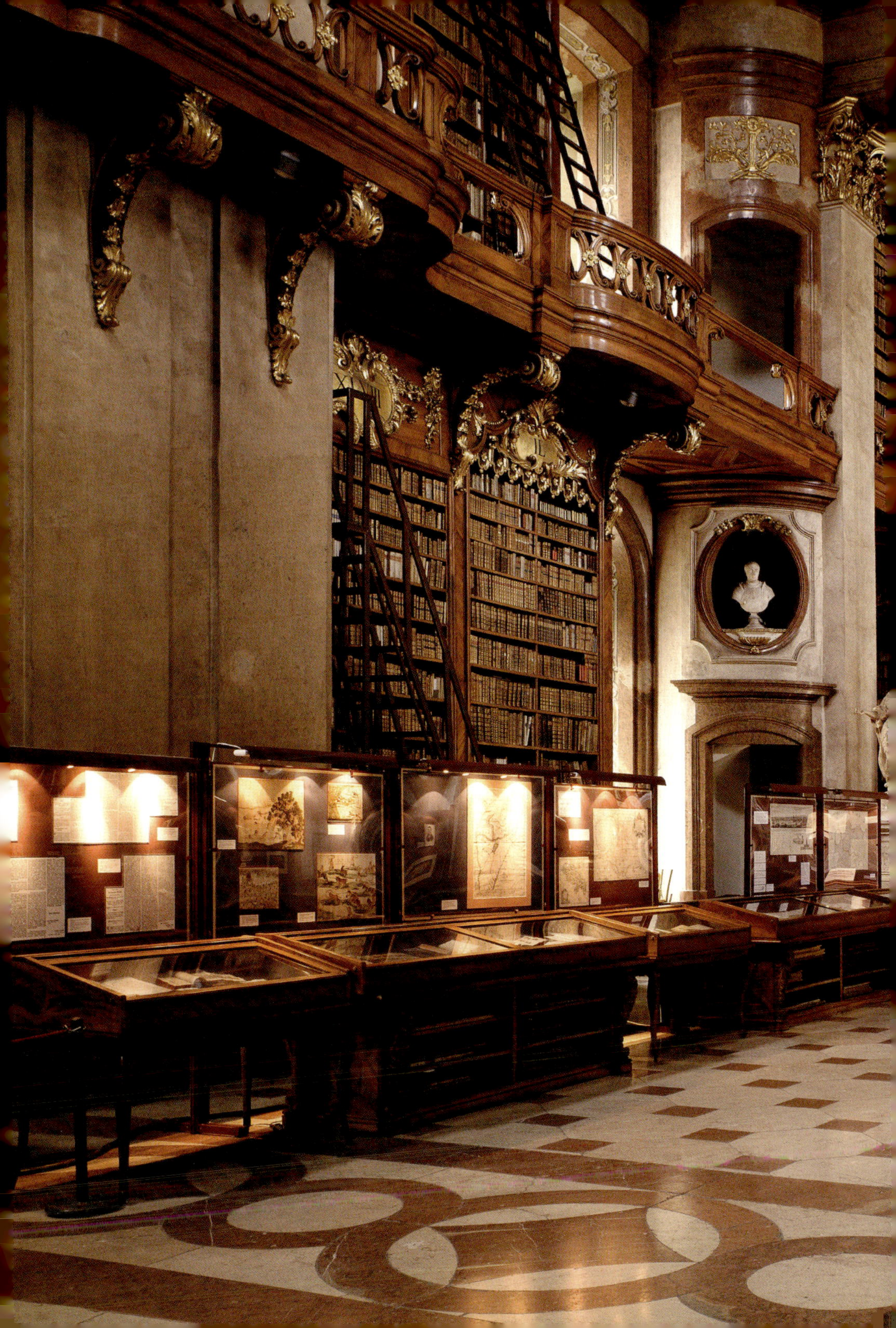

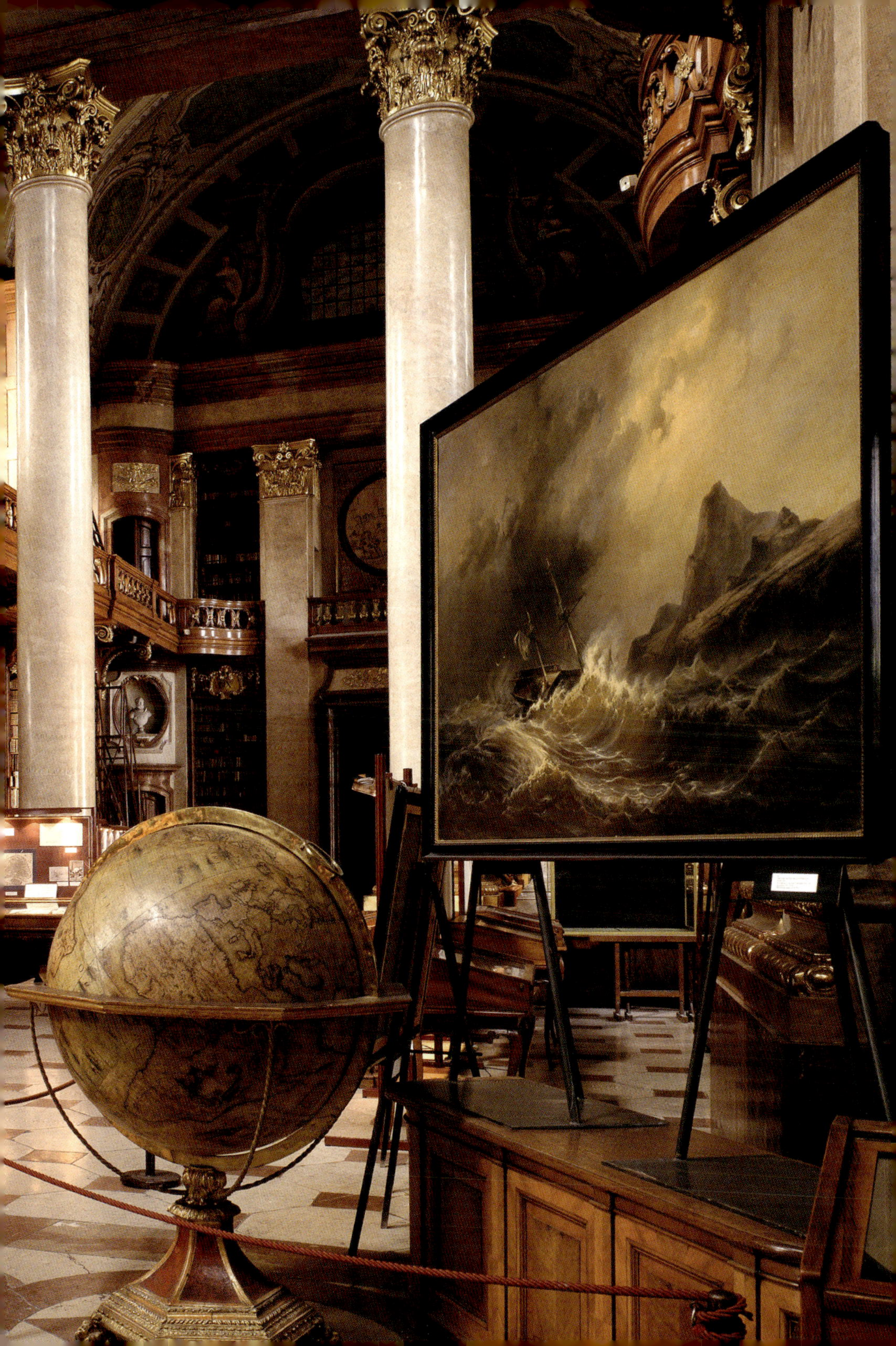

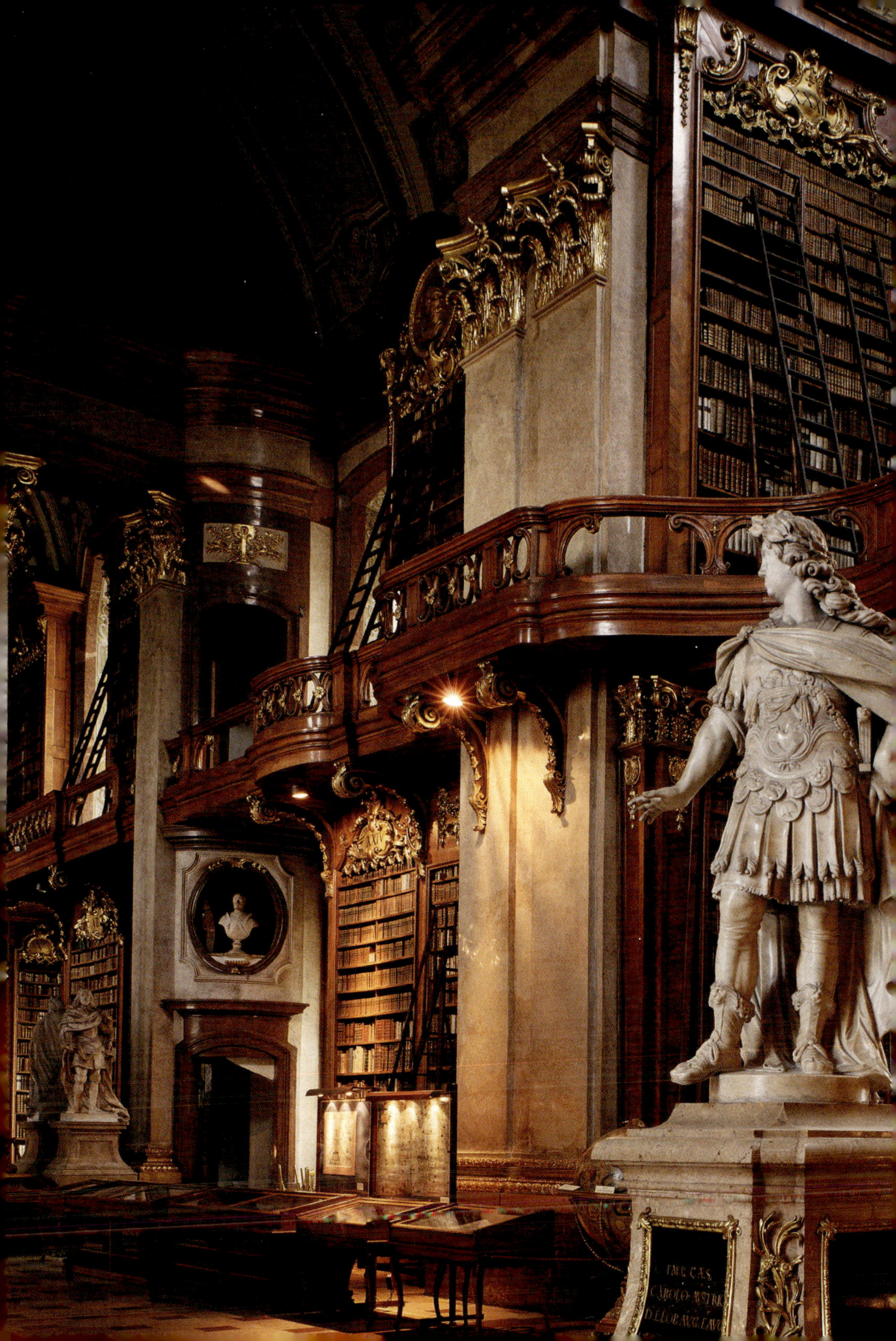

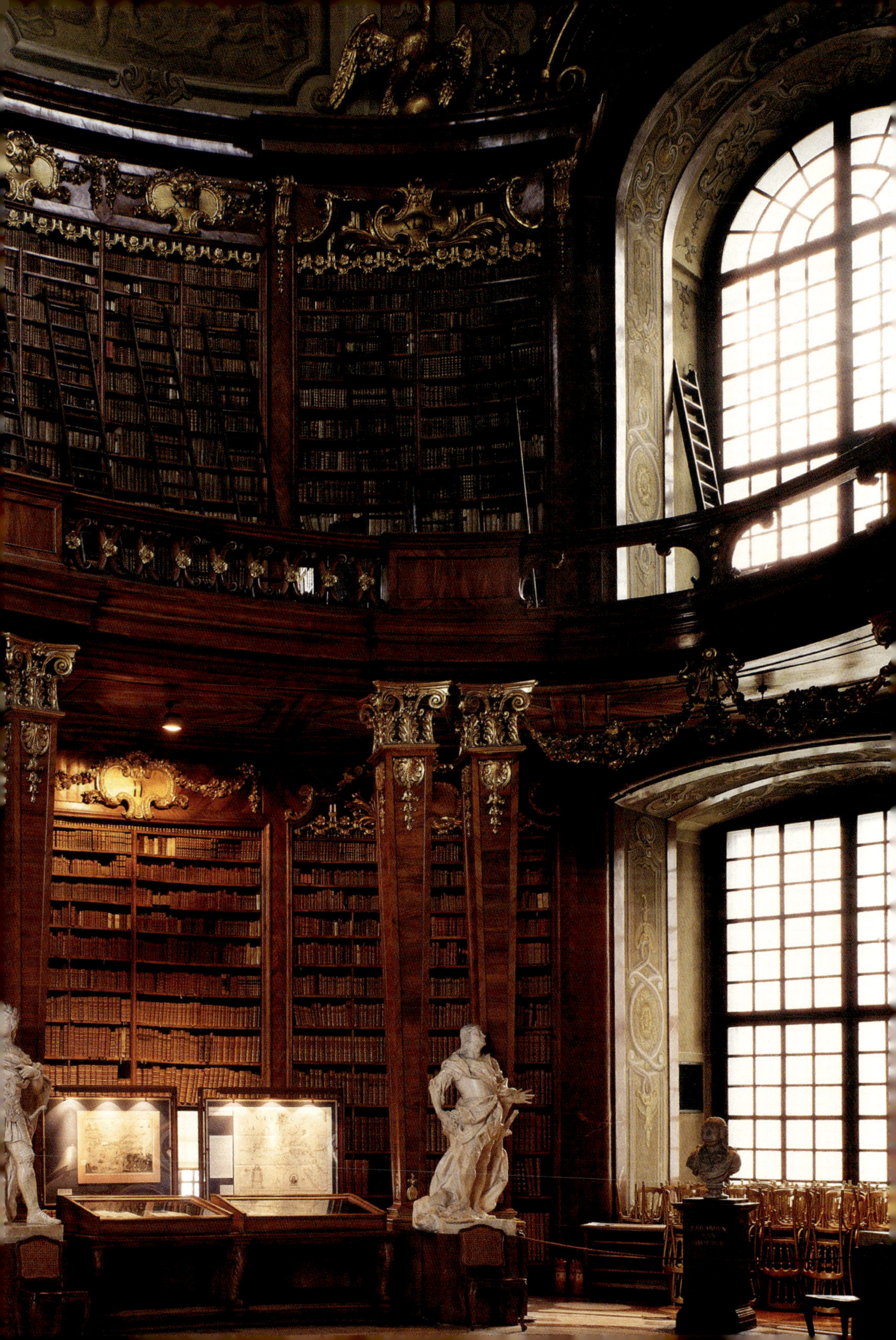

Strahovská Knihovna

The Royal Canonry of Premonstratensians at Strahov in Prague's Hradčany district is one of the oldest Premonstratensian monasteries in the world. Founded in 1143 by the powerful Bishop of Olomouc, Jindřich Zdík (c. 1080–1150), and granted royal privileges by the Přemyslid King of Bohemia Vladislaus II (c. 1110–1174) and his wife Gertrude, Strahov Abbey soon became the spiritual counterweight to the royal residence that originally stood nearby. A library and scriptorium formed an integral part of the monastery right from the start, as witnessed by the library's earliest holdings from the middle of the 12th century, which still carry the ownership mark "Mons Sion" (the Latin equivalent of the Bohemian "Strahov") and were in some cases produced in-house. Even older codices, such as the *Strahov Evangeliary* of 860/865, entered the library in later years as a result of endowments, bequests and specific acquisitions. These last became necessary after the loss of valuable holdings as a result of fire, wars and plundering. Thanks to Strahov's close contacts with Prague's Charles University, the library also acquired important works of academic and scientific literature. Unique documents relating to the Prague activities of Johannes Kepler (1571–1630) and Tycho Brahe (1546–1601) originate from the library of the astronomer and director of the Prague Observatory Anton Strnad (1746–1799). By the end of the 18th century the Bibliotheca Strahoviensis was considered the most important monastic library in Bohemia. Its comprehensive holdings and the broad spectrum of topics covered by its books even led its librarian, Václav Urban (1752–1787), to propose opening it to the academic public as a national library, in keeping with the enlightened thinking of the day. The Theological Hall, designed in the Baroque style and housing 18,000 volumes, was complemented during the Enlightenment by the Philosophical Hall, with its 42,000 volumes on philosophy and the natural sciences. The first of these monumental halls was commissioned in 1671 by the philosopher and Abbot of Strahov, Jeroným Hirnhaim (1637–1679), who also formulated the principles of faith, study, human knowledge and divine providence illustrated in the paintings and inscriptions making up the interior decoration. Built by Giovanni Domenico Orsi de Orsini (1634–1679), an architect of Italian extraction who had trained under Carlo Lurago (1615–1684), the Theological Hall is fitted with shelves with a reddish hue and its codices uniformly bound in white combine with the gleaming white stucco

Founded 1143; Theological Hall built from 1671 by Giovanni Domenico Orsi de Orsini, Philosophical Hall from 1783 by Ignác Jan Palliardi
Holdings c. 200,000 volumes, of which 1,500 incunabula
Type of library monastic library
Highlights *Strahov Evangeliary*, Trier, c. 860/865, with Ottonian miniatures that were bound into the codex, c. 980 (DF III 3); Abdal-Rahmanal al-Sūfī, *Book of Fixed Stars, Atlas of Stars, Sufi Latinus Corpus*, 14th century (DA II 13); *Liber Pontificalis of Albrecht of Sternberg*, 1376 (DG I 19); *Spis o nových zemiech a o novém světě (On the new lands, and the new world)*, 1503–1504 (DR IV 37a); Karel von Hinterlangen, *Xylothek* in 68 vols., c. 1825

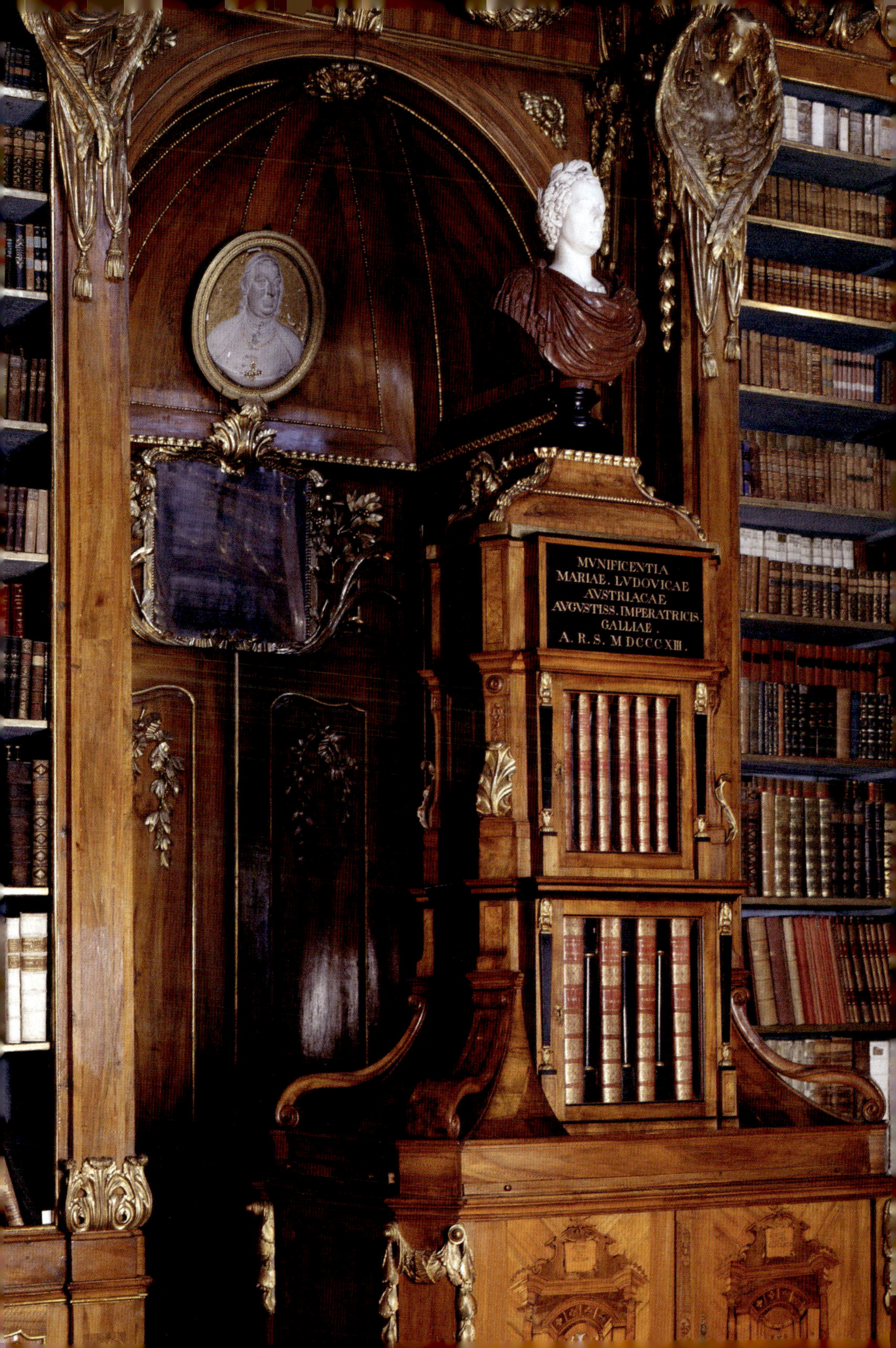

MVNIFICENTIA
MARIAE. LVDOVICAE
AVSTRIACAE
AVGVSTISS. IMPERATRICIS.
GALLIAE.
A. R. S. M DCCC XIII.

décor and framed frescos to form a decorative whole in the Bohemian Baroque style. The Philosophical Hall, by contrast, built starting in 1783 by Ignác Jan Palliardi (1737–1824), is a neoclassical ensemble with an interior which is characterised by magnificent book cabinets, galleries and wall fittings in walnut, all of which came from the dissolved Premonstratensian abbey of Louka, near Znojmoin in southern Moravia. Just one book cabinet – installed in a niche and containing a collection of rare French encyclopaedias – has an imperial provenance: it was a gift from the Empress of the French, Marie-Louise of Austria (1791–1847) on the occasion of her visit to the Royal Canonry in 1812. The development of the sciences from Antiquity to the 18th century is traced in the illusionistic ceiling fresco, one of the last works by Franz Anton Maulbertsch (1724–1796) and dating from 1794. Following its appropriation

by the Czechoslovakian State in 1950, Strahov's library was incorporated into the Museum of National Literature. In 1991 it was restituted to the Premonstratensians, who continue to run the canonry today. Its historical library rooms and accompanying cabinet of curiosities can today be visited as a museum.

✳ ✳ ✳

Auf dem Prager Hradschin befindet sich eine der ältesten Prämonstratenser-Niederlassungen der Welt, die seit ihrer Gründung im Jahr 1143 über eine Bibliothek und eine Schreibstube verfügte. Vom mächtigen Bischof von Olmütz, Heinrich Zdík (um 1080–1150), gefördert und von Vladislav II. (um 1110–1174) aus der Dynastie der Přemysliden und seiner Frau Gertrude mit königlichen Privilegien ausgestattet, bildete das Stift von Strahov bald den geistlichen Gegenpol zu der damals unweit

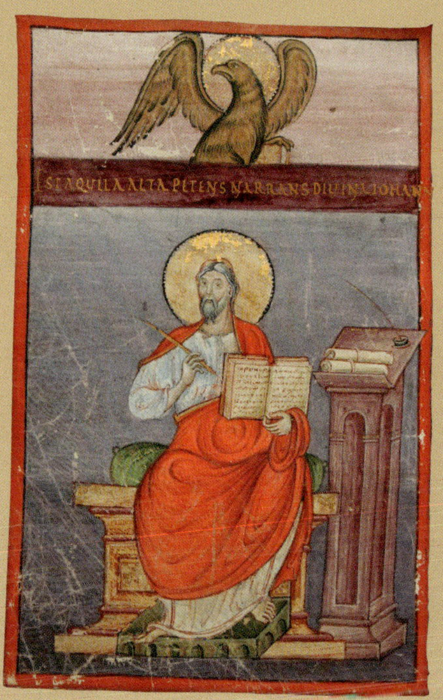

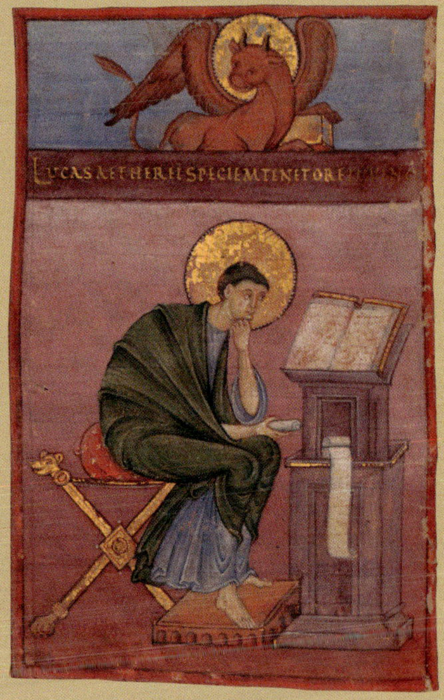

davon eingerichteten Residenz. Die frühesten,
teils im hauseigenen Skriptorium gefertigten
Bestände aus der Mitte des 12. Jahrhunderts
tragen noch heute den handschriftlichen
Eigentumsvermerk „Mons Sion", was gleich-
bedeutend mit dem böhmischen „Strahov"
ist. Noch ältere Kodizes, wie das *Strahover
Evangeliar* von 860/865, kamen in den Folgejahren durch Stiftungen, Nachlässe und
gezielte Ankäufe dazu. Diese hatten sich insbesondere nach dem Verlust wertvoller Bestände
durch Feuer, Kriege und Plünderungen als
notwendig erwiesen. Dem engen Kontakt
zur Prager Karls-Universität ist der Eingang
bedeutender wissenschaftlicher Fachliteratur
zu verdanken. Einzigartige Dokumente zur
Prager Tätigkeit von Johannes Kepler (1571–
1630) und Tycho Brahe (1546–1601) stammen
aus der Bibliothek des Astronomen und
Direktors der Prager Sternwarte, Anton Strnad
(1746–1799). Am Ende des 18. Jahrhunderts galt
die Bibliotheca Strahoviensis als bedeutendste
Ordensbibliothek in Böhmen. Ihr Bibliothekar
Václav Urban (1752–1787) schlug sogar vor, sie
dem Zeitgeist entsprechend als Nationalbibliothek dem gelehrten Publikum zu öffnen, denn
ihre Bestände waren umfassend und das
Themenspektrum der Bücher weit. Dem in
barocken Formen gestalteten Theologischen
Saal mit 18 000 Bänden wurde in der Zeit der
Aufklärung der Philosophische Saal zur Seite
gestellt, wo Philosophie und Naturwissenschaften in 42 000 Bänden abgehandelt sind.
Glaube, Studium, menschliches Wissen und
göttliche Vorhersehung sind die in Bild und
Text der Ausstattung vorgeführten Grundsätze, die der Philosoph und Abt von Strahov

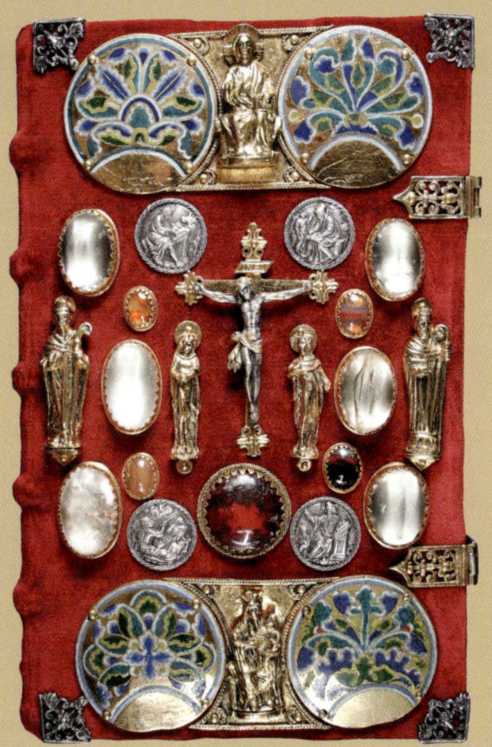

Strahov Evangeliary, Trier, c. 860/865,
sig. DF III 3, fol. 176v: *John the Evangelist*

Strahov Evangeliary, Trier, c. 860/865,
sig. DF III 3, fol. 107v: *Luke the Evangelist*

Strahov Evangeliary, Trier, c. 860/865,
sig. DF III 3: *Treasure binding with representation
of the Crucifixion and Saints.* Enamel and coin
appliqués, semi-precious stones

Hieronymus Hirnhaim (1637–1679) formuliert
hat. Er beauftragte 1671 Giovanni Domenico
Orsi de Orsini (1634–1679), einen bei Carlo
Lurago (1615–1684) ausgebildeten Architekten
italienischer Abstammung, mit der Errichtung
des ersten monumentalen Büchersaals. Seine
rot getönten Regale mit den einheitlich weiß
gebundenen Kodizes bilden mit dem leuchtend
weißen Stuckdekor und seinen ihm eingeschriebenen Freskenmalereien eine dekorative
Einheit im Stil des böhmischen Barock. Ein
klassizistisches Raumensemble hat sich hingegen in dem ab 1783 von Johann Ignaz Palliardi
(1737–1824) gestalteten Philosophischen Saal
erhalten. Raumprägend sind hier die prächtigen Bücherschränke, Laufgänge und Wandver-
bauten in Nussholz, die aus dem aufgelösten
Prämonstratenserstift Klosterbruck bei Znaim
in Südmähren übernommen wurden. Einzig
der einer Nische eingestellte Kabinettschrank

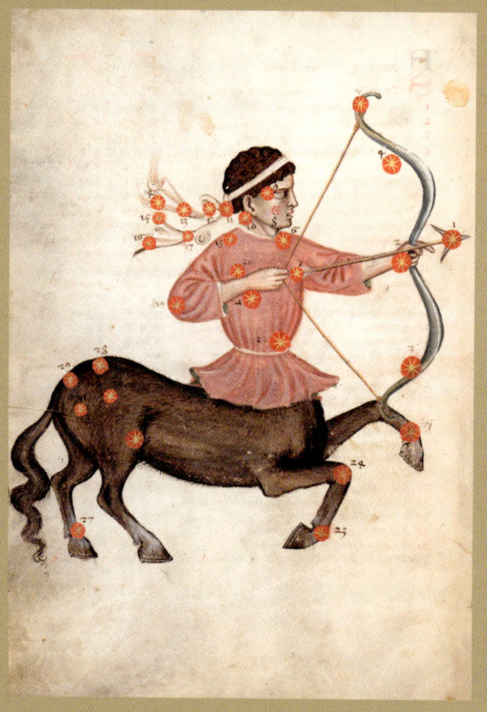

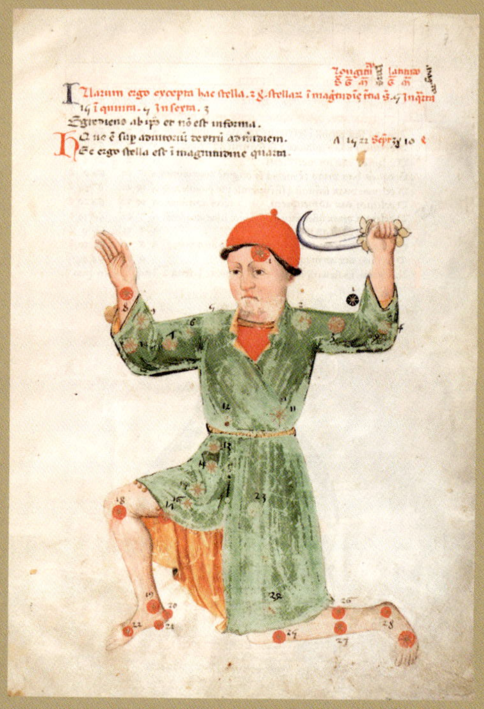

mit einer Sammlung seltener französischer Enzyklopädien ist kaiserlicher Provenienz, ein Geschenk der Kaiserin der Franzosen Marie-Louise von Österreich (1791–1847) anlässlich ihres Besuches der königlichen Kanonie im Jahr 1812. Im illusionistischen Deckenfresko wird der Entwicklung der Wissenschaften von der Antike bis zur Gegenwart Raum gegeben. Es ist eines der letzten Werke von Franz Anton Maulbertsch (1724–1796) aus dem Jahr 1794. Nach der Enteignung der Bibliothek im Jahr 1950 durch den tschechoslowakischen Staat wurde die interim vom Böhmischen Museum für Literatur verwaltete Büchersammlung 1991 wieder an den Prämonstratenserorden restituiert, der das Stift weiterhin betreut. Seine historischen Büchersäle und eine zugehörige Wunderkammer sind heute als Museum zu besichtigen.

❋❖❋

Sur la colline pragoise du château Hradčany se trouve l'un des plus anciens sites de Prémontrés au monde, qui disposa d'ailleurs d'une bibliothèque et d'un salon d'écriture dès sa création en 1143. Fondé par le puissant évêque d'Olomouc, Jindřich Zdík (vers 1080–1150), et doté de privilèges royaux par Vladislav II (vers 1110–1174) de la dynastie de Přemyslides et sa femme Gertrude, le couvent de Strahov devint rapidement l'antithèse spirituelle de la résidence dont il était voisin. Les fonds les plus anciens, remontant au XIIe siècle et en partie réalisés dans le scriptorium attenant, portent aujourd'hui encore la note manuscrite « Mons Sion », l'équivalent du terme bohémien « Strahov ». Des codex encore plus anciens comme l'*Évangéliaire de Strahov* de 860/865 s'y ajoutèrent peu après par le biais de donations, legs et achats ciblés. La perte de fonds très précieux, causée par des incendies, des guerres ou des pillages, avait rendu ces acquisitions indispensables. D'importants ouvrages scientifiques sont parvenus à la bibliothèque par liaison avec l'université Charles de Prague. Des documents exceptionnels sur les activités de Johannes Kepler (1571–1630) et Tycho Brahe (1546–1601) à Prague proviennent de la bibliothèque d'Anton Strnad (1746–1799), astronome et directeur de l'observatoire de Prague. À la fin du XVIIIᵉ siècle, la Bibliotheca Strahoviensis était la bibliothèque ecclésiastique la plus importante de Bohême. Son bibliothécaire Václav Urban (1752–1787), très au fait de son époque, proposa même de l'ouvrir au public instruit en l'instituant bibliothèque nationale tant ses fonds étaient considérables et couvraient un vaste éventail de thèmes. À l'époque des Lumières, une salle où la philosophie et la science sont traitées en 42 000 volumes fut adjointe à la salle théologique au décor baroque abritant 18 000 ouvrages. Le décor de cette dernière transpose en mots et en images les fondements de Hieronymus Hirnhaim (philosophe et abbé de Strahov, 1637–1679) que sont la foi, l'étude, les humanités et la Providence divine. En 1671, il charge Giovanni Domenico Orsi de Orsini (1634–1679), un architecte de souche italienne formé auprès de Carlo Lurago (1615–1684), de réaliser la première salle de lecture monumentale. Les étagères rouges supportant des codex, pour la plupart reliés en blanc, s'intègrent dans un décor de style baroque agrémenté de fresques et de moulures en stuc blanc reflétant la lumière. La salle de philosophie, en revanche, a été aménagée dans l'esprit classique par Johann Ignaz Palliardi (1737–1824) en 1783. Elle est généreusement rehaussée par le bois de noyer dans lequel les somptueux corps de bibliothèque, coursives et vitrines ont été réalisés. Le mobilier provient de l'abbaye, aujourd'hui disparue, des Prémontrés de Znojmo, dans le sud de la Moravie. Seul le cabinet (placé devant une niche) comportant un recueil d'encyclopédies françaises rares est de source impériale, cadeau de l'impératrice Marie-Louise d'Autriche (1791–1847) au couvent royal lors de sa visite en 1812. Le trompe-l'œil au plafond rend compte de l'évolution du

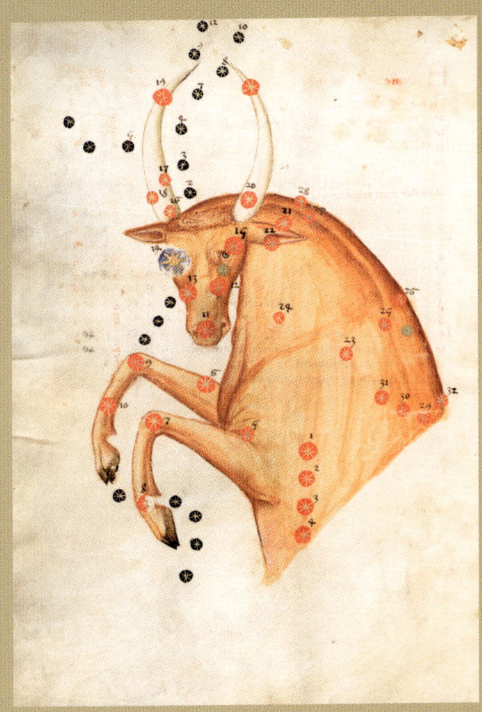

savoir depuis l'Antiquité jusqu'à l'époque moderne. Exécuté en 1794, c'est l'un des derniers travaux de Franz Anton Maulbertsch (1724–1796). L'État tchécoslovaque expropria la bibliothèque en 1950, puis, en 1991, la collection de livres temporairement administrée par le musée de la littérature nationale fut restituée à l'ordre des Prémontrés qui continue de s'occuper du couvent. De nos jours, un musée permet de visiter les salles historiques et la salle du trésor attenante.

Abd al-Rahmanal al-Sūfī, *Book of Fixed Stars*, 14th century, sig. DA II 13, fol. 29v: *Sagittarius* (*"The Archer"*)

Abd al-Rahmanal al-Sūfī, *Atlas of Stars*, 14th century, sig. DA II 13, fol. 7r: *Hercules* (*"The Kneeling Man"*)

Abd al-Rahmanal al-Sūfī, *Atlas of Stars*, 14th century, sig. DA II 13, fol. 21v: *Taurus* (*"The Bull"*)

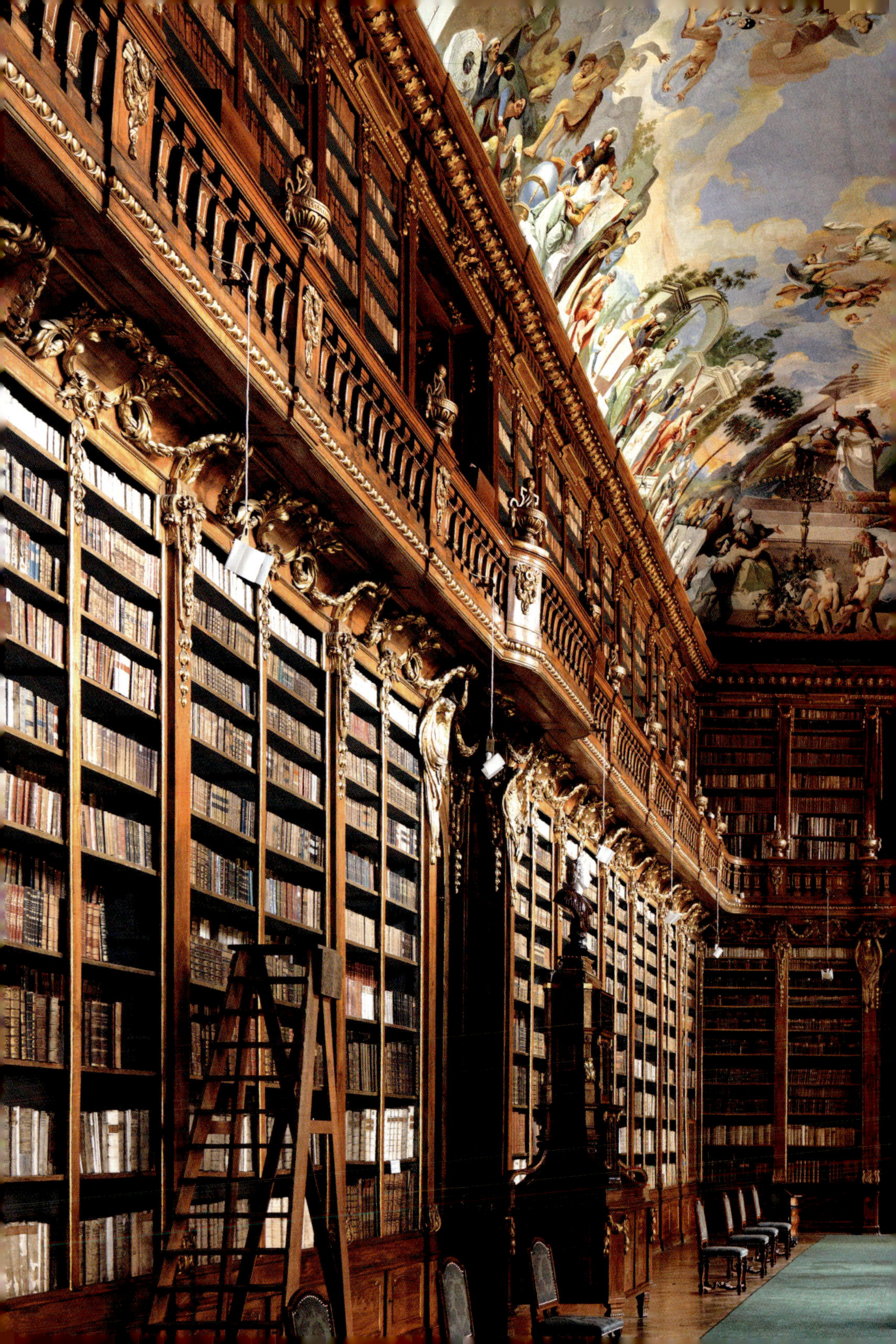

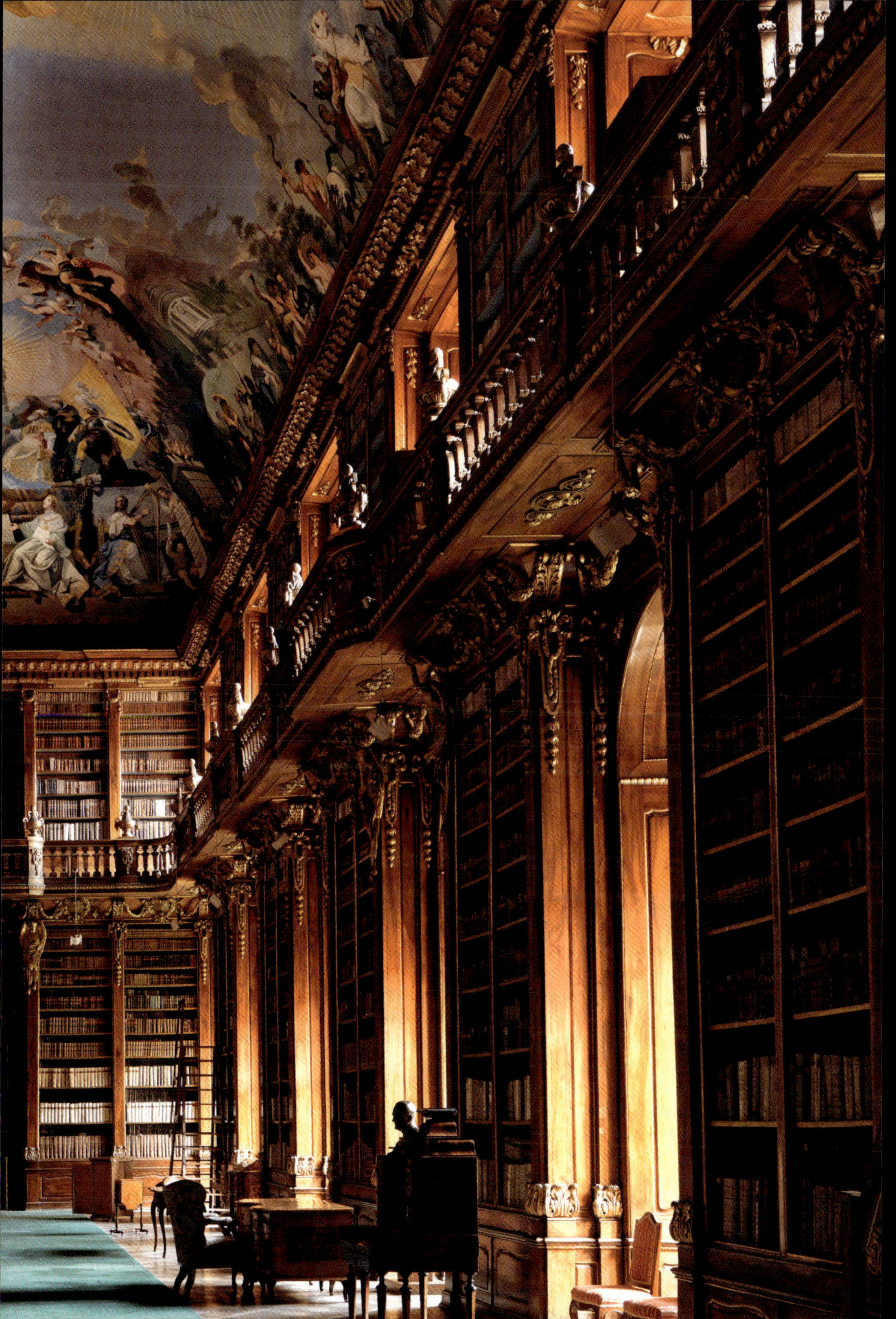

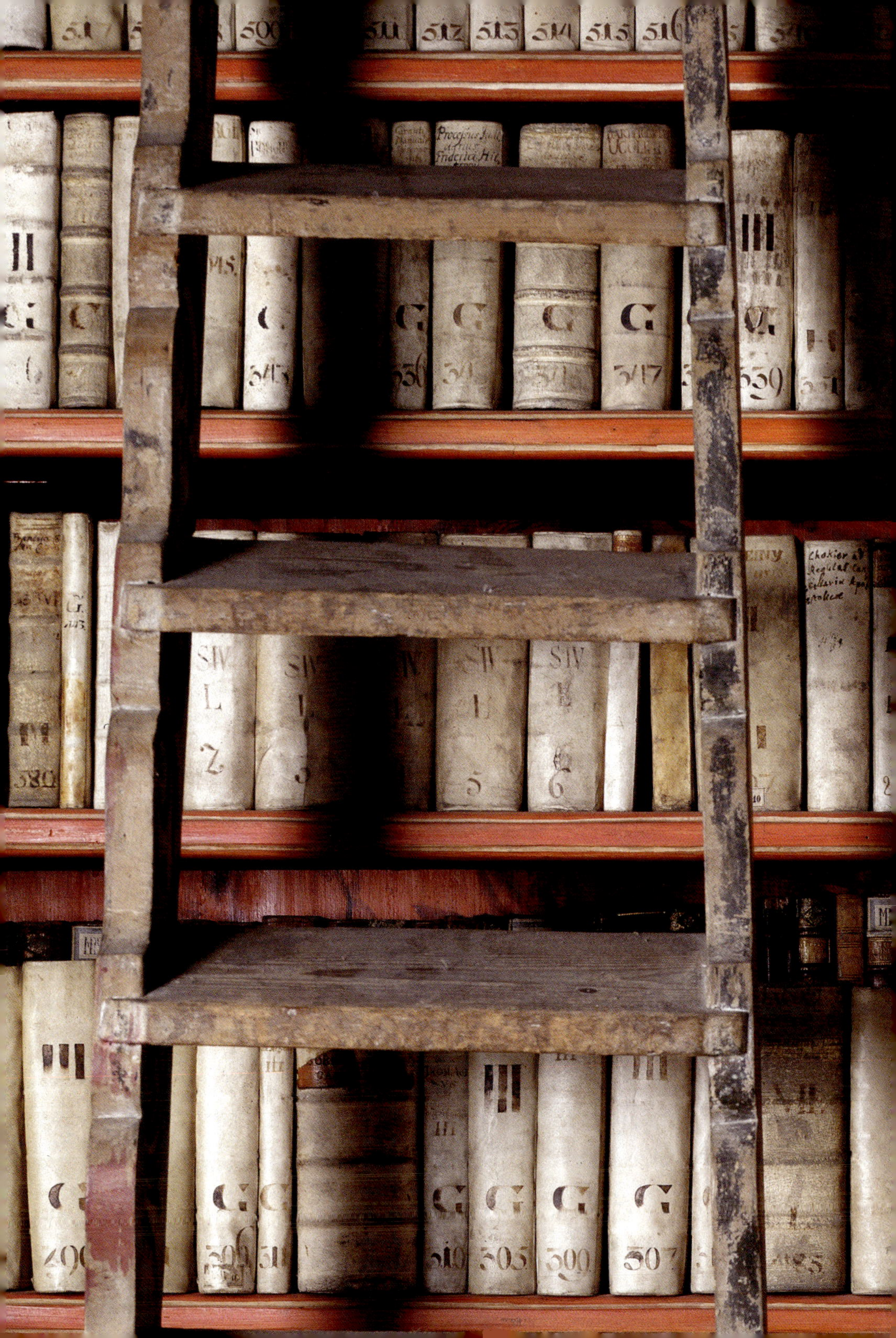

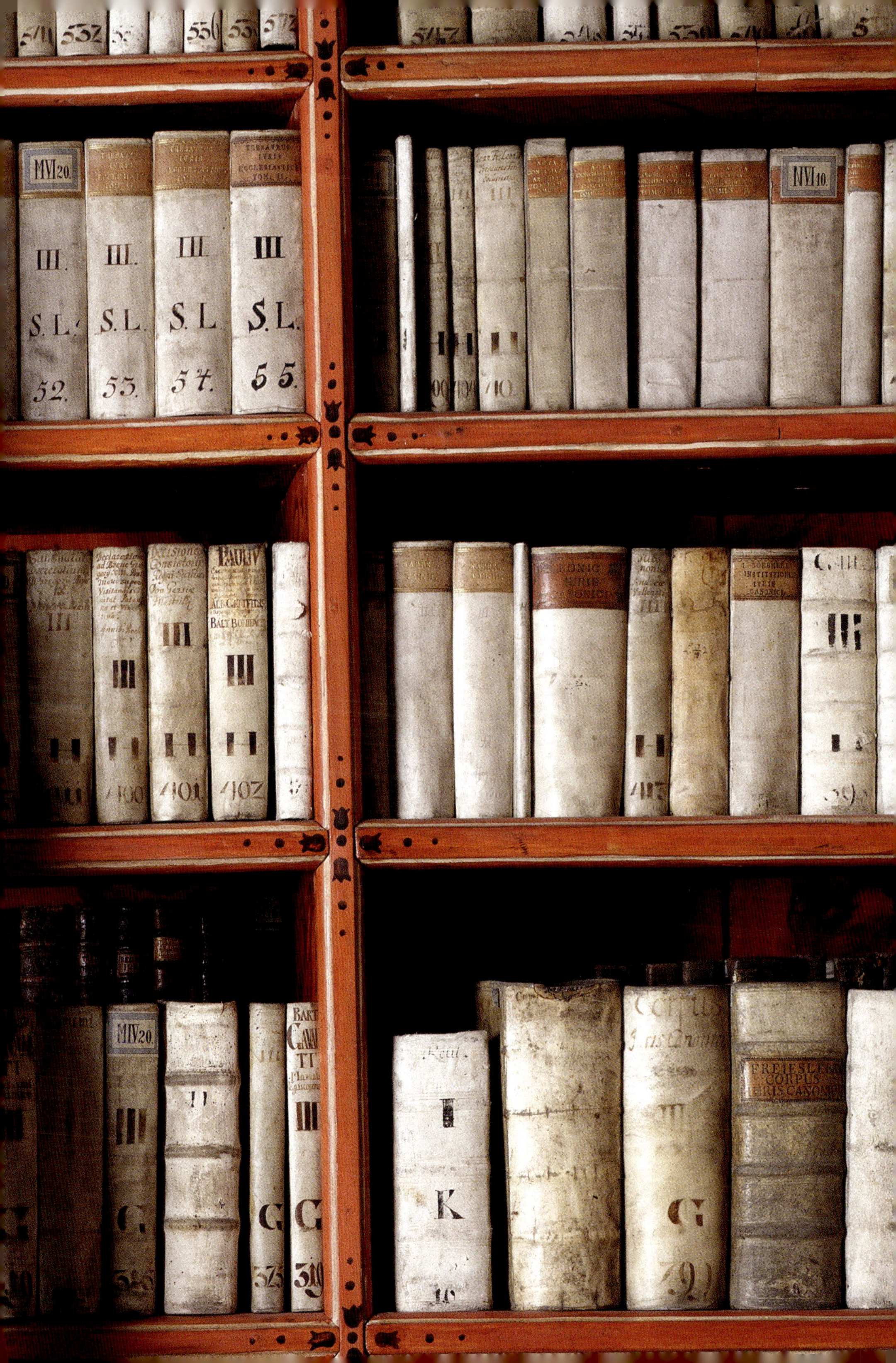

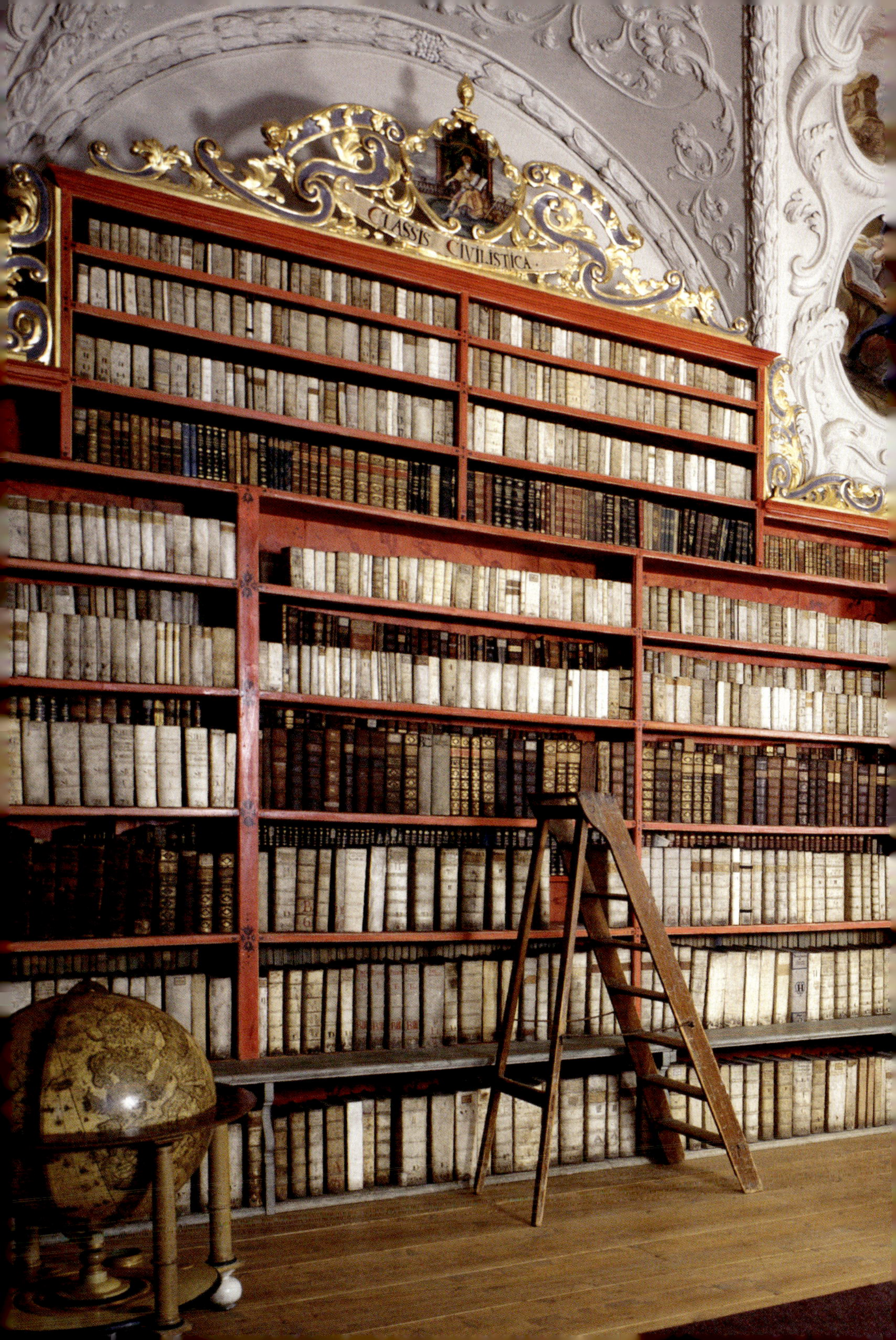
CLASSIS CIVILISTICA

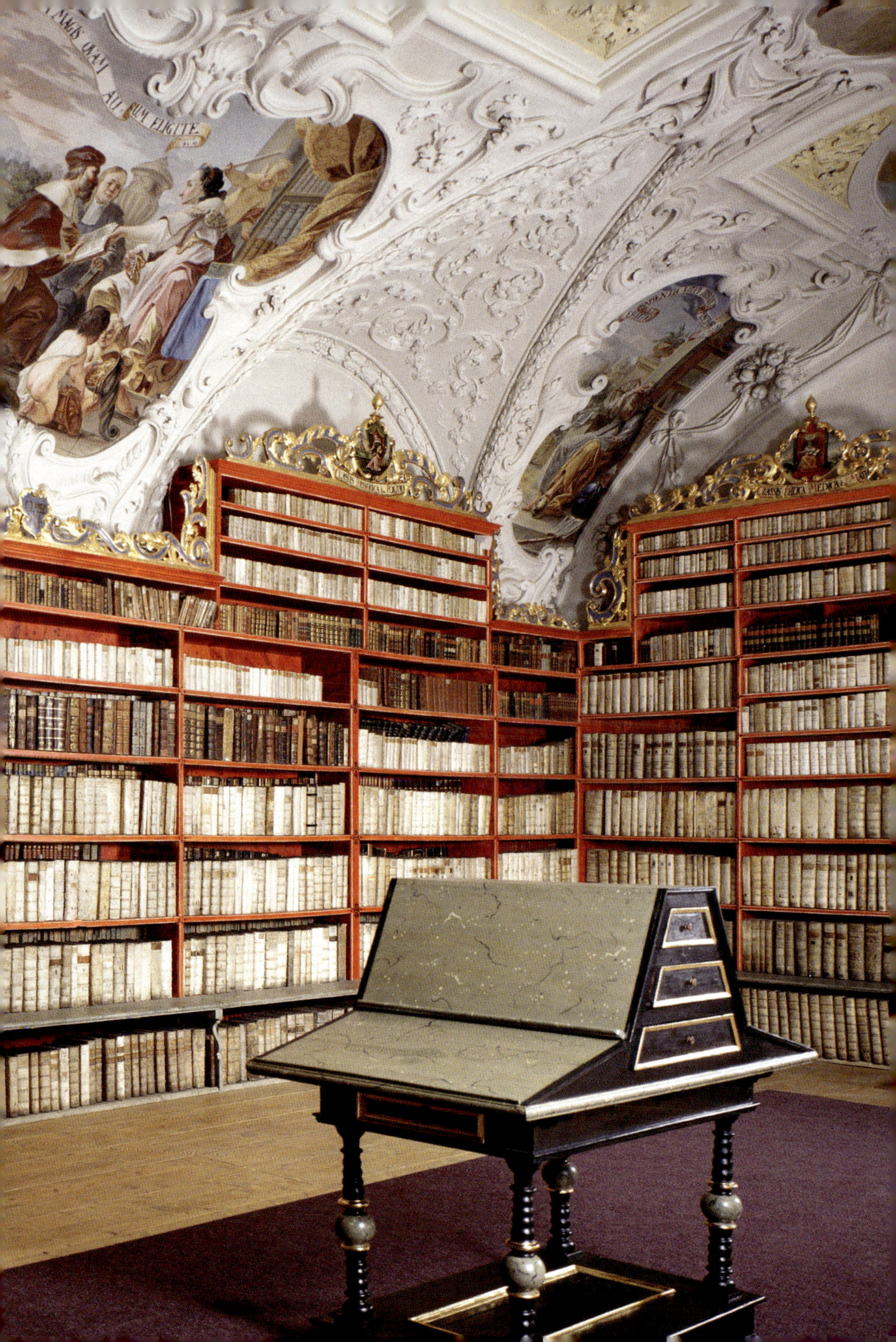

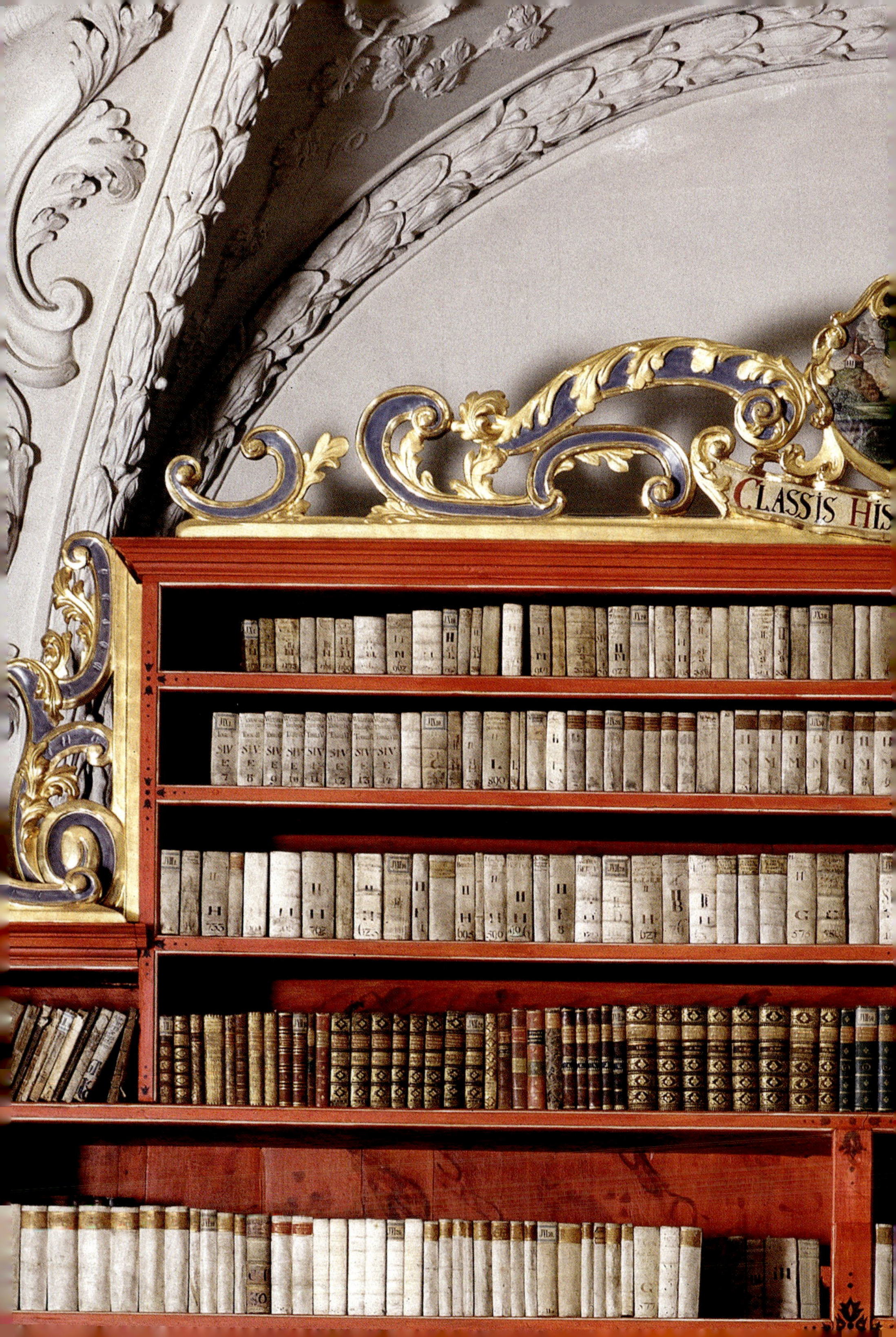
CLASSIS HIS

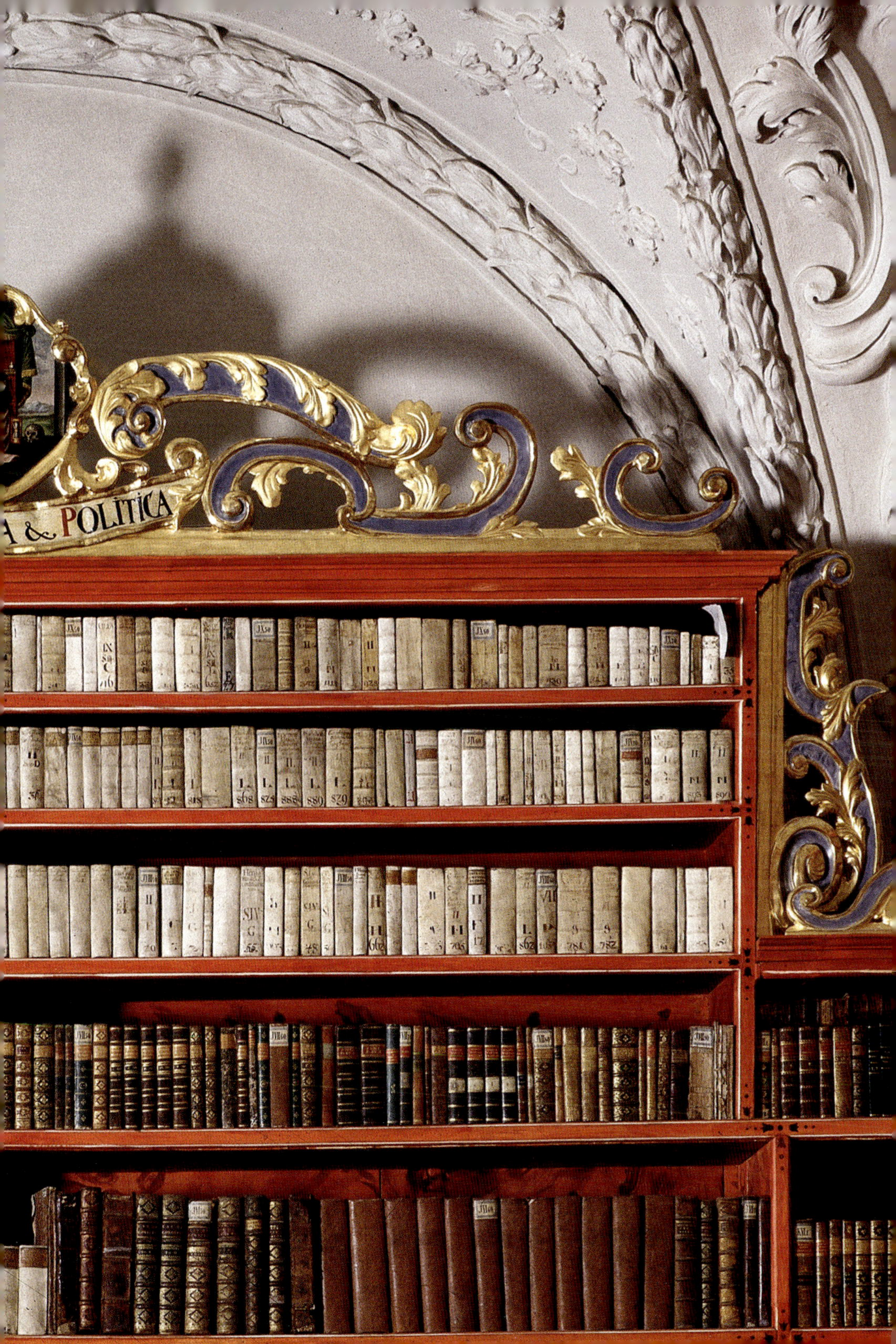
A & POLITICA

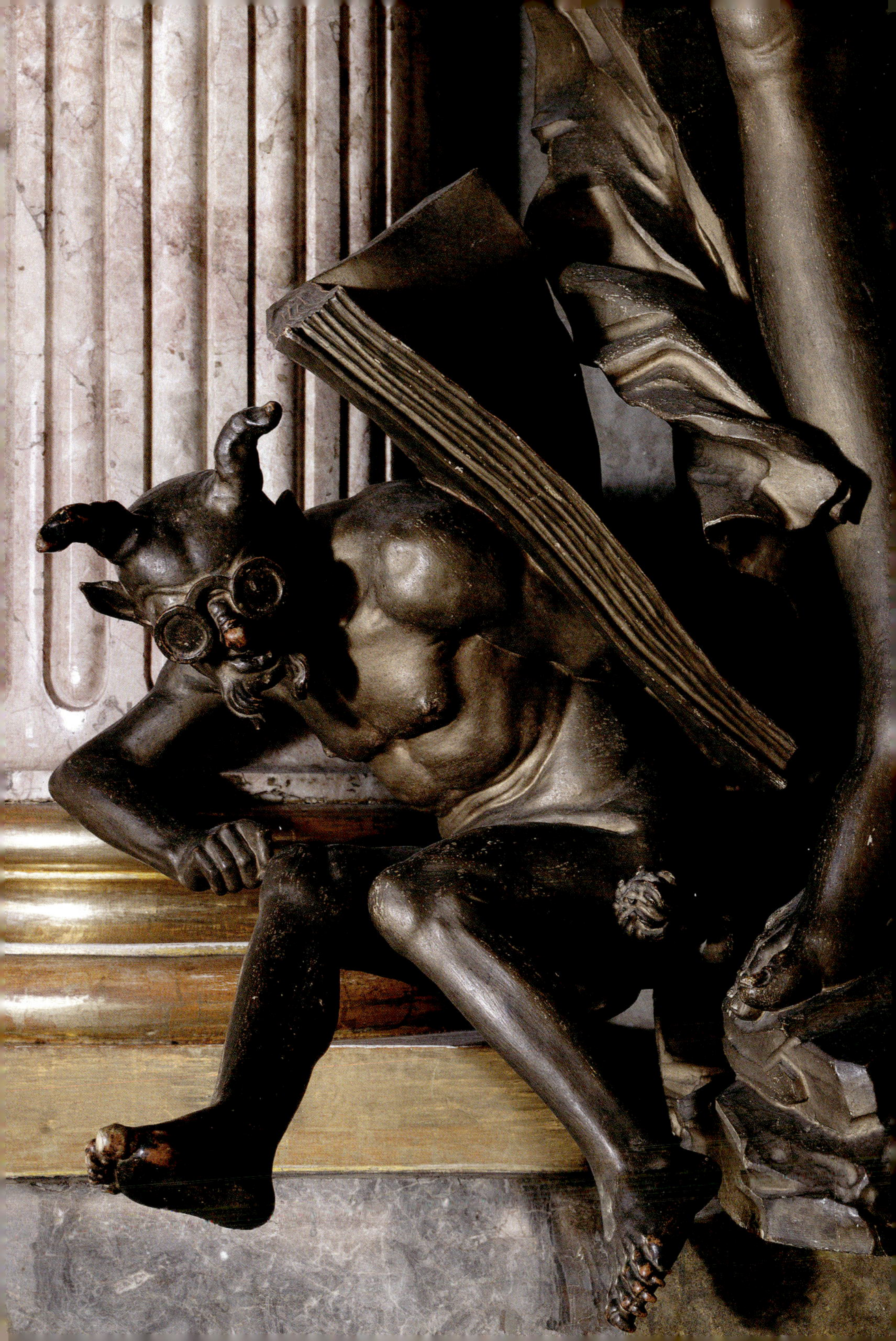

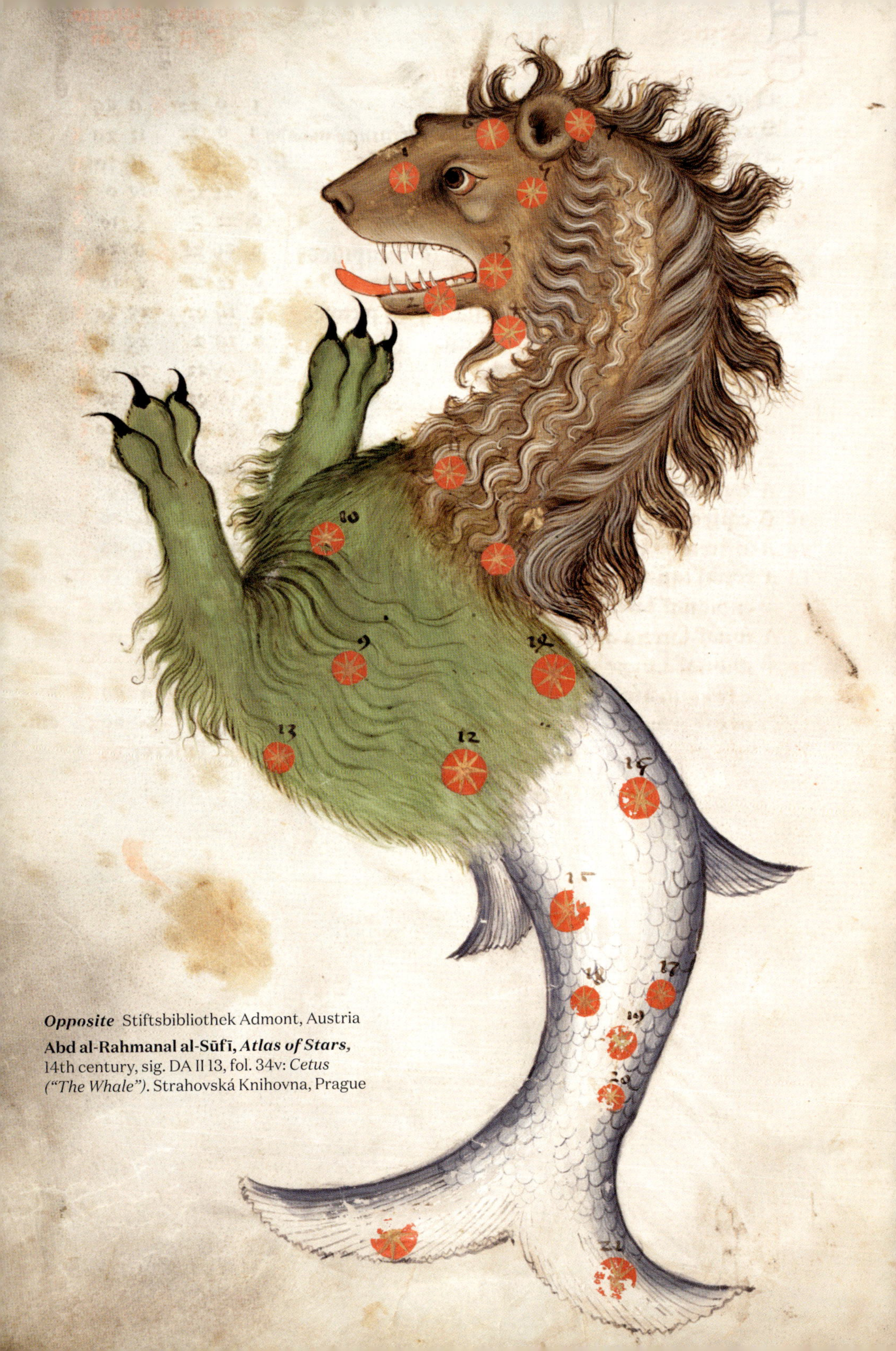

Opposite Stiftsbibliothek Admont, Austria

Abd al-Rahmanal al-Sūfī, *Atlas of Stars,* 14th century, sig. DA II 13, fol. 34v: *Cetus* ("The Whale"). Strahovská Knihovna, Prague

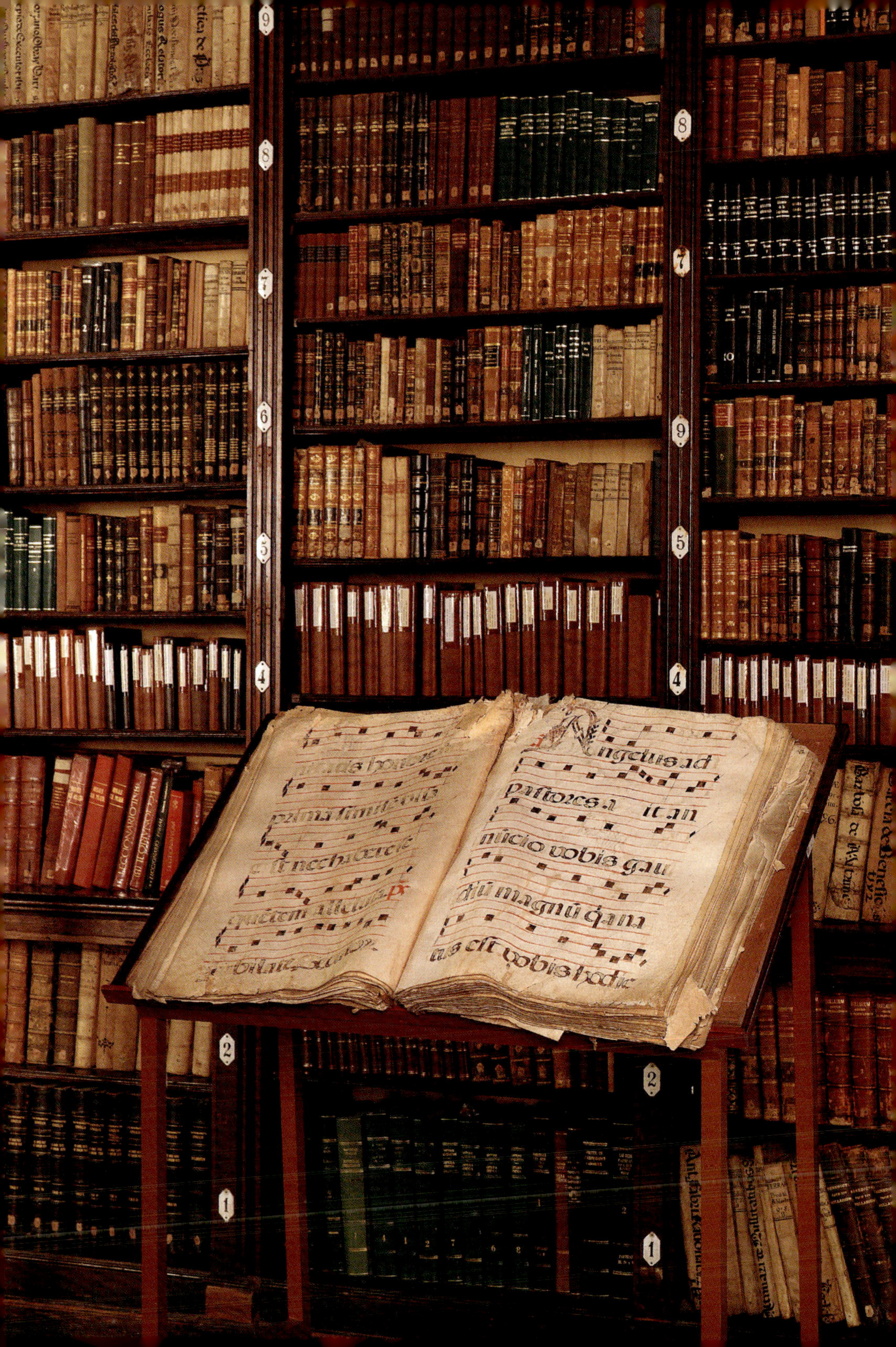
ngelus ad
pastores a. it an
nucio vobis gau
diu magnu quia
us est vobis hodie

THE AMERICAS

United States
Mexico
Brazil
Peru

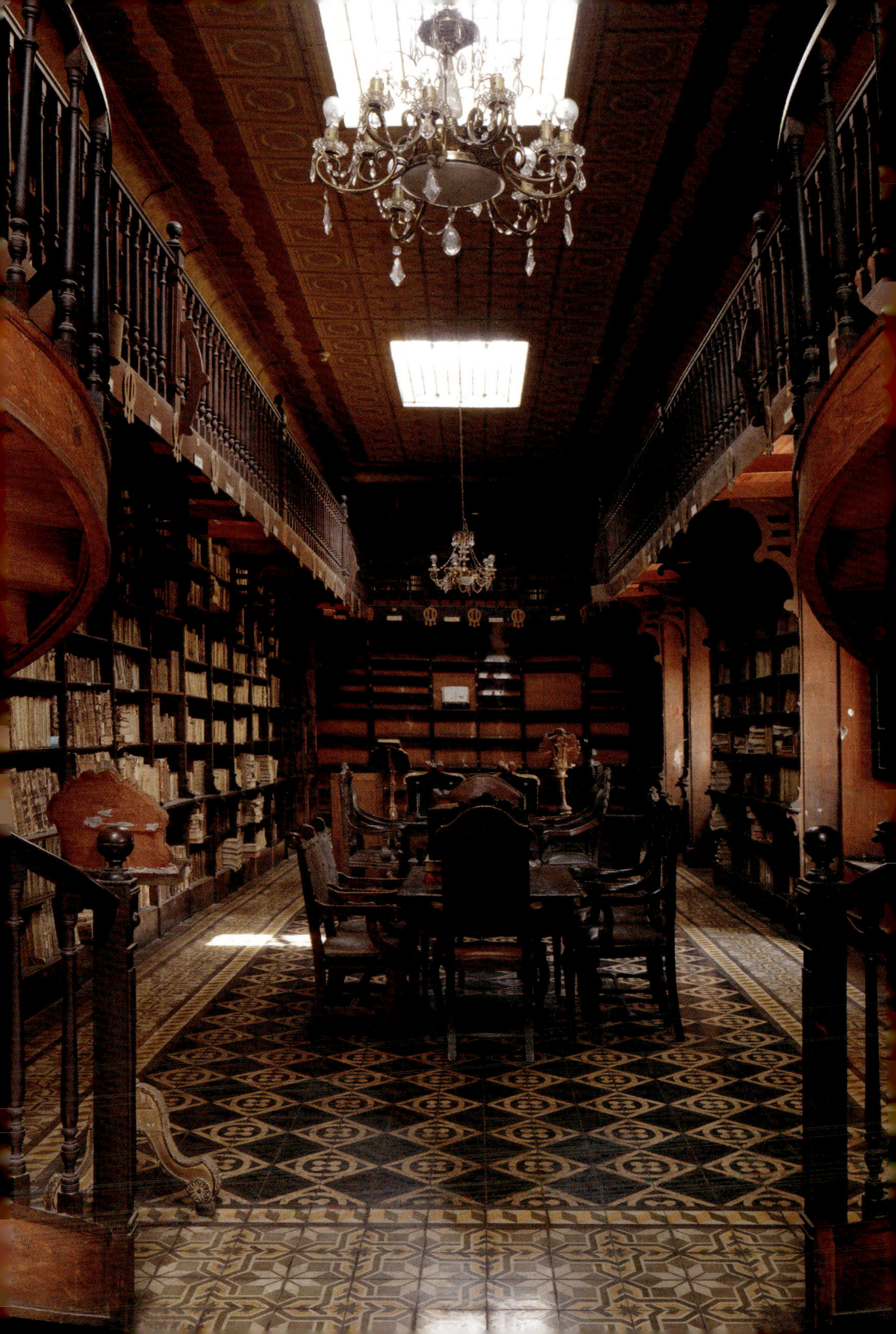

UNITED STATES

The Morgan Library, New York 468–473

MEXICO

Biblioteca Palafoxiana, Puebla 474–483

BRAZIL

Real Gabinete Português de Leitura, Rio de Janeiro 484–491

PERU

Biblioteca del Convento de San Francisco de Asís, Lima 492–503

Text by Elisabeth Sladek

Page 464 Biblioteca del Convento de Santo
Domingo, Lima, Peru

Opposite Biblioteca del Convento de San Francisco
de Asís, Lima, Peru

The Morgan Library

Between 1902 and 1906 two of the most important libraries in New York were built in the centre of Manhattan: Mr Morgan's and the New York Public Library, although they could not have been more different. The public lending library was created from the merger of the formerly private Astor and Lenox libraries and introduced an innovative open-stack system whose operational design is credited to the first librarian, John Shaw Billings (1838–1913). By contrast, John Pierpont Morgan (1837–1913) created a magnificent new building right next to his private residence on Madison Avenue, in which his lavish art collection was housed in an intimate palazzo-like structure that is indebted to European art and architecture. The European-educated banker and industrialist, who from 1904 was also President of the Metropolitan Museum of Art, pursued his passion for collecting in a wide range of areas and his library is correspondingly laid out as a treasury of precious objects. The architect he engaged for the project, Charles Follen McKim (1847–1909), had made a name for himself with new buildings in the style of the Italian Renaissance and had already built a library a few years earlier for Columbia University in New York. McKim based the façade of the Morgan Library on the Nymphaeum (the garden loggia) of the Villa Giulia in Rome, whilst inside the marble-clad building the visitor is greeted by a shrine to erudition, furnished with historical fittings of European provenance. These include Renaissance coffered ceilings as well as Baroque wall-coverings (today replaced by copies) and items of furniture that embed the precious books and artworks in an appropriate historical framework. In the middle of New York,

Morgan thus created a Temple of the Muses with a predominantly European atmosphere, in which the greatest minds of the past are gathered together and represented in portraits and aphorisms. He was particularly interested in medieval and Renaissance manuscripts, valuable illuminations, first editions and luxury bindings. Other specialist areas of the Morgan collection include papyrus fragments and music manuscripts. Mr Morgan's Library is the largest and grandest room in the McKim building and lies at the centre of the complex. The walls are lined floor to ceiling with triple tiers of walnut shelving and the decorative scheme contains numerous iconographical references to the founder. Morgan's sumptuous study,

Founded as public institution in 1924.
Built in 1906 by Charles Follen McKim for John Pierpont Morgan; Library Annex completed 1928; Morgan House acquired 1988; extension 2006 by Renzo Piano
Holdings c. 500,000 objects
Type of library originally a private library, today a public museum and research library
Highlights *Lindau Gospels*, St Gallen, c. 870–880 (MS. M. 1); *Crusader Bible*, Paris, c. 1244–1254 (MS. M. 638); *Ramsey Psalter*, London or East Anglia, c. 1303–1310 (MS. M. 302); *Black Hours*, Bruges, c. 1480 (MS. M. 493). Original manuscripts by John Milton, John Keats, Lord Byron, Jane Austen, the Brontës, Robert Burns, Charles Dickens, John Ruskin, Oscar Wilde, Henry David Thoreau, Mark Twain, John Steinbeck, and Albert Einstein; letters and documents by George Washington, Thomas Jefferson, and Abraham Lincoln

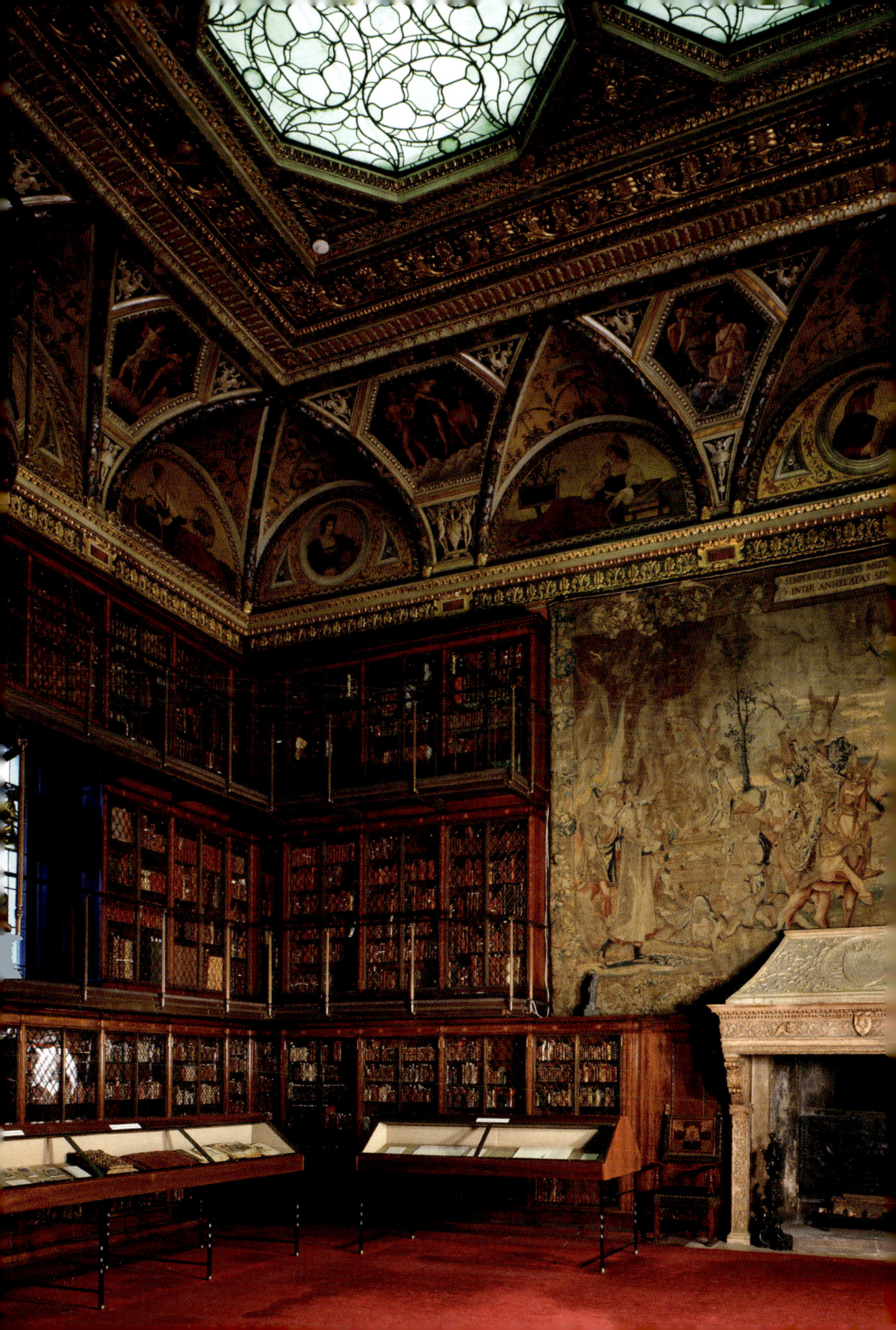

known as the West Room, lies close by, along with the office used by Belle da Costa Greene (1883–1950), an internationally acclaimed art dealer and Morgan's librarian. In 1924 Pierpont Morgan's son transferred the Morgan collection of books and art to public ownership and in 1928 constructed the Annex – containing a reading room, an exhibition room and additional storage rooms – on the site of Morgan's home. His own brownstone residence was acquired by the Morgan in 1988 and added to the complex. In 2006 Renzo Piano created a new entrance area that has opened up additional display spaces.

❋❋❋

Zwischen 1902 und 1906 entstanden im Zentrum von Manhattan zwei der bedeutendsten Bibliotheken in New York, die unterschiedlicher nicht sein könnten: Mister Morgan's und die New York Public Library. In der öffentlichen Leihbücherei, deren Grundstock aus den früheren Privatbibliotheken Astor und Lenox besteht, wurde ein innovatives Magazinsystem verwirklicht, dessen Ablaufplanung deren erstem Bibliothekar, John Shaw Billings (1838–1913), zugeschrieben wird. John Pierpont Morgan (1837–1913) aber schuf sich und seiner reichen Kunstsammlung direkt neben seinem Wohnhaus an der Madison Avenue einen repräsentativen Rahmen, dessen intime, palastähnliche Struktur europäischer Kunst und Architektur verpflichtet ist. Seine Bibliothek ist als Schatzkammer angelegt, ganz in Entsprechung zu den vielfältigen Sammelinteressen des in Europa ausgebildeten Bankiers und Industriellen, der seit 1904 auch Präsident des Metropolitan Museum of Art war. Der von ihm beauftragte Architekt, Charles Follen McKim (1847–1909), hatte sich mit Neuschöpfungen im Stil der italienischen Renaissance einen Namen gemacht. Für die Fassade der Morgan Library diente ihm das Nymphäum der Villa Giulia in Rom als Vorbild. Eine Bibliothek hatte er bereits wenige Jahre zuvor für die Columbia University in New York errichtet. Im Inneren des mit Marmor verkleideten Baus eröffnet

sich dem Besucher ein Schrein der Gelehrsamkeit, der mit historischen Versatzstücken europäischer Provenienz ausgestattet ist. Dazu zählen Kassettendecken der Renaissance ebenso wie barocke Wandtapeten (die heute durch Kopien ersetzt sind) und Möbel, die die kostbaren Buchschätze und Kunstwerke in einen historisch adäquaten Rahmen einbetten. Mister Morgan hatte sich mitten in New York einen europäisch geprägten Musentempel erschaffen, in dem die größten Geister der Vergangenheit in Porträts und Sinnsprüchen versammelt sind. Sein besonderes Interesse galt Handschriften des Mittelalters und der Renaissance, wertvollen Illustrationen, Erstausgaben und kostbaren Einbänden. Weitere Schwerpunkte stellen die Papyrussammlung und eine Kollektion von Musikautografen dar. Der monumentale Büchersaal, dessen Wände komplett von prächtigen Nussholzregalen in drei Geschossen überzogen sind, nimmt das Zentrum des Baukomplexes ein. An seiner Seite lag das üppig ausgestattete Arbeitszimmer des Gründers, der sogenannte West Room, auf den vielfältige ikonografische Bezüge im Dekorationsprogramm weisen. Daneben wirkte Belle da Costa Greene (1883–1950), eine international anerkannte Kunsthändlerin, als Leiterin der Bibliothek. 1928 sollte an der Stelle des Morgan'schen Wohnhauses der sogenannte Annex der Bibliothek entstehen. Dort ließ der Sohn des Gründers, der die Bücher- und Kunstsammlung seit 1924 der Öffentlichkeit zugänglich gemacht hatte, einen Lesesaal, eine Ausstellungshalle und neue Magazinräume einrichten. 1988 wurde auch dessen ehemaliges Wohnhaus von der Bibliothek erworben. Über Renzo Pianos neuen Eingangsbereich werden seit 2006 zusätzliche Ausstellungsflächen erschlossen.

❋❋❋

Entre 1902 et 1906, deux bibliothèques majeures (la New York Public Library et celle de Monsieur Morgan) ont vu le jour dans le centre de Manhattan. Elles ne pouvaient pas

être plus différentes. L'établissement public, qui
rassemble les anciennes bibliothèques privées
Astor et Lenox, bénéficia d'un système d'ordonnancement innovant mis en place par le premier
bibliothécaire John Shaw Billings (1838–1913).
John Pierpont Morgan (1837–1913), en revanche,
installa son inestimable collection d'art dans
un édifice majestueux attenant à sa résidence
de Madison Avenue. La structure palatiale et
le caractère intime de cet édifice rendent hommage à l'art et à l'architecture européens. La
bibliothèque s'apparente à un trésor dévoilant
les divers centres d'intérêts du collectionneur,
qui bénéficia d'une formation de banquier et
d'industriel en Europe et devint président du
Metropolitan Museum of Art en 1904. L'architecte qu'il commandita, Charles Follen McKim
(1847–1909), s'était forgé une réputation pour
ses demeures dans le goût de la Renaissance
italienne. Ainsi, la façade de la Morgan Library
s'inspire du nymphée de la Villa Giulia à Rome.
Quelques années auparavant, McKim avait
conçu la bibliothèque de la Columbia University
à New York. Habillé de marbre, l'intérieur de « la
Morgan » se présente comme un temple d'érudition agrémenté de pièces et objets historiques
en provenance d'Europe. Le visiteur admirera
des plafonds à caissons Renaissance, des tapisseries baroques (aujourd'hui remplacées par
des copies) ainsi qu'un mobilier servant d'écrin
idoine aux inestimables trésors imprimés et
œuvres d'art exposés. Monsieur Morgan fit
donc ériger au cœur de New York un temple des
muses d'inspiration européenne où les génies de
l'histoire étaient rassemblés sous forme de portraits et de bons mots. Inestimables estampes,
éditions originales et volumes rares séduisaient
Monsieur Morgan qui vouait un intérêt tout
particulier aux manuscrits du Moyen Âge et de
la Renaissance. La présence de papyrus et de
partitions originales témoigne de centres d'intérêt très divers. Au centre de l'édifice se trouve
un magasin de livres monumental dont les murs
sont en totalité recouverts par de somptueux
rayonnages. Réalisés en bois de noyer, ces derniers s'étalent sur trois niveaux. L'éblouissant

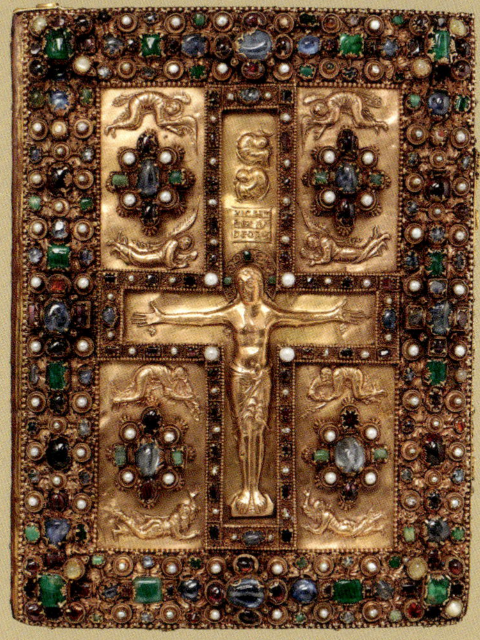

bureau du fondateur, appelé West Room, lui
était contigu. Il donne aussi à voir l'éventail des
acquisitions iconographiques décoratives. Dans
une autre pièce adjacente travaillait Belle da
Costa Greene (1883–1950), négociante en art
mondialement célèbre et première directrice de
la bibliothèque. Les appartements de la famille
Morgan devinrent l'annexe de la bibliothèque en
1928. C'est là que le fils du fondateur, qui rendit
public l'accès aux livres et aux collections d'art
en 1924, fit aménager une salle de lecture, un
hall d'exposition et des nouveaux dépôts. La
bibliothèque a fait l'acquisition de la résidence
privée en 1988. Une extension réalisée en 2006
par Renzo Piano permet de disposer d'une plus
grande surface d'exposition.

Lindau Gospels, St Gallen, c. 870–880,
sig. Ms. M. 1: *Carolingian jewelled front cover
with repoussé figure of Christ crucified.*
Chased sheet gold and semi-precious stones

CONTES
DES FÉES
1830

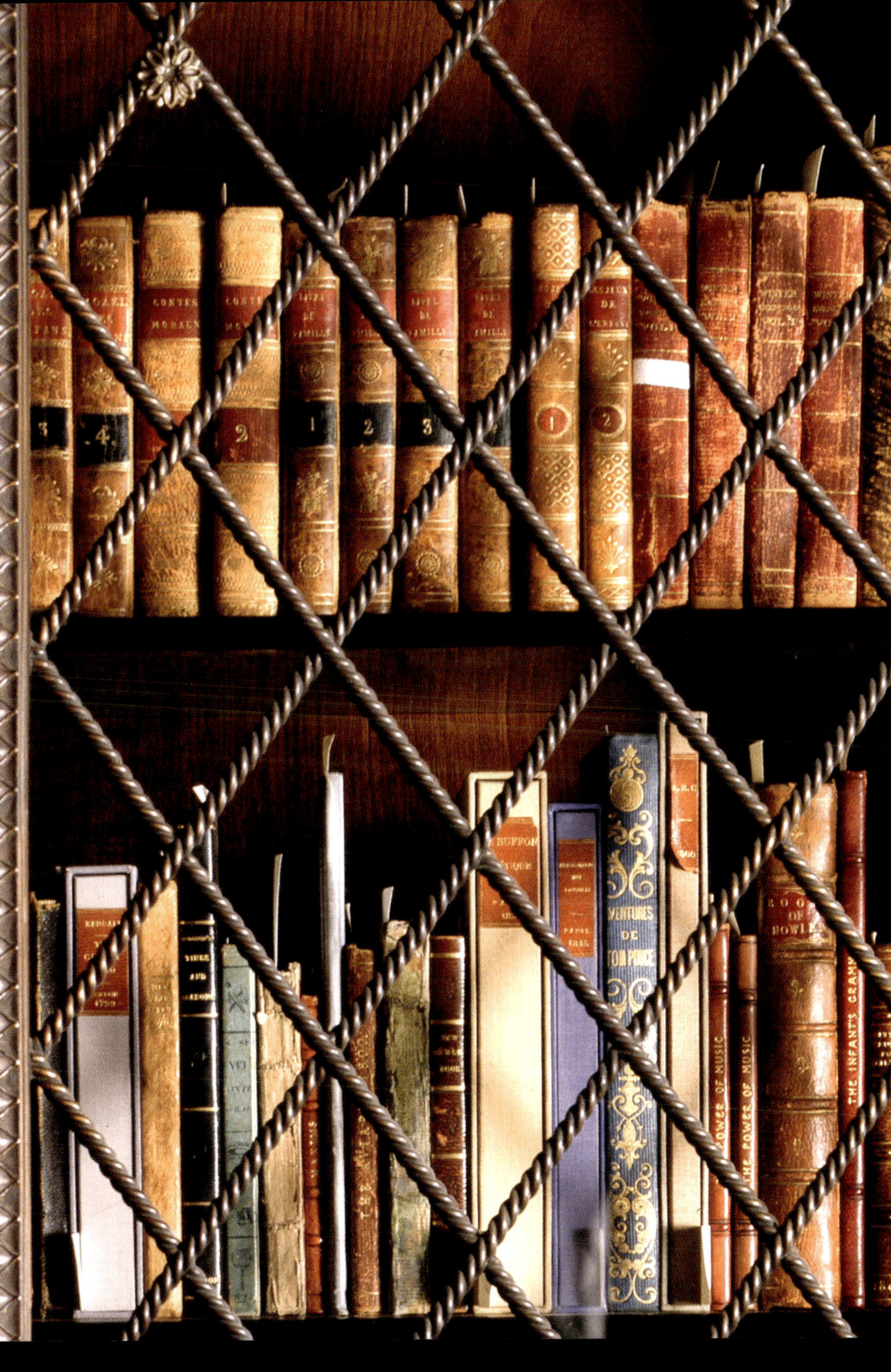

Biblioteca Palafoxiana

Juan de Palafox y Mendoza (1600–1659) spent almost ten years in his bishopric of Puebla de los Ángeles, one of the most important colonial cities in the viceroyalty of New Spain, on the central plateau of modern-day Mexico. Prior to leaving Spain, he had worked in the service of the Spanish crown as chaplain to Maria Anna of Austria (1606–1646), who in 1642 even appointed him temporary viceroy of New Spain. In his idealistic efforts, as General Visitor, to introduce European standards into the administration, finances, religious practice and general culture, he encountered considerable resistance from the entrenched colonial authorities and religious orders, in particular the Jesuits, who had built up their own centres of power. In his correspondence with Pope Innocent X (1574–1655), which still survives, Palafox denounces this deplorable state of affairs. All of these things may have been what prompted him to found, next to his episcopal palace (today the Casa de la Cultura), a theological college oriented strictly towards the precepts of the Council of Trent, and a school. In 1646 he provided the college with the first public library in the country, whose substantial nucleus included 5,000 books from his personal collection. With its current holdings of almost 50,000 books, atlases and globes, the Biblioteca Palafoxiana is the most important library dating from the colonial era in Mexico and Latin America and for this reason has been incorporated into UNESCO's Memory of the World register. Following the expulsion of the Jesuits – with whom Palafox had clashed bitterly in his own day – from the Spanish colonial empire beginning in 1767, the books from their colleges also passed into the Palafoxiana. The monumental library hall, completed in 1773, on the first floor of the college is furnished with carved ebony bookshelves and has a typical Mexican Talavera-tiled floor.

❋❋❋

Founded 1646, library hall completed 1773
Holdings over 41,000 volumes
Type of library research library
Highlights Franciscus de Bobio, *Gentilis de febribus*, n.d. (second half of the 15th century; NL R412); Abraham Ortelius, *Theatrum oder Schawbuch der gantzen Welt*, Antwerp, 1602 (NL 41575); Henrico y Cornelio Verdussen, *Obras de Francisco Quevedo Villegas*, 1699

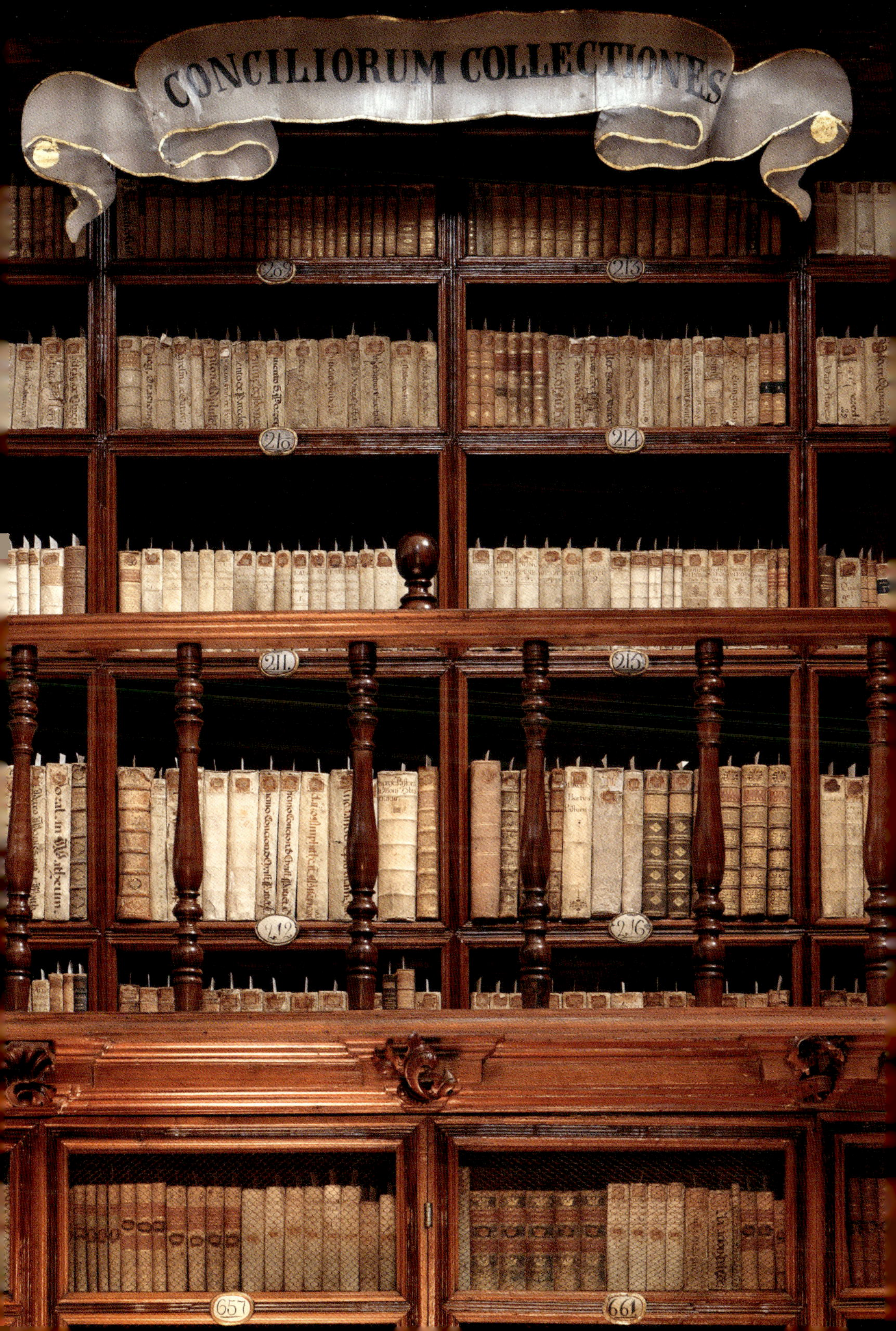

CONCILIORUM COLLECTIONES

Juan de Palafox y Mendoza (1600–1659) verbrachte annähernd zehn Jahre in seinem Bistum Puebla de los Ángeles, einer der wichtigsten Kolonialstädte im Vizekönigreich Neu-Spanien, im zentralen Hochland des heutigen Mexiko gelegen. Vor seiner Abreise aus Spanien hatte er als Kaplan der Maria von Österreich (1606–1646) in den Diensten der spanischen Krone gestanden, die ihm im Jahr 1642 vorübergehend sogar das Amt des Vizekönigs von Neu-Spanien übertrug. In seinem von Idealismus erfüllten Bestreben, als Generalvisitator europäische Maßstäbe in der Verwaltung, im Finanzwesen, in der religiösen Praxis und der allgemeinen Kultur einzuführen, stieß er auf beträchtlichen Widerstand bereits alteingesessener kolonialer Instanzen und religiöser Orden, insbesondere der Jesuiten, die eigene Machtzentren gebildet hatten. Bekannt ist sein Briefwechsel mit Papst Innozenz X. (1574–1655), in dem er diese Missstände anprangert. All dies bewog ihn möglicherweise, nächst

seiner Bischofsresidenz – der heutigen Casa de la Cultura – ein streng an den Vorgaben des Tridentinischen Konzils orientiertes Bildungskolleg sowie eine Schule einzurichten. Ihm stellte er ab 1646 die erste öffentliche Bibliothek des Landes zur Seite, die den beachtlichen Grundbestand von 5 000 Büchern aus seinem Privatbesitz aufwies. Heute bewahrt die Biblioteca Palafoxiana mit fast 50 000 Büchern, Atlanten und Globen die bedeutendste Sammlung Mexikos und Lateinamerikas der Kolonialzeit und wurde deswegen von der UNESCO in die Liste des Weltdokumentenerbes aufgenommen. Auch die Bücher aus den Jesuitenkollegien, die Palafox aufs Äußerste bekämpft hatte, befinden sich seit der Vertreibung des Ordens aus dem spanischen Kolonialreich (ab 1767) in der Palafoxiana. Der 1773 vollendete, monumentale Bibliothekssaal im Obergeschoss des Kollegs ist mit geschnitzten Bücherregalen aus Ebenholz ausgestattet und mit ortstypischen Talavera-Fliesen verlegt.

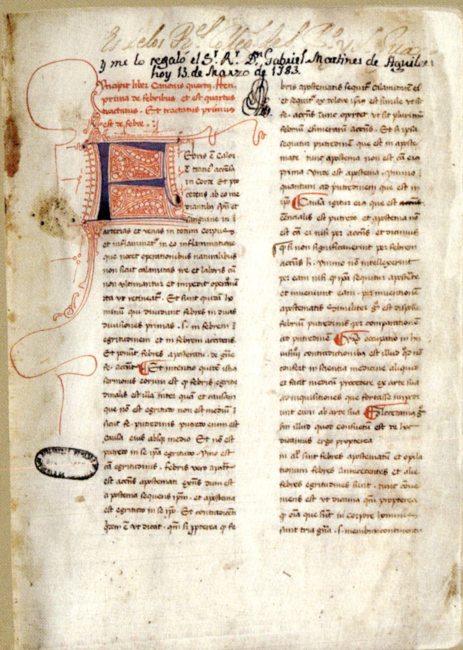

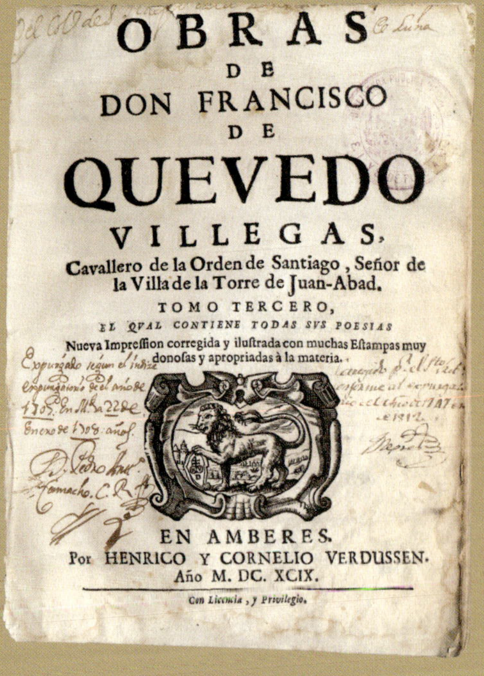

Juan de Palafox y Mendoza (1600–1659) passa
près de dix ans dans l'évêché de Puebla de los
Ángeles, ville coloniale importante de l'ancien
vice-royaume de la Nouvelle-Espagne, situé
sur les plateaux centraux du Mexique actuel. Il
avait été promu, avant son départ, chapelain de
Marie-Anne d'Autriche (1606–1646) au service
de la Couronne espagnole, qui lui confia alors,
à titre temporaire, la fonction de vice-roi de
Nouvelle-Espagne en 1642. Dans son effort de
visitador general pétri d'idéalisme souhaitant
introduire une dimension européenne dans
l'administration, la finance, la pratique religieuse
et la culture générale, il se retrouva en rupture
totale avec les instances coloniales et ordres religieux installés de longue date, et notamment les
Jésuites aux puissantes institutions. Il dénonce
ces abus dans une célèbre correspondance avec
le pape Innocent X (1574–1655). Tous ces désac-
cords l'amenèrent vraisemblablement à fonder
un collège fortement axé sur les directives du
concile de Trente ainsi qu'une école à proximité
de sa résidence épiscopale (la Casa de la Cultura
actuelle). Il créa aussi dès 1646 la première bibliothèque publique du pays, qu'il dota d'un fonds
initial considérable de 5 000 livres, issus de sa
collection particulière. La biblioteca Palafoxiana
abrite aujourd'hui près de 50 000 ouvrages,
atlas et globes, et représente la collection la plus
importante du Mexique et de l'Amérique latine
sur l'époque coloniale. L'UNESCO l'a inscrite au
patrimoine de l'humanité. Même les livres des
collèges jésuites, que Palafox avait âprement
combattus, ont rejoint la Palafoxiana dès 1767
après l'expulsion de l'ordre du royaume colonial
d'Espagne. Achevée en 1773, la salle de bibliothèque monumentale située à l'étage du collège
est entièrement habillée de bois d'ébène sculpté
et carrelée de *talavera*, typiques de la région.

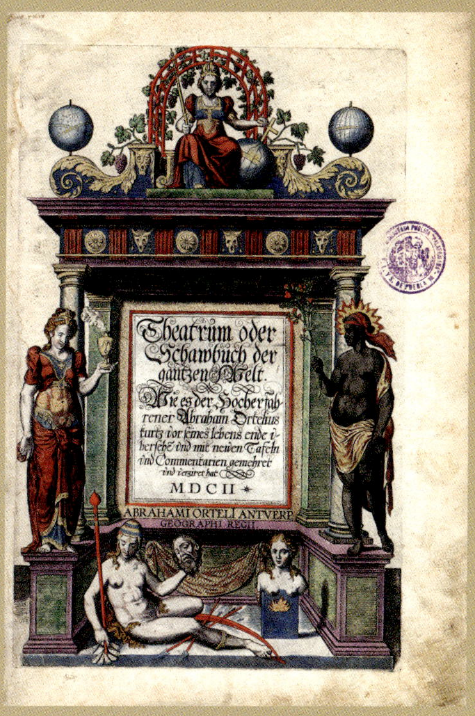

Abraham Ortelius, *Theatrum oder
Schawbuch der gantzen Welt*, Antwerp,
1602, sig. NL 41575: *Frontispiece*

Franciscus de Bobio, *Gentilis de febribus*,
n.d. (second half of the 15th century),
sig. NL R412, fol. not numbered

Henrico y Cornelio Verdussen,
Obras de Francisco Quevedo Villegas,
1699, vol. 3: *Frontispiece*

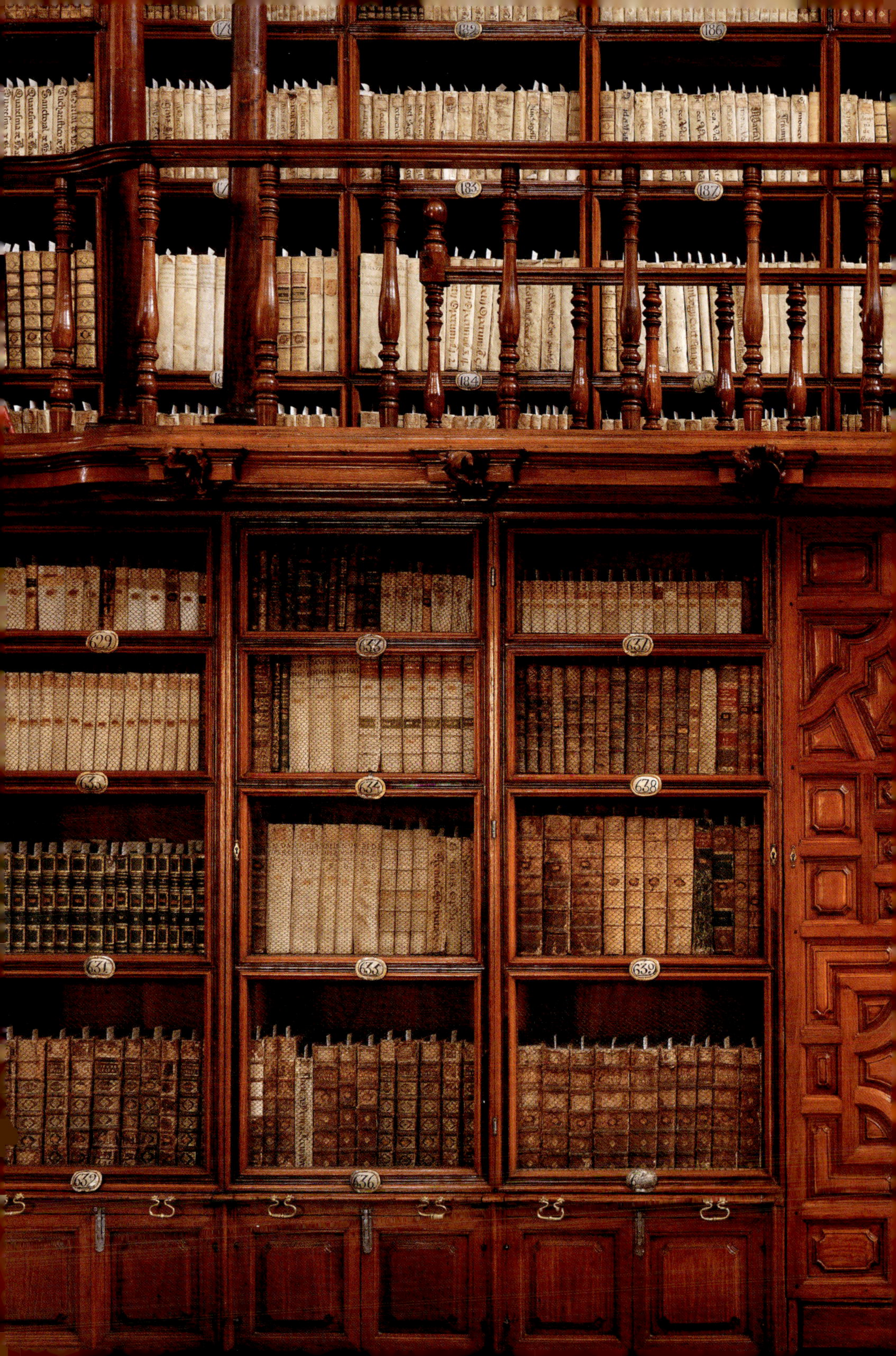

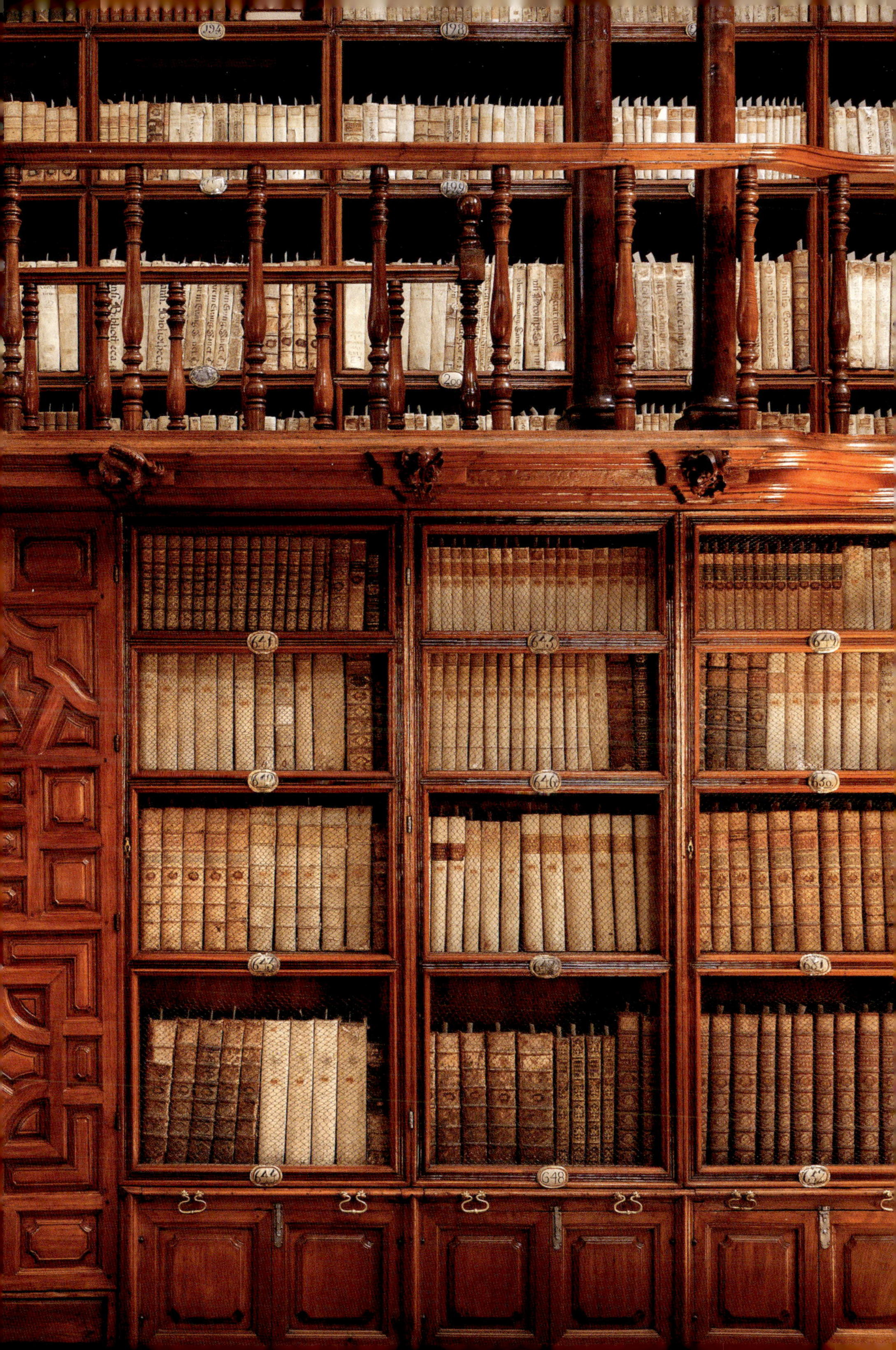

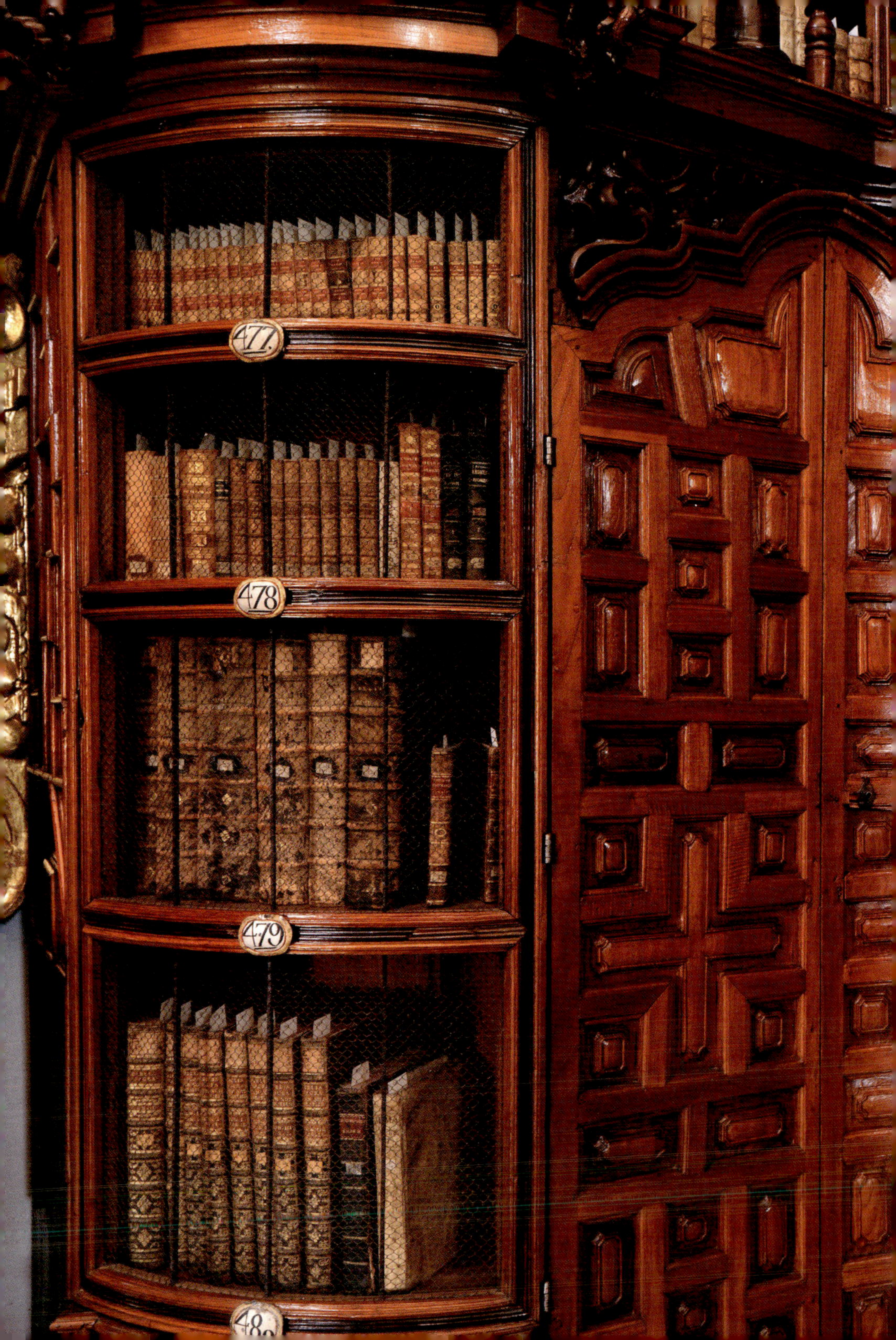

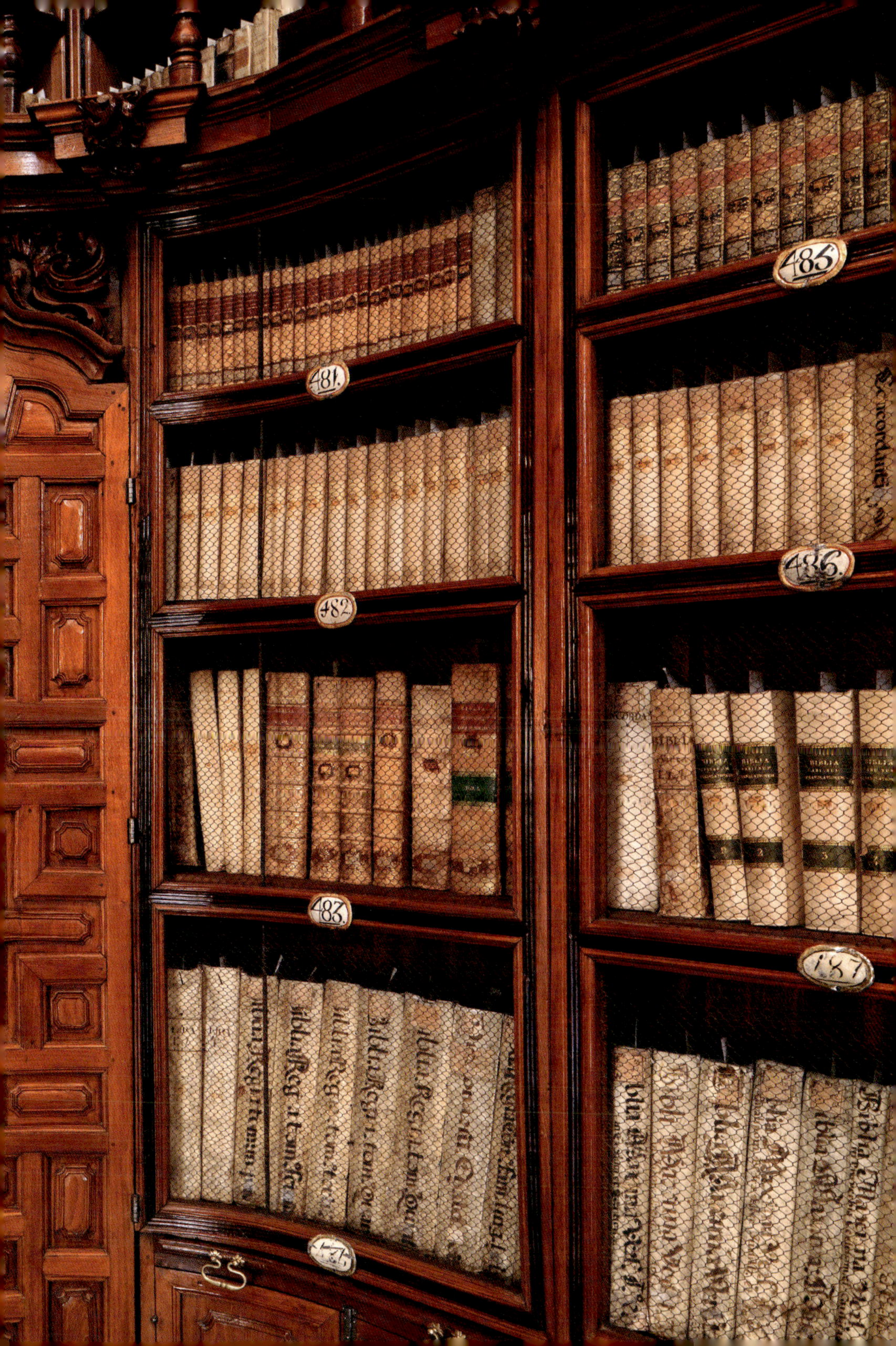
481.
482.
483.
485.
486.
487.

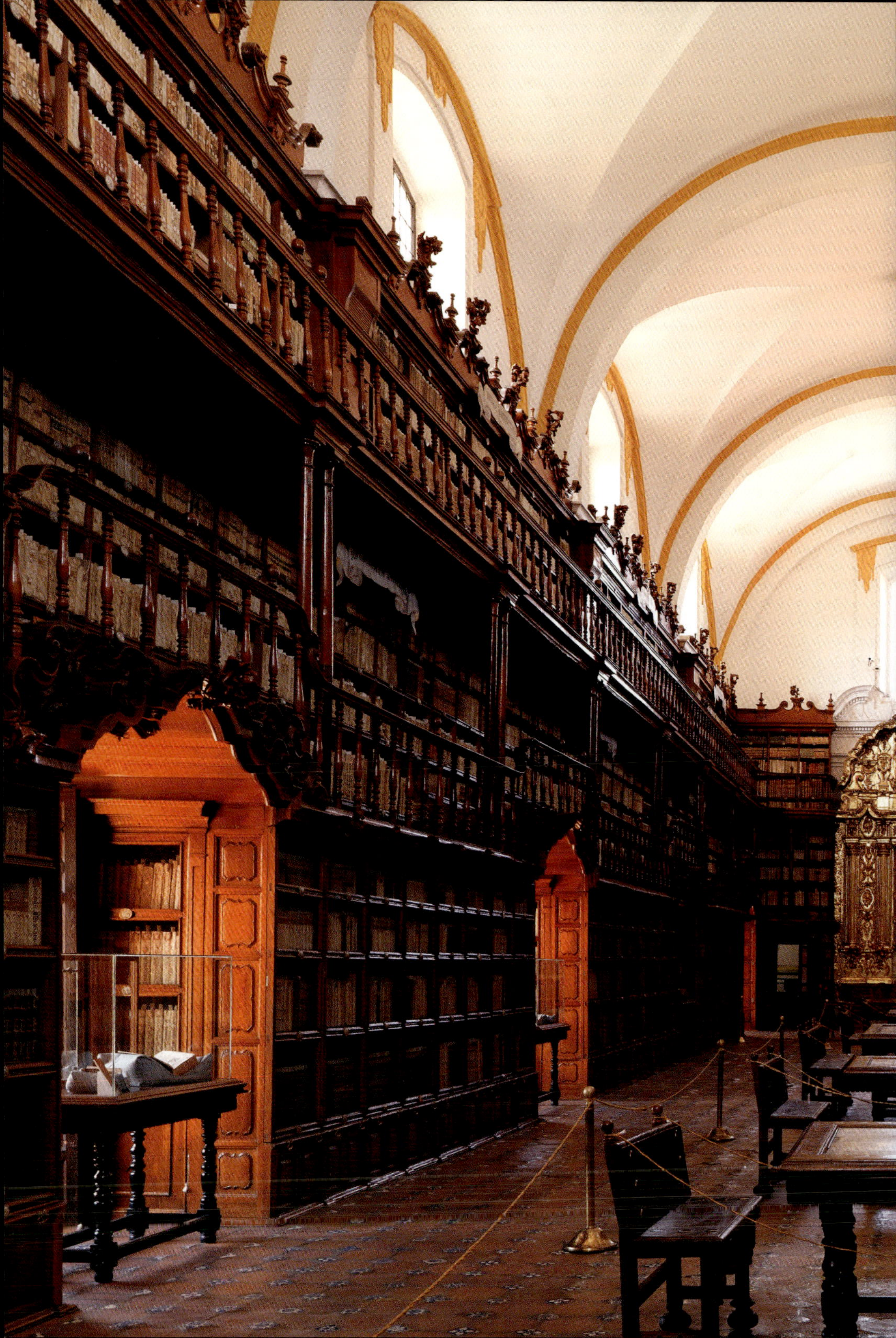

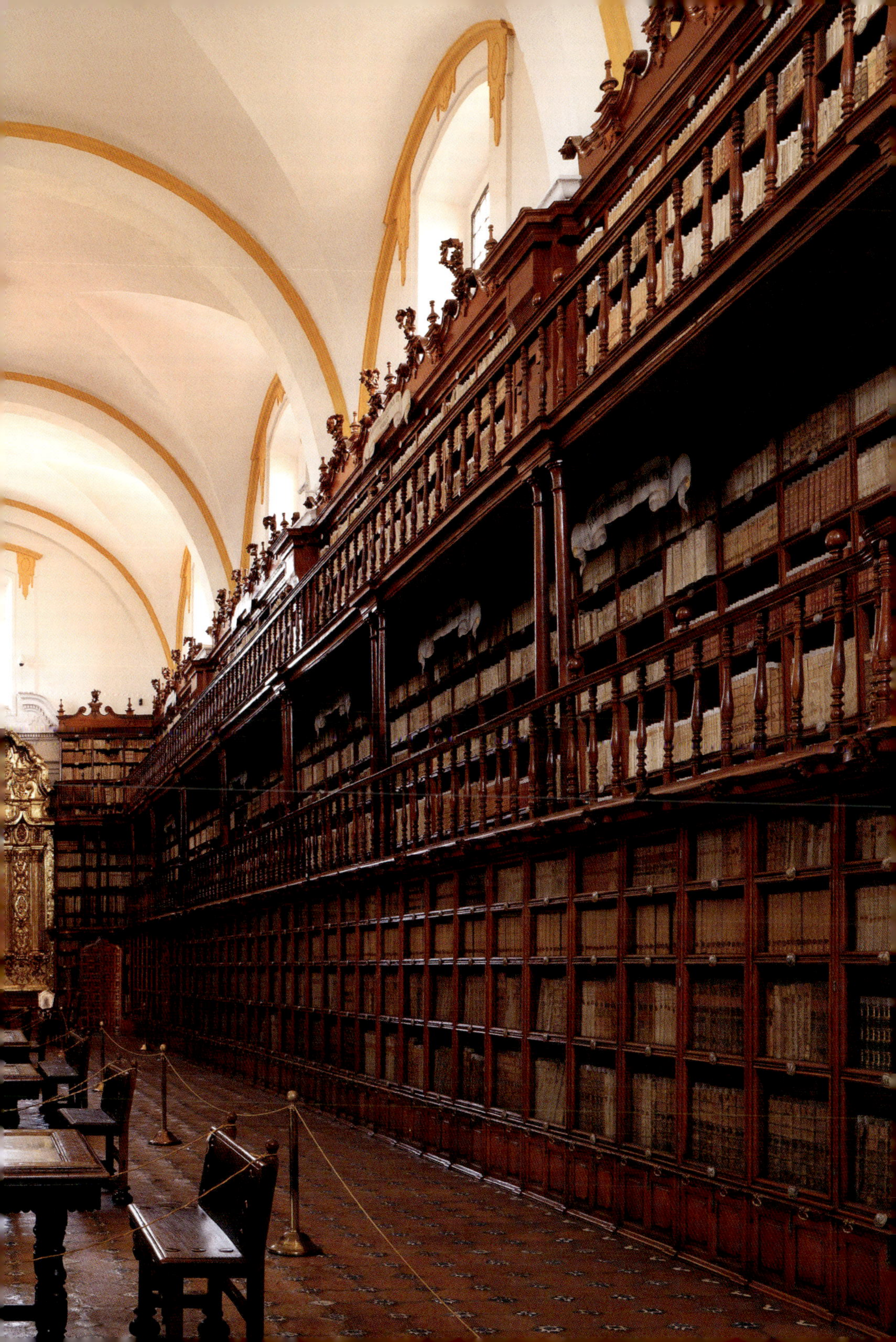

Real Gabinete Português de Leitura

In 1880 work began on a magnificent new library in the centre of Rio de Janeiro, the former capital of the Empire of Brazil, independent since 1822. The library was built to mark the tercentenary of the death of Luís de Camões (1524–1580), the Portuguese national poet after whom the street on which it stands is named. The aim was to nurture and spread Portuguese culture, just as the first Gabinete Português de Leitura had done since its foundation in 1837. At that time a group of 43 Portuguese immigrants, made up chiefly of merchants but also including a number of political refugees, had joined forces to establish a reading room in their native language – a *boutique à lire* as had become the fashion in post-Revolution France and which found expression in America in Masonic libraries. In the new library built between 1880 and 1887, however, a new aspect played a role: *memoria*. For the Portuguese colony of Brazil, its European roots had by now probably become an idealised memory and the heroic period of Portuguese voyages of discovery was now to be evoked for future generations by way of a magnificent work of historicist architecture. The entire building is hallmarked by sumptuous Manuelline ornamentation and an architecture that recalls particular aspects of the Portuguese Late Gothic. Inside the library, which is laid out over two storeys, these characteristics are found not only in the carved décor of the bookshelves and the galleries running right around the walls, but also in the cast-iron roof construction, through which the interior is lit from above. The decorative architectural elements, carved in limestone,

were produced in Portugal and shipped to Brazil ready for installation. The façade of the Brazilian library is in fact a copy of probably the most famous building in Portugal, the early 16th-century monastery of the Hieronymites in Lisbon. A symbol of national identity, the monastery houses the funerary monuments of King Manuel I (1469–1521) and his family, as well as those of Vasco da Gama (c. 1469–1524) and Luís de Camões (c. 1524–c. 1579). A first edition of the latter's main work, the Portuguese epic poem *Os Lusíadas* (*The Lusiads*), is one of the Reading Room's greatest treasures. The library also houses historically valuable original editions of chronicles of Portuguese discoveries. Since the Reading Room – distinguished by the title "Royal" since 1906 – receives deposit copies of every book published in Portugal, it today houses the largest collection of Portuguese books outside Portugal.

⁂

Founded 1837; built 1880–1887 by Rafael da Silva e Castro
Holdings c. 350,000 volumes
Type of library library specialised in Portuguese culture and history
Highlights Jacob Cromberger, *O primeiro (-quinto) liuro das Ordenações*, Lisbon, 1521; *Capitolos de Cortes e Leys que sobre alguu(n)s delles fizeram*, Lisbon, 1539; Francisco Álvares, *Ho preste Ioam das Indias: Verdadera informaçam das terras do Preste Ioam*, Lisbon, 1540 (CRES 412v); Luís de Camões, *Os Lusíadas* (epic poem), first edition of 1572

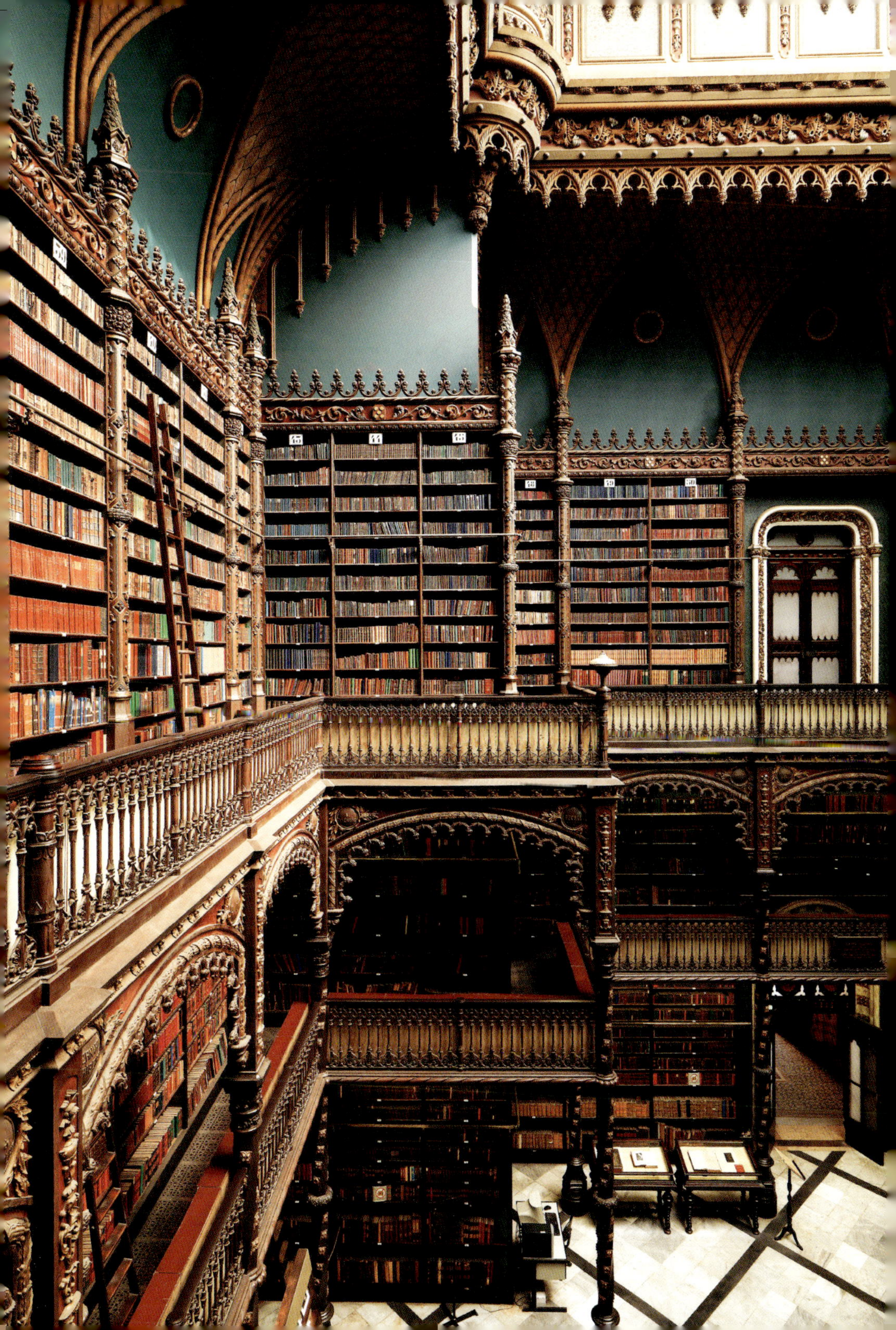

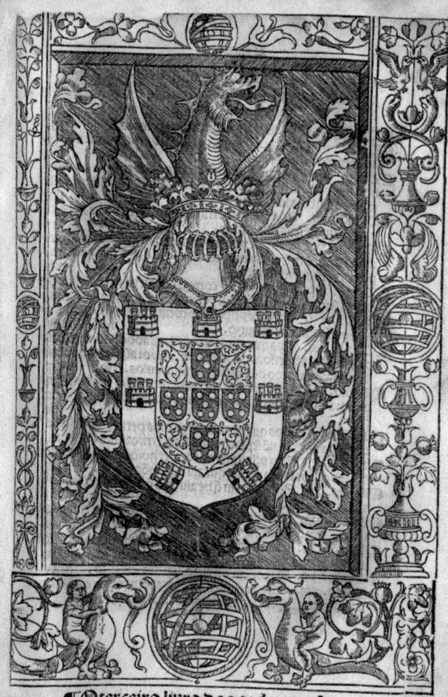

Im Zentrum von Rio de Janeiro, der ehemaligen Hauptstadt des seit 1822 unabhängigen Kaiserreichs Brasilien, wurde zum 300-jährigen Todestag des portugiesischen Nationaldichters Luís de Camões (1524–1580), nach dem heute auch die Straße benannt ist, ein prächtiges Bibliotheksgebäude errichtet. Portugiesische Kultur sollte hier gepflegt und vermittelt werden, wie bereits seit der Gründung des ersten Gabinete Português de Leitura im Jahr 1837. Damals hatte sich eine Gruppe von 43 portugiesischen Einwanderern, zumeist Händler, aber auch in ihrem Herkunftsland politisch Verfolgte, zusammengeschlossen, um eine Lesestube in ihrer Muttersprache zu gründen. Eine „boutique à lire", wie sie im nachrevolutionären Frankreich zur Mode geworden und in Amerika in den Lesestuben der Freimaurer eingelöst war. Mit dem Neubau in den Jahren 1880 bis 1887 kam aber ein neuer Aspekt zum Tragen, jener der *Memoria*. Ihre europäischen

Wurzeln waren der portugiesischen „Kolonie" Brasilien wohl mittlerweile zur idealisierten Erinnerung geworden, den künftigen Generationen sollte nun mit einem Prachtbau in historisierendem Stil die heroische Epoche der portugiesischen Entdeckungsreisen evoziert werden. Prunkvolle manuelinische Ornamentik und eine an Sonderformen der Spätgotik gemahnende Architektur kennzeichnen den gesamten Bau. Im Innenraum der über zwei Geschosse angelegten Bibliothek trägt nicht nur das Schnitzwerk der Bücherregale samt umlaufender Galerien diese Charakteristika, sondern auch die Gusseisenkonstruktion der Decke, durch die Oberlicht den Raum erhellt. Die aus Kalkstein gemeißelten Architekturdekorationen wurden sogar direkt in Portugal hergestellt und als Fertigteile nach Brasilien verschifft. Denn die Fassade der brasilianischen Bibliothek ist eine Kopie des wohl berühmtesten identitätsstiftenden Bauwerks in Portugal, des Hieronymusklosters aus dem frühen 16. Jahrhundert. Dort befinden sich die Grabdenkmäler König Manuels I. (1469–1521) und seiner Familie sowie auch jene von Vasco da Gama (um 1469–1524) und Luís de Camões (um 1524–um 1579). Eine Erstausgabe seines Hauptwerks, des portugiesischen Heldenepos *Os Lusíadas (Die Lusiaden)*, zählt zu den Prunkstücken der Bibliothek. Auch finden sich historisch wertvolle Originalausgaben von Zeitdokumenten der portugiesischen Entdeckungen. Da die seit 1906 mit dem Titel „Königlich" ausgezeichnete Bibliothek seit damals Pflichtexemplare jedes in Portugal veröffentlichten Buches erhält, besitzt das Real Gabinete heute die größte portugiesische Büchersammlung außerhalb Portugals.

Jacob Cromberger, *O primeiro (-quinto) liuro das Ordenações*, Lisbon, 1521:
Frontispiece of the third book
Capitolos de Cortes e Leys que sobre alguu(n)s delles fizeram, Lisbon, 1539

Dans le centre de Rio de Janeiro, ancienne capitale de l'Empire du Brésil indépendant depuis 1822, un magnifique bâtiment fut inauguré à l'occasion du 300ᵉ anniversaire de la mort du poète portugais Luís de Camões (1524–1580), qui donna aussi son nom à la rue où l'édifice est situé. À l'instar du premier Gabinete Português de Leitura fondé en 1837, la bibliothèque se voulait un centre de transmission et de conservation de la culture portugaise. 43 immigrés portugais, négociants pour la plupart, mais aussi réfugiés politiques pour d'autres, s'étaient associés pour obtenir une salle de lecture d'ouvrages édités dans leur langue maternelle. Une sorte de « boutique à lire », comme il était de coutume de rencontrer dans la France post-révolutionnaire, ou de salon de lecture que les francs-maçons affectionnaient en Amérique. Le nouveau bâtiment de 1880–1887 prit un aspect inédit en considération : celui de la mémoire. Les racines européennes de la « colonie » portugaise étant devenues un souvenir idéalisé, l'époque héroïque des grandes découvertes portugaises devait être rappelée aux générations futures par un bâtiment grandiose dans un style historisant. L'extérieur se distingue par sa fastueuse ornementation manuéline et ses formes architecturales spécifiques rappelant le gothique tardif. À l'intérieur, ces traits caractéristiques ne se retrouvent pas seulement dans les étagères ouvragées des deux niveaux et de la galerie, mais aussi dans la construction en fonte du plafond qui laisse filtrer la lumière éclairant la salle. Le décor architectural en pierre à chaux fut sculpté au Portugal et convoyé vers le Brésil, une fois prêt. En fait, la façade de la bibliothèque brésilienne est une copie d'un célèbre édifice, fondateur de l'identité portugaise : le monastère des Hiéronymites érigé au début du XVIᵉ siècle. Ce dernier abrite d'ailleurs la nécropole de la famille royale de Manuel Iᵉʳ (1469–1521), ainsi que les tombeaux de Vasco de Gama (vers 1469–1524) et de Luís de Camões (vers 1524–1579). Une édition originale de son œuvre maîtresse, le poème épique *Les Lusiades (Os Lusíadas)*, fait partie des joyaux de la bibliothèque de Rio. Elle est accompagnée d'éditions originales de documents historiques précieux datant de l'époque des grandes découvertes portugaises. Comme la bibliothèque, qualifiée de « royale » dès 1906, reçoit depuis lors un exemplaire de chaque ouvrage publié au Portugal, le Real Gabinete contient aujourd'hui la plus grande collection de livres portugais en dehors du Portugal.

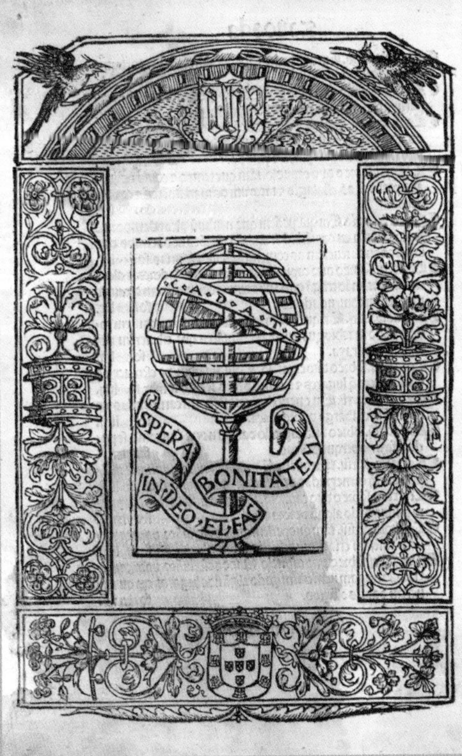

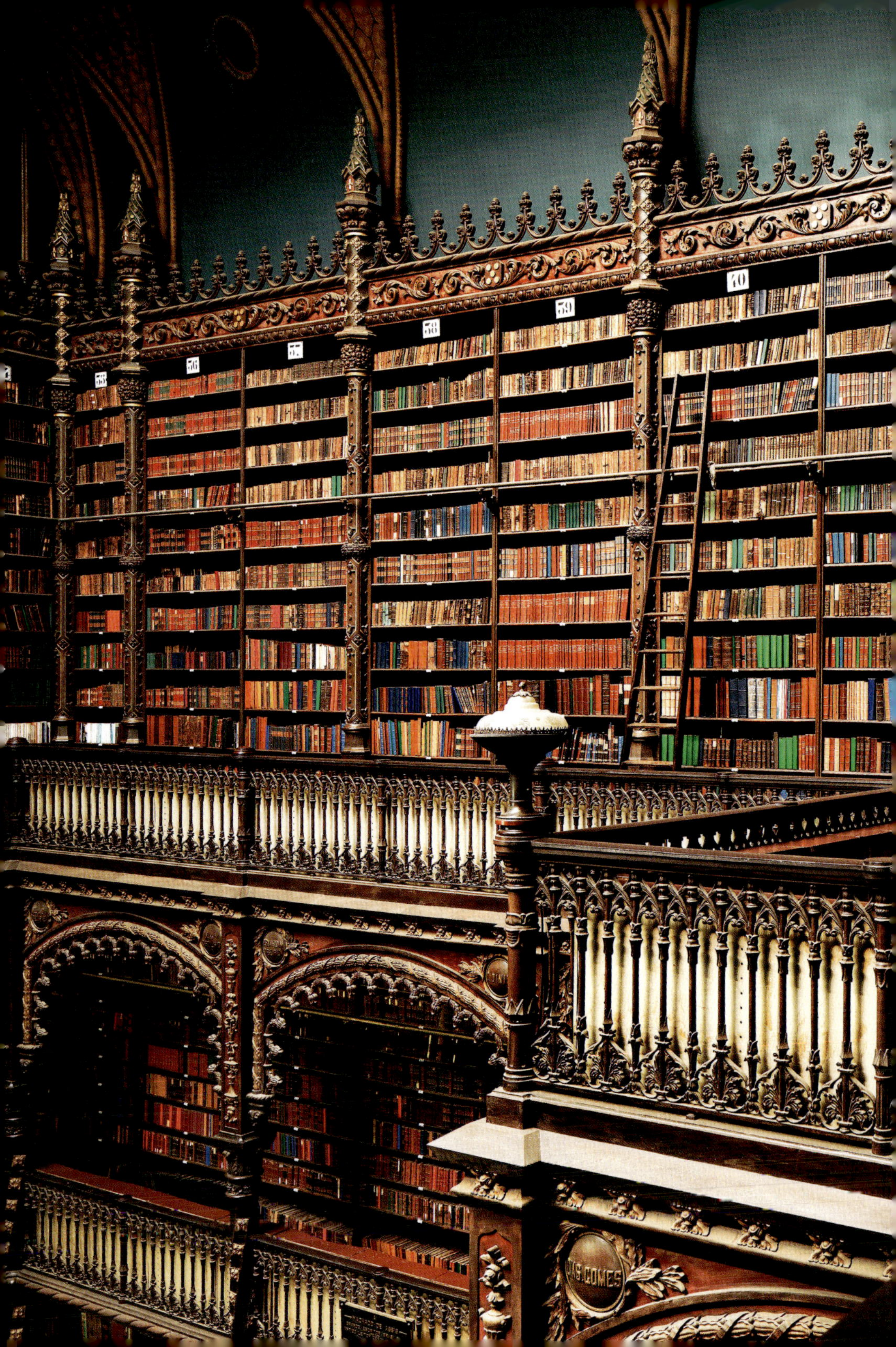

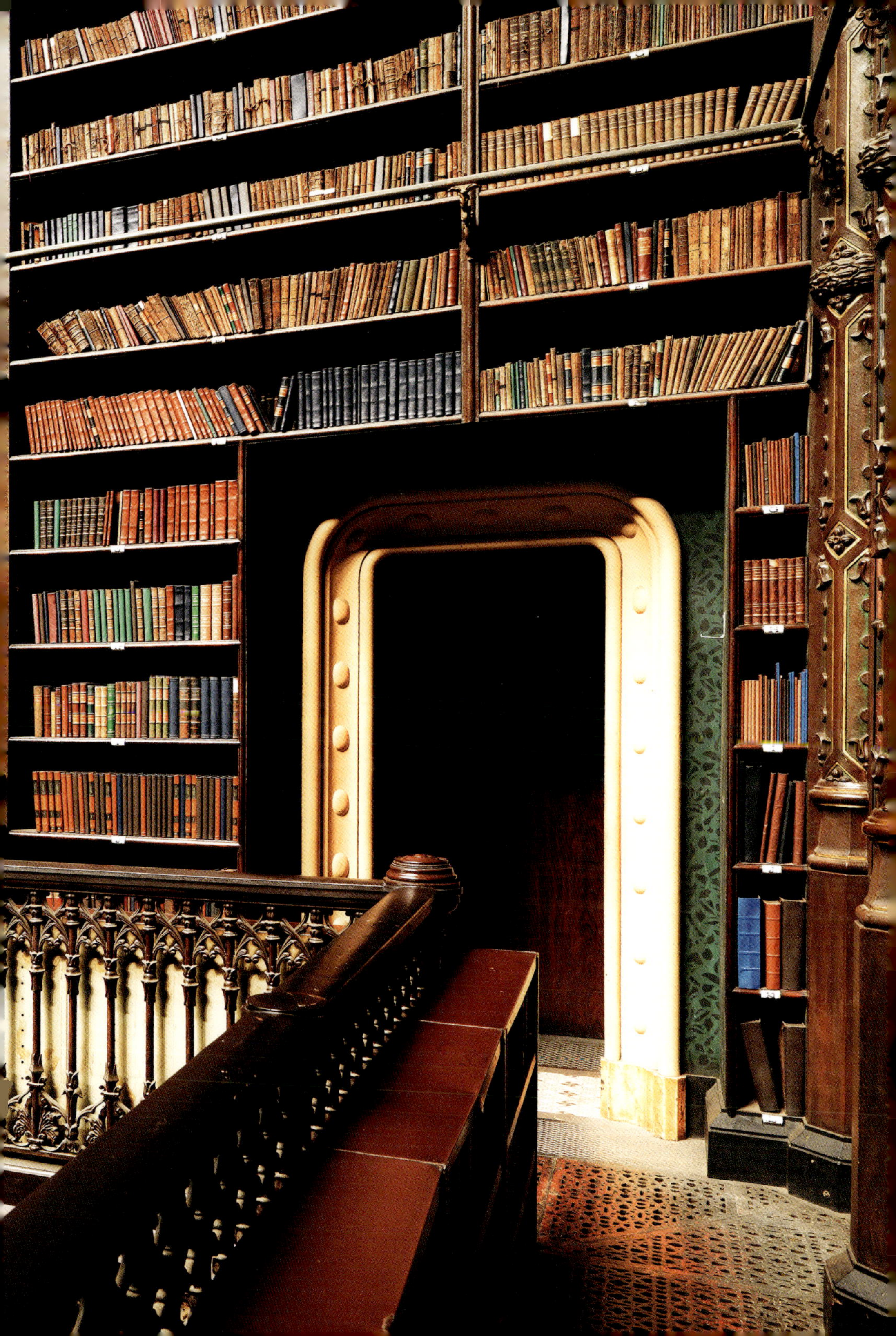

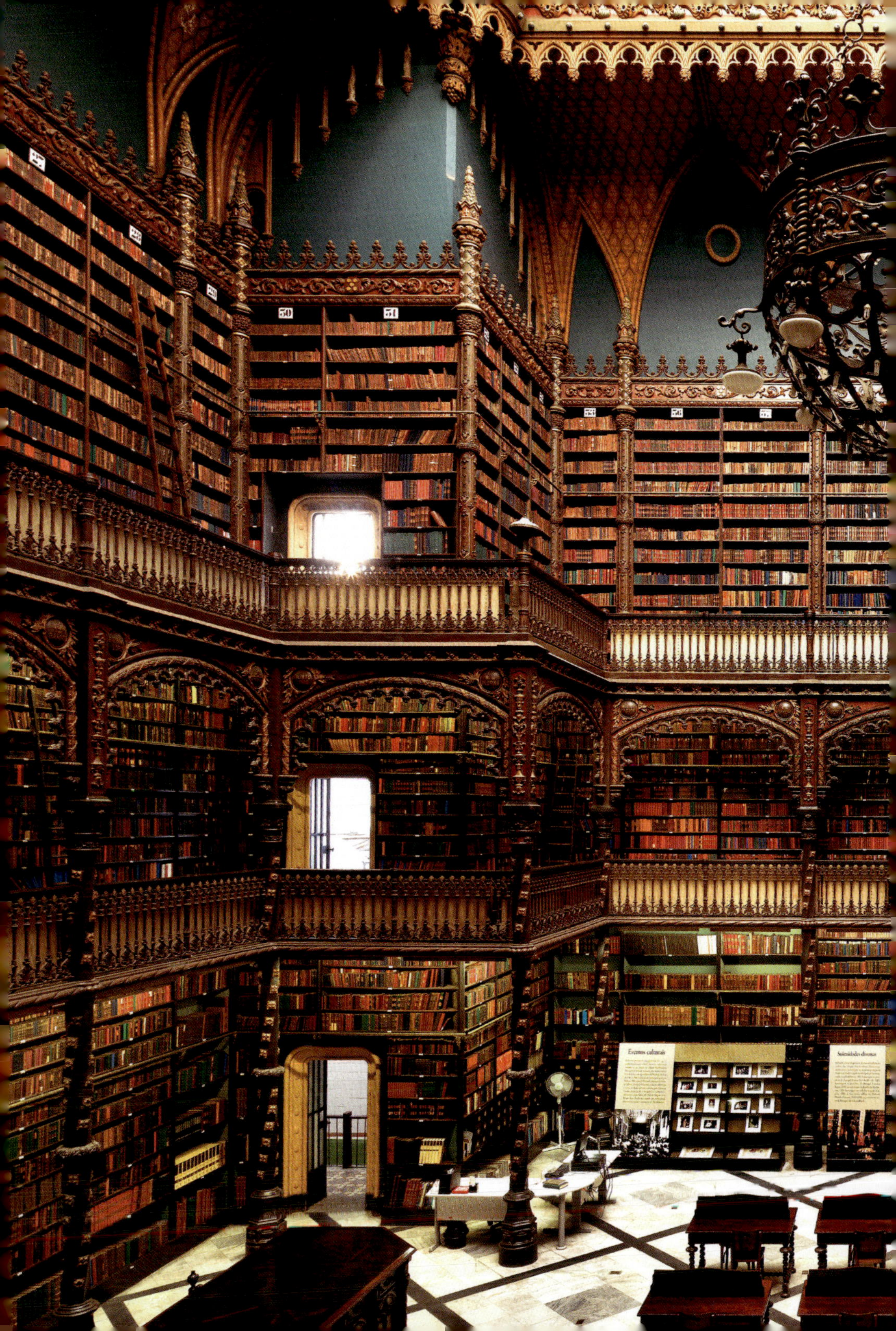

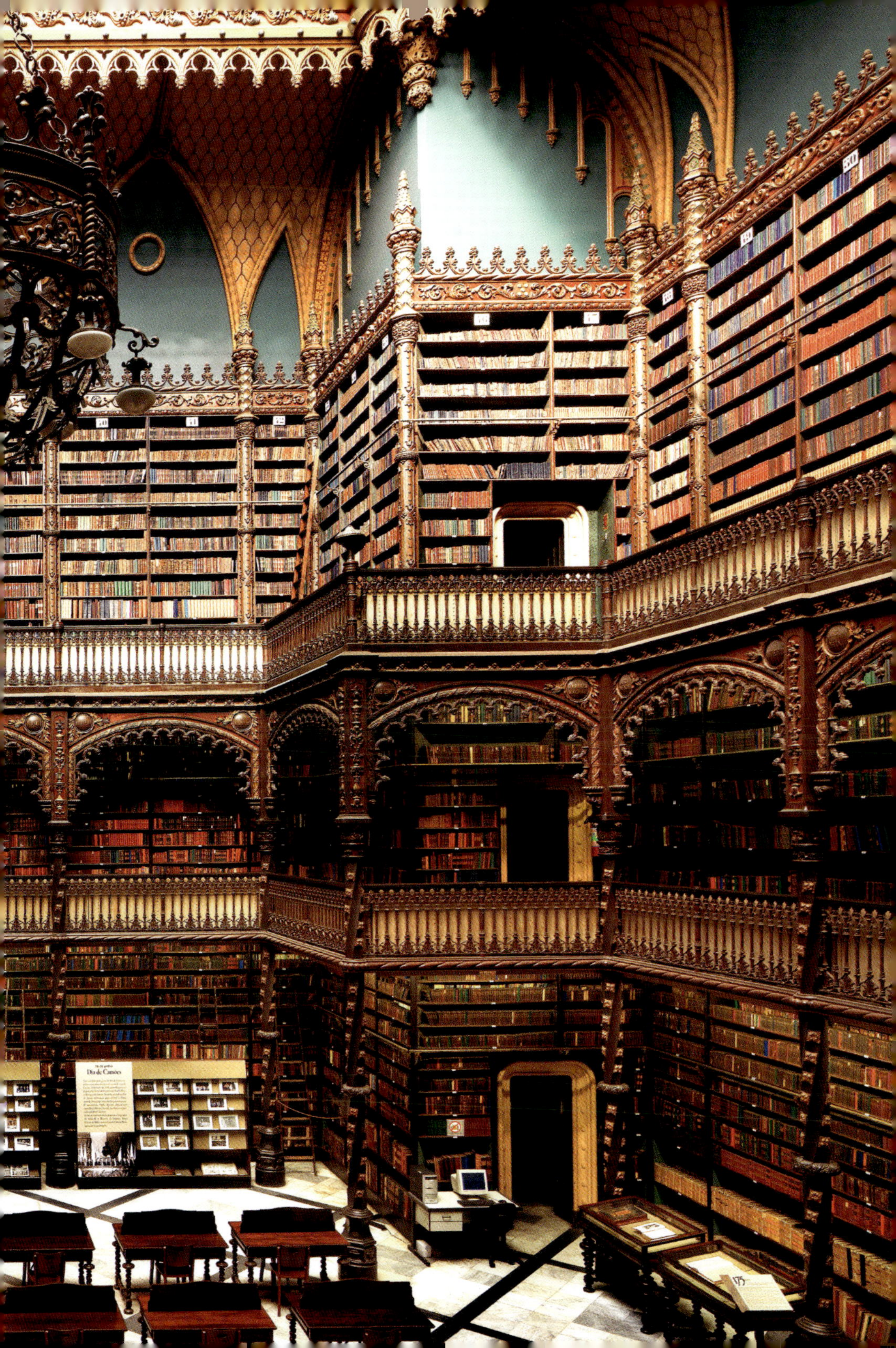

Biblioteca del Convento de San Francisco de Asís

The magnificent Franciscan convent built in the Spanish Baroque style in the historical heart of Lima is not only one of the largest monuments to Lima's colonial past, but perhaps also its most characteristic. It was a centre of the mission with which the Franciscans were charged on behalf of the Spanish crown and for which they were suitably equipped – books having always been considered the monk's spiritual tools. Faced with the challenge of conquering new territories, a monastery without a library would have struck the Franciscans as a fortress without an armoury. The convent was thus furnished upon its foundation with a basic stock of codices that were sent across from Europe, and which enabled it to develop into a Spanish centre of expertise in multiple spheres of learning. The library was an expression of the complex association which at that time existed between religion and rule, and served as an educational resource for the whole city, newly founded by the Spaniards on the ruins of the destroyed Inca Empire. Its holdings comprise not only standard works on Church history and theology, philosophy and the sciences, but also late medieval hymnbooks, Bibles and dictionaries, including the first dictionary of the Spanish language compiled by the Royal Spanish Academy. Numerous documents and archival materials attest to the administrative-type functions performed by the Franciscans at Inquisition trials. The monastery is thought to have been connected to the archbishop's palace and the Inquisition tribunal via secret underground passages, probably part of the extensive network of catacombs beneath the church of San Francisco. Today, the imposing library with its documents and papers bears witness to this complex history. Books and files, in some cases loosely stacked, line the walls of the room, which is situated on the top floor and is lit via overhead windows. Spiral staircases and low doors in the corners of the room provide access to the upper galleries. The floor tiles, like those in the cloisters, come from Seville and provide a colourful contrast to the dark cedar furnishings.

* * *

Founded 1673, monastery and library completed in 1776; restored several times after earthquake damage, most recently in 1970
Holdings c. 25,000 volumes
Type of library monastic library, research library

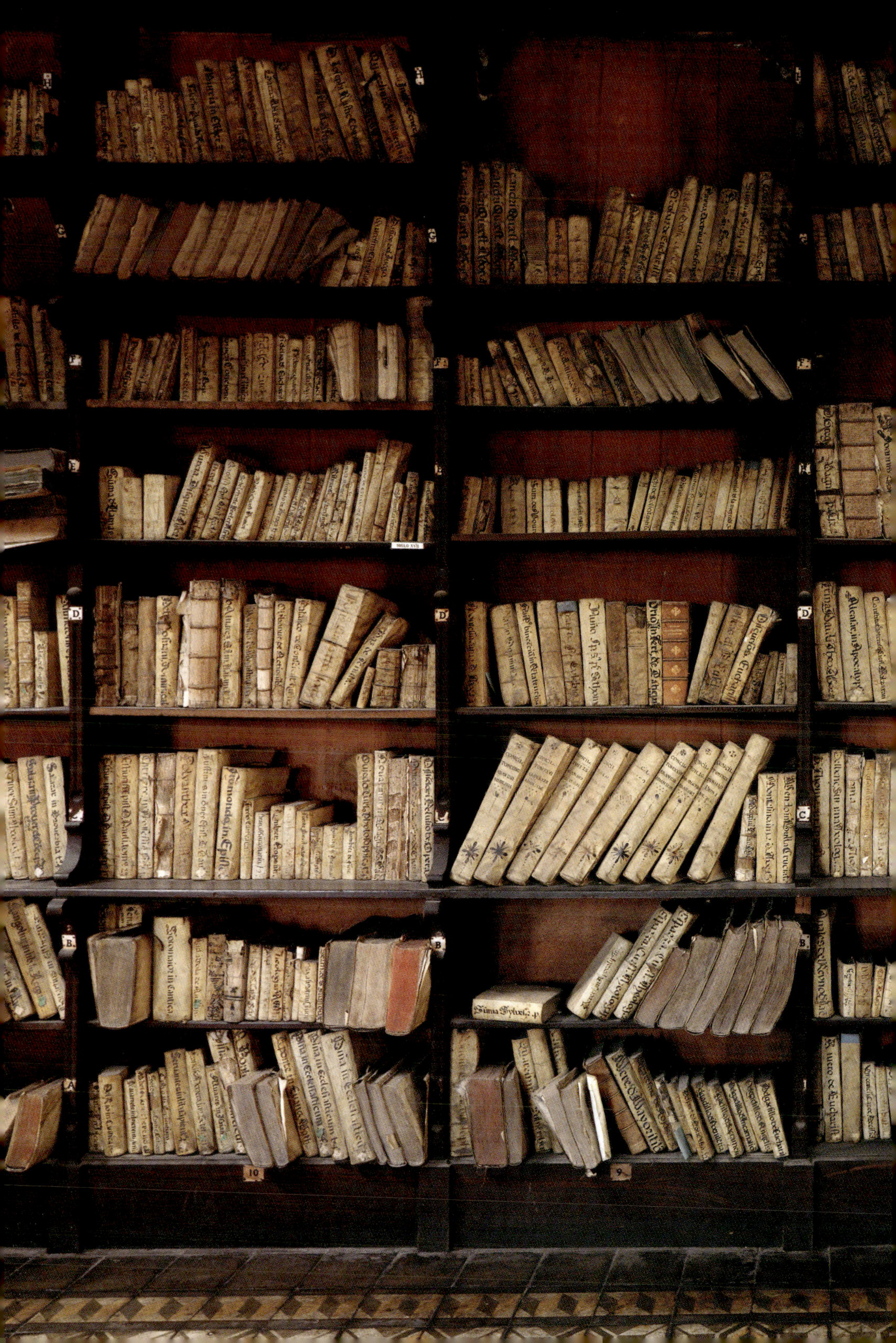

Der Gebäudekomplex des in spanischem Barockstil errichteten, prächtigen Franziskanerklosters zählt nicht nur größenmäßig zu den bedeutendsten Denkmälern der Kolonialzeit im historischen Stadtkern von Lima, er ist auch der vielleicht charakteristischste. Ein Zentrum der Mission, zu der die Franziskaner im Auftrag der spanischen Krone berufen und entsprechend ausgestattet wurden – galten doch die Bücher seit jeher als das geistige Rüstzeug der Ordensleute. Ihnen mag gerade zur Zeit der Eroberung des Territoriums ein Kloster ohne Bibliothek wie eine Festung ohne Rüstkammer erschienen sein. Seit der Gründung der Niederlassung besaß die Klosterbibliothek einen aus Europa transferierten Grundstock von Kodizes, mithilfe dessen sie sich zu einem spanischen Kompetenzzentrum für mannigfaltige Bereiche entwickeln konnte. Sie war Ausdruck der komplexen Verbindung, die damals zwischen Religion und Herrschaft bestand, sowie Bildungszentrum für die gesamte von den Spaniern auf den Trümmern des zerstörten Inkareiches neu gegründete Stadt. Ihre Bestände umfassen nicht nur Standardwerke zu Kirchengeschichte und Theologie, zu Philosophie und den Wissenschaften, sondern auch spätmittelalterliche Choralbücher, alte Bibelausgaben und Wörterbücher, unter diesen das erste von der königlichen spanischen Akademie edierte Wörterbuch der spanischen Sprache. Zahlreiche Schriftstücke dokumentieren die Inquisitionsprozesse, in denen den Franziskanern behördenähnliche Funktionen zukamen. Über unterirdische Geheimgänge, die wohl in Zusammenhang mit den weitläufigen Katakomben unterhalb der Franziskanerkirche entstanden sind, soll das Franziskanerkloster mit dem Sitz des Erzbischofs und dem Inquisitionstribunal verbunden gewesen sein. Heute

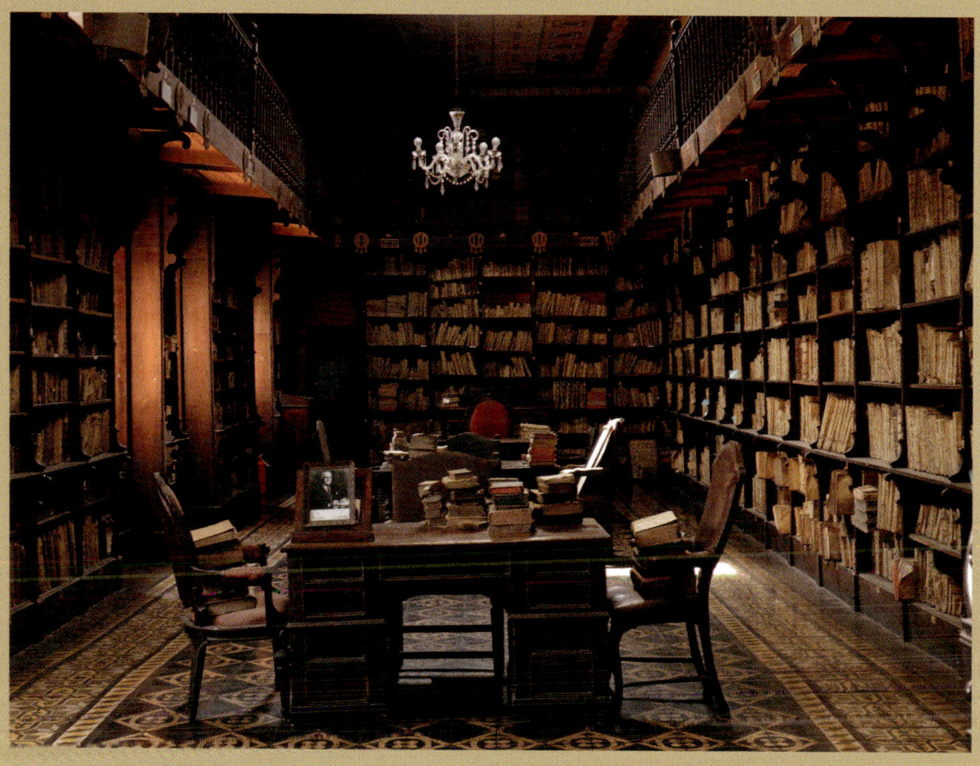

zeugt der imposante Büchersaal mit seinen
Dokumenten von dieser komplexen Geschichte.
Oberlicht fällt in den im Obergeschoss des
Klosters gelegenen Saalraum, dessen Wände
umlaufend von teilweise lose gestapelten Akten
und Büchern überzogen sind. Zwecks besserer
Erreichbarkeit befinden sich Wendeltreppen
oder kleine Türen in den Ecken, die zu den Galerien emporführen. Dem dunklen Zedernholz
des Mobiliars wirkt der buntfarbig leuchtende
Fliesenboden entgegen, dessen Kacheln ebenso
wie jene der Kreuzgänge aus Sevilla stammen.

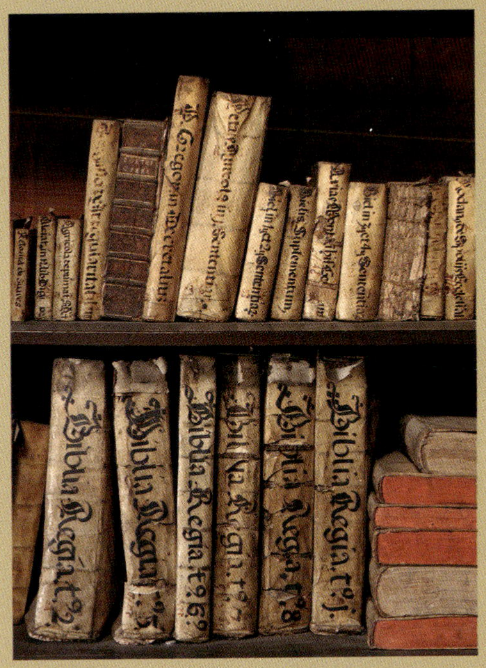

✳ ✳ ✳

Le couvent franciscain et ses dépendances
de style baroque espagnol s'inscrit, de par
ses dimensions parmi les monuments les plus
significatifs de l'époque coloniale du noyau
historique de Lima, et parmi les plus emblé-
matiques. Au cœur de la mission assignée
aux Franciscains par la prodigue Couronne
espagnole, les livres ont toujours incarné l'arme
spirituelle des hommes de foi. À l'époque de
la conquête du territoire, un monastère sans
bibliothèque aurait ressemblé à une forteresse
sans salle d'armes. Dès la fondation de l'édifice,
la bibliothèque monacale a bénéficié d'un fonds
de codex en provenance d'Europe, ce qui lui
a permis de devenir par la suite un centre de
compétences espagnol dans des domaines très
divers. Elle était à la fois l'incarnation du lien
complexe existant à l'époque entre religion et
pouvoir, ainsi qu'un centre d'enseignement
pour la ville récemment construite par les
Espagnols sur les décombres de l'Empire
inca anéanti. Ses fonds ne se composent pas
seulement d'ouvrages standards concernant
l'histoire de l'Église et la théologie, la philosophie et la science, mais aussi de livres de chants
liturgiques médiévaux, d'anciennes éditions de
la Bible et de dictionnaires, dont le tout premier
dictionnaire de langue espagnole publié par
l'Académie royale espagnole. De nombreux
documents et manuscrits renseignent sur les
procès menés par l'Inquisition, pour lesquels les
Franciscains remplissaient une fonction d'autorité. Il se peut que le couvent San Francisco ait
été relié au siège de l'épiscopat et au tribunal de
l'Inquisition par des voies souterraines secrètes,
vraisemblablement creusées en même temps
que les vastes catacombes situées en dessous
de l'église franciscaine. Avec ses écrits et documents, l'imposante salle de lecture témoigne
aujourd'hui encore de cette histoire complexe.
La salle située à l'étage est éclairée par le
plafond. Ses murs sont entièrement couverts
d'ouvrages et de dossiers parfois disposés en
vrac. Des escaliers en colimaçon et des petites
portes insérées dans les coins garantissent un
accès aux galeries. Le mobilier en bois de cèdre
contraste avec le dallage chamarré au sol dont
les carreaux proviennent de Séville (à l'instar de
ceux du cloître).

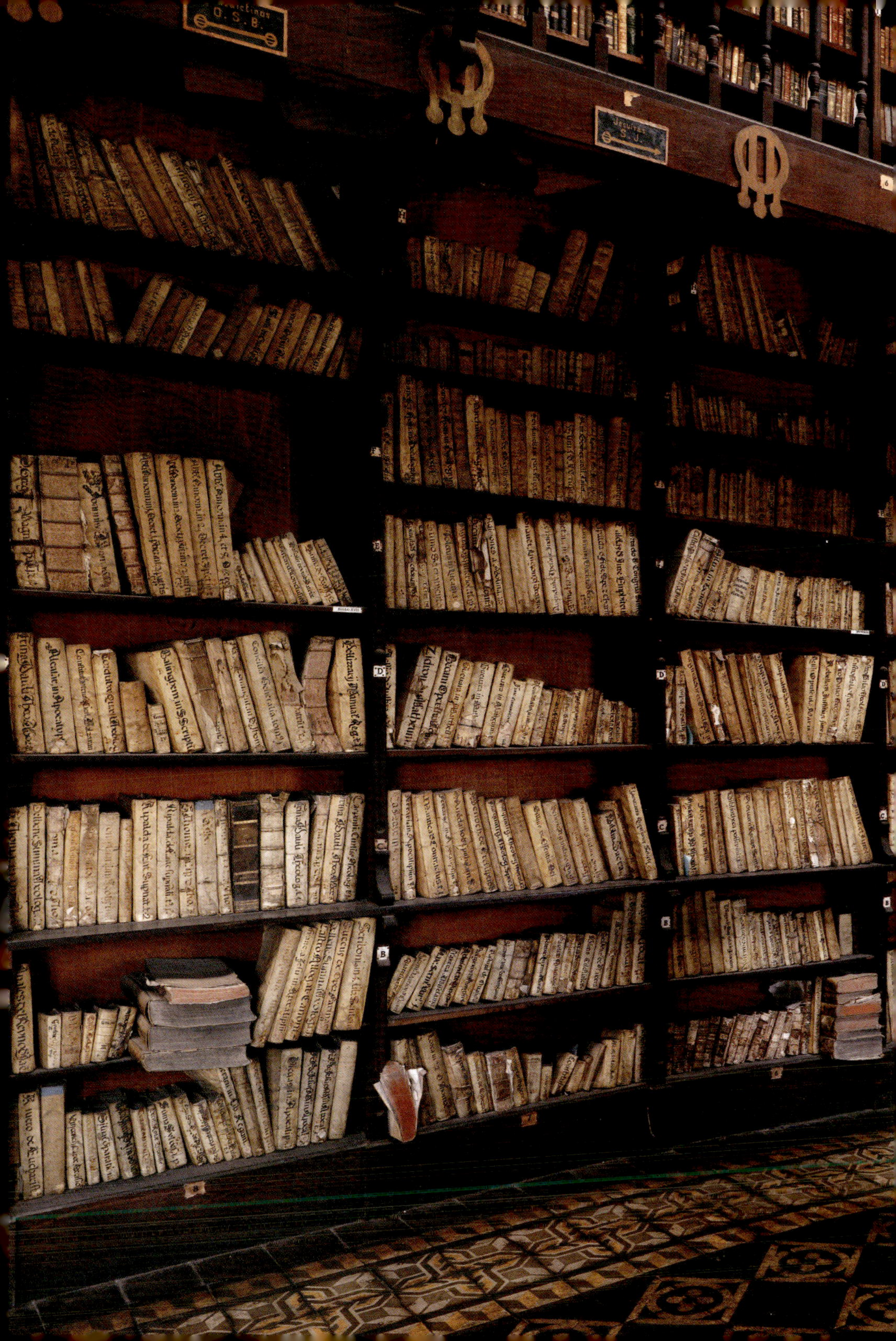

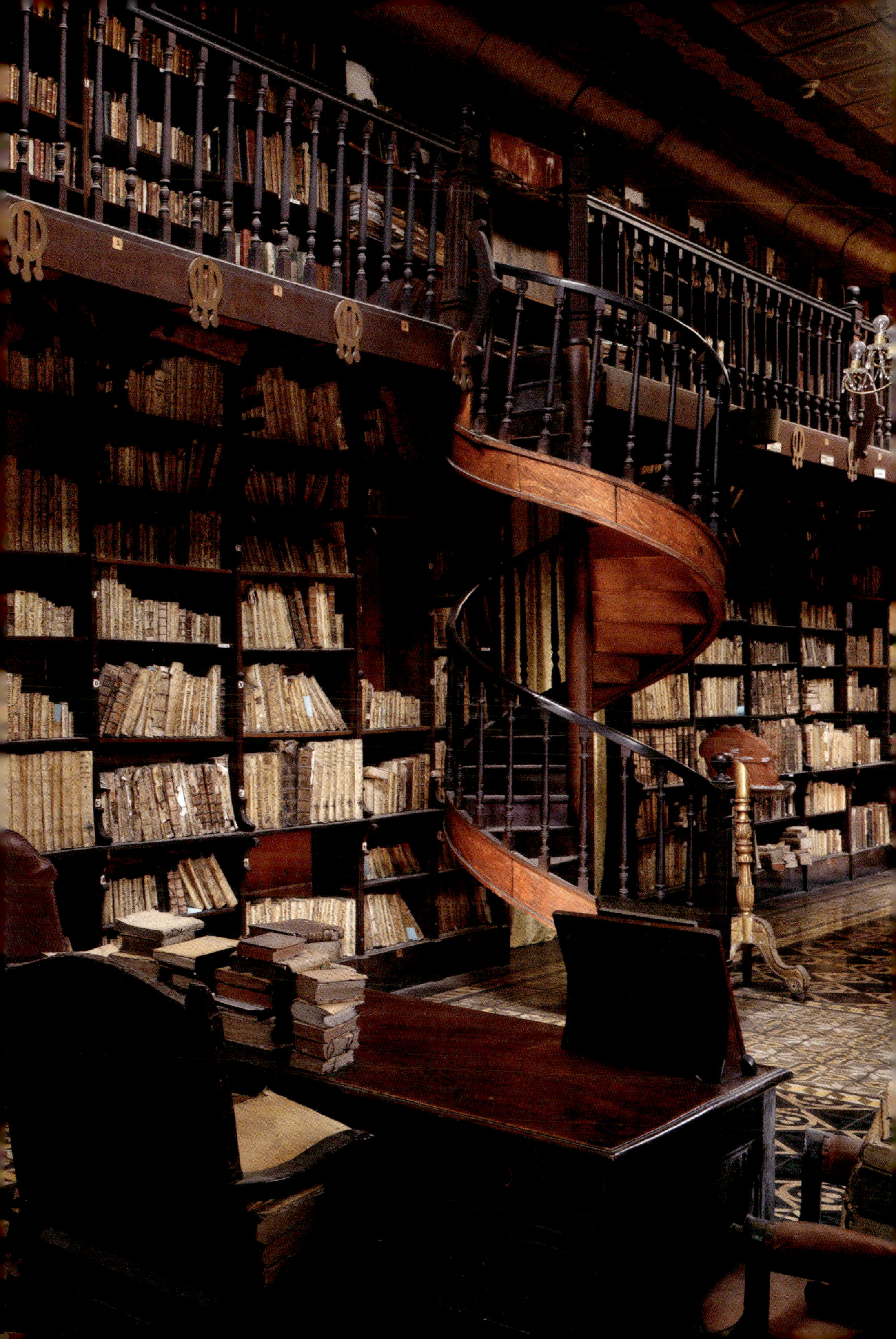

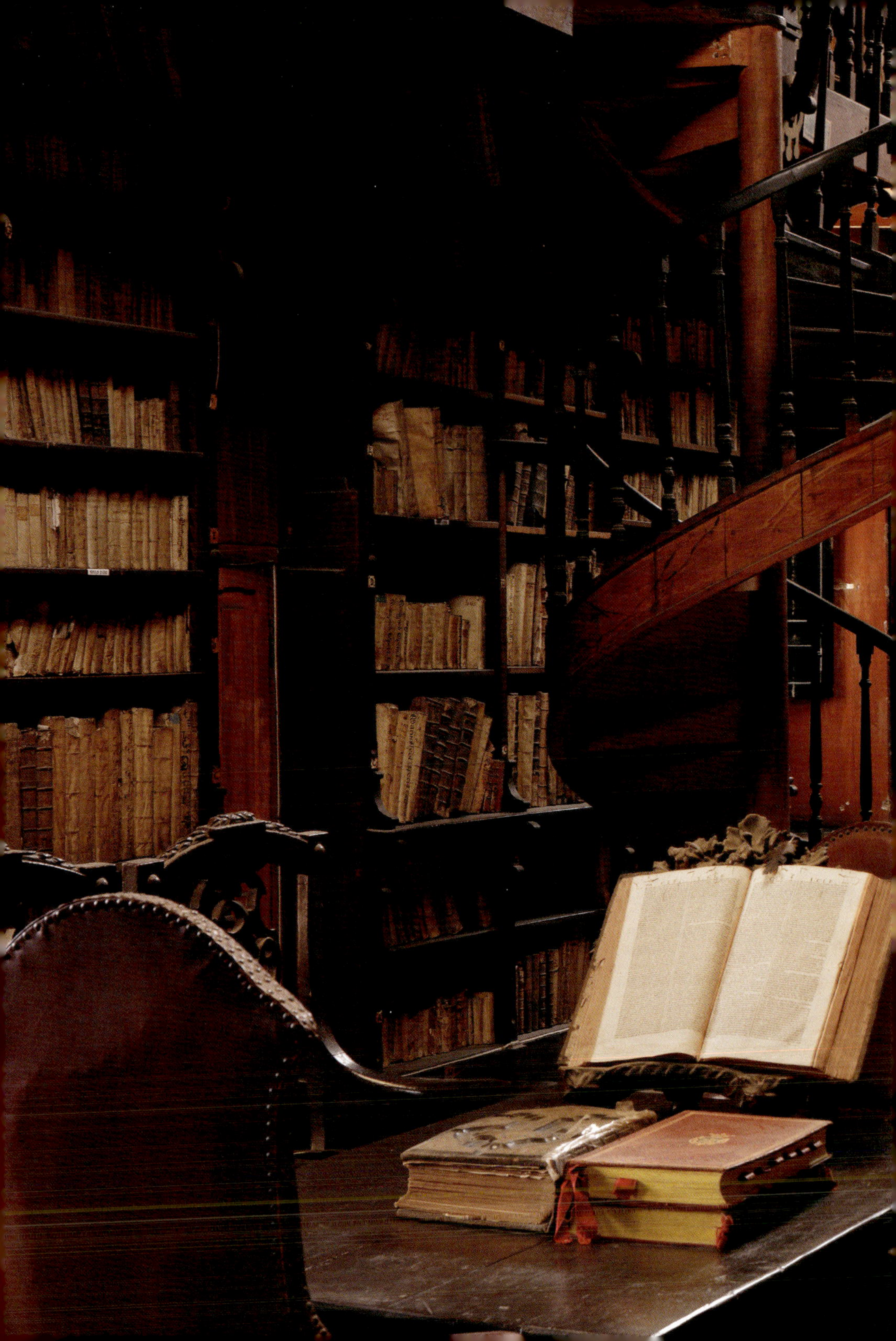

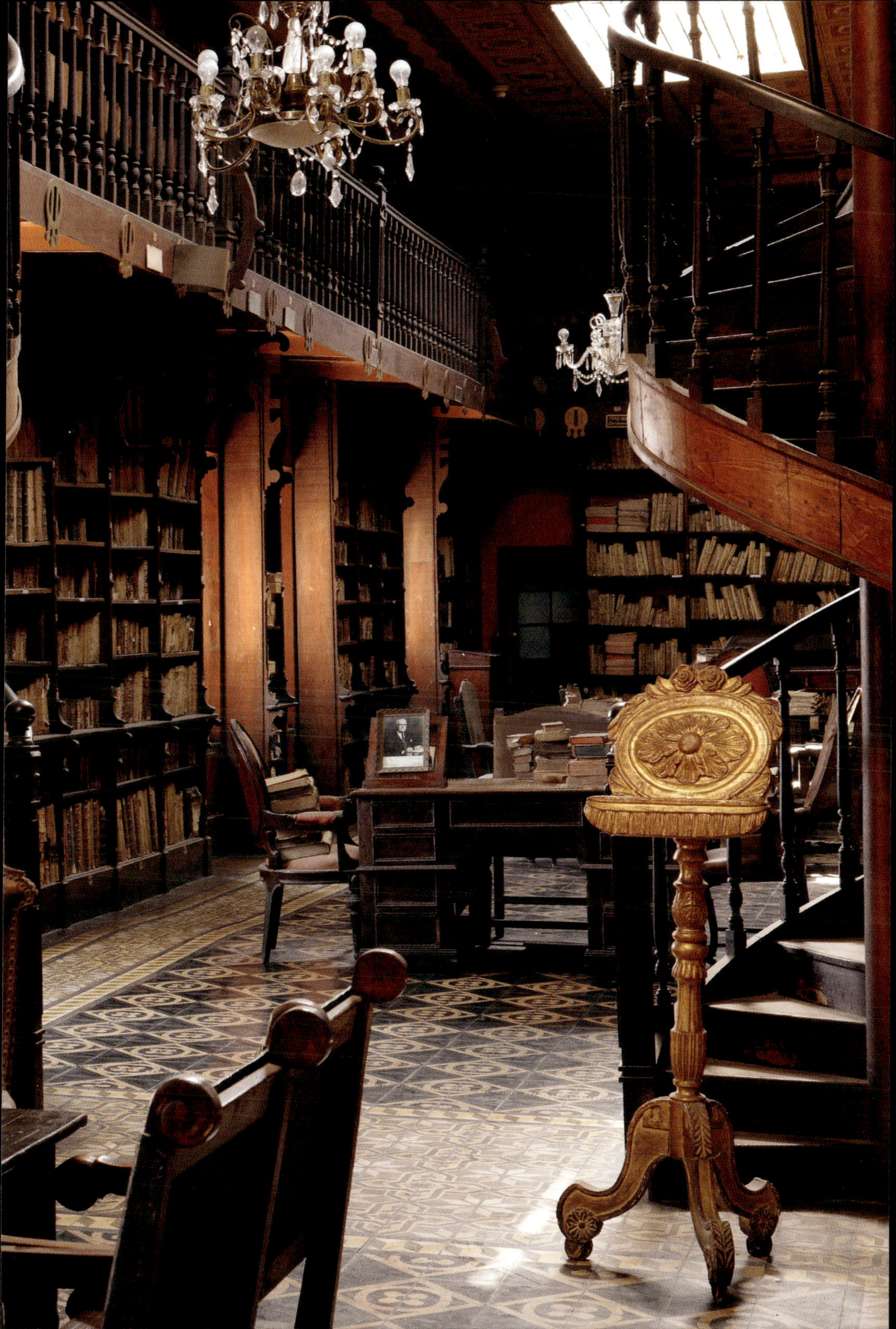

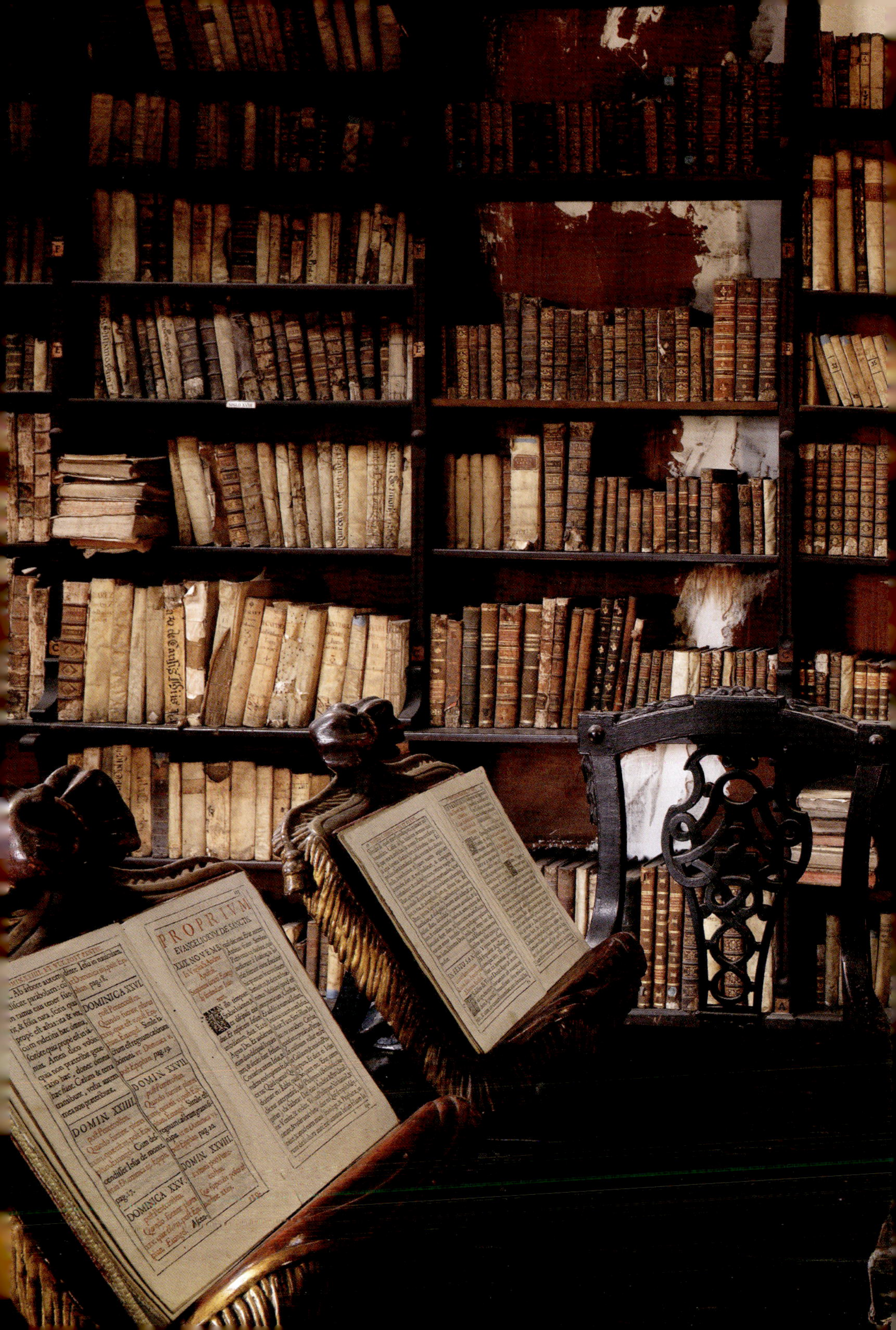

PROPRIVM
EVANGELIORVM DE SANCTIS
DOMINICA XXVI
DOMIN XXVII
DOMIN XXVIII
DOMINICA XXV
DOMIN XXVIII

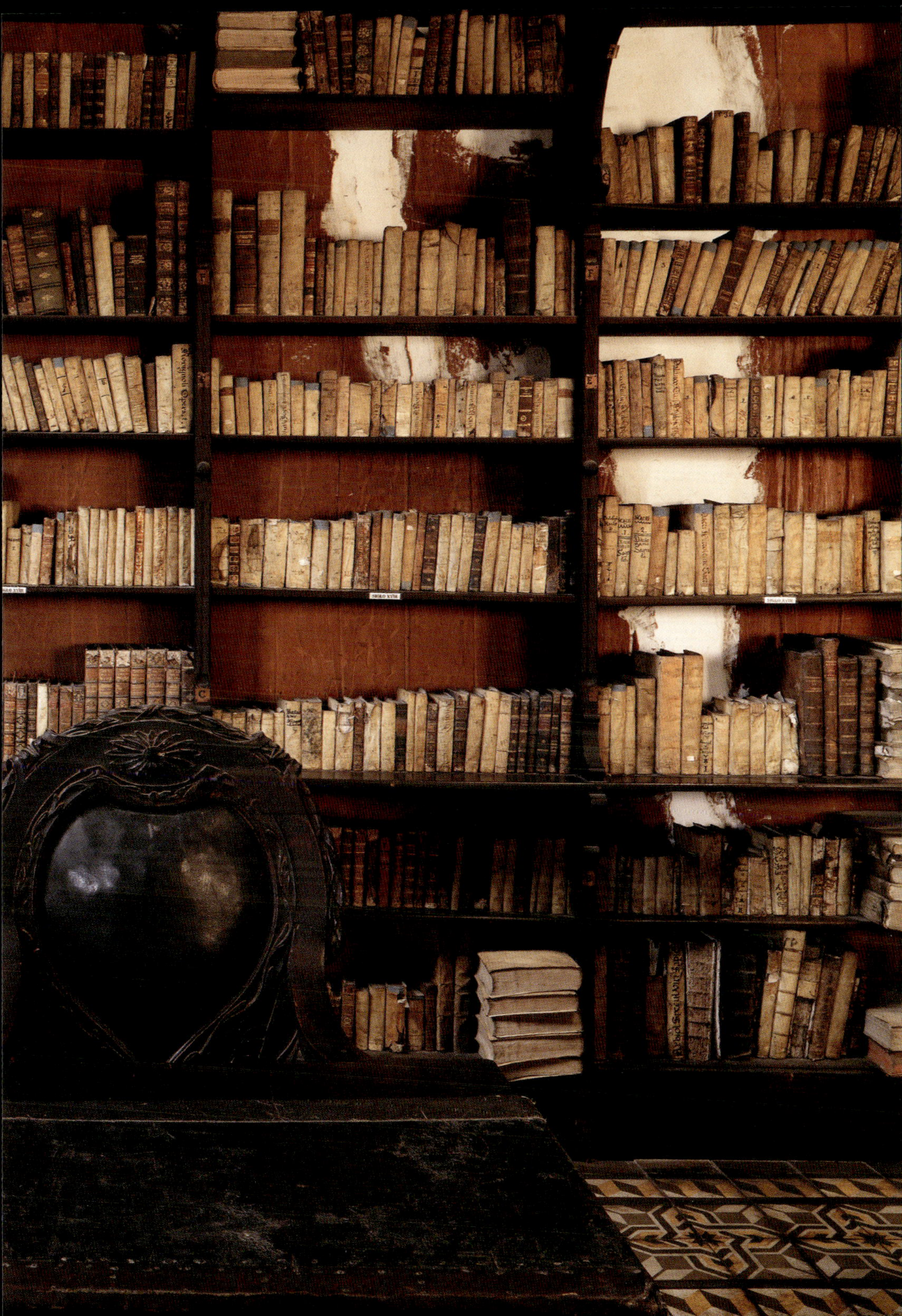

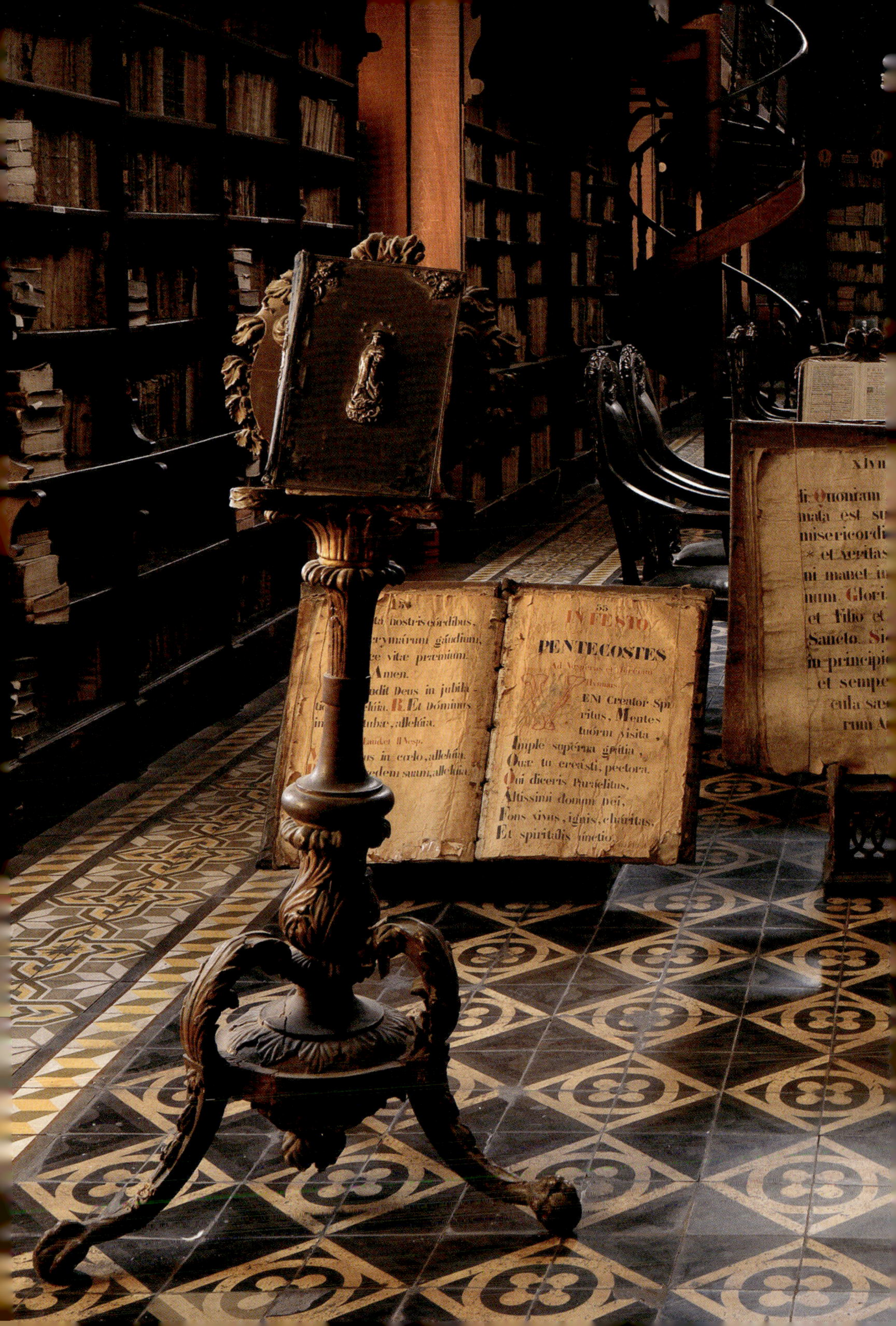

55
IN FESTO
PENTECOSTES

VENI Creator Spiritus, Mentes tuórum visita
Imple supérna grátia, Quæ tu creásti, péctora.
Qui díceris Paráclitus, Altíssimi donum Dei,
Fons vivus, ignis, cháritas, Et spiritális únctio.

XLVII

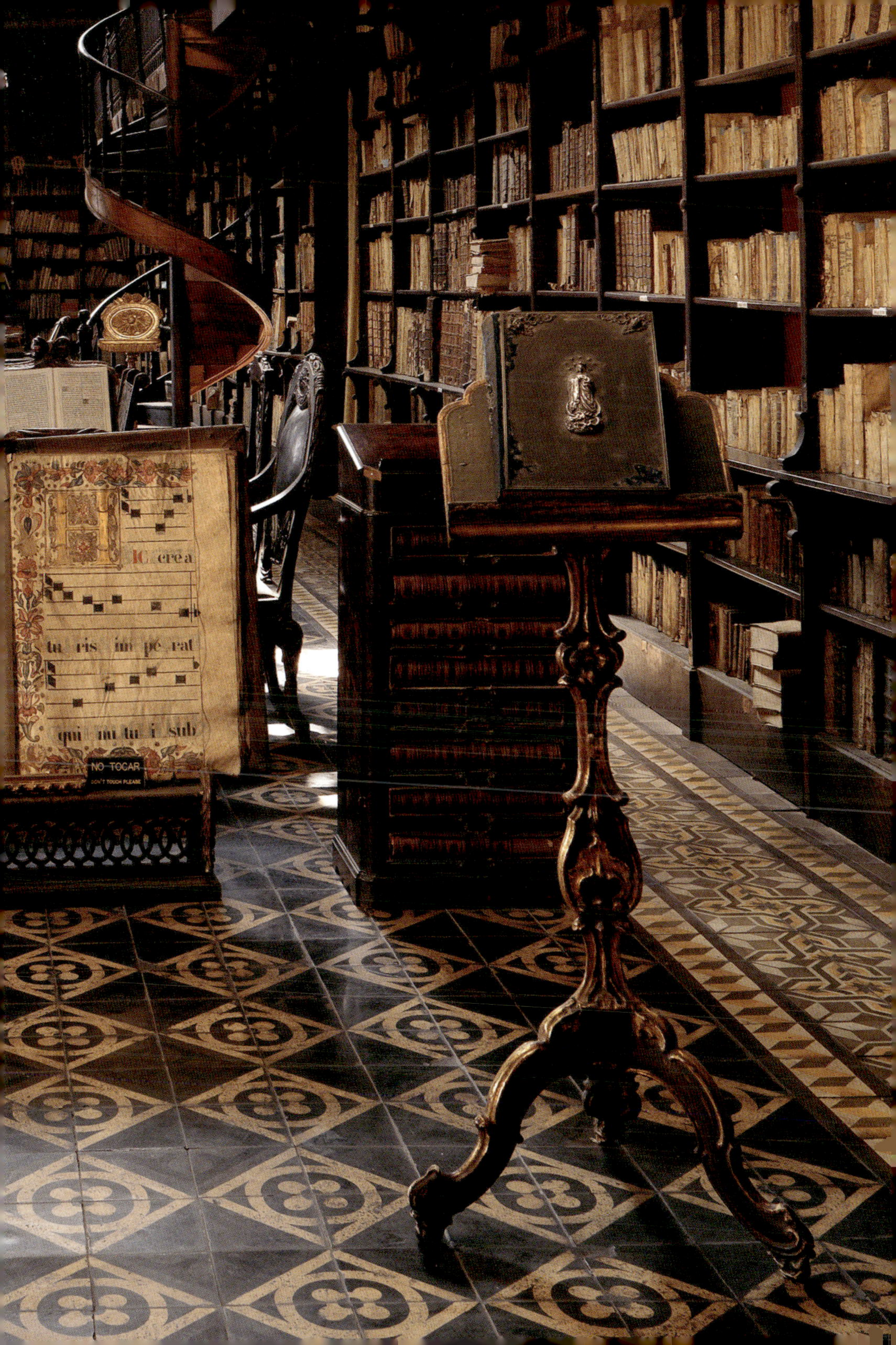
IC erea
tu ris im pe rat
qui ni tu i sub
NO TOCAR
DON'T TOUCH PLEASE

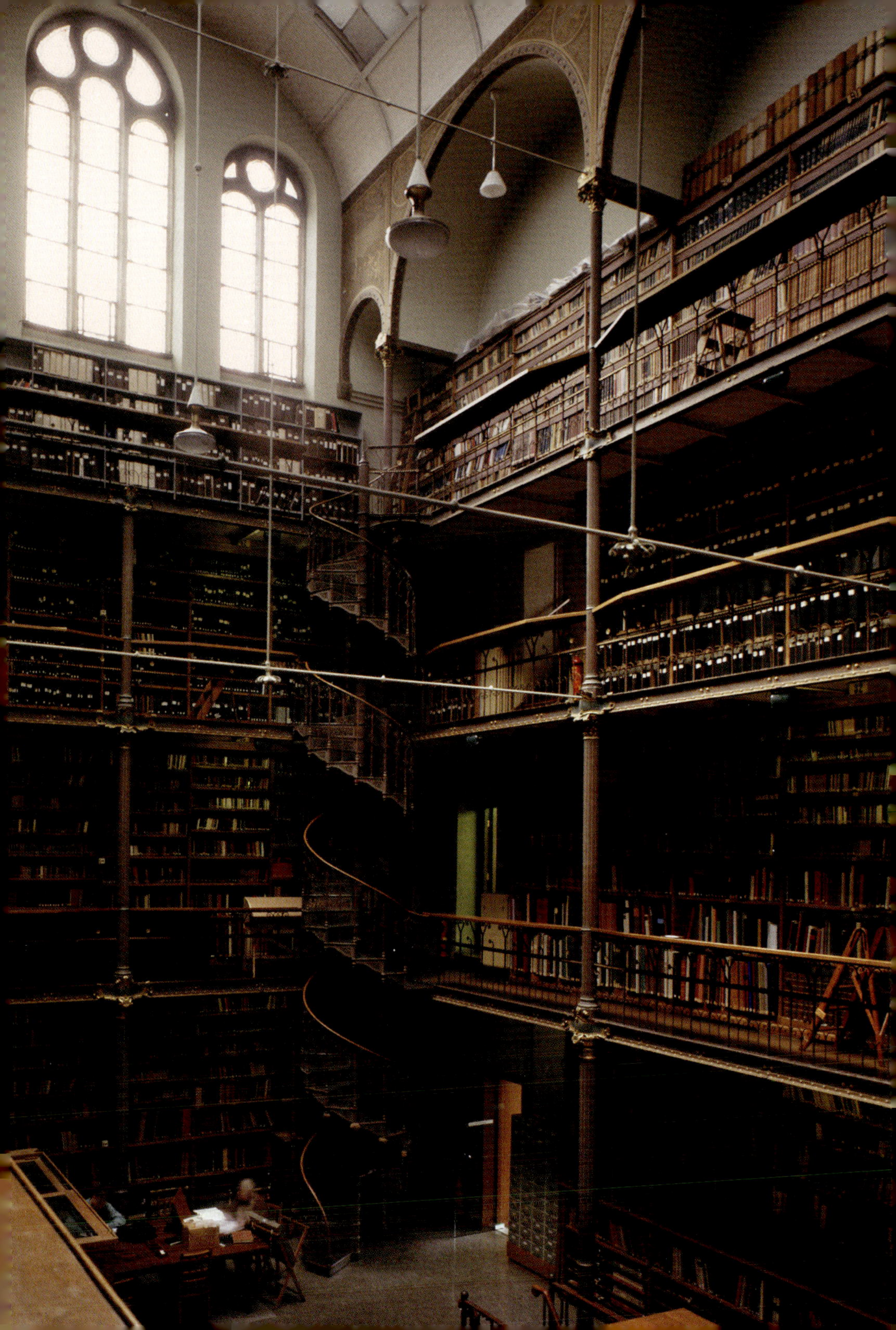

Bibliography

Battles, Matthew, Die Welt der Bücher. *Eine Geschichte der Bibliothek*, Düsseldorf 2007

Baur-Heinhold, Margarete, *Schöne alte Bibliotheken. Ein Buch vom Zauber ihrer Räume*, 2nd edn., Hamburg 2000

Becker, Peter Jörg, "Bibliotheksreisen in Deutschland im 18. Jahrhundert", in: *Archiv für die Geschichte des Buchwesens*, vol. 21, 1980, pp. 1361–1534

Blumenberg, Hans, *Die Lesbarkeit der Welt*, Frankfurt a.M. 1981

Brawne, Michael, *Libraries: Architecture and Equipment*, London 1970

Buzas, Ladislaus, *Deutsche Bibliotheksgeschichte*, 3 vols., Wiesbaden 1975–1978 (*Elemente des Buch- und Bibliothekswesens*, vols. 1–3)

Ertuğ, Ahmet, *Temples of Knowledge. Historical Libraries of the Western World*, Istanbul 2010

Gaberson, Eric, *Eighteenth-Century Monastic Libraries in Southern Germany and Austria. Architecture and Decorations*, Baden-Baden 1998

Goethe, Johann Wolfgang, "Tag- und Jahres-Hefte als Ergänzung meiner sonstigen Bekenntnisse, von 1749 bis 1806", in: *Goethes Werke*, publ. on behalf of Princess Sophie of the Netherlands, vol. 35, Weimar 1892 (English: "Annals; or, Day and Year Papers", trans. Charles Nisbet, in: *The Autobiography of Goethe. Truth and Poetry: From My Own Life. Books XIV–XX*, London 1884; Français: *Œuvres de Goethe, Mélanges*, traduction: J. Porchat, Paris 1863)

Handbuch Bibliothek. Geschichte, Aufgaben, Perspektiven, ed. Konrad Umlauf and Stefan Gradmann, Stuttgart and Weimar 2012

Heinemann, Otto von, *Die Herzogliche Bibliothek zu Wolfenbüttel. Ein Beitrag zur Geschichte deutscher Büchersammlungen*, 2nd edn., Wolfenbüttel 1894

Hutten, Ulrich von, *Gesprächbüchlein Ulrichs von Hutten* (first published Strasbourg 1521), ed. Hugo Angermann, Dresden 1905 (gutenberg.spiegel.de/buch/gesprachbuchlein-ulrichs-von-hutten-5999/2, accessed 14.09.2016)

Jochum, Uwe, *Kleine Bibliotheksgeschichte*, 3rd edn., Stuttgart 2007

Jochum, Uwe, *Geschichte der abendländischen Bibliotheken*, 2nd edn., Darmstadt 2012

Kloepfer, Inge, "Der irre Boom der Bibliotheken. Alles redet von der Digitalisierung – und Berlin plant für 300 Millionen Euro eine Bibliothek voller Papier. Ist das verrückt? Von wegen: Kein Platz ist den Menschen lieber als die Bücherei", in: *Frankfurter Allgemeine Sonntagszeitung*, 16 March 2014

Lehmann, Edgar, *Die Bibliotheksräume der deutschen Klöster im Mittelalter*, Berlin 1957

Lehmann, Edgar, *Die Bibliotheksräume der deutschen Klöster in der Zeit des Barock*, Berlin 1996

Lerner, Fred, *The Story of Libraries. From the Invention of Writing to the Computer Age*, London 2009

Luther, Martin, "An die Ratherren aller Städte deutschen Lands, daß sie christliche Schulen aufrichten und halten sollen", in: *Martin Luthers Werke. Kritische Gesamtausgabe*, vol. 15, Weimar 1899, pp. 9–53 (English: "To the Councilmen of All Cities in Germany That They Establish and Maintain Christian Schools", in: Albert Steinhauser (trans.), *Luther's Works*, vol. 45, Philadelphia 1962, pp. 347–378)

Masson, André, *Le décor des bibliothèques du Moyen Âge à la Révolution*, Genf 1972

Medvedková, Olga (ed.), *Bibliothèques d'architecture / Architectural Libraries*, Paris 2009

Nerdinger, Winfried (ed.), *Die Weisheit baut sich ein Haus. Architektur und Geschichte von Bibliotheken*, Munich 2011

O'Gorman, James F., *The Architecture of the Monastic Library in Italy 1300–1600*, New York 1972

Stockhausen, Johann Christoph, *Critischer Entwurf einer auserlesenen Bibliothek für die Liebhaber der Philosophie und schönen Wissenschaften. Zum Gebrauch akademischer Vorlesungen*, Berlin 1771.

Warncke, Carsten-Peter (ed.), *Ikonographie der Bibliotheken*, Wiesbaden 1992

Wiegand, Wayne A. and Donald G. Davis, *Encyclopedia of Library History*, New York 1994

"Wir sind Teil eines großen Werkes, das über jeden Einzelnen hinausweist." Prominente Begegnungen mit Büchern und Bibliotheken, ed. Georg Ruppelt (published on behalf of the Friends and Patrons of the Gottfried Wilhelm Leibniz Library to mark the 350th anniversary of the library's foundation in 2015 and the 300th anniversary of the death of its namesake in 2016), Hanover 2015

Willms, Johannes, *Bücherfreunde – Büchernarren. Entwurf zur Archäologie einer Leidenschaft*, Wiesbaden 1978

Addresses

AUSTRIA
Österreichische
Nationalbibliothek
Josefsplatz 1
1015 Vienna
Phone: +43 1 534 10
onb@onb.ac.at
www.onb.ac.at

Stiftsbibliothek Admont
Kirchplatz 1
8911 Admont
Phone: +43 3613 2312-0
info@stiftadmont.at
www.stiftadmont.at/bibliothek

Stiftsbibliothek Kremsmünster
4550 Kremsmünster
Phone: +43 7583 5275-0
bibliothek@stift-kremsmünster.at
www.stift-kremsmuenster.at

Stiftsbibliothek Melk
Abt-Berthold-Dietmayr-Straße 1
3390 Melk
Phone: +43 2752 555-342
bibliothek@stiftmelk.at
www.stiftmelk.at

Stiftsbibliothek Seitenstetten
Am Klosterberg 1
3353 Seitenstetten
Phone: +43 7477 423 00
stift@stift-seitenstetten.at
www.stift-seitenstetten.at

Stiftsbibliothek Zwettl
3910 Zwettl
Phone: +43 2822 20202-441
bibliothek@stift-zwettl.at
www.stift-zwettl.at

BRAZIL
Real Gabinete Português
de Leitura
Rua Luís de Camões 30
20051-020 Rio de Janeiro,
Centro
Phone: +55 212221-3138
gabinete@realgabinete.com.br
www.realgabinete.com.br

CZECH REPUBLIC
Strahovská Knihovna
Strahovské nádvorí 1/132
118 00 Prague 1, Hradčany
Phone: +420 233 107 710
info@strahovskyklaster.cz
www.strahovskyklaster.cz

ENGLAND
The Codrington Library
All Souls College
High Street, Oxford OX1 4AL
Phone: +44 1865 279 318
codrington.library@
all-souls.ox.ac.uk
www.asc.ox.ac.uk/the-library

Eastnor Castle Library
Eastnor Castle, Ledbury
Herefordshire HR8 1RL
Phone: +44 1531 633 160
enquiries@eastnorcastle.com
www.eastnorcastle.com

FRANCE
Bibliothèque du Château
de Chantilly
Château de Chantilly
7, rue Connétable
60500 Chantilly
Phone: +33 3 4462 6269
bibliotheque@domaine
dechantilly.com
www.bibliotheque-conde.fr

Bibliothèque Mazarine
23, quai de Conti, 75006 Paris
Phone: +33 1 4441 4406
contact@bibliotheque-mazarine.fr
www.bibliotheque-mazarine.fr

Bibliothèque Paul Marmottan
7, place Denfert-Rochereau
92100 Boulogne-Billancourt
Phone: +33 1 5518 5761
bibliothequemarmottan@
mairie-boulogne-billancourt.fr

Bibliothèque Sainte-Geneviève
10, place du Panthéon,
75005 Paris

Phone: +33 1 4441 9797
bsgmail@univ-paris1.fr
www-bsg.univ-paris1.fr

GERMANY
Bibliothekssaal Kloster
Schussenried
Neues Kloster 1
88427 Bad Schussenried
Phone: +49 7583 9269-140
info@kloster-schussenried.de
www.kloster-schussenried.de

Klosterbibliothek Fürstenzell
Marienplatz 15, 94081 Fürstenzell
Phone: +49 8502 802-0
info@fuerstenzell.de

Klosterbibliothek Metten
94526 Metten
Phone: +49 991 9108-125
Benediktinerstift-metten@
t-online.de
www.kloster-metten.de

Klosterbibliothek Ottobeuren
Sebastian Kneipp-Straße 1
87724 Ottobeuren
Phone: +49 8332 7980
webmaster@abtei-ottobeuren.de
www.abtei-ottobeuren.de

Klosterbibliothek Wiblingen
Schlossstraße 38, 89079 Ulm
Phone: +49 731 502 89 75
info@kloster-wiblingen.de
www.kloster-wiblingen.de

Stiftsbibliothek Waldsassen
Basilikaplatz 2, 95652 Waldsassen
Phone: +49 9632 9200-25
info@abtei-waldsassen.de
www.abtei-waldsassen.de

IRELAND
Marsh's Library
St Patrick's Close
Wood Quay, Dublin 8
Phone: +353 1 4543 511
keeper@marshlibrary.ie
www.marshlibrary.ie

Trinity College Library
College Green
Dublin 2
Phone: +353 1896 1127
library@tcd.ie
www.tcd.ie/library

ITALY
Biblioteca Angelica
Piazza Sant'Agostino, 8
00186 Rome
Phone: +39 06 684 0801
b-ange@beniculturali.it
www.bibliotecaangelica.
beniculturali.it

Biblioteca Apostolica Vaticana
Cortile del Belvedere
00120 Vatican City
Phone: +39 06 6987 9411
bav@vatlib.it
www.vatlib.it

Biblioteca Casanatense
Via di Sant'Ignazio, 52
00186 Rome
Phone: +39 06 697 6031
b-casa@beniculturali.it
www.casanatense.it

Biblioteca Civica Gambalunga
Via Alessandro Gambalunga, 27
47921 Rimini
Phone: +39 0541 704 486
gambalunghiana@comune.rimini.it
www.bibliotecagambalunga.it

Biblioteca comunale di Imola
Via Emilia, 80, 40026 Imola
Phone: +39 0542 602 636
bim@comune.imola.bo.it
www.bim.comune.imola.bo.it

Biblioteca Nazionale Braidense
Via Brera, 28, 20121 Milan
Phone: +39 02 8646 0907
b-brai@beniculturali.it
www.braidense.it

Biblioteca Nazionale Marciana
Piazzetta San Marco, 7
30124 Venice
Phone: +39 041 240 7211
biblioteca@marciana.venezia.
sbn.it
www.marciana.venezia.sbn.it

Biblioteca Palatina
Strada alla Pilotta, 3,
43100 Parma
Phone: +39 0521 220 411
b-pala@beniculturali.it
www.bibpal.unipr.it

Biblioteca Riccardiana
Palazzo Medici Riccardi
Via Ginori, 10
50123 Florence
Phone: +39 055 212 586
b-ricc@beniculturali.it
www.riccardiana.firenze.sbn.it

**Biblioteca Statale
Oratoriana dei Girolamini**
Via Duomo, 114, 80138 Naples
Phone: +39 081 294 444
bmn-gir@beniculturali.it
www.bibliotecadeigirolamini.
beniculturali.it

MEXICO
Biblioteca Palafoxiana
Av 7 Ote 3, Centro, 72000 Puebla
Phone: +52 222 232 3483
b.palafoxiana@gmail.com
www.palafoxiana.com

THE NETHERLANDS
Rijksmuseum Research Library
Museumstraat 1
1070 DN Amsterdam
Phone: +31 20 6747-267
bibliotheek@rijksmuseum.nl
library.rijksmuseum.nl

PERU
**Biblioteca del Convento de
San Francisco de Asís**
Plazuela San Francisco
Lima
Phone: +51 1427 1381
info@museocatacumbas.com
www.museocatacumbas.com

PORTUGAL
**Biblioteca do Convento
de Mafra**
Palácio Nacional de Mafra
Terreiro D. João V
2640 Mafra
Phone: +351 261 817 550
geral@pnmafra.dgpc.pt
www.palaciomafra.gov.pt

Biblioteca Joanina
Largo da Porta Férrea
3000-447 Coimbra
Phone: +351 239 242 744/5
reservas@uc.pt
www.uc.pt/informacaopara/visit/
paco/biblioteca

SPAIN
Archivo General de Indias
Avenida de la Constitución, 3
41071 Seville
Phone: +34 954 500 528
agi2@mecd.es
www.mecd.gob.es/cultura-mecd/
areas-cultura/archivos/mc/
archivos/agi/portada.html

**Real Biblioteca del Monasterio de
San Lorenzo de El Escorial**
Avenida D. Juan de Borbón y
Battenberg, 1
28200 San Lorenzo de El Escorial
(Madrid)
Phone: +34 91 890 5011
biblioteca.escorial@
patrimonionacional.es
rbme.patrimonionacional.es

SWEDEN
Skoklosters Slotts Bibliotek
Skoklosters Slott
746 96 Skokloster
Phone: +46 8402 3060
samlingar@lsh.se
www.skoklostersslott.se

SWITZERLAND
Stiftsbibliothek Sankt Gallen
Klosterhof 6D
9004 St Gallen
Phone: +41 71 227 3416
stibi@stibi.ch
www.stibi.ch

USA
The Morgan Library
225 Madison Avenue
New York, NY 10016
Phone: +1 212 685 0008
visitorservices@themorgan.org
www.themorgan.org

Photo Credits

All images © Massimo Listri with the exception of:

Agenzia Photografica Scala, Antella, Florence © 2018 Photo Scala, Florence: pp. 17, 34, 100

© akg-images: p. 11; akg-images / Bible Land Pictures / Jerusalem Photo by Z. Radovan: p. 8; akg-images / Erich Lessing: p. 25

American Propaganda / Universal History Archive / UIG / Bridgeman Images: p. 73

Fredrik Andersson: p. 305

Antiquariat Kunsthandel Joseph Steutzger: p. 326

Archive of the publisher, collector or author: pp. 282, 377

© Bayerische Staatsbibliothek München: p. 369

© Benediktinerstift Admont, Archiv und Bibliothek: pp. 398, 399

© Benediktinerstift Kremsmünster, Stiftsbibliothek: pp. 386, 387

© Biblioteca Angelica, Rome. Authorised by the Ministero per i Beni e le Attività Culturali. Mario Setter: pp. 128, 129

© 2018 Biblioteca Apostolica Vaticana, Vatican City State: pp. 61, 82, 83

© Biblioteca Casanatense, Rome. Authorised by the Ministero dei Beni e delle Attività Culturali e del Turismo: pp. 152, 153

© Biblioteca Civica Gambalunga, Rimini: pp. 142, 143

© Biblioteca comunale di Imola, Imola: pp. 162, 163

Biblioteca Geral da Universidade de Coimbra: pp. 217, 218

© Biblioteca Nacional de Portugal: pp. 486, 487

© Biblioteca Nazionale Braidense, Milan. Authorised by the Ministero per i Beni e le Attività Culturali: pp. 182, 183

Bibliotec Nazionale Centrale, Florence. Authorised by the Ministero dei Beni e delle Attività Culturali e del Turismo: p. 58

Biblioteca Palafoxiana, photo Rocio Jaramillo: pp. 476, 477

© Biblioteca Palatina, Parma. Authorised by the Ministero dei Beni e delle Attività Culturali e del Turismo: pp. 172, 173

© Biblioteca Riccardiana, Florence: p. 121

© Bibliothèque Paul-Marmottan, Ville de Boulogne-Billancourt, Académie des Beaux-Arts, France / Bridgeman Images: pp. 288, 289

© BnF, Dist. RMN-Grand Palais / image BnF, Paris: pp. 45, 57

© The Board of Trinity College, Dublin, Ireland / Bridgeman Images: pp. 242, 243

Peter Böttcher, Allhartsberg: pp. 416, 417

© bpk: pp. 16, 55; Ägyptisches Museum und Papyrussammlung, SMB | Andreas Paasch: pp. 14–15; bpk | Alinari Archives | Magliani Mauro for Allinari: p. 37; bpk | Bayerische Staatsbibliothek: pp. 3, 48; bpk | British Library Board: p. 63; bpk | The Trustees of the British Museum: p. 19; bpk | Vorderasiatisches Museum, SMB | Olaf M. Teßmer: p. 12

© De Agostini Picture Library | Scala, Florence: pp. 100, 101

© España. Ministerio de Educación, Cultura y Deporte. Archivo General de Indias. Archivo General de Indias: pp. 207, 209

General Collection, Beinecke Rare Book and Manuscript Library, Yale University: p. 49

Göttingen, Niedersächsische Staats- und Universitätsbibliothek: pp. 38, 64

The Israel Museum, Jerusalem / Bridgeman Images: pp. 20–21

© Kunsthistorisches Museum, Vienna: p. 31

© Jean-Luc Lacroix / Musée de Grenoble © domaine public: p. 41

© Marsh's Library, Dublin: pp. 252, 253

© Mary Evans Picture Library: p. 265

Roland and Sabrina Michaud / akg-images: p. 33

© The Morgan Library & Museum, New York: p. 471

National Gallery, London: p. 32

Biographies

Massimo Listri

Born in Florence in 1953, Massimo Listri began his professional career as a photographer at the young age of 17, working for art and architecture magazines. Thanks to publisher Franco Maria Ricci, he had the opportunity to produce the early great photo features for the magazine *FMR* dedicated to the most beautiful palaces, the most extraordinary villas and architecture, as well as memorable books of photographs. During the course of his career he has created over 70 books collaborating with the most prestigious European and international publishers. For the last few years he has devoted himself to exhibiting his art around the world. His most recent shows have taken place at the Morgan Library & Museum in New York, Palazzo del Quirinale in Rome, Museo de Arte Moderno in Buenos Aires, Benaki Museum in Athens, Kunsthistorisches Museum in Vienna, National Museum of San Carlos in Mexico City, National Central Library of Taipei, Schusev State Museum of Architecture in Moscow.

Georg Ruppelt

After studying history, German language and literature, education and philosophy, Georg Ruppelt gained his PhD with a doctoral thesis on "Friedrich Schiller in National Socialist Germany". He subsequently worked as a librarian, becoming deputy director of the Herzog August Bibliothek in Wolfenbüttel in 1987, and director of the Gottfried Wilhelm Leibniz Bibliothek in Hanover from 2002 to 2016. Ruppelt has published over 400 essays and 40 monographs on the subject of books, library science, and cultural history.

Elisabeth Sladek

Elisabeth Sladek studied art history in Vienna, classical archaeology and Judaic studies and wrote her dissertation at the Max Planck Institute in Rome. Her specialisation is the history of Baroque art and architecture and she is an active researcher and teacher in Vienna, Rome and Zurich, among others. She also publishes regularly on these themes.

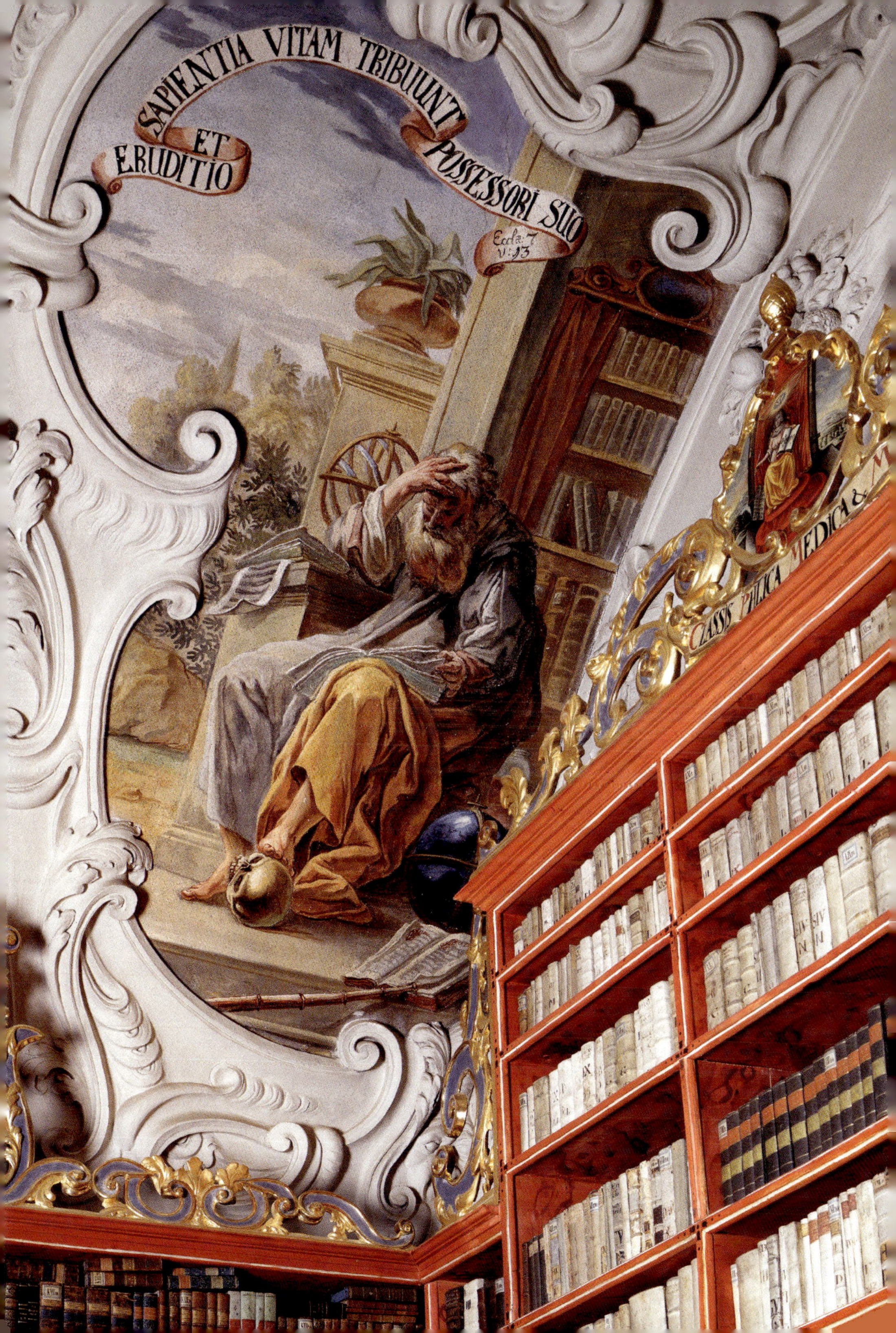

SAPIENTIA VITAM TRIBUUNT
ET
ERUDITIO
POSSESSORI SUO
Eccla:7 v:13
CLASSIS PHILICA MEDICA &

Imprint

EACH AND EVERY TASCHEN BOOK PLANTS A SEED!
Each year, we offset our annual carbon emissions with carbon credits at the
Instituto Terra, a reforestation program in Minas Gerais, Brazil, founded by
Lélia and Sebastião Salgado. To find out more about this ecological partnership,
please check: www.taschen.com/institutoterra.
Inspiration: unlimited. Carbon footprint: (almost) zero

Want to see more? Visit taschen.com to view our current publications, browse
our latest magazine, and subscribe to our newsletter.

Publisher's acknowledgements
We are much indebted to all the libraries, archives and other institutions cited in
the picture captions and in the photo credits for their kind assistance in the publication
of this volume. Ecclesiastical authorities, librarians, photographers and photo agencies
have contributed decisively to the success of our undertaking.

© 2025 TASCHEN GmbH
Hohenzollernring 53, D–50672 Köln
www.taschen.com

English translation
Karen Williams, Rennes-le-Château
French translation
Aude Fondard, Gérardmer

Printed in Bosnia-Herzegovina
ISBN 978–3–8365–9381–6

Temples of Knowledge

Exceptional access to the world's illustrious libraries

Bibliophiles, rejoice! In this rapturous photographic journey, Massimo Listri travels to some of the oldest and finest libraries to celebrate their architectural and historical wonder. From medieval to 19th-century, from private to monastic, this is a cultural-historical pilgrimage to the heart of our halls of learning and the stories they tell.

Kathedralen des Wissens

Zu Besuch in den schönsten Bibliotheken der Welt

Massimo Listris Fotos führen Sie zu den ältesten und schönsten Bibliotheken weltweit. Entdecken Sie die architektonisch und historisch einzigartigen Bauwerke und deren einladenden Lesesäle. Vom Mittelalter bis zum 19. Jahrhundert, von Privat- bis zu Klosterbibliotheken – begeben Sie sich auf eine kulturgeschichtliche Fotoreise und gelangen Sie in das Herz dieser oft geheimnisvollen Orte des Wissens.

Temples de la connaissance

Une plongée unique au cœur des bibliothèques les plus prestigieuses au monde

Dans ce voyage en images, Massimo Listri parcourt les plus anciennes et les plus belles bibliothèques pour en célébrer les merveilles architecturales et historiques. Du Moyen Âge au XIXe siècle, entre les collections privées et monastiques, voici un pélerinage culturel et historique au cœur de ces lieux de savoir et des histoires qu'ils racontent.

> "Prepare to be transported to heaven on earth."
> BBC

> "Listri's meticulous attention to minutiae and details is exquisite. One can practically smell the dust on these ancient books."
> Artology

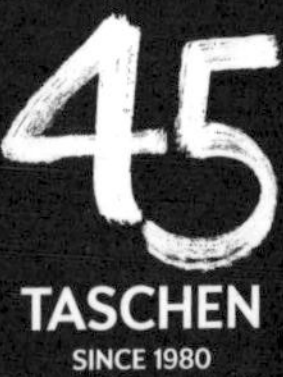

MOSER
MOSER
MOSER
MOSER
MOSER
MOSER
MOSER
MOSER
MOSER
PAUL
PAUL
PAUL
PAUL
PAUL
LE BRET STAATSGESCH. DER REPUBLIK VENE.
LE BRET STAATSGESCH. DER
LE BRET STAATSGESCH. DER
GOLDASTI MONARCH. ROM. IMPER. TOM. II.
GOLDASTI MONARCH. ROM. IMPER. TOM. III.
GOLDASTI COLLECT. CONSTIT. IMPERIAL. TOM. II.
GOLDASTI COLLECT. CONSTIT. IMPERIAL. TOM. III. IV.
GOLDAST REICHS SATZUNGEN
KÖNIG CORPS JURI GERMAN. TOM. I.
KÖNIG CORPS JURI GERMAN. TOM. II.
SIM. SCHARD. Scriptores Rerum Germ. TOM. I. II. III. IV.